No. 9
Handbook of Latin American Studies: 1943

A SELECTIVE GUIDE TO MATERIAL PUBLISHED IN 1943 ON ANTHROPOLOGY, ARCHIVES, ART, ECONOMICS, EDUCATION, FOLKLORE, GEOGRAPHY, GOVERNMENT, HISTORY, INTERNATIONAL RELATIONS, LABOR AND SOCIAL WELFARE, LANGUAGE AND LITERATURE, LAW, LIBRARIES, MUSIC, AND PHILOSOPHY

No. 9

HANDBOOK OF LATIN AMERICAN STUDIES: 1943

EDITED FOR

THE LIBRARY OF CONGRESS

AND

THE JOINT COMMITTEE ON LATIN AMERICAN STUDIES

OF

THE NATIONAL RESEARCH COUNCIL

THE AMERICAN COUNCIL OF LEARNED SOCIETIES

AND

THE SOCIAL SCIENCE RESEARCH COUNCIL

BY

MIRON BURGIN

62218

1963

UNIVERSITY OF FLORIDA PRESS

GAINESVILLE

MEMPHIS
THEOLOGICAL SEMINARY
LIBRARY
168 EAST PARKWAY SOUTH
MEMPHIS, TN. 38104

COPYRIGHT © 1946 BY THE PRESIDENT AND FELLOWS
OF HARVARD COLLEGE

COPYRIGHT TRANSFERRED TO THE BOARD OF COMMISSIONERS
OF STATE INSTITUTIONS OF FLORIDA, 1962

LIBRARY OF CONGRESS CATALOGUE CARD NO. 36-32633

LITHOPRINTED EDITION, 1963

DOUGLAS PRINTING COMPANY, INC.
JACKSONVILLE, FLORIDA

LIST OF CONTRIBUTING EDITORS

Francisco Aguilera, *Library of Congress*, LITERATURE
Ralph L. Beals, *University of California*, ANTHROPOLOGY
Ralph Steele Boggs, *University of North Carolina*, FOLKLORE
Miron Burgin, *Department of Commerce*, HISTORY
Manuel S. Canyes, *Pan American Union*, INTERNATIONAL RELATIONS
James B. Childs, *Library of Congress*, GOVERNMENT
Helen L. Clagett, *Library of Congress*, LAW
Donald Collier, *Chicago Natural History Museum*, ANTHROPOLOGY
Adolfo Dorfman, ECONOMICS
Gordon F. Ekholm, *The American Museum of Natural History*, ANTHROPOLOGY
Russell H. Fitzgibbon, *University of California*, GOVERNMENT
Risieri Frondizi, *Universidad Nacional de Tucumán, Argentina* PHILOSOPHY
Charles C. Griffin, *Vassar College*, HISTORY
Arthur E. Gropp, *American Library at Montevideo*, LIBRARIES
Clarence H. Haring, *Harvard University*, HISTORY
Roscoe R. Hill, *The National Archives*, ARCHIVES
Roland D. Hussey, *University of California*, HISTORY
Preston E. James, *Syracuse University*, GEOGRAPHY
Clarence F. Jones, *Northwestern University*, GEOGRAPHY
James F. King, *University of California*, HISTORY
George Kubler, *Yale University*, ART
Sturgis E. Leavitt, *University of North Carolina*, LITERATURE
Irving A. Leonard, *University of Michigan*, LITERATURE
Allen H. Lester, *Office of Foreign Agricultural Relations, Department of Agriculture*, ECONOMICS
M. B. Lourenço Filho, *Instituto Nacional de Estudos Pedagógicos, Rio de Janeiro, Brazil*, EDUCATION
George McCutchen McBride, *University of California*, GEOGRAPHY
Merle Alexander McBride, *Library of Congress*, GEOGRAPHY
Alexander Marchant, *The Johns Hopkins University*, HISTORY
Anyda M. Marchant, *Library of Congress*, LAW
Alfred Métraux, *Smithsonian Institution*, ANTHROPOLOGY
Sanford A. Mosk, *The University of California*, ECONOMICS
Dana Munro, *Princeton University*, HISTORY
Rafael Picó, *Puerto Rico Planning, Urbanizing and Zonig Board, Santurce, Puerto Rico*, GEOGRAPHY
Samuel Putnam, LITERATURE
Gustavo-Adolfo Rohen y Gálvez, LABOR AND SOCIAL WELFARE
Charles Seeger, *Pan American Union*, MUSIC
Earl B. Shaw, *State Teachers' College, Worcester, Massachusetts*, GEOGRAPHY
Charmion Shelby, *Library of Congress*, BIBLIOGRAPHIES
Roberto Simonsen, *Escola Livre de Sociologia e Política, São Paulo, Brazil*, ECONOMICS
Robert C. Smith, *Sweet Briar College*, ART
T. D. Stewart, *United States National Museum*, ANTHROPOLOGY
Bryce Wood, *Swarthmore College*, INTERNATIONAL RELATIONS
Kathryn H. Wylie, *Office of Foreign Agricultural Relations, Department of Agriculture*, ECONOMICS

TABLE OF CONTENTS

	PAGE
TABLE OF CONTENTS	vii
INTRODUCTION	xvi
BIBLIOGRAPHIES . . . . *Charmion Shelby*	1
GENERAL STATEMENT	
BIBLIOGRAPHY	
GENERAL WORKS	11
ANTHROPOLOGY	18
GENERAL	18
MIDDLE AMERICA: ARCHAEOLOGY . . . . . . *Gordon F. Ekholm*	21
General Statement	
Bibliography	
General; Mexican and Mayan History and Epigraphy; Mexico; Maya Area; Southern Central America and the Antilles; Addenda (General, Mexican and Mayan history and epigraphy, Mexico, Maya area, Southern Central America and the Antilles)	
MIDDLE AMERICA: ETHNOLOGY . . . . *Ralph L. Beals*	31
General Statement	
Bibliography	
Bibliographies; Monographs and Special Papers (General, Mexico, except Yucatán, the Yucatán peninsula, Guatemala, Honduras, Nicaragua, Panama, El Salvador, the West Indies); Addenda	
SOUTH AMERICA: ARCHAEOLOGY . . . . *Donald Collier*	35
General Statement	
Bibliography	
General; Argentina; Bolivia; British Guiana; Chile; Colombia; Ecuador; Peru; Uruguay; Venezuela; Addenda	
SOUTH AMERICA: ETHNOLOGY . . . . *Alfred Métraux*	41
General Statement	
Expeditions	
Bibliography	
General; Argentina; Bolivia; Brazil; Chile; Colombia; Ecuador; Paraguay; Peru; Venezuela; Addenda (Argentina, Brazil, Peru)	

ANTHROPOLOGY—Continued

MIDDLE AND SOUTH AMERICA: PHYSICAL ANTHROPOLOGY
T. D. Stewart — 51
General Statement
Bibliography
General: Middle America and the Antilles; Argentina; Bolivia; Brazil, Colombia and Chile; Peru, Venezuela; Addenda

ARCHIVES . . . . *Roscoe R. Hill* — 57

GENERAL STATEMENT

NATIONAL ARCHIVES
Argentina; Bolivia; Brazil; Colombia; Costa Rica; Cuba; Dominican Republic; Guatemala; Haiti; Honduras; Mexico; Panama; Paraguay; Peru; Uruguay; Venezuela

OTHER ARCHIVES
Argentina; Brazil; Mexico; Venezuela

DOCUMENTARY PUBLICATIONS

PUBLICATIONS ON ARCHIVOLOGY

ADDENDA
National Archives (Chile, Peru); Documentary Publications; Publications on Archivology

SPANISH AMERICAN ART . . . . *George Kubler* — 72

GENERAL STATEMENT

BIBLIOGRAPHY
General; Colonial Architecture, Painting and Sculpture; Nineteenth Century Architecture, Painting and Sculpture; Contemporary Architecture, Painting and Sculpture; Artists by Countries (Argentina, Bolivia, Colombia, Cuba, Mexico, Peru, Uruguay)

BRAZILIAN ART . . . . *Robert C. Smith* — 85

GENERAL STATEMENT

BIBLIOGRAPHY
General; Colonial; Nineteenth Century; Modern

ECONOMICS 100

General 100

THE CARIBBEAN AREA . . . . *Sanford A. Mosk* — 107
General Statement
Bibliography
General; Mexico (General, Banking and public finance, Industry and trade, Mining and petroleum, Population, Trans-

TABLE OF CONTENTS

ECONOMICS—Continued   PAGE

portation, Miscellaneous); Central America (General, Costa Rica, Guatemala, Honduras, Nicaragua, Panama, El Salvador); The Islands (General, Cuba, Dominican Republic, Haiti, Puerto Rico); Colombia (General, Industry and trade, Mining and petroleum, Population, Transportation, Miscellaneous); Venezuela; Addenda

AGRICULTURE: THE CARIBBEAN AREA . . . . . *Kathryn H. Wylie*   122
    Bibliography
        Mexico; Central America (Costa Rica, Guatemala, Honduras, Nicaragua, Panama, El Salvador); The Islands (Cuba, Dominican Republic, Jamaica); Colombia; Venezuela

SOUTH AMERICA (EXCEPT BRAZIL, COLOMBIA AND VENEZUELA)
                                                                                 Adolfo Dorfman   128
    General Statement
    Bibliography
        General; Argentina; Bolivia; Chile; Ecuador; Paraguay; Peru; Uruguay; Addenda

AGRICULTURE: SOUTH AMERICA (EXCEPT BRAZIL, COLOMBIA AND VENEZUELA) . . . . *Allen H. Lester* and *Kathryn H. Wylie*   146
    Bibliography
        Argentina; Chile; Ecuador; Paraguay; Peru; Uruguay

BRAZIL . . . . *Roberto Simonsen*   150
    General Statement
    Bibliography
        General; Production and Natural Resources; Coffee; Money; Foreign Trade; Transportation and Communication; Labor and Social Legislation; Immigration; Miscellaneous; Statistics and Statistical Series; Journals

AGRICULTURE: BRAZIL . . . . *Allen H. Lester*   161
    Bibliography

EDUCATION . . . . *M. B. Lourenço Filho*   163
    BIBLIOGRAPHY
        General; Brazil

FOLKLORE . . . . *Ralph S. Boggs*   167
    GENERAL STATEMENT

    BIBLIOGRAPHY
        General and Miscellaneous; Mythology, Legend and Tradition; Folktale; Folk Poetry, Music, Dance and Game; Custom and Festival; Drama; Art, Craft, Architecture, Dress and Adornment; Food and Drink; Belief, Witchcraft, Medicine and Magic; Folkspeech; Proverb; Riddle; Addenda (General and

TABLE OF CONTENTS

FOLKLORE—Continued

    miscellaneous, Mythology, Legend, and tradition, Folktale, Folk poetry, music, dance and game, Custom and festival, Drama, art, craft, architecture, Dress and adornment, Food and drink, Belief, Witchcraft, Medicine and Magic, Folkspeech, Proverb)

GEOGRAPHY 183

  GENERAL 183

  THE CARIBBEAN AREA ..... *C. F. Jones, E. B. Shaw* and *R. Picó*   185
    General Statement
    Bibliography
      General; Mexico; Central America (Costa Rica, Guatemala, Honduras, Panama, El Salvador); Colombia; Venezuela; West Indies (General, Greater Antilles, The Bahamas, Lesser Antilles); Addenda

  SOUTH AMERICA (EXCEPT BRAZIL, COLOMBIA AND VENEZUELA)
                       George M. McBride and *Merle A. McBride*   193
    General Statement
    Bibliography
      General; East Coast; West Coast; Addenda

  BRAZIL .... *Preston E. James*   201
    General Statement
    Bibliography
      General; Physical and Mathematical Geography; Economic and Regional Geography

GOVERNMENT ... *James B. Childs* and *Russell H. Fitzgibbon*   206

  GENERAL STATEMENT

  BIBLIOGRAPHY
    General; Argentina; Bolivia; Brazil; Chile; Colombia; Costa Rica; Cuba; Dominican Republic; Ecuador; Guatemala; Haiti; Honduras; Mexico; Nicaragua; Panama; Paraguay; Peru; El Salvador; Uruguay; Venezuela; Addenda (Brazil, Chile, Ecuador, Peru)

  CHANGES IN PUBLIC ADMINISTRATION AUTHORIZED IN 1943
                                    James B. Childs   222
    Argentina; Bolivia; Chile; Colombia; Costa Rica; Cuba; Dominican Republic; Ecuador; Guatemala; Haiti; Mexico; Nicaragua; Panama; Paraguay; Peru; El Salvador; Uruguay; Venezuela

HISTORY 242

  GENERAL 242

TABLE OF CONTENTS

	PAGE
HISTORY—CONTINUED	
SPANISH AMERICA: THE COLONIAL PERIOD	
Roland D. Hussey and *James F. King*	246
General Statement	
Bibliography	
General; Addenda; Middle America and The Islands (Lists and indices, Documents, Other works, Addenda); South America (Documentary indices and guides, Documents, Other Works, Addenda)	
SPANISH AMERICA: THE REVOLUTIONARY PERIOD . *Charles C. Griffin*	277
General Statement	
Bibliography	
General; Mexico and Central America; Northern South America; Southern South America; Addenda	
CARIBBEAN AREA: THE NATIONAL PERIOD .... *Dana G. Munro*	288
General Statement	
Bibliography	
Mexico; Central America; Cuba; Dominican Republic; Addenda	
SPANISH SOUTH AMERICA: THE NATIONAL PERIOD	
Clarence H. Haring and *Miron Burgin*	293
General Statement	
Bibliography	
Argentina; Bolivia; Chile; Colombia; Ecuador; Paraguay; Peru; Uruguay; Venezuela; Addenda	
BRAZIL . . . . *Alexander Marchant*	304
General Statement	
Bibliography	
General; Colonial and Revolutionary Periods; The Empire and the Republic; Addenda	
INTERNATIONAL RELATIONS	313
INTERNATIONAL RELATIONS SINCE 1830 . . . . *Bryce Wood*	313
General Statement	
Bibliography	
General; Pan Americanism; Monroe Doctrine; Good Neighbor Policy; Hemisphere Defense; Axis Influence; Political Questions; Post War Problems; Boundaries; Addenda	
TREATIES, CONVENTIONS, INTERNATIONAL ACTS, PROTOCOLS, AND AGREEMENTS . . . . *Manuel S. Canyes*	323
General Statement	
Bilateral Treaties; Addenda; Multilateral Treaties and Conventions	

LABOR AND SOCIAL WELFARE
Gustavo-Adolfo Rohen y Gálvez — 350

BIBLIOGRAFÍA

América Latina (General, Derecho y legislación del trabajo, Organismos oficiales, asociaciones patronales y obreras, Empleo y desocupación, Migración y colonización, Salarios, horas, descansos y costo de la vida, Seguro social, Vivienda, nutrición y otros standards de bienestar obrero, Trabajo de mujeres y menores y otras categorías especiales de trabajadores); Argentina (General, Derecho y legislación del trabajo, organismos oficiales, asociaciones patronales y obreras, Relaciones industriales, Empleo y desocupación; Migración y colonización, Salarios, horas, descansos y costo de la vida, Seguro social, Vivienda, nutrición y otros standards de bienestar obrero, Trabajo de mujeres y menores, y otras categorías especiales de trabajadores); Bolivia (General, Derecho y legislación del trabajo, Salarios, horas, descansos y costo de la vida, Seguro social, Vivienda, nutrición y otros standards de bienestar obrero, Trabajo de mujeres y menores y otras categorías especiales de trabajadores); Brasil (General, Derecho y legislación del trabajo, Organismos oficiales, asociaciones patronales y obreras, Empleo y desocupación, Migración y colonización, Salarios, horas, descansos y costo de la vida, Higiene y seguridad del trabajo, Seguro social, Vivienda, nutrición y otros standards de bienestar obrero, Trabajo de mujeres y menores y otras categorías especiales de trabajadores, Miscelánea); Chile (General, Empleo y desocupación, Salarios, horas, descansos, y costo de la vida, Seguro social, Vivienda, nutrición y otros standards de bienestar obrero); Colombia (General, Organismos oficiales, asociaciones patronales y obreras, Salarios, horas, descansos y costo de la vida, Seguro social); Costa Rica (General, Organismos officiales, asociaciones patronales y obreras, Seguro social); Cuba (General, Organismos oficiales, asociaciones patronales y obreras, Empleo y desocupación, Seguro social, Miscelánea); Ecuador (General, Organismos oficiales, asociaciones patronales y obreras, Seguro social); El Salvador (Miscelánea); Guatemala (Miscelánea); Haiti (Miscelánea); Honduras (Miscelánea); México (General, Organismos oficiales, asociaciones patronales y obreras, Relaciones industriales, Empleo y desocupación, Migración y colonización, Salarios, horas descansos y costo de la vida, Higiene y seguridad del trabajo, Seguro social, Vivienda, nutrición y otros standards de bienestar obrero, Trabajo de mujeres y menores y otras categorías especiales de trabajadores); Nicaragua (Miscelánea); Panamá (Miscelánea); Paraguay (General, Salarios, horas, descansos y costo de la vida, Miscelánea); Perú (General, Relaciones industriales, Salarios, horas, descansos y costo de la vida, Seguro social, Vivienda, nutrición

LABOR AND SOCIAL WELFARE—Continued

y otros standards de bienestar obrero, Trabajo de mujeres y menores y otras categorías especiales de trabajadores); República Dominicana (Miscelánea); Uruguay (Miscelánea); Venezuela (General, Vivienda, nutrición y otros standards de bienestar obrero); Addenda

LANGUAGE AND LITERATURE 368

Spanish American Literature: The Colonial Period
Irving A. Leonard 368

General Statement
Bibliography
Bibliographical Works; Texts; Individual Figures; Essays, Criticism, Miscellaneous Studies; Addenda

Spanish American Literature: The National Period
Sturgis E. Leavitt and *Francisco Aguilera* 374

General Statement
Bibliography
Bibliographical Works; Literature other than Poetry (Essays, criticism and biography, Prose fiction, Drama, New editions, Translations, Addenda); Poetry (Books of verse, Biography and criticism, New editions, Translations, Addenda)

Brazilian Literature .... *Samuel Putnam* 392

General Statement
Bibliography
Linguistics, Dictionaries, Encyclopedias, Bibliographies; Criticism, Essays, Biographies, Memoirs, Travels, Anthologies, Miscellaneous Prose, Collected Works; Novels, Short Stories, Prose Sketches; Verse; Drama; Translations; Children's Books, Addenda

LAW .... *Helen L. Clagett* and *Anyda M. Marchant* 416

General Statement

Bibliography

Collections of Laws and Bibliographies (Argentina, Chile, Costa Rica, Cuba, Mexico, Nicaragua, Peru); Philosophy of Law, History of Law, Jurisprudence (General, Argentina, Brazil, Colombia, Dominican Republic, Mexico, Peru, Venezuela); Courts and Judicial Procedure (Argentina, Brazil, Chile, Colombia, Cuba, Guatemala, Haiti, Mexico, Uruguay, Venezuela); Administrative and Constitutional Law (Argentina, Brazil, Chile, Cuba, Mexico, Uruguay, Venezuela); Civil Law (Argentina, Brazil, Chile, Colombia, Cuba, Mexico, Uruguay, Venezuela); Criminal Law (Argentina, Brazil, Colombia, Cuba, Peru, Uruguay); Commercial Law (Argentina, Brazil, Chile, Colombia, Cuba, Mexico, Peru, Uru-

LAW—CONTINUED
  guay); International Law, Private (Argentina, Brazil, Colombia, Ecuador, Mexico, Venezuela); International Law, Public (Argentina, Chile, Dominican Republic); Other Topics (Argentina, Brazil, Colombia, Mexico, Uruguay, Venezuela).

LIBRARIES . . . . *Arthur E. Gropp*   433
  NOTES OF EVENTS AND TRENDS
  BIBLIOGRAPHY

MUSIC . . . . *Charles Seeger*   444
  GENERAL STATEMENT
  BIBLIOGRAPHY
    Music (General, Argentina, Brazil, Bolivia, Chile, Colombia, Costa Rica, Cuba, Dominion Republic, El Salvador, Mexico, Nicaragua, Uruguay, Venezuela); Records (Bibliography, Records); Publications (General, Argentina, Bolivia, Brazil, Chile, Colombia, Costa Rica, Cuba, Dominican Republic, Ecuador, Guatemala, Mexico, Nicaragua, Panama, Paraguay, Peru, Uruguay, Venezuela, Puerto Rico); Addenda (Music, Publications)

PHILOSOPHY . . . . *Risieri Frondizi*   462
  OJEADA GENERAL
  BIBLIOGRAFÍA
    Reediciones y Estudios Críticos; Obras Generales y Miscelánea; Lógica y Epistemología; Ética y Filosofía Social y Política; Apéndice (Filosofía antigua y medieval, Filosofía moderna, Filosofía contemporánea); Addenda

ABBREVIATIONS   473

INDEX   489

INTRODUCTION

The present volume of the Handbook of Latin American Studies appears under the joint auspices of the Library of Congress and the Joint Committee on Latin American Studies of the National Research Council, the American Council of Learned Societies and the Social Science Research Council. The Library of Congress assumed responsibility for the maintenance and operation of the editorial office of the Handbook as an integral part of the Hispanic Foundation. The Joint Committee on Latin American Studies has retained the responsibility for the publication and distribution of the Handbook through the Harvard University Press.

The character and objectives of the Handbook remain unchanged. It endeavors to record with descriptive and critical notes the more important publications of the year in the fields of the humanities and the social sciences. The Handbook is a selective guide; it is not a comprehensive list of publications in disciplines represented in the volume.

Several changes have occurred on the editorial board. Sanford A. Mosk succeeded Leland H. Jenks in editing the section on Economics, The Caribbean Area; Adolfo Dorfman assumed charge of the section on Economics, South America, formerly edited by Miron Burgin; publications relating to agriculture in Latin America are treated separately by Kathryn H. Wylie and Allen H. Lester; Dana G. Munro assumed the editorship of the section on History, Caribbean Area, National Period; the section on law previously prepared by Crawford M. Bishop is now under the editorship of Helen L. Clagett (Spanish America) and Anyda M. Marchant (Brazil); and Charles Seeger succeeded Gilbert Chase in editing the section on Music. The editor regrets that it has been necessary to omit in this volume the sections on Spanish American Education and Spanish American Language. For reasons beyond the control of the editors material on cartography had to be relegated to the tenth volume of the Handbook.

Numerous persons and institutions have continued to take interest in the Handbook. The editor is glad to have this opportunity to express his profound appreciation for the invaluable assistance he and his staff have received from members of the staffs of the Library of Congress, the Columbus Memorial Library of the Pan American Union, and the Library of the Department of Agriculture. For aid in the various phases of the preparation of the Handbook the editor wishes to extend his thanks to Evelyn Beam, Teodoro Becú, Louise O. Bercaw, Janeiro V. Brooks, Frances Greer Brown, Cuca Alvarado Clark, Juan Comas, Carmen Couvillion, Alice Dugas, Leila Fern, Marian Forero, Manuel Gamio, Bernhard Goldberg, Madge Goolsby, Annie M. Hanney, Marion T. Loops, Helen Kaufman, Mary Ann Martinik, Louise T. Mayhugh, Elizabeth C. Mearns, Gaye W. Moore, Margarita Obregón Loría, Elsie Rackstraw, Carmelo Sáenz de Santa María, William C. Sturgis, Edith M. Wise and Harriet Woodring. He would pay special tribute to Doris Havener, Charmion Shelby, Margaret S. Bowie, and Consuelo G. Talkington who as members of the editorial staff have borne their share of the burden of preparing the volume and seeing it through the press.

Publishers, institutions and authors throughout the Americas have assisted the editorial office and the contributing editors by sending their publications to the Handbook. The editor has found this assistance most useful. He hopes that the flow of material suitable for listing in the Handbook will continue to increase and in this manner contribute to as complete a coverage as possible.

The editor regrets that because of difficulties engendered by the war and reconversion to peace the publication of the volume has been retarded. To bring the Handbook up to date is among the major preoccupations of the editor and he hopes within the near future to reduce to a minimum the interval between the publication of the volume and the year it covers.

MIRON BURGIN

WASHINGTON, D. C.

BIBLIOGRAPHIES

BY

CHARMION SHELBY
Library of Congress

GENERAL STATEMENT

A notable trend in the bibliographical field in Latin America, as revealed in the year's publications, is the interest in national and local bibliographies. Among those in the first group, new in the field, is Jorge Fidel Durón, *Repertorio Bibliográfico Hondureño* (no. 30). Fermín Peraza y Sarausa, *Segundo Congreso Nacional y Panamericano de Prensa. Exhibición de la Prensa Cubana Contemporánea* (no. 76), deals with Cuban journalism. In Mexico, the Segunda Feria del Libro was the occasion for preparation of a series of bibliographies and histories of the press of the several states, as Francisco R. Almada, *La Imprenta y el Periodismo en Chihuahua* (no. 2); Joaquín Fernández de Córdoba, *Nuevos Documentos para la Historia de la Imprenta en Morelia* (no. 32); Héctor R. Olea, *La Primera Imprenta en las Provincias de Sonora y Sinaloa* (no. 69); and Héctor Pérez Martínez, *Bibliografía del Estado de Campeche* (no. 78). Bibliographies of various of the federal government agencies also were prepared on the same occasion, as the *Bibliografía, 1821–1942*, of the Secretaría de Hacienda y Crédito Público (no. 58).

An addition to the list of bibliographies of bibliographies is Agustín Millares Carlo and José Ignacio Mantecón, *Ensayo de una Bibliografía de Bibliografías Mexicanas* (no. 65). Another such compilation now (1945) ready for the press is Fermín Peraza y Sarausa, *Bibliografías Cubanas*. This work will initiate a series of Latin American bibliographies of bibliographies to be issued by the Hispanic Foundation of the Library of Congress. It was prepared by Dr. Peraza while he was acting as consultant in Cuban bibliography at the Library of Congress in 1944.

Among guides to periodical literature, mention should be made of "Latin American Periodicals Dealing with Labor and Social Welfare," in *Handbook of Latin American Studies, No. 8, 1942*, by G. A. Rohen y Gálvez (no. 86). Also, it may be noted that the comprehensive guide prepared by the Hispanic Foundation of the Library of Congress, *Latin American Periodicals Currently Received in the Library of Congress and in the Library of the Department of Agriculture* is now (1945) off the press.

BIBLIOGRAPHY

(*See also items* 209, 460, 477, 516, 1210, 2155a, 3033, 3159, 3373, 3832–3841, 4107a, 4109, 4116)

Albornoz (h.), Alejandro. Fuentes para el estudio de la historia hispanoamericana. Documentos y libros existentes en la Biblioteca nacional de Buenos Aires. Descubrimiento de América; conquista y colonización (*Rev. bibl. nac.*, Buenos Aires, tomo 8, no. 25, primer trim., p. 243–252; no. 26, segundo trim., p. 493–500;

tomo 9, no. 27, tercer trim., p. 241-252; no. 28, cuarto trim., p. 491-500). [1
Continuation of item 1 in *Handbook, no. 8, 1942*, comprising items 317-585. Most of titles 317-437 deal with Columbus' voyages. Items 437-585 cover Spanish exploration and colonization in both North and South America.

Almada, Francisco R. La imprenta y el periodismo en Chihuahua. México. Publ. del Gobierno del estado de Chihuahua. 49 p. [2
A history of printing and journalism in Chihuahua from the establishment of the first press in 1825. Title pages of early imprints are reproduced. There are chapters on journalism in Chihuahua City and elsewhere in the state, and on the *Periódico Oficial* of Chihuahua.

Argentina. Córdoba. Universidad nacional. Biblioteca mayor. Catálogo de la Librería jesuítica. Córdoba. Imp. de la Univ. nac. de Córdoba. 311 p. [4
The great library amassed by the Jesuits at their center of instruction at Córdoba during the 17th and 18th centuries was dispersed following the expulsion of the Order in 1767. Many of the books were taken to Buenos Aires in the early years of independence to become a part of the newly-formed Biblioteca Pública. Others were widely scattered, many falling into the hands of private persons. In later years efforts have been made to restore at least a portion of the library to Córdoba, as a part of the library of the Universidad Nacional. Some 2000 works are now assembled. The present first part of the catalog, extending through the letter F, lists the books by author or title. All were published prior to 1767, and are "for the most part . . . works on philosophy, theology and moral treatises, many of them of singular importance."

Behrendt, Richard F. Selected bibliography of books, pamphlets, and periodicals in English in the field of economics, politics, and sociology of Latin America. Third rev. ed. Albuquerque. Univ. of New Mexico, School of inter-American affairs. (Inter-Americana series, Bibliographies, 1). 36 p. [5
Listing material, mostly of recent date, available in the Library of the University of New Mexico, this bibliography is somewhat broader in scope than the title indicates. The first section includes handbooks, historical, geographical and other works of a general nature. The rest of the bibliography is arranged regionally, some entries having brief comments. Periodicals and serials are included.

BIBLIOGRAFIA BRASILEIRA (*Cultura política*, ano 3, no. 27, maio, p. 171-179; no. 28, junho, p. 210-218; no. 30, agôsto, p. 191-205; no. 32, set., p. 239-250; no. 33, out., p. 237-244; no. 34, nov., p. 254-263; no. 35, dez., p. 278-286). [6
Continuation of the monthly bibliographical lists, including works in translation.

The entries are arranged under subject headings. The September issue contains the "Bibliografia sôbre o Estado Nacional e o Pensamento do Presidente." See also item 83.

BIBLIOGRAFÍA DE AUTORES NACIONALES (*Bol. bibl. archivo nac.*, año 3, no. 6, oct. 31, p. 81-109). [7
Prepared by Miguel A. Ramos, director of the Archivo y Biblioteca Nacionales, the works are listed alphabetically by author's name. There are occasional comments. Literature, geography, history, political science, foreign relations, and other fields are represented, and a number of textbooks for lower schools are included as well as notices of works in preparation. To be continued.

BIBLIOGRAFÍA DE HISTORIA DE AMÉRICA, 1941-1943 (*Rev. hist. Amér.*, no. 16, dic., p. 225-424). [8
Continuation of this monumental historical bibliography, which now numbers 4169 titles. Arrangement is regional under subject headings and the reviews are contributed by editors from all the American republics.

BIBLIOGRAFÍA HISPANOAMERICANA (*Rev. hisp. mod.*, año 9, no. 1-2, enero-abril, p. 144-180; no. 3, julio, p. 245-267; no. 4, oct., p. 325-362). [9
A classified bibliography which covers a wide field, including much more than literature. [S. E. Leavitt]

BIBLIOGRAFÍA MARTIANA DE 1941 (*Arch. José Martí*, año 3, no. 1, enero-dic., 1942 [i.e., 1943], p. 166-188). [10
Writings of the year about Martí and new editions of his works. See also item 74.

Biblioteca nacional de Venezuela. Catálogo de la Exposición de libros bolivarianos. 16 de diciembre de 1942-20 de enero de 1943. Caracas. C. A. artes gráf. 237 p. [11
The exposition was held as one of the commemorative acts of the centenary of the removal of the remains of Bolívar to Caracas. 1546 imprints were included—books, pamphlets, etc., all relative to Bolívar and all found in the Biblioteca Nacional, the Academia Nacional de la Historia, or the Casa Natal del Libertador. Titles are listed alphabetically by author, with bibliographical information but no annotations. There is a title index.

BOLETIM BIBLIOGRÁFICO. Publicação da Biblioteca pública municipal de São Paulo. São Paulo. Ano 1, vol. 1, out./dez.—. [12
Designed to record the activities of the library as a cultural center. Sections are: Colaboração original (including bibliographies of selected authors); Autores e livros (book reviews and bibliographical essays); Bibliografia (books received in the library, June 1-October 31, 1943). See item 82.

BOLETÍN BIBLIOGRÁFICO. Ministerio de agricultura. Buenos Aires. Enero/marzo–oct./dic. [13

Entries, chiefly periodical articles, are listed by author under a number of subject headings within the general field of agriculture. Among the sections of general as well as agricultural interest are: Economía Política y Rural, Industrias, Inmigración, Tierras, Colonización. There are no comments.

BOLETÍN BIBLIOGRÁFICO. Publicado por la Biblioteca de la Cámara de diputados. Lima. Año 1, no. 1, nov.—. [14

BOLETÍN BIBLIOGRÁFICO. Universidad mayor de San Marcos. Lima. Año 16, no. 1/2, julio–3/4, dic. [15

BOLETÍN BIBLIOGRÁFICO. NÓMINA DE LOS LIBROS ENTRADOS. Univ. nac. de Cuyo, Biblioteca. Mendoza. 41; 58 p. [16

Vol. 1 covers the period November, 1942–March, 1943; Vol. 2, April–September, 1943. Arranged under more than 20 subject headings, listing separately books, pamphlets and periodicals, with the usual bibliographical information. The works cover a wide range of materials in belles-lettres, the sciences, economics, history, agriculture, etc., including many of foreign origin and translations from other languages.

BOLETÍN BIBLIOGRÁFICO ARGENTINO. Min. de justicia e instrucción pública de la nación, Comisión nacional de cooperación intelectual. Buenos Aires. No. 13–14, enero–dic. 5–171 p. [17

As the publication of the Comisión Nacional de Cooperación Intelectual, gives a comprehensive list of titles appearing in Argentina during the year. Arranged alphabetically by author's name under forty-seven subject hearings. There is an author index, and an appended article, "Seis años de cooperación intelectual," giving a review of the activities of the Comisión.

BOLETÍN BIBLIOGRÁFICO MEXICANO. Instituto panamericano de bibliografía y documentación. México, D. F. Año 4, no. 37, enero–no. 47/48, nov./dic. [18

Published by the Librería de Porrúa hnos. Each monthly issue has three sections: "Crítica de libros," with reviews of several current books; "Libros recibidos," Mexican and foreign, the latter arranged by subject; and "Libros del mes," current publications also listed by subject. Prices when given are in Mexican pesos.

BOLETÍN DE BIBLIOGRAFÍA YUCATECA. Universidad de Yucatán. Mérida. No. 16, enero/marzo–no. 18, julio/sept. [19

No. 16 is devoted to a history of printing and of journalism in Yucatán, beginning with the introduction of the first printing press in 1813. No. 17 contains a bibliography of Yucatán imprints for 1942, arranged under several subject headings; with occasional annotations. There are 61 entries. No. 18 contains a list of works on *henequén*, found in the Biblioteca "Crescencio Carrillo y Ancona." The titles are arranged chronologically, the first being of the year 1830. Some are annotated. A useful compilation on the subject.

Brazil. **Ministério da justiça e negócios interiores.** Relatório. Atividades da Imprensa nacional no quatrienio 1939–1942. Rio de Janeiro. Imp. nacional. 559 p. [20

The report of the Director of the official press of Brazil for the period 1939–1942 is submitted under heads of Administration, Control and Statistics, Accounting, Personnel, Production, Publications, etc. Includes graphs and statistical tables. The Appendix lists by title all government publications of those years.

Burgin, Miron (ed.). Handbook of Latin American studies, no. 8. A selective guide to the material published in 1942 on anthropology, archives, art, economics, education, folklore, geography, government, history, international relations, labor and social welfare, language and literature, law, libraries, music, and philosophy. Cambridge, Mass. Harvard univ. press. xv, 521 p. [22

The eighth number of this annual lists 4954 items, arranged by subject in nineteen sections, with comments by the respective contributing editors. A special article is "Latin American Periodicals Dealing with Labor and Social Welfare," by G. A. Rohen y Gálvez (p. 449–479). See item 86.

CATÁLOGO ADICIONAL DE LA EXPOSICIÓN DEL LIBRO VENEZOLANO. Quito. Imp. del Min. del gobierno. (El Grupo América). 1943? viii p. [23

The *Catálogo Adicional* includes books presented to the Grupo América of Ecuador by the Venezuelan government on the occasion of the Exposición del Libro Venezolano. The entries are listed alphabetically by author. See item 31.

CERVANTES. Revista bibliográfica mensual ilustrada. Habana. Año 18, no. 1–2, enero/feb.–no. 9–12, sept./dic. [24

Brief articles of criticism, biographical sketches and notes of authors, book reviews, publishing news, and a bibliography, arranged by author's name under subject headings, of "Obras recibidas en las librerías 'La Moderna Poesía' y 'Cervantes'" for the current period. Descriptive notes are included, and prices.

Chávez, Tobías (comp.). Notas para la bibliografía de las obras editadas o patrocinadas por la Universidad nacional autónoma de México. Contiene además las notas bibliográficas de las tesis presentadas por los graduados, durante los años de 1937 a 1942, y una breve noticia histórica de la Universidad. México. Imp. univ. xiv, 260 p. [25

One of the bibliographical series of the Feria del Libro. It is described as "only a contribution for a bibliography of works edited, sponsored, or otherwise published" by the University, as a complete list would require more extensive research. In three parts: I. Books, pamphlets, reviews. II. Theses of graduates of 1937–1942, by discipline. III. Indexes. A brief historical sketch of the University precedes the bibliography. There are 4501 items, listed by author.

Chicago public library. Books of the Americas in Spanish and Portuguese. Chicago. 19 p. [26
Spanish and Portuguese works are listed separately under various heads: Literature, Poetry, Travel, Biography, Books for children. Most are fairly recent publications, but the collection is uneven and seems to have been assembled by chance rather than according to plan.

Childs, James B. Venezuelan government publications. A brief survey of the present situation (*Int. amer. bibliog. rev.*, vol. 3, no. 2, summer, p. 120–125). [27

Claremont colleges. American hemispheric solidarity. Library resources. Claremont, Calif. 49 p. [28
A list that should be useful to teachers and others planning programs on this topic. Divided into twelve subject headings, among which are: The arts, Minority and racial groups, Economic aspects, Instructional implementation, Conferences and conference reports. Both books and periodical and pamphlet material are listed, including a number of official publications.

Córdoba Flores, Cristina. Selección de artículos publicados en revistas y periódicos nacionales llegados a la biblioteca . . . (*Bol. bibliog., Lima*, año 16, vol. 13, no. 1–2, p. 79–102; no. 3–4, dic., p. 198–228). [29
Continuation of this valuable analysis of current periodical literature of Peru. The articles are listed by author under more than forty subject headings, with bibliographical data but no descriptive annotations. The first installment covers the period December 1, 1942–May 15, 1943. The second article refers to the period May 15, 1943–September 15, 1943.

Durón, Jorge Fidel. Repertorio bibliográfico hondureño. Tegucigalpa. Imp. Calderón. (Inst. hondureño de cultura interamericana). viii, 68 p. [30
This "primero tentativo . . . para la bibliografía nacional" is a catalog of books, pamphlets, etc., assembled for the Exposición y Feria del Libro Hondureño, held under the Instituto's auspices. Some 900 titles, listed by author, include works by Honduran writers, and works about Honduras, some of which were sent from other countries for purposes of the Exposition. A detailed list of the contents of the *Bibliografía de Don José Cecilio del Valle*, by Rafael Heliodoro Valle, is a useful feature. There is an author index.

Exposición del libro venezolano. Quito. Imp. del Min. del gobierno. (El Grupo América). 32 p. [31
In honor of the visit to Ecuador of President Isaías Medina Angarita of Venezuela the Grupo América prepared the Exposición del Libro Venezolano, consisting of Venezuelan books in its library. The present catalog of this collection is arranged by subject and gives only the author's name and the title, with no other bibliographical information. See also item 23.

Fernández de Córdoba, Joaquín. Nuevos documentos para la historia de la imprenta en Morelia. Impresores e impresos morelianos del siglo 19. México. Bibl. Benjamín Franklin. 62 p., ilus. [32
An account of the early presses of Morelia, with sketches of the three leading printers, Ignacio Arango, Octaviano Ortiz and José Rosario Bravo, including examples of their work. Published on the occasion of the Exposición Bibliográfica de Michoacán, organized by the Sociedad de Geografía e Historia of the state and held under the auspices of the Biblioteca Benjamín Franklin, Mexico City.

González, Silvino M. (comp.). Algunas fichas para una bibliografía general de la Secretaría de la defensa nacional. México. Tall. Nigromante de González, Martínez y cía. 206 p. [34
A bibliography of official publications of this Secretaría, prepared on the occasion of the Feria del Libro. The list is chronological, beginning in 1821, and contains 847 items. There is an author index.

Guía del libro, 1935–1942. Buenos Aires. Ed. Papel, libro, revista. 373, lxviii p. [35
"The purpose of this work is to place in reach of all persons and institutions concerned with books, a general selected catalog in which appear almost all books in Spanish of all publishers issued from the year 1935 to 1942." Arrangement is by subject and a section on textbooks is included. Prices are given in some cases, and there is an author index.

Herrera, Moisés. Contribución para una bibliografía de obras referentes al estado de Puebla? 112 p. [36
According to the compiler, a "simple contribution" toward the bibliography of Puebla, hitherto not attempted. The largest section, "General Works," lists almanacs, calendars and guide books. There are short sections on Philosophy, Religion and Social Science. A supplement lists official publications of the church and the state. Name and subject indexes are included. A large proportion of the entries are of religious works.

Iguíniz, Juan B. Disquisiciones bibliográficas. Autores, libros, bibliotecas, artes gráficas. México. El Colegio de México, ed. 310 p. [38
A volume of bibliographical memorabilia of particular interest. Part I, "Autores,"

contains fifteen bio-bibliographical sketches, beginning with the 16th century Jesuit theologian, Padre Jerónimo de Ripalda, and ending with Genaro Estrada. Part II, "Libros y periódicos," is composed of commentaries on important Mexican publications over a period of centuries. Part II, "Bibliotecas," is a series of sketches of outstanding libraries of Mexico. Part IV, "Artes gráficas," contains historical accounts of printing in Mexico and in Guadalajara during the colonial period.

Índice de los artículos publicados en la *Revista de la Universidad de Buenos Aires,* primera época: 1904–1923 *(Rev. univ. Buenos Aires,* tercera época, año 1, no. 1, julio–sept., p. 117–126). [39

A guide to works of a number of important writers not obtainable elsewhere, among them being: Carlos O. Bunge, José L. Alberdi, José Ingenieros, Alejandro Korn, Ricardo Rojas, Emilio Ravignani, Ernesto Quesada. The titles are arranged under subject heads: Educación, Cuestiones universitarias, Filosofía, Letras, Artes, Antropología, etc.

Informativo bibliográfico. Universidad nacional del Litoral. Facultad de ciencias económicas, comerciales y políticas. Biblioteca "Estanislao S. Zeballos." Rosario. Año 12, no. 43, oct./dic., 1942 [i.e., 1943]—año 13, no. 46, agosto/oct. [40

Contains, in addition to titles in the fields indicated, sections on law, mathematics, history and geography, philosophy and religion, education, literature and others. Analysis of contents is given for some of the more important titles.

James, Florence. Recent articles of bibliographical interest *(Int. amer. bibliog. rev.,* vol. 3, no. 1, spring, p. 9–11; no. 2, summer, p. 74–77). [41

Continuation of item no. 37, *Handbook, no. 8, 1942.*

Jones, C. K., John Englekirk, and **Madaline W. Nichols.** Latin Americana. Selected reading on the good neighbors *(Sat. rev. lit.,* vol. 26, no. 15, April 10, p. 24–25). [42

A list of key works from and about Latin America, in English or in English translation. The authors range in point of time from Peter Martyr to Ciro Alegría. Would be extremely useful as the basis for selecting a general library of Latin Americana.

Kiddle, Lawrence B. Bibliografía adicional para la obra de la señorita Nichols *(Rev. iberoamer.,* vol. 7, no. 13, nov., p. 221–240). [43

An analytical and critical review of the work followed by 141 additional items presented by way of supplement to the original, *A Bibliographical Guide to Materials on American Spanish* (see *Handbook, no. 7, 1941,* item 4467). It may be noted that, as the bibliography is a selective one, the inclusion of some of the additional items suggested might be questioned.

Kinnaird, Lucia Burk, and **Madaline W. Nichols.** Bibliography of articles in political science from *Nosotros,* of Buenos Aires, volumes 1–76 (concluded) *(Int. amer. bibliog. rev.,* vol. 3, no. 1, spring, bibliog. supplement, p. 55–63). [44

Conclusion, comprising items 400–468, of this annotated list which makes available a useful body of material on the subject indicated by the title.

Kraft, Guillermo. Cumplió 38 años de fundada la Sección artes gráficas de la Unión industrial argentina *(Biblos,* año 1, no. 6, enero–marzo, p. 7–8). [45

An address delivered on the occasion of the celebration of the thirty-eighth anniversary of the founding of the organization, praising its past accomplishments and its position of prestige in the field of book making and bibliography in general.

Ledesma Medina, Luis A. Adición a la biobibliografía de Andrés A. Figueroa. Buenos Aires. 61 p. [45a

Separate from *Bol. inst. invest. hist.,* tomo 26, no. 89–92, julio, 1941–junio, 1942.

Lelevier, Armando I. Historia del periodismo y la imprenta en el territorio norte de la Baja California. México. Tall. gráf. de la Nación. 29 p. [46

The first *Periódico Oficial* of the territory appeared in 1873 in Real del Castillo, where the first press was established. There are historical sketches of printing in the territory as a whole and also in Tijuana and Mexicali. A list of periodicals which have appeared in the territory, with dates and place of publication, is at the end.

Lewis, Beatrice Fleischman. Recent U. S. government publications dealing with Latin America *(Int. amer. bibliog. rev.,* vol. 3, no. 1, spring, p. 11–17; no. 2, summer, p. 77–84; no. 3, fall, p. 145–153; no. 4, winter, p. 206–210). [47

Continuation of item no. 33, *Handbook, no. 8, 1942.*

Library of international relations, Chicago. Titles chosen as representative of the collection on Central and South America. Chicago. 1943? 35 p., illus. [49

An annotated list of the Library's collection of pamphlets, magazines, newspapers and maps, as well as books in the field. Arranged topically and by country. The collection is devoted primarily to social, economic and political aspects of current international affairs.

Libros editados en México de julio a diciembre de 1943 *(Cult. México,* año 2, no. 2, julio–dic., p. 105–119). [50

Arranged in ten sections under subjects: Obras generales; Filosofía; Religión; Ciencias sociales; Filología; Ciencias aplicadas; Bellas artes; Literatura; Historia, geografía, biografía. There are occasional annotations.

A LIST OF MEXICAN ARTICLES APPEARING IN *Inter-America,* 1917-1926 (*Mexicana rev.,* vol. 3, no. 2, summer, p. 6-8). [52
Founded in 1917 by the Carnegie Endowment for International Peace, and published monthly alternately in Spanish and in English, the purpose of *Inter-America* was "to contribute to the establishment of a community of ideas between all the peoples of America; . . . it is . . . made up of articles translated from the periodical literature of the American countries." The present bibliography lists all articles on Mexican topics which appeared up to the time that *Inter-America* ceased publication in 1926. Over half are concerned with literature; the rest deal with varied cultural and political topics.

M. P. de A. [Mireya Priego de A.?]. Índice de las obras que tratan sobre el henequén, existentes en la Biblioteca "Crescencio Carrillo y Ancona" (*Bol. bibl. yucateca,* no. 18, julio-sept., p. 2-24). [53
A valuable compilation for the study of the industry. Arrangement of the titles is chronological, from the *Reglamento de la Compañia para el Cultivo y Beneficio del Jenequén,* of 1830, to theses presented at the University of Yucatán in 1940. There are notes on the contents of the more important titles.

Macedo, Roberto. Apuntamentos para uma bibliografia carioca. Rio de Janeiro. Ed. do Centro carioca. 112 p. [53a

Manrique de Lara, Juana, and **Guadalupe Monroy** (comps.). Seudónimos, anagramas, iniciales, etc. de autores mexicanos y extranjeros. México. Tall. gráf. de la Sría. de educ. públ. 78 p. [54
Several hundred names and the corresponding pseudonyms, anagrams, initials, etc. are listed for Mexican and foreign authors.

México. Departamento agrario. Publicaciones del Departamento. México (Bibl. de la Feria del libro y exposición nacional del periodismo, 1943). 8 p. [55

————. **Departamento de salubridad pública.** Bibliografía que el Departamento de salubridad pública presenta en la Feria del libro y exposición nacional del periodismo. Dirección general de educación higiénica. México. Tall. gráf. de la nación. 63 p. [56
Includes also the publications of the former Consejo Superior de Salubridad. [J. B. Childs]

————. **Secretaría de comunicaciones y obras públicas.** Bibliografía, 1941-1943. México. Tip. La nacional. 189 p., ilus. [57
One of the useful series of bibliographies of official publications compiled on the occasion of the Feria del Libro y Exposición Nacional del Periodismo. The bibliography is preceded by a directory of the personnel of the Secretaría, and is divided into seventeen parts, one for each of its administrative sections, whose functions are outlined in a preliminary note. The 444 entries are an admittedly incomplete representation of the publications of the Secretaría since its establishment in 1891. There is an author index.

————. **Secretaría de hacienda y crédito público.** Bibliografía, 1821-1942. México. 226 p. [58
One of the series prepared for the Feria Nacional del Libro. The bibliography is in two parts: I. Publicaciones hechas por la Secretaría de Hacienda o con su Autorización, in which the items are listed cronológicamente, beginning in 1821, for each of the functional divisions of the Secretaría. II. Publicaciones Relativas a los Asuntos Encomendados a la Secretaría de Hacienda y Crédito Público, Hechas por Otros Órganos del Gobierno y por Particulares. The listing is by author. In some instances indication is given of the libraries in which the titles are to be found.

————. **Secretaría de la defensa nacional.** Algunas fichas para una bibliografía general de la Secretaría de la defensa nacional, recopiladas por el cor. de inf. ret. Silvino M. González. México, D. F. Tall. lino-tip. Nigromante de González, Martínez y cía. (Bibl. de la Feria del libro y exposición nacional del periodismo). 206 p. [59
Before Nov. 1, 1937, Defensa Nacional was known as Guerra y Marina. [J. B. Childs]

————. **Secretaría de la economía nacional.** Publicaciones oficiales, Secretaría de la economía nacional, 1933-1942. México. Tall. gráf. de la nación. 75 p. [60
Excludes periodical publications which are to be described in a separate publication. The Secretaría succeeded the Secretaría de Industria, Comercio y Trabajo in 1933. [J. B. Childs]

————. **Secretaría del trabajo y previsión social. Departamento de informaciones sociales y estadística. Biblioteca.** Feria del libro y exposición nacional del periodismo, 1943. México. Tall. gráf. de la nación. 32 p., ilus. [61
Descriptive bibliography of the publications of the Secretaría, including pamphlets, books, periodicals, etc. There is an analysis of the Ley de Seguro Social of December 31, 1941. Illustrated with photographs of safety posters.

————. **Servicio de bibliotecas.** Exposición retrospectiva del libro mexicano. México, D. F. Bibl. de la Segunda feria del libro y exposición nac. del periodismo. 15 p., ilus. [62
A description of the historical exhibition of bookmaking in Mexico from 1539 to 1870. Included are a description of the plan and contents of the pavilion, chrono-

logical list of works exhibited, pictures of leading Mexican bibliophiles, title pages of rare works, posters, etc. Also lists of the leading printers and authors of each century.

Millares Carlo, Agustín. Algunos documentos sobre tipógrafos mexicanos del siglo 16 (*Fil. letras,* tomo 5, no. 12, oct.-dic., p. 303–324). [63

Notes on a collection of sixty-seven documents from Spanish and Mexican archives, including the Archivo de Notarías del Distrito Federal and the Archivo del Sagrario de la Catedral de México. They deal with four Mexican printers of the sixteenth century: Juan Pablos (1539–1560); Antonio de Espinosa (1559–1576); Pedro Ocharte 1563–1592) and Pedro Balli (1574–1600). A brief indication is given of the contents of the more important documents, and fourteen are reproduced in whole or in part in the appendix. An interesting body of material on the early history of printing in Mexico.

———. Las obras de carácter bibliográfico publicadas con ocasión de la Segunda feria del libro y exposición nacional del periodismo (*Fil. letras,* tomo 5, no. 12, oct.-dec., p. 362–370). [64

Bibliographies and studies prepared on this occasion deal primarily with books, printing, and periodicals, usually on a regional basis with the collaboration of the various states. Also included are bibliographies of official publications of various agencies of the federal government. There are thirty-six entries in the present list, with a brief note on the contents of each.

———, and **José Ignacio Mantecón.** Ensayo de una bibliografía de bibliografías mexicanas. La imprenta, el libro, las bibliotecas, etc. México. (Departamento del Distrito federal, Dirección de acción social, Oficina de bibliotecas). xvi, 224 p. [65

The purpose of this compilation is to "complete and bring up to date the works of Cecil K. Jones, Nicolás León and Juan B. Iguíniz, which constitute the antecedents of the present essay." There are two main divisions: General bibliographies of America referring to Mexico, and Bibliographies of Mexico. Within these divisions are sections on special topics, printing, periodicals, book catalogs, etc. There are 1740 items listed, with bibliographical information, and comments for the more important titles. A helpful guide to Mexican bibliography.

Moliner, Israel M. Índice bio-bibliográfico de Bonifacio Byrne. Matanzas. Imp. Carreño. 11 p. [66

A list of the author's poems, prose writings, and unpublished works, as well as writings about him.

New England institute of inter-American affairs. An informal list of books on Latin America for the general reader and a directory of Latin American collections in New England libraries. Boston. Silver Burdett & co. 16 p. [67

A briefly annotated list of books, chiefly of recent date, arranged by subject and followed by selected works for each country. There are also notes on research materials on Latin America to be found in more than twenty University and other libraries in New England.

NOTICIAS BIBLIOGRÁFICAS (*Bol. inst. invest. hist.,* año 21, tomo 27, no. 93–96, julio, 1942—junio, 1943, p. 367–938). [68

This extensive bibliographical survey of the field of history in general includes (1) Books, (2) Periodicals, (3) Newspaper articles, (4) Pamphlets and minor works. Each section is arranged by country of publication. Bibliographical information is followed by a listing of the table of contents in the case of books, and of articles in the case of periodicals and newspapers. The latter feature is particularly useful.

Pan American union. Columbus memorial library. The Pan American book shelf. Washington, D. C. Vol. 6, no. 1, Jan.—no. 12, Dec. [70

Continuation of the monthly listing of books and pamphlets received in the Columbus Memorial Library. The titles are arranged under twenty or more subject headings with full bibliographical information and in some cases analyses of contents or notes on authors. There is an author and country index.

Partido de la revolución mexicana. Selección bibliográfica revolucionaria. México, D. F. Imp. S. Turanzas del Valle. 46 p. [71

Contains a selection of 155 titles from the *Bibliografía de la Revolución Mexicana,* by Roberto Ramos, and an appended list of works on the Partido Nacional Revolucionario and its successor, the Partido de la Revolución Mexicana. The compilation was made to accompany an exhibition of works on the Revolution at the Feria del Libro.

Peixoto, Sílvio. Roteiro bibliográfico da República (*Cultura política,* ano 3, no. 33, out., p. 245–260; no. 34, nov., p. 264–273). [72

"An investigation of all the books published about the history of the Republic, from its inception at the end of the second reign, to the present time." To be published in instalments. There is a descriptive comment, often of some length, for each title. There seems to be no systematic arrangement, either chronological or by author or title.

Peraza Sarausa, Fermín. Anuario bibliográfico cubano, 1942. Habana. 184 p. [73

The present number completes the sixth year of publication. Cuban books and pamphlets of 1942 are listed by author and under seventeen subject heads. There are in addition supplementary lists for 1937–1941, and sections on lectures, periodicals and newspapers founded in 1942, new libraries, and a Bibliografía Martiana. There is also a general author index.

———. Bibliografía martiana (1941). Habana. Ed. Molina y cía. (Bibl. municipal de la Habana, Serie C, Guías bibliográficas no. 7). 40 p. [74
Books and articles relative to Martí appearing in the year 1941. Included are vols. 29–38 of the *Obras Completas de Martí*, issued by Editorial Trópico, and devoted to his *Escenas Norteamericanas*.

———. Ignacio Agramonte y Loynaz. Habana. Municipio de La Habana, Depto. de cult. (Publ. de la Bibl. municipal de La Habana, Serie C, Guías bibliográficas 6). 7 p. [75
A list of "books and pamphlets for the study of the life and work" of the Cuban patriot, found in Havana libraries. Two works are by Agramonte; the rest are about him. The bibliography is preceded by a biographical sketch.

———. Segundo congreso nacional y panamericano de prensa. Exhibición de la prensa cubana contemporánea. Catálogo. Habana. Imp. Alfa. 45 p. [76
A list of periodical publications appearing currently throughout the Republic, arranged by province and by city. Founding date, director's name, address and frequency are given. The exhibition was arranged by the Hemeroteca Pública Americana "Colón."

Pérez Galaz, Juan de Dios. Reseña histórica del periodismo en Campeche. Campeche. Tall. linotip. del Gobierno del estado. 45 p. [77
Preceded by a historical sketch of journalism in Campeche, from its beginning in about 1823. There follows a list of periodicals that have appeared in the state, with dates and a full description of the successive official periodicals. The present *Periódico Oficial* began in 1883.

Pérez Martínez, Héctor, and Juan de Dios Pérez Galaz. Bibliografía del estado de Campeche. Campeche. 377 p. [78
A catalog of imprints from Campeche, or concerning it, dating from the time of the introduction of printing there in 1815. The bibliography is preceded by a sketch of the history of printing in the state and a note on libraries and publications consulted. There is an appended list of periodicals and official publications issued in the city of Campeche, 1823–1943. One of the state bibliographies prepared for the Segunda Feria del Libro.

PUBLICACIONES GUATEMALTECAS . . . ENVIADAS POR LA TIPOGRAFÍA NACIONAL DE GUATEMALA (*Bol. mus. bibl.*, Guatemala, segunda época, año 2, no. 4, enero, p. 123–128; año 3, no. 3, oct., p. 106–111). [79
The first part lists works received under the national copyright law from June 16 to December 15, 1942. In two sections: 1.

Books, listed without order, giving author's name, title, place and date of publication. Official publications are included. 2. Newspapers and periodicals; particularly useful as a source of information on this type of material.
Part 2, covering publications received from December 16, 1942 to September 30, 1943, is confined to books, and gives size as well as author, title, and date and place of publication.

RASGOS BIOGRÁFICOS DE MONSEÑOR N. E. NAVARRO. RESUMEN DE SUS LABORES. Caracas. Ed. Venezuela. 23 p. [80
Over eighty works are included in the list, for the most part on religious subjects. The section "Historia" contains titles on political as well as ecclesiastical history. A biographical sketch precedes the bibliography.

Rasmussen, Wayne. Recent articles relating to inter-American affairs in periodicals published in English (*Int. amer. bibliog. rev.*, vol. 3, no. 1, spring, p. 26–46; no. 2, summer, p. 91–110; no. 3, fall, p. 163–182; no. 4, winter, p. 218–226). [81
Continuation of item 79, *Handbook, no. 8, 1942*.

REGISTRO BIBLIOGRÁFICO DAS OBRAS ENTRADAS NA BIBLIOTECA PÚBLICA MUNICIPAL DE SÃO PAULO DE 1 DE JUNHO A 31 DE OUTUBRO DE 1943 (*Bol. bibliog.*, São Paulo, ano 1, vol. 1, out.–dez., p. 121–177). [82
The titles, with full bibliographical information, are arranged by subject according to the decimal classification system.

Reis, António Simões dos. Bibliografia brasileira (*Cultura política*, ano 3, no. 24, feb., p. 77–94; no. 25, março, p. 202–210; no. 26, abril, p. 184–190). [83
"Movimento bibliográfico" is recorded by months, the titles being arranged according to subject. Both books and magazine articles are included, as well as translations from other languages. In the issue for February is a section, "Bibliografía sôbre o Estado Nacional e o Pensamento do Presidente." There are no annotations. See also item 6.

———. Bibliografia nacional, 1942. Vols. 6–8. Rio de Janeiro. Ed. Zélio Valverde. 3 vols. [84
Continuation of the series initiated in 1942, in which year five installments appeared. (See *Handbook, no. 8, 1942*, item 83). Includes, through vol. 8, 2222 titles of Brazilian publications, with bibliographical data and occasional biographical notes on the authors. The material is arranged under more than thirty subject headings and there is an author index.

———. Bibliografia nacional, 1943. Vol. 1. Rio de Janeiro. Ed. Zélio Valverde. 92 p. [85
Continuation of the above, with 490 additional titles arranged according to the same bibliographical scheme.

Rohen y Gálvez, Gustavo-Adolfo. Latin American periodicals dealing with labor and social welfare (*Handbook of latin american studies*, no. 8, 1942, p. 449–479). [86

The bibliography lists 120 current Latin American periodicals dealing with these subjects, received in various Washington libraries. Arrangement is by country, and there are extensive bibliographical, descriptive and critical notes.

Romero Flores, Jesús. La imprenta en Michoacán. México. 134 p. [87

The bibliographical contribution of the state of Michoacán to the Segunda Feria del Libro. The first part is an historical account of printing, cultural centers, and outstanding writers of the state, and gives a bibliography of works printed there during the colonial and revolutionary periods, including official and unofficial journals. The second part is a general bibliography of works printed in the state since 1821, arranged by year and by author. There are 571 items in this section.

Saldívar, Gabriel. Bibliografía de la Secretaría de relaciones exteriores. México. Tall. gráf. de la nación. (Bibl. de la Feria del libro y exposición nacional del periodismo, 1943, Series bibliográficas mexicanas, no. 2). 96 p. [88

Covers from 1821 to date. [J. B. Childs]

Sánchez, Luis-Alberto, and Alfredo M. Saco. Aprista bibliography (*Hisp. amer. hist. rev.*, vol. 23, no. 3, Aug., p. 555–585). [89

A timely bibliography on this significant political movement. The compilers explain that only books and pamphlets are included, periodical and newspaper material being reserved for separate treatment. Divided as follows: I. González Prada, the Precursor. II. Formative period. III. Political struggle. IV. Non-Aprista books which take up Aprismo. V. Books of Aprista authors. VI. Anti-Aprista publications. Leading works of González Prada, Haya de la Torre, and Luis-Alberto Sánchez appear, as well as official publications of the Aprista party.

Schwab, Federico. Libros y folletos peruanos publicados en 1942 (*Bol. bibliog.*, Lima, año 16, vol. 13, no. 1–2, julio, p. 110–154). [90

Bibliographical data and in most cases comments on 291 titles published in Peru in 1942. The list is arranged under some forty subject headings and is followed by an author index.

———. Los *Textos millcayac* del P. Luis de Valdivia y la antigua Biblioteca de los jesuítas del Cuzco (*Bol. bibliog.*, Lima, año 16, vol. 13, no. 3–4, dic., p. 268–277). [91

Discovery of the *Textos Millcayac* of Padre Luis de Valdivia settles the controversy as to time and place of publication of these works on the Indian languages of the Province of Cuyo. The imprint is Lima, 1609. The *Revista del Museo de la Plata*, nueva serie, tomo 2, p. 61–223, contains a reproduction of the original with commentaries upon it. The rest of the article is devoted to a description of the "Biblioteca de los Jesuítas," now a part of the library of the University of Cuzco. A printed inventory lists some 4500 works on theology, law, history, and other topics.

Soto Paz, Rafael. Antología de periodistas cubanos. 35 biografías, 35 artículos. Habana. Ed. de publ. 256 p., ilus. [92

An historical statement on the Cuban press, followed by biographical sketches and examples of the writings of 35 persons chosen as representatives of Cuban journalism. An interesting survey of the subject from 1764 to the present.

STRATEGIC INDEX OF THE AMERICAS. TENTATIVE LIST OF REFERENCES ON VENEZUELA. Washington? Coordinator of inter-American affairs. 11 p. [93

A mimeographed list to be submitted to specialists for correction and comment, in order to compile a definitive list of sources. References are grouped regionally, for six regional subdivisions of the country. The list includes 113 titles, concerned largely with economics and geography.

Torre Revello, José. Biobibliografía de Félix F. Outes (*Bol. inst. invest. hist.*, año 21, tomo 27, no. 93–96, julio, 1942—junio, 1943, p. 939–1063). [94

Preceded by a biographical sketch of his distinguished career in anthropology and allied disciplines, the works of the author, to the number of 293 titles, are listed in sections: books, addresses, works edited, monographs, in the fields of anthropology, geology, ethnology, archaeology, prehistory, etc. The more important titles have comments of some length.

———. Contribución a la biobibliografía de Emilio A. Coni (*Bol. inst. invest. hist.*, año 21, tomo 27, no. 93–96, julio, 1942—junio, 1943, p. 1063–1090). [95

A brief account of the writer's attainments as an agronomist, historian and economist precedes the bibliography of his works, numbering 48 titles, in these and other fields. Descriptive comments are included.

Tumba Ortega, Alejandro. Revistas peruanas publicadas en el segundo semestre de 1942 y en el año 1943 (*Bol. bibliog.*, Lima, año 16, vol. 13, no. 3–4, dic., p. 278–308). [96

Current installments of a valuable annual guide to Peruvian periodicals, containing 208 items arranged by subject. "Esta Biblioteca recibe casi todas las revistas publicadas en el Perú, de modo que la presente recopilación puede considerarse completa."

Ugarteche, Félix de. Pequeña historia de la imprenta en América. Buenos Aires. Imp. López. 35 p. [97

Brief accounts of the establishment of the first presses in various countries of

Spanish America, and of early books issued by them.

U. S. Library of Congress. Division of bibliography. Puerto Rico. A selected list of recent references. Washington, D. C. 44 p. [97a

"Primarily a supplement to the . . . list of 1939 which is now obtainable only from Public Affairs Information Service in New York City." Includes 381 items divided as follows: Bibliographies; General, description and travel; Economic and social conditions; Education; Industry, resources and commerce; Politics and government; Defenses. An author index, with occasional subject entries, is appended.

Urioste, Antero. Algunas papeletas bibliográficas de Rocha. Montevideo. Imp. L. I. G. U. 35 p. [98

An annotated list of historical, descriptive and other works relative to the Department of Rocha, selected from materials assembled for a more complete bibliography to be published in the future.

Valle, Rafael Heliodoro. Documentos de la sociología en Hispano-América (*Rev. mex. soc.*, año 5, vol. 5, no. 1, primer trimestre, p. 133–150; no. 2, segundo trimestre, p. 277–293; no. 4, cuarto trimestre, p. 569–580). [99

Chiefly works by Hispanic American authors. The usual bibliographical information, descriptive notes or lists of chapter headings, and notes on many of the authors are included. The number and variety of works listed indicates the activity of scholars in this field throughout Hispanic America.

Vargas Ugarte, Rubén. Bibliografía de santos y venerables peruanos (*Bol. bibliog.*, Lima, año 16, vol. 13, no. 3–4, dic., p. 253–267). [100

Thirty-nine works on Peruvian hagiography, published in other countries and not hitherto listed in any bibliography on the subject. The list is chronological, beginning with the *Vida y Martirio del Glorioso Padre Fray Diego Ruiz Ortiz* . . . of Nicolás Suárez (Madrid, 1569) and including a number of titles relating to St. Rose of Lima. Works on the topic published in Peru are reserved for a later bibliography.

Velasco Ceballos, Rómulo. Fichas bibliográficas sobre asistencia pública en México. México. 86 p. [101

"Contribución de la Secretaría de Asistencia Pública a la Segunda Feria del Libro y Exposición Nacional del Periodismo, 1943."
Covers not only the Secretaría which dated from 1937, but earlier agencies. [J. B. Childs]

Wilgus, Alva Curtis. Recent publications in the United States dealing with Latin American affairs and related fields (*Int. amer. bibliog. rev.*, vol. 3, no. 1, spring, p. 18–26; no. 2, summer, p. 84–91; no. 3, fall, p. 154–162; no. 4, winter, p. 211–217). [102

Continuation of item no. 101, *Handbook, no. 8, 1942*.

Wilson, Charles Morrow. Books about Middle America. A selected bibliography. New York. The Middle American information bureau conducted by the United fruit co. 1943? 23 p. [103

Composed of "standard publication in English," chiefly, but not wholly, of recent date. Arranged by country, with descriptive annotations.

ADDENDA

Peraza y Sarausa, Fermín. Antonio Bachiller y Morales. Habana. Municipio de la Habana, Depto. de cult. (Publ. de la. Bibl. municipal de La Habana, Serie C, Guías bibliográficas 5). 1942. [104

Preceded by a biographical sketch, the works of the "father of Cuban bibliography" are listed as found in four libraries of Havana: the Biblioteca Municipal, The Biblioteca Nacional, the Biblioteca de la Sociedad Económica de Amigos del País, and the Biblioteca de la Universidad de la Habana. Works about the writer are included also.

GENERAL WORKS

(*See also items* 992, 2534, 3849)

Alayza y Paz Soldán, Luis. Mi país. Lecturas peruanas. Segunda serie. Lima. Imp. Publicidad americana. 470 p., mapa. [105
Continuation of the author's earlier volume of the same title. Upon a geographical framework are hung many observations about things Peruvian. [G. M. McBride]

Allen, Devere. The Caribbean, laboratory of world cooperation. New York. League for industrial democracy. 40 p. [106
A review of the problems facing the Anglo-American Caribbean Commission, in Puerto Rico and the British West Indies. [B. Wood]

Amunátegui R., Miguel Luis. La Real academia española i sus relaciones con sus hijas de América. Santiago, Chile. Dirección general de prisiones. 154 p. [107

Argentina. Ministerio de relaciones exteriores y culto. Guía de "Informaciones argentinas." Buenos Aires. 39 p. [108
A brief official directory, accompanied by lists of newspapers, magazines and radio stations. [J. B. Childs]

Ávila, Federico. Tierra y alma boliviana. Segunda ed. Asunción. Ed. La Colmena. 278 p. [109
A sociological and historical study, but built upon a geographical frame work, of inter-Andean plateaus, mountain valleys, and forested plains. [G. M. McBride]

Azevedo, Fernando de. A cultura brasileira. Recenseamento geral do Brasil. 1940. Vol. 1: Introdução, tomo 1. Rio de Janeiro. 535 p. [109a
A large and authoritative review of the elements of the Brazilian civilization. The land and race; an outline of economic history; settlement, and the growth of cities; social and political evolution; the psychology of the Brazilian people; and chapters on the various aspects of Brazilian life—religion, intellectual life, literature, science, art and education. [P. E. James]

Basadre, Jorge. ¿Han existido históricamente influencias de origen americano en la cultura occidental? (*Proc. eighth amer. scien. cong.*, vol. 9, p. 247–250). [110
An introduction to the Hispanic American influences upon European culture. In particular the author concludes that "much can be said regarding the connections between the utopian dreams and the American soil." Numerous European writers are mentioned who utilized the American theme. The influences declined during the National period. [Roscoe R. Hill]

Beals, Carleton. Dawn over the Amazon. New York. Duell, Sloan & Pearce, publ. 536 p. [111
A romantic and unreal novel about the resistance by South American patriots of the left to a hypothetical attack by Japan and Germany on Chile and Brazil. [B. Wood]

———. Río Grande to Cape Horn. Boston. Houghton Mifflin co. vi, 377 p., maps. [112
Popular résumé of Latin America today. Interpretation of backgrounds, glimpses of personalities, notes on travel, and attempts at prophecy. The author's point of view is of course well known from his many books on Latin America. This volume is no exception to his sympathetic treatment of Latin American problems. [A. Marchant]

BOLETÍN DEL INSTITUTO DE SOCIOLOGÍA. Universidad de Buenos Aires. Facultad de filosofía y letras. Buenos Aires. No. 2, 1943—. [113
This periodical publishes articles on methodology, theory and applied sociology. Permanent sections include note on sociologists in the Americas, reports on studies prepared in the Instituto de Sociología, book reviews, and news on the activities of sociological centers abroad. [Ed.]

BOLETÍN DEL SEMINARIO DE CULTURA MEXICANA. Secretaría de educación pública. México, D. F. Tomo 1, no. 1, julio. [114
"En el instante excepcional que vivimos, tres datos destacan, impresionantes, en el panorama de México: Contamos con grupos selectos de sabios, filósofos y artistas que colocan a nuestro país, culturalmente, en un plano envidiable; Frente a esos grupos dispersos un pueblo heróico sufre sed de conocimientos, lucha por lograr su auténtica expresión y hallar el sentido de su existencia; Es preciso crear formas que permitan organizar los esfuerzos de esas valiosas minorías y trazar, con urgencia, caminos de contacto entre ellas y nuestras grandes masas incultas."
Main fields of interest are: history, literature, philosophy and art in all its forms.

Brenner, Anita. The wind that swept Mexico. The history of the Mexican revolution, 1910–1942. New York, London. Harper bros. 302 p., illus. [115
Anita Brenner has written a hundred page sketch of the Mexican Revolution (1910–1942) to accompany a chronologically arranged series of 184 photographs illustrating the Revolution. The latter assembled by George R. Leighton, are largely news shots of scenes and participants in the

Revolution, and form an unusually interesting "photo-history" of the period. The captions, largely taken from the text, are frequently unfortunate in their employment of sarcasm and a heavy sort of humor. The book provides a valuable graphic addition to anyone's "book-larnin'" about the only American social revolution. [B. Wood]

Burden, W. A. M. The struggle for airways in Latin America. New York. Council on foreign relations. 245 p. [116

The story of the growth and rivalry of commercial airlines in Latin America from 1920 to the early period of World War II. A discussion of future possibilities. An authoritative work, beautifully printed and illustrated. [P. E. James]

Carneiro Leão, A. El sentido de la sociología en las Américas (*Rev. mex. soc.*, año 5, vol. 5, no. 1, primer trim., p. 27–37). [117

No area in the world is more propitious to the development of sociology than the Western Hemisphere.

Chile. Biblioteca nacional. Chile. Santiago. Imp. Universo. 86 p. [118

General description. [G. M. McBride]

Comisión cubana de cooperación intelectual. América ante la crisis mundial. Habana. Ed. Ucar, García. 301 p. [119

Papers presented to a *plática* in Habana in November 1941, with transcription of the discussions. [A Marchant]

Coney, Donald. The materials of intellectual interchange (*Int. amer. intel. interchange*, p. 19–26). [120

A sketch of the materials—"the institutions, the channels, and the machinery for transferring books from one country to another, for bringing them to the attention of the proper persons, for making them best available to the largest number of users."

CONFERENCE ON LATIN AMERICA IN SOCIAL AND ECONOMIC TRANSITION, ALBUQUERQUE, NEW MEXICO, 1943. PROCEEDINGS. Albuquerque. Univ. of New Mexico press. (New Mexico univ., School of inter-American affairs, Inter-Americana series, Short papers, 5). 104 p. [121

Papers presented at the conference are grouped under the following three headings: "The Common People Claim their Share" (3 contributions by Richard F. Behrendt, Michel Pijoan and Donald P. Brand); "Latin America's Changing Role in World Affairs" (3 papers by Richard F. Behrendt, Donald P. Brand and Stuart Cuthbertson); "Individual Countries" (2 contributions by Erna Fergusson on Chile, and George I. Sánchez on Mexico). Important articles are reviewed elsewhere in this volume. [Ed.]

Costa, João Angyone. Paisagens do Chile. Rio de Janeiro. Inst. brasileiro-chileno de cultura. (Publ., no. 1). 114 p. [122

With the present work, this new series, designed to promote a Brazilian-Chilean cultural *rapprochement*, makes a propitious start. At once informative and entertaining, it is written in an easy-reading style. [S. Putnam]

CUATRO SIGLOS DE LA HISTORIA DE SANTIAGO. Santiago. Emp. Ziz-zag. 323 p., ilus. [123

A history of the growth and development of the capital of Chile, issued in commemoration of the four hundredth anniversary of the founding of the city. Profusely illustrated. [Ed.]

Díaz Doin, Guillermo. 236 biografías sintéticas, políticos y militares. Buenos Aires. Ed. Mundo atlántico. 235 p. [125

Encyclopedia americana. Latin America. New York, Chicago. Americana corporation. 126 p. [126

Reference data on Latin America compiled from the latest edition of the *Encyclopedia Americana*. Contains information on the history, natural resources, industries, ethnology and the political and cultural relations. It also has sections on art, music and literature as well as a brief "who's who." A convenient reference work. [Roscoe R. Hill]

Figueiredo, Lima. A conquista do Brasil pelos brasileiros. Rio de Janeiro. Conselho nac. de geografia. 150 p. [127

Lectures delivered in the Conselho Nacional de Geografia; analysis of the beginnings of the settlement in the country, the defense problems of the territory, the unsatisfactory spacial distribution of population and the necessity of internal colonization. [R. Simonsen]

First national and Pan American press congress, May, 1942. Records. Translated by Annelies Morgan and M. H. Austin. México. Dept. of the Federal District. 255 p., illus. [128

Fischlowitz, Estanislau. As migrações, problema internacional (*Rev. serv. públ.*, ano 6, vol. 4, no. 3, dez., p. 43–49). [129

Population mobility and international problems; its connection with the present conflict, the migration phenomena following the present war and the influence it will have upon future migration. [R. Simonsen]

Frank, Waldo. South American journey. New York. Duell, Sloan & Pearce, publ. xvii, 404 p., maps. [130

There is a good deal too much Waldo Frank and not enough South America in this travelogue of a public appearance tour. [B. Wood]

Franklin, Albert B. Ecuador. Garden City. Doubleday Doran, publ. 236 p., illus. [131

With its subtitle, "Portrait of a People," this is a readable account of the author's experiences and observations as he traveled about the country, into which is woven something of the nation's history, bits of its geography and some discussion of the problems faced by the Ecuadoreans. [G. M. McBride]

Gandía, Enrique de. Orígenes de la democracia en América, y otros estudios. Buenos Aires. Ed. Argentinas. (Col. Continente, 1). 318 p. [132
The title essay is only one of eighteen. The others are historical in character but on a wide variety of topics, from the "*sentido de argentinidad*" to a study of numismatics as an auxiliary science of history. [R. H. Fitzgibbon]

Garcés, V. Gabriel. Tiempo y espacio de la cultura (*Rev. mex. soc.,* año 5, vol. 5, no. 1, primer trim., p. 39–47). [133
On geographic-historic concepts in understanding Latin American cultural developments and the problem of synchronizing rapid-urban-plains-Hispanic and slow-rural-mountainous-Indian cultures. [R. S. Boggs]

Garrido Alfaro, Vincent. Síntesis histórica del *Boletín de la Sociedad mexicana de geografía y estadística* (*Proc. eighth amer. scien. cong.,* vol. 9, p. 315–320). [134
A brief statement of the ideals and objectives of the *Boletín,* with an indication of the numbers which appeared during the first century of its existence. [Roscoe R. Hill]

Gómez Haedo, Juan Carlos. El centenario del Instituto histórico y geográfico del Uruguay (*Rev. nac.,* Montevideo, año 6, tomo 23, no. 67, julio, p. 33–41). [135
An outline of the program and objectives of the original Institute with brief sketches regarding the founders and their contributions to historical and geographical studies. [Roscoe R. Hill]

Green, Philip L. Haiti's new horizons (*Agric. Americas,* vol. 3, no. 2, Feb., p. 34–36). [136
Describes the trend toward diversification of agricultural production and the efforts of the government of Haiti to improve the standard of living and sanitation in rural areas. [Ed.]

———. El Salvador. Beehive of activity (*Agric. Americas,* vol. 3, no. 1, Jan., p. 10–12). [137
A sympathetic account of economic, social and cultural achievements in recent years. [Ed.]

Gunther, John. L'Amérique latine. Trad. par Albert Pascal. Montréal. Ed. de l'Arbre. 549 p. [138
Translation into French of *Inside Latin America.* [A. Marchant]

Hanke, Lewis. Americanizing the Americas (*Mexican life,* vol. 19, no. 12, Dec., p. 35, 48–58). [139
A brief statement of the trends in the development of a Latin American culture, divorced largely from European influence. [Roscoe R. Hill]

Hanson, Earl Parker (ed.). The new world guides to the Latin American republics. Vol. 1: Mexico and Central America. Vol. 2: South America. New York. Duell, Sloan and Pearce, publ. (Office of the U. S. Coordinator of inter-American affairs). 2 vols., illus., maps. [140
The two volumes are divided into 20 chapters, one for each of the Latin American countries. Each chapter contains a brief survey of political history and a geographical description with maps, a section on art and architecture, informative notes of practical value to tourists and travellers, and a regional guide. Each volume contains in addition brief statements on the area as a whole dealing with the following topics: Latin America's cultural and historic foundations; Latin American art; Bibliographic notes; Maps; the Pan American Union; Principal Catholic holidays; Educational opportunities in Latin America; the Pan American highway; Mountaineering; and Weights and measures. [Ed.]

Hanson, Elliott S. Mexican trade trainees in United States "earn as they learn" (*For. com. weekly,* vol. 10, no. 5, 30 Jan., p. 10, 35, illus.). [141
Para ayudar a la industrialización de 17 países latinoamericanos y en especial de México, la Oficina del Coordinador de Asuntos Interamericanos de Washington, D. C., estableció un programa interamericano de becas técnicas cuyo funcionamiento se describe e ilustra aquí.
Resúmen español en *Bol. unión panamer.,* vol. 77, no. 8, agosto, p.442–446. [G. A. Rohen y Gálvez]

Herring, Hubert Clinton. México. La formación de una nación. México, D. F. Ed. Minerva. 106 p. [143
A concise review for popular consumption of Mexico's political and economic development. [Ed.]

Herron, Francis. Letters from the Argentine. New York. G. P. Putnam's sons, publ. 307 p. [144
By an associate of the Institute of Current World Affairs who made a sincere and in many ways successful effort to know Argentina. The letters are published as they were originally written to Walter S. Rogers, director of the Institute.
The topics discussed are for the most part confined to matters with which the author was in direct contact. In addition to the letters the volume contains notes and memoranda on the following topics: Social attitudes in Argentina; Conflicts between provincial and cosmopolitan attitudes; The role of the *estanciero;* Education in Argentina; Argentina's prudent neutrality. There is also a useful glossary of terms. [Ed.]

Horne, Bernardino C. El infraconsumo de productos alimenticios en América (*Rev. mex. soc.,* año 5, vol. 5, no. 3, tercer trim., p. 391–394). [145
Calls attention to the fact that a large proportion of the population of Latin

America is undernourished, although Latin America produces large surpluses of foodstuffs. [Ed.]

HUMANIDADES. Órgano de los alumnos de la Facultad de filosofía y letras. Universidad nacional autónoma de México. México, D. F. Tomo 1, no. 1, julio—. [146

Humphreys, R. A. Latin America and the post war world (*Agenda*, vol. 2, no. 1, Feb., p. 80–92). [147
A thoughtful statement of the problems that will confront Latin America after the war. The author streses the trend in Latin America toward industrialization and diversification of production and he points out that the war has demonstrated the need of inter-American cooperation, both economic and political. [Ed.]

Hernández de León, Federico. Viajes presidenciales. Breves relatos de algunas expediciones administrativas del general D. Jorge Ubico. Tomo 2. Guatemala. Imp. El Liberal progresista. v, 546 p., ilus. [148
These accounts afford an insight into local economic and administrative problems. The volume covers travels in 1941, 1942 and 1943. [Ed.]

IDEARIO COSTARRICENSE, RESULTADO DE UNA ENCUESTA NACIONAL. San José, C. R. Ed. Surco. (Publ. no. 2). 437 p. [149
In an effort to crystallize the economic and political problems facing the country, prominent Costa Ricans were asked to state their views. The replies which constitute the bulk of the volume provide a cross section of enlightened public opinion. [Ed.]

Inman, Samuel Guy. Backgrounds and problems in intellectual exchange (*Int. amer. intel. interchange*, p. 3–18). [150
A brief historical sketch of what has been done up to and including the State Department programs. The essence of the problem is how to improve our knowledge of each other. [A. Marchant]

INSTITUTO DE AMÉRICA. México, D. F. Año 1, tomo 1, no. 5, enero–no. 12, agosto; año 2, tomo 2, no. 1, sept.–no. 4, dic. [151
This periodical publishes brief articles and informative notes designed to foster inter-American understanding and cooperation. [Ed.]

INTER-AMERICAN CHRONOLOGY FOR 1942 (*Int. amer. affairs*, 1942, p. 211–238). [152
Arranged by month and day. Covers events in international relations as well as internal politics.

Kelsey, Vera, and Lilly de Jongh Osborne. Four keys to Guatemala. New York, London. Funk & Wagnalls co. 332 p. [154
An illustrated guide to the people and country of Guatemala. Special attention is given to the customs of the Indians. [B. Wood]

Leavitt, Sturgis E. Permanent values of intellectual interchange (*Int. amer. intel. interchange*, p. 27–32). [155
Although a good deal has been achieved in strengthening cultural relations between the United States and Latin America there is room for improvement. The author specifically mentions Latin American collections in University libraries, exchange of students and professors, summer sessions, and research. [Ed.]

Leonard, Irving A. A survey of the personnel and activities in Latin American aspects of the humanities and social sciences at twenty universities of the United States (*Notes latin amer. studies*, no. 1, April, p. 7–51). [156

LIBERTAD CREADORA. Revista trimestral. Publicada por los amigos de Alejandro Korn. Buenos Aires. Tomo 1, no. 1, enero/marzo—. [157
This well edited quarterly is devoted to the propagation of democratic ideals in politics as well as in the arts. The review promises to continue "un imperativo militante cumplido desde mucho tiempo atrás por los amigos de Alejandro Korn que trabajan, piensan y luchan confortados por su influencia filosófica." [Ed.]

Lombardo Toledano, V. La segunda vuelta de Martín Fierro. 25 mayo, 1810–1943. México. Univ. obrera de México. 31 p. [158
An address given by the CTAL president on the occasion of the Argentine anniversary of independence. It is the duty of organized workers, Lombardo says, to fight vigorously against the Axis and to oppose domestic reaction. [R. H. Fitzgibbon]

Mac-Lean y Estenós, Roberto. Discursos parlamentarios. Lima. Lib. Gil. 675 p. [159
Speeches given in the Chamber of Deputies in the years 1929–30 and 1939–42 on international affairs, foreign relations, education, national problems, administrative organization and industrialization. The author held numerous important positions, under Leguía and Benavides. [R. H. Fitzgibbon]

Normano, J. F., and Antonello Gerbi. The Japanese in South America. New York. Inst. of Pacific relations. x, 135 p. [160
A detailed and documented study of the Japanese in Brazil and Peru and of the reactions of the two governments and their people to the problems created by Japanese immigration. [B. Wood]

NOTES ON LATIN AMERICAN STUDIES. Joint committee on Latin American studies. Washington, D. C. No. 1, April—. [161
The first issue of a periodical publication of the Joint Committee on Latin American Studies. It contains a brief statement of the work of the Committee and notes re-

garding activities of institutions and individuals interested in the Latin American field of studies. The major portion of the first number is devoted to a survey of personnel and activities in Latin American aspects of the humanities and social sciences at twenty universities of the United States by Irving A. Leonard. [Roscoe R. Hill]

O'Brien, John A. Discovering Mexico. A country in transition. Huntington, Ind. Our Sunday visitor press. 151 p. [162

An illustrated book of travel and comment intended apparently for use in Catholic secondary schools. The author is critical of the Mexican anti-clerical legislation, but he notes that under the present administration, "the church in Mexico is enjoying a breathing spell of peace and liberty." He fears a return to power by Lázaro Cárdenas and his view of Mexico's future is indicated by the title of Chapter XVII; "Synarchism: the Hope of Mexico." [B. Wood]

OUTLINE OF RESEARCH IN THE STUDY OF CONTEMPORARY CULTURE PATTERNS IN LATIN AMERICA (*Notes latin amer. studies*, no. 2, Oct., p. 3–26). [163

The committee which devised the outline was careful to point out that the plan is neither definitive nor complete. It is intended merely to suggest the kind of broad problems that might be profitably investigated. Under each of the nine broad headings a number of specific topics is listed. [Ed.]

Padilla, Ezequiel. El hombre libre de América. Un augurio para la postguerra. México, D. F. Ed. Nuevo mundo. 288 p. [164

A resounding expression of faith in, and hope for, the cause of democracy, the solidarity of the American Republics, and the continuity of the good neighbor policy. The Mexican Foreign Minister ranges widely in time and subject in an eloquent and significant survey of the problems of the Americas.

Under the title *Free Men of America* a complete English translation of the Spanish edition was published by Ziff-Davis, Chicago, 1943, 173 p. [B. Wood]

Pan American union. Documentary material for the Good neighbor tour. An imaginary visit to the republics of Latin America. Vols. 1–10. Washington, D. C. 10 vols. [165

A course on Latin America for study clubs. Part of the material is in the form of travelogues, but there are also general articles on political and social subjects, as well as on art and folklore. The material appears well designed for introducing North Americans to Latin American affairs. The volumes are mimeographed, however, and there are no pictures. [B. Wood]

PAN-AMERICANA. THE SATURDAY REVIEW OF LITERATURE. A special issue. New York, N. Y. Vol. 26, no. 15, April 10, p. 1–43. [166

In addition to a considerable number of reviews of books dealing with Latin America, this issue carries special articles of unusual significance, such as "An American publisher tours South America," by Blanche Knopf; "The story of *Selecciones* and *Seleções*," by Norman Cousins; "The activities of the A.L.A. in Latin America," by Carl M. Milam and Marion A. Milczewski; and "Latin Americana, Selected reading on the Good Neighbors," unsigned. [S. E. Leavitt]

PRORSUS. Órgano del Instituto superior de pedagógica y letras de Guayaquil. Guayaquil. Año 1, no. 1, set.—. [167

Publishes papers in the various disciplines taught at the Instituto, and news about the Instituto. [Ed.]

Quintanilla, Luis. A Latin American speaks. New York. Macmillan co., publ. x, 268 p., tables. [168

A well-written, frank and important book, in which the former Mexican ambassador to the United States presents a Latin American viewpoint on many issues that North Americans usually fail to see in the round. [B. Wood]

RECOMENDACIONES INTERAMERICANAS SOBRE LA PLANIFICACIÓN DE LA POSTGUERRA (*Rev. int. trab.*, vol. 27, no. 2, feb., p. 241–244). [169

Cumpliendo con las resoluciones sobre problemas de la postguerra tomadas por la Tercera Reunión de los Ministros de Relaciones Exteriores de las Repúblicas Americanas (véase *Handbook, no. 8, 1942*, ítems 3571, 3578, 3579 y 3667), el Comité Jurídico Interamericano preparó, y el Consejo Directivo de la Unión Panamericana aprobó, recomendaciones sobre política económica (tendiente a la eliminación del "imperialismo y el nacionalismo económicos," explotación de los territorios poco desarrollados bajo la vigilancia de la comunidad internacional, coordinación de la economía mundial mediante una fórmula que combine la autodeterminación nacional con el interés primordial de toda la comunidad, disminución de las barreras aduanales y otras restricciones al comercio y "desarme económico" por medio de la eliminación de "la implacable concurrencia y rivalidad comercial") y sobre política social tendiente a eliminar los factores sociales de la guerra, (elevación del nivel de vida de la población obrera por medio de la acción nacional e internacional y desenvolvimiento de la Oficina Internacional del Trabajo).

Texto inglés en *Int. lab. rev.*, vol. 47, no. 2, Feb., p. 211–213. [G. A. Rohen y Gálvez]

Reissig, Luis. Una política cultural para toda América. Buenos Aires. Colegio libre de estudios superiores. 14 p. [170

From *Cursos y Conferencias*, año 12, vol. 33, no. 138, sept., 1943, p. 499–510. Also published in *Atenea*, año 20, tomo 73, no. 218, agosto, 1943, p. 122–141.

Suggests that problems confronting each nation be examined and solved collectively. Each country might establish a "School of National Studies" whose work should be closely related to problems of direct interest to the community. [Ed.]

REVISTA DE LA UNIVERSIDAD DEL CAUCA. Popayán. No. 1, enero/feb.—. [171
Publishes studies in various disciplines represented in the curriculum of the University. The more important contributions are listed separately under the appropriate heading. [Ed.]

REVISTA UNIVERSITARIA DE LA ASOCIACIÓN DE POST-GRADUADOS DE LA UNIVERSIDAD AUTÓNOMA DE GUADALAJARA. Guadalajara. Tomo 1, no. 1, feb./abril—. [172

Reyes, Alfonso. Posición de América (*Cuad. amer.*, año 2, vol. 8, no. 2, marzo-abril, p. 7–23). [173
The time has come for America to play its part in the development of cultural values, now that Europe cannot be expected to emerge from the war unscarred. [Ed.]

Rivet, Paul. Reflexiones sobre la América latina (*Cuad. amer.*, año 2, vol. 12, no. 6, nov.–dic., p. 129–137). [174
The distinguished ethnologist corrects certain misconceptions about Latin America among Europeans and North Americans. [Ed.]

THE ROLE OF BOOKS IN INTER-AMERICAN RELATIONS. New York. Book publ. bureau. The American textbook publishers inst. 108 p. [175
The report prepared at the request of the Department of State by representatives of the book industry in the United States deals with the following problems: the distribution of books in English published in the United States; the Latin American publishing industry and books of United States origin in Spanish or Portuguese translation; the distribution of works of Latin American origin in the United States; problems of particular classes of books; the general question of export techniques. [Ed.]

Sayán de Vidaurre, Alberto. Cómo resolver los problemas del nuevo mundo. Iniciativas y proyectos dedicados a la próxima conferencia interamericana. Estudio prologar por Ana Rosa S. de Martínez Guerrero. Buenos Aires. Tall. Gadola. 40 p. [177
The solution to the problem is to be found in greater democracy in each of the American Republics, and in close cooperation of all. Suggests among other things that the next Inter-American Conference recommend to the governments of the American Republics measures which would consolidate true democracy based upon law and justice. [Ed.]

Seoane, Manuel. The Japanese are still in Peru (*Asia and the Americas*, vol. 43, no. 12, Dec., p. 674–676). [179
An Aprista comments on the fact that, despite post-Pearl Harbor restrictions on the Japanese, many remain active in Peruvian commercial life as Peruvian citizens. Concludes that the Peruvian Japanese are now secure because the most anti-Japanese elements in Peru—the Apristas—are still outlawed or forced into exile. Translated by Lloyd Mallan. [A. Marchant]

Sievers Wicke, Hugo Konrad. Rutas patagónicas. Santiago. Ed. Orbe. [1943?] 251 p., tablas, mapa. [180
Travels by automobile from Santiago to Punta Arenas and north to Comodoro Rivadavia, Mar del Plata and Buenos Aires, and then west to Santiago. Description of the country traversed, state of highways, facilities, etc. [Ed.]

Solari, Juan Antonio. Ser argentinos. Comentarios y reflexiones. Buenos Aires. Ed. La Vanguardia. 189 p. [181
Collection of articles and speeches on current political events in Argentina. [Ed.]

Stockdale, Frank. Development and welfare of the West Indies, 1940–1942. London. Great Britain colonial office. (Colonial no. 184). 93 p. [183
A survey of social and other problems in the West Indies. [C. F. Jones]

Tannenbaum, Frank. Agrarismo, indianismo y nacionalismo (*Hisp. amer. hist. rev.*, vol. 23, no. 3, Aug., p. 394–423). [184
The 450 years of Spanish domination has not brought about the integration of the Indian into the European culture. Present efforts to improve the material and intellectual equipment of the Indians in order to facilitate their incorporation into the European stratum of Hispanic America may in the opinion of the author be self-defeating. The Indian is apt to use this equipment to oppose European culture more effectively than ever before. One must, therefore, expect the emergence of Indian nationalism "more vigorous and self conscious than existed before the Conquest." [Ed.]

Tomlinson, Edward. The other Americans. Our neighbors to the South. New York. Charles Scribner's sons, publ. vi, 456 p., illus. [185
A travel book, emphasizing "color" and eschewing economics, politics and geography. [B. Wood]

United States. Department of state. Report of the Anglo-American Caribbean commission to the governments of the United States and Great Britain for the years 1942–1943. Washington. Govt. print. off. 94 p. [186
The first report of the Anglo-American Caribbean Commission, which was established March 9, 1942 for the purpose of cooperation in the social and economic development of the area. The report presents the organizational set-up and discusses the details of both the immediate and long range aspects of its program. The appendices include the Joint *Communiqué* of March 9, 1942, report of five meetings and a conference held by the Commission, and extracts from a special report entitled *The*

Caribbean Islands and the War. [Roscoe R. Hill]

———. **Office of the coordinator of inter-American affairs.** Guide to the inter-American cultural programs of non-government agencies in the United States. Washington. 181 p. [187
For each of the organizations listed the information supplied includes, whenever possible, address, name of principal officer, date of establishment, membership, source of funds, purpose, inter-American activities, and fields of interest. [Ed.]

Universidad nacional de La Plata. Instituto iberoamericano. Resolución del presidente de la Universidad, doctor Alfredo L. Palacios, de 18 de enero de 1943. La Plata. 30 p. [188
Objectives and organization. The Instittute proposes among other things to publish an Ibero-American bibliographical bulletin. [Ed.]

University of Texas. Institute of Latin American studies. Inter-American intellectual interchange. Austin. 188 p., illus. [189
Papers presented at the third annual conference in the field of Latin American studies held at the University of Texas, June 16–17, 1943. The contributions are grouped under the following general headings: The Development of Intellectual Interchange; Philosophy, Literature and Science; the Need for Cultural Understanding Between the Americas; History—The Teaching of History as a Vehicle of Intellectual Interchange; Fine Arts in the Americas; Old and New Argentine Universities. The more significant contributions are listed under the appropriate headings. [Ed.]

WEST INDIES YEAR BOOK, INCLUDING ALSO THE BERMUDAS, THE BAHAMAS, BRITISH GUIANA AND BRITISH HONDURAS. New York. Thomas Skinner of Canada. 456 p., illus., maps. [189a
An excellent reference on the West Indies. [C. F. Jones]

Whitaker, Arthur P. (ed.). Inter-American affairs, 1942. An annual survey. No. 2. New York. Colombia univ. press. ix, 252 p., illus. [190
The second volume of this valuable survey, which, as the editor states, is published because the first has made its way. This is the best single source of information on the yearly development of Inter-American affairs. [B. Wood]

Zuloaga, Manuel Antonio. Nuestra raza y los problemas de posguerra en la Argentina. Buenos Aires. Ed. La Facultad. 363 p. [191
Part of this volume was first published in 1931 under the title "Nuestra Raza y la Condición del Extranjero en la Argentina." Part I is a detailed study of the demographic pattern of Argentina. Part II deals in a rather general way with a variety of sociological and economic problems.

Zum Felde, Alberto. El problema de la cultura americana. Buenos Aires. Ed. Losada. (Cristal del tiempo). 233 p. [192
A "discussion of the non-existence of a distinctively [Spanish] American culture and the reasons therefor, of the foreign currents dominant in Latin America, and of the sociological aspects which must enter into the development of its culture." [Roscoe R. Hill]

ADDENDA

Castillo Jácome, Julio. La provincia del Chimborazo en 1942. Riobamba. Ed. J. Castillo y J. Ignacio Paredes. 1942. 474 [i.e. 506], 28 p., ilus. [193
A useful manual. Covers history, economic development, political organization, and cultural activities. [Ed.]

REGISTRO DE CULTURA YUCATECA. México, D. F. Año 1, no. 1, dic., 1942—. [194

ANTHROPOLOGY: GENERAL

Acta americana. Review of the Inter-American society of anthropology and geography. Washington, D. C. Vol. 1, no. 1, Jan./March—. [195
This new journal is designed to strengthen international cooperation in the Americanist field and should serve greatly to stimulate research. Preference is given to articles on problems of more than local interest, and of scientific or historical rather than applied significance. Complete bibliographic coverage is not attempted in view of existing bibliographic tools and emphasis is placed on abstracts of the more significant literature. All articles, reviews, abstracts. and other communications are published in the language in which they are submitted. The first volume contained 550 pages. The index is published in the first issue of the following volume. [R. L. Beals]

Anderson, Edgar D. Races of Zea Mays II. A general survey of the problem (*Acta amer.*, vol. 1, no. 1, Jan.–March, p. 58–68). [196
This lucid summary of the genetic problems of Zea Mays indicates clearly the importance of genetic research to the history of American Indian cultures. A definitive resolution of many problems is possible and the anthropologist may be of great aid by proper collecting techniques. [R. L. Beals]

Bennett, W. C., P. A. Means, W. D. Strong, and G. C. Vaillant. Preliminary report of the Institute of Andean research program (*Acta amer.*, vol. 1, no. 2, April–June, p. 221-239). [197
A summary of field work in Middle and South America. [D. Collier]

Boletín del museo arqueológico de Colombia. Ministerio de educación naciónal. Extensión cultural y bellas artes. Servicio de arqueología. Bogotá. Año 1, no. 1—. [198

Brand, Donald D. Special anthropological and geographical problems in Latin America (*Notes latin amer. studies*, no. 2, Oct., p. 27-31). [199
Points out a number of needed research tools for anthropologists and geographers and some special problems. Emphasis is placed on collaborative aspects of research and the need for small unit regional studies. Specific areas of such studies are suggested. [R. L. Beals]

Comas, Juan. La asistencia pública y el desarrollo biológico del indígena (*Amér. indígena*, vol. 3, no. 4, oct., p. 337-344). [200
A vigorous plea for improved health services. Summary materials are presented to show the extent of biological deficiency in various groups. Health and dietary conditions rather than congenital or hereditary inferiority are responsible. [R. L. Beals]

———. El mestizaje. México, D. F. (Primer congreso demográfico interamericano). 12 p. [201
A good discussion of the biological and social problems of hybridization as they affect the Indian countries of the Americas. Severely criticizes the work of some biologists and gives a devastating answer to "racist" ideas. [R. L. Beals]

Hernández de Alba, Gregorio. La antropología y la geografía en Colombia (*Acta amer.*, vol. 1, no. 4, Oct.–Dec., p. 464–470). [202
Excellent summary of activities in Colombia in the fields of archaeology and ethnography. List of recent publications. [A. Métraux]

Imbelloni, José. The peopling of America (*Acta amer.*, vol. 1, no. 3, July–Sept., p. 309-330). [204
A general exposition of the author's theories concerning the origin and spread to the New World of the eight morphological groups in which he places the Indian populations of North and South America. [D. Collier]

Kirchoff, Paul. Mesoamérica (*Acta amer.*, vol. 1, no. 1, Jan.–March, p. 92-107). [206
This is an important attempt to delineate a major culture area in Mexico and Central America. The method used is primarily the systematic comparison with other areas in terms of culture traits. The author makes a good case for the separation of the region from the Chibchan and Andean areas and sets provisional boundaries for Meso-America. [R. L. Beals]

Kuczynski-Godard, Maxime H. Civilización del indio selvícola (*Amér. indígena*, vol. 3, no. 4, oct., p. 313-321). [207
Present exploitative relations with the forest Indians are asserted to be hampering acculturation. Group educational programs adapted to each group are recommended. Strict control of economic developments is urged to protect the Indian and prevent wasteful and destructive exploitation of the forests. [R. L. Beals]

Larco Herrera, Rafael. Internacionalidad del problema indígena en América (*Amér. indígena*, vol. 3, no. 3, julio, p. 191-197). [208
Points out features of the Indian problem common to many American countries. Urges parallel government action on behalf of the Indian and creation of an Inter-American Institute of Indian Psychology. [R. L. Beals]

Lines, Jorge A. Bibliografía antropológica aborigen de Costa Rica. Incluye especialmente arqueología, cartografía, etnología, geografía, historia y lingüística. San José. Ed. Lucem Aspicio. xiv, 263 p. [209

This comprehensive bibliography includes 1262 items—books, pamphlets, articles, periodicals, maps, etc. Some entries have descriptive notes and there are valuable analyses of certain titles, such as *Colección de Documentos para la Historia de Costa Rica* (10 vols.), and *Revista de Costa Rica; Historia, Geografía, Geología, Arqueología,* . . . (4 vols.). At the end are lists of kings of Spain, 1492–1821, of discoverers and conquerors of Costa Rica, 1502–1566, and of governors of Costa Rica, 1508–1819. [C. Shelby]

Mason, J. Alden. Idiomas indígenas y su estudio (*Amér. indígena*, vol. 3, no. 3, julio, p. 231–244). [210

A relatively non-technical discussion and plea for the study of Indian languages. The tentative character of linguistic classifications is pointed out and there is some discussion of various classifications for North America and Meso-America. Of most importance to the specialist is the outline of the views of Whorf and a revision of Mason's own classification. [R. L. Beals]

Noguera, Eduardo. Áreas geográficas de las ruinas arqueológicas (*Rev. mex. geog.*, tomo 4, no. 1–2, enero–junio, p. 103–105). [211

Maintains that the high cultures of ancient Mexico developed in the most favorable geographic locations. [G. F. Ekholm]

REVISTA DEL INSTITUTO ETNOLÓGICO NACIONAL. Bogotá. Vol. 1, entrega primera—. [212

Rivet, Paul. Los orígenes del hombre americano. Trad. de José Recasens. México. Ed. Cultura. (Ed. Cuads. amer., 5). 244 p. [213

Spanish translation of Rivet's *Origines de l'Homme Américain* in which he summarizes the results of his research in the fields of physical anthropology, archaeology and linguistics. [A. Métraux]

Roberts, Jr., Frank H. H. Evidence for a Paleo-Indian in the New World (*Acta amer.*, vol. 1, no. 2, April–June, p. 171–201). [214

Half of this article deals with Middle and South America. [D. Collier]

Rodríguez Aragón, Ismael. Técnica de la educación indígena (*Méx. agrario*, vol. 5, no. 4, oct.–dic., p. 247–258). [215

Points out historical, social, linguistic and other factors which create a different psychology for the Indian. Development of successful educational techniques requires adequate knowledge of native psychology and the causative factors. [R. L. Beals]

Rondón, Cándido M. da Silva. Problema indígena (*Amér. indígena*, vol. 3, no. 1, enero, p. 23–37). [216

This report of the mixed commission on the settlement of the Leticia dispute between Peru and Colombia reveals that the notorious exploitation of the natives of the Putumayo region is still continued. Specific recommendations for legal measures and the maintenance of a joint frontier inspection service on Brazilian model and spirit to protect Indians. [R. L. Beals]

Steward, Julian H. Acculturation and the Indian problem (*Amér. indígena*, vol. 3, no. 4, oct., p. 323–328). [217

All American Indians have been influenced by European culture and there are no more entirely pure native cultures. Every innovation produces some disturbance in a culture, but later a process of reintegration begins. [A. Métraux]

———. Anthropological research needs and opportunities in South America (*Acta amer.*, vol. 1, no. 1, Jan.–March, p. 20–37). [218

Attempts to list the areas where fieldwork could be done. See on the same subject *Handbook of Latin American Studies*, no. 7, 1941, p. 61–66. [A. Métraux]

Strong, William Duncan. Cross sections of new world prehistory. Washington. Smithsonian institution. (Smithsonian misc. collections, vol. 104, no. 2, publ. 3739.) 46 p., plates. [219

A summary report on the work of the ten archaeological expeditions sent to Latin America during 1941–42 by the Institute of Andean Research. The results of each project are reviewed and evaluated in connection with a brief summary of the present status of archaeological studies in Latin America. [G. F. Ekholm]

Trimborn, Hermann. Tres estudios para la etnografía y arqueología de Colombia (*Rev. Indias*, Madrid, año 4, no. 11, enero–marzo, p. 43–92; no. 12, abril–junio, p. 331–347; no. 13, julio–sept., p. 441–456; no. 14, oct.–dic., p. 629–682). [220

El presente trabajo, primero de los tres que anuncia el autor, versa sobre la cultura de los Reinos Guaca y Nore. Tras la enumeración de las fuentes, que aquí son Vadillo, Robledo, Benálcazar y el famoso Cieza de León (todos protagonistas de la expedición guerrera que acabó con los Reinos), que como tantos otros, demostraron tanta habilidad en la pluma en su edad madura cuanto con la espada en sus años mozos. Los encuadres geográficos e históricos, determinados por el autor con verdadero escrúpulo germánico, nos llevan a colocar los Reinos en la intrincada red de valles que vierten sus aguas en el Río Sucio afluente del Atrato, aunque ya muy cerca de la divisoria del Cauca. En estos rincones, opina el autor, habían quedado restos de indios chibchas, isla etnográfica rodeada por todos lados de pueblos chocoes mas recientes.

El estudio etnológico basado casi exclusivamente en datos históricos, los pocos indios actuales son resultado de mezclas posteriores a la Conquista, no da a juicio del autor resultados concluyentes ni se puede hablar de un tipo perfectamente delimitado. A falta de generalizaciones, tal vez aventuradas, prefiere enumerar detalladamente las características familiares y sociales enumeradas por los cronistas. Pueblos agricultores, comerciantes que obedecían a un cacique y hacían la guerra conforme a normas bastante adelantadas, buscando en ella la satisfacción de instintos sexuales y antropófagos que han de considerarse, dice el autor, de sentido mágico. El mismo sentido predomina en sus relaciones religiosas, con un Dios prácticamente olvidado y una serie de ceremonías funerales que indican la creencia general en muchos pueblos primitivos de la supervivencia del individuo, de un modo que se ha dado en llamar, el del "cadáver viviente."

El trabajo que evita cuidadosamente las generalizaciones aventuradas es un compendio minucioso y ordenadísimo de los datos etnológicos de los cronistas. [C. Sáenz de Santa María]

Valcárcel, Luis E. Historia de la cultura antigua del Perú. Lima. Imp. del Museo nac. [220a

Mimeographed course on Peruvian archaeology and ethnography with frequent digressions into philosophy. The material is very abundant and clearly presented. [A. Métraux]

Zum Felde, Alberto. La tragedia del indio en Suramérica (*Cuad. amer.*, año 2, vol. 9, no. 3, mayo–junio, p. 129–141). [221

Sound protest against the cheap romantic *indianista* literature which glorifies the Indian without seriously attempting to know him. The psychology and culture of modern Indians must be interpreted in the light of 400 years of cruel Spanish domination. [A. Métraux]

ADDENDA

Martínez del Río, Pablo. The antiquity of maize cultivation in America (*Actas primera sesión 27 cong. int. amer.*, tomo 1, 1942, p. 92–95). [222

Individual treatment in seed selection and the individual cultivation of plants may have been factors which speeded the evolution of cultivated maize. [G. F. Ekholm]

MIDDLE AMERICA: ARCHAEOLOGY

BY

GORDON F. EKHOLM

The American Museum of Natural History

GENERAL STATEMENT

Relatively little field work was accomplished in Middle America during 1943, but rather significant progress was nevertheless made in the development of the field as a whole. The list of the publications which appeared during the year is a long one, and, although most of the articles are short, a number of them are of outstanding importance. Despite the difficulties and restrictions in travel and the fact that many workers were in the war services, the Third Round Table Conference of the Sociedad Mexicana de Antropología, held from August 25th to September 2nd in Mexico City, was well attended and was in all respects a highly successful meeting. The subject of discussion was northern Mexico and the relations between the cultures of Middle America and those of the Southeast and Southwest of the United States. The important but much neglected area of northern Mexico was subjected to various studies in preparation for the conference, particularly by Mexican scholars, and it was discussed from all the points of view of history, ethnology, linguistics, archaeology and physical anthropology. The most important result of these deliberations was primarily the clarification of the many anthropological problems of the area which must be subjected to extensive research in the future.

The fifth National Geographic Society—Smithsonian Institution expedition was the only regular expedition to Middle America supported by any United States institution during the year. Dr. Matthew Stirling, this time accompanied by Dr. Waldo Wedel, made further excavations at La Venta and also surveyed an area further inland on the isthmus. Outstanding finds at La Venta were two large tiger mask mosaics made of blocks of green serpentine and a number of jade objects, some of which are of a finer quality jade than any previously known in America. Four monographs on previous work in this area by Stirling, Weiant, and Drucker are important publications of the year.

Many of the members of the Carnegie Institution staff are in the war services, while the remainder have been devoting themselves largely to the writing of reports. No excavation was undertaken, but E. M. Shook and R. E. Smith had the opportunity of doing a certain amount of reconnaissance in the field, the former in western Guatemala and the latter in Alta Verapaz. They recorded a number of new sites and studied and photographed several important private collections.

The archaeologists of the Instituto Nacional de Antropología of Mexico have continued their field explorations in many parts of their country, for a full account of which the author is indebted to a communication from Sr. Eduardo Noguera. These studies are largely continuations of projects which have been in progress for some time. Dr. Caso with a group of students continued his manifold work at Monte Albán, and late in the year Lorenzo Gamio excavated a tomb at Zaachila where he is reported to have found an important stone carving. Exploration in the interior of the pyramid of Cholula was continued, as well as further preparation of the local museum. Sr. Pedro Armillas made great strides in his excavations at Teotihuacan, clearing a number of buildings in the "Avenida de los Muertos" and achieving very promising results from his stratigraphic studies. The work at Tula, Hidalgo, has proceeded steadily with continued spectacular finds. During the latter part of the year the area to the south of the Temple of the Moon was cleared, revealing a colonnade and walls exactly like those of the Temple of the Warriors at Chichen Itzá. From this section also is reported a sculptured frieze of warriors in procession and on one side of the pyramid a sculptured frieze of eagles and tigers, again notably like that of the Temple of the Warriors.

Sr. Noguera and others continued their excavations at Xochicalco, clearing and consolidating the ball court and some other buildings and making stratigraphic studies. In eastern Mexico Juan Valenzuela recovered many fine objects from tombs at the site of Tlacuache, Vera Cruz, and during the latter part of the year made excavations at Acatlán de Pérez and Malinaltepec in the same State. Wilfrido du Solier continued his work in the Huasteca in the State of Hidalgo, clearing both rectangular and circular buildings containing tombs at Huichapa, Huejutla, and at the site of Vinasco. An important find was also made within the city of Mexico on the corner of La Palma and Cuba streets where foundations for modern buildings were under construction. Here Juan Valenzuela cleared a number of plaster floors and found in association with them a burial and a number of small objects as well as five beautiful stone sculptures placed in a row. Two of these are coiled serpents, reported to be as fine as any in the collections of the National Museum, and the others, besides being fine examples of the stone carving art of the Aztecs, show a symbolism connecting them with the New Fire ceremony. Finally, the work of clearing and reconstruction was continued at Palenque and Uxmal.

In the Central American Republics the only field work accomplished outside of the several brief surveys by Carnegie Institution personnel was in El Salvador. Here work at Tazumal was continued by the National Museum under the direction of Stanley Boggs. Three small structures and one tomb were cleared, the latter containing a rich series of offerings.

American institutions did not engage in any work in the West Indies during 1943, but the various local institutions and societies continued their studies as in the past.

An important publication event of the year was the appearance of the first volume of the papers presented at the Twenty-seventh International Congress of Americanists held in Mexico City in 1939. Two new journals of potential importance to Middle American archaeology began their careers, *Acta Americana* and *Tlalocan*. The first of these is meant to deal with the broader aspects of Americanist studies while the second will publish the written source materials on the native cultures of Mexico. Both therefore are of real interest to this field and should reinforce the present tendency toward a closer alignment of purely archaeological studies with those of related fields.

BIBLIOGRAPHY

GENERAL

Carnegie institution of Washington. Year book no. 42, 1942–1943. Washington. [223
The report of the Division of Historical Research by A. V. Kidder contains a brief account of the activities of the Institution during 1942–1943.

Deevey, Jr., Edward S. Intento para datar las culturas medias del valle de México, mediante análisis de polen (*Ciencia*, vol. 4, no. 4–5, oct. 20, p. 97–105). [224
A preliminary study of the possible use of pollen analysis in Mexico.

Ekholm, Gordon F. A selective guide to the material published in 1942 on anthropology: Middle America: archaeology (*Handbook of latin american studies, no. 8, 1942*, p. 16–20). [225

Kelly, Isabel. Notes on a west coast survival of the ancient Mexican ball game (*Notes on middle amer. arch. ethnol.*, vol. 1, no. 26, Nov. 10, p. 163–175). [226
Details of a ball game played on the west coast of Mexico. A contribution of great importance for the interpretation of the ancient game and ball courts.

Mason, John Alden. The American collections of the University museum. The ancient civilizations of Middle America (*Univ. mus. bull.*, vol. 10, no. 1–2, p. 1–64, illus.). [227
An up-to-date popular survey of Middle American prehistory, copiously illustrated with objects in the University Museum.

———. Archaeological work in Middle America in 1941–43 (*Amer. antiquity*, vol. 9, no. 1, July, p. 2–10). [228
A summary of field work.

Noguera, Eduardo. Resultado y consecuencias de la conferencia de Tuxtla (*Acta amer.*, vol. 1, no. 1, Jan.–March, p. 50–57). [229
A summary of the most important aspects of the second round-table conference.

Von Hagen, Victor Wolfgang. The Aztec and Maya papermakers. Introd. by Dard Hunter. New York. George Grady press. 115 p., plates. [230
This beautifully printed book deals with many aspects of paper making among the ancient and modern Indians of Middle America. It is shown that paper was not made from the maguey plant, as has been commonly supposed, but from the bark of the fig tree. Samples of papers made by present-day Indians of Mexico are included in the book.

MEXICAN AND MAYAN HISTORY AND EPIGRAPHY

Anderson, Edgar D., and R. H. Barlow. The maize tribute of Moctezuma's empire (*An. Missouri botanical garden*, vol. 30, no. 4, Nov., p. 413–420). [231
A concise and valuable study of the amount of maize paid as tribute to Moctezuma and the location of the provinces from which it came.

Barlow, R. H. The *Mapa de Huilotepec* (*Tlalocan*, vol. 1, no. 2, p. 155–157, illus.). [232
Brief description of a post-conquest pictorial document from Oaxaca.

———. The periods of tribute collection in Moctezuma's empire (*Notes on middle amer. arch. ethnol.*, vol. 1, no. 23, Oct. 30, p. 152–155). [233
Suggests that certain provinces paid tribute six times yearly. An addition to the studies of R. C. E. Long in the same series.

Berlin, Heinrich. Notes on glyph C of the lunar series at Palenque (*Notes on middle amer. arch. ethnol.*, vol. 1, no. 24, Nov. 10, p. 156–159). [235
A technical discussion.

Bourgeois, Julia F. Los verdaderos años del calendario azteca y maya y el verdadero sistema cronológico maya. Ed. revisada. Trad. por M. Miguel Ramos G. México, D. F. Ed. Cultura. 28 p. [236
A discussion of the methods of counting time. A translation from the English edition published in 1942.

Caso, Alfonso. The calendar of the Tarascans (*Amer. antiquity*, vol. 9, no. 1, July, p. 11–28). [237
A valuable detailed analysis of the Tarascan calendar which shows that it agreed day by day with the Aztec calendar.

———. The codices of Azoyu (*Dyn*, no. 4–5, p. 3–6). [238
Brief description of these two new codices from Guerrero with two pages reproduced in full color.

Cirerol Sansores, Manuel. Uinal-el mes de veinte días de los antiguos mayas (*Orbe*, segunda época, no. 20, nov., p. 18–29; no. 21, dic., p. 5–14). [239
A description of each of the twenty day signs as found on the monuments, in the codices, and in Landa.

Escalona Ramos, Alberto. Los aztecas no eran mexicanos. Identificación del legendario Chicomoztoc y posible filiación étnica de los aztecas (*Bol. soc. mex. geog.*

estad., tomo 58, no. 3–6, mayo–dic., p. 359–384). [240

An attempt to clarify the legendary accounts of Aztec history.

Guzmán, Eulalia. El arte cartográfico entre los antiguos mexicanos (*Rev. mex. geog.*, tomo 4, no. 1–2, enero–junio, p. 79–94, ilus.). [241

A discussion of three aboriginal maps and of the possible importance of map making in pre-Spanish Mexico.

Imbelloni, J. La "Essaltatione delle Rose" del Códice vaticano mexicano 3738, el "Nicté-katun" de las fuentes maya y el "Pecado nefando" de la tradición peruana más remota. Mendoza. Ed. Best hnos. (Religiones de América, no. 11). 47 p., láms. [242

Reprinted from *Anales del Instituto de Etnografía Americana*, Univ. Nacional de Cuyo, tomo 4, p. 161–205.

A detailed study of that part of the codex, Vaticanus A, which treats of the four ages of man, and a comparison, indicating basic parallels, with similar myths of the Maya and of the Indians of Peru.

———. El "génesis" de los pueblos protohistóricos de América. Buenos Aires. Ed. Coni. (Religiones de América, nos. 3, 4, 5, 7, 10). [243

Reprinted from *Boletín de la Academia Argentina de Letras*, vols. 8–11, 1940–1943.

An analytical study of Mexican and Central American religions. Five of proposed nine sections have been published.

Makemson, Maud Worcester. The astronomical tables of the Maya (*Contrib. amer. anthrop. hist.*, vol. 8, no. 42, p. 183–221). [244

The astronomical tables of the Dresden codex and the correlation problem are examined by an astronomer.

———. The enigma of Maya astronomy (*Dyn*, no. 4–5, p. 47–52). [245

Important comments on the correlation problem by an astronomer.

Margain Araujo, Carlos R. The painting in Mexican codices (*Dyn*, no. 4–5, p. 59–61, ilus.). [246

Analyses of the differing art styles in the Aztec, Mixtec, and Maya codices.

Martín del Campo, Rafael. El más antiguo parque zoológico de América (*An. inst. biol.*, tomo 14, no. 2, p. 635–643). [247

A collection of historical data concerning the Aztec knowledge of plants and animals and the zoological collection in the Aztec capitol.

Pavón Abreu, Raúl. Cronología maya. Campeche. Museo arqueológico etnográfico e histórico de Campeche. 248 p. [248

A good brief explanation of the Maya calendar in Spanish and a long series of tables giving the Gregorian equivalent for every day in the Maya era according to the Goodman-Martínez Hernández-Thompson correlation.

Sánchez Ventura, Rafael. Flores y jardines del México antiguo y del moderno (*Cuad. amer.*, año 2, vol. 7, no. 1, enero-feb., p. 127–148, ilus.). [249

A collection of data from the codices and from history on the use of flowers in Mexico.

Satterthwaite, Jr., Linton. New photographs and the date of stela 14, Piedras Negras (*Notes on middle amer. arch. ethnol.*, vol. 1, no. 28, Nov. 22, p. 182–188). [250

A refutation of Thompson's reading of this stela.

Thompson, J. Eric S. The initial series of stela 14, Piedras Negras, Guatemala, and a date on stela 19, Naranjo, Guatemala (*Notes on middle amer. arch. ethnol.*, vol. 1, no. 18, March 30, p. 113–116). [251

A new reading is suggested.

———. Maya epigraphy: a cycle of 819 days (*Notes on middle amer. arch. ethnol.*, vol. 1, no. 22, Oct. 30, p. 137–151). [252

A technical discussion.

———. Maya epigraphy: directional glyphs in counting (*Notes on middle amer. arch. ethnol.*, vol. 1, no. 20, May 1, p. 122–126). [253

A technical discussion.

Toscano, Salvador. Los códices Tlapanecas de Azoyu (*Cuad. amer.*, año 2, vol. 10, no. 4, julio-agosto, p. 127–136, ilus.). [254

An account of the discovery and a brief description of two new codices from Guerrero.

Vaillant, George C. Aztec craftsmanship (*Mexican life*, vol. 19, no. 5, May, p. 23–25, 42–47). [255

A general popular review of Aztec crafts.

———. Aztec social system (*Mexican life*, vol. 19, no. 7, July, p. 19–20, 48–56). [256

A brief summary of Aztec economics and social organization.

MEXICO

Acosta, Jorge R. Los colosos de Tula (*Cuad. amer.*, año 2, vol. 12, no. 6, nov.-dic., p. 138–146, ilus.). [257

Details of the remarkable sculptures recently discovered in the ruins at Tula. The great similarity between the art of Tula and Chichen Itzá is made evident.

Apenes, Ola. The "tlateles" of Lake Texcoco (*Amer. antiquity*, vol. 9, no. 1, July, p. 29–32). [258

Archaeologic sites within and along the shores of Lake Texcoco in the Valley of

Mexico. The large mounds or *tlateles* are thought to be the remnants of *chinampas* or "floating gardens."

Brand, Donald D. The Chihuahua culture area (*New Mex. anthrop.*, vol. 6–7, no. 3, whole no. 27, July–Sept., p. 115–158). [259
Valuable notes locating and describing a large number of archaeologic sites and with a discussion of the pottery types found on each one.

Covarrubias, Miguel. Tlatilco, archaic Mexican art and culture (*Dyn*, no. 4–5, p. 40–46, illus.). [261
Many figurines and other objects from a new "archaic" site in the Valley of Mexico are briefly described and beautifully illustrated.

Drucker, Philip. Ceramic sequences at Tres Zapotes, Veracruz, Mexico. Washington, D. C. U. S. Govt. print. office. (Smithsonian institution, Bureau of American ethnology, bull. 140). ix, 155 p., plates. [262
A detailed stratigraphic study by which the occupation of the site is divided into four periods.

———. Ceramic stratigraphy at Cerro de las Mesas, Veracruz, Mexico. Washington, D. C. U. S. Govt. printing office. (Smithsonian institution, Bureau of American ethnology, bull. 141). 95 p., plates. [263
A detailed study of pottery and figurines dividing the occupation of the site into four phases and allowing a correlation with the Tres Zapotes and the Central Mexican sequences.

Du Solier, Wilfrido. A reconnaissance on Isla de Sacrificios, Veracruz, Mexico (*Notes on middle amer. arch. ethnol.*, vol. 1, no. 14, March 30, p. 63–80). [264
Contains new data on this very important late site. Some elaborate pottery vessels as well as other objects are well illustrated.

Enciso, Jorge. Seals of the ancient Mexicans (*Dyn*, no. 4–5, p. 54). [265
Reproductions of some designs.

García Payón, José. Interpretación cultural de la zona arqueológica de El Tajín, seguida de un ensayo de una bibliografía antropológica del Totonacapan y región sur del Estado de Veracruz. México. Imp. universitaria. [266
An attempt to clarify the complicated historical problems of Vera Cruz. Contains a handy bibliography.

———. Interpretación de la vida de los pueblos matlatzincas (*México antig.*, tomo 6, no. 4–6, feb., p. 93–119). [267
The second and concluding portion of a paper begun in vol. 6, no. 1–3, 1942.
An attempt to reconstruct Matlatzinca culture from the historical sources.

Goggin, John M. An archaeological survey of the Río Tepalcatepec Basin, Michoacán, Mexico (*Amer. antiquity*, vol. 9, no. 1, July, p. 44–58). [268
Results of a surface survey with descriptions of pottery, and other artifacts.

Hendrichs, P. R. Tlachtemalacates y otros monumentos de la zona arqueológica de La Soledad, Guerrero (*México antig.*, tomo 6, no. 4–6, feb., p. 120–130, ilus.). [269
Description of four ball court rings of a unique type.

Melgarejo Vivanco, José Luis. Totonacapan. Xalapa, Veracruz. Tall. gráf. del Gobierno del Estado. 249 p., ilus. [270
A collection of various data on the Totonacs and on the region of central Veracruz.

Moedano Koer, Hugo. Tizatlan asiento del Señor Xochipilli (*Cuad. amer.*, año 2, vol. 11, no. 5, sept.–oct., p. 133–142, ilus.). [271
Evidence is presented to show that two building periods are present in the ruins at Tizatlan and that during both periods the temples were devoted to the god Xochipilli.

Müllerried, F. K. G., and **H. von Winning.** El "Cerrito" al este de Tepotzotlán, México, en el valle de México (*México antig.*, tomo 6, no. 4–6, feb., p. 131–139). [272
A brief description of some pottery, figurines, and obsidian artifacts combined with a geological study.

Noguera, Eduardo. Excavaciones en El Tepalcate, Chimalhuacán, México (*Amer. antiquity*, vol. 9, no. 1, July, p. 33–43). [273
A site in Lake Texcoco is shown to be of Teotihuacan I date.

Ochoa Campos, Moisés. El descubrimiento arqueológico más importante de 1943 (*Cult. México*, año 2, no. 2, julio-dic., p. 30–34). [274
An account of the Chac Mool recently found in Mexico City.

Orozco Muñoz, Francisco. El arte totonaca del antiguo México (*Hijo pródigo*, año 1, vol. 1, no. 2, mayo, p. 94–96). [275
Contains several good photos of stone and clay objects.

Osborne, Douglas. An archaeologic reconnaissance in southeastern Michoacán, Mexico (*Amer. antiquity*, vol. 9, no. 1, July, p. 59–73). [276
A description of ruins and of several carved stone monuments.

Paalen, Wolfgang. Birth of Fire, a mythological hypothesis suggested by the ap-

pearance of a new volcano (*Dyn*, no. 4–5, p. 71). **[277**
Suggests that the pyramid might be the mythological representation of the volcano.

Saldívar, Gabriel. Los indios de Tamaulipas. México. (Insto. panamericano de geografía e historia, Publ. no. 70). 36 p. **[278**
An account including both historic and archaeologic data.

Stirling, Matthew William. Stone monuments of southern Mexico. Washington, D. C. U. S. Govt. print. office. (Smithsonian inst., Bureau of American ethnology, bull. 138). 84 p., plates. **[279**
A description and brief analysis of all the stone monuments at Tres Zapotes, Cerro de las Mesas, La Venta, and Izapa. An extremely important addition to our knowledge of Middle American stone carving.

———. La Venta's green stone tigers (*Nat. geog. mag.*, vol. 84, no. 3, Sept., p. 321–332, illus.). **[280**
A brief account of the 1943 expedition with photographs of the more important finds. Outstanding is a mosaic floor of serpentine blocks representing a jaguar.

Toscano, Salvador. La cerámica tarasca (*Hijo pródigo*, año 1, vol. 1, no. 5, agosto, p. 296–298). **[281**
The art of the Tarascan figurines. Contains eight good photos.

Vaillant, George C. The Aztecs. Their cultural and historical position in Middle American archaeology (*Proc. amer. phil. soc.*, vol. 86, no. 2, Feb. 10, p. 320–322). **[282**
A general review of Central Mexican history with emphasis on the last or Aztec period.

Valle, Cipriano. Archaeological discoveries at Tula (*Mexican life*, vol. 19, no. 10, Oct., p. 13–15). **[283**
A brief text accompanying seven good photographs.

Weiant, Clarence Wolsey. An introduction to the ceramics of Tres Zapotes, Veracruz, Mexico. Washington, D. C. U. S. govt. printing office. (Smithsonian institution, Bureau of American ethnology, Bull. 139). 144 p., plates. **[284**
Detailed studies of the ceramic material from the excavations of the first season at the site.

MAYA AREA

Andrews, Edward Wyllys. The archaeology of southwestern Campeche (*Contrib. amer. anthrop. hist.*, vol. 8, no. 40, Jan., p. 1–100, illus.). **[285**
An account of a survey in this region and a discussion of archaeological problems of the northern Maya area.

Baratta, Augusto. La unidad de medida en nuestra raza aborigen (*Tzunpame*, año 3, no. 1, oct., p. 89–103). **[286**
A discussion of possible standards of measurement in prehistoric America.

Boggs, Stanley H. Notas sobre las excavaciones en la hacienda "San Andrés," Departamento de La Libertad (*Tzunpame*, año 3, no. 1, oct., p. 104–126). **[287**
Contains a description of the ruins with plans and cross sections, details of the most important pottery types, and a general statement of the known chronology of this site and of Salvador as a whole.

———. Observaciones respecto a la importancia de "Tazumal" en la prehistoria salvadoreña (*Tzunpame*, año 3, no. 1, oct., p. 127–133). **[288**
A general statement of the work being done and of the known history of the site.

———. Tazumal en la arqueología salvadoreña (*Rev. min. instr. públ.*, vol. 2, no. 7, julio–sept., suplemento). **[289**
American prehistory in general and some details on the site of Tazumal.

Dutton, Bertha P., and Hulda R. Hobbs. Excavations at Tajumulco, Guatemala. Santa Fe, N. M. School of American research and Museum of New Mexico. (School of American research, Monograph, no. 9). 124 p., illus. **[290**
A study of a site in southwestern Guatemala belonging primarily to the "Mexican" Period. The study is particularly important in regard to Plumbate pottery.

Fernández, Miguel Ángel. New discoveries in the Temple of the Sun in Palenque (*Dyn*, no. 4–5, p. 55–58, illus.). **[291**
Notes on three caches found underneath the floor, one containing a beautiful stucco mask, here illustrated in color.

Gann, Thomas. Painted stucco heads from Louisville, British Honduras (*Middle amer. research records*, vol. 1, no. 4, March, p. 13–16, illus.). **[292**
Describes a series of forty-one life sized heads of stucco which had covered the wall of a temple.

Kidder, A. V. Grooved stone axes from Central America (*Notes on middle amer. arch. ethnol.*, vol. 1, no. 29, Dec. 20, p. 189–193). **[293**
An interesting occurrence of six grooved stone axes far outside their normal known range.

———. Pottery from the Pacific slope of Guatemala (*Notes on middle amer. arch. ethnol.*, vol. 1, no. 15, March 30, p. 81–91). **[294**
A description of several pottery collections which show possible relationship with wares from other parts of Middle America.

———. Spindle whorls from Chichen Itzá, Yucatan (*Notes on middle amer. arch. ethnol.*, vol. 1, no. 16, March 30, p. 92–99). [295
Description and many good illustrations.

Kurtz, Benjamin T. The great American palace at Sayil (Zayi), Yucatán (*Bull. nat. hist. soc. Maryland*, vol. 13, no. 4, April–June, p. 56–62, illus.). [296
Various comments on the site.

Lunardi, Federico. Los misterios maya del valle de Otoro (*Rev. geog. amer.*, año 9, vol. 20, no. 118, julio, p. 11–24). [297
A brief description of sites in this valley in western Honduras.

McDougall, Elsie. A vase from Sanimtaca, Alta Verapaz, Guatemala (*Notes on middle amer. arch. ethnol.*, vol. 1, no. 30, Dec. 20, p. 194–197). [298
Description and illustration of a beautifully carved but fragmentary Maya vase.

Mimenza Castillo, Ricardo. El arte y la cultura mayas. Estudios arqueológicos. México, D. F. Ed. Ibero-americanas. (Col. Estudios mexicanos, vol. 1.) 122 p. [299
A brief and fragmentary summary of Maya art and history.

Morley, Sylvanus Griswold. Archaeological investigations of the Carnegie institution of Washington in the Maya area of Middle America, during the past twenty-eight years (*Proc. amer. phil. soc.*, vol. 86, no. 2, Feb. 10, p. 205–219). [300
A summary of the research program carried out.

Mota, Otoniel. Interrogações na cultura máia (*Rev. arq. mun.*, São Paulo, ano 8, vol. 88, jan.–fev., p. 159–166). [301
Questions in regard to the correct identification of the animal variously called tiger, jaguar or ocelot in Maya and Mexican studies.

Ruppert, Karl. The Mercado, Chichen Itzá, Yucatan (*Contrib. amer. anthrop. hist.*, vol. 8, no. 43, Oct., p. 223–226, illus.). [302
A full description and illustration of the building known as the Mercado.

———, and **John H. Denison, Jr.** Archaeological reconnaissance in Campeche, Quintana Roo, and Petén. Washington, D. C. (Carnegie institution of Washington, Publ. 547.) 156 p., 126 figs., 75 plates. [303
Contains a large quantity of basic information on architecture and inscriptions from a number of sites.

Satterthwaite, Jr., Linton. Animal-head feet and a bark-beater in the middle Usumacinta region (*Notes on middle amer. arch. ethnol.*, vol. 1, no. 27, Nov. 22, p. 176–181). [304
A discussion of the possible continued occupation of the Central Maya area up into the Mexican Occupation Period.

———. Notes on sculpture and architecture at Tonala, Chiapas (*Notes on middle amer. arch. ethnol.*, vol. 1, no. 21, May 25, p. 127–136). [305
Brief notes made on a short visit. Contains sketches and photographs of stelae.

———. Piedras Negras archaeology: Architecture. Part 1, no. 1: Introduction. Philadelphia. Univ. of Pennsylvania, Univ. museum. 32 p., illus. [306
This is the first section of the University Museum's study of Piedras Negras which will appear in parts as ready. This number contains a large scale and complete map of the entire site as well as cross section profiles and a reconstruction drawing.

Smith, A. L., and **A. V. Kidder.** Explorations in the Motagua Valley, Guatemala (*Contrib. amer. anthrop. hist.*, vol. 8, no. 41, June, p. 101–182, illus.). [307
Important source material on a previously unknown portion of the Maya area, beautifully presented and illustrated.

Thompson, J. Eric S. A figurine whistle representing a ballgame player (*Notes on middle amer. arch. ethnol.*, vol. 1, no. 25, Nov. 10, p. 160–162). [308
A clay figurine shown with a heavy belt and holding a ball under the arm.

———. Representations of Tlalchitonatiuh at Chichen Itzá, Yucatan, and at Baul, Escuintla (*Notes on middle amer. arch. ethnol.*, vol. 1, no. 19, March 30, p. 117–121). [309
Figures in the sculptured friezes of the Temple of the Warriors are identified as a special form of the Aztec sun god rather than as Tlaloc.

———. Some sculptures from southeastern Quezaltenango, Guatemala (*Notes on middle amer. arch. ethnol.*, vol. 1, no. 17, March 30, p. 100–112). [310
Contains description and illustration of sculpture and other objects and also a discussion of the possible use of the 400 day year in Vera Cruz as well as in the southern highlands of Guatemala.

———. A trial survey of the southern Maya area (*Amer. antiquity*, vol. 9, no. 1, July, p. 106–134). [311
A valuable general summary of Maya archaeology in which Maya history is divided into four great periods. The southern portion of the area is treated in considerable detail, and there is much information on as yet unpublished material.

SOUTHERN CENTRAL AMERICA AND THE ANTILLES

(See also item 51)

Fisher, Kurt A. Une amulette jumelée en os de la section d'archeologie du bureau d'ethnologie de la République d'Haïti (*Bull. bur. d'ethnologie*, p. 31-32). [312
Brief description of an amulet.

Lacaille, A. D. A mortar and a rock-carving in Jamaica (*Man*, vol. 43, no. 66, July-August, p. 87-88). [313
A brief description.

Lehmann, Walter. Arqueología costarricense (*Rev. arch. nac.*, Costa Rica, año 7, no. 1-2, enero-feb., p. 66-87). [314

Roumaine, Jacques. L'outillage lithique des ciboney d'Haïti (*Bull. bur. d'ethnologie*, p. 22-27). [315
Description of some new specimens and a general discussion of the Ciboney culture.

Stone, Doris. A preliminary investigation of the flood plain of the Río Grande de Térraba, Costa Rica (*Amer. antiquity*, vol. 9, no. 1, July, p. 74-88). [316
Description of sites, pottery, and a number of immense stone balls, the latter being the most outstanding feature of the area.

ADDENDA

GENERAL

Gillan, Crosby Lee. Los juegos de pelota en Arizona (*Actas primera sesión 27 cong. int. amer.*, tomo 1, 1942, p. 209-216). [317
A brief comparison of Southwestern and Middle American ball courts.

MEXICAN AND MAYAN HISTORY AND EPIGRAPHY

Barrera Vásquez, Alfredo. El pronóstico de los 20 signos de los días del calendario maya, según los libros de Chilam Balam de Kaua y de Maní (*Actas primera sesión 27 cong. int. amer.*, tomo 1, 1942, p. 470-481). [318
A study of the names in the Maya equivalent of the *tonalpohualli*.

Beyer, Hermann. Algunos datos sobre los dinteles mayas de Tikal en el Museo etnográfico de Basilea (*Actas primera sesión 27 cong. int. amer.*, tomo 1, 1942, p. 338-343). [319
On the proper arrangement of the separate portions of the Tikal lintels.

―――. The long count position of the serpent number dates (*Actas primera sesión 27 cong. int. amer.*, tomo 1, 1942, p. 401-405). [320
A technical discussion.

―――. The Maya hieroglyph "ending day" (*Actas primera sesión 27 cong. int. amer.*, tomo 1, 1942, p. 344-351). [321
An interpretation of a glyph common in the inscriptions at Piedras Negras.

Dieseldorff, E. P. Cronología del calendario maya (*Actas primera sesión 27 cong. int. amer.*, tomo 1, 1942, p. 305-321). [322
A discussion of problems concerning the adjustment of the calendar year to the tropical year.

Escalona Ramos, Alberto. Cronología y astronomía maya méxica (*Actas primera sesión 27 cong. int. amer.*, tomo 1, 1942, p. 623-630). [323
A presentation of the 11.3.0.0.0 correlation.

García Granados, Rafael. Estudio comparativo de los signos cronográficos en los códices prehispánicos de Méjico (*Actas primera sesión 27 cong. int. amer.*, tomo 1, 1942, p. 419-469). [324
A valuable statistical comparison of the day signs in the Mexican codices. Contains a useful series of illustrations of the variant forms of the twenty signs.

Linné, Sigvald. El mapa más antigua del valle de México (*Actas primera sesión 27 cong. int. amer.*, tomo 1, 1942, p. 492-500). [325
A discussion of the early map attributed to Alonzo de Santa Cruz.

Lizardi Ramos, César. Cómputo de fechas mayas (*Actas primera sesión 27 cong. int. amer.*, tomo 1, 1942, p. 356-359). [326
A quick method for computing calendar round dates without the use of tables.

―――. El glifo B y la sincronología maya-cristiana (*Actas primera sesión 27 cong. int. amer.*, tomo 1, 1942, p. 360-374). [327
An attempt to prove that the Maya counted their lunar periods from the beginning of the new moon.

Margain, Carlos R. El culto fálico en México (*Actas primera sesión 27 cong. int. amer.*, tomo 1, 1942, p. 375-390). [328
The partial publication of an extensive analytical study of Aztec religion from this point of view.

Mateos Higuera, Salvador. Cien códices del Museo nacional de México (*Actas primera sesión 27 cong. int. amer.*, tomo 1, 1942, p. 546-549). [329
A list of the codices with their catalog numbers.

Rickards, Constantine G. An interpretation of the Mexican year sign as a life

symbol (*Actas primera sesión 27 cong. int. amer.*, tomo 1, 1942, p. 612-622). [330
The interlaced A and O of the year sign are considered to be the male and female life symbols.

Satterthwaite Jr., Linton. Opposed interpretations of dates and hieroglyphs styles at Chichen Itzá (*Rev. mex. estud. antrop.*, tomo 6, no. 1-2, 1942, p. 19-35). [330a
An analysis of the methods used by Beyer and Thompson in their interpretations of the inscriptions at Chichen Itzá.

Schulz, R. P. C. Apuntes sobre algunas fechas del Templo de la Cruz de Palenque y sobre astronomía y cronología de los antiguos mayas (*Actas primera sesión 27 cong. int. amer.*, tomo 1, 1942, p. 352-355). [331
Brief notes.

Tompkins, John Barr. Codex Fernández Leal (*Pac. art rev.*, summer, 1942, p. 39-59). [331a
A short commentary on this important codex now in the Bancroft Library of the University of California. Includes a small but good photographic reproduction of the codex.

MEXICO

Brand, Donald D. Recent archaeologic and geographic investigations in the basin of the Río Balsas, Guerrero and Michoacán (*Actas primera sesión 27 cong. int. amer.*, tomo 1, 1942, p. 140-147). [332
A general preliminary account of a survey conducted by Dr. Brand and his students.

Linné, S. Mexican highland cultures: archaeological researches at Teotihuacan, Calpulalpan and Chalchicomula in 1934-35. Stockholm. (The ethnographical museum of Sweden, Stockholm, New series, Publ. no. 7). 1942. 223 p., illus. [333
An account of extensive excavations at Teotihuacan and minor ones in the states of Tlaxcala and Puebla. Important material, well illustrated.

Moedano Koer, Hugo. Estudio general sobre la situación de la fortaleza de Oztuma (*Actas primera sesión 27 cong. int. amer.*, tomo 1, 1942, p. 557-563). [334
A brief description of the ruins.

Noguera, Eduardo. Exploraciones de "El Opeño," Michoacán (*Actas primera sesión 27 cong. int. amer.*, tomo 1, 1942, p. 574-586). [335
Description of three tombs near Zamora, Michoacán. The figures and other objects found indicate affinity with the "archaic" cultures of the Valley of Mexico.

Núñez y Domínguez, José de J. La colección de objetos mexicanos antiguos del "Museo del hombre" de Paris (*Rev. mex. estud. antrop.*, tomo 6, no. 1-2, 1942, p. 5-18). [335a
Description and illustration of the more notable Mexican objects in the Musée de l'Homme.

Palacios, Enrique Juan. Hallasgos arqueológicos afectuados en México (*Rev. mex. estud. antrop.*, tomo 6, no. 1-2, 1942, p. 51-61). [335b
A carving from Xochimilco is seen to throw light on the meaning of the so-called Aztec calendar stone.

———. Los "yugos" y su simbolismo (*Actas primera sesión 27 cong. int. amer.*, tomo 1, 1942, p. 509-545). [336
The classification, distribution, and symbolism of stone yokes. Contains twenty-five illustrations.

Rickards, Constantine G. Coleoptero grabado en jadeita, de la mixteca, estado de Oaxaca, México (*Rev. mex. estud. antrop.*, tomo 6, no. 1-2, 1942, p. 102-108). [336a
Carvings of insects are rare in Mexican materials.

Rodríguez, Blas E. Una escultura huasteca (*Actas primera sesión 27 cong. int. amer.*, tomo 1, 1942, p. 587-600). [337
Description and illustration of a magnificent sculptured figure.

Sieck Flandes, Roberto. ¿Cómo estuvo pintada la piedra conocida con el nombre de "el calendario azteca"? (*Actas primera sesión 27 cong. int. amer.*, tomo 1, 1942, p. 550-556). [338
A restoration from various sources of the original colors of the calendar stone shown in a colored plate.

Wardle, H. Newell. Clay cultus (?) objects from (Tuxtla) Vera Cruz, Mexico (*Actas primera sesión 27 cong. int. amer.*, tomo 1, 1942, p. 501-508). [339
A description and analysis of five small clay objects.

MAYA AREA

Berlin, Heinrich. Un templo olvidado en Palenque (*Rev. mex. estud. antrop.*, tomo 6, no. 1-2, 1942, p. 62-90). [339a
Study of a temple no more than briefly described in the previous literature. An architectural sequence of three periods is suggested for Palenque.

Cirerol Sansores, Manuel. La realidad de las fachadas mayas (*Actas primera sesión 27 cong. int. amer.*, tomo 1, 1942, p. 406-418). [340
Speculations as to the original appearance of the facades of Maya buildings when plastered and painted.

Fernández, Miguel Ángel. Los dinteles de zapote y el secreto de cómo fueron tallados (*Actas primera sesión 27 cong. int. amer.*, tomo 1, 1942, p. 601–611). [341

Principally a description of the lintel from Tikal in Basle.

Mariscal, Federico E. La escultura maya y la figura humana (*Acta primera sesión 27 cong. int. amer.*, tomo 1, 1942, p. 482–491). [342

A study of body proportions in Maya sculpture.

Thompson, J. Eric S. Las llamadas "fachadas de Quetzalcouatl" (*Actas primera sesión 27 cong. int. amer.*, tomo 1, 1942, p. 391–400). [343

Proves that the large mask façades of certain Maya buildings have been wrongly attributed to Quetzalcoatl.

Wauchope, Robert. Cremations at Zacualpa, Guatemala (*Actas primera sesión 27 cong. int. amer.*, tomo 1, 1942, p. 564–573). [344

A preliminary statement on the excavations at Zacualpa and a discussion of cremation burial in Middle America.

SOUTHERN CENTRAL AMERICA
AND THE ANTILLES

Lines, Jorge A. Esbozo arqueológico de Costa Rica (*Actas primera sesión 27 cong. int. amer.*, tomo 1, 1942, p. 217–222). [345

A brief résumé of the prehistoric remains of Costa Rica.

———. Estatuaria Huetar del sacrificio humano (*Rev. mex. estud. antrop.*, tomo 6, no. 1–2, 1942, p. 36–50). [345a

Figures holding human heads are identified as persons making human sacrifices. It is also suggested that the elaborate so-called metates were meant to hold the hearts of victims.

Stone, Doris. A delimitation of the Paya area in Honduras and certain stylistic resemblances found in Costa Rica and Honduras (*Actas primera sesión 27 cong. int. amer.*, tomo 1, 1942, p. 226–230). [346

A review of archaeological materials in Honduras tending to show that the remains in the Paya area are related to the south.

MIDDLE AMERICA: ETHNOLOGY

BY

RALPH L. BEALS

University of California

GENERAL STATEMENT

The year 1943, as was to be expected, saw a virtual cessation of ethnological field work in Mexico save for activities of Mexican scholars. Alfonso Villa Rojas continued his studies in Chiapas for the Carnegie Institution. Some work was done by members of the staff of the Instituto Nacional de Antropología e Historia and advanced students of the Escuela Nacional de Antropología. Roberto Weitlaner continued his numerous but rather brief studies in Guerrero and Oaxaca. Carlos Basauri and others also made short field excursions. Among students, the most notable work was that of Arturo Monson among the Huave. In Central America work was initiated by the Instituto Indigenista Inter-Americano on problems of diet and health.

The declining field activities of the previous two years were reflected in lessened publication. Publication was mostly in the form of short articles. The most extended publications in Mexico were by sociologists and others; a number were recapitulations of documentary material rather than reports of field work.

The Third Round Table sponsored by the Sociedad Mexicana de Antropología, which met in Mexico City in September, 1943, was perhaps the most significant of these gatherings from the standpoint of ethnology. The theme was the problem of relations between Middle America and Northern Mexico with the Southeastern and Southwestern areas of the United States. Many more ethnologists attended and much more discussion centered about ethnological data and problems than was the case in preceding Round Tables. The meeting was highly successful in bringing about an exchange of views and in clarifying the major problems. Plans were laid for a Fourth Round Table on the problems of the Santiago-Lerma and Balsas drainages. This conference would also have included many ethnological problems but circumstances made holding of the conference in 1944 impossible.

Another important development was the organization of the Institute of Social Anthropology in the Smithsonian Institution with support from the Division of Cultural Relations of the State Department. The Institute laid plans for the establishment of a number of cooperative institutes to carry on teaching, field training, and research in various Latin American countries. The first institute to get under way (in 1944) was that in Mexico. Field work and field training were scheduled to begin late in 1944.

BIBLIOGRAPHY
(See also section on FOLKLORE)

BIBLIOGRAPHIES

Beals, Ralph L. A selective guide to the material published in 1942 on anthropology: Middle America: ethnology (*Handbook of latin american studies, no. 8, 1942,* p. 21–25). [347

MONOGRAPHS AND SPECIAL PAPERS

GENERAL

Beals, Ralph, Robert Redfield, and **Sol Tax.** Anthropological research problems with reference to the contemporary peoples of Mexico and Guatemala (*Amer. anthrop.,* vol. 45, no. 1, Jan.–March, p. 1–21). [348

An attempt to summarize briefly existing knowledge of each major native group in Mexico and Guatemala and to suggest the various research projects that may be successfully pursued with each group. In addition to specific suggestions, discusses the broad general problems of the area and the opportunities for research related to general anthropological theory.

Jongh Osborne, Lilly de. La cerámica indígena en Centro América (*Amér. indígena,* vol. 3, no. 4, oct., p. 351–358). [349

A review of prehistoric, colonial, and modern pottery techniques, together with a good sketch of localities making pottery today.

Whorf, Benjamin Lee. Loan-words in ancient Mexico. New Orleans. Tulane univ. of Louisiana, Middle American research inst. (Philological and documentary studies, vol. 1, no. 1.) 13 p. [350

Interesting discussion of the possible uses of linguistic techniques to throw light on historical and archaeological problems. Illustrated mainly by Mayan and Uto-Aztecan examples.

MEXICO, EXCEPT YUCATÁN

(See also items 267, 2769)

Beals, Ralph L. The aboriginal culture of the Cáhita Indians. Berkeley. Los Angeles. Univ. of California press. (Ibero-Americana, 19). vii, 86 p., plates. [351

An attempt to achieve the fullest possible reconstruction of an aboriginal culture through the use of documents, comparative methods, and field studies of the modern culture of the group.

———. The population of northwest Mexico (*Amer. anthrop.,* vol. 45, no. 1, July–Sept., p. 486–488). [352

Reviews the evidence for the population of the Cáhita-speaking area and concludes the large figure given by Carl O. Sauer must be accepted despite doubts expressed by A. L. Kroeber.

———, and **Evelyn Hatcher.** The diet of a Tarascan village (*Amér. indígena,* vol. 3, no. 4, oct., p. 295–304). [353

A quantitative and qualitative study of diet in a relatively prosperous village, showing deficiencies and possible improvements. Emphasizes need of improved techniques of dietary studies and suggests changing of food habits may sometimes be more important than increasing food budgets.

Brand, Donald D. An historical sketch of geography and anthropology in the Tarascan region: Part 1. (*New Mex. anthrop.,* vol. 6–7, no. 2, whole no. 26, April–June, p. 37–108). [354

Synthesizes a large mass of documentary material. There will be disagreement with some of the conclusions. The very large bibliography is not specifically oriented to the Tarascan problem but is primarily a general bibliography for central Mexico.

———. Primitive and modern economy of the middle Río Balsas, Guerrero and Michoacán (*Proc. eighth amer. scien. cong.,* vol. 9, p. 225–231). [354a

Mainly devoted to modern conditions, pointing out location of various exploitive activities.

Cabeza de Vaca. Apuntes sobre la vida de los tarahumaras. México, D. F. Ed. Vargas Rea. (Bibl. Aportación histórica). 49 p. [355

Cerda Silva, Roberto de la. Los coras (*Rev. mex. soc.,* año 5, vol. 5, no. 1, primer trim., p. 89–117). [356

Continuation of a series of sketches of contemporary native groups in Mexico, now in its fourth year.

———. Los tarahumaras (*Rev. mex. soc.,* año 5, vol. 5, no. 3, tercer trim., p. 403–436). [357

———. Los tepehuanes (*Rev. mex. soc.,* año 5, vol. 5, no. 4, cuarto trim., p. 541–567). [358

Comas, Juan. Crítica del libro "Pescadores y campesinos tarascos" del Dr. José Gómez Robleda. México, D. F. 385–391 p. [360

Justly asserting that the day of the encyclopedist is past, the author gives concrete criticisms of biometric techniques in a useful and well-intentioned book.

Reprint from *América Indígena,* vol. 3, no. 4, oct., 1943.

Hatch, D. Spencer. Rural reconstruction in Mexico (*Applied anthrop.*, vol. 2, no. 4, Sept., p. 17-21). [362
Discussion of methods and results of a rural mission near Tepoztlan, Morelos.

Hostos, Adolfo de. Valor de la cultura indígena (*Amér. indígena*, vol. 3, no. 1, enero, p. 49-54). [363
Urges extension of all types of scientific study of native cultures to show that they are intrinsically similar to other cultures.

Johnson, Jean Bassett. A clear case of linguistic acculturation (*Amer. anthrop.*, vol. 45, no. 3, July-Sept., p. 427-434). [364
A technical discussion showing the influence of Spanish on all aspects of Yaqui speech, including morphology.

Loyo, Gilberto. Redistribución de grupos indígenas en México (*Amér. indígena*, vol. 3, no. 1, enero, p. 39-47). [365
A sane discussion of resettlement problems by a distinguished demographer, considering determination of resettlement needs; integration with social, political and economic organization of country is objective; psychological and cultural obstacles are recognized and suggestions for overcoming them are made.
Problems of organization in communities such as credit and administration are discussed.

Mendieta y Núñez, Lucio. Política cultural indigenista (*Amér. indígena*, vol. 3, no. 3, julio, p. 227-230). [366
Urges establishment of separate policies and educational systems for each Mexican Indian group, based on detailed study of ethnography and biotypology of each society. Points to failure of education unrelated to the cultural peculiarities, social goals, and practical necessities of the Indian societies.

Meyer L'Epée, Consuelo. La agricultura de México en la época precortesiana (*Investig. econ.*, tomo 3, no. 4, cuarto trim., p. 375-385). [367
A useful introduction for non-specialists.

Passin, Herbert. The place of kinship in Tarahumara social organization (*Acta amer.*, vol. 1, no. 3, July-Sept., p. 360-383; no. 4, Oct.-Dec., p. 471-495). [368
The most detailed analysis of kinship, made along functional lines, that has been made for any Mexican group. Part one deals with the structure of the system, part two describes it in action.

Sady, Rachel Reese. Usefulness of Mexican government records to ethnologists (*Acta amer.*, vol. 1, no. 3, July-Sept., p. 389-395). [369
Mexican government records may serve the ethnologist if checked carefully with field work.

Spicer, Edward H. Linguistic aspects of Yaqui acculturation (*Amer. anthrop.*, vol. 45, no. 3, July-Sept., p. 410-426). [370
A valuable discussion of both linguistic processes in an acculturated group and the use of linguistic evidence to understand acculturation phenomena.

TLALOCAN. A journal of source materials on the native cultures of Mexico. Publ. by the House of Tlaloc. Sacramento, California. Vol. 1, no. 1—. [371
A unique project, *Tlalocan* will be of value to specialists on conquest and colonial problems of Mexico's native cultures. Material so far published is mainly in native languages with translations or discussions of important colonial documents such as the *Relaciones Geográficas*. The editors hope to make available a considerable body of hitherto untranslated documents written in native languages which will be of value not only to the anthropologist but to the colonial historian.

Vega, J. La raza tarahumara y el medio geográfico y social en que vive (*Bol. soc. mex. geog. estad.*, tomo 58, no. 1-2, enero-abril, p. 103-121). [372

Vivó, Jorge A. Rasgos tribales y nacionales del problema indígena (*Cuad. amer.*, año 2, vol. 9, no. 3, mayo-junio, p. 155-163). [373
A survey of the historic and present social organization of the various types of American Indian societies with a plea for self-determination for surviving groups.

Warner, Ruth E. Yaquis of Mexico and their folk literature (*Kiva*, vol. 8, no. 3, March, p. 18-22). [374a
Brief introduction to a subject needing more extended treatment.

Weitlaner, R. J., and **Irmgard Weitlaner de Johnson.** Acatlán y Hueycantenango, Guerrero (*México antig.*, tomo 6, no. 4-6, feb., p. 140-204). [375
Discussion of surviving material culture and linguistic problems for the primarily Mexican speaking region east of Chilpancingo, Guerrero. Based on field work and documentary sources.

THE YUCATÁN PENINSULA

Barrera Vásquez, Alfredo. La lengua maya y su influencia en el español de Yucatán (*Yikal maya than*, año 4, tomo 4, no. 44, abril, p. 79, 92-95). [377
Brief, but by a highly qualified writer.

Hernández, Juan J. Costumbres de las indias de Yucatán (*Bol. arch. gen.*, México, tomo 14, no. 2, abril-junio, p. 267-280). [379

Morley, Silvanus Griswold. El nuevo imperio maya (*Yikal maya than*, año 4, tomo 4, no. 41, enero, p. 9–10; no. 43, marzo, p. 62–65). [380

Muntsch, Alberto. Some magico-religious observances of the present-day Maya Indians of British Honduras and Yucatán (*Primitive man,* vol. 16, no. 1–2, p. 31–43). [381

Negrón Pérez, Porfirio. Leyenda del Ahau-Dzon (*Yikal maya than,* año 4, tomo 4, no. 42, feb., p. 36–38). [382

Pérez Galaz, Juan de Dios. Derecho y organización social de los mayas. Campeche. Gobierno constitucional del Estado de Campeche. 106 p. [383

GUATEMALA

Gillin, John. Houses, food, and the contact of cultures in a Guatemalan town (*Acta amer.,* vol. 1, no. 3, July–Sept., p. 344–359). [384
A significant approach to acculturation problems. In Guatemala marked cultural dichotomy exists in matters of housing and food.

Redfield, Robert. Culture and education in the midwestern highland of Guatemala (*Amer. jour. soc.,* vol. 48, no. 6, May, p. 640–648). [385
The school is important only in formal education and as an agency of culture change. Most education is informal, supplemented in Indian culture by myths, tales, and service in the mixed social-religious-political organization.

Ries, Maurice. The ritual of the broken pots (*Amér. indígena,* vol. 3, no. 3, julio, p. 245–252). [386
A somewhat popular account of a Quiche ceremony in Guatemala performed every 260 days. Knowledge of the Tzolkin persists.

Teletor, Celso Narciso. Toponimia guatemalteca (*An. soc. geog. hist. Guatemala,* año 19, tomo 19, no. 2, dic., p. 116–124). [387
Etymology of native place names in the vicinity of Rabinal, Baja Vera Paz.

HONDURAS

Von Hagen, V. Wolfgang. The Jicaque (Torrupan) Indians of Honduras. New York. Museum of the American Indian, Heye foundation. (Indian notes and monographs, no. 53.) ix, 112 p., illus. [389
A brief but fairly systematic account. Best on material culture.

NICARAGUA

Álvarez Lejarza, Emilio. El problema del indio en Nicaragua. Managua. Ed. Nuevos horizontes. (Folleto no. 2.) 8 p. [390

PANAMA

Hooper, Ofelia. Possibilities for improvement among rural Panamanians (*Applied anthrop.,* vol. 2, no. 4, Sept., p. 4–10). [391
Discusses not only possibilities of environment and markets, but cultural obstacles to change and proposes mechanisms for accomplishing improvements.

EL SALVADOR

Lardé y Larín, Jorge. Distribución geográfica de los pueblos pokomanes y chortíes de la república de El Salvador (*Tzunpame,* año 3, no. 1, oct., p. 134–143). [392
Analysis of documentary materials. Apparently a reprint from *Revista del Archivo y Biblioteca Nacionales,* Tegucigalpa, tomo 21, no. 8, enero, 1943, p. 547-555.

THE WEST INDIES

Ortiz Fernández, Fernando. Las cuatro culturas indias de Cuba. Habana. Ed. Arellano. (Bibl. de estudios cubanos, vol. 1.) 176 p., ilus. [393
A scholarly review of past theories regarding the native cultures and a synthesis and interpretation of modern archaeological and ethnological data.

———. Nuevas teorías sobre las culturas indias de Cuba (*Rev. bim. cub.,* vol. 52, no. 1, julio-agosto, p. 5–17). [394
A summary of the author's recent book on Cuban cultures. See no. 393.

ADDENDA

Córdoba, Juan de. Vocabulario castellano-zapoteco. Introd. de Wigberto Jiménez Moreno. México, D. F. Inst. nac. de antropología e historia. (Bibl. lingüística mexicana, 1.) 1942. 37 p. [395
Facsimile reproduction of a work by one of the best of the colonial students of native languages.

Díaz-Bolio, José. Mayas antiguos y modernos (*Reg. cult. yuc.,* año 1, no. 1, dic., 1942, p. 5–20). [396

SOUTH AMERICA: ARCHAEOLOGY

BY

DONALD COLLIER

Chicago Natural History Museum

GENERAL STATEMENT

As was expected, war conditions during 1943 made it impossible for North American archaeologists to carry out field work in South America, with the exception of the work in Peru by Samuel K. Lothrop and John H. Rowe. The volume of field work done by South Americans was also reduced.

A number of South American journals carrying articles on archaeology were delayed in publication and distribution, and consequently are not in this volume of the *Handbook*. The following report on field work is incomplete because of difficulties encountered in gathering information.

Publication of the results of the Institute of Andean Research projects in South America (cf. *Handbook, no. 7, 1941*, and *Handbook, no. 8, 1942*) was brought nearly to completion during 1943. Two preliminary general reports and ten final reports on individual projects appeared (see items 197, 205, 410, 426, 432, 436, 437, 443, 444, 446–448).

EXPEDITIONS

In Colombia the active tempo of field work of recent years was maintained during 1943, and the founding of two new anthropological publications gave promise of expanding research activities. The Instituto Etnológico Nacional in Bogotá, under the direction of Paul Rivet, began publication of a *Revista*, the first volume of which contained several articles on archaeology. The Museo Arqueológico de Colombia, directed by Gregorio Hernández de Alba, issued the first volume of its *Boletín*.

During an exploration of the Guayabetal region near Villavicencio, Gregorio Hernández de Alba found cylindrical stone tombs associated with Chibcha ceramics and another type of pottery which he attributes to the Guayapes Indians, who inhabited the Meta plains at the time of the Conquest. Also, as the result of a study of a collection of pottery from the vicinity of Honda on the Río Magdalena, he was able to extend the distribution for the culture formerly called Mosquito but now renamed the Río Magdalena culture.

Luis Duque Gómez excavated tombs at San Agustín from which he recovered stone slabs, characteristic pottery, and ornaments of beaten and soldered gold. Luis Alfonso Sánchez carried out reconstructions of previously excavated monuments at the same site.

Eliécer Silva Celis, for the Instituto Etnológico, excavated a probably post-Conquest Indian cemetery at Soacha on the *altiplano* of Bogotá. He also explored several burial caves in the valley of Valleza (Boyacá) from which he removed skeletal material and artifacts.

Gerard Reichel-Dolmatoff, also of the Instituto Etnológico, discovered Chibcha burials and chronologically later Carib burials in the region of the

Páramo of Sumapaz (Cordillera Central). His excavations in Tolima revealed Carib urn burials and Quimbaya tombs containing ceramics.

Henri Lehman, of the University of Cauca, continued work in the Cauca region. In the vicinity of Moscopán, which lies midway between San Agustín and Tierradentro, he found a stone statue showing close similarities to San Agustín sculpture.

In Peru Rafael Larco Hoyle continued work on El Salinar and Cupisnique sites, and also excavated pottery of the Negativo style.

Julio C. Tello, of the Universidad de San Marcos, continued his work of restoration and reconstruction at Pachacamac.

Samuel K. Lothrop continued his study of the archaeological sites and collections of coastal Peru.

Under the direction of John H. Rowe, archaeological work in the Cuzco region was continued by the Section of Archaeology of the Universidad de Cuzco. The Site Catalogue of southern Peru was expanded, and the surface reconnaissance added to taxonomic and chronological knowledge of the area. It was possible on the basis of the new data to set up three ceramic series for the Cuzco region; namely, Chanapata (Pre-Inca), Killke (Early Inca), and Cuzco (Late Inca). Surface associations of pottery types further confirmed the temporal position of the Killke series. The distribution of the Chanapata culture was expanded.

In Chile, María de las Mercedes Constanzó, of the Museo Etnográfico in Buenos Aires, and Eduardo Casanova, of the Museo Argentino de Ciencias Naturales, studied the archaeological collections in Santiago, examined sites at Cartagena and Tiltil, and excavated at Chiu-Chiu near Antofagasta.

In Argentina, Francisco de Aparicio, of the Museo Etnográfico in Buenos Aires, carried out a reconnaissance in the Calchaquí and Santa María valleys. Of the many sites located the most important was a very large prehistoric town near Tolombón (Salta), where it is planned to excavate. Later, excavations were resumed at Pampa Grande (Salta), where three types of burial were found in caves.

Eduardo Casanova made a survey in the Valle Grande region in eastern Jujuy, and excavated at Doncellas (Puna de Jujuy) with good results.

Antonio Serrano, of the Instituto Arqueológico of the Universidad Nacional de Córdoba, carried out investigations in the departments of Cruz de Eje, Soto, Minas and Pocho.

BIBLIOGRAPHY

GENERAL

Collier, Donald. A selective guide to the material published in 1942 on anthropology: South America: archaeology (*Handbook of latin american studies, no. 8, 1942*, p. 26–32). [397

ARGENTINA

(*See also item* 466)

Canals Frau, Salvador. Las ruinas de Malargüé en la Provincia de Mendoza, (*An. inst. etnog. amer.*, tomo 4, p. 11–46, 4 láms.). [398
 Prehistoric and historic stone structures in southern Mendoza.

Rex González, Alberto. Arqueología del yacimiento indígena de Villa Rumipal. Córdoba. Univ. nacional de Córdoba. (Inst. de arqueología, lingüística y folklore "Dr. Pablo Cabrera," Publ. 4). 71 p., figs., láms. [400
 Published also, under the same title, in *Rev. univ. nac. Córdoba*, año 30, no. 7-8, sept.–oct., p. 916–973.

―――. Las figuras arcáicas de los yacimientos de Córdoba (*Rev. geog. amer.*, año 9, vol. 19, no. 117, junio, p. 345-350, ilus.). [401
Description of prehistoric clay figurines from Córdoba.

Salas, Alberto Mario. La labor arqueológica argentina en estos últimos años (*Acta amer.*, vol. 1, no. 2, April-June, p. 202-205). [402

Serrano, Antonio. El arte decorativo de los diaguitas. Córdoba. Imp. de la Universidad. (Univ. nac. de Córdoba, Inst. de arqueología, lingüística y folklore "Dr. Pablo Cabrera," Publ. 1). 137 p., 20 figs., 43 láms. [403
Discussion of four art styles of the Diaguita area, namely, Calchaquí, Sanagasta, Chaco-Santiagüeño, and Draconiform (Barreal). The so-called dragon in the last named style is nothing but a conventionalized feline figure.

Tabbush, Bertha J. Lobet de. Figuritas humanas en terracota del territorio argentino (*An. inst. etnog. amer.*, tomo 4, p. 249-343, 123 figs., 8 láms.). [404
Typological and distributional study of figurines from six different localities situated between Córdoba and Salta.

BOLIVIA

Casanova, Eduardo. Dos yacimientos arqueológicos en la península de Copacabana, Bolivia (*An. mus. arg. cien. nat.*, tomo 40, p. 333-399, 52 figs., 8 láms.). [405
Exploration and excavation in the region of Macachi and Copacabana. One test pit yielded the stratigraphic sequence: Inca, Decadent, Tiahuanaco, Classic Tiahuanaco.

Posnansky, Arthur. La gigantesca cabeza monolítica de Tihuanacú, hoy en el templete Tihuanacú en la plaza del "Hombre americano" (*An. arq. Bol.*, vol. 1, no. 1, p. 15-16). [406

―――. Los hieroglíficos lunares de Puma Punku (*An. arq. Bol.*, vol. 1, no. 1, p. 23-26). [407

Uhle, Max. Alter und herkunft der ruinen von tiahuanaco (*Rev. mus. nac.*, Lima, tomo 12, no. 1, primer semestre, p. 14-18). [408
Comments on the origin and antiquity of Tiahuanaco. Spanish translation by J. C. Muelle (p. 19-23).

BRITISH GUIANA

Carter, J. E. L. An account of some recent excavations at Seba, British Guiana (*Amer. antiquity*, vol. 9, no. 1, July, p. 89-99, 3 figs., 2 plates). [409
Test excavation on the Demarara River yielding stone and pottery artifacts.

CHILE

Bird, Junius B. Excavations in northern Chile. New York. American museum of natural history. (Anthrop. papers, vol. 38, part 4). 179-318 p., 46 figs. [410
Survey and excavations on the coast from Pisagua to Coquimbo. Establishes stratigraphically two non-agricultural, pre-pottery, fishing cultures, and a subsequent horizon with pottery and agriculture in which Tiahuanaco influences appear to be relatively late.

Mostny, Grete. Chilean archaeology (*Andean quart.*, summer, p. 23-30). [411

―――. Informe sobre excavaciones en Arica (*Bol. mus. nac.*, Chile, tomo 21, p. 79-117, 12 láms.). [412
Description of 13 graves with complete list of associated artifacts by grave.

COLOMBIA

(*See also item* 502)

Barbosa, Enrique. La cerámica en Popayán (*Rev. univ. Cauca*, no. 1, enero-feb., p. 205-208). [413

Duque Gómez, Luis. Excavación de un sitio de habitación en Supía (*Rev. inst. etnol. nac.*, Bogotá, vol. 1, entrega 1, p. 95-115, 4 figs., 2 láms.). [414
Test excavation in Departamento de Caldas.

―――. Informe de la Comisión arqueológica del Departamento de Caldas (*Bol. mus. arq. Col.*, año 1, no. 2, nov., p. 15-31). [415
Part I of report on an archaeological survey in Caldas, including inventory of private collections in the region.

Hernández de Alba, Gregorio. Guía arqueológica de San Agustín o del macizo central de los Andes. Bogotá. Imp. nacional. (Min. de educación nacional, Extensión cultural y bellas artes, Servicio arqueológico.) 40 p., 27 láms. [416

―――. Momias de Chiscas, Boyacá (*Bol. mus. arq. Col.*, año 1, no. 1, feb., p. 3-9). [417
Description of removal of textile wrappings from a mummy.

Lehman, H. Notas arqueológicas sobre el Cauca (*Rev. univ. Cauca*, no. 1, enero-feb., p. 196-201). [418

Ochoa Sierra, Blanca. Una técnica en la decoración de cerámicas (*Bol. mus. arq. Col.,* año 1, no. 1, feb., p. 9-14). [419
Deeply cut or excavated designs on Quimbaya pottery.

Pérez de Barradas, José. Arqueología agustiniana. Excavaciones arqueológicas realizadas de marzo a diciembre de 1937. Bogotá. Imp. nacional. (Bibl. de cultura colombiana.) 169 p., 179 figs., 189 láms., 1 mapa, 1 plan. [420
An account of the geography and history of the locality and a detailed and well illustrated description of explorations and excavations within and near San Agustín National Park. An important addition to the literature on San Agustín culture.

Polanía Puyo, Jaime. Cultura precolombina (*Bol. hist. antig.,* vol. 30, no. 342-343, abril-mayo, p. 489-494). [421
Remarks relating to San Agustín culture and to the archaeology of Plata Vieja. [A. Métraux]

Reichel-Dolmatoff, Gérard. Apuntes arqueológicos de Soacha (*Rev. inst. etnol. nac.,* Bogotá, vol. 1, entrega 1, p. 15-25, 3 láms.). [422
Surface collection of sherds, spindle whorls, and miscellaneous artifacts from a Chibcha (?) site on the *altiplano* of Bogotá.

————, and Alicia Dussan de Reichel. Las urnas funerarias en la Cuenca del Río Magdalena (*Rev. inst. etnol. nac.,* Bogotá, vol. 1, entrega 1, p. 209-281, 11 figs., 11 láms.). [423
Funeral urns from the lower, middle and upper Magdalena. Some description of associated artifacts.

Rivet, Paul. Metalurgía del platino en la América precolombina (*Rev. inst. etnol. nac.,* Bogotá, vol. 1, entrega 1, p. 39-45). [424
Deals with platinum artifacts from Ecuador and Colombia.

Silva Celis, E. La arqueología de Tierradentro (*Rev. inst. etnol. nac.,* Bogotá, vol. 1, entrega 1, p. 117-130). [425
Part I of a report on an archaeological survey of Tierradentro.

ECUADOR

Collier, Donald, and John V. Murra. Survey and excavations in southern Ecuador. Chicago. Field museum of natural history. (Anthropological series, vol. 35, Inst. of Andean research, Paper no. 9 b.) 108 p., 18 figs., 54 pl. [426
A reconnaissance in the provinces of Chimborazo, Cañar, Azuay and Loja, and stratigraphic excavations in Cañar revealing two pre-Inca periods and an Inca horizon. A Spanish translation by Aníbal Buitrón Chávez of the concluding chapter appeared under the title "Arqueología Ecuatoriana" in *Bol. acad. nac. hist.,* Quito, vol. 23, no. 61, enero-junio, p. 127-132.

PERU

(*See also item* 1938)

Bennett, Wendell C. The position of Chavin in Andean sequences (*Proc. amer. phil. soc.,* vol. 86, no. 2, Feb. 10, p. 323-327). [427
An appraisal of the chronological aspect of the Chavin problem.

Clothier, II, William J. Recuay pottery in the lower Santa valley (*Rev. mus. nac.,* Lima, tomo 12, no. 2, segundo semestre, p. 239-242). [428
Negative painted pottery from cemetery near Tanguche.

Cornejo Bouroncle, Jorge. El templo del sol (*Rev. geog. amer.,* año 9, vol. 20, no. 119, agosto, p. 81-88). [429
A description of the temple of the Sun with a good photograph. [A. Métraux]

Cuadros E., Manuel E. Las nuevas e importantes ciudades milenarias descubiertas en la región de Machupicchu. Cuzco. Tall. gráf. La Económica. (Bibl. Cultura, Centro Inca Garcilaso, vol. 1.) 16 p. [430
Also published in *Garcilaso,* set., p. 24-38.

Delgado Flores, Carmen. Area del imperio del Gran Chimú (*Alpha,* año 3, no. 4, set., p. 14-17). [431

Kidder, II, Alfred. Some early sites in the northern Lake Titicaca basin. Cambridge, Mass. (Harvard univ., Peabody museum of American archaeology and ethnology, Papers, vol. 27, no. 1, Expeditions to southern Peru, Report no. 1.) 48, vii p., 7 figs., 5 plates. [432
A reconnaissance in the Puno region. Suggests a Pucara phase for this area as distinguished from a Tiahuanaco phase to the south, both being manifestations of an early Titicaca Basin culture.

Llanos, Luis A. Hallazgo en el Cusco (*Rev. mus. nac.,* Lima, tomo 12, no. 1, primer semestre, p. 109-114). [433
Inca pottery and silver objects from three tombs discovered in Cuzco.

Muelle, Jorge C. Concerning the middle Chimú style. Berkeley, Los Angeles. Univ. of California press. (Univ. of Calif. publs. in American archaeology and ethnology, vol. 39, no. 3). p. 203-221, illus., plates. [434
Proposes the thesis that the stylistic transition from Early to Late Chimú resulted from the transfer of Early Chimú

forms in clay to Middle Chimú vessels of metal, and the subsequent retransfer to late Chimú clay vessels.

Navarro de Águila, Víctor. Los pukullos de Huayanay (*Rev. mus. nac.*, Lima, tomo 12, primer semestre, p. 97–108). [435
Stone tombs in Ayacucho.

Strong, W. D., and J. M. Corbett. A ceramic sequence at Pachacamac (*Archaeological studies in Peru, 1941–1942*. New York. Columbia univ. press. p. 27–121, 20 figs., 6 pls.). [436
A stratigraphic cut in refuse 10 meters deep revealed the following sequence of ceramic periods: Inca, three-color Geometric, Tiahuanacoid, Early Lima, Interlocking, Chancay White-on-red.

———, and G. R. Willey. Archaeological notes on the central coast (*Archaeological studies in Peru, 1941–1942*. New York. Columbia univ. press.) p. 5–25, 5 pl. [437
Report on surveys to north and south of Lima and on excavations in the early shell heaps at Ancon and Supe.

———, ———, and John M. Corbett. Archeological studies in Peru, 1941–1942. New York. Columbia univ. press. (Columbia studies in archaeology and ethnology, vol. 1.) 222 p., illus. [438

Swanton, John R. The quipu and Peruvian civilization. Washington, D. C. Smithsonian inst. (Bureau of American ethnology, Bull. no. 133, Anthropological papers, no. 26.) 589–596 p. [439

Tello, Julio C. Discovery of the Chavin culture in Peru (*Amer. antiquity*, vol. 9, no. 1, July, p. 135–160, 14 plates). [440
General account and illustrations of Tello's Chavin finds of the past twenty-five years, with special emphasis on discoveries in the valleys of Nepeña and Casma. Translation, with additional illustrations, of an article entitled "Sobre el Descubrimiento de la Cultura Chavin del Perú," in *Proc. int. cong. amer.*, Mexico, vol. 1, p. 231–252. The Spanish version also appeared in *Letras*, Lima, tercer cuatrimestre, p. 326–373.

Villar Córdoba, P. E. Las ruinas de Ascona y Maranga (*Actas acad. nac. cien. exac. fis. nat. Lima*, vol. 5, parte 5, p. 160–177, 5 figs.). [441
Adobe pyramids near Lima.

Willey, G. R. Excavations in the Chancay valley (*Archaeological studies in Peru, 1941–1942*, New York, Columbia univ. press, p. 123–196, 13 figs., 9 plates, 9 tables). [443
Stratigraphic proof that Chancay White-on-red pottery is older than the Interlocking style. A culture sequence for the central coast is presented.

———. A supplement to the pottery sequence at Ancon (*Archaeological studies in Peru, 1941–1942*, New York, Columbia univ. press, p. 200–211). [444
Analysis of pottery from twenty graves excavated from the Ancon Necropolis. The material falls stylistically between Middle Ancon II and Late Ancon I.

URUGUAY

Freitas, Carlos A. Alfarería del delta del río Negro (Reprint from *Rev. hist.*, Montevideo, segunda época, año 36, tomo 13). [445
Well illustrated report on plain, painted and incised pottery from a site at the junction of the Río Negro and the Río Uruguay.

VENEZUELA

Howard, George Delvigne. Excavations at Ronquín, Venezuela. New Haven. Yale univ. press; London. Oxford univ. press. (Inst. of Andean research, Publ. 5A; Yale univ. publ. in anthrop., no. 28.) 90 p., 11 figs., 7 pl. [446
This stratigraphic excavation on the middle Orinoco established an earlier period with pottery resembling the earliest known ceramics in Trinidad, and a later period typical of the middle Orinoco region.

Osgood, Cornelius. Excavations at Tocorón, Venezuela. New Haven. Yale univ. press; London. Oxford univ. press. (Inst. of Andean research, Publ. 5 B; Yale univ. publ. in anthrop., no. 29.) 72 p., 16 figs., 16 pl. [447
Excavations of mounds in the Lake Valencia area revealing two successive ceramic periods, the earlier of which resembles early pottery of the Orinoco area and Trinidad.

———, and George D. Howard. An archaeological survey of Venezuela. New Haven. Yale univ. press; London. Oxford univ. press. (Inst. of Andean research, Publ. 5 D; Yale univ. publ. in anthrop., no. 27.) 153 p., 27 figs., 15 pl. [448
Establishes six ceramic areas for Venezuela. A relationship in pottery styles is found between the Orinoco region and the West Indies.

ADDENDA

Aparicio, Francisco de. La tambería del rincón del Toro (*Publ. mus. etnog.*, Buenos Aires, serie A, vol. 4, 1942, p. 239–251, 7 figs., 6 láms.). [450

Canals Frau, Salvador. El límite austral de los diaguitas (*Publ. mus. etnog.*, Buenos

Aires, serie A, vol. 4, 1942, p. 117-139). **[451**

Estevão, Carlos. O ossuário da "Gruto-do-Padre," em Itaparica, e algumas noticias sobre remanescentes indígenas do nordeste (*Bol. mus. nac.*, Rio, vol. 14–17, 1942, p. 153–184, 27 láms). **[451a**
Cave burials on the Rio São Francisco in the state of Pernambuco. Stone implements, textile fragments, and bone and shell implements were recovered from the graves. Appendix by Bastos de Ávila on two of the human teeth.

Greslebin, Héctor. Sobre el descubrimiento de una forma de techar los recientes pircados, rectangulares, realizados en la tambería del Inca, Chilecito, Provincia de La Rioja, República Argentina (*Actas primera sesión 27 cong. int. amer.*, tomo 1, 1942, p. 261–276, 15 figs.). **[452**

Lehmann, Henri. Note sur une statue en pierre de Tiahuanaco (*Actas primera sesión 27 cong. int. amer.*, tomo 1, 1942, p. 253–260, 6 figs.). **[453**
Description of a feline figure collected by d'Orbigny at Tiahuanaco in 1833, and recently brought to light in Paris.

Oramas, Luis R. Prehistoria y arqueología de Venezuela. Construcciones y petrografías artísticas en una región de Venezuela (*Actas primera sesión 27 cong. int. amer.*, tomo 1, 1942, p. 277–302, 14 figs.). **[454**
Stone structures and petroglyphs in the Vigirima Valley, state of Carabobo.

Vellard, J. A. Archéologie des Andes vénézuéliennes (*Bol. mus. nac.*, Rio, vol. 14–17, 1942, p. 363–380). **[454a**
General discussion of the archaeology of the Andes of Mérida.

SOUTH AMERICA: ETHNOLOGY

BY

ALFRED MÉTRAUX

Smithsonian Institution

GENERAL STATEMENT

The anthropological bibliography for 1943 is somewhat larger than for the preceding years. Unfortunately our knowledge of the South American Indians has gained very little by this increase in publications. Once more we are overwhelmed by anthologies reproducing the same well known passages, by naïve and unscholarly compilations and by lyrical outbursts about the virtues of the Indians and their future grandeur in the New World. In the meantime few of those who live near the Indians make any attempt to save for posterity a vision of their vanishing culture. If those who indulge in literary exercises would rather turn their attention to the reality around them, they would serve science and even help the Indians.

Those in South America who conceive of anthropology as something different from an antiquarian pastime are far too few. Again and again men, conscious of the urgency of original field work, must muster their energy to save the debris of native cultures and they must provoke in others awareness of the need for trustworthy observations of the still living Indians. Even today South American ethnology is in its infancy. The number of tribes which are well known is ridiculously small. Since Europe for years will be unable to send scientists to the field and since it is doubtful whether sufficient funds will be available for North American anthropologists to accomplish by themselves the essential survey of the unknown areas of South America, South Americans must contribute to the study of their own native populations. This they will be able to accomplish only when they give up writing eulogies or pointless compilations. There is no substitute for field work and painstaking research by serious minds. The appropriate time for essays and inspirational articles will come when more factual material about the Indian population is accumulated.

EXPEDITIONS

The war brought to a standstill anthropological field research in South America. The only news about field trips had reached us from Brazil and Colombia.

During 1943, the Museu Nacional of Rio de Janeiro, under the direction of Dra. Heloisa Torres, sent out on a field expedition Mr. and Mrs. James Watson of the Department of Anthropology, University of Chicago, and Mr. Nelson Texeira and Eduardo Galvão, who planned to study a group of Caiuá (Guaraní) Indians in the State of Matto Grosso. There is as yet no information about the results of this expedition.

Henri Lehmann, of the Instituto Etnológico Nacional of Bogotá, accompanied by Alberto Ceballos and Milcíades Cháves visited the Kwaiker Indians in Southwestern Colombia. Measurements and blood tests were made of about 150 Indians; linguistic materials also were recorded and artifacts were assembled.

During 1943 appeared the first issue of the *Revista del Instituto Etnológico Nacional* of Bogotá founded by Paul Rivet. The articles which it contains are reviewed below. This new journal sets a very high standard of scholarship and brings out important contributions to Colombian ethnology and archaeology.

BIBLIOGRAPHY

(See also section on FOLKLORE*)*

GENERAL

Costa, João Angyone. Indiologia. Rio de Janeiro. Gráf. Laemmert. (Bibl. militar, vols. 66–67). 272 p. [455
Essays on various topics of South American ethnography. Among other things the author discusses the sense of modesty among the Indians, domestication of animals, native foods, the African origin of the word *tanga*. American readers will be especially pleased by the chapter about American contribution to Brazilian ethnology. A chapter is dedicated to bibliography. There is also a long article about Easter Island and its significance for South American ethnology. The whole constitutes a worthwhile contribution to many important problems.

Gandía, Enrique de. Problemas indígenas americanos. Buenos Aires. Col. Buen Aire. 113 p. [456
Essays on South American ethnology. Erudite compilation of the known data on the Indians of the Province of Buenos Aires in the sixteenth century. Documents on the deportation of Indian groups during the colonial period. Interesting hypothesis about the function of the mysterious mounds of the region of Salta which the author interprets as cultivation plots. He also explains the enigmatic holes in rocks so common in certain regions of Argentina (Córdoba, San Luis) as small gardens for planting cassava, melons and other plants. Comparison between the drive hunts of the Inca empire and those of India. See item 518.

Métraux, Alfred. Le caractère de la conquête jésuitique (*Acta amer.*, vol. 1, no. 1, Jan.–March, p. 69). [457
The Jesuits succeeded in forming their reductions by offering the Indians obvious economic advantages, such as iron tools. They also were assimilated to shamans and chiefs. All these factors facilitated their peaceful conquest of vast regions in South America.

———. A selective guide to the material published in 1942 on anthropology: South America: ethnology (*Handbook of latin american studies, no. 8, 1942*, p. 33–40). [458

Rojas, Ricardo. El problema indígena (*Sustancia*, año 4, no. 14, marzo–abril, p. 354–371). [459
Generalities about the Indian problem in America. Lengthy exposé of the policy of the United States toward the Indians. The author asks for land and schools for the Indians.

Schaden, Egon. Bibliografia do P. Wilhelm Schmidt, S. V. D. (*Bol. bibliog.*, São Paulo, ano 1, vol. 1, out.–dez., p. 21–39). [460
Valuable bibliography of the famous Catholic anthropologist, editor of *Anthropos*. Short biography.

Vivante, Armando. Pueblos primitivos de Sudamérica. Buenos Aires. Ed. Emecé. (Col. Buen aire). 103 p. [461
The title is misleading. The book is an anthology of selected pages from various chroniclers describing the Indians of Peru and of the Argentine. The choice is very limited. This anthology aims perhaps at showing that our only information about Indians is confined to what may be found in early chronicles.

ARGENTINA

Caillet-Bois, Teodoro. El fin de una raza de gigantes (*Bol. inst. invest. hist.*, año 21, tomo 27, no. 93–96, julio, 1942–junio, 1943, p. 7–41). [462
Travels of Musters among the Patagonian (Tehuelche) Indians. Tragic fate of several Tehuelche bands in the second half of the last century. In 1917 there were still about 300 Tehuelche mixed with other groups.

Canals Frau, Salvador. Los aborígenes del valle de Salta en el siglo 16 (*An. inst. etnog. amer.*, tomo 4, p. 207–248). [463
The author considers the La Candelaria culture as "Amazonian" with Andean influences. However, no evidence is given for that hypothesis. The rest of the article contains interesting historical data on the Pulares, Guachipas and other groups of Northwestern Argentina. The Lule may well have been distinct from the Tonocoté who in the reviewer's opinion are the carriers of La Candelaria culture.

———. El "habitat" de los antiguos querandíes (*Gaea,* tomo 7, entrega 1, p. 123-130). [464

Harrington, Tomás. El keñewe o yamjatrráwich. Córdoba. Imp. de la Univ. (Univ. nac. de Córdoba, Inst. de arqueología, lingüística y folklore, publ. 2.) 12 p. [465
Interesting note about the preparation of skins among the Indians of Patagonia. Elaborate description of the scratchers.

Márquez Miranda, Fernando. Los diaguitas y la guerra (*An. inst. etnog. amer.,* tomo 4, p. 207-248). [466
The second part of an article reviewed in *Handbook of Latin American Studies, no. 8, 1942,* item 293. It contains a study on the weapons of the Diaguita. These Indians used bows and arrows, spearthrowers, slings, maces, spears, shields.

Métraux, Alfred. Suicide among the Matako of the Argentine Gran Chaco (*Amér. indígena,* vol. 3, no. 3, julio, p. 199-209). [467
History of about 14 cases of suicides which occurred among the Matako Indians and an attempt to analyze the psychological factors behind the suicidal epidemics among these Indians. The Matako kill themselves by eating a fruit called the *sachasandia* (*Capparis salisifolia*) which is also used as food after it has been properly cured. It is still uncertain whether the suicidal epidemics took place in aboriginal conditions as frequently as they do now. Suicide among the Matako has often a very aggressive character.

Paucke, Florián. Hacia allá y para acá. Una estada entre los indios mocobíes, 1749-1767. Trad. por Edmundo Wernicke. Tucumán, Buenos Aires. Imp. Coni. xii, 322 p., ilus. [468
Second part of the work by the German Jesuit Paucke. See *Handbook of Latin American Studies, no. 8, 1942,* item 372.

Rojas, Ricardo. El problema indígena en Argentina (*Amér. indígena,* vol. 3, no. 2, abril, p. 105-114). [469
The famous Argentine writer asks for better treatment of the Indians and for better understanding of their problems. Stresses the part played by the Indian in Argentine history.

Strube E., León. Técnica etimológica y etimología andina (*Rev. univ. nac. Córdoba,* año 30, no. 5-6, julio-agosto, p. 419-459). [470
The author calls attention to the very inaccurate transcription of native sounds in ancient chronicles and documents. An elementary knowledge of phonetics is necessary to indulge in the joys of etymology.
Also published separately: Córdoba. Imp. de la Univ. (Univ. nac. de Córdoba, Inst. de arqueología, lingüística y folklore, publ. 3.) 45 p.

Tebboth, Tomás. Diccionario castellano-toba (*Rev. inst. antrop. univ. nac. Tucumán,* vol. 3, no. 2, p. 35-221). [471
Fairly extensive Spanish-Toba dictionary composed by a British missionary. It represents the dialect spoken by the Toba of Sombrero Negro (Formosa, Argentina).

BOLIVIA

Camacho, José María. Los aymaras. Cap. 7-8 (*Bol. soc. geog. La Paz,* año 54, no. 65, junio, p. 13-48). [472
Ethnography of the ancient Aymara, their political organization, army, and land tenure. The author is prone to idealize and to simplify the complexity of the culture. First hand observations would have been more useful.

Escalante, José Ángel, and others. Cómo puede ser la escritura del qheshwa, sus dialectos, y el aymara (*Rev. ling. farm. ind.,* vol. 1, no. 1, p. 3-9). [473
The author deciphers the symbolic meanings of designs on Tiahuanaco vases! He follows Dr. Posnansky's path.

Markham, Clemente H. La impropiedad del nombre Aymara (*Kollasuyo,* año 5, no. 50, agosto-sept., p. 112-133). [474
Translation of an article by the English erudite published 60 years ago. The name Aymara is improperly used since it originally applied to a small Quechua group.

Posnansky, Arthur. Los dos tipos indigenales en Bolivia y su educación (*Amér. indígena,* vol. 3, no. 1, enero, p. 55-60). [475
The author again reveals his naïve racist theories about Bolivia: the Indians of the *altiplano* belong to two races, one, the Kholla, is intelligent and light skinned, the other, the Arawak, is stupid and, of course, dark skinned. Such unwarranted and fantastic theories may cause a great deal of harm with people who are not aware of scientific anthropology.

Sapahaqui, David F., and **Manuel Sapahaqui.** De la naturaleza, calidades, y grados de árboles, frutos, plantas, flores, animales y otras cosas exquicitas y raras del nuevo orbe del Perú y pa. más claridad pr. el Orn. de A.B.C. (*An. arq. Bol.,* vol. 1, no. 1, Sección farmacopeia indiana, p. 1-15). [476
Manuscript of 1699 discovered by Arturo Posnansky which deals with medicinal herbs. Valuable information about the preparation of drugs and their effects.

BRAZIL

Ayrosa, Plínio. Etnografia e lingua tupí-guaraní. São Paulo. Univ. de São Paulo,

Facultad de filosofia, ciencias e letras. (Bol. 33). 333 p. [477

Dr. Plínio Ayrosa has undertaken one of the most difficult tasks of South American erudition, namely to establish an exhaustive bibliography of the Tupí-Guaraní linguistic family. As he himself warns the reader, gaps and omissions were unavoidable, but this volume will prove of great help to linguists and anthropologists. Each of the 585 books and publications listed by Ayrosa is carefully described and briefly analyzed. The volume contains also a good bibliography of bibliographies of Tupí-Guaraní. It is to be hoped that Dr. Plínio Ayrosa will complete this bibliography by including the list of articles dealing with Tupí-Guaraní languages which have been published in Europe and South America. He seems to have overlooked the *Revista de Etnología de la Universidad de Tucumán* and the *Revista del Museo de la Plata*, as well as the *Zeitschrift für Ethnologie* and *Anthropos*.

————. Hispanismos no tupí-guaraní (*Rev. acad. paulista let.*, ano 6, no. 23, set., p. 19–28). [478
Spanish influences on Tupí-Guaraní dialects.

Baldus, Herbert. Ensáio sôbre a história da etnologia brasileira (*Bol. bibliog.*, São Paulo, ano 1, vol. 1, out.–dez., p. 59–69). [479
History of anthropological studies in Brasil from the sixteenth century to our days. Serious and well documented essay. Spanish translation published in *Rev. mex. soc.*, año 5, vol. 5, no. 2, segundo trim., p. 171–183.

Costa, João Angyone. A alimentação de nossos índios (*Amer. indígena*, vol. 3, no. 3, julio, p. 221–226). [480
The author makes the rather amazing statement that the Indians of the Brazilian coast did not have any agriculture in the sixteenth century. He mentions as his sources authors who give excellent descriptions of Indian farming.

————. Conversa sôbre os idiomas do índio (*Rev. bras.*, ano 3, no. 5, março, p. 95–106). [481
Historical survey of studies of native languages in Brazil from the sixteenth century down to the present.

————. O sentimento do pudor entre os índios do Brasil e da América (*Rev. bras.*, ano 3, no. 7, set., p. 74–83). [482
See *Indiologia*, item 455.

Cruz, Manuel. O exorcismo da caça, do peixe e das frutas entre os borôro (*Rev. arq. mun.*, São Paulo, ano 8, vol. 89, março–abril, p. 151–156). [483
Valuable article on the magic rites performed by Bororo shamans to remove from foods obnoxious influences.

————. Mitologia borora (*Rev. arq. mun.*, São Paulo, ano 9, vol. 91, julho, p. 159–166). [484
The first myth is about a certain kind of beings, half men, half spirits who made the first necklaces of fruit shell, invented ritual songs and finally were changed into various species of birds. The *urucu*, the cotton and the gourd were born from their ashes. The second myth tells us of a time when spirits had in their care fields in which maize grew spontaneously. A woman's unkind remark ended the spontaneous growth of maize and henceforth men were obliged to sow it. However, they may still obtain good crops if they invoke the benevolent spirit.

Drumond, Carlos. Designativos de parentesco no tupí-guaraní (*Sociologia*, vol. 5, no. 4, out., p. 328–354). [485
List of the relationship terms used by the Tupí-Guaraní. Unfortunately the author does not attempt to establish their relationship system.

Freitas, Newton. Amazonia. Leyendas ñangatú. Buenos Aires. Ed. Nova. (Col. Mar dulce.) 90 p. [486
Anthology of legends of modern Indians of the Amazon. These tales were collected by Brandão de Amorim and published in 1928 in the *Revista de Instituto Histórico e Geográfico do Brasil*.

Krause, Fritz. Nos sertões do Brasil (*Rev. arq. mun.*, São Paulo, ano 8, vol. 88, jan.–fev., p. 183–205; vol. 89, março–abril, p. 157–172; vol. 90, maio–junho, p. 179–193; ano 9, vol. 91, julho, p. 167–180; vol. 92, agôsto–set., p. 161–173; vol. 93, out.–dez., p. 131–142). [487
Portuguese translation of Fritz Kraus' *In den Wildnissen Brasiliens*, published in Leipzig, in 1911. The volume contains an account of the author's trip to the Araguaya in 1908 and very detailed description of the material culture of the Shavajé, Kayapó, Karajá and Tapirapé.

Lévi-Strauss, Claude. The social use of kinship terms among Brazilian Indians (*Amer. anthrop.*, vol. 45, no. 3, July–Sept., p. 398–409). [488
The Nambikuára have a simple classificatory kinship system. Cross-cousin marriage prevails. Actual and prospective brothers-in-law observe a special set of behaviors and are aften bound by homosexual ties. When a new group joins force with another, the newcomers are assimilated to brothers-in-law. A similar kinship structure and marriage rules obtained among the ancient Tupinamba. Relationships between brothers-in-law were also very close and determined by special behavior. The European assimilated the brother-in-law relationship to that of "compères" which in the Mediterranean world is endowed with special significance and also serves to create a tie with strangers taken into a community.

Magalhães, Amílcar A. Botelho de. O problema de civilização dos índios no

Brasil (*Amér. indígena*, vol. 3, no. 2, abril, p. 153-160; no. 4, oct., p. 329-335). [489
Pages from a diary of the 1907 expedition under Colonel Rondon to the country of the Nhambiquaras. The author mentions anthropological publications on these Indians. He also quotes an official report showing that the Indians were employed as telegraphers and workers a few years after the line was established.
The second part of the study is the history of the pacification of the Kaingang in Southern Brazil. It shows the remarkable results of the method advocated by General Rondon. Fair treatment, justice and generosity achieved more than the old brutal measures against the natives.

Pinto, Estevão. O franciscano André Thevet (*Cultura política*, ano 3, no. 32, set., p. 118-136). [490
Remarkable study on the famous French traveller and cosmographer André Thevet who visited Brazil in 1554. Biographical data, analysis of his talent and appreciation of his contributions to Brazilian ethnology.

Ramos, Arthur. Introdução a antropologia brasileira. Primeiro vol. As culturas não-européias. Rio de Janeiro. (Col. Estudos brasileiros da C.E.B. I., Série B.) 540 p. [491
The modest title "introduction" does not do justice to this comprehensive handbook of Brazilian ethnology. The author has not only included Indian cultures, but also the African cultures, a subject on which he is an authority. The author discusses the general theories about the origin of the Indians, then he examines separately the various linguistic groups: Tupí-Guaraní, Gê, Aruak, Carib, Bororo, Nambikwára and Carajá.
The section devoted to the Negro elements in Brazil, begins with an outline of the African background and then examines the cultural survivals of the main African groups in Brazil.
An extensive and up-to-date bibliography is attached to each chapter.
This handbook is probably one of the most important contributions to ethnography published in South America in recent years.

Vieira, Gastão. Vocabulário caiapó (*Cultura política*, ano 3, no. 23, jan., p. 120-122). [492
Short vocabulary of the Caiapó language.

Wagley, Charles. Notas sobre aculturação entre os guajajara (*Bol. mus. nac.*, Rio, nova série, antropologia, no. 2, 15 de junho, p. 1-12). [493
Short, but very precise description of the present state of the culture of the Guajajara-Tenetehara. Customs centering around life cycle have remained almost unimpaired. Child betrothal still exists. Their religion is based on shamanism and some villages still have from six to seven shamans. Shamans are possessed by spirits and act according to the characteristics of that spirit.

Thus a man taken by the spirit of the deer will eat leaves.
The mythology shows Negro and White influences.

———. Xamanismo tapirapé (*Bol. mus. nac.*, Rio, nova série, antropologia, no. 3, 15 de set., p. 1-94). [494
One of the year's best contributions to South American ethnology. Short description of the cultural background of the Tapirapé. Knowledge of the supernatural world is gained chiefly through dream experiences of the shamans. The soul of the shaman frees itself and has many adventures. It receives power from spirits who become his familiars. Shamans destroy enemies by capturing their souls and perform cures by sucking out of the patient's body some pathogenic object. They protect people against ghosts, control pregnancy of women and bring them children. They also provide the people with abundant food and see that they are not attacked by dangerous animals. They have power of prophecy and every year, at the beginning of the rainy season, they fight against thunder and his minions in order to protect the gardens and even the people themselves from its violence. The article contains a detailed description of the ceremony during which shamans fight thunder.

Wirth, D. Mauro. A mitologia dos vapidiana do Brasil (*Sociologia*, vol. 5, no. 3, agôsto, p. 257-268). [495
Careful analysis of Wapidiana folklore. The Wapidiana are Arawakan Indians who live across the border of Brazil and British Guiana. Most of the motifs analyzed by the author occur in the mythology of other Guiana tribes.

CHILE

Oyarzún, Aureliano. La institución de la iniciación entre los yaganes (*Rev. chil. hist. geog.*, no. 102, enero-junio, p. 318-362). [496
The initiation ceremonies of the Yaghan of Tierra del Fuego based on Gusinde's detailed information published in several articles and in his great work *Die Yamana* (St. Gabriel, 1937).

COLOMBIA

Arboleda, José Rafael. El centro de investigaciones lingüísticas y etnográficas de la Amazonía colombiana (*Rev. javeriana*, tomo 19, no. 94, mayo, p. 178-183). [497
Justified homage to the work realized by Father de Castellví to save the Amazonian languages and the traditions of the Indians of the Putumayo and Caquetá.

Friede, Juan. Los indios del Alto Magdalena. Vida, luchas y exterminio. 1609-1931. Bogotá. Ed. Centro. (Inst. indigenista de Colombia). 40 p. [498
Valuable history of the Indians of San Agustín after the conquest. It is based on

local archives and throws interesting light on the stubborn but futile efforts made by the Indians to keep some of their ancestral lands.

Ortiz, Sergio Elías. Lingüística colombiana (*Bol. hist. antig.*, vol. 30, no. 347–348, sept.–oct., p. 825–842). [499

Quechua is spoken in Colombia by about 4,000 people in the Departments of Nariño and Cauca, and in the Comisarías of Caquetá and of Putumayo. It is known as Ingano or Napeño. The differences between the Ingano and Napeño are not sufficiently great to warrant their separation into two separate dialects. Quechua has influenced not only Spanish but other native languages of Colombia.

There is little doubt that Quechua was introduced into Colombia after the conquest by Spanish missionaries.

———. Lingüística colombiana: familia goahibo (*Univ. cat. bolivariana*, vol. 9, no. 30–31, abril–junio, p. 155–181). [500

Study of the Guahibo linguistic family. The author analyses the literature, gives comparative vocabularies and adds a new dialect to the family, the Guayabero, spoken by the Cunimias Indians. These Indians are nomads who live between the Ariari River and its tributary the Guejar and an imaginary line from Puerto Limón to the mouth of the Cano Acacias on the Guejar. They also reach the Guayabero River.

Pacheco Quintero, Ricardo. Ligeras observaciones sobre los indígenas del Sarare (*Bol. hist. antig.*, vol. 30, no. 347–348, sept.–oct., p. 930–933). [501

A few general data on the Pedrazas and Tunebo Indians.

Rivet, Paul. La influencia karib en Colombia (*Rev. inst. etnol. nac.*, vol. 1, entrega 1, p. 55–93, 283–295). [502

Minute analysis of culture traits which indicate Carib influences in Colombia. The author begins by stressing the wide distribution of the deformation of the calves which seems to be peculiar to the Carib tribes. Then he examines the distribution of languages spoken in Colombia related to the Carib linguistic family. He lists among them the Choco, the Quimbaya, the languages spoken in the Cauca Valley, the Motilon, Yarigui, Carare, Colima and Muzo. He considers the inclusion of Palenque, Panche and Pijao within the same family as possible but not entirely proved. In the second part of this monograph, Rivet points out the fact that the word *caracoli* designating metal in many Carib dialects was applied in Colombia to a specific ornament worn principally in the region of the Cauca Valley where Carib influence seems to have been strong.

———. La lengua choco (*Rev. inst. etnol. nac.*, vol. 1, entrega 1, p. 131–196). [503

First part of a comparative study of the Choco language which was considered to be independent. Numerous grammatical similarities between Choco and Carib dialects justify the inclusion of that language within the extensive Carib family to which so many Colombian Indians belong.

ECUADOR

Garcés, V. Gabriel. La comunidad indígena (*Prev. soc.*, Quito, no. 14, set.–dic., p. 46–55). [504

Lecture about the land system in ancient Peru and during the colonial period. Brief reference to the modern *ayllu*.

Jaramillo Alvarado, Pío. Situación política, económica y jurídica del indio en el Ecuador (*Prev. soc.*, Quito, no. 12, enero–abril, p. 35–58; no. 13, mayo–agosto, p. 19–34). [505

Ecuador has 3,000,000 Indians—that is to say that the Indian element represents three fourths of the total population. The present land system is feudal. The author advocates some sort of collective land ownership to take its place.

The second part is an interesting study of the Indian in the past and in the present. South America will head world civilization if it takes account of the *"alma de la raza."* Lyrical racism mixed with good intentions.

Ministerio de previsión social. El día del indio, 19 de abril de 1943. Quito. Tall. gráf. de educación. 22 p. [506

Text of the decree creating a Servicio de Asuntos Indígenas, and a speech translated into Quechua.

PARAGUAY

Baldus, Herbert. Sinopse da cultura guayakí (*Sociologia*, vol. 5, no. 2, mayo, p. 147–153). [507

Compilation of available data on the little known Guayakí tribe of Paraguay. The Guayakí, a Guaraní speaking tribe, are among the most primitive Indians of South America. They have been hounded for centuries first by the Guaraní, then by the Mestizos, and have become therefore extremely shy and elusive. Very little is known about their culture.

Métraux, Alfred. A myth of the Chamacoco Indians and its social significance (*Jour. amer. folklore*, vol. 56, no. 220, April–June, p. 113–119). [508

Description of men's feast and initiation rites of boys into manhood, with texts of related myth and comparative study, of these Indians of the Paraguayan Chaco. [R. S. Boggs]

Schmidt, Max. Los paressís (*Rev. soc. cient. Paraguay*, tomo 6, no. 1, agosto, p. 1–296). [509

One of Max Schmidt's most important contributions to South American ethnology was a monograph published in 1914 on the Paressí-Kabishí Indians who form one of the three branches of the formerly large and powerful Paressí tribe. In 1928 the author visited the Paressí proper and, though he was unable to study their culture which had disappeared by that time, he collected a large vocabulary and a few mythological texts. He gives us here his linguistic material and compares it with other vocabularies and texts. The linguistic study is preceded by a compilation of all the available data on the history and ethnography of the Paressí. Especially valuable is the chapter about the relations between the Paressí and the Whites.

The Paressí belong to the Arawakan linguistic family and together with the Mojo and Chané form the southernmost part of that widely extended linguistic group. They are divided into three sub-tribes: the Kachiníti, Uaimaré and Kozariní or Paressí-Kabishí. Their religion centers around the cult of spirits symbolized by trumpets, which women are not allowed to see.

PERU

(See also item 3827)

Auza Arce, Carlos. Cosco (*Rev. mus. nac.*, Lima, tomo 12, no. 2, segundo semestre, p. 212-224). [510
Various etymologies based on toponymy.

Cornejo Bournoncle, Jorge. Los indios mashcos (Perú) (*Rev. geog. amer.*, año 9, vol. 19, no. 117, junio, p. 331-338). [511
This short article is one of the few sources on the still little known Mashco Indians who live on the Río Colorado, a tributary of the Upper Madre de Dios. They are typical Montaña Indians who belong to the Panoan linguistic family. They wear tunics of barkcloth, cultivate sweet manioc, plantains and pineapples. Curiously enough, women carry children fastened to a kind of papoose made of light wood. This type of cradle, so well known among North American Indians occurs in South America only in Tierra del Fuego, Patagonia and Chile. Father Álvarez, on whose reports the article is based, mentions large Mashco villages that are still unexplored. The article ends with a fragment of Mashco myth recorded by Father Álvarez: the first man and his wife climbed through a rope down to this earth. Their former companions on the stars provoked a flood so that they might return with the rising waters. The couple survived and remained on earth.

Dávila, Víctor M. Los grupos lingüísticos de la Amazonía peruana (*Alpha*, año 3, no. 4, set., p. 24-27). [512
Short note mentioning a few linguistic families of the upper Amazon.

Farfán, José M. B. La lengua quechua. Lima. Imp. del Museo nac. [513
Generalities about the Quechua language which, according to the author, is still spoken by about ten million people. The pamphlet contains also a very interesting Quechua folk tale which is given in Quechua, Spanish and English. It deals with the visit of Fox to the sky where he steals a queñua grain. He descends through a rope which is cut by a parrot. This tale is probably a vestige of an Andean myth about the origin of food plants.
Also published in *Rev. mus. nac.*, Lima, tomo 12, no. 1, primer semestre, p. 115-118.

———. Una leyenda del mes de agosto en sus versiones quechua, castellana e inglesa (*Rev. mus. nac.*, Lima, tomo 12, no. 2, segundo semestre, p. 235-238). [515
Folktale about a stupid boy and a clever old woman.

———. El quechua bibliográfico (*Rev. mus. nac.*, Lima, tomo 12, no. 2, segundo semestre, p. 228-234). [516
Note about some outstanding works on Quechua.

Fejos, Paul. Los indios yaguas. New York. Viking fund. (Publ. in anthropology, no. 1.) 144 p., láms. [517
An important contribution to the ethnology of the little known Montaña region of Peru. The monograph is not definitive and is somewhat weak on the non-material side but substantially expands knowledge of the group. Reviewed in *Rev. mus. nac.*, Lima, tomo 12, no. 2, segundo semestre, p. 253-254. [R. L. Beals]

Gandía, Enrique de. Orígenes de las cacerías denominadas "Chacu" (*Rev. geog. amer.*, año 10, vol. 20, no. 120, p. 171-176). [518
Quotations from ancient sources concerning the collective drive hunts of the ancient Peruvians. Comparisons with similar hunts in India.

Herrera Gray, Enriqueta. Influencia mítica en la ceremonía educativa del Guarachico (*Letras*, Lima, no. 24, primer cuatrimestre, p. 115-126). [519
Religious influences on the initiation rites of the Peruvians. Naïve, evolutionary interpretation.

Horkheimer, Hans. Historia del Perú. Época prehispánica. Trujillo. Imp. Gamarra. 193 p. [520
Textbook based on a course given by the author at the University of Trujillo. Praiseworthy effort to give in a systematic form all that is known about ancient Peru from the beginnings of time to the Conquest. Each chapter has a short bibliography.

Ibarra Grasso, Dick Edgar. El "Ave María" en la escritura quichua (*Rev. geog. amer.*, año 9, vol. 19, no. 116, p. 287-293). [521
More details on the ideographic and sometimes phonetic symbol used by some Quechua Indians to memorize religious texts. Some of the texts are represented by modelled clay figures set in rows.

Larco Hoyle, Rafael. La escritura peruana sobre pallares (*Rev. geog. amer.*, año

11, vol. 20, no. 122, nov., p. 277-292; no. 123, dic., p. 345-354). [523
The author states again that painted beans were elements of a pictographic writing and at the origin of Maya writing. He refuses to accept the theory that beans represented on Chimu pots were markers of games.

Lira, Jorge A. Fundamentos de la lengua kkechuwa (*Waman puma,* año 3, vol. 3, no. 15, primer semestre, p. 43-48). [524
Phonetic analysis of Quechua. The system should be compared with Rowe's excellent treatment of the same subject.

Mac-Lean y Estenós, Roberto. Significado sociológico de la educación en el imperio de los incas (*Bol. inst. soc.,* no. 2, p. 65-80). [525
Education in the Inca empire. A more anthropological approach to the problem would be preferable.

Navarro del Águila, Víctor. Pukllay taki (*Peruanidad,* vol. 3, no. 12, enero-feb., p. 914-935). [526
From *Revista del Instituto Americano del Arte,* Cuzco.
Carnival songs in Quechua collected in the province of Andahuailas, Depto. de Apurimac. Description of musical instruments, words of songs and musical texts.

Poma de Ayala, Felipe Huamán. Guaman Poma. Buenos Aires. Ed. Nova. (Col. Mar dulce.) 84 p. [527
Reproduces without comment the drawings of the manuscript by Guaman Poma published in facsimile edition by the Institute of Ethnology of Paris.

Posnansky, Arthur. Chaskis y kipus. El correo de los incas (*Bol. soc. geog. La Paz,* año 54, no. 66, oct., p. 66-73, ilus.). [528
Reproduces several pictures of Guaman Poma de Ayala showing Indians (couriers) with quipu.

——— (ed.). Tercera y cuarta partes de la obra de Phelipe Guamán Pomá de Ayala El primer nueva corónica y buen gobierno, fojas 560-1169 (*Bol. soc. geog. La Paz,* año 54, no. 65, junio, anexo; no. 66, oct., anexo). [529
Continuation of the famous chronicle of Guamán Poma edited by Posnansky.

Reiser, Hans. Indios. Braunschweig. Verlag Wenzel und sohn. 232 p. [530
Travel account describing the jungle of eastern Peru. Few and superficial data on the Amoisha and Campa Indians.

Rowe, John H., and **Gabriel Escobar M.** Los sonidos quechuas de Cuzco y Chanca (*Waman puma,* año 3, vol. 3, no. 15, primer semestre, p. 21-34). [531
Valuable phonetic and phonemic analysis of the Quechua dialects. The author proposes a simplified and logical system of transcription.

Schedl, Armando. El quipu peruano según Martín de Morúa (*Rev. geog. amer.,* año 9, vol. 20, no. 118, julio, p. 37-42). [532
Analysis and quotations of passages of Morúa's chronicle concerning the function of the quipus and the training of the *quipocamayoc.*

Schwab, Federico. La fiesta de las cruces y su relación con antiguos ritos agrícolas (*Historia,* Lima, vol. 1, no. 4, set.-oct., p. 363-385). [533
Generalities about the survival of primitive beliefs. Description of the feast of the Santa Cruz as it is still celebrated at Huancayo. One of the salient features of the feast is the presence of men disguised as women or wearing masks. The dancers are divided into two groups and each one fells a tree with axes. The man who causes the tree to fall has to pay the expenses of the next feast. The author describes various Inca feasts after the chroniclers and then compares them with the modern ceremony. He rightly assumes that the two groups of dancers represent two former moieties.

Valcárcel, Luis E. La agricultura entre los antiguos peruanos (*Rev. mus. nac.,* Lima, tomo 12, no. 1, primer semestre, p. 1-7). [534

———. Cultura de pueblos agrícolas (*Rev. mus. nac.,* Lima, tomo 12, no. 2, segundo semestre, p. 141-166). [535
Sociological interpretation of Peruvian cultures based on economic considerations.

Yépez Arangua, Edgar, and **Gabriel Chacón.** Exploración de las tribus de los huachipaires (*Bol. soc. geog. Lima,* tomo 40, segundo trim., p. 115-119). [537
Short account of a trip to the Huachipaire Indians in the region of San Juan de Oro. A few vague anthropological data. Some obvious misstatements.

VENEZUELA

Antolínez, Gilberto. El demonio del bosque (*Bitácora,* vol. 1, cuad. 2, abril, p. 35-41). [538
Short monograph on the famous Curupira, a favorite character of Brazilian folklore.

———. Kanaimé. El vengador de la sangre (*Acta amer.,* vol. 1, no. 2, April-June, p. 240-245). [539
The author repeats well known legends about the *kanaima,* who is either a man practicing vengeance or a bad spirit. The article is spiced with Freudian jargon.

Armellada, Cesáreo de. Gramática y diccionario de la lengua pemón. Arekuna, taurepán, kamarakoto, familia caribe. Caracas. C. A. artes gráfs. [540
The author, a Capuchin missionary, calls Pemon, the Indians known before as Are-

kuna, Taulipang and Kamarakoto. They all speak the same language which is a Carib dialect. Both grammar and vocabularies show extensive linguistic knowledge and awareness of modern methods.

CUESTIONES ETNOGRÁFICAS Y LINGÜÍSTICAS DEL ARCHIVO DE LISANDRO ALVARADO (*Rev. nac. cultura*, año 5, no. 37, marzo–abril, p. 46–56). [541
Letters by the erudite Tavera Acosta about various anthropological subjects such as spelling of native names and linguistic affinities.

López Ramírez, Tulio. Algunos datos sobre los barbascos de Venezuela (*Acta amer.*, vol. 1, no. 4, Oct.–Dec., p. 503–505). [542
List of vegetable poisons used by natives to drug fish. Native names and scientific determinations.

———. Demografía indígena venezolana (*Acta amer.*, vol. 1, no. 3, July–Sept., p. 335–343). [543
Excellent analysis of demographic data concerning the native population of Venezuela. According to the 1936 census the Indian population was about 103,147. The article ends with an appeal in favor of the mistreated and misunderstood Indians.

Pinilla, Gaspar María de. Etnografía guaraúna (*Rev. nac. cultura*, año 6, no. 41, nov.–dic., p. 150–167). [544
Monograph on the Warrau Indians of the Orinoco Delta. They still number about 10,000. The author believes that flogging is the best way to civilize Indians. He does not hide a strong and prejudiced dislike of the Indians and appears to advocate a policy of "bread and whip."

Rivet, Paul, and **Víctor Oppenheim.** La lengua tunebo (*Rev. inst. etnol. nac.*, vol. 1, entrega 1, p. 47–53). [545
On the basis of a vocabulary collected by Víctor Oppenheim among the Pedraza Indians, who live in Venezuela between the Río Magua and the Río Cutufi, at the foot of the Andes, Rivet was able to link these Indians with the Tunebo of eastern Colombia. The Tunebo language belongs to the Chibchan linguistic family.

Tamayo, Francisco. El mito de María Lionza (*Bol. centro hist. Larense*, año 2, no. 5, primer trim., enero–marzo, p. 1–8). [546
María Lionza is an important character in the folklore of western Venezuela. She is a sylval deity who protects game animals. She is surrounded by a court including all kinds of characters with Spanish names. Local people—the author unfortunately does not specify who they are—render homage to her in order to obtain various favors. Some Negro influences may be assumed in the formation of her legend.

ADDENDA

ARGENTINA

Ferrario, Benigno. Revisión gramatical y la lengua tsoneca (*Actas trab. cient. del 27 cong. int. amer.*, tomo 2, 1942, p. 41–46). [547
Short grammatical analysis of the Tsoneca language. The author is to be commended for asking for more scientific and painstaking studies of South American languages.

Palavecino, Enrique. Breves noticias sobre algunos nuevos elementos en la cultura de los indios del Chaco (*Actas trab. cient. del 27 cong. int. amer.*, tomo 2, 1942, p. 313–314). [548
A short note about a few artifacts collected by the author.

BRAZIL

Colbacchini, Antonio. Os boróros orientais, orarimogodogue do planalto oriental de Mato Grosso. São Paulo. Cia. ed. nacional. (Bibl. ped. bras., Serie 5a, Brasiliana, vol. 4). 1942. 454 p., ilus. [549
Translation of Colbacchini's classic work on the Bororo Indians, published under the title "*I Bororos Orientale, Orarimugudoge, del Matto Grosso, Brasile*, Soc. Ed. Internazionale, Torino, 1926. The Portuguese edition of this masterpiece equals the original in the beautiful presentation and the abundance of photographs.

PERU

(Two items which appeared in 1941 are listed here. The information about these items did not reach the editor in time for inclusion in vol. 8).

Álvarez, José. Mitología, tradiciones y creencias religiosas de los salvajes huarayos (*Actas trab. cient. del 27 cong. int. amer.*, tomo 2, 1942, p. 153–161). [550
The so-called Huarayo Indians are the same as the Tiatinagua, a tribe of the Takanan linguistic family. According to their origin myth, their ancestors came from the sky by means of a rope which broke. A great many animals are transformed men, all the food plants came from a Tree of Life. They believe in a supreme being, speak of two helpful spirits (twin culture heroes?). Their religion seems to be based on extensive animism: all the plants have a spirit (shahua). Every person has three souls, one which becomes a ghost, a second which goes to the Supreme God and a third which settles in a beautiful country. The flood was caused by a sudden rising of the rivers. A family escaped to the top of a mountain.

Baudin, Louis. La actualidad del sistema económico de los incas (*Actas trab. cient. del 27 cong. int. amer.*, tomo 2, 1942, p. 175–187). [551
Stresses the fact that the Inca empire was a unique socio-economic experience in the history of mankind. Advocates its study.

Eckert, Georg. Die menschenhauttrommel in Alt Peru (*Zeit. ethn.*, jahr 73, 1941, no. 4–5. p. 133–145). [552
Careful compilation of the data concerning drums made of human skin used as trophies in ancient Peru and in neighboring countries. The human skin drum was found in the Cauca Valley, among the Lile Indians, and among the Huanca of the Xauxa Valley. Several Incas ordered the skins of their slain enemies to be turned into drums.

Escalante, José Ángel, John Ritchie, J. Félix Silva, Alejandro Franco, and **J. M. B. Farfán.** Cómo puede ser la escritura del qheswa, sus dialectos y el aymara (*Actas trab. cient. del 27 cong. int. amer.*, tomo 2, 1942, p. 33–36). [553
A new system to transcribe the Quechua language.

Farfán, J. M. B. Epitetos "lapidarios" del quechua. El realismo descarnado del humorismo quechua. Una interpretación tentativa de su contenido psicológico (*Actas trab. cient. del 27 cong. int. amer.*, tomo 2, 1942, p. 37–40). [554
List of some epithets in Quechua which the author finds particularly succulent and humorous. It is "genial adjectivation."

Franco Inojosa, José María. Mit-maj. Esquema para un ensayo retrospectivo de la colonización inca (*Actas trab. cient. del 27 cong. int. amer.*, tomo 2, 1942, p. 211–227). [555
Quotes passages of the ancient chronicles about the mitimae or deported colonists. The author thinks the sadness of Indian music derives from the nostalgia of these defeated groups transplanted to new lands.

Garcés Bedregal, Miguel. Evolución técnica de la música peruana gama eptafónica (*Actas trab. cient. del 27 cong. int. amer.*, tomo 2, 1942, p. 25–32). [556
A technical article on the evolution of tones in Peruvian music. Assumes the existence of an eptaphonal gamut in ancient Peru.

García, Secundino. Mitología de los salvajes machiguengas (*Actas trab. cient. del 27 cong. int. amer.*, tomo 2, 1942, p. 229–237). [557
Interesting collection of Campa myths. Creation of men by Tasorinchi. The Moon brings the first cultivated plants. He is the father of the 3 Suns (our Sun, the Sun of the country of the dead, the Sun of the Upper sky). Myth of the first Tasaronchi, one of whom is both the Trickster and Culture hero. Origin of the comets.

Grain, José María. Los machiguengas (*Actas trab. cient. del 27 cong. int. amer.*, tomo 2, 1942, p. 239–244). [558
Some notes on the agriculture, the food and the dress of the Machiguenga (Campa) Indians.

Imbelloni, J. La "weltanschauung" de los amautas reconstruida: formas peruanas del pensamiento templario (*Actas trab. cient. del 27 cong. int. amer.*, tomo 2, 1942, p. 245–271). [559
Attempts at reconstructing the cosmogony of the ancient Peruvians by means of parallels with the Old World and the cultures of Centro-América. The Universe was divided into 3 floors, each subdivided into four compartments. The ancient Peruvians probably knew different "ages" or "suns" corresponding to different humanities. The author makes much of the parallel established by Krickeberg between the episode of the rebellion of the objects collected by Dávila and also reproduced on a fresco of the temple of Moche and on Chimu pots and a famous passage of the Popul-Vuh. The author does not mention the fact that the same myth was found in 1929 by the reviewer among the Chiriguano Indians. Had he done so, he would have discovered the parallel between the Peruvian, Chiriguano and Mayan versions of the myth.

Latcham, Ricardo E. Algunos factores básicos para el estudio de la sociología prehistórica andina (*Actas trab. cient. del 27 cong. int. amer.*, tomo 2, 1942, p. 273–283). [560
The old frazerian system applied to Peru.

López Albújar, Enrique. Exegesis de la justicia penal chupana (*Actas trab. cient. del 27 cong. int. amer.*, tomo 2, 1942, p. 285–294). [561
Law and order in the community of Chupán.

Pulgar Vidal, Javier. Algunos elementos de las culturas del Ande y la Amazonia peruanos en la cuenca del río Huallaga (*Actas trab. cient. del 27 cong. int. amer.*, tomo 2, 1942, p. 315–323). [562
Ethnography of the tribes of the Upper Huallaga as it survives in the modern mestizo population. These survivals consist mainly of dances and games. Some legends. Worthwhile contribution to Peruvian folklore.

Trimborn, H. Dämonen und zauber in Inkareich (*Zeit. ethnol.*, jahr 73, 1941, no. 4–5, p. 146–162). [563
Text and translations of folio 105v to 114 r. of Francisco de Ávila's famous manuscript found recently in Madrid. These pages did not appear in the complete German edition of the manuscript published by Trimborn in 1939.

MIDDLE AND SOUTH AMERICA: PHYSICAL ANTHROPOLOGY

BY

T. D. STEWART

United States National Museum

GENERAL STATEMENT

The increased number of bibliographical items listed below for this year (45 as compared to 38 at most for any one of the past five years) reflects somewhat the intensive work carried on recently in Latin America. At the same time, perhaps, it reflects the rush to get the results published ahead of war restrictions. Since obviously there was much data on hand, and much of it of high quality, it was fortunate for the science that some new journals appeared at this time to facilitate publication. One of these, the New Series of the *American Journal of Physical Anthropology*, brought out a first issue devoted almost exclusively to Latin American subjects. Indeed, during the year, this journal published nine important articles in the Latin American field. Among other journals which were initiated this year, and which include articles on physical anthropology, the following are especially noteworthy: *Acta Americana* and *Revista del Instituto Etnológico Nacional* (Bogotá). But for the most part, articles in this field were printed as usual in many different places. This situation handicaps exhaustive compilation and review.

On the debit side, offsetting the receipt of rich new data, must be mentioned two losses by death among notable contributors from the older generation. Aleš Hrdlička [1] died on September 5, and within less than two months—on October 16—he was followed by Ricardo E. Latcham.[2] These two men were born in the same year (1869)—one in Bohemia and the other in England; both came to the New World (United States and Chile) in the 1880's; and both settled down to a career in anthropology around the beginning of this century. In their respective adopted countries these men were leaders in the field of physical anthropology, and Latcham was besides a leader in cultural anthropology. Hrdlička made only brief visits to Latin America, but his writings, especially those relating to ancient man in America, have been very influential throughout the hemisphere. Latcham, on the other hand, confined his activities largely to Chile, where he labored to put on record the physical and cultural characteristics of the native groups, both modern and prehistoric.

The published proceedings of anthropological societies are usually a good and sometimes the only source of information about the activities of physical anthropologists. Unfortunately, however, these proceedings from societies in

---

[1] The following obituary is especially informative: Wells, J. Robert. Aleš Hrdlička † 5 de septiembre de 1943 (*Rev. mus. nac.*, Lima, tomo 12, p. 265–270).
[2] Schwab, Federico. Ricardo E. Latcham † 16 de octubre de 1943 (*Rev. mus. nac.*, Lima, tomo 12, p. 271–279, bibliog.).

Latin America are not always published promptly or in full. This year the Sociedad Argentina de Antropología alone supplies us with such information. Below are listed the papers in physical anthropology given at the fourth and fifth annual "Anthropological Weeks" (Nov. 3-7, 1942; Nov. 15-20, 1943).[3]

[3] *Bol. soc. arg. antrop.*, no. 3, 1942, p. 38-42 (Also in *An. inst. etnog. amer.*, tomo 4, p. 351-354); *Bol. soc. arg. antrop.*, no. 5-6, p. 75-85. These proceedings contain abstracts of the papers read at the meetings.
Luis A. Chillida. Anotaciones previas sobre la tibia en los aborígines del territorio argentino. 1942; Luis A. Chillida. Dos fémures de un indígena del Chubut. 1943; María de las Mercedes Constanzó. Restos óseos de Purmamarca (Jujuy). 1942; María de las Mercedes Constanzó. Observaciones sobre momia del norte de Chile. 1943; José Imbelloni. Sobre algunos caracteres anátomo-fisionómicos de los Yámana. 1942.

BIBLIOGRAPHY

GENERAL

Hrdlička, Aleš. Pan-American anthropology (*Acta amer.*, vol. 1, no. 2, April-June, p. 246-251). [564
Sketches the main lines of future research in American physical anthropology.

Imbelloni, José. Los artistas plásticos y la antropología (*Bol. soc. arg. antrop.*, no. 4, p. 52-55). [565
In addition to discussing the classical canons of body proportions, the writer calls attention to the failure of American artists to recognize the true proportions of the Indian body type.

Montagu, M. F. Ashley. Genetics and the antiquity of man in the Americas (*Man*, vol. 43, no. 105, Nov.-Dec., p. 131-135). [567
Concludes that the Indian population of this hemisphere is progressively from north to south less mongoloid and more caucasoid. This is taken to prove "that the genetic approach holds more than a promise of throwing an appreciable light upon the problem of the antiquity of man in America."

Romero, Javier. Los prejuicios raciales (Primer congreso demográfico interamericano, Secretaría de gobernación. México, reprint of 11 p.). [568
Shows that physical anthropology has destroyed the basis for the idea of superiority of one human group over others.

Steggerda, Morris. Stature of South American Indians (*Amer. jour. phys. anthrop.*, new series, vol. 1, p. 5-20). [569
Summarizes literature giving averages by regions and by size. Shows on a map the distribution of four classes of stature.

Stewart, T. D. Distribution of cranial height in South America (*Amer. jour. phys. anthrop.*, new series, vol. 1, p. 143-155). [570
The average mean height indices of 30 South American cranial series are listed to show the geographical distribution of the high and low heads. The latter are shown to be located mainly in the northern parts. The theory is advanced that these low heads connect with those of western North America.

―――. Relative variability of Indian and white cranial series (*Amer. jour. phys. anthrop.*, new series, vol. 1, p. 261-270). [571
Mean sigmas for a number of measurements and indices are listed for as many as 15 South American series having a minimum number of 25 specimens. Comparisons are made with North American and European series.

―――. A selective guide to the material published in 1942 on anthropology; Middle and South America: physical anthropology (*Handbook of latin american studies, no. 8, 1942*, p. 41-46). [572

MIDDLE AMERICA AND THE ANTILLES

Comas, Juan. La antropología física en México y Centro-América. México. Ed. Stylo. (Inst. panamericano de geografía e historia, Publ. no. 68.) 131 p. [573
Lists anthropometric mean measurements on the living, according to sex, by tribe, number of subjects and author. Maps show the distributions of the more important characters. Full bibliography.

―――. El metopismo: sus causas y frecuencia en los cráneos mexicanos (*An. inst. etnog. amer.*, tomo 4, p. 121-159). [574
Extensive review of the literature with summation of frequency of this anomaly in various racial groups. In addition the author contributes new data, especially on Mexican groups. Here he finds the anomaly in 4.1% of 430 modern skulls and in 1.2% of 409 prehispanic skulls. Those with the anomaly are described in detail and illustrated.

Goldstein, Marcus S. Demographic and bodily changes in descendants of Mexican

immigrants. Austin, Texas. Inst. of Latin American studies. 103 p. [575
Detailed measurements of some 2000 subjects from 305 families (176 in Texas—mainly San Antonio—and 129 in Mexico—Celaya, Guanajuato, Monterrey and Saltillo). About 40 pages are given over to a general summary of the findings.

———. Observations on Mexican crania (*Amer. jour. phys. anthrop.*, new series, vol. 1, p. 83–93). [576
Based on 274 crania from the modern ossuaries at Guanajuato and Saltillo. The variability of this mestizo, but predominantly Indian, population is about average as compared to Europeans and somewhat higher than North American Indians.

Gómez Robleda, José. Pescadores y campesinos tarascos. México. Ed. de la Sría. de educación pública. xlvi, 433 p. [577
Anthropometric, physiologic and psychologic observations on 116 fishermen from Janitzio, 47 "peasants" from the neighborhood of Paracho, and 45 students from the agricultural school in Paracho. Of the students 15 are female. Analyses by a group of 6 collaborators stress body and constitutional types. Mean measurements with their statistical constants are listed. Types are illustrated by photographs.

Guilbert, Henry D. The Mayan skulls of Copán (*Amer. jour. orthodontics and oral surgery*, oral surgery section, vol. 29, no. 4, April, p. 216–222). [578
Describes the teeth of the only two skulls thus far found at Copán. One of these has all of the anterior teeth, upper and lower, inlaid with iron pyrites and jade. Some teeth have two inlays each. Illustrations.

Johnson, Frederick. Tooth mutilation among the Guaymi (*Amer. anthrop.*, new series, vol. 45, p. 327–328). [579
An addendum to item no. 448 in *Handbook, no. 8, 1942.*

Martínez, Liborio. Estudio biotipológico de cien niños de Izúcar de Matamoros, Puebla (*An. inst. biol.*, tomo 14, no. 2, p. 455–485). [580
Presents measurements and observations according to long, broad and mixed types of body build. Makes comparisons with Viola's standards and touches on familial inheritance.

Stewart, T. D. Skeletal remains from Tajumulco, Guatemala (Appendix I in *Excavations at Tajumulco, Guatemala* by Bertha P. Dutton, and Hulda R. Hobbs. Santa Fe, New Mexico. Monographs of the School of American research, no. 9, p. 111–114). [581
Description of 10 lots of material (mostly tooth crowns) from nine tombs. Includes a case of fronto-vertico-occipital cranial deformity and a case of dental multilation.

ARGENTINA

Castellanos, Alfredo. Antigüedad geológica del yacimiento de los restos humanos de la "Gruta de Candonga," Córdoba. Rosario. Inst. de fisiografía y geología. (Publ., tomo 4, no. 14). 108 p., 66 figs. [582
Description of a fragmentary deformed skull belonging to a 6 or 8 year old child. The remains are attributed to the uppermost Bonaerense or basal Platense geological ages, which correspond to the interval between the Riss and Würm glacial periods in European chronology. Accompanying animal remains and cultural objects (some of recent date) are also described.

Chillida, Luis Alberto. Características métricas y morfológicas del húmero en los aborígenes argentinos (*Rev. inst. antrop. univ. nac. Tucumán*, vol. 3, no. 1, 35 p.). [583
Measurements on 349 humeri from 14 sites. Material located at Museo Argentino and Museo Etnográfico in Buenos Aires and at the Museo de La Plata. Sex and site not distinguished.

Constanzó, María de las Mercedes. Las investigaciones antropológicas y etnográficas en la Argentina (*Acta amer.*, vol. 1, no. 3, July–Sept., p. 331–334). [584
General statements about the scope of the work in physical anthropology.

Paulotti, Osvaldo L., and Luis González Alegría. Grupos sanguíneos de los nativos de la Puna Jujeña (*An. mus. arg. cien. nat.*, tomo 41, p. 21–28). [585
A sample of 209 Indians, selected for racial purity, were examined mainly in the departments of Humahuaca, Cochinoca and Yavi. These yielded the following: 94.73% group O, 4.54% A, 0% B and 0.71% AB (r=0.973, p=0.024, q=0.001). The serological technique is described.

Rusconi, Carlos. Fracturas óseas en indígenas prehispánicos de Mendoza (*Rev. asoc. méd.*, tomo 57, no. 519, julio 30, p. 830–831). [586
Description of the left radius and ulna of an old male. This specimen, which was found at Uspallata and bears the number "245 An." in the Museo de Historia Natural de Mendoza, shows evidence of having been fractured twice. Drawings and x-rays.

BOLIVIA, BRAZIL, COLOMBIA, AND CHILE

Arcila Vélez, Graciliano. Grupos sanguíneos entre los indios Páez (*Rev. inst. etnol. nac.*, vol. 1, entrega 1, p. 7–14). [587
Based upon 303 observations made in various localities in Tierradentro. Of the subjects 246 are pure bloods and 57 mestizos; 269 males and 34 females. Of the pure bloods 92.7% are group O, 4.1% A, and 3.2% B.

Ávila, J. Bastos d'. Alguns dados de cefalometria no escolar (*Arq. mus. nac.*, vol. 37, p. 289-329). [588
Reports 17 measurements and 8 indices for a sample of 1366 children of both sexes between 6 and 14 years of age. Some data are given on 308 Negroes. Few comparisons.

———. Os tipos de Kretschmer na infancia escolar (*Rev. educ. públ.*, Rio, vol. 1, no. 1, p. 51-56). [589
Reconhecimento dos tipos constitucionais de Kretschmer nas populações escolares, sugerindo o autor para os mesmos as denominações de "astenoide, atletoide e picnoide." [M. J. Pourchet]

Henckel, Carlos, and Eduardo Skewes. El peso de algunos órganos internos (*Bol. soc. biol. Concepción*, tomo 17, p. 39-56). [590
Absolute and relative weight by age periods of the heart, lungs, liver, spleen and kidneys in 175 males. All individuals had two Spanish names and had died by accident. The main statistical constants are given.

Hernández de Alba, Gregorio. Momias de Chiscas, Boyacá (*Bol. mus. arq. Colombia*, vol. 1, no. 1, feb., p. 3-9). [591
Includes measurements of two skulls.

Lehmann, H., L. Duque, and M. Fornaguera. Grupos sanguíneos entre los indios Guambiano-Kokonuko (*Rev. inst. etnol. nac.*, vol. 1, entrega 1, p. 197-208). [592
Based upon 584 observations (457 males, 127 females) from three municipalities in the department of Cauca. Findings: 84.2% group O, 8.6% A, 6.2% B, 1.0% AB. A postscript gives 10 additional observations (90% O, 10% A).

Oppenheim, Víctor. La cuenca fosilífera de Tarija, Bolivia (*Notas mus. La Plata*, tomo 8, geología, no. 24, p. 179-190). [593
Maintains that the human remains found among the fossil animals in this locality are nothing more than the accidental inclusions of recent burials.

Posnansky, Arthur. Qué es raza? La Paz. Inst. "Tihuanacu" de antropología, etnografía y prehistoria. 52 p. [594
Separates mankind into brachycephalic or superior and dolichocephalic or inferior races. Discusses the "Khollas" and "Arawakes" as examples of these two divisions respectively.

Pourchet, Maria Julia. Considerações sobre o crescimento (*Formação*, no. 58, p. 29-32). [595
A autora sugere observações periódicas do crescimento, lembrando os estudos de Boas e Godin. [M. J. Pourchet]

Souza, Odorico Machado de. Fundamentos e métodos de classificação dos tipos humanos constitucionais (*Arq. pol. civil São Paulo*, vol. 6, segundo semestre, p. 163-224). [596
O autor apresenta uma sintese dos fundamentos doutrinarios indispensaveis para a pesquisa e classificação dos tipos constitucionais. Em seguida faz o estudo crítico das diferentes escolas, pugnando por uma unificação dos métodos empregados, e sugerindo o método de Viola como o mais perfeito. [M. J. Pourchet]

Tinoco Filho, Mário. O serviço médico-escolar de São Gonçalo e o índice ACH (*Vida médica*, ano 11, no. 2, p. 13-32). [597
Observações do estado de nutrição de 1066 creanças de São Gonçalo, Estado do Rio de Janeiro, pelo índice de Franzen e Palmer. [M. J. Pourchet]

Wenger, Franz. Racial differences in the colon in natives of Bolivia (*Amer. jour. phys. anthrop.*, new series, vol. 1, p. 313-333). [598
Eighty-nine unselected autopsy cases of Indians and mestizos showed the sigmoid colon to be unusually long (average length 74.8 cm.; range 37-115 cm.). The enlargement was due to the length of the pelvic and not of the iliac portion.

Whitaker, Edmur de Aguiar. A orientação biotipológica em antropologia: Definição do argumento, evolução, estado atual (*An. paulistas medicina e cirurgia*, vol. 45, no. 6, p. 440-442). [599
Abstract of paper read before the Associação Paulista de Medicina in which the author concludes that Sheldon's method is an advance over those of Viola and Kretschmer. In the discussion of Coriolano R. Alves defends the method of Viola, whereas Edgard Pinto César adds a criticism of the method of Kretschmer.

PERU, VENEZUELA

Candela, P. B. Blood group tests on tissues of Paracas mummies (*Amer. jour. phys. anthrop.*, new series, vol. 1, p. 65-67). [600
Fifteen tissue samples from 14 mummies gave no dependable or reproducible reactions. It is pointed out that the only reported sample of pureblood modern Peruvian Indians is entirely group O.

Hrdlička, Aleš. Skull of a midget from Peru (*Amer. jour. phys. anthrop.*, new series, vol. 1, p. 77-81). [601
Further description of the specimen reported in item 474 in *Handbook, no.8, 1942*.

López Ramírez, Tulio. Alteraciones dentarias intencionales entre los indios de Venezuela (*Acta amer.*, vol. 1, no. 1, Jan.-March, p. 88-91). [602
Summary of the methods used in shaping and coloring the teeth.

Navarro del Águila, Víctor. Los pukullos de Huayanay (*Rev. mus. nac.*, Lima, tomo 12, no. 1, primer semestre, p. 97–108). [603

Includes a brief description of five trephined skulls from this highland site in the Province of La Mar, Department of Ayacucho.

Newman, Marshall T. A metric study of undeformed Indian crania from Peru (*Amer. jour. phys. anthrop.*, new series, vol. 1, p. 21–45). [604

Compares five series—identified as Chancay, Miscellaneous Chicama, San Damian, Paucarcancha and Machu Picchu—after the elimination of deformity and after making corrections for differences in measuring techniques. Finds two highland types (San Damian and Paucarcancha) and a coastal type. The San Damian series is the least variable, the Machu Picchu series the most.

Quevedo A., Sergio A. [Reply to reviews of author's "Ensayos de antropología física" (1941–42)] (*Rev. univ.*, Cuzco, año 32, no. 85, segundo semestre, p. 195–197). [605

Confirms the absence of cranial deformation at the Calca site. Gives a new calculation of stature that accords with earlier studies.

———. La trepanación incana en la región del Cuzco (*Rev. univ.*, Cuzco, año 32, no. 85, segundo semestre, p. 1–191; also in *Rev. mus. nac.*, Lima, tomo 12, no. 1, primer semestre, p. 8–13; no. 2, segundo semestre, p. 181–211). [606

Reviews most of the published data on the subject. Adds observations on specimens available locally. One of the more important new observations concerns the nature of the tissues covering trepan openings in mummies. Numerous illustrations. Large bibliography.

Stewart, T. D. Skeletal remains from Paracas, Peru (*Amer. jour. phys. anthrop.*, new series, vol. 1, p. 47–63). [607

Reviews the subjects of mummification, deformation, trephining, pathology and physical type as they relate to these remains. Gives observations on 11 skeletons, all but two of which have skulls, and three other skulls from the Tello collection in Lima.

——— Skeletal remains with cultural associations from the Chicama, Moche and Virú Valleys, Peru (*Proc. U. S. nat. mus.*, vol. 93, p. 153–185). [608

Based primarily upon a Cupisnique series (8 males, 5 females) and a Mochica series (13 males, 8 females) from the Larco collection at Chiclín. Comparisons are made with an undeformed series (50 of each sex) from the Chicama Valley in the collection of the U. S. National Museum. Discussion of type classifications. Illustrations.

Trotter, Mildred. Hair from Paracas Indian mummies (*Amer. jour. phys. anthrop.*, new series, vol. 1, p. 69–75). [609

The form and size of the hair of 10 mummies showed wide variation. This may be the result of obtaining the samples from different parts of the scalp.

ADDENDA

Barrientos R., Juvenal. Antropología constitucional de 116 araucanos actuales de Temuco y sus alrededores (*Rev. mus. hist. nac. Chile*, año 1, no. 3, 1942?, p. 270–418). [610

Detailed observations of mestizos between the ages of 17 and 28 years. No comparisons.

———. Consideraciones generales sobre antropología constitucional (*Rev. mus. hist. nac. Chile*, año 1, no. 3, 1942?, p. 217–235). [611

Definitions and outline of observations.

Beeche Cañas, L., Mariano Salazar B., and Pablo Luros. Promedio de las medidas externas de la pelvis de la mujer costarricense (*Rev. médica*, San José, vol. 5, no. 94, 1942, p. 127–129). [612

External obstetrical measurements of the pelvis in 20,987 women, representing 15% of the female population of Costa Rica between the ages of 15 and 45. The racial composition of the sample is not stated.

Comas, Juan. Aportación a la bibliografía y estadística serológica racial americana (*Bol. bibliog. antrop. amer.*, vol. 5, no. 1–3, enero–dic., 1941 [i.e., 1942], p. 29–37). [613

Lists 81 references and gives in tabular form the percentage of each blood group (O, A, B, AB) according to racial group and author. The table is subdivided by country.

———. El hueso interparietal, epactal o inca en los cráneos mexicanos (*An. escuela nac. cien. biol.*, vol. 2, no. 4, 1942, p. 469–490). [614

"Different names given to interparietal bone, as well as its homologies with similar formations in mammals, and theories on its ossification centers, are discussed. The names 'inca bone' and 'epactal bone' are discarded. Then a description of 14 Mexican skulls (increased to 16 in a 'nota adicional' accompanying the reprint) with interparietal bones is given, comparing them with other series and establishing the percentage of interparietal bones in relation to sex, cranial deformation, race and metopism." [Author's abstract]

———. El problema de la existencia de un tipo racial Olmeca (*Mayas y Olmecas. Segunda reunión de mesa redonda sobre problemas antropológicos de México y*

Centro América, Tuxtla Gutiérrez, Chiapas, 1942, p. 69–70). [615
States that the skeletons from Cerro de las Mesas do not correspond to a single somatic type. Doubts that the sculptured faces so characteristic of "Olmec" art represent the physical type of the "Olmecs."

Girard, Rafael. Caracteres antropométricos de los Chortís (*An. soc. geog. hist. Guatemala,* año 17, tomo 17, 1942, p. 412–423). [616
Individual measurements on 23 males and 9 females, together with general statements on non-metrical characters. Broad comparisons for stature and the indices of the head.

Imbelloni, José. Acotaciones al mapa de los pueblos deformadores de la región andina central (*An. mus. arg. cienc. nat.,* tomo 40, 1942, p. 253–268). [617
Revises an earlier distribution map as a result of new data published by Latcham.

Pretto, Julio C., and **Noe Huamán Oyague.** Desarrollo antropométrico del lactante en Lima (*La crónica médica,* año 59, 1942, p. 117–119). [618
General results of studies on infants in the Refectoría Maternal. Comparisons with the findings of Suárez (1935) in the "Gotas de Leche."

Rubín de la Borbolla, Daniel F. Las representaciones olmecas desde el punto de vista antropológico (*Mayas y Olmecas,* Segunda reunión de Mesa redonda sobre problemas antropológicos de México y Centro América, Tuxtla Gutiérrez, Chiapas, 1942, p. 70–73). [619
In collaboration with Comas, Maldonado, Hanna Kirchhoff, and Dávalos, the author outlines arguments used in criticism· of Caso's classification and for use in arriving at a new classification.

Santiana, Antonio, and **José D. Paltán.** Contribuciones al estudio de la antropología ecuatoriana. La dentadura de los indios de Imbabura y Chimborazo (*An. univ. cent. Ecuador,* tomo 67–68, no. 314–315, 1942, p. 575–641). [620
Detailed observations on 144 skulls, mostly modern, from the Museo del Instituto de Anatomía, and on 1182 living. The latter were derived about equally from the two provinces, with the males outnumbering the females 854 to 328. Except for a few mestizos in the Chimborazo series, the subjects are regarded as full blood Indians. Analysis of the data occupies 35 tables.

Saunders, G. M., and **Huldah Bancroft.** Blood pressure studies on Negro and White men and women living in the Virgin Islands of the United States (*Amer. heart jour.,* vol. 23, 1942, p. 410–423). [621
Data are reported on 4374 Negroes (perhaps 20% colored) and 539 Whites. Negroes had a higher blood pressure than Whites, but the average for both is higher than that of residents of the U. S. The roles of climate and poverty are discussed.

ARCHIVES

BY

ROSCOE R. HILL

The National Archives

GENERAL STATEMENT

This survey of Latin American archives marks the beginning of the second lustrum of its appearance in the *Handbook*. Perhaps this affords occasion to briefly review the more outstanding features of the archives and their contribution to archivology during the years.

The eighteen national archives are essentially historical and in each the emphasis is on the colonial and independence periods, although there is an increasing tendency for the governments to transfer to the archives documents of the national period. Relatively they are small institutions and for the most part they have been inadequately housed.

During recent years the movement for the provision of more suitable surroundings for the records has been very noticeable. Argentina, the Dominican Republic and Ecuador reconditioned relatively modern structures for their archives. Cuba on the other hand constructed a completely new building and repairs were effected in other countries. Throughout the years the budgets provided have not been impressive and the staff of each archive has been small.

In general the direction of the archives has been in the hands of men of scholarly tastes and attainment. In addition there has been a notable amount of lengthy tenure. This has tended to afford excellent service which is revealed in the extensive use which has been made of the records by the many scholars, who have found occasion to seek for information in these archives.

Perhaps the most outstanding feature, which has been recorded in these surveys, is the excellent character of the publications issued by the archives. Some of these have been appearing for a long time, but many others are of more recent date. They are of two types, either serial publications or volumes in series or singly. The content varies, consisting of documents, indexes or more general historical information, or else a combination of these. In format and presentation the publications maintain a high standard. In fact even during the war regular appearance has continued, so that the several countries have made very worth-while contributions to archivology.

A reading of the statements presented below records that the year 1943 saw advancement along many lines. The bibliography includes many valuable contributions and the reviews presented the usual amount of interesting material. Instruction of staff members was continued in several countries. New accessions were reviewed and arrangement of records was carried forward. Cataloguing and carding were given much attention.

The editors of the *Handbook* regret that information was lacking regarding several archives. It is believed that for each institution there are items which would be of general interest and should be chronicled. Perhaps on another occasion the necessary data can be secured.

NATIONAL ARCHIVES

ARGENTINA

ARCHIVO GENERAL DE LA NACIÓN

LEANDRO N. ALÉM 250, BUENOS AIRES

Director: HÉCTOR C. QUESADA

The accessions during 1943 while not extensive included some very interesting groups of documents. Among these are: (1) Papers of the astronomer Nicolás Descalzi comprising letters, diaries, meteorological and astronomical studies and notes regarding the exploration of the Río Negro in 1833-1834; (2) collection of documents of General Juan José Viamonte; (3) documents of the noted historian Carlos Ernesto Roberts, 57 items of originals and copies, relating to the British occupation, and the imprisonment and flight of Beresford consisting of correspondence with outstanding persons of the epoch; (4) a group of typed copies of documents dealing with the preparation and organization of the expedition of Pedro de Mendoza as well as with events connected with the first founding and abandonment of Buenos Aires; (5) a plan of the posts of the Province of Córdoba, 1771-1820; and (6) some 300 letters of prominent Argentines, among whom may be mentioned General Justo José de Urquiza, Ambrosio Funes, Narciso Lozano, Juan José Larramendi, Juan José Paso, Salvador M. del Carril, José Gregorio Calderón, Nicasio Moreau, and others.

The director of the Archive was authorized to grant permission to individuals to carry on investigation in the archive. A new assistant was added and the budget for the year amounted to 170,740 pesos m/n.

Arrangement of collections and making of catalogue cards continued during 1943. The card catalogues greatly facilitate the use of the records. During the year 239 persons consulted 3000 *legajos* in the archive.

PUBLICATIONS

No volumes appeared in 1943.

BOLIVIA

ARCHIVO GENERAL DE LA NACIÓN

SUCRE

Director: ALFREDO GUTIÉRREZ VALENZUELA

PUBLICATIONS

REVISTA DE LA BIBLIOTECA Y ARCHIVO NACIONALES. Sucre. No. 24-30. 155 p. [622

The Sección de Archivo contains: *Un interesante litigio sucesorio en el año 1785—La personalidad de don Pedro Murillo—Una fé de bautismo auténtica e importantes documentos de gran valor histórico*, by Alfredo Gutiérrez Valenzuela, p. 1-13, based on documents from the Archivo; *Los archivos de la América pre-colombina*, by Manuel M. Arce T., p. 60-71; *La historia de Potosí*, by N. Arzanz y Vela, being two additional chapters of this inedited work with an editorial note, p. 103-111; the chapters are: 43, *De como se comenzó a sacar la plata de los metales del cerro con azogue y el grandísimo provecho que de esto resultó;* and 44, *De la venida del exmo. señor don Francisco de Toledo Virey del Perú a esta villa; de como inventó la famosa fábrica de ingenios y las muchas admirables y provechosas ordeananzas que dictó.*

There is also a *Catálogo-cronológico de expedientes de la época colonial, año 1780*, p. 151-155.

The remainder of the *Revista* is composed of articles about libraries. There are lists of books and publications acquired by the library during the year, p. 132-150.

BRAZIL

ARQUIVO NACIONAL

PRAÇA DA REPÚBLICA 26, RIO DE JANEIRO

Director: EUGENIO VILHENA DE MORAIS

At the end of 1943, Dr. Vilhena de Morais had completed five and one half years of service as director of the Arquivo Nacional. During that period he had contributed much to its advancement and thus had carried forth most meritoriously the excellent work of his predecessors. The building was repainted and extensive improvements were made which served to better the physical surroundings of the valuable records. Electric lighting was installed and fire extinguishers were provided.

During this period considerable bodies of records were accessioned. These pertained to the Administrative Section and included: 1939—Documents of the Alfândega do Estado do Espírito Santo, 1300 documents; 1940—Documents of the various divisions of the Ministério da Justiça e Negócios Interiores, 1246 documents; 1942—Papers in cases of the Diretória de Justiça, 6690 documents; Papers in naturalization cases, 10,320 documents; Papers on cases of various states, 625 documents; Papers in miscellaneous cases of the Diretória de Justiça, 9088 documents; Papers in expulsion cases, 1031 documents; 1943—Papers on miscellaneous cases, 6932 documents; Papers in cases of concession of medals, 1023 documents; Correspondence of the Secretary of State with various Ministries, 60,000 documents. Work on classification and cataloguing was carried on to make the records more accessible. Cards were prepared for cases in the Judicial Section and for documents in the Coleção Portugal. Numerous studies were conducted in the Archive by various scholars. The Archive participated in several expositions and inaugurated a series of lectures in the Sala Cairú.

PUBLICATIONS

No volumes appeared in 1943.

CHILE

ARCHIVO NACIONAL

BIBLIOTECA NACIONAL, SANTIAGO

Director: RICARDO DONOSO

In conformity with existing legislation the various administrative departments of the government deposited in the archive their records corresponding to the year 1937. The Sección Histórica y Judicial received the following: *Copiadores de correspondencia de los jefes de la frontera con la Intendencia de Concepción, 1819–1826* (4 vols.); *Resultas y cargos de la tesorería de Valdivia, 1724–1740* (1 vol.); *Correspondencia del Intendente de Concepción con el Gobernador de Valdivia, 1786–1788* (1 vol.); *Autos formados sobre las diligencias practicadas en el establecimiento de la Población de Santa Ana de Bribiesca, 1780* (1 vol.). Also there were accessioned 215 volumes of older notarial protocols and registers of real property from ten municipalities; 112 volumes from the Intendency of Atacama dated prior to 1885; and 125 *legajos* from the Judicial Archive of Iquique comprising 1697 *expedientes* in civil and criminal cases, 1900–1910.

Work continued on the arrangement of the documents of the Contaduría Mayor, which resulted in the formation of 397 volumes. The important O'Higgins collection presented to the archive in 1942 (see *Handbook, no. 8, 1942*, p. 51) was arranged and bound in 20 volumes.

Although pressure of other work retarded the cataloguing, some real progress was made in this essential labor particularly with reference to documents which are consulted most frequently. The card index of the notaries of Santiago now covers 38 volumes; and cards have been made for the volume of Samuel Donoso of Antofagasta for the year 1906. During the year there were also catalogued 1697 *expedientes* of the Judicial Archive of Iquique; additional documents of the Colección de Papeles Varios; and part of the Morla Vicuña collection of copies of historical documents from the archives at Seville, Simancas and Madrid.

The commission appointed in 1942 to prepare the documents of the O'Higgins collection for publication (see *Handbook, no. 8, 1942*, p. 51) worked actively during 1943 and had materials ready for three volumes at the end of the year.

To fill the vacancy created by the retirement of Luis Ignacio Silva Arriagada, Gustavo Opazo, who has been on the staff since 1925, was named section chief. The statistics for the year show that there were 4057 requests for information, 1718 certified copies were made and 2078 *expedientes* were loaned to or copied for the several ministries. The sum of 13,821 pesos was received for services rendered.

PUBLICATIONS

CATÁLOGO DEL ARCHIVO DE LA REAL AUDIENCIA. Santiago. Vol. 4. [623

Feliú Cruz, René. Índice de los cien primeros números [de la] *Revista chilena de historia y geografía*, 1911–1942. Santiago. Imp. Universitaria. 128 p. [624

REVISTA CHILENA DE HISTORIA Y GEOGRAFÍA. Santiago. No. 102, enero–junio, 419 p.; no. 103, julio–dic., 254 p. [625

Among the historical articles of these numbers the following may be mentioned: *El catecismo político cristiano*, by Ricardo Donoso; *El Dr. don Santiago de Tordesillas*, by Aniceto Almeyda; *La encomienda sin tierra*, by F. A. Kirkpatrick; *Pretendió el gobierno francés tomar posesión del Estrecho de Magallanes*, by Benjamín Valdés A.; *Diario de viaje de Lima a Chiloé, 1796–1797*, by Tomás O'Higgins; *Relaciones comerciales de Gran Bretaña con Chile, 1810–1830*, by Charles W. Centner, and *Alonso de Hojeda y el descubrimiento de Venezuela*, by Albert Harkness.

COLOMBIA

ARCHIVO HISTÓRICO NACIONAL

MINISTERIO DE EDUCACIÓN NACIONAL
BOGOTÁ

Director: ENRÍQUE ORTEGA RICAURTE

A visit of the director, Dr. Ortega Ricaurte, to various cities of the republic was made in 1943 for the purpose of preparing for the transfer to Bogotá of the protocols of the Notarios de Circuito prior to 1800. Difficulties were encountered, but some volumes were received by the Archive and the basis for future transfers was laid. In the course of this visit numerous inventories of provincial documents were made and provision for the better care locally of the records in several municipalities was provided. In other places the records are to be arranged and shipped to Bogotá. Also during the year the older records of the Ministry of Education were moved into the archive. As soon as these papers are arranged they will be catalogued.

In order to control more effectively the records of the provincial and municipal archives as well as to provide for the concentration in Bogotá of the records necessary to tell properly the history of the country it was proposed to create a National Directorship of the National Archives which would be in charge of the Director of the Archivo Histórico Nacional. Another important project under consideration was the new draft of Regulations for the Archivo Nacional prepared by Dr. Ortega Ricaurte. This was submitted to a committee of the Academy of History consisting of Enrique Otero D'Costa and Miguel Aguilera. After approval by the Academy the project will be submitted to the Minister of Education for study and final approval.

Work of cataloguing was carried on during 1943. At the end of the year there were ready for publication the catalogues of the following collections: *Aguardientes*, 55 vols.; *Negros y Esclavos*, 56 vols.; *Tabacos*, 36 vols.; and *Impuestos*, 54 vols.; making a total of 201 volumes completed during the year. Over 3900 requests for information were made, mostly relating to land titles.

The number of persons making investigations was somewhat less than in other years, nevertheless various important studies were in progress. Special mention should be made of the following, with an indication of their subjects of study: José María Restrepo Sáenz, biographies of the Governors of Antioquia; Roberto Botero Saldarriaga, *La dictadura de Urdaneta;* Raimundo Rivas, *Genealogías de Santafé de Bogotá* (tomo 2); José María Ots Capdequí, *El derecho español en América en la época de la colonia;* Guillermo Hernández de Alba, *Crónica del muy ilustre Colegio mayor de Nuestra Señora del Rosario;* and Juan R. Granados de la Hoz, historical monograph on the founding of his native city of Sincelejo.

The importance of the publications of the archive is indicated in the list below. Preparation of additional volumes of the *Genealogías de Nuevo Reino de Granada* and of the first volume of *Hojas de servicio de los militares que iniciaron su carrera en 1810* was carried forward. Dr. Ortega, in addition to the work involved in these items, was also engaged in collaboration with Guillermo Hernández de Alba and Ignacio Rivas Putnam in editing for the Academia Colombiana de Historia the papers of Domingo Caycedo, which are largely from the Archive. The first volume was published in 1943 (see below) and others were in preparation.

Finally it should be added that Dr. Ortega Ricaurte was named by the Venezuelan Government member of the commission to edit the papers of the Gran Mariscal de Ayacucho, General José Antonio de Sucre.

The distinguished guests who were entertained by the Archive during 1943 included: Mr. Henry Wallace, Vice-President of the United States; General Enrique Peñaranda, President of Bolivia; General Isaías Medina Angarita, President of Venezuela; Dr. Alfonso López, President of Colombia; Dr. Dario Echandía, first designate to the presidency; Dr. Ricardo J. Alfaro, ex-President of Panamá; Dr. Roberto Picón Lares, Prime Minister of Venezuela; Dr. Gonzalo Zaldumbide, Ambassador of Ecuador; and Dr. Carlos Arenas Loayza, Ambassador of Perú.

The budget for 1943 amounted to 21,225.44 pesos, of which $14,425 was for personal services, $2,000 for furniture and supplies, and $4,800 for publications. It may be added that the personnel received an additional 36% of their salaries each month.

PUBLICATIONS

Flórez de Ocariz, Juan. Genealogías del Nuevo Reyno de Granada. Tomo 1. Segunda ed. Bogotá. Prensas de la Biblioteca nacional. Publicación del Archivo histórico nacional, Enrique Ortega Ricaurte, ed. xiii, 477 p. [626

This seventeenth century work on New Granada contains an introductory essay on nobility, rank and heraldry, lists of early settlers, genealogical sketches of 92 notables, and notes on 80 cities and towns giving information on the founding, history, and coats of arms of each. The volume is illustrated particularly with drawings of family and municipal coats of arms.

Ortega Ricaurte, Enrique. Villavicencio, 1842–1942: Monografía histórica. Bogotá. Prensas de la Biblioteca nacional. 142 p., ilus. [627

A well documented study of the city of Villavicencio, issued in commemoration of the centenary of its founding.

REVISTA DEL ARCHIVO NACIONAL. Bogotá. Tomo 5, no. 45-56, enero–diciembre. 415 p. [628

Contents: No. 45-46, enero-febrero, comprises an advance printing of the first 94 pages of the monograph on Villavicencio, noted above.

No. 47, marzo, contains two groups of documents from the archive: *Probanza de servicios de Rodrigo de Santander*, p. 161-204; and *Nuevos y desconocidos documentos para la historia de la conspiración del 25 septiembre de 1828*, p. 205-224.

No. 48-49, abril-mayo, contains two documents regarding San Josef de Cúcuta: *Título de muy noble, valerosa y leal villa*, p. 227-242, and *Padrón del vecindario*, taken in November 1792, p. 242-279.

No. 50-52, junio-agosto, contains a reprint of a chapter from *Genealogías del Nuevo Reyno de Granada*, noted above, entitled "Autoridad y distrito de la Real Audiencia y sus poblaciones," p. 294-342.

No. 53-56, septiembre-diciembre, contains documents from the Archive relating to Gonzalo Jiménez de Quesada, p. 359-375 and to the town of La Palma, p. 376-397.

Each issue also has reprints of reviews of and articles about the publications of the archive which appeared in the press of Colombia and other countries.

COSTA RICA

ARCHIVOS NACIONALES

AVENIDA 2ª ESTE, SAN JOSÉ

Director: JORGE VOLIO Y JIMÉNEZ

During 1943 a number of important accessions were received by the Archive. From the Congress and its secretariat a large number of *expedientes* corresponding to the years 1932-1935 were transferred to the Archive. The Secretary of Public Instruction deposited 24 volumes of correspondence of the Jefatura de Educación for 1937 and 11 volumes of lists of persons employed in the Secretaría and in colleges and schools during the years 1936 to 1937. The Oficina del Tribunal Superior de Arbitraje transmitted 7153 *expedientes* concerning accidents to laborers. Also 114 *protocolos* of *notarios* of the Province of San José and *juzgados* of other provinces were received.

Work of cataloguing this new material was carried on actively. 252 *expedientes* of Congress for 1932-1933 were carded and the volumes from the Secretaría de Instrucción Pública were catalogued. Some 15,000 cards were made for the records of the Tribunal Superior de Arbitraje and 571 older *expedientes* regarding administrative matters were studied for which there were made 571 principal cards and 2876 auxiliary cards.

As usual the Sección Jurídica showed great activity. Searches were made upon requests of individuals, documents were furnished to the courts, certificates were issued, some 30,000 cards were made and 40,000 *expedientes* were arranged and sewed.

In the Sección Histórica work continued on the listing of the colonial documents and installments were regularly published in the *Revista*. Nevertheless much work of revision is said to be necessary before the documents will be fully available.

Considerable work has also been done on the records of the national period, but little attention has been given as yet to the municipal records.

In March a reorganization of the sections of the Archive was effected in conformity with Decree no. 54. The purpose was to provide a more efficient and logical arrangement of the work of the Archive. All the benefits had not been secured by the end of the year.

The director in his annual report pointed out the need for more adequate quarters and more suitable equipment which would serve to facilitate the work of the employees.

PUBLICATIONS

REVISTA DE LOS ARCHIVOS NACIONALES. San José. Bimestral. Año 7, nos. 1-12, p. 1-672; índice, p. 589-680. [629

Contents: The *Índices de la Sección colonial de los Archivos nacionales de Costa Rica* is continued from the preceding volume with separate pagination, p. 589-680. The instalments give a calendar of colonial documents covering the period from June 4, 1812 to December 11, 1820.

The principal documentary publication comprises a part of the *Libro copiador de comunicaciones del ministro general Saravia, 1842* (continued from preceding volume; to be continued), p. 109-112, 168-185, 542-558. Other documents from the Archive are: *Privilegio concedido a la iglesia de Nuestra Señora de Los Ángeles, decreto de 1862*, p. 104; *Circular a los Gobiernos de los Estados, abril 1842* (Morazán), p. 193-196; *Comunicaciones a los emigrados, 1840-41* (Carrillo), p. 196-198; *Decreto para trasladar el pueblo de Tucurrique, 1839*, p. 215-222. There is also a document from the Archivo General de Indias: *Provanzas del capitán don Gonzalo de Alvarado, conquistador de Guatemala*, p. 3-16.

The several numbers contain numerous historical and other articles most of which are very brief. The more important items are: Emmanuel Thompson, *Defensa de Carrillo*, tercera parte (to be continued), p. 454-474; Norberto de Castro, *Fundadores de casas hidalgas en Costa Rica*—genealogical data—(continued from preceding volume), p. 105-108, 186-193, 325-330, 434-443, 507-515; Aniceto Playa, *Reliquias de España*—historical notes and impressions with illustrations—, p. 99-104, 149-156, 279-

286, 423–430, 487-494, 584–593; and Roscoe R. Hill, *Marinos americanos en Nicaragua 1912-1925*,—translation by José Dávila S. of a chapter from Wilgus (ed.), *Hispanic American Essays* (Chapel Hill, 1942),—p. 20–34.

CUBA

Archivo Nacional

Compostela y Fundición, La Habana

Director: Joaquín Llaverías y Martínez

The principal event of 1943 was the continuation of the work of construction of the new building for the Archive, of which the corner stone was laid in October, 1942. In view of the facts that the new building was erected on the site of the old home of the Archive and that the records were not removed during construction, a considerable amount of shifting of the records was necessary and this interfered somewhat with the regular work of the Archive. However, there were about the usual number of visitors seeking information and the members of the staff carried on their work of organization and cataloguing. As a part of the centennial program, the publication of a new series of volumes on archivology was inaugurated in 1943.

PUBLICATIONS

Boletín del archivo nacional. Habana. Tomo 40, enero-dic., 1941 [published in 1943]. 236 p. [630
The texts of important documents appear in this issue as follows: *Carta importantísima del general Antonio Maceo al Secretario del exterior de la República de Cuba en armas, 1896*, p. 150–151; three letters regarding English attacks on Cuba, 1762–1764, p. 57–58; *Comunicación dirigida a José Pablo Valiente sobre la remisión hecha por el gobernador de Nueva Orleans de treinta y siete indivíduos de color y blancos complicados en una sublevación proyectada, 1795*, p. 59–62; *Comunicación . . . relativo a las ideas del Ministro inglés y sobre las medidas convenientes para la aprehensión del famoso general Francisco de Miranda, 1798*, p. 62; *Expediente donde se decreta la retención de dos obras de Gertrudis Gómez de Avellaneda, 1844*, p. 103–108; *Expediente académico de José Martí y Pérez en el Instituto de segunda enseñanza de La Habana*, p. 112–127; *Memoria de un presentado, 1869*, p. 127–135; *Primera sublevación importante de los indios-cubanos, 1534*, p. 38–55; *Proclama suscrita por el intendente José Domingo Díaz anunciando las operaciones de los realistas y exhortando al pueblo venezolano a la submisión, 1827*, p. 90–103; *Real cédula dándole gracias al gobernador de Cuba por las noticias que ha dado de haber abandonado los ingleses el terreno que ocupaban cerca de la Bahía de Guantánamo, 1742*, p. 55–57; *Relación de los servicios prestados por la Jefatura de policía del Gobierno de la Provincia de La Habana, 1896*, p. 151–164; *Testimonio de las diligencias . . . sobre el combate que tuvo nuestra lancha cañonera titulada Nuestra Señora del Carmen . . . con dos fragatas de guerra inglesas, 1798*, p. 62–90.
In this volume there are continued from vol. 37–38, 1938–1939 (see *Handbook, No. 6, 1940*, item 614), the following indexes of records in the archive: *Inventario general de la Delegación del Partido revolucionario cubano en Nueva York, 1892–1898*, p. 166–211, covers documents no. 15255–16074, of *cajas* 115–117; and *Índice del libro diez y seis de reales órdenes*, p. 212–234, covers the orders of the year 1803. These two indexes are to be continued.
There are also several historical articles, reprints of some articles about the Archive and a reprint of the annual report of the Director of the Archivo Nacional de Venezuela for 1941, p. 15–23.

Catálogo de los fondos del Real Consulado de Agricultura, Industria y Comercio y de la Junta de Fomento. Habana. Imp. El Siglo XX. (Archivo nacional de Cuba, publ., 1). xliv, 655 p. [631
This is the first volume of a new series of publications inaugurated in connection with the celebration of the centenary of the founding of the archive. It is an alphabetical index of subjects in the papers of the Real Consulado and the Junta de Fomento. The collection catalogued comprises 209 *legajos* and 211 volumes. There is an historical introduction by Joaquín Llaverías and a foreword by Emeterio S. Santovenia.

Correspondencia diplomática de la Delegación cubana en Nueva York durante la guerra de independencia de 1895 a 1898. Tomo primero. Habana. Imp. El Siglo XX. (Archivo nacional de Cuba, publ., 2). xlviii, 171 p. [632
A collection of 204 letters mostly written by Tomás Estrada Palma. They treat of subjects connected with the prosecution of the war. The historical introduction is by Joaquín Llaverías and the foreword by José Agustín Martínez.

DOMINICAN REPUBLIC

El Archivo General de la Nación

Calle Arzobispo Nouel, no. 52
Ciudad Trujillo

Director: Emilio Rodríguez Demorizi

The regular accessions during 1943 comprised the records of the various governmental offices for the year 1938. A large number of photocopies were received from the Archivo de las Indias at Sevilla, the

Biblioteca Nacional at Madrid and various libraries in the United States. Private gifts of documents were made by Dr. Manuel de J. Troncoso de la Concha, Pedro Spignolio, José Ortega V., Fernando Amiama Tió, R. A. Jorge Rivas, Luis E. Pou and Enrique Abréu.

During the year courses on classification and cataloguing of documents, and on paleography and diplomatics were conducted by Lic. María Ugarte de Brusiloff. Forty-seven students successfully completed these courses in archivology and were presented with certificates by the Secretary of State for Interior and Police, Lic. Arturo Despradel on December 17.

Cataloguing of the documents of the Ministry of Foreign Relations was continued. Plans were formulated for the publication of a series of volumes of documents in connection with the celebration of the centenary of the republic in 1944. Many documents were furnished by the Archive for inclusion in the *Colección de Obras Históricas* to be published under the direction of Lic. M. A. Peña Batlle, member of the Dominican Academy of History. Sr. Luis Rodríguez Guerra, as the representative of the Archivo General, continued the investigations in Cuba.

Members of the staff continued their historical studies. As a result the following publications appeared during the year: by Emilio Rodríguez Demorizi, *El acta de la separación dominicana y el acta de independencia de los Estados Unidos de América* (Ciudad Trujillo, 53 p.) and *Del romancero dominicano* (Santiago, R. D., 115 p.); and by Luis E. Alemar, *Santo Domingo, Ciudad Trujillo* (Santiago, R. D., 350 p.).

The budget for 1943 amounted to $13,770.

PUBLICATIONS

BOLETÍN DEL ARCHIVO GENERAL DE LA NACIÓN. Ciudad Trujillo. Vol. 6, nos. 26–31. 410 p. [633

The first issue, no. 26–27, is dedicated to the commemoration of the centenary of the revolutionary activities of 1843. There are two leading articles: *La Municipalidad de Santo Domingo ante el golpe libertador del 27 de febrero*, by Guido Despradel y Batista, p. 3–27, and *La revolución de 1843, apuntes y documentos para su estudio*, by Emilio Rodríguez Demorizi, p. 28–109. This last article comprises an introductory essay and the text of eleven important documents with extensive footnotes.

The major portion of the other two issues, no. 28–29, 30–31, is devoted to the publication of a collection of documents from the Archives du Ministère des Affaires Extrangères in Paris under the title *Correspondencia del Consul de Francia en Santo Domingo, 1844–1846*, p. 142–243, 273–403. The collection of 83 documents was copied by Dr. Salvador E. Paradas in 1931–1933. The introductory statement and the footnotes are by Emilio Rodríguez Demorizi. These documents serve to throw much light on the events in the first years of Dominican independence.

There are two additional articles: *Publicación de la ley en Santo Domingo durante el período de la dominación española* by María Ugarte de Brusiloff, and *El estilo imperial de Felipe II y las edificaciones del siglo XVII en la Española*, by Erwin Walter Palm.

There are continuations from the preceding volume of the following: *Colección Lugo*, p. 110–115, 254–268, 404–408 (to be continued), entries from the notebooks of Américo Lugo comprising data from the Archivo de las Indias relating to Santo Domingo; and *Indice general de los libros copiadores de la sección de relaciones exteriores*, p. 116–118, 269–270, 409–410 (to be continued).

Each issue also contains editorial notes about the archive and its activities, p. 1–2, 119–120, 271–272.

ECUADOR

ARCHIVO NACIONAL DE HISTORIA

APARTADO 826, QUITO

Director of the Archive and Museum:
JORGE PÉREZ CONCHA

Secretary in Charge of the Archive:
JESÚS VAQUERO DÁVILA

GUATEMALA

ARCHIVO GENERAL DEL GOBIERNO

4ᴬ AVENIDA NORTE, NO. 4, GUATEMALA

Director: J. JOAQUÍN PARDO

PUBLICATIONS

BOLETÍN DEL ARCHIVO GENERAL DEL GOBIERNO. Guatemala. Tomo 8, no. 1–4, p. 1–447; índice separately paginated, p. 503–522. [634

Contents: No. 1 is dedicated to the celebration of the fourth centenary of the founding of the city of Antigua Guatemala. It comprises selected extracts from the *Actas de Cabildos, 1542–1820*, which serve to give a picture of the life and progress of the city.

The other numbers contain groups of interesting documents from the Archive relating to various educational institutions. These are: Eight documents relating to the founding and early years of the Colegio de Santo Tomás de Aquino, which was the predecessor of the Universidad de Guatemala (no. 2, p. 227–292; no. 3, p. 295–

315); three documents pertaining to the Colegio de la Compañía de Jesús (no. 3, p. 315-359); and one regarding the expulsion of the Jesuit Order from Guatemala in 1767 (no. 3, p. 359-367; no. 4, 371-375); two documents respecting the Colegio de Recogimiento de Doncellas (no. 4, p. 395-402); ' two documents dealing with the founding and suppression of the Colegio de San Jerónimo (no. 4, p. 402-442).

The *Indice de los documentos existentes en el Archivo general del Gobierno* is continued in no. 2-4 for 1943, p. 503-522. The entries cover classification A 1.5, Real Consulado de Comercio, *legajos* 2408-2440, 2443, 2444, for the years 1804-1821, with a few documents earlier than 1804, and A 1.6, Real Sociedad Económica, *legajos* 2006-2007, for the years 1796-1798.

HAITI

ARCHIVES NATIONALES

PORT-AU-PRINCE

Director: MENTOR LAURENT

HONDURAS

ARCHIVO NACIONAL DE HONDURAS

TEGUCIGALPA

Director: MIGUEL ÁNGEL RAMOS

The annual report for 1942-1943 of the director of the Archive presented to the Minister of Public Education (*Boletín*, año 3, no. 5, p. 10-14) gives an account of the activities of the year.

The accessions in the section of Registro Civil comprised 95 duplicate volumes from various municipalities of the republic. The section of Hemeroteca received many current newspapers and periodicals particularly those issued in Honduras. No changes were registered in the sections of Historia and Tierras. The need for the arrangement and cataloguing of the documents of the section of Historia was emphasized and it was indicated that this work cannot now be undertaken due to lack of adequate personnel.

During the year, 3,984 visits were made to the Archive for the purpose of consulting the records. Esteban Guardiola and Félix Salgado regularly assembled inedited documents for publication in the *Revista del Archivo y Biblioteca Nacionales*, the organ of the Sociedad de Geografía e Historia de Honduras. Father La Madrid assembled data regarding the Orden de la Merced and Ernesto Alvarado García continued his studies regarding the members of the Cuban colony in Honduras.

The Archive participated in the First Exposition and Fair of Books held in Tegucigalpa in September. The materials exhibited included eleven volumes of the original manuscript *Actas* of the Legislature for the years between 1824 and 1859, four *expedientes* of the Sección de Tierras of the years 1585, 1606, 1672 and 1673, and four volumes from the collection of duplicates of the Registro Civil.

The director of the Archive also called attention in his report to the importance of the archives of the municipalities and churches for the history of the country and the need for their protection against fire, insects and other injurious factors. He made an effort to assemble information regarding these archives throughout the Republic in order to have it available in the Archivo Nacional for use by scholars interested in local history.

PUBLICATIONS

BOLETÍN DE LA BIBLIOTECA Y ARCHIVO NACIONALES. Tegucigalpa. Año 3, nos. 5 and 6. 157, 191 p. [635

Contents: No. 5 is a special edition dedicated to the centenary of the cities of Santa Rosa de Copán, la Sultana de Occidente, and Danlí, la Ciudad de las Colinas. It comprises various historical articles and numerous documents relating to the cities which serve to give an interesting and intimate picture of these two Honduran communities. There are also included in Spanish translation the documents relating to the efforts of the United States and the Central American Republics to reestablish constitutional government in Honduras which appear in *Foreign Relations of the United States, 1924*, vol. 1.

Besides the information given in the introductory statement, no. 6 contains the following historical articles based largely on materials from the Archive: *Los símbolos de la República de Honduras*, p. 17-34; *Los payas, documentos curiosos y viajes*, by Federico Lunardi, p. 43-80; *Escudos de armas de la Provincia de Honduras y banderas de Centro América, Archivo general de Indias*, by George Ypsilanti, p. 131-156; and *Estudio, custodia, restauración y conservación de las ruinas de Honduras*, by Miguel A. Ramos, p. 175-182.

REVISTA DEL ARCHIVO Y BIBLIOTECA NACIONALES. Tegucigalpa. Tomo 21, nos. 7-12, p. 433-818; tomo 22, nos. 1-6, p. 1-384. [636

The historical portion of this organ of the Sociedad de Geografía e Historia de Honduras, as in other years, contains documents and articles relating to the history of the country. Inserted in installments in various numbers are the following: *Lempira —El héroe de la epopeya de Honduras*, by Federico Lunardi; *Don Francisco Cruz y la Botica del pueblo*, by José Reina Valenzuela; *Documentos y escritos de 1821—*

1822, published by Rafael Heliodoro Valle; *Anales parlamentarios, Asamblea ordinaria del Estado de Honduras, año 1830, actas números 33-40;* and *Sucesos relacionados con la expedición del Gral. Ricardo Streber al puerto de Omoa y con el bombardeo de la Fortaleza de San Fernando, por la fragata inglesa 'Niove' al mando de Sir Lambton Loraine, el 19 de agosto de 1873.* In several numbers there are materials regarding General Francisco Morazán which serve to compliment those published in the preceding year. Finally tomo 21, number 10 is devoted to the celebration of the centenary of the towns of Santa Rosa de Copán, Danlí y Ocotepeque. Most of the material of this number deals with Santa Rosa.

MEXICO

Archivo General de la Nación

PALACIO NACIONAL, MÉXICO, D. F.

Director: Julio Jiménez Rueda

In 1943 there were received from the Private Secretary of the Presidency the records of that office corresponding to the administration of General Lázaro Cárdenas, 1934–1940 and consisting of 305 *legajos*. Also the private papers of Fernando Iglesias Calderón were deposited in the Archive as a donation.

The work of cataloguing in the sections of Historia and Tierras was continued actively. During the period from September 1, 1942 to August 31, 1943, indexing was completed in the Sección de Historia on *ramos* as follows: Ramo de Inquisición, 68 *tomos;* Justicia e Instrucción Pública, 10 *tomos;* Correspondencia de Virreyes, 4537 cards; General de Parte, 200 cards; Provincias Internas, 16 *tomos;* and in the Sección de Tierras on *ramos:* Tierras, 70 *volúmenes;* Reales Cédulas, 4819 *expedientes;* Indios, 2300 *expedientes;* Civil, 30 *volúmenes;* and Marquesado del Valle, Hospital de Jesús, 34 *volúmenes*. Numerous certificates of land titles and of services of federal, civil and military personnel of the Federal government were issued as requested. In addition the members of the staff transcribed and studied numerous important historical documents of the colonial period.

Student fellows of the Colegio de México carried on studies in the archive on subjects dealing with 18th century colonial history. Joaquín Ramírez Cabañas and Luis Chávez Orozco examined documents relating to colonial commerce.

By a decree of December 31, 1943 the Archive is empowered to grant permits for the exportation of documents and rare books from Mexico. Plans regarding more suitable quarters for the Archive were formulated. It is proposed to remodel the building known as La Ciudadela, which it is considered will provide an adequate locale for the valuable records in the Archive.

The budget for 1943 amounted to 100,000 pesos, which was a decided increase over the preceding year.

PUBLICATIONS

Boletín del archivo general de la nación. México, D. F. Vol. 14, nos. 1–4. 716 p. [637

As in preceding volumes most of the space in the *Boletín* is devoted to the publication of the text of documents from the Archive with brief introductory notes by members of the staff. No. 1, p. 9–184, is dedicated to the State of Vera Cruz and comprises five documents selected and transcribed by Luis G. Ceballos, chief paleographer, with a prefatory note "Vera Cruz en la historia," by Teodoro Hernández. The other documents are: *Un auto de fe en el siglo XVII,* p. 215–259; *El Convento de la Concepción,* p. 261–266; *Costumbres de las indias de Yucatán,* by Juan J. Hernández, p. 267–280; *Auxilios a Campeche y Yucatán por el Virrey Marqués de Croix,* p. 281–285; *La nobleza colonial, último tercio del siglo XVIII* (continued from vol. 13), p. 287–315, 441–476; *El pleito de las borlas,* p. 527–590; *La vida en la colonia, cuaderno de apuntes de un ministro del Santo Oficio,* 1606–1617, p. 591–615; *Busca de tesoros precortesianos en el cerro de Chapultepec,* p. 617–632.

The *Catálogo de pobladores de Nueva España,* prepared by Edmundo O'Gorman and described in the *Handbook, no. 8, 1942,* no. 490, is continued and concluded in this volume with a note on the corresponding three alphabetical indexes and part of the index of names, p. 317–351, 477–501, 659–713. There are 872 entries in the *Catálogo*.

The *Índice del ramo de tierras* is continued from preceding volumes, p. 187–198, 355–364, 503–512, 633–642, and covers the *expedientes* relating to lands in volumes 1423 to 1454 of the collection.

Each number contains a list of publications received by the Archive during the preceding quarter, p. 199–205, 355–364, 513–519, 649–656 and there is a bibliographical note regarding the *Handbook, no. 7, 1941,* p. 645–646.

PANAMA

Archivo Nacional

PANAMÁ

Director: Juan Antonio Susto

PARAGUAY

Archivo General de la Nación

ASUNCIÓN

Director: José Doroteo Bareiro

PERU

Archivo Nacional del Perú

CALLE ESTUDIOS NO. 492, LIMA

Director: Horacio H. Urteaga

During the fire of May 10, which destroyed the Biblioteca Nacional, the Archive suffered considerable damage from water. The locale was made completely unusable and the Archive was temporarily closed. The appeal of the director to the President resulted in making immediately available space in the Palacio de Justicia, which was assigned to the Archive but had been occupied by another office since the earthquake of 1940. As a result the records were moved to the new quarters between May 31 and June 18. The Archive was reopened on June 21, in its more modern and adequate surroundings.

PUBLICATIONS

Revista del Archivo Nacional del Perú. Lima. Tomo 16, entregas 1–2. 240 p. [638

Contents: Documents from the archive with introductory notes by J. Zevallos Quiñones as follows: *Para la historia de la imprenta en Lima*—a contract of 1625, and lease and transfer of print shop in the Convent of Santo Domingo, 1645—p. 5–16; *José de Boqui y la emancipación del Perú*—will and special instructions—p. 17–25; *Una licencia del Presidente La Gasca, 1550*—granting Pedro de Quirós license to travel —p. 123–126; and *Sobre don Toribio Rodríguez de Mendoza*—power of attorney, 1803, and will, 1818—p. 131–142. *Traslación de la Villa de Pisco, año de 1688*,—begun in the 1940 issues (see *Handbook, nos. 6* and *7*) is concluded in this volume, p. 27–57, 143–147.

The *Índice del Libro becerro de escrituras*, prepared by Guillermo Lohman Villena is continued from the preceding volumes (see *Handbook, no. 7*) and comprises 446 entries from the notarial register for the years 1536 and 1537, p. 59–100, 175–219 (to be continued).

The section *Índice del Archivo nacional del Perú*, continues the inventory of the Archivo de la Real Junta de Temporalidades covering: Títulos de la Hacienda La Macacona, 2 *legajos*, 1767–1818, p. 101–102; and Títulos de la Hacienda San José de La Nasca, 2 *legajos*, 1763–1804, p. 221–238.

URUGUAY

Archivo General de la Nación

MONTEVIDEO

Director: Ángel Vidal

PUBLICATIONS

(See also item 3348)

Acuerdos del extinguido Cabildo de Montevideo. Anexo. Vol. 18. Montevideo. Ed. Botella. 304, xxii p. [639

This volume comprises the entries from the third *Libro de anexos*, covering the period from January 6, 1792 to July 20, 1795. It concludes the series of volumes of the *actas* from the founding of the city down to 1829, which presents an excellent picture of the activities of the colonial municipality.

VENEZUELA

Archivo Nacional

OESTE 1, NO. 7, CARACAS

Director: Luis Yépez

Due to the resignation of Dr. Mario Briceño-Iragorry, who had served as director since August, 1941, Luis Yépez was appointed to the position by a resolution of the Minister of National Education of November 23.

The seminar in colonial paleography was continued under the direction of María Teresa Bermejo, the technical adviser of the archive. Its principal work consisted of the correction of the proofs of the *Actas del Cabildo de Caracas*, the transcription of 16th century documents and the cataloguing of early manuscripts of the Sección Real Hacienda. Among the documents transcribed were the act of the founding of Caracas, the *Libro copiador de cédulas*, two discourses of Bolívar before the Congress of Angostura and the oldest *Libro de real hacienda de Trujillo* (1595).

A three day conference on archivology was held in October, which was attended by employees of the archives of the Ministries, the Congress, the Principal Registry Office, and the National Library as well as by those of the National Archive. The discussions and practical exercises of this conference served to better prepare the archivists for effecting their tasks.

The technical adviser in her report insisted on the necessity of adopting the reforms proposed in the previous year for the law relating to the National Archive and pointed out the importance of the creation of a Superior Council of Archives. She also indicated the difficulty in proceeding with classification and cataloguing of the documents on the modern sections due to the presence of duplicates, triplicates, quadruplicates and even quintuplicates at times, adding that "only the originals should be kept," in order to save space.

Work of classification, cataloguing and indexing was carried on in various sections of the archive. The formation of summaries of the Sección Encomiendas was completed for volume 48 and volume three of this list is ready for publication. A volume of documents relating to the founding of the Villa de San Luis de Cura was selected. Index notes were made of the *expedientes* in civil and criminal cases from the Archivo de Barquisimeto.

In 1943 a total of 339 volumes of the Sección Real Hacienda had been bound and fifty more were ready to be bound early the following year. It was proposed to terminate this work in the latter year. In the arrangement of the documents of Real Hacienda, eleven volumes of papers belonging to Real Consulado were separated and transferred to the latter section. The alphabetical index of the Sección Toma de Razón was continued. The separation of papers for the Sección Filiaciones, the continuation of *Próceres y servidores de la República,* progressed and four volumes were ready for binding.

In the Sección Gobernación y Capitanía General, tomos 130 to 141 and 171 to 218 were completed and made available for study. Also in the Sección Secretaría del Interior y Justicia, tomos 375 to 424 were finished and placed in their respective document boxes. The documents for tomos 225 to 254 of this section were chronologically arranged. Documents of the Ministerio de Guerra y Marina for the year 1810 were put in order and a card catalogue was made of them. Finally the card index of the Sección Diversos, a miscellaneous collection, was completed for 22 of the volumes.

Two accessions were received during the year. One consisted of 500 packages of documents regarding projects of Obras Públicas Nacionales effected down to 1925. These papers were easily handled since each package had its corresponding index. The second accession consisted of 42 packages of documents and 123 *libros copiadores* from the Ministerio de Guerra y Marina.

It was impossible to use all the additional space provided by the improvements to the Archive mentioned in the previous *Handbook,* since shelving could not be secured.

Sr. Yépez in concluding his annual report reiterated what the technical adviser had said as to the necessity of a new law for the Archive. He urged that the project included in the report of his predecessor should be put into force in order to "preserve the invaluable treasure of the national documents" in a more fitting manner.

The budget for the year amounted to 152,122 bolívares.

A decree of President Isaías Medina Angarita, dated December 9, 1942, provided for the publication of the papers of Mariscal José Antonio de Sucre. The bulk of these documents are originals recently acquired by the Venezuelan government and will be supplemented by copies of others presented by Jacinto Jijón y Caamaño of Ecuador. The Ministers of Interior Relations and National Education, acting under authority of the presidential decree appointed, on April 16, 1943, a committee to prepare and edit the documents. This committee includes Mario Briceño Iragorry, Sra. Lucila L. de Pérez Díaz, José Antonio Calcaño and Jacinto Jijón y Caamaño, with Héctor García Chuecos, of the Archive, as secretary. The collaborating members are Carlos Blanco Galindo, Bolivia; Enrique Ortega Ricaurte, Colombia; José Lefebre, Panamá; and Carlos Enrique Paz Soldán, Perú.

PUBLICATIONS

Actas del cabildo de Caracas. Tomo 1, 1573–1600. Caracas, Ed. Elite. 616 p., ilus. [641

The *actas* in this volume were transcribed and edited by members of the seminar in paleography under the direction of the technical adviser of the Archive, María Teresa Bermejo. The introduction is by Mario Briceño Iragorry, formerly director, and the valuable study *Cuadro de gobernadores, alcaldes y otros cargos capitulares* is by Julio Febres Cordero G., a member of the staff of the Archive. The volume covering the municipal activities from 1573 to 1600 gives a vivid picture of colonial life in Caracas.

Boletín del archivo nacional. Caracas. Tomo 29, no. 114–116, p. 247–438; tomo 30, no. 117–119, p. 1–192. [642

As in preceding years most of the space in the *Boletín* is given to successive installments of the indexes to the various sections of the Archive. The numbers for 1943 contain the following: *Enomiendas,* tomo 32, folio 44–189; *Gobernación y Capitanía general,* tomo 18, folio 170–370, tomo 19, folio 1–242; *Reales provisiones,* tomo 22, folio 102–481, tomo 23, folio 1–498; *Intendencia de ejército y Real hacienda,* tomo 18, folio 48–337, tomo 19, folio 1–329, tomo 20, folio 1–247; *Compañía Guipuzcoana,* tomo 10, folio 15–350, tomo 11, folio 1–51; *Hojas militares,* tomo 10, folio 269 (Letra R)—342 (Letra S); *Causas de infidencia,* tomo 22, folio 342–528; *República de Venezuela, Secretaría de interior y justicia,* tomo 34, folio 289–360, tomos 35–49, tomo 50, folio 1–192.

In each number of the *Boletín* there is included the text of one or more documents from the various sections of the Archive.

The titles are as follows: *Título de lugarteniente de gobernador de los indios cumanagotos,* no. 114, p. 247–248; *Informe sobre el estado de la provincia de Maracaibo, 1784,* no. 114, p. 249–254; *Estadística de la provincia de Barquisimeto en 1834,* no. 114, p. 255–263; *Descripción corográfico-mixta de la provincia de Guayana, 1788,* no. 115, p. 311–326; *Estadística de la provincia de Barinas en 1831,* no. *116,* p. 375–386; *Jueces que vinieron a la provincia,* no. 117, p. 1–4; *Reconstrucción de las casas reales, 1698–1699,* no. 117, p. 5–9; *El Rey ordena varias obras públicas en la cuidad,* *1733,* no. 118, p. 66–69; *Las tiendas de los escribanos en la Plaza Real, 1745–1750,* no. 118, p. 70–80; *El primer puente sobre el arroyo Caroata, 1736,* no. 119, p. 129–134; *El Cabildo de la ciudad de Valencia pide la remoción de un teniente, 1785,* no. 119, p. 135–141.

The report of the director of the archive, for the year 1942 appears in no. 115, p. 363–374, under the title *Informe . . . al Ministro de relaciones interiores sobre las labores del Instituto en el año 1942.* There are also bibliographical and other notes in some of the issues.

OTHER ARCHIVES

ARGENTINA

Archivo Histórico de la Provincia de Buenos Aires

LA PLATA

PUBLICATIONS

Heras, Carlos. Orígenes de la Imprenta de Niños expósitos. Con una introducción sobre *Los primeros trabajos de la Imprenta de Niños expósitos.* La Plata. Tall. de impresiones oficiales. (Documentos del Archivo, tomo 10). xxii, 363 p. **[643**

Contains the text of two *expedientes* of 1780 and 1783, from the Archive of the colonial Audiencia de Buenos Aires, regarding the activities of the Portuguese José de Silva y Aguiar as administrator of the first printing press in Buenos Aires. The introduction discusses the early imprints and lists those of the press down to 1783.

Biblioteca Nacional

CALLE MÉXICO 564, BUENOS AIRES

Director: G. Martínez Zuviría

PUBLICATIONS

Revista de la biblioteca nacional. Buenos Aires. Tomo 8, nos. 25–26, p. 1–500; tomo 9, nos. 27–28, p. 1–500. **[644**

The issues of this review are devoted to the publication of documents from the various valuable and interesting collections of the Archive.

Contents: General section: *Las montoneras del caudillo General Ángel Vicente Peñalosa (El Chacho), 1863,* tomo 8, p. 15–101, 293–381—64 letters of General Wenceslao Paunero to General Juan A. Gelly y Obes; *El general Justo José de Urquiza, campaña contra la dictadura de Rosas, 1846–1856,* tomo 8, p. 261–292—10 letters of Valentín Alsina to Félix Frías; *Política argentina, asuntos varios, 1849–1867,* tomo 8, p. 382–428—17 letters of Mariano Balcarce to Félix Frías; *Rebelión de Entre Ríos, Ricardo López Jordán, 1870,* tomo 9, p. 11–72—42 letters from the papers of Gelly y Obes; *Política interna argentina, 1853–1859,* tomo 9, p. 73–104—7 letters of Félix Frías to various persons; *Política interna argentina, 1862–1906,* tomo 9, p. 263–299—15 letters, correspondence of José Benjamín Gorostiaga, Domingo F. Sarmiento, Bernardo Solveyra, Julio A. Roca, Bartolomé Mitre, Miguel Juárez Celman, Guillermo Rawson and Eduardo Wilde; *Muerte de Félix Frías,* tomo 9, p. 309–315—5 letters; *Últimos años del general San Martín,* tomo 9, p. 316–325—4 letters.

Sección colonial: The following items described in the *Handbook, no. 8, 1942,* are continued in the issues of 1943 and will be continued in 1944: *Materia médica misionera del hermano Pedro Montenegro, 1710,* tomo 8, p. 142–178, 429–448; tomo 9, p. 119–158, 396–441; *Las "Memorias curiosas" o "Diario" de Beruti, 1717–1807,* tomo 8, p. 179–193, 449–465; tomo 9, p. 159–178, 442–448; *Libro de matrícula de estudiantes de los reales estudios del Colegio de San Carlos de Buenos Aires, 1773–1818,* tomo 8, p. 194–198, 446–470; tomo 9, p. 179–184, 449–453. There are also the following documents in this section of the *Revista: El virrey caballero de Croix al bailío frey Antonio Valdés, sobre inconveniencia de aplicación de las ordenanzas de intendentes, año 1790,* tomo 8, p. 105–141—a document from the Archivo General de Indias; *Vestigios de cultura en la provincia de Salta antes de su conquista,* tomo 9, p. 105–118—a report of Filiberto de Mena; *Informe de Pedro Esteban Dávila manifestando el número y la clase de reducciones de indios,* tomo 9, p. 326–335—copied from the National Library at Rio de Janeiro; *Relación hecha al virrey del Perú por don Francisco Álvarez sobre el carácter y la organización de los indios,* tomo 9, p. 336–365; *Capitulación con el mariscal Diego de Almagro,* tomo 9, p. 366–374; *Testamento otorgado por Don Pedro de Mendoza,* tomo 9, p. 375–381; *Información sobre Nueva Castilla,* tomo 9, p. 382–390; *Carta del licenciado Matienzo referente a desórdenes en Cuzco,* tomo 9, p. 391–395—the last four documents are from the Archivo General de Indias.

Sección Internacional: *Relación histórica de las misiones diplomáticas argentinas, embajadas y legaciones,* by Abelardo Arenas Fraga, tomo 8, p. 199–208, 471–480; tomo 9, p. 217–240, 454–464 (continued from preceding year; to be continued); *Correspondencia del Deán Funes referente al Congreso de Panamá* tomo 8, p. 209–222 (continued from tomo 7); there are also under various titles 38 letters from the papers of Félix Frías relating to international problems, tomo 8, p. 223–242, 481–492; tomo 9, p. 185–216, 466–490.

The *Revista* in publishing the documents gives in the heading an indentification and summary of the content. In a note at the end of each document there is a complete description including size and character of paper, handwriting, state of conservation, whether original or copy, name of collection to which it belongs, and the document number, as well as any other special features of the document.

BRAZIL

ARQUIVO MUNICIPAL

SÃO PAULO

Director: FRANCISCO PATI

PUBLICATIONS

REVISTA DO ARQUIVO MUNICIPAL. São Paulo. Ano 8, vols. 88–90; ano 9, vols: 91–93. 288, 290, 256, 204, 195, 280 p. **[645**

The *Revista* is published bi-monthly by the Departamento Municipal de Cultura being edited by its Division of Historical and Social Documentation. It is also the organ of the Sociedade de Etnografia e Folclore and of the Sociedade de Sociologia. Each issue contains installments of documents from the Archive as follows: *Ordens régias*, 1739–1740, no. 397–432; *Papeis avulsos*, 1820–1821, no. 88–139; *Atas da Câmara de Santo Amaro*, 1902–1904; *Decretos municipais*, 1943, no. 379–480; *Decretos-leis municipais*, 1943, no. 190–239. The remainder of each issue is devoted to historical, social and cultural articles.

MEXICO

ARCHIVO HISTÓRICO DE HACIENDA

MÉXICO, D. F.

PUBLICATIONS

GUÍA DEL ARCHIVO HISTÓRICO DE HACIENDA. SIGLOS XVI A XIX. México, D. F. Secretaría de hacienda y crédito público. 1940—. **[646**

During the year 1942, there were added to the *Ramo Consulados*, hojas 35–51, and a new *Ramo Filipinas*, hojas 1–23, was begun.

LA LIBERTAD DEL COMERCIO EN LA NUEVA ESPAÑA EN LA SEGUNDA DÉCADA DEL SIGLO XIX. Introducción de Luis Chávez Orozco. México, D. F. Secretaría de hacienda y crédito público. (Col. de documentos, vol. 1). 203 p. **[647**

The first of a series of volumes issued in inexpensive form, to make available important documents from the Archive. It contains nine documents, 1810–1819 "relating to the proposal to open the ports of Mexico to trade of foreign countries and the conversion of Habana into a center for illicit trade with the Spanish Indies."

VENEZUELA

ARCHIVO HISTÓRICO DE LA MUNICIPALIDAD DE VALENCIA

VALENCIA

PUBLICATIONS

BOLETÍN DEL ARCHIVO HISTÓRICO DE LA MUNICIPALIDAD DE VALENCIA. Valencia. Cuad. primero, dic. 62 p. **[648**

Published by the Consejo Municipal de Valencia under the editorship of Dr. Ulrich Leo. The first part of the issue explains the importance of the documents in the Archive and method followed in their publication. The second part contains the text of documents relating to the colonial history of Nueva Valencia del Rey.

ARCHIVO HISTÓRICO DE LA PROVINCIA DE MÉRIDA

MÉRIDA

In 1941 the National Government of Venezuela established in the Oficina Principal de Registro in Mérida an archive to preserve adequately the rich collection of records relating particularly to the colonial period. The archive with a view of furthering its cultural activities established a *Boletín* in 1943 under the editorship of Luis Spinetti Dini and José Rafael Febres Cordero.

PUBLICATIONS

BOLETÍN DEL ARCHIVO HISTÓRICO DE LA PROVINCIA DE MÉRIDA. Mérida. No. 1–5, feb.-oct. **[649**

Contents: Indexes of *Reales cédulas, Reales ordenes,* and *Decretos;* documents concerning the conspiracy of Gual y España; documents relating to patriotic movements of 1816; and indexes of *encomiendas y reales provisiones.* There is also an article entitled *Noticia histórica y jurisdicciones de Mérida* by Dr. Tulio Febres Cordero.

DOCUMENTARY PUBLICATIONS

(See also item 2652a)

ANALES DEL INSTITUTO DE INVESTIGACIONES HISTÓRICAS. Universidad nacional de Cuyo. Tomo 1: 1941. Mendoza. Best hnos. xix, 666 p. [650
Contains the text of a volume of documents from the Archivo Nacional de Chile entitled *Gobierno i agentes diplomáticos de la República Arjentina en Chile, 1836–1847*, p. 3–523. There are four historical articles and a number of book reviews, p. 525–632. There is also a list of documentary collections of the Instituto, p. xiii–xix.

ARCHIVO EPISTOLAR DEL GRAL. DOMINGO CAYCEDO. TOMO 1, 1804–1830. Bogotá. Ed. A. B. C. (Bibl. de historia nac., vol. 67). xxiii, 308 p. [651
The volume, a publication of the Academia Colombiana de Historia, comprises 310 letters addressed to Caycedo. They "deal with events in connection with the achievement of independence and the activities of Caycedo as Governor of the Province of Neiva, Chargé d'Affaires of Central America and Senator of the Republic."

DESCRIPCIÓN DE LA CIUDAD DE TUNJA SACADA DE LAS INFORMACIONES HECHAS POR LA JUSTICIA DE AQUELLA CIUDAD EN 30 DE MAYO DE 1610 (*Bol. hist. antig.*, vol. 30, no. 342–343, abril–mayo, p. 451–486). [652
This document from the Archivo General de Indias is reprinted from *Colección de Documentos del Archivo de Indias* (Madrid, 1868), tomo 9, p. 393–451. The modern shelf number is not given.

DOCUMENTOS HISTÓRICOS. Vol. 59, Provisões, patentes, alvarás, 1699–1711. Vol. 60, Provisões, patentes, alvarás, 1711–1713. Vol. 61, Provisões, patentes, alvarás, 1713–1715. Vol. 62, Provisões, patentes, alvarás, 1715–1716; Tombo das terras pertencentes a'Igreja de Santo Antão da Companhia de I.H.S., Bahia, Livro 5. Rio de Janeiro. Typ. Baptista de Souza. 4 vols.: 399, 400, 399, 394 p. [653
Texts of colonial documents relating to Brazil from the Biblioteca Nacional.

ERECCIÓN DE LA SANTA IGLESIA CATEDRAL METROPOLITANA. DOCUMENTACIÓN HISTÓRICA. SEGUNDO CENTENARIO DEL ARZOBISPADO DE GUATEMALA, 1743, 16 DE DICIEMBRE, 1943. Guatemala. Tip. nacional. xx, 173 p. [654
Documents from the *Expediente sobre Erigir en Metropolitana la Yglesia Catedral de Guatemala, años 1717 a 1743*, which is in the Archivo General de Indias at Sevilla.

Feliú Cruz, G. (ed.). Expediente relativo al desgraciado suceso de las armas reales en Maipó, el 5 de abril de 1818. Santiago. Tall. gráf. de la Nación. (Bibl. nac., Col. de historiadores y de documentos relativos a la independencia de Chile, tomo 31). 460 p., ilus. [655

Hernández de Alba, Guillermo. El Cedulario del Cabildo de Bogotá (*Bol. hist. antig.*, vol. 30, no. 342–343, abril–mayo, p. 367–385). [657
An index of *reales cédulas* of the Cabildo, 16th to 18th centuries, the originals of which were destroyed by fire in 1900. The original of this index is in the Archivo Nacional.

Otero Muñoz, Gustavo. Archivo Santander. Erratas sustanciales en los veinticuatro tomos (*Bol. hist. antig.*, vol. 30, no. 339–340, enero–feb., p. 1–222). [658
A list of errors in the published papers of Santander made by comparing the printed text with the original manuscripts.

Pivel Devoto, Juan E., and Rodolfo Fonseca Muñoz (comps.). Archivo histórico diplomático del Uruguay. Tomo 3, La diplomacia de la patria vieja, 1811–1820. Montevideo. xvi, 407 p. [659
A collection of documents regarding the personality of Artigas and the development of national autonomy. The documents are arranged in groups dealing with various diplomatic missions and treaty negotiations.

PUBLICATIONS ON ARCHIVOLOGY

Cortés Vargas, Carlos. Noticias sobre el Archivo de las Juntas de temporalidades de las colonias españolas con referencia a la expulsión de los Padres Jesuítas (*Bol. hist. antig.*, vol. 30, no. 344–345, junio–julio, p. 699–702). [661
A brief account of the collection of documents regarding the Jesuits, which were acquired by the Archivo Nacional de Chile in 1877.

Cortés González, J. J. Documentos coloniales de la Nueva Veracruz. Veracruz. 47 p. [662
Contains an account of the colonial records in the Archivo de Veracruz.

Hill, Roscoe R. A selective guide to the material published in 1942 on archives (*Handbook of latin american studies, no. 8, 1942*, p. 47–64). [663

Ledesma Medina, L. A. El Archivo general de la Provincia de Santiago del Estero y sus existencias documentales (*Rev. junta estud. hist. Santiago del Estero*, vol. 1, p. 217-232). [664

Páez Brotchie, L. La importancia de nuestros archivos (*Estud. hist.*, año 1, no. 1, enero, p. 93-96). [665

Pérez Martínez, Héctor. Catálogo de documentos para la historia de Yucatán y Campeche. Campeche. Museo arqueológico, histórico y etnográfico de Campeche. viii, 133 p. [666

Lists documents relating to Campeche in various archives and libraries in Mexico and in other countries.

ADDENDA

NATIONAL ARCHIVES

CHILE

REVISTA CHILENA DE HISTORIA Y GEOGRAFÍA. Santiago. Tomo 92, no. 100, enero-junio, 1942, 421 p.; no. 101, julio-diciembre, 1942, 298 p. [667

This volume contains the following documents: *Autobiografía de Juan García del Río*, no. 100, p. 5-54; *Diez cartas inéditas de Juan Bautista Alberdi*, no. 100, p. 55-67; *Cartas de don José Eusebio de Llano Zapata a don José Perfecto de Salas, 1761-1770*, no. 100, p. 160-238; *Carta inédita del director supremo don Bernardo O'Higgins sobre su abdicación*, no. 101, p. 22-32; *Diario del viaje del captán D. Tomás O'Higgins de Lima a Chiloé, 1796-1797*, no. 101, p. 42-97; *Tres cartas del general San Martín a O'Higgins*, no. 101, p. 98-101.

PERU

REVISTA DEL ARCHIVO NACIONAL DEL PERÚ. Lima. 1942. Tomo 15, entregas 1-2. [668

The principal articles of this volume are listed in the section History: Spanish America: Colonial Period in *Handbook*, no. 8, 1942.

DOCUMENTARY PUBLICATIONS

ACTAS CAPITULARES DE CORRIENTES. Tomo 3, años 1659-1666. Buenos Aires. Acad. nac. de la historia. 1942. 621 p. [669
Edited by Hernán F. Gómez.

PUBLICATIONS ON ARCHIVOLOGY

Levene, R. Fundamentos y ante-proyecto de ley sobre archivos históricos. Buenos Aires. Acad. nac. de la historia. 1942. 12 p. [670

A suggested law regarding the organization and proper administration of the archives in the Republic. Proposes the establishment of a National Commission on Historical Archives.

SPANISH AMERICAN ART

BY

GEORGE KUBLER

Yale University

GENERAL STATEMENT

A substantial increase in the number of articles and books over preceding years may be observed for 1943. The listing, furthermore, contains a high proportion of durable works, including several fundamental catalogues (items 673, 692, 742, 785, and 792), whose value as primary sources will never be superseded.

That the most valuable work in Latin American art is currently being done by the Library of Congress and a few great museums is significant of a change in the tactics of study. The universities, with their departmental restrictions and budgetary limitations, have been reluctant to subsidize ambitious new investigations. The museums, on the other hand, have relied upon group workmanship and extensive collaboration in the formation of collections and the preparation of catalogues. In effect, several museums have become such centers of Latin American studies that it may be questioned whether the universities can recover their lost opportunity. The situation contrasts sharply with the state of affairs in classical archaeology or American archaeology, where the North American universities took the lead at the end of the nineteenth century. At that time, the major contributions to learning in these fields came from academic environments. Today the centers of scientific study, at least in the history of Latin American art, are located in non-academic institutions such as the Library of Congress, Brooklyn Museum, the Museum of Modern Art, or the Taylor Museum, in Colorado Springs. It might appear, in the long run, that it makes no difference where the work is done, so long as it gets done. But in the long run again, only the university has the facilities for recruiting badly needed new workers, while the museum rarely is equipped to train and subsidize them in any numbers.

An important step towards achieving a center of studies in Latin American art was taken this year with the formal inauguration of a central repository of visual documents, in the Archive of Hispanic Culture in the Library of Congress. The Keeper, Dr. Robert C. Smith, and his assistants are currently engaged in collecting a master file of negatives and prints; in the compilation of a monumental *Guide to the Art of Latin America;* and in the preparation of teaching sets suitable for the various levels of study.

Students now have access to a first-class collection of Latin American art at Brooklyn Museum (item 675). Assembled by H. J. Spinden, the materials represent a wide range of colonial and nineteenth-century work in various materials and techniques. It is the earliest permanent collection in this country to be gathered by a major museum. At Brooklyn again, the loan exhibition, "America South of U. S.," held in 1941, was antedated only by the World's Fair display, held at the Roerich Museum on Riverside Drive in New York

City, and by the remarkable loan exhibition in 1939 at the Institute of Latin American Studies in Ann Arbor, Michigan.

As Mr. Barr noted in the Foreword to Lincoln Kirstein's catalogue (item 785), the Museum of Modern Art, in New York City, now possesses 293 works of recent art from the various republics. New York City is, therefore, the seat of the most abundant collections of Latin American art in the U. S. A. Students will find the library resources equally rich, distributed between the Metropolitan Museum of Art (item 680) and the New York Public Library.

In the Latin American countries, vigorous scholarship is shown in the rediscovery and documentation of such important nineteenth-century artists as José María Velasco in Mexico (items 753, 760, 767). The general interest evoked by modern religious painting (item 807) may also be noted. For the rest, the large number of articles and books dealing with colonial architecture is striking. With respect to folk art, a notable event was the catalogue published by the Museo de Bellas Artes in Santiago, Chile (item 673).

BIBLIOGRAPHY

(*See also sections on* Anthropology *and* Folklore)

GENERAL

Arenas Betancur, Rodrigo. Las obras maestras de la escultura (*Rev. educ.*, Medellín, segunda época, no. 2, oct., p. 17-24). [671
An analysis of the factors hindering the development of Latin American sculpture.

Cash, M. C. Mexico through her arts (*Design*, vol. 44, June, p. 11-13, illus.). [672

Chile. Museo de bellas artes. Catálogo de la exposición de artes populares americanas. Santiago. Imp. El Esfuerzo. (Univ. de Chile, Comisión chilena de cooperación intelectual). 221 p., ilus. [673
A valuable survey, with brief introductory essays upon the popular arts in Argentina, Bolivia, Chile, Colombia, Mexico, Peru, and Venezuela. The catalogue is unprecedented for completeness and historical documentation.

Iriarte, Agustín F. La pintura en Guatemala (*Ars*, México, vol. 1, no. 5, mayo, p. 9-20). [674
Review of pre-Columbian, colonial, and modern painting in Guatemala. Illustrations of paintings by Antonio de Montúfar, Tomás de Merlo (obit 1739), Francisco de Villalpando; Iriarte (nineteenth century). Brief notes on contemporary artists.

LATIN-AMERICAN GALLERIES OF THE BROOKLYN MUSEUM (*Museum news*, vol. 20, Feb. 15, p. 1). [675
A report on the path-breaking new installation of colonial art in Brooklyn. If not the first of its kind, this collection stands out as the most important display of Latin-American colonial and nineteenth-century art in the country.

Lazo, Agustín. Voz de la pintura mexicana (*Hijo pródigo*, año 1, vol. 1, no. 4, julio 15, p. 211-218, ilus.). [676
An essay upon the values of colonial, nineteenth-century, and modern Mexican painting.

Leipziger, Hugo. Architecture in the Americas, its significant forms and values (*Int. amer. intel. interchange*, p. 137-150). [677
The author defends the thesis of psychic unity among the races of man to account for "the spontaneous recurrence of symbolic figures in many parts of the world." The examples range from pre-Columbian monuments to Frank Lloyd Wright.

León, Pedro. El arte decorativo en el Ecuador (*América*, Habana, vol. 20, no. 1-2, oct.-nov., p. 31-34). [678
A discussion of the history of taste in the nineteenth and twentieth centuries in Ecuador.

Méndez Dorich, Rafael. Ubicación del arte en la cultura. Diversos ensayos para la introducción de una interpretación materialista de la cultura. Lima. Imp. gráf. Stylo. 216 p. [679
A Marxist interpretation of artistic activity. Incidental references to Latin America.

Montignani, John B. (comp.). Books on Latin America and its art in the Metropolitan museum of art library. New York. Metropolitan museum of art. 63 p. [680
A classified list of some 350 volumes in the Museum Library, bearing specifically upon the art of all periods. A useful guide for students and teachers. Lacks critical comment.

Nel Gómez, Pedro. Por la pintura americana (*Rev. educ.,* Medellín, segunda época, no. 2, oct., p. 13–16). **[681**
Brief criticism of contemporary commentaries upon painting and an appeal for mural painting which shall reveal social conscience.

Smith, Robert C. The evolution of Latin-American art (*Int. amer. intel. interchange,* p. 151–160). **[682**
Discussion of the materials necessary for an adequate text in the history of colonial Latin-American art.

Toussaint, Manuel. A defense of baroque art in America (*Int. amer. intel. interchange,* p. 161–175). **[683**
A discussion of Hispanic character in America and its inclination to baroque expression, defined as "the classic art itself which has been transformed through the influence of an internal ferment of fantasy and luxury," and as a unifying factor of Latin-American culture. Printed in Spanish and English.

Yankas, Lautaro. Síntesis de la pintura chilena (*Atenea,* año 20, tomo 71, no. 211–212, enero–feb., p. 60–71). **[684**
Brief review of the history of colonial, republican, and modern painting in Chile.

COLONIAL ARCHITECTURE, PAINTING AND SCULPTURE

(*See also item* 2999)

Álvarez Urquieta, Luis. Los primeros pasos de las bellas artes en Chile (*Saber vivir,* año 4, no. 37, agosto–sept., p. 48–51). **[685**
Well illustrated, general survey of colonial art in Chile.

Angulo Iñíguez, Diego. Las catedrales mejicanas del siglo 16 (*Bol. real acad. hist.,* vol. 113, no. 1, julio–set., p. 137–194, ilus.). **[686**
A fundamentally important article, presenting new documents and an analysis of the cathedrals with relation to Peninsular models. Plans, photographs, bibliography.

Argentina. Academia nacional de bellas artes. Documentos de arte argentino. La región andina y del Tucumán. Buenos Aires. Ed. Peuser. 37 p., xcvi láms. **[687**
The text by Martín Noel continues this magnificent series upon the colonial architecture and art of Argentina.

————. Documentos de arte argentino. Región de Cuyo. Buenos Aires. Ed. Peuser. 53 p., cxxvi láms. **[688**
A remarkably complete survey of the entire artistic culture of the colonial period in the provinces of Cuyo, originally part of the Captaincy-General of Chile. Text by Alfredo Villalonga.

————. Documentos de arte colonial sudamericano. Vol. 1. La villa imperial de Potosí. Buenos Aires. Tall. gráf. de la Casa J. Peuser. 159 p., 136 láms. **[689**
This new series is intended to complement the *Documentos de Arte Argentino* in providing well illustrated and well documented monographs on colonial cities beyond the present boundaries of Argentina. The present volume with its magnificent illustrations, deals with the civil buildings of Potosí in Bolivia; a second volume will present the religious architecture. Others will treat of Chuquisaca and Upper Peruvian towns. The text of the Potosí volume is by Martín Noel.

Argos (pseud.). El Palacio Torre Tagle, sede de la Cancillería del Perú (*Perú,* segunda época, año 1, no. 2, julio, p. 26–30, ilus.). **[690**
Built about 1730, the mansion became government property in 1918. Brief enumeration of present furnishings.

Bay Sevilla, Luis. El convento de Santa Catalina de Sena (*Arquitectura,* Habana, año 11, no. 124–125, nov.–dic., p. 427–451). **[691**
Destroyed to make way for a bank building, the convent is here studied and published in great detail. Documents.

Bello, José Luis, and Gustavo Ariza. Pinturas poblanas, siglos 17–19. México, D. F. Tall. gráf. de la nación. 152 p., 52 láms. **[692**
A fundamental study of the painting of Puebla, largely illustrated from the Bello Collection. Biographical notices, analyses of style, measurements, provenances, and bibliographies are given with exemplary fullness and accuracy.

Buschiazzo, Mario J. La iglesia de Yavi (*Bol. com. nac. mus. mon. hist.,* año 5, no. 5, p. 143–151). **[693**
A masterly study, supported by documents and comparisons, of the important little church at Yavi near the Bolivian border, built in the seventeenth century.

Campos, Mauricio M. La arquitectura religiosa en México (*Arquitectura,* México, no. 14, nov., p. 211–215, ilus.). **[694**
Brief discussion of colonial architecture. Measured drawings of the open chapel at Teposcolula (Oaxaca).

UNA CARTA DEL ARQUITECTO IGNACIO DE CASTERA (*An. inst. invest. est.,* vol. 3, 10, p. 82–83). **[695**
A letter from the architect, Ignacio de Castera, pertaining to the construction of the Oratorio in Querétaro, written in 1786.

Castro, Martha de. La arquitectura barroca del virreinato del Perú (*Univ. Habana,* año 8, no. 50–51, sept.–dic., p. 145–176). **[696**
An ambitious study treating chiefly the monuments of Lima and Cuzco, and of cer-

tain towns in the *altiplano.* The author designates sixteenth-century architecture as Barroco Español, modified by indigenous influences, i. e., "hispano-incaic." The critique of pure visibility expounded by Wölfflin is followed.

———. Plazas y paseos de La Habana colonial (*Arquitectura,* Habana, año 11, no. 115, feb., p. 63–70). [697
An important study for the urban history of the Cuban capital, by a sensitive and scrupulous historian of art.

Contreras y López de Ayala, Juan, Marqués de Lozoya. Zurbarán en el Perú (*Arch. español arte,* no. 55, enero–feb., p. 1–6). [698
Publication of Spanish paintings attributed to Zurbarán and his school in Lima, in the sacristy of San Francisco and in the Casa de los Hijos de San Camilo de Lelis.

Dorta, Enrique Marco. Arquitectura colonial. Francisco Becerra (*Arch. español arte,* no. 55, enero–feb., p. 7–15). [699
New information about the Mexican and Peruvian architect extracted from an unpublished *probanza,* used earlier by Ceán.

———. La arquitectura del renacimiento en Tunja (*Bol. hist. antig.,* vol. 30, no. 344–345, junio–julio, p. 531–560). [700
Founded in 1539, the city was provided with a Cathedral in 1569, of which the main facade, executed 1598–1600, is carefully studied. Other religious edifices in Tunja, as well as the civil architecture of the sixteenth and seventeenth centuries are examined. A documentary appendix is provided. An important study of a colonial urban style of architecture.

Enciso, Jorge. Los frescos cortesianos del Hospital de Jesús (*Hijo pródigo,* año 1, vol. 1, no. 6, set., p. 344–345, ilus.). [701
Founded before 1524, the Cortés hospital is housed today in a building which is one of the few sixteenth-century remains of Mexico City, perhaps the work of Juan de Arrué, a creole architect born in Colima province *c.* 1565. The frescoes of the patio walls probably represent members of the family of Martín Cortés, second Marqués del Valle.

Escalona Ramos, Alberto. Algunas construcciones de tipo colonial en Quintana Roo (*An. inst. invest. est.,* vol. 3, 10, p. 17–40, ilus.). [702
An important study, the first of its kind, presenting exact imformation upon the colonial edifices of eastern Yucatán. Photographs and measured drawings.

Fernández, Justino. Rubens y José Juárez (*An. inst. invest. est.,* vol. 3, 10, p. 51–57, ilus.). [703
A painting of the Sagrada Familia by José Juárez, now in the Academia de Bellas Artes in Puebla, and painted in 1655, is based upon a painting by Rubens *c.* 1609. The author suggests that Juárez had access to contemporary engravings, such as that by Martinus van der Enden.

———. Tiepolo, Mengs and Don Rafael Ximeno y Planes (*Gazette des beaux arts,* series 6, vol. 23, June, p. 345–362, illus.). [704
An important study of the neo-classic style of the last of the great academic painters of colonial Mexico, and of the Royal Academy of San Carlos.

Flores Araoz, José. La pintura colonial en América, siglo 18 (*Cultura peruana,* año 3, vol. 3, no. 12, enero–julio). [705
A further installment of a history of Latin American colonial painting. Illustrations of paintings by José de Ibarra, Juan Correa, Cristóbal Lozano, Francisco Martínez, Pedro Díaz, Cristóbal de Aguilar.

Furlong, Guillermo, and Mario J. Buschiazzo. Arquitectura religiosa colonial. Historia y análisis de unos planos. Buenos Aires. 26 p., láms. [706
Important publication and commentary of colonial plans preserved in the Colegio de la Immaculada, Santa Fe, Argentina, identified as by the Jesuit architect, Antonio Forcada (1701– ?), active in America 1745–1767. From *Archivum,* tomo 1, cuad. 2.

García, Juan Crisóstomo. Guía de las principales iglesias bogotanas (*Bol. hist. antig.,* vol. 30, no. 342–343, abril–mayo, p. 416–450). [707
A useful summary of the building dates and principal furnishings of the chief churches of Bogotá.

González Garaño, Alejo B. Iconografía argentina anterior a 1820. Con una noticia de la vida y obra de E. E. Vidal. Buenos Aires. Ed. Emecé. (Col. Buen aire, 29.) 76 p. [708
Chiefly illustrations from the work of Emeric Essex Vidal.

Govantes, Evelio. La ciudad de Trinidad (*Arquitectura,* Habana, año 11, no. 114, enero, p. 13–15). [709
Brief history of the colonial Cuban city.

Greenleaf, R. Ecuador was long a center of painting (*Amer. collector,* vol. 12, August, p. 8–77, illus.). [710
Illustrations of paintings by Miguel de Santiago (died 1673), José Cortez, Gorivar (died 1698), J. M. Mora, and Antonio Salas (died 1860), all in the author's collection.

Harth-Terré, Emilio. Un artífice del siglo 17. Ascensio de Salas, escultor (*Peruanidad,* vol. 3, no. 12, enero–feb., p. 945–950). [711
An excellent study of a Spanish woodcarver, active in Lima in the mid-seventeenth century. His work has nearly all disappeared although many documents al-

low its historical reconstruction. From *El Comercio*, Lima.

———. Entalladores del siglo 17. Capítulo de historia del arte virreinal en Lima (*Bol. inst. invest. hist.*, año 21, tomo 27, no. 93-96, julio, 1942-junio, 1943, p. 131-154). **[712]**
The author continues preparing the foundations for a thorough study of the ornamentalists of the seventeenth century. New documents bring many forgotten craftsmen of Lima to light again.

———. Fray Cristóbal Caballero. El alarife y escultor mercedario (*Mercurio peruano*, año 18, vol. 25, no. 197, agosto, p. 383-388). **[713]**
Works of ornamental sculpture by Fray Cristóbal are dated between 1650 and 1698, when he was *maestro mayor de fábricas* for the Cathedral of Lima.

———. La obra de la Compañía de Jesús en la arquitectura virreinal peruana (*Arquitectura*, Habana, año 11, no. 118, mayo, p. 172-176, 199-204). **[714]**
New documents and interpretations of Jesuit building in Peru, by the foremost historian of Peruvian architecture.

———. Renacimiento de una campana (*Mercurio peruano*, año 18, vol. 25, no. 192, marzo, p. 99-104). **[715]**
Useful essay upon the history of the casting of colonial church-bells in Peru.

———. Los tesoros de la catedral de Lima (*Arquitectura*, Habana, año 11, no. 122, sept., p. 341-344, 370-373). **[716]**
New documents upon the decorative arts of the seventeenth century in Peru.

Hewett, Edgar L., and **Reginald Fisher.** The mission monuments of New Mexico. Albuquerque. Univ. of New Mexico press. 270 p., illus. **[717]**
Published as one of the New Mexico *Handbooks of Archaeological History*, the volume offers a digest of many primary and secondary sources, mainly concerning the religious history of New Mexico. Abbreviated reports from the supervisors of projects to restore the missions will interest students of architecture.

Jaramillo, Gabriel Giraldo. Introducción a la estética colonial (*Bol. hist. antig.*, vol. 30, no. 344-345, junio-julio, p. 686-698). **[718]**
The author notes the lack of exalted aesthetic intentions among colonial craftsmen; their limited technical equipment; the primacy of religious art; the indifference to the particulars of their environment; the standardization of colonial political and economic life; the rigorous Hispanization of all forms of artistic expression. He concludes that colonial art is a debased copy of Spanish art.

Kendrick, A. F. Carpets and tapestry from South America (*Burlington mag.*, vol. 82, no. 479, Feb., p. 41-42, illus.). **[719]**
Three woollen carpets, probably made in Peru in the seventeenth century, and now located in the Victoria and Albert Museum.

Kubler, George. Two modes of Franciscan architecture: New Mexico and California (*Gazette des beaux arts*, series 6, vol. 23, Jan., p. 39-48, illus.). **[720]**
The two campaigns of Franciscan missionary activity, separated by a century and a half, differ radically from one another: the New Mexican campaign reflects a humanist philosophy; the Californian campaign was strategic and absolutist.

Lehmann, H. Colonial art at Popayán (*Gazette des beaux arts*, series 6, vol. 24, July, p. 41-54, illus.). **[721]**
A systematic review of the important colonial works of art in the Colombian city. Santo Domingo was rebuilt 1740-1750. Discussion of the eighteenth-century work of José María Burbano, c. 1780.

Levene, Ricardo. Labor realizada por la Comisión nacional de museos y monumentos históricos (*Bol. com. nac. mus. mon. hist.*, año 5, no. 5, p. 7-46). **[722]**
Report upon works of restoration and preservation; lists of historic monuments; reports upon museums.

Marian, Dagmar. The art of Peru (*The Pan American*, vol. 4, no. 7, Dec., p. 35-37). **[723]**
Description of a private collection of colonial and modern Peruvian painting, now in New York City.

Marín García, Segundo. La iglesia mayor de Sancti Spíritus (*América*, Habana, vol. 20, no. 1-2, oct.-nov., p. 43-48). **[724]**
The Cuban town of Sancti Spíritus, founded by Diego Velázquez, contains several churches of which the Iglesia Mayor is the subject of special study.

Maza, Francisco de la. El proceso de Adrian Suster (*An. inst. invest. est.*, vol. 3, 10, p. 41-49). **[725]**
The Flemish sculptor of several choirstalls in Mexico was the subject of inquisitorial examination in 1598-1600, on account of his heretical declarations and friendships.

———. Simón Pereyns, el primer gran pintor colonial (*Rev. univ.*, Guadalajara, tomo 1, no. 2, mayo-julio, p. 75-77, ilus.). **[726]**
A brief study based mainly upon the work of Manuel Toussaint.

Mendoza Zeledón, Carlos. Los primeros constructores de la villa de La Habana (*Arquitectura*, Habana, año 11, no. 115,

feb., p. 53–56; no. 116, marzo, p. 107–110; no. 117, abril, p. 154–157). **[727]**
A valuable discussion of sixteenth-century builders and buildings in Havana.

Nadal Mora, Vicente. La arquitectura tradicional de Buenos Aires, 1536–1870. Buenos Aires. Imp. F. y M. Mercatali. 165 p., ilus. **[728]**

O'Bourke, Juan E. Tres iglesias de Cholula (*Arquitectura*, Habana, año 11, no. 115, feb., 44–47). **[729]**
An appreciation of S. Francisco Acatepec, S. Bernardino Tlascalancingo and S. María Tonancintla.

Onetto, Carlos L. Bóveda y cúpula de la iglesia de la Compañía de Jesús en Córdoba (*Tecné*, año 1, no. 2, 8 p., fotos.). **[730]**
The Jesuit church in Córdoba has a wooden roof built after 1645 by the Jesuit naval architect Felipe Lemer, recalling the wooden ceilings invented by Philibert de L'Orme in the sixteenth century.

Pach, Walter. Aspectos desconocidos de la pintura mexicana (*Hijo pródigo*, año 1, vol. 1, no. 3, junio, p. 157–162, ilus.). **[732]**
The critic attributes the portrait of Doña Agustina Teresa de Arosqueta, now in the Chapultepec Museum, to Miguel Cabrera. Other problems of attribution to Barreda and Tresguerras are discussed. English version entitled "Unknown aspects of Mexican painting" published in *Gazette des beaux-arts*, series 6, vol. 24, Oct., 1943, p. 209–220, illus.

Palm, Erwin Walter. El estilo imperial de Felipe II y las edificaciones del siglo 17 en la Española (*Bol. arch. gen.*, Ciudad Trujillo, año 6, vol. 6, no. 28–29, mayo-agosto, p. 244–253). **[733]**
A discussion of the question of Renaissance and Baroque style in American architecture. The author proposes that the fixed quantity in the architectural styles of the colonial epoch is the "substratum" of Herreran severity common to them all. Several buildings in Ciudad Trujillo are analyzed in this sense: La Merced, San Francisco, and the Cathedral.

Restrepo Posada, José. La primitiva Catedral de Santafé de Bogotá (*Bol. hist. antig.*, vol. 30, no. 349, nov., p. 1065–1076). **[734]**
An older Cathedral, prior to the present edifice built in 1806, was begun in 1572, and remained incomplete at the time of the earthquake of 1785. An even earlier edifice, begun c. 1553, may also be identified from documents. In 1556 little had been built, and its construction continued slowly until 1565, when it was found inadequate.

Ribón, Segundo Germán. Santa Cruz de Mompox (*Bol. hist. antig.*, vol. 30, no. 347–348, sept.-oct., p. 965–981, ilus.). **[735]**
Description of the religious and public monuments of the city of Mompox. Of special interest is the Church of Santa Barbara, founded in 1613, built in 1630.

Roig de Leuchsenring, Emilio. Iglesias, conventos y cementerios de la ciudad de La Habana (*Architectura*, Habana, año 11, no. 120, julio, p. 266–269). **[736]**
A compact study of various colonial buildings, by the municipal historian of Havana.

Romero de Terreros y Vinent, Manuel. El "Calvario" de Jimeno (*An. inst. invest. est.*, vol. 3, 10, p. 80–81). **[737]**
Discussion of a Calvary painted by Rafael Jimeno y Planes, now located in the Museum of the Monte de Piedad in Mexico City, and related to a sketch in the Academia de San Carlos.

———. Principal painters of New Spain (*Gazette des beaux-arts*, series 6, vol. 23, March, p. 161–172, illus.). **[738]**
A brief survey of Mexican colonial painting.

LAS RUINAS DE SAN IGNACIO, EN MISIONES (*La Prensa*, año 74, no. 26.944, 19 dic., ilus.). **[739]**
Photographic studies of the important Jesuit mission buildings of the eighteenth century.

SEGUNDO CENTENARIO DE LA FUNDACIÓN DE SAN JAVIER (*La Prensa*, año 74, no. 26.770, 27 junio, ilus.). **[740]**
Photographic record of the present condition of the Jesuit *reducción* founded in 1743 for the Mocoví Indians northeast of Santa Fe.

Spota, Felipe. ¿Existió el estilo colonial? (*Rev. univ. Puebla*, año 1, no. 2, agosto). **[741]**
Brief review of colonial architectural history in Mexico.

Toussaint, Manuel. Mexican colonial paintings in Davenport (*Gazette des beaux arts*, series 6, vol. 24, Sept., p. 167–174, illus.). **[742]**
The large Ficke collection donated to the city of Davenport in 1925, contains fifty-seven colonial Mexican paintings. About half these are important canvasses, by Echave y Rioja, Sebastian de Arteaga (attributed), Ximeno, and others.

———. Retratos de monjas (*Hijo pródigo*, año 1, vol. 2, no. 7, oct., p. 32, ilus.). **[743]**
Brief essay upon five important eighteenth-century Mexican portraits of nuns, by José de Alcíbar, Cabrera and others. The full length figure attributed to Cabrera is one of the masterpieces of Mexican colonial painting.

Viñas, Julia MacLean. A sentimental journey in Peru. 4: Jauja and Ocopa (*Bull. pan amer. union*, vol. 77, no. 11, Nov., p. 611–617, illus.). **[744]**
A valuable if brief description of the important Franciscan church at Ocopa.

Waterman, Thomas Tileston. The Gothic architecture of Santo Domingo (*Bull. pan amer. union,* vol. 77, no. 6, June, p. 312-325, illus.). [745

An important study of the palace of Diego Columbus, the fortifications, and the churches. Catalonian influences are suggested for the structural system of the churches. The cathedral of San Juan, Puerto Rico, is compared with the Ciudad Trujillo buildings. Excellent ground plans, measured and drawn by the author.

NINETEENTH CENTURY ARCHITECTURE, PAINTING AND SCULPTURE

Abad, Plácido. Una casa patricia suntuosa. El palacete Montero-Regalia (*Rev. nac.,* Montevideo, año 6, tomo 22, no. 66, junio, p. 438-444, ilus.). [746

The building history of one of the great urban residences of Montevideo, built for Antonio Montero between 1825-1831, from the designs of an unidentified European architect, possibly the Portuguese, Juan Dos Reis.

Berro, Román. Blanes, pintor de historia (*Rev. nac.,* Montevideo, año 6, tomo 22, no. 64, abril, p. 21-29). [747

An analysis of nine historical paintings and projects for historical paintings by the eminent nineteenth-century portraitist, Juan Manuel Blanes.

Buceta Basigalup, Juan Carlos. Carlos Morel, un ilustrador del pasado argentino. Buenos Aires. Tall. del diario Norte. 94 p., láms. [748

Carlos Morel (1813-1894), the *costumbrista* lithographer of Argentina, also produced occasional oil paintings and watercolors. This biographical and critical study presents a compact, serviceable treatment of an artist whose talents exceeded his training.

Buschiazzo, Mario J. La catedral de Buenos Aires. Prólogo por Martín Noel. Buenos Aires. Ed. artísticas argentinas. (Monografías históricas de las iglesias argentinas, vol. 1.) 69 p., 45 láms. [749

A fundamental study by the distinguished professor of the History of Architecture at the University of Buenos Aires. Created in 1620, the diocese received a fitting Cathedral in 1671, augmented with a façade by Blanqui and Primoli in 1727, and rebuilt after 1821 following the design of Catelin and Benoit. The present façade recalls the Palais Bourbon in Paris. The illustration of the church furnishings is exemplary.

Contreras y López de Ayala, Juan, Marqués de Lozoya. Un siglo de pintura peruana (*Peruanidad,* vol. 3, no. 12, enero-feb., p. 978-981). [750

Following brief remarks on colonial painting, nineteenth-century Peruvian artists are discussed, especially Ignacio Merino (1817-1876), and Francisco Lazo (1823-1869), both schooled in Paris. José Sabogal is discussed briefly. From *El Comercio,* Lima. Illustrated version published in *Perú,* segunda época, año 1, no. 2, julio, 1943, p. 26-30, ilus.

Díaz de León, Francisco. Gabriel Vicente Gahona (*Dyn,* no. 4-5, p. 68-70, illus.). [751

Gahona, a precursor of Posada in Yucatán, was trained in Italy 1856-1857. He produced woodblock engravings of satirical content. The author is the Director of the Escuela de las Artes del Libro in Mexico City.

————. Gahona y Posada, intérpretes del pueblo (*Bol. sem. cult. mex.,* tomo 1, no. 2, oct., p. 8-35, ilus.). [752

The discoverer of Gahona's forgotten engravings compares them with those of J. G. Posada (1852-1913), for whose life new information is presented.

Encina, Juan de la. Velasco y el sentido del paisaje moderno (*Letras de México,* año 7, vol. 1, no. 15, nov. 11, p. 5-6). [753

Velasco's negative relationship to European impressionism is discussed.

Gaya, Ramón. El grabador Posada, 1852-1913 (*Hijo pródigo,* año 1, no. 1, abril, p. 32, ilus.). [754

An appreciation of the *tranche de vie* represented in Posada's journalistic woodcuts. Eight reproductions.

Giménez Lanier, Joaquín. La ciudad de San Juan de los Remedios (*Arquitectura,* Habana, año 11, no. 121, agosto, p. 305-311). [755

Founded c. 1515, the town of San Juan contains many nineteenth-century buildings of considerable interest.

González Garaño, Alejo B. El pintor Juan León Pallière, ilustrador de la vida argentina del 1860. Buenos Aires. Imp. A. Baiocco. 25 p. [756

Pallière (1823-1887), the son of a painter, was born in Rio de Janeiro. Trained among the French artists at the Brazilian court, and in France and Italy, he settled in Buenos Aires in 1856. His skillful drawings, lithographs, and paintings of Argentine life are unsurpassed in his period. This study is a definitive biographical survey.

Gutiérrez, Ricardo. El pintor de la pampa: Eduardo Sívori (*La Prensa,* año 74, no. 26,741, 30 mayo, ilus.). [757

Sívori (1847-1918) was trained in Paris, painted the Argentine landscape, and taught in the Taller Libre de Dibujo y Pintura.

Montero Bustamante, Raúl. Las últimas confidencias de Juan Manuel Blanes (*Rev.*

nac., Montevideo, año 6, tomo 22, no. 66, junio, p. 344-358). [758
The letters written by the academic painter, Blanes, to his friend Juan Mesa, between 1895 and 1901, pertaining to family troubles.

Morillo, Manuel M. El más grande pintor dominicano (*América*, Habana, vol. 17, no. 1-2, enero-feb., p. 71-74). [759
Biographical notice and appreciation of the historical paintings by Luis Desangles (1861-1943).

O'Gorman, J. Velasco: painter of time and space (*Magazine of art*, vol. 36, Oct., p. 202-207, illus.). [760
Juan O'Gorman, the gifted architect, who continues the tradition of landscape painting defined in Mexico by Velasco, here offers a solid study of his predecessor's great talent. Foreword by Alfred H. Barr, Jr.

Ontañón, Mada. México en los grabados de Posada (*Hoy*, abril 24, p. 48-49, ilus.). [761
An appreciation of the great exhibition of Posada's work, held in the Palacio de Bellas Artes.

Ossandón Guzmán, Carlos. Cerámica popular chilena (*Saber vivir*, año 4, no. 37, agosto-sept., p. 62-63, ilus.). [762
The author describes his collection of perfumed pottery made by the nuns of Santa Clara in Santiago, Chile, from the late eighteenth century until recent years.

Pach, W. A newly found American painter: Hermenegildo Bustos (*Art in America*, vol. 31, Jan., p. 32-43, illus.). [763
Anecdote and critical appreciation of the gifted portrait painter of Guanajuato (1832-1907).

Pérez Montero, Carlos. La iglesia Matrız, 1855-1867 (*Rev. nac.*, Montevideo, año 6, tomo 22, no. 64, abril, p. 69-94). [764
The present façade of the Cathedral of Montevideo is shown as the design of a Swiss-Italian architect, Bernardo Poncini, in 1858-1859, working in the rigid neoclassic manner of the Brera Academy. Documentary appendix.

Prati, Edmundo. Una visita a la casa del pintor Baltasar Verazzi, en Lesa (*Rev. nac.*, Montevideo, año 6, tomo 21, no. 61, enero, p. 90-116). [765
Discussion of the South American paintings by Baltasar Verazzi (1819-1886), the North Italian muralist active in Brazil, Argentina, and Uruguay between 1853 and 1868. Biography and catalogue.

Rivas, Guillermo. A century of Mexican portraiture (*Mexican life*, vol. 19, no. 5, May, p. 27-30). [766
Review of the exhibition held at the Benjamin Franklin Library in Mexico City.

Romero de Terreros y Vinent, Manuel. Paisajistas mexicanos del siglo 19. México. Imp. univ. 28 p., 45 láms. [767
In this new addition to the excellent series sponsored by the Instituto de Investigaciones Estéticas, the great distinction of nineteenth-century Mexican landscape painting is made public. Previously ignored, these painters, Gualdi, Landesio, Jiménez, Coto, Serrano, Álvarez, Dumaine, Murillo, Velasco, Saldaña, Almanza, and Rivera (Carlos) are made known by judicious selections from their works, biographical notices, and critical evaluations. A basic study.

Sabogal, José. Pancho Fierro, pintor peruano (*Cuad. amer.*, año 2, vol. 8, no. 2, marzo-abril, p. 153-156, ilus.). [768
Born 1803, Fierro recorded Peruvian life in water colors, oils, murals, and prints. Sabogal designates him as the first Peruvian artist to attend to the affairs of his own land.

Westheim, Paul. Pincheta, artista ignorado (*Hoy*, abril 3, p. 48-49, 82 ilus.). [769
Gabriel Gaona lived in Mérida in the nineteenth century under the pseudonym of Pincheta, producing satirical wood-engravings which remind the author of Gavarni. Gaona was self-taught and approached the vigor of expression attained by the later craftsman, Posada.

CONTEMPORARY ARCHITECTURE, PAINTING AND SCULPTURE

Alfaro Siqueiros, David. Un hecho artístico embrionariamente trascendental en Chile (*Hoy*, feb. 20, p. 48-50, ilus.). [770
An analysis by Siqueiros of the mural produced by three of his followers (José Venturelli, Erwin Wenner, Alipio Jaramillo) in the Alianza de Intelectuales in Santiago, Chile. An important if confused record of Siqueiros' views upon politics and painting.

ART FOR HEMISPHERE SOLIDARITY; PAN AMERICANISM AND THE IMPORTANCE OF CULTURAL EXCHANGE IN WARTIME (*Design*, vol. 44, March, p. 7-9, illus.). [771

BELLAS ARTES. REVISTA DE LA SOCIEDAD DE BELLAS ARTES DEL PERÚ. Lima. Año 3, no. 3, dic. [772
Articles of appreciation dealing with the sculpture by Luis F. Agurto and Artemio Ocaña, and the paintings by Teófilo Castillo and Patricio Gimeno. Report upon the activities of the Sociedad de Bellas Artes del Perú.

Caillet-Bois, Horacio. El Museo provincial de bellas artes "Rosa Galisteo de Rodríguez" (*Saber vivir*, año 4, no. 39, nov., p. 20-21). [773
Opened at Santa Fe in 1922, the Gallery contains some 450 works of modern art from various countries.

Cash, M. C. Mexico through her arts (*Design*, vol. 44, June, p. 11–13, illus.). [774

Díaz Morales, Ignacio. Report from Mexico (*Liturgical arts*, vol. 11, May, p. 60–63, illus.). [775
Good illustrations of recent religious art and architecture in Mexico. Paintings by Orozco, Cantú, Ricardo Martínez; architecture by the author.

Espinosa Saldaña, Antonio. ¿Puede hablarse de un arte peruano? (*Historia*, Lima, vol. 1, no. 2, mayo–junio, p. 82–86). [776
An essay discussing the limitations of modern Peruvian art. The cult of *feísmo*, or ugliness is blamed, although qualities of vigor and spirit are mentioned favorably.

LA EXPOSICIÓN DE PINTURA PANAMERICANA (*Cultura peruana*, año 3, vol. 3, no. 12, enero–julio). [777
Review of the exhibition sponsored by the International Business Machines Corporation.

Fernández, Justino. Arte mexicano como relación cultural (*Cult. Méx.*, año 2, no. 2, julio–dic., p. 36–39). [778
A reprint of a brief newspaper article discussing the attainment of cultural understanding by works of art.

————. Catálogo de exposiciones, 1942 (*An. inst. invest. est.*, vol. 3, 10, p. 85–123). [779
A report upon art exhibitions held in Mexico City during 1942.

Gallagher de Parks, Mercedes. La escultura monumental en el Perú (*Mercurio peruano*, año 18, vol. 25, no. 200, nov., p. 540–548, 4 ilus.). [780
Nineteenth- and twentieth-century public monuments in Lima are discussed, together with Ocaña's model for the monument to Grau.

Gayne, Jr., C. Art of the people, by the people, and for the people of Latin America (*Design*, vol. 44, March, p. 12–13, illus.). [781

Guerrero Galván, J. Modern Mexican painting (*Design*, vol. 44, March, p. 17). [782
A statement by one modern Mexican painter.

Hunter, R. V. Latin-American art in U.S.A. (*Design*, vol. 44, March, p. 20–21, illus.). [783

Instituto interamericano de historia municipal e institucional. Exposición de grabados mexicanos contemporáneos. Habana. Ed. Fernández y cía. 16 p., ilus. [784
An exhibition catalogue of the Mexican prints shown in Cuba.

Kirstein, Lincoln. The Latin-American collection of the Museum of modern art. New York. Museum of modern art. 110 p., illus. [785
A masterpiece of catalogue preparation, Indispensable both to research and general instruction. Works from the countries are illustrated. General historical essay, biographical notices, and bibliography.

Kraus, H. Felix. Mexico's fighting artists (*The Pan American*, vol. 4, no. 3, June, p. 14–18, illus.). [786
A report upon the work of the Taller de Gráfica Popular in Mexico City.

Meléndez, Luis. Artistas y críticos de arte (*Atenea*, año 20, tomo 74, no. 220, oct., p. 65–69). [787
A discussion of the conflict between artists and critics in modern Chile.

Mora, Enrique de la. Iglesia de la Purísima en Monterrey, México (*Arquitectura*, México, no. 14, nov., p. 228–229, ilus.). [788
Project for a modern church with parabolic vaults and cross-vaults.

Pan American union. Division of intellectual cooperation. Thirty Latin American artists. Biographical notes. Washington. 15 p. [789
Short notices of the careers of painters from thirteen republics.

Pani, Mario. Iglesia de Cristo Rey, México, D. F. (*Arquitectura*, México, no. 14, nov., p. 230–231, ilus.). [790
Another project for a modern church, now in construction.

Perotti, J. Fine arts in Chile; an interpretation of the present show (*Carnegie mag.*, vol. 16, no. 8, Jan., p. 233–238, illus.). [791

Philadelphia museum of art. Mexican art today. Organized by the Philadelphia museum of art, with the collaboration of the Dirección general de educación extraescolar y estética, México. Philadelphia. 104 p., illus. [792
Catalogue of an exhibition held in the Philadelphia Museum of Art in 1943 in answer to the question "What are Mexican painters doing today?" Introduction by Henry Clifford. Essay in Spanish and English by Luis Cardoza y Aragón, entitled "Contemporary Mexican Painting." Chronology of Mexican painters by generations, from Dr. Atl to Juan Soriano. 82 illustrations, 66 artists represented. An indispensable and unique survey of the present status of Mexican painting.

Prieto, Julio. Esquema del desarrollo del grabado contemporáneo en México (*Letras de México*, año 7, vol. 1, no. 15, sept. 9, p. 8). [793
A brief history and bibliography of Mexican print-making.

Real de Azúa, Exequiel M. Problemas estéticas de la edificación de Buenos Aires (*La Prensa*, año 74, no. 28.874, 10 oct., segunda sección, ilus.). [794
Analysis of some problems in the silhouette and perspective compositions of the streets of Buenos Aires.

Rivas, Guillermo. Annual prints exhibit at "Decoración" (*Mexican life*, vol. 19, no. 10, Oct., p. 27–31, illus.). [795
Short review of the graphic arts in Mexico from Samuel Estradamus (17th century) to the present.

———. Whither Mexican art? (*Mexican life*, vol. 19, no. 9, Sept., p. 31–34, illus.). [796
The critic observes that the exhibit of the Decoración Galleries in Mexico City reveals a "marked tendency toward the more conventional and less conspicuous norms." Illustrations of work by Monroy, Barthez, Tejeda, O'Higgins, Martínez, Fabregat, and others.

Rivera, Diego. Carta (*Bol. sem. cult. mex.*, tomo 1, no. 2, oct., p. 53–57). [797
The painter takes issue with Bergamín's views on Velasco, and Orozco, providing his own views of the art of these colleagues.

Silva Valdés, Fernán. Temas de la pintura uruguaya (*Le Prensa*, año 74, no. 26.895, 31 oct., ilus.). [798
Discussion of Uruguayan painting from Blanes to Figari and Cúneo.

Sociedad central de arquitectos, Buenos Aires. Anuario 1943. Buenos Aires. 48, 31, 48, 34 p., ilus. [799
Yearbook of the Argentine Architectural Society. Index of publications, lists of members, competitions. Budget and records of meetings.

SOUTH AMERICANS IN NORTH AMERICA; MUSEUM OF MODERN ART'S PERMANENT COLLECTION ON TOUR (*Magazine of art*, vol. 36, Oct., p. 220–223, illus.). [800
Captions to selected paintings, written by Alfred H. Barr, Jr.

EL TRIGÉSIMOTERCERO SALÓN NACIONAL DE BELLAS ARTES (*Saber vivir*, año 4, no. 38, oct., p. 18–21). [801
Review; illustrations of work by López Claro, Capdepont, Amicarelli, Cobresman, Alonso, Aráoz Alfaro, March, Bonome, and others.

Velarde, Héctor. La arquitectura actual en el Perú (*Mercurio peruano*, año 18, vol. 25, no. 190, enero, p. 6–29). [802
A witty essay upon nineteenth-century currents of taste, decrying electicism, and explaining the "neo-Peruvian" style of colonial antecedents, created c. 1920 by Piqueras, the Spanish sculptor.

Vidussi, J. Alrededor del cuarto salón de artistas rosarinos (*Cultura*, año 14, no. 101, julio–set., p. 68–73). [803

EL VIGÉSIMONOVENO SALÓN DE ACUARELISTAS Y GRABADORES (*Saber vivir*, año 4, no. 39, nov., p. 46–48). [804
Review of the remarkably varied showing at the Society presided by Alfredo González Garaño. Illustrations of work by Miraglia, Longarini, Chale, Manzorro, Castagna, Gambartes, Dell'Acqua, and Moncalvo.

Villaurrutia, Xavier. Retratistas mexicanos (*Hoy*, enero 30, p. 44–47, ilus.). [805
A review of a century of portraiture in Mexico, an exhibition held in the Biblioteca Franklin in Mexico City.

Westheim, Paul. El arte de México es ignorado en México (*Hoy*, feb. 6, p. 44–50, ilus.). [806
The author maintains that the Mexican people are insufficiently aware of the prolific and world-famous works of art produced by Mexican artists in the past two decades. Excellent illustrations of little-known works, such as the portrait by Goitia.

Zárraga, Ángel. Arte religioso. Notas de un pintor (*Ábside*, vol. 7, no. 1, enero–marzo, p. 3–88, 30 láms.). [807
The opinion of a painter of religious themes, long resident in Paris, upon the problem of modern religious painting. Also published separately: México, Ed. Ábside, 27 p., ilus.

———. Discurso a los maestros (*Bol. sem. cult. mex.*, tomo 1, no. 1, julio, p. 48–60). [808
An eloquent speech by the religious painter on art and education, to the Congress of Rural Teachers in Cuernavaca.

ARTISTS BY COUNTRIES

ARGENTINA

Anganuzzi, Mario
EL PINTOR MARIO ANGANUZZI (*La Prensa*, año 74, no. 26.762, 20 junio, ilus.). [809
Born in 1888, Anganuzzi is a teacher and painter, whose work records the customs and peoples of Mendoza and La Rioja.

Beristayn, Jorge
Pagano, José León. Jorge Beristayn. Buenos Aires. Ed. Espasa-Calpe argentina. 200 p., 60 láms. [810
Text in English, French, and Spanish. The critic is not concerned with the "external biography," but with Beristayn's "fervent, lavish, and plural" qualities, with his "receptive organism." Colored reproductions of the painter's work.

Gómez Cornet, Ramón
RAMÓN GÓMEZ CORNET. Buenos Aires. Ed. G. Kraft. (Col. de arte argentino.) 19 p., 20 ilus. [811
Born in 1898 in Santiago del Estero, Ramón Gómez Cornet's work evokes

French nineteenth-century antecedents. Introduction by Julio E. Payró.

Guttero, Alfredo
Payró, Julio E. Alfredo Guttero. Buenos Aires. Ed. Poseidón. (Bibl. argentina de arte.) 64 p., 39 ilus. [812
Alfredo Guttero (1882–), born in Argentina, lived in France and Spain from 1904 until 1922. His work is well-reproduced, and shows abundant contact with the masters of European painting.

Pettoruti, Emilio
Kraus, H. Felix. Argentina's Pettoruti (*The Pan American*, vol. 3, no. 10, March, p. 15–19). [813
Brief appreciation of the Argentine painter and educator.

Suárez Marzal, Julio. Pettoruti, vanguardista y clásico. La Plata. Ed. El Sol. 14 p., port. [814
The artist is described in terms of his cubist and futurist achievement as well as by his "conquest of profundity through plastic evaluation."

Santo, Francisco de
Korn, Guillermo. Las pinturas murales de Francisco de Santo (*Nosotros*, segunda época, año 8, tomo 22, no. 90, set., p. 300–304, ilus.). [815
Appreciation of the murals for children in the Escuela y Colonia de Vacaciones de Punta Lara, by a painter resident in La Plata.

Soto Avendaño, Ernesto
Neyra, Joaquín. Una ciclópea obra del escultor Soto Avendaño (*Sustancia*, año 4, no. 13, enero–feb., p. 91–121, ilus.). [816
The Argentine sculptor, Ernesto Soto Avendaño, won a competition in 1928 for the great national monument to be erected at the ravine of Humahuaca. His studies for the monument are abundantly illustrated.

BOLIVIA

Núñez del Prado, Marina
Iglesias, Antonio. Chisel with a soul (*The Pan American*, vol. 4, no. 1, April, p. 24–26). [817
An interview with the Bolivian sculptor, Marina Núñez del Prado, reporting biographical data.

COLOMBIA

Correa, Carlos
Gómez Jaramillo, Ignacio
Engel, Walter. Dos pintores antioqueños (*Rev. Indias*, segunda época, no. 50, feb., p. 325–342). [818
Critique of the exhibitions held by Ignacio Gómez Jaramillo, who was schooled in Paris and worked in Mexico; and by Carlos Correa (born 1912, Medellín) trained in Colombia by Colombian and European painters.

CUBA

Carreño, Mario
Kraus, H. Felix. Cuba's nationalist artist (*The Pan American*, vol. 4, no. 4, July–Sept., p. 20–22, illus.). [819
Notice of the Cuban painter, Mario Carreño, schooled in Spain, Mexico, and Paris.

MEXICO

Alfaro Siqueiros, David
Alfaro Siqueiros, David, and **Lincoln Kirstein.** La reciente obra mural de Siqueiros en el conjunto del muralismo mexicano (*Hoy*, junio 26, p. 46–47, ilus.). [820
Siqueiros not only admits to having learned much from Rivera and Orozco, but insists that such personal situations are of little consequence, since the modern Mexican school constitutes a collective movement.

Kirstein, Lincoln. Siqueiros in Chillán (*Magazine of art*, vol. 36, no. 8, Dec., p. 282–287, ilus.). [821
History, analysis, and evaluation of the murals in Chile. The basic article upon these paintings, supplementing Siqueiros' own remarks.

Anguiano, Raúl
Fernández, Justino. Anguiano pintor realista (*Hoy*, sept. 11, p. 64–65, ilus.). [822
Raúl Anguiano, born in Jalisco in 1915, was trained in Guadalajara, and has developed a style of painting showing relationship both to Orozco and Picasso.

Domínguez Bello, Arnulfo
CUATRO OBRAS DEL ESCULTOR ARNULFO DOMÍNGUEZ BELLO (*Bol. sem. cult. mex.*, tomo 1, no. 1, julio, p. 84–88, ilus.). [823
Trained at San Carlos Academy and in Europe, Domínguez Bello is associated with the Mexican Academy of Fine Arts.

Guerrero, Xavier
Neruda, Pablo. Los frescos de Xavier Guerrero en Chillán (*Ars*, México, vol. 1, no. 5, mayo, p. 61–62, ilus.). [824
Brief note upon the murals in Chile. See *Handbook, no. 8, 1942*, item 816.

Guerrero Galván, Jesús
Fernández, Justino. Un regalo a los Estados Unidos (*Hoy*, oct. 9, p. 63–80, ilus.). [825
Discussion of the career of Jesús Guerrero Galván (born 1910), whose re-

cent murals in the University of New Mexico treat of the union of America.

Izquierdo, María
Fernández, Justino. La poesía salvaje de María Izquierdo (*Hoy*, sept. 25, p. 66–67, ilus.). [826]
Born in Jalisco in 1907, María Izquierdo was originally trained in the Academy of San Carlos, and later came within the sphere of Diego Rivera.

Kahlo, Frida
Rivera, Diego. Frida Kahlo y el arte mexicano (*Bol. sem. cult. mex.*, tomo 1, no. 2, oct., p. 89–101, ilus.). [827]
An imaginative and stimulating account of the history of Mexican art, brilliantly written around the subject of Frida Kahlo's psychiatric paintings. The essay is a most important evaluation of the Mexican school by one of its deacons.

Leal, Fernando
Izquierdo, María. El pintor muralista Fernando Leal (*Hoy*, julio 17, p. 62, ilus.). [828]
Short discussion of state-subsidized artists; review of new murals by Leal for the Sindicato de Ferrocarrileros.

Macías Báez, Leopoldo
Rivas, Guillermo. Leopoldo Macías Báez (*Mexican life*, vol. 19, no. 7, July, p. 25–28). [829]
Brief appreciation of the watercolors of the young artist whose work is directly pictorial, in the tradition of J. M. Velasco.

Meza, Guillermo
Fernández, Justino. Meza, pintor de lo imposible (*Hoy*, agosto 7, p. 64–65, ilus.). [830]
Guillermo Meza (1919–) has produced paintings abounding in surrealist images, and depending as well upon Blake and Beardsley.

Montenegro, Roberto
Fernández, Justino. La obra de Montenegro (*Hoy*, nov. 27, p. 47–49, ilus.). [831]
Recent paintings by Roberto Montenegro (1885–), whose early work stood under the influence of Aubrey Beardsley, and whose most notable activity in Mexico has been in connection with the Museo de Arte Popular. Surrealist tendencies are strongly evident in his work of the last years.

O'Gorman, Juan
Rivas, Guillermo. Juan O'Gorman (*Mexican life*, vol. 19, no. 12, Dec., p. 31–34). [832]
Illustrations of the important and skillful landscapes by Juan O'Gorman. The critic believes that landscape painting, before O'Gorman, had almost become extinct.

Orozco, José Clemente
Fernández, Justino. Obras recientes (*Hoy*, oct. 30, p. 59–61, ilus.). [833]
A review of the recent work by Orozco, exhibited in the Colegio Nacional in Mexico City.

Orozco, José Clemente. Si pintas ¿Para qué hablas? (*Cult. México*, año 2, no. 2, julio–dic., p. 36–37). [834]
A newspaper interview in which Orozco expounded a doctrine of esthetic autonomy.

Rodríguez, Lozano. Política y arte (*Hoy*, sept. 4, p. 62). [835]
An attack upon Orozco's recent statements concerning the relationship between politics and art.

Valdés, Octaviano. Exégesis a una "Crucifixión" de José Clemente Orozco (*Ábside*, vol. 7, no. 3, julio–sept., p. 311–317). [836]
A recent canvas by Orozco is the subject of an essay purporting to define the painter's relation to mysticism.

Ortiz Monasterio
Zárraga, Ángel. Notas sobre el arte de Ortiz Monasterio (*Bol. sem. cult. mex.*, tomo 1, no. 2, oct., p. 102–109, ilus.). [837]
Appreciation of the sculpture by Ortiz Monasterio, defined as "classic" by a painter.

Rodríguez Lozano, Manuel
Altolaguirre, Manuel. La pintura quemante (*Hoy*, nov. 20, p. 55–57, ilus.). [838]
An appreciation of recent paintings and drawings by Manuel Rodríguez Lozano.

Ruiz, Antonio
Bergamín, José. La pintura de Antonio Ruiz (*Bol. sem. cult. mex.*, tomo 1, no. 1, julio, p. 25–32, ilus.). [839]
An appreciation of the romantic naturalism of Antonio Ruiz.

Serrano, Alfredo
Izquierdo, María. El pintor Alfredo Serrano (*Hoy*, junio 5, p. 48, ilus.). [840]
The critic points out Serrano's gifts, as well as his occasional abuse of decorative facility.

Zárraga, Ángel
Prats, Alardo. Galería de nuestro tiempo (*Hoy*, oct. 23, p. 28–33, ilus.). [841]
Recent portraits by Ángel Zárraga, now painting in Mexico after his long residence in Paris.

PERU

Núñez Ureta
Gallagher de Parks, Mercedes. La exposición de acuarelas de Núñez Ureta

(*Mercurio peruano,* año 18, vol. 25, no. 195, junio, p. 257-258). [842

Review of a current exhibition in Lima. The reviewer compares Núñez Ureta's watercolors to contemporary British work.

Sabogal, José

Ontañón, Mada. José Sabogal en México (*Hoy,* enero 23, p. 96-97, ilus.). [843

An interview with the Peruvian *indigenista,* who announces his intention to practice fresco-painting in his own country after seeing the work of the Mexican school.

URUGUAY

Laroche, Ernesto

Museo y archivo Ernesto Laroche. Ficha biográfica de Ernesto Laroche. Su representación en galerías oficiales del país y del extranjero; su labor cultural; su labor administrativa. Montevideo. Ed. Morales hnos. 7 p. [844

Ernesto Laroche (1879-1940) occupied an important position in the Uruguayan academic and museum professions. A prolific writer upon art, he was also a landscape painter.

Telmo, Manacorda. Presencia de Ernesto Laroche. Montevideo. (Publ. Museo Ernesto Laroche, año 3, no. 6.) 15 p., ilus., 23 grabs. [845

Pastor, Adolfo

Vitureira, Cipriano Santiago. El dibujo de Adolfo Pastor (*Rev. nac.,* Montevideo, año 6, tomo 23, no. 67, julio, p. 94-103, ilus.). [846

An appreciation of the "lyrical realism" manifested in drawings and prints by Adolfo Pastor.

BRAZILIAN ART

BY

ROBERT C. SMITH

Sweet Briar College

GENERAL STATEMENT

Two exhibitions held at the Museum of Modern Art in New York did more than anything else during the year to attract attention to Brazilian art. The careful preparations for these exhibitions, mentioned in last year's *Handbook*, bore splendid fruit. The first of these, Brazil Builds, was a survey of Brazilian architecture concentrating upon colonial and contemporary monuments. The vehicle of presentation was a collection of photographs made by G. E. Kidder Smith. Dramatically posed with brilliant contrasts of light and dark and rich, expressive textures, they are among the finest architectural photographs ever made. They brought out eloquently the virtues of the simply constructed but vividly decorated baroque buildings of Pernambuco, Bahia, and Minas Gerais, and revealed a subtle connection between these colonial structures and the breath-takingly beautiful modern architecture of Brazil. The catalogue of this exhibition, also called Brazil Builds (item 849), written by the architect Philip Goodwin who had accompanied the photographer to Brazil. It is an exceptionally handsome and well prepared volume in which Mr. Kidder Smith's photographs with some others from the Serviço do Patrimônio Histórico e Artístico Nacional were as effectively illustrated as they were displayed in the exhibition.

Shortly after the conclusion of the New York showing in January the exhibition began a tour of the country. At Boston, the first stopping place, a valuable symposium on Brazilian architecture was held at the Museum of Fine Arts (item 949). During the summer the exhibition visited Mexico (item 934) and later it was shown in Rio de Janeiro and in London (item 924) with enthusiastic receptions from the general public and from local architects. The exhibition and the catalogue demonstrated beyond question that colonial Brazilian architecture has more than a picturesque appeal, and that the recent buildings of Oscar Niemeyer, Lúcio Costa, the Roberto's and other Brazilian architects are among the most distinguished for their ingenuity and beauty in the world today.

Brazil Builds was followed by another exhibition in the spring of 1943 at the Museum of Modern Art, in which contemporary Brazilian painting formed a part of a general show of modern Latin American painting gathered the previous year for the Museum's permanent collection by Mr. Lincoln Kirstein. In spite of the absence of several important canvases which did not arrive in time for the exhibition, the work of the best Brazilian artists was well represented and was judged to compare favorably with the other outstanding schools of Latin America, those of Mexico, Cuba and Argentina. The well known grandeur and versatility of Portinari, the forceful drawing and brilliant coloring of José Pancetti, the decorative inventions of Alberto da Veiga Guignard, and the sheer fine painting of Paulo Rossi entirely destroyed the unfavorable impression produced by previous exhibitions in New York of more conservative Brazilian painting. Mr. Kirstein added to his catalogue of the exhibition a fine essay (item 850) on the development of Brazilian painting. This together with a more general account of the growth of Brazilian art published in the second volume of a guide to Latin America sponsored by the Coordinator of Inter-American Affairs (item 856), a special issue (September) of the London *Studio* devoted to Brazil (items 852, 859, 894, 923, 926), and a long well illustrated essay in Portuguese (item 847), furnished a body of information on the subject never before available in English.

Another exhibition held in the Spring of 1943 at the Valentine Gallery in New York, presented the recent sculptures of Maria (Mme. Carlos Martins Pereira e Sousa). These small bronzes of complicated and impressionistic surfaces showed a decided contrast to the smooth surfaces and grand proportions of much of the previous work of this Brazilian sculptress (item 917). Photographs made the year before in Brazil by Genevieve Naylor were also shown at the Museum of Modern Art. Differing in subject matter and technique from those of Kidder Smith they offered a wide range of unusual material, including religious processions in Ouro Preto, studies of shop fronts and mosaic pavements in Rio de Janeiro, river traffic and villages in the *sertão* of Bahia and some dynamically patterned views of crowds in Belo Horizonte. Copies of these photographs, those of Brazil builds and others greatly increased during the year the Brazilian section of the Archive of Hispanic Culture at the Library of Congress.

Also in the spring of 1943 the Brooklyn Museum opened its new galleries of Latin American colonial art, in which several pieces of Brazilian silver and wood carving were shown. The sparse representation of Brazil in this exhibition, where Mexico and Peru shone with so many examples of fine craftsmanship, served to recall once again how little of the baroque art of Portuguese America can be seen in United States museums. These are, to be sure, a few paintings in the Oliveira Lima Library at the Catholic University of America in Washington, among them the Pernambucan landscape of Frans Post, another fine Post at Detroit, a silver coffee pot in Boston. But nowhere has this editor been able to find examples of what was possibly Brazil's finest artistic achievement during the colonial period—the sculptured D. João V and D. Maria I furniture of *jacarandá* wood. To suggest that any of these 18th century treasures be exported to this country from Brazil is a delicate matter. The Brazilian government has very wisely acted to prevent the scattering abroad of the national patrimony of colonial art, just as it has prevented the destruction of 18th century architecture in such important sites as Ouro Preto. But with the interest in Brazilian culture that now obtains here it would be of great advantage if two or three important and strategically placed museums could display some outstanding examples of the colonial painting and minor arts of Brazil, perhaps against the special setting of a period room. Only in this way can the 17th and 18th century civilization of Olinda, Salvador, Rio de Janeiro and Minas Gerais be fully understood. The suggestion that the Brazilian museums exchange with several key institutions in this country duplicates from their collections deserves careful study.

From the standpoint of exhibitions in the United States 1943 was a wonderful year for Brazilian art. At home one great national showing in the capital of the work of the São Paulo painter Lasar Segall took place. A fine catalogue with contributions from several Brazilian writers was published (item no. 943) and widely circulated. In the field of publications the year was no less memorable.

A great deal of new source material for the study of colonial art is exposed in the third and fourth volumes of Father Sarafim Leite's monumental *História dos Jesuitas no Brasil*, where Jesuit buildings of the extreme north are discussed extensively in the light of important documents from a variety of sources (item 877). The official monograph on the Rio de Janeiro church of N. S. da Glória offers a combination of good photographs of the recently restored building, sound deductions about its construction, and charming old *costumista* views of the monument (item 886). The tendency to use 19th century prints for documentation of colonial buildings, which has happily been developing in recent years, is carried further in some valuable essays on old city fountains by José Marianno (item 882). The Wolfgang Hoffman Harnisches, father and son, have discussed with distinction the colonial sculptures of the Jesuit missions of Rio Grande do Sul, praised over a century ago by the first historian of Brazilian art, Manoel Araújo Pôrto-Alegre and illustrated their findings with some striking photographs (items 872 and 873). The Russian-born critic, Michel Benisovich, now residing in New York, whose Brazilian reseaches have several times been noted in this section, makes a valuable contribution to our knowledge of Frans Post in an article in the *Burlington Magazine* in which he deals with the influence of Portuguese America on some Gobelins tapestries (item 866).

It is always a pleasure to call attention in this section to the excellent publications of the Serviço do Patrimônio Histórico e Artístico Nacional, and to commend that organization for its work of preserving and documenting colonial art in Brazil. This year's issue of the *Revista do Serviço do Patrimônio Histórico e Artístico Nacional*, the seventh in the series, is without doubt the finest of all. The quality of its nine contributions, both from the standpoint of subjects treated and the careful, scholarly presentation is outstanding. Emphasis is placed this year on domestic architecture. The principal essay is a Portuguese translation of a collection of letters on the houses of Pernambuco written by L. L. Vauthier and published in a French architectural journal in the middle of the 19th century (item 898). This, to a certain extent, sets the tone for the rest of the publication. Another important article deals with old country houses in the district around Rio de Janeiro (item 867). One of these buildings is discussed in a separate study (item 884). Balconies of Pernambucan town houses like those described by Vauthier are the subject of still another of the articles in this issue of the *Revista* (item 883). Cônego Trindade's well documented history of the church of the Third Order of St. Francis in Mariana is a basic monograph for the study of the colonial architecture of Minas Gerais (item 897). There is some valuable new information on early furniture of that state (item 890) and a fascinating analysis of some of the famous tiles in the Franciscan convent of Bahia (item 885). The article by Michel Benisovich on designs by Dutch artists for Gobelins tapestries (item 866), published this year also in England, introduces a new note, the influence of Brazil on European art. The late 18th century report on the fortifications of Pará (item 888), while perhaps of more interest to political historians than students of Brazilian art, is important for the list of forts it contains, which will be of great assistance to whoever undertakes to study the military architecture of Brazil, a subject which deserves careful analysis because of its relation to the official constructions of the old Portuguese empire. It should be noted also that all the articles in this issue have full bibliographical references to the works consulted by their authors; the paper and printing are exceptional; and most of the illustrations are well reproduced. During 1943 important articles on problems of colonial art by S.P.H.A.N.'s gifted director, Rodrigo Melo Franco de Andrade (items 860-864) also appeared.

Monographs on the great figures of 19th century Brazilian art, which this editor considers a basic need, continued to appear. This year we have a far from perfect but very useful study of the versatile Manoel Araújo Pôrto-Alegre (item 901) which contains a good list of his writings on Brazilian art. A new edition of a late 19th century biography of Pedro Américo, although it does not evaluate the painter according to modern standards, is an interesting period piece, which the publishers are justified in making available (item 908). More important, however, are the reprints of 19th century albums of views of Rio de Janeiro, original copies of which are rare even in great libraries (items 902 and 904). It is interesting to note that the Buvelot prints were used in the monograph on N. S. da Glória mentioned above. Hercules Florence, long an enticing but inaccessible figure, has been abundantly disclosed in a fine publication of his sketch book (item 915). Francisco Marques dos Santos has added another of his brilliant essays on the art and social history of the empire. This year he has written about the wedding of D. Pedro II.

Several outstanding publications on modern art have been noted above. One other deserves special attention. This is an album of reproductions of drawings by Lasar Segall of São Paulo, handsomely printed by the *Revista Acadêmica* and issued in a limited edition with interpretative notes and four signed prints (item 941). It is a collector's item that is worth possessing not alone for its rarity as an example of fine production but also for the excellent material, both graphic and literary, that it contains. It is a source of satisfaction to know that the *Revista*, which has long been a protagonist for the best of modern Brazilian art, is again active. The list of future publications that this press has announced, promises some exceptional books on the contemporary art of Brazil which, thanks to the exhibitions which have made this year outstanding, is now known to the international public.

BIBLIOGRAPHY

(*See also sections on* Anthropology, Folklore, *and* History: Brazil)

GENERAL

Azevedo, Fernando de. A cultura artística (In *Cultura brasileira: recenseamento geral do Brasil*. Rio de Janeiro. Instituto brasileiro de geografia e estatística. Vol. 1, tomo 1, p. 245–286, ilus.). [847

An interesting statement on the history of Brazilian art. A general criticism is that almost no examples are cited in the section dealing with colonial art and the bibliography is erratic. Many basic works, like L. Costa's paper on Jesuit building (see *Handbook, no. 7, 1941*, item no. 667a are not listed.

Specific criticism can be directed to the inadequate treatment of 16th and 17th century architecture, including that of the Jesuits, and the practical exclusion of contemporary architecture, a field in which Brazil is preeminent.

FEIRAS DO NORDESTE (*Ilus. bras.*, ano 21, no. 98, junho, p. 37-39, 7 ilus.). [848

Fine photographs, published anonymously, of country fairs in northern Brazil.

Goodwin, Philip L. Brazil builds. Architecture new and old, 1652–1942. New York. Museum of modern art. 198 p., 305 illus., 4 in color. [849

This beautiful catalog of the exhibition Brazil builds is an excellent introduction to the colonial and contemporary architecture of Brazil. Mr. Goodwin's text is full of the keen observations of a distinguished modern architect. The photographs of Mr. G. E. Kidder Smith are outstanding. The volume, which is published in both English and Portuguese, is also illustrated with many valuable plans and drawings by contemporary architects.

Kirstein, Lincoln. The Latin-American collection of the Museum of modern art. New York. Museum of modern art. 110 p., illus. [850

A fine example of catalogue preparation, indispensable both to research and general instruction. Works from the countries are illustrated. General historical essay, biographical notices, and bibliography.

The catalog to the Museum's exhibition of modern Latin American painting presents a survey of the development of that art from the Conquest to 1900 and individual essays on its contemporary expression in a number of countries, including Brazil. It is the first serious attempt to trace the history, even in broad terms, of Latin American painting and is extremely successful.

In dealing with colonial art in Brazil Mr. Kirstein makes a few errors. On page 7, in writing of the Dutch painter, Albert van Eckhout, he speaks of "full-length standing portraits of distinguished Dutch soldiers and mulatto planters." He really means half length portraits of Negroes in Dutch costumes. On page 10 he says that "Aleijadinho" worked at Congonhas do Campo from 1757 almost until his death in 1814, whereas he seems not to have gone to the pilgrimage church until much later in the century. Furthermore the statues to which he refers do not represent apostles but prophets, which accounts for the "tragic Old Testament monumentality" which he sees in them. One would like to know more about his "series of careful documentary portraits . . . showing the subtle variants of blood mixture, Indian. Negro, mestizo, mulatto and lesser combinations" of the late eighteenth-century (p. 9–10). Where do they exist? His description of the impression of the Post landscape (p. 7) is admirable.

In the nineteenth century he rightly stresses the importance of the Brazilian Imperial Academy of Fine Arts (p. 11) in the formation of a national school. In the same section he speaks of hand colored lithographs in Debret's book. These were not tinted in the regular edition. It is difficult to find the influence of Trumbull's *Bunker Hill* in the *Battle of Guararapes* by Victor Meireles. Almeida Junior, who appears only in a list of names, deserves longer treatment (p. 16).

Mr. Kirstein's section on modern painting (p. 34–36) gives a rather one-sided account of the present situation. He omits an analysis of the present style of Segall, the most influential painter of São Paulo. The effect of Portinari's influence is not properly considered nor is there any estimate of his accomplishment as a whole. But what is most important is that he does not mention the conservative painters of Brazil, who although one may not greatly admire their work, still wield great power on the local scene, as this section has so often pointed out in past years.

The bibliography which concludes the volume leaves out the art sections of the *Handbook of Latin American Studies*, although they have been for the last half dozen years probably the richest source for information on publications concerning Latin American art of all periods.

Koseritz, Carl von. Imagens do Brasil. Tradução, prefácio e notas de Afonso Arinos de Melo Franco. São Paulo. Livr. Martins. (Bibl. histórica bras., vol. 13). 292 p., ilus. [851

Magno, Paschoal Carlos. Brazilian painting (*Studio*, vol. 126, no. 606, Sept., p. 98–105, 28 illus., 8 in color). [852

This is a careful and valuable statement. It correctly points out the weakness of colonial painting. Then follows a long section on the nineteenth century, in which, on the whole, the many names and facts are handled with skill and a just feeling for what was most important. Here one would like to see more attention given the work of Almeida Júnior.

Senhor Magno writes with understanding of the modern conservatives, who are still dependent upon a Europe that has vanished. The future of Brazilian painting, he feels, is in the hands of Portinari and a small group of other artists, whom he barely mentions. One wishes that he had included more influential modern painters in this group and that he had offered more illustrations of their work. As it is there is only one reproduction of a Portinari, none of the other moderns. On the other hand the many illustrations of the work of conservative artists gives the impression, until the text is carefully read, that the author esteems only their work.

Marianno Filho, José. Viagem pitoresca a Araruama e Cabo Frio (*Dom Casmurro*, no. 331–332, 25 dez., segundo cad., p. 3, 1 ilus.). [853

This article includes some notes on the present appearance of S. Pedro da Aldeia, a Jesuit construction of the late 17th century. It contains also criticism of S.P.H.A.N.'s methods of restoration. The author jibes at Brazilian "sociologists," and complains of a lack of local color in Brazil.

Santa Rosa, Tomás. Esquema das artes do Brasil (*Atlântico*, no. 4, p. 143–145). [854
A few lines are devoted to each of the outstanding painters, print makers, architects and sculptors of Rio de Janeiro and São Paulo. In the last category it is surprising not to find the name of Bruno Georgi.

Santos, José de Almeida. Introdução ao mobiliário artístico brasileiro (*Estud. bras.*, ano 5, vol. 10, no. 29–30, março–junho, p. 223–237, 4 ilus.). [855
This article presents a number of interesting observations concerning 18th century furniture resulting from the author's comparison of Brazilian pieces with the contemporary English production. He speaks of 3 styles: (1) *Mineiro-goiano* of the 18th century which corresponds to Louis XV and Chippendale; (2) *colonial*, or *D. Maria I brasileiro*, 1790–1820; (3) *Béranger*, used in Pernambuco 1820–1850, which is like the French Empire style. One wonders why the author limits the first to the inland provinces, when there was so much of it produced on the coast, and why is only the *D. Maria I* called *colonial?* To illustrate the style are a bed and table that look like a combination of Sheraton and Empire. Why is the *D. Maria I* of Brazil so different from the *D. Maria I* of Portugal which is still rococo? Generally in colonial Latin America just the opposite happened. A style of the mother country was pretty much out of date before it was widely imitated in the colonies.
All this perplexes the reader and makes him long for a thorough study of Portuguese seventeenth- and eighteenth-century furniture to fix the styles of the period detail by detail and bring together all the available information on craftsmen. Then with this solid background we could approach Brazilian furniture with assurance and try to settle once and for all these vexing questions of style and nomenclature.

Smith, Robert C. Art and architecture [of Brazil] (*New world guides to the Latin American republics*, vol. 2, South America, The United States of Brazil, p. 22–33). [856
This is an attempt to bring together in a concise statement the outstanding developments and monuments of Brazilian art of the colonial, nineteenth-century, and modern periods. Since the material has never been thoroughly studied, many details of the account will probably prove incorrect as research by the Brazilian government and private individuals continues. It is, however, the fullest statement on the subject in English. It is marred by two inexcusable errors, a mistake of ten years in the date of the removal of the capital to Rio de Janeiro and a reference to the statues at Congonhas do Campo as "apostles" instead of "prophets."

———. Brazil builds on tradition and today (*Art news*, vol. 41, no. 18, Feb. 1–14, p. 14–18, 33, 8 illus., 1 in color). [857
These comments on the exhibition Brazil builds attempt to bring out certain stylistic relationships between colonial Brazilian architecture and the distinguished contemporary work of Niemeyer, Costa and others.

———. A selective guide to the material published in 1942 on Brazilian art (*Handbook of latin american studies, no. 8, 1942*, p. 87–98). [858

ARCHAEOLOGY

Costa, Angyone. Manifestations of art in Brazilian archaeology (*Studio*, vol. 126, no. 606, Sept., p. 119–120, 4 illus.). [859
A short survey of the ceramics of Santarém, Marajó, and Cunani (Brazilian Guiana) which is clear but entirely too brief, for the last group is not adequately described. There is no discussion of the motifs in Marajó ware, beyond a description of the *tanga*. The small drawings are attractive but do not take the place of photographs.
The translator unfortunately used the word "porcelain" instead of "ceramics" throughout the article, thus creating an entirely erroneous impression.

COLONIAL

(*See also item* 130)

Andrade, Rodrigo Melo Franco de. O decano de nossos arquitetos (*A Manhã*, 17 out.). [860
The writer quotes 16th century documents relative to the buildings of Luiz Dias in Salvador between 1549 and 1554. Among them was a town hall and prison which had two stories, stone walls and a tile roof. Dr. Andrade suggests that this was the prototype for other colonial town halls, some of which exist, more or less unchanged.

———. Dois arquitetos franciscanos (*A Manhã*, 12 nov.). [861
The author calls attention to two early Franciscan arquitects in Brazil. The first, Frei Francisco dos Santos is mentioned by Frei Antônio de Santa Maria Jaboatão in his *Novo Orbe Seráfico Brasílico*. He built the monastery of Nossa Senhora das Neves at Olinda, which was founded in 1585. He was then ordered to erect the Franciscan house in Paraíba (João Pessoa) in 1590. Transferred to Bahia that same year Frei Francisco dos Santos designed the retables for the church of his Order at São Salvador. In 1640 he began to direct the construction of a Franciscan monastery in São Paulo, and nine years later that of Paraguassú in the Recôncavo of Bahia. Father Jaboatão does not inform us as to where and when Frei Francisco was born or died.
In a note dated 1740 in the Franciscan archives at Rio de Janeiro Nair Batista of S.P.H.A.N. has found reference to the Mestre do Obras Frei Antônio da Natividade "comquem os mais officiaes da cidade se vem enformar para as suas obras."

———. Francisco Xavier de Brito, mestre de Aleijadinho (*A Manhã,* 27 agôsto). **[862**
Joaquim José da Silva, writing in 1790, said that Aleijadinho had had 3 masters. The first was his father, Manuel Francisco, the architect. The second was the distinguished medalist from Lisbon, J. Gomes Batista, while the third was a sculptor, F. X. de Brito. The article calls attention to resemblances between the style of Brito's altars at S. Francisco da Penitência in Rio de Janeiro and other work in Ouro Preto, where he remained from 1741 until his death in 1758, and the peculiar manner of Aleijadinho. Dr. Andrade mentions documents that strengthen the relationship.

———. A igreja de São Pedro (*A Manhã,* 23 nov.). **[863**
A plea from the distinguished director of S.P.H.A.N. to the prefect of Rio de Janeiro to move the eighteenth-century church of São Pedro dos Clérigos directly from its original site in the path of the new Avenida Getúlio Vargas to a different location. This project, which the prefect had suggested, was opposed by other municipal authorities on the grounds that the historical and architectural value of the church was not sufficient to justify the considerable cost involved. The writer points out that a number of distinguished Brazilians were buried in São Pedro dos Clérigos and that its curvilinear plan had a considerable influence on later buildings in Minas Gerais, while its cupola is unique in Brazil. He warns that the counter-proposal, to take the church apart and rebuild it when convenient, is dangerous. Unfortunately the prefect's plan seems not to have been carried out. Recent photographs give the impression that the church has been demolished.

———. Informação sôbre o pintor José de Oliveira (*A Manhã,* 6 junho). **[864**
Important note on a mysterious colonial artist. José de Oliveira Rosa, author of paintings in the Capela das Relíquias of the Mosteiro de São Bento, Rio de Janeiro, and a portrait of Madre Jacinta de São José in the Convento das Recolhidas de Santa Teresa in Rio. Examination of documents in the convent show that both works date from 1769, the year in which the artist died. Since his mother was still living at this time, it is assumed that José de Oliveira died young.

UMA ANTIGA CATEDRAL BRASILEIRA (*Cultura política,* ano 3, no. 27, março, p. 162–163, 8 ilus.). **[865**
A note on the construction of this Jesuit church of São Miguel near Sto. Ângelo, Rio Grande do Sul, by the Milanese Giovanni Primoli during the years 1735 to 1749, which has recently been restored by S.P.H.A.N. The photographs are good and there are reproduced a drawing by Demersey of the ruins made in 1846 and a 19th century reconstruction of the façade by the painter Júdicis de Mirandole.

Benisovich, Michael. The history of the *Tenture des indes* (*Burlington mag.,* vol. 83, no. 486, Sept., p. 216–225, 2 illus.). **[866**
A delightful and well documented account of 5 tapestries: *L'Eléphant et le cheval Isabelle; Les deux taureaux; Le cheval rayé; L'indien à cheval;* and *Les pecheurs indiens;* at the Musée des Gobelins, Paris, which were made for Louis XIV after paintings by Albert Eckhout which Maurice of Nassau had sent to France in 1679. The author sees in the background the influence of the landscapes of Frans Post, that other Dutch painter whom the Count of Nassau Siegen had taken with him to Brazil.
Published also in *Rev. serv. patr. hist. art. nac.,* no. 7, p. 35–56.

Cardoso, Joaquim. Um tipo de casa rural do Distrito federal e estado do Rio (*Rev. serv. patr. hist. art. nac.,* no. 7, p. 209–253, 46 ilus., 10 drawings). **[867**
This is primarily a thorough investigation of a type of *fazenda* in the region of Rio de Janeiro dating from the second half of the eighteenth century or early nineteenth. These houses have a *loggia* or *varanda* as the principal element of the main façade. This porch is ornamented with short round or cylindrical columns of general Doric derivation which are very similar to those in the upper stories of cloisters of Franciscan convents of northeastern Brazil and the porches or *alpendres* of a few remaining colonial chapels. The author admits that it is impossible to prove whether this kind of column was first used in plantation houses or in churches. Certainly both uses were traditional in Portugal. There is also a discussion of stairs, plans, and position of chapels in the 3 principal fazendas of this group, Columbandê, Engenho d'Água, and Viegas.
Three other types of plantation house in this region are also briefly mentioned and illustrated. The first has a long unbroken façade and may be derived from Jesuit constructions. The second has a curious break in the roof line, creating almost a hip-roof profile. The third, which is very Portuguese, has a high center façade flanked by lower wings on either side. The article is lavishly illustrated with well reproduced photographs.

O CHAFARIZ DO PAÇO (*Dom Casmurro,* no. 331–332, 25 dez., segundo cad., p. 7, 2 ilus.). **[868**
A description of the famous late eighteenth-century fountain in Rio de Janeiro dedicated to D. Maria I.

Cúrio, Nestor Wanderley. O precursor da arte de gravar no Brasil (*Dom Casmurro,* no. 331–332, 25 dez., terceiro cad., p. 27, 1 ilus.). **[869**
Interesting note on the engraver Romão Eloy de Almeida, thought to have come to Brazil from Portugal in 1808, who worked at the Impressão Régia. Some of his engravings for books have been preserved at the Imprensa Nacional.

Fazenda, Viera. O mosteiro e a igreja de São Bento (*Dom Casmurro*, no. 331–332, 25 dez., segundo cad., p. 2, 1 ilus.). [870
Republication of an old description of the church of the Benedictine Order in Rio de Janeiro with a pen drawing by George Wambach.

Gomes, Antônio Osmar. Caixa-Pregos (*Rev. semana*, ano 44, no. 28, 10 julho, p. 16–17, 6 ilus.). [871
The article describes a town on the Bahia de Todos os Santos and includes a photograph of an important Jesuit church of the 17th century (S. Lourenço).

Hoffmann-Harnisch, Wolfgang. Viagem através das missões brasileiras (*Cultura política*, ano 3, no. 29, julho, p. 111–120). [872
Contains a description of the Jesuit ruins at S. Miguel and the new museum of the S.P.H.A.N. there.

Hoffmann-Harnisch Júnior, Wolfgang. Arte antiga das missões brasileiras (*Cultura política*, ano 3, no. 33, out., p. 216–217, ilus.). [873
The author, who has photographed from dramatic angles 400 mid-eighteenth-century wood and clay sculptures from the Jesuit missions of Rio Grande do Sul, points out convincingly German, Italian, and Indian, as well as Portuguese influences in the technically excellent work. If the figures are as fine as they seem from these photographs to be, they are, indeed a high point of sculpture in the Americas.

A IGREJA DOS REMÉDIOS (*Ilus. bras.*, ano 21, no. 104, jan., p. 26, 1 ilus.). [874
Aspects of the history of this now demolished São Paulo church.

Kamenka, Michel B. Franz Post, o brasileiro (*Ilus. bras.*, ano 21, no. 103, nov., p. 8–9, 4 ilus.). [875
A description of the style, color, and subjects of Post's paintings on the occasion of the opening of a new gallery in the Museu Nacional de Belas Artes. This Sala Frans Post contains the landscapes purchased recently by the Brazilian government and a portrait of Maurício de Nassau by Frans Post after Pierre Nazon which was presented to the nation by the Dutch.

Krull, Germaine. Uma cidade antiga do Brasil: Ouro Preto. Lisboa. 38 p., 39 ilus. [876
A volume of photographs by G. Krull with text by Raul Lins and Ribeiro Couto.

Leite, Serafim. História da Companhia de Jesús no Brasil. Vols. 3 and 4. Rio de Janeiro. Imp. nacional. 2 vols.: xxviii, 487; xxv, 440 p., 46 ilus. [877
In the two new volumes of his great work Father Leite continues to reveal the fruits of long digging in the archives of Portugal, Brazil, and Rome to find the true story of what the Jesuits accomplished in colonial Brazil. There is new information about all the Company's foundations in the north, and in some cases names of craftsmen and specific information on the construction of such important churches as N. S. da Luz at Maranhão, S. Francisco Xavier at Belém, and N. S. Mãe de Deus at Vigia. Among the illustrations are many hitherto unpublished details of Jesuit buildings, a wonderful map of Fortaleza at the colonial archive in Lisbon which shows the earliest structures in remarkable detail (circa 1726), and the handsome view of the Jesuit church and seminary in Belém from the *Viagem Filosófica* of Alexandre Rodrigues Ferreira.

Lemoine. Um pouco de história sob as arcadas do convento de Santo Antônio (*Cultura política*, ano 3, no. 33, out., p. 207–215). [878
Some description of the Franciscan convent building in Rio de Janeiro with a good deal of historical detail.

Macieira, Anselmo. Moveis do Brasil antigo (*Rev. semana*, ano 44, no. 14, 3 abril, p. 16–17, 10 ilus.). [879
Presents excellent photographs of the colonial furniture of the Museu Histórico of Rio de Janeiro by Arnoldo Vieira.

Marianno Filho, José. Duas obras que se devem excluir do inventário artístico do Aleijadinho (*Jornal do commércio*, ano 116, no. 84, 10 jan., p. 3). [880
The doors of the Capela do Senhor Bom Jesús de Matosinhos in Ouro Prêto and the parish church of S. João do Morro Grande, often attributed to Aleijadinho, are not stylistically his work, the author feels.
This is a selection from a book *O Aleijadinho e a Sua Arte* to be published later.

———. Influências muçulmanas na architectura tradicional brasileira. Rio de Janeiro. Ed. A Noite. 47 p., 33 ilus. [881
This book is about the shuttered windows and over-hanging latticed balconies of colonial Brazil. In Rio de Janeiro almost all of them were destroyed by a decree in 1809 to modernize the city. In Ouro Prêto, Recife and Olinda a few have survived.
It is true that these latticed windows in one form or another are found in Spanish America, Spain, and Portugal. Similar arrangements occur in Islamic countries. The Brazilian examples may derive from Moorish prototypes as part of the Iberian *mudéjar* inheritance (like the use of tiles and enclosed courtyards with wells or fountains in their centers). But those that have survived in Brazil do not have any strongly marked Moorish or Islamic ornament. This the writer fails to notice in his attempt to prove their Islamic inspiration. A sounder explanation might be that the Brazilian windows and balconies are the product of a climate and way of life that also resulted in the *muxarabís* of Mohammedan civilization.
The book is beautifully printed and illustrated with old views and some fine pen drawings by Pacheco.

———. Os tres chafarizes de mestre Valentim. Rio de Janeiro. 68 p., 42 ilus. **[882**

In this carefully written and effectively documented study of three colonial fountains in Rio de Janeiro—Marrecas (1785); Carmo (1789); and Saracuras (1795)—the author continues his investigations of the work of the distinguished 18th century sculptor Valentim da Fonseca. He has made use of the great 19th century topographical works and the many fine prints of the fountains of the same period. The work, like the N. S. da Glória monograph (item no. 886) shows the value of this kind of material for research in the history of Brazilian art.

MUXARABÍS E BALCÕES; ENSÁIO SÔBRE ANTIGOS ELEMENTOS ARQUITETÔNICOS NOS QUAIS SE PODERÃO VER TRAÇOS DE INFLUÊNCIA MOURISCA (*Rev. serv. patr. hist. nac.*, no. 7, p. 309–340, 48 ilus.). **[883**

The Arabic word *muxarabí* is used here to describe the wooden latticed balconies so common in Brazilian town houses in the colonial period and now almost non-existent. Two still survive in incomplete form in Olinda. These are studied with great care in this article as are the houses which they decorate.

Plans are provided. The author, who unfortunately remains anonymous, has made good use of old lithographs and descriptions by travelers. He brings out, and this is of the greatest interest, that although the wooden screens have disappeared on many old houses in both Recife and Olinda, the stone supports of the original balconies still remain. This is not true of Rio de Janeiro or Bahia. These stone supports are generously illustrated by photographs and a drawing of various types.

Nigra, Clemente Maria da Silva. A antiga fazenda de S. Bento em Iguaçu (*Rev. serv. patr. hist. art. nac.*, no. 7, p. 257–282, 5 ilus.). **[884**

Iguaçu, in the region of Guanabara, was the first Benedictine foundation in Brazil. A house with a church attached is still standing there. Careful searching of the Benedictine archives in Rio de Janeiro indicates that the church is the original structure erected by the abbot Frei Mauro das Chagas between 1645 and 1648 while the house was rebuilt in 1754. The woodcarving of the Virgin and Child known as Nossa Senhora de Iguaçu is identified on stylistic evidence, and quite rightly, it appears, as a work of the first half of the 17th century.

The author publishes also certain documents relative to the acquisition of the land by the members of his order, inventories and notes on colonial Benedictines who administered and built up S. Bento de Iguaçu.

Ott, Carlos Fidelis. Os azulejos do convento de São Francisco da Bahia (*Rev. serv. patr. hist. art. nac.*, no. 7, p. 7–34, 14 ilus.). **[885**

The author, who is a Franciscan of Bahia identified the blue and white painted tiles of the lower floor of the cloister of his convent as illustrations of themes from Horace. He proves this by comparing photographs of some of the tiles with a series of engravings by the Flemish artist Otto van Veen published in 1608 with the title *Emblems from Horace*. They are almost exactly the same. Occasionally, according to the author, the Portuguese tile painter improved on the models. Further documentation is provided by a 17th century Spanish *Theatro Moral* which gives descriptions of the scenes. Ott dates these tiles in the 1740's and suggests that they may be the work of the Portuguese Bartolomeo Antunes, who signed and dated in the year 1737 one of the tiles in the chancel of the adjacent church of S. Francisco.

The article opens with a brief account of the history of tile making from ancient times to the 18th century in Portugal. Father Ott points out the need for further study of the Portuguese industry, especially for its relation to Brazil. A valuable and very readable contribution.

Peixôto, Afrânio. A igreja de Nossa Senhora da Glória do Outeiro. Rio de Janeiro. Min. da educação e saúde. (Publ. do Serviço do patrimônio histórico e artístico nac., no. 10.) 59 p., 44 ilus., 1 plano, 1 debuxo. **[886**

An excellent monograph on an important church of Rio de Janeiro which is here attributed to the Portuguese military engineer, José Cardoso Ramalho and assigned to the second decade of the 18th century. The building, which has an octagonal plan closely related to those of several early churches in Minas Gerais, has been well restored by S.P.H.A.N. The introduction by Afrânio Peixoto analyses the published material on the church from contemporary accounts through the writings of 19th century European travelers and local historians. This is followed by a group of 24 fine reproductions of 19th century prints and paintings showing the church, brought together by the collector and custodian of N. S. da Glória, Dr. Raymundo de Castro Maya, a description of its careful restoration and finally photographs of the structure as it is today. A most valuable and useful publication.

PRESERVAÇÃO DE DUAS IGREJAS DO VELHO RIO (*Ilus. bras.*, ano 21, no. 100, agôsto, p. 8–9, 4 ilus.). **[887**

In addition to the church of S. Pedro dos Clérigos that of the Bom Jesús do Calvário begun in 1719 will be moved to make way for the Avenida Getúlio Vargas in Rio de Janeiro.

Reis, Arthur Cézar Ferreira. Das condições defensivas da capitania do Pará ao findar o século XVIII (*Rev. serv. patr. hist. art. nac.*, no. 7, p. 283–308). **[888**

Presents in its entirety a *Memória* of February 14, 1795 in the Biblioteca Pública of Belém, describing in detail the fortifications of the State of Pará during the administration of Captain-General D. Francisco Inocêncio de Sousa Coutinho. A number of forts are mentioned, information about their equipment is given, but there is really no discussion of their architecture.

REVISTA DO SERVIÇO DO PATRIMÔNIO HISTÓRICO E ARTÍSTICO NACIONAL, NO. 7. Rio de Janeiro. 340 p., 126 ilus. [889

A yearbook consisting of nine important monographs dealing principally with colonial art and architecture. These articles are separately listed in this section.

Rodrigues, José Wasth. Móveis antigos de Minas Gerais (*Rev. serv. patr. hist. art. nac.*, 7, p. 79-97, 18 debuxos). [890

Senhor Rodrigues, who has recently begun to publish measured drawings of details of the colonial architecture of São Paulo presents here a useful selection of well drawn designs of authentic beds, chests, wardrobes and tables of the 18th century found in Minas Gerais. They are accompanied by a graceful essay describing the contents of old houses in Mariana before antique hunting became an industry in Brazil. The author mentions some of the outstanding collectors in Minas Gerais.

Sepp, Antônio. Viagem as missões jesuíticas e trabalhos apostólicos. São Paulo. Ed. Martins. (Bibl. histórica bras., no. 11.) 256 p., 50 ilus. [891

This is a translation of the writings of an Austrian Jesuit who built the church at São João (Rio Grande do Sul) in 1698. The value of this edition for the art historian lies in its introduction by Wolfgang Hoffmann Harnisch and the photographs of Jesuit sculptures taken by his son.

Harnisch has brought together a good deal of valuable information on the early appearance of the now ruined Jesuit missions, especially that of São Miguel. He classifies the 200 or more statues made at these missions in 4 groups: (1) masterpieces by distinguished European craftsmen; (2) minor works; (3) statues that combine European and Indian features; (4) Indian production. Each photograph is accompanied by a judicious note giving dimensions and provenance of the piece and a stylistic analysis. Among the European sculptures Germanic and Italian influences predominate, for many of the Jesuit craftsmen had come from those countries. There are no distinctly Portuguese elements, Rio Grande do Sul having been added to Brazil only after the treaty of 1750 between Spain and Portugal. The architecture and sculptures of this region can only be considered Brazilian in a geographic sense. Spiritually and stylistically they are foreign to the Luso-Brazilian tradition.

Silva, Nogueira da. Mestre Valentim, o creador da escultura nacional (*Dom Casmurro*, no. 331-332, 25 dez., segundo cad., p. 7, 1 ilus.). [892

A well-worded tribute.

Smith, Marinobel. The colonial period in Brazilian art (*Think*, vol. 9, no. 1, Jan., p. 20, 43, 44, 12 illus.). [893

A general description of the richness and Portuguese flavor of Brazilian colonial art.

One statement, that there is French influence in the architecture of Maranhão, is challengeable.

Also published in *Brazil*, Feb., p. 12-13, 21; March, p. 8-9.

Sousa-Leão, Joaquim (filho). Brazilian colonial architecture (*Studio*, vol. 126, no. 606, Sept., p. 113-118, 11 illus.). [894

An attractive description of 18th century Brazilian architecture with some splendid illustrations.

———. Frans Post: a postscript (*Barlington mag.*, vol. 83, no. 486, Sept., p. 217, 3 illus.). [895

In this article the well known authority on the Dutch 17th century master examines some paintings by Post in English collections.

Taunay, Affonso de E. Galeria do Museu paulista; ruinas da capela de Antônio Raposo Tavares em Quitarina (*Jornal do commércio*, ano 117, no. 21, 24 out.). [896

Valuable discussions of a number of minor works of art in the gallery of São Paulo.

Trindade, Cônego Raimundo. A igreja de S. Francisco de Assis de Mariana (*Rev. serv. patr. hist. art. nac.*, no. 7, p. 57-76, 3 ilus.). [897

A valuable detailed history of the construction of one of the finest and best preserved of the eighteenth-century churches of Minas Gerais. It was compiled by an authority on the ecclesiastical history of Mariana from the original books of the local Third Order of St. Francis. The following are the most important presented.

In 1761 plans for the church by the architect José Pereira dos Santos were accepted. Work was begun in 1763, with José Pereira Arouca entrusted with the construction. In 1781 the latter modified the design of the towers and frontispiece. Work on the church was not completed until the 19th century. In the course of the undertaking Aleijadinho was invited to inspect the portals. This is of great importance because it indicates his preeminence in the carving of door frames and suggests that he really was the author of the portal of the church of the Third Order of St. Francis in Ouro Preto which is so abundantly apparent from stylistic evidence if not from documents. Manuel da Costa Ataíde, the best known colonial decorative painter of Minas, who also worked in the latter church, painted a hanging and colored and gilded certain figures in the church at Mariana during 1794 and 1795. The article also contains a great many names of craftsmen, in certain cases with indications of what they did and when.

This monograph, a pendant to one published by S.P.H.A.N. on the church of N. S. do Carmo in Sabará, (see *Handbook, no. 6, 1940*, item 657) calls for a second study analyzing the architecture of the building and treating in detail of the decoration on the basis of Cônego Trindade's findings. The author is curator of the recently opened Museu da Inconfidência at Ouro Preto.

Vauthier, Louis L. Casas de residência no Brasil (*Rev. serv. patr. hist. art. nac.*, no. 7, p. 98–208, 16 ilus.). [898

One of the great documents on the architecture and social history of the first half of the 19th century in the northeast of Brazil, this series of letters written in French by the engineer and architect Vauthier has been hidden for almost a hundred years in the Paris *Revue de l'Architecture et des Travaux Publics*. These letters have now been effectively translated into Portuguese by Vera Andrade, and, equipped with superlative notes by Gilberto Freyre, are published with the original illustrations. One of these, it is interesting to note, shows a house in Recife with its *muxarabí* or projecting wooden balcony. The stone supports for this balcony appear to be of the same sort still found in Pernambuco and discussed in item 883.

The letters deal in considerable detail with traditional building in Recife, Olinda and other parts of the State of Pernambuco and to some extent with Vauthier's own architecture.

In a brilliant introduction Senhor Freyre, who has written before on the diary of Vauthier, compares his accounts with those of other foreign visitors and brings to light new documents from the archives of Pernambuco relative to this French engineer who was in Recife from 1840 to 1846, where he exercised a profound influence.

UMA VISITA À IGREJA DE SÃO PEDRO (*Cultura política*, ano 3, no. 33, out., p. 218–224, 10 ilus.). [899

A reporter's account of the important Rio de Janeiro church of São Pedro dos Clérigos, completed in 1738 in circular form, which is to be moved to make way for the Avenida Getúlio Vargas. According to this article, the building, which has long been hidden by surrounding structures, will be set in a square of its own where its unusual, severe architecture will be visible from all directions.

NINETEENTH CENTURY

Almeida, Horácio de. Pedro Américo. Paraíba. A União, ed. 63 p., ilus. [900

Brief biographical sketch of the painter of Paraíba (1843–1905). [S. Putnam]

ANGELO AGOSTINI (*Rev. semana*, ano 44, no. 14, 3 abril, p. 24–25, 10 ilus.). [900a

A famous caricaturist (1843–1910), born in Piemonte, whose illustrations appeared in *Diabo Coxo* and *Cabrião* of São Paulo in 1864. In 1866 he came to Rio de Janeiro where he worked principally for the *Revista Illustrada* (1876–1896) but also for *Semana Illustrada, Mosquito, Dom Quichote, Malho,* and *Vida Fluminense*.

Antunes, Dioclécio de Paranhos. O pintor do romantismo. Vida e obra de Manoel de Araújo Pôrto-Alegre. Rio de Janeiro. Ed. Zélio Valverde. (Bibl. de grandes biografias, 3.) 238 p., 18 ilus. [901

An important biography of one of the founders of the nineteenth-century tradition of Brazilian art. Among other things Pôrto-Alegre was a painter, architect, art critic and Americanist whose career is full of surprises. He was probably the first art historian in the modern sense in South America. The value of this book lies chiefly in its wide use of old journals and newspapers to reveal minor aspects of Pôrto Alegre's accomplishment, in its attempt to make a catalog of his works of art and publications and in its large bibliography.

Buvelot, Louis-Auguste, and Louis-Auguste Moreau. Rio de Janeiro pitoresco. São Paulo. Ed. Martins. (Albuns do Brasil, no. 1). 19 ilus. [902

The first of a series of reprints of picturesque views of old buildings in Rio de Janeiro. Originally published between 1842 and 1845, these lithographs have always been considered among the rarest of 19th century *costumista* material and have long been esteemed for their usefulness in tracing the history of Brazilian architecture. Their reproduction here on coated paper is not quite as clear as one would wish. It would not be possible to make satisfactory photographs from them, which is an important criterion in judging reproductions of prints.

Francisco Marques dos Santos has contributed a short factual introduction which is as useful and as elegant as all his writing on 19th century Brazilian art.

O CARICATURISTA PEDRO AMÉRICO (*Rev. semana*, ano 44, no. 17, 24 abril, p. 16–18, 15 ilus.). [903

A little known aspect of the painter's work was his caricatures for the Rio de Janeiro journal *Comédia Social* of the 1870's. The article reproduces some of the charming sketches of young girls and old women that are so closely related in arrangement to Goya and in style to Gavarni and Constantin Guys. There is also illustrated a caricature self-portrait made by the artist in 1867, which is now at the Museu Nacional de Belas Artes.

Chamberlain, Henry. Vistas e costumes da cidade do Rio de Janeiro em 1819–1820. Segundo desenhos feitos pelo Tte. Chamberlain, da artilharia real, durante os anos de 1819 a 1820, com descrições. Tradução e prefácio de Rubens Borba de Moraes. Com o texto do original inglês. Rio de Janeiro. Livr. Kosmos. (Col. de temas brasileiras, vol. 1.) 235 p., 42 ilus. [904

This is a reprint of one of the handsomest collections of colored prints of early 19th century Brazil. The reproduction is quite good.

Gomes, Tapajoz. Artistas de outros tempos: M. Teixeira da Rocha (*Ilus. bras.*, ano 21, no. 99, julho, p. 38–39, 4 ilus.). [905

Brief notes, with good photographs, on a little known genre painter and impressionist (b. 1863 in Alagôas) on the occasion of an exhibit of his work at the Museu Nacional de Belas Artes.

INTERIORES DO PALÁCIO DO CATETE ONDE FOI HOSPEDADO O PRESIDENTE DA BOLÍVIA (*Ilus. bras.*, ano 21, no. 99, julho, p. 28-29, 4 ilus.). [906
Excellent photographs by Carlos of the 19th century neo-classic palace.

Lobato, Monteiro. Pedro Américo (*Rev. semana*, ano 44, no. 17, 24 abril, p. 24-25, 4 ilus.). [907
He is here presented as a victim of 19th century academism. Yet the author singles out his *Ipiranga*, one of Américo's most conventional canvases, as his finest work.

Oliveira, J. M. Cardoso de. Pedro Américo; sua vida e suas obras. Ed. especial comemorativa do centenário do seu nascimento, reimpressão da primitiva, revista e completada pelo autor. Rio de Janeiro. Imp. nacional. 203 p., 36 ilus. [908
A new edition of a biography by a friend of the artist brought out to commemorate the anniversary of Américo's birth. The text appears to be the same, but many well reproduced illustrations have been added. The book is full of anecdotes about the glamorous painter and *littérateur*, who is chiefly known for his large battle pictures, but who was equally renowned for a long series of sentimental figure pieces and religious canvases. What criticism there is in the book is lyrical praise of Américo, the romantic expatriate who lived in Paris and Florence. The work, which was originally published in 1898, is valuable both as a source of information and as an example of late nineteenth-century Brazilian art history. Many of the illustrations represent little known works by Pedro Américo in the possession of Ambassador Cardoso de Oliveira.

Rêgo, José Lins do. Notas sôbre Pedro Américo (*Rev. semana*, ano 44, no. 17, 24 abril, p. 23, 3 ilus., 1 de color). [909
The distinguished novelist and Américo's compatriot discounts the battles and allegories and praises a few portraits by the painter which are little known and esteemed. A sensitive self-portrait of 1895 is illustrated.

Santos, Francisco Marques dos. O casamento de Dom Pedro II (*Estud. bras.*, ano 5, vol. 10, no. 29-30, março-junho, p. 166-222, 6 ilus.). [910
In the course of a brilliant essay on Dom Pedro II's wedding, filled with delectable social details taken from diaries and newspapers of the day, the author has supplied notes on the artists who pictured the Empress and her voyage from Naples, lithographs of the pair, medals, triumphal arches and similar architecture *de gala*.

Little by little in his publications in this journal and others Francisco Marques dos Santos is telling the story of Brazilian painting, sculpture and minor arts in relation to the two emperors. He is a keen critic with a gifted pen and his descriptions are not only precious historically, but make delightful reading. It is to be hoped that they will be brought together some day in the form of a volume on nineteenth-century Brazilian art.

———. Contrastes de prateiros no Rio de Janeiro (*Estud. bras.*, ano 5, vol. 10, no. 29-30, março-junho, p. 289-290, 2 ilus.). [911
More hall marks with the names of silversmiths who used them and the addresses of these craftsmen between 1841 and 1880.

Smith, Robert C. The imperial family of Brazil in 1831 (*Gazette des beaux-arts*, series 6, vol. 23, no. 911, Jan., p. 49-56, 6 illus.). [912
An English version of an article on 4 portraits by Simplício de Sá now in the Oliveira Lima collection, Catholic University of America (*Handbook*, no. 8, *1942*, item 908). The new version has more illustrations and is accompanied by notes.

Taunay, Affonso de E. Miguel Arcanjo Benício Dutra e sua obra (*Ilus. bras.*, ano 21, no. 93, jan., p. 6-7, 3 ilus.). [913
An interesting "primitive" who died at Piracicaba (São Paulo) in 1875, Dutra was a piano maker who painted a series of views of *fazendas*, examples of which, dated 1835 and 1840, are illustrated.

———. Velhos panoramas de São Paulo (*Ilus. bras.*, ano 21, no. 98, junho, p. 11, 2 ilus.). [914
Of particular interest is the delightful view by A.-J. Pallière in the collection J. F. (Yan) de Almeida Prado.

VIAGEM FLUVIAL DO TIETÊ AO AMAZONAS DE 1825 A 1829. São Paulo. Ed. Melhoramentos. 1943? 218 p., 112 ilus., 8 de color. [915
Hercules Florence, a French artist who accompanied the Baron von Langsdorff expedition into the interior of Brazil as second draughtsman (Amado Adriano Taunay was the first), left a diary and a large number of pencil drawings and water colors of the landscapes and Indians he saw. This is the first time they have been made available in good reproductions which permit careful study of the extremely delicate and detailed observations of this artist, whose landscapes often resemble in technique those of Turner. His pictures of Indians refuse to be "dated." They are as modern as Portinari's. Indeed this wealth of material is a natural link between the paintings and drawings of the Dutch group of the seventeenth century and the numerous artists like Portinari, Alfredo Guigard and Percy Lau who are today recording the appearance of Brazil in much the same way as Florence and Taunay did over a century ago. Several of the latter's sketches are included among the illustrations.

The book bears no imprint date but seems to have appeared either in 1943 or 1944. It is here assigned arbitrarily to 1943.

A VIDA CINEMATOGRÁFICA DE PEDRO AMÉRICO (*Rev. semana*, ano 44, no. 17, 24 abril, p. 20–21, 4 ilus.). [916
A good biography of the painter of Paraíba (1843–1905). The town of Areia, where he was born, is illustrated.

MODERN

(*See also item* 4159)

AMAZONIA BY MARIA. New York. Valentine gallery. March 22. 16 illus. [917
A portfolio of plates of sculpture representing figures from the folklore of the Amazon by Maria Martins. These bronzes in various sizes have rough uneven surfaces that suggest clay models. Around the totem-like figures are spun the complicated forms of tropical tree trunks, vines and flowers in a highly original fashion. A brief text by Jorge Zarur relates the legends associated with the figures.

ARCHITECTURE OF BRAZIL (*Architect. record*, vol. 93, no. 1, Jan., p. 34–56, 50 illus.). [918
A large section of Brazil builds is here presented in a new layout.

A ARTE DO PORTINARI (*Rumo*, terceira fase, ano 1, vol. 1, no. 2, terceiro trim., p. 86–89, 2 ilus.). [919
After general comments on Portinari's recent exhibition it is announced that he will teach at the Casa do Estudante in Rio de Janeiro and decorate the building.

A ARTE HARMONIOSA DE MARQUES JÚNIOR (*Rev. semana*, ano 44, no. 21, 22 maio, p. 2, 7 ilus.). [920
Reproductions of portraits, landscapes, and still life.

ARTES E ARTISTAS (*Ilus. bras.*, ano 21, no. 98, junho, p. 34–35, 5 ilus.; no. 100, agôsto, p. 22, 1 ilus.). [921
The first article is a bitter attack on "modernist art," using as its point of departure the government sponsored exhibition of Lasar Segall. The second article contains notes on the exhibit of the sculptor J. B. Ferri.

Avila, Jefferson. Antônio Parreiras (*Jornal do commércio*, ano 117, no. 21, 24 out.). [922
A brief, but succinct biography of one of the most esteemed of modern landscape painters whose home in Niterói has recently become a museum.

Boavista, Paulo T. Modern architecture (*Studio*, vol. 126, no. 606, Sept., p. 121–129, 14 illus.). [923
A vivid account by a young engineer of what has been achieved in Brazil. Photographs from Brazil builds.

BRAZIL BUILDS (*Jour. roy. inst. British architects*, third series, vol. 50, no. 7, May, p. 155–158, 14 illus.). [924
This review of Mr. Goodwin's book is typical of the enthusiastic reception it received in England. A special note is made of the technical competence of Brazilian builders.

BRAZILIAN ARCHITECTURE: LIVING AND BUILDING BELOW THE EQUATOR (*New pencil points*, vol. 1, no. 1, Jan., p. 55–64, 26 illus.). [925
A number of handsome pages of photographs, plans and elevations of the Pampulha buildings, the Rio Press Building, and the Instituto Vital Brazil in Niterói assembled from the photographs of G. E. Kidder Smith and text of Philip Goodwin.

Callado, A. C. Brazilian sculpture (*Studio*, vol. 126, no. 606, Sept., p. 132–134, 5 illus.). [926
A journalist's article, loosely written. Many names are mentioned, but sculpture is seen to culminate with V. Brécheret and Maria Martins.

O CASINO ATLÂNTICO EM SUA NOVA TEMPORADA (*Ilus. bras.*, ano 21, no. 98, junho, p. 41, 3 ilus.). [927
Photographs of a newly redecorated Rio de Janeiro night club. The elegant restaurant recalls in certain details that of the Statler Hotel in Washington.

Chateaubriand, Assis. Anabase (*O jornal*, 15 set.). [928
A sparkling address at the inauguration of Portinari's new São Paulo frescoes in which the speaker pointed out an "about face" of the painter not only in technique but in subject matter.

50 ANOS DE VIDA ARTÍSTICA E BOÊMIA (*Rev. semana*, ano 44, no. 16, 17 abril, p. 20–21, 7 ilus.). [929
On a retrospective exhibition of paintings and drawings by Hélios Selinger.

Estrada, Gonzaga-Duque. Pedro Américo (*Rev. semana*, ano 44, no. 17, 24 abril, p. 26–29, 8 ilus.). [930
Republication of a critique published on the painter's death in 1905. Several of his paintings in the Cardoso de Oliveira collection are illustrated.

Etchegoyen, Félix E. Pintura brasileira (*Jornal do commércio*, ano 116, no. 234, 7 julho). [931
Remarks on the occasion of the exhibition in the Galería Moody in Buenos Aires of 75 modern Brazilian paintings organized by Paul Biró. The speaker stresses the fabulous landscapes of the group, so typical of Brazil, and singles out several for measured, academic praise. This is fitting in as much as the exhibit was almost entirely the work of conservative academic painters. The paintings later visited Lima, where they were shown by the Sociedad "Entre Nous" during September.

EXPOSIÇÃO DE AZULEJOS DA OSIRARTE DE SÃO PAULO NO MUSEU NACIONAL DE BELAS ARTES DO RIO DE JANEIRO DE 13 A 27 DE JULHO DE

1943. Rio de Janeiro. Museu nac. de belas artes. Folder, 1 ilus. [932
This is the catalog of an exhibition of glazed tiles representing Brazilian landscape and folklore subjects by Paulo Rossi Osir. This artist of São Paulo was commissioned by the Ministério da Educação e Saúde to develop a technique for colored tiles similar to that used in colonial work. He states in his introduction that he was unable to reproduce exactly the characteristic 18th century blue which he believes the Portuguese prepared from a cobalt imported by them from Angola. He has, however, achieved a satisfactory substitute. These tiles, freed of the cliché subjects which so long hampered the industry in Brazil, promise an unusual and important vehicle for modern painters.

EXPOSIÇÃO JOSÉ MARIA DE ALMEIDA (*Rev. semana*, ano 44, no. 25, 19 junho, p. 23, 6 ilus.). [933
Contained some interesting paintings of modern Rio de Janeiro.

Fanda, Lorenzo. Sólo esperamos la oportunidad! dijo el arquitecto Félix Sánchez B. en su plática de la exposición "Brasil construye" (*Excelsior*, México, año 27, tomo 4, no. 9,497, 25 julio, segunda sección, p. 5, 2 ilus.). [934
Speech made at the opening of the exhibition Brazil builds at the Palacio de Bellas Artes in Mexico.

Gomes, Tapajoz. O carnaval na pintura brasileira (*Ilus. bras.*, ano 21, no. 94, fev., p. 18–20, 9 ilus., 1 de color). [936
Paintings by Rodolfo Chambelland, Armando Vianna, Haydea Santiago, Manuel Faria, Santa Rosa, Jurandyr Paes Leme, Euclides Fonseca, and Gilberto Trompowski, are illustrated.

———. São Paulo e a pintura brasileira (*Ilus. bras.*, ano 21, no. 104, dez., p. 56–58, 8 ilus.). [937
A choice of the works of a number of painters of São Paulo.

Goodwin, Philip L. New architecture at Belo Horizonte, Brazil (*Magazine of art*, vol. 36, no. 3, March, p. 90–93, 9 ilus.). [938
A detailed description of Oscar Niemeyer's three pleasure buildings which the author finds "full of variety and charm." He criticizes only the weak design of some decorative tiles in the casino. It is Mr. Goodwin's opinion that modern architecture cannot live on "functionalism" alone and must seek decorative expedients of an original character to relieve its monotony. These he finds in such characteristic motives of the new Brazilian architecture as the flaring concrete ramps.

Honig, Edwin. Portinari's New World murals (*New Mexico quart. rev.*, vol. 12, no. 1, spring, p. 5–9, 2 illus.). [939
A fine description of the murals in the Hispanic Foundation in the Library of Congress.

O INTERVENTOR AMARAL PEIXOTO E SEUS AUXILIARES DE GOVÊRNO VISITAM O INSTITUTO DE RESSEGUROS DO BRASIL (*Ilus. bras.*, ano 21, no. 100, agôsto, p. 37, 7 ilus.). [940
Photographs of interiors of an interesting new building in Rio de Janeiro.

LASAR SEGALL. MANGUE. Rio de Janeiro. Ed. Rev. acadêmica. 46 lâms. [941
This is a portfolio of reproductions of drawings and watercolors together with an original lithograph and three woodcuts, all signed by the artist. Made in 1924, these works all relate to a disreputable quarter of Rio de Janeiro known as the Mangue. They are excellent examples of Segall's early Brazilian production.

Machado, Anibal M. A arte de Lasar Segall (*Rumo*, terceira fase, ano 1, vol. 1, no. 2, terceiro trim., p. 53–59). [942
A profound series of remarks about art made on June 5, 1943 on the occasion of the closing of the Lasar Segall exhibition in Rio de Janeiro. Machado writes of the precarious position of the modern painter, of the power of penetrating representation over the public and of the career of Segall. For him the war has brought a return of melancholy moods and subjects after the gay sunlit years in Brazil. In closing Machado deplores the protests against modern art which this exhibition provoked.

Ministério da educação e saúde. Lasar Segall. Rio de Janeiro. 47 p., 12 ilus. [943
The current work of this fine painter was presented in an exhibition sponsored by the Ministério da Educação e Saúde. The handsome catalog contains good reproductions, many press notices and an essay by Mário de Andrade, which is an extremely sensitive appraisal of Segall's evolution. One is inclined to accept his interpretation of some of the painter's attitudes rather than those of Paul Fierens.

O MONUMENTO AO BARÃO DO RIO BRANCO (*Ilus. bras.*, ano 21, no. 102, out., p. 4–8, 13 ilus.). [944
Publishes photographs of the monument consisting of colossal figure standing before an obelisk. There are two high relief panels showing diplomatic triumphs of the great statesman and a cascade with conventional water gods. The monument, the work of the sculptor H. Leão Veloso and the arquitect A. da Rocha Miranda, was recently dedicated.

Nunes, Osório. Que nome deve ter o movimento surgido com a "Semana de arte moderna"? (*Dom Casmurro*, 5 fev.). [945
Prof. Figueira de Almeida suggests "*brasilianismos*," while Augusto Frederico Schmidt wants no new term. Others vote for "expressionism" or "Clube do que já estava feito."

PAULO ROSSI RETOMA, NO BRASIL, COM UM SENTIDO EMINENTEMENTE NACIONAL, A ARTE DO AZULEJO (*A Manhã*, 13 julho). [946
In an interview the distinguished painter of São Paulo describes his experiments to

revive the Portuguese colonial art of painting scenes on enameled tiles. Since receiving a commission to decorate a part of the new Ministry of Education building with a composition of tiles several years ago, Senhor Rossi has developed some 82 subjects. See also *Handbook, no. 7, 1941,* item 720.

Pinto, Almir. Raimundo Brandão Cela (*Rev. semana,* ano 44, no. 25, 19 junho, p. 28–29, 6 ilus.). [947
An artist who since winning the European travel fellowship in 1917 has preferred to remain in his native Ceará painting *costumista* sketches of great charm.

Rubens, Carlos. The history of painting in Brazil. Rio de Janeiro. Imprensa nacional. (Ministry of state for foreign affairs, Division of intellectual cooperation, résumé no. 3.) 47 p. [948
This is a condensation in English of the author's *Pequena História da Pintura Brasileira* (*Handbook no. 7, 1941,* item 752). The translation is at times awkward.

Rudofsky, Bernard. On architecture and architects (*New pencil points,* vol. 1, no. 4, April, p. 62–64, 4 illus.). [949
A brilliant address delivered at a Brazilian symposium in the Boston Museum of Art, Philip Goodwin presiding. The speaker, one of the outstanding architects of São Paulo, explains the early dependency of contemporary Brazilian architects on Italy, the official character of much of their work, methods of work, importance of climate and a number of other factors to be taken into consideration when discussing modern architecture in Brazil. The illustrations attempt to show the inferiority of United States official architecture to that of Brazil. A different choice might have been more effective.

QUARENTA FIGURAS DE SEIS METROS DE ALTURA IMORTALIZANDO A AUDÁCIA DOS BANDEIRANTES (*Ilus. bras.,* ano 21, no. 104, dez., p. 27, 2 ilus.). [950
Details of the enormous monument to the Bandeirantes of São Paulo now being executed by Victor Brécheret are described and illustrated.

O SALÃO DE BELAS ARTES (*Ilus. bras.,* ano 21, no. 102, out., p. 25–27, 5 ilus.; no. 103, nov., p. 35–37, 12 ilus.). [951
First part is a general report of exhibitors before the award of prizes. Second part concerns the first prize won by J. J. Rescala's *Aguas,* a *costumista* scene of Ceará, and the second prize won by Armando Pacheco with a protrait.

Seth. O Brasil pela imagem. Desenhos de Seth (Álvaro Marins). Rio de Janeiro. Ed. Indústria do livro. 188 p. [952

Smith, Robert C. Murals by Cândido Portinari in the Hispanic Foundation of the Library of Congress. Washington. U. S. government printing office. 31 p., 8 illus. [953
Contains a biography of the artist, a bibliography, the history of this Washington commission and a description of the murals.

Teódulo, José. O momento é para arquitetura (*Cultura política,* ano 3 no. 29, julho, p. 96–98). [954
As a result of the interest of the Museum of Modern Art, contemporary Brazilian architecture is justified, according to the author, who explains some of its characteristics.

TIPOS E ASPECTOS DO BRASIL (*Rev. bras. geog.,* ano 5, no. 1, jan.–março, p. 279–282, 2 ilus.; no. 2, abril–junho, p. 127–130, 2 ilus.). [955
An interesting new series of regional drawings by the distinguished draughtsman, Percy Lau. They represent *rendeiras do nordeste, carnaubais, ervais, ervateiros.*

WATERCOLORS BY GEORGE WAMBACH (*Dom Casmurro,* no. 331–332, 25 dez., primeiro cad., 5 ilus. de color). [956
A series of watercolors of well known buildings in Rio de Janeiro made in 1939 and reproduced in color illustrate this section of the paper.

ECONOMICS: GENERAL

(See also item 121)

ACCIÓN COOPERATIVA. Órgano de la Superintendencia nacional de cooperativas. Bogotá. Año 1, no. 1, mayo—. [957

Aguirre González, Juan Manuel. Situación y perspectivas para la organización del intercambio comercial interamericano. Montevideo. Tall. gráf. del Banco de la República oriental del Uruguay. 61, 35 p., cuads. [958
Examines the pattern of inter-American commerce and suggests means whereby such trade may be encouraged. The author argues that since Europe will not be able to regain her pre-war position in the markets of the Western Hemisphere, a new economic equilibrium in the continent must be looked for.
The study is followed by an extensive statistical appendix. [Ed.]

Alarcón M., Adolfo. La guerra y el comercio de exportación de productos agropecuarios de Latino-América (Estadística, vol. 1, no. 1, March, p. 119–131). [959
Studies the effect of the World War upon the agricultural exports of the Latin American countries, particularly for the years 1939 and 1940. [Ed.]

Antonioletti, Mario. Panorama económico. El sistema cooperativo en el mundo de hoy y de mañana (Econ. finan., año 7, no. 85, nov., p. 4–12). [960
Includes brief notes on cooperatives in Argentina, Colombia and Chile. [Ed.]

Barcos, Julio R. Segunda etapa de la emancipación americana (Atenea, año 20, tomo 71, no. 213, marzo, p. 181–214). [961
Proposes an economic union of Chile, Argentina, Paraguay, Uruguay and Bolivia to form a Federation of the South. Mexico, Peru and the Caribbean might form a Federation of the Center. These with Brazil and the United States of America might be prepared to establish a continental customs union. [Ed.]

Behrendt, Richard F. Inter-American economic cooperation problems, recent developments and prospects; a syllabus. Third ed., revised. Albuquerque. Univ. of New Mexico. 31 p. [962
Contains Latin-American trade data and statistics.

———. Inter-American economy and postwar reconstruction (World affairs, vol. 106, no. 1, March, p. 53–58). [963
Inter-American economic cooperation during the war shows what can be achieved by a larger program of world-wide economic cooperation in the postwar period. The author enters a strong plea for the establishment of a world-wide, truly international economy after the war, rather than a hemisphere bloc, as the best means of insuring economic progress in the western hemisphere as well as elsewhere. [S. Mosk]

———. Land for the people. Toward greater economic stability. Albuquerque. Univ. of New Mexico. 23 p. [964
Land for the People. A good analysis of the economic, social, and political problems arising out of latifundismo in Latin America. The necessary land reforms should proceed by peaceful and gradual means, and they should be adapted to the social and physical conditions found in each country.
Toward Greater Economic Stability. An interesting statement of characteristic economic features in Latin America. Major trends in current economic transition are 1) diversification of export products, 2) expansion of production for domestic markets, 3) nationalistic policies. The author points out dangers inherent in these trends, and reaches the conclusion that economic progress and higher standards of living in Latin America can best be attained by full participation in a relatively free (but somewhat "planned") world economy. [S. Mosk]

Bellegarde, Dantès. Organisation et la solidarité économique interaméricaine (Proc. eighth amer. scien. cong., vol. 10, p. 115–124). [965
The eminent Haitian statesman proposes the setting up of a permanent inter-American agency of economic coordination, looking forward to the day when an all-American customs union may be established. [B. Wood]

Belzoni, Guido C. Las vías férreas internacionales en América del Sud (Bol. asoc. internac. perm., año 27, no. 80, set.–oct., p. 11–42). [966
After presenting general considerations and charts dealing with the development of railroads in various countries of America, the author lists and comments briefly upon the following international railroads: Colombia-Venezuela, Peru-Bolivia, Chile-Peru, Chile-Bolivia, Argentina-Bolivia, Bolivia-Brazil, Chile-Argentina, Argentina-Paraguay, and Argentina-Brazil. [A. Dorfman]

Bidwell, Percy W. Good neighbors in the war, and after (For. affs., vol. 21, no. 3, April, p. 524–534). [967
A well-informed survey of economic good-neighborism during the war. The problem of the regional, as compared to the uni-

versalist trend of United States policy is discussed in a manner which suggests the argument of Professor Whitaker in item no. 3516. [Bryce Wood]

BOLETÍN DEL INSTITUTO SUDAMERICANO DEL PETRÓLEO. Montevideo. Vol. 1, no. 1, abril—. [968
Contains a notice about the constitution and functions of the Institute, general information concerning petroleum industry in South America, notes on Uruguay and Argentina. December issue (vol. 1, no. 2) contains notes on Colombia, Argentina, Bolivia, Uruguay and Ecuador. [A. Dorfman]

Brand, Donald D. Latin America as a source of strategic materials (*L. A. social econ. trans.*, p. 53–72). [969
A compact survey of Latin American resources, including foodstuffs, for the supply of materials vital to the war effort. [S. Mosk]

Bryan, C. R. Natives' return—Many Western-hemisphere products, once world migrants, feel again the stimulus of heightened effort in America (*For. com. weekly*, vol. 11, no. 11, June 12, p. 8–9, 38–39). [970
The "rebirth of production" in the Americas of many products native to them, namely rubber, kapok, henequen and sisal, cassava, cocoa, capsicum plants, quinine, vanilla, cashews, and peanuts. [Ed.]

Carson, James S. The post-war significance of our loans and investments in Latin America (*Export trade and shipper*, vol. 47, no. 17, May 31, p. 3–5, 16, 18–19). [972
Advocates industrialization of Latin America as one way of developing foreign markets for United States manufactures. Industrialization will require large scale dollar financing which, the author believes, should be done through private enterprise. [Ed.]

Chalmers, Henry. Wartime controls and stimuli upon the foreign trade of Latin America (*For. com. weekly*, vol. 11, no. 4, April 24, p. 3–5, 37). [973
Discusses Latin American import and export controls, limitations on inter-American trade because of shortages of shipping, and the United States decentralization plan. [Ed.]

Colombia. Federación nacional de cafeteros. Informe del gerente al XIII Congreso nacional de cafeteros, junio de 1943. Bogotá. Ed. Antena. 216 p. [974
Report contains data on the inter-American agreement on coffee export quotas, the coffee warehouses, Colombian coffee in Argentina, Chile and Uruguay, the Pan American Coffee Bureau, and rural health activities.

Consejo permanente de asociaciones americanas de comercio y producción. Contenido económico de las constituciones de América. Montevideo. 117 p. [975
Largely a compilation of pertinent passages in the constitutions of the twenty-one American Republics arranged by topics and countries. The principal topics are: private property, industry and commerce, freedom of movement and communications, money and banking, public finance, public debts, natural resources, public service, economic activities of the state, and labor. [Ed.]

———. Encuesta continental sobre el consumo de productos de alimentación y vestido y sobre la vivienda popular. Respuesta-tipo referente a la república de Chile. Montevideo. 155 p. [976
A detailed study of consumption of foodstuffs, clothing and of low cost housing in Chile prepared at the request of the Permanent Council. The study considers the degree of underconsumption, examines the principal causes and lists some of the measures devised to improve existing conditions. [Ed.]

———. Comisión ejecutiva. Plan de trabajo de la Comisión ejecutiva. Acta de la primera sesión celebrada por la misma los días 9 y 10 de diciembre de 1942. Montevideo. 87 p. [977
Contains in an appendix resolutions of the Conferencia Americana de Asociaciones de Comercio y Producción held in Montevideo in 1941 as revised and expanded by the first plenary session of the Council.

¿CONVIENE APOYAR LA CREACIÓN DE UN BANCO INTERAMERICANO? (*Acción económica*, año 3, no. 33, julio, p. 11–13). [978
The establishment of an inter-American Bank is advised, and its different functions are sketched. The article stresses the necessity for economic cooperation. [A. Dorfman]

Council of the corporation of foreign bondholders. Sixty-ninth annual report, for the year ending December 31, 1942. London. 1943. Williams, Lea, publ. 90 p., tables. [979
Contains information on external debt operations and agreements of several Latin American countries. [S. Mosk]

Dewey, L. H. Fiber production in the Western Hemisphere. Washington. U. S. Department of agriculture. (Misc. publ. no. 518.) 95 p. [980
Spanish edition of this material issued as: *Fibras Vegetales y Su Producción en Américas*. Translated by María A. Ruisánchez Masters. Unión Panamericana, Oficina de Cooperación Agrícola (Publ. agr., nos. 137–140). 101 p.

Dorfman, Adolfo. Etapas del desarrollo industrial de América Latina (*Rev. prob. arg. amer.*, no. 2, julio, p. 53–61). [981
Summary of a book published by the author concerning the development of

manufacturing industries in Latin America. [A. Dorfman]

——. La técnica y la economía (*Ciencia y técnica*, vol. 100, no. 492, p. 497–502). [982

The relation between the study of engineering and economics.

ESTADÍSTICA. Journal of the Inter-American statistical institute. México, D. F. Vol. 1, no. 1, March—. [983

First volume of the quarterly journal of the Inter American Statistical Institute. This publication is intended to be primarily a forum for the discussion of problems encountered by statisticians and governmental statistical agencies, and consequently most of the articles deal with techniques and methods of compiling and analyzing statistical data. Notes on statistical developments and publications in the various American countries are given in each issue. Articles are published in Spanish, English, Portuguese, or French. [S. Mosk]

Fabra Ribas, A. The cooperative movement in Latin America: its significance in hemisphere solidarity. Transl. by Ann Light. Introd. by Richard F. Behrendt. Albuquerque. Univ. of New Mexico. (Inter-American short papers, 3.) 62 p. [984

A well-known authority takes an optimistic view of the future of the cooperative movement in Latin America, for which a favorable basis already exists in legislation and national policies. Recommends a program of student exchange among centers for the study of cooperation in the Americas, which will promote a wholesome hemispheric solidarity as well as bring about an expansion in the cooperative movement. [S. Mosk]

——. Hacia un nuevo orden económico (*Univ. Antioquia*, tomo 15, no. 59–60, julio–agosto, p. 329–343). [985

A sturdy plea for the extension of the Cooperative Movement in various sectors of economic life, as the best means of achieving social welfare within a framework of democracy. [S. Mosk]

Galarza, Ernesto. Labor trends and social welfare in Latin America, 1941 and 1942. Washington. Pan American union, Div. of labor and social information. 153 p., processed. [986

Includes such topics as cost and standard of living, labor and wages in agriculture, popular restaurants, and land settlement in the various countries.

García Montes, Oscar. Necesidad de una organización económica interamericana para asegurar la solidaridad continental (*Proc. eighth amer. scien. cong.*, vol. 11, p. 49–57). [987

A very general statement of the advantages that may be expected to result from setting up inter-American consultative machinery on economic questions. [S. Mosk]

Girón Cerna, Carlos. La nueva paz del indio. México, D. F. Primer congreso demográfico interamericano. 24 p. [988

Suggests measures to implement and extend the various policies recommended by the Pátzcuaro Congress, for the economic and social improvement of indigenous peoples in the Americas. The author properly emphasizes the relation between the economic problems of the indigenous groups and the general economic problems of Latin America. [S. Mosk]

Haag, Alfred H. A quarter century of ocean transport between the United States and other American republics (*Proc. eighth amer. scien. cong.*, vol. 11, p. 161–168). [989

The situation of ocean shipping since the outbreak of the First World War is studied in a rather general way. The establishment of a strong network of maritime services is advocated. [A. Dorfman]

Hall, Melvin. Intercontinental air transportation (*Proc. eighth amer. scien. cong.*, vol. 11, p. 151–159). [990

Mainly a summary of the development of air traffic between the United States and Latin America, with an optimistic outlook on future air transport for freight, as well as passengers and mail. [S. Mosk]

Harris, Seymour E. Price control as a hemisphere problem (*Mex. amer. rev.*, vol. 11, no. 7, July, p. 42–43). [991

Contends that export price control has made it impossible for United States exporters to charge excessively high prices for goods shipped to Latin America; lack of adequate controls in the importing countries, therefore, is responsible for such prices. Published in *For. com. weekly*, vol. 11, no. 7, May 15, 1943. [S. Mosk]

——. Price control in South America (*For. com. weekly*, vol. 13, no. 4, Oct. 23, p. 12–13, 42). [991a

Complementando el anterior artículo (item 991) el autor presenta una encuesta personal acerca de las causas de la "seria situación" de los precios en América del Sur.

Texto español en *Rev. econ.*, México, vol. 6, no. 11, 30 nov., p. 21–24. [G. A. Rohen y Gálvez]

Haussmann, Frederick. Latin American oil in war and peace (*For. affs.*, vol. 21, no. 2, Jan., p. 354–361). [992

New kinds of arrangements, involving compromises on both sides, are needed between foreign oil companies and Latin American governments, in order to insure further development of the industry without prejudice to economic and social conditions in the countries concerned. [S. Mosk]

Horne, Bernardino C. La agricultura y la economía en el continente americano (*Rev. prob. arg. amer.*, no. 2, julio, p. 49–52). [993

Stresses the importance of closer economic cooperation of the countries of the

American continent. Broader markets in the Western Hemisphere for foodstuffs and other agricultural products provides the proper basis for sustained prosperity of all. [Ed.]

Inter-American financial and economic advisory committee. Actas de las sesiones del Comité consultivo económico financiero interamericano. Vol. 18, de la Sesión ordinaria no. 106 del 11 de febrero de 1943 a la Sesión ordinaria no. 115 del 5 de agosto de 1943. Washington. Unión panamericana. v, p. 2207-2337. [994

Reports and minutes of discussions covering a wide range of economic questions. [S. Mosk]

——. Handbook of its organization and activities, 1939-1943. Washington. 1943? 117 p. [995

Also published in Spanish: "Manual de su organización y actividades, 1939-1943."

Inter-American statistical institute. The Inter-American statistical institute. Its origin, organization, and objectives. Second ed. Washington, D. C. Census bureau, 48 p. [996

Contains a summary of organization, activities and publications, statutes, a list of members, and committees. Text in English, Spanish, and Portuguese.

Lecron, James D. Cooperative movement in South America (*Commer. Amer.*, vol. 40, no. 1, July, p. 13-14, 19). [998

A brief but informative sketch of the principal developments of a cooperative character. [S. Mosk]

Lorwin, L. L. Postwar plans of the United Nations. New York. Twentieth century fund. 307 p. [999

Outlines agricultural plans of farmers' organizations in the United States and of the United States Government, as well as those of the British Government and the Governments-in-Exile, Latin American countries, Canada, Australia, New Zealand, the Union of South Africa, India, China, and the U. S. S. R.

McClintock, John C. Food for the Americas (*For. com. weekly*, vol. 10, no. 8, Feb. 20, p. 3-5, 11, illus.). [1000

Un "panorama hemisférico" de los problemas, reajustes y objetivos derivados de la guerra en relación con el intercambio de productos alimenticios en América Latina. [G. A. Rohen y Gálvez]

Mac-Lean y Estenós, Roberto. El primer congreso demográfico inter-americano (*Letras*, Lima, no. 26, tercer cuatrimestre, p. 292-325). [1001

Account of the work of the First Interamerican Population Congress, with particular reference to racial problems. Resolutions introduced by the Peruvian delegation are given special attention. [Ed.]

McQueen, Charles A. Latin America postwar monetary standards. New York. The Monetary standards inquiry. 23 p. [1002

A brief survey of monetary experiences of the Latin American Republics. Because of the specific problems facing these countries the author suggests the advisability of establishing an institution along the lines of the proposed Inter-American Bank. [Ed.]

Maffry, August. Foreign trade classification problems of the American Republics (*Estadística*, vol. 1, no. 3, Sept., p. 108-114). [1003

Indicates typical purposes for which foreign trade statistics are used; purposes, obviously, must guide countries in adopting classification systems. [S. Mosk]

Márquez Blasco, Javier. Bloques económicos y excedentes de exportación. México. Banco de México. (Informaciones económicas, 1). 87 p. [1004

A thoughtful study of the problem of customs unions in the Western Hemisphere. The author points to the many economic difficulties which stand in the way of the realization of customs unions in general, and especially in the Western Hemisphere. [Ed.]

Migone, Raúl C., and Marcelo F. Aberastury. Introducción a los cuadros de computaciones estadísticas sobre el crecimiento argentino (*Proc. eighth amer. scien. cong.*, vol. 11, p. 197-201). [1006

A table comprising figures related to production, industries, trade, transports, demography, finance covering the period from 1914 through 1938. [A. Dorfman]

Moore, R. E. Inter-American advance through collaboration (*Land pol. rev.*, vol. 6, no. 2, summer, p. 16-19). [1007

Inter-American cooperation in the field of agriculture and the agreements for the establishment of cooperative agricultural development stations.

——. What shall the Americas grow? (*Agric. Americas*, vol. 3, May, p. 83-85). [1008

Agricultural collaboration between the Americas.

Mortara, Giorgio. Estudos de demografia interamericana (*Estadística*, vol. 1, no. 3, Sept., p. 65-88, no. 4, Dec., p. 89-96). [1009

The first of these two items is the Portuguese text of an article also published in the *An. econ. estad.* (Colombia), analyzing mortality tables for Colombia. The second gives an analysis and critique of the mortality tables for Lima, Peru, prepared by Franz Schruefer. [S. Mosk]

National policy committee. Inter-American progress and problems. Washington, D. C. 17, 28 p. [1010

Nieto Arteta, Luis E. El régimen de compensación y el comercio americano (*Trim.*

econ., vol. 9, no. 4, enero–marzo, p. 560-590). **[1011**

This article is devoted mainly to an examination of the foreign economic policies of Nazi Germany, with comparative observations on the principles and structure of the traditional English free-trade economy. A number of other questions are discussed incidentally or as extensions of the main topic, but not systematically. [S. Mosk]

Normano, J. F. Attitudes towards settlement in Latin America (*World econ.,* vol. 1, no. 1-2, Jan., p. 57-63). **[1012**

Latin America can no longer be considered as welcoming mass immigration. The trend is now toward a policy of organized and selective immigration. The author suggests that the problem of migration after the war will be at best a complicated one, and that a solution should be sought now. [Ed.]

Oficina internacional del trabajo. El movimiento cooperativo en las Américas. Montreal. 56 p. **[1013**

Textos de una serie internacional de emisicnes radiofónicas sobre el movimiento cooperativo, organizadas en 1942 por la Oficina Internacional del Trabajo y la Liga Cooperativa de los Estados Unidos. Incluye: *La cooperación en la Argentina* por Bernardo Delom; *La cooperación en Colombia* por A. Fabra Ribas; *Origen e importancia del movimiento cooperativo en México* por José González Padilla; y *Origen del movimiento cooperativo en el Perú* por F. Alvarino Herr. [G. A. Rohen y Gálvez]

Olson, Paul R., and **C. Addison Hickman.** Pan American economics. New York. John Wiley & sons. v, 479 p., illus. **[1014**

This book is devoted to a description and, in much lesser degree, an analysis of the economic relations of Latin America with the rest of the world, especially the United States. Following are the main topics covered: foreign trade; foreign investment; commercial policies; Pan American economic cooperation. The few observations made on internal economic structures and problems are incidental to these external questions. Excessive detail and reluctance to suggest even tentative generalizations reduce the value of the book to the level of a reference work for mature students in the field, and also weaken it as a text for students who are being introduced to Latin American economic problems.

For a more extensive review of the study see *The Pacific Historical Review,* vol. 13, no. 2, June, 1944, p. 211-212. [S. Mosk]

Pan American union. Ata final da Segunda conferência interamericana de agricultura celebrada na cidade do México do dia 6 ao dia 16 de julho de 1942. Washington. (Série de congressos e conferências, no. 27). iii, 58 p. **[1015**

Contains list of delegates and resolutions approved by the Conference.

————. Report on the proposed inter-American agricultural credit bank. Resolution 9 of the Second inter-American conference of agriculture, Mexico, D. F., Mexico, July 6-16, 1942. Washington. 1943? 15, 4 p., tables. **[1016**

Objectives and functions of the proposed bank and general economic considerations justifying the project.

————. **Governing board.** La cooperación económica interamericana. Principios fundamentales. Medidas de emergencia. Planes para la post guerra. Washington. 67 p. (Spanish and Portuguese editions: mimeographed. English edition, "Recent trends in inter-American economic cooperation"). 40 p. **[1017**

The study is divided into three parts. The first part notes the principles which govern Inter-American economic relations. Part two examines the manner in which these principles are applied. In part three consideration is given to post war plans. [Ed.]

————. **Oficina de información obrera y social.** Lista de sindicatos obreros de América. Washington, D. C. 22 p. **[1018**

A list of labor organizations, with addresses, which receive publications of the Division of Labor and Social Information of the Pan American Union. Arranged alphabetically by countries.

Patterson, Gardner. The Export-import bank (*Quart. jour. econ.,* vol. 58, no. 1, Nov., p. 65-90). **[1019**

History of the bank and its operations, touching on its aid to international trade in agricultural products, and outlining its aid to Central and South American countries.

Pearl, Raymond. Un examen comparativo de ciertos aspectos de las poblaciones del nuevo mundo (*Estadística,* vol. 1, no. 4, Dec., p. 29-66). **[1020**

Spanish translation of an article originally published in *Human Biology,* September, 1940, comparing population features and trends of the Western Hemisphere with those of the Eastern Hemisphere. The New World as a whole shows a lower population density, and more favorable indexes for natural increase and age composition. [S. Mosk]

Platt, Robert S. Development and problems of land transport in Latin America (*Proc. eighth amer. scien. cong.,* vol. 11, p. 131-150). **[1021**

A sketch of the transport pattern of Latin America, stressing the orientation of railroad construction toward overseas markets rather than toward the objective of national unification. [S. Mosk]

Rasmussen, W. D. Agriculture in war (*Agric. Americas,* vol. 3, June, p. 103-106). **[1022**

Work of the United States Department of Agriculture in the field of Inter-American cooperation.

Recomendaciones interamericanas sobre la planificación de la postguerra (*Rev. int. trab.*, vol. 27, no. 2, feb., p. 241-244). [1022a

Cumpliendo con las resoluciones sobre problemas de la postguerra tomadas por la Tercera Reunión de los Ministros de Relaciones Exteriores de las Repúblicas Americanas (véase *Handbook, no. 8, 1942*, items 3571, 3578, 3579, y 3667), el Comité Jurídico Interamericano preparó, y el Consejo Directivo de la Unión Pan-americana aprobó, recomendaciones sobre política económica (tendiente a la eliminación del "imperialismo y el nacionalismo económicos," explotación de los territorios poco desarrollados bajo la vigilancia de la comunidad internacional, coordinación de la economía mundial mediante una fórmula que combine la autodeterminación nacional con el interés primordial de toda la comunidad, disminución de las barreras aduanales y otras restricciones al comercio y "desarme económico" por la eliminación de "la implacable concurrencia y rivalidad comercial") y sobre política social tendiente a eliminar los factores sociales de la guerra (elevación del nivel de vida de la población obrera por medio de la acción nacional e internacional y desenvolvimiento de la Oficina Internacional del Trabajo)). Texto inglés en *Int. lab. rev.*, vol. 47, no. 2, Feb., p. 211-213. [G. A. Rohen y Gálvez]

Rodríguez Goicoa, J. Replicando: 1) A los fundamentos del "Bancor" como patrón monetario internacional. 2) A la creación del banco interamericano. Buenos Aires. Tall. gráf. Gadola Gadola. 16 p. [1023

Doubts that the establishment of an Inter-American Bank could solve the economic problems of the Hemisphere. The basic problem according to the author is one of balancing production and consumption, on the one hand, and exports and imports, on the other. [Ed.]

Roigt, Honorio E. La unión económica del río de la Plata (*Rev. econ. arg.*, año 25, tomo 42, no. 295, enero, p. 17-25). [1024

Analyzes briefly the economic problems of Argentina, Uruguay, Paraguay and Bolivia. An economic union of these countries would in the author's opinion be advantageous to all. [A. Dorfman]

Sapriza Carrau, Héctor M. Proyectos de grandes uniones aduaneras americanas (*Rev. econ. arg.*, año 25, tomo 42, no. 299, mayo, p. 150-174). [1025

Describes briefly various proposals recommending the establishment of customs unions, beginning with the proposals considered at the First Conference of the American States. Other proposals discussed include those formulated by L. V. de Abad, M. Pelliza, F. Bilbao, G. Subercaseaux, and A. Planet. There is also a brief consideration of regional customs unions. [Ed.]

Terán Gómez, Luis. Ponencias para el Congreso demográfico interamericano realizado en México el 11 de octubre de 1943 (*Protec. soc.*, año 6, no. 68, sept., p. 25-30). [1026

Suggests measures dealing with post war immigration and recommends the establishment of an Inter-American agency for the study of the absorptive capacity of the American Republics for the purpose of regulating post-war flow of immigrants. [Ed.]

United States. Bureau of the census. General censuses and vital statistics in the Americas. An annotated bibliography of the historical censuses and current vital statistics of the 21 American republics, the American sections of the British commonwealth of nations, the American colonies of Denmark, France and the Netherlands, and the American territories and possessions of the United States. Prepared under the supervision of Irene B. Traeuber. Washington. Govt. printing office. 151 p. [1027

The usefulness of this valuable reference work is enhanced by an historical sketch of the census experience of each country, giving background information on the various census compilations. [S. Mosk]

———. Library of congress. Censuses and vital statistics of the Americas. Washington, D. C. Government printing office. [1027a

An annotated bibliography covering the historical censuses and current vital statistics for the 21 American Republics, the British Dominions, the British French, Dutch and United States colonies and possessions. [C. F. Jones]

———. **Tariff commission.** Commercial policies and trade relations of European possessions in the Caribbean area. A report on recent developments in the trade of the European possessions in the Caribbean area with special reference to trade with the United States. Under the provisions of title 3, part 2, section 332 of the tariff act of 1930. Washington. U. S. Govt. printing office. (Report no. 151, Second series). 324 p., illus. [1028

Contains good brief sketches of economies of the individual European possessions in the Caribbean area, as well as analyses of their foreign trade and commercial policies. [S. Mosk]

Universidad nacional de Córdoba. Escuela de ciencias económicas. Sistemas monetarios latino-americanos. I. Córdoba. Imp. de la Universidad. 502 p. [1029

This volume, first in a series, presents essays on the monetary systems in Brazil, Paraguay, Venezuela, Colombia, Peru, Chile, Mexico and Argentina. Nearly two hundred pages of the volume are given over to Argentina, while Colombia is allocated less than twenty pages. There is no uniformity in the period covered. Some essays cover the period since independence while others do not go beyond the last decades. The treatment, too, of the problem is uneven. [Ed.]

Urquidi, Víctor L. Problemas de cambios de América Latina (*Investig. econ.*, tomo 3, no. 2, segundo trim., p. 117–138). [1030

A good analysis of the changing factors affecting Latin American balances of payments and exchange rates in the period 1937–1942. The problems common to all Latin American nations, as exporters of raw materials and foodstuffs, are stressed; however, observations are made on the experience of individual countries, both as to problems and policies adopted to solve them. [S. Mosk]

Wallich, H. C. The future of Latin American bonds (*Amer. econ. rev.*, vol. 33, no. 2, June, p. 321–335). [1031

An interesting and suggestive analysis of the broad economic questions involved in the Latin American dollar-bond problem, leading to important recommendations on principles and methods to be followed in settling this problem. [S. Mosk]

Wickizer, V. D. The world coffee economy with special reference to control schemes. Stanford univ. Food research inst. 258 p. [1032

This lengthy review of coffee production, trade, and marketing control is a useful catalogue of information, but it is scarcely marked by analytical subtlety or sophisticated writing. [S. Mosk]

Wythe, George. The United States and Latin America (*Int. amer. affairs*, 1942, p. 53–87). [1033

A compact and informative survey of economic developments in Latin America during 1942 with special emphasis upon the part played by the United States. The survey covers developments in agriculture, industry, mining, commerce, finance, transportation. Of particular interest are references to Development Corporations and industrialization projects. [Ed.]

ADDENDA

Cuarto congreso panamericano de carreteras, México, D. F., 1941. Memoria. Tomos 1–3. México, D. F. 1942. 3 vols.: 758, 806, 622 p., cuads., ilus. [1034

ECONOMICS: THE CARIBBEAN AREA *

BY

SANFORD A MOSK

University of California

GENERAL STATEMENT

The theme of adjusting to wartime conditions is to be found in virtually all the literature concerned with economic conditions in the Caribbean region in 1943. Writers dealing with the past, the present, or the future, with narrow or broad questions, with descriptive material or analysis—almost without exception, they have introduced some observations on the problems which their countries have been obliged to face as a consequence of the war. This, of course, is to be expected, in view of the seriousness and complexity of the problems and of the issues in public policy involved. Dislocations in trade, in price structures, and in the production of goods for domestic consumption as well as strategic materials for export, have occurred in one degree or another and in one form or another in all the countries of the area. The very nature of these problems and the lack of even the normal complement of published official statistics (a casualty of wartime restrictions) have made comprehensive and extended analysis virtually impossible, but this should not be allowed to detract from the merit of what has been done.

Wartime economic reactions in Mexico were brought out by Eduardo Villaseñor (item 1052), in a paper read at the National University, in a series of discussions on "Economic Problems of the Americas." His special concern was the inflationary development in Mexico, but occasional odd twists in the argument combined with heavy stress on the urgency of getting more capital equipment from the United States suggest that the paper was intended to attract attention to the issues which the Mexican-American Commission for Economic Cooperation was subsequently set up to consider. Undoubtedly Villaseñor's paper enlivened the negotiations and influenced the report of this Commission (item 1047). A more prosaic, but valuable, statement of the effect of the war on Mexico's economy can be found in the annual report of the Secretaría de la Economía Nacional (item 1049). In Cuba, the designation of a Junta de Economía de Guerra gave rise to a series of discussions featuring problems of a wartime character (item 1138). As final illustrations of publications dealing with wartime adjustments in an over-all manner, we may cite two reports of the Anglo-American Caribbean Commission (items 1125, 1126) on the United States and British possessions in this area.

On the more specific question of inflation, in addition to the article of Eduardo Villaseñor already noted, attention should be called to two interesting (and different) viewpoints on the relations between monetary supply and prices in the context of the Venezuelan economy, for which we are indebted to Carlos A. D'Ascoli (item 1207) and Ernesto Pelzer (item 1214). For

---

* Publications on agriculture are listed separately under the heading Agriculture: The Caribbean Area (items 1221–1307).

Colombia, Eugenio J. Gómez (item 1178) pointed out the inflationary impulses in the existing economic situation, from the perspective gained by an analysis of that country's inflationary experience in 1923–1928.

It is encouraging to observe that economic questions of long-run importance to the countries of this area have continued to provoke discussion during the war period, when there is a temptation to brush them aside. Social security is one of these questions. In Colombia, Ernesto Herrnstadt (item 1196) not only contributed an excellent statement of the principles and problems of social security, but he also made a thorough appraisal of the Colombian system and pointed out its shortcomings. The newly instituted social security program in Mexico was favorably viewed in two articles published in the journal *Investigación Económica* (items 1087, 1090). Agricultural credit, especially for small farmers, is another question of continuing interest in the region; it is frequently discussed in connection with agricultural development in general, but special studies were not lacking. New advances in rural credit in El Salvador were described by José Valle (item 1122) and in the first report of the Federación de Cajas de Crédito (item 1120), while the administration of Mexico's program of agricultural credit was subjected to exceedingly sharp criticism by Moisés T. de la Peña (item 1244). The vital question of reducing the dependence of the Cuban economy upon an uncertain market for sugar led Herminio Portell Vilá (item 1143) and Rogelio Pina (item 1140) to outline programs of economic reorganization for that country. In Puerto Rico, the sugar cane industry was made the subject of a comprehensive study by the Minimum Wage Board (item 1159), covering social as well as economic features. The perennial interest of Mexico in silver production is illustrated by an article written by Raúl Salinas Lozano (item 1075), who has a modestly optimistic outlook on the future world demand for the metal. Two studies concerning agriculture are worthy of special note because of the field investigations involved; one is the survey of Colombian agriculture by F. R. Pound (item 1202), and the other is the report of the United States Soil Conservation Mission to Venezuela (item 1220).

Serious efforts are being made in the countries of the region to improve and amplify their statistics of economic and social conditions. The need for an agricultural census in Colombia was strongly urged by Hernán Montoya (item 1172) and Álvaro Pineda de Castro (item 1201), while José Abdiel Arias F. (item 1110) stressed the usefulness of getting more complete figures on Panama's balance of payments, and Chester W. Young (item 1156) pointed out the defects in Haiti's population data and vital statistics. In Mexico, the accuracy of official agricultural statistics was questioned by Moisés T. de la Peña (item 1244), but improvement in the price index of the Secretaría de la Economía Nacional was recorded by Federico Bach and Margarita Reyna (item 1079).

Almost everything written about the coming postwar period was general and abbreviated in character. An article by Víctor L. Urquidi (item 1072), anticipating Mexico's postwar economic problems in specific terms, is a notable exception. Apart from the war, a number of writers gave interpretations of broad economic trends in the world as a whole, and thereby were led to offer suggestions for the principles which should guide governments in questions of economic policy; these writers included Antonio García (items

1166, 1167) and Gregorio Sánchez Gómez (item 1174) in Colombia, Rodrigo Facio (item 1102) in Costa Rica, and Luis Montes de Oca (item 1045) in Mexico. A plea for the Cooperative Movement as a mechanism of promoting social progress in the Americas was voiced by the well-known authority, A. Fabra Ribas (items 984, 985).

BIBLIOGRAPHY

(*See also sections on* Agriculture: the Caribbean Area; Geography: the Caribbean Area; *and* Labor and Social Welfare)

GENERAL

Labell, Milton J. Yesterday, today and tomorrow in Caribbean fisheries. (*Bull. pan amer. union,* vol. 77, no. 3, March, p. 134–139). [1035

Suitable government policies to encourage technical improvement and to reorganize marketing can lead to a substantial development of the fishing industry in the Caribbean, although the aggregate resources are not great.

Middle American information bureau. Background, information on Middle America, Mexico, Guatemala, El Salvador, Honduras, Nicaragua, Costa Rica, Panama, Cuba, Haiti, Dominican Republic. New York. 32 p. [1036

Has a section on Middle American agriculture.

———. Middle America and the United States. Proceedings of the one day institute April 12, 1943, held under the joint auspices of The Middle American information bureau (Conducted by The United fruit company, and the Latin-American section, New York Board of trade). New York. viii, 101 p. [1037

A collection of speeches, most of which deal with economic relations between Middle America and the United States. [B. Wood]

MEXICO

GENERAL

(*See also item* 354a)

Alanís Patiño, Emilio. La riqueza de México (*Estadística,* vol. 1, no. 1, March, p. 34–53; no. 2, June, p. 131–147). [1038

The writer continues his studies of the national wealth of Mexico, earlier results of which were published in *México en Cifras–1938.* In the first article he gives a preliminary estimate of national wealth for 1940, and compares figures for the various component elements with earlier figures for similar items. The second article gives sources for his data and methods of making estimates.

Armijo, Leoncio. El porvenir económico del Estado de Guerrero (*Rev. econ., México,* vol. 6, no. 4, abril 30, p. 34–36). [1039

Discusses average annual production of agricultural products, means of communication, irrigation works, and the system of agricultural fields, and makes recommendations. [K. H. Wylie]

Boletín de estadística. Departamento del Distrito federal. Oficina de estadística y estudios económicos. México, D. F. Enero–[dic.?] [1040

Boletín mensual de la dirección de economía rural. Secretaría de agricultura y fomento. México, D. F. No. 200, jan.–no. 211, dic. [1041

In addition to agricultural statistics and reports on current legislation, credit developments, etc., these monthly bulletins contain very valuable special studies (*monografías comerciales*) on Mexican agricultural products.

González Gallardo, Alfonso. La orientación de la agricultura mexicana (*Trim. econ.,* vol. 9, no. 4, enero-marzo, p. 506–535). [1042

An address, attempting to indicate the ideals behind the agricultural program of the present Mexican administration, apart from the war effort—1) security in the possession of land, 2) remunerative prices for farm products, 3) an assured market for agricultural output. Achievements are summarized, and suggestions are made for further elaboration of policies to reach the desired objectives.

Hediger, Ernest S. Impact of war on Mexico's economy (*For. pol. rep.,* vol. 19, no. 7, June 15, p. 78–87). [1043

A good factual survey, compactly presented, of wartime economic developments and problems.

Mexico: one year at war (*Fortune,* vol. 28, no. 2, August, p. 120–121, 151–152, 154, 156, 158, 160, 162). [1044

An analysis of recent unfavorable economic conditions in Mexico, with evidence that the "gringo" is being held primarily to blame. It is suggested that the United States should enlarge its health and food program in Latin America. [B. Wood]

Montes de Oca, Luis. La intervención del estado en la actividad económica (*Investig. econ.*, tomo 3, no. 3, tercer trim., p. 223-264). [1045

An erudite plea for a return to the guiding principles of nineteenth-century economic liberalism, the advantages of which are discussed at length on an abstract level. World-wide trends toward greater state intervention in economic affairs hold dangers for personal liberty and for democracy; these trends, it is contended, can and should be reversed after the war. Growth of state intervention in Mexico since about 1900 is briefly outlined.

PLANIFICACIÓN ECONÓMICA. Secretaría de la economía nacional. México, D. F. No. 1, marzo 6—. [1046

This new series of publications offers brief but informative articles and notes on economic problems in Mexico. Special attention is given to the question of stimulating production, with reference to appropriate governmental policies.

REPORT OF MEXICAN-AMERICAN COMMISSION FOR ECONOMIC COOPERATION (*Bull. pan amer. union*, vol. 77, no. 12, Dec., p. 676-681). [1047

Text of the report, with brief summary comment. The Commission, which held a number of meetings in May-June, 1943, made recommendations on measures designed to alleviate Mexico's wartime economic problems and gave preliminary consideration to specific projects of a long run developmental character in food production, industry, public works, sanitation, and transportation.

REVISTA DE ESTADÍSTICA. Secretaría de la economía nacional. Dirección general de estadística. México, D. F. Vol. 6, no. 1, enero-no. 12, dic. [1048

A very valuable monthly compilation of statistical data on production, prices, cost of living, foreign trade, transportation and communication, monetary and banking operations.

Secretaría de la economía nacional. Memoria, septiembre de 1942-agosto de 1943. México. Tall. de la Nación. 269 p., ilus. [1049

This report gives analyses of recent economic trends and problems, as well as a summary of the work performed by the various divisions of the Secretaría. Especially valuable are the discussions of problems arising out of wartime conditions, in price control, foreign trade, and industrial development.

United States. Office of the coordinator of inter-American affairs. Mexico; next door neighbor. Washington. 26 p. [1051

Includes discussion of the land reform and the agricultural resources of Mexico. [K. H. Wylie]

Villaseñor, Eduardo. La economía de guerra en México (*Investig. econ.*, tomo 3, no. 1, primer trim., p. 7-33). [1052

Discussion of various elements in the wartime inflationary situation in Mexico. Urges the United States to release more capital goods for export to Mexico.

Also published separately and in English translation by the Asociación de Banqueros. de México.

BANKING AND PUBLIC FINANCE

Bauer, Walter, and **Julia L. Wooster.** Agricultural credit in Mexico. Kansas City, Mo. (Farm credit administration, bull. no. CR-4). 56 p. [1053

A brief summary of the development of rural credit legislation since 1926, and of the present structure of agricultural credit institutions.

PLAN DE AJUSTE Y PAGO DE LA DEUDA EXTERIOR DE MÉXICO (*Trim. econ.*, vol. 9, no. 4, enero-marzo, p. 487-505). [1054

Text of a message from Pres. Ávila Camacho to the Chamber of Deputies on the 1942 debt agreement between the Mexican Government and the International Committee of Bankers. The message lists the bond issues outstanding in 1914, when debt service was suspended, surveys the principal attempts to negotiate settlements after 1922, summarizes the terms of the 1942 agreement, and explains certain of its features.

Rosado de la Espada, Diego. El crédito agrícola oficial (*Méx. agrario*, vol. 5, no. 3, julio-sept., p. 160-164). [1055

Urges a more liberal public credit policy for small farmers.

Sorrell, Vernon G. Problems of exchange between the United States and Mexico (*Proc. eighth amer. scien. cong.*, vol. 11, p. 59-73). [1056

Examination of principal factors affecting the dollar-peso exchange rate in recent years (United States silver purchase program, oil expropriation, foreign investment, tourist trade).

United States. Office of price administration. Inflation and inflation controls in Mexico. Washington. 31 p. [1057

Includes controls over food sales and lists food price indexes. [K. H. Wylie]

Villaseñor, Eduardo. El problema de la escasez de moneda fraccionaria (*Investig. econ.*, tomo 3, no. 3, tercer trim., p. 213-222). [1058

A lucid and largely non-technical discussion of the shortage of silver coins in Mexico, and of the means taken to alleviate this condition; principal step was suspension of the silver agreement with the United States.

Wooster, Julia L. The Mexican agricultural credit system (*For. agric.*, vol. 7, no. 2, Feb., p. 27-38). [1059
A descriptive sketch; no appraisal of the system is attempted.

INDUSTRY AND TRADE (FOREIGN AND DOMESTIC)

Aramburu, Marcelo G. La pesca, futura fuente de riqueza (*Investig. econ.*, tomo 3, no. 1, primer trim., p. 95-116). [1060
Examination of Mexican fishing resources and fishing operations in recent years. Advantages and possibilities of expansion are stressed, and outlines of a development program suggested.

Dirección general de estadística. Anuario estadístico del comercio exterior. 1941. México. Tall. gráf. de la Nación. (Sría. de la economía nacional). 632, xxix p., ilus. [1061

Gleason Álvarez, Miguel. Maquinaria agrícola. México. Monografías industriales del Banco de México. 227 p. [1063
Includes the historical development of the agricultural machinery industry in Mexico, the present status of the industry, production, and importation of machinery. [K. H. Wylie]

LA INDUSTRIA DEL HUARACHE EN MÉXICO (*América*, Habana, vol. 18, no. 3, junio, p. 18-21). [1064
A household industry is faced with wartime problems arising out of a shortage of leather and shoe rationing in the United States.

Llamosa, Rafael. El comercio exterior de México y el estado de guerra (*Investig. econ.*, tomo 3, no. 1, primer trim., p. 63-80). [1065
Describes Mexico's system of wartime import controls; believes that the information obtained in this connection will be of permanent value for economic planning.

Mejía Fernández, Miguel. El problema de la pesca en México (*Méx. agrario*, vol. 5, no. 4, oct.-dic., p. 263-295). [1067
Analysis of available statistics on fishing resources and economics of fishing industry. High prices are held responsible for small domestic consumption, especially of canned fish. Recommends adoption of C. T. M. plan for development of the industry.

Poore, Charles. Building boom stimulates Mexican tile industry (*Mex.-amer. rev.*, vol. 11, no. 5, May, p. 6-9). [1068

REVISTA DEL COMERCIO EXTERIOR. Secretaría de relaciones exteriores. México, D. F. Tomo 8, no. 1, enero-no. 12, dic. [1069

United States. Tariff commission. Trade agreement between the United States and Mexico. Digests of trade data with respect to products on which concessions were granted by the United States. Washington. lxvi, 355 p. [1070
Text and principal features of the agreement; statistical and other data on production and United States trade in commodities on which concessions were granted to Mexico.

Uribe Romo, Emilio. Ensayo estadístico sobre la industria del calzado en México (*Bol. soc. mex. geog. estad.*, tomo 58, no. 1-2, enero-abril, p. 35-55). [1071
A good description of the shoe industry in Mexico. The author notes that in recent years small scale, non-mechanized production has increased at the expense of factory output. [Ed.]

Urquidi, Víctor L. La postguerra y las relaciones económicas internacionales de México (*Trim. econ.*, vol. 10, no. 2, julio-sept., p. 320-344). [1072
An excellent discussion of the broad problems arising out of international trade conditions and foreign investment that are likely to face the Mexican economy in the postwar period. A number of tentative but pointed suggestions for policy are made. The author writes from a good theoretical background as well as an extensive knowledge of the literature on international economic questions.

Villafuerte Flores, Carlos. El censo comercial en México (*Proc. eighth amer. scien. cong.*, vol. 8, p. 241-247). [1073
Discussion of methods and problems of Mexico's first commercial census.

Wylie, Kathryn H. The United States-Mexican trade agreement (*For. agric.*, vol. 7, no. 2, Feb., p. 39-48). [1074
Discusses the application to agriculture of the terms of the reciprocal trade agreement concluded between the United States and Mexico on December 23, 1942. Agricultural concessions granted by the United States to Mexico and by Mexico to the United States are listed.

MINING AND PETROLEUM

MEXICAN PETROLEUM INDUSTRY (*For. com. weekly*, vol. 12, no. 1, July 3, p. 9, 32). [1074a
Brief statement on petroleum production. Photographs. [C. F. Jones]

Salinas Lozano, Raúl. El mercado de la plata (*Trim. econ.*, vol. 9, no. 4, enero-marzo, p. 614-635). [1075
Examination of the principal forces affecting world demand for silver in recent years, including special wartime uses. The author is faintly optimistic about the future for silver.

Population

Dirección general de estadística. Sexto censo de población, 1940. México. Sría. de la economía nacional. 19 vols., tablas. **[1076**
Census of the following states: Campeche (51 p.), Chihuahua (160 p.), Coahuila (106 p.), Colima (49 p.), Distrito Federal (87 p.), Durango (94 p.), Estado de México (213 p.), Guanajuato (140 p.), Guerrero (149 p.), Hidalgo (160 p.), Morelos (75 p.), Nayarit (56 p.), Puebla (418 p.), Quintana Roo (32 p.), San Luis Potosí (123 p.), Tabasco (162 p.), Tlaxcala (72 p.), Yucatán (216 p.), Zacatecas (119 p.).

Transportation

Núñez Brian, Joaquín. La red ferroviaria mexicana (*Bol. asoc. internac. perm.*, año 27, no. 77, marzo-abril, p. 57-68). **[1077**
A good description with adequate statistical documentation. [Ed.]

The railways of mexico (*Railway gaz.*, vol. 79, no. 10, March 5, p. 241, 251). **[1078**
A good brief review of the technical and organizational status of the Mexican railroads.

Miscellaneous

(*See also item* 3728)

Bach, Federico, and **Margarita Reyna.** El nuevo índice de precios al mayoreo en la Ciudad de México de la Secretaría de la economía nacional (*Trim. econ.*, vol. 10, no. 1, abril-junio, p. 1-63). **[1079**
Description of the method and data used in constructing the new price index of the Secretaría de la Economía Nacional; comparisons are made with other price indexes. An analysis of price fluctuations, as shown by the new index, is made for the period 1918-1942.
Also published separately.

Benítez Gámez, Santos. Iniciativa que propone la creación y función de la Sociedad catastral y del Banco catastral de México (*Bol. soc. mex. geog. estad.*, tomo 58, no. 3-6, mayo-dic., p. 399-424). **[1080**
Advances fiscal and other reasons for preparing a comprehensive cadastral survey of Mexico, and suggests measures to organize such a survey.

Dirección general de estadística. Segundo censo ejidal de los Estados Unidos Mexicanos, 6 de marzo de 1940. Morelos. México, D. F. 209 p. **[1081**

Fernández, Ramón. Land tenure in Mexico (*Jour. farm econ.*, vol. 25, no. 1, Feb., p. 219-234). **[1082**
Nature and experience of Mexico's agrarian program are briefly examined; excessively small holdings are an unfortunate outcome of agrarian reform thus far.

Flores Zavala, Leopoldo. Los problemas de la agricultura en México (*Rev. mex. soc.*, año 5, vol. 5, no. 1, primer trim., p. 63-72). **[1083**
Wartime shortage of farm machinery imposes severe limitations on agricultural development; recommends a government program to establish and stimulate production of farm equipment, and price controls.

Frola, Francisco. Los ejidos colectivos en México (*América*, Habana, vol. 19, no. 1, julio, p. 39-41). **[1084**
High praise for the Mexican agrarian program, as carried forward by the Cárdenas and Ávila Camacho administrations. Refers especially to accomplishments in the Yaqui Valley.

González Padilla, José. Origen e importancia del movimiento cooperativo en México (*Coopecarril*, año 18, no. 221, nov., p. 15-17). **[1085**
Discusses the different forms of cooperatives in Mexico, their legislative background, as well as problems and possibilities for the future. [K. H. Wylie]

Gutiérrez, Alfredo F. La verdad sobre el cooperativismo en México. México. Unión distribuidora de ediciones. 93 p. **[1086**
A collection of articles on different phases of the cooperative movement in Mexico. [K. H. Wylie]

El instituto mexicano del seguro social (*Investig. econ.*, tomo 3, no. 2, segundo trim., p. 195-211). **[1087**
An unsigned article discussing the long-felt need for social security in Mexico and expressing a favorable judgment on the organization set up to administer for the new social security program.

Loyo, Gilberto. Notas sobre la habitación en México (*Investig. econ.*, tomo 3, no. 3, tercer trim., p. 265-304). **[1088**
Analysis of data collected in housing census of 1939, including comparisons with 1929 figures. Inferences drawn are significant for an understanding of Mexican social conditions, but they are somewhat lost in the discussion, which is heavily laden with detailed statistics.

Merla, Pedro. Estadística de salarios. México. Tall. de la nación. (Sría. del trabajo y previsión social). **[1089**

Rangel Couto, Hugo. Legislación de México sobre las cooperativas de consumo (*Investig. econ.*, tomo 3, no. 2, segundo trim., p. 155-193). **[1091**
Summary of legislation and work of government agencies dealing with cooperatives.

Rojas Coria, Rosendo. Las sociedades cooperativas de productores. Prólogo de

Roberto Lira Leyva. México. Ed. Promex. 239 p. [1092
The author, an enthusiastic advocate of cooperative organization, discusses the theory and history (European) of the Cooperative Movement in a somewhat unsophisticated manner; most of the publication (Part II) is devoted to legal and administrative aspects of organizing producers' cooperatives under the Mexican law.

CENTRAL AMERICA

GENERAL

Carrillo, Alfonso. Aspectos generales de la economía centroamericana (*Economista*, año 5, tomo 9, no. 103, junio 1, p. 16–22; no. 104, junio 16, p. 17–22). [1093
A light sketch of economic developments in Central America in the prewar and war periods.

Pollan, A. A. The United fruit company and Middle America. New York. Middle America information bureau. 1943? 27 p. [1094
The vice-president of the United Fruit Company tells of the accomplishments and plans of his organization.

THE RAILWAYS OF GUATEMALA AND SALVADOR (*Railway gaz.*, vol. 79, no. 13, March 26, p. 333, 346, map). [1095
Relevant technical and organizational information, neatly assembled.

COSTA RICA

Becker, Henry F. Land utilization in Guanacaste province of Costa Rica (*Geog. rev.*, vol. 33, no. 1, Jan., p. 74–85). [1096
An interesting account of the nature of cattle ranching in this tropical area; less important forms of land use are logging and farming.

Chacón, Lucas Raúl. Las condiciones económicas y sociales de Costa Rica (*Proc. eighth amer. scien. cong.*, vol. 11, p. 203–210). [1097
The unique qualities of Costa Rica's social and economic structure are explained, in the familiar manner, by the institution of small land holdings; these came to prevail in the colonial period because the absence of natives and extensive areas with appropriate climatic conditions made large holdings impossible.

Dirección general de estadística. Anuario estadístico. Vol. 41: año 1937; vol. 42: año 1938. San José. Imp. nacional. 2 vols.: 291; 282 p. [1098

———. Boletín de exportación. No. 2. Año 1942. San José. Imp. nacional. 23 p., cuads. [1099

———. Importación por artículos. Volumen, precio y procedencia. Complemento al informe de 1942. Año 1942. San José. Imp. nacional. 39 p., ilus., cuads. [1100

Escalante, Carlos Manuel. Memoria de la Secretaría de hacienda: 1941, 1942. San José. Imp. nacional. 2 vols.: 378; 252 p. [1101

Facio, Rodrigo. Un programa costarricense de rectificaciones económicas (*Surco*, año 3, no. 38, julio, p. 8–12). [1102
Advocates a "centrist" program of economic reform in Costa Rica, involving an extension of government ownership or control in certain sectors of the economy, and a revitalized "free market" sector based on small farms and small-scale industrial establishments.

GUATEMALA

FUNCIÓN ECONÓMICA DEL CONSORCIO SALINERO DE GUATEMALA (*Rev. econ. nac.*, año 7, no. 79–80, julio–agosto, p. 8–19). [1103
Nature and operations of the official salt cartel are explained and praised, although some difficulties are pointed out.

HONDURAS

Bradley, David H. British Honduras under war economy (*For. com. weekly*, vol. 10, no. 6, Feb. 6, p. 5, 8–9). [1104

———. Honduras faces its "unsold bananas" problem (*For. com. weekly*, vol. 11, no. 1, April 3, p. 5–8, 34, photographs). [1104a
The effect of the war on the production and shipment of bananas, strategic minerals, coffee and other products. [C. F. Jones]

Burgos, Joaquín. El sistema monetario de Honduras (*Rev. econ. estad.*, Córdoba, año 5, no. 4, cuarto trim., p. 505–532). [1105
A brief and rather sketchy account of the monetary system in Honduras since the pre-Hispanic era.

Rodríguez, Jesús María. Datos sobre las condiciones económicas y etnográficas de Honduras (*Proc. eighth amer. scien. cong.*, vol. 11, p. 245–251). [1106
Brief notes on economic and geographic conditions are assembled here, but without apparent "point."

NICARAGUA

DeBayle, León. La cooperación financiera de los Estados Unidos en Nicaragua. Managua. Tip. Gurdian. 16 p. [1107
What the United States has done to insure the financial and economic stability of Nicaragua. [Ed.]

ECONOMÍA Y FINANZAS. Órgano de la Superintendencia de bancos, de la Dirección general de estadística y de la Junta de control de precios y comercio. Managua. Año 1, tomo 1, no. 1, dic.—. [1108
Devoted to the publication of news and articles relating to the country's economic, social and financial problems. [Ed.]

Recaudador-general de aduanas y alta comisión. Memoria, 1 de enero al 31 de diciembre de 1942. Managua. 168 p., ilus., cuads. [1109

PANAMA

Arias F., José Abdiel. El comercio de Panamá y la estadística (*Proc. eighth amer. scien. cong.*, vol. 8, p. 153–159). [1110
Stresses the need for more complete statistics of the items entering into Panama's balance of payments, as a means of securing commercial development of the country along the most desirable lines.

Jiménez, Georgina. El censo de población de 1940 de la República de Panamá (*Estadística*, vol. 1, no. 2, June, p. 53–64). [1111
A somewhat abbreviated version of the report published in Oficina del Censo. *Censo de Población, 1940; Informe Preliminar*, item 1114.

Ministerio de hacienda y tesoro. Memoria. Panamá. Imp. de la acad. lxxv, 769 p., ilus. [1112

Oficina del censo. Censo de población, 1940. Panamá. Imp. nacional. (Contraloría general de la República). 3 vols., cuads., mapas. [1113
Vol. 1. Provincia del Darién. 83 p. Vol. 2. Provincia de Panamá y Ciudad de Panamá. 211 p. Vol. 3. Provincia de Colón. 169 p.

———. Censo de población, 1940. Informe preliminar. Panamá. Imp. nacional. 36 p., ilus. [1114
Seven summary tabulations of 1940 census data, preceded by a report on the arrangements for taking the census.

THE RAILWAYS OF PANAMA (*Railway gaz.*, vol. 79, no. 21, May 21, p. 512). [1115
Relevant technical and organizational information, neatly assembled.

Scott, Warner H. H. War's effect on Panama's economy (*For. com. weekly*, vol. 11, no. 13, June 26, p. 15–19, 44–45). [1116

EL SALVADOR

Brannon, Maximiliano P. Desarrollo histórico de la estadística en El Salvador (*Proc. eighth amer. scien. cong.*, vol. 8, p. 263–278). [1117
Historical notes on efforts to gather statistics in El Salvador since pre-colonial times, arranged in chronological order but without "point."

Dirección general de estadística. Anuario estadístico correspondiente al año de 1942. Tomos 1–2. San Salvador. Imp. nacional. (Min. de hacienda). 2 vols.: 291; 301 p., cuads., tablas. [1118

Federación de cajas de crédito. Legislación del crédito rural, 1943. San Salvador. Imp. nacional. 220 p. [1119
Texts of laws, decrees, and other documents relating to rural credit institutions.

———. Memoria de las labores de la institución desde el 12 de febrero hasta el 31 de mayo de 1943. Primer ejercicio. San Salvador. 20 p. [1120
Report on the organization and first operations of the Federación.

Ministerio de hacienda, crédito público, industria y comercio. Gestión, 1942. San Salvador. Imp. nacional. 911 p., cuads. [1121

Valle, José. Rural credit in El Salvador. Washington, D. C. Pan American union, Division of agricultural cooperation. (Series on cooperatives, no. 20). 17 p. [1122
Describes the organization of a credit cooperative for small farmers in Izalco, established by the Banco Hipotecario de El Salvador. The experiment proved successful, and similar institutions were planned for other areas.

Vásquez, Juan Ernesto. Ciencia de la hacienda pública. Tomo 1. San Salvador. Banco hipotecario de El Salvador. 170 p. [1123
A standard statement, with frequent references to practices currently in use in El Salvador. [Ed.]

THE ISLANDS

GENERAL

Latin American economic institute. Economic problems of the Caribbean area. New York. (Pamphlet series, no. 7). 60 p. [1124
Contains texts or abstracts of papers presented at a conference in New York, dealing with wartime adjustments and likely postwar problems of the Caribbean islands. The theme of "problem area" runs through most of the papers.

REPORT OF THE ANGLO-AMERICAN CARIBBEAN COMMISSION TO THE GOVERNMENTS OF THE

UNITED STATES AND GREAT BRITAIN FOR THE YEARS 1942–1943. Washington. 94 p. [1125
Official summary of the emergency programs and long-range plans of the Commission for the United States and British possessions in the Caribbean.

United States. Department of state. Anglo-American Caribbean commission. United States section. The Caribbean islands and the war. Washington. U. S. Govt. printing office. (Dept. of state, publ. no. 2023). v, 85 p., illus. [1126
Summary of non-military problems and adjustments of the war period in the Caribbean area, principally in the United States and British possessions.

CUBA

Abad, Luis V. ¿Banco nacional o banco del estado? (*Rev. bim. cub.,* vol. 52, no. 1, julio–agosto, p. 35–48). [1127
Advocates the establishment of a central bank, with non-political management.
Also published in *Rev. Habana,* año 1, tomo 2, no. 12, agosto, p. 565–576.

———. Proyecto de aumentos en la tributación y la crisis fiscal del estado (*Rev. bim. cub.,* vol. 51, no. 2, marzo–abril, p. 226–238). [1128
Criticism of government's fiscal policy.

Arrendondo, Alberto. El café cubano ante cinco guerras (*Rev. agric.,* Cuba, año 26, vol. 26, no. 20, julio, 1942–enero, 1943, p. 61–69). [1129
Traces the story of coffee in Cuba through five wars. Tables give exports of coffee from 1804 to 1941, imports from 1902 to 1941, and consumption by months from 1937 to 1941. [K. H. Wylie]

———. La ruta: 100 milliones por la banca nacional (*Rev. nac.,* Habana, año 2, no. 15, feb., p. 9–12). [1130
Recommends banking and other fiscal policies to minimize Cuba's dependence upon foreign capital for investment needed to promote economic development.

Barro y Segura, Antonio. The truth about sugar in Cuba. Corrections to and explanations of the pamphlet entitled "The sugar industry and its future," by Herminio Portell Vilá. Habana. Ed. Ucar, García & cía. 45 p. [1131
A vigorous criticism of Portell Vilá's thesis that the sugar industry in Cuba is "parasitic," and of the various corollaries of this thesis; the writer points out a number of alleged errors of fact as well as of interpretation in Portell Vilá's pamphlet.

Cosio, J. B. La Comisión nacional de propaganda y defensa del tabaco habano. Apuntes sobre sus principales actividades durante sus quince años de existencia. Habana. Imp. Muñiz. 50 p. [1132
Includes a brief survey of the agricultural services rendered by the commission. [K. H. Wylie]

CUBAN BEEF INDUSTRY (*For. com. weekly,* vol. 12, no. 7, August 14, p. 7, 32). [1133
Basic conditions and future progress. [C. F. Jones]

CUBA'S CHEESE INDUSTRY (*For. com. weekly,* vol. 11, no. 10, June 5, p. 5, 21). [1133a
A short study of one of Cuba's little known industries. [C. F. Jones]

Dirección general del censo. Censo de 1943. Ley del censo. Instrucciones generales a los enumeradores. Instrucciones para la identificación dactiloscópica. Instrucciones para llenar el modelo número 10 (informe de población). Habana. Imp. Cultural. 74 p. [1134

González Rodríguez, Miguel. El azúcar en las conferencias de la paz; Cuba en la guerra y en la post-guerra (*Ind. azuc.,* año 49, no. 596, junio, p. 340–346, 348). [1135
Reprinted from *Cuba Económica y Financiera,* Habana, marzo, 1943.
Importance of the sugar industry in the Cuban economy, development of the industry, its wartime position, and post-war future. [K. H. Wylie]

Hernández, Carlos. La industria ganadera e industrias derivadas de la ganadería desde el punto de vista económico (*Rev. soc. cub. ing.,* vol. 38, no. 3, mayo, p. 336–360). [1136
Examines the state of development of Cuba's livestock industry, and stresses the need for improvements in pasturage, breeds, etc., with a view toward exports as well as larger domestic consumption of animal products.

JORNALES QUE ANUALMENTE PAGAN LOS GANADEROS EN PERSONAL FIJO, CHAPEAS Y MENCIÓN DE LOS JORNALES NO CALCULADOS (*Rev. ganadera,* Habana, vol. 3, no. 4–5, abril–mayo, p. 12–13). [1137
An estimate of annual wages in the Cuban cattle and dairy industry.

Junta de economía de guerra. La economía al servicio de la nación. Habana. Ed. Cultural. (Publ. no. 1). 71 p. [1138
The principal address published in this pamphlet is one by the head of the Junta de Economía de Guerra, Dr. Ramón Zaydín, reviewing the problems of adjusting Cuba's economy to war conditions, describing the measures so far adopted, and discussing the general question of governmental intervention in economic affairs. The function of labor in a war economy is discussed by Carlos Fernández R., and the function of capital by Estanislao S. Crespo.

Mendigutía, Fernando. La organización sindical en Cuba (*Trabajo,* segunda época,

año 2, vol. 3, no. 5, mayo, p. 655–660). [1139
A brief but informative statement.

Pina, Rogelio. Estudios sobre problemas de la post-guerra (*Rev. Habana*, año 1, tomo 2, no. 9, mayo, p. 270–277). [1140
Brief outline of an economic and social program for post-war Cuba, including government purchase of unused land of sugar companies for settlement of small farmers.

Pla, Gil. Estado actual de la industria de alcohol etílico en Cuba y sus posibilidades (*Rev. soc. cub. ing.*, vol. 38, no. 3, mayo, p. 361–412). [1141
A résumé of the technical status and economic problems of alcohol production in Cuba.

Portela, Gerardo. Los problemas económicos de Cuba en la post-guerra. Habana. Tall. de la Sría. gen. (Univ. de la Habana). 37 p. [1142
After the war Cuba must increase production of goods consumed in the country, find new markets for exportable surplus, reexamine its system of taxation, reorganize its hauling system. [Ed.]

Portell Vilá, Herminio. La industria azucarera en Cuba (*Economista*, año 4, tomo 8, no. 93, enero 1, p. 11–16, 35–36). [1143
An interesting and suggestive development of the thesis that the sugar industry in Cuba has always been, and is, of a "parasitic" character, in its dependence upon special concessions and privileges and its failure to contribute to national well-being; recent United States policy suggests that Cuban sugar will no longer enjoy its highly favored position, and the industry is also faced with the threat of competition from synthetic sugar substitutes. The author outlines a program of readjustment, including development of industrial by-products of sugar output and release of land to small farmers for raising other crops. If the Cuban sugar industry cannot suitably readjust itself, he argues, it should be allowed to decline.

Sociedad económica de amigos del país. Memoria de las actividades y de los trabajos realizados . . . durante el año 1942. Habana. Ed. Molina. 91 p., cuads. [1144

Universidad de la Habana. Facultad de ciencias sociales y derecho público. Economía política. Trabajos realizados por los alumnos de economía política en el curso académico de 1939 a 1940. Habana. Imp. Berea, Cuba y Luz. (Publ. de la revista *Universidad de la Habana*). 164 p. [1145
The second part (p. 69–159) contains several brief studies dealing with various aspects of the Cuban economy, including mining, merchant marine, the fishing industry, and diversification of production.

DOMINICAN REPUBLIC

Dirección general de estadística. Estadística bancaria, segundo semestre de 1942, vol. 7, no. 2. Ciudad Trujillo. Sección de publ. 44 p., cuads. [1146
Gives texts of laws and decrees relating to banking, as well as banking statistics.

———. **Sección de producción y economía.** Exportación de la República Dominicana, año 1942. Ciudad Trujillo. 463–532 p., ilus., cuads. [1147

———. Exportación de la República Dominicana. Estadística comparativa entre los años 1942 y 1941. Año 11, no. 1–6, enero–junio; no. 7–12, julio–dic. Ciudad Trujillo. 2 vols.: 1–226; 227–462 p., ilus., cuads. [1148

———. Importación de la República Dominicana, año 1942. Ciudad Trujillo. 423–476 p., ilus., cuads. [1149

———. Importación de la República Dominicana. Estadística comparativa entre los años 1942 y 1941. Año 3, no. 1–6, enero–junio; no. 7–12, julio–dic. Ciudad Trujillo. 2 vols.: 1–215; 216–422 p., ilus., cuads. [1150

———. Sacrificio de ganado, año 1942. Ciudad Trujillo. Sección de publ. 61 p., ilus., cuads. [1151

Harding, Jane, and **John A. E. Orloski.** Dominican Republic tackles war problems (*For. com. weekly*, vol. 10, no. 3, Jan. 16, p. 6–9, 26–28). [1152

Registro público. Estadística de operaciones registradas, 1942. Ciudad Trujillo. Sección de publ. 62 p., ilus., cuads. [1153
Mortgage statistics for 1942, classified in various ways; comparisons with 1939, 1940, and 1941; data on new business establishments, and on those dissolved.

HAITI

Banque nationale de la république d'Haïti. Département fiscal. Annual report for the fiscal year, October, 1942–September, 1943. Port-au-Prince. Imp. de l'état. 1943? 110 p., tables. [1154
A valuable compilation of trade as well as fiscal statistics; text gives a summary of economic developments during the period.

Kernisan, Clovis. Mémoire sur les conditions de bases économiques et sociales d'Haïti et sur les problèmes les plus importants qui se posent à son gouvernement dans les mêmes domaines (*Proc. eighth*

amer. scien. cong., vol. 11, p. 235–243). [1155
Brings out the related economic and social problems of Haiti, and summarizes recent measures to solve them.

Young, Chester W. Observations relatives a la population de la république d'Haïti (*Estadística*, vol. 1, no. 3, Sept., p. 21–25). [1156
Since a complete census has not been taken in Haiti, only estimates are available for population data. The author gives an estimate of 2,700,000 for total population in 1941, and compares it with other available figures. The vital statistics collected so far are found to be unsatisfactory, but improvement is expected.

PUERTO RICO

Descartes, S. L. Land reform in Puerto Rico (*Jour. land pub. util. econ.*, vol. 19, no. 4. Nov., p. 397–417). [1157
A study of land policy in Puerto Rico from the time of United States Occupation down to the present day. [C. F. Jones]

Insular board for vocational education. Socio-economic conditions in Puerto Rico. San Juan. 37 p. [1157a
Facts brought out in other studies regarding population, families, income, health conditions, food consumption, housing, etc. are summarized and brought together in this publication.

Junta de salario mínimo. División de investigaciones y estadísticas. La industria de cerveza y gaseosas en Puerto Rico. San Juan. 39 p. [1158
Data on the beverage industry are compiled and briefly analyzed, as a basis for minimum wage regulation.

Minimum wage board. The sugar cane industry in Puerto Rico. San Juan, Sept. 1942. San Juan. Insular procurement office, Print. div. 215 p. [1159
A comprehensive study of both agricultural and industrial phases of sugar production, undertaken to provide a basis for the regulation of minimum wages, hours of work, and working conditions. Social, as well as economic, aspects are treated. The data presented on the cost of production of sugar cane are especially interesting because very little information on this subject was previously available.

Rivera-Santos Luis. Rural taxation in Ponce, Puerto Rico. Santurce. P. R. planning board. 68 p., tables, bibliography. [1159a
A study of taxation and agricultural and rural life in a section of the south coast of Puerto Rico, showing influence of farm sizes and land classification on assessments and taxes paid. Submitted in partial fulfillment of the requirements for the degree of Master of Science of Agriculture, at the University of Georgia. [C. F. Jones]

Truesdell, Leon E. The population census of Puerto Rico (*Estadística*, vol. 1, no. 3, Sept., p. 26–32). [1160
Description of the methods used in taking this census, and of its main characteristics.

United States. Bureau of the census. Censo décimosexto de los Estados Unidos: 1940. Puerto Rico. Viviendas. Características generales. Washington. U. S. Govt. printing office. 121 p. [1161
Tabulations of housing data, similar to those published for continental U. S.

Vélez, Martín. Financial analysis and membership problems of Cooperative Pozuelo, Inc. Río Piedras. Agricultural experiment station. (Mimeographed report 22). 14 p. [1161a
An analysis of a fishing and handicraft cooperative organized by Redemptorist Father Goetten with laborers living in Guayama. Recommendations are made for greater training of members in the administrative and operational phase of the business. [C. F. Jones]

COLOMBIA

GENERAL

(*See also item* 2478)

Araujo, Alfonso. El plan fiscal y económico del gobierno de Colombia (*Economista*, año 4, tomo 8, no. 93, enero 1, p. 21–24). [1162
Text of a message by the Minister of Finance making various recommendations on fiscal legislation.

Bogotá. Contraloría municipal. Anuario municipal de estadística: 1942. Bogotá. Imp. municipal. (Depto. de estadística e investigación social, no. 3, julio). xiv, 240 p., ilus., cuads., gráfs., mapas. [1163

Caro, Miguel Antonio. Escritos sobre cuestiones económicas. Bogotá. Imp. del Banco de la República. 122 p. [1164
A commemorative volume, containing a number of articles and papers on monetary questions written by Miguel Antonio Caro in the period 1890–1903.

Correa Arango, Iván. Estímulo económico en guerra y post-guerra (*Univ. Antioquia*, tomo 15, no. 58, abril-mayo, p. 179–191). [1165
The author believes that agriculture is the proper basis for the Colombian economy, and recommends policies to insure a large and stable rural population; selective immigration should be used after the war to colonize and develop agriculture in suitable regions now sparsely populated.

García, Antonio. La autarquía y el orden nacional (*An. econ. estad.*, año 6, tomo 6,

no. 13, julio 5, p. 13-17; no. 14-15, agosto 5, p. 11-16). [1166
An interesting interpretation of the changing structure of capitalism; policies of economic nationalism, it is contended, symbolize a new stage of capitalist development.

———. La crisis de la libertad económica (*An. econ. estad.*, año 6, tomo 6, no. 12, junio 20, p. 39-42). [1167
Extension of governmental regulation in economic affairs is held to be a result of the nature of capitalist development; in particular, of the accumulation and concentration of capital.

García Cadena, Alfredo. Unas ideas elementales sobre problemas colombianos. Preocupaciones de un hombre de trabajo. Bogotá. Ed. Voluntad. 303 p. [1168
The author, a professor of economics at the Universidad Javeriana, assembles in this volume his speeches and articles on economic and other problems of Colombia. The material is grouped under the following headings: Cuestiones económicas y sociales; Por los predios de la política; Una política cafetera; Agricultura y ganadería colombianas; En la Sociedad de agricultores de Colombia. [Ed.]

Medellín. Oficina de caminos, catastro y estadística. Anuario estadístico, 1942. No. 28. Medellín. Imp. Municipal. 1943? 199 p., ilus., cuads. [1169

Mira Restrepo, Jorge. Índices del movimiento económico de Colombia (*An. econ. estad.*, año 6, tomo 6, no. 1-12, enero 20, p. 32-51; no. 10, mayo 20, p. 40-50; no. 11, junio 5, p. 31-44). [1170
Statistics on monetary and banking operations; prices; cost of living; rents; foreign trade; production; property transactions. Text merely points out changes in figures for most recent months available in 1942.

Montoya, Hernán. El censo de 1938 fué admirablemente realizado (*An. econ. estad.*, año 6, tomo 6, no. 5, marzo 5, p. 29-37). [1171
Methods used in taking the 1938 census, and summary results, are briefly discussed.

———. Plan general para el levantamiento del primer censo agropecuario (*An. econ. estad.*, año 6, tomo 6, no. 19-20, oct. 20, p. 17-51). [1172
The author, Director de la Oficina Preparatoria del Censo Agropecuario, argues that an agricultural census is vitally needed as a guide to socio-economic policy. Proposed organization and methods for taking such a census are given in detail.

Muñoz, Laurentino. Estudios sobre realidad colombiana (*Univ. Antioquia*, tomo 14, no. 56, enero, p. 315-334). [1173
Stresses the need for two measures, in order to improve health conditions in Colombia: 1) effective public health institutions; 2) development of agriculture, in order to insure fuller employment and thereby raise living standards.

Vidales, Luis. La organización estadística actual (*An. econ. estad.*, año 6, tomo 6, no. 23, dic. 20, p. 25-31). [1175
Sketch of the statistical work being carried on in Colombia; organizational structure, kinds of data gathered, problems, plans.

Vuelvas, Luis Matías. Estudio agrícola y económico de la tercera zona arrocera de Bolívar (*An. econ. estad.*, año 6, tomo 6, no. 19-20, oct. 20, p. 52-57). [1176
Principally a compilation of statistics on agricultural operations, without analysis.

BANKING AND PUBLIC FINANCE

Contraloría general. Informe financiero, 1942. Bogotá. Imp. nacional. lxxxv, 229 p., ilus., cuads. [1177
Fiscal statistics, with an introduction containing observations on the nature of the various fiscal operations.

Gómez, Eugenio J. En previsión del futuro (*An. econ. estad.*, año 6, tomo 6, no. 10, mayo 20, p. 26-31). [1178
Recalls the inflationary experience of Colombia in 1923-1928, followed by severe deflation, points out the inflationary elements in the current economic situation, and suggests means to offset them.

Revisoría fiscal de instituciones oficiales de crédito. El crédito agrario en Colombia. Informe, 1943. Bogotá. Ed. Santafé. 168 p. [1178a
A report of the organization and operation of government agricultural credit institutions; includes legislative authority for the principal agencies. [K. H. Wylie]

———. El crédito agrario regional. Suplemento a El crédito agrario en Colombia. Informe a la Cámara de representantes. Bogotá. Ed. Santafé. 151 p. [1178b
A detailed survey of agricultural credit institutions available by regions, together with an analysis of their operation. [K. H. Wylie]

Valenzuela, Eduardo. Régimen tributario de Bogotá. Industria y comercio. Bogotá. Imp. municipal. 293 p. [1179
A compilation of *acuerdos*, *decretos* and *resoluciones* which regulate the imposition and collection of taxes in Bogotá. The author finds that the tax pattern is rather complicated, but that at the same time the system in force is inadequate. [Ed.]

INDUSTRY AND TRADE

Angarita R., Roberto. El Ingenio central del Tolima (*An. econ. estad.*, año 6, tomo 6, no. 16-17, sept. 5, p. 24-26). [1180
Descriptive data on this sugar mill.

Camargo Gámez, Eduardo. Colombia exporta artículos de primera necesidad (*An. econ. estad.,* año 6, tomo 6, no. 7, abril 5, p. 27–28). [1181
Summary of 1942 statistics on exports of foodstuffs, most of which were directed toward nearby countries. Such exports suggest a tendency for Colombia to become self-sufficient in food production.

Contraloría general. Anuario de comercio exterior. Colombia, 1942. Bogotá. Imp. nacional. xxxiv, 680 p., ilus., cuads. [1182
Statistics on foreign trade for 1942, by commodities, by countries, and by customs districts, including some comparative figures for earlier years, especially 1940 and 1941.

Herrán, Alberto L. Posibilidades de exportación de ganado a la zona del Canal de Panamá (*An. econ. estad.,* año 6, tomo 6, no. 23, dic. 20, p. 45–51). [1183
Analysis of relevant statistics leads to the conclusion that cattle exports have not appreciably reduced Colombia's livestock supply.

Ministerio de fomento. Dirección general de estadística. Estadística mercantil y marítima. Año 1941; año 1942. Ed. oficial. Caracas. Tip. Americana. 2 vols.: 457; 435 p., ilus. [1184
Foreign trade statistics, by countries, by commodities, and by customs districts; shipping statistics, by ports.

MINING AND PETROLEUM

Abadía Arango, Sergio. Las concesiones mineras en Colombia (*An. econ. estad.,* año 6, tomo 6, no. 1–2, enero 20, p. 66–71; no. 3, feb. 5, p. 5–10). [1185
A critique of the mining code and mining policy.

Cock A., Víctor. Colombia minera en los arreglos internacionales de la post-guerra (*Rev. minería,* Medellín, vol. 21, no. 123–125, sept.–nov., p. 9820–9823). [1186
Stresses need for Colombia to participate in post-war international agreements or cartels relating to minerals.

Martínez Syro, Lázaro. Importancia de la industria minera en la economía colombiana (*Rev. minería,* Medellín, vol. 21, no. 123–125, sept.–nov., p. 9824–9835). [1187
Examines the position of mining (especially gold mining) in the Colombian economy since 1931, with respect to exports, foreign exchange, employment, and public finance. Suggests measures to expand mining activity.

Ministerio de minas y petróleos. Informe al Congreso nacional en sus sesiones ordinarias de 1942. Anexo al tomo 1. Bogotá. Imp. nacional. 346 p., ilus. [1188
Annual report of the work of the Ministerio; special reports on mineral resources and their exploitation are included, together with data about the operating companies.

Ospina Racines, E. La explotación del petróleo en Colombia (*Economista,* año 5, tomo 10, no. 112, oct. 16, p. 28–32). [1189
Contends that the petroleum industry in Colombia will decline unless laws regarding subsoil property rights are modified, thus stimulating investment.

———. La industria del petróleo en Colombia (*Economista,* año 4, tomo 8, no. 95, feb. 1, p. 11–16). [1190
Main theme of this article is that tax laws and other legislation relating to the petroleum industry must be modified in order to stimulate further investment and development.

POPULATION

Rodríguez, Jorge. Población probable de Colombia (*An. econ. estad.,* año 6, tomo 6, no. 9, mayo 5, p. 13–14). [1191
Gives reasons for belief that the population estimate published in *Anuario Estadístico Nacional* for 1941 is too low.

———. Tabla de mortalidad de Colombia (*An. econ. estad.,* año 6, tomo 6, no. 6, marzo 20, p. 23–29). [1192

TRANSPORTATION

Ortega, Alfredo. Vías interoceánicas por Colombia (*Bol. asoc. internac. perm.,* año 27, no. 79, julio–agosto, p. 85–86). [1193
River and railroad transportation facilities in Colombia, briefly stated. [A. Dorfman]

MISCELLANEOUS

CREADA LA INTERVENTORÍA DE PRECIOS (*Rev. nac. agric.,* año 37, no. 467, mayo, p. 13–15). [1194
Text of a decree of May 11, 1943 which provides for the establishment of an Interventor de Precios in Colombia with power to fix maximum and minimum prices for all commodities and to set up a system of rationing. [K. H. Wylie]

González Couttin, H., and **Guillermo Navarro.** Las investigaciones demográficas y sanitarias en los años de 1939, 1940 y 1941 (*An. econ. estad.,* año 6, tomo 6, no. 13, julio 5, p. 9–12). [1195
Summary and brief interpretation of vital statistics.

Mira Restrepo, Jorge. La alimentación, los precios y los salarios (*An. econ. estad.,* año 6, tomo 6, no. 11, junio 5, p. 3–8). [1197
Estimates of minimum dietary standards for various kinds of workers and their

families. Average wages in Bogotá in December 1942 fell considerably short of enabling workers to maintain such standards.

Mortara, Jorge. Tabla de mortalidad y supervivencia para Colombia (*An. econ. estad.*, año 6, tomo 6, no. 13, julio 5, p. 18-25). [1198
Critique of Prof. Jorge Rodríguez' mortality table for Colombia.

Neira Martínez, Policarpo. Causas del aumento del costo del control fiscal (*An. econ. estad.*, año 6, tomo 6, no. 1-2, enero 20, p. 83-95). [1199
Description of the auditing functions performed for the various government agencies.

Osorio Lizarazo, J. A. Algunas intimidades sobre la industria del trigo en Colombia (*An. econ. estad.*, año 6, tomo 6, no. 18, sept. 20, p. i-iii). [1200
A plea for the collection of statistics on wheat production, yields, etc., as a necessary basis for the development of the wheat industry.

Pineda de Castro, Álvaro. Importancia del censo agropecuario en la economía de los Estados Unidos (*An. econ. estad.*, año 6, tomo 6, no. 1-2, enero 20, p. 61-65). [1201
A special plea for taking an agricultural census in Colombia, in terms of the need for precise information as a basis for wartime agricultural cooperation in the Americas.

Pound, F. P. Algunos aspectos de la agricultura en Colombia con especial referencia a la producción de cacao (*An. econ. estad.*, año 6, tomo 6, no. 16-17, sept. 5, p. 33-51; no. 18, sept. 20, p. 31-44). [1202
Dr. Pound, of the Department of Agriculture for Trinidad and Tobago, conducted a survey of various aspects of agriculture in Colombia, at the request of the Colombian Government. His report gives detailed recommendations for the agricultural development of certain regions, especially on soil conservation, irrigation, and cultivation and preparation of cacao.

Soto, Jorge N. La ganadería (*An. econ. estad.*, año 6, tomo 6, no. 4, feb. 20, p. 11-15; no. 9, mayo 5, p. 17-20; no. 11, junio 5, p. 14-19; no. 12, junio 20, p. 13-18). [1203
Continuation of item 1367 *Handbook, no. 5, 1942.* Carne, sal, transportes, los llanos, navegación.—Irrigación, parcelación, abonos, los llanos, la navegación del meta.—Agricultura, los llanos.—Desarrollo agrícola, los llanos.

VENEZUELA

Banco central de Venezuela. Memoria, 1942. Caracas. Lit. del comercio. 1943? lxxxiii p., ilus. [1204
Statistics and non-analytical commentaries on 1942 commercial and central banking operations; price indexes, 1938-1942.

Boletín del Banco Central de Venezuela. Caracas. Año 2, no. 7, enero-no. 8, abril; año 3, no. 9, julio-no. 10. oct. [1205
Statistics and analysis of current developments in money, banking, foreign exchange, public finance, prices, and security markets in Venezuela; special articles on economic topics (articles on international monetary stabilization featured in 1943).

Cárdenas C., Luis A. Balance de pagos de Venezuela en 1942 (*Rev. hacienda*, Venezuela, año 8, no. 14, set., p. 31-36). [1206
Estimates of the various items in Venezuela's 1942 balance of payments are briefly explained.

D'Ascoli, Carlos A. El actual problema monetario venezolano (*Rev. hacienda*, Venezuela, año 8, no. 14, set., p. 9-30). [1207
Notes currency expansion and rises in certain sectors of the price level, but concludes that the statistics available are not adequate to show that the former is responsible for the latter; undeveloped state of credit machinery is held to cushion inflationary effect of larger currency issues.

Dirección de estadística. Anuario estadístico de Venezuela, 1942. Caracas. Ed. Grafolit. 573 p., cuads. [1208
Contains data (mostly for 1941 and 1942) on the following: meteorology; population; postal and telegraph operations; transportation; production; prices; monetary and banking operations; public finance; foreign trade; education; crime.

Febres-Cordero G., César. El cooperativismo y la ley venezolana de cooperativas. Santiago. Imp. Relámpago. 61 p. [1209
Discusses the cooperative movement and the different classes of cooperatives in connection with the cooperative law of Venezuela promulgated in September 1942. Includes a short summary of two Chilean laws dealing with agricultural cooperatives. [K. H. Wylie]

Grases, Pedro. Contribución a la bibliografía venezolana de temas agropecuarios. Caracas. Tip. Garrido. (Publ. del Min. de agricultura y cría). 176 p. [1210
A tentative bibliography listing 469 titles.

Hernández Ron, Ramón. La política económica venezolana (*Proc. eighth amer. scien. cong.*, vol. 11, p. 93-106). [1211
A schematic presentation of the technical and administrative features of Venezuela's commercial policy; economic analysis is lacking.

Moll, Roberto. Lecciones de economía venezolana (*Rev. fomento*, año 5, no. 50, enero-marzo, p. 79-111). [1212
Observations, in semi-outline form, on various aspects of the economy of Venezuela in the colonial period.

Monsanto, Luis E. Los artesanos y nuestra economía. Caracas. Tall. Patria. 92 p. [1213

Recommends a program to develop skilled handicraft industries in Venezuela, especially for wood, leather, and clay products; European artisans should be encouraged to immigrate and to teach their skills to Venezuelan craftsmen.

Peltzer, Ernesto. Algunos aspectos del desarrollo monetario en Venezuela (*Rev. hacienda,* Venezuela, año 8, no. 15, dic., p. 9–30). [1214

An interesting and debatable analysis of the relations of money income, real income, monetary supply, and prices, in the context of the Venezuelan economy, 1938–1943. The main question which the author attempts to answer is—Why has the rise in prices been so small compared to the increase in money supply?

PUERTO LIBRE (*Rev. hacienda,* Venezuela, año 8, no. 15, dic., p. 31–37). [1215

Text of a report advising against the establishment of a free port in Venezuela.

Rasmussen, Wayne D. Colonia Tovar, Venezuela. Washington. 11 p. [1216

Account of the development of a German settlement, established in 1843, which still maintains its cultural identity and is largely isolated from the remainder of Venezuela.

Also published in *Agricultural History,* vol. 17, July, p. 156–166.

Salazar Maza, T. C. Evolución del sistema fiscal venezolano (*Rev. hacienda,* Venezuela, año 8, no. 15, dic., p. 39–57). [1217

First part of a brief sketch of fiscal history, covering the colonial and early independence periods.

Vandellós, José A. El petróleo en la economía venezolana (*Proc. eighth amer. scien. cong.,* vol. 11, p. 37–48). [1218

Sketch of certain changes in the Venezuelan economy, relating to the shift from dependence mainly on coffee to petroleum (after 1936).

Veloz, Ramón. Historia del cambio en Venezuela desde 1830–1831 hasta 1942–1943 (*Rev. hacienda,* Venezuela, año 8, no. 14, set., p. 57–96). [1219

Consists mainly of brief statements about balance of trade and gold movements in each fiscal year of the period 1831–1943, compiled from official documents and publications.

ADDENDA

VENEZUELA

United States. Soil conservation mission to Venezuela. Land conditions in Venezuela and their relation to agriculture and human welfare. Washington. U. S. Dept. of agriculture, Soil conservation service. 1942. 154 p., illus. [1220

At the request of the Venezuelan Government, the Mission made a field study of erosion conditions in relation to methods of land use in various regions, and gave field demonstrations of soil conservation methods. This report on the findings and work of the Mission also contains recommendations for the organization of a soil conservation program.

AGRICULTURE: THE CARIBBEAN AREA

BY

KATHRYN H. WYLIE

Office of Foreign Agricultural Relations,
Department of Agriculture

BIBLIOGRAPHY

(See also sections on Economics: the Caribbean Area; Geography: the Caribbean Area; and Labor and Social Welfare)

MEXICO

LOS ALMACENAMIENTOS DE GRANO EN MÉXICO (*Planificación econ.*, no. 6, agosto 6, p. 1-8). [1221
Notes the need for increased facilities for warehousing of grain in Mexico.

Banco nacional de crédito agrícola. Un trienio de ayuda financiera al pequeño agricultor (*Bol. mens. dir. econ. rural*, no. 210, nov. 15, p. 1178-1181). [1222
Describes activities of this bank during the past three years, a period of serious economic upset.

Crawford, D. M. Mexico's banana business experiencing revival (*For. com. weekly*, vol. 12, no. 3, July 17, p. 6-9). [1223
Discusses the evolution of the industry, production and producing states, export tax and duties, banana by-products, and prospects for the future.

Escobar, Abelardo. Costo medio del cultivo del algodón por hectárea en el valle de Juárez (*Agricultor mex.*, tomo 59, no. 7, julio, p. 25-27). [1224
Estimates given of the cost of cotton production per hectare under "normal conditions."

García de León, Jr., Porfirio. La producción ganadera (*Méx. agrario*, vol. 5, no. 3, julio-sept., p. 171-186). [1226
Quantity and value of livestock production in the State of Michoacán, Mexico, the effect of the land legislation on the industry, taxation of livestock, and the need for experimental stations.

González H., Gonzalo. Agricultura mexicana: productos de importancia actual (*Estadística*, vol. 1, no. 3, sept., p. 89-107). [1227
Discusses the extent to which the various crops are produced in Mexico. Tables show area, volume and value of production, as well as imports and exports.

Klinge, Gerardo. El crédito agrícola en México (*Vida agríc.*, vol. 20, no. 236, julio, p. 497, 499, 501, 503, 505, 507, 509, 511, 513, 515, 517-518; no. 237, agosto, p. 625-632; no. 238, set., p. 705-712; no. 239, oct., p. 769-776; no. 240, nov., p. 845-850; no. 241, dic., p. 917-925). [1228
A comprehensive discussion of agricultural credit in Mexico.

MONOGRAFÍAS COMERCIALES: EL CAMOTE (*Bol. mens. dir. econ. rural*, no. 211, dic., p. 1313-1331). [1229
Discussion, with statistics, of Mexican production, consumption, and trade, and world production and trade.

MONOGRAFÍAS COMERCIALES: CAÑA DE AZÚCAR Y AZÚCAR (*Bol. mens. dir. econ. rural*, no. 200, enero, p. 1022-1062). [1230
An economic study of sugar and sugarcane in Mexico. Includes volume and trends in production, producing states and regions, consumption, prices, and foreign trade, as well as world production and consumption, international world trade, and conditions in world markets. Contains numerous graphs and statistical tables.

MONOGRAFÍAS COMERCIALES: LA CEBOLLA (*Bol. mens. dir. econ. rural*, no. 207, agosto, p. 743-769). [1231
Production and producing regions, harvesting time, marketing specifications, trade, and world production and trade.

MONOGRAFÍAS COMERCIALES: CHICLE (*Bol. mens. dir. econ. rural*, no. 201, feb., p. 44-64). [1232
Production, producing states, domestic and foreign commerce, and domestic consumption; and world production, consumption and trade.

MONOGRAFÍAS COMERCIALES: CHILE SECO (*Bol. mens. dir. econ. rural*, no. 203, abril, p. 267-284). [1233
Principal producing states and regions, domestic consumption, distributing centers, prices, foreign trade and tariffs, and world production and market conditions.

MONOGRAFÍAS COMERCIALES: CHILE VERDE (*Bol. mens. dir. econ. rural*, no. 203, abril, p. 246-266). [1234
Volume of production, chief producing states and regions, varieties, consumption, domestic and foreign trade, tariffs, and world production and market conditions.

Monografías comerciales: la copra (*Bol. mens. dir. econ. rural,* no. 202, marzo, p. 136-161). [1235
Production and producing areas, consumption, domestic trade, prices, and foreign trade; world production and consumption; and international trade.

Monografías comerciales: la higuerilla (*Bol. mens. dir. econ. rural,* no. 201, feb., p. 65-80). [1236
Producing states, commercial varieties, consumption of beans, foreign and domestic trade in beans and oil, world production of beans, world trade in castor beans and oil, and conditions for beans and oil in world markets. Mexican production of castor oil is also included.

Monografías comerciales: el melón (*Bol. mens. dir. econ. rural,* no. 209, oct., p. 1027-1045). [1237
Production, grades, consumption, domestic and foreign trade, and tariffs, and world production and trade.

Monografías comerciales: la naranja (*Bol. mens. dir. econ. rural,* no. 210, nov., p. 1147-1177). [1238
Producing regions, varieties, grades and standards, consumption, foreign and domestic trade, and world production, consumption and trade.

Monografías comerciales: la uva (*Bol. mens. dir. econ. rural,* no. 208, sept., p. 878-909). [1239
Production, consumption, domestic and foreign trade, prices, and tariffs. World markets and countries importing wine and raisins are noted.

Monografías comerciales: vainilla (*Bol. mens. dir. econ. rural,* no. 204, mayo, p. 372-390). [1240
Producing states, regions and counties, varieties, consumption, domestic and foreign trade, tariffs, and world production and trade.

Necesidad de fomentar la ganadería en México (*Planificación econ.,* no. 10, dic. 6, p. 1-7). [1241
Discusses the causes of low production of livestock in Mexico and the measures needed to increase it. Credit is noted as the greatest need.

Ortega Ruiz, Francisco J. El henequén de Yucatán; antecedentes y perspectivas económicas. México. Ed. América. (Col. Nuevos economistas, 4). 129 p. [1242
A comprehensive study of the henequen industry including prices, cost of production, and trade. Contains bibliographical references.

Pan American union. Inter-American collaboration policy of the Republic of Mexico (*Commer. pan. Amer.,* vol. 12, no. 11-12, Nov.-Dec., p. 1-35). [1243
Includes wartime development and policy in agriculture. Tables show acreage and production of chief agricultural products, 1937-1942.

Peña, Moisés T. de la. La agricultura y los técnicos (*Investig. econ.,* tomo 3, no. 4, cuarto trim., p. 305-321). [1244
The official rural credit program is held to be a failure because of poor administration, not because of defects in the law. The administrative set-up is severely criticized for bureaucratic delays, unwillingness to supply adequate credit, errors with respect to the size of rural credit groups, etc. A second section of the article questions the accuracy of production and other statistics compiled by the Secretaría de Agricultura. [S. Mosk]

El problema de la maquinaria agrícola (*Planificación econ.,* no. 2, abril 6, p. 3-7). [1245
Summary of suggestions made by the Secretaría General de la Comisión Federal de Planificación Económica to deal with the problem of scarcity and high prices of agricultural machinery and equipment.

Secretaría de agricultura y fomento. Informe de labores . . . del 1 de septiembre de 1942 al 31 de agosto de 1943. México. 394 p. [1246
Report on the work of the Secretaría de Agricultura y Fomento, including experimentation, extension, credit, irrigation, and production.

———. Plan de movilización agrícola de la República Mexicana. Cotejo de los resultados obtenidos en 1942 y modificaciones impuestas para 1943 y años subsecuentes. México, D. F. Tall. gráf. de la nación. 23 p., gráfs. [1247
Statistics of agricultural production in 1942 are compared with the goals set by the plan instituted in June, 1942 for wartime expansion. Mexican agriculturists are warned of the dangers of producing for the transitory markets of the war period, and are urged to devote more effort to products for which imports have been necessary in recent years; these include wheat, copra, wool, rubber, cotton, lard, hides, and hops. [S. Mosk]

———. Dirección de economía rural. Preámbulo (*Bol. mens. dir. econ. rural,* no. 200, enero, suplemento, p. 1092-1106). [1248
This supplementary report has as its purpose to give a comprehensive picture of the development, structure and functioning of the Dirección de Economía Rural in general, and of the Servicio de las Estadísticas Contínuas Agropecuarias in particular.

Tabasco; riqueza agrícola y humana potencial (*Méx. agrario,* vol. 5, no. 2, abril-junio, p. 151-156). [1249
Based upon a report written by Enrique G. Nájera of the Banco Nacional de Crédito Ejidal.
A description of agricultural conditions in Tabasco, the extent to which the *ejido*

system is in operation, the potential wealth of the State, rudimentary agricultural methods, the yields which might be obtained in sugar-cane and rice, and other crops which should be encouraged.

Ulloa S., A. G. Estudios agrícolas desde México (*Bol. consorcio centros agríc. Manabí*, año 5, no. 35, julio-sept., p. 49-51; no. 36, oct.-dic., p. 12-14). [1250

The first article discusses the Mexican *ejido* and the second touches on the problems of land tenure and credit.

CENTRAL AMERICA

Costa Rica

Hernández, A. E. El crédito rural en Costa Rica (*Vida agríc.*, vol. 20, nov., p. 817, 819, 821, 823-832). [1251

Reviews the development of agricultural credit in Costa Rica.

Hodgson, R. E., and **A. C. Dahlberg.** The dairy industry of Costa Rica. Washington. U. S. Bureau of dairy industry. 44 p. [1252

With the assistance of the U. S. Office of Foreign Agricultural Relations.

An analysis of the dairy industry, including measures to be taken to increase production and improve processing, distribution, and sanitary control.

León, Jorge. La agricultura y la colonización en Sarapiquí (*Rev. inst. defensa café Costa Rica*, tomo 13, julio, p. 445-452). [1253

Agriculture and settlement in the Costa Rican district of Sarapiquí, including roads and markets, history of agriculture, types of crops, types of farming, forest utilization, and settlement policy.

————. Informe sobre los cultivos de adlay en la región de Tilarán (Guanacaste), 1942 (*Rev. inst. defensa café Costa Rica*, tomo 13, no. 107-108, oct., p. 601-612). [1254

A survey of the cultivation of adlay in the Tilarán region, including a discussion of soils, climate, cultivation and processing methods, and uses of the product.

Luján, E. R., and **Edwin Navarro Bolandi.** Efectos de la ley del 31 del mayo de 1932 (*Rev. agríc.*, Costa Rica, año 15, abril, p. 157, 159-163, 165-167). [1255

A report on the results of the livestock assistance law in Costa Rica of May 31, 1932, under which imports of livestock were taxed so as to eliminate foreign competition.

Muñoz. M. A. Informe acerca del Cantón de Poás de la Provincia de Alajuela, en sus aspectos agrícola e industrial (*Rev. agríc.*, Costa Rica, año 15, no. 10, oct., p. 435, 437-440, 442-444, 446, 448; no. 11, nov., p. 483-485, 487; no. 12, dic., p. 549-556). [1256

The agriculture and industry of the Cantón del Poás, including the crops produced, soil types, and agricultural policies.

Nichols, R. A. El establecimiento de pequeños fundos (*Rev. inst. defensa café Costa Rica*, tomo 13, no. 98-99, dic., 1942-enero, 1943, p. 69-74). [1257

Discusses the factors involved in determining various systems of small holdings in Costa Rica, and concludes that results are almost always bad, especially in the Western Hemisphere.

Picado, Teodoro. La industria del café desde el punto de vista de la nueva política económica (*Rev. agríc.*, Costa Rica, año 15, dic., p. 535-537, 539-543, 546-547). [1258

The coffee industry in the Costa Rican economy.

Popenoe, Wilson. Cinchona. San Pedro de Montes de Oca. Depto. nac. de agricultura. (Bol. técnico, 42). 23 p. [1259

The history and cultivation of cinchona.

Powell, J. S. Agriculture in Costa Rica. Washington. Pan American union. (American agriculture series, 3). 51 p. [1260

History, crop pattern, and government policies affecting agriculture.

Velázquez Fernández, Raúl. Proyecto de cooperativa del cacao (*Agric. costarricense*, año 1, no. 2, julio, p. 59-62). [1261

The rise of the cacao industry in Costa Rica and the needs of the small farmers who produce 53 percent of the total crop. Cooperation is needed to prevent them from being victimized by speculators.

Guatemala

Ippisch, Franz. La contribución de Guatemala en la nueva fase de colaboración agrícola-económica de las Américas (*Rev. agríc.*, Guatemala, vol. 20, no. 3-4, abril 15, p. 8-11, 34, 54; no. 5-6, mayo-junio, p. 16-19, 49; no. 10-12, oct.-dic., p. 50-53). [1262

Discusses rubber, cinchona, essential oils, woods, vegetable oils and spices produced in Guatemala. To be continued.

Redención de las fincas de café gravadas en favor del Banco Central de Guatemala (*Rev. econ. nac.*, año 7, no. 81-82, sept.-oct., p. 8-17). [1263

Discusses the intervention of the Central Bank in the field of agriculture.

Secretaría de agricultura. Memoria . . . de 1942, presentada a la Asamblea legislativa en sus sesiones ordinarias de 1943.

Guatemala. Tip. nacional. 377 p., ilus. [1264
The annual report of the Secretaría de Agricultura; includes production statistics, reports of the various commissions, institutes, and national experiment stations concerned with agriculture.

Wylie, K. H. Agricultural production in Guatemala (*For. agric.*, vol. 7, Sept., p. 195–211). [1265
Discusses food crops, export crops, livestock, foreign trade, and government policies and plans for agriculture.

HONDURAS

Hodgson, R. E., and A. C. Dahlberg. The dairy industry of Honduras. Washington. U. S. Bureau of dairy industry. 30 p. [1266
With the assistance of the U. S. Office of Foreign Agricultural Relations.
An analysis of the dairy industry, including measures to be taken to increase production and improve processing, distribution, and sanitary control.

NICARAGUA

Dahlberg, A. C., and R. E. Hodgson. The dairy industry of Nicaragua. Washington. U. S. Bureau of dairy industry. 30 p. [1267
With the assistance of the U. S. Office of Foreign Agricultural Relations.
An analysis of the dairy industry, including measures to be taken to increase production and improve processing, distribution, and sanitary control.

Guest, P. L. Nicaraguan agriculture looks ahead (*Agric. Americas,* vol. 3, Oct., p. 187–190). [1267a
Discusses scientific improvement of agriculture, and the principal agricultural areas and their products.

PANAMA

Dahlberg, A. C., and R. E. Hodgson. The dairy industry of Panama. Washington. U. S. Bureau of dairy industry. 34 p. [1268
With the assistance of the U. S. Office of Foreign Agricultural Relations.
An analysis of the dairy industry including measures to be taken to increase production and improve processing, distribution and sanitary control.

Hooper, Ofelia. Land and rural people on the Isthmus link (*Land pol. rev.,* vol. 6, no. 2, summer, p. 12–15). [1269
Brief discussion of land tenure, agricultural development, rural life, cooperative labor through the "junta," and land traditions in Panama.

Ministerio de agricultura y comercio. Sección de economía agrícola. Censo agropecuario, 1942, por provincias y distritos. Panamá. Cía. ed. nac. 57 p. [1270
An agricultural and livestock census including production and area cultivated in important crops and numbers of livestock by provinces.

PROGRAMA DE AGRICULTURA (*Rev. agric. com.*, Panamá, año 3, no. 23, julio, p. 1–38). [1271
Entire issue is given over to the 1943/44 agricultural program for Panama, the purpose of which is to produce enough to supply the domestic market and the Canal Zone.

Wylie, K. H. Recent agricultural policy developments in Panama (*For. agric.*, vol. 7, Nov., p. 256–264). [1272
Includes a brief survey of the crop and livestock pattern as well as recent government measures affecting agriculture.

EL SALVADOR

Hodgson, R. E., and O. F. Hunziker. The dairy industry of El Salvador. Washington. U. S. Bureau of dairy industry. 32 p. [1273
An analysis of all phases of the industry, including measures to be taken to increase production and improve processing, distribution, and sanitary control.

O SALVADOR E SUA INDÚSTRIA CAFEEIRA (*D.N.C.,* ano 11, março, p. 375–379). [1274
Translated from *El Nacional,* México, julio 26, 1942.
The development of El Salvador's coffee industry, including agricultural conditions in the country, the coffee zones, and erosion control.

THE ISLANDS

CUBA

AGRO CUBANO. Revista de economía y política agraria. Colegio nacional de maestros agrícolas. Habana. Año 1, no. 1, [enero?]—. [1275
This review publishes short popular articles of technical and economic nature. [Ed.]

Arango, Rodolfo. Cultivos obligatorios de emergencia (*Rev. agric.,* Cuba, año 26, vol. 26, no. 20, julio, 1942–enero, 1943, p. 25–33). [1276
An account of the provisions of the decree-law of February 4, 1942 which makes obligatory increased production of basic foods for domestic consumption, particularly rice, peanuts and other oilseeds and also increased production of hogs. Seeds are distributed and the equivalent of "victory gardens" encouraged.

DATOS DE LA SIEMBRA DE ARROZ CON OBJETO DE PRODUCIR SEMILLA, POR EL MINISTERIO DE

AGRICULTURA, BAJO LA DIRECCIÓN DEL INGE-NIERO FÉLIX MALBERTI (*Rev. agric.*, Cuba, año 26, vol. 26, no. 23, sept.-oct., p. 6–7). [1277
Includes data on yields and cost of production.

Lamar Roura, Justo. La industria ganadera, factor de economía nacional (*Rev. ganadera*, Habana, vol. 3, no. 10, oct., p. 3–16). [1278
A survey of the Cuban cattle industry, showing value of exports in animal and dairy products, labor and wages involved, cattle stocks, consumption of meat, milk and butter, possibilities of increasing the milk production of Cuban cows, and possible expansion of the industry.

Martínez Sáenz, Joaquín. El catastro nacional (*Rev. agric.*, Cuba, año 26, vol. 26, no. 24, nov.-dic., p. 97–105). [1279
Scope and value of the Cuban land cadaster and the membership of the Comisión del Catastro Nacional.

Ministerio de agricultura. Hacia la revolución agraria. 1. La reconquista de la tierra. Habana. Ed. Guerrero. 30 p. [1280
Contains legislation aimed at guaranteeing the existence of the small farm in Cuba and facilitating the acquisition of land by farmers. Two statements by J. Martínez Sáenz, the Minister of Agriculture, on the subject are included.

Sánchez Mouso, J. M. La ganadería cubana y sus industrias (*Rev. agric.*, Cuba, año 26, vol. 26, no. 20, julio, 1942–enero, 1943, p. 48–60). [1281
Discusses Cuba's livestock industry and its expansion since World War I.

LA SIGNIFICACIÓN SOCIAL Y ECONÓMICA DE LA GANADERÍA CUBANA (*Diario de la marina*, abril 15, suplemento diario en rotograbado, 4 p.). [1282
This is a supplementary issue to the *Diario de la Marina* of Havana showing the social and economic importance of the livestock industry in Cuba.

Vivó, Hugo. Algunas consideraciones estadísticas sobre el problema del arroz en Cuba; estudio sobre la probabilidad matemática de obtener determinados rendimientos en las cosechas (*Rev. agric.*, Cuba, año 26, vol. 26, no. 23, sept.-oct., p. 20–35). [1283
A statistical study of the Cuban rice market and yields of rice.

DOMINICAN REPUBLIC

Berrios, R. H. A. Costo de producción de plátanos (*Rev. agric.*, Dom. Rep., vol. 34, no. 150, sept.-oct., p. 528–532). [1284
Describes production techniques and estimates cost of production for plantains.

Powell, Jane. Agriculture in the Dominican Republic. Washington, D. C. Pan American union, Division of agricultural cooperation. (American agriculture series, no. 2). 27 p. [1285
History, crop pattern, and government policies affecting agriculture. The second of the Pan American Union series on the Agriculture of Latin American countries.

JAMAICA

Wakefield, A. J. Memorandum of agricultural development in Jamaica (*Jour. Jamaica agric. soc.*, vol. 47, June–August, p. 155–217). [1286
Surveys the various elements in Jamaican agriculture and recommends a policy to be followed. Includes crops and livestock, soil erosion, forestry, farming systems, agricultural education, marketing and cooperatives, and land tenure and settlement.

COLOMBIA

Beltrán, P. P. Cundinamarca necesita grandes recursos para fomento agrícola y pecuario (*Vida rural*, año 4, no. 45, abril, p. 31–32). [1287
Discussion of Cundinamarca's needs for the promotion of her agriculture and what is being done in this line, based upon a report of the Director de Agricultura y Ganadería of Cundinamarca.

CUNDINAMARCA INICIA UN PLAN DE POSTGUERRA PARA PRODUCCIÓN RURAL (*Vida rural*, año 5, no. 51, oct., p. 6–11). [1288
Discusses a program for development of rye production, the growing of kikuyu, increase of cooperation in agriculture, and development of the livestock industry.

Díaz Rodríguez, Justo. Informe anual del señor Director del Departamento de tierras, al señor Ministro de la economía nacional (*Tierras y aguas*, año 5, no. 57–58, sept.-oct., p. 3–18). [1289
Includes discussion of public lands, Indians, and progress in land settlement and forestry, in Colombia.

———. Política agraria y colonización (*Tierras y aguas*, año 5, no. 55–56, julio-agosto, p. 3–62). [1290
A survey of the urban and rural population of Colombia and population movements is followed by an examination of the country's land tenure legislation and problems of colonization.

Galán Gómez, Mario. El tabaco—algo sobre su historia (*Bol. cont. dept.*, año 9, no. 35, nov., p. 3–32). [1291
A history of the tobacco industry in Colombia including statistics on production, prices, and trade in the 19th century.

García R., José María. La cooperación en la industria cafetera (*Rev. fac. nac. agron.*,

Medellín, año 5, vol. 5, no. 20, p. 25-31, 33). [1292
The need for cooperation in the coffee industry in Colombia and the way in which cooperatives should be formed.

Hauzer, René. Una nueva variedad de ajonjolí (*Vida rural,* año 4, no. 43, feb., p. 13-14, 15). [1293
Describes a new variety of sesame (the "Papare" variety) found in the Department of Magdalena, and its economic importance.

Ortiz R., Guillermo. Cultivo del tabaco en el Valle del Cauca, 1943. Cali. Imp. departamental. 43 p., ilus. [1294
Discusses tobacco production in the Cauca Valley, including varieties, methods of cultivation, and costs of production.

Otoya Arboleda, F. J. La erosión y la conservación de suelos en Colombia (*Rev. fac. nac. agron.,* Medellín, año 5, vol. 5, no. 20, p. 80-196). [1295

Pound, F. P. A bird's eye view of agriculture in Colombia (*Proc. agric. soc. Trinidad Tobago,* vol. 43, Sept., p. 191, 193, 195, 197, 199, 201, 203). [1296
Describes briefly the agricultural pattern and the economic policy of Colombia.

Rivas Camacho, Santiago. El plan nacional del Ministerio de la economía (*Vida rural,* vol. 4, no. 44, marzo, p. 3-4, 6-8). [1297
The Minister of National Economy of Colombia outlines a four-year plan for agriculture.

Romero Manrique, Alfonso. Situación actual de la industria arrocera nacional (*Rev. nac. agric.,* año 37, no. 471, sept., p. 17-18). [1298
Includes statistical data on area cultivated, per hectare yields, production, number of consumers, and consumption of rice in Colombia by departments.

Secretario de agricultura y fomento. Informe . . . al sr. gobernador del Departamento del Valle del Cauca. Cali. 46 p. [1299
Contains a plan for the economic development of the Cauca Valley and outline of a study of agriculture and industries derived from it, prepared by Carlos E. Chardón.

Valle del Cauca (Depto.). Secretaría de agricultura y fomento. Informe, 1941/1942. Cali. Imp. Moreno. 46 p. [1300
A report of the activities of the Secretaría de Agricultura y Fomento of the Department of Valle del Cauca.

Varela Martínez, Raúl. Acción agraria (*Rev. nac. agric.,* año 37, no. 471, sept., p. 27-28, 36). [1301
Suggests a program for government aid to Colombian agriculture.

VENEZUELA

Calzadilla Valdez, Fernando. Por los llanos de Apure; los económicos llaneros (*Bol. cam. comercio Caracas,* segunda época, año 32, julio, p. 8891-8897). [1302
Describes the organization of a ranch in Apure, buildings and equipment and their costs, livestock, and labor.

Henao Jaramillo, J. El café en Venezuela (*Agric. ven.,* año 7, no. 83-84, marzo-abril, p. 20-23, 26-31, 33-37). [1304
Contains a brief history of the coffee industry, methods of cultivation, varieties, diseases of the plant, processing, and the importance of the industry in Venezuela.

Mendes, J. E. T. A lavoura cafeeira na Venezuela (*Bol. sup. serv. café,* ano 18, março, p. 154-158). [1305
Gives a résumé of census data concerning coffee in Venezuela.

Nass, Hermann. El Banco agrícola y pecuario de Venezuela (*Bol. unión panamer.,* vol. 77, nov., p. 622-628). [1306
Discusses the need for agricultural credit; gives history and operation of the Agricultural and Livestock Bank of Venezuela.

United States. Department of state. Development of foodstuffs production in Venezuela; agreement between the United States of America and Venezuela, effected by exchange of notes signed at Caracas May 14, 1943. Washington. (U. S. Dept. of state, publ. 2001, Executive agreement series, no. 333). 13 p. [1307

ECONOMICS: SOUTH AMERICA (EXCEPT BRAZIL, COLOMBIA AND VENEZUELA)*

BY

ADOLFO DORFMAN

GENERAL STATEMENT

Two problems dominated the economic literature of 1943. One was the question of adjustment to changes in the pattern of production and trade occasioned by the war. The other was the continued expansion of government participation in the field of economic endeavor. In many countries governments assumed functions which until recently remained almost entirely within the realm of private enterprise. As the scope of economic activities of the governments increased the number of agencies multiplied and the system of economic controls and regulations became more complex. It is not surprising therefore to find that an increasing number of publications have been either sponsored by governments or devoted to economic activities controlled or managed by government agencies.

Outstanding works have been few and far between. It would seem that most economists were concerned primarily with the problem of putting into operation the programs and plans formulated in government bureaus. It may not be without significance that in many countries reports of central banks are the best examples of economic analysis produced in the course of the year.

BIBLIOGRAPHY

(See also sections on Agriculture: South America, except Brazil, Colombia and Venezuela; Geography: South America except Brazil, Colombia and Venezuela; Labor and Social Welfare)

GENERAL

Echeverría, Ruperto. Ferrocarriles trasandinos entre Chile y Bolivia (*An. inst. ing. Chile*, año 56, no. 10–11, oct.-nov., p. 355–378). [1308]
The various railroads linking Chile with Bolivia and their commercial importance. The Bolivian railroad policy in relation to her neighbors is analyzed. Detailed account and map of the projected line from Arica to Santos is presented.

Jiménez Correa, Carlos P. Estadísticas económicas comparadas. Chile-Perú (*Estadística*, vol. 1, no. 2, June, p. 103–115). [1309]
Comparative figures for the more important fields of economic activities in Chile and Peru including production, transportation, trade, and finance.

Mullen, A. J. Dried-fruit industry in Argentina and Chile (*For. com. weekly*, vol. 11, no. 8, May 22, p. 10–12, 38–39). [1310]

———. South America's wine industry (*For. com. weekly*, vol. 11, no. 11, June 12, p. 5–7, 40–41). [1311]
The countries considered are Argentina, Chile, and Peru.

Ponce de León, Carlos. Vías de comunicación entre Chile y Argentina. Santiago. Imp. El Imparcial. 43 p. [1312]
The author analyzes the condition and economic characteristics of railroad and highway transportation between Chile and Argentina.

Terán Gómez, Luis. Los enlaces ferroviarios entre Argentina y Bolivia (*Amé-*

---

* Publications on agriculture are listed separately under the heading Agriculture: South America (except Brazil, Colombia and Venezuela), items 1553–1604.

rica, Habana, vol. 19, no. 1, julio, p. 22–24). [1313

The geographic and economic conditions of the Bolivian region of Santa Cruz to be crossed by a long-projected rail junction between Argentina and Bolivia, through Yacuíba.

ARGENTINA

Administración general de vialidad nacional. Séptimo censo de tránsito realizado en la red nacional de caminos, año 1940. Buenos Aires. 18 p., mapa. [1314

Statistical results of the census with a detailed account of how the census was levied.

Almazán Rodríguez, Ángel. Exportación. Recopilación metódica, compilada por orden alfabético de las disposiciones en vigor sobre el comercio de exportación. Buenos Aires. Imp. Busnelli. [1315

Compilation, by commodities, of the various decrees governing exports from Argentina. A useful guide for business men which would give the scholar an appreciation of the intricacies of custom regulations.

Alonso, José. Población de la provincia de Santa Fe (*Bol. oficial bolsa com. Rosario,* año 31, no. 746, feb. 15, p. 3–14). [1316

Having reviewed the national demographic situation and stressed the downward trend in rural population, the author studies in some detail the problem in Santa Fe.

Anaya, Laureano O. El problema nacional del combustible en la paz y en la guerra (*Bol. inform. petrol.,* año 20, no. 227, julio, p. 1–26). [1317

Detailed analysis of conditions in Argentina with particular emphasis upon the importance and possibilities of petroleum derivatives. Attention is also given to coal and other fuels, especially those of domestic origin.

Angelelli, Victorio. San Juan y sus minas (*Ingeniería,* año 47, no. 826, agosto, p. 551–560). [1318

Mining in San Juan since 1932, by commodities; present status and future possibilities.

ANTE LAS DIFICULTADES FINANCIERAS DEL ESTADO (*Acción económica,* año 3, no. 33, julio, p. 9–10). [1319

Examination of the national budget followed by a suggestion that, with the help of producers, a balanced budget is possible.

Armour research foundation, Chicago. Technological and economic survey of Argentine industries with industrial research recommendations. Chicago. xv, 381, 14 p. Lithoprinted. [1320

"Report to the Corporación para la Promoción del Intercambio, s. a."

Studies Argentine economic structure, analyzes selected industries, reviews technical education and applied technology in Argentina, and proposes the establishment of an Argentine research institute. [J. B. Childs]

Banco central de la República Argentina. Memoria anual. Octavo ejercicio, 1942. Buenos Aires. Imp. Luis L. Gotelli. 100 p. [1321

This important document analyzes economic conditions in Argentina during 1942, giving due weight to maladjustments brought about by the war. Value of agricultural and industrial production is given for the first time. Stresses changes in the volume and value of foreign trade (especially imports), and examines prospects of industrial expansion.

Published also in English.

Banco de la Nación Argentina. Memoria y balance general de cincuenta y un ejercicio correspondiente al año 1942. Buenos Aires. Ed. Guillermo Kraft. 132 p., cuads. [1322

Data related to operations of the Bank (the most important Argentine institution of its kind with branches throughout the country); an appraisal of the general economic situation; and an outlook for the future.

Barrau, José. La situación económica porqué atraviesa la República Argentina (*Economista,* año 4, tomo 8, no. 94, enero 16, p. 29–32). [1323

General economic and budgetary situation is reviewed. Concludes that the situation is one of growing distress.

Barres, Francisco. Reseña de los ferrocarriles argentinos (*Bol. asoc. internac. perm.,* año 27, no. 77, marzo–abril, p. 25–32; no. 78, mayo–junio, p. 41–58; no. 80, set.–oct., p. 43–56). [1324

A survey of the railway system in Argentina, with tables and graphs depicting the general characteristics of the various railroads and data pertaining to their operation (movement of merchandise, costs, revenues, etc.).

Blaisten, Raúl J. Carburante nacional. Sus posibilidades (*Sustancia,* año 4, no. 13, enero–feb., p. 46–61). [1325

The use of ethylic alcohol, for blending with gasoline, is recommended in view of the shortage of the latter and the good qualities of the blend. Its importance to the Tucumán sugar refineries is mentioned.

Bormida, Alfredo. La industria del ácido tartárico en Mendoza (*Rev. econ. arg.,* año 25, tomo 42, no. 296, feb., p. 56–59). [1326

Development of the tartaric acid industry in the wine growing region of Mendoza.

Bose, Walter B. L. El correo en la Constitución nacional de 1853. Antecedentes sobre la nacionalización del correo argentino. Buenos Aires. Imp. Amoretti. 22 p. [1327]

Historical review of the beginnings of the postal services in Argentina from colonial times to 1853.

Buenos Aires (prov.). Departamento del trabajo. Condiciones de vida de la familia obrera. La regulación colectiva del trabajo. Buenos Aires. Min. de gobierno. 189 p., diags. [1328]

A special study of living conditions and economic status of workers in the Province of Buenos Aires. Detailed information about officially sponsored collective bargaining.

———. **Ministerio de gobierno.** Anuario estadístico, 1940. La Plata. Imp. oficiales. (Anuario 5, La Plata, 1 de enero de 1941, no. 276; Min. de gobierno de la provincia de Buenos Aires, Registro general y censo permanente de la población, inmuebles, comercio e industrias). 884 p., ilus., cuads. [1329]

A detailed description of the general economic and demographic situation in the province of Buenos Aires. Contains numerous graphs and tables.

Bunge, Alejandro Ernesto. Impacto de la industrialización sobre las relaciones comerciales y en las políticas nacionales de los países de la Cuenca del Plata (*Proc. eighth amer. scien. cong.*, vol. 11, p. 31–36). [1330]

Argentine industrialization has been made necessary by international economic conditions since 1914. Progressive industrial development will lead to an expansion of imports, as soon as the international economy makes larger exports possible. [S. Mosk]

Carbajales, Eduardo. Algunos aspectos generales del impuesto a la renta (*Rev. cien. econ.*, serie 2, año 31, no. 268, nov., p. 1195–1214). [1331]

What is meant by income and income tax; its evolution in Argentina; the problems arising from it.

Carranza Pérez, R. El sistema monetario argentino (*Rev. econ. estad.*, año 5, no. 1–2, primero y segundo trim., p. 21–208). [1332]

Evolution of currency from the colonial period to the creation of the Central Bank. The principal banks, agencies, measures, laws are reviewed in detail. Many graphs and tables complete the study.

Also published separately: Buenos Aires, Lib. Depalma, 1943, 195 p.

Catalano, Luciano R. Plan argentino de movilización industrial. Las fuentes de energía hidráulica y las posibilidades mineras y metalúrgicas argentinas como elementos de liberación económica, balance de la riqueza minera nacional. Primera aproximación. Buenos Aires. Tall. gráf. V. Matera. 191 p. [1333]

Potential expansion of mining and metalurgical production in Argentina. The author is inclined to view the situation with optimism.

Colombo, Luis. Política económica argentina (*Rev. econ. arg.*, año 25, tomo 42, no. 295, enero, p. 7–9). [1334]

The president of the Unión Industrial Argentina stresses those aspects of Argentina's economic policy which look toward industrial expansion.

Consejo permanente de asociaciones americanas de comercio y producción. El control de cambios en la república Argentina. Montevideo. 76 p., mimeographed. [1335]

A concise statement of the evolution of foreign exchange control. The author distinguishes four stages in Argentine control policies: October 1931–November 1933, November 1933–November 1938, November 1938–November 1940, November 1940—.

Contraduría general de la nación. Memoria, año 1942. Anexo de la Memoria del Ministerio de hacienda. Tomos 1–4. Buenos Aires. Ed. Gerónimo J. Pesce. 4 vols., ilus. [1336]

La Corporación argentina de productores de carnes. Defensa de los productores y ordenación del consumo interno (*Rev. parlamentaria*, año 11, no. 135, junio, p. 3–88). [1337]

A brief historical résumé of the constitution and activities of the C.A.P. followed by a more intensive study of current development, starting with the decree of February, 1943. Considers especially domestic activities as well as the struggle for foreign markets (United States). Detailed tables supplement this comprehensive study.

Crespo, Eduardo. La tierra pública y la población de algunos territorios nacionales (*Rev. econ. arg.*, año 25, tomo 42, no. 298, abril, p. 111–114). [1338]

Advocates extension of general and special rural education coupled with sound economic measures designed to utilize migratory rural population for the peopling of underpopulated areas in Argentina.

Cristiá, Pedro J. Comercio exterior argentino (*Rev. parlamentaria*, año 11, no. 136, julio, p. 5–13). [1339]

Brief outline of the pattern of Argentine foreign trade as a background for the analysis of present conditions. Foreign trade must be fitted into a general plan of national economic development.

Departamento nacional del trabajo. Adaptación de los salarios a las fluctuaciones del costo de la vida. Problemas que suscita. Normas de aplicación práctica. Buenos Aires. 86 p. [1340]

———. **División de estadística.** Investigaciones sociales, 1942. Buenos Aires. 273 p., 121 p. [1341
As usual this publication deals with economic and social problems related to labor. Includes statistics on strikes, cost of living, wages, etc. An attempt to measure the economic loss resulting from absenteeism.

DESARROLLO DEMOGRÁFICO EN LOS TERRITORIOS NACIONALES DESDE 1933 HASTA 1941 (*Rev. parlamentaria,* año 11, no. 132, marzo, 18–21). [1342
Brief review.

Dirección general de ferrocarriles. Estadística de los ferrocarriles en explotación. Tomo 47–49, ejercicio 1938/39–1940/41. Buenos Aires. Tall. gráf. del Min. de obras públicas. 3 vols., tablas. [1343
This regular report gives statistical data on the activities of Argentine railroads: mileage, rolling stock, tonnage, kilometers run, costs, etc. A different set of tables is presented for each company both private and government owned.

Dirección general de navegación y puertos. Anuario del movimiento de los puertos de la República Argentina correspondiente a 1941 y noticia sumaria del período 1937–1941. Buenos Aires. Tall. del Min. de obras públicas. xviii, 529 p., ilus. [1344
Data on shipping and trade for 1941, with a historical notice for earlier periods. Spheres of economic influence of different ports with a comparison between railroads and highways as outlets for agricultural production.

Dirección general del impuesto a los réditos. Memoria, año 1942. Buenos Aires. 94 p., ilus. [1345
The regular annual report on income taxes collected during 1942, broken down by groups of taxpayers and comparison with returns in preceding years.

Dorfman, Adolfo. La industria en la economía argentina de postguerra (*Acción económica,* año 3, no. 34, agosto, p. 19–21)'. [1346
An analysis of the present condition of Argentine industries. A general guide for encouragement of sound industries in the future is also presented.

———. El precio de costo industrial (*Acción económica,* año 3, no. 32, junio, p. 18–25). [1347
A detailed study of the cost structure of Argentine industries.

Ernesto Tornquist & co., ltda. Business conditions in Argentina. Buenos Aires. Quarterly report no. 237, Jan.–no. 240, Oct. [1348
Statistical tables and comments on the most important economic activities in Argentina in various fields such as agricultural production and prices, foreign trade, manufacturing industries, railways, stock exchange, banks, etc.

Federación argentina de cooperativas de consumo. Almanaque de la cooperación, 1943. Buenos Aires. 208 p., ilus. [1349
Statistics related to the subject, explanation of its basic principles, various articles covering achievements in different fields.

Fenoglio Preve, Simón. El azufre y sus industrias en la Argentina (*Ingeniería,* año 47, no. 826, agosto, p. 536–550). [1350
Imports and use of sulphur in Argentina; full account of its consumption by different industries; a policy of fostering domestic production advocated.

———. Estadística minera de la Nación, año 1942. Buenos Aires. Dirección general de minas, geología e hidrología. (Publ. no. 128). 104 p., tablas. [1351
This comprehensive study presents a survey of the output of the mining industries, both in volume and value; export figures, as well as some descriptive data; graphs and tables.

Ferrer, Juan M., and **Ángel Valle C.** El balance de pagos de la República Argentina (*Proc. eighth amer. scien. cong.,* vol. 11, p. 181–196). [1352
Argentine balance of payments is studied from 1927 through 1937 by principal items. Tables.

Ferreyra, Miguel A. El carburante nacional (*Acción económica,* año 3, no. 30, abril, p. 18–22). [1353
The consumption of gasoline in Argentina. The author advocates increased use of ethylic alcohol.

Figuerola, José. Las condiciones sociales y económicas de la clase obrera argentina (*Proc. eighth amer. scien. cong.,* vol. 11, p. 171–180). [1354
Tables and graphs depict series of index numbers covering cost of living (broken down by mean constituents), prices and wages, employment. Some series go as far as 1914; most go back to 1929 or 1933.

Fornaciari, Mario. Las finanzas del Estado y el Banco central (*Rev. econ. estad.,* año 5, no. 3, tercer trim., p. 323–439). [1355
After stating that central banks belong to the general pattern of governmental economic intervention, the author surveys the various functions of this agency, giving particular attention to those concerning financial and monetary problems. Their relations with and impact upon the national economy is also studied. Presents many figures dealing with the operation of central banks in different countries.

FUEL SUBSTITUTES IN ARGENTINE INDUSTRY (*Comments on arg. trade,* vol. 22, no. 10, May, p. 18–20, 23–24, 27, 48). [1356
Problems involved in the use of the corn surplus for fuel. [A. H. Lester]

Fürnkorn, Dívico Alberto. El problema de post-guerra es la cuestión social (*Rev. cien. econ.*, serie 2, año 31, no. 267, oct., p. 931–934). [1357]
The author insists that the most important and all but forgotten problem of the postwar reconstruction period is the launching of basic social reforms and redistribution of income.

García-Mata, Carlos. La ganadería del norte y el mercado norteamericano (*Rev. econ. arg.*, año 26, tomo 42, no. 304, oct., p. 399–400). [1358]
Notes the impossibility of levying embargo upon Argentine meat for U. S. markets; states, however, that many opportunities are still open, especially for salted meat, which could well be exported from the northern region. The responsibility for the lack of this kind of exports is attributed to packers and, above all, to the producers themselves.

García-Mata, Rafael. La situación del algodón en la Argentina (*Algodón*, no. 95, marzo, p. 165–168). [1359]
Brief historical statement of the cotton industry in Argentina.

Gil, Enrique. Relación entre el concepto de "seguridad social" y la integración económica de los territorios. Buenos Aires. Ed. Guillermo Kraft. 28 p. [1360]
The author argues that economic integration of the countries of southern South America is likely to bring about improved social organizations.
From *Revista de Economía Argentina*, tomo 42, junio, 1943.

Glover, Tomás B., and Boris Traucki. Algunos conceptos sobre la industrialización de los carbones argentinos (*Ingeniería*, año 47, no. 825, julio, p. 484–498). [1361]
This study, presented to the First Congress of Mining Industries in Argentina, deals with the technical and economic possibilities of the use of domestic coal for industrial purposes. It is based on a series of experiments which are also reviewed.

Godwin, Francis W. Empleo industrial del maíz (*Rev. bolsa cereales*, año 31, no. 1618, oct. 2, p. 6–8, 23, 25–26; no. 1619, oct. 9, p. 8, 23, 25–26). [1362]
On the utilization of corn for the manufacture of fuel and other industrial uses. [A. H. Lester]

González Arzac, Rodolfo A. Nuestra marina mercante requiere leyes urgentes (*Acción económica*, año 3, no. 32, junio, p. 14–17). [1363]
Concludes that a national merchant marine would serve the best interests of the country and urges adoption of adequate legislation.

González Galé, José. Los problemas de la post-guerra (*Rev. cien. econ.*, serie 2, año 31, no. 267, oct., p. 935–936). [1364]
Solution of problems arising out of the postwar readjustment requires an adequate system of social security.

GUÍA ESPECIALIZADA DE FABRICANTES Y EXPORTADORES DE LA REPÚBLICA ARGENTINA. Buenos Aires. 1410 columnas. [1365]
Furnishes information related to commercial aspects of the most important firms operating in this field in Argentina.

Guido, Mario M. ¿La carne antes que el trigo? (*Rev. cien. econ.*, serie 2, año 31, no. 267, oct., p. 993–995). [1366]
The problem of foodstuffs, especially meat, is the most outstanding for the postwar period. Argentina should try to retain the British market.

Gutiérrez Castel, Luis Alberto. Descentralización industrial y aprovechamiento de materias primas (*Acción económica*, año 3, no. 37, nov., p. 11–17). [1367]
Decentralization of manufacturing industries will permit more rational utilization of domestic raw material and will thus strengthen national economy.

Hileret, René. Estudio sobre el consumo de azúcar en la Argentina (*Ind. azuc.*, año 49, no. 595, mayo, p. 248–252). [1368]
Statistics of production and consumption of sugar in Argentina during the last 11 years with brief comments.

Hofmannsthal, Emil von. Un estudio sobre el llamado "Plan Pinedo." Buenos Aires. Tall. gráf. J. Rosselli. 36 p. [1369]
Critique of the so-called "Plan Pinedo" formulated by Federico Pinedo, while Minister of Finance in 1940. The author points out that the plan is inflationary in character, and that the construction program is not realistic. He objects also to the suggestion that domestic industry be encouraged by means of protectionist legislation. In the author's opinion Pinedo's plan would create more problems than it proposed to solve, and he suggests instead more traditional remedies, such as immigration, reduction of international trade barriers, liberalization of regulations relating to inflow of foreign capital and skills. The study was prepared in 1940, but published in 1943. [Ed.]

LA INDUSTRIA DE PRODUCTOS MEDICINALES EN NUESTRO PAÍS (*Acción económica*, año 3, no. 34, agosto, p. 8–10). [1370]
A study of the economic and social aspects of the growing pharmaceutical industry in Argentina.

LA INDUSTRIA DEL PETRÓLEO EN LA REPÚBLICA ARGENTINA. CARACTERÍSTICAS GENERALES DE LA PRODUCCIÓN PETROLERA DURANTE EL AÑO 1942 (*Bol. inst. sudamer. petról.*, vol. 1, no. 2, dic., p. 96–117). [1371]
Review of petroleum mining and refining in Argentina during 1942; figures on out-

put, yield in different products, wells drilled, etc. by zones and companies.

LA INDUSTRIA DEL VIDRIO EN LA REPÚBLICA ARGENTINA (*Ingeniería,* año 47, no. 821, marzo, p. 188–193). [1372
Account of a new and important glass factory in Argentina.

Instituto agrario argentino. Reseña general, histórica, geográfica y económica del partido de San Isidro. Buenos Aires. 203 p. [1373

Instituto de estudios económicos del transporte. El problema argentino de los combustibles (*Rev. econ. arg.,* año 26, tomo 42, no. 302, agosto, p. 337–342). [1374
Summary notice of an extensive and extremely valuable study concerning the use of fuels in Argentina. An exhaustive breakdown by class of fuels, source and use for a period of years, as well as special mention of substitutes.

Instituto movilizador de inversiones bancarias, Buenos Aires. Memoria, ejercicio 7—1942. Buenos Aires. Tall. de la Casa Peuser. 41 p., ilus. [1375
Detailed account of the financial operations of the Instituto (with breakdown by types, etc.). Comparative data for the preceding five years.

Junta reguladora de granos. Memoria, septiembre de 1940–diciembre de 1942. Buenos Aires. 103 p. [1376
Established by decree of November 28, 1933, and its first period of activity ceased in December 1936. This covers the second period of activity arising from the great crop of wheat in 1938/39. [J. B. Childs]

Lanús, Carlos E. La industria sericícola en la Argentina (*Acción económica,* año 3, no. 27, enero, p. 32–35). [1377
A brief review of the silk industry in Argentina with suggestions for its further development.

Lisdero, Alfredo. Índice de precios en los últimos 10 años (*Bol. inform. petrol.,* año 20, no. 221, enero, p. 36–40). [1378
Price indexes since 1929 are tabulated and compared with the movement of prices of different petroleum products.

Llorens, Emilio, and Pío I. Monteagudo. Acerca del censo general (*Rev. econ. arg.,* año 26, tomo 42, no. 305, nov., p. 432–434). [1379
Dispositions of the recent law calling for the fourth general census in Argentina are analyzed and its overall importance stressed. Particular attention is paid to administrative problems.

————, and Rafael García-Mata. Geografía económica argentina (*Proc. eighth amer. scien. cong.,* vol. 11, p. 211–219). [1380
Description of various economic regions in Argentina defined on the principle of "economic capacity." Tables and maps.

Mendive, Pedro I. Nuestra historia monetaria es rica en enseñanzas y en sugestiones (*Acción económica,* año 3, no. 29, marzo, p. 20–24). [1381
The author examines some aspects of Argentine monetary history in the light of their effect upon foreign trade and cost of living.

Mendoza. Ministerio de economía, obras públicas y riego. Censo general de población y riqueza de Mendoza. Ley 1398. Ganadería—1942. Mendoza. 60 p. [1382
Data on population, agriculture, cattle, and other resources of the Province of Mendoza with detailed breakdown. Deals specifically with the cattle industry.

Ministerio de hacienda. Memoria del Departamento de hacienda correspondiente al año 1942. Tomos 1 y 3. Buenos Aires. Ed. Gerónimo J. Pesce. 3 vols., ilus., cuads. [1383
The Argentine budget for 1942. Analysis of sources of revenue.
At end of vol. 1 (p. 246–252) is a table of the messages and budget laws, 1871–1943.

————. Dirección general de estadística de la nación. El comercio exterior argentino en los primeros semestres de 1943 y 1942. Buenos Aires. (Boletín no. 232). 154 p. [1384
This volume belongs to a series of quarterly reports reviewing the major characteristics of Argentina's foreign trade: imports and exports by volume and value, by countries (detailed breakdown by important commodities).

————. El comercio exterior argentino en 1942 y 1941 y estadísticas económicas retrospectivas. Buenos Aires. (Boletín no. 231). 259 p. [1385
Detailed information about export and import trade during 1941–1942, by commodities and countries; tariff rates; and a brief historical summary.

————. El comercio exterior argentino en 1942 y su comparación con él de 1941. Buenos Aires. Ed. Guillermo Kraft. (Informe no. 92, Serie C, no. 68, Comercio exterior). 75 p., ilus. [1386
Summary information about Argentine foreign trade in 1942 and 1941, by classes of commodities, and by countries of origin and destination. General data on shipping, demography, trade in earlier years, etc.

————. Dirección general de estadística y censos de la nación. La pobla-

ción y el movimiento demográfico de la República Argentina en los años 1942 y 1941. Buenos Aires. (Informe no. 94, Serie D, no. 11, Demografía). 75 p. [1387]
Estimate of the growth of Argentina's population by states and federal districts. No census figures since 1914 are available.

Moreno Quintana, Lucio M. La integración de la economía nacional (*Rev. cien. econ.*, serie 2, año 31, no. 263, junio, p. 483–503). [1388]
After an analysis of the present "crucial" economic situation (in regard to trade, industries, cost of living, etc.) the author considers the idea of the reconstruction of the Virreynato del Río de la Plata as a method of establishing a better balanced economy. He suggests also that more attention be given to the domestic market.

Mozo, Sadí H., and Jaime Bermejo. Argentina petrolera, 1943. Legislación, técnica, estadística. Buenos Aires. Ed. Cultura. 190 p. [1389]
A useful reference source with adequate statistical documentation. Lacks cost analysis. [Ed.]

Nürenberg, Zacarías. Problema de los combustibles (*Bol. oficial bolsa com. Rosario*, año 31, no. 755, junio 30, p. 19–22). [1390]
Describes hardships caused by the scarcity of imported fuels, particularly to the electrical utilities; emphasizes new trends in the use of substitutes.

Ortiz, Ricardo M. Valor económico de los puertos argentinos. Buenos Aires. Ed. Losada. (Bibl. de estudios económicos). 242 p. [1391]
The first systematic treatise on Argentine ports and their economic spheres of influence. The study describes the history and characteristics of Argentine ports in the last hundred years. In the last chapter the author presents an outline of a new law of ports. It is a remarkably thorough and solid piece of research.

Peña Guzmán, Solano. El nuevo conflicto cañero industrial (*Ind. azuc.*, año 48, no. 594, abril, p. 208–212). [1392]
Analysis of the dispute between sugar growers and refiners in Tucumán. Economic and social factors.

Pereda, José A. La producción porcina. Su relación con el problema maicero en Argentina (*Rev. cien. econ.*, serie 2, año 31, no. 263, junio, p. 531–554). [1393]
The evolution of the hog industry in the last 50 years; The author urges improvement in quality of production.

Repetto, Nicolás. Estudios cooperativos. Buenos Aires. Tall. La Vanguardia. (Federación argentina de cooperativas de consumo). 137, vi p. [1394]
The cooperative movement in Argentina is studied in a series of articles, covering especially housing and agriculture. Pertinent legislation is explained.

Reti, Ladislao. El problema del caucho y su solución nacional (*Rev. econ. arg.*, año 26, tomo 42, no. 302, agosto, p. 343–349). [1395]
The author, manager of an important chemical concern, points out the lack of natural rubber in Argentina and the possibility of manufacturing synthetic rubber based on the country's resources of ethylic alcohol.

REVISTA DEL BANCO DE LA NACIÓN ARGENTINA. Órgano oficial de la Institución. Buenos Aires. Vol. 7, no. 1–3. [1396]
Deals specifically with financial activities of the Bank, the most important institution of its kind in Argentina. Detailed account of the loans and other operations performed by all branches, with breakdown by kind, amount, etc. Full statistical documentation.

Rodríguez Arias, Julio C. Los intereses de la nación, los servicios públicos y el capital extranjero (*Rev. econ. arg.*, año 26, tomo 42, no. 305, nov., p. 435–437). [1397]
Advocates the creation of "mixed" establishments in which private foreign and domestic capital would participate with public investment.

Rosario. Dirección general de estadística del municipio. Anuario estadístico, 1941. Rosario. Ed. Emilio Fenner. 139 p. [1398]
Tables presenting data for 1941 on area, climate, building activities, population, health and sanitation, prices, transports, education, finances.

Saavedra Lamas, Carlos. Consejo económico nacional (*Rev. econ. arg.*, año 25, tomo 42, no. 295, enero, p. 10–16). [1399]
Text of a speech delivered by the author at the Unión Industrial Argentina, in which he analyzes the earlier attempts to create a centralized coordinating economic agency and proposes bases for its constitution.

Sánchez de Bustamante, Teodoro. ¿Estatización o industria privada en materia de servicios públicos de transportes y comunicaciones? (*Rev. cien. econ.*, serie 2, año 31, no. 267, oct., p. 963–973). [1400]
After reviewing the economic and legal situation of railroad and telephone companies in Argentina, the author concludes that those services should be publicly owned and administered.

Santamarina, Jorge A. El desarrollo de la industria y el crédito industrial. Decreto de creación del sistema de crédito industrial y sus fundamentos. Buenos Aires. Imp. Gerónimo J. Pesce. 32 p. [1401]
The former Undersecretary of the Department of Agriculture considers the need

of capital and credit for Argentine manufacturing industries.

———. Las finanzas nacionales y las fuerzas activas de la economía (*Rev. cien. econ.*, serie 2, año 31, no. 264, julio, p. 605–616). [1402
Speaking as Minister of Finance, the author stresses the difficult budgetary situation of the Argentine government. Examines possible solutions and asks cooperation of private business.

Saubidet Bilbao, Eduardo. Un sistema de protección selectiva a la industria argentina (*Bol. oficial bolsa com. Rosario*, año 31, no. 760, set. 15, p. 6–10). [1403
Advocates setting different measures to assure the growth of necessary industries, which would complement mere tariff protection, which the author considers insufficient.

Shellenberger, J. A. Argentine grain survey (*Comments on arg. trade*, vol. 23, no. 4, Nov., p. 22–24, 26, 28, 30). [1403a
Condensation of the first half of a "Report on Grains" written for the Corporación para la Promoción del Intercambio. Deals with trends affecting production, consumption, marketing, and exportation of Argentine cereals, storage problems; and uses of the various grains. [A. H. Lester]

Soler Sanuy, Juan. Producción y consumo de energía hidroeléctrica en la Argentina (*Bol. inform. petrol.*, año 20, no. 225, mayo, p. 23–28). [1404
Production of hydro-electric energy in Argentina as compared with the one which relies on fuels. Emphasizes the disparity between potential capacity and utilization.

Stadler, Remigio N. D. Los ferrocarriles del estado en la República Argentina (*Bol. asoc. internac. perm.*, año 27, no. 81, nov.–dic., p. 16–46). [1405
Present situation of government owned railroads in Argentina.

Steinfeld, Eduardo R., and José A. Andicoechea. El régimen financiero argentino durante los años 1931 a 1943. Buenos Aires. Ed. E. Perrot. 63 p. [1406
The author reviews briefly exchange control, the Central Bank, gold revaluation and other financial measures taken since 1934, loans and budgets. There is a chapter devoted to the evolution of tax systems during the last 12 years.

SUPLEMENTO ESTADÍSTICO DE LA *Revista económica.* Banco central de la República Argentina. Oficina de investigaciones económicas. Buenos Aires. No. 66, enero–no. 77, dic. 1407
This publication contains neither comments nor studies which were usually placed in the Bank's review, discontinued for the last 6 years. As a statistical supplement it gives, however, valuable data (some of it original or unique) on banking, foreign trade, industrial activity, agriculture and cattle, finance, building, etc.

Taylor, Carl C. La explotación agropecuaria y la vida rural en las principales zonas de producción en la Argentina (*Rev. econ. arg.*, año 26, tomo 42, no. 305, nov., p. 425–431). [1408
An American agricultural expert who spent a year in Argentina studies the different agricultural regions in Argentina, pointing out the reasons underlying their specialization.
Translated from *Foreign Agriculture*, July, 1943.

Torres Gigena, Carlos (comp.). Tratados de comercio concluídos por la República Argentina . . . 1812–1942. Buenos Aires. Ed. Centurión. 329 p. [1409
A collection of commerce and navigation treaties concluded between Argentina and other nations, with notes by the compiler. The material is arranged alphabetically by countries. [H. Clagget]

Tortorelli, Lucas A. Los bosques argentinos en la industria del papel de diarios. Buenos Aires. Imp. de la Univ. (Univ. de Buenos Aires, Facultad de agronomía y veterinaria, Inst. de frutivicultura y silvicultura, tomo 1, fascículo 3). 58, 23 p., ilus. [1410
The author considers the possible use of forest resources for manufacturing pulp and paper. Economic and technological factors are reviewed and a favorable conclusion is reached.

Trevisán, Egidio C. Estudio sobre la ley argentina de impuesto a los réditos (*Rev. cien. econ.*, serie 2, año 31, no. 265, agosto, p. 707–719). [1411
The second part of this study on income tax analyzes thoroughly the different aspects of the corresponding law. See *Handbook*, no. 8, 1942, item 1555.

Universidad nacional del Litoral. Facultad de ciencias económicas, comerciales y políticas. Trabajos de seminario. Tomo 17. Rosario. Min. de justicia e instrucción pública. 468 p. [1412
The volume contains three studies on insurance with detailed statistics and economic appraisal and one study of telephone companies operating in Santa Fe Province.

Volpi, Carlos A. La economía nacional de la energía en la República Argentina (*Ingeniería*, año 47, no. 829, nov., p. 981–988). [1413
Consumption and domestic output of various kinds of fuels; policy in the field of electrical services, The example of the United States is brought out and a general plan advocated.

Zanetta, Alberto. Algunos aspectos de la industria de los combustibles en nuestro

país (*Bol. inform. petrol.,* año 20, no. 221, enero, p. 20-35). **[1414**
Use of fuels by kind is presented and domestic deposits thoroughly studied. Takes into account technological characteristics and economic factors pertaining to both production and transport. Tables and sketches.

BOLIVIA

Antezana Paz, Franklin. Estabilización del peso boliviano (*Economista,* año 4, tomo 8, no. 94, enero 16, p. 17-18; no. 96, feb. 16, p. 25-28). **[1415**
After analyzing related factors (especially prices, currency, indebtedness and cost of living) the author advocates continued accumulation of gold holdings and foreign exchange as a stabilizing agent.

―――. El problema del oro. Algunos aspectos de la cooperación económica de EE.UU. Cochabamba. Imp. universitaria. (Univ. autónoma de Cochabamba, Facultad de derecho, Cuads. sobre derecho y ciencias sociales, no. 20). 184 p., ilus. **[1416**
The first of these two lectures deals with problems of currency and monetary policy; the second with questions of economic collaboration between the United States and Bolivia as exemplified by the Bolivian Development Corporation. The author is a strong proponent of the gold standard.

Ballivián C., René. The Bolivian development corporation (*Bolivia,* vol. 8, no. 14, Jan.-Feb., p. 6, 20). **[1417**
A brief sketch of the creation of the Bolivian Development Corporation and of its aims for furthering agricultural development through improved transportation. [A. H. Lester]

―――. El comercio de exportación de Bolivia (*Trim. econ.,* vol. 9, no. 4, enero-marzo, p. 536-559). **[1418**
A comprehensive account of Bolivia's foreign trade and its position in the national economy.

Banco hipotecario nacional. El Banco hipotecario nacional en su cincuentenario, 1 de enero de 1893-1 de enero de 1943. 105-106 memoria anual presentada por el Consejo general de administración a los señores accionistas correspondiente a la gestión del año 1942. Cochabamba. Ed. América. 68 p. **[1419**

Banco mercantil, La Paz. Vigésima memoria que presenta el Directorio a la consideración de la Junta anual de accionistas, celebrada en la ciudad de La Paz, el día 27 de enero de 1943. La Paz. 12 p. **[1420**

Banco minero de Bolivia. Sexta memoria, 1942. La Paz. Imp. Artística. 54 p., cuads. **[1421**
Production, exports and prices of the chief minerals of Bolivia. Analysis of activities of the Bank.

Belmont Arias, Jorge. La estadística en Bolivia (*Econ. bol.,* año 1, no. 1, oct., p. 31-37). **[1422**
Historical sketch of the evolution of population statistics in Bolivia, with mention of other statistical activities.

Burgaleta, Vicente. La reconstrucción económica de Bolivia (*Econ. bol.,* año 1, no. 1, oct., p. 15-23). **[1423**
Formulation of a five year plan of economic development with detailed account of investments in different fields. Participation of the government in economic activities is advocated.

Chávez, Cástulo. Dos ferrocarriles de vital importancia (*Rev. inst. soc. bol.,* año 2, no. 2, 1942-1943, p. 37-43). **[1424**
Examines the advisability of constructing the Cochabamba-Santa Cruz and Sucre-Camirí railroads.

CORPORACIÓN BOLIVIANA DE FOMENTO. SUS ORÍGENES, ORGANIZACIÓN Y ACTIVIDAD. La Paz. Ed. Universo. 127 p. **[1425**
The establishment of the Bolivian Development Corporation. Full account of the findings and recommendations of the United States economic mission to Bolivia. General characteristics of the objectives of the Corporation. Laws and decrees related to this institution.

Cuadros, Alfredo. Compendio de hacienda pública. Cochabamba. Imp. universitaria. (Univ. autónoma de Cochabamba, Facultad de derecho, Cuads. sobre derecho y ciencias sociales, no. 24). 231 p. **[1426**
A detailed study of public finance and taxation in Bolivia.

Davalillo, Clemente. Bolivia, país productor de petróleo (*Bol. inst. sudamer. petról.,* vol. 1, no. 2, dic., p. 118-128). **[1427**
Brief description of the various oil deposits with mention of output and products, during 1942 and part of 1943.

Dirección general de presupuesto. Presupuesto general para 1943. La Paz. Escuela tip. Salesiana. 714 p. **[1428**
Detailed budget as approved by executive decree of January 16, 1943. [J. B. Childs]

ECONOMÍA BOLIVIANA. Revista de economía y finanzas. La Paz. Año 1, no. 2, dic. **[1429**
Contains articles on economic conditions in Bolivia, Paraguay and Uruguay.

EL FUTURO DE LA INDUSTRIA DEL ESTAÑO (*Econ. bol.,* año 1, no. 2, dic., p. 5-10). **[1430**
Present situation and future possibilities of the tin mining industry in Bolivia.

INFORME DE LA COMISIÓN PARLAMENTARIA SOBRE EL FERROCARRIL CORUMBÁ-SANTA CRUZ (*Rev. jurídica,* año 5, no. 22, marzo, p. 47-71). **[1431**
Report of a special Parliamentary Commission, charged with the study of this

proposed railroad. Technical and economic problems.

International labor office. Los problemas del trabajo en Bolivia. Informe de la Comisión mixta boliviano-estadounidense del trabajo. Montréal. 45 [i.e. 90] p. [1432
Spanish and English text given. Text of the report and recommendations of the Magruder mission which visited Bolivia early in 1943. The Commission rejects the argument that low productivity of the Bolivian worker accounts fully for his low wages. On the other hand the Commission believes that a considerable effort will be necessary in "a large number of different fields in order to raise the standard of living for the workers." [Ed.]

Mariaca, Guillermo. Reseña sobre la industria petrolífera de Bolivia. La Paz. Ed. Kollasuyo. 73 p., tablas, láms, mapas. [1433
The ex-president of YPFB reviews the main aspects of the Bolivian oil industry. The present stage of development is discussed in some detail and current problems are related to future development. Statistical tables and various production data.

Paz Estenssoro, Víctor. Ideas y hechos económicos en Bolivia (*Econ. bol.*, año 1, no. 2, dic., p. 11–20). [1434
Currency situation is discussed in relation to production of tin and balance of payments.

Peñaloza, Luis. Bancos de rescate y fomento minero. Prólogo de Santiago Schulze. La Paz. Imp. artística. viii, 143 p., cuads. [1435
The history of credit institutions for mineral industries in Bolivia. Extension of such credits under government direction is strongly advocated. A more detailed study of the characteristics and functioning of the Mining Bank of Bolivia is given.

Riera Fernández, José, and Jaime Palenque Ceballos. Hacia la creación en Bolivia de un Banco de crédito industrial (*Econ. bol.*, año 1, no. 2, dic., p. 37–40). [1436
General characteristics of a proposed industrial credit institution for the fostering of national industrial development.

Rocha, Federico A. Política ferroviaria y el oriente boliviano (*Rev. jurídica*, año 5, no. 22, marzo, p. 33–46). [1437
Historical review of Bolivian railroads and policy. Stresses the importance of railroads linking the two main Bolivian regions.

Superintendencia de bancos. Memoria de la Superintendencia de bancos correspondiente a los años 1939-1940-1941. La Paz. Ed. Sport. 1942 i.e. 1943. vii, 263 p. [1438
Includes banking legislation and regulations. [J. B. Childs]

Terán Gómez, Luis. En torno del ferrocarril Sucre-Camirí (*Bol. asoc. internac. perm.*, año 27, no. 81, nov.–dic., p. 63–67). [1439
Construction of this line in the shortest possible time is strongly advocated.

Videla, Carlos J. Bolivia ponders a labor problem (*The Pan American*, vol. 3, no. 10, March, p. 7–9). [1440
Working conditions and general economic background of tin miners in Bolivia briefly presented with more detailed account of a recent pledge for increased wages.

CHILE

Álvarez González, Humberto (Pedro. J. Vargas A.). Problemas económico-financieros nacionales, 1942-1943. Santiago. Imp. El Imparcial. 370 p., ilus., cuads. [1441
These articles published in 1942 through 1943 deal with problems of salaries, cost of living, money, inflation, budgets, and finance. The author's chief concern is to prevent inflation.

Álvarez Vázquez de Prada, Enrique. El problema del fierro en la economía chilena. Un estudio técnico de la necesidad, posibilidad y futuro de la industria pesada en Chile. Santiago. Ed. Ercilla. 119 p. [1442
Advocating the establishment of an iron and steel industry in Chile, the author points out the possibilities the country offers in this field and its future importance.

Antonioletti, Mario. Fundamentos para una política económica nacional. Santiago. 17 p. [1443
Brief account of the major economic activities in Chile; proposal of a working plan for the development of agriculture on a cooperative basis; the establishment of an adequate iron and steel industry and a plan of public works.

———. La inflación en Chile (*Economista*, año 4, tomo 8, no. 96, feb. 16, p. 11–14). [1444
A discussion of inflationary trends in Chile and the manner in which they might have been checked.

Arriagada H., Carlos. A circunstancias económicas extraordinarias, expedientes económicos extraordinarios (*Econ. finan.*, año 7, no. 85, nov., p. 13–26). [1445
As a means of improving the general economic situation of Chile credits should be granted, through an appropriate agency, to foster the development of planned basic economic enterprises such as metallurgy, electrical energy, public works, etc.

Artigas Soriano, Rosa. La industria algodonera. Santiago. Tall. gráf. Millantun. 52 p. [1446
Mainly an appraisal of the textile industry in Chile, stressing the desirability of promoting the production of raw cotton.

Báguena Visconti, Enrique. El problema del petróleo en Chile. [Santiago?] Ed. Garay y Alániz. 51 p. [1447
Discussion of the economic and political importance of oil, with particular reference to Chile. Various economic and legislative measures are advised and further explorations of oil deposits in Chile is strongly advocated.

Banco central de Chile. Balanza de pagos de Chile, año 1942. Santiago. Imp. El imparcial. 67 p., tablas. [1447a
A detailed discussion of the balance of payments of Chile for 1943 and a comparison with 1929.

———. Memoria anual, no. 17, presentada . . . 1942. Santiago. Imp. San Germán. 220 p., ilus., cuads. [1448
Brief analysis of economic conditions in Chile reflected in the activities of the Banco Central. Currency and various operations are presented. A comprehensive supplement (containing laws and decrees issued in 1942) completes the report.

Banco hipotecario de Chile. Consejo de administración. 98ª memoria semestral, segundo semestre de 1942. Santiago. Imp. Ex-Lathrop. 6 p., cuads. [1449
Balance sheet of the Bank without further comment.

BOLETÍN MENSUAL DEL BANCO CENTRAL DE CHILE. Santiago. Año 16, no. 179, enero–no. 190, dic. [1450
An introductory survey is followed by a much more detailed review of mining, agriculture, manufacturing industries, foreign trade, prices, cost of living, banking, stock exchange, etc.

Bulnes Aldunate, Luis. La Corporación de fomento de la producción. Santiago. Tip. La Gratitud nac. 270 p. [1451
Origins, scope of activities and achievements of the Corporation. A brief outline of earlier Chilean attempts and of foreign experiences. Legal and administrative aspects with a full discussion of special features of the economic plan by activities, investments and results.

Caja autónoma de amortización de la deuda pública. Informe al Ministerio de hacienda sobre las operaciones realizadas en el año 1942. Santiago. Imp. La Sud-América. 93, iii p., ilus., cuads. [1452
Full review of amount and movement of the public debt with detailed breakdown both by types and sources.

———. Servicio de la deuda externa. Año 1942. Santiago. Imp. La Sud-América. 29 p., ilus. [1453
Foreign indebtedness of the country with a breakdown by type (pounds, dollars, Swiss francs).

Caja de crédito agrario. Memoria . . . 1941-1942. Santiago. Ed. La Nación. 105 p. [1453a
Report on the operations of the Bank of Agricultural Credit during 1941 and 1942. [A. H. Lester]

Caja de crédito hipotecario. Memorial anual, 1942. Santiago. Ed. Artes y letras, N. Avaria e hijo. 157 p., ilus. [1454
Annual report covering the activities of the Caja (loans, housing, agrarian credit, etc.) A detailed account of operations is followed by pertinent laws and decrees.

Chilean nitrate sales corporation. Chilean nitrate, 1941-1943. New York. 15 p., illus. [1454a
This booklet describes production and export of nitrates during the war. Special attention is given to the part played by the government in insuring uninterrupted production.

Cifuentes S., Alberto (comp.). Bolsa de comercio. Estadísticas bursátiles, 1920-1930-1943. Santiago. Imp. Universo. 34 p., ilus. [1455
A collection of tables and graphs picturing the evolution of major financial factors in Chilean economic life. It covers banks, exchanges, insurance, commercial and industrial enterprises, etc. A comparison between 1920, 1930 and 1943 is drawn.

Confederación de la producción y del comercio. Segunda convención de la producción y del comercio, celebrada en Santiago de Chile los días 30 y 31 de agosto y 1 de septiembre de 1942. Organizada por la Confederación de la producción y del comercio. Santiago. Tall. gráf. Casa nacional del niño. 1943? 265 p. [1455a
In addition to resolutions approved by the convention, the volume contains essays on a number of topics, such as production, social problems, state intervention in economic activities, taxes. The conference was attended by representatives of the principal industrial and commercial organizations in the country.

Corporación de fomento de la producción. Plan de electrificación del país de la Corporación de fomento de la producción, Chile; directivas generales y plan de electrificación primaria del país. Santiago. Imp. Universo. 1942 i.e. 1943. 211 p., mapa. [1456

Cruz-Coke, Eduardo. Fundamentos de la economía nacional. Santiago. Imp. El Imparcial. 23 p. [1457
A study of economic and social problems in Chile, stressing low purchasing power and widespread malnutrition. Attention is also directed to broad aspects of commercial and monetary policies.

Dirección general de estadística. Anuario de industria, año 1940. Valparaíso. Imp. Universo. 72 p., cuads. [1458
Manufacturing industries in 1939 by major groups. Number of firms, employees, value of production, raw materials, fuels, and capital invested. Some industries are reviewed in greater detail.

―――. Estadística bancaria. Resumen de los estados de situación al 17 de febrero de 1943. No. 81. Santiago. Imp. La SudAmérica. 36 p., ilus., cuads. [1459
This publication deals with the financial condition of banking institutions in Chile. Full and detailed account is presented with tables and graphs.

―――. Secretaría general del censo. El censo económico general de 1943. Antecedentes sobre su organización. Santiago. Imp. Universo. 10, viii p., ilus. [1460
Forms used in the census of 1943 are presented and their use and significance explained. They cover population, mining, agriculture, and industries.

Durán, Fernando. Sociedad explotadora de Tierra del Fuego, 1893-1943. Valparaíso. Imp. Universo. 128 p., ilus. [1461
Reviews the origin and evolution of the powerful firm Sociedad Exploradora de Tierra del Fuego. In Chapter XI the author appraises the economic significance of this enterprise as a producer and exporter of wool, leather, meat and other products. Illustrated by many photographs.

ESTADÍSTICA CHILENA. Dirección general de estadística. Santiago. Año 16, no. 1/2, enero/feb.–no. 12, dic. [1462
Series of economic indexes covering, in some detail, exports, imports, production, etc. Special studies on budget, finances, mining, agriculture, manufacturing industries, foreign trade (very detailed table), demography, and social security. Graphs and tables. The December issue contains a general synopsis of economic events in 1943, whereas No. 6 gives special data related to real estate and Nos. 1 through 12 partial tables of the last population census.

FACULTADES ECONÓMICAS ESPECIALES. PROYECTO ECONÓMICO. Tomo 1. Historia fidedigna de su establecimiento (*El consultor práctico de las leyes*, año 1, no. 5, p. 1-302). [1462a
A discussion of proposal to grant special economic powers to the President of Chile. Important data on the economic situation in the country will be found throughout the text.

Gutiérrez Forno, María Antonieta. Política y legislación caminera en Chile. Santiago. Imp. Relámpago. 104 p. [1463
This valuable study deals with the background of transportation in Chile and in other countries, with particular attention to highways. Pertinent laws and economic factors are discussed.

Ibáñez, Bernardo. Defensa de la clase obrera. Santiago. Imp. Yungay. 44 p. [1464
Some speeches delivered by the Secretary General of the Confederación de Trabajadores de Chile, stating the aims and purposes of the trade union movement in Chile, and dispelling the fear aroused by some periodicals about its activities.

INFORME DE LA COMISIÓN GUBERNATIVA SOBRE LA INDUSTRIA SIDERÚRGICA EN CHILE (*An. inst. ing. Chile*, año 56, no. 1, enero, p. 21-39; no. 2, feb., p. 67-84). [1465
These reports deal with a vital question for the Chilean economy: the enlargement of the existing facilities for the production of iron and steel and the establishment of new units. Considers the location of several plants, with regard to iron ore, coal, hydroelectric resources, port facilities; the best suited zones for the purpose; technological and economic factors.

Instituto de fomento minero e industrial. Nómina de los trabajos presentados al Primer congreso de la economía de las provincias de Tarapacá y Antofagasta, marzo de 1943. Iquique. 9 p. [1466
A list of studies grouped under general headings, including agriculture, fishing, industries, and power.

Ivovich, Esteban. La producción de Chile y los nuevos órganos de política económica del estado. Santiago. Comisión chilena de cooperación intelectual. 1943? 112 p., tablas. [1466a
A review of the organization, activities and achievements of the Ministry of National Economy, the National Council of Foreign Trade and the Corporation for the Development of Production.

Krassa, Pablo. Sobre las posibilidades de desarrollo de algunas industrias químicas en el país. Concepción. Tip. Salesiana. 10 p. [1467
The possible development of some chemical industries in Chile. Mention of important inorganic and some organic chemicals.

Ministerio de hacienda. Exposición sobre el estado de la hacienda pública, presentada a la Comisión mixta de presupuestos en octubre de 1943. Santiago. Imp. Universo. 50 p., cuads. [1468
A general survey of the financial situation, with a detailed analysis of revenues and expenditures.

Narizzano, Hugo. La solución inmediata del problema ferroviario chileno (*Econ. finan.*, año 7, no. 85, nov., p. 27-36). [1469
Advocates the necessity of improving railroad transportation to the South.

Nehgme Rodríguez, Elías. La economía nacional y el problema de las subsistencias

en Chile. Tomos 1-2. Santiago. Imp. Condor. 2 vols. 955 p. [1470
A detailed description of the economy of Chile profusely documented with statistical data. [Ed.]

Pacull T., Luis M. Control de precios. Santiago. Imp. Nascimento. 120 p., tablas. [1471
The central thesis of this study is that government intervention in regulating prices is, under the present circumstances, both desirable and unavoidable.

Primer congreso de la economía de las provincias de Tarapacá y Antofagasta, Iquique, 1943. Reglamento. Antofagasta, Iquique. Imp. Chile. 15 p. [1472
Resolutions and recommendations relating to the nitrate industry, mining, agriculture, fishing industry, fuel and power industry, public utilities, economic development, credit and other economic problems. [Ed.]

———. Resumen de conclusiones y ponencias aprobadas durante su celebración. Iquique. Sría. general. 24 p. [1473
A brief outline of the work of the Congress and its recommendations, dealing with mining, transportation, agriculture, industries, and credit.

El proyecto económico en el congreso nacional. Santiago. Ed. La Nación. 55 p. [1474
Congressional discussion of the project of a law regulating the financial aspects of economic policy. Contains valuable data on Chilean economy in relation to taxes, and national income.

Ruiz Bourgeois, Julio. La minería en la vida de Chile. El individual (la minería chilena hasta 1880). La empresa (la minería chilena desde 1881 a 1930). El estado (la minería chilena desde 1931 hasta el presente). Santiago. Imp. Universo. 35 p., ilus., cuads. [1475
The history of the development of Chilean mining industries with emphasis upon the pioneering action of the "discoverers." The period of the big enterprises and state intervention is fully discussed.

Saleh Sada, Félix. Política pesquera. Santiago. Ed. Molina Lackington. 57 p. [1476
The possibilities for fisheries in Chile compared to development in other countries. Present situation (economic and legal aspects) and recommendation for improvement.

Simón, Raúl. El concepto de industria nacional y la protección del estado (*Proc. eighth amer. scien. cong.*, vol. 8, p. 213–239). [1477
General economic pattern of Chile with detailed study of manufacturing industries and working population. Favors protection of industry by means of high custom duties and import quotas coupled with freedom of enterprise within the country.

———. Oro, moneda, salarios y precios (*An. inst. ing. Chile*, año 56, no. 7-8, julio-agosto, p. 244–249; no. 9, sept., p. 312–327; no. 10–11, oct.–nov., p. 392–400). [1478
The author tries to embody, in a single formula, the relationship between the volume of currency, national income, wages, and prices. Gold standard, inflation and deflation are also considered, and the formula is applied to the economy of the United States.
Also published separately.

Superintendencia de la Casa de moneda y especies valoradas. Memoria de la Superintendencia de la Casa de moneda y especies valoradas de Chile de los años 1940-1941-1942. Santiago. Tall. de especies valoradas. 65 p. [1479
Contains a table showing production of fine gold in Chile, 1920–1942.

Tapia Villarroel, Noel Guillermo. El movimiento cooperativo en Inglaterra y en Chile. Santiago. Imp. Cultura. 107 p. [1480
The history and social implications of the cooperative movement. The author gives a full account of what has been already achieved in Chile and outlines a proposed plan for its improvement.

Trabajos de estadística de la dirección general de Santiago de Chile (*Estadística*, vol. 1, no. 1, March, p. 104–112). [1481
This office presents industrial, financial and other statistics for the years 1939–1941. Special attention is given to manufacturing industries.

Vassallo Rojas, Emilio, and **Carlos Matus Gutiérrez.** Ferrocarriles de Chile: historia y organización. Primera ed. Santiago. Ed. Rumbo. 448 p. [1483

Vergara, Roberto. Los censos de población en Chile (*Proc. eighth amer. scien. cong.*, vol. 8, p. 95–108). [1484
Historical review of the earlier population censuses, with special reference to the methods followed in 1930.

Wilson, J. P. Chilean cooperatives (*Agric. Americas*, vol. 3, Dec., p. 236–237). [1484a
Discussion of a few of the many agricultural cooperatives being established. [A. H. Lester]

ECUADOR

Albán Mestanza, Ernesto. La industrialización del cloruro de sodio en el Ecuador (*An. univ. cent. Ecuador*, tomo 60, no. 317–318, enero–junio, p. 83–106). [1485
A detailed technical and economic study of the possibilities of developing this industry in Ecuador.

Andrade, César D. Aspectos de la economía ecuatoriana (*Proc. eighth amer. scien. cong.,* vol. 11, p. 221–233). [1486
Taxes, currency, prices, production, foreign trade, with some tables and graphs. Stresses the necessity for inter-American cooperation.

Banco central del Ecuador. Memoria anual, 1942. Quito. Tall. del Banco central. 36, xxxi p., cuads. [1487
The activities of the Bank with special attention to currency, inflation and related problems. Graphs and tables.

BOLETÍN MENSUAL DEL BANCO CENTRAL DE ECUADOR. Quito. Año 16, no. 185/186, dic., 1942/enero, 1943–no. 191/192, junio/julio; año 17, no. 193/194, agosto/sept.–no. 197/198, dic., 1943/enero, 1944. [1488
Some periodical indexes, chiefly concerning finance, the annual report of the Bank for 1942 (with an analysis of economic conditions), and articles on taxation, investments, etc.

Cámara de comercio de Guayaquil. Memorandum sobre el descenso de la producción de balsa debido a la decisión de la Junta de guerra contra los productores ecuatorianos. Guayaquil. Lit. La Reforma. 8 p. [1489
Conditions prevailing in the production and commerce of balsa wood. The Cámara recommends abolition of trade monopoly in this commodity.

Castillo Vélez, Othón. Nuestro suelo (*Rev. univ. Guayaquil,* año 14, tomo 14, no. 1, enero–abril, p. 225–260). [1490
Advocates measures designed to encourage settlement and to stimulate efficient farming.

Contraloría general. Informe al Congreso nacional y al Ministro de hacienda, julio de 1942–junio de 1943. Quito? Tall. gráf. del Min. de hacienda. 25, viii p., ilus. [1491
An account of the budget for 1942. Includes a comparative table for 1940, 1941 and 1942.

Ministerio de hacienda. Informe al Congreso nacional, 1943. Quito. Imp. del Min. de hacienda. 48 p. [1492
Report on the financial situation of Ecuador covering sources of revenue and a discussion of economic conditions in the country.

Saad, Pedro A. El Ecuador y la guerra. Guayaquil. Imp. Emporio gráf. 40 p. [1493
An outline of social and economic problems confronting the country of special concern to workers. This outline was submitted to a Congress of Workers.

Samaniego, Juan José. Bioestadística en el cosmos ecuatoriano. Quito. Tall. gráf. de educación. (Publ. del Min. de previsión social). 23 p. [1494
Total amount, geographic distribution, urban and rural settlements and other demographic indices of Ecuador. Special mention on education and health.

Superintendencia de bancos. Informe del superintendente de bancos por el año de 1942. Quito. Imp. del Min. de hacienda. xviii, 67 p. [1495
Includes report on insurance companies as well as banks.

PARAGUAY

Antezana Paz, Franklin. La reforma monetaria paraguaya (*Econ. bol.,* año 1, no. 2, dic., p. 26–32). [1496
The text and implication of the decree-law of October, 1943. Questions the possibility of similar changes in Bolivia.

BOLETÍN DEL MINISTERIO DE AGRICULTURA, COMERCIO E INDUSTRIAS. Asunción. Año 4, vol. 4, no. 1, primer trim. 45 p., mimeographed. [1497
The *Boletín* publishes statistics of production and trade, as well as decrees and laws relating to the economic life of the country. [Ed.]

Dirección general de estadística. Anuario estadístico de la República del Paraguay, 1940–1941. Asunción. Imp. nacional. 293 p. [1498
This yearbook reviews the output of the more important agricultural industries. Figures related to trade and other economic activities are also presented.

Martínez Díaz, Nicasio. El sistema impositivo paraguayo (*Rev. cien. econ.,* serie 2, año 31, no. 258, enero, p. 27–44). [1499
The tax system in Paraguay, general principles which underlie it and specific component items, such as income tax, inheritance tax, consumption tax, etc.

EL RÉGIMEN MONETARIO ORGÁNICO DE LA REPÚBLICA DEL PARAGUAY. Asunción. Ed. Guaranía. 43 p. [1500
A discussion of the present monetary situation in Paraguay followed by an analysis of projected reforms. Text of the pertinent law is given.

United States. Office of price administration. Foreign information branch. Latin American section. Paraguay. A study of price control, cost of living and rationing. Washington. vi, 40 p., tables. [1501
Analysis and full text of laws dealing with price control and the situation with respect to prices of both imported and domestic commodities. Cost of living and agricultural development programs, commodity control and rationing complete this valuable survey.

PERU

Arca Parró, Alberto. El inventario del potencial económico de la nación peruana (*Estadística*, vol. 1, no. 4, Dec., p. 122–127). [1502

———. Problemas y soluciones para el censo demográfico peruano de 1940 (*Proc. eighth amer. scien. cong.*, vol. 8, p. 17–28). [1503
After reviewing the experiences of the past censuses the author explains the methods to be followed in the census of 1940.

Arrús, Oscar F. El índice de precios en el Perú (*Estadística*, vol. 1, no. 1, March, p. 76–89). [1504
Wholesale price indices in Peru since 1914; explanation of the method used in its composition in its present form, which dates from 1920.

Banco central de reserva del Perú. Memoria, 1942. Imp. Torres Aguirre. 1943? 71 p., ilus. [1505
Full account of the financial situation and activities of the Bank and member banks with special studies covering currency, types of loans and investments, prices, and cost of living.

Banco central hipotecario del Perú. Memoria, 1942. Lima. Imp. Torres-Aguirre. 32, v p., cuads. [1506
Detailed account of mortgage loans (by area and type) with a review of present financial situation of the Bank.

Banco del Perú y Londres en liquidación. Memoria anual de la superintendencia de bancos al 31 de diciembre de 1942. Lima. Imp. Torres Aguirre. 30 p., cuads. [1507
Detailed account of operations during 1942.

BOLETÍN DEL BANCO CENTRAL DE RESERVA DEL PERÚ. Lima. Enero–dic. [1508
A comprehensive and very condensed survey of economic conditions, followed by tables and graphs covering chief items, such as banks, currency, foreign trade, prices, cost of living. Detailed attention to imports and exports by countries and commodities.

Cámara de diputados. Plan de acción de la Comisión de post-guerra, presentado a la Cámara por el presidente de dicha comisión, señor ingeniero don Juvenal Monje, diputado por Paucartambo, en las sesiones de los días 8 y 9 de setiembre de 1943. Lima. Ed. Gil. 27 p. [1509

COOPERATIVISMO (*Div. agric.*, no. 46, 24 p.). [1509a
Discusses agricultural cooperatives in Peru and consumers' cooperatives, giving a model constitution for a consumers' cooperative. [A. H. Lester]

Departamento de estadística general de aduanas. Anuario del comercio exterior del Perú correspondiente a 1942. Lima. Emp. ed. Peruana. lxxx, 414 p. [1510

Dirección de caminos y ferrocarriles. Cuadros sobre inversiones, trabajos efectuados y costos en la construcción y conservación de carreteras, en el año 1941. Lima. Imp. del Min. de guerra. 1942? xxx, 146 p., ilus., cuads. [1511
Detailed account by type and geographical location of all highway works executed, with financial statements.

Ferrero, Rómulo A. Perspectivas económicas de la post-guerra (*Mercurio peruano*, año 18, vol. 25, no. 201, dic., p. 586–608). [1512
A review of the economic disturbances created by the war and its aftermath. Advocates state intervention and economic planning in certain fields, of economic activity.
The author reviews Peru's position in world economy and examines the country's prospects in the fields of foreign trade and industrialization.

———. La realidad económica de Perú (*Trim. econ.*, vol. 9, no. 4, enero-marzo, p. 591–613). [1513
Chief aspects of Peruvian economy; special attention to policies thus far applied; industrialization strongly advocated.

Gerbi, Antonello. El Perú en marcha. Lima. Ed Banco italiano. 412 p. [1514
A glorification of present-day Peruvian progress, with much worthwhile information.

Hobagen, Jorge. Anuario de la industria minera en el Perú en 1942. Lima. Imp. Americana. (Dirección de minas y petróleos, Bol. 72). 211 p. [1515
The value of mineral production for 1942 was Soles 374,732,746, as compared with Soles 333,651,287 for 1941.

Jiménez Correa, Carlos P. El impuesto sobre la renta en el Perú (*Estadística*, vol. 1, no. 3, Sept., p. 115–118). [1516
Comparative table of income tax receipts in 1941–1942. Supplemented by brief comments.

Junta nacional de la industria lanar. Memoria, 1942. Lima? 109 p., tablas. [1517
Annual report of accomplishments through 1942 with a detailed financial account. Statistical table and special technical reports.

Moll, Bruno, and Emilio G. Barreto. El sistema monetario del Perú. Córdoba. Univ. nac. de Córdoba. 88 p. [1518
From *Revista de economía y estadística*, año 4, no. 3.
An historical appraisal of the evolution of the monetary policy in Peru, from 1900 through 1940, followed by a discussion of

the establishment of the Central Bank and current policies. Criticizes the plan proposed by Kemmerer and suggests new policies.

Pareja, José. Importancia y valor económico de la costa peruana (*Mercurio peruano*, año 18, vol. 25, no. 192, marzo, p. 105–116). [1519

The economy of the coastal strip of Peru with special reference to agriculture, petroleum, sulphur, guano, fisheries. The industrial development of this region and its importance in foreign trade. A comparison is drawn between this and other areas.

Paulet, Pedro E. Información sobre las condiciones económicas y sociales del Perú y sus problemas fundamentales (*Proc. eighth amer. scien. cong.*, vol. 11, p. 253–268). [1520

After a brief study of economic resources of the country the author discusses the balance of payments and national income. The development of iron and steel industry is envisaged as a means of reorganizing the economy of the country.

Quiroga, Oscar. Estado general de los campos petrolíferos del Perú al finalizar el año 1941 (*Bol. inst. sudamer. petról.*, vol. 1, no. 1, abril, p. 69–73). [1521

General information on production of petroleum in 1940/41 by fields and companies; the number of wells, output, productivity, etc.

Regal, Alberto. Política ferroviaria peruana (*Rev. univ. cat. Perú*, tomo 11, no. 6–7, set.–oct., p. 264–270). [1522

A brief analysis of the development of railroads in Peru. Considers the rôle of railroads paramount to the economic development of the country.

Sociedad nacional agraria, Lima. Memoria que la Junta directiva presenta a la asamblea general ordinaria, año 1942–43. Lima. Lib. Gil. 131 p., cuads., mapa. [1523

Deals chiefly with the economic situation during the period covered, and with the production of cotton, sugar, lime, seed, grains, and other commodities which the Sociedad Nacional Agraria puts on the market. Includes statistical tables and charts.

Superintendencia de bancos. Balances de las empresas bancarias y compañías de seguros, al 30 de junio de 1942. No. 54. Lima. Imp. Gil. 40 p., ilus., cuads. [1524

Detailed accounts for the Central Bank, Agricultural Bank, Industrial Bank, Mining Bank, along with commercial banking institutions and mortgage banks, and insurance companies.

———. Memoria de la superintendencia de bancos y estadística bancaría de seguros y capitalización, 1942. Lima. Imp. Gil. 590 p., ilus., cuads. [1525

Activities of the Superintendencia, measures taken, operations performed by private establishments in the field. Detailed tables.

Tappy, Elizabeth B. Peruvian guano (*For. agric.*, vol. 7, August, p. 185–192). [1526

Conditions surrounding the production of this fertilizer, used even in Inca days. [A. H. Lester]

Vignolo Murphy, Carlos. Vías de comunicación en el Perú (*Bol. asoc. internac. perm.*, año 27, no. 80, set.–oct., p. 91–96). [1527

Means of transportation in Peru (highways, railroads, air, water), accomplishments, drawbacks and future possibilities. Suggests a coordinated plan to promote development of more adequate transportation facilities.

URUGUAY

Asociación nacional de contadores. Instituto de economía. Las industrias del mar. Montevideo. 29 p., diag. [1528

Analysis of the potential development of fishing industries.

Aznárez, Julio Gregorio. La industria azucarera en el Uruguay. Montevideo. Ed. Urta y Curbelo. 76 p. [1529

Uruguay can and should grow and refine the sugar it consumes. The government should formulate and follow a sound policy designed to encourage the growth of an adequate sugar industry.

This concise study is amply documented with statistical data. [Ed.]

Banco de la República Oriental del Uruguay. Memoria 1938–1942. Balances de situación y resultados e información estadística correspondiente al ejercicio terminado el 31 de diciembre de 1942. Montevideo. Tall. gráf. del Banco de la República Oriental del Uruguay. 129 p., ilus. [1530

Review of the economic maladjustments brought about by the outbreak of the war with special reference to Uruguay. The report is documented with statistical tables, some carrying back as far as the end of nineteenth century.

Basabe Castellanos, Carlos. Organización de la estadística económica en el Uruguay (*Proc. eighth amer. scien. cong.*, vol. 8, p. 161–168). [1531

A review of the current statistical appraisals in Uruguay, covering industrial census (every 5 years), indexes of industrial production, occupation, wages, disputes (every 3 months), monthly statistics of foreign and domestic trade, prices, and living costs.

Boletín mensual del banco de la república oriental del Uruguay. Departamento de investigaciones económicas. Montevideo. No. 1, enero?–no. 12, dic. [1532
Brief surveys of important aspects of Uruguayan economic life, economic series and transcription of regulations dealing with exchange available for imports and exports. Balance of payments, trade, banking, currency, stocks, revenues, prices are adequately discussed.

Christophersen, Ricardo. El consumo interno de productos agrarios en el Uruguay (*Mercados del mundo,* año 7, no. 33, julio, p. 1–10, tablas, gráfs.). [1533
Consists chiefly of tables and graphs showing consumption of various products and relation of consumption to production, p. 3–10. [A. H. Lester]

Comercio exterior. Datos estadísticos. Contralor de exportaciones e importaciones. Montevideo. No. 12, enero–no. 23, dic. [1534
This official publication covers Uruguay's foreign trade (imports and exports) by months, commodities and countries; pays special attention to foreign exchange; presents some retrospective data.

Cosío, Ricardo. La situación de las finanzas ordinarias y extraordinarias del estado. Conferencia pronunciada por el señor ministro de hacienda . . . el 21 de junio de 1943 en el salón de actos de la institución, al instalar la Comisión creada por decretos de 4 y 18 del mismo mes. Montevideo. Bolsa de comercio. Cámara nacional de camercio. 15 p. [1535

Dupont Aguiar, Mario. El Uruguay en la post guerra. La gran crisis. El futuro del mundo. Las fuerzas morales y materiales de la República. Montevideo. Ed. Independencia. (Col. Economía y política). 162 p. [1536
A useful study of Uruguayan economy in relation to post-war readjustments. A good part of the discussion, however, is not particularly relevant to the issue at hand. [Ed.]

Freire, Omar R. Estudio sintético de la gestión económica cumplida por el Frigorífico nacional (*Rev. fac. cien. econ. adm.,* año 4, no. 5, nov., p. 661–680). [1537
Financial and economic features of the National Meat Packing Plant and its contribution to the national economy.

Martínez Lamas, Julio. Economía uruguaya. Montevideo. Ed. G. García. 262 p. [1538
First part of a two volume study of the economic resources and organization of Uruguay. This volume reviews the geographic, ethnic and cultural aspects of the national economy.
A useful reference source. [Ed.]

Milans, Jeremías. Observaciones sobre el cultivo de la caña de azúcar en la región de Tranqueras, departamento de Rivera, Uruguay, en las cosechas de los años 1941 y 1942 (*Ind. azuc.,* año 48, no. 593, marzo, p. 115–125). [1539
Agricultural aspects of the cane sugar industry.

Ministerio de ganadería y agricultura. Dirección de agronomía. El Uruguay como país agropecuario. Montevideo. 57 p. [1540
A special study of agriculture and cattle by products follows an analysis of exports. All related factors are considered. Comparative tables and graphs complete this brief but valuable report.

Monteverde, Manuel. El Banco central del Uruguay y la situación financiera del momento. Proyecto de estatutos y exposición de motivos. Montevideo. Ed. A. Monteverde. 110 p. [1541
The author proposes a law for the establishment of a central bank in Uruguay. Supports his plan with various considerations of economic and financial character, and with examples from other countries.

———. Lo que se vió y lo que no se vió. Examen crítico retrospectivo de algunos aspectos de la política financiera y monetaria adoptada por el país. Montevideo. Imp. A. Monteverde. 282 p. [1542
In this collection of brief studies the author attempts to discuss the prevailing financial and monetary situation in Uruguay. He examines measures already promulgated, tracing their relationships to loans, taxation, national income, and balance of payments, and sets forth principles for the establishment of a sound economic and monetary policy.

Morató, Octavio. El estado industrial y sus funcionarios. Montevideo. Ed. Ceibo. 59 p. [1543
Sketch of the evolution of government-sponsored economic agencies in all fields. Discusses in more detail legal and functional characteristics. The status of personnel of such agencies (especially of banks) is studied with particular respect to pensions.

Ochoa, Raúl. Contralor de cambios en el Uruguay (*Rev. fac. cien. econ. adm.,* año 4, no. 5, nov., p. 217–529). [1544
A detailed study of the background, establishment and functioning of exchange control in Uruguay. Analyzes fully currency, indebtedness, various related legal measures. Present conditions are covered in great detail. Tables and graphs.

Revista del banco de la república oriental del Uruguay. Departamento de investigaciones económicas. Montevideo. Año 1,

no. 4, enero; año 2, no. 5, abril–no. 7, oct. [1545
This very valuable quarterly periodical statistical series on foreign trade, revenues, cost of living, agriculture, finance, etc., and detailed information on foreign trade, balance of trade, balances of banks, monetary matters, exchange control, etc.

Silveira Zorzi, Fermín. Preparación del país para afrontar la post-guerra (*Rev. nac.*, Montevideo, año 6, tomo 24, no. 71, nov., p. 216–243). [1546
The author analyzes thoroughly the monetary problem in Uruguay, which, linked to trade and production, constitutes the clue to the readjustments necessary to improve the country's preparedness for the post-war world.

Simoens Arce, F. El problema cambiario en el Uruguay. Resumen terórico. Montevideo. Ed. A. Barreiro y Ramos. 130 p. [1547
The chief features of the foreign trade of Uruguay from 1914 through 1942, broken down into three cycles. Special attention is devoted to the last one, starting in 1931 when the controls were launched and enforced.

TEXTO DEL DISCURSO PRONUNCIADO POR EL ING. GONZÁLEZ VIDART (*Rev. asoc. rural Uruguay*, año 70, no. 10, oct., p. 14–16). [1548
Uruguay's Secretary of Agriculture expresses the opinion that unification of foreign trade operations by the governments of the United States and Great Britain during war-time points to likely postwar trends, and that centralized control over various of her products which enter foreign trade is especially opportune for Uruguay under the circumstances. [A. H. Lester]

ADDENDA

Asociación peruana de ingenieros agrónomos, Lima. Anales de la primera convención agronómica y regional. Provincia Litoral de Tumbes y departamentos de Piura, Lambayeque y La Libertad. Realizada en la ciudad de Chiclayo del 26 al 29 de julio de 1942. Lima. Imp. Americana. 1942. vi, 202 p., ilus., cuads., figs. [1549
Proceedings of the convention, with reprints of the studies submitted, speeches and recommendations. Problems of crops, irrigation, experimental stations, etc. are discussed.

Melo, Leopoldo. La postguerra y algunos de los planes sobre el nuevo orden económico. Buenos Aires. Unión industrial argentina, Inst. de estudios y conferencias industriales. 1942. [1550
This lecture, delivered under the auspices of the Unión Industrial traces in broad outline the proposed world wide solutions for coping with post-war economic problems. Melo reviews the measures adopted during the depression of the thirties and comments briefly upon the Argentine situation. He advocates a balance between state intervention and free enterprise.

Peña Guzmán, Solano. La autarquía en la economía argentina. Tucumán. Ed. La Raza. 1942. 270 p. [1551
The author's purpose is to develop an autarchic national economy free from foreign investments. To back his proposals he presents a factual economic analysis of the Argentine situation in major fields (production, trade, demography, etc.) complemented by a review of chief features of economic policies in the past and a theoretical chapter in defense of protectionism.

Perú. Dirección nacional de estadística. Extracto estadístico del Perú, 1941. Lima. Imp. Americana. (Min. de hacienda y comercio). 1942? 534 p., ilus., cuads. [1552
This publication contains historical tables brought up to date related to mining, trade, population, banks, etc. Physical output and value figures are presented.

Yriart, Juan F. La movilización económica nacional. Montevideo. 1942. 16 p. [1552a
Taking as his text the resolution approved at the meeting of Foreign Ministers at Rio de Janeiro 1942, calling for the mobilization of the economic resources of the American Republics the author considers ways and means to increase production in Uruguay. He suggests that extensive use be made of the Interamerican Development Commission.

AGRICULTURE: SOUTH AMERICA (EXCEPT BRAZIL, COLOMBIA AND VENEZUELA)

BY

ALLEN H. LESTER

AND

KATHRYN H. WYLIE

*Office of Foreign Agricultural Relations,
Department of Agriculture*

BIBLIOGRAPHY

(See also sections on Economics: South America, except Brazil, Colombia and Venezuela; Geography: South America, except Brazil, Colombia and Venezuela; and Labor and Social Welfare)

ARGENTINA

THE ARGENTINE VEGETABLE OIL INDUSTRY (*Comments on arg. trade,* vol. 23, no. 1, August, p. 10–14). [1553
Adaptation of report made by scientists of the Armour Research Foundation working for the Corporación para la Promoción del Intercambio, S. A.

Argerich, Guillermo. Cómo está resolviendo la Argentina el problema del almacenamiento de cereales (*La Hacienda,* año 38, oct., p. 423–426). [1554
Argentina's handling of the problem of grain storage.

Belaúnde, C. H. La propiedad de la tierra en la Argentina. (*Rev. econ. arg.,* año 25, tomo 42, junio, p. 274–282). [1555
A study of land tenure in Argentina since 1914, showing a decrease in the percentage of rural properties worked by their owners and discussing the reasons for this.

Correa Ávila, Carlos. Informe primario sobre la producción agropecuaria de Tucumán. Tucumán. Tall. gráf. M. Violetto. (Col. La grande Argentina, Serie Investigaciones y estudios económico-sociales). 63 p. [1556
Changes in agriculture including livestock raising in the Province of Tucumán between 1937 and 1942.

Croce, Francisco M. Desecación natural de frutas. Mendoza. Min. de economía, obras públicas y riego (Bol. 29). 177 p. [1557
First briefly pointing out statistically the significance of fruits to Argentina and to the Province of Mendoza, the author discusses drying methods for various types in relation to local conditions.

García-Mata, Rafael, and **R. A. Franchelli.** El costo de la cosecha mecánica del algodón (*Bol. mens. junta nac. algodón,* no. 93, enero, p. 15–22). [1558
Gives details of costs of mechanical harvesting of cotton.

Mason, D. I. El costo de los arrendamientos y el valor ficticio o especulativo de la tierra ha perturbado el desenvolvimiento de una agricultura más estabilizada (*Noticioso,* año 8, nov. 25, p. 133–136). [1559
The Argentine Minister of Agriculture discusses agricultural rents, their effect on cost of production, and other phases of agricultural policy.

———. Nuestra economía agraria puede realizar una contribución de inapreciable valor a la política de panamericanismo efectivo en que se encuentra empeñado el gobierno (*Noticioso,* año 8, agosto 10, p. 85–86, 88). [1560
Discusses Argentina's new agricultural policy, described as aimed at expansion of production in contrast to previous restriction, and at protection of the producer.
Summarized in English in the *Review of the River Plate,* August 13, 1943, p. 13–14.

———. La palabra oficial en la exposición ganadera de Palermo (*Bol. oficial bolsa com. Rosario,* año 31, no. 759, agosto 31 p. 24–28). [1561
Discusses government agricultural policy with especial regard to the livestock industry in Argentina.

Ministerio de agricultura. Almanaque 1943. Año 18. Buenos Aires. Dirección de propaganda y publicaciones. 447 p. ilus. [1562
A source of a wide range of information on Argentine agriculture, and physical and institutional conditions affecting it.

EL PLAN DE COLONIZACIÓN QUE REALIZA EL BANCO HIPOTECARIO NACIONAL (*Inform. arg.*, no. 71, feb. 15, p. 47, 48–52). **[1563**
Account of the colonization program of the Argentine National Mortgage Bank, including selection of settlers, technical assistance, land utilization, price, and economic and financial organization of the plan. A table shows the colonies established, giving name, province, department, area, number of parcels, and price at which sold to settlers.

Shellenberger, J. A., and **J. A. Hopkins.** The Argentine dairy industry. Condensed report (*Comments on arg. trade*, vol. 22, no. 12, July, p. 12–17, 30, 32, 34, 36). **[1565**
Study made by members of the Armour Research Foundation working under contract to the Corporación para la Promoción del Intercambio, S. A. Full report to be published in Spanish by the Corporation.
Treats institutional influences upon dairying, problems of farm sanitation and equipment, the location and size of the dairy manufacturing industry, and the manufacture and industrial uses of dairy products.

Taylor, C. C. Land-ownership and status in Argentina (*Land pol. rev.*, vol. 6, no. 2, summer, p. 25–30). **[1567**
An analysis of land tenure in Argentina, giving a history of its evolution to date, and suggesting possible future developments.

CHILE

Bastida R., Luis. Porvenir de nuestra fruticultura. Necesidad que hay de que el Gobierno la estimule y proteja en forma decidida y perseverante. Argentina nos da un ejemplo que debemos imitar (*Unión agríc. sur*, año 1, no. 8, nov., p. 23–26). **[1568**
Discussing markets for Chilean fruits, the author claims that Chile enjoys natural competitive advantages over Argentina, and that the government should take measures to encourage fruit-growing.

Chaparro Ruminot, Leoncio. Fomento racional de la agricultura chilena (*Simiente*, año 13, no. 3, tercer trim., julio-sept., p. 115–126). **[1569**
A program for the planning of Chilean agriculture and the organization for carrying it out.

Correa Vergara, Luis. Posibilidades de la agricultura en Chile. ¿Cuánta es nuestra capacidad agrícola? (*Campesino*, vol. 75, no. 1, enero, p. 45–50, 52). **[1570**
A study of the capacity of Chile's agricultural production, to refute the idea that Chile cannot feed herself. The writer states that the land will sustain the people if intelligently worked. He takes up the cultivable area and the amounts that can be produced of meat, fodder, wheat, rice hemp, vineyards, fruits, sugar beets, and forests. He believes mechanization advisable.

Gho Elizondo, Sigifredo. Crianza artificial de terneros. Contribución al estudio del problema de la carne (*Simiente*, año 13, no. 2, segundo trim., abril-junio, p. 65–70). **[1571**
Considers the effect upon the Chilean meat supply of prohibiting the slaughter of calves and discusses cost of raising calves with skimmed milk as compared with whole milk.

Hepp D., Ricardo, and **Juan Jirkal H.** El problema forestal en Chile. Generalidades sobre el problema de la erosión del suelo en Chile. Plantas forrajeras. Concepción. Lit. Concepción. (Univ. de Concepción, Depto. agrícola). 40 p., ilus. **[1572**
Contains considerable information on the extent of soil erosion in Chile, the types of forestation adapted to the various areas concerned.

Jaramillo Bruce, Rodolfo. Estudio sobre costo, precio y fomento de producción de la leche; aspectos generales del problema y condiciones especiales de la producción lechera en Santiago (*Campesino*, vol. 75, junio, p. 360–365). **[1573**
A discussion of the development of the dairy industry, and its costs and price structure, by a former cabinet officer. Makes especial reference to the Santiago area.

Labarca Letelier, René. Subproducción agrícola y sistema de propiedad ante la estadística chilena. Santiago. Imp. El Esfuerzo. 90 p. **[1574**
An historical treatment of Chilean agriculture and land-holding, submitted as a thesis at the Universidad de Chile.

Maige Abarca, José. Colonización y reestructuración agraria del Valle del Río Lluta (*Simiente*, año 13, no. 4, cuarto trim. oct.–dic., 164–168, 170–171). **[1575**
Surveys agricultural conditions in the Río Lluta Valley in Chile, including size and value of farms, population, and market for products, and proposes a plan of settlement. Notes the existence of malaria and the necessity for public health measures before colonization could be encouraged.

Risopatrón M., Daniel. Problemas de la ganadería nacional (*Campesino*, vol. 75, nov., p. 746–748). **[1576**
Discusses the problems of Chile's livestock industry and asks for state intervention for the industry by price control and other measures, including tariff protection, control of diseases, improvement of fodder production, and subsidies for production of high-grade cattle. Notes a trend away from meat breeds toward combined meat and dairy types.

Sindicato nacional vitivinícola. Situación de la industria vitivinícola. Conclusiones del Congreso de vinicultores celebrado en Talca (*Campesino*, vol. 75, julio, p. 410-421). [1577

The Syndicate, in presenting the case of the vineyards against the incidence of a new freight rate schedule upon wine, describes conditions in the industry.

Wolnitzky B., Alfredo. Nuevamente el problema del trigo (*Agricultor*, no. 18-19, marzo-abril, p. 27-28, 30-32). [1578

Chilean wheat prices, price policy, and cost of production.

ECUADOR

Alcívar Castillo, Gonzalo. Estudio sintético acerca de las sociedades cooperativas (*Bol. consorcio centros agríc. Manabí*, año 5, no. 33, enero-marzo, p. 5-16; no. 34, abril-junio, p. 10-20; no. 35, julio-sept., p. 34, 35-45; no. 36, oct.-dic., p. 30-35). [1579

"Tesis Previa al Grado de Doctor en Jurisprudencia. Universidad de Guayaquil, 1941."

This study of cooperative societies takes up the concept of cooperation, a general history of the cooperative movement, and a history of the movement in Ecuador. To be continued.

Burbano, Jaime, and **Cristóbal Ruiz P.** Monografía agrícola de la Provincia de Imbabura. Quito. Depto. de agricultura, División de economía y cooperación agrícola. (Bol. 26). 118 p. [1580

A comprehensive agricultural survey of the Province, including soils, climate and vegetation, factors entering into the profitability of farming, crops produced and costs and amount of production, land tenure and land values, rural legislation, the native family, wages, and future of agriculture in the Province.

Cheesman, E. E. Informe relacionado con una visita a los cacaoteros del Ecuador y sobre las investigaciones científicas necesarias para cualquier rehabilitación de la industria. Quito. Tall. tip. del Min. de hacienda. (Depto. de agricultura, Bol. 23). 31 p. [1581

An account of a trip to the cacao-producing areas of Ecuador and suggestions for the improvement of the industry. Published also in *Bol. consorcio centros agríc. Manabí*, año 5, no. 35, julio-sept., p. 5-14, 16-20, 21.

Clark, J. M. Revival in El Oro (*For. com. weekly*, vol. 12, no. 8, August 21, p. 5-8, 31). [1582

Reconstruction of El Oro Province in Ecuador which was damaged by the war between Peru and Ecuador. The agricultural program is described.

Ministerio de agricultura. Crédito agrario. Memorandum del Ministerio de agricultura para un plan de fomento y reajuste agrícola. Quito. (Min. de agricultura, Bol. 24). 13 p. [1584

Describes a plan of agricultural development, based on a period of at least ten years, which was worked up as a result of an offer of a loan by the Export-Import Bank of Washington. The loan was to be chiefly for the development of food products, raw materials, and other vital necessities.

Muñoz, J. E. Esquema de organización de la producción nacional. (*Rev. cám. agric. primera zona*, año 6, no. 47-48, julio-agosto, p. 753-761; no. 49-50, set.-oct., p. 823, 824; no. 51-52, nov.-dic., p. 878-885). [1585

Coordination and promotion of production under the Centro de Investigaciones Técnicas. Contains an agricultural program for Ecuador.

Pérez, A. R. La cascarilla y su importancia económica (*Prev. soc.*, Quito, no. 13, mayo-agosto, p. 35-50). [1586

History of cinchona in Ecuador and other producing countries.

Viver, G. E. Aportes para el conocimiento agrológico de la Provincia de Pichincha. (*Rev. cám. agric. primera zona*, año 6, no. 41-42, enero-feb., p. 556-559). [1587

"En colaboración con el Práctico Agrícola Manuel Silva King." This installment is a survey of the agriculture of the Conocoto and Amaguana zone of the Province of Pichincha, Ecuador.

PARAGUAY

Avellar Marques, J. Q. de. El problema de la conservación del suelo paraguayo (*Rev. min. agric. com. ind.*, año 2, no. 10, junio, p. 24-38). [1588

Briefly indicates Paraguay's soil erosion problems, drawing upon foreign source in discussing the nature of soil erosion and remedies for it.

PERU

Alberts, H. W. Wheat in Peru (*Agric. Americas*, vol. 3, Dec., p. 233-235). [1589

Difficulties found in efforts to increase production.

Higbee, E. C. Rotenone production in the Amazon Valley (*For. com. weekly*, vol. 12, no. 4, July 24, p. 8-9, 30). [1590

Increase in plantings and advances in production of derris and lonchocarpus, two of the complementary products whose production in the Western Hemisphere the U. S. Department of Agriculture has been encouraging.

Klinge, Gerardo. Crédito agrícola (*Vida agríc.*, vol. 20, no. 230, enero, p. 49, 51-58;

no. 231, feb., p. 123–126, 129–134; no. 232, marzo, p. 211–216; no. 233, abril, p. 292–298; no. 234, mayo, p. 367–368, 370–374). **[1592**
A five-installment edition of a report presented to the Agricultural Bank of Peru on agricultural credit in general and the specific applications of its principles to conditions in Peru.

Mac-Lean y Estenós, Alejandro. The agricultural cooperative movement in Perú. Washington. Pan American union, Div. of agricultural cooperation. (Series on cooperatives, no. 21). 16 p. **[1593**
Urges an increase in Peruvian agricultural cooperatives, traces governmental policy regarding them, and mentions some existing ones.

Moore, R. E. Tingo María (*Agric. Americas*, vol. 3, June, p. 107–108). **[1594**
This agricultural experiment station, the first of a series set up with United States cooperation in the other American Republics, attacks problems incident to the increased production of necessary crops.

Pesce, Vicente. La agricultura en el Oriente Amazónico (*Vida agríc.*, vol. 20, sept., p. 677–686). **[1595**
Includes labor supply and practical details on types of crops grown including cost of producing them, in the Departments of Loreto and San Martín, Peru.

Solar, Enrique M. del. El paiche y la piscicultura en la selva. Lima. Min. de agricultura, Dirección de asuntos orientales, colonización y terrenos de Oriente. (Depto. de ganadería tropical, caza y pesca, Bol. 3.) 15 p., ilus., láms., fotos, dibujo, gráf., mapa. **[1596**
Description of a food fish of the Peruvian forest region and efforts for its propagation.

Wille, J. E. Entomología agrícola del Perú. Lima. Min. de agricultura, Dirección de agricultura. (Estación experimental agrícola de La Molina). 468 p. **[1597**
Decribes Peru's insect pests and notes their economic importance to agriculture.

Záferson Macedo, S. La quinua; el alimento de los incas (*Rev. fac. cien. econ.*, no. 28, dic., p. 70–114). **[1598**
Contains sections on cultivation, utilization, cost of production, and history of the plant.

URUGUAY

Dirección de agronomía. El Uruguay como país agropecuario, su desarrollo actual, perspectivas para el futuro. Años 1937–1941. Montevideo. Imp. nacional. 57 p. **[1599**
Indicates the place of livestock and crops in Uruguay's production and trade, discussing past trends and the future by individual lines of activity.

DISCURSO DEL MINISTRO DE GANADERÍA Y AGRICULTURA INGENIERO AGRÓNOMO ARTURO GONZÁLEZ VIDART (*Diario rural*, año 4, no. 312, sept. 15, p. 12, 13). **[1600**
Discusses various aspects of agricultural policy in Uruguay, including improvement of the rural cultural level, meat marketing, prices, and coordination of production among the countries of the continent.

LA PRODUCCIÓN DE UVA Y VINO EN EL URUGUAY (*Mercados del mundo*, año 7, no. 31, mayo, p. 2–8). **[1601**
Graphs and tables show trends in production and foreign trade.

LA PRODUCCIÓN Y EL CONSUMO DE AZÚCAR EN EL URUGUAY (*Mercados del mundo*, año 7, no. 30, abril, p. 2–5). **[1602**
Surveys trends. Includes statistics.

EL XXVII CONGRESO ANUAL DE LA FEDERACIÓN RURAL; DETALLE COMPLETO DE SU DESARROLLO (*Diario rural*, año 3, no. 274, mayo 5, p. 1, 8, 10). **[1603**
Account of proceedings of the 27th Annual Congress of the Federación Rural at Fray Bentos. Among topics discussed were reforms in the rural code, soil erosion, cattle transportation, cattle recovery, agrarian reform, wool production and marketing, and national policy. Conclusions were summarized.

Vercesi, D. R. La erosión de los suelos. Montevideo. Min. de ganadería y agricultura, Dirección de agronomía. (Cartilla 67). 15 p. **[1604**
A general discussion of the problems of soil erosion in Uruguay.

ECONOMICS: BRAZIL *

BY

ROBERTO SIMONSEN

Escola Livre de Sociologia e Política, São Paulo, Brasil

GENERAL STATEMENT

Brazil's participation in the war has led her economists to fix their attention on problems of the country's economic mobilization. All literature bearing on the subject reflects this trend which is characterized by the extreme purposefulness of its aims.

Monetary inflation, which the government could not duly control, seriously perturbed the harmonious relationship between production and the cost of living, thereby making it difficult to appreciate thoroughly the character of the economic evolution of the country.

Many of the technical advisory committees appointed by the Government, on which the producing classes are represented, worked most efficiently, and a great number of the conclusions deserve to be recorded.

But an event of major importance was the Primeiro Congresso Brasileiro de Economia convoked by the Rio de Janeiro Commercial Association and held during the last two months of 1943 in the Federal Capital.

There were 145 theses submitted indicative of a carefully elaborated program, and the Congress approved 256 resolutions embracing the fundamental problems of the Brazilian economy.

The program itself comprised eight sections with numerous subdivisions.

In the first section, fundamental problems were dealt with in regard to the country's agricultural and industrial development. Recommendations of this section refer to the protection of natural resources, utilization of electric water power, exploitation of national fuel resources and mineral deposits, utilization of waterways suitable for navigation, and to extractive industries in general. Regarding agriculture, the creation of an organization for the cultivation of foodstuffs along lines compatible with the country's characteristics was strongly recommended. As for industrial expansion, certain measures connected with the installation of basic and transformative industries were recommended, while suggestions for improvement in production, industrial reconstruction, professional training, and technical assistance, also financing of industries assumed a highly significant aspect.

In the second section, problems of transportation received attention. A criticism of the inadequacy of these services in Brazil was approved, and a number of comprehensive measures were formulated with a view to provide and improve transport facilities. In addition, the section considered tariff policy, the institution of exchanges for manufactured goods, and the norms to be observed in connection with international trade.

The third section examined problems relating to money and banking. Vari-

---

* Publications on agriculture are listed separately under the heading Agriculture: Brazil (items 1750–1774).

ous measures were suggested for combating inflation, and norms were formulated for the expansion of credit and control of monetary policy.

The fourth section dealt with the application of foreign capital in this country and the bases for investment and transfer of funds. It concluded by recognizing the advantages to be derived from foreign capital investment in this country and recommended the establishment of a free exchange market to facilitate transfers in payment of interest, dividends and amortization. In order to prevent any hindrance to such transfers, a recommendation to the government was approved in the sense of conducting the country's commercial policy along lines aiming to create a favorable balance of foreign trade so that the credit balances arising therefrom may provide the means for payments abroad.

The fifth section discussed public finance and taxation systems in general. An appeal was made to the government to maintain its taxation policy in accord with Brazil's economic realities without regard to the guiding principles applicable to overcapitalized countries.

The sixth section of the Congress was devoted to problems of planning. With regard to Brazil, for instance, it was recommended that a careful inquiry be made into the nature of goods exchanged with foreign countries and that a careful scrutiny be made of the relative index values of imports and exports. It was also recognized that the flow of immigrants into the country should be intensified.

The Congress also dealt with questions pertaining to social insurance, economic studies and research, as well as a number of problems relating to Brazil's economic expansion.

Finally, in the eighth section, the problems of State intervention in economic activities were studied. A resolution was approved which recognized that the State's activities should as a rule be supplementary, guiding and auxiliary. Only in very exceptional cases of highest national import should the State's action be direct and immediate, always subordinated, however, to a previous and necessary consultation with Class Associations.

The conclusions approved and the speeches delivered at the inauguration of the Congress have already been published in book form under the auspices of the Commercial Association of Rio de Janeiro. Other volumes, now in press, contain the theses and debates.

The archives of the First Brazilian Congress, which are available for reference in the Commercial Association of Rio de Janeiro afford a vast amount of information to all those who wish to keep themselves posted not only on the current state of the Brazilian economy but also on the thinking that prevails among the country's producing groups.

BIBLIOGRAPHY

(*See also sections on* Agriculture: Brazil; Geography: Brazil; and Labor and Social Welfare)

GENERAL

Almeida, A. Tavares de. Oeste Paulista: a experiência etnográfica e cultural. Rio de Janeiro. Ed. Alba. 220 p. [1605

Study based upon the 1940 census of the region in the West of the State of São Paulo having as center the town of Rio Preto. Analysis of the immigration problem in general and of the Japanese immigrants in particular.

Almeida, Rômulo de. A mobilização econômica e o planejamento da expansão do

país (*Cultura política*, ano 3, no. 27, maio, p. 55–62). [1606]
Suggests different means for the purpose of dispersing large clusters of population in Brazil: cattle grazing, extractive industry, settlement due to population growth and introduction of machinery in agriculture. Points out the necessity of planning for such expansion from the viewpoint of economics, administration and means of communication.

ANAIS DO PRIMEIRO CONGRESSO BRASILEIRO DE ECONOMIA. Primeiro vol. Rio de Janeiro. Associação comercial. 198 p. [1607]
First volume of the proceedings of the Primeiro Congresso Brasileiro de Economia held in Rio de Janeiro from November 25, to December 18, 1943. Includes both the opening and the closing speeches, resolutions, program of the proceedings, list of members, institutions which were represented in it, composition of the different sections, and a list of the papers presented.

ANÁLISE DOS RESULTADOS DOS CENSOS DEMOGRÁFICOS (*Bol. min. trab. ind. com.*, ano 9, no. 108, agôsto, p. 296–306). [1608]
Comparative study of the fertility index of married women in different Brazilian towns, based upon the 1940 census. Statistical tables.

Araujo, Oscar Egídio de. Pesquisas e estudos econômicos (*Rev. arq. mun.*, São Paulo, ano 9, vol. 93, out.–dez., p. 7–21). [1609]
Suggestions for the organization of statistical data considered necessary for the study and orientation of the Brazilian economy; standard of living indexes. Appraisal of population needs as to food, working facilities and welfare.

ASPECTOS ECONÔMICOS DA PARAÍBA (*Cultura política*, ano 3, no. 35, dez., p. 146–162). [1610]
Government-controlled economic measures studied against the background of land and people in the State of Paraíba. [P. E. James]

Augusto, José. Aspectos históricos e econômicos do Rio Grande do Norte (*Cultura política*, ano 3, no. 30, agôsto, p. 63–68). [1611]
The founding of the city of Natal. Economy of the State of Rio Grande do Norte, based on salt, cotton, sugar and carnauba.

———. A região do Seridó (*Cultura política*, ano 3, no. 26, abril, p. 24–35). [1612]
"Cattle brought civilized man to Seridó (Rio Grande do Norte) and cotton pushed out the cattle and attached the settlers to the land."

Banco do Brasil. A situação econômica e financeira do Brasil (*Bol. min. trab. ind. com.*, ano 9, no. 107, julho, p. 163–183). [1613]
Report of the Banco do Brasil for the year 1942, with a review of the country's economic and financial situation, emphasizing home and foreign trade, production and exchange, currency and the financial market.

Barros, Richomer. Natureza e dados econômicos do município de Princesa Isabel, Estado de Paraíba (*Bol. min. agric.*, Rio, ano 32, no. 2, fev., p. 47–154). [1614]
A quite detailed study of a county of the State of Paraíba, giving much information about the agricultural economy of the region, and the environment in which it exists. [A. H. Lester]

Bentenmüller, Gustavo Linhares. Contrôle específico da produção, da exportação e da importação. Rio de Janeiro. Cia. bras. de artes gráf. 16 p. [1615]

BRASIL 1942, RECURSOS, POSSIBILIDADES. Rio de Janeiro. Min. das relações exteriores. 643 p. [1616]
Report on the geographical, economic and social conditions of Brazil up to 1942. Includes statistical data.

Carvalho, Daniel de. Equilíbrio da produção brasileira (*Rev. ciên. econ.*, São Paulo, ano 5, vol. 5, no. 2, fev., p. 59–62). [1617]
The author calls attention to the part played by agriculture and industry in the Brazilian economic system.

Carvalho, João Luiz. Subsídios para a história dos estudos econômicos no Brasil. Rio de Janeiro. 115 p. [1618]
A series of articles analysing various economic problems confronting the country.

Carvalho, Mário Orlando de. As conjunturas de guerra, a economia nacional e o Banco do Brasil (*Cultura política*, ano 3, no. 31, agôsto 22, p. 106–118). [1619]
Historical study of Banco do Brasil's evolution from its beginning up to the present; the war's influence on its activities.

Cavalcanti, Carlos de Lima. Past and present economy of Brazil. Forces and trends responsible for the different stages of economic development of the Republic of Brazil (*Commer. pan. Amer.*, vol. 12, no. 1–2, Jan.–Feb., p. 1–14). [1620]
Résumé of the economic history of Brazil. [P. E. James]

Costa, Fernando. Problemas econômicos do Brasil. São Paulo. Imp. oficial do Estado. 318 p. [1621]
Collection of speeches and press interviews.

Costa Filho, Miguel. Civilização brasileira e açucar (*Bras. açucar.*, ano 11, vol. 21, junho, no. 6, p. 63–67). [1622]
The influence of sugar plantations on the settlement of Brazil either directly through the conquest of soil or indirectly through the importation of slaves.

Herrmann, Lucila; Gioconda Mussolini; Nair Ortiz; Cecilia Castro Paiva; and **Rita de Freitas.** Alterações da estrutura demográfico-profissional de São Paulo, da capital e do interior, num periodo de 14 anos: 1920–1934 (*Rev. arq. mun.*, São Paulo, ano 8, vol. 89, março-abril, p. 9–104). [1623

Results of a research carried on in the State of São Paulo analysing the demographic-occupational and absolute occupational changes in ten agricultural districts. Determination of three different ecological areas. Deals also with the interior of the State, the evolution of the occupational structure in the City of São Paulo from 1872 to 1940, and studies mobility of workers in different industries.

Jobim, José. Brazil in the making. New York. Macmillan co. 318 p. [1624

A factual survey of Brazilian economy. Nearly three quarters of the volume is given over to a description of manufacturing in Brazil by industries. [Ed.]

Lacerda, Pedro Paulo Sampaio. O Brasil na economia de guerra (*Cultura política*, ano 3, no. 31, agôsto 22, p. 87–105). [1625

War-time finance, economic mobilization, price control, rationing, priorities, transportation, production and trade.

Lewinsohn, Richard. O Brasil, berço de um grande princípio econômico (*Cultura política*, ano 3, no. 35, dez., p. 115–121). [1626

Insists on the development and export of economic ideas and procedures, such as the valorization of coffee. [P. E. James]

Lourenço, João de. Quadro geral das atividades do Serviço de estatística econômica e financeira, sob o regime de centralização pelo I. B. G. E. (*Rev. bras. estat.*, ano 4, no. 14, abril-junho, p. 201–216). [1627

Article showing how economic and financial statistics are collected and used by the Serviço de Estatísticas Econômicas e Financeiras under the direction of the Instituto Brasileiro de Geografia e Estatística.

Meneses, Djacir. A economia corporativa e o meio social brasileiro (*Cultura política*, ano 3, no. 33, out., p. 97–101). [1628

The corporative economy in Brazil; its historical evolution and present trends.

Mesquita, José de. A política nacional do Rumo a Oeste (*Bol. min. trab. ind. com.*, ano 10, no. 111, nov., p. 259–275). [1629

The "Westward" policy and its several trends. The different aspects according to which it is put into effect at present (the transcontinental, the Paraguayan area, the southern Mato Grosso, etc.).

Mortara, Giorgio. Estatísticas necessárias ao estudo e orientação da economia brasileira (*Rev. bras. estat.*, ano 4, no. 16, out.-dez., p. 653–660). [1630

Paper presented at the Primeiro Congresso Brasileiro de Economia held in Rio de Janeiro in 1943, pointing out some statistical data which would be necessary for the study of the Brazilian economy.

Oliveira, Carlos Gomes de. Economia do mate. Rio de Janeiro. Inst. nac. do mate. [1632

Discussion of problems relating to the mate industry.

Pierson, Donald. A distribuição especial das classes e das raças na Baía (*Bol. min. trab. ind. com.*, ano 9, no. 105, maio, p. 285–297). [1633

Article showing the relation between higher and lower classes and races, the classes corresponding to an ecological distribution in Baia (Cidade do Salvador). The author concludes that social organization rests upon class rather than caste.

Potsch, Waldemiro. Brasil e suas riquezas. Décimo nona ed. Rio de Janeiro. Ed. Alves. 392 p. [1634

A simply written book, nearly half of which is devoted to discussion of individual agricultural products of Brazil. [A. H. Lester]

Ross, Lee. Building Brazil (*For. com. weekly*, vol. 11, no. 13, 26 Jan., p. 3–9, 40–41; vol. 12, no. 1, 3 July, p. 6–8, 11, illus.). [1635

La expansión industrial, el desarrollo y movimiento de la población industrial y agrícola, la política de la vivienda popular de las Cajas de Previsión Social y la modernización de edificios gubernamentales han dado una extraordinaria expansión a la industria de la construcción brasileña, cuyos aspectos económicos y sociales están seriamente estudiados, documentados e ilustrados en estos artículos. [G. R. Rohen y Gálvez]

Simonsen, Roberto Cochrane. Alguns aspectos da política econômica mais conveniente ao Brasil no periodo de após-guerra. São Paulo. Federação das indústrias do estado de São Paulo. 22 p. [1636

The economic situation of the belligerent countries, the U. S. A. and Brazil in particular. The different economic policies; analysis of the present social, agricultural and industrial conditions and suggestions concerning Brazil's future policies.

———. Ensáios sociais, políticos e econômicos. São Paulo. Emp. gráf. da Revista dos tribunais. (Ed. da Federação das indústrias do estado do São Paulo). 303 p. [1637

Essays on a number of social, political and economic topics, including a paper presented to the Eighth American Scientific Meeting held in Washington on the economic resources and population movements in the New World.

Soares, José Carlos de Macedo. Recent statistical developments in Brazil (*Estadística*, vol. 1, no. 1, March, p. 64–75). [1638

Article describing the Instituto Brasileiro de Geografia e Estatística, the official statistical organization in Brazil which directed the 1940 census.

PRODUCTION AND NATURAL RESOURCES

A BORRACHA: PASSADO, PRESENTE E FUTURO (*Obs. ecôn. fin.*, ano 8, no. 89, junho, p. 119–149). [1639

Long and detailed editorial, well documented with photographs, graphs and statistical data on the rubber exploitation in Brazil. Historical background, present situation and the problems to be dealt with in the future.

Boudot, Eugenio. Carvão mineral no Brasil (*Obs. ecôn. fin.*, ano 8, no. 93, out., p. 18–31). [1640

Historical background, producing areas, enterprises and output of coal in Brazil.

O BRASIL E OS ÓLEOS VEGETAIS (*Bol. min. trab. ind. com.*, ano 9, no. 107, julho, p. 116–159; no. 108, agôsto, p. 128–154; ano 10, no. 109, set., p. 158–168; no. 110, out., p. 165–195; no. 111, nov., p. 172–194; no. 112, dez., p. 173–189). [1641

A survey of the vegetable oil industry. to be continued. [A. H. Lester]

Bueno, Zei, and Lourenço Pereira da Cunha. A usina de chumbo e prata de Apiaí (*Bol. min. trab. ind. com.*, ano 9, no. 108, agôsto, p. 119–127). [1642

Article giving information on the recently erected lead and silver mill in Apiaí, State of São Paulo.

Correia Filho, Virgilio. A borracha em Mato Grosso (*Obs. ecôn. fin.*, ano 8, no. 89, junho, p. 41–56). [1643

Geographical area, production, and economic conditions of rubber exploitation in the State of Mato Grosso.

De Carli, Gileno. Ensáio sobre a eficiência da indústria açucareira no Brasil. Rio de Janeiro. Ed. Irmãos Pongetti. 59 p. [1644

Essay presenting data on the number of workers, hours of work, wages and production. The importance of the human element in sugar production and the efficiency of the sugar industry.

———. Gênese e evolução da indústria açucareira paulista. Rio de Janeiro. Ed. Irmãos Pongetti. [1645

Evolution and present position of the sugar industry in the State of São Paulo. Wartime supply problems.

Federação das indústrias do estado de São Paulo. A cidade do aço. Impressões de Volta Redonda. São Paulo. 218 p. [1646

Articles, lectures, press interviews and statements on the iron and steel plant at Volta Redonda, dealing with the geographical aspect of the area, the history of the Brazilian iron and steel plant and the different economic aspects of the new undertaking. Photographs.

Gusmão, Clovis. Gloria e tragédia da borracha (*Obs. ecôn. fin.*, ano 8, no. 85, p. 67–75). [1647

Rubber production in the Amazon Valley; settlement and conditions of exploitation.

INDUSTRIAS DE PERNAMBUCO. O CAROÁ (*Bol. min. trab. ind. com.*, ano 9, no. 104, abril, p. 217–226). [1648

A statement on the cultivation and trade of caroá. Statistical data.

INQUÉRITO SÔBRE O PROBLEMA DO FERRO NO BRASIL (*Obs. ecôn. fin.*, ano 8, no. 93, out., p. 35–51, 55–88, 90–103, 107–131). [1649

Series of four editorials, largely documented with photographs, maps and graphs, covering the following aspects of the iron problem in Brazil: (1) "Do Brasil Colônia ao Brasil República," a historical account of its exploitation (p. 35–51); (2) "A Companhia Vale do Rio Doce," an account of the largest ore mining enterprise in Brazil (p. 55–88); (3) "Companhia Siderúrgica Nacional," the large iron and steel mill at Volta Redonda (p. 90–103); and (4) "A Iniciativa Privada na Siderurgia," the operation of the different private companies in iron and steel production (p. 107–140).

Jurandyr, Dalcidio. A ilha de Marajó (*Obs. ecôn. fin.*, ano 8, no. 89, junho, p. 77–87). [1650

Stock raising on Marajó Island.

Lacerda, Pedro Paulo Sampaio. O babaçú na economia brasileira (*Cultura política*, ano 3, no. 34, nov., p. 118–126). [1651

Licínio, Aluízio. Mica, o mineral da vitória (*Obs. ecôn. fin.*, ano 8, no. 94, nov., p. 51–58). [1652

Varieties and technical properties of mica, its occurrence, mining, processing and trade in Brazil.

Lima, Herman. História do diamante no Brasil (*Obs. ecôn. fin.*, ano 8, no. 94, nov., p. 19–31). [1653

Location of diamond mines, working conditions, production and trade.

Lima Sobrinho, Barbosa. Os fundamentos nacionais da política do açucar. Rio de Janeiro. 32 p. [1654

Discusses problems of supply, transportation, ceiling prices of sugar cane in the State of São Paulo, production controls and the formulation of national policy with respect to sugar.

———. Problemas econômicos e sociais de lavoura canaviera. Segunda ed. Rio de Janeiro. Ed. Z. Valverde. 292 p. [1655
Economic and labor problems in the production of sugar cane in Brazil. [P. E. James]

Mendes, Amando. A borracha no Brasil. São Paulo. Ed. Difusão. (Sociedade impressora brasileira). 2 vols. [1656
Historical review of transplantation of rubber from Brazil to the East Indies. Labor immigration in the Amazon region. Rubber extraction and its future. Agricultural-industrial organization of rubbergroves. The Ford project and rubber exploitation in the Amazon. The American view as to the supply of rubber in the international market and prices in the Brazilian-American agreement.

Pereira, Moacir Soares. Plano de produção da gasolina sintética e acetona no Brasil (*Bras. açucar.*, ano 11, vol. 21, no. 1, jan., p. 105–110). [1657
Analysis of the possibilities of using alcohol for obtaining gas and acetone in Brazil; technical and financial possibilities.

A pesca na amazônia (*Obs. ecôn. fin.*, ano 8, no. 89, junho, p. 69–76). [1658
Different types of fishing and fishermen in the Amazon.

São Paulo (Estado). Departamento estadual de estatística. Catálogo das indústrias do estado de São Paulo, exclusive o município da capital. São Paulo. xxx, 1188 p. [1659
Directory of industrial concerns in the interior of the State of São Paulo. Data collected in November, 1940–March, 1941, by *municípios* and listed by industrial groups. Classification of industries and indexes according to products and *municípios* in alphabetical order.

———. Catálogo das indústrias do município da capital. São Paulo. xxvi, 477 p. [1660
Directory of industrial concerns in the *município* of São Paulo, State of São Paulo. Data collected in November 1940–March 1941. Group classification key to industries and indexes by groups and by products in alphabetical order.

———. Estatística industrial. 1938 e 1939. São Paulo. xlviii, 375 p. [1661
General statistical data on investment, value of production, raw materials used, consumption of fuel and electricity, number of workers, and taxes. Index of tables. Classification of industries. Alphabetical index of products.

Silva, Edmundo de Macedo Soares e. Volta Redonda e o desenvolvimento industrial no Brasil (*Estud. bras.*, ano 6, vol. 11, no. 31–33, julho–dez., p. 59–90). [1662
Industries consuming steel. The need for the training of technicians. Photographs.

Silveira, Artur Leite. Pequena história do cacáu (*Obs. ecôn. fin.*, ano 8, no. 90, julho, p. 36–48). [1663
Cocoa in Brazil and especially in Bahia. Economic, social and political aspects of exploitation. Statistical data.

Zink, Sidney. Brazil's industry. War's emergencies spur unprecedented activity (*For. com. weekly*, vol. 12, Sept. 11, p. 3–10, 25). [1664
A factual summary of Brazil's wartime expansion of manufacturing industries. [P. E. James]

COFFEE

Andrade, Theophilo de. A execução do acôrdo de outubro (*D. N. C.*, ano 20, abril, p. 503–505). [1665
Discusses an exchange of notes in March 1943 relating to the carrying out of the coffee agreement signed October 1942 between Brazil and the United States. Brings out the importance of the agreement for the coffee market. [A. H. Lester]

Anuário estatístico, 1942. Superintendência dos servicos do café. São Paulo. Sria. de fazenda do estado de São Paulo. 192 p. [1666
Statistical data on coffee production, shipping, coffee exports, consumption markets, prices, duties. Graphs.

Guedes, Jaime Fernandes. O café brasileiro em 1942. Rio de Janeiro. Depto. nac. do café. 80 p. [1667
Annual report of the Departmento Nacional do Café; presents situation of Brazilian coffee production and trade.

Mendes, J. E. Teixeira. A pequena propriedade cafeeira (*Bol. sup. serv. café*, ano 18, no. 196, junho, p. 426–432). [1668
Small coffee farms in the State of São Paulo and the quality of its production.

Superintendência dos serviços do Café. Relação dos cafeicultores do estado de São Paulo. São Paulo. Sria. da fazenda do estado de São Paulo. 420 p. [1669
Complete listing up to June, 1941, of all coffee growers in the State of São Paulo indicating the place of farm by *município* and railway district, distance, area, topography, quality of soil and processing equipment.

Vidal, Bento A. Sampaio. O café na economia brasileira (*Obs. ecôn. fin.*, ano 8, no. 88, maio, p. 70–89). [1670
Article analyzing production and trade problems of coffee in Brazil.

MONEY

Azevedo, Aldo M. de. Em tôrno da inflação (*Bol. min. trab. ind. com.*, ano 10, no. 110, out., p. 211–219). [1671
Considerations of the problem of inflation with reference to Brazil.

Franke, H. Análise do perigo inflacionista no Brasil em 1941 (*Bol. min. trab. ind. com.*, ano 9, no. 104, abril, p. 245–257). [1672

Analysis of the problem of inflation in Brazil and the development of currency circulation in 1941. Differences between inflation in Brazil and other countries such as the United States and Canada.

Gudin, Eugenio. Princípios de economia monetária. Rio de Janeiro. Ed. Civilização brasileira. 400 p. [1673

Currency and banking. Inflation and exchange problems in Brazil. Inflation, exchange and foreign trade in relation to trade.

Vale, J. Rodrigues. Considerações contra a inflação monetária. Rio de Janeiro. 22 p. [1674

Analysis of the difficulties caused by the progressive increase in currency circulation without the necessary technical precautions. The situation in Brazil and in other countries.

FOREIGN TRADE

COMPOSIÇÃO DO COMÉRCIO EXPORTADOR DO BRASIL (*Bol. min. trab. ind. com.*, ano 9, no. 108, agôsto, p. 158–163). [1675

Article showing the composition of export trade of Brazil.

Melo, J. C. O comércio brasileiro no primeiro semestre de 1943 (*Bol. sup. serv. café*, ano 18, no. 200, out., p. 808–811). [1676

Statistical data with commentaries concerning Brazilian imports and exports up to June, 1943.

———. A exportação paulista em 1942 (*Bol. sup. serv. café*, ano 18, no. 202, dez., p. 1068–1072). [1677

Statistical data, with commentaries concerning total exports of coffee from the State of São Paulo by countries of destination.

REGIÕES ECONÔMICAS DO BRASIL NO COMÉRCIO EXTERIOR (*Bol. min. trab. ind. com.*, ano 9, no. 106, junho, p. 155–162). [1678

Analysis of economic regions in Brazil in relation to foreign trade.

TRANSPORTATION AND COMMUNICATION

Acre (Território). Departamento estadual de geografia e estatística. Tábuas itinerárias acreanas. Rio Branco. [1679

Record of all means of transportation in the Território do Acre, its extent and time needed in travelling. Maps of the *municípios* showing the means of transportation.

Figueiredo, Lima. A ferrovia Corumbá-Santa Cruz de La Sierra (*Rev. bras. geog.*, ano 5, no. 1, jan.–março, p. 61–76). [1680

The construction of Corumbá-Santa Cruz de La Sierra railway uniting the port of Santos and Bolivia. Review of past efforts. Technical details. Maps and photographs.

Minas Gerais (Estado). Departamento estadual de estatística. Belo Horizonte. Oficinas gráf. de estatística. 350 p. [1681

Means of communication in the State of Minas Gerias. Graphs.

Viana, João de Segadas. Sistema ferroviário brasileiro (*Cultura política*, ano 3, no. 23, jan., p. 123–135). [1682

Study of the Brazilian railway system with reference to physical aspects and different economic areas of the country and economic value of the railways. The different railway networks, its mileage and indexes according to area and number of inhabitants are considered.

Vieira, Flavio. Classificação regional das estradas de ferro brasileiras (*Rev. bras. geog.*, ano 5, no. 1, jan.–março, p. 99–103). [1683

Classification by the Departamento Nacional de Estradas de Ferro of Brazilian railroads in four large regions based on railway density.

LABOR AND SOCIAL LEGISLATION

Araujo, Oscar Egidio de. O operário industrial (*Bol. min. trab. ind. com.*, ano 9, no. 103, março, p. 130–138). [1684

Relation between worker's wages and efficiency, as reflected in cost of production. Analysis based upon data assembled in the city of São Paulo.

———. Salário mínimo no Brasil (*Bol. min. trab. ind. com.*, ano 9, no. 106, junho, p. 63–70). [1685

The effect of minimum wages in Brazil upon standard of living of labor.

Catharino, José Martins. Proteção ao trabalhador rural no Brasil (*Rev. trabalho*, ano 11, no. 125, nov., p. 5–8). [1686

The author notes the exclusion of rural workers from the benefits of the law regulating conditions of work in industry and commerce and proposed solution of the problem within the framework of present legislation.

CENSO SINDICAL CARIOCA EM 1941 (*Bol. min. trab. ind. com.*, ano 9, no. 108, agôsto, p. 99–115). [1687

Article on the census in the capital of Brazil concerning the trade union organization.

Cruz, Salviano. Problemas econômicos e sociais dos trabalhadores brasileiros (*Cul-*

tura política, ano 3, no. 33, out., p. 48-60). [1688]
Plan for research on the standard of living of the rural worker, his mobility, his efficiency and quality of his production. and labor conditions.

Fischolowitz, Estanislau. Ação contra os acidentes do trabalho (*Bol. min. trab. ind. com.,* ano 9, no. 102, fev., p. 213-227). [1689]
The problem of safety in work as a field for research in Brazilian social legislation; the present situation and the preliminary steps already taken.

————. O salário familiar (*Rev. serv. públ.,* ano 6, vol. 4, no. 1, out., p. 13-18). [1690]
Article on family wages, a recent development in Brazilian labor legislation.

Lacerda, Dorval. A guerra e a legislação brasileira do trabalho (*Rev. trabalho,* ano 11, no. 119, maio, p. 19-26). [1691]
The wartime social legislation in Brazil. Includes a list of all decree-laws concerning the subject with an alphabetical and cross reference index.

Lopes, R. Paula. A evolução social do Brasil (*Bol. min. trab. ind. com.,* ano 9, no. 103, maio, p. 120-139). [1692]
An attempt to show how social problems surpass the framework of labor legislation in Brazil.

Pimenta, Joaquim. Sociologia jurídica do trabalho. Rio de Janeiro. Ed. Max Limonad. 200 p. [1693]
Synthesis and criticism of labor legislation in Brazil before and after 1930.

Pinheiro, Maria Esolina. Os parques proletários (*Bol. min. trab. ind. com.,* ano 10, no. 112, dez., p. 127-145). [1694]
Report on living conditions in two proletarian sections in Rio de Janeiro.

AS REALIZAÇÕES DO ESTADO NACIONAL NO SETOR SOCIAL-TRABALHISTA (*Cultura política,* ano 3, no. 24, fev., p. 156-165). [1695]
An article quoting statistical data (for 1938) giving the number of syndicates and professional associations in existence in each Brazilian state and the value of production in each of them. Wages paid to adult workers in each state. Maps indicating average wages, number of state enterprises by states. Graph showing number of invention copyrights authorized in the period 1935-1939.

SINDICATOS E FEDERAÇÕES EM 1943 (*Bol. min. trab. ind. com.,* ano 10, no. 109, set., p. 111-123). [1696]
Article on Brazilian syndicates and federations of syndicates in 1943.

Torres, Vasconcellos. Padrão de vida do trabalhador rural (*Bras. açucar.,* ano 11, vol. 21, no. 6, junho, p. 81-88). [1697]
Study of the standard of living of one thousand families employed in the sugar cane mills in Brazil.

Viana, Oliveira. Problemas do direito sindical. Rio de Janeiro. Ed. Max Limonad. [1698]
Analysis of Brazilian trade union organization; legislation and administration and comparison with foreign legislation.

IMMIGRATION

Barreto, Castro. A imigração no após-guerra (*Estud. bras.,* ano 5, vol. 10, no. 29-30, março-junho, p. 141-165). [1699]
Past and present immigration into Brazil; the effect of the war on future admission of aliens into the country.

————. Resposta ao questionário do Latin American economic institute, sôbre problemas demográficos da América Latina no após-guerra (*Estud. bras.,* ano 6, vol. 11, no. 31-33, julho-dez., p. 53-58). [1700]
Miscellaneous aspects of immigration in Brazil: legislation, its importance, nationalities.

Departamento nacional de imigração. Estatística de 1941 e dados comparativos dos exercícios de 1939 e 1940. Rio de Janeiro. 1943? 204 p. [1701]
Continued by mimeographed tables for 1942 and 1943. [J. B. Childs]

Gonzaga, Antônio Galvão. Contribuição para o estudo das imigrações no Brasil (*Bol. min. trab. ind. com.,* ano 9, no. 108, agôsto, p. 263-269). [1702]
Japanese settlement in the State of São Paulo. Statistical data.

Oliveira, Beneval de. As populações brasileiras e seus movimentos (*Cultura política,* ano 3, no. 28, junho, p. 67-74). [1703]
Distribution of population in Brazil. Past and present internal population movements. Problems of settling the hinterland of the country.

Vidal, Ademar. Os movimentos nordestinos de emigração (*Cultura política,* ano 3, no. 23, jan., p. 51-56). [1705]
Economic, social and geographic conditions affecting movement of rural populations from northeastern Brazil to three principal areas: São Paulo (coffee), Amazon (rubber) and seaside towns. Suggests measure to prevent this movement.

MISCELLANEOUS

Amaral, F. Pompeu do. A alimentação da população paulistana (*Rev. arq. mun.,* São Paulo, ano 8, vol. 90, maio-junho, p. 55-87). [1706]
Nutrition of the inhabitants of the City of São Paulo. Findings and questionnaires used in the study.

Apocalipse, Geraldo G. M. O custo da vida e o cooperativismo (*Cultura política,* ano 3, no. 34, nov., p. 154-158). [1707]

Chavez, Arlindo. Propriedades rurais e posses em terras devolutas (*Bol. min. trab. ind. com.*, ano 9, no. 104, abril, p. 287-294). [1707a
The land tenure problem in Minas Gerais. [P. E. James]

Costa, J. Wilson. Mercado de aves e ovos da capital de São Paulo. Diretoria de publicidade agrícola. 108 p. [1708
Publication issued by the Secretaria da Agricultura. Production, trade and consumption of poultry and eggs in the City of São Paulo. Includes legislation on the subject, photographs, statistical tables and graphs.

ESTABLISHMENT OF PRICE CEILING IN BRAZIL, 1943 (*Month. labor rev.*, vol. 56, no. 4, April, p. 610-611). [1708a
Control de precios, al nivel de diciembre 1 de 1942, para mercancías, productos y transportes, según resoluciones de enero 8 y 10 de 1943. [G. A. Rohen y Gálvez]

ESTATÍSTICAS DEMOGRÁFICAS (*Bol. min. trab. ind. com.*, ano 9, no. 104, abril, p. 309-324). [1709
Birth rate in the States of Mato Grosso and São Paulo based upon the 1940 census; statistics and population mobility, its reconstruction and correction.

Gonçalves, Álvaro. Aristocracia rural e pequena propriedade no sul do Brasil (*Cultura política*, ano 3, no. 25, março, p. 66-73). [1709a
The large landowner vs. the small farmer in South Brazil. A study of origins and trends. [P. E. James]

Heller, Fréderico. O êxodo do campo como fator de desenvolvimento (*Sociologia*, vol. 5, no. 1, p. 57-64). [1710
The different causes leading to the migration of rural population to towns and the danger inherent in a restrictive immigration policy.

ÍNDICE DO CUSTO DE VIDA DA FAMÍLIA OPERÁRIA NA CIDADE DE SÃO PAULO (*Rev. arq. mun.*, São Paulo, ano 9, vol. 92, agôsto-set., p. 7-30). [1711
Study of the cost of living of workers' families presenting data collected in the City of São Paulo. Data on different types of family expenses and types of work. Each expense item is analyzed.

ÍNDICES BRASILEIROS DO CUSTO DA ALIMENTAÇÃO (*Bol. min. trab. ind. com.*, ano 9, no. 108, agôsto, p. 285-295). [1712
Food cost indexes in several Brazilian states; the siuation in 1942 and changes in the period 1935-1942. Statistical tables.

Kafuri, Jorge. Aspectos nacionais e internacionais do problema da alimentação (*Bol. min. trab. ind. com.*, ano 10, no. 110, out., p. 223-242). [1713
The people of Brazil expect their government to contribute to Brazilian progress in the postwar world by such means as fostering mechanization of agriculture, carrying out recommendations of the Hot Springs Conference regarding nutrition, and assuring a living wage. [A. H. Lester]

Mortara, Giorgio. Mortalidade e sobrevivência no Rio de Janeiro e em São Paulo (*Bol. min. trab. ind. com.*, ano 9, no. 106, junho, p. 289-307). [1714
Analysis of mortality and survival tables in the municipality of São Paulo according to 1940 census as compared with those for the Distrito Federal and both places with cities of foreign countries.

———. A riddle resolved: Brazil's population (*Estadística*, vol. 1, no. 1, March, p. 142-147). [1715
Article giving historical information on the censuses in Brazil, since the first attempt of population estimate in 1776, until the last census undertaken in 1940. Some commentaries upon the preliminary results of the last census are included.

Oliveira, Beneval de. Variações sôbre povoamento e política demográfica (*Cultura política*, ano 3, no. 33, out., p. 61-72). [1716
Study of different questions in relation to settlement: the "Westward" march, the results of the 1940 census and the unequal population distribution.

Prazeres, T. Alves. O viajante comercial na economia do Brasil (*Bol. min. trab. ind. com.*, ano 10, no. 111, nov., p. 197-211). [1717
Article pointing out the rôle of the traveling salesman in the economy of Brazil.

O PROBLEMA DA CARNE; MEDIDAS TOMADAS PELA COOPERATIVA INSTITUTO DE PECUÁRIA E OUTROS INTERESSADOS SÔBRE O MOMENTOSO PROBLEMA QUE PREOCUPA O GOVERNO E POPULAÇÃO DO ESTADO (*Bol. coop. inst. pecuária Bahia*, ano 6, no. 38, abril-junho, p. 53-71). [1718
A collection of documents related to the meat supply problem including its causes and remedies. They contain data on costs, and discuss such matters as credit, transportation facilities, the need for statistics, regulation of the fresh meat market, and disadvantages arising from the region's considerable dedication to fattening. (See also an analysis on pages 9-10 of the same issue). [A. H. Lester]

Torres, José Garrido. O mercado interno do Brasil (*Rev. ciên. econ.*, São Paulo, ano 5, vol. 5, no. 1, jan., p. 21-30). [1719
Development of the home market offers a solution of the difficulties resulting from the war.

STATISTICS AND STATISTICAL SERIES

BOLETIM DO DEPARTAMENTO ESTADUAL DE ESTATÍSTICA. São Paulo. No. 1, jan.-no. 12, dez. [1720
Founded in 1939. Statistical tables showing industrial and trade development in the

State of São Paulo. Demographic conditions. Education, recreational facilities. Official acts. Graphs and tables.

BOLETIM ESTATÍSTICO. Instituto brasileiro de geografia e estatística, Conselho nacional de estatística. Rio de Janeiro. Ano 1, no. 1/2, jan./junho—. [1721
M. A. Teixeira de Freitas, editor. Papers and commentaries on demographic data, monthly and annual statistics concerning economic activities.

BOLETIM ESTATÍSTICO. Instituto nacional do sal. Rio de Janeiro. Ano 1, no. 43/5, jan.– 43/12, agôsto; ano 2, no. 43/13, set.–43/16, dez. [1722
Monthly. Statistical tables on distribution, deliveries, production, prices, etc. of salt in Brazil.

BOLETIM ESTATÍSTICO. Ministério da fazenda, Diretoria de rendas aduaneiras. Rio de Janeiro. Ano 6, no. 1–12. [1723
Monthly. Odilon da Silva Conrado, editor. Statistical tables on customhouse revenues. Official acts concerning customhouse revenues and its control.

COMÉRCIO DE CABOTAGEM PELO PORTO DE SANTOS. São Paulo. Departamento estadual de estatística, Diretoria de estatística, indústria e comércio. [1724
Monthly. Cumulative statistics of coastal trade. Products are classified: data on weight and value in cruzeiros.

COMÉRCIO DE CABOTAGEM PELO PORTO DE SANTOS. BIÊNIO DE 1940–1941. São Paulo. Departamento estadual de estatística, Diretoria de estatística, indústria e comércio. 545 p. [1725
Statistics of coastal trade. Products are classified; data on weight and value in cruzeiros.

COMÉRCIO EXTERIOR DO BRASIL. Ministério da fazenda. Serviço de estatística econômica e financeira. Rio de Janeiro. [1726
A monthly bulletin. Publishes statistical data on exports and imports by countries and major commodities.

ESTATÍSTICA DO COMÉRCIO DO PORTO DE SANTOS COM OS PAÍSES ESTRANGEIROS. Departamento estadual de estatística, Diretoria de estatística, indústria e comércio. São Paulo. [1727
Monthly. Cumulative statistical publication on imports and exports. Quantity and value in cruzeiros on board ship in Santos.

JOURNALS

BOLETIM DA INDÚSTRIA ANIMAL. Publicação do Departamento da produção animal. Secretaria da agricultura, indústria e comércio. São Paulo. Ano 12, nova série, vol. 6. [1728
Irregular. A. Mello, editor. Founded in 1929. Until 1941 published under the title Revista da Industria Animal. Authoritative papers on animal industry by members of the Departamento. News. Reviews of books and journals.

BOLETIM DA SUPERINTENDÊNCIA DOS SERVIÇOS DO CAFÉ. Publicado em continuação a "Revista do Instituto do café." Secretaria da fazenda do estado de São Paulo. São Paulo. Ano 18, no. 191, jan.–no. 202, dez. Gratis. [1729
Monthly. J. Testa, editor. Founded in 1926. Technical articles on coffee production and marketing. Statistics. Legislation.

BOLETIM DO CONSELHO NACIONAL DE GEOGRAFIA (BOLETIM GEOGRÁFICO). Instituto brasileiro de geografia e estatística. Rio de Janeiro. Ano 1, no. 1, abril—. 60 cruzeiros per year, foreign subscription. [1730
Monthly. Christovão Leite de Castro, editor. In the July issue (ano 1, no. 4) the title was changed to Boletim Geográfico. Information, news, book reviews and legislation.

BOLETIM DO INSTITUTO NACIONAL DO MATE. Rio de Janeiro. [1731
Founded in 1940. The review publishes essays and statistics relating to the production of trade in this commodity.

BOLETIM DO MINISTÉRIO DA AGRICULTURA. Rio de Janeiro. Serviço de informação agrícola. Ano 32, no. 1, jan.–no. 12, dez. Gratis. [1732
Monthly. Founded in 1911. Publishes articles on economic and technical subjects. Legislation and public administration relating to the Ministério da Agricultura, Indústria e Comércio.

BOLETIM DO MINISTÉRIO DO TRABALHO, INDÚSTRIA E COMÉRCIO. Serviço de estatística da previdência e trabalho. Rio de Janeiro. Ano 9, no. 101, jan.–no. 108, agôsto; ano 10, no. 109, set.–no. 112, dez. Gratis. [1733
Monthly. Founded in 1934. An official publication devoted to all aspects of contemporary problems in the social sciences in Brazil. Official decrees, news on the industrial and labor front. Legal aspects of arbitration in Brazil and abroad. Occasional historical studies.

BOLETIM DO SERVIÇO DE ECONOMIA RURAL. Ministério da agricultura, Serviço de informação agrícola. Rio de Janeiro. Ano 1, no. 1—. Gratis. [1734
Quarterly. Founded in 1943. Journal devoted to the publication of material relating to rural economy.

BOLETIM DO SETOR DA PRODUÇÃO INDUSTRIAL. Coordenacão da mobilização econômica. Rio de Janeiro. No. 1, agosto—. [1735
Quarterly. Founded in 1943. Journal devoted to the publication of material relating to rural economy.

BOLETIM SEMANAL. Associação comercial. São Paulo. [1736
Weekly. R. Fonseca, editor. Pocket size digest of economic and financial information for the use of members of the Association.

BRASIL AÇUCAREIRO. Instituto do açucar e do alcool. Rio de Janeiro. Ano 11, vol. 21, no. 1, jan.–no. 6, junho; vol. 22, no. 1, julho–no. 6, dez. 35 cruzeiros per year, foreign subscription. [1737
Monthly. Miguel Costa Filho, editor. Founded in 1932. A journal printing most important data on sugar and alcohol production and trade in Brazil. Statistical tables and articles by government and private experts on sugar and alcohol.

BRAZIL TODAY. Brazilian government trade information bureau. New York. [1738
Monthly. Founded in 1940. Francisco Silva, editor.

D. N. C. REVISTA DO DEPARTAMENTO NACIONAL DO CAFÉ. Rio de Janeiro. Ano 11, no. 115, jan.–no. 126, dez. Gratis. [1739
Monthly. Founded in 1933. Benedito Mergulhão, editor. Articles on the production, trade and consumption of coffee. Statistical tables and news on the activities of D. N. C.

JUSTIÇA DO TRABALHO. Rio de Janeiro. 50 cruzeiros per year. [1740
Monthly. Ernesto Machado, editor. Devoted to labor legislation.

O OBSERVADOR ECONÔMICO E FINANCEIRO. Rio de Janeiro. Ano 7, no. 84, jan.; ano 8, no. 85, fev.–no. 95, dez. 100 cruzeiros per year, foreign subscription. [1741
Monthly. Founded in 1936. Valentim F. Bouças, editor.
An unusual journal both in regard to format and comprehensiveness. Three sections: Notas Editoriais; Política Internacional; and Comércio Exterior. Short contributions most of which deal with various aspects of Brazilian social and economic life. The articles on international affairs are informative rather than analytical. Abundant statistical data and financial news.

ORIENTADOR FISCAL. São Paulo. Ano 7, no. 86–ano 8, no. 96. [1742
Monthly. Samuel Ferra de Camargo, editor. Essays on taxation. Tax legislation. No. 96-A includes alphabetical and cross-section index for the whole year.

REVISTA BRASILEIRA DE ESTATÍSTICA. Órgão oficial do Conselho nacional de estatística e da Sociedade brasileira de estatística. Rio de Janeiro. Ano 4, no. 13, jan./março–no. 16, out./dez. 40 cruzeiros per year. [1743
Quarterly. Mario Augusto Teixeira de Freitas, editor. Founded in 1940. Very well printed journal. Articles by well known writers on theoretical & applied statistics. Competent information on Brazilian economic and social phenomena. Book reviews.

REVISTA BRASILEIRA DE GEOGRAFIA. Órgão oficial do Conselho nacional de geografia. Rio de Janeiro. Ano 5, no. 1, jan./março–no. 4, out./dez. 40 cruzeiros per year. [1744
Quarterly. Founded in 1939. Cristovão Leite de Castro, editor. Handsome publication of the Instituto Brasileiro de Geografia e Estatística. Authoritative articles on Brazilian geography with summaries in Spanish, French, German, Italian, English and Esperanto. Minutes of the meetings of the activities of the Instituto. Legislation related to geographical questions. Occasional book reviews. Good illustrations and maps.

REVISTA DE CIÊNCIAS ECONÔMICAS. São Paulo. 50 cruzeiros per year, foreign subscription. [1745
Monthly. Founded in 1939. Frederico Herrmann Junior, editor. A journal devoted to the study of economic theory. Book reviews.

REVISTA DE IMIGRAÇÃO E COLONIZAÇÃO. Órgão oficial do Conselho de imigração e colonização. Ministério das relações exteriores. Rio de Janeiro. Ano 4, no. 1, março–no. 4, dez. [1746
Quarterly. Founded in 1940. Tenente Coronel Aristóteles de Lima Camara, editor. Publishes scholarly articles on ethnographic, sociological and anthropolgical problems of Brazil, with special emphasis on the demographic aspect of these questions. The articles are followed by excellent summaries in French. Often a statistical appendix is published with good diagrams and graphs. Sections set apart for the publication of laws and decrees affecting the status of foreigners in Brazil, and for reports on new developments in the field. Very attractive format and printing.

REVISTA DO TRABALHO. Rio de Janeiro. Ano 11, no. 115, jan.–no. 126, dez. 50 cruzeiros per year. [1747
Monthly. Founded in 1933. Gilberto Flores, editor. Information on current labor problems, accident insurance and compensations, court decisions, trade unionism, minimum wages, labor regulation. Index in the last issue of the year.

REVISTA FISCAL E DE LEGISLAÇÃO DA FAZENDA. Rio de Janeiro. 110 cruzeiros per year. [1748
Fortnightly. Regular appendices on customhouse subjects, stamp tax, business and minor taxes, and miscellaneous tax legislation. Index in the last issue of the year.

SOCIOLOGIA. Revista didáctica e científica. São Paulo. Vol. 5, no. 1, março–no. 4, out. 35 cruzeiros per year, foreign subscription. [1749
Quarterly. Founded 1939. Romano Barreto and Emilio Willems, editors. Journal devoted to social sciences, teaching and research. Original articles are published in each issue. It has one section under Dr. Herbert Baldus devoted to ethnology and another under Dr. Donald Pierson to sociology. News and book reviews.

AGRICULTURE: BRAZIL

BY

ALLEN H. LESTER

*Office of Foreign Agricultural Relations,
Department of Agriculture*

BIBLIOGRAPHY

(See also sections on Economics: Brazil; Geography: Brazil; and Labor and Social Welfare)

Adames, George E. Babassú—A hard nut to crack (*Agric. Americas*, vol. 3, Oct., p. 193-196). [1750
The potential wealth of Brazilian babassu nuts staggers the imagination. Yet full utilization of nature's lavish gift is prevented by problems difficult to solve under present conditions.

———. Brazil expands its silk culture (*Agric. Americas*, vol. 3, August, p. 146-149). [1751
Silk is needed for the war effort, Brazilian agriculture needs diversification, and the country's climate and soil conditions are favorable.

Azevedo, Raúl de. O babaçú do Brasil (*Cultura política*, ano 3, no. 33, out., p. 120-123). [1752
A short but interestingly written article on the babassu, pointing out its many uses.

Bastos, A. M. A castanha do Pará (*Bol. min. trab. ind. com.*, ano 9, no. 101, jan., p. 162-178). [1753
Notes high costs of production of the Brazil nut as well as expensive freight costs. Among suggestions made is planting of the trees in accessible places.

Bittencourt, H. V. de C. O controle à erosão nos cafezais, sulcos e cordões em contorno (*Bol. sup. serv. café*, ano 18, abril-junho, p. 230-237, 322-330, 418-425). [1754
The importance of erosion control on São Paulo coffee plantations, its history, a critique of methods, and details of a system deemed advantageous.

Carvalho, P. P. de. Aspectos de nossa economia rural, a lavoura cafeeira e o fomento á policultura. São Paulo. Ed. Martins. 57 p. [1755
Brazil's agricultural problems, with a program sketched for crop diversification, and for direct action by the government to secure for the farmer agricultural credit, storage and processing facilities to replace what the author deems a predatory system now operated by middlemen.

Ceccatto, G. do N. O pinho brasileiro [*Araucaria angustifolia*]. Rio de Janeiro. Min. da agricultura, Serviço florestal. 39 p. [1756
Dealing chiefly with method of growing, this includes sections describing habitat in Brazil, plantation costs, and uses of Paraná pine.

Instituto do açucar e do alcool. Conferência canavieira de 1941. Rio de Janeiro. Ed. Zélio Valverde. 303 p. [1757
Proceedings of the meetings held at the Instituto do Açucar e do Alcool in Rio de Janeiro in July and August 1941 for discussing legislation regulating the relations between sugar mill owners and sugar cane suppliers. [R. Simonsen]

Jor, J. O. de Souza. O custo de produção no setor agro-pecuário (*Ouro branco*, ano 9, no. 3, julho, p. 12-14; no. 4, agôsto, p. 11-12). [1758
Discusses factors in the farmer's costs of production and in agricultural development in general, proposing a comprehensive agricultural program.

Jorim, Labieno. Erosão dos solos (*Bol. min. trab. ind. com.*, ano 10, no. 112, dez., p. 161-173). [1759
Article analysing the causes and more frequent types of erosion in the country and suggesting solutions. [R. Simonsen]

Maia, Alvaro. Na vanguarda da retaguarda (campanha da produção da borracha). Manáus, Amazonas. D. E. I. P. 354 p. [1760
A series of articles and addresses on various aspects of the Amazon development program for rubber production, including the rural code and the Amazonas Agricultural Colony.

Marques, J. de O. Colônias agrícolas nacionais (*Rev. imig. col.*, ano 4, no. 4, dez., p. 88-99). [1761
A brief description by the Director of the Division of Lands and Colonization of inspection trips through agricultural colonies in four states.

Paiva, Ruy Miller, and Mario D. Homem de Mello. Estudo sôbre a agricultura dos sitiantes (*Rev. arq. mun.*, São Paulo, ano 8, vol. 86, out.–nov., p. 67–110). [1762
A study of agricultural and animal production of the *"sitiante"* (small farmer) in the Município of Campinas (State of São Paulo). Analysis of rural techniques and economy. Photographs and statistical data. [R. Simonsen]

Paz, Ataliba de Figueiredo. Discurso pronunciado . . . ao ser instalado o décimo terceiro congresso rural (*Rev. agron.*, ano 7, no. 80, agôsto, p. 455–464). [1763
An account of accomplishments of the Ministry of Agriculture, Industry and Commerce of the quite important State of Rio Grande do Sul during the 5-year period 1938–1942.

Pôrto, Hannibal. A noz do Brazil (castanha do Pará). Rio de Janeiro. (Min. da agricultura, Serviço de informação agrícola, no. 7). 19 p. [1764
Treats collection, processing, and marketing. Has several full-page photographs.

Resende, Antonio. Conservação do solo, erosão e seu combate (*Ceres*, vol. 5, no. 25, set.–out., p. 27–45). [1765
A plea that Brazilians follow soil conservation practices, and specific methods suggested.

São Paulo (estado). Secretaria da agricultura, indústria e comércio. Diretoria de publicidade agrícola. Notas agrícolas (Coletânea de communicados, notas e informações enviados a imprensa pela Diretoria de publicidade agrícola, durante o periodo de 1° de janeiro de 1941 ate o 1° semestre de 1942). Vol. 6. Organizada pela Secção de divulgação agrícola. São Paulo. 615 p. [1766
A very convenient source for developments in the agriculture of the State of São Paulo.

Schmidt, C. B. Aspectos da vida agrícola no vale do Paraitinga (*Sociologia*, vol. 5, no. 1, março, p. 35–55). [1767
A description of the agriculture of this region, including tenure, techniques, crops and livestock, and occupations of the women and children.

———. Systems of land tenure in São Paulo (*Rural sociology*, vol. 8, Sept., p. 242–247). [1768
This brings out changes to which the development of cotton farming in the last ten years has contributed.

———, and José Reis. Rasgando horizontes; a Secretaria da agricultura no seu cinquentenário. São Paulo. Sria. da agricultura, indústria e comércio, Diretória de publicidade agrícola. 420 p. [1769
Activities of the various agencies of the Department of Agriculture of the State of São Paulo, and a history of the Department.

Slifko, C. W. Commercial possibilities in Brazil's forest wealth (*For. com. weekly*, vol. 10, no. 1, April 3, p. 10–11, 35). [1770
A thumbnail sketch of the stage of development of Brazil's forest resources.

United States. Department of state. Development of foodstuffs production in Brazil; agreement between the United States of America and Brazil signed at Rio de Janeiro September 3, 1942, effective September 3, 1943. Washington. (U. S. Dept. of state publ. 1898, Executive agreement series 302). 9 p. [1771
Text, in English and Portuguese, outlines the scope of the program, and the obligations of the two governments.

Vidal, Ademar. A política de produção agrícola (*Cultura política*, ano 3, no. 34, nov., p. 247–253). [1773
Political problems in the development of Paraíba due to the difficulty of securing the support of the people of the south of Brazil. [P. E. James]

Witt, Lawrence W. Changes in the agriculture of south central Brazil (*Jour. farm econ.*, vol. 25, August, p. 622–643). [1774
The nature of and reasons for changes in quantities of agricultural products grown in Minas Gerais, Rio de Janeiro, and São Paulo, with special reference to the decline of coffee and the expansion of cotton.
Published also in *Brazilian Business*, vol. 23, Oct., 1943, p. 382–384.

EDUCATION *

BY

M. B. LOURENÇO FILHO

Instituto Nacional de Estudos Pedagógicos, Rio de Janeiro, Brasil

BIBLIOGRAPHY

GENERAL

Chacón y Calvo, José María. Hacia la unidad continental (*Rev. cub.*, vol. 17, no. 2, abril–dic., p. 250–274). [1774a
A review, from the Cuban point of view, of the work of the First Conference of Ministers and Directors of Education of the American Republics, Panama, September 27–October 4, 1943. [Bryce Wood]

Lourenço Filho, M. B., and George I. Sánchez. A selective guide to the material published in 1943 on education (*Handbook of latin american studies, no. 8, 1943*, p. 161–167). [1775

BRAZIL

(*See also item 3651*)

Alencar, Meton de, and Gloria Quintela. Estudo sôbre o quociente intelectual na infância desvalida (3.000 menores) (*Arq. serv. assist. menores*, vol. 2, dez., p. 129–175). [1776
Causas gerais da sub-normalidade entre os menores desvalidos.

Aquino, Ivo d'. Nacionalização do ensino. Aspectos políticos. Florianópolis. Imp. oficial, 184 p. [1777
O autor, que desempenha as funções de Secretário da Justiça e Educação, no Estado de Santa Catarina, justifica a política de nacionalização do ensino adotada no país; expõe as providências postas em prática, naquele Estado, para a execução da legislação sôbre o assunto, e junta, por fim, abundante documentação sôbre as escolas nas zonas de colonização estrangeira.

Arruda, Joy. Contribuição para o estudo da fantasia excessiva na criança (*Bol. serv. soc. menores*, São Paulo, vol. 3, no. 1, julho, p. 5–25). [1778
Estudo de 9 casos de fantasia excessiva, em crianças; causas provaveis; meios corretivos.

Azevedo, Fernando de. Velha e nova política. São Paulo. Cia. ed. Nacional. (*Atualidades pedagógicas*, vol. 40). 188 p. [1779
Coletânea de artigos e discursos produzidos de 1932 a 1941, sôbre aspectos e figuras da educação nacional.

Backheuser, Everardo. Do espírito universitário no Brasil (*Formação*, ano 5, no. 65, dez., p. 9–25). [1780
O problema da liberdade de ensino, nas universidades; importância dos trabalhos de pesquisa; especialização e cooperação.

Bahr, Carlos, and J. Pinto Lima. Clubes agrícolas. Rio de Janeiro. Imp. nacional. (Serviço de informações agrícolas do Min. da agric.). 40 p. [1781
A organização dos clubes agrícolas, no Brasil, e a dos Clubes "4-H," nos Estados Unidos.

Barbosa, M. A. Caldas. O problema da orientação e seleção profissionais em face do ensino superior (*Rev. serv. públ.*, ano 5, vol. 1, no. 2, 17 p.). [1782
Importância de orientação prévia e do exame médico dos candidatos as escolas superiores.

Bartholomeu, Hermes. Especificações do Pôsto de puericultura. Rio de Janeiro. Imp. oficial. (Col. do Depto. nac. da criança, 77). 25 p. [1783
Normas para construção de um posto padrão de puericultura, estabelecidas pelo Departamento Nacional da Criança.

————. Um sistema regional de proteção à infância e à adolescencia (*Bol. trim. depto. nac. criança*, ano 3, no. 12, março, p. 24–31). [1784
Bases para a organização de um Serviço de Assistência Social.

Bassewitz, Maria Pavão V. O problema dos menores abandonados e delinquentes. Como resolver entre nós. Pôrto Alegre. Serv. ed. 20 p. [1785
Causas da delinqüência; conceito de responsabilidade de menores delinqüentes; proteção social á infância.

---

* The bibliography on Education in Spanish America is omitted this year.

Bastide, Roger. Educação dos educadores (*Estud. educ.*, ano 3, no. 4, junho, p. 3–20). [1786
Os fatores de formação do professor secundário; observações sôbre o problema na França e no Brasil.

Boisson, Cardoso Ofélia. Contribuição ao estudo da orientação profissional (*Rev. educ. públ.*, Rio, vol. 1, no. 2, abril–junho, p. 152–177). [1787
Resultados do exame de 175 candidatos a cursos intensivos de preparação profissional.

Caracas, Raul de, and others. O que deve ser o ensino de engenharia no Brasil. Por Raul de Caracas, Francisco Lessa, Dulcidio Pereira, e Paulo Sá. Rio de Janeiro. Imp. nacional. (Publ. do Conselho nac. de tecnologia). 88 p. [1788
Opiniões sôbre o ensino de engenharia no Brasil por um professor, um administrador, um diretor e um engenheiro de laboratório.

Carvalhal, José Francisco. A autonomia na escola e o problema da liberdade em educação (*Arq. serv. assist. menores*, vol. 2, dez., p. 199–210). [1789
Conceito de liberdade; liberdade dos educandos e disciplina escolar; ensáios de disciplina autônoma.

Carvalho, José Zacarias de Sá. Alguns aspectos sociais no planejamento da escola rural (*F. N. F.*, ano 3, no. 5–7, p. 208–224). [1790
Condições de vida social nos núcleos urbanos e rurais; sua importância na organização educacional.

Clark, Oscar. Jardins de infância e escolas —hospitais. Rio de Janeiro. Livr. Acadêmica. 157 p. [1791
Importância do papel médico-social da escola primária no Brasil; necessidade de que a pedagogia se baseie na medicina preventiva.

Clozel, José. Plano para instalação de colônias escolares. Araraquara. Ed. Industrias reunidas irmãos. 14 p. [1792
Tese apresentada ao Primeiro Congresso Brasileiro de Saúde Escolar, reunido em São Paulo, em 1943.

Congresso pan-americano da criança. Aspectos atuais do problema da criança. Sergipe. Livr. Regina. (Depto. de saúde). 41 p. [1794
Conclusões e recomendações do Oitavo Congresso Panamericano da Criança, realizado em Washington, de 2 a 9 de maio de 1942.

Correia, Jonas. Educação pública (*Rev. educ. públ.*, Rio, vol. 1, no. 1, jan.–março, p. 5–20). [1795
Professores e programas; a estatística e a educação na Prefeitura do Distrito Federal; tipos de ensino; o plano de matrícula nas escolas municipais, em 1943; despesas com o ensino primário e construções escolares em 1943.

Departamento nacional de educação. Divisão de educação física. Regimento do primeiro Congresso panamericano de educação física, julho de 1943. Rio de Janeiro. Imp. nacional. (Min. da educação e saúde). 34 p. [1796

O ENSINO NO BRASIL EM 1937. Rio de Janeiro. Serv. gráf. do Inst. bras. de geografia e estatística. (Min. da educação e saúde, Serviço de estatística da educação e saúde, Órgão do Inst. bras. de geografia e estatística). [1797
Estatística do ensino primário geral; organização didática e movimento escolar; resultados regionais resultados nacionais.

OS EXERCÍCIOS FÍSICOS E A SUA ADAPTAÇÃO PROFISSIONAL. Rio de Janeiro. Serv. ed. (Min. da educação e saúde, Depto. nac. da educação, Div. da educação física). 47 p. [1798
Instruções sôbre a prática de exercícios físicos compensadores dos distúrbios orgânicos provocados pelas atividades especializadas de cada profissão.

Figueiredo, Gastão de. Creche. Rio de Janeiro. Imp. nacional. (Min. da educação e saúde, Col. do Depto. nac. da criança, no. 95). 26 p. [1799
Histórico, fins e organização das creches.

Goiânia. Colégio Santa Clara. A freqüência regular à escola; o problema da deserção escolar; assistência aos alunos; transporte; internatos e semi-internatos (*Rev. educ.*, Goiânia, ano 8, no. 20). [1799a
Tese apresentada pelo Colégio Santa Clara, de Goiânia, ao Oitavo Congresso de Educação, reunido em junho de 1943, nessa capital.

GUIA DA FACULDADE DE FILOSOFIA, CIÊNCIAS E LETRAS PARA 1943. São Paulo. Ed. Rev. dos Tribunais. (Univ. de São Paulo). 326 p. [1800
Informações sôbre a constituição, finalidades e organização da Faculdade referida.

A IGREJA E A EDUCAÇÃO FÍSICA. Rio de Janeiro. Tip. Batista de Souza. (Min. da educação e saúde, Depto. nac. da educação, Div. de educação física). 16 p. [1801
A colaboração dos colégios religiosos de São Paulo no Plano Nacional de Educação Física.

Jubé Júnior, J. R. R. Diagnóstico das aptidões profissionais pelos índices de capacidade mental (*Rev. serv. públ.*, ano 6, vol. 1, no. 2, 18 p.). [1802
Análise factorial de Thurstone e sua aplicação á seleção profissional.

Katzenstein, Betti. Observações e estudos sôbre ajustados e desajustados (*Rev. arq. mun.*, São Paulo, ano 9, vol. 93, out.–dez., p. 145–161). [1803
O comportamento de 189 crianças, entre 4 a 7 anos, no primeiro dia de frequência a um jardim da infância.

Leite, João Barbosa, and others. Pioneiros da educação física no Brasil. Rio de Janeiro. Tip. Batista de Souza. (Min. da educação e saúde, Depto. nac. da criança, Div. de educação cívica). 22 p. [1804
Discursos na solenidade comemorativa do vigésimo aniversário da morte de Rui Barbosa, por J. B. Leite, A. J. Lacombe e J. de Morais.

Lopes, Luciano. O professor ideal. Rio de Janeiro. Ed. Francisco Alves. 121 p. [1805
Estudo dos requisitos para a formação do professor modelo.

Lopes, Tomás de Vilanova Monteiro. Técnica geral de organização de provas objetivas (*Rev. serv. públ.*, ano 6, vol. 1, no. 2, fev., p. 22–32). [1806
Condições, especificação e construção de uma prova objetiva.

Magalhães, Lucia. A atual organização do ensino secundário brasileiro (*Formação*, ano 5, no. 63, out., p. 24–35). [1807
Resumo das aulas ministradas no curso de Organização do Ensino Secundário, da Universidade do Ar (Rádio Nacional) em maio de 1943.

Maia, Jacyr. As provas de nível mental e aptidão na seleção ao serviço público (*Formação*, ano 5, no. 62, set., p. 7–20). [1808
Indicação geral dos processos de análise estatística, utilizados para a habilitação dos candidatos ao serviço público, em provas de nível mental, organizadas pelo Instituto Nacional de Estudos Pedagógicos.

Maia, Silvia Tigre. A evolução intelectual da mulher no Brasil (*Formação*, ano 5, vol. 62, set., p. 45–51; vol. 65, dez., p. 33–39). [1809
Sumário histórico da instrução feminina no Brasil, seus processos e resultados.

Marinho, Inezil Pena. Contribuição para a história da educação física no Brasil. Brasil colônia, Brasil império, Brasil república. Rio de Janeiro. Imp. nacional. (Min. da educação e saúde, Depto. nac. da educação, Div. da educação física). c/570 p., gravs. [1810
Documentação sôbre a evolução da educação física no Brasil.

Mendes, Figueiredo. Alimentação na infância. Algumas sugestões úteis. Rio de Janeiro. Imp. nacional. (Min. da educação e saúde, Col. do Depto. nac. da criança, 85). 19 p. [1811
Alimentação racional da criança; papel da escola na educação alimentar; carater supletivo da merenda escolar.

Montesenti, M. Lourdes Macuco. O papel dos professores do Serviço social dos menores e seus problemas (*Bol. serv. soc. menores*, São Paulo, vol. 3, no. 1, julho, p. 49–64). [1812
Salienta a necessidade do estudo do menor e do meio social em que haja vivido até a entrada para o abrigo, e assim tambem, os problemas de adaptação.

Moreira, J. Roberto. O equipamento original do homem em face do comportamento coletivo (*Estud. educ.*, ano 3, no. 4, junho, p. 33–46). [1813
Exposição sôbre a necessidade de uma psicosociologia educacional.

———. A escola e o abandono. Florianópolis. Depto. estadual de imprensa e propaganda. 17 p. [1814
Conferência por ocasião da Semana da Criança, em Santa Catarina.

Neiva, Alvaro. Educando para a vida. Vol. 5, Cruzeiro. Ed. Bibl. de educação "João Neiva." (Col. Inst. Cruzeiro). 39 p. [1815
Princípios e resultados de uma experiência realizada pelo autor por vários anos, no Instituto Cruzeiro, de Cruzeiro (São Paulo), para educação integral dos adolescentes.

Oitavo congresso panamericano da criança. Ata final. Washington, D. C., 2–9 de maio de 1942 (*Bol. trim. depto. nac. criança*, ano 3, no. 12, março, p. 5–20). [1816
Resoluções e recomendações aprovadas.

Oliveira, Olinto. Discurso inaugural na sessão de abertura da Semana da criança no. Palácio Tiradentes. Rio de Janeiro. Imp. nacional. (Depto. nac. da criança, Bol. no. 11, suplemento). 8 p. [1817
Papel do Departamento Nacional da criança; problemas relativos á infancia, entre os quais se destaca o da alimentação.

Otão, José. Aprender e ensinar (*An. fac. educ. ciên. let. Pôrto Alegre*, p. 89–94). [1818
Aula inaugural do Curso de Didática, na mencionada Faculdade.

Pinheiro, Maria Esolina. Reações anti-sociais de menores abandonados. Segunda ed. Rio de Janeiro. Imp. nacional (Min. da educação e saúde, Col. do Depto. nac. da criança, 94). 43 p. [1819
Pesquisas das causas das reações anti-sociais dos menores desvalidos; medidas para proteção, adaptação social e profissional dos menores abandonados.

Potsch, Waldemiro. Os pareceres da Seção de ciências físicas e naturais da Comissão nacional do livro didático. Rio de Janeiro. 1130 p. [1820]
Réplica ao parecer da Comissão Nacional do Livro Didático e Miltido pelo livro *Zoologia,* do mesmo autor.

Ribeiro, Carolina. Os parques infantis como centros de educação extra-escolar (*Rev. arq. mun.,* São Paulo, ano 8, vol. 89, março–abril, p. 229–264). [1822]
Objetivos dos parques infantis; na capital de São Paulo; organização e funcionamento.

Sá, Carlos. Higiene e educação da saúde. Rio de Janeiro. Gráf. Barbero. (Min. de educação e saúde, Serv. nac. de educação sanitária, Publ.). 195 p. [1823]
Palestras sôbre educação da saúde realizadas na Associação Brasileira de Educação em janeiro de 1942.

Santos, Francisco Martins dos. O moderno ensino industrial brasileiro (*Rev. serv. públ.,* ano 6, vol. 4, no. 1, out., p. 46–56). [1824]
Descrição das atividades da Escola Industrial Escolástica Rosa, da Cidade de Santos, Estado de São Paulo.

A SEMANA DA CRIANÇA EM 1943, 10–17 DE OUTUBRO. SUGESTÕES PARA SUA COMEMORAÇÃO. TEMA: A INFÂNCIA ABANDONADA. Rio de Janeiro. Imp. nacional. (Min. de educação e saúde, Col. do Depto. nac. da criança, 88). 13 p. [1825]

A SEMANA NACIONAL DA CRIANÇA DE 1943. Espírito Santo (Vitória). Imp. oficial. 53 p. [1826]
Palestras radiofônicas: O direito da infância abandonada viver em ambiente familiar, por E. da S. Guimarães; Menores abandonados nas cidades, por M. A. Freire; O conceito moderno da delinqüência juvenil e o seu tratamento, por E. de Salles; Os deveres dos pais na prevenção do abandono, por A. Lins; Profilaxia e tratamento da conjuntivite do recem-nascido, por J. Martins; A escole e a infância abandonada, por M. L. P. dos Santos; Menores abandonados nas zonas rurais, por O. Rocha; e Amparo material, moral e social, eficiente e carinhoso a criança abandonada, por J. M. de Araujo.

Sete, Mario. Escolas e colégios (*Cultura política,* ano 3, no. 32, set., p. 170–180). [1827]
Reminiscencias da vida escolar.

SUBSÍDIOS PARA A HISTÓRIA DA EDUCAÇÃO BRASILEIRA. 3: ANO DE 1942. Rio de Janeiro? (Min. de educação e saúde, Inst. nac. de estudos pedagógicos, Bol. no. 26). 139 p. [1828]
Súmula dos atos governamentais e indicação dos fatos de maior importância na vida educacional do país, no ano de 1942.

Venâncio Filho, Francisco. A educação de após-guerra (*Estud. bras.,* ano 6, vol. 11, no. 31–33, dez., p. 129–139). [1829]
Comentários sôbre a educação atual no Brasil; o autor sugere para a educação de após guerra, as normas estabelecidas no manifesto publicado em 1932 por um grupo de educadores.

Viana, Gaspar. A transformação do ensino secundário (*Formação,* ano 5, no. 54, jan., p. 16–28). [1830]
Notas sôbre a evolução do ensino secundário no Brasil, e importância da reforma de 1942.

Vieira, Oldegar. Educação extra-escolar e educação prémilitar. Rio de Janeiro. Ed. A. Coelho Branco. 249 p. [1831]
Necessidade de sistematização da educação extraescolar. Educação física, moral e nacional da juventude brasileira.

Zobrozek, Jerzy. Para uma reforma do ensino superior das ciências sociais (*Formação,* ano 5, no. 64, nov., p. 27–42). [1832]
Contribuição para a reforma da Faculdade Nacional de Filosofia.

FOLKLORE

BY

RALPH STEELE BOGGS

University of North Carolina

GENERAL STATEMENT

Despite the war Latin American publications in our field show, if anything, a tendency to increase. None of the regular folklore periodical publications of the New World appear to have suspended publication.

Folklore scholars have been active as usual. Augusto Raúl Cortázar, member of Folklore Américas in Buenos Aires, made a folklore trip to Salta, and reported to the Sociedad Argentina de Antropología on the festival of Nuestra Señora de la Candelaria in Molinos and the process of making a Carnival *caja*. Cortázar is continuing zealously his bibliographic activities in the Museo Etnográfico of the Universidad de Buenos Aires. Luis Heitor Corrêa de Azevedo, member of Folklore Américas in Rio de Janeiro, in cooperation with the Library of Congress in Washington, D. C., recorded Brasilian folkmusic in 1942 in Goyaz and in 1943 in Ceará. To develop this work more amply, he is organizing a center of folklore research in the Escola Nacional de Música in Rio de Janeiro. Oreste Plath and Oribe Echeverría, of Chile, have been in Rio de Janeiro on fellowships, studying folklore with Corrêa de Azevedo. Oreste Plath, who was giving a course in folklore in School no. 7 in Valparaíso, Chile, already in 1934, has now been made secretary of the Instituto de Arte Folklórico in Santiago de Chile. Corrêa de Azevedo and Renato Almeida lectured on folklore demonstrations of Goiânia, illustrated with films and recordings, before the Sociedade Brasileira da Antropologia e Etnografia in Rio de Janeiro, December 9, 1942. Eugenio Pereira Salas, member of Folklore Américas in Santiago de Chile, taught during the summer of 1943 in the University of Chicago, Illinois. Vicente T. Mendoza, member of Folklore Américas in Mexico City and president of the Sociedad Folklórica de México, gave a course on Mexican literature with special attention to works reflecting folk life and customs, another course on Hispanic folk music and poetry, a series of Monday and Wednesday evening sessions at which students were taught to sing Mexican folksongs, ending with an audition of 20 Latin American folksongs, and on August 4, 1943, a lecture on the characteristics of Mexican folkmusic, all well illustrated with songs and pictures, in the 1943 summer term of the Spanish Department of Columbia University in New York City. On April 15, 1943, Raúl G. Guerrero, member of the Sociedad Mexicana de Antropología, gave this Society a report on his trip of folklore investigation (especially in music and dance) in Chiapas, with color film and recordings made in the Zoque, Chiapanec, Tzotzil and Tojolabal regions. At the Sexto Congreso Mexicano de Historia in September 1943 at Jalapa, Veracruz, he spoke on choreographic folklore of Veracruz, analyzing current dances there for their pre-Hispanic and European elements. On October 2, 1943, he lectured on ethnographic and musical notes of Chiapas, at the inauguration of the Ateneo de Ciencias y Artes of Tlaxcala. Narciso R. Colman, of Ybitimí and Asunción, Paraguay, was named honorary president of the Folklore Section of the Academia de Cultura Guaraní. Víctor Navarro del Águila, member of Folklore Américas in Cuzco, Peru, has been appointed to a newly created professorship of folklore in the Universidad de Cuzco.

Regular folklore organizations have continued their group meetings and some new ones have been formed. Folklore Americas added a new member during the year: B. A. Botkin, in charge of the Archive of American Folksong, Library of Congress, Washington, D. C. The Departmento de Folklore of the Instituto de Cooperación Universitaria of the Cursos de Cultura Católica in Buenos Aires had a series of interesting lectures. July 4, 1942, Juan Alfonso Carrizo, member of Folklore Americas and director of the Department, gave one on poetic folklore of La Rioja. July 21, 24, 28 and 31, José Imbelloni gave a cycle: Doctrine of *patrimonio*, its analysis and reconstruction; Doctrine of *pervivencia*, basis of folklore; Contingent problems of folklore in America; and Problems inherent in mythographic interpretation. August 8, in commemoration of the 25th anniversary of the death of the great Argentine folklorist, Juan B. Ambrosetti, Julián B. Cáceres Freyre spoke on Ambrosetti, precursor of folklore studies in Argentina, and María Delia Millán de Palavecino on aboriginal medicine in the Chaco region of Salta. September 2, 9, 16, 23, and 30, Enrique Palavecino gave a short course on cultural areas and circles, with special reference to South America. The Instituto de Arqueología, Lingüistica y Folklore "Dr. Pablo Cabrera" of the Universidad de Córdoba, Argentina, was created by an order of December 10, 1941, to organize and classify materials of the Córdoba region, build up a card file, library and museum, and to train specialists in the field. A promising series of publications was initiated in 1943 with *El Arte Decorativo de los Diaguitas*, by Antonio Serrano, director of the Instituto. National Indian institutes, as affiliates of the Instituto Indigenista Interamericano, have been created in Ecuador, Salvador, Nicaragua and the United States. Article XII of the statutes of the Ecuadorean Institute provides especially for the study of belief, music, dance, custom and other materials of folklore interest. All these Institutes have a general interest in American Indian folklore, though they are primarily concerned with the improvement of the Indian's welfare. A Haitian society of folklore was founded in Port-au-Prince, Haiti, May 24, 1942, with Dr. Price-Mars as president. The Instituto Interamericano de Estudios Músico-Folklóricos, under the Facultad de Humanidades y Educación of the Universidad de Panama, was formed in 1943, under the directorship of Myron Schaeffer, and is to become a department of the Inter-American University there. By making recordings in Panama and by exchange of records with other American republics, it hopes to build a large archive of New World folkmusic, which it will study and diffuse through schools and musical composition. It is anxious to establish relations with scholars and cultural centers of similar interest in all parts of the New World and to exchange publications as well as records with them.

Museums, exhibits and festivals continue with undiminished vigor. Under the able leadership of Rafael Jijena Sánchez, member of Folklore Americas and chief of the Folklore Section in the Universidad de Tucumán, Argentina, a provincial folklore museum is to be organized by the government in Tucumán, rich north Argentine cultural and historic center, where aboriginal and Spanish cultures early met and adapted to their new environment. Jijena Sánchez is also preparing a riddle classification with comparative notes based upon his collection from Tucumán. The Instituto Indigenista Interamericano of México, D. F., received from the Mexican government a collection of Indian art, and another from the Ministerio de Agricultura y Comercio of Panamá. Another is ready to be given by the Indian Arts and Crafts Board of the Department of Interior of the United States. Argentina, Bolivia, Nicaragua and Peru are expected to make similar contributions. The president of Mexico has promised a suitable location for these exhibits. The Museum of Modern Art in New York City exhibited in May 1943 religious folk art of the Spanish southwest (New Mexico and Colorado), 1725–1875. The Brooklyn Museum of New York has established a permanent collection of Latin American colonial and folk art, to be used in a course for teachers, assembled largely through the effects of Herbert J. Spinden, whose *America South of U. S. As Revealed by Art* has been published by this Museum's press.

Folklore archives are also growing. The Ministerio de Educación Nacional in Bogotá, Colombia, in resolution 572 of May 5, 1942, issued a folklore questionnaire covering materials, indication of provenience and background data, and instructed teachers in schools all over the country to send in all such data to the Ministry's Section of Folk Culture. Luis David Peña is director of the Section. Materials have now been received from almost all municipalities of the country, and shortly they are to be classified, analyzed and selected for publication by a commission of folklorists. The Comité de Investigaciones del Folklore Nacional y de Arte Típico Salvadoreño of the Ministerio de Instrucción Pública in El Salvador sent groups during the year to visit various villages rich in traditional culture, named fifteen collaborators and took other steps to establish a network over the country for collecting folklore materials. It also considered publication of folklore books by Gavidia and Baratta.

A few new publications are appearing. Vol. I, no. 1, of the *Boletín de Folklore, Folkvisa y Folkway de Bolivia* appeared in La Paz in 1942, in conjunction with the *Revista de Antropología de Bolivia*, sponsored by the Tihuanacu Institute, under the leadership of Arthur Posnansky, member of Folklore Américas in La Paz, and as the organ of the Sociedad de Folklore, Folkvisa y Folkway de Bolivia, founded in 1940. This first number contains the act of founding of the Society, definition of the terms in the title, and several articles, with illustrations and music. *Tlalocan*, a journal of source materials on the native cultures of Mexico, is issued by the House of Tlaloc, Sacramento, California, under the editorship of R. H. Barlow and G. T. Smisor, chiefly for publishing native language texts and translations, various colonial Spanish reports, notes and bibliographies pertaining to various phases, past and present, of the aboriginal traditional cultures of Mexico. (See its report in the *California Folklore Quarterly*, vol. 2, 1943, p. 225–226.) The *Boletín de la Sociedad Venezolana de Ciencias Naturales*, Venezuela, announced the inauguration of a permanent folklore section.

The radio and phonographic recordings are helping to preserve and diffuse knowledge of folklore. The Instituto Indigenista Interamericano of Mexico City has prepared nine radio programs of recordings of music of indigenous groups and of contemporary composers using native music in their compositions, from various parts of Latin America, the United States and Canada. Transcriptions of this series are to be sent to all the American countries for rebroadcast. A Library of Congress project for recording Indian music in Mexico and Guatemala, with collaboration of the Instituto Indigenista Interamericano of Mexico City, the music section of the Mexican department of education, and the government of Guatemala, and personnel consisting of Luis Sandi and Roberto Téllez Girón, of this music section, and Henrietta Yurchenco, of this Institute, will begin with a two months' trip in Tzotzil, Tzeltal and Lacandon regions in Chiapas, Mexico, followed by a two months' trip in Guatemala. Investigation of large groups in central and northern Mexico will follow later.

BIBLIOGRAPHY

(See also sections on Anthropology, Art, and Music)

GENERAL AND MISCELLANEOUS

(See also item 2338)

Asociación folklórica argentina. Principios, bases, estatutos, reglamentaciones, organización técnica y administrativa. Buenos Aires. (Cuad. folklórico, no. 1). 120 p. [1833
New edition of the no. 1 issued in 1938. Contains largely the same material, revised, expanded and brought up to date, though each edition has items not found in the other. On organization, activities, plans and membership.

Beesley, Claude A. Religion of the Maya (Palacio, vol. 50, no. 1, Jan., p. 8-21). [1834
Describes various folklore, chiefly of Yucatán, Mexico.

Bellani Nazeri, Rodolfo. Del folklore indiano (Rev. geog. amer., año 11, vol. 20, no. 122, nov., p. 259-266). [1835

Boggs, R. S. Una bibliografía general del folklore (Folklore Americas, vol. 3, no. 2, Dec., p. 9-12). [1836
Some 50 titles suggested as a basis for any folklore library.

―――. Folklore: materials, science, art (Folklore Americas, vol. 3, no. 1, June, p. 1-8). [1837
Brief attempt to define folklore and to indicate its place among the sciences and arts, to help in orientation of this field. Spanish translation of this article in Waman Puma, 1943, año 3, vol. 3, no. 15, primer trim, p. 35-42, and in Cuad. tall. San Lucas, no. 3, 1943, p. 85-92.

―――. Folklore bibliography for 1942 (South. folk. quart., vol. 7, no. 1, March, p. 13-73). [1838

Bravo, Carlos. Chontales, la tierra de mi madre (Cuad. tall. San Lucas, no. 2, p. 3-18, 1 ilus.). [1839
On the chontales 'foreigners,' their background, traits, customs, beliefs, songs, etc., in Guatemala.

Cascudo, Luiz da Câmara. Lição etnográfica nas "Cartas chilenas" (Rev. arq. mun., São Paulo, ano 8, vol. 89, março-abril, p. 193-202). [1840
Cites text excerpts from these Cartas portraying life in the capital of Minas Gerais, Brasil, in 1788, which refer to dress, customs, proverbs, sayings, food, drink, dance, festivals and words of folk interest.

Cortázar, Augusto Raúl. Breve esquema de los estudios folklóricos en la Argentina (Acta amer., vol. 1, no. 4, Oct.-Dec., p. 437-441). [1842

Dufourcq, Lucila. Estudio del folklore de Lebu (An. fac. filos. educ., sec. filol., tomo 3, 1941-1943, p. 225-294). [1843
52 proverbs and phrases, 149 beliefs, 51 riddles and riddle tales, words only of 24 folksongs and 10 ballads, 3 children's games, 6 cures, burial beliefs and customs, a tradition, on witchdoctors and 3 "cases," 5 tales. Some comments and comparative notes. Informants not cited.

Imbelloni, J. El folklore de América y sus dificultades contigentes (Rev. geog. amer., año 10, vol. 20, no. 120, sept., p. 133-142). [1844

INFORME DE LAS LABORES DESARROLLADAS POR EL PODER EJECUTIVO EN EL RAMO DE INSTRUCCIÓN PÚBLICA DURANTE EL AÑO DE 1942, RENDIDO ANTE LA HONORABLE ASAMBLEA NACIONAL LEGISLATIVA POR EL PROFESOR JOSÉ ANDRÉS ORANTES, SUBSECRETARIO DE ESTADO,

EL 13 DE ABRIL DE 1943. San Salvador. Imp. nacional. 181 p. [1845
Report on the Comité de Investigaciones del Folklore Nacional y de Arte Típico Salvadoreño, p. 51–53.

Lullo, Orestes di. El folklore de Santiago del Estero; material para su estudio y ensayos de interpretación; fiestas, costumbres, danzas, cantos, leyendas, cuentos, fábulas, casos, supersticiones, juegos infantiles, adivinanzas, dichos y refranes, loros y cotorras, conocimientos populares. Tucumán. (Univ. nac. de Tucumán, Depto. de investigaciones regionales, Insto. de historia, lingüística y folklore, Sección de folklore, publ. 3.) 446 p. [1846
Rich body of these various types of folklore from this archaic region of north Argentina, which has well preserved the indigenous and Spanish colonial cultures which came down from Peru and Bolivia. Texts, descriptions, informants, interpretation. Parts previously published in newspapers.

Magalhães, Basílio de. Trabalhos folklóricos e parafolklóricos (*Cultura política*, ano 3, no. 29, julho, p. 90–95). [1847
Miscellany of notes on recent Hispanic American folklore publications.

Manríquez, Cremilda. Estudio del folklore de Cautín (*An. fac. filos. educ., sec. filol.*, tomo 3, 1941–1943, p. 5–131). [1848
Words only of 72 ballads, cradle songs, *coplas, zamacueca* verses and other folksongs, 141 riddles, 7 riddle tales, 22 prayers, charms and incantations, 119 beliefs, 25 cures, 20 items of witchcraft and description of various witchdoctors' dens in Carahue, Chile. Some comments and comparative notes. Informants not often cited.

Meléndez, Concha. El mito de los ríos en dos novelas hispanoamericanas; orígenes del mito (In *Asomante, estudios hispanoamericanos*, San Juan, P. R., p. 101–107). [1849
This is publication 1 of the series Publicaciones de la Universidad de Puerto Rico under the auspices of the Instituto Interamericano of the University of Puerto Rico.
Eternal life-giving rivers have been deified since the Nile and Ganges by ancients. Studies two South American novels published in 1935 and motivated chiefly by river mythology: Rómulo Gallegos, *Canaima* (the Orinoco) and Ciro Alegría, *La Serpiente de Oro* (the Marañón)

Muñoz, Lucila. Estudio del folklore de San Carlos (*An. fac. filos. educ., sec. filol.*, tomo 3, 1941–1943, p. 133–183). [1851
Words only of 6 ballads, 17 folksongs, biographic sketches of 2 folk poets, verses of 3 *cuecas*, 39 riddles, 2 prayers and 23 beliefs and incantations. Some comments and comparative notes. Informants not cited.

Núñez y Domínguez, José de J. Importancia del folklore (*An. soc. folk. México*, vol. 2, 1941 [*i.e.* 1943], p. 255–261). [1852
Definition of folklore and its place among sciences; classification of its materials. Erroneously regards it as a branch of anthropology, parallel to ethnography, which, he says, studies material and intellectual culture of primitive peoples, while folklore studies same among "popular" classes of "civilized" countries.

Parsons, Elsie Clews. Folklore of the Antilles, French and English; part 3. New York. American folklore society. (Memoirs of the American folklore society, vol. 26, part 3.) xvi, 487 p. [1853
Comparative notes and English summaries of 404 tales, many with several variants, citing texts in first 2 vols. Alphabetical list of solution words, with some comparative notes, followed by some 1,200 riddles in English and French. English and French texts of 657 proverbs, with notes. Only citation of provenience is name of island.

Peixoto, Afrânio. Pelo folclore (*Rev. acad. bras. let.*, ano 42, vol. 65, jan.–junho, p. 203–209). [1854

Pinto, Luis C. El gaucho y sus detractores; defensa de las tradiciones argentinas; reivindicación del gaucho. Buenos Aires. Ed. Ateneo. 213 p. [1855
Admirable defense of this Argentine folktype, born of the country's early struggles, symbol of its nationality and enriched by a growing tradition.

Quijada Jara, Sergio. Del folklore huancavelicano: tres supersticiones y una fiesta (*Cinófono*, año 11, no. 107–108, julio, p. 29–30). [1856
Describes beliefs current among Indians in Huancavelica, Peru, about *jarjaria* (a condemned wandering spirit) and *jayacoj* (diviner), retells a ghost legend of the "Molino" of Izcuchaca, and describes festival of "Niño perdido" of January 15.

Ramírez, Guadalupe. Las artes populares en las pulquerías de México (*An. soc. folk. México*, vol. 2, 1941 [*i.e.* 1943], p. 225–238). [1857
Colorful description of these native drink shops, their paper decorations, drink containers, paintings and verses, music and dances, their names, gifts and prizes for customers, and part they play in festivals.

Robledo, Emilio. De nuestro folklore (*Rev. javeriana*, no. 100, nov., p. 266–269). [1858

Saavedra, Alfredo M. La expresión folklórica militar (*An. soc. folk. México*, vol. 2, 1941 [*i.e.*, 1943], p. 207–223). [1859
Alphabetical list of folk words of Mexican soldier, and words only of ballad "Despedimiento de un militar ascendido."

———. Opinión sobre la labor de la Sociedad folklórica de México (*An. soc. folk. México*, vol. 2, 1941 [*i.e.*, 1943], p. 249–253). [1860
Fine discourse on the viewpoint of the folklorist and the excellent work of the Sociedad Folklórica de México befitting of its aims.

Saubidet, Tito. Vocabulario y refranero criollo, con textos y dibujos originales y láminas en colores. Buenos Aires. 426 p. [1861

Villablanca, Celestina. Estudio del folklore de Chillán (*An. fac. filos. educ., sec. filol.*, tomo 3, 1941–1943, p. 185–223). [1862
Words only of 6 ballads, 14 prayers and praises, 16 folksongs, 16 riddles, 2 traditions, 1 tale. Some comments and comparative notes. Informants sometimes given.

MYTHOLOGY

Gámiz, Abel. Quetzalcóatl (*An. soc. folk. México*, vol. 2, 1941 [*i.e.*, 1943], p. 91–107). [1863
Rather lyrical discussion and retelling of this bit of Mexican myth.

Rosado Ojeda, Vladimiro. Ritos del fuego entre los aztecas (*Ars*, México, vol. 1, no. 5, mayo, p. 3–8, 7 ilus.). [1864
Examines the significance of fire in Aztec mythology of ancient Mexico, its symbolism and representation, especially with vivid description of related festivals.

Siegel, Morris. The creation myth and acculturation in Acatán, Guatemala (*Jour. amer. folklore*, vol. 56, no. 220, April–June, p. 120–126). [1865
English text and analysis of this myth, dictated by an Indian of San Miguel Acatán, showing fusion of European Catholic and Maya Indian elements and adaptation to modern local environment. "Acculturation" is a word come into vogue among those anthropologists fond of technical terminology, and apparently means little more than 'adaptation' applied to culture in its normal morphological evolution in adapting itself to ever changing conditions, especially those arising from its contact with another cultural tradition.

LEGEND AND TRADITION

(*See also item* 3802)

Carreño, Ángel. La taberna del diablo (*Waman puma*, año 3, vol. 3, no. 15, primer semestre, p. 87–91). [1867
Tradition of origin of cross on Picchu hill near Cuzco, Peru, marking spot where San Francisco Solano in 16th century dragged Satan disguised as a woman keeping tavern nearby. Cross is taken to San Francisco church every May 3.

Raposo, Inácio. Lendas maranhenses (*Cultura política*, ano 3, no. 23, jan., p. 79–87). [1868
Some 20 legends and traditions retold in brief, from Maranhão, Brasil.

Río, Alfonso del. Leyendas de la Guadalupana en Chavinda, Michoacán (*An. soc. folk. México*, vol. 2, 1941 [*i.e.* 1943], p. 57–67, 4 ilus.). [1869
Retells 7 Mexican Virgin of Guadalupe legends.

Rodríguez Rivera, Virginia. Tesoros escondidos (*Prev. segur.*, p. 69–70). [1870
General observations on traditions of buried treasures in Mexico, with a few illustrative examples.

FOLKTALE

Beals, Ralph L. Problems in Mexican Indian folklore (*Jour. amer. folklore*, vol. 56, no. 219, Jan.–March, p. 8–16). [1872
Inspiring for folktale student. Notes lack of usable folktale collections from Spain and Mexico, prevalence of tales of Spanish origin and lack of those of Indian origin, as well as lack of historical and comparative and functional studies. Outlines periods of Mexican cultural history, noting break between pre-Conquest and modern mestizo tradition. Notes especially lack of tales among western Mixe of Oaxaca

Cascudo, Luiz da Câmara. Um conto africano que é europeu (*Diario de noticias*, Rio, junho 6). [1873
Considers tale type 105 (*FFC* 74), Cat's only trick, and gives variants from Brazil and U. S. A.

Guerra, Fermina. Mexican animal tales (*Texas folk. soc. pub.*, no. 18, p. 188–194). [1874
Lists about a dozen general traits, and illustrates with 3 tales in English: Little ant, ox and horse, Good deed repaid by evil one.

Guerrero, Raúl G. Folklore: cuentos indígenas (*Tiras de colores*, vol. 1, no. 1, mayo 31, p. 4). [1875
Otomí tale of Flor de San Juan from Alfajayucan, Hidalgo, Mexico.

Radin, Paul. Cuentos y leyendas de los zapotecas (*Tlalocan*, vol. 1, no. 1, p. 3–30; no. 2, p. 134–154). [1876
Examines Zapotecan Indian language of Oaxaca, Mexico, as seen in Juan de Córdoba's *Arte* and *Vocabulario*, 1578, and as reported by modern scholars. General observation on Zapotecan folk narratives. Zapotecan texts and literal Spanish translations of 4 folktales.

Simpson, George Eaton. Traditional tales from northern Haiti (*Jour. amer. folklore*, vol. 56, no. 222, Oct.–Dec., p. 255–265). [1877
English texts of 7 tales, with names of informants.

FOLK POETRY, MUSIC, DANCE AND GAME

Angulo A., José. El improvisador, verdadero precursor de la poesía nacional (*An. soc. folk. México*, vol. 2, 1941 [*i.e.* 1943], p. 117–123). [1878
Identifies 5 of these improvising bards, apparently chiefly of the 19th century, of Chile, with some of their verses (no music).

———. Música folklórica chilena (*An. soc. México*, vol. 2, 1941 [*i.e.* 1943], p. 125–131). [1879
Says Chilean folkmusic is sad and is of the mountains and valleys, not of the sea. Defines and illustrates with verses (no music) the *cueca, tonada, esquinazo* and *canción*. Also mentions briefly the *estilo criollo* and *mapuchinas* or *araucanas*.

Azevedo, Luiz Heitor Corrêa de. A Escola nacional de música e as pesquisas de folklore musical no Brasil (*Cultura política*, ano 3, no. 30, agôsto, p. 153–155). [1880
On its teachings of folklore; on trips to Goiaz and Ceará where 18 and 75 disk recordings were made, and on plans for collecting, analyzing and classifying folkmusic recordings by disk or MS., musical instruments, films and photographs of instruments and dances, and bibliography.

———. A "moda de viola" no Brasil central (*Cultura política*, ano 3, no. 32, set., p. 181–184). [1881
Brief indications of character of this music of northern São Paulo, western Minas Gerais, southern Mato Grosso and Goiás, sung by 2 voices or more, accompanied by this string instrument. The *moda* is a ballad (kind of folk newspaper) or folk-song (sentimental lyrics), whose music does not follow precisely its melodic line or tempo.

Brondo Whitt, E. Hilitos de oro (*An. soc. folk. México*, vol. 2, 1941 [*i.e.*, 1943], p. 113–116). [1882
Description and verses of this children's game. No music nor indication of provenience.

Cardenal Argüello, Salvador. Música indígena para marimba (*Cuad. tall. San Lucas*, no. 3, p. 82–83). [1883
Initiates a series of marimba folk dance music from Diriomo, Nicaragua. I. Musical transcription and descriptive notes on execution of *Jarabito suelto*.

Castañeda, Daniel. El corrido mexicano, su técnica literaria y musical. Mexico, D. F. Ed. Surco. 124 p. cartas, música. [1884
Good, detailed, well illustrated investigation of its metrical and rhythmical forms, contrasted with ballad in Spain; also observations on the creative procedure of the *corredista*, his literary formulas and language and origin, themes and classification of *corridos*.
2 tables, one of metrical, one of music notation.

Fogelquist, Donald F. La figura de Pancho Villa en los "corridos" de la revolución mexicana (*América*, Habana, vol. 17, no. 3, marzo, p. 59–66). [1885
Reviews his life story as told in Mexican ballads, from which he cites numerous verses, showing that Villa has become a folk hero of considerable importance.

FOLKLORE: POESÍA DE DICIEMBRE (*Cuad. tall. San Lucas*, no. 2, p. 19–23). [1886
Words only of 7 Christmas songs current in Guatemala.

Freitas, Newton. Música popular del Brasil (*Rev. mus. mex.*, vol. 3, no. 8, agosto 7, p. 176–178). [1887
General observations on its Afro-Brazilian nature and present development.

Galván de del Río, Carmen. Folklore en la propaganda comercial (*An. soc. folk. México*, vol. 2, 1941 [*i.e.* 1943], p. 181–194, 4 ilus.). [1888
Reproduces and comments on signs in a large secondhand store in Guadalajara, Jalisco, Mexico, which advertises various types of merchandise in verse, in the style of street vendor's cries.

Garrido, Pablo. Biografía de la cueca. Santiago, Chile. Ed. Ercilla. 135 p. [1889
This Chilean musician examines in detail the development of this national folk dance of Chile: its origin, historical references to it in Chile from the early 19th century descriptions and definitions of it, its place in Chilean society, analysis of its verses and music, illustrated with numerous citations of verses and previous literature about it.

Hellmer, Joseph R. Is it really Latin American? (*The Pan American*, vol. 4, no. 1, April, p. 15–18). [1890
Discusses popular music of Mexico, Puerto Rico, Cuba, Argentina Brazil which has become popular in the United States.

Kahn, Máximo José. El cante jondo (*Rev. mus. mex.*, vol. 3, no. 8, agosto 7, p. 171–176). [1891
On origin, nature and types of this category of Andalusian folksong, called *cante flamenco* or *cante hondo*, from Hebrew *jom tob* 'good day, religious festival'.

Kennedy, Stetson. La paloma in Florida (*South. folk quart.*, vol. 7, no. 3, Sept., p. 163–164). [1892
Cites Ortega's opinion that this contemporary Mexican folksong derives from an ancient Aztec funeral song, and 1717 report of Spanish governor of Florida that Indians there had a song by this name, and wonders if the two are related.

Lima, Emirto de. La copla popular colombiana (*An. soc. folk. México*, vol. 2, 1941 [*i.e.* 1943], p. 243-247). [1893

Words only of various *coplas* illustrating different varieties found in Tolima and Huila.

Liscano, Juan. Folklore venezolano (*Rev. mus. mex.*, vol. 3, no. 5, mayo 7, p. 99-103). [1894

Reprinted from *Boletín del Instituto Cultural Venezolano-Británico* (Caracas), 1942, no. 6, p. 5-13. General observations on folkmusic in Venezuela.

Luna, Lisandro. Folklore puneño: danzas vernaculares de Santiago de Pupuja (*Waman puma*, año 3, vol. 3, no. 15, primer semestre, p. 59-63). [1895

Describes Novenante and Saraqquena dances, and September 14th festival when they are performed, in commemoration of appearance of Christ child dressed as an Indian.

Mendoza, Vicente T. Una canción isabelina en México (*Div. hist.*, vol. 4, no. 4, feb. 15, p. 214-220, lám.). [1896

Gives verses and examines variants of the ballad "¿Dónde vas, Isabel?" from Jalisco, Michoacán, Sinaloa and Nuevo León, Mexico. (Music notations for the first and fourth are given, together with verse and notation for the song "Isabelita" from a Spanish source. [C. Seeger]). Compares it with an Andalusian children's game "La ponchada" printed in Mexico first c. 1840. Concludes that this ballad, of political implications, refers to queen Isabel II, was produced c. 1837, and became current in Mexico, also with political implications, toward the middle of the century.

———. Música indígena; teorías migratorias, influencias asiáticas, de las islas del océano Pacífico, posibles influencias del oriente y del sur, instrumentos exóticos que aparecen en México, el por qué de su persistencia (*Rev. univ.*, Guadalajara, tomo 1, no. 3, agosto-oct., p. 27-31, ilus., mapa). [1897

Study of surviving musical instruments and their portrayal on pottery, etc. of ancient Indians of Mexico shows a complex cultural pattern, with movement from north to south and west to east. Sees Oriental influences (Chinese, Polynesian), also African, Egyptian and Palestinian parallels, most plainly among Indians who have resisted Spanish influence.

———. Origen de dos canciones mexicanas (*An. soc. folk. México*, vol. 2, 1941 [*i.e.* 1943], p. 145-172). [1898

Studies developments of the ten commandments in Mexican folksong and its antecedents in Spain. 4 music notations.

———. Origen de tres juegos mexicanos (*An. soc. folk. México*, vol. 2, 1941 [*i.e.*, 1943], p. 77-89). [1899

Gives description, music and words of 3 children's games current in Mexico: La víbora, víbora del mar; Al ánimo; Pasen, pasen, caballeros; which vary in text but are played alike. Believes they are, in essence, all the same, and traces their antecedents to Spain. 9 music notations.

———. Simbolismo femenino en la lírica popular mexicana (*Prev. segur.*, p. 77-79). [1900

Studied through numerous verses cited from Mexican folksongs.

Miranda, Nicanor. Jogos motores para crianças de 4 a 6 anos (*Rev. arq. mun.*, São Paulo, ano 8, vol. 88, jan.-fev., p. 237-268, 12 láms.). [1901

Describes 53 Brazilian children's games.

Nieto, Luis. Charango. Romancero cholo. Cuzco. Ed. H. G. Rozas sucs. (Inst. amer. de arte del Cuzco, Bibl., vol. 1). 160 p. [1902

Olivares Figueroa, R. El "folklore" en la escuela; canciones de cuna venezolanas (*Educación*, Caracas, año 4, no. 25, junio-julio, p. 13-15). [1903

Observations on the cradle song in general, in school, in Spain and Venezuela, with verses of Venezuelan examples.

———. Folklore guayanés: juegos infantiles en el Orinoco (*Onza, tigre y león*, año 5, no. 50, agosto, p. 4-5, 14). [1904

Describes Venezuelan children's games related chiefly to fish and animals of the Orinoco river: *baba, chigüire, tonina, pescao, pilón, caimán, perro y chigüire, concha en el agua.*

———. Folklore merideño: burlas y dicharachos infantiles (*Onza, tigre y león*, año 5, no. 51, sept., p. 11-12). [1905

14 texts in verse of satiric and humoristic sayings of children, from oral tradition of the capital of Mérida, Venezuela.

Pan American union. Folk songs and stories of the Americas. Washington, D. C. 64 p. [1906

Reprinted from *Bulletin of Pan American Union*, February, 1937.

Pardo, Isaac J. Viejos romances españoles en la tradición popular venezolana (*Rev. nac. cultura*, año 5, no. 36, enero-feb., p. 35-74). [1907

Gives words only of 9 ballads from Venezuela, some previously published, others not, with notes of provenience and comparisons with versions from Spain. To stimulate further collection, indicates nature and content of other such ballads likely to be found in Venezuela.

Santelices, Sergio. La cueca—Chile's national dance (*The Pan American*, vol. 4, no. 1, April, p. 22–23). [1908
Chiefly on this folkdance, also *huasos* and *chinas* who dance it, and *chicha* they drink and folkfoods they eat on September 18, Chile's independence day, in Santiago's Cousiño park.

Secades, Eladio. La conga (*Prev. segur.*, p. 68). [1909
Observations on this folkdance in relation to the social life and character of the Cuban folk.

Tamayo, Francisco. La fulía (*Bol. soc. venez. cien. nat.*, tomo 8, no. 54, enero–marzo, p. 181–184). [1910
Is a type of folksong sung at *velorios* of babies, saints and the Cross, with drum or *cuatro* accompaniment, in eastern and central Venezuela, usually in *copla* form with religious or secular subject, of Spanish origin. Gives verses of three.

Travesari, Pedro P. Orientación folklórica: influencia de la música de los árabes y de otras de las artes moriscas evocadoras del "folklore de las Américas" (*Oasis*, año 1, no. 1, mayo, p. 23–27). [1911
On influence of Arabic on Spanish folklore, hence Arabic element in Latin American folklore. Considers especially folkmusic. Believes Chilean *zamacueca* is of Arabic origin.

CUSTOM AND FESTIVAL

Brondo Whitt, E. Del viejo folklore (*An. soc. folk. México*, vol. 2, 1941 [*i.e.* 1943], p. 109–112). [1913
On Mexican calendar customs. Also brief mention of children's games.

Doria, João. "Água, com muita fé, aos pés do Senhor do Bonfim" (*Rev. Brasil*, ano 6, terceira fase, no. 54, junho, p. 76–83). [1914
A contribution to the folklore of the Bahian region, dealing with the "Quintafeira do Bonfim" festival, or cleansing of the church. [S. Putnam]

Hoffmann-Harnisch, jr., Wolfgang. O carnaval gaúcho (*Cultura política*, ano 3, no. 24, fev., p. 139–140, 6 fotos). [1915
Pictures costumed, playing, singing and dancing groups, celebrating rustic carnival in Rio Grande do Sul, Brasil.

Medina Álvarez, Cesáreo. La fiesta de los quiatlaxpes (*An. soc. folk. México*, vol. 2, 1941 [*i.e.* 1943], p. 139–140). [1916
Describes this May third Mexican festival.

Michaca, Pedro. La procesión del "Divino Pastor" en la hacienda de la Sauceda, Durango (*An. soc. folk. México*, vol. 2, 1941 [*i.e.* 1943], p. 239–242). [1917
Description of this ritual to bring rain.

Passin, Herbert. Comparative note on sorcery (*Jour. amer. folklore*, vol. 56, no. 222, Oct.–Dec., p. 266–271). [1918
Studies custom of sharing with others, enforced by negative sanction of sorcery, especially in case of Tarahumara Indian chief of Chihuahua, Mexico, who refused cattle donation to Guadalupe festival of December 12.

Quijado Jara, Sergio. Del folklore huancavelicano: fiesta de las cruces (*Comercio*, junio 30, p. 6). [1919
Huancavelica, Peru, has many crosses: Cruz de Potojchi, Santa Cruz, Cruz del Espíritu, de Oropesa, de San Antonio, de Balcón Pata, Pata, de Phyhuán, Soltera. Describes their typical May third festival.

Río, Alfonso del. Impresiones de romería (*An. soc. folk. México*, vol. 2, 1941 [*i.e.* 1943], p. 69–75). [1920
Description of May Cross festival on Cerro Alto, near Chavinda, Michoacán, Mexico, May 3.

Rodríguez Rivera, Virginia. Calendas (*Prev. segur.*, p. 185, 190). [1921
Describes festival of Nativity of Virgin, September 8, in Oaxaca, Mexico.

Val, Gorki del. Del folklore tambobabino: cutipay (*Waman puma*, año 3, vol. 3, no. 15, primer semestre, p. 76–80). [1923
Describes this rustic festival following communal cultivation of fields, with Spanish verses of some *wifalas* sung there.

DRAMA

Cuadra, Pablo Antonio, and **Francisco Pérez Estrada.** Teatro popular: original del jigante, anónimo de Diriamba (*Cuad. tall. San Lucas*, no. 3, p. 93–104). [1924
Reproduces text of this gem folkdrama portraying, in vivid style found only in folklore, with traces of verse and untroubled by anachronisms, the Biblical battle between David and Goliath, with a bit of Moors and Christians thrown in, as faithfully copied by Pérez Estrada from a MS. of Diriamba. In this and other villages of southeast Nicaragua it has been performed until recently. Excellent notes on language and content of text by Cuadra.

Gillmor, Frances. Dance dramas of Mexican villages. Tucson, Arizona. Univ. of Arizona. (Univ. of Arizona bull., vol. 14, no. 2). 28 p. [1925
Describes and summarizes in English the Spanish texts of 3 dance dramas and describes the festivals at which they are given: Moors and Christians, Conquest of Mexico, Plume dance.

PASTORELA; ORIGINAL DE PASTORES PARA OBSEQUIO AL NIÑO DIOS EN LAS PASCUAS, ANÓNIMO DE LA VILLA DE NIQUINOHOMO (*Cuad. tall. San Lucas*, no. 2, p. 25–34). [1926
Interesting text from Guatemala of this widely diffused Epiphany folkdrama of

shepherds' adoration and presentation of gifts to Christ Child, said to be performed there still; copy of Carlos Sotelo MS.

ART, CRAFT, ARCHITECTURE, DRESS AND ADORNMENT

Biró de Stern, Ana. Alfarería de Itatí (*An. inst. etnog. amer.*, tomo 3, p. 351–355, 3 figs.). **[1927**
Brief historical survey of this indigenous and colonial pottery center of Corrientes, Argentina, and description of its methods.

Carroll, Charles D. Miguel Aragon, a great santero (*Palacio*, vol. 50, no. 3, March, p. 49–64). **[1928**
On this woodcarver and painter of saints' images, altars and other religious objects, who lived in Cordova, New Mexico, U. S. A., about a century ago.

Chávez González, Rodrigo A. El arte maya en América; ensayo para el estudio de la sociología prehistórica de América (*Rev. mun.*, Guayaquil, año 17, no. 95–97, 1942, p. 137–144; no. 98–100, p. 173–180; no. 101–103, p. 191–193; año 18, no. 104–106, 1943, p. 145–151; año 18, no. 107–109, p. 157–165). **[1929**
Continuation. Cosmogony and astronomy, decorative art, architecture and sculpture, pottery, music, Mayan influence in North, Central and South America, ancient Peruvian cultures, Tiahuanacu, decadence of American cultures and social motives thereof.

Delboy, Emilio. El manhuaré de nuestros salvajes, precursor de la radiotelefonía (*Historia*, Lima, vol. 1, no. 4, sept.–oct., p. 303–306). **[1930**
Describes this pair of hollow wood cylinders, struck with rubber mallet, giving 4 note scale, keyed in various combinations to transmit any message by sound, used by Indians along Putumayo river border country between Peru and Colombia.

Jongh Osborne, Lilly de. Cerámica indígena en Centro América (*Amér. indígena*, vol. 3, no. 4, oct., p. 351–358). **[1932**
Describes modern practices of potter's art, which show a combination of pre-Columbian and colonial European survivals.

―――. Influencias de la época colonial sobre la indumentaria indígena de Guatemala (*An. soc. geog. hist. Guatemala*, año 18, tomo 18, no. 4, junio, p. 425–435). **[1933**
Short descriptive survey of Guatemalan dress, especially in colonial period, under Spanish influence, types, weaving processes, designs.

Lehmann-Nitsche, Robert. La bota de potro (*Aberdeen angus*, no. 17, p. 33–51, 7 figs.; no. 18, p. 33–48; no. 19, p. 49–63, 25 figs.; no. 20, p. 17–27, 1 fig.). **[1934**
Excellent historic, descriptive and linguistic study on this rustic or gaucho leather boot, its names, in Argentina, Uruguay, Chile, Bolivia and Brazil, proverbs, folk expressions and poetry referring to it. Also discusses *chiripá*, a shawl used as a kind of loose, short trousers, meanings and origin of the word, in Argentina, Uruguay, Brazil and Chile. Traces origin and evolution of *bota de potro* from ancient Greeks through medieval Europe to colonial times, when it was brought to America and survives in La Plata, southern Brazil and Chile. Etimological study of *bota, huesa, estibal, zueco, coturno, calzado*.

Lobet de Tabbush, Bertha J. Figuritas humanas en terracota del territorio argentino; esbozo de clasificación y distribución (*An. inst. etnog. amer.*, tomo 4, p. 249–343, 8 láms., 123 figs., cartas). **[1935**
Good geographic study and classification of this ceramic art in northwest and central Argentina, with abundant illustrations actually examined.

Tamayo, Francisco. Exposición indígena (*Bol. soc. venez. cien. nat.*, tomo 8, no. 54, enerzo–marzo, p. 129–133). **[1936**
Lists objects of aboriginal Venezuelan folk culture from eight private collections exhibited in December 1942–January, 1943, during which five lectures were given on folkmusic and dance, and mythology.

Walker, Edwin F. A real Mexican Atlatl (*Masterkey*, vol. 17, no. 3, May, p. 91–94). **[1937**
Describes one of these spear throwers used in duck hunting, from Tarascan Indians, Jaracuaro Island, Lake Pátzcuaro, Michoacán, Mexico.

Watkins, Frances E. A silver fish from Peru (*Masterkey*, vol. 17, no. 3, May, p. 88–90). **[1938**
On this modern example of fine metal work, a shawl pin from Chucuito, Puno, Peru, and the tradition of the craft from Inca times.

FOOD AND DRINK

Calasans, José. Aspectos folclóricos da cachaça. Separata da *Revista de Aracajú*, no. 1, 1942. **[1939**
An interesting and hitherto more or less neglected folklore theme. [S. Putnam]

Pereira Salas, Eugenio. Apuntes para la historia de la cocina chilena. Santiago, Chile. Imp. universitaria. 84 p. **[1940**
Reprinted from *Boletín de Educación Física*, Institute of education, University of Chile. Excellent historical description of traditional foods, drinks, their preparation, manner of serving, tableware, eating customs, etc., showing fusion of three traditions: indigenous, Spanish and foreign.

Ramos Espinosa, Alfredo. El folklore y la alimentación (*An. soc. folk. México*, vol. 2, 1941 [*i.e.* 1943], p. 195–205). **[1941**
Observations by a doctor of medicine on nutritive value, good taste, etc. of various Mexican folkfoods.

Rodríguez Rivera, Virginia. Algunas comidas de México de fines del siglo 19 (*An. soc. folk. México,* vol. 2, 1941 [i.e. 1943], p. 173–180). [1942
Description of preparation of 14 dishes, and various other notes on Mexican folkfoods.

BELIEF, WITCHCRAFT, MEDICINE AND MAGIC

Barrera Vásquez, Alfredo. Horoscopos mayas, o el pronóstico de los 20 signos del tzolkin, según los libros de Chilam Balam, de Kaua y de Mani (*Reg. cult. yuc.,* año 1, no. 6, oct.–nov., p. 4–33). [1943
On the signs in the *tzolkin* or *tonalamatal* book of 260 days of the ritual calendar, and their use in fore-telling future of children born on the day of each sign, among ancient Mayans.

González Sol, Rafael. Farmacoterapia prealvaradeana en Centroamérica. San Salvador? 52 p. Typed carbon copy. [1943a
Excellent contribution assembling data gleaned from colonial Spanish chronicles on medicinal use of drugs (vegetable, animal, mineral), by early Indians, including a surprising amount of detailed information on specific cures, and a few notes on methods, with description of a sweat bath treatment.

Ibarra (h.), Alfredo. Majoma; leyenda de Sinaloa (*An. soc. folk. México,* vol. 2, 1941 [i.e. 1943], p. 7–21, 6 ilus.). [1944
On belief in this virtue which enables one to get what one wants, with vivid background sketch of this region of Mexico.

Jiménez Borja, Arturo, and Hermógenes Colán Secas. Mates peruanos [Área Huaral-Chancay, Depto. de Lima] (*Rev. mus. nac.,* Lima, tomo 12, no. 1, primer semestre, p. 29–35). [1945
Name, illustration and use of 19 types of gourd, reference to two colonial chronicles on ritualistic use of *mates* among early Peruvian Indians, and one case of their use in modern witchcraft.

Lastres, Juan B. Medicina aborigen peruana (*Rev. mus. nac.,* Lima, tomo 12, no. 1, primer semestre, p. 61–80). [1946
Indicates types of evidence (language, pottery, folklore, colonial Spanish chronicles, bones and mummies) for investigating medicine in Inca Peru, their advantages and limitations, with critical survey of scholars' work, and results to be obtained along these lines.

Magalhães, Basílio de. Ainda os mitos aquáticos do Brasil (*Cultura política,* ano 3, no. 30, agôsto, p. 161–167). [1947
Various notes on imaginary beings associated with water: *jemanjá, mãe-d'água (do rio), minhocão, boiuna* and *bói-açú, cabeça-de-cuia, barba-ruiva, cabocolo-d'água, ururau.*

———. Mitos aquáticos (*Cultura política,* ano 3, no. 28, junho, p. 190–195). [1948
Surveys beliefs in Brazilian folklore about water spirits: *iara, bôto* and the like. Further note on *mboitatá.* Note on St. Amaro in Brazilian folk cure of arm and leg pains.

———. Mitos ígneos (*Cultura política,* ano 3, no. 24, fev., p. 134–138; no. 27, maio, p. 164–167). [1949
Surveys various manifestations of fire beliefs in Brazilian folklore: *mboitatá, mãe-do-ouro, zelação, cumacanga, carneiro-de-ouro, carbúnculo, salamanca, cerro-bravo.* Also comments on recent publications.

———. Santos Padroeiros no dominio folclórico (*Cultura política,* ano 3, no. 35, dez., p. 269–274). [1950
On the saints in Brazilian folklore.

Pereda Valdés, Ildefonso. Medicina popular y folklore mágico del Uruguay. Montevideo. Ed. Galien. 117 p. 13 láms. [1951
General survey of folk medicine, in picaresque novel of Spain and indigenous South America. 65 recipes from notebook of a folk-curer, with identification of medicaments used and other explanatory notes. Survey of method of medicine man in sympathetic magic. Eight curative and preventive prayers. Detailed case history of "professor" Noufrof. Fine broad study of this field for Uruguay.

FOLKSPEECH

Buentello, Humberto. Origen o significado de algunos nombres geográficos de América (*Prev. segur.,* p. 117–118, 120–122, 124–127). [1952
On original meaning and origin of some 214 New World place names.

Dávila Garibi, J. Ignacio. Algunas disquisiciones acerca del vocablo "tapatío" (*Fil. letras,* tomo 6, no. 11, julio–sept., p. 91–110). [1953
On origin and meaning of this word (most commonly referring to something of Guadalajara or even whole state of Jalisco, Mexico), citing two legendary accounts of its origin and verses of folksongs, proverbs and expressions containing this word.

Kany, C. E. American Spanish *amalaya* to express a wish (*Hisp. rev.,* vol. 11, no. 4, Oct., p. 333–337). [1954
Traces currency and variants of this curious semantic development through Spanish American folkspeech: *ah mal haya* gives *amalaya,* equivalent to *ojalá;* and *amalayar,* to *anhelar.*

———. Temporal conjunction *a lo que* and its congeners in American Spanish (*Hisp. rev.,* vol. 11, no. 2, April, p. 131–142). [1955
Considers its use in various Spanish American dialects.

Magalhães, Basílio de. Filologia folklórica: amerindianismos (*Cultura política*, ano 3, no. 23, jan., p. 88–92). [1956
Examines Tupí Indian origin of Brazilian place names *Caxambú* and *marabá* 'halfbreed of White-Indian parents.' Miscellaneous comments on recent folklore publications.

Malaret, Augusto. Españolerías (*Univ. cat. bolivariana*, vol. 9, no. 29, feb.–marzo, p. 11–33). [1957
Alphabetical list of words, their meaning and region, selected at random from published dialect vocabularies of various regions of Spain, for the pointed consideration of those purists who would restrict to a minimum American contributions to general Spanish vocabulary.

———. Semántica americana; notas. Cataño, Puerto Rico. Imp. San José. 128 p. [1958
Peculiarities of American Spanish: word formation, verbs, adverbs, interjections, meaning, spread and survival of Americanisms from Fernández de Oviedo's *Historia General y Natural de las Indias*, 1535, and Herrera's *Descripción de las Indias Occidentales*, 1601, tendencies of folkspeech in pronunciation and morphology common to various countries, and borrowed words, especially from modern English.

Navarro Tomás, Tomás. Cuestionario lingüístico hispanoamericano. 1: Fonética, morfología, sintaxis. Buenos Aires. Ed. Coni. (Univ. de Buenos Aires, Facultad de filosofía y letras, Inst. de filología.) 113 p. [1959
Lists 518 points for field worker to look for, with examples; also general advice on procedure. Should prove a fine stimulus and guide to work in Spanish American folkspeech.

Osorio, Pedro Miguel. Expresiones del "caló" salvadoreño (*Bol. of. policía*, San Salvador, año 11, no. 123–124, sept.–oct., 1942, p. 39–43; no. 125–126, nov.–dic., p. 27–31; año 12, no. 127–128, enero–feb., 1943, p. 38–41). [1960
Alphabetical list of Spanish words and phrases current in underworld slang of Salvador, with meanings, by a police agent. In behalf of this contribution, see Rafael Gonzáles Sol, "Folklore salvadoreño auténtico," in *Diario de hoy*, año 8, no. 3070, sept. 15, 1943, p. 6.

Pearce, Thomas M. New Mexican folk etymologies (*Palacio*, vol. 50, no. 10, Oct., p. 229–234). [1961
Río de las ánimas perdidas en purgatorio to *Purgatoire* to *Picket-wire*. *L'eau de mort* to *Lo de Mora* to *Mora*. *U. S. Hill*. "Simmer on" to *Cimmarrón*. "Sock a row" to *Socorro*. "Lam the tar" to *Lemitar*. *Pie Town*. "Green grow" to *gringo*. *Greaser*. *Belén*. Gives stories supposed to account for these names.

Plath, Oreste. El sentido oceánico en el hablar del pueblo chileno (*Rev. marina mercante nac.*, no. 34, p. 7–8). [1962
Sea terms that have come ashore and acquired new meanings and established themselves in proverbial phrases and comparisons among the Chilean folk.

Rojas Carrasco, Guillermo. Chilenismos y americanismos. Valparaíso. Dirección general de prisiones. 229 p. [1963

Saavedra, Alfredo M. El "caló" de la delincuencia y la expresión sexual (*An. soc. folk. México*, vol. 2, 1941 [*i.e.* 1943], p. 23–38). [1964
Alphabetical lists of words and phrases from underworld and sex slang, interpreting former as defense mechanism, latter as inferiority complex.

PROVERB

Malaret, Augusto. Paremiología americana (*Univ. cat. bolivariana*, vol. 9, no. 33, julio–sept., p. 347–377). [1966
List of proverbs alphabetized by keyword, names of countries in which they are found, explanation of their meanings and of words of Indian origin in them. Proverbs from Spain current in America are excluded; only those thought to be of New World origin are included. Compiler is to be praised for listing by keyword and explaining meaning, practices not followed by many. More specific data on provenience should appear.

RIDDLE

Jijena Sánchez, Rafael (comp.). Adivina adivinador; 500 de las mejores adivinanzas de la lengua española. Buenos Aires. Ed. Albatros. 200 p. [1967
500 Spanish texts, with answers at end of book, selected from cited published and MS. sources of Spain and Spanish America, for children.

ADDENDA

General and Miscellaneous

Barata, Mário. Proteção ao nosso património histórico e artístico no quinquenio 1937–1942 (*Cultura política*, ano 2, no. 21, nov., 1942, p. 327–354). [1968
Good survey of recent state of museums and other archiving of documents, photographs, etc. recording and preserving Brazilian culture, much of it of folklore interest.

Boggs, Ralph Steele. Folklore democrático y cultura aristocrática (*Folklore Americas*, vol. 2, no. 2, Dec., 1942, p. 17–20). [1969
With decadence of European aristocratic culture, New World nations are finding

their true nationalism, panamericanism and artistic inspiration in the democratic tradition of their own folklore.

Cáceres Freyre, Julián B. Juan B. Ambrosetti, precursor de los estudios de folklore en la Argentina. Buenos Aires. Ed. Coni. 1942. 14 p. [1970
Reprinted from *Bol. acad. arg. let.*, tomo 10, p. 673–687. Surveys Ambrosetti's folklore publications since 1893.

Canal Feijóo, Bernardo. El norte. Buenos Aires. Ed. Emecé. 1942. 107 p., 8 láms. [1971
Selections from chronicles of 16th to 19th centuries, with folk songs and tales from Santiago del Estero, Argentina.

Carneiro, Edison. Candomblés da Baía (*Rev. arq. mun.*, São Paulo, ano 7, vol. 84, julho–agôsto, 1942, p. 127–137). [1972
Study of these Negro religious societies, especially in relation to their African influences.

Cortázar, Augusto Raúl. Guía bibliográfica del folklore argentino; primera contribución. Buenos Aires. Imp. de la Univ. (Univ. de Buenos Aires, Facultad de filosofía y letras, Inst. de literatura argentina, Sección de bibliografía, tomo 1, no. 1.) 1942. 293 p. [1973
Exhaustive introduction on folklore bibliography and preparation of this one, with help of folklore bibliography seminar students at Instituto de Literatura Argentina. Has sections on bibliography, collections, works of folklore, literature, language, ethnography, history, travel and diverse. Lists books and pamphlets only (not articles). Sometimes indicates contents, library in Buenos Aires where work may be consulted. One of best folklore bibliographies for any American country.

———. Panorama y perspectivas de nuestro folklore. Buenos Aires. 1942. 32 p. [1974
Published in *Verbum*, Buenos Aires, nueva época, no. 2–3, December, 1942. Vivid and generally sound view of serious Argentine folklore study, past, present and future. Errs in excluding indigenous groups, in trying to make folklore conform to lines of social classes, and in regarding upper class as chief source of folklore. Surveys advantages and disadvantages for folklorist of materials from colonial chroniclers, local color writers, scholars in related fields, poorly trained collectors, travelers, intellectuals who occasionally turn to folklore, "folkloric" artists; present pioneer status of Argentine scientific folklorists; and sound program for future of Argentine folklore studies in preparing scholars, collecting, classifying, studying, libaries, bibliographies, archives, museums, cooperation with other agencies, and ultimate goals of social betterment.

FOLKLORE DE LOS URUS Y CHIPAYAS (*Bol. folklore, folkvisa y folkway*, vol. 1, no. 1, 1942, p. 8–9). [1975

García y García, Elvira. Cuzco: su tradición y su leyenda (*Bol. soc. geog. La Paz*, año 53, no. 64, julio, 1942, p. 35–36). [1976
On Incaic Cuzco, Peru: tradition, dress, festival, augurers, etc.

González, N. Bases y tendencias de la cultura paraguaya (*Cuad. amer.*, año 1, vol. 5, no. 5, sept.–oct. 1942, p. 87–106). [1977
Guaraní and Spanish contributions. Mestizaje. Genesis of Paraguayan culture. Dwellings, food.

Inchauspe, Pedro. Elementos tradicionales de la región central para nuestro teatro (*Cuad. cult. teatral*, no. 16, 1942, p. 25–28). [1978
Lecture given August 12, 1940. Advocates use of gaucho folk tradition in Argentine drama. Indicates wealth of material for dramatist in this tradition.

Jacovella, Bruno. Memoria del año 1942 del Departamento de folklore (*Folklore*, no. 8, 1942, p. 69). [1979
Excellent warning against 5 plagues which the scientific folklorist must fight: dilettantism, aestheticism, traditionalism, romanticism, evolutionism.

Lachatañeré, Rómulo. Manual de santería; estudios afrocubanos; el sistema de cultos "lucumís." Habana. Ed. Caribe. 1942. 94 p., mapa, tablas. [1980
Santería is the religious system of Afro-Cubans and derives from Lucumí slaves from Yoruba, with other African and Hispanic elements, in a particularly Cuban mixture. Describes its gods, beliefs, customs, ritual, organization, altar equipment, associated witchcraft, table of gods with corresponding Catholic saint, symbol and image, etc.

Ladrón de Guévara, Blanca. El folklore en las Américas y su relación con el signo escalonado (*Bol. folklore, folkvisa y folkway*, vol. 1, no. 1, 1942, p. 3–5, 6 fig.). [1981
Also in *Boletín de la Sociedad geográfica de La Paz*, Bolivia, año 53, no. 64, 1942, p. 60–66, 6 fig. On general significance of folklore and stairstep design in indigenous Latin American Indian folk art, suggested by terraces cultivated on slopes of the Andes.

Lullo, Oreste di. Contribución del folklore al teatro nacional (*Cuad. cult. teatral*, no. 16, 1942, p. 101–129). [1982
Lecture given September 23, 1940. Affirms that only intelligent use of Argentine folklore will develop a truly national drama. Advises in some detail on problems in use of this material, from viewpoint of both drama and folklore materials.

Magalhães, Basílio de. O elemento religioso afro-brasileiro (*Cultura política*, ano 2, no. 19, set., 1942, p. 155–159). [1983
Notes on Brazilian Negro gods: Obztalá Ifá, Ogún, Iemanjá, Oxó-oxí, Dadá, Orixáocó, Exú. Words only of 3 folksongs. Note

on identity of Mané Dantas, who issued sentence against image of St. Anthony.

————. Folklore religioso afro-brasileiro (*Cultura política*, ano 2, no. 20, out., 1942, p. 136–140). [1984]
Notes on Brazilian Negro gods, compared with Catholic saints, on Paraguaya ballad in Ismael Moya's *Romancero 1941*, on words *quiriri, ibituruna, juruparí, tapé*.

Ortiz Dueñas, Jorge, and others. Chancay, provincia nuestra. Huacho, Peru. Ed. La Libertad. 1942. 226 p. [1985
Narratives and descriptions, including custom, festival, tradition, dialect, etc. of this region of Peru.

Quijada Jara, Sergio. Del folklore huancavelicano: algunas leyendas (*Comercio*, sept. 23, 1942, p. 6). [1986
5 legends of Huancavelica, Peru, retold: Virgen del Rosario of Manzanayoj, Virgen de Cocharcas of Izcuchaca, Virgin Purísima of Pampas, San Francisco of Querco and Miñito of Lachoj.

Tupí Caldas, J. A. L. Etnologia sul-riograndense; esbôço fundamental (*Rev. inst. hist. geog. Rio Grande do Sul*, ano 22, no. 86, 1942, p. 303–380, 20 figs., 2 mapas). [1987
Describes dwelling, food, drink, pottery, textile, speech and other folklore of Tupí-Guaraní Indian tribes of Rio Grande do Sul, Brasil.

MYTHOLOGY

Cascudo, Luiz da Câmara. Juruparí (*Cultura política*, ano 2, no. 19, set., 1942, p. 160–175). [1988
Good study of this Brazilian Indian deity.

LEGEND AND TRADITION

Colán Secas, Hermógenes. Tres leyendas de Chancay (*Folklore*, no. 8, 1942, p. 75–76). [1989
3 traditions from Peru: Descansamuerto, Cerro del águila, Toro huanco.

Gutiérrez Colombres, Benjamín. Notas sobre el familiar (*Folklore*, no. 8, 1942, p. 76). [1990
Sketches a legend from a sugar refinery in Tucumán, Argentina, of Devil pact and various forms taken by *familiar*.

Sanz, Rafael. Folklore referente al advenimiento del inca en la isla del Sol (Titicaca), recogido por . . . en 1858 (*Bol. folklore, folkvisa y folkway*, vol. 1, no. 1, 1942, p. 5–8, 2 figs.). [1991
A legendary account.

Vidal de Battini, Berta Elena. Leyenda de la ciudad perdida (*Rel. soc. arg. antrop.*, tomo 3, 1942, p. 119–150). [1992
Cites variants from Latin America and many other parts of the world of tradition of lost or disappeared city. It is hoped author will continue this valuable work with a comparative study of this theme.

FOLKTALE

Jijena Sánchez, Rafael. Un cuento de adivinanza: Elena morada o El niño sabio (*Folklore*, no. 7, 1942, p. 63–64). [1993
Examines antecedents of *Elena morada* riddle in Spain and its variants in Puerto Rico, Nicaragua, Venezuela, Peru, Uruguay and Argentina, and gives a folktale containing it, collected by author in Tucumán, Argentina.

FOLK POETRY, MUSIC, DANCE AND GAME

Almeida, Renato. O brinquedo da capoeira (*Rev. arq. mun.*, São Paulo, ano 7, vol. 84, julho–agôsto, 1942, p. 155–162). [1994
Description of this game of skill, as seen in Santo Antonio de Jesús, Baía, Brazil, with verses and music.

————. O bumba-meu-boi de Camassarí (*Cultura política*, ano 2, no. 19, set., 1942, p. 193–197, 2 láms.). [1995
Description of this popular Brazilian folkdance as seen at Camassarí, Baía, at Epiphany, including verses and music.

Alvarenga, Oneyda. A discoteca pública municipal (*Rev. arq. mun.*, São Paulo, ano 8, vol. 87, dez., 1942, p. 7–98). [1996
Report on organization and services of the municipal library of phonographic recordings of São Paulo, Brazil, founded 1935. This library has considerable material on folk song and dance on disks and films, as well as a museum of folk musical instruments.

Carrizo, Juan Alfonso (comp.). Cancionero popular de La Rioja. Buenos Aires. Ed. A. Baiocco. 1942. 3 vols.: 301, 462, 446 p. 26 láms., 27 figs. [1997
Excellent and enormous collection of folkpoetry from La Rioja, Argentina. Geographic, social and historic survey (123p.) from Diaguita and Araucanian Indians on down, illustrated with maps and documents. Account of author's collecting trip and informants. Roots, transmission and survivals from Spain. Words only of 5,735 items, including 4,251 *coplas*, 528 riddles, 75 children's rimes, 102 carols, 15 tongue twisters, ballads, folksongs of love, parting, scorn, grief, etc., prayers, charms, verses from dance songs and tales, etc., citing sources and parallels from Spain and America.

Delgado Vivanco, Edmundo. El forasterito en el folklore (*Waman puma*, año 2, vol. 2, no. 11–14, agosto–nov., 1942, p. 25–30). [1998

Quechua texts and Spanish translations of numerous folklyrics on variations of the wanderer theme: his homesickness, loneliness, hardships, passing friendships, loves, etc. Also appeared in *Peruanidad, 1943*, vol. 3, no. 14, junio–agosto, p. 1095–1102.

Franco, Alberto. Cancionerillo de amor. Buenos Aires. Ed. Emecé. 1942. 101 p., 4 láms. [1999

Popular anthology of 132 Argentine folksongs, words only, including *canciones* and dance songs, *vidalas, coplas, glosas* and 10 in Quechua with Spanish translation, from *cancioneros* of Juan Alfonso Carrizo, Orestes di Lullo, Juan Draghi Lucero, Jorge M. Furt and others, with 2 pages of music, notes and bibliography.

———. Retablo de Navidad; cantares y villancicos. Buenos Aires. Ed. Emecé. 1942. 92 p., 5 láms. [2000

Texts of 92 Argentine Christmas songs and carols, some with music, selected from *cancioneros* of Juan Alfonso Carrizo, Orestes di Lullo, Juan Draghi Lucero, Rafael Jijena Sánchez, Consejo Nacional de Educación, Francisco Rodríguez Marín (Spain).

INSTRUMENTOS DE MÚSICA Y DANZAS AFROVENEZOLANAS (*Venezuela*, año 1, no. 9, dic., 1942, [4 p.], 7 ilus.). [2001

Brief descriptive notes in Spanish and English on drums, dances and festivals of Negroes in valleys of Tuy and Barcelona, Venezuela.

Lima, Emirto de. Folklore colombiano. Barranquilla. 1942. 210 p. [2002

Collection of essays and lectures on various phases of Colombian folkmusic, musical instruments, songs, dances, street cries, festivals, riddles, etc., with illustrative music and verses. 50 music notations.

Posnansky, Arthur, and others. ¿Qué es folkvisa?; himno al sol; asnu kallu; mariposa de oro (*Bol. folklore, folkvisa y folkway*, vol. 1, no. 1, 1942, p. 10–16. [2003

Indian and Spanish words and music of songs.

Vivante, Armando. La escritura de los mochica sobre porotos; los habitantes prehispánicos del norte del Perú habrían poseído un sistema de escritura sobre la cutícula de los porotos, según el descubrimiento del Sr. Larco Hoyle, pero es más probable que no se trate más que de un juego, según lo atestigua la compulsa de los cronistas (*Waman puma*, año 2, vol. 2, no. 11–14, agosto–nov., 1942, p. 11–17). [2004

Interprets certain beans (*pallares*) portrayed on ancient Indian pottery of northern Peru as those used in game.

CUSTOM AND FESTIVAL

CINCO AÑOS EN BUENOS AIRES, 1820–1825, por "un inglés." Prólogo de Alejo B. González Garaño. Buenos Aires. Ed. Solar. 1942. xix, 247 p. [2005

Spanish translation of *A Five Years' Residence in Buenos Aires during the Years 1820–1825*, by an Englishman, London, G. Herbert, 1925. González Garaño believes author was John Laccock and not Thomas George Love. This vivid account of life in Buenos Aires describes much of folklore interest, especially customs and festivals.

Posnansky, Arthur. Aspectos generales del folkway; el ekeko y la fiesta de "Alacitas"; el kjucho; la wilancha (*Bol. folklore, folkvisa y folkway*, vol. 1, no. 1, 1942, p. 17–22, 12 figs.). [2006

Indicates scope and ramifications of "folkway." Relates modern Bolivian *Alacitas* to older Indian *Ekeko*, good luck new year festivals. *Kjucho* and *challar* foundation rites on beginning construction of a building. Rites against drought and hail. *Wilancha* blood sacrifice of propitiation to spirits.

DRAMA

HISTORIA FAMOSA TITULADA DEL TRIUNFO DE LA INMACULADA CONCEPCIÓN. San Salvador. Min. de gobernación. 1942. 21 p. [2007

Apparently text of Moors and Christians, as known in Salvador.

ART, CRAFT, ARCHITECTURE, DRESS AND ADORNMENT

FINE AND FOLK ARTS OF THE OTHER AMERICAN REPUBLICS. A bibliography of publications in English, prepared by the Archive of Hispanic culture, Hispanic foundation, Library of Congress, for the Division of inter-American activities in the United States, Office of the Coordinator of inter-American affairs. Washington, D. C. 1942. 18 p. [2008

Cites 28 titles at end on folk art.

Szaffka, Tihamér. Sôbre construções navais duma tribu de índios desconhecidos do rio das Mortes (*Rev. arq. mun.*, São Paulo, ano 8, vol. 87, dez., 1942, p. 171–181, 2 láms. fig.). [2009

On primitive present day *balsas* of Chavante Indians of Brazil.

FOOD AND DRINK

Castillo de Luca, Antonio. Refranero médico de la olla castellana (*Folklore*, no. 7, 1942, p. 67–68). [2010

On this classic folkfood of Spain: its elements, varieties, manners of preparation, eating, nutritive values and proverbs about it.

Belief, Witchcraft, Medicine and Magic

Carrizo Valdés, Jesús María. Supersticiones medicinales de La Rioja Chilecito y Valle de Catamarca (*Folklore*, no. 7, 1942, p. 64; no. 8, p. 70). [2011
Lists some 30 folk cures, alphabetized by keyword, from Argentina.

Lira, Jorge A. De la medicina tradicional peruana: diagnóstico y curación por medio del "kkollpa" (*Folklore*, no. 7, 1942, p. 65–66). [2012
Excellent detailed description of folk cure with these alkaline minerals, based on data from Marangani, Sikuwani, Cuzco, Peru.

Quijada Jara, Sergio. Tres supersticiones del folklore huancavelicano (*Folklore*, no. 7, 1942, p. 66). [2013
Describes beliefs of *jarjaria, jayacoj* and *condenao*, from Huancavelica, Peru.

Vellard, Juan Alberto. Animales en el folklore y la medicina popular del Alto Amazonas (*Folklore*, no. 8, 1942, p. 71–75). [2014
Folk cures, good luck charms, fiesta of seven dogs on November 2, care and nourishment of pregnant women, and other beliefs of immigrants in upper Amazon region, who came chiefly from northeast Brazil and appear in process of forming a new folklore, modified by their new environment.

Folkspeech

Ardissone, Romualdo. Influencia del ombú en la toponimia sudamericana (*Publ. mus. etnog.*, Buenos Aires, 1940–1942, serie A, vol. 4, p. 41–115, 8 pl. map.). [2015
Excellent study of more than 300 occurrences of name of this tree in place names of Argentina, Uruguay, south Brazil and Paraguay, chiefly those of ranches, islands, streams and other small places and natural features, rather than large administrative divisions, which usually bear names of historic events and persons.

Berro García, A. Gentilicios uruguayos (*Bol. filol.*, Montevideo, tomo 3, no. 18–19, sept., 1941–marzo, 1942, p. 362–372). [2016
Directed by Berro García, chief of philology section of Instituto de Estudios Superiores, a seminar group gathered and analyzed the adjectival suffixes preferred to designate people and things from various places from all regions of Uruguay. Results recorded here. To be continued.

Campanella, Andrés. Tucumán (*Bol. filol.*, Montevideo, tomo 3, no. 18–19, sept. 1941–marzo, 1942, p. 358–361). [2017
Derives it from Aymara *tuku-huaña* 'end, limit,' *i. e.* of Inca empire.

Fein Pastoriza, Delia. Frases figuradas (*Bol. filol.*, Montevideo, tomo 3, no. 18–19, sept., 1941–marzo, 1942, p. 343–351). [2018
General observations on structure and popular origin of these gems of folkspeech: idioms, crystallized and figurative phrases.

Gómez Haedo, Juan Carlos. Origen del "che" rioplatense (*Bol. filol.*, Montevideo, tomo 3, no. 18–19, sept., 1941–marzo, 1942, p. 319–326). [2019
Derives it from Castilian *ce*, found in *Celestina* and on through Golden Age, used as call to attract person's attention, and cites doublet developments like *cisme* and *chisme* from *cimice*, but ignores chronology of this development and has no proof of one of type *cisme* to *chisme* nor a *che* doublet contemporary to *ce*. I still suggest Galician *che* from Latin *te*, used as pleonastic dative.

Magalhães, Basílio de. Africanismos (*Cultura política*, ano 2, no. 22, dez., 1942, p. 156–160). [2020
Banana, candombe (candomblé), mandinga, monjolo: surveys previous discussion of these words, their use in Portuguese of Brazil and Spanish of other South American countries, and ascertains their African origin. In note at end cites various folklore articles recently received.

Navarro del Águila, Víctor. Folklore peruano: literatura i lingüística, a) insultos populares, b) vocabulario tetralingüe (*Waman puma*, ano 2, vol. 2, no. 11–14, agosto–nov., 1942, p. 5–8). [2021
Indian texts, literal and free Spanish translations and explanations of 10 insults, with general analysis, from Huamanga, Peru. List of 38 words in Spanish, Chinchai simi, Kcoskco simi and Aimara simi, with observations.

Spalding, Walter. Com respeito ao uso da palavra "macanudo" (*Bol. filol.*, Montevideo, tomo 3, no. 18–19, sept., 1941–marzo, 1942, p. 352–354). [2022
Reports this popular word of folkspeech of Plata region is also current in Rio Grande do Sul, Brazil, meaning 'strong,' and has spread to São Paulo and Rio de Janeiro. Believes it is of Guaraní origin: *macana* 'club.'

Proverb

Colman, Narciso R. Folklore guaraní: ñe'êngá rovï (refranes verdes); diccionario carape; ogüerecó va jhetá pucá sororó. Tercera ed. corregida y aumentada; para hombre solamente. Asunción. Col. Rosicrán. 1942. 56 p. [2023
Some 400 vulgar proverbs, alphabetized by first word, in Guaraní, untranslatable, to preserve this portion of Paraguayan proverbial lore which otherwise might be lost.

GEOGRAPHY: GENERAL

(See also items 1680, 2660)

Cabrera la Rosa, Augusto. Características geomorfológicas de los ríos en la región amazónica (*Bol. soc. geol. Perú*, tomo 14-15, p. 28-58). [2024

Unusually informative notes on the behavior of streams and resulting land forms, with local terminology, and some biological and human relations. Maps and air photographs. [G. M. McBride]

Camacho, José María. Urus, changos y atacamas (*Bol. soc. geog. La Paz*, año 54, no. 66, oct., p. 9-35). [2025

Contains data regarding their habitat.

Carlson, Fred A. Geography of Latin America. New York. Prentice-Hall. xxiii, 566 p., maps, illus. [2026

A revised and enlarged edition of this well-known text. [G. M. McBride]

Caballero Calderón, Eduardo. El hombre y el paisaje en América (*Rev. Indias*, segunda época, tomo 17, no. 53, mayo, p. 185-202). [2027

Analysis of the general effects of geographic conditions upon man in America (Latin America), particularly the stamp which the Andes, the pampa, the selva and the llanos, have set upon the people, their towns and cities. [G. M. McBride]

Crist, Raymond E. The Caracas-Quito highway (*Bull. pan amer. union*, vol. 77, no. 1, Jan., p. 4-12). [2028

Continuation of article begun in vol. 76, no. 11, Nov., 1942, p. 601-609 (*Handbook*, no. 8, *1942*, item 2316). Good details of road condition and areas traversed. Part II, The Colombian and Ecuadorian sections of highway. [M. A. McBride]

Franck, Harry A. Rediscovering South America. Philadelphia, New York. J. B. Lippincott, publ. 435 p. [2030

Readable travelogue. [G. M. McBride]

Giuffra, Elzear Santiago. La circulación de la atmósfera en el hemisferio sur. Montevideo. Ed. A. Monteverde y cía. 85 p. [2031

New meteorological conceptions applied to South American climatic conditions. [M. A. McBride]

Haskins, Caryl P. The Amazon. The life history of a mighty river. Garden City, N. Y. Doubleday, Doran & co. viii, 415 p., map, illus. [2032

From Gondwanaland to the Rio de Janeiro Conference, and from the Sechura Desert on the Peruvian coast to Belém, Pará, is what this volume attempts to cover, and to "show the continuity of geography and history" over such a time and such an area! [G. M. McBride]

Jakob, Cristofredo. El pichiciego (*Rev. geog. amer.*, año 9, vol. 19, no. 117, junio, p. 307-314). [2033

Zoogeographical statement on the armadillo-related animal. [M. A. McBride]

Mangelsdorf, P. C., and R. G. Reeves. El origen del maíz indio y sus congeres. Trad. del inglés por Epamínondas Quintana. Guatemala. Tip. nacional. 377, xii p., mapas, ilus. [2035

Spanish version of this authoritative study. [G. M. McBride]

Marmer, H. A. Tidal investigations on the west coast of South America (*Geog. rev.*, vol. 33, no. 2, April, p. 299-303). [2036

Summarizes the internationally coordinated program. [M. A. McBride]

NUEVO ATLAS GEOGRÁFICO DE LAS AMÉRICAS. 24 láminas originales en colores con 76 mapas y diagramas de geografía física, política y económica, ajustados a los programas de enseñanza secundaria, normal y profesional y, por sus detalles, apropiados también para consulta. Buenos Aires. Ed. J. Anesi. [2037

General world, but with special coverage of Latin America. [M. A. McBride]

Platt, Raye R. Milestones in American cartography (*Proc. eighth amer. scien. cong.*, vol. 9, p. 55-63). [2038

Evolution of cartography in the Western Hemisphere, discusses influential factors, important individuals and institutions and outstanding works. [M. A. McBride]

———. Some recent works on the Latin-American republics (*Geog. rev.*, vol. 33, no. 2, April, p. 304-311). [2039

Recommends 17 dependable up-to-date books for general reading, evaluates each. [M. A. McBride]

Platt, Robert S. Latin America. Countrysides and united regions. New York, London. McGraw-Hill, publ. 564 p., maps, illus. [2040

"A collection of simple field studies in a frame of complex generalizations"; "not a complete geography of Latin America," yet telephoto views of so many bits of the landscape as it is organized into farm, village, mine, fishing settlement or pastoral community, as to give, together with the generalizations which fuse the units into "united regions," a very fair concept of Latin America as a whole—all richly illustrated with detailed maps and photographs taken with such definite purpose as to become actually a part (an important part) of the text. [G. M. McBride]

Villar, G. E. Informaciones relativas a la industria petrolera de la América del Sur (*Bol. inst. sudamer. petról.*, vol. 1, no. 1, abril, p. 50–63). **[2041**

Wernicke, Edmundo. Confusión de los conceptos geográficos, toponímicos y gentilicios en la época del descubrimiento y en tiempos modernos (*Gaea,* tomo 7, entrega 1, p. 119–122). **[2042**

GEOGRAPHY: THE CARIBBEAN AREA

BY

CLARENCE F. JONES
Northwestern University

EARL B. SHAW
State Teachers' College, Worcester, Massachusetts

RAFAEL PICÓ
*Puerto Rico Planning, Urbanizing and Zoning Board,
Santurce, Puerto Rico*

GENERAL STATEMENT

As in the past few years, the list of publications continues to reflect the effect of the war on geographical publications on the Caribbean in 1943. Many articles discuss the production of commodities needed to aid in the war effort and analyze the effects of the war on different regions. The contributions of geographers of the United States are very few; especially noticeable is the lack of articles based even on reconnaissance field observations, not to mention detailed field work.

Worth noting in the list of publications is the increasing number of articles in Latin American magazines and of Latin American government publications. While most of these publications are still descriptive in character, many show a tendency towards increasing geographic analysis.

BIBLIOGRAPHY

(*See also sections on* Economics: the Caribbean Area; Agriculture: the Caribbean Area)

GENERAL

Benítez Delorme, Carlos. Geografía humana, social y económica. Quinta ed., corregida y reformada. México, D. F. Lib. Porrúa. 334 p. [2043]
General human, social and economic geography.

Cooke, C. Wythe, and others. Correlation of the cenozoic formations of the Atlantic and Gulf coastal plains and the Caribbean region (*Bull. geol. soc. America,* vol. 54, no. 11, Nov. 1, p. 1713-1722). [2044]
Contains a two-page bibliography on Caribbean geology.

Deutschman, Z. Malaria in North America and the Caribbean regions. Apropos of "A symposium on human malaria" (*Geog. rev.,* vol. 33, no. 3, July, p. 487-491). [2045]
A brief discussion of the relation of malaria incidence to temperature, rainfall and other conditions; comments on publications in the field.

MEXICO

Antúnez Echegaray, Francisco. Informe acerca de los recursos naturales del territorio norte de la Baja California y exposición de las condiciones de ésta (*Bol. minas petról.,* México, tomo 14, no. 5, mayo, p. 3-16; tomo 14, no. 6, junio, p. 3-13). [2047]

Araujo, Juan. México y las colonias extranjeras (*Rev. mex. geog.,* tomo 4, no. 3-4, julio-dic., p. 43-54). [2048]

Blasques L., L. La edad glacial en México (*Bol. soc. mex. geog. estad.,* tomo 58, no 3-6, mayo-dic., p. 263-305). [2049]
A somewhat detailed discussion of glaciation in Mexico.

Brodkorb, Pierce. Birds from the Gulf Lowlands of Southern Mexico. Ann Arbor, Michigan? Univ. of Michigan. (Museum

of zöology, Misc. publ. no. 55). 88 p., maps. [2050
A detailed study of the birds of this region. Contains considerable geographical information.

Castillo y Piña, José. Otra excursión a los pueblos del sur (*Rev. mex. geog.,* tomo 4, no. 1-2, enero-junio, p. 1-27). [2051

Díaz, Severo. La geodesia en la carta del valle de Guadalajara (*Bol. junta aux. jalis.,* tomo 8, no. 2, oct., p. 51-61). [2052

Flores, Teodoro. Posibilidades de la existencia y producción de sales de potasa en la República Mexicana (*Bol. soc. mex. geog. estad.,* tomo 58, no. 3-6, mayo-dic., p. 307-337). [2053
Analysis by regions of the existence and possibilities of production of potash in Mexico.

Galindo Mendoza, Alfredo. Apuntes geográficos y estadísticos de la República y de la iglesia mexicana. México. Imp. Aldina. 59 p. [2054

González, Pedro A. Las cuencas del Usumacinta y del Grijalva (*Rev. mex. geog.,* tomo 4, no. 3-4, julio-dic., p. 19-29). [2055

González Ortega, José. El volcán de Parícutin (*Rev. geog. amer.,* año 9, vol. 20, no. 119, agosto, p. 75-80). [2056
See also items 2062, 2064, 2075.

Hernández, Timoteo L. Geografía del estado de Nuevo León. Monterrey. 90 p., ilus., mapas. [2057
A general treatment of the physical and economic geography of the state.

Irigoyen, Ulises. Carretera transpeninsular de la Baja California (*Bol. soc. mex. geog. estad.,* tomo 58, no. 3-6, mayo-dic., p. 339-358). [2058

López, Víctor M., and **John H. Brineman.** Estudio geológico y minero del yacimiento de mercurio de San Jacinto, Estado Lara (*Rev. fomento,* año 5, no. 50, enero-marzo, p. 29-61). [2059
The geology and mineralogy of the mercury deposits of San Jacinto.

Müllerried, Federico K. G. La geografía y geología del valle de Tixtla, Guerrero (*Bol. soc. mex. geog. estad.,* tomo 58, no. 1-2, enero-abril, p. 139-148). [2060
Brief analysis of the geography and geology of the Valle de Tixtla.

Muñoz Lumbier, Manuel. El estado de Jalisco (*Rev. mex. geog.,* tomo 4, no. 1-2, enero-junio, p. 37-55). [2061

Ordóñez, Ezequiel. The new volcano of Parícutin (*Int. amer. intel. interchange,* p. 62-78). [2062
An account of the development of the volcano of Parícutin and some effects of its growth on the surrounding country.

Orive Alba, Adolfo. Water for the thirsty lands of Mexico (*For. com. weekly,* vol. 11, no. 10, June 5, p. 6-7, 34). [2063
Brief excellent statement on irrigation developments in Mexico. Photographs.

Pough, Frederick H. Parícutin is born (*Nat. hist.,* vol. 52, no. 3, Oct., p. 134-142). [2064
An interesting, somewhat detailed account of the growth of the volcano of Parícutin. Photographs.

Quinn, Vernon. Picture map geography of Mexico, Central America and the West Indies. New York, Philadelphia. Frederick A. Stokes, publ. 114 p., illus. [2065

Ruiz de Velasco, Tomás. La cuenca del río Balsas y río del Marqués en los estados de Guerrero y Michoacán (*Rev. mex. geog.,* tomo 4, no. 1-2, enero-junio, p. 29-36). [2066

Sánchez Miguel, J. Xalapa, racial y bella. Ensayos o nuevos modos de ver la vieja ciudad veracruzana. Xalapa-Enríquez. Ed. Génesis. 192 p. [2067

Sociedad mexicana de geografía y estadística. Estudios de geografía. México. 104 p. [2068

Steggerda, Morris. Some ethnological data concerning one hundred Yucatan plants (*Bull. bur. amer. ethnol.,* no. 136, p. 189-226). [2069
Brief descriptions of many plants and their distribution.

Valencia Rangel, Francisco. Regreso al Cuiyutziro (*Rev. mex. geog.,* tomo 4, no. 3-4, julio-dic., p. 31-42). [2070

————. El volcán de Cuiyutziro (*Rev. mex. geog.,* tomo 4, no. 1-2, enero-junio, p. 59-77). [2071

————. Guanajuato. México. Tall. gráf. de La Nación. 32 p., ilus. [2073

Vidal, Esther. Apuntes de geografía física. Con los datos más importantes acerca de la República Mexicana. Novena ed. corr. y aumentada. México, D. F. Imp. Algarin. 258 p. [2074

Waitz, Paul. El nuevo volcán de Parícutin, Mich. (*Rev. soc. geog. Cuba,* año 16, no. 1, enero-marzo, p. 5-14). [2075
The growth of the volcano of Parícutin and its effects on the surrounding countryside.

———. Reseña geológica de la cuenca del Lerma (*Bol. soc. mex. geog. estad.,* tomo 58, no. 1-2, enero–abril, p. 123-138). [2076
A brief sketch of the geology of the Lerma basin.

Wetmore, Alexander. The birds of southern Veracruz, Mexico (*Proc. U. S. nat. mus.,* vol. 93, no. 3164, p. 215-340) [2077
A detailed study of the birds of the region. Contains a great deal of geographic information.

Zilli, Juan. Geografía del estado de Veracruz. México. Bibl. del maestro de El Nacional. 181 p. [2078
Detailed descriptive physical and economic geography of the state.

CENTRAL AMERICA

Costa Rica

León, Jorge. Nueva geografía de Costa Rica. San José. Imp. Española. (Serie escolar "Costa Rica," no. 4). 172 p. [2079
A physical, economic and human geography of the country.

Merker, C. A., and others. The forest resources of Costa Rica. Washington, D. C. U. S. Forest service. 48 p. [2080
Analysis of present forest situation, principal forest types and their distribution, lumbering methods and a description of the principal forest trees and their distribution. Map showing forest areas. Illustrations.

Monge Alfaro, Carlos. Geografía social y humana de Costa Rica. Segunda ed. San José. Imp. Universal. 129 p. [2081
A social and human geography of the country.

Secretaría de gobernación. División territorial electoral de la república. San José. Imp. Nacional. 32 p. [2082
Territorial electoral divisions of the country.

Stone, Doris. A preliminary investigation of the flood plain of the Río Grande de Terraba, Costa Rica. San José. 88 p. [2083

Guatemala

Sociedad de geografía e historia. Guía turística de las ruinas de la antigua Guatemala. Guatemala. Tip. nacional. 180 p. [2084
A detailed guide to the ruins of old Guatemala for use by tourists.

Sterling, E. A. Beating the "bush" for chewing gum (*Amer. forests,* vol. 49, no. 7, July, p. 338-341). [2085
Description of the production, preparation and transportation of *chicle* in Guatemala. Photographs.

Honduras

Bobadilla, Perfecto H. Monografía del departamento de Cortés (*Rev. arch. bibl. nac.,* Tegucigalpa, tomo 21, no. 11, mayo, p. 733-740; no. 12, junio, p. 791-798; tomo 22, no. 2, agosto, p. 93-100; no. 3, sept., p. 151-158; no. 4, oct., p. 229-236). [2086

Panama

División territorial de la república de panamá en 1943. Panamá. Imp. Nacional. 19 p. [2087
Discussion of the territorial divisions of Panama.

Oficina del censo de 1940. La provincia del Darién (*Bol. acad. panameña hist.,* segunda época, no. 1, enero–junio, p. 101-134). [2088

Wagner, Moritz. Bosquejo físico-geográfico de la provincia de Chiriquí en Centroamérica (*Rev. arch. nac.,* Costa Rica, año 7, no. 5-6, mayo–junio, p. 228-271). [2089
Description of the physical geography of the province of Chiriquí.

El Salvador

González Sol, Rafael. Balsam of El Salvador (*Amer. forests,* vol. 49, no. 4, April, p. 158-159). [2090
Notes on production, preparation and uses of balsam. Photographs.

Osborne, Lilly de Jongh. Trees of El Salvador (*Bull. pan amer. union,* vol. 77, no. 5, May, p. 262-267). [2091
Pictures and descriptions of trees.

COLOMBIA

Bruet, Edmond, and **Aubert de la Rue.** La hoya del río Naya (*Rev. univ. Cauca,* no. 1, enero–feb., p. 137-160). [2092

Castro, Luis Gabriel. La capital de la gran Colombia. Cúcuta. Imp. departamental. 381 p. [2093

Contraloría general de la república. Geografía económica de Colombia. Tomo 6, Choco. Bogotá. 692 p., fotos, mapas. [2094
A descriptive economic geography of the Choco of Colombia.

Dóndoli, César. La región de El General. Condiciones geológicas y geoagronómicas de la zona. San Pedro Montes de Oca. Depto. nac. de agricultura. (Bol. técnico, no. 44, Geología 6). 16 p. [2095

Miles, Cecil W. Estudio económico y ecológico de los peces de agua dulce del

Valle del Cauca. Cali. Sría. de agricultura y fomento del Departamento. 97 p. [2096]

Montón Blasco, Juan. El azufre en la región volcánica de Purace. Ensayo sobre su procedencia (*Rev. univ. Cauca*, no. 1, enero–feb., p. 179–195). [2097]
Analysis of the character and occurrence of sulphur in the volcanic region of Purace.

Royo y Gómez, José. El territorio de Manizales y la estabilidad de su suelo (*Rev. acad. col. cien. exact. fís. nat.*, vol. 5, no. 19, dic., p. 337–343). [2098]
Brief excellent statement of the causes of rapid soil erosion in the Manizales region and its consequences.

Trumpy, D. Pre-cretaceous of Colombia (*Bull. geol. soc. amer.*, vol. 54, no. 9, Sept. 1, p. 1281–1304, maps, stratigraphic sections). [2099]
Brief notes on the rocks and stratigraphy in several different localities.

Vidales, Luis. Geografía ecónomica de Colombia (*Rev. educ.*, Medellín, segunda época, no. 1, sept., p. 25–35). [2100]
Brief sketchy treatment of the economic geography of Colombia.

Vila, Pablo. Nuevos aspectos de la geografía colombiana (*Rev. univ. Cauca*, no. 1, enero–feb., p. 161–178). [2101]
Brief treatment of certain aspects of Colombian geography.

VENEZUELA

Badel, Dimas. Diccionario histórico-geográfico de Bolívar. Una síntesis movida de su paisaje físico y de su ambiente histórico. Corozal. Bibl. municipal. 478 p. [2102]

Bundy, P. A. Some gold lodes of Bolívar, Venezuela (*Engin. mining jour.*, vol. 144, no. 1, Jan., p. 43–45, maps, photos.). [2103]
A brief statement of the geology, ore bodies and outlook for development of the gold lodes of this district.

Crist, Raymond E. Cattle ranching in the tropical rainforest (*Sci. month.*, vol. 56, no. 6, June, p. 521–527). [2104]
A brief excellent account of cattle ranching in the area to the south of Lake Maracaibo. Photographs.

Felipe, Luis, and **Armando Vegas.** Notas geográficas sobre la gran sabana. Caracas. Tip. Casa de especialidades. 201–204 p. [2105]
From *Boletín de la Sociedad Venezolana de Ciencias Naturales*, tomo 8, no. 55, abril–junio, 1943.

Liddle, R. A., G. D. Harris, and **J. W. Wells.** The Rio Cachirí section in the Sierra de Perija, Venezuela (*Bull. amer. paleontology*, vol. 27, no. 108, April 6, p. 270–368). [2106]
A description of the rocks in a small section of the Sierra de Perija; stratigraphy, topographic relationships and paleontology. Maps, fossil plates, and illustrations.

López, Víctor Manuel, E. Mencher, and **J. H. Brineman, Jr.** Geología del sureste de Venezuela. Caracas. Tip. del Comercio. 65 p. [2107]
An excellent detailed study of the geology of the southeastern part of Venezuela.

Pittier, H. Una contribución más al estudio de la flora venezolana (*Bol. soc. venez. cien. nat.*, tomo 8, no. 54, enero–marzo, p. 135–145). [2108]

THE GUIANA COLONIES

Scott, Winthrop R. War economy of the Guianas (*For. com. weekly*, vol. 11, no. 3, April 17, p. 5–10). [2109]
The basic economy of the Guianas and the effects of the war on the colonies. Photographs.

Smith, Nicol. Color glows in the Guianas, French and Dutch (*Nat. geog. mag.*, vol. 83, no. 4, April, p. 459–480). [2110]
Brief notes on economic resources and activities. Photographs.

WEST INDIES

General

Climate and weather in the West Indies (*Geog. rev.*, vol. 33, no. 3, July, p. 499–501). [2112]
Comments on recent publications devoted to weather and climate in the West Indies; references.

Duncan, David D. Capturing giant turtles in the Caribbean (*Nat. geog. mag.*, vol. 84, no. 2, August, p. 177–190). [2113]
An illustrated story of catching turtles near the Cayman Islands.

Faulkner, O. T., and **C. Y. Shephard.** Mixed farming, the basis of a system for West Indies peasants (*Tropical agric.*, vol. 20, no. 6, July, p. 136–142). [2114]
A plea for more mixed farming among the peoples of the West Indies.

Hiss, Philip Hanson. The Dutch territories in the west, Netherlands America. New York. Duell, Sloan and Pearce. 225 p., 64 p. of photographs. [2115]
A study of the territories of the Netherlands in the Western Hemisphere from the discovery of the New World to the present day.

NOTES OF THE CRYPTOSTEGIA PLANT (*Tropical agric.*, vol. 20, no. 10, Oct., p. 195–197). [2116
Comments on recently published studies on the culture of Cryptostegia in the West Indies.

Tobell, Milton F. Yesterday, today and tomorrow in the Caribbean fisheries (*Bull. pan amer. union*, vol. 77, no. 3, March, p. 134–139). [2117
Notes on the catching and consumption of fish in the region.

GREATER ANTILLES

Shaw, Earl. The food front in the Greater Antilles (*Econ. geog.*, vol. 19, no. 1, Jan., p. 55–76). [2117a
A comparison of the islands as regards types of food shortages and food surpluses.

United States. Bureau of foreign and domestic commerce. Highways of Haiti and the Dominican Republic. Washington. 55 p., maps. [2117b
A study showing types of roads now available as well as those under construction. A short treatment of the geography of each country.

CUBA

Corral, José Isaac. El níquel cubano (*Rev. soc. geog. Cuba*, año 16, no. 1, enero–marzo, p. 50–57). [2118
Brief description of Cuba's nickel deposits and production of nickel.

CUBA SUGAR YEAR BOOK. Habana. Cuba económica y financiera. [2119
A good reference on Cuba's major crop with many maps containing worthwhile geographic information.

García Vázquez, Ricardo, and Pedro Cabrer Mestre. Clave para conocer los suelos de Cuba. Habana. Imp. La Milagrosa. 46 p. [2120

Gastón, Francisco José. Cuba y sus puertos. Comentarios por Juan Manuel Planas, Pablo Urguiaga Padilla y Oliverio García. Havana. Cía. ed. de libros y folletos. 53 p. [2121
Brief descriptions of the ports of Cuba.

Millás, José Carlos. La lluvia en la Habana. Habana. Imp. O'Reilly. 34 p. [2122
An analysis of the rainfall of Havana.

Peón Aloy, Pura. Las aguas minerales de Cuba. Su importancia en el futuro económico del país (*Rev. soc. geog. Cuba*, año 16, no. 1, enero–marzo, p. 25–34). [2123
A brief statement on the importance of the mineral waters of Cuba to its economy.

Waibel, Leo. Place names as an aid in the reconstruction of the original vegetation of Cuba (*Geog. rev.*, vol. 33, no. 3, July, p. 376–396). [2124
A detailed scientific analysis of the use of place names in the reconstruction of the original vegetation of Cuba. An excellent map of vegetation of Cuba.

DOMINICAN REPUBLIC

Secretaría del tesoro y comercio. Informe . . . correspondiente el año 1942. Ciudad Trujillo. Ed. La Nación. 124 p. [2125
A good statistical reference on the economy of the Dominican Republic.

HAITI

Fennell, Thomas A. Activities and purposes of SHADA (*For. com. weekly*, vol. 10, no. 12, March 20, p. 4–5, 21). [2126
The origin, functions and objectives of SHADA are discussed. Photographs.

———. Cryptostegia and related new activities of Haiti's SHADA (*For. com. weekly*, vol. 13, no. 6, Nov. 6, p. 3–5, 29). [2127
A short analysis of rubber growing and other agricultural activities. Photographs.

Pressoir, C. Eléments de géologie d'Haiti. Port-au-Prince. Imp. du College Vertieres. (Publ. du Bureau d'ethnologie de la république d'Haïti, no. 2). 131 p., ilus. [2128
Rather detailed study of the geology of Haiti.

Sharp, Roland Hall. Cryptostegia and hevea (*Christian science monitor*, Oct. 21, second section, p. 11). [2129
A popular treatment of SHADA's rubber growing activities in Haiti.

JAMAICA

Hutchinson, J. B. The cottons of Jamaica (*Tropical agric.*, vol. 20, no. 3, March, p. 56–58). [2131
An analysis of cotton growing in the island.

Raw, Frank, and C. A. Matley. Some altered palagonite tuffs from Jamaica and the origin and history of their chlorites (*Jour. geol.*, vol. 51, no. 4, May–June, p. 215–243, maps, photos.). [2132
The deposits of the old San Antonio mine have yielded chiefly lead and silver, but tin and vanadium ores have been produced commercially. Detailed descriptions of the tin and vanadium ores are given.

Theaman, John R. Tropical downpours of Jamaica. Indianapolis. 21 p., map. [2133
A pamphlet giving the maximum precipitation in Jamaica for various periods.

PUERTO RICO

Alberts, H. W., and **García-Molinare.** Ovidio pastures of Puerto Rico and their relation to soil conservation. Washington. U. S. Dept. agric. (Miscellaneous publ. no. 513). [2134
Distribution and physical requirements of the major, minor and supplementary pasture grasses in Puerto Rico and the relation of the grasses to soil erosion; notes on types of pasture land and livestock. Map of distribution of predominating native pasture grasses.

Colón, Ramiro L. Report of the present critical situation of the coffee farmers in Puerto Rico. San Juan. Coffee growers cooperative association. 15 p. [2135

Díaz-Pacheco, Santiago, and **Mariano Roses.** La distribución de carnes en Puerto Rico. Río Piedras. Agricultural experiment station. (Bull. 65). 42 p., tables. [2136
Covers business operations of 11 meat wholesalers, 127 meat retailers, and 39 grocery stores selling meat in Puerto Rico during February 1942. It analyzes profits, expenses, and general information. Sources of meat supply are studied with regard to the type and quality of meat sold at marketing outlets.

——, **Martín Vélez,** and **Pablo B. Vásquez Calcerrada.** Practices and operating costs of Puerto Rican fishermen. Río Piedras. Agricultural experiment station. (Mimeographed report 21, January). 30 p., tables. [2137
This report covers one phase of a survey made jointly by the Agricultural Experiment Station, Insular Department of Agriculture and Commerce, and the U. S. Fish and Wildlife Service. It covers fishing practices and expenses of commercial fishermen from August to September 1942 in practically all fishing localities of Puerto Rico.

Gándara, Raúl. Land and liberty. La Fortaleza, San Juan. Office of information. 44 p., tables, maps, illus. [2138
A brief history of Puerto Rico's long battle to solve its land tenure problem. Translated from the Spanish, edited, and annotated.

González Ruiz, Ricardo. Geography of Puerto Rico. Also the rudiments of astronomical, physical, social and political geography. Transl. by Artemio P. Rodríguez, Julia E. Rodríguez and Iris M. Rodríguez. Second ed. San Juan. Imp. Venezuela. 142 p. [2139

Griffin, Donald F. Water and power in Puerto Rico. San Juan. National resources planning board, Field office, region 11. 44 p., maps, tables, bibliography, mimeo. [2140
A survey of water and power resources, their use and possible future development. Domestic water supply, sewage disposal, irrigation and electric power.

Heath, S. Burton. Our American slum, Puerto Rico (*Harper's mag.*, vol. 187, no. 1117, June, p. 56–63). [2141
A portrayal of the widespread poverty on the island of Puerto Rico.

Institute of tropical agriculture. Annual report, 1942–1943. Mayguez. 69 p., tables. [2142

Izquierdo, Luis A. Proposición de un programa de acción económico-social para Puerto Rico rural y agrícola. San Juan. Department of agriculture and commerce. 21 p., mimeo. [2143
Recommendations for a program to better conditions of the rural population through education, organization of cooperatives, training in efficient methods of farm administration, provision of agricultural credit facilities, housing and health measures, reforms in land tenure, and marketing.

Martínez Rivera, E. A note on the development of public health in Puerto Rico. Reprint from *Boletín de la Asociación Médica de Puerto Rico*, October. 10 p. [2144
A brief history of public health in Puerto Rico from Spanish times to the present. Development of the program of public health units throughout the island and an explanation of their personnel and organization.

Morales Otero, Pablo. Nuestros problemas. San Juan. Imp. Venezuela. Bibl. de autores puertorriqueños. 224 p. [2145
A general background study of the major problems of Puerto Rico, and information on the following topics: history, population, natural resources, agriculture, industry, commerce, living standards, nutrition, vital statistics and social problems.

Office of information. Puerto Rico: The story of a warbase. La Fortaleza, San Juan. 39 p. [2146
Brief résumé of the location, climate, and economic and social developments of the Island up to 1942, with statistical appendices detailing important aspects of Puerto Rico's economy.

——. General district hospitals for Puerto Rico. Santurce. 16 p., mimeo. [2147
A section of the Master Plan for the Development of Puerto Rico, presenting information on existing general hospital facilities and recommendations for the establishment of five new district hospitals, specifying capacities, location, and areas to be served.

REPORT OF THE COMMITTEE APPOINTED BY THE GENERAL SUPPLIES ADMINISTRATOR OF PUERTO RICO TO STUDY THE ACTUAL COFFEE SITUATION OF THE ISLAND. Río Piedras. Agricultural experiment station. (Mimeographed report). 8 p. [2148
Report on a study of the economics of coffee farming.

REPORT ON THE POSSIBILITIES OF UTILIZING NAVY LANDS IN VIEQUES ISLAND FOR A RESETTLEMENT PROJECT. Río Piedras. Agricultural experiment station. (Mimeographed report 23). 32 p. [2149
An investigation of the economic situation confronting the inhabitants of the island of Vieques, Puerto Rico, as a result of the expropriation by the Navy of nearly two-thirds the island's area and the stagnation of economic activity caused by the termination of Naval construction. A study of nonrestricted lands was made, including soil characteristics, precipitation, past and present utilization. A complete resettlement plan is outlined with specific recommendations made for the use of these lands.

THREE-FOURTHS ILL-FED, ILL-CLOTHED, ILL-HOUSED. La Fortaleza, San Juan. Office of information. 28 p., tables, illus. [2150
A description of present living conditions and diet of low-income families in Puerto Rico, with suggestions for improvement. Based on a report "Minimum Decent Living Standards for Puerto Rico" by the Committee on Living Standards of the National Resources Planning Board, Field Office, Region 11, San Juan.

United States. Department of commerce. Bureau of the census. Population. Bulletin no. 2: characteristics of the population, Puerto Rico, census of 1940. 82 p., tables. [2151
Statistics on population by age, sex, color, urban and rural, school attendance, marital status, literacy and employment by municipalities and large cities and towns.

Water resources authority. Annual report, 1941–1942. San Juan. 285 p., tables, charts. [2152

———. Report on Caonillas hydro-electric project. San Juan. 41 p., mimeo., maps, tables, charts. [2153
A report of the chief engineer of the WRA on the possibilities of constructing a dam at Caonillas, P. R. including estimates of water available, energy out-put, construction features, and costs.

THE BAHAMAS

Stark, Harry N. The Bahamas look to the future (*For. com. weekly*, vol. 11, no. 6, May 8, p. 8–10, 36). [2154
An article presenting up-to-date facts about the economic and commercial situation in the Bahamas. Photographs.

LESSER ANTILLES

Hardy, F. Studies on aeration and water supply in some cacao soils of Trinidad (*Tropical agric.*, vol. 20, no. 4, May, p. 89–104). [2155
A study of cacao reactions to clay, sand and other soil types in Trinidad. Tables and graphs.

Hiss, Philip Hanson. A selective guide to the English literature on the Netherlands West Indies; with a supplement on Guiana. New York. Netherlands information bureau. 129 p. [2155a
A bibliography of special importance to students of the Netherlands West Indies.

Hodge, W. H. The vegetation of Dominica (*Geog. rev.*, vol. 33, no. 3, July, p. 349–375). [2156
A regional treatment of Dominica's vegetation, well illustrated with photographs and maps. A short but excellent treatment of the four main types of vegetation in Dominica: the tropical coastal thickets, the xerophytic vegetation of the low leeward slopes; the mesophytic vegetation of the mountain slopes and the mossy forest of the high peaks.

Jolly, A. L. The effect of age of field on cacao yields in Grenada compared with the Montserrat district of Trinidad (*Tropical agric.*, vol. 20, no. 3, March, p. 47–50, tables, graphs). [2157
Detailed analysis of yields in relation to age of trees.

Moore, W. Robert. Curaçao and Aruba on guard (*Nat. geog. mag.*, vol. 83, no. 2, Feb., p. 169–192). [2158
An illustrated article on the economy and defense of the Netherlands West Indies.

Olschki, Leonardo. The Columbian nomenclature of the Lesser Antilles (*Geog. rev.*, vol. 33, no. 3, July, p. 397–414). [2159
An analysis of the survival of some place names and the abandonment of others in the Lesser Antilles.

Roche, Jean Cazenave de la. Tension in the French West Indies (*For. affs.*, vol. 21, no. 3, April, p. 560–565). [2160
The stratification of the population and problems of political administration.

Stark, Harry N. Martinique and France's other West Indian islands (*For. com. weekly*, vol. 10, no. 13, March 27, p. 3–7, 34–35). [2161
Pertinent facts on the geography, commerce, basic economy and prospects of the French West Indies. Photographs.

———. Peace and war in the Netherlands West Indies (*For. com. weekly*, vol. 10.

no. 9, Feb. 27, p. 6-13, 39, maps, photos). [2161a

A brief statement on the geography of the northern and southern groups of islands and the effects of the war on them.

ADDENDA

Williams, L. Natural resources of Venezuela (*Chron. bot.*, vol. 7, no. 2, March, 1942, p. 75-77). [2162

Very brief discussion of the rubber, oils, and palm fibers of Venezuelan Guayana.

Wilson, Charles Morrow. Cultural America: challenge and opportunity. London. George Allen and Unwin, publ. 1942. 294 p., maps, photos. [2163

A combination of sound, carefully selected information on the Central American republics, British Honduras, the West Indies and Colombia. The book is divided into three parts: countries, crops, and the future. Separate chapters deal with the six principal crops of the areas as a whole—coffee, bananas, coconuts, cacao, chicle, and rubber.

GEOGRAPHY: SOUTH AMERICA
(EXCEPT BRAZIL, COLOMBIA AND VENEZUELA)

BY

GEORGE McCUTCHEN McBRIDE
University of California

AND

MERLE ALEXANDER McBRIDE
Library of Congress

GENERAL STATEMENT

Except for Platt's volume of detailed studies (accumulated during past years and widely distributed over Latin America) neither Latin American nor foreign professional geographers have contributed much in this region during the year. Even the organized geographical institutions have produced little in the field. Foreign agencies, of course, have been engrossed in other activities, and war conditions have hampered the numerous geographical societies in the various Latin American countries.

On the other hand, botanists, geologists, oceanographers and general writers have made some valuable contributions in fields marginal to geography proper. Schweigger's continued work along the coast of Peru, Brüggen's writings on the seismology of Chile and numerous books and papers on the upper Amazon area have added decidedly to geographical knowledge.

As to the regions in which contributions were made: in Peru interest was focused largely upon the *montaña* and *selva;* in the Argentine, as in other recent years, attention centered mainly upon Patagonia and the northern provinces. Neither Bolivia, Chile, Ecuador, Paraguay nor Uruguay evinced much interest in their frontier regions, and, probably the first time for many years, there appeared no important studies upon individual international boundaries. Curiously enough for these times, two important contributions were published on the Antarctic region.

The year was marked by the reproduction, in translation or otherwise, of some important works, such as those of Azara, Haenke, Reiche, Goodspeed, Bowman and Subercaseaux.

All in all, the year added no very distinguished fresh gains but a variety of more or less substantial ones in this section of Latin America.

BIBLIOGRAPHY

(*See also sections on* Economics: South America, except Brazil, Colombia and Venezuela; Agriculture: South America, except Brazil, Colombia and Venezuela)

GENERAL

McBride, George McCutchen, and Merle Alexander McBride. A selective guide to the material published in 1942 on geography: South America (except Caribbean countries and Brazil) (*Handbook of latin american studies, no. 8, 1942,* p. 197-202). [2164

Maes, Ernest E. Soil conservation in South America (*Agric. Americas,* vol. 3, no. 7, July, p. 123–217). [2165

Pleiss, Paul. A motor journey round South America (*Geog. jour.,* vol. 51, no. 2, Feb., p. 66–78, map, illus.). [2166
Notes on a trip from Caracas to Magallanes and up to Rio de Janeiro following, as far as possible, the Pan American highway, with many good geographical notes.

United States hydrographic office. Sailing directions for Antarctica including the off-lying islands south of latitude 60°. H. O. 138. Washington. U. S. govt. print. off. xiii, 312 p., illus. [2168
Description of coasts, review of explorations, account of living conditions.

EAST COAST

ALGUNOS ASPECTOS DE LA PATAGONIA (*Rev. geog. amer.,* año 9, vol. 20, no. 119, agosto, p. 89–104). [2169
General discussion of the area, paleontological discoveries, history, economic potentialities.

Argentina. Instituto geográfico militar. Catálogo del material cartográfico. Buenos Aires. 64 p. [2171

Besio Moreno, E. Rosario de Santa Fe. Cartografía y población, 1744–1942 (*Rev. mus. La Plata,* nueva serie, sección geológica, tomo 1, p. 259–298). [2172

Biloni, José Santos. Lianas caracteristicas del bosque ribereño bonaerense (*Rev. geog. amer.,* año 11, vol. 20, no. 123, dic., p. 312–320). [2173

Bracaccini, O. El problema de la exploración petrolera en la República Argentina (*Gaea,* tomo 6, sept., p. 3–6). [2174

Bosch, B. Informe preliminar sobre la habitación en el delta del Paraná (*Gaea,* tomo 7, primera entrega, p. 113–117). [2175

Calcagno, Alfredo D. Creación del Instituto de investigaciones geográficas argentinas en la Universidad nacional de La Plata (*Gaea,* tomo 7, primera entrega, p. 137–140). [2176

———. Los estudios geográficos en la Universidad nacional de La Plata (*Gaea,* tomo 7, primera entrega, p. 131–136). [2177

Daus, Federico A. Los recientes estudios geográficos en la Argentina (*Acta amer.,* vol. 1, no. 1, Jan.–March, p. 83–87). [2178
A brief statement of the agencies operating in the geographic field, with a few citations of outstanding productions.

Deasy, George F. Distribution of flax production in Argentina (*Econ. geog.,* vol. 19, no. 1, Jan., p. 45–54). [2179

———. A tentative growing-season map of Argentina (*Jour. geog.,* vol. 42, no. 6, Sept., p. 225–229, table, maps). [2180

Dupuy, Daniel Hammerly. La "Fortaleza protectora argentina" (*Rev. geog. amer.,* año 9, vol. 19, no. 115, abril, p. 187–194). [2181
Historical account of construction of Bahía Blanca (1805–1828) as a strategic sea base to protect Buenos Aires from Indian attack.

Frenguelli, Joaquín. Vestigios de una fase lacustre reciente, en La Cuenca de la Salina Chica en península Valdez (Chubut) (*Gaea,* tomo 7, primer entrega, p. 65–71). [2182

García Castellanos, Telasco. Reconocimiento geológico de la parte central de la Sierra Norte de Córdoba (*Rev. univ. nac. Córdoba,* año 30, no. 1–4, marzo–junio, p. 131–140; no. 5–6, julio–agosto, p. 571–616). [2183

Goison, Christopher H. Through Paraguay and southern Matto Grosso (*Nat. geog. mag.,* vol. 84, no. 4, Oct., p. 459–488). [2184

Instituto agrario argentino. Reseña general, histórica, geográfica y económica del partido de Las Conchas (pcia. de Buenos Aires). Buenos Aires. (Reseñas, año 3, no. 14). 69 p. [2185
A concise description with statistical data relating to the economy of the district. [Ed.]

———. Reseña general, histórica, geográfica y económica del partido de San Isidro. Buenos Aires. (Reseñas, año 3, no. 18). 203 p. [2186

Jakob, Cristofredo. Hacia los penitentes pigmeos (*Rev. geog. amer.,* año 9, vol. 19, no. 112, enero, p. 1–10). [2187
Snow formations near the transandean railway.

Jakob, Ricardo. Los saltos del Río Uruguay (*Rev. geog. amer.,* año 9, vol. 19, no. 114, marzo, p. 121–126). [2188
The waterfalls as potential tourist attraction.

Keidel, J. El ordovício inferior en los Andes del norte Argentino y sus depósitos marino-glaciales (*Bol. acad. nac. cien.,* Córdoba, tomo 36, entrega 2–3, p. 140–229, mapas, perfiles, ilus.). [2189

Kühn, Franz, and **Guillermo Rohmeder.** Estudio fisiográfico de las sierras de Tucumán. Tucumán. Univ. nac. de Tucumán, Facultad de filosofía y letras, Insto. de estudios geográficos. (Monografías del Insto. de estudios geográficos, 3). 96 p., mapas, ilus. [2190

A new, much revised edition of Kuhn's well known study of these mountains, first published in 1924. Rohmeder, during 1941–1943, extended the investigations, particularly toward the western side of the area, and adds data on climate and vegetation resulting from recent studies. The maps are revised and excellent photographs added.

Latzina, Francisco. Calendario pluvial para Buenos Aires y sus alrededores más próximos, basado sobre una experiencia de cuarenta años (*Bol. acad. nac. cien.*, Córdoba, tomo 36, entrega 2–3, p. 97–105). [2191

Indicates how many times in forty years it has rained on each day of the year, thus giving an index of frequency of rainfall.

Lázaro, Juan F. de. Un pleito secular entre Santiago del Estero y Tucumán, 1685–1788 (*An. soc. cient. arg.*, tomo 136, entrega 3, sept., p. 125–139; entrega 4, oct., p. 179–192; entrega 5, nov., p. 216–232). [2192

Litigation over tolls collected along the historic highways from Buenos Aires to Perú.

Lazzari de Pandolfi, Carolina. Estudio petrográfico y bosquejo geológico de la región de Chaján, Córdoba. Buenos Aires. Dirección de minas y geología. (Bol. no. 54). 46 p., ilus. [2193

Levín, Enrique. Determinación de la diferencia de gravedad La Plata—Potsdam. La Plata. Univ. nac. de La Plata, Observatorio astronómico. (Serie geodésica, tomo 3). 68 p., gráfs. [2194

Niklison, Carlos A. El puerto de Santa Fe (*Rev. geog. amer.*, año 9, vol. 19, no. 117, junio, p. 301–306). [2195

The Paraná River port.

Núñez, José Ramón. De Corrientes a la Asunción (*Rev. geog. amer.*, año 9, vol. 19, no. 115, abril, p. 181–186). [2196

Trip up the Paraguay River.

———. Viajando por el Río Paraná (*Rev. geog. amer.*, año 9, vol. 19, no. 112, enero, p. 11–28; no. 113, feb., p. 85–104). [2197

Buenos Aires to Iguassú Falls; travelogue with good details; well illustrated.

Paraguay. Dirección de hidrografía y navegación. Anuario hidrográfico, año 3, 1942. Asunción. Imp. Nacional. 22 p., mapas, gráfs. [2198

Parodi, L. R. La vegetación del departamento de San Martín en Corrientes (Argentina) (*Darwiniana*, tomo 6, no. 2, sept., p. 127–178, ilus.). [2199

Much ecological data.

Pellerano, Glorialdo. Recuerdos de un viaje por el noroeste argentino (*Rev. geog. amer.*, año 9, vol. 19, no. 117, junio, p. 339–344). [2200

To the north of the Río Uruguay, the Corrientes region.

Rohmeder, Guillermo. Observaciones meteorológicas en la región encumbrada de las Sierras de Famatina y del Aconquija, República Argentina (*An. soc. cien. arg.*, tomo 136, entrega 3, sept., p. 97–124). [2201

———. El paisaje entre Jujuy y La Quiaca: Un cuadro sinóptico de la Quebrada de Humahuaca y de la parte adyacente de la puna jujeña (*Gaea*, tomo 7, entrega 1, p. 93–97, gráf., mapa, tabla). [2202

It is this *quebrada* which provides the natural avenue for an important section of the historic highway between Lima and Buenos Aires and of the Argentine-Bolivia railway.

Santillán, Luis A., and **S. Heredia Luna.** Tucumán. Su suelo y su clima (*Rev. fac. agron.*, Montevideo, no. 32, mayo, p. 33–72). [2203

Rainfall map and graphs of precipitation and temperature.

Sgrosso, Pascual. Contribución al conocimiento de la minería y geología del noroeste argentino. Buenos Aires. Dirección de minas y geología. (Bol. no. 53). 180 p., ilus. [2204

Spangenberg, Guillermo. Características ecológicas y forma de explotación de una estancia entrerriana (*Rev. fac. agron.*, Montevideo, no. 33, agosto, p. 185–240, mapas, ilus.). [2205

Detailed study of land utilization, soils, water, natural and introduced vegetation, communications, etc., of a 15,000 acre *estancia*, in the Departamento de Gualeguaychú, Distrito Pehuajó Norte.

Torres, Ana Palese de. Las actividades del Instituto geográfico militar (*Gaea*, tomo 7, entrega 1, p. 49–59). [2206

The Instituto is devoted mainly to the mapping of the national territory.

Yepes, José. Ambientes faunísticos de la Sierra de Velasco (*Gaea*, tomo 7, entrega 1, p. 81–91, ilus.). [2207

WEST COAST

(*See also items* 2535, 2987)

Acosta Solís, M. Breves anotaciones sobre la historia de la climatología del Ecuador

(*Flora*, vol. 3, no. 7–10, dic., p. 10–45). [2208
Brief comparison of data recorded by observers from early colonial times to the present.

Aguilar Revoredo, J. F. Relieve primitivo y evolución fisiográfica de los Andes (*Bol. mus. hist. nat. "Javier Prado,"* año 7, no. 24–25, primer y segundo trim., p. 9–24). [2209

Amunátegui Solar, Domingo. Influencia de la ocupación de la tierra en la estructura de la sociedad chilena (*Proc. eighth amer. scien. cong.,* vol. 9, p. 221–224). [2210

Andia, Teófilo. La reforma agraria en las comunidades indígenas de Bolivia (*Rev. jurídica,* año 6, no. 25, dic., p. 69–72). [2211
Geographical in treatment.

Armendaris, Luis A., and **Darío C. Guevara.** Monografía del cantón Rumiñahue. Quito. Imp. Ecuador. 304 p., ilus. [2212
Like many other "monografías" of regions in Latin America, this contains much data of little interest outside of the immediate district, but includes some detailed description not found elsewhere. The student of Latin America may pick up many fragments from such monographs. The Cantón of Rumiñahue lies in the Valley of Los Chillos, a few miles south of Quito.

Aslakson, Carl I., and **Clarence H. Swick.** Gravity observations in Perú and Colombia. Washington. U. S. Dept. of commerce, Coast and geodetic survey. (Special publ. no. 233). 18 p., illus. [2213

Avellaneda, Jacinto. Monografía de la provincia de Yauyos (*Bol. soc. geog. Lima,* tomo 60, segundo trim., p. 146–158). [2214
This paper, on one of the provinces of the Department of Lima, contains a few data of value and much that has merely local interest.

Banda C., Francisco. Ecuador's balsa goes to war (*Agric. Americas,* vol. 3, no. 11, Nov., p. 211–213). [2215

Bolivia. Ministerio de hacienda. Dirección general de estadística. Demografía, 1940. La Paz. Ed. Argote. 191 p. [2216

———. Estadística agro-pecuaria, 1939–1940, 1941. La Paz. Ed. Fénix. 117 p. [2217
Statistics regarding public lands, farms, Indian communities, crops, stock, and some meteorological data.

Broggi, J. A. La desglaciación actual de los Andes del Perú (*Bol. soc. geol. Perú,* tomo 14–15, p. 59–90, ilus.). [2218

———. La desglaciación andina y sus consequencias (*Rev. ciencias,* Lima, año 45, no. 444, junio, p. 159–173). [2219
Discusses a supposed general retreat of glaciers in the Central Andes of Peru, with a consequent increase of water in the chains of glacial lakes, resulting in the breaking of morainal dams, first in the uppermost ones, then in those lower down, thus accounting for the disastrous floods of recent years, particularly in the Cordillera Blanca about the great snow fields of Huascarán.

———. Geología del embalse del río Chotano en Lajas (*Bol. soc. geol. Perú,* tomo 12, fasc. 1, p. 1–23, mapas). [2220
A study made to ascertain the possibility of turning the waters of the Chotano from the Huancabamba-Marañón system into the coastal stream of Chancay-Reque to augment irrigation in the desert Lambayeque region.

———. Historia y geología de los yacimientos minerales del Perú (*Bol. mus. hist. nat. "Javier Prado,"* año 7, no. 26–27, tercer y cuarto trim., p. 181–209). [2221

———. Sobre geomorfología y climatología de Huacachina, Ica (*Bol. soc. geol. Perú,* tomo 14–15, p. 91–98, mapa). [2222
Study of a little lake among the sand dunes near Ica, now frequented as a resort by the people of Lima.

———, and **A. J. Indacochea Gárate.** Observaciones atmológicas en un viaje a Piaz, Parcoy y Ariabamba (*Bol. soc. geol. Perú,* tomo 14–15, p. 17–27, mapas, gráf.). [2223
Weather observations on flight from Lima, along the coast and over the Western Cordillera.

Brüggen, Johannes Otto. Contribución a la geología sísmica de Chile. Santiago. Imp. universitaria. 132 p., ilus., mapas. [2224
Basic general survey of the subject, technical but attempts explanation for non-technical reader.

———. Los geisers de los volcanes del Tatio. Santiago. Imp. univ. 23 p., ilus. [2225
The geysers about head waters of Laja River, south-central Chile.

Buero, Juan Antonio. Los tres Perú (*Peruanidad,* vol. 3, no. 15, set.–oct., p. 1198–1210). [2226
Brief over-all description of the three main regions of the country.

Bullón Noroña, Gustavo. Monografía de Ataura. Ataura (Jauja), Perú. 275 p., ilus. [2227
General description of an Andean town, Province of Jauja, Departamento de Junín, Perú, with much data useless to anyone outside of the vicinity.

Bustos Pérez, Vicente. Geografía de Chile, política y económica. Santiago. Imp. Universo. 142 p. [2228

Cárdenas, Fortunato E. Tarma, Palca, Chanchamayo, El Pichis, El Río Negro. Tarma, Perú. Imp. La Voz de Tarma. 295 p., ilus. [2229
A few geographical facts.

Carrera Andrade, Jorge. Mirador terrestre. La república del Ecuador; encrucijada cultura de América. Forrest Hills, N. Y. Las Américas publ. co. 62 p., ilus. [2230
General description.

Castillo V., Julio. La sierra ecuatoriana (*Rev. geog. amer.*, año 9, vol. 20, no. 118, julio, p. 43–49). [2231

Chile. Instituto geográfico militar. Anuario, no. 4, 1939–1942. Santiago. 134 p., mapas, ilus. [2233

———. **Oficina meteorológica.** Anuario meteorológico de 1942. Santiago. Ed. La Ilustración. (Sección climatológica, publ. 59). 293 p. [2234

Chira, Magdaleno C. Tingo María, ensayo monográfico. Lima. Imp. Miranda. 53 p. [2235
A brief description of the conditions of climate, soil, vegetation, communications, organization, etc. of the colony being formed on the upper Huallaga River in the Ceja de Montaña of Perú.

Delgado Barrenechea, José C. Geografía económica del Perú; monografía sobre "El carbón vegetal." (*Rev. fac. cien. econ.*, no. 27, agosto, p. 98–118). [2236

Eguiguren, Luis Antonio. Invincible Jaén. Notes on the territorial question between Peru and Ecuador. Lima. 829 p., illus., maps. [2237
Historical and geographical data regarding the Province of Jaén and its relation to Peru; documented but rambling.

Elhueta G., Manuel, and Juan Jirkal H. Erosión de los suelos en Chile. Santiago. Imp. Sud América. (Min. de agricultura, Dirección general de agricultura, Depto. de genética y fitografía, Bol. técnico, no. 4). 27 p., ilus. [2238

Escobar V., Ismael. Contribución al estudio del tiempo en Bolivia. La Paz. 50 p. [2239

———. Los tipos del tiempo y la predicción del mismo sobre La Paz. La Paz. (Dirección general de agricultura, Min. de agricultura, ganadería y colonización Bol. mensual, Servicio meteorológico de Bolivia, no. 12, año 2, mapas, grafs.). 30 p. [2240

Fergusson, Erna. Chile. New York. Alfred A. Knopf. 341, vi p., illus. [2241
Easy reading narrative style, authentic personal account with important observations regarding the country in general and its basic regions. Thoughtful comments on Chile-American relations.

Fiedler, Reginald H., Norman D. Jarvis, and M. J. Lobell. La pesca y las industrias pesqueras en el Perú, con recomendaciones para su futuro desarrollo. Lima. Cía. administradora de guano. 371 p., mapas, ilus. [2242
Thirteen pages given to description of oceanographic conditions.

Fuenzalida Villegas, Humberto. El Cerro Azul y el Volcán Quizapú. Estudios sobre el volcanismo de la Cordillera de Talca, no. 3. (*Bol. mus. nac.*, Chile, tomo 21, p. 37–53). [2243

García Méndez, Carlos A. Conceptos sobre condensación y precipitación según las ideas de Sverol Petersen y Bergeron, aplicados a las características de las masas aéreas de la costa peruana (*Agronomía*, año 7, no. 28, 1942, p. 135–140; año 8, no. 31, 1943, p. 45–54). [2244

Greenbie, Sydney. Between mountain and sea. Chile. Evanston, Ill., New York. Row, Peterson and co. (The good neighbor series). 84 p. [2245

Gridilla, Alberto. Un año en el Putumayo. Lima. (Col. Descalzos, no. 5). 111 p. [2246
Events of 1913 in the region (rubber exploitation scandals, boundary conflicts, etc.) and geographical exploration of the Franciscan missionaries in the Amazon region.

Harrison, J. V. Geología de los Andes Centrales en parte del departamento de Junín, Perú (*Bol. soc. geol. Perú*, tomo 16, p. 3–97). [2247
Final report, in Spanish and English. Maps, profiles and photographs.

Heilborn, Ott. Contribución a la ecología de los páramos ecuatorianos (*Flora*, vol. 3, no. 7–10, dic., p. 67–82). [2248
Translated from *Sartryck ur Svensk Batanisk Tidskrift*, February, 1925, by Blanca de Acosta Solís.

Herrera, F. L. Nomenclatura fitonímica (*Rev. mus. nac.*, Lima, tomo 12, no. 1, primer semestre, p. 41–60; no. 2, segundo semestre, p. 167–180). [2249
"Clasificación de los nombres vulgares de las plantas del Cuzco atendiendo a la índole de las lenguas de su origen.—Sinonimias vulgares de los nombres vernaculares de las plantas del Cuzco."

Higbee, E. C. Agriculture across the Andes (*Agric. Americas*, vol. 3, no. 1, Jan., p. 3–7). [2249a
Zones along the new highway Lima-Pucallpa. [G. M. McBride]

Hoempler, Armin. Apuntes sobre la región azufrera de Cano (*Bol. soc. geol. Perú*, tomo 14–15, p. 99–103, mapa). [2250
Sulphur deposits in the volcanic region in the Department of Tacna.

Ibáñez C., Donaciano. Historia mineral de Bolivia. Antofagasta. Imp. Macfarlane. 258 p., ilus. [2251

Katz, Carlos. Estudio de praderas y potreros en la ganadería ecuatoriana. Ecuador. Min. de agricultura. (Bol. no. 22). 94 p., ilus. [2252

Klein, Enrique. Pastos naturales del Departamento de Piura (*Bol. dir. gen. agric. ganad.*, año 14, tomo 16, no. 48–51, enero-feb., p. 197–220). [2253

Kuczynsky-Godard, Máximo. Alba sobre la Amazonía (*Historia*, Lima, vol. 1, no. 3, julio–agosto, p. 192–206). [2254
Geographical and sociological study of the Amazon plain, particularly the Peruvian part: Kinds of lands usable, resources, food supply, diseases, ways of life in relation to the habitat, by a government public health official who has devoted many years to the area.

Macbride, James Francis. Flora of Peru. Chicago. (Field museum of natural history, Publ. 531, Botanical series, vol. 13, part 3, no. 1, Oct. 11). 507 p. [2255
An additional volume of this monumental work.

Maldonado, Ángel. Las lagunas de Boza, Chilca y Huacachina y los gramadales de la costa del Perú. Reimpreso de las *Actas y trabajos del Segundo congreso peruano de química*. Lima. 143 p., mapa, ilus. [2256
A careful, detailed scientific study of the numerous desert lakes, ponds and grassy marshes along and near the coast of Perú.

Marín Madrid, Alberto. Topografía. Santiago. Inst. geográfico militar. 373 p. [2257

Mejía Baca, José. El hombre del Marañón. Vida de Manuel Antonio Mesones Muro. Lima. Ed. San Martí. 149 p. [2259
This biography of one of Peru's most noted recent explorers, edited under the auspices of the Comité del Cuarto Centenario del Descubrimiento del Amazonas, contains much geographical data regarding the Andes of northern Peru and the Pongo de Manseriche on the upper Marañón. It describes the discovery of the Porculla Pass, the lowest gap across the Andes between northern Colombia and southern Chile.

Meneses, Rómulo. El imperativo geográfico en la mediterraneidad de Bolivia. Prólogo de Enrique Baldivieso. La Paz. Ed. Renacimiento. 90 p. [2260

Miller, O. M. La expedición al Perú de la American geographical society, en 1927–1928 (*Bol. minas petról.*, Lima, año 21–22, no. 70–71, junio, p. 20–41, mapas, ilus.). [2261
Translated from the *Geog. rev.*, Jan., 1929, by C. Nicholson.

Moravsky, Bernardo. Satipo. Notas monográficas (*Bol. soc. geog. Lima*, tomo 60, primer trim., p. 3–19, ilus.). [2262
Detailed notes on this new area of colonization in the Ceja de Montaña region, east of Lima.

Newell, Norman D., and Isaac A. Tafur H. Ordovícico fosilífero en la selva oriental del Perú (*Bol. soc. geol. Perú*, tomo 14–15, p. 5–16, mapa, ilus.). [2263

Oppenheim, Víctor. Bibliografía geológica de Bolivia (*Bol. soc. geog. La Paz*, año 54, no. 65, junio, p. 90–106). [2264
A valuable list for students of the geology and the geography of Bolivia.

———. Geología de la sierra de Cucutú, frontera Perú-Ecuador (*Bol. soc. geol. Perú*, vol. 14–15, p. 104–111, ilus.). [2265
Brief notes on this seldom-visited region.

———. Las terrazas del río de La Paz (*Bol. soc. geog. La Paz*, año 54, no. 65, junio, p. 88–89). [2266
Mere noting of seven terraces between 3,100 and 4,150 meters, attributed to uplift in quaternary times.

Ortiz de Zevallos, Luis. La geografía como base de todo estudio urbano (*Historia*, Lima, vol. 1, no. 3, julio–agosto, p. 215–219). [2267
An architect analyzes the relation of geography to urban development with special reference to Peruvian cities.

Osgood, Wilfred H. The mammals of Chile. Chicago. Field museum of nat. hist. (Zool. series, vol. 30, Publ. 542). 268 p. [2268

Paredes, Manuel Rigoberto. Ligera descripción del distrito minero La Chacarilla (*Bol. soc. geog. La Paz*, año 54, no. 65, junio, p. 7–12). [2269

Pareja Paz Soldán, José. Geografía del Perú. Curso universitario. Segunda ed. Lima. Lib. D. Miranda. 474 p., ilus., mapas. [2270
Systematically arranged data regarding the physical and human elements that make up the nation, with some discussion of the historical development of the Peruvian people; useful for reference as well as university study.

Pérez, Aquiles. Patria y geografía. Quito. Tall. gráf. de educación. 23 p. [2272

PERUVIAN YEARBOOK, 1942–1943. Lima. Peruvian times. 124 p., maps, illus. [2273
A very useful review of activities in Peru during the year, including lumbering; mining; agriculture; city improvement; roadbuilding; construction of port works at Callao, Chimbote and Matarani; the building of new hydroelectric plants; a report on the census of 1940; description of rubber exploitation, public health service, etc.

Petersen, George. Sobre el petróleo de Islaycocha (*Bol. soc. geol. Perú*, tomo 12, fasc. 2, p. 1–32, mapas). [2274
This district is in the Province of Espinar, Department of Cuzco. Bibliography.

Pulgar Vidal, Javier. Verdadero origen del río Huallaga (*Bol. soc. geog. Lima*, tomo 60, segundo trim., p. 133–145, mapa). [2275
Complex consideration of a much discussed subject among Peruvian geographers, with the conclusion that, of the ten pretended sources, the true head of the Huallaga is in the Pichiucocha and Raura lakes, and that the Chaupihuaranga, not the Huariaca, constitutes the real upper Huallaga.

Raimondi, Antonio. Notas de viajes para su obra *El Perú*, segundo volumen, publicado por el Ing. Alberto Jochamowitz. Lima. Imp. Torres Aguirre. 288 p., mapas, láms. [2276
Observations made during travels in Peru, during the years 1860 and 1861.

Ramos, Ignacio. Termalismo en el Perú (*Bol. escuela nac. ing.*, serie 3, tomo 16, julio-set., p. 3–97, ilus.). [2277
Detailed study of distribution, character and uses.

Ribadeneira, Jorge A. Estudio geológico del Archipiélago de Colón, Galápagos (*Flora*, vol. 3, no. 7–10, dic., p. 147–162). [2278
Notes resulting from an excursion to the islands, taken by the Comisión Científica Nacional, in August, 1937.

Risopatrón, Oscar. Camino longitudinal de Nos a Talca (*An. inst. ing. Chile*, año 56, no. 9, sept., p. 328–336). [2279

Schweigger, Erwin. La bahía de Pisco (*Bol. soc. geol. Perú*, tomo 13, p. 1–97, mapas). [2280
An oceanographical study; one of the three papers included in the author's *Tres Estudios*, noted below. A summary of this paper is given by Dr. Jorge A. Broggi in the *Actas de la Academia Nacional de Ciencias Exactas, Físicas y Naturales de Lima*, año 5, vol. 5, fasc. 4.

———. Pesquería y oceanografía del Perú y proposiciones para su desarrollo futuro. Lima. Imp. Gil. xi, 356 p., 4 anexos, (statistical) 8 gráfs. pleg., 69 mapas. [2281
Contains an eight page summary, in English. A volume developed by the author independently of the work issued by the American Mission in the service of the Peruvian government, but reaching generally similar conclusions. Of the four parts, the second is of particular geographical interest, as it deals with oceanographic conditions along the Peruvian coast. The author is fisheries expert who has been with the Peruvian government Guano Administration Company for some five years. An important contribution to knowledge of the Peruvian Current and its effect upon sea life and bird life and upon the climate of the coastal region.

———. Tres estudios referentes a la oceanografía del Perú. Lima. Imp. Gil. 189 p., mapas, gráfs. [2282
The three studies are, "Los fenómenos en el mar desde 1925 hasta 1941, en relación con observaciones meteorológicas efectuadas en Puerto Chicama"; "La bahía de Pisco" and "La bahía de Chimbote." All of them were made in connection with the work of the Compañía Administradora del Guano and had been published in abbreviated form; the first in the *Boletín de la Sociedad Geográfica de Lima*, the others in the *Boletín de la Compañía Administradora del Guano*. Each is a definite contribution to the all too scant knowledge of ocean conditions along the Peruvian (Humboldt) Current.

Seijas Rodríguez, Antenor. Tingo María (*Bol. soc. geog. Lima*, tomo 60, segundo trim., p. 89–114). [2283
General data regarding this site of recent colonization in the Ceja de Montaña, on the upper Huallaga. The author, for nearly two years government medical and sanitary officer at this post, plans two other monographs, dealing with health conditions there.

Soler, Enrique M. del. El paiche y la piscicultura en la selva. Lima. Min. de agricultura, Dirección de asuntos orientales, colonización y terrenos de oriente, Depto. de ganadería tropical, caza y pesca. (Bol. no. 3). P. 3–15, ilus., mapa. [2284
Most of this paper is biological, but there are detailed descriptions of streams and lakes (largely the ox-bow lakes, called cochas).

Szyszlo, Vitold de. Problemas de la colonización de nuestra montaña (*Bol. soc. geog. Lima*, tomo 60, tercer y cuarto trim., p. 176–196). [2285
Treats mainly of the Huallaga Valley.

———. La selva del Huallaga (*Bol. mus. hist. nat. "Javier Prado,"* año 7, no. 26–27, tercer y cuarto trim., p. 236–239). [2286

Valcárcel, Luis E. Cuzco. Lima. Emp. gráf. T. Scheuch. 37 p., ilus. [2287
A guide in English for tourists, prepared by the Director of the National Archaeological Museum.

Valdivia Dávila, Víctor. El Perú turístico. Lima. Emp. Ed. Rimac. 206 p., mapas, ilus. [2288
Tourist guide.

Villarejo, Avencio. Así es la selva. Estudio geográfico y etnográfico de la Provincia de Bajo Amazonas. Prólogo por Víctor Andrés Belaunde. Lima. Cía. de impresiones y publicidad. 252 p., ilus., mapa. [2290

Weberbauer, Augusto. Principios de clasificación aplicables a las formaciones vegetales del Perú (*Bol. mus. hist. nat. "Javier Prado,"* año 7, no. 26–27, tercero y cuarto trim., p. 210–218). [2291
Ecological treatment.

———. La protección de la vegetación y de la flora del Perú (*Bol. mus. hist. nat. "Javier Prado,"* año 7, no. 24–25, primero y segundo trim., p. 3–8). [2292
Brief description of vegetation by natural regions and methods for its protection.

ADDENDA

Acosta Solís, M. Anotaciones sobre la vegetación del norte de Quito. Contribuciones a la geobotánica ecuatoriana. Quito. Imp. univ. 1942. 120 p., mapa, ilus. [2294
An ecological study, containing brief descriptions of topographic features, soil conditions, climatic factors and present land uses, with a botanical inventory of the region.

Bergeiro, José M. Contribución al mejor conocimiento del clima. Montevideo. Imp. García. (Inst. de estudios superiores, Sección de investigaciones meteorológicas, Ent. no. 3). 1942. 48 p., ilus., mapas. [2295
Deals mainly with conditions in Uruguay.

Carral Tolosa, Esther W. de. Observaciones geológicas en el oeste del Chubut. Argentina. Tall. cartog. (Min. de agric., Dir., min. y geol.). 1942. 73 p., mapa, ilus. [2296

Díaz, Juvenal A. Tierra, agua y cultivos en el valle de Piura. Piura, Peru. 1942. 61 p., ilus. [2297
Largely a discussion of the water problem.

Fernández Usubillaga, Jorge. Monografía agrícola sintética del Ecuador. Quito. Imp. min. de relaciones exteriores. 1942. 41 p. [2298
A very condensed, authoritative statement regarding agricultural conditions, treating the country by natural regions.

Lermitte, Carlos. Algo sobre climatología médica en sus relaciones con la geografía integral (*Bol. sec. inv. geog.,* tomo 2, no. 5–8, dic., 1942, p. 31–48). [2299

Seuánez y Olivera, R. Riberas de los ríos y arroyos navegables o flotables (*Bol. sec. inv. geog.,* tomo 2, no. 5–8, dic., 1942, p. 109–127). [2300
Deals largely with Uruguayan rivers.

Silva Ferrer, Manuel. Climatopatología. La inadaptación climática del niño y del adulto. Los inadaptados climáticos. Montevideo. Instituto de estudios superiores del Uruguay, Sección de investigaciones geográficas. Tall. gráf. del libro inglés. 1942. 27 p. [2301

Wile, Raymond S. En las montañas entre las cuales corre el Mapiri (*Bol. sec. inv. geog.,* tomo 2, no. 5–8, dic., 1942, p. 131–137). [2302

GEOGRAPHY: BRAZIL

BY

PRESTON E. JAMES

Syracuse University

GENERAL STATEMENT

During the war year of 1943 the contributions of Brazilian writers in the field of geography continued the trend of the past few years by showing a notable increase in both quantity and quality. That geographical studies written philosophically in an office chair are likely to be of second-rate importance, and that field observations carefully recorded and mapped are the basis of all scientific geography are beginning to be widely recognized in Brazil.

The leaders of the profession in Brazil recognize that Brazil needs, first, good, large-scale base maps. The mapping program under Christovam Leite de Castro, secretary of the *Conselho Nacional de Geografia* has been progressing on sound lines, but a very great deal remains to be done. When the necessary large scale maps become available, field studies, which are already being planned, will collect the data and produce the analyses on which the settlement of the land can be guided. Brazil is in the happy position of being able to organize its "regional authorities" largely in advance of settlement.

During the year the very excellent *Revista Brasileira de Geografia* has dropped behind in its schedule of publication. It is earnestly to be hoped that, when world conditions again permit, this excellent periodical will be returned to its schedule with the same high quality.

Meanwhile the Conselho Nacional de Geografia has started the publication of a monthly information bulletin, the *Boletim do Conselho Nacional de Geografia* or, beginning in July 1943, the *Boletim Geográfico*. It is to contain information about geographical studies in Brazil and items of interest to any one who is engaged in the study of Brazilian geography. In each number there will be an extensive bibliography of publications and maps, partly covering older materials and partly dealing with current items. There is the usual long list of decree laws and official resolutions.

BIBLIOGRAPHY

(*See also sections on* Economics: Brazil; *and* Agriculture: Brazil)

GENERAL

Alves, José. O código de minas e o incremento da mineração no Brasil em 1941. Rio de Janeiro. Min. da agricultura, Depto. nacional da produção mineral, Div. de fomento da produção mineral. (Avulso 49). [2303
The mining code of Brazil, and list of concessions granted in 1941.

Barbosa, Octavio, and **Glycon de Paiva.** Relatório da Diretória. Rio de Janeiro. Min. da agricultura, Depto. nacional de produção mineral, Div. de fomento da produção mineral. (Bol. 57). [2304
Report on geologic activities and mineral developments in 1940.

Freitas, M. A. Texeira de. Instituto geográfico e estatístico e os problemas de base do Brasil (*Estadística*, vol. 1, no. 2, June, p. 27-47). [2305
A summary of the objectives and problems of the Instituto Brasileiro de Geografia e Estatística.

Castro, Christovam Leite de. Conselho
nacional de geografia: organização, e realizações (Proc. eighth amer. scien. cong.,
vol. 9, p. 295-313). [2306
Report on the Brazilian Conselho Nacional de Geografia—its organization and accomplishments, by its able secretary.

Marchant, Annie d'Armond. Brazilian
spelling and geographic names (Bull. pan
amer. union, vol. 57, no. 5, May, p. 253-
261). [2307
An attempt to bring order out of chaos.
Reprinted in Jour. geog., vol. 42, no. 6,
Sept., p. 208-215.

Oliveira, Beneval de. No limiar da antropogeografia catarinense (Cultura política,
ano 3, no. 35, dez., p. 163-172). [2308
Notes on geographical studies in Santa
Catarina. Emphasizes need for field studies,
and points to special areas where studies
have been made or are needed.

Os NOVOS TERRITÓRIOS FEDERAIS (Bol. min.
trab. ind. com., ano 10, no. 112, dez., p.
276-293). [2309
Report on the newly created federal territories of Brazil.

Sampaio, Theodoro. Interpretação de alguns nomes tupis usados na geografia nacional (Rev. inst. hist. geog. Rio Grande
do Sul, ano 23, no. 89, primeiro trim., p.
20-65). [2310
On the Indian origin of place names in
Brazil.

Zarur, Jorge. Aspeitos da geografia brasileira (Acta amer., vol. 1, no. 1, Jan.-
March, p. 38-42). [2311
Observations on the development of geographical studies in Brazil.

PHYSICAL AND MATHEMATICAL GEOGRAPHY

Abreu, Frois. Feições morfológicas e
demográficas do litoral do Espírito Santo
(Rev. bras. geog., ano 5, no. 2, abril-junho,
p. 215-234, mapas). [2312
Physical features and geology of the
coast of Espírito Santo. Thin population
of the region attributed to the unattractive
nature of the land.

Almeida, Fernando Flávio Marques de.
Geomorfologia da região de Corumbá
(Bol. assoc. geog. bras., ano 3, no. 3, nov.,
p. 8-18). [2313
Physiographic studies around Corumbá.

Barbosa, Otávio. Geomorfologia da região
de Apiaí (Bol. assoc. geog. bras., ano 3,
no. 3, nov., p. 19-24). [2314
Brief treatment of the landforms of a
part of São Paulo State.

BRASIL 1942. RECURSOS MINERAIS. Rio de
Janeiro. Min. da agricultura, Depto. nacional da produção mineral, Div. de
fomento da produção mineral. (Bol.
56). [2315
Summary of mineral resources in Brazil
for 1942, with map of minerals.

Campos, Luiz Felipe Gonzaga de. Fisiografia da zona ferrífera de Minas Gerais
(Rev. bras. geog., ano 5, no. 2, abril-junho,
p. 241-249). [2316
Brief discussion of the iron-ore region of
Minas Gerais.

A CARTOGRAFIA BRASILEIRA NOS PERIÓDICOS
ESTRANGEIROS, 1836-1885 (Bol. con. nac.
geog., ano 1, no. 1, abril, p. 131-132). [2317
The mapping of Brazil.

Guimarães, Fábio de Macedo Soares.
Esbôço geológico do Brasil (Bol. con. nac.
geog., ano 1, no. 3, junho, p. 40-46). [2318
A brief sketch of the geological formations of Brazil, with simplified sketch map
—a valuable summary.
Reprinted in Bol. min. trab. ind. com.,
ano 10, no. 111, nov., 1943, p. 247-259.

Instituto geográfico e geológico. Compensação dos erros nos trabalhos de triangulação. Nivelamento de precisão. São
Paulo. Sria. da agric. ind. e com. (Bol.
no. 30). 71 p. [2319
A work in technical cartography.

MINAS GERAIS, CENTRO PRODUTOR DE CASSITERITA (Cultura política, ano 3, no. 34,
nov., p. 150-153). [2320
Discusses tin ores of Minas Gerais and
the need for action in their development.

Moura, Pedro de. Bacia do alto Paraguai
(Rev. bras. geog., ano 5, no. 1, jan.-março,
p. 3-38). [2321
A description of the physical geography
of a little-known region—the upper Paraguay Valley—with map.

―――. O relêvo da Amazônia (Rev. bras.
geog., ano 5, no. 3, julho-set., p. 323-
342). [2322
The Amazon terrain.

Oliveira, Américo Leónidas Barbosa de.
O vale Tocantins-Araguaia (Bol. min.
trab. ind. com., ano 9, no. 101, jan., p. 276-
304; no. 102, fev., p. 265-275; no. 103,
março, p. 251-274; no. 104, abril, p. 295-
305; no. 105, maio, p. 298-323; no. 106,
junho, p. 277-285). [2323
A report on the navigability and obstructions to navigation in the Tocantins-Araguaia system. Maps and graphs. Bibliography.

Rambo, Balduino. Aspectos do Brasil,
viagens de estudo (Rev. inst. hist. geog.
Rio Grande do Sul, ano 23, no. 91-92,
tercer trim., p. 21-76). [2324

Rosa, José Vieira da. Serras e litorais do Brasil meridional (*Rev. soc. geog. Rio de Janeiro*, tomo 50, p. 36-49). [2325
A report on the coastal terrain of southern Brazil.

Rosa, Otelo. Rio Pardo (*Rev. inst. hist. geog. Rio Grande do Sul*, ano 23, no. 91-92, segundo seméstre, p. 97-104). [2326

Roxo, Matias G. de Oliveira. Considerações sôbre as formações permo-carboníferas brasileiras (*Rev. bras. geog.*, ano 5, no. 1, jan.-março, p. 39-50). [2327
Characteristics and distribution of permocarboniferous strata in Brazil.

Soares, Lúcio de Castro. Posição geográfica do Brasil (*Bol. con. nac. geog.*, ano 1, no. 2, maio, p. 27-29). [2328
Brazil's position in latitude and longitude. Map of official time zones.

Sousa, Henrique Cáper Alves de. As bêtas e a cassiterita de São João del Rei (*Rev. bras. geog.*, ano 5, no. 2, abril-junho, p. 195-214). [2329
Tin ores near São João del Rei.

―――. Crômo em Piuí. Rio de Janeiro. Min. da agricultura, Depto. nacional da produção mineral, Div. de fomento da produção mineral. (Avulso 50). [2330
Occurrence of chrome ore in Minas Gerais.

Spalding, Walter. La laguna de los Patos y la barra del Río Grande (*Rev. geog. amer.*, año 9, vol. 19, no. 113, feb., p. 111-113). [2331

Teixeira, Emilio Alves. Zircônio em Poços de Caldas. Rio de Janeiro. Min. da agricultura, Depto. nacional da produção mineral, Div. de fomento da produção mineral. (Bol. 55). [2332
Occurrence of zirconium in Minas Gerais.

Várzea, Afonso. Relêvo do Brasil (*Bol. min. trab. ind. com.*, ano 10, no. 110, out., p. 282-298). [2333
Outline of the surface configuration of Brazil.

Vieira, Nuno R. Passado e presente da mineração (*Obs. econ. fin.*, ano 8, no. 94, nov., p. 33-50). [2334
Geographical distribution and different types of mines of metallic and non-metallic minerals in Brazil. [R. Simonsen]

ECONOMIC AND REGIONAL GEOGRAPHY

Alexander, J. L. The Matto and Campos of southern Brazil (*Geog. mag.*, vol. 15, no. 10, Feb., p. 492-499, map). [2335
Description of a brief visit.

Broca, Brito. Diamantina (*Cultura política*, ano 3, no. 29, julho, p. 133-138). [2336
Report on the town of Diamantina.

Carvalho, Maria Conceição Vicente de. O pescador no litoral leste do estado de São Paulo (*Rev. arq. mun.*, São Paulo, ano 9, vol. 92, agôsto-set., p. 31-46). [2337
Notes on the way of living of a little-known group of fishing people on the São Paulo littoral.

Cidade, F. de Paulo. Aspectos geo-humanos de Mato Grosso: Corumbá (*Rev. bras. geog.*, ano 5, no. 2, abril-junho, p. 3-21). [2338
The communication between São Paulo and Corumbá: the geographical environment and communication facilities. Corumbá, the chief population center in the region of the *pantanal* (swamp). Description of the town and of the human element. [R. Simonsen]

A CIDADE DO AÇO (*Cultura política*, ano 3, no. 32, set., p. 224-238). [2339
Good report on the steel center of Volta Redonda.

A COLONIZAÇÃO AGRÍCOLA (*Cultura política*, ano 3, no. 35, dez., p. 184-195). [2340
Report on several agricultural colonies of Brazil.

CUIABÁ (*Cultura política*, ano 3, no. 33, out., p. 225-236). [2341
Report on the city of Cuiabá.

DADOS DEMOGRÁFICOS SÔBRE O ESTADO DE MATO GROSSO (*Bol. con. nac. geog.*, ano 1, no. 2, maio, p. 34-36). [2342
Population of Mato Grosso.

DIVISÃO REGIONAL DO BRASIL (*Bol. con. nac. geog.*, ano 1, no. 1, abril, p. 35-40). [2343
Further discussion of the regional divisions of Brazil.

Fairbanks, João Carlos. A altitude geográfica como fator de povoamento (*Bol. min. trab. ind. com.*, ano 10, no. 110, out., p. 265-281). [2344
Relation of lines of communication and centers of settlement to the landforms of Brazil.

Franca, Arí. Aspectos do povoamento da noroeste. A região de Pirajuí (*Bol. assoc. geog. bras.*, ano 3, no. 3, nov., p. 49-57). [2345
Types of people and settlement in the Northeast.

Gibson, Christopher H. Through Paraguay and southern Matto Grosso (*Nat. geog. mag.*, vol. 84, no. 4, Oct., p. 459-488, map). [2346
The story of a trip through the southern part of interior Brazil.

Giovanetti, Bruno. Esboço histórico da Alta Sorocabana. São Paulo. Ed. do autor. [2347

Collection of a series of articles published in the press of the Alta Sorocabana District on the development of this area in the State of São Paulo, emphasizing the geographical environment, the settlement and the evolution of its towns. [R. Simonsen]

Graves, Norma Ryland. The rubber metropolis of the Amazon (*Travel*, vol. 81, no. 6, Oct., p. 6–9). [2348

Description of Manaus.

Henius, Frank. Oil from the Amazon. From the trees of the great Amazon Valley may come the vegetable oils for the western hemisphere (*Amer. forests*, vol. 49, no. 2, Feb., p. 60–62). [2349

Sketch of the vegetable oil sources potentially available in the Amazon region.

Instituto histórico e geográphico brasileiro. Tipos e aspectos do Brasil. Rio de Janeiro. Serviço gráfico IBGE. [2351

Descriptive.

Leitão, Cândido de Melo. Fauna amazônica (*Rev. bras. geog.*, ano 5, no. 3, julho–set., p. 343–370). [2352

Animals of the Amazon.

Lima, Araújo. A explotação amazônica (*Rev. bras. geog.*, ano 5, no. 3, julho–set., p. 371–418). [2353

Development of Amazon resources.

Mendes, Renato da Silveira. A conquista do solo na Baixada Fluminense (*Rev. arq. mun.*, São Paulo, ano 8, vol. 89, março–abril, p. 175–189). [2354

Reclamation of wet lands in Rio de Janeiro State.

Monbeig, Pierre. Comentário em tôrno do mapa da evolução da população do Estado de São Paulo entre 1934 e 1940 (*Bol. assoc. geog. bras.*, ano 3, no. 3, nov., p. 42–48). [2355

Population changes in São Paulo.

———. Notes relatives à l'évolution des paysages ruraux dans l'état de São Paulo (*Proc. eighth amer. scien. cong.*, vol. 9, p. 175–179). [2356

Notes on the rural landscapes of São Paulo State.

Müller, João Pedro. Madeiras do Brasil (*Cultura política*, ano 3, no. 25, março, p. 100–111). [2357

Brazilian forest resources.

Namm, Benjamin H. São Paulo, the fastest-growing city in the world (*Bull. pan amer. union*, vol. 77, no. 10, Oct., p. 541–550). [2358

Description of São Paulo.

NITEROI (*Cultura política*, ano 3, no. 32, set., p. 192–206, mapa). [2359

Report on the capital of Rio de Janeiro State.

Oliveira, Avelino Inácio de. Recursos minerais da Amazônia (*Obs. econ. fin.*, ano 8, no. 89, junho, p. 18–30). [2360

Minerals obtained in the Amazon Valley. Places and conditions of production. [R. Simonsen]

Oliveira, Beneval de. O Brasil e a floresta (*Cultura política*, ano 3, no. 30, agôsto, p. 69–84). [2361

The forests of Brazil—their use and destruction by man.

———. Faces da economia destrutiva e o problema da ocupação do solo (*Cultura política*, ano 3, no. 26, abril, p. 43–50). [2362

Remarks on the economy of destructive exploitation in Brazil and its results in the pattern of settlement.

———. Pontos de apoio para o aproveitamento do São Francisco (*Cultura política*, ano 3, no. 34, nov., p. 159–165). [2363

Lack of development of São Francisco valley due to neglect of large landowners.

Pan American union. Travel division. Recife. Washington. (Ports and harbors of Brazil series). 14 p., illus. [2364

Descriptive.

Pereira, Altamirano Nunes. As matas e as madeiras do Brasil (*Cultura política*, ano 3, no. 26, abril, p. 51–68). [2365

Forests and timber of Brazil.

Pinto, Luis. O rio Paraíba-do-Norte fixador humano (*Rev. soc. geog. Rio de Janeiro*, tomo 50, p. 76–87). [2366

Settlement in the Northeast.

Simmons, Anna G. E. Babassu nut. (*Econ. geog.*, vol. 19, no. 3, July, p. 279–282, maps). [2367

Description of the distribution and exploitation of the babassu nuts.

Soper, F. L., and D. B. Wilson. *Anopheles gambiae* in Brazil, 1930 to 1940. New York. Rockefeller foundation. 262 p., maps, photos. [2368

A complete account of the invasion of *anopheles gambiae* from Africa, its spread in the Northeast of Brazil, and the measures taken to combat and eliminate it. A detailed glimpse of the complex factors in the geography of disease.

O VALE DO RIO DOCE (*Cultura política*, ano 3, no. 35, dez., p. 122–133). [2369

An important study of the development of the Rio Doce route for the export of the iron ores of central Minas Gerais. Illustrated by maps. Brings history of negotiations for use of this route up to 1930. Later negotiations to be included in January number of 1944.

Varzea, Afonso. Alta bacia do São Francisco (*Obs. econ. fin.*, ano 8, no. 90, julho, p. 68–79). [2370
The geographical environment and its possibilities in the upper São Francisco basin. [R. Simonsen]

——. Geografia do açucar no leste do Brasil. Rio de Janeiro. Gráf. Rio arte. 462 p. [2371
Human geographical study of the sugar area extending from Baia de Todos os Santos to Ceará analysing the agricultural economical and social situation of this crop.

Geographical discription of the region. Maps and photographs. [R. Simonsen]

——. O tempo na bacia do São Francisco (*Obs. econ. fin.*, ano 8, no. 95, dez., p. 59–72). [2372
The São Francisco Basin; the geographical environment, settlement possibilities and economic exploitation. [R. Simonsen]

Vidal, Ademar. A mineração do ouro no Nordeste (*Cultura política*, ano 3, no. 32, set., p. 34–43). [2373
Gold mining in the Northeast.

GOVERNMENT

BY

JAMES B. CHILDS

Library of Congress

AND

RUSSELL H. FITZGIBBON

University of California at Los Angeles

GENERAL STATEMENT

It is possibly the exigencies of publication during wartime that appear to have reduced the number of items dealing with Government in the Latin American States that were published during 1943. Not only has the volume of such publication been reduced but on the whole the various items present little in the way of pronounced trends.

Perhaps as distinguishing a feature as any during the course of the year was the publication of several items dealing with the celebration of the ninetieth anniversary of the Argentine Constitution. This occurred in April and May of 1943, just a few weeks, ironically, before a further departure from the practice of constitutional government in that country.

Developments in the field of public administration in Brazil continue to attract the attention of writers. It is in order to note, perhaps, that plans are under way for the translation and publication of some of these studies in the United States, but nothing is yet available for inclusion in the appropriate issue of the *Handbook*.

The undersigned is indebted to Mr. Joe Toyoshima, for assistance in examination of some of the materials recorded in this section. [Russell H. Fitzgibbon]

As a part of the preparation for the Second Book Fair at México, D. F., in the spring of 1943, a presidential instruction requested the cooperation of the *Secretarías* and other agencies of the government of Mexico in producing catalogs of their official publications. The two most pretentious of these cover the Secretaría de Relaciones Exteriores and Secretaría de Hacienda beginning with the period of independence. That for the Secretaría de Comunicaciones y Obras Públicas covers the period from its establishment in 1891 to 1943. That for the Secretaría de la Economía Nacional begins with its establishment in 1933. That for the Secretaría de la Defensa Nacional is also extensive. And there are several others. Taken as a whole these catalogs or checklists represent one of the most substantial recent contributions made to government document bibliography in any of the other American republics. In México, the following still remain to be covered: official gazette, Congreso Nacional, Secretaría de Agricultura y Fomento, Secretaría de Educación Pública, Secretaría de Gobernación, Secretaría de Marina, and the Poder Judicial.

Another contribution is to be found in the *Relatório* of the Imprensa Nacional of Brazil for the years 1939–1942, which lists by title all publications of the Brazilian government printed by it during those years.

Argentina in 1943 has undergone a very considerable number of changes in governmental organization. These have in good part revolved about the Ministerio de Agricultura and the various agencies connected with it. That reorganization has continued well along into 1944. Extensive welfare and charitable functions attached to the Ministerio de Relaciones Exteriores y Culto have been transferred to Ministerio del Interior and merged with the Departamento Nacional de Higiene to form the Dirección Nacional de Salud Pública y Asistencia Social. Since the number of ministries has been fixed in the Constitution, the device of "Secretaría" set up with the rank of Ministry by executive decree, has been used to deal with problems of increasing importance. The Secretaría de la Presidencia was organized to have control over information, press and propaganda. The Secretaría del Trabajo y Previsión incorporated the Departamento Nacional del Trabajo, the Comisión Nacional de Casas Baratas, la Dirección de Inmigración, and other agencies from the Ministerio del Interior as well as the social security funds from the Ministerio de Hacienda.

In Peru the Ministerio de Agricultura was authorized and organized. The Ministerio de Aeronáutica, which had been authorized in 1941 as an offshoot from the Ministerio de Marina y Aviación was also organized at the beginning of the war.

In Paraguay the ministries were reorganized, the Ministerio de Industria y Comercio being created as the ninth executive department.

In México, the Secretaría de la Asistencia Pública was through the incorporation of the autonomous Departmento de Salubridad Pública transformed into the Secretaría de Salubridad y Asistencia.

In Nicaragua the Secretaría de la Presidencia was created with the rank of a cabinet department.

In Colombia, the law of March 2, 1943, gave the President of the republic authority to reorganize the various branches of the administration.

The government corporation seems increasingly favored as a means of handling problems demanding considerable flexibility. In Peru two such corporations have been organized. One of these, the Corporación Peruana del Santa, was formed for the development of the Santa Valley north of Lima. The other, Corporación Peruana de Aeropuertos y Aviación Comercial, is to develop commercial aviation and facilities on a nationwide scale. In Brazil a soda industry company was formed, and in Paraguay a meat industry company. On the other hand, in Venezuela the coffee institute was liquidated and its functions transferred to existing agencies.

In the field of social security organizations there is continuing development. Paraguay created a national social security institute. In Cuba the number of special funds was increased by the establishment of the Retiro Médico.

In the field of education some changes may be mentioned. In México a Colegio Nacional was authorized to consist of twenty eminent Mexicans to lecture in their special fields. In Haiti a university council was formed consisting of representatives of the professional and scientific schools, being preliminary to the establishment of a national university. In Ecuador the Junta Universitaria at Loja was raised to the rank of a University. In Uruguay, a faculty of humanities was added to the University of the Republic.

In Panama the recently established national university was designated as an Inter-American university. National Indian institutes were created in Nicaragua and in El Salvador corresponding to the Inter-American Indian Institute in México. More and more these changes call attention to the need in many ways for detailed study and analysis, not only of national governmental organization but also of the Inter-American instrumentalities in various fields. [J. B. Childs]

BIBLIOGRAPHY

(See also sections on History, International Relations, and Law)

GENERAL

(See also item 158)

Betancourt, Félix. Sobre reglamentación legal de los partidos políticos (*Univ. Antioquia*, tomo 15, no. 57, feb.–marzo, p. 43–49). [2374]
The mission of the democratic state, in contrast to the nazi-fascist system, is to safeguard and improve the individual. Between extreme individualism and absolute *etatismo* is a compromise condition involving legal regulation of the political parties.

Ireland, Gordon. Las constituciones latinoamericanas (*Rev. parlamentaria*, año 11, no. 134, mayo, p. 3–18). [2375]
Brief summaries of the constitutional development of Argentina, Brazil, Colombia, Cuba, Chile, Mexico, Panama, Paraguay, Peru, Uruguay, and Venezuela.

Lorca Rojas, Gustavo. La administración comunal. Valparaíso. 169, vi p. [2376]
A thesis presented to the University of Chile. The author discusses such subjects as general concepts of administration; municipal agencies, powers, property, and revenues; the position of the *alcalde*; the municipal civil service. The short bibliography is drawn almost entirely from Chilean, Argentine, Spanish, and French materials. The study is not documented.

Maglione, Eduardo F. La autonomía municipal es la base de la organización política del país (*Bol. hon. consejo deliberante*, año 5, tomo 8, no. 37–38, p. 13–17). [2377]
The author argues for municipal autonomy because "all the world appears headed toward governments based on unification and force."

Moran, Carlos M. Intermunicipal cooperation in the Americas (*Publ. management* Chicago, vol. 25, no. 12, Dec., p. 354–356). [2378]

Pasquel, Leonardo. Las constituciones de América: textos íntegros vigentes. México. 2 vols. [2379]
A handy compilation of the Spanish texts of all the American constitutions including those of Canada and Puerto Rico. For Dominican Republic reproduces the constitution of 1934 instead of 1942, and for a few countries such as Brazil, Guatemala and Uruguay omits the more recent constitutional amendments.

Serrato, José. Concepto de gobierno y los problemas contemporáneos (*Rev. nac.*, Montevideo, año 6, tomo 24, no. 70, oct., p. 25–29). [2380]
State intervention in various phases of life will free man and release creative enterprise.

Silva, Benedicto. Teoria dos departamentos de administração geral (*Rev. serv. públ.*, ano 6, vol. 1, no. 1, jan., p. 10–13; vol. 2, no. 2, maio, p. 11–14). [2381]

Uriarte, Amanda Cajina. Dinámica de la democracia americana. Síntesis histórico-política de todamérica. Habana. Ed. Ucar, García & cía. 281 p., ilus. [2383]
The study is divided into five parts: the United States, Bolivarian America, the Nations of the South, Mexico and the Antilles, and Central America. It offers a convenient summary, though not much more than that, of historical development and political ideas.

Wainer, Jacobo. Racionalización administrativa. Buenos Aires. Ed. Argentina de finanzas y administración. 161 p. [2384]
Contains three addresses, an article and supplementary material. The first address deals with general principles, the second with "Estatuto de empleado público," and the third with "La misión de los técnicos en ciencias económicas."

ARGENTINA

Amadeo, Santos P. Argentine constitutional law. The judicial function in the maintenance of the federal system and the preservation of individual rights. Foreword by L. S. Rowe. New York. Columbia univ. press. (Columbia univ., Faculty of law, Columbia legal studies, no. 4). 243 p. [2385]
An excellent study by a member of the faculty of the University of Puerto Rico

of the Argentine courts' decisions in the fields of federal-provincial government relations, criminal procedure, civil liberties and economic interests. The dissimilarities in theory and practice of the Argentine constitution from that of the United States are emphasized, although Argentine recurrence to United States Supreme Court decisions is marked, particularly in regard to property rights. A table of the cases referred to is appended.

Andrea, Miguel de. Justicia social, estado corporativo o democracia corporativa? Buenos Aires. Ed. Difusión. 22 p. [2386
A brief address given by the Bishop of Temnos to the Argentine Federation of Professional Catholic Associations of Nurses at Buenos Aires, November 22, 1943.

Andreozzi, Manuel. Facultades implícitas de investigación legislativa y privilegios parlamentarios. Buenos Aires. Ed. Ideas. 611 p. [2387
An examination of the situation at national as well as state and provincial levels that should do much to the understanding of the common parliamentary problems of the American countries. The author is a professor of administrative law at Tucumán, a former speaker of the Tucumán provincial chamber of deputies. and a former member of the Argentine chamber of deputies.

Barros Hurtado, César. Hacia una democracia orgánica. Contribución al estudio de una ley reglamentaria de las actividades de los partidos. Prólogo de B. Mirkine-Guetzevitch. Buenos Aires. Ed. Impulso. 366 p. [2388
A study of Argentine political parties and their internal organization, particularly since 1931. Various proposed plans of reform are reviewed, and the Argentine parties are compared to those of the United States. He wants the state to regulate their activities in order to save them from themselves and to promote an "organic democracy." Draft of law is given.

Bielsa, Rafael. El órden político y las garantías jurisdiccionales. Separación de poderes y vigencia del derecho. Buenos Aires. Imp. de la Univ. nac. del Litoral. 194 p. [2389
In this volume the author, a well-known Argentine scholar, studies the principle of the division of powers, the differentiation between powers and functions, problems of sovereignty and legality, the question of the legitimacy of *de facto* power, judicial independence, and other topics.

Carulla, Juan E. Genio de la Argentina. Deberes frente a la crisis político-social de nuestro pueblo. Buenos Aires. Distr. R. Medina & cía. 231 p. [2390
A synthesis of the thought and work of a well-known Argentine journalist and writer. It includes essays on doctrine and politics, international policy, the Argentine family, and problems of the population.

Catamarca (prov.). Gobernador. Mensaje del gobernador de Catamarca, Ernesto M. Andrada, al inaugurar el período ordinario de sesiones de la h. Legislatura 1943. Catamarca. 71 p. [2391

Córdoba (prov.). Gobernador. Mensaje leído por s. e. el señor gobernador de la provincia, dr. Santiago H. del Castilla, ante la h. Legislatura el 1° de mayo de 1943. Córdoba. 77 p. [2392

Díaz Doin, Guillermo. Diccionario político de nuestro tiempo; político-biográfico-económico-sociológico. Buenos Aires. Ed. Mundo atlántico. 557 p. [2394

ESTATUTO DEL SERVICIO CIVIL DE LA NACIÓN. Buenos Aires. Imp. del Congreso nacional. 64 p. [2395
The text of the decree no. 16,672, December 16, 1943, and decree no. 16,673, December 16, 1943, making the *Estatuto* applicable also in the provincial and the local governments. Preceded by a report from Carlos Gabriel Delfino, Auditor General de Guerra y Marina to the Secretaria de la Presidencia de la Nación.
The new *Estatuto* is applicable to all permanent civil personnel. Each of the agencies is to appoint a Junta de Calificación, and there is to be a national body, the Consejo del Servicio Civil de la Nación (Ministerio del Interior), with five members. The chairman of the Consejo is to be appointed by the Executive branch of the Government.

Fayt, Carlos S. Fuentes de la constitución argentina. Juicio crítico de A. Walter Villegas. Prólogo de Jorge Eduardo Coll. Buenos Aires. Ed. Dovile. 94 p. [2396
After tracing many social and other factors of Argentine life and the constitutional models used, the author concludes that the Constitution is venerable but not venerated and is in need of modernization.

Gollán (h.), Josué. Elogio a la Constitución nacional. Santa Fe. Univ. nac. del Litoral. (Insto. social, Col. La Constitución argentina, no. 6). 13, v p. [2397
A eulogy of the constitution of 1853 by the rector of the Universidad Nacional del Litoral. The university began a series of studies of the Argentine constitution in 1936.

———. Homenaje a la constitución nacional en su nonagésimo aniversario. Santa Fe. Imp. de la Univ. nac. del Litoral. 22 p. [2398
Record of the proceedings of a commemorative session April 3, 1943, honoring the 90th anniversary of the Argentine constitution. Remarks by the rector, Dr. Gollán, and by Dr. Carlos Saavedra Lamas, rector of the Universidad de Buenos Aires

and former Minister of Foreign Relations of Argentina.

Greca, Alcides. Derecho y ciencia de la administración municipal. Segunda ed. Santa Fe. Imp. de la Univ., 4 vols. [2399
This is a very important work dealing in comprehensive fashion with the various phenomena of urbanism; the first edition was published in 1937. Vol. 1 considers sociological and demographic aspects of cities; vol. 2 treats of historical antecedents, administration, and social welfare; vol. 3 deals with juridical and financial aspects, and public services; and vol. 4 with Argentine municipalities.

Loza Colomer, Carlos A. El problema de la intermunicipalidad (*Rev. prob. arg. amer.*, no. 2, julio, p. 69–80). [2400
Taking as his starting point the First Pan-American Congress of Municipalities at Havana in 1938, the author discusses problems of organization of an intermunicipal association in Argentina.

Melo, Carlos R. Los partidos políticos argentinos. Córdoba. Imp. de la Univ. nac. de Córdoba. 54 p. [2401
The study is principally historical. It traces party development from the time of Alberdi in the 1850s. The treatment of the last few years is sketchy.

Mendoza (prov.). Gobernador. Mensaje del Gobernador de Mendoza, Adolfo A. Vicchi al inaugurarse el período ordinario de sesiones de la h. Legislatura. Mendoza, junio de 1943. Mendoza. Imp. oficial. xliii, 352 p. [2402
Principally a summary of the reports of the provincial ministries for the previous year.

Ministerio del interior. Anteproyecto de código político. Buenos Aires. Imp. del Congreso nac. 203 p. [2403
Proposed electoral code prepared for public discussion.

Molinas, Nicanor. La constitución nacional. Santa Fe. Univ. nac. del litoral, Insto. social (La Constitución argentina, no. 7). 21 p. [2404
Lecture delivered on May 26, 1943, on the 90th anniversary of the promulgation of the national constitution.

Podestá, Roberto A. Antecedentes y puntos de vista para una revisión constitucional. Buenos Aires. Ed. Inti. 199 p. [2405
The winner of a 1942 prize established by the Comisión Nacional de Cultura expounds his evolutionist views and suggests constitutional changes. Includes drafts of proposed revisions of various sections of the constitution.

Rabuffetti, Luis Ernesto. El dogma radical. Buenos Aires. Tall. gráf. J. Hays Bell. 350 p. [2406
Prof. Rabuffetti traces briefly the historical development of the Unión Radical, but most of the volume is devoted to an analysis of its political and economic doctrines.

Rodríguez Arias, Julio C. Relaciones de las entidades autárquicas con la administración central. Mendoza. Ed. Best hños. 77 p. [2407
The legal, financial, and administrative relationship of independent government agencies to the central administration. Argentine examples are cited.

Salta (prov.). Gobernador. Mensaje leído ante la h. Asamblea legislativa por el excmo. señor gobernador de la provincia de Salta, dr. Ernesto M. Araoz, el día 1° de mayo de 1943. Salta. Tall. gráf. Cárcel penitenciaria. 206 p. [2408
Principally a summary of the reports of the provincial ministries for the previous year. On pages 35–37 there is mention of the conference between federal provincial representatives concerning police coordination.

Santa Fe (prov.). Gobernador. Mensaje del gobernador de Santa Fe, dr. Joaquín Argonz, al inaugurarse el período ordinario de sesiones de la honorable Legislatura, el 10 de abril de 1943. Santa Fe. Tall. gráf. de la provincia. 204 p. [2409
Includes a table of elections in December, 1942.

Sayán de Vidaurre, Alberto. De la llamada democracia a la verdadera democracia. Prólogo por Juan Estéban Vacarezza. Estudio prologar por Ricardo Carrasco. Buenos Aires. Union nac. y democrática interamericana. 223 p. [2410
By social action on a national and inter-American scale, centered around the United States, the author proposes to attain true democracy and put an end to social upheavals.

Seco Villalba, José Armando. Fuentes de la constitución argentina. Prólogo de Alberto Padilla. Buenos Aires. Ed. Depalma. 295 p., ilus. [2411
One of the several volumes commemorating the ninetieth anniversary of the Argentine Constitution. The author's early chapters deal with questions of libertarian ideas and their expansion, natural law, public constitutional law. He then deals with early constitutional ventures in Argentina, 1813, 1815, 1819, 1826, and 1852–1854. The Constitution is reprinted with an article-by-article annotation of sources and antecedents.

Silva, Carlos Alberto. El poder legislativo de la nación argentina. Tomo 4: Organización nacional, 1854–1861. Gestión económico-financiera (primera parte). Buenos Aires. Imp. del Congreso nac. 780 p., láms. [2412
Takes up first the Estatuto para la Organización de le Hacienda y Crédito

Público, then banks, next money, further budgets and finally revenue.

Storni, Horacio Julio. El parlamentarismo y la representación corporativa. Buenos Aires. Ed. Valerio Abeledo. 130 p. [2413

Unión cívica radical. Memoria del H. Comité nacional a la H. Convención nacional (abril 1942 a enero 1943). Buenos Aires. 35 p. [2414

Universidad nacional del Litoral. Instituto de investigaciones jurídico-políticas. Estudios sobre la constitución nacional argentina. Santa Fe. Imp. de la Univ. nac. del Litoral. 639 p. [2415
A series of papers delivered at the Universidad Nacional del Litoral, Santa Fe, on the occasion of the nineteeth anniversary of the Argentine Constitution of 1853. The topics discussed include "The National Constitution and Political Rights," "Constitutional Limits of the Police Power," "The State of Siege," and "The State of Law and Equilibrium among the Branches in the Argentine Constitution."

Vigo, Salvador C. El régimen municipal de la constitución y las leyes orgánicas municipales. Santa Fe. Imp. de la Univ. nac. del Litoral. 35 p. [2416
A survey of the pattern of municipal government, as to organization, suffrage, councils, powers, fiscal control, incorporation, etc. Draft of proposed changes in the constitution of Santa Fe, as it affects "municipios."

BOLIVIA

BOLETÍN OFICIAL. Sección compiladora del Ministerio de gobierno. La Paz. Ed. del Estado. Año 1, no. 1, enero—. [2417
Includes laws, decrees and ministerial orders of permanent character. Monthly official gazette. There has been no official gazette since the suspension of the *Gaceta Oficial de la República de Bolivia* with año 5, no. 131, julio 2, 1928.

Montellano, Carlos, and **Julián V. Montellano.** La justicia boliviana al servicio de la masonería. Acusación contra tres miembros de la Corte suprema de justicia. Prólogo de Augusto Céspedes. La Páz. Ed. Trabajo. 68 p. [2418
Concerning cases arising from the article proposed for the 1938 Constitution prohibiting membership by public officials in secret entities or domestic or international groups that the State does not recognize.

Presidente. Mensaje al h. Congreso ordinario de 1943. La Paz. Imp. ed. Universo. 238 p. [2419
This message of President Enrique Peñaranda is mainly a summary of the activities of the ministries.

Revilla Q., Alfredo. Ponencia presentada al Congreso de municipalidades (*Universidad*, Potosí, año 6, no. 9, abril-junio, p. 855-863). [2420

BRAZIL

ADMINISTRAÇÃO PÚBLICA. Órgão do Departamento do serviço público do estado de São Paulo. São Paulo. Imp. do Estado. Año 1, no. 1, março—. ' [2421
A public administration monthly stressing to a considerable extent problems facing São Paulo.

Amazonas (estado). Departamento estadual de estatística. Prontuário geral da divisão administrativa e judiciária do estado. Manáus. 26 p. [2422
Gives tables of the administrative and judicial districts in accordance with decree-laws 176, December 1, 1938, and 984, February 2, 1943.

———. **Interventor federal.** Exposição ao excelentíssimo senhor doutor Getúlio Vargas, presidente da república, por Alvaro Maia, interventor federal. Maio de 1942-maio de 1943. Manáus. Ed. Depto. estadual de imprensa e propaganda. 138 p. [2423

Andrade, Almir de. As diretrizes da nova política do Brasil (*Cultura política*, ano 3, no. 23, jan., p. 7-19). [2424
A lecture delivered before the National Institute of Political Science on December 19, 1942. A philosophical consideration of various Brazilian domestic and international political problems with special reference to democracy and liberty.

Arrais, Monte. Aspectos da constituição brasileira (*Cultura política*, ano 3, no. 32, set., p. 10-24). [2425
Arrais in this article considers various features of the Brazilian constitutional system of 1937 and compares them with that of 1891 and with corresponding features of the United States system.

———. Da origem e estrutura dos poderes na constituição de 1937 (*Cultura política*, ano 3, no. 35, dez., p. 79-98). [2426
On the differences between the constitutional system of 1937 and its predecessor, the organization of the legislature, suffrage, and electoral norms and processes.

———. A forma federativa e a constituição de 10 de novembro de 1937. A posição constitucional das fôrças armadas (*Cultura política*, ano 3, no. 33, out., p. 34-37). [2427
A documented article in which the author, a former federal deputy considers the structure of the branches of government, federal competence, interstate relations, and various problems relating to the

armed forces. Most of his references are to United States publications.

Conselho nacional de geografia. Boletim do Conselho nacional de geografia. Instituto brasileiro de geografia e estatística. Informações, notícias, bibliografia, legislação. Mensário. Rio de Janeiro. Ano 1, no. 1, abril—. [2428
Monthly information bulletin containing a "Quadro geral da administração pública brasileira," being a current but brief directory of the national government, the state governments, and the municipal governments. Also includes each month a list of all Brazilian decree-laws with references to the *Diário oficial*.

CONSTITUIÇÃO DA REPÚBLICA DOS ESTADOS UNIDOS DO BRASIL, PROMULGADA EM 10 DE NOVEMBRO DE 1937, COM AS EMENDAS ODENADAS PELAS LEIS CONSTITUCIONAIS NOS. 1-2-3-4-5-6-7 E 8, ACOMPANHADA DE UM ÍNDICE REMISSIVO E ALFABÉTICO. Quarta ed. São Paulo. Livr. académica, Saraiva & cia. (Legislação brasileira, Bibl. da Livr. académica). 136 p. [2429

Costa, Odorico. A dissolução dos partidos políticos brasileiros (*Cultura política*, ano 3, no. 34, nov., p. 166–176). [2430
The writer, director of the Official Press of the State of Goiaz, defends the dissolution of Brazilian political parties in 1937.

———. Os municípios goianos no estado nacional (*Cultura política*, ano 3, no. 32, set., p. 28–33). [2431
A short article dealing with the municipalities in the state of Goiaz. The author briefly traces developments from the first legislation in 1828. "The Brazilian municipality," he says, "was born with a sad sense of inferiority."

Curitiba. Prefeitura municipal de Curitiba. Decretos-leis e decretos de 1942. Curitiba. Emp. gráf. Paranaense. 179 p. [2432
Annual volume of municipal ordinances and regulations.

Departamento administrativo do serviço público. Circulares da secretaria da presidencia da república, 1937–1942. Rio de Janeiro. Imp. nacional. 100 p. [2433

———. Relatório, 1942. Rio de Janeiro. Imp. nacional. xv, 645 p. [2434
Considers organizational changes in the various agencies, budgetary problems, personnel problems, material and supply problems, and various other matters handled by the general administrative department in 1942.

Espírito Santo (estado). Interventor federal. Relatório apresentado ao excelentíssimo senhor presidente da república, pelo major João Punaro Bley, interventor federal no estado do Espírito Santo. Vitória. Imp. oficial. 228 p. [2435
Apparently covers the period November, 1937 through 1942. Includes at end (p. 213–228) a report on the city of Vitória.

Leite, João Barbosa. O aperfeiçoamento físico do funcionário público. Rio de Janeiro. Tip. Batista de Souza. (Min. da educação e saúde, Depto. nac. da educação, Div. da educação física). 30 p. [2436
Conferência realizada em 28 de março de 1943; debates pelos srs. A. de C. Fernandes, M. C. de Mendonça e E. Cruz. [M. B. Lourenço Filho]

Macedonia, Leonardo. Notícia sôbre a organização política, administrativa e judiciária do Rio Grande do Sul (*Rev. inst. hist. geog. Rio Grande do Sul*, ano 23, no. 90, segundo trim., p. 159–167). [2437
A study "written in 1934" of the organization and distribution of powers in the state under the monarchy and the republic.

Machado, Alexandre Marcondes. O momento constitucional brasileiro. Rio de Janeiro. Imp. Nacional. 27 p. [2438
A lecture by a Cabinet minister before the administrative council of State on some of the problems emanating from the Constitution of 1937—the plebiscite, the economic order, presidential powers, national sovereignity, etc.

Magalhães, Celso de. O I. B. G. E. (*Rev. serv. públ.*, ano 6, vol. 4, no. 1, out., p. 31–36). [2439
A consideration of the status of the Instituto Brasileiro de Geografia e Estatística in connection with the use of the term *para-estatal*.

Magalhães, Lucia. Educação e funcionalismo (*Formação*, ano 5, no. 59, junho, p. 15–29). [2440
Estudo dos problemas que á educação propõem as provas práticas de seleção e aperfeiçoamento dos servidores públicos.[M. B. Lourenço Filho]

Maranhão (estado). Interventor federal. Relatório apresentado ao exmo. sr. Presidente da república, pelo interventor federal no estado. Exercício—1942. San Luiz. Ed. do Diretória de estatística e publicidade. 215 p. [2441

Medeiros, Océlio de. Um caso objetivo de análise: a reorganização administrativa do territorio do Acre (*Rev. serv. públ.*, ano 6, vol. 4, no. 1, oct., p. 19–30). [2442
"Excerto dos originais do livro *Política Territorial*."

Pará (estado). Interventor federal. Relatório apresentado ao excmo. sr. presidente da república pelo dr. José Carneiro da Gama Malcher, interventor federal do Pará, 1940–1941. Belém, Para. Oficinas

gráf. do Insto. Lauro Sodré. 228 p., láms., cartas. [2443
Covers the two years 1940 and 1941, and includes "Reorganização da administração pública," p. 41–45.

Pessôa Sobrinho, Eduardo Pinto. Administração de pessoal nos estados e municípios (*Rev. serv. publ.,* ano 6, vol. 2, no. 1, abril, p. 51–54). [2444
The author is an administrative technician.

Prazeres, Oto. As dissoluções do Parlamento brasileiro (*Cultura política,* ano 3, no. 34, nov., p. 195–210). [2445

Ramos, Arlindo Vieira. Notas sôbre o estudo da personalidade em administração (*Rev. serv. públ.,* ano 6, vol. 1, no. 3, março, p. 16–36). [2446
Importância do problema em face dos princípios e das práticas da administração. [M. B. Lourenço Filho]

Ramos, Floriano Augusto. Departamento administrativo do estado de São Paulo (*Rev. serv. publ.,* ano 6, vol. 2, no. 1, abril, p. 43–50). [2447
An analysis, in outline form. Some of the departmental forms used in São Paulo are reproduced. General administrative departments were installed in the states of Brazil by decree law 1,202, April 8, 1939.

REVISTA DO SERVIÇO PÚBLICO. Órgão de interesse da administração. Rio de Janeiro. Ano 6, vol. 1, no. 1–3, jan.–março; vol. 2, no. 1–3, abril–junho; vol. 3, no. 1–3, julho–set.; vol. 4, no. 1–3, out.–dez. 100 cruzeiros per year, foreign subscription. [2448
Monthly. Founded in 1937. Paulo Lopes Corrêa, editor. Voluminous monthly journal. Furnishes official interpretation of the development and political tendencies of the "New State." Articles on social progress, labor legislation, housing, international affairs. Reports on the decisions of the state controlled syndicalist system; also statistical information covering all the government departments. [R. Simonsen]

Ribeiro, Adalberto Mário. O Departamento nacional de imigração. Rio de Janeiro. Imp. nacional. 22 p. [2449
"Separata da *Revista do Serviço público,* año 6, vol. 2, no. 2, maio de 1943."
A study of the organization of the Immigration department, published by the Departamento Administrativo do Serviço Público.

Rio Grande do sul (estado). Estatuto dos funcionários públicos civís do estado do Rio Grande do Sul, Decreto-lei no. 311 de dezembro de 1942. Pôrto Alegre. Oficinas gráf. da Imp. oficial. 51 p. [2450

Rocha, Germano Carvalho, and others. À margem da reforma administrativa cearense (*Rev. serv. públ.,* ano 6, vol. 3, no. 2, agôsto, p. 41–47). [2451
Concerned chiefly with the salaries of government workers in Ceará and their high cost of living. Family bonuses or allowances are suggested.

Santa Catarina (estado). Interventoria federal. Exercício de 1942. Relatório apresentado ao exmo. sr. presidente da república, pelo dr. Nereu Ramos, interventor federal no estado de Santa Catarina. Florianópolis. Imp. oficial. 224 p. [2452

Sergipe (estado). Administração sergipana. Relátorio apresentado ao exmo. snr. presidente da república—dr. Getúlio Vargas—pelo interventor federal no estado de Sergipe, coronel Augusto Maynard Gomes, referente ao atividades da administração sergipana, durante o ano de 1942. Aracajú. Imp. oficial. 85 p. [2453

Tannenbaum, Frank. A note on Latin American politics (*Pol. sci. quart.,* vol. 58, no. 3, Sept., p. 415–421). [2454
Caudillism, especially as it affects Brazil, is difficult to view out of its Latin American context and milieu in either European or United States terms.

Uruguaiana. Prefeitura municipal. Relatório apresentado ao exmo. sr. interventor federal, cel. Osvaldo Cordeiro de Farias, pelo prefeito Francisco Maria Piquet, 1941. Pôrto Alegre. Livr. do Globo. 229 p. [2455

Vargas, Getulio. A obra de proteção ao servidor público. Rio de Janeiro. Imp. nacional. 107 p. [2456

Vargas Viriato, and **Monte Arrais.** O estado novo e sua doutrina. Conferencias realizadas no Instituto nacional de ciência política. Rio de Janeiro. Gráf. Milone. 47 p. [2457

Veiga, A. César. A democracia e o estado nacional (*Cultura política,* ano 3, no. 34, nov., p. 35–67). [2458
The writer is professor of educational sociology in special courses in the Ministry of Agriculture. He deals with various problems of the family, the race question, capitalism and socialism and religion. A three-and-one-half page bibliography is included.

Vitória (prefeitura municipal). Administração Américo Monjardim. Síntese geral das obras realizadas no quinquenio 1937— 2 de dezembro—1942. Vitória. 22 p. [2459
"Separata da edição especial de *A Tribuna*".

CHILE

Álvarez Álvarez, Manuel. De las divisiones territoriales administrativas. Ancud. Tip. y enc. La Cruz del Sur. 188 p. [2460
Thesis, Facultad de Ciencias Jurídicas y Sociales, Universidad de Chile. Takes up various types of administrative divisions, in Chile—judicial, financial, public health, electoral, maritime, customs, postal, etc.

Amunátegui Lecaros, Miguel Luis. Las constituciones liberales. Santiago. Imp. La Tarde. 45 p. [2461
A thesis dealing with the Chilean constitutions of 1828, 1833, and 1925. Brief bibliography.

Bernaschina G., Mario (ed.). Constitución política de la República de Chile, promulgada el 18 de septiembre de 1925. Santiago. Ed. de la Univ. de Chile. 167 p. [2462
Constitution of 1925 annotated with references to *Actas, Concordancias* and *Jurisprudencia* under this and the constitution of 1833.

———. Fuentes para el estudio de la Constitución política promulgada el 18 de septiembre de 1925. Santiago. Univ. de Chile. 34 p. [2463
The bibliography of 520 numbers is referred to on p. 3–12 by section of the Constitution.

ESTATUTO ORGÁNICO PARA LOS FUNCIONARIOS DE LAS INSTITUCIONES SEMIFISCALES Y DE ADMINISTRACIÓN AUTÓNOMA. Decreto no. 235,683 de 14 de octubre de 1942. Santiago. Tall. gráf. La Nación. 43 p. [2464

Partido socialista. Cuarto Congreso extraordinario del Partido socialista. Antecedentes, informes, acuerdos y conclusiones. Realizado en Valparaíso en agosto de 1943. Santiago. Tall. gráf. Olmos. 64 p. [2465

———. Informe sobre posición política del Partido socialista. Santiago. Tall. Claridad. 24 p. [2466
The report discusses the international situation caused by the war, its consequences for Chilean politics and economy, its effect on the Socialist part, the dangers and possibilities of the post-war period, and the party's "plan of action."

Presidente. Mensaje de s. e. el presidente de la república, don Juan Antonio Ríos, en la apertura de las sesiones ordinarias del Congreso nacional 21 de mayo de 1943. Santiago. Imp. fiscal de la penitenciaría. xxx, 299 p. [2467
Contains reference to the extensive administrative reorganizations made in 1942.

COLOMBIA

Antioquia (depto.). Gobernador. Mensaje del gobernador de Antioquia a la honorable Asamblea en sus sesiones de 1943. Medellín. Imp. departamental. 30 p. [2468

———. **Secretaría de gobierno.** Informe. 1943. Medellín. Imp. departamental. 149 p. [2469
Includes the election returns, March 21, 1943.

Bolívar (depto.). Secretaría de gobierno. Reseña y prospecto de labores de la Secretaría de gobierno, 1943. Cartagena. Imp. departamental, Bolívar. 107 p. [2470

Cardozo, Antonio M. Derecho municipal colombiano. Bogotá. Lib. Camacho Roldán. 240 p. [2471
Chapters: Indicaciones históricas; Historia legislativa del municipio en Colombia; Situación jurídica del municipio en Colombia; Gobierno municipal; Estatuto jurídico de los funcionarios municipales; Hacienda municipal; De los servicios municipales; Contratos municipales; Obras públicas municipales; La expropiación forzosa en la administración municipal; Tutela administrativa y control jurisdiccional del municipio; Régimen de la ciudad de Bogotá. This is a ground-breaking study.

Gibson, William Marion. The Colombian Council of state, a study in administrative justice (*Jour. pol.*, vol. 5, no. 3, August, p. 291-311). [2472

Ministerio de gobierno. Código de elecciones. Compilación agrupada por materias, de todas las disposiciones electorales vigentes hasta la fecha. Edición ordenada por el ministro de gobierno, doctor Darío Echandía. Revista por el secretario general del ministerio, doctor Enrique Acero Pimentel. Coordinada y dirigida por Ramón Rosales. Bogotá. Imp. nacional. vii, 267 p. [2473

———. Informes de los jefes de departamento y de sección al ministro de gobierno, para la Memoria de 1943. Bogotá. Imp. nacional. 207 p. [2474
Includes election returns.

Plata Uricoechea, Fernando. El régimen constitucional en Colombia y en los Estados Unidos. Bogotá. Ed. Cromos. 169 p. [2475
A thesis. It is a comparative study of public law, individual liberties and social guarantees, the presidency, the congress, parties and elections, and the judiciary in Colombia and the United States.

Presidente. Mensaje presidencial al Congreso de 1943. Bogotá. Imp. nacional. 119 p. [2476

This annual message of President López presented in August, 1943 contains sections on the *código electoral*, on judicial reform, and on the revision of the *código de régimen político y municipal*.

Riveros, Bernabé. América y la democracia colombiana (*Rev. Indias*, segunda época, tomo 18, no. 56, ogosto, p. 224–232). [2477

A lecture delivered by Dr. Riveros at the Club de Lengua Castellana in Bogotá on July 20, 1943.

Sánchez Gómez, Gregorio. Sociología política colombiana. Ensayo crítico. Cali. Ed. Sánchez Gómez hnos. 114 p. [2478

Essays on political parties, the status of labor, suffrage, the professions and politics, the press, *caudillaje*, public life, etc. A significant contribution.

Santander (depto.). Informe del ejecutivo de Santander a la Asamblea departamental, 1943. Bucaramanga. Imp. del Departamento. 359 p. [2479

The message of Governor Arturo Santos presented in April, 1943, and the "informes" of the Secretarías de Gobierno, Hacienda Obras Públicas, and Agricultura e Industrias and also of the director for education for the year 1942. On page 15 the Governor mentions the need for a Secretaría de Higiene y Asistencia Social. On pages 55–56 and 134–136 are given details of the transfer of the Oficina de Catastro Departamental to the national government as a regional office of the Instituto Geográfico Militar y Catastral.

Tolima (depto.). Gobernador. Mensaje a la Asamblea departamental en sus sesiones ordinarias de 1943. Ibagué. Imp. departamental. 7 p. [2480

———. **Secretaría de gobierno.** Informe al señor gobernador, 1943. Ibagué. Imp. departamental. 97 p. [2481

COSTA RICA

AL PUEBLO. QUIÉNES SON LOS LIBERALES? San José. (Opúsculos de la Junta central). 16 p. [2482

CUBA

CÓDIGO ELECTORAL; ESTA OBRA CONTIENE EL TEXTO DE LA EDICIÓN OFICIAL DE LA LEY NO. 17 DE 31 DE MAYO DE 1943, *publicada* EN LA *Gaceta oficial* DE 19 DE JUNIO DE 1943 . . . ANOTADA POR GUSTAVO GUTIÉRREZ SÁNCHEZ. Habana. Ed. Lex. 469 p. [2484

Gschwind, Eduardo P. La novísima constitución de Cuba (*Rev. cien. jur. soc.*, tercera época, año 8, no. 38, p. 127–149). [2485

An analysis and discussion of a portion (through the articles dealing with constitutional guarantees) of the Cuban Constitution of 1940.

Martínez, José Agustín (ed.). Reglamento provisional para la organización de la carrera administrativa. Habana. Ed. J. Montero. (Col. legis. cubana, vol. 3). 47 p. [2486

Núñez Portuondo, Emilio. Una campaña democrática. Habana. Ed. Niños. 381 p. [2487

A series of articles, most of them printed originally in the Habana newspaper *Luz*, dealing with four main topics, Cuba and the War, comments on the policies of the Cuban communists, problems of internal politics, and democratic solidarity.

Oriente (prov.). Gobierno de la provincia de Oriente. Memoria de los trabajos efectuados por el gobierno provincial de Oriente durante los ejercicios económicos de 1940, 1941 y 1942. Santiago de Cuba. Imp. Arroyo. 88 p. [2488

Contains notice of organization of the Asociación de Alcaldes Municipales de Oriente in January 1942.

Roca, Blas [Francisco Calderío]. Los fundamentos del socialismo en Cuba. Habana. Ed. Páginas. 155 p. [2489

Senado. Comisión de derecho político y constitucional. Dictamen sobre el proyecto de ley de los oficios públicos. Habana. Imp. P. Fernández. 169 p. [2490

Sosa de Quesada, Arístides. Por la democracia y por la libertad. Habana. Ed. P. Fernández. 180 p. [2491

Addresses by the author as minister of national defenses, February 26, 1942.–February 26, 1943.

Torra, A. Como cumple Batista su plataforma de gobierno. Habana. Prensa indoamericana. 77 p. [2492

DOMINICAN REPUBLIC

Santo Domingo (distrito). Memoria que presenta al señor secretario de estado de lo interior y policía y al Consejo administrativo del distrito de Santo Domingo, su presidente el señor lic. don Ángel Fremio Soler relativa a las labores realizadas durante el año 1942. Ciudad Trujillo. Ed. La Nación. 435 p. [2494

Unión democrática antinazista dominicana. Trujillo es un nazi (pruebas documentales). Habana. 52 p. [2495

A very severely critical pamphlet by a refugee group.

ECUADOR

Ministerio de gobierno. Informe a la nación, 1943. Quito. Imp. del Min. de gobierno. 104 p. [2496

———. Nómina de los señores senadores y diputados al Congreso nacional ordinario del año de 1943 (*Reg. oficial,* no. 884, agosto 11, p. 5709–5712.) [2497

Presidente. Mensaje que el excmo. señor presidente constitucional de la república, doctor don Carlos A. Arroyo del Río, presenta al Congreso nacional ordinario de 1943. Quito. Imp. del Min. de gobierno. 40 p. [2498

GUATEMALA

Presidente. Mensaje del presidente de la república, general Jorge Ubico a la Asamblea nacional legislativa al abrir sus sesiones ordinarias del 1º de marzo de 1943. Guatemala. Tip. nacional. 155 p. [2499

Secretaría de gobernación y justicia. Memoria de las labores del poder ejecutivo en el ramo de gobernación y justicia durante al año administrativo de 1942, presentada a la Asamblea legislativa en sus sesiones ordinarias de 1943. Guatemala. Tip. nacional. 227 p. [2500
Only summaries of the *Memoria de la Policía Nacional* and of the *Memoria de Sanidad Pública* are included, since the full reports are issued separately.

HAITI

EXPOSÉ GÉNÉRAL DE LA SITUATION PRESENTÉ AU PEUPLE HAITIEN EN UN MESSAGE DU PRÉSIDENT DE LA RÉPUBLIQUE LE 1er JANVIER 1943 ET DÉPOSÉ DEVANT LE CORPS LÉGISLATIF LE 22 JANVIER 1943. Port-au-Prince. Imp. de l'état. 66 p. [2501
The annual report of President Élie Lescot on the activities of the government. The executive departments do not ordinarily issue separate annual reports.

HONDURAS

DECRETOS DEL CONGRESO NACIONAL, 1942–1943. Tegucigalpa. Tall. tip. nacional. 139 p. [2502
Decree no. 2, December 11, 1942, amends articles 171 and 173 of the Constitution relating to military service.

Tegucigalpa. Distrito central. Consejo. Cinco años de labor administrativa. Tegucigalpa. Imp. Honduras. 121 p., ilus. [2503
Public works, mortality records, etc. for the Central District (Tegucigalpa) for a five-year period.

Presidente. Mensaje del sr. presidente de la república, doctor y general Tiburcio Carías A., al soberano Congreso nacional, 1943. Tegucigalpa. Tall. tip. nacional. 23 p. [2504

Secretaría de gobernación. Informe de los actos realizados por el poder ejecutivo en los ramos de gobernación, justicia, sanidad y beneficencia presentado al Congreso nacional por el secretario de estado, ing. Abraham Williams, año fiscal de 1941 a 1942. Tegucigalpa. Tall. tip. nacional. 335 p. [2505
Includes a full report on police activities.

Zúñiga Huete, Ángel. Carta abierta a Tiburcio Carías Andino, dictador de la república de Honduras. México, D. F. 11 p. [2506
Prepared by Zúñiga Huete, Heliodoro Valle, and other Honduran political exiles.

———. Regalos del exilio. ¿Por qué es inconstitucional el gobierno de Tiburcio Carías Andino, dictador de Honduras? México. 39 p. [2507
The foreign representative of the Liberal Party cites reasons for his beliefs in reply to the government's position as given in "Ángel Zúñiga Huete. Líder en descomposición." The latter work was written as a refutation of Zúñiga's "Un gobierno de facto," written for the Unión Democrática Centro-Americana in Mexico.

MEXICO

Adame, Enrique Bautista. Democracia y dictadura como formas de estado. México, D. F. 93 p. [2508
The author places particular stress on the democratic state and the Mexican constitution.

Álvarez Basurto, Herminio. La eficacia de las atribuciones del poder ejecutivo en los regímenes parlamentario y presidencial. México, D. F. (Univ. nac. autónoma de México, Escuela nac. de jurisprudencia). [2509

Campeche (estado). Gobernador. Informe rendido por el ... gobernador ante la honorable XXXVII legislatura ... el día siete de agosto de 1943. Campeche. Oficina de prensa y publicidad. 99 p. [2510

CONSTITUCIÓN POLÍTICA REFORMADA DEL ESTADO DE NAYARIT. Promulgada el 5 de febrero de 1918. Tepic. Imp. del gobierno. 20 p. [2510a

Davis, Harold E. The enigma of sinarquism (*Mexican life,* vol. 19, no. 6, June, p. 13–15, 51–55). [2511
The rise of Sinarquism since its founding in 1937 and its reactionary note during the present Ávila Camacho administration.

Guanajuato (estado). Constitución política del estado libre y soberano de Guanajuato. Guanajuato? 48 p. [2512
Text of the 1918 Constitution, adopted in pursuance of the Federal Constitution of 1917, including forty-nine amendments voted by the legislature.

Hidalgo (estado). Gobernador. Informe que rinde . . . ante la XXXVII legislatura del estado . . . en el período comprendido del 1° de marzo de 1942 al 28 de febrero de 1943. Pachuca, Hgo. Tall. linotip. del Gobierno del estado. 62 p. [2513

Jalisco (estado). Gobernador. Informe que el c. gobernador constitucional . . . rindió ante la XXXVI legislatura, en el cuarto año de su gestión administrativa. Guadalajara. 108 p., láms. [2514
Covers the year 1943, and includes a summary for his term 1939–1943. A map of the "División política electoral" of the state faces p. 8.

Lombardo Toledano, Vicente. Definición de la nación mexicana. México. Univ. obrera de México. 28 p. [2515
An address given by the well known labor leader on January 21, 1943, in commemoration of Lenin. The address deals particularly with an analysis of the concept of the nation and the development of the Mexican nation from its origins to the present.

Nuevo León (estado). Gobernador. Informe que rinde el . . . gobernador constitucional del estado de Nuevo León al h. Congreso del estado sobre su labor administrativa llevada a cabo durante el año de 1942–1943, y memoria anexa, Monterrey. 151 p. [2517

Partido de la revolución mexicana. 33 meses al servicio de la revolución. Memoria del Partido de la revolución mexicana. 1940–1943. México, D. F. 214 p. [2518
"Ciclo histórico del régimen del presidente Ávila Camacho y del Partido de la Revolución Mexicana, 1940–1943."

Presidente. Informe que rinde al h. Congreso de la Unión sobre la acción desarrollada por la administración pública, del 1° de septiembre de 1942 al 31 de agosto de 1943. México. Sría. de gobernación. 90 p. [2519
On p. 77–78 is a report on extraordinary powers.

San Luis Potosí (estado). Constitución política del estado libre y soberano de San Luis Potosí. San Luis Potosí. Tall. gráf. del estado. 42 p. [2520
"Suplemento al núm. 93 del *Periódico Oficial* de fecha 4 noviembre de 1943."

TRES AÑOS DE GOBIERNO EN MÉXICO PRESENTADA POR *Hoy* COMO HOMENAJE DE LA NACIÓN AL PRESIDENTE ÁVILA CAMACHO EN EL TERCER ANIVERSARIO DE SU PATRIÓTICO GOBIERNO (*Hoy*, no. 357, dic. 25). [2521

Velásquez Carrasco, Luis. Breve estudio sobre la democracia y el ejercicio del sufragio en México. México. Tip. Virginia. (Univ. nac. autónoma de México, Facultad de derecho y ciencias sociales). 55 p. [2522
The P. R. M., the author argues, should be dissolved, since, as constituted, it is undemocratic. With the revision of the election laws, fair and secret ballots are possible, resulting from improvements in technique.

NICARAGUA

Barahona López, Ernesto. Realidades de la vida nicaragüense. Comentarios de problemas nacionales que necesitan solución. Managua. Tip. Excelsior. 111 p. [2523
A discussion of various semi-political problems, such as illiteracy, immigration and colonization, new doctrines of social welfare, etc.

Granada. Labores de la municipalidad de Granada en el período del 1° de julio de 1941 al 31 de diciembre de 1942. Granada. Tip. Salesiana. 56 p. [2524

Lacayo B., Gilberto. El pueblo de Granada pide al soberano congreso nacional la reforma de la Constitución política. Granada. 47 p. [2525

Ministerio de gobernación. Ley reglamentaria de jefes políticos. Managua. Tall. nac. de imp. 20 p. [2526

———. Segundo congreso de municipalidades de Nicaragua, realizado en León el 8 y 10 de diciembre de 1942 auspiciado por la Secretaría de gobernación y anexos. Managua. Tall. nac. de imp. 213 p. [2527

Presidente. Mensaje del presidente de la república, general de división Anastasio Somoza, al honorable Congreso nacional al inaugurar su V período constitucional de sesiones ordinarias el 15 de abril de 1943. Managua. Tall. nacional. xlvii, 64 p. [2528

EL PUEBLO DE LEÓN REUNIDO EN SOLEMNE CABILDO ABIERTO PIDE AL SOBERANO CONGRESO NACIONAL LA REFORMA DE LA CARTA FUNDAMENTAL DE NICARAGUA. León. Tip. El Cronista. 45 p. [2529

PANAMA

Ministerio de gobierno y justicia. Memoria que el ministro de gobierno y justicia presenta a la honorable Asamblea nacional en sus sesiones ordinarias de 1943. Panamá. xix, 1317 p. [2530]
Includes the decrees, *resoluciones* and *acuerdos*, as well as the reports of the bureaus and of the provincial governors, for the preceding biennial period.
By decree 156 of September 10, 1941 the Departamento de Correos y Telecomunicaciones was shifted from Relaciones Exteriores to Gobierno y Justicia.

Presidente. Mensaje del presidente de la república a la Asamblea nacional en sus sesiones ordinarias de 1943. Panamá. Imp. nacional. [2531]

Quijano, Manuel de Jesús. En la ruta liberal y democrática. Tomo 1. Una campaña antifascista, 1937–1940. Panamá. Ed. La Moderna. (Bibl. de "La prensa ilustrada"). xv, 173 p. [2532]
A collection of many very brief articles published over a four-year period.

PARAGUAY

Presidente. Mensaje presidencial leído en el palacio de gobierno por el exmo. general don Higinio Morínigo M. en el acto de prestar juramento para asumir la presidencia de la república por el período constitucional 1943–1948. Asunción. Depto. nac. de prensa y propaganda. 8 p. [2533]

Stefanich, Juan. El Paraguay nuevo, por la democracia y la libertad hacia un unevo ideario americano. Buenos Aires. Ed. Claridad (Colección Claridad, vol. 198). 186 p. [2534]
The Foreign Minister during the Chaco war gives his ideas in speeches and articles on a new *"solidarista"* democracy and the relationship of Man to Society.

PERU

Cavero Egusquiza, Ricardo. Demarcación política de Loreto. Compilación de leyes y otros documentos. Lima. Imp. del Ministerio de guerra. 146 p. [2535]
Documents from 1802 concerning boundaries of this department on the headwaters of the Amazon. Partial texts of treaties with Brazil (1851, 1909), Colombia (1922) and Ecuador (1942) are also given.

Concha, Carlos. Proyectos y discursos parlamentarios. Lima. Imp. Torres Aguirre. 2 vols. [2536]
A miscellaneous collection of decrees, parliamentary addresses, reports, open letters, and other documents, dated 1938 to 1943, by a former Peruvian foreign minister.

McNicoll, Robert Edwards. Intellectual origins of aprismo (*Hisp. amer. hist. rev.*, vol. 23, no. 3, Aug., p. 424–440). [2537]
The literary and political precursors of Aprismo, particularly Manuel González Prada and José Carlos Mariátegui.

Martínez de la Torre, Ricardo. De la reforma universitaria al partido socialista. Apuntes para una interpretación marxista de historia social del Perú. Lima. Ed. Frente. 136 p. [2538]
"Hemos reproducido los documentos más importantes de la histórica polémica que, en torno a la cuestión de 'alianza o partido' efectuó el grupo de Lima, bajo la dirección de Mariátegui, que desde el primer momento luchó en defensa de la independencia doctrinaria, táctica y política, del proletariado, sosteniendo su indiscutible derecho a organizarse en un partido propio, de clase"

Núñez Valdivia, Jorge E. Presente y porvenir de la democracia en el Perú (*Historia*, Lima, vol. 1, no. 4, set.–oct., p. 334–339). [2539]
Essay on what Peru needs in political and economic affairs to develop into a full-fledged democratic commonwealth.

Patrón Taura, Pedro. Legislación peruana sobre empleados públicos. Leyes, decretos y resoluciones vigentes sobre funcionarios y empleados públicos y disposiciones de la constitución y los códigos, relacionadas con todas las actividades de los servidores civiles del estado. Clasificada por materias y en orden cronológico. Lima. 216 p. [2540]

Presidente. Mensaje presentado al Congreso por el señor doctor Manuel Prado, presidente constitucional de la república. Lima. 293 p. [2541]
Covers the administrative period 1942–1943.
Also printed in *El Peruano*, año 103, no. 785, julio, 1943, p. 1–15.

Rimac. Memoria de la administración comunal del Rimac correspondiente al año 1942 leída por el alcalde del distrito, sr. Jorge E. Albertini, en la sesión solemne del Concejo del 1°. de enero de 1943. Lima. Imp. Segrestan. 63 p. [2542]
Annual report of the city government of Rimac.

EL SALVADOR

Presidente. Mensaje presidencial. San Salvador. Imp. nacional. 19 p. [2544]

San Salvador. Alcaldía municipal. Segundo congreso de municipalidades. República de El Salvador, 1943. San Salva-

dor. Ed. Ahora. (Publ. de la Municipalidad de San Salvador). 48 p., ilus. [2545
The record of the Second Congress of Municipalities of the Republic held at San Salvador, November 4–7, 1941.

URUGUAY

Azarola Gil, Luis Enrique. La entraña histórica de los partidos tradicionales. Montevideo. Ed. A. Barreiro y Ramos. 32 p. [2546

CONSTITUCIÓN: TEXTO CONTENIENDO LAS DISPOSICIONES RATIFICADAS EN EL PLEBISCITO DE 29 DE NOVIEMBRE DE 1942. CONCORDADO Y ANOTADO CON LOS ANTERIORES TEXTOS CONSTITUCIONALES, POR EL DR. EDUARDO JIMÉNEZ DE ARÉCHAGA (HIJO). Segunda ed. corr. y aum. Montevideo. Casa A. Barreiro y Ramos, ed. 168 p. [2547

Presidente. Mensaje del presidente de la república, general arquitecto don Alfredo Baldomir a la Asamblea general al inaugurarse el 1er período de la XXXIV legislatura, 25 de febrero de 1943. Montevideo. 32 p. [2549
Contains just a brief mention of the amendment to the Constitution.

Universidad. Facultad de derecho y ciencias sociales. La comisión permanente. Montevideo. Imp. Peña. (Facultad de derecho y ciencias sociales de Montevideo, Seminario de derecho constitucional, Bibl. de publ. oficiales, Sección 3, 16). 497 p. [2550
A comprehensive study of the "Permanent Committee" (of Congress), tracing its development through Spanish law, in Argentina, Chile, and Uruguay. The second part of the volume is a comparative study of the Latin American states (a) that have permanent committees, and (b) that do not have them. Post-war European constitutional organization is also considered. The volume is a very useful study.

VENEZUELA

Anzoátegui (estado). Presidente. Informe que el presidente del estado Anzoátegui presenta a la Asamblea legislativa en sus sesiones ordinarias de 1943. Barcelona. Tip. Americana. 1942 [i.e., 1943]. 24 p. [2551

——. **Secretaría general de gobierno.** Memoria que presenta el ciudadano secretario general de gobierno del estado Anzoátegui a la Asamblea legislativa, en sus sesiones ordinarias del presente año. Barcelona. Imp. del estado. xxxii, 325 p. [2552

Aragua (estado). Presidente. Mensaje que . . . presenta a la Asamblea legislativa de Aragua en sus sesiones ordinarias de 1943. Maracay? C. A. Artes gráf. 16 p. [2553

Barinas (estado). Presidente. Mensaje que el . . . presidente del estado Barinas, presenta a la Asamblea legislativa, en sus sesiones ordinarias de 1943. Barinas. Imp. oficial del estado. 11 p. [2554

——. **Secretaría general de estado.** Memoria que el . . . secretario general de gobierno del estado Barinas, presenta a la Asamblea legislativa en sus sesiones ordinarias de 1943. Barinas. Imp. oficial del estado. 247 p. [2555

Bolívar (estado). Presidente. Mensaje presentado por el . . . presidente del estado Bolívar, a la Asamblea legislativa en sus sesiones ordinarias de 1943. Tip. La Empresa, J. Suegart. 16 p. [2556

——. **Secretaría general.** Memoria y cuenta que presenta el secretario general de gobierno del estado Bolívar a la Asamblea legislativa en su reunión de 1943. Ciudad Bolívar. Tip. La Empresa, J. Suegart. vi, 233 p. [2557

Carabobo (estado). Presidente. Mensaje que presenta a la Asamblea legislativa del estado Carabobo en el año de mil novecientos cuarentitrés el . . . presidente del estado. Caracas. C. A. Artes gráf. 1942 [i.e., 1943] 31 p. [2558

——. **Secretaría general de gobierno.** Memoria que el ciudadano secretario general de gobierno del estado Carabobo, presenta a la Asamblea legislativa en sus sesiones ordinarias de 1943. Valencia. Tip. Venezuela. 150 p. [2559
Includes a plan of the city of Valencia.

Cojedes (estado). Presidente. Mensaje presentado por el . . . presidente del estado Cojedes, a la Asamblea legislativa en sus sesiones ordinarias del año 1943. Valencia. Tip. Valencia. 16 p. [2560

——. **Secretaría general de gobierno.** Memoria que el secretario general de gobierno del estado Cojedes presenta a la Asamblea legislativa en sus sesiones ordinarias de 1943. Valencia. Tip. Venezuela. 59 p. [2561

Distrito federal. Gobernador. Exposición del gobernador al Concejo municipal del Distrito federal en enero de 1943. Caracas. Tip. Garrido. xi, 300 p. [2562
Includes the reports of the various bureaus of the Federal District.

Falcón (estado). Presidente. Mensaje del presidente del estado Falcón a la Asamblea legislativa 1943. Coro. Tip. Bolívar. 3 p. [2563

———. Secretaría general de gobierno. Memoria que el secretario general de gobierno del estado Falcón presenta a la Asamblea legislativa en sus sesiones ordinarias de 1943. Coro. Tip. Ramírez. 509 p. [2564

Gabaldón Márquez, Joaquín. Los partidos políticos en Venezuela (*Bitacora*, vol. 2, cuad. 8, oct.–dic., p. 3–22). [2565

Guárico (estado). Presidente. Mensaje que el ... presidente del estado Guárico, presenta a la Asamblea legislativa en sus sesiones ordinarias de 1943. San Juan de los Morros. Imp. del estado. 7 p. [2566

Lara (estado). Presidente. Mensaje que presenta León Jurado, presidente del estado Lara a la Asamblea legislativa en sus sesiones ordinarias, 1943. Barquisimeto. Ibérica imp. 18 p. [2567

Mérida (estado). Presidente. Mensaje a la Asamblea legislativa del estado en sus sesiones ordinarias de 1943. Mérida. Imp. oficial. 31 p. [2568

———. Secretaría general de gobierno. Memoria que el secretario general de gobierno del estado Mérida, presenta a la Asamblea legislativa en sus sesiones ordinarias de 1943. Mérida. Imp. oficial. 101, 314, 30 p. [2569

Medina Angarita, Isaías. La nueva lucha y la acción nueva. Caracas. Oficina nac. de prensa. 38 p. [2570
"El ideario político del señor general Isaías Medina Angarita, presidente de la república, tomado de sus principales documentos públicos."

Ministerio de relaciones interiores. Memoria y cuenta que el Ministerio de relaciones interiores presenta al Congreso nacional en sus sesiones ordinarias del año de 1943. Caracas. Imp. nacional. xi, cii, 482 p. [2571

Miranda (estado). Presidente. Mensaje que el ... presidente del estado Miranda, presenta a la Asamblea legislativa del estado en sus sesiones ordinarias de 1943. Caracas. Tip. Ayacucho. 21 p. [2572

———. Secretaría general de gobierno. Memoria y cuenta que el ... secretario general de gobierno del estado Miranda, presenta a la Asamblea legislativa en sus sesiones ordinarias de 1943. Los Teques. 73 p. [2573
Contains only the titles of decrees accompanied by financial statements and a table of traffic report.

Nueva Esparta (estado). Presidente. Mensaje que el ... presidente del estado Nueva Esparta presenta a la Asamblea legislativa en sus sesiones ordinarias de 1943. La Asunción. Imp. del estado. 8 p. [2574

———. Secretaría general. Memoria y cuenta que el ciudadano secretario general del estado Nueva Esparta presenta a la Asamblea legislativa en sus sesiones ordinarias de 1943. La Asunción. Imp. del estado. 70, 241 p. [2575
Decrees and orders with a few statistical tables at the end.

Portuguesa (estado). Presidente. Mensaje que el ... presidente del estado Portuguesa, presenta a la Asamblea legislativa en sus sesiones ordinarias de 1943. Guanare. Imp. del estado. 15 p. [2576

———. Secretaría general de gobierno. Memoria y cuenta que el ... secretario general de gobierno del estado Portuguesa presenta a la Asamblea legislativa del estado en sus sesiones ordinarias de 1943. Guanare. Imp. del estado. 331 p. [2577

Presidente. Mensaje que el ciudadano general Isaías Medina A., presidente de los Estados Unidos de Venezuela, presenta al Congreso nacional en sus sesiones ordinarias de 1943. Caracas. Lit. del Comercio. 48 p. [2578

Sucre (estado). Presidente. Mensaje que presenta el ... secretario general de gobierno, encargado de la Presidencia del estado Sucre, a la Asamblea legislativa en la sesión del 5 de enero de 1943. Cumaná. Ed. Renacimiento. 51 p. [2579
On p. 11–13 contains sections on municipal councils and on elections.

———. Secretaría general de gobierno. Memoria de la Secretaría general, 1942. Cumaná. Ed. Renacimiento. 240 p. [2580
Contains a statistical section at the end.

Táchira (estado). Presidente. Mensaje presentado por el ... presidente del estado Táchira, a la Asamblea legislativa en sus sesiones ordinarias del año de 1943 el día 3 de enero de dicho año, en la sesión extraordinaria celebrada para tal fin. San Cristóbal. Imp. del estado. 33 p., láms. [2581
Mentions on p. 30 the Asamblea de Municipaladades of the state which met on December 20, 1942.

———. **Secretaría general de gobierno.** Memoria y cuenta que el . . . secretario general de gobierno, presenta a la Asamblea legislativa del Táchira, en sus sesiones ordinarias de 1943. San Cristóbal. Imp. del estado. 56, cxxviii, 18 p. [2582
Includes some statistical tables.

Trujillo (estado). Presidente. Mensaje presentado por el . . . presidente del estado Trujillo, a la Asamblea legislativa, en sus sesiones ordinarias de 1943, el día 3 de enero de dicho año, en la sesión extraordinaria celebrada para tal fin en el Palacio de gobierno. Trujillo. Imp. del estado. 13 p. [2583

———. **Secretaría general.** Memoria y cuenta que el . . . secretario general de gobierno, presenta a la Asamblea legislativa del estado Trujillo en sus sesiones ordinarias de 1943. Trujillo. Imp. del estado. 347 p., láms., mapa. [2584
Mainly decrees and orders for 1942. The map depicts the route of the Trujillo-San Lázaro highway. Scale 1:20,000.

Zulia (estado). Presidente. Mensaje que el . . . presidente del estado Zulia, presenta a la Asamblea legislativa dal mismo en su reunión de 1943. Maracaibo. Emp. Panorama. 21 p. [2585

ADDENDA

BRAZIL

Branco, Plinio A. A experiéncia da municipalidade de São Paulo como subsídio para a regulamentação dos serviços públicos concedidos. São Paulo. Prefeitura do município. 1942. [2586
"Trabalho submetido ao Segundo Congresso Interamericano de Municípios, reunido em Santiago de Chile, em Setembro de 1941."

Instituto brasileiro de geografia e estatística. Divisão territorial dos Estados Unidos do Brasil (Quadro territorial—administrativo e judiciário—das unidades da federação fixado para o quinquênio de 1939–1943, em virtude da lei orgánica nacional n° 311, de 2 de março de 1938). Segunda ed. Rio de Janeiro. Serviço gráf. do I. B. G. E. 1942. xvi, 451 p. [2587

CHILE

Rosselot Borden, Fernando. El veto presidencial. Santiago. Dirección general de prisiones, imp. 1942. 114 p. [2588
Thesis. Facultad de Ciencias Jurídicas y Sociales, Universidad de Chile.

Senado. Manual del Senado, 1810–1942. Santiago, Chile. Imp. universitaria. 1942. 362 p. [2589
The first edition was published in 1923. This includes Constitution of 1925, accompanied section by section with that of 1833, text of laws relating to members of Congress, *reglamento del Senado,* the cabinets from 1810 to 1942 and members of the Senate, 1812–1942.

ECUADOR

Ecuador. Partido socialista. Un año de lucha socialista; informe presentado por el compañero dr. Juan Isaac Lovato, secretario general del Partido socialista ecuatoriano, al VIII Congreso de éste, realizado del 29 de noviembre de 1941 al 7 de diciembre del mismo año, en la ciudad de Quito. Ed. socialista. 1942. 70 p. [2590

PERU

Partido comunista del Perú. Resoluciones del primer Congreso nacional del Partido comunista del Perú. Lima, 29 de setiembre al 5 de octubre de 1942. Lima. 1942? 22 p. [2591

CHANGES IN PUBLIC ADMINISTRATION AUTHORIZED IN 1943

BY

JAMES B. CHILDS

Library of Congress

ARGENTINA

ACADEMIA NACIONAL DE CIENCIAS MORALES Y POLíTICAS

By decree 11,426, October 10, 1943, the Academia de Ciencias Morales y Políticas established at Buenos Aires since December 28, 1938, was given official status under the above name, similar to the other official academies. Its statutes to be presented for approval within 60 days.

CÁMARA DE AQUILERES DE LA CAPITAL FEDERAL

A rent control office under the Ministerio del Interior set up by decree 1,580, June 29, 1943, and regulated by decree 3,862, July 29, 1943.

CÁMARA INFORMATIVA DE SALARIOS

An advisory board of ten created by decree 8,923, September 17, 1943, to report on salaries in relation to the cost of living. Presided over by the Minister of the Interior. Functions in connection with the Departamento Nacional del Trabajo.

CENTRO DE ALTOS ESTUDIOS

Created as of January 1, 1943, in the Ministerio de Guerra under the Inspector General del Ejército by decree 141,264, January 21, 1943.

COMISIÓN ASESORA PARA LA VIVIENDA POPULAR

Created by decree 2,746, July 13, 1943 attached to the Ministerio de Hacienda, and by decree of November 27, 1943 attached to the new Secretaría de Trabajo y Previsión.

COMISIÓN DE ARANCEL Y CONTRALOR DE PRODUCTOS MEDICINALES

Created under the Departamento Nacional de Higiene by decree 8,891, September 15, 1943, in place of the Comisión de Especialidades.

COMISIÓN DE CITRICULTURA

Created by order no. 41,691 of the Ministerio de Agricultura, April 2, 1943, to advise about citrus diseases.

COMISIÓN HONORARIA DE LAS FUERZAS ACTIVAS DE LA ECONOMíA NACIONAL

Created by decree 1,859 of July 6, 1943. Met for first time on August 9, 1943.

COMISIÓN INTERMINISTERIAL COORDINADORA EN MATERIA POLICIAL Y JUDICIAL

Set up in connection with the Ministerio de Relaciones Exteriores y Culto by decree 1,058, July 6, 1943.

COMISIÓN INVESTIGADORA DE LOS SERVICIOS PÚBLICOS DE ELECTRICIDAD

Created under the Ministerio del Interior by decree 4,910, August 6, 1943, to investigate light and power situation in Buenos Aires.

COMISIÓN NACIONAL DE CASAS BARATAS

Decree 11,596, October 13, 1943, extends the activity of the Commission to the whole territory of the republic.

COMISIÓN NACIONAL DE RECONSTRUCCIÓN ECONóMICO-SOCIAL

Created by decree 1,859, July 3, 1943, along the pattern of the Comisión Interministerial Permanente de Política Económica. The División Uniones Internacionales of the Subsecretaría de Relaciones Exteriores acts as secretariat for the Commission.

DEPARTAMENTO NACIONAL DEL TRABAJO

Transfered from Ministerio del Interior directly to Presidency about November 30 under the newly established Secretariat of Labor and Social Security which is to have control over public health, rent control, labor relations, immigration, postal savings, unemployment, housing, etc. Merged with the Secretaría del Trabajo y Previsión.

A Registro Nacional de Colocaciones created in the Departamento by decree 2,928, July 21, 1943, to coordinate and regulate throughout the country the supply of and demand for labor.

DIRECCIÓN DE CONSTRUCCIÓN DE ELEVADORES

Transferred from the Ministerio de Agricultura to the Ministerio de Obras Públicas by decree 5,373, August 13, 1943.

DIRECCIÓN DE INMIGRACIÓN

Transferred from the Ministerio de Agricultura to the Ministerio del Interior by decree 10,790, October 8, 1943, effective November 1, 1943. By decree of November 30, 1943, became a part of the new Secretaría de Trabajo y Previsión.

DIRECCIÓN DE INVESTIGACIONES

Established in the Ministerio de Agricultura by decree 15,317, November 27, 1943, and by decree 16,846/44 June 27, 1944, given the status of an *entidad autárquica*. Administered by a *consejo* consisting of the directors of the institutes of rural engineering, vegetable pathology, soils, and *agrotecnia*.

DIRECCIÓN DE PISCICULTURA Y PESCA

Established under Ministerio de Agricultura by decree 148,119, April 19, 1943. Formerly a División de Pesca y Piscicultura. Decree 86,793, creating the Comisión Nacional de Oceanografía y Pesca Marítima was revoked by decree 148,119.

DIRECCIÓN DE TIERRAS

The decree of August 4, 1942, which provided for the incorporation of the Dirección de Tierras of the Ministerio de Agricultura with the Consejo Agrario Nacional as of September 2, 1943, was revoked by decree 151,074, May 29, 1943, and "nacional" added to the name of the "Dirección." Apparently the addition of "nacional" did not become effective, and the incorporation was suspended by decree 6,447, August 26, 1943.

DIRECCIÓN DE VITIVINICULTURA

By decree 1,298, June 28, 1943, the Junta Reguladora de Vinos, created as an emergency measure by law 12,137 and Comisión Nacional Antifiloxérica, created by decree 127,175, August 12, 1942, was abolished and the duties transferred to the Dirección General de Vitivinicultura of the Ministerio de Agricultura. Name changed to Dirección de Vitivinicultura by decree of November 27, 1943.

DIRECCIÓN GENERAL DE AERONÁUTICA CIVIL

Transferred from the Ministerio del Interior to the Ministerio de Guerra by decree 38, June 10, 1943.

DIRECCIÓN GENERAL DE ESTADÍSTICA Y CENSOS DE LA NACIÓN

Decree 10,783, October 6, 1943, provided for the taking of a fourth national census within the period of a year from the date of the decree under the Dirección General de Estadística which is henceforth designated Dirección General de Estadística y Censos de la Nación.

DIRECCIÓN GENERAL DE LA MARINA MERCANTE

Created in the Ministerio de Marina by decree 149,858, May 12, 1943, the Flota Mercante del Estado having recently been organized in that Ministry.

DIRECCIÓN GENERAL DE SUMINISTROS DEL ESTADO

By decree 10,113, September 27, 1943, all supply services for the agencies of the government were centralized in the above which was created under the Ministerio de Hacienda by decree of June 26, 1941. By decree 10,114, September 28, 1943, the ministries of war and marine were excepted from its jurisdiction.

DIRECCIÓN NACIONAL DE ENERGÍA

Created as an *entidad autárquica* under the Ministerio de Agricultura by decree 12,648/43, October 28, 1943, published in the *Boletín Oficial*, July 10, 1944 to regulate the production, distribution and consumption of all fuel resources in the country. Administered by a Directorio composed of a chairman who is to be an "oficial superior del Ejército o de la Armada," and six other members, one each for the Ministries of war, marine, treasury, and public works, and two for the Ministry of Agriculture. Chairman appointed by decree 9,180, April 11, 1944 and the other directors by decree 16,847/44, June 27, 1944.

DIRECCIÓN NACIONAL DE SALUD PÚBLICA Y ASISTENCIA SOCIAL

Established under the Ministerio del Interior by decree 12,311, October 21, 1943 which assigned all matters relating to "beneficencia, hospitales, asilos, asistencia social, sanidad e higiene" to that Ministry as of that date. This Dirección Nacional is formed by the Departamento Nacional de Higiene, the Comisión Asesora de Asilos y Hospitales Regionales, the Instituto Nacional de la Nutrición, the Sociedad de Beneficencia de la Capital Federal, the Registro Nacional de Asistencia Social, the Dirección de Subsidios, and all the public health and welfare organizations and medical services of the ministries and other agencies of the government. By decree 18,524, December 31, 1943, the Comisión Nacional de Ayuda Escolar was also transferred to the Dirección.

FLOTA MERCANTE DEL ESTADO

The provisional organization by decree 103,316, October 16, 1941, was replaced by permanent organization under the Ministerio de Marina through decree 145,734, March 24, 1943, the Comisión Administradora being replaced by an Administrador General.

The statutes of the Flota were promulgated by decree 12,941, October 29, 1943.

INSTITUTO DE LA TRADICIÓN

By decree 15,951 of December 20, 1943, the Instituto was created under the Ministerio de Justicia e Instrucción Pública to study folk language and literature, folk music and dances, social and material aspects of folk culture.

INSTITUTO MOVILIZADOR DE INVERSIONES BANCARIAS

Terminated by decree 17,800 of December 28, 1943, and placed in liquidation.

MINISTERIO DE AGRICULTURA

By decree 15,317/43, November 27, 1943, a comprehensive reorganization of the Ministry was promulgated, the decree being printed in the *Boletín Oficial,* February 7, 1944. Under the Minister and directly responsible to him is a Subsecretaría which has supervision over (1) the four Direcciones Generales (Agricultura, Ganadería, Industria and Comercio), over (2) the eight Direcciones independent of these (Administración, Asuntos Jurídicos, Estadística, Investigaciones, Enseñanza, Parques Nacionales y Turismo, Meteorología, Geofísica e Hidrología, and Forestal), and over (3) the following autarchic entities: Consejo Agrario Nacional, Dirección Nacional de Energía, Junta Nacional de Carnes, Junta Reguladora de Granos, and the Comisión Nacional de Granos y Elevadores.

The Subsecretaría is to have the following sections: Inspección General, Despacho, Personal, Informaciones; Biblioteca, Traductores; Asesoría de Obras; Registro; Servicios Médicos; Mesa de Entradas y Salidas; Archivo; Comisión de Estudios y Coordinación.

Dirección General de Agricultura has the following Direcciones: Agronomías Regionales; Estaciones Experimentales; Política Social Agraria; Fiscalización y Lucha contra las Plagas; Cereales, Linos y Forrajes; Vitivinicultura; Cultivos Especiales; Frutas, Hortalizas y Flores; Algodón; Tabaco; and Yerba Mate.

Under the Dirección General de Ganadería are the Direcciones: Sanidad Animal; Zootecnia; Lanas; Lechería; Granjas; Piscicultura y Pesca; and Patología Animal.

Under the Dirección General de Industria are the following Direcciones: Economía y Política Industrial; Siderurgía y Metalurgía; Industrias Químicas; Industrias de Elaboración; Minas, Geología y Hidrogeología; Patentes y Marcas. Under this Dirección are the following autarchic organizations: Fábrica Nacional de Envases de Algodón; Fábrica de Productos Químicos; and the Corporación Argentina de Tejeduría Doméstica.

Under the Dirección General de Comercio are the following Direcciones: Política Comercial; Contralor Comercial; Abastecimiento; Créditos Prendarios; and the Comité de Exportación.

A Director General de Industria was appointed on October 11, 1943 and Dirección Général organized as of that date.

MINISTERIO DE JUSTICIA E INSTRUCCIÓN PÚBLICA

By decree 18,411 of December 31, 1943, religious instruction in the schools is made obligatory. A Dirección General de Instrucción Religiosa and an Inspección General de Instrucción Religiosa were created in the Ministry to care for these matters.

MINISTERIO DE OBRAS PÚBLICAS

By decree 2,743, July 14, 1943, the *directorios* of the Obras Sanitarias de la Nación and of the Dirección Nacional de Vialidad were replaced by Consejos de Administración the chairman of the Consejo in both cases being designated Administrador General and the names of the organizations being changed to Administración General de Obras Sanitarias de la Nación and to Administración General de Vialidad. Both thus have an organization corresponding to that of the Ferrocarriles del Estado set up by law 6,757.

By decree 4,173, August 3, 1943, the Dirección General de Estudio y Obras del Riachuelo was merged in the Dirección General de Navegación y Puertos.

MINISTERIO DE OBRAS PÚBLICAS

By resolución ministerial 505, October 29, 1943, the Asesoría Letrada y Sumarios of the Ministry was designated División de Asuntos Legales.

MINISTERIO DE RELACIONES EXTERIORES Y CULTO

Reorganized in part by decree of December 7, 1943. Established the position of Director General of the Ministry. Since Beneficencia, Asistencia Social, Asilos y Hospitales Regionales were transferred to the Dirección Nacional de Salud Pública y Asistencia Social (Ministerio del Interior) by decree of October 21, the Subsecretaría de Culto was replaced by a Dirección General de Culto.

The organic Reglamento of the ministry dates from August 25, 1934.

A Dirección de Personal created on the basis of the existing División de Personal by decree 143,601 of February 23, 1943. The División had been set up by decree of October 25, 1941.

MINISTERIO DEL INTERIOR

By decree 13,525, November 12, 1943 the functions assigned to the Dirección General de Territorios Nacionales by arts. 15 and 16 Reglamento General del Ministerio del Interior, decree 109,594, December 31, 1941, are to be distributed among the other branches of the Ministry.

POLICÍA FEDERAL

Created by decree of December 24, 1943, directly under the President, the chief of the Policía Federal is to be at the same time chief of the Policía de la Capital. Action to be coordinated with the Gendarmería Nacional and with Prefectura Marítima. The *Estatuto Orgánico* was promulgated by decree 17,550, December 24, 1943.

PROCURADOR DEL TESORO

Decree 14,546, November 20, 1943, regulates the functions of the general counsel of the Treasury.

REGISTRO NACIONAL DE IDONEIDAD PERSONAL

A registry of national aptitudes. Created by decree 2,745, July 13, 1943, in connection with the Ministerio del Interior. To be in direct charge of the Vicepresidencia de la República.

SECRETARÍA DE LA PRESIDENCIA

By decree 12,937, October 21, 1943 the Secretario de la Presidencia was given a rank equal to that of a Minister, and the following Subsecretarías established (1) General, (2) de Informaciones y Prensa, and (3) de Coordinación. Decree 13,644, October 21, 1943 sets forth the functions of the Subsecretaría de Informaciones y Prensa, and decree 18,406, December 31, 1943, organizes it in detail as follows:

Dirección General de Subsecretaría;
Dirección General de Prensa;
Dirección General de Propaganda;
Dirección General de Espectáculos Públicos;
Dirección General de Radiodifusión.

As of January 1, 1944, the following services are transferred to this Subsecretaría: Consejo Supervisor y Oficina de Trámite y Fiscalización de Programas of the Dirección de Radiocomunicaciones, Instituto Cinematográfico del Estado, Archivo Gráfico de la Nación, Boletín Oficial, Oficina de Radio Control Central, and Instituto Nacional de Locutores. The Servicio Oficial de Radiodifusión (Radioemisoras del Estado) is also to be transferred, the technical sections to continue in Dirección General de Correos y Telégrafos.

SECRETARÍA DE TRABAJO Y PREVISIÓN

Established under la Presidencia de la Nación by decree of November 27, 1943, by the incorporation of the following: Departamento Nacional del Trabajo, sections of Higiene Industrial y Social and

Leyes de Previsión Social of the Dirección Nacional de Salud Pública y Asistencia Social; Sección Accidentes of the Caja Nacional de Pensiones y Jubilaciones Civiles; the Comisión Nacional de Casas Baratas; the Cámara de Alquileres; the Comisión Asesora de Vivienda Popular; the Dirección de Inmigración; Tribunal Bancario; Comisión Honoraria de Reducción de Indios; and the Junta Nacional para Combatir las Desocupaciones. Also all labor conciliation and arbitration services. Further, the following are transferred to the new Secretaría mostly from the Ministerio de Hacienda: Caja Nacional de Jubilaciones y Pensiones Civiles; Caja Nacional de Jubilaciones y Pensiones Ferroviarias; Caja Nacional de Jubilaciones y Pensiones Bancarias; Caja Nacional de Jubilaciones y Pensiones de Empleados y Obreros de Empresas Particulares; Caja Nacional de Ahorro Postal; Caja de Maternidad; Caja Nacional de Jubilaciones y Pensiones de Periodistas; and Caja Nacional de Jubilaciones y Pensiones de la Marina Mercante Nacional. Organized with the following:

Dirección general de Servicios Técnico-administrativos
Dirección General de Trabajo
Dirección General de Acción Social
Dirección General de la Vivienda
Dirección General de Migraciones
Dirección General de Estadistica
Dirección General de Administración
Asesor Legal

An advisory Consejo Superior de Trabajo y Previsión set up. Provincial labor offices transfered to the new Secretaría, and made regional offices.

BOLIVIA

INSTITUTO DE FOMENTO AZUFRERO

By decree of July 22, 1943, the Banco Minero was authorized to establish an agency to be called Instituto de Fomento Azufrero.

INTERVENCIÓN FISCAL DE PRECIOS

Created under Ministerio de la Economía. May 18, 1943.

BRAZIL

Federal territories of Amapá, Rio Branco, Guaporé, Ponta Porã and Iguassú were created by decree-law 5,812, September 12, 1943, from parts of the states of Pará, Amazonas, Mato Grosso, Paraná, and Santa Catarina. Decree-law 5,839 provides for the administration of these territories, the change becoming effective on January 1, 1944. The governor of each territory is appointed by the President of the Republic. Amapá is the capital of Amapá, Boa Vista of Rio Branco, Porto Velho of Guaporé, Ponta Porã of Ponta Porã, and Iguassú of Iguassú.

ADMINISTRAÇAO DO PORTO DE LAGUNA

The A. P. L. was created by decree-law 5,460, May 5, 1943, as an autonomous body, "com personalidade jurídica própria," located at Laguna, to function under the Ministério de Viação e Obras Públicas in industrial and commercial development, and improvement of Porto de Laguna.

CAIXA DE CRÉDITO COOPERATIVO

Created by title V of decree-law 5,893, October 19, 1943 (on cooperatives) under the supervision of the Ministério de Agricultura to finance and develop cooperatives in Brazil, the government to guarantee the operations of the Caixa, and making available a credit of cr. $300,000,-000 to begin operations.

CENTRO NACIONAL DE ENSINO E PESQUISAS AGRONÓMICAS

The centro which was set up under the Ministério de Agricultura by decree-law 982, November 23, 1938, was reorganized by decree-law 6,155, December 30, 1943. It is to be made up hereafter of the Universidade Rural (U. R.), Serviço Nacional de Pesquisas Agronômicas (S. N. P. A.), Serviço Médico (S. Méd.), Superintendéncia de Edifícios e Parques (S. E. P.), Serviço de Administração (S. A.) and Biblioteca (B). The Universidade Rural is comprised of the existing Escola Nacional de Agronomia, the existing Escola Nacional de Veterinâria, the existing Cursos de Aperfeiçoamento e Especialização, the Cursos de Extensão, Serviço Escolar, and Serviço de Desportos. The S. N. P. A. is to be composed of the existing Institutos de Ecologia e Experimentação Agrícolas (I. E. Exp. A.), of the existing Instituto de Química Agrícola (I. Q. A.), of the existing Instituto Nacional de Óleos (I. N. O.) to be known as Instituto de Óleos (I. O.), of the existing Laboratorio Central de Enologia to be called Instituto de Fermentação, of the existing Instituto Agronômico do Norte, of the Instituto Agronômico do Nordeste, of the Instituto Agronômico do Sul, of the Instituto Agronômico do Oeste, the latter three to be installed.

COMISSÃO ADMINISTRATIVA DO ENCAMINHAMIENTO DE TRABALHADORES PARA AMAZONIA

The C. A. E. T. A., consisting of three members, was created by decree-law 5,813, September 14, 1943, approving the agreement relative to the recruiting, transportation and location of workers for Amazonia.

COMISSÃO CENSITÁRIA NACIONAL

The commission in charge of the census of 1940 by decree-law 969, December 31, 1938, was continued in existence until December 31, 1944, by decree-law 5,561, June 9, 1943.

COMISSÃO CENTRAL DE REQUISIÇÕES

Established by decree-law 5,275, February 24, 1943, with representatives from war, navy, aeronautics and other ministries.

COMISSÃO DE FINANCIAMENTO DA PRODUÇÃO

The C. F. P. is a commission of five members, with the finance minister as chairman, set up by decree-law 5,212, January 21, 1943, to stimulate production. Under the C. F. P. is a Serviço de Controle e Recebimento de Produtos Agrícolas e Matérias Primas (S. C. R. P.).

COMISSÃO NACIONAL DO GASOGENIO

Decree 13,333, September 3, 1943, approves the Regimento of the Commission which was created in the Ministério de Agricultura by decree-law 1,125, February 28, 1939.

COMISSÃO TÉCNICA ORIENTAÇÃO SINDICAL

Established in connection with the Ministério do Trabalho Indústria e Comércio by decree-law 5,199, January 16, 1943 (Cf. decree-law 4,298, May 14, 1942).

COMPANHIA NACIONAL DE ALCALIS

Decree-law 5,684, July 20, 1943, authorizes the Instituto Nacional do Sal (I. N. S.) to organize the above named company to implant the soda industry in Brazil. The capital is 50,000,000 cruzeiros, 26,000,000 being in ordinary shares, and 24,000,000 in preferred. The I. N. S. is to subscribe for the ordinary shares, and jointly with the social security funds for that portion of the preferred shares for which there are no subscribers in the open market.

CONSELHO DE ADMINISTRAÇÃO DE PESSOAL

Created in connection with the Departamento Administrativo do Serviço Público by decree-law 5,937, October 28, 1943, to promote better coordination and greater efficiency in the federal civil service, being composed of the directors of four divisions of the D. A. S. P. and of the directors of personnel in the ministries.

CONSELHO DE ADMINISTRAÇÃO DO MATERIAL

The C. A. M. was established in connection with the Departamento Administrativo do Serviço Público by decree-law 5,715, July 31, 1943, the object being "promover melhor coordenação e maior eficiência dos órgãos interessados na administração de material do serviço civil federal."

CONSELHO NACIONAL DE POLÍTICA INDUSTRIAL E COMERCIAL

An advisory body under the chairmanship of the Minister of Labor, Industry and Commerce, created by decree-law 5,982, November 10, 1943. Two members represent commerce, two industry, one each for the Ministério da Fazenda, Ministério de Agricultura, Ministério da Viação e Obras Públicas, and Ministério do Trabalho, Indústria e Comércio, and five prominent representatives of the social and political sciences.

CONSELHO NACIONAL DE SERVIÇO SOCIAL

The C. N. S. S. of seven members is organized under the Ministério da Educação e Saúde by decree-law 5,697, July 22, 1943, as a coordinating and advisory body in matters of welfare and social service, as referred to in decree-law 525, July 1, 1938. Decree-law 5,698, July 22, 1943, regulates the financial cooperation of the federal government with private agencies.

DEPARTAMENTO DO INTERIOR E DA JUSTIÇA

The Diretoria da Justiça e do Interior of the Ministério da Justiça e Negócios Interiores was transformed into the above named department in the same Ministry by decree-law 5,630, June 29, 1943. Competence in reference to the Corpo de Bombeiros and Polícia Militar of the Distrito Federal was transfered to the Departamento de Administração of the Ministry.

ESCOLA MILITAR DE REZENDE

Created by decree-law 6,012, November 19, 1943 as of January 1, 1944 at the city of Rezende, state of Rio de Janeiro, for the training of combat officers of the army, the existing Escola Militar at Realengo to be continued until December 31, 1944.

FUNDAÇÃO BRASIL CENTRAL

By the decree-law 5,878, October 4, 1943, the Federal Government was authorized to establish the above foundation for colonization purposes in central and western Brazil. The Federal Government is to be represented by the Coordinador da Mobilização Econômica.

INSTITUTO BENJAMIN CONSTANT

Decree-law 6,066, December 3, 1943, defined the purpose and functions of the above agency for the blind under the Ministério da Educação e Saúde. The *regimento* of the I. B. C. was approved by decree 14,165, December 3, 1943.

INSTITUTO NACIONAL DE SURDOS-MUDOS

Decree-law 6,074, December 7, 1943, defined the objectives of the I. N. S. M., an organism of the Ministério da Educação e Saúde for the aid of deaf-mutes, and decree 14,199, December 7, 1943 approves its *regimento*.

LABORATÓRIO NACIONAL DE ANÁLISES

The L. N. A. of the Ministério da Fazenda, subordinate to the Direção Geral da Fazenda Nacional, was reorganized by decree-law 6,067, December 3, 1943, and given a *regimento* by decree 14,168, December 3, 1943.

MINISTÉRIO DA GUERRA

Decree-law 5,311, March 10, 1943, deals with the organization of the Ministry, and supersedes decree-law 279, February 16, 1938.

Decree law 5,388, April 12, 1943, replacing decree-law 556, July 12, 1938, deals with the organization of the army. All references to the air forces are eliminated since the new Ministry of aeronautics has taken over that function.

MINISTÉRIO DA JUSTIÇA E NEGÓCIOS INTERIORES

A Serviço de Documentação (S. D. J.) in the Ministry was created by decree-law 5,971, November 5, 1943, consisting of Secçao de Documentação, Secção de Referência Legislativa, Biblioteca, and the *Arquivos do Ministerio da Justiça e Negócios Interiores.*

MINISTÉRIO DA MARINHA

Decree-law 5,558, June 8, 1943, created directly under the Ministro de Estado the Serviço de Documentação da Marinha, comprising the Secção da História Marítima do Brasil, Biblioteca da Marinha, Arquivo Histórico, and *Revista Marítima Brasileira.*
The S. D. M. takes the place of the Quarta Divisão (E M-4) of the Estado Maior da Armada.

SERVIÇO DE DEFESA CIVIL

The Serviço de Defesa Pasiva Anti-Aérea, created by decree-law 4,624, August 26, 1942, is by decree-law 5,861, September 30, 1943, designated as above.

SERVIÇO DE NAVEGAÇÃO DA BACIA DO PRATA

The shipping of the rivers Paraguay and Paraná and their tributaries, under control of Lloyd Brasileiro is by decree law 5,252, February 16, 1943, to be administered by the above, set up as "entidade autárquica com personalidade própria," subordinate to the Ministerio de Viação e Obras Públicas. The S. N. B. P. has headquarters at Corumbá, Mato Grosso.

SERVIÇO DE METEOROLOGIA

Decree-law 5,995, November 17, 1943, establishes the organization of this service in the Ministério de Agricultura as follows: Divisão de Pesquisas Meteorológicas (D. P. M.); Divisão de Meteorologia Aplicada (D. M. A.); Divisão de Coordenação e Informações Meteorológicas (D. C. I.); Biblioteca (B.); and Secção de Administração.
The S. M. has jurisdiction over the whole national territory which is divided into eight districts. Each is to be under the supervision of an Instituto Regional de Meteorologia; located as follows: 1st dist., Distrito Federal; 2nd dist., São Paulo; 3rd dist., Coussirat de Araujo; 4th dist., Belo Horizonte; 5th dist., Salva-

dor; 6th dist., Recife; 7th dist., Belém; 8th dist., Cuiabá. The I. R. M. of the 2nd, 3rd, 4th, 5th, and 6th districts are to begin functioning immediately. The other as the opportunity occurs. The *regimento* of the Serviço de Meteorologia was approved by decree 14,020, November 17, 1943.

CHILE

CAJA DE LA HABITACIÓN POPULAR

Law 7,600, October 8, 1943 (Ministerio del Trabajo) is a substitute for the text of law 5,950, October 10, 1936, creating the Caja de la Habitación Popular for low cost housing.

COLEGIO DE ARQUITECTOS DE CHILE

Reglamento of law 7,211, July 30, 1942, creating the above, was approved by decree 1,214, July 22, 1943 (Ministerio de Obras Públicas y Vías de Comunicación).

CONSEJO NACIONAL DE BOSQUES

Created by decree 607, August 13, 1943, under the Ministerio de Economía y Comercio to orient, coordinate and formulate the forestry policy and to consist of representatives of the Ministerio de Economía y Comercio, of the Ministerio de Obras Públicas y Vías de Comunicación, Ministerio de Agricultura, Ministerio de Tierras y Colonización, Dirección General de Carabineros, Corporación de Fomento de la Producción, Sociedad Amigos del Árbol, Consorcio Nacional de Productores de Maderas, Asociaciones de Productores de Maderas, and Sociedades de Comerciantes o Exportadores de Maderas y Productos Forestales.

CONSEJO SUPERIOR DE LA HÍPICA NACIONAL

Set up by decree 1,588, May 17, 1943 to advise the Ministerio de Hacienda on the obligations signaled in art. 5 of law 5,055, February 12, 1932.

DEPARTAMENTO DE PREVISIÓN SOCIAL

Decree 458, March 26, 1943, approves the *reglamento* of this department.

DIRECCIÓN GENERAL DE CORREOS Y TELÉGRAFOS

Decree 2,203, April 30, 1943, approves the *reglamento* of the "Ley Orgánica de Correos y Telégrafos."

INSTITUTO GEOGRÁFICO MILITAR

By decree 458 (Ministerio de Defensa Nacional) April 6, 1943, the Servicio Catastral (en su Rama Agrícola) is organized in connection with the Instituto Geográfico Militar with autonomous administration responsible directly to the director of the Institute.

PATRONATO NACIONAL DE REOS

By decree 542, February 5, 1943, both a national *patronato* and *patronatos* for each of the penal institutions were established. The Patronato Nacional is organized by the Minister of Justice (chairman), the Subsecretary of the Ministry of Justice, a member of the Corte de Apelaciones, Santiago, President of the Instituto de Ciencias Penales, Director General of prisons, the medical director of the Instituto de Criminología, Visitadora Social, Jefe de los Servicios de Prisiones, and two members appointed by the President of the Republic.

SERVICIO MÉDICO NACIONAL DE EMPLEADOS

The reglamento orgánico was approved by decree 1, 960, November 22, 1943.

COLOMBIA

Law 7 of March 2, 1943, gives the chief executive among other things authorization to reorganize the various branches of the administration. Art. 12 invests him with this authority until December 31, 1944.

CAJA DE CRÉDITO AGRARIO, INDUSTRIAL Y MINERO

A special section "Sección de Fomento Agrícola" is created by decree 1,599.

COMISIÓN DE LA DEFENSA ECONÓMICA NACIONAL

A commission of five members authorized by law 7, March 2, 1943.

CORTE SUPREMA DE JUSTICIA

Law 67 of December 21, 1943 makes certain changes in the organization of the Supreme Court.

CUERPO AUXILIAR DEL ÓRGANO JUDICIAL

Reorganized by decree 650 of March 30, 1943, under the Departamento de Justicia.

CUERPO ESPECIAL DE GUARDIA RURAL

Created by decree 924 of May 11, 1943, under law 4 of February 27, 1943 as a special section of the Policía Nacional.

DEPARTAMENTO DE CONTROL DE BIENES DE EXTRANJEROS

An alien property office under the Ministerio de Hacienda y Crédito Público established by decree 1013, May 24, 1943.

DIRECCIÓN GENERAL DE TURISMO

By law 48 of December 10, 1943, the Sección de Turismo in the Ministerio de la Economía Nacional became the Dirección General de Turismo. In normal times the seat of the Dirección General is to be at Cartagena.

ESCUELA DE POLICÍA GENERAL SANTANDER

Organized by decree 85 of January 18, 1943.

POLICÍA JUDICIAL (CUERPO AUXILIAR DEL ÓRGANO JUDICIAL)

Reorganized by decree 650 of March 30, 1943.

PREFECTURA DE CONTROL DE CAMBIOS

By decree 2,631 of December 30, 1943, the above is to function as a dependency of the Banco de la República in the same form as the Oficina de Control de Cambios y Exportaciones.

REVISOR PRESIDENCIAL

Authorized by art. 11 of law 7 of March 2, 1943, as a means of reorganizing and improving public administration.

SERVICIO COOPERATIVO INTERAMERICANO DE SALUD PÚBLICA

Established as a section of the Ministerio de Trabajo, Higiene y Previsión Social by decree 41 of January 13, 1943, carrying out an agreement between the Government of Colombia and the Office of the Coordinator of Inter-American Affairs.

SERVICIO MÉDICO DE LOS MINISTERIOS

Set up by decree no. 250 of February 5, 1943, under the Ministerio de Trabajo, Higiene y Previsión Social to furnish medicinal, surgical, dental and pharmaceutical service for employees of all the Ministries except the Ministerio de Guerra, and of the Policía Nacional and Prisiones.

COSTA RICA

AUDITORÍA GENERAL DE HACIENDA

Created in connection with the Secretaría de Hacienda y Comercio by executive decree no. 62, September 27, 1943.

CAJA COSTARRICENSE DE SEGURO SOCIAL

The social security agency set up by law 17, November 1, 1941, is now governed by law 17, October 22, 1943.

INSTITUTO NACIONAL DE HIGIENE

The Institute attached to the Secretaría de Salubridad Pública was designated Instituto Nacional de Higiene Clodomiro Picado by decree no. 1, April 15, 1943 in honor of its first director and founder.

JUNTA CENTRAL DE ABASTOS

A price control agency of three members set up by legislative decree of July 12, 1943. There are also provincial *juntas*. The *reglamento* of this agency under the Secretaría de Trabajo y Previsión Social was proclaimed by decree no. 5, November 3, 1943.

JUNTA NACIONAL DE CARRETERAS

Created by legislative decree no. 4, May 15, 1943, to have charge of highway construction under the loan of the Export-Import Bank. The Secretario de Fomento is the chairman, and the managers of the Banco Nacional de Costa Rica and of the Banco Nacional de Seguros are members.

JUNTA NACIONAL DE CONTROL DE DROGAS

Created by executive decree no. 2, May 1, 1943, to continue acting in its restricted field with the attributions given in general to the Junta Central de Abastos by law no. 37, July 13, 1943.

LIGA SOCIAL ANTIVENÉREA

Created by executive decree no. 7, July 14, 1943, to collaborate with the campaign of the Departamento de Lucha Antivenérea of the Secretaría de Salubridad Pública y Protección Social.

SECRETARÍA DE TRABAJO Y DE PREVISIÓN SOCIAL

Under the Código de Trabajo signed August 27, 1943, effective September 15, the Secretaría is given the following organization: a. Oficina General de Trabajo; b. Dirección General de Previsión Social; c. Instituto Nacional de Investigaciones y de Estudios Sociales; and d. Inspección General de Trabajo. Justice in labor matters is handled by a. Juzgados de Trabajo; b. Tribunales de Conciliación y de Arbitraje; c. Tribunal Superior de Trabajo; and d. Sala de Casación de la Corte Suprema de Justicia.

The Oficina de Investigación y Control de Precios and the Patronato Nacional de la Infancia are also included with the Secretaría.

CUBA

ASOCIACIÓN NACIONAL DE CAFICULTORES DE CUBA

Under authorization of decree 1,396, May 5, 1943, *estatutos* of this Association recognized as official and national in character including all coffee growers were proclaimed by decree 2,891, October 7, 1943. Under supervision of the Ministerio de Agricultura.

ASOCIACIÓN NACIONAL DE COMERCIANTES-ALMACENISTAS DE CAFÉ

Authorized under the supervision of the Ministerio de Comercio by decree 2,218, July 23, 1943, the *estatutos* being approved by decree 774, October 23, 1943.

ASOCIACIÓN NACIONAL DE GANADEROS DE CUBA

The *estatutos generales* were approved by decree 1,861, June 24, 1943, on the proposal of the Minister of Agriculture. As soon as the official association of cattle raisers has been organized, the Comisión de Defensa de la Ganadería is to cease.

ASOCIACIÓN NACIONAL DE INDUSTRIALES TOSTADORES DE CAFÉ

An official organization set up by decree 2,705, August 30, 1943, under the supervision of the Ministerio de Agricultura.

ASOCIACIÓN NACIONAL DE MEDIADORES DEL COMERCIO DE CAFÉ

Authorized under the supervision of the Ministry of Commerce by decree 3,921, December 9, 1943.

CAJA GENERAL DE JUBILACIONES Y PENSIONES DE EMPLEADOS Y OBREROS DE FERROCARRILES Y TRANVÍAS

Reglamento was adopted by decree 2,191 July 2, 1943, replacing that of decree 1,853, June 23, 1930.

CAJA DE RETIRO Y ASISTENCIA SOCIAL DE OBREROS Y EMPLEADOS DE LA INDUSTRIA AZUCARERA

Authorized by law 20, 1941, arts. 7 and 12, and regulated under the Ministerio del Trabajo by decree 3,383, November 16, 1943.

CENTRO DE ORIENTACIÓN INFANTIL

The Centro created by law of June 23, 1938, which had been taken over and directly controlled by the Ministerio de Salubridad y Asistencia Social through decree 3,117, October 30, 1940, was again given autonomous status through decree 3,217, November 11, 1943.

COLEGIO NACIONAL DE PERIODISTAS DE CUBA

The *estatutos* of this professional organization were promulgated by decree 3,382, November 16, 1943.

COMISIÓN DE ESTUDIOS DEL PLAN DE SEGURIDAD SOCIAL

A special committee authorized in connection with the Ministerio del Trabajo by decree 1,099, April, 1943.

COMISIÓN DEL CATASTRO NACIONAL

Established in connection with the Ministerio de Agricultura by decree 1,539, May 21, 1943 to prepare a general plan and specific rules for taking a national cadastral survey. *Reglamento* of the Commission approved by *resolución* 184, February 18, 1944.

COMISIÓN NACIONAL DE AVIACIÓN

An advisory body of five members established in connection with Defensa Nacional by decree 1,834, June 17, 1943, carrying out the recommendation of the Interamerican Technical Conference on Aviation, Lima, 1937.

COMISIÓN NACIONAL INTERMINISTERIAL COORDINADORA

Established in connection with the Ministerio de Estado, by decree 1,901, June 9,

1943 to cooperate with the Consultative Emergency Committee for Political Defense, Montevideo. Composed of representatives of the Ministries of Estado, Gobernación, Justicia, Hacienda, Defensa Nacional and President of the Comisión Marítima Cubana.

COMISIÓN NACIONAL PARA EL ESTUDIO DE LOS PROBLEMAS DE LA POST-GUERRA

An interministerial committee created in connection with the Ministerio de Estado by decree 1,584, May 22, 1943. *Reglamento* proclaimed by decree 2,297, July 27, 1943.

CONSEJO SUPERIOR DEL TRABAJO

Established under Ministerio del Trabajo to take care of questions arising from decree 1,983, July 2, 1943, declaring certain services essential to national defense. The Comisión Nacional de Cooperación Social set up by decree-law 3, 1934, has been taken over in the composition of the Consejo.

CORPORACIÓN NACIONAL DE ASISTENCIA PÚBLICA

By decree 2,432, August 21, 1943, the Corporación is to function in the future as an autonomous and independent organization, according to original plan of its establishment in 1936. It has been-attached to the Ministerio de Salubridad y Asistencia Social in October, 1940.

DIRECCIÓN GENERAL DE RELACIONES CULTURALES

The functions of this bureau in the Ministerio de Estado are defined by decree 2,710, September 14, 1943.

ESCUELA PROFESIONAL DE PERIODISMO

The *reglamento* of this school under the Ministerio de Educación was promulgated by decree 1,588, May 7, 1943.

INSTITUTO CUBANO DE ESTABILIZACIÓN DEL CAFÉ

By decree 1,811, June 17, 1943, the *estatutos* and *reglamento* were suspended for 120 days, the Junta Consultiva was dissolved, and the Institute was to be governed, represented and administered by a Director General appointed by the President of the Republic on the nomination of the Minister of Agriculture.

All functions of price control relating to coffee transferred from Oficina de Regulación de Precios y Abastecimiento by decree 3,312, November 10, 1943.

JUNTA DE ECONOMÍA DE GUERRA

Established by decree 1,437, April 1, 1943, and presided over by the Primer Ministro. The Ministers of State, Finance, Agriculture, Commerce, Labor, two Ministers without portfolio, the Chairman of the Comisión de Fomento Nacional, the Director of the Oficina de Regulación de Precios y Abastecimiento, Agente General de Importación y Exportación, the Chairman of the Comisión Marítima Cubana, the Interventor de la Propiedad Enemiga, and the Chairman of the Comisión Nacional de Transporte are the other members of the Junta. By decree 3,509, November 30, 1943, the following are attached to the Junta: Oficina de Regulación de Precios y Abastecimento; Agencia de Importación y Exportación; and Comisión Marítima Cubana.

JUNTA NACIONAL DEL CENSO

A committee of five members created under the Ministerio de Justicia by the Ley del Censo, April, 1943.

MINISTERIO DE EDUCACIÓN

A "reglamento de la educación rural" was proclaimed by decree 3,450, November 10, 1943, taking the place of the "reglamento para el régimen y gobierno de la educación cívico-rural" December 29, 1938, which was in charge of the Cuerpo de Cultura of the Ejército Constitucional.

OFICIAL NACIONAL DEL CENSO Y ESTADÍSTICA ELECTORAL

By article 154 of the 1943 Código Electoral the work of the decennial census as well as the registration of voters is placed in charge of the above under the Tribunal Superior Electoral. The Oficina Nacional del Censo attached to the Ministerio de Justicia is transferred to form a part of the new office.

PATRONATO PARA LA PROFILAXIS DE LA LEPRA, ENFERMEDADES CUTÁNEAS Y SÍFILIS

Estatutos y reglamento general promulgated by decree 2,116, July 8, 1943. The Patronato which was organized under Law of February 1, 1938, and decree 265, December 5, 1938, functions in connection with the Ministerio de Salubridad y Asistencia Social.

RETIRO MÉDICO

The *reglamento* of the Retiro Médico set up under supervision of the Ministerio de Salubridad y Asistencia Social by law 2, February 20, 1943, was approved by decree 2,434, August 23, 1943. Operates as a "corporación de interés público." Semiannual balances are to be published in the *Gaceta Oficial*.

DOMINICAN REPUBLIC

By decrees 1,048 and 1,049, March 17, 1943 the civil governors of the provinces of Trujillo and of Santiago were given the status of Secretaries of State.

BANCO DE RESERVAS DE LA REPÚBLICA

The Junta Consultiva as provided in art. 31 of law 586, October 24, 1941, was constituted by decree 939, January 20, 1943.

COMISIÓN NACIONAL DEL SERVICIO CIVIL

Law 472, December 30, 1943, concerning the organization and functioning of the Comisión, repeals and takes the place of law 43, July 17, 1942 as amended by law 89, October 3, 1942, and law 284, May 19, 1943.

COMISIÓN NACIONAL PARA EL ESTUDIO DE LOS PROBLEMAS DE LA POST-GUERRA

Created by decree 1,545, November 20, 1943, under the chairmanship of the Secretary of State for foreign relations.

COMISIÓN MARÍTIMA NACIONAL

Decree 951, January 30, 1943 replaced by decree 1,079, April 2, 1943, places under control of the government all ships of more than 20 tons of national registry, to be administered and operated by a commission of five members attached to the Secretaría de Guerra y Marina.

CONSEJO NACIONAL DE TUBERCULOSIS

A council of seven members created under the Secretaría de Sanidad y Asistencia Pública by law 450, December 15, 1943, taking over the activities conducted by the Liga Nacional Antituberculosa (established by law 338, September 30, 1940).

DIRECCIÓN GENERAL DE DEPORTES

Set up under the Secretaría de Educación y Bellas Artes by law 463, December 23, 1943, to promote the better organization and practice of the sports. Law 298, May 30, 1919 and Law 437, March 25, 1920 are repealed.

MARINA NACIONAL

Decree 1,081, April 3, 1943, creates a military marine force under the Comandancia de la Marina Nacional.

SECRETARÍA DE EDUCACIÓN Y BELLAS ARTES

Reglamento for the department promulgated by decree 1,128, May 4, 1943.

ECUADOR

BANCO NACIONAL DE FOMENTO PROVINCIAL

The Banco Hipotecario del Ecuador was converted into the above as of January 1, 1944, by legislative decree approved October 14, 1943, to promote agricultural production, national industry, especially small industry, the means of cultivation, the extension of technical education and agricultural experimentation, organizing the interchange of products, the promotion of savings, colonization and parcelling out of lands, and organization and financing of agricultural and industrial cooperatives. A Banco Provincial Asociado is to be established in each province except Orientales.

CAJA DEL SEGURO

Estatutos of the Caja del Seguro approved by decree 2052, December 28, 1943, to become effective April 1, 1944.

DIRECCIÓN DE ESTADÍSTICA AGROPECUARIA

The organization of this national service in the Ministerio de Agricultura was provided for by decree 722, April 17, 1943.

DIRECCIÓN GENERAL DE BELLAS ARTES

Created under the Ministerio de Educación Pública by decree 713, May 15, 1943.

DIRECCIÓN GENERAL DE ORIENTE

Created in the Ministerio de Gobierno as of January 1, 1944, by legislative decree approved October 19, 1943.

GERENCIA GENERAL DE LOS FERROCARRILES DEL ESTADO

A "reglamento para administración de los ferrocarriles del estado, subordinados al Ministerio de Obras Públicas," was approved by decree 17, January 15, 1943.

INSTITUTO CULTURAL ECUATORIANO

Created by decree 1,755, November 11, 1943 in connection with the Ministerio de Educación, having nine members including representatives of the academies and universities. To continue the Biblioteca de Clásicos Ecuatorianos to organize expositions, trips, lectures, concerts, etc., and to promote cultural matters. Supported by a tax on exports.

MINISTERIO DE DEFENSA NACIONAL

The decree 972, June 30, 1943 changes the name of Tercero Departamento Servicios to Intendencia General de las Fuerzas Armadas.

SERVICIO COOPERATIVO INTERAMERICANO DE SALUD PÚBLICA

Created in cooperation with the Coordinator of Inter-American Affairs and with the Ministerio de Previsión Social by decree 119, February 1, 1943.

SERVICIO DE ASUNTOS INDÍGENAS

Decree 511-bis of April 2, 1943, provides for the organization of this service in the Ministerio de Previsión Social y Trabajo.

UNIVERSIDAD DE LOJA

By decree 1,553, October 9, 1943, the Junta Universitaria de Loja was raised to the rank of Universidad de Loja there having been recently added a Facultad de Ciencias to the original Facultad de Jurisprudencia y Ciencias Sociales.

GUATEMALA

INSPECCIÓN GENERAL DEL EJÉRCITO

For the duration of the war, the duties of inspection were by decree of April 27, 1943, separated from the Secretaría de Guerra and placed directly under the President of the Republic.

SOCIEDAD DE GEOGRAFÍA E HISTORIA

The "attributes" of the Sociedad were transferred from the Secretaría de Educación Pública to the Secretaría de Relaciones Exteriores by decree of June 30, 1943, and it is expected that its program will include publications of a different nature from those published to the present.

HAITI

BUREAU DES MINES

Decree-law 337, December 22, 1943 amending the mining legislation, creates a Bureau des Mines in the Département des Travaux Publics.

CONSEIL DE L'UNIVERSITÉ D'HAITI

Created by *arrêté* of March 31, 1943, to coordinate the schools of higher learning with a view to formation of a university. These schools of higher learning are the Faculté de Droit; École des Sciences Appliquées; École Nationale d'Agriculture; Faculté de Médicine, Pharmacie et d'Art Dentaire.

MEXICO

BANCO DE MÉXICO

By a decree of June 15, 1943, a "fondo nacional de garantía" was set up in the amount of $5,000,000 for agricultural credit operations, the administration to be entrusted to the Banco de México. Amended by decree of September 21, 1943.

CÁMARA DE LA PROPIEDAD RÚSTICA Y URBANA DEL DISTRITO FEDERAL

An "institución pública autónoma con personalidad jurídica" set up by law of May 21, 1943, to represent the interest of all proprietors in the Federal District. By decree of November 19, 1943 the law of May 21, 1943 was revoked.

CASA DEL MARINO DE LOS ESTADOS UNIDOS MEXICANOS

Considered as a national institution by *acuerdo* of April 28, 1943, functioning under the administration of the Secretaría de Marina. Has "personalidad jurídica." First building opened at Vera Cruz. *Reglamento general* approved May 12, 1943. Collection of funds originally authorized by decree of March 4, 1941.

COLEGIO NACIONAL

Established by decree of April 8, 1943 to consist of twenty eminent Mexicans conducting courses of lectures during ten months of the year, free from the limitations of the universities. To publish a review. The Secretaría de Educación Pública will designate the first 15 members.

COMISIÓN CONSULTIVA DE FIANZAS

The *reglamento* of the Commisión to advise the Secretaría de Hacienda y Crédito Público in procedural matters under the first chapter of title 5 of the Ley de Instituciones de Finanzas was proclaimed by order of June 12, 1943.

COMISIÓN NACIONAL DE CARRERAS DE CABALLOS

An advisory commission established under the Secretaría de Gobernación by decree of October 6, 1943, to promote the breeding of full-blooded stock.

COMISIÓN NACIONAL DE EMERGENCIA PARA LA DEFENSA POLÍTICA

Established by decree of July 22, 1943, with representatives from the Secretarías of Gobernación, Relaciones Exteriores, Defensa Nacional, Comunicaciones y Obras Públicas, Marina, and from the Procuraduría General, in accordance with a resolution of the Comité Consultivo de Emergencia para la Defensa Política. The representative of Secretaría de Gobernación to be the chairman.

CONSEJO NAVAL

A commission established in Secretaría de Marina by decree of August 1, 1943, to deal with matters of compensation and promotions for the officers and to serve as a Consejo de Honor Superior de la Armada.

CUERPO DE ESPECIALISTAS DE EDUCACIÓN FÍSICA MILITAR

Set up under the Secretaría de la Defensa Nacional by decree of March 22, 1943.

DIRECCIÓN DE ORGANIZACIÓN EJIDAL

Instituted in the Secretaría de Agricultura in September, 1943 to increase farm production.

DIRECCIÓN DEL SEGURO DE VIDA MILITAR

Established by Ley del Seguro de Vida Militar, April 6, 1943.

DIRECCIÓN GENERAL DE CONSTRUCCIONES NAVALES

Created in the Secretaría de Marina by decree of December 13, 1943.

DIRECCIÓN GENERAL DE OBRAS PÚBLICAS

An *acuerdo* of February 28, 1944 provides for the consolidation in the Secretaría de Comunicaciones y Obras Públicas of the Departamento de Obras Hidráulicas and of the Departamento de Edificios under the above designation.

ESCUELA DE AVIACIÓN NAVAL DE LA ARMADA

Created in the Secretaría de Marina, Dirección General de la Armada, as of September 1, 1943, by decree of August 29.

FONDO DE AHORRO DEL EJÉRCITO

Decree of June 21, 1943, orders that this fund set up by decree of January 1, 1936, be administered by a Consejo Directivo del Seguro de Vida Militar. Seguro de Vida Militar had been established under the Secretaría de la Defensa Nacional by law published in the *Diario Oficial* of May 11.

INSTITUTO NACIONAL DE CARDIOLOGÍA DE MÉXICO

Set up by law of May 19, 1943.

JUNTA DE ECONOMÍA DE EMERGENCIA

Set up by decree of May 12, 1943, as a temporary advisory board consisting of the Secretaries of Treasury, National Economy, Agriculture, Foreign Relations, with the Coordinator of Production and the Secretary of the President. Abolished by decree of February 11, 1944.

SECRETARÍA DE SALUBRIDAD Y ASISTENCIA

Created by decree of October 15, 1943, through the fusing of the Secretaría de Asistencia Pública (originally Departamento de Asistencia Social Infantil by decree of June 30, 1937, and Secretaría by decree of December 31, 1937) and the Departamento de Salubridad Pública (decree of December 25, 1917).

SERVICIO DE TRANSPORTES (EJÉRCITO)

Established in the Army as of November 1 by decree of October 30, 1943.

NICARAGUA

Legislative decree 276, August 28, 1943, relating to the control and expropriation of alien property, provides for the creation of a Comisión Consultiva sobre Bienes Controlados, attached to the Secretaría de Hacienda y Crédito Público composed of the Ministro de Hacienda y Crédito Público, the Ministro de Relaciones Exteriores, the Gerente General del Banco Nacional and a representative of the Secretaría de Hacienda.

INSTITUTO INDIGENISTA NACIONAL

Established by executive decree 923, November 26, 1943, as an affiliated organization of the Instituto Indigenista Interamericano. Not attached to any Ministry. The Executive Committee is composed of the Secretaries of State and the Director General de Sanidad.

SECRETARÍA DE LA PRESIDENCIA

By decree of May 12, 1943, the reglamento del poder ejecutivo was amended with a section organizing the above service, the Secretario de la Presidencia to have all the prerogatives of the Secretarios de Estado. The decree was effective as of July 1, 1943.

PANAMA

CAJA DE SEGURO SOCIAL

Law 134 of April 27, 1943 takes the place of law 23 of 1941 which establishes the social security.

JUNTA NACIONAL DE NUTRICIÓN

Created by decree 218, October 30, 1943, in accordance with the United Nations Conference on Food and Agriculture under the Ministerio de Agricultura y Comercio to consist of the Gerente of the Banco Agro-Pecuario y Industrial and six persons competent in education, health, nutrition, economics and agriculture.

LOTERÍA NACIONAL DE BENEFICENCIA

Reorganized by law 109, February 8, 1943. Under the Ministerio de Salubridad y Obras Públicas. Law 29, April 1, 1941, secs. 13–42 dealing with this institution repealed.

MUSEO COLONIAL HISTÓRICO SAMUEL LEWIS

To be established in one of the old edifices of Old Panama City under the Ministerio de Educación by law 113, March 16, 1943.

OFICINA GENERAL DE TRABAJO

By decree 195, July 30, 1943, the Sección de Organización Obrera of the Ministerio de Agricultura y Comercio was designated as above, the duties being those assigned in decree-laws 38 of 1941 and 34 of 1942.

TRIBUNAL DE LO CONTENCIOSO-ADMINISTRATIVO

Created by art. 7 of law 135, April 30, 1943, consisting of three magistrates named directly by the President of the Republic for terms of six years. Until an organ is selected, the decisions are to appear in the *Gaceta Oficial*. The court was installed on June 1, 1943.

UNIVERSIDAD INTERAMERICANA

Law 122, April 9, 1943, authorized the executive branch to institute and organize the above University. The institution was created by decree of August 1943, which is of temporary nature until the statutes are ratified by the competent bodies in the other countries.

PARAGUAY

Decree 19,392, of August 13, 1943, reorganizes the Ministries, transferring Justicia to Interior, Culto to Relaciones Exteriores, Instrucción Pública becoming a separate department as Educación, Industria y Comercio being separated from Agricultura, Guerra y Marina being renamed Defensa Nacional, and Salud Pública being called Salud Pública y Previsión Social. There are now nine ministries instead of eight, as follows: 1. Interior y Justicia; 2. Relaciones Exteriores y Culto; 3. Hacienda; 4. Educación; 5. Agricultura; 6. Industria y Comercio; 7. Obras Públicas; 8. Defensa Nacional; and 9. Salud Pública y Previsión Social. The functions are restated in decree 387, September 20, 1943.

COMISIÓN DICTAMINADORA DE SALARIOS MÍNIMOS

Appointed by decree October 4, 1943, for the provisional fixing of wages.

INSTITUTO AGRONÓMICO NACIONAL

Established by decree 18,422.

INSTITUTO DE ENSEÑANZA DEL PERSONAL FEMENINO AUXILIAR DE SALUD PÚBLICA "DOCTOR ANDRÉS BARBERO"

Created under the Ministerio de Salud Pública by decree 17,865, April 5, 1943, absorbing the Escuela de Visitadores de Higiene, founded about 1940.

SERVICIO TÉCNICO INTER-AMERICANO DE COOPERACIÓN AGRÍCOLA

Decree 16,507, January 13, 1943, approved the contract of December 24, 1942, between the Minister of Agriculture, Commerce and Industries and the Institute of Inter-American Affairs setting up the above-named service.

INSTITUTO DE PREVISIÓN SOCIAL

Established by decree law 17,071 of February 18, 1943 as an autonomous organization under the supervision of the Ministry of Public Health. *Reglamento* approved by decree 1,371, November 26, 1943.

PERU

ACADEMIA NACIONAL DE DERECHO Y CIENCIAS POLÍTICAS

This Academy organized by the Facultad de Derecho of the Universidad Nacional Mayor de San Marcos by University resolution of August 10, 1943, is recognized by supreme decree of August 17, 1943, as a national academy functioning as an advisory body to the government after the pattern of the Academia Nacional de Ciencias Exactas Físicas y Naturales organized by the Facultad de Ciencias of the same University and recognized officially by supreme resolution of October 23, 1939.

ARCHIVO NACIONAL AEROFOTOGRÁFICO

Created in the Dirección General de Aerofotografía of the Ministerio de Aeronáutica by supreme decree of July 1, 1943.

COMITÉ DE ACCIÓN SOCIAL

Created by decree of January 8, 1943, the Minister of Public Health and Welfare being the chairman.

COMITÉ NACIONAL DE LUCHA ANTI-TUBERCULOSA

Established in connection with the Ministerio de Salud y Asistencia Social by supreme decree of August 3, 1943.

CONSEJO DIRECTIVO DE LA CULTURA MUSICAL

The *reglamento* of the Consejo under the Ministerio de Educación Pública was approved by supreme resolution 2,075, July 21, 1943, in accordance with supreme decree of June 10, 1943. The Consejo has control over the Orquesta Sinfónica Nacional, and is to transform the existing Academia de Música Alcedo into a Conservatorio Nacional.

CONSEJO DIRECTIVO DE LAS BELLAS ARTES

Created under the Ministerio de Educación Pública by supreme decree of August 5, 1943.

CORPORACIÓN PERUANA DE AEROPUERTOS Y AVIACIÓN COMERCIAL

Created in connection with the Ministerio de Hacienda and the *estatutos* approved by supreme decree of June 25, 1943 under authority of law 9,577, March 1943, to conduct commercial air service and to promote the construction of air materiel in Peru. The capital of 10,000,000 soles is subscribed entirely by the Government.

CORPORACIÓN PERUANA DEL SANTA

Created in connection with the Ministerio de Hacienda and the Estatutos approved by supreme decree of June 4, 1943, to develop iron and steel industry and to exploit hydroelectric power in the Santa Valley, north of Lima. The capital of 100,000,000 soles is to be subscribed entirely by the government.

CORTE SUPERIOR

Law 9,882, December 31, 1943, provides that the Corte Superior de Justicia de Lima be made up of three *salas en lo civil* and of three *tribunales correccionales*, and increases the membership to 19. Law 9,883 of same date provides that the Corte Superior del Distrito Judicial del Cuzco be organized into two *tribunales correccionales* and a single *sala civil*. Law 9,884 of same date provides that the Corte Superior de Justicia function as two *salas en lo civil* and as a *tribunal correccional*.

DEPARTAMENTO DE ASUNTOS TEXTILES

Created in the Ministerio del Trabajo at end of December, 1943.

DEPARTAMENTO DE ESTADÍSTICA AGRO-PECUARIA

Transferred from the Dirección de Alimentación Nacional to the Dirección de Agricultura by *resolución suprema* 15, January 26, 1943.

DEPARTAMENTO DE PESCA Y CAZA

Established in the Dirección de Asuntos Orientales of the Ministerio de Agricultura, September, 1943.

DIRECCIÓN DE INFORMACIONES

Supreme decree of July 6, 1943, organizes this bureau in the Ministerio de Gobierno y Policía in three sections: 1. Técnica y Administrativa; 2. Prensa; and 3. Propaganda.

INSPECCIÓN GENERAL DE FARMACIA

Created by supreme decree of July 15, 1943 as a part of the Ministerio de Salud Pública y Asistencia Social, to supervise the practice of the profession as well as the manufacture of drugs.

INSTITUTO DE PROBLEMAS INTERNACIONALES DE POST GUERRA

Set up under the Ministerio de Relaciones Exteriores y Culto by supreme decree of March 15, 1943.

INSTITUTO NACIONAL DE METEOROLOGÍA E HIDROLOGÍA

Transferred from Dirección de Agricultura to the Ministerio de Aeronáutica by decree of January 19, 1943.

INSTITUTO PERUANO DE ESTADÍSTICA

Organized May 20, 1943 as a technical professional association, and recognized officially by *resolución* of August 12, 1943.

LIGA PERUANA CONTRA EL REUMATISMO

Recognized as having official character by supreme resolution of September 21, 1943.

MINISTERIO DE AERONÁUTICA

A minister for aeronautics was appointed by decree of January 3, 1943. The Ministry was authorized by law 9,416, October 27, 1941, as an offshoot from the Ministerio de Marina y Aviación. Although the Ministerio de Aeronáutica was to have been set up on January 1, 1942, action was delayed a year for various reasons.

A decree of February 26, 1943, fixes the provisional organization of the Ministry as follows, the Cuerpo Aeronáutico del Perú being transferred to the Ministry: Estado Mayor General de Aeronáutica; Dirección General de Aeronáutica Civil; Dirección General de Administración de Aeronáutica; Dirección General de Comunicaciones y Meteorología Aeronáutica (created by decree of February 3, 1943), including the former Instituto Nacional de Meteorología e Hidrología; Dirección General de Aerofotografía; Consejo Superior de Aeronáutica; Inspección General de Aeronáutica.

MINISTERIO DE AGRICULTURA

Established by law 9,711, January 2, 1943, with the following subdivisions: Dirección de Agricultura; Dirección de Ganadería; Dirección de Aguas e Irrigación; Dirección de Asuntos Orientales, Colonización y Terrenos de Oriente; and Dirección de Alimentación Nacional. By decree of April 20, 1943, the Dirección de Aguas e Irrigación was transferred to the Ministerio de Fomento.

By supreme decree 545, July 2, 1943, all activities related to the fisheries industries were centralized in this Ministry. The Ministerio de Marina through its Dirección de Capitanías is to care for the police of the maritime fisheries.

OFICINA DEL CONTRALOR DEL PETRÓLEO Y DERIVADOS Y COORDINADOR GENERAL DE TRANSPORTE NACIONAL

Created by Resolución Suprema of April 24, 1943.

SERVICIO COOPERATIVO INTERAMERICANO DE PRODUCCIÓN ALIMENTICIA

The contract with the government of the United States with reference to the establishment of this service under the Ministerio de Agricultura was approved by supreme resolution 266, May 20, 1943.

SERVICIO NACIONAL DE PROTECCIÓN MATERNO-INFANTIL

Constituted by the Instituto Nacional del Niño under the Dirección General de Salubridad of the Ministerio de Salud Pública y Asistencia Social by supreme decree of July 2, 1943.

EL SALVADOR

DIRECCIÓN GENERAL DE EDUCACIÓN FÍSICA

The *reglamento* of this bureau in the Ministerio de Instrucción Pública was promulgated by decree 8, September 22, 1943 (printed in the *Diario Oficial*, enero 25, 1944).

INSTITUTO INDIGENISTA NACIONAL

In accordance with legislative decree 18, March 18, 1941, ratifying the convention creating the Inter-American Indian Institute the executive decree 11, November 13, 1943 (Secretaría de Instrucción Pública) creates the above-named Instituto consisting of the Subsecretary of Public Instruction, of the Salvadorean member of the Executive Committee of the Interamerican Institute, one or more officials of "empresas públicas," and one or more officials of "empresas privadas."

INSTITUTO TECNOLÓGICO DE EL SALVADOR

The legislative decree 38, July 31, provides for the establishment of a corporation "de utilidad pública" under the above name, to carry on technical and scientific investigations and studies relating to agriculture, mining, and other economic activities. The following are the initial supporting members of the Instituto: Mejoramiento Social; S. A., Banco Hipotecario; Asociación Cafetalera de El Salvador; Compañía Salvadoreña del Café, S. A.; Cooperativa de Cajas de Crédito Rural Ltda.; and Asociación de Ganaderos de El Salvador.

JUNTA DE VIGILANCIA DE BANCOS Y SOCIEDADES ANÓNIMAS

Legislative decree 32, April 3, 1943, which repeals decree 124 of September 10, 1936, regulates the function of this body which is composed of the Director General del Presupuesto and of four other members from the Ministerio de Hacienda.

LOTERÍA NACIONAL DE BENEFICENCIA

The *reglamento* was promulgated by decree 2, September 1, 1943. At the same time the *reglamento general* of the Lotería del Hospital Rosales y Hospicio, San Salvador, dated May 1, 1912, was abrogated. The Junta Directiva is composed of the Director of the Hospital Rosales (chairman), the Director of the Casa Nacional del Niño (vice-chairman), the Director General de Contribuciones, the Oficial Mayor of the Ministerio de Asistencia Social and the Interventor of the Lotería (secretario). Reports annually to the Ministerio de Asistencia Social.

PROVEEDURÍA GENERAL DE LA REPÚBLICA

Established under the Ministerio de Hacienda as the general supply office of the government by legislative decree 101, December 13.

URUGUAY

CAJA DE JUBILACIONES BANCARIAS

The Caja de Jubilaciones y Pensiones de los Empleados de las Instituciones Bancarias y Bolsa de Comercio was designated as above, and had its organic act modified by decree law 3,050/942, January 29, 1943.

CAJA DE TRABAJADORES RURALES

Created by decree law 2,685/939, January 20, 1943, as a section of the Instituto de Jubilaciones y pensiones del Uruguay.

CAJA NACIONAL DE AHORROS Y DESCUENTOS

A *reglamento general* was proclaimed by decree of February 19, 1943, replacing the decree of June 29, 1934. The Caja is managed in connection with the Banco de la República.

COMISIÓN DE EXPORTACIONES E IMPORTACIONES

The Consejo Honorario Asesor of the Dirección de Asuntos Comerciales of the Ministerio de Relaciones Exteriores created by decree of April 1, 1936 was by decree of July 28, 1943, given the above name, and organized as of that date.

COMISIÓN NACIONAL COORDINADORA DE TRANSPORTE

Constituted in connection with the Ministerio de Obras Públicas by decree of July 8, 1943.

COMISIÓN NACIONAL DE COOPERACIÓN INTELECTUAL

The Comisión created by decree of June 1, 1937 was reorganized by decree of August 4, 1943. The Comisión by the decree of August 4, 1943, has 28 members representing cultural institutions and 57 members designated by the Poder Ejecutivo. The Comisión actually functions through a Consejo Ejecutivo of nine members with headquarters at the Ministerio de Relaciones Exteriores.

COMISIÓN INTERMINISTERIAL PARA LA DEFENSA POLÍTICA

Established in connection with the Ministerio del Interior by decree of March 29, 1943, to assemble and furnish data to the Comité de Emergencia para la Defensa Política del Continente.

CONTRALOR DE EXPORTACIONES E IMPORTACIONES

Decree 373/1940 of January 29, 1943 promulgated the Reglamento Interno of the Comisión Honoraria del Contralor de Exportaciones e Importaciones.

DIRECCIÓN DE RELACIONES CULTURALES

Created in the Ministerio de Relaciones Exteriores by decree of August 4, 1943. The director is to be charged with the secretariat of the Comisión Nacional de Cooperación Intelectual and with its Consejo Ejecutivo.

FACULTAD DE HUMANIDADES

Created in the Universidad de la República by decree-law of February 11, 1943, for research and higher education in philosophy, letters, history and pedagogy.

INSTITUTO NACIONAL DE VIVIENDAS ECONÓMICAS

Decree of October 15, 1943 determines that the Instituto, created by law of November 19, 1937, is not a decentralized service, but a dependency of the Ministerio de Obras Públicas.

VENEZUELA

ADMINISTRACIÓN GENERAL DEL IMPUESTO SOBRE LA RENTA

Created under the Ministerio de Hacienda by decree 46, March 16, 1943 in accordance with the income tax law, July 17, 1942.

BANCO CENTRAL

Amendments to the "ley de Banco Central" by law of July 10, 1943.

COLEGIO DE ODONTÓLOGOS DE VENEZUELA

Created as a professional association by Ley de Ejercicio de la Odontología, October 1, 1943, to which all members of the profession must belong. To serve as an advisory organization and to represent the profession before the public authorities. The law of October 1, 1943, repeals the Ley de Ejercicio de la Dentistería of July 19, 1926.

COMISIÓN INTERMINISTERIAL COORDINADORA

Established by decree September 2, 1943.

COMISIÓN PARA EL ESTUDIO DE LAS CUESTIONES DE LA POSGUERRA

Created by decree 197, October 6, 1943, and composed of Ministers of Foreign Relations, Finance, War and Marine Development, Public Health and Welfare, Agriculture and Cattle Raising, Labor and Communications, and in addition the Judicial Adviser of the Secretary of the Presidency, the President of the Banco Central, the President of Comisión de Control de Importaciones, and the Director of the Instituto Técnico de Inmigración y Colonización. Attached to the Ministry of Foreign Relations.

COMISIÓN PREPARATORIA DE LA REFORMA AGRARIA

Set up in December, 1943 in the Ministry of Agriculture to study agricultural problems. Alfredo Machado Hernández, ex-Finance minister, the chairman.

GRAN FERROCARRIL DE VENEZUELA

Nationalized late in 1943. Formerly belonged to a German company.

INSTITUTO DE LA CIUDAD UNIVERSITARIA

Created by decree 196, October 2, 1943, under the Ministerio de Obras Públicas, to carry out the plans and work on the Ciudad Universitaria. To be liquidated upon completion of the work.

INSTITUTO NACIONAL DE OBRAS SANITARIAS

By decree 71, April 15, 1943, established in connection with the Ministerio de Obras

Públicas, having "personalidad jurídica autónoma y patrimonio propio distinto e independiente del Fisco Nacional." To be administered by a *junta* of five containing representatives from ministries of finance, public works, and health. *Reglamento* promulgated by decree 104, May 22, 1943. Began to function July 1.

INSTITUTO NACIONAL DEL CAFÉ

To be liquidated as of June 30, 1943, in accordance with decree 76, April 16, 1943, the activities to be divided between the Ministerio de Agricultura y Cría, and the Banco Agrícola y Pecuario.

OFICINA COOPERATIVA INTERAMERICANA DE SALUD PÚBLICA

Established at Maracay under the Ministerio de Sanidad y Asistencia Social by decree 58, March 26, 1943, in accordance with the exchange of notes on February 18, 1943, with the United States Government relative to intensifying the antimalarial campaign in Venezuela.

OFICINA TÉCNICA DE HIDROCÁRBUROS

Created in the Ministerio de Fomento by decree 58, March 31, 1943, the following being abolished as of April 1, 1943: Dirección de Hidrocárburos; Inspección Técnica General de Hidrocárburos; Sala Técnica de Minas; and the Fiscalía de Rentas. Some of the functions of the Sala Técnica de Minas were transferred to Servicio Técnico de Minería y Geología.

ORGANIZACIÓN DE BIENESTAR ESTUDIANTIL VENEZUELA

Created in the Universidad Central by decree 279 December 13, 1943, and attached to the Ministerio de Educación Nacional as an autonomous official institute. The Vicerector of the University is the chairman.

PROCURADOR GENERAL

A law of July 16, 1943, redefines the functions of the attorney general and repeals the previous law of June 14, 1916.

HISTORY: GENERAL

Amunátegui Solar, Domingo. Formación de la nacionalidad chilena. Ed. de la Univ. de Chile. 170 p. [2592
A concise statement. Covers the colonial period and the years of emancipation. [Ed.].

Arce, Henrique J., and Ernesto J. Castillero R. Guía histórica de Panamá. Segunda ed. Panama. Cía. ed. nacional. 216 p. [2593
Official text book; history to 1942. [R. D. Hussey]

ARCHIVUM. Revista de la Junta de historia eclesiástica argentina. Buenos Aires. Tomo 1, cuad. 1, enero–junio—. [2594
New publication devoted to Argentine ecclesiastical history, the result of a resolution adopted at the Episcopal Conferences of 1938 for the creation of a nation-wide organization to encourage such studies. The impressive volume of more than 300 pages contains monographs, commentaries, and book reviews and notices. [C. Shelby]

Arévalo Martínez, Rafael. Influencia de España en la formación de la nacionalidad centroamericana. Guatemala. Tip. Nacional. 29 p. [2595
An essay intended to demonstrate that Central American nationality, which persists despite present political divisions owes to Spain its distinctive character: predominant race, political unity (in colonial times and later), geographical unity, religion, law, language, culture. The history of attempts at political unification since 1821 is sketched. [C. Shelby]

Baldwin, Leland Dewitt. The story of the Americas: the discovery, settlement, and development of the New World. New York. Simon and Schuster. 720 p. [2597
A textbook, and a poor one. It is completely out of proportion (there are 465 pages on the colonial period), rather over-popularized, far from objective in its judgments, and not irreproachable as to factual accuracy. It is, however, readable, and on the whole sympathetic to the Latin cultures and settlements. [R. D. Hussey]

Behrendt, Richard F. Aspectos sociales y económicos del Istmo de Panamá durante la época del tráfico interoceánico primitivo, 1519–1848 (*Rev. mex. soc.*, año 5, vol. 5, no. 1, primer trim., p. 49–61). [2598
Suggests that except for the first, the dates 1519, 1821, and 1903, traditional milestones in the political history of Panama, have little significance for the social and economic history of the Isthmus. The writer believes that a more meaningful division of Panamanian history comprises the following periods: 1519–1848, before modern traffic developed; 1849–1913, during which the Gold Rush and the Panama Railway gave impetus to land transportation across the Isthmus; and 1914 to the present, the period dominated by the traffic through the Canal. The author discusses in detail the first period and on the basis of a wide variety of secondary and original sources, presents a picture of stagnation and decreasing population, particularly after the mid-eighteenth century. [J. F. King]

Besson, Juan. Historia del estado Zulía. Maracaibo. Ed. Hnos. Belloso Rossell. [2599
The first volume of a projected three-volume history of the Venezuelan state of Zulía. This portion covers the period 1499–1800, and gives attention to social and economic as well as to political history—approximately half the book is given over to the text of documents, chiefly from Spanish archives. [C. Shelby]

BOLETÍN DEL ARCHIVO HISTÓRICO DE LA PROVINCIA DE MÉRIDA. Mérida, Venezuela. Año 1, no. 1, feb.—. [2600
The Archivo Histórico, created in 1942, has been inventoried, and the present publication is designed to make its contents known to the public. Six numbers issued in 1943 contain brief articles, documents, and indices. [C. Shelby]

Carbia, Rómulo D. Historia de la leyenda negra hispanoamericana. Buenos Aires. Ed. Orientación española. 240 p. [2601
Not a complete or objective history of this fascinating subject. Carbia brings few new facts to light, and is not as satisfactory as Constantino Bayle, but this volume is itself a source revealing the attitude of a contemporary conservative Argentine who believes that the "leyenda negra" had no sound basis. His thesis is not helped by the twenty five reproductions of Spanish cruelty from various editions of Las Casas. [L. Hanke]

Cervera Andrade, Alejandro. Breve historia de la cirugía en Yucatán (*Orbe*, segunda época, no. 11, feb., p. 6–14). [2602
From Maya days to the present. Little more than a list of names with a line or two concerning the achievements of the person mentioned, but fuller detail is given for the last half century. [R. D. Hussey]

ESTUDIOS HISTÓRICOS. Guadalajara. Año 1, no. 1, enero—. [2603
This semi-annual publication, edited by Dr. Luis Medina Ascensio, proposes to publish original studies, documents and descriptions of archives, and notes and reviews of recent publications of interest to historians. [Ed.]

Ferrari Rueda, Rodolfo de. Córdoba histórica. Prólogo de Rodolfo Martínez. Cordóba. Tall. gráf. Biffignandi. 376 p. [2604

A retired member of the provincial judiciary reviews the development and growth of the province since the conquest. The survey is based on published material. [Ed.].

Furlong, Guillermo. La historiografía eclesiástica argentina, 1536-1943 (*Archivum*, tomo 1, cuad. 1, enero-junio, p. 58–92). [2605

A careful survey, beginning with the work of Antonio Rodríguez, a soldier who accompanied Mendoza in 1536, and who later became a Jesuit. Many other early chroniclers of the Río de la Plata were ecclesiastics whose works emphasized religious topics, and travel books of the next three centuries also touched upon them. The author remarks that provincial historians were more peroccupied with ecclesiastical matters than were authors of ambitious national histories. Works devoted to church history as such seem to be a comparatively recent development. The article constitutes a valuable bibliography on the subject. [C. Shelby]

Gallegos, Gerardo. Venezuela. Las Américas. Habana. Ed. La República. (Cuadernos de divulgación histórica, vol. 1, no. 1). 64 p. [2606

Sketches in a popular style of historical places, personages and events of colonial Venezuela, ending with a discussion of the racial composition of the country and its social implications. Number 2 of the series will deal with the period of the Republic. [C. Shelby]

Gamio, Manuel. Static and dynamic values in the indigenous past of America (*Hisp. amer. hist. rev.*, vol. 23, no. 3, Aug., p. 386–393). [2607

The "static" values of the ancient Indian culture—by which the author means those values which have disappeared, though not necessarily beyond revival—seem more valuable than the "dynamic" values which have survived. Static values include the arts, mythology, and the democratic spirit. [R. D. Hussey]

Gangotena y Jijón, Cristóbal de. Bustamante. Estudio genealógico (*Bol. acad. nac. hist.*, Quito, vol. 23, no. 62, julio-dic., p. 207–220). [2608

Genealogical notes on a still-existing Ecuadoran family of colonial origin. Traces the family from the sixteenth century to the present. [J. F. King]

Greve, Ernesto. Historia de la amalgamación de la plata (*Rev. chil. hist. geog.*, no. 102, enero-junio, p. 158–259). [2609

Founded on a wide variety of archival and secondary material, this lengthy article primarily concerns silver mining in Chile in the colonial period and in the nineteenth century. Particular attention is given to the introduction and development of the "patio process" of silver amalgamation. [J. F. King]

Humphreys, Robert Arthur. Latin American history. London. P. S. King & Staples, publ. (Historical association pamphlet, no. 127). 18 p. [2610

Thumbnail sketch of Latin American history for the general reader. A list of a dozen books suitable to form the basis of a school library on the subject is appended. [C. Shelby]

Kemble, John Haskell. The Panama route, 1848–1869. Berkeley and Los Angeles. Univ. of California press. (Univ. of California publ. in history, vol. 29). 316 p. [2611

A sketch of steamship transportation by way of the Panama route in the twenty years preceding the opening of the transcontinental railway in 1869. [C. Shelby]

Leiva, Elío, and Edilberto Marbán. Curso de historia de Cuba. Segunda ed. Habana. Casa Montero. 2 vols., ilus. [2612

The second volume discusses events from the accession of Tacón (1834) to the Constitution of 1903, with a few pages only as to the succeeding forty years. [R. D. Hussey]

López Portillo y Weber, José. Programa para la formación de un atlas de geografía e historia mexicanas (*Mem. acad. mex. hist.*, tomo 2, no. 2, abril-junio, p. 158–188). [2613

The author presents his plan for an historical atlas of Mexico, in the belief that it is possible to synthesize in maps an "objective interpretation of historical events, and that making in this form a parallel study of the actors and the scene, we may better understand the history of the country, and up to a certain point, from a general opinion on its future development." Within four divisions (1) Precortesian, (2) Spanish conquest, (3) Spanish dominion, (4) Independent Mexico, illustrative maps are proposed, covering not only geography and history, but economic, social, ethnic, and other cultural aspects as well. [C. Shelby]

Martínez y Díaz, José F. Historia de la educación pública en Cuba desde el descubrimiento hasta nuestros días, y causa de su fracaso. Pinar del Río. Imp. de la Casa Villalba. 231 p. [2614

Primarily a criticism of the present day educational system of Cuba. As history, it has almost nothing on the era before 1808, and is not too complete on the nineteenth century. It is, however, practically a "source" for the era since 1898. [R. D. Hussey]

Métraux, Alfred. Le caractère de la conquête jésuitique (*Acta amer.*, vol. 1, no. 1, Jan.–March, p. 69–82). [2616

The success of the Jesuits in erecting their famous "empire" on the Paraguay and the Amazon is attributed to the fact that they were beneficiaries of "economic and political factors which were products of the savage encounter between whites and Indians," as well as to certain beliefs and institutions of the natives, and to the courage, good sense and devotion of the missionaries themselves. [C. Shelby]

Mitchell, Julio. Comercio marítimo y puertos del país (*Div. hist.*, vol. 4, no. 6, abril 15, p. 324–332). [2617

An analysis of the non-rare work *Comercio Exterior de México*, by Miguel Lerdo de Tejada, who at the time of its publication (1853) was a member of Santa Ana's cabinet. The discussion is prefaced by remarks on the author's political career. [C. Shelby]

Moreno, Delfino C. Noticia histórica de la Biblioteca "Lafragua" de la Universidad de Puebla (*Rev. univ. Puebla*, año 1, no. 3, nov., p. 67–79). [2618

Formally established in 1871 by adding the 2300 volumes left by José María Lafragua to the 6000 already owned from the old Jesuit library. Later bequests, gifts and purchases have brought the holdings to some 45,000 volumes, with much historical value. (Each issue of the Revista of the University lists current acquisitions). [R. D. Hussey]

NUEVA HISTORIA DE LOS PAÍSES COLONIALES Y DEPENDIENTES. AMÉRICA LATINA. Bajo la redacción de los profesores S. N. Rotovski, I. M. Reisner, G. S. Kara-Murza, B. K. Rubtzov. Habana. Ed. Páginas. 171 p. [2619

A publication of the Institute of History of the Academy of Sciences of the U. S. S. R. (*Akademia nauk, Institut istorii*). Straight Marxist interpretation. Not entirely without value as a corrective to common overemphasis on non-causal political history, but it created such disfavor by its evaluation of the characters of certain great leaders that it is said to have been withdrawn from sale soon after publication. [R. D. Hussey]

Orico, Osvaldo. Hombres de América. Héroes civiles y militares del continente. Prólogo de Octavio R. Amadeo. Buenos Aires. Ed. Claridad. (Bibl. Los Andes, vol. 1). 235 p., ilus. [2620

Popular biographical sketches of sixteen national heroes of the Americas, including the United States. Translation of the first Portuguese edition of 1943. [C. Shelby]

Padilla D'Onís, Luis. Historia de Santo Domingo. Primera parte: Prehistoria dominicana. México. Inst. panamer. de geog. e hist. (Publ. no. 71). 315 p., ilus., mapas. [2621

Historical geology, geography, anthropology, and archeology, intended as the start of a series. [R. D. Hussey]

PRIMER CONGRESO NACIONAL DE HISTORIA, LA HABANA, OCT. 8–12, 1942. Habana. Inst. cívico militar, Sección de artes gráf. del C. S. T. 2 vols. [2623

The two volumes contain proceedings of the sessions of the Congress, lists of those in attendance, among whom are representative historians from all parts of America, and *résumes* of the papers presented. The latter deal with general history. American history and Cuban history. Among the nearly 100 titles may be mentioned: Ramón A. Catalá, *Colón y el Descubrimiento;* Duvon C. Corbett, *Cuba y el Sistema Administrativo en las Floridas;* George Kubler, *Movimientos de Población en México durante el Siglo XVI;* Herminio Portell Vilá, *Bolívar y la Democracia;* Enrique Gay-Calbó, *El General Serrano en Cuba;* Francisco Pérez de la Riva, *Apuntes para Servir a la Historia del Café en Cuba;* Emillio Roig de Leuchsenring, *Revalorización de la Guerra Libertadora Cubana de 1895.* [C. Shelby]

Robertson, William Spence. History of the Latin-American nations. Third ed. New York. D. Appleton-Century, publ. xviii, 560 p., illus. [2624

A new edition of this textbook, bringing it up to date. No important changes. [L. Hanke]

Rubio, Ángel. Proyecto de atlas de historia general de América y de la cultura americana y de mapas murales de los grandes descubrimientos geográficos, exploración y conquista de América (*Bol. acad. panameña hist.*, segunda época, no. 1, enero-junio, p. 227–289). [2625

The project for the atlas was first presented to the Congreso Hispano-Americano de Geografía e Historia, held in Seville, May, 1930, and was endorsed by the First Conference of Ministers and Directors of Education of the American Republics, Panama, 1943. The outline given is that prepared in Seville in 1929, though the present article points out certain shortcomings of the plan. It is in three sections: I. Text. II. Plates. III. Photographic illustrations. The text consists of descriptions of the plates, 23 in number, which will be maps illustrative of political, military, social and economic features of American history from pre-conquest times to the present. These are described in detail. In addition, two wall maps of the exploration and conquest are planned. There will be 8 or 10 photographs of the most important monuments of American art and of historical personages. [C. Shelby]

Saiz de la Mora, Santiago. Consideraciones sobre el gobierno del general Tacón en Cuba (*Rev. bim. cub.*, vol. 52, no. 2, sept.–oct., p. 293–303; no. 3, nov.–dic., p. 384–457). [2626

An account of the four-year term (1834–1838) of Don Miguel Tacón y Rosique as governor and captain-general of Cuba, which stresses his activity in supressing liberal movements, intellectual as well as political. Many Cuban leaders were exiled, among them the publicist José Antonio Sacó and the poet Francisco de Orgaz, for opposing the régime. Tacón's accomplishments as an administrator also are reviewed. [C. Shelby]

Sánchez, Luis Alberto. A new interpretation of the history of America (*Hisp. amer. hist. rev.*, vol. 23, no. 3, Aug., p. 441-456). [2627

A brief and not wholly organized interpretation of the significance of Aprismo for history writing in America.

Tovar y Ramírez, Enrique Demetrio. El apóstol de Ica, fray José Ramón Rojas, el padre Guatemala. Lima. Cía. de impr. y publ. 308 p. [2628

Fray José Ramón Rojas de Jesús María was born in Quetzaltenango, Guatemala, in 1775. He lived in Guatemala, Costa Rica, or Honduras until 1831, when he was compelled to leave Central America due to his resistance to the anti-clericalism of Morazán. About half the present book treats of those early years. The rest is essentially a new edition of the author's *Bosquejo Biográfico*, published in the *Anales* of the Guatemalan Sociedad de Geografía e Historia in 1933. [R. D. Hussey]

Universidad nacional de Cuyo. Instituto de investigaciones históricas. Anales. Tomo 1. 1941. Mendoza. 666 p. [2629

A large part of this volume of the *Anales* (p. 3–523) is given over to diplomatic correspondence copied from documents in the Archivo Nacional de Chile assembled in a folio entitled "Gobierno i Ajentes Diplomáticos de la República Arjentina, en Chile, 1836–1847." The remainder of the volume contains four short articles. Three of these by Juan Draghi Lucero, director of the Instituto de Investigaciones Históricas of the Universidad Nacional de Cuyo, deal with the date of San Martín's return from Peru, with San Martín's chacra, and with a diary by O'Higgins covering the period July 3–31, 1816. The fourth article is a brief study of the Jofré family in Argentina. [Ed.]

Wilgus, A. Curtis, and Raul d'Eça. Outline history of Latin America. Foreword by James A. Robertson. Third ed. New York, Barnes & Noble, publ. (College outline series). 420 p. [2630

Most recent revision of this useful concise text intended for secondary schools and colleges. New material, including bibliographical references, is incorporated. A separate supplement entitled "Teaching aids for use in secondary schools," by Beatrice Fleischman Lewis accompanies the text. [C. Shelby]

Zúñiga, Neptalí. Vicente León. Quito. Tall. gráf. de educación. 340 p., ilus. [2631

Prize-winning biography in a contest held on occasion of the centenary of the Colegio de San Vicente de Latacunga. The early life of Dr. León and his career as philanthropist, publicist and educator are treated in detail. Following his death in 1839 the Colegio de San Vicente was founded in accordance with the terms of his will. [C. Shelby]

ADDENDA

Lanz Margalli, Luis. Apuntes para una cartografía general de Tabasco (*Bol. soc. mex. geog. estad.*, tomo 56, no. 1, enerofeb., 1942, p. 121-151). [2633

Lists 217 items, 1813 to date, of which only five antedate 1874. [R. D. Hussey]

Pastor, R. A. La guerra con el indio en la jurisdicción de San Luis. Prólogo de Héctor R. Ratto. Buenos Aires. Bibl. de la Sociedad de historia argentina, vol. 13. 1942. xx, 569 p., láms., ilus. [2634

Reviewed in *Rev. hist. Amér.*, no. 16.

HISTORY: SPANISH AMERICA
THE COLONIAL PERIOD

BY

ROLAND D. HUSSEY

University of California, Los Angeles

AND

JAMES F. KING

University of California, Berkeley

GENERAL STATEMENT

1943 was a valuable year for productions on the colonial history of Mexico and the Caribbean areas, somewhat against the trend of the earlier war years. The 1942 anniversary of various discoveries and explorations continued to influence output, the bicentennial of the Guatemala cathedral inspired valuable items, and the year was also marked by the appearance of two full length devoutly Marxist interpretations of Latin American history (nos. 2619, 2674).

Four Mexican periodicals of some historical interest started in 1943. *Estudios Históricos*, a thoroughly scholarly semi-annual published in Guadalajara, emphasizes but is not confined to materials dealing with its region. It has something of a clerical flavor. Three quarterlies which are not primarily historical, but publish some historical articles: *Revista de la Universidad de Puebla*, *Boletín del Seminario de Cultura Mexicana*, published by the Secretaría de la Educación, and *Humanidades, Órgano de los Alumnos de la Facultad de Filosofía y Letras* of the University of Mexico. The last should not be confused with *Humanidades*, long published in Buenos Aires. Also to avoid confusion, note that although volume forty of the *Boletín* of the Cuban National Archive is dated 1941, it appeared only in 1943. Finally, scholars will welcome the reappearance of the *Boletín de la Academia Panameña de la Histora*, last published in 1939.

At the risk of seeming to slight other valuable studies, one cannot refrain from singling out a few items. Three excellent bibliographies or finding tools are those of Agustín Millares Carlo and José Ignacio Mantecón (no. 65), not of course confined to the colonial period, of the exceedingly rich archive of the former Cuban Consulado (no. 2687), and of Father Steck (no. 2696). Outstanding additions were made to our printed documentary materials in the compilations by Conway (no. 2711) and Hanke (no. 2652). The project started in Spain, represented in 1943 by the work edited by Cebreiro Blanco (no. 2643) may become very useful, though this particular item seems to offer no previously unprinted text. It is understood that the Spanish *Consejo de la Hispanidad* also began in 1943 with an ambitious project, of facsimile reproductions, but specific data has not so far come to hand. [R. D. Hussey]

Publication in the field of Spanish South American colonial history in 1943 continued at a reduced rate that reflected war-time shortages of printing supplies, equipment, and labor. It is significant, though not surprising, that except for several periodical contributions by Spanish scholars and the merest handful of similar items by North Americans, work in this field during the war year of 1943 was written and published entirely in South America. The year apparently witnessed the publication of no really major original work in Spanish South American colonial history. As usual, a relative abundance of documents of varying value saw the light of day. Periodical articles, which formed the great bulk of the original studies, tended to be local in character and sometimes rather antiquarian in approach. Of the few books published, several were new editions of older works. In short, the 1943 output in the field was heavily weighted with raw material and studies of a primarily local nature, which, if they are to have the greatest possible interest and value to the larger world of scholarship require synthesis and a greater relation to the history of mankind as a whole. [J. F. King]

BIBLIOGRAPHY

(*See also sections on* Archives; Spanish American Art; History: Revolutionary Period; *and* Spanish American Literature: the Colonial Period)

GENERAL

Álvarez López, Enrique. La filosofía natural en el padre José de Acosta (*Rev. Indias*, Madrid, año 4, no. 12, abril–junio, p. 305–322). [2635

This interpretive article discusses the thinking of the great Jesuit naturalist as illustrative of the encouragement which the exploration of the New World gave to the development of the exact sciences in the period of the Spanish conquest. [J. F. King]

Arciniegas, Germán. Germans in the conquest of America, a sixteenth century venture. Transl. by Ángel Flores. New York. Macmillan co., publ. ii, 217 p., illus. [2636

Interprets German participation in the Spanish conquest, not as a series of unconnected episodes, but as a manifestation of the concerted Teutonic penetration of the Spanish world under Charles V. "The Emperor put at the disposition of the German bankers all this part of the continent [South America], reserving for the Spaniards only two or three points on the Caribbean coast and that which Pizarro had conquered. . . . To the Welsers he gave the conquest of Venezuela . . . and to the Fuggers the territory from Magallanes to the equator. . . . The main idea was to give the Germans the opportunity, every opportunity they might demand, to participate in the great conquering expedition, and on terms even more favorable than those given to governors of Spanish origin. When we read the contracts that were made with Vido Herll, Fugger's agent, and with Heinrich Ehinger and Hieronymus Seiler, Welser's agents, Pizarro seems to be no more than the slice of chicken between the two walls of a sandwich. And the fact remains that if the Fuggers had been energetic and had taken control of the situation in America, and if the Welsers had been less prudent, it is extremely doubtful that the world which Columbus put beneath the banner of Castile would have remained under the banner of Castile" (p. 200–201).

This book, written mostly in the present tense to give a sense of reality to the story, seeks to re-create the color and pageantry of sixteenth century Europe and America for the intelligent popular audience. Specialists will nevertheless find the volume stimulating because of its interpretations, though they may regret the restriction of references to sources to sketchy chapter bibliographies at the end of the volume. The omission there of K. Häbler's fundamental monograph, *Die Überseeischen Unternehmungen der Welzer* is particularly notable. [J. F. King]

Ballesteros Gaibrois, Manuel. Juan Caboto en España (*Rev. Indias*, Madrid, año 4, no. 14, oct.–dic., p. 607–628). [2638

Tres documentos hallados por el autor, en el Archivo del Reino de Valencia, arrojan luz insospechada sobre el paréntesis 1476–1496, abierto hasta, ahora en la vida del descubridor y que se habían esforzado en llenar sus biógrafos de la manera mas honrosa para él y para sus patronos los Reyes ingleses.

De los documentos (dos cartas del Rey D. Fernando al Bayle General de Valencia y otra de éste al Rey, sobre la construcción de un puerto según los planos de Caboto) se deduce que el piloto estuvo en España los años 1490 a 1493, con las consiguientes influencias sobre él del viaje de Colón, y en franca incompatibilidad con su supuesto viaje descubridor en 1480 o 1494. Por último el apellido Caboto y Montecalunya tal como aparece en los documentos es un nuevo argumento a favor de su origen italiano y tal vez gaetano, como quiere Bellemo. Copiosa bibliografía y la trascripción de los documentos completan el valor histórico del trabajo. [S. Sáenz de Santa María]

Barreda Laos, Felipe. Cronistas de Indias (*Rev. bibl. nac.*, Buenos Aires, tomo 9, no. 28, cuarto trim., p. 253-262). [2639

Interpretive notes on the personal backgrounds and formative influences of colonial *cronistas*, with special attention devoted to the following: Miguel Estete, Juan de Betanzos, Antonio de Herrera y Tordesillas, Pedro Cieza de León, and the Inca Garcilaso de la Vega. [J. F. King]

Basadre, Jorge. América en la cultura occidental (*Mercurio peruano*, año 18, vol. 25, no. 196, julio, p. 283-301). [2640

A lecture delivered in Buenos Aires discussing European literary productions of the sixteenth, seventeenth and eighteenth centuries which have America as their theme. [Roscoe R. Hill]

Bayle, Constantino. La comunión entre los indios americanos (*Rev. Indias*, Madrid, año 4, no. 12, abril-junio, p. 197-254). [2641

This substantial article, based in large part upon contemporary documents and accounts, describes the practices and customs relating to the giving of holy communion to the Indians. Emphasizes the sixteenth century, and within that, the period of the conquest. Gives considerable attention to the opposition among certain Spaniards to permitting the Indians to share in communion. [J. F. King]

Canoutas, Seraphim G. Christopher Columbus, a Greek nobleman. A disquisition concerning the early life of the great discoverer, and a refutation of the charges against him. New York. The author. xvi, 288 p. [2642

A brief by a Greek, trained member of the New York and Massachusetts bars, absolving Columbus of the "charge" that he was the son of a plebeian weaver of Genoa. As he and his son claimed, he really was a kinsman of the fifteenth century noble corsair with whom he sailed. Using Greek sources, the author "proves" that he was George Paleologus of Bissipat, driven from Constantinople about 1453. [R. D. Hussey]

Cebreiro Blanco, Luis. Colección de diarios y relaciones para la historia de los viajes y descubrimientos. Madrid. Ed. C. S. I. C. (Inst. histórico de marina). 2 vols.: 168; 150 p., mapas. [2643

El Instituto Histórico de Marina bajo la dirección de D. Julio Guillén ha comenzado la publicación de todos los diarios o relaciones de los marinos españoles que con pretensiones geográficas o con intentos colonizadores recorrieron los mares en siglos pasados. La colección ha de ir apareciendo, nos dice el director en pequeños volúmenes, a cada uno de los cuales acompañarán en forma fácilmente desgajable los mapas de las derrotas respectivas y a cada grupo de nueve tomitos el conjunto de índices que le corresponda.

En el primer volumen aparecen los diarios de Alonso de Camargo (1539) enviado por el Obispo de Plasencia en expedición, que fracasó, rumbo al Perú, pero a través del Estrecho de Magallanes; sigue el diario de Rodríguez Cabrillo que en 1542 llegó siguiendo órdenes del gran virrey D. Antonio de Mendoza, hasta más arriba del Cabo Blanco en las costas de California; el tercero es el de Pedro de Valdivia (1542) a tierras de Chile; el cuarto y el quinto corresponden a Antonio de Vea y Pascual de Iriarte (1676) que bojaron las costas de Chile en busca de pretendidos establecimientos ingleses en las cercanías del estrecho de Magallanes, y se concluye el primer volumen con la interesante y circunstanciada relación del cosmógrafo jesuita José Quiroga (1745) sobre el viaje que hizo a los Patagones, en compañía del célebre Padre Cardiel, que buscaba sitio apropiado para el establecimiento de una misión entre aquellos salvajes.

En el segundo se coleccionan los diarios de Pedro de Valdivia a las costas de Chile en 1540; el interesantísimo de Pedro Menéndez de Avilés a la Florida, con la destruccion de los fuertes franceses allí establecidos; uno muy breve de la fracasada expedición de Flores Valdés y Alonso de Sotomayor a tierras del Magallanes y por último la legendaria expedición de D. Juan Francisco de la Bodega y Quadra, realizada en una goleta de 10 metros de eslora y que sin embargo ha dejado tantas huellas de su paso a lo largo de la toponimia californiana hasta más allá de los 58 grados Norte, año 1775.

La colección bien editada y de fácil lectura nos hace descar la salida de los siete volúmenes que con los presentes constituyen el primer tomo con los copiosos índices que los completan. [C. Sáenz de Santa María]

Chanetón, Abel. Un pedagogo colonial (*Bol. soc. geog.* Sucre, tomo 39, no. 393-395, agosto, p. 130-157). [2644

This scholarly article on Fray José Antonio de San Alberto, Bishop of Córdoba and later Archbishop of La Plata, is republished from the *Boletín del Instituto de Investigaciones Históricas*. [J. F. King]

Díaz Durán, José Constantino. Breve noticia de la vida de Fray Bartolomé de las Casas (*An. soc. geog. hist. Guatemala*, año 19, tomo 19, no. 1, sept., p. 8-19). [2646

A well written résumé of standard printed sources. [R. D. Hussey]

Gandía, Enrique de. Las ideas políticas en la historia colonial (*Nosotros*, segunda época, año 8, tomo 23, no. 93, dic., p. 252-255). [2647

Vigorously decries the alleged tendency on the part of Latin-American writers to assume that there was no political thought in the Spanish colonies merely because there is a lack of documents explicitly concerned with the subject. On the contrary, believes this author, there were many and basic political ideas, which in the colonies as elsewhere shaped events. Calls for a re-

García Franco, Salvador. La geografía astronómica y Colón (*Rev. Indias*, Madrid, año 4, no. 11, enero-marzo, p. 93-116). [2648

Sin ánimo de oscurecer la figura del Almirante estudia el autor alguno de los datos astronómicos consignados por él en su diario para llegar a la conclusión que si es verdad que Colón no fué ningún genio de la astronomía como lo fué de la geografía, sus equivocaciones eran del mismo orden de las que solían cometer los marinos sus contemporáneos. [C. Sáenz de Santa María]

Gay Calbó, Enrique. Fray Bartolomé de las Casas (*Rev. Habana*, año 1, tomo 2, no. 10, junio, p. 392-400). [2649

An appreciation of Las Casas' moral leadership as to Indians. [R. D. Hussey]

Graham, Robert Bontine Cunninghame. Bernal Díaz del Castillo. Semblanza de su personalidad a través de su *Historia verdadera de la conquista de Nueva España*. Buenos Aires. Ed. Inter-americana. 249 p. [2650

Translated from the English, apparently without changes or additions. [R. D. Hussey]

Guillén y Tato, Julio (comp.). Monumenta chartográphica indiana. 1. Regiones del Plata y Magallánica. Entrega primera. Madrid. Sección de relaciones culturales del Ministerio de estado. 135 p., láms. [2651

Esta monumental colección, que comprenderá, nos dice su preparador, 60 volúmenes con cerca de 15.000 láminas, se ideó como consecuencia de la fracasada Exposición Geográfica del Plata que hubo de suspenderse en Buenos Aires a causa de la guerra. España que acudía con lo mejor de sus archivos decidió, antes de proceder a la devolución de los documentos, fotocopiarlos todos. Esas copias llevadas ahora a la imprenta y prologadas y comentadas por la primera autoridad en la materia, D. Julio Guillén, constituyen la presente y magnífica edición.

En una breve y enjundiosa exposición nos adiestra D. Julio Guillén en las palabras y signos más usados en cartografía y a renglón que es el comentario detallado de todos y cada uno de los mapas que han de ir presentándose. La distribución de estos hecha con amplio criterio geográfico comienza por las regiones del Plata y Magallánica, y en esta primera entrega se describen hasta el más mínimo detalle, los correspondientes a la región entera; y los particulares de la tierra del Magallanes y sus portulanos correspondientes.

Bajo nueva carátula y con índice independiente se ofrece al público la primera colección de láminas—127—algunas a todo color, ordenadas conforme a su procedencia bibliográfica. De primer orden, tanto la presentación fotográfica, cuanto el comentario. [C. Sáenz de Santa María]

Hanke, Lewis. Cuerpo de documentos del siglo 16 sobre los derechos de España en las Indias y las Filipinas. Ed. por Agustín Millares Carlo. México. Fondo de cultura económica. lxvi, 364 p., ilus. [2652

The ten carefully edited treatises here printed for the first time range in date from about the middle to the end of the sixteenth century and were copied from manuscripts found by the editor in various Spanish archives. Taken as a whole, these writings accurately reflect contemporary Spanish preoccupation with the legal bases of dominion over the peoples and lands of the Indies. It is significant that Spanish thinkers, as represented by these learned opinions, held varying and frequently contradictory theories concerning imperial dominion after half a century of colonization. The editor's introduction, which contains an essay on the emergence and background of Spanish theories of conquest to about 1550 as well as short analyses of the ten writers here represented, is itself a useful addition to the literature in this field. Those who wish to pursue the subject further will find at the end of the volume a detailed bibliography of "los más importantes tratados del siglo XVI y demás escritos sobre cuestiones teóricas de autor conocido." The introduction to this volume was also published in *Revista de las Indias*, tomo 19, no. 58, oct., p. 50-89; no. 59-60, nov.-dic., p. 197-238. [J. F. King]

Harkness, Jr., Alberto. Alonso de Hojeda y el descubrimiento de Venezuela (*Rev. chil. hist. geog.*, no. 103, julio-dic., p. 197-213). [2653

This succinct and scholarly article reexamines the activities of Ojeda from his departure from Spain on his first independent voyage along the Venezuelan coast in 1499 to the eve of his attempt to colonize the Urabá region in 1509. The account is based upon a critical use of standard sources, here cited in detail. In reconstructing the voyage of 1499, the author is inclined to accept Vespucius' famed letter to Soderini as an account of this expedition, believing with other writers that the date 1497 assigned to the letter is probably a mistake. The present article devotes almost as much attention to Ojeda's activities in Española during the period under consideration as it does to his Venezuelan explorations. [J. F. King]

Iraizoz, Antonio. Cristóbal Colón Se llamaba Salvador González Zarco? (*Rev. arch. nac.*, Costa Rica, año 7, no. 3-4, marzo-abril, p. 144-146). [2654

Recounts with some sympathy the theory which two Portuguese advanced in 1927, that the Discoverer was the illegitimate son of a highly placed family, born in the Madeiras in 1456. [R. D. Hussey]

Johnson, John J. The introduction of the horse into the western hemisphere (*Hisp. amer. hist. rev.*, vol. 23, no. 4, Nov., p. 587-610). [2655

Scholarly account of the introduction of horses into Española and the other Greater Antilles and their multiplication there during the first two decades after the discovery of America. Based upon the colonial historians, published documentary collections, and pertinent modern monographs. [J. F. King]

Jos, Emiliano. Centenario del Amazonas. La expedición de Orellana y sus problemas históricos (*Rev. Indias*, Madrid, año 3, no. 10, oct.-dic., 1942, p. 661-710; año 4, no. 11, enero-marzo, p. 5-42; no. 12, abril-junio, p. 256-304; no. 13, julio-sept., p. 479-523). [2656

En esta serie de artículos nos ofrece el Sr. Jos, ya conocido en el mundo erudito hispanoamericano por sus trabajos sobre Orellana, un avance bibliográfico sobre la obra que piensa dedicar a la maravillosa expedición de Orellana y sus compañeros desde tierras de Quito hasta la desembocadura en el Atlántico del gran río que infiel a su descubridor ha cambiado su nombre por el más poético de Amazonas. El libro que ha de conmemorar el cuarto centenario de esta hazaña ha de contribuir, piensa el autor, a resolver problemas ya geográfico-políticos como la prioridad de los descubrimientos sobre los portugueses, ya de naturaleza mítica como el del origen de la fábula de las mujeres amazonas y el de la localización en aquellas selvas del Dorado. En este primer capítulo dedicado a la bibliografía pasa revista a la multitud de autores antiguos y modernos que han tratado el asunto y los va situando en los dos campos que desde un principio se enfrentaron, de los entusiastas y de los denigradores del explorador. El trabajo es interesantísimo e imprescindible para quien en lo sucesivo quiera tocar temas amazónicos. [C. Sáenz de Santa María]

Juderías y Loyot, Julián. La leyenda negra. Estudios acerca del concepto de España en el extrangero. Segunda ed. completamente refundada. Barcelona. Ed. Araluce. 395 p. [2657

First edition in 1918. A useful work, and not badly biased in view of its subject and purpose. [R. D. Hussey]

King, James Ferguson. Descriptive data on Negro slaves in Spanish importation records and bills of sale (*Jour. negro hist.*, vol. 28, no. 2, April, p. 204-230). [2658

States the need for supplementing political and economic accounts of the slave trade with studies of the social aspects of the traffic, emphasizing such matters as tribal origins of slaves, ages and relative numbers of the sexes in cargoes, diseases of slaves, etc. Suggests that the *palmeo* records (documents recording import formalities) and bills of sale by which title of slaves was conveyed by the importers to the first buyers in the Indies are prime sources for such information. Presents in a documentary appendix examples of these two types of documents. [J. F. King]

Kirkpatrick, F. A. La encomienda sin tierras (*Rev. chil. hist. geog.*, no. 102, enero-junio, p. 363-374). [2659

Translated from the original article, which appeared in *The Hispanic American Historical Review*, vol. 22 (November, 1942), under the title, "The Landless Encomienda." See *Handbook, no. 8, 1942,* item 2907. [J. F. King]

León Pinelo, Antonio de. El paraíso en el nuevo mundo. Comentario apologético, historia natural y peregrina de las Indias Occidentales, islas de tierra firme del mar océano. Tomos 1 y 2. Publícalo, con un prólogo, Raúl Porras Barrenechea, bajo los auspicios del Comité del cuarto Centenario del descubrimiento del Amazonas. Lima. Imp. Torres Aguirre. 2 vols., ilus. [2660

An example of the incredibly pedantic erudition of which a really good scholar could be guilty in the seventeenth century. [R. D. Hussey]

Lewin, Boleslao. Tupac Amarú, el rebelde. Su época, sus luchas y su influencia en el continente. Buenos Aires. Ed. Claridad. (Bibl. de grandes biografías, vol. 5). 496 p. [2661

Reviewed in *Rev. hist. Amér.*, no. 16, dic., 1943, p. 314-315.

Luelmo, Julio. Los judíos y el descubrimiento de América (*Bol. hist. antig.*, vol. 30, no. 347-348, sept.-oct., p. 894-901). [2662

A popularization of ideas brought out by Kayserling (as quoted by Herbert B. Adams) and Kohen, some time ago. [R. D. Hussey]

Márquez, Javier. El mercantilismo de Saavedra Fajardo (*Trim. econ.*, vol. 10, no. 2, julio-sept., p. 247-286). [2663

Extracts from works of Diego de Saavedra Fajardo (1584-1648) showing his economic thought, with commentary. Saavedra's thought was rather advanced, though he is less well known in the economic field than in others. He barely mentions America. [R. D. Hussey]

Martínez Dalmau, Eduardo. La política colonial y extranjera de los reyes españoles de la casa de Austria y de Borbón y la toma de la Habana por los ingleses. Habana. Imp. El siglo XX. (Acad. de la historia de Cuba). 103 p. [2664

A somewhat wandering, but useful discussion, of background factors in the British seizure of Havana in 1762, with [p. 65-101] the text of a diary by some unidentified Spanish official. [R. D. Hussey]

Mateos, S. I. F. En el centenario de las leyes nuevas de Indias 1542-1543 (*Razón y fe*, fascs. 3-4, no. 548-549, sept.-oct., p. 202-221). [2665

En cuatro apartados se describen: las fases preliminares; la promulgación de las nuevas leyes con los efectos desastrosos que produjeron, sobre todo en el Perú; y el final arreglo con que el tacto político de Mendoza y después de La Gasca prepararon la final estabilización, aprobada después por el Emperador. El artículo no aporta datos nuevos, pero es un compendio util por su claridad y esquematismo. [C. Saenz de Santa María]

Mello, Astrogildo Rodrigues de. As encomiendas e a politica colonial de Espanha. São Paulo. (Univ. de São Paulo, Fac. de filosofia, ciéncias e letras, Boletim 39). 88 p. [2666

An excellently done synthesis, making full use of the recent work of such students as Silvio Zavala, Lesley Byrd Simpson, and Lewis Hanke. [R. D. Hussey]

——. O regime de trabalho dos indígenas na América Espanhola (*Sociologia*, vol. 5, no. 4, out., p. 293-304). [2667

Molina, Raúl A. Las finanzas municipales en la colonia (*Rev. der. admin. munic.*, no. 166, dic., p. 1169-1191). [2668

Brief description of the sources of municipal revenues. [Ed.]

Olschki, Leonardo. Hernán Pérez de Oliva's "Ystoria de Colón" (*Hisp. amer. hist. rev.*, vol. 23, no. 2, May, p. 165-196). [2669

A manuscript now in private possession in New York, apparently written or copied about 1583. It is probably about the same as, but not identical with, one owned by Fernando Colón. The introduction discusses the known facts about Pérez de Oliva.

(Students might like to add that the Barcelona book dealer Babra offered a Pérez de Oliva MS. history of the Mexican conquest, in 1933, with a facsimile of the first page; present whereabouts unknown to this reviewer.) [R. D. Hussey]

Ots Capdequí, José María. Manual de historia del derecho español y del derecho propiamente indiano. Buenos Aires. Tall. graf. de A. Baiocco. (Inst. de hist. del derecho arg., Col. de estudios para la hist. del derecho arg., vol. 3, 4). 2 vols. [2670

A synthesis of the author's many earlier monographs. Emphasizes the development of the law in the Indies. [R. D. Hussey]

Quinzio Figueiredo, Jorge Mario. La colonización española y su espíritu, según la Recopilación de leyes de Indias. Santiago, Chile. Dirección general de prisiones, imp. 77 p. [2671

A philosophical interpretation of the Spanish Laws of the Indies. [R. D. Hussey]

Quiroz, Juan B. de. El contenido laboral en los códigos negros americanos (*Rev. mex. soc.*, año 5, vol. 5, no. 4, cuatro trim., p. 473-510). [2671a

Comparative analysis of the content of the first American "Black code," the French of 1685, and of the principal Spanish code, the Código Carolino Negro, dated in Santo Domingo City, December 14, 1784. Some references are made to other laws on the subject. [R. D. Hussey]

Romero, Fernando, and Emilia Romero de Valle. Probable itinerario de los tres primeros viajes marítimos para la conquista del Perú (*Rev. hist. Amér.*, no. 16, dic., p. 1-23). [2672

The authors make use of two seldom exploited contemporary maps, that which Oviedo obtained from the pilots Bartolomé Ruiz and Fernando Pérez Peñate, and the "Carta Universal" of Rivero, on which, so they believe, the West Coast of South America is delineated according to data brought to Spain by Pizarro. In the light of this cartographic evidence they reconstruct the itineraries of the three voyages of Almagro and Pizarro. In *Notas a Posteriori* there are comments on the points of agreement and discrepancy between the present account and Robert Cushman Murphy, "The Earliest Spanish Advances Southward along the West Coast of South America," in *The Hispanic American Historical Review*, vol. 21, no. 1, Feb., 1941 (See *Handbook, no. 7, 1941*, item 2851). [J. F. King]

Rosen, Edward. Copernicus and the discovery of America (*Hisp. amer. hist. rev.*, vol. 23, no. 2, May, p. 367-371). [2673

Copernicus' only reference to the discovery of the new world (in a book printed in 1543) has been interpreted by good students as implying his acceptance of Vespucci as the discoverer. The present author, an authority on Copernicus, attempts to prove this a misinterpretation. His proof requires the reader to depart pretty far from common sense. [R. D. Hussey]

Teitelboim, Volodia. El amanecer del capitalismo y la conquista de América. Santiago, Chile. Ed. Nueva América. 203 p. [2674

A highly provocative work, which exploits a large documentation in the light of the teachings of Marx and Engels. [R. D. Hussey]

Tobar Donoso, Julio. La organización jurídico-territorial de las colonias españolas (*Bol. acad. nac. hist.*, Quito, vol. 23, no. 61, enero-junio, p. 55-96). [2675

An effort to cover the whole colonial period in Spanish America, though emphasizes South America. Makes good use of documents gathered for boundary disputes. Not too well synthesized, but valuable. [R. D. Hussey]

Torre Revello, José. Merchandise brought to America by the Spaniards, 1534-1596 (*Hisp. amer. hist. rev.*, vol. 23, no. 4, Nov., p. 773-781). [2676
A classified list of the commodity names (without reference to quantities) which appear in cargo lists of ships going to America from Spain. A brief introductory note comments chiefly as to the inclusion of goods from many foreign countries. [R. D. Hussey]

Valentini, F. J. J. Cuarto viaje de Colón. Cap. 5. De Cariari a Caramburú y Portobelo (*Rev. arch. nac.*, Costa Rica, año 7, no. 7-8, julio-agosto, p. 353-368). [2677
A careful description and comment, with regard to the Costa Rican coast. The author, born in Berlin in 1824, was prominent in Costa Rica as an archeologist and in other ways such as founding Port Limon, from 1854 until he went to New York to live about 1876. He was naturalized in the United States and died there in 1899. [Ibid., p. 344-352] [R. D. Hussey]

─────. Cuarto viaje de Colón. Traducción de Víctor Sanabria M. San José. Imp. Lehmann. 120 p. [2677a
Presumably a lengthier work from which the above item was extracted, but has not been seen. [R. D. Hussey]

Valle, Rafael Heliodoro. Algunos franceses en México (*Fil. letras*, tomo 5, no. 11, julio-sept., p. 153-159). [2678
List of names, with a few notes, on various Frenchmen in Mexico, mostly eighteenth century or first half of the nineteenth. Apparently from printed works. [R. D. Hussey]

Viñas y Mey, Carmelo. La sociedad americana y el acceso a la propiedad rural (*Rev. int. soc.*, vol. 1, no. 1, p. 103-148; no. 2-3, p. 257-284; no. 4, p. 159-178). [2679
Aunque las cuestiones de la propiedad rural en Indias han sido tratadas con frecuencia y el mismo autor ha publicado trabajos sobre el mismo tema, estos artículos pretenden adentrarse en el espíritu de la legislación y percibir sus ideales en el punto concreto del acceso a la propiedad privada. Cuatro partes tiene el estudio: una priliminar sobre los pueblos de indios y sus características principales de religiosidad, hermandad, moralidad e higiene todo bajo el alto patronato del encomendero o del corregidor; siguen dos, una sobre la curiosa situación jurídica del agro americano considerado propiedad del Rey y dado en "comisión" a los españoles y en "resguardo" a los indios; y otra la más interesante sobre el sentido familiar que se quiso dar a estos "resguardos"; se pretendía que el indio pudiera sacar de su terreno todo lo necesario para sí y para su familia; de este modo el terreno familiar sustituiría en todo o en parte al salario (p.e. en los yanaconas); se obligaba al encomendero o al contratador de trabajo indígena a dejar libre al indio cuatro veces al año y dos días a la semana; y se buscaba como un ideal que los indios mineros pudiesen establecerse en las cercanías de las minas y que en un radio de varios kilómetros se establecieran los pueblos con suficiencia de terrenos para que allí mismo tuvieran posibilidad de hacer sus sementeras y sustentar sus familias. Todo ello complementado por la institución de las tierras comunales para los casos de enfermedad o vejez.
El acceso a la propiedad queda más confirmado por el respeto que siempre hallaron los indios en las autoridades superiores españolas respecto a sus bienes propios o apropiados, pues no faltaron entre ellos los que se aprovecharon de su situación de verdadera excepción jurídica para arrojar a los españoles de los terrenos que les convenían.
Unas breves consideraciones sobre la evolución que se fué efectuando en los indios acostumbrados al rígido colectivismo incásico y sobre su alegre adaptación al individualismo español corona el interesante trabajo.
El estudio hecho a base de documentos inéditos del Archivo Histórico Nacional de Madrid, rompe los estrechos moldes de las Leyes de Indias, de las que no suelen pasar los cantores de la Legislación española en América. [C. Sáenz de Santa María]

Vives Buchaca, Lorenzo. Descubriendo a un descubridor. ¿Colombo, Colomo, Colom o Colón? (*An. soc. geog. hist. Guatemala*, año 19, tomo 19, no. 2, dic., p. 106-115). [2680
The author believes that the name Colon came from a Catalan Jewish family named Colom. [R. D. Hussey]

Zavala, Silvio. New viewpoints on the Spanish colonization of America. Philadelphia. Univ. of Pennsylvania. 118 p. [2681
A series of lectures, synthesizing and interpreting the considerable body of knowledge about Spain's Indian policy in America, which Zavala and others have been bringing out in recent years. [R. D. Hussey]

ADDENDA

Bermúdez Plata, Cristóbal. Catálogo de pasajeros a Indias, 1535-1538. Vol. 2. Sevilla. Ed. C. S. I. C. 1942. 507 p. [2682
Bajo las mismas normas que el anterior ha salido este segundo volumen en que para un lapso de 3 años se nos presenta un total de 5620 papeletas, que equivalen a cerca de 6000 pasajeros, comprendidas en los libros 3, 4 y 5 de asientos existentes en el Archivo de Indias.
Años excepcionalmente activos en la emigración española, debido, sobre todo, a tres famosas expediciones que por entonces zarparon de Sevilla, rumbo al Nuevo Mundo. La de Pedro de Mendoza (fichas 1374-2109) que cuenta entre sus haberes la fundación del primer núcleo urbano que llevó el nombre de Santa María del Buen Aire, humilde cuna de la magnífica metró-

poli argentina. La organizada por el noble y caballeroso Hernando de Soto (fichas 3914-4717) a tierras de Florida, que después de tantas penalidades acabó con la muerte de su organizador a orillas del Misisípi. Y la fracasada de Alvarado a las Islas de la Especieria; (fichas 5099-5620); en ésta aparece arrebolada con tintes de catástrofe la ficha 5510 en que se enumera el acompañamiento del Adelantado y en primer lugar los nombres de las nueve damas que acompañaban a su mujer Doña Beatriz y que tan pronto habían de encontrar la muerte en la noche en que quedó sepultada bajo las aguas del Volcán la Guatemala de Almolonga.

Tres copiosos índices; nombres y profesiones, el primero; de nombres geográficos, el segundo y de patrones de navío el tercero nos abren la puerta de este monumental catálogo que honra a sus autores, el director y empleados del Archivo de Indias. [C. Sáenz de Santa María]

Gandía, Enrique de. Historia de Cristóbal Colón. Buenos Aires. Ed. Claridad. 1942. 493 p., ilus. [2683
A critical and scholarly survey of everything—it would seem—that has ever been written about the discoverer. [R. D. Hussey]

Sierra, Vicente D. El sentido misional de la conquista de América. Prólogo de Carlos Ibarguren. Buenos Aires. Ed. Orientación española. 1942. 406 p. [2684
An extensively documented work, advancing the thesis that the most important conquest of America by Spain was through the church, not the military or the capitalist. The author's apparent acceptance of the ideas associated with Hispanidad will handicap the reception of his ideas by many historians. [R. D. Hussey]

MIDDLE AMERICA AND THE ISLANDS

BY

ROLAND D. HUSSEY

Lists and Indices

Barlow, R. H. Los manuscritos de la Biblioteca Bancroft que pertenecieron a la antigua colección de D. José Fernando Ramírez (*Mem. acad. mex. hist.*, tomo 2, no. 2, abril-junio, p. 189-200). [2685
A discussion of some of the most important items for the history of colonial Mexico, in the form of a running text. The author points out that Bancroft acquired nearly all the manuscripts from the Ramírez collection.

Colección Lugo. Archivo general de Indias. continuación del libreta 36 (*Bol. arch. gen.*, Ciudad Trujillo, año 6, vol. 6, no. 28-29, mayo-agosto, p. 254-268). [2686
Abstracts and extracts of documents concerning the English attack on Santo Domingo and the Dominican attack on Tortuga, 1654. To be continued.

Cuba. Archivo nacional. Catálogo de los fondos del real consulado de agricultura, industria y comercio y de la junta de fomento. Prefacio de Emeterio S. Santovenia. Habana. Imp. El Siglo XX. 655 p. [2687
Catalogs over 9000 *expedientes*, by subjects, dealing with a great variety of matters which were handled by the Cuban Consulado (or its successor from 1832, the Junta de Fomento) from 1794 to 1854.

Subject matter is by no means confined to the strictly economic, and areas dealt with include parts of Latin America other than Cuba (especially Mexico, the West Indies), and the United States.

Debien, G. Notes bibliographiques sur l'histoire de Saint-Domingue (*Rev. soc. hist. géog. Haïti*, vol. 14, no. 48, janv., p. 25-42). [2688
44 items on *Histoire medicale* and 67 items on *Expedition de 1802*, published in the later 18th and early 19th centuries. (They primarily concern French, not Spanish, Santo Domingo).

Index to the Spanish judicial records of Louisiana (*La. hist. quart.*, vol. 26, no. 1, Jan., p. 257-305; no. 3, July, p. 842-909; no. 4, Oct., p. 1187-1236). [2689
Compiled by Laura L. Porteous, with notes by Walter Pritchard. These installments center around the years 1784-1785.

Índice del libro diez y seis de reales órdenes (*Bol. arch. nac.*, Habana, tomo 40, enero-dic., 1941 [i.e., 1943], p. 212-234). [2690
This installment lists documents dated 1803.

Índice del ramo de tierras. Vols. 1423-1454 (*Bol. arch. gen.*, México, tomo 14, no. 1, enero-marzo, p. 187-198; no. 2, abril-junio, p. 355-364; no. 3, julio-sept., p. 503-512; no. 4, oct.-dic., p. 633-642). [2691
The documents listed range from 1616 to 1846, but in the first issue most are from 1816-1832, and in the other three issues most are from 1701-1735.

Moore, Ernest Richard. Adiciones a la Biblioteca de Beristain (*Div. hist.*, vol. 4, no. 8, junio 15, p. 414-423). [2692
Notes, while mentioning a few examples, that he has seen about a thousand additions himself, in passing, among the "thousands of imprints and manuscripts in libraries of the United States."

O'Gorman, Edmundo (ed.). Catálogo de pobladores de Nueva España (*Bol. arch. gen.*, México, tomo 14, no. 2, abril-junio, p. 319-411; no. 3, julio-sept., p. 477-501). [2693
These installments include items no. 766-872, and a nearly complete *Indice de*

nombres. For earlier installments, see *Handbook no. 7, 1941,* no. 2876, and *no. 8, 1942,* no. 2939.

Peraza y Sarausa, Fermín. Índice del "Papel periódico de la Havana" (*Rev. bim. cub.*, vol. 51, no. 1, enero–feb., p. 134–136; no. 2, marzo–abril, p. 287–289; no. 3, mayo–junio, p. 450–456; vol. 52, no. 1, julio–agosto, p. 137–145; no. 2, sept.–oct., p. 304–313; no. 3, nov.–dic., p. 468–470). [2694

An index prepared cooperatively by students of history in the Universidad de la Habana, of the whole periodical, 1790–1804. It is most unfortunate that the index is by the first words of titles, but a note is added to explain the contents. To be continued.

Pérez Martínez, Héctor (comp.). Catálogo de documentos para la historia de Yucatán y Campeche que se hallan en diversos archivos y bibliotecas de México, y del extranjero. Campeche. Ed. Triay hnos. (Museo arqueológico histórico y etnográfico de Campeche). vi, 133 p. [2695

A very useful gathering up of lists of maps and documents in various depositories of Mexico, the United States, and Europe, already published in scattered books and pamphlets. Most concern the colonial period.

Steck, Francis B. A tentative guide to historical materials on the Spanish borderlands. Washington, D. C. Catholic university of America. 106 p. [2696

The "Borderlands" are, of course, those now part of the United States. Although the author modestly calls his work "tentative," it seems able satisfactorily to serve historians for a long time before fundamental revision will be needed. Periodicals and books from many countries are included.

Susto, Juan Antonio. Cartografía colonial panameña (*Bol. acad. panameña hist.*, segunda época, no. 1, enero–junio, p. 137–199). [2697

A product of the author's three years in the Archivo de Indias, 1923–1926. Lists 131 items in that depository, dated by him from 1541 to 1804 (and one of 1892). The following sixteen items do not appear in the well known catalogs of Pedro Torres Lanzas: 25 (dated 1632), 32, 33, 34, 43, 44, 67, 74, 75, 79, 94, 97, 104, 105, 106, 109 (dated 1784).

Ugarte, Salvador. Notas de bibliografía mexicana. México. Imp. Aldina por el autor. 104 p., 7 facs. [2698

One hundred copies printed, for private distribution. Precise collations, with some discussion, of sixty items in the author's collection, either not previously known, or incorrectly or incompletely described by bibliographers. Most are of the *Doctrina Cristiana* or *Vocabulario* type. There is a notable group in the "lengua Mixe," and emphasis on Puebla printing.

DOCUMENTS

(*See also item* 4904)

Aguilar, Francisco de. Relato breve de la conquista de la Nueva España. México. Ed. Vargas Rea. (Bibl. Aportación hist.). 73 p. [2699

One hundred numbered copies reprinted from *Anales del Museo Nacional*, 1903, which used the copy made by Francisco del Paso y Troncoso in 1892, of the original in the Escorial.

UN AUTO DA FE EN EL SIGLO XVII (*Bol. arch. gen.*, México, tomo 14, no. 2, abril–junio, p. 215–259). [2700

The auto da fe, an unusually important and solemn one, was on April 11, 1649.

[AUTOS ACERCA DE LA UTILIDAD DE LA FUNDACIÓN DEL COLEGIO DE SAN JERÓNIMO POR PARTE DE LOS RELIGIOSOS MERCEDARIOS] (*Bol. arch. gen.*, Guatemala, tomo 8, no. 4, dic., p. 402–442). [2701

Petition, with *testimonio*, for its founding, dated 1739, and legal documents of 1763–1768 concerning its closing because founded without proper license.

AUXILIOS A CAMPECHE Y YUCATÁN POR EL VIRREY MARQUÉS DE CROIX (*Bol. arch. gen.*, México, tomo 14, no. 2, abril–junio, p. 281–285). [2702

Documents of 1770, establishing *comercio libre* and *estancos de pólvora y naipes*, and granting aid to the starving.

Barlow, R. H., and **George T. Smisor.** Nombre de Dios, Durango. Two documents in Nahuatl concerning its foundation. Sacramento, House of Tlaloc. xxv, 103 p. [2703

130 numbered copies. Two documents in Nahuatl, 1563 and 1585, with English and Spanish translations. Appendices of six other documents, concerning the foundation of Nombre de Dios. A thoroughly scholarly piece of work.

The value of the texts here translated and edited is as great as the novelty of their character. The Spanish and English texts are on opposite pages, with the Nahuatl text and then the notes below them.

Berlin, Heinrich. Una carta de fray Francisco de Viana (*An. soc. geog. hist. Guatemala*, año 19, tomo 19, no. 2, dic., p. 128–131). [2704

Dated at the Dominican monastery, Coban, September 18, 1577. As a result of inquisitorial edict of 1576, forbidding translation of Scriptures into Indian tongues and ordering extant versions gathered up, Viana sends a list of the books in such tongues then at Coban. All were by himself or by the great linguist Fray Domingo de Vico, who died same year (1566) that Viana entered monastery. The list has great value for clarifying previous knowledge of Vico's work.

BUSCA DE TESOROS PRECORTESIANOS EN EL CERRO DE CHAPULTEPEC (*Bol. arch. gen.*, México, tomo 14, no. 4, oct.–dic., p. 617–632). [2705
Documents dated throughout most of the 18th century, in connection with a treasure seeking project of 1796.

Coiscou Henríquez, Máximo. Documentos para la historia de Santo Domingo (*An. univ. Santo Domingo*, año 7, no. 1, enero-marzo, p. 119–132; no. 3–4, julio-dic., p. 410–427). [2706
Items of 1571 and 1768 concerning the origin and state of the Hospital de San Nicolás de Bari.

[EL COLEGIO DE LA COMPAÑÍA DE JESÚS] (*Bol. arch. gen.*, Guatemala, tomo 8, no. 3, sept., p. 315–359). [2707
Documents of 1621–1646, presenting testimony in favor of the Jesuit college's right to grant degrees.

EL COLEGIO DE SANTO TOMÁS DE AQUINO (*Bol. arch. gen.*, Guatemala, tomo 8, no. 2, junio, p. 227–292; no. 3, sept., p. 295–315). [2708
Documents of 1577–1646. The Colegio opened in 1622, based on a Dominican college established in 1562 and Bishop Marroquín's bequest of 1563. It was the origin of the later Universidad de San Carlos.

COMUNICACIÓN DIRIGIDA A JOSÉ PABLO VALIENTE SOBRE LA REMISIÓN HECHA DEL GOBERNADOR DE NUEVA ORLEANS DE TREINTA Y SIETE INDIVÍDUOS DE COLOR Y BLANCOS COMPLICADOS EN UNA SUBLEVACIÓN EN AQUELLA PROVINCIA (*Bol. arch. nac.*, Habana, tomo 40, enero–dic., 1941 i.e. 1943, p. 59–62). [2708a
Documents of 1795.

COMUNICACIÓN DIRIGIDA AL GOBERNADOR DE CUBA QUE SE REFIERE A LA CONDUCTA DEL PRESBÍTERO JOSÉ ANTONIO SACO, ACUSADO DE OPOSITOR A LA PROPRIEDAD (*Bol. arch. nac.*, Habana, tomo 40, enero–dic., 1941, [i.e. 1943], p. 59). [2709
Royal order of February 18, 1794, telling the governor to interpose his veto in case the bishop should name Saco to an unnamed post.

EL CONVENTO DE LA CONCEPCIÓN (*Bol. arch. gen.*, México, tomo 14, no. 2, abril–junio, p. 261). [2710
An undated document setting forth the main facts in the history of this famous convent in Mexico City, from 1522 to 1655.

Conway, George Robert Graham. La noche triste. Documentos. Segura de la Frontera en Nueva España, año de 1520, que se publican integramente por primera vez con un prólogo y notas. México, D. F. Gante press. 105 p. [2711
Testimony of 19 participants, two months after the event. Printed from a photostat made in 1926, while original documents were still in private archive of Marquesado del Valle de Oaxaca. Present location unknown.

Dávila Caribi, José Ignacio. Un manuscrito histórico desconocido, contribución para la historia de Tonala (*Estud. hist.*, año 1, no. 2, julio, p. 49–57). [2713
A document of 1759, concerned with the royal grants and privileges of the Jaliscan town.

———. Prevenciones tomadas por el Gobierno de la Nueva Galicia ante el temor de un ataque de los piratas ingleses a las costas del Pacífico. (*Mem. acad. mex. hist.*, tomo 2, no. 4, oct.–dic., p. 346–371). [2714
A document of 1740 from the parish archive of Compostela, with annotations.

DEL ESTADO Y ABONO DE FIADORES EN QUE ESTABAN LOS SUBDELEGADOS DE LA INTENDENCIA Y CAJA PRINCIPAL DE MÉRIDA, YUCATÁN, EN 1809 (*Bol. arch. gen.*, México, tomo 14, no. 3, julio–sept., p. 431–439). [2715
Documents signed at Mérida on February 20, 1809, as ordered in 1792 (!) listing the names, titles, etc. of the officials.

DIARIO DEL VIAGE QUE HIZO EL VIRREY ITURRIGARAY A VERACRUZ, 1805 (*Bol. arch. gen.*, México, tomo 14, no. 1, enero–marzo, p. 153–169). [2716
Inspection trip, especially as to road conditions. The document is accompanied by Luis Martín's "Notas mineralógicas."

[DOCUMENTOS DEL ARCHIVO DEL AYUNTAMIENTO PARA LA HISTORIA DE LA CIUDAD] (*Bol. arch. gen.*, Guatemala, tomo 8, no. 1, marzo, p. 9–224). [2718
Dated from the earlier sixteenth century to the early nineteenth, upon a variety of subjects. Generally speaking, they concern matters dealt with by the *ayuntamiento*, and not the processes of government.

DOCUMENTOS SOBRE OCUPACIÓN DE LA HABANA POR LOS INGLESES (*Bol. arch. nac.*, Habana, tomo 40, enero–dic., 1941 i.e. 1943, p. 57–59). [2718a
Three short documents, respectively 1762, 1763 and 1764.

ERECCIÓN DE LA SANTA IGLESIA CATEDRAL EN METROPOLITANA. Documentación histórica. Segundo centenario del arzobispado de Guatemala, 16 de diciembre, 1743–1943. Guatemala. Tip. nacional. xx, 173 p. [2719
César Brañas signs the introductory statement. The work reproduces the text of an *expediente* from the Archivo· de Indias (Audiencia de Guatemala, exp. 66–5–1), dated from 1718 to 1743. The book is the result of an initiative by the Archbishop of Guatemala.

[ESCRITURA DE DOTACIÓN Y FUNDACIÓN DEL COLEGIO DE RECOGIMIENTO DE DONCELLAS]

(*Bol. arch. gen.*, Guatemala, tomo 8, no. 4, dic., p. 395–402). [2720]
Escritura by three *vecinos* of Santiago de los Caballeros, July 5, 1591, and petition to king from the *cabildo*, May 2, 1604.

[Expulsión de los padres de la Compañía de Jesús] (*Bol. arch. gen.*, Guatemala, tomo 8, no. 3, sept., p. 359–367; no. 4, dic., p. 371–395). [2721]
Expediente by Governor and Captain General Pedro Salazar, opened at Guatemala City on June 8, 1767.

Fernández, Justino. El origen de la Biblioteca de la antigua Academia de San Carlos (*Div. hist.*, vol. 4, no. 6, abril 15, p. 292–298; no. 7, mayo 15, p. 345–350). [2722]
A list of books etc. Reprinted from Diego Angulo Iñiguez. *La Academia de Bellas Artes de México* (Sevilla, 1935).

Fragmento de la última voluntad de Juan de Pasco, año 1625 (*Rev. arch. nac.*, Costa Rica, año 7, no. 3–4, marzo–abril, p. 209–211). [2723]
Document. Paso was a *vecino* of Cartago.

Fundación del pueblo de San Carlos Chachalacas (*Bol. arch. gen.*, México, tomo 14, no. 1, enero–marzo, p. 49–152). [2724]
Documents of 1764–1773, dealing with establishment of the village named, two and a half leagues from Veracruz, by Indians who left Pensacola with the Spanish.

King, James Ferguson. Admiral Vernon at Portobelo: 1739 (*Hisp. amer. hist. rev.*, vol. 23, no. 2, May, p. 258–282). [2726]
The full text of the important portions of a lengthy *expediente*, now preserved in the Archivo Histórico Nacional of Bogotá. A very great addition to the printed materials either in English or Spanish.

La libertad del comercio en la Nueva España en la segunda década del siglo XIX. Introducción de Luis Chávez Orozco. México. Sría. de hacienda y crédito público. (Dirección de estudios financieros, Archivo hist. de hacienda, vol. 1). 201 p. [2727]
Nine documents, dated 1810–1818, opposing the grant of freedom to England to trade with Spain and its possessions. The introduction traces the efforts of foreigners to encroach upon the trade of the Indies, from the 16th century.

Lunardi, Federico. Los payas. Documentos curiosos y viajes (*Bol. bibl. archivo nac.*, año 3, no. 6, oct. 31, p. 43–82 bis). [2728]
A very scholarly, though somewhat poorly organized, study of the Indian mission frontier of eastern Honduras, with special reference to the eighteenth and first half of the nineteenth centuries. The documents come, in several cases, from parochial or other little used archives.

Navarro y Noriega, Fernando. Catálogo de los curatos y misiones de la Nueva España. Seguido de la Memoria sobre la población del reino de Nueva España, primer tercio, siglo 19. México. Publ. del Inst. mex. de invest. hist.-juríd. 69 p. [2729]
Two items, originally published in Mexico by Arizpe, respectively in 1813 and 1820. The second was written in 1814. Both have value for conditions at the very end of the eighteenth century and start of the nineteenth. The editing is by J. Ignacio Rubio Mañé.

El pleito de las borlas (*Bol. arch. gen.*, México, tomo 14, no. 4, oct.–dic., p. 527–590). [2730]
Documents of 1762–1764, concerning a dispute with the *claustro* of the Universidad de México, over a proposed chair of Oriental languages. The dispute was in large part about the doctors' *propinas*.

Primera sublevación importante de los indios cubanos bajo la dirección del cacique Guama (*Bol. arch. nac.*, Habana, tomo 40, enero–dic., 1941 [i.e. 1943], p. 38–55). [2731]
Unannotated document of 1534, from the Archivo General de Indias.

Probanças del capitán don Gonzalo de Alvarado (*Rev. arch. nac.*, Costa Rica, año 7, no. 1–2, enero–feb., p. 3–16). [2732]
A document dated in Guatemala in 1555, original in Archivo General de Indias, Sevilla. Don Gonzalo came with Pedro de Alvarado.

Real cédula a los capitanes que fueren a descubrir tierra firme, para que puedan capturar los canibales sino quisieren obedecer y venderlos pagando la parte que perteneciere a sus altezas (*Bol. arch. nac.*, Habana, tomo 42, enero–dic., p. 7–9). [2732a]
Undated document, of 1503.

Real cédula dándole gracias al gobernador de Cuba por las noticias que ha dado de haber abandonado los ingleses el terreno que ocupaban cerca de la bahía de Guantánamo y por lo que en esta ocasión ha ejecutado (*Bol. arch. nac.*, Habana, tomo 40, enero–dic., 1941 [i.e. 1943], p. 55–57). [2733]
Documents of 1742.

Salinas Alanís, Miguel. Bienes y tributos del estado y marquesado del valle de Oajaca (*Mem. acad. mex. hist.*, tomo 2, no. 4, oct.–dic., p. 321–334). [2736]
An account of 1569, with comments. The annual tribute amounted to 48,280 pesos de oro comun (e.g., of 300 maravedí each), plus 28,815 fanegas of corn worth on the average one peso each. The properties are discussed only in rather general terms.

Sobre exploraciones y fundaciones de la costa septentrional de las Californias en tiempo del Excmo. Sr. Virrey don Martín de Mayorga (*Bol. arch. gen.*, México, tomo 14, no. 3, julio–sept., p. 409–421). [2737
Documents of 1779, concerning the ceremonial taking of possession of the port of Santiago Apostol in Ensenada de Nuestra Señora de Regla, in February.

Tamayo, Jorge L. La minería de Nueva España en 1794 (*Trim. econ.*, vol. 10, no. 2, julio–sept., p. 287–319). [2738
After long search, the author in 1934 found the archives of the Colegio de Minería and Real Tribunal de Minería in the Palacio de Minería. They are almost complete, 1771–1867.
He prints here a careful description of the *minería*, *diputación* by *diputación*, signed by Fausto de Elhuyer on February 17, 1794. The document was used by Humboldt. Tamayo's notes point out differences in the data.

Testimonio de las diligencias que se han formado de orden del Gobernador y Capitán General sobre el combate que tuvo nuestra lanche cañonera en la costa de Barlovento con dos fragatas de guerra inglesas (*Bol. arch. nac.*, Habana, tomo 40, enero–dic., 1941 i.e. 1943, p. 62–90). [2738a
Documents of 1798 and 1799, which show that the lanche cañonera "fought" with rather excessive circumspection.

Tributos para el hospital real de indios (*Bol. arch. gen.*, México, tomo 14, no. 3, julio–sept., p. 423–429). [2739
Document of 1603, which orders compliance with earlier orders about contributions of maize for the hospital.

Uranga H., Javier. Don Vasco de Quiroga. Lo que hay que hacer por los indios (*Rev. arch. nac.*, Costa Rica, año 7, no. 3–4, marzo–abril, p. 202–206). [2740
Abstract of Quiroga's rules, established in the mid-sixteenth century, for hospital in Michoacán.

Vázquez de Espinosa, Antonio. La audiencia de Guatemala. Primera parte. Libro quinto del *Compendio y descripción de las Indias Occidentales.* Año 1629. Guatemala. Tip. lib. Sánchez y de Guise. (Cuarto centenario de la fundación de la Antigua Guatemala). ix, 73 p. [2741
For the whole work of which this is a part, but in English translation, see *Handbook no. 8, 1942,* no. 2931. This extract is edited by Adrián Recinos, from the photocopy of the original in the Smithsonian Institution. There is a useful introduction.

La vida en la colonia. Cuaderno de apuntes de un ministro del Santo Oficio, 1606–1617 (*Bol. arch. gen.*, México, tomo 14, no. 4, oct.–dic., p. 591–615). [2742
A sort of diary by Pedro de Fonseca, who died in 1622. Primarily as to formal attendance by Inquisitors at the burials of various important persons, but has considerable value for the social history of Mexico City, especially as to public ceremonials and fiestas, and the earthquakes of 1611 and 1616.

Visita a la congregación de Chumatlán (*Bol. arch. gen.*, México, tomo 14, no. 1, enero–marzo, p. 13–48). [2743
Document, by Juez Comisario Rodrigo de Zárate y Villegas, 1599. Contains a description by various witnesses of an entirely Indian pueblo or *congregación*.

Other Works

(*See also items* 733, 4920)

Aguilar, Juan María. La Iglesia de San Francisco de la Montaña (*Bol. acad. panameña hist.*, segunda época, no. 1, enero–junio, p. 45–50). [2744
Architectural description of the church of San Francisco de la Montaña de Veraguas, the tower of which fell completely in October, 1941. The author advocates its reconstruction. See also the item by Samuel Lewis, no. 2797.

Alemar, Luis E. Santo Domingo. Ciudad Trujillo. Apuntaciones históricas . . . Historia de sus calles, plazas, paseos . . . edificios públicos y privados. Santiago, R. D. Ed. El Diario. 350 p., ilus. [2745
As its full name implies, a discussion of the names old and new, the buildings, the episodes and personalities, associated with the various streets of the ancient city of Santo Domingo. The arrangement is somewhat unfortunate for narrative historians, but there are excellent indices, sources are cited, and the arrangement will be overlooked by anyone capable of interest in such matters. A fascinating book, the spoil of wide and long reading.

Alessio Robles, Vito. Condiciones sociales del norte de la Nueva España (*Bol. sem. cult. mex.*, tomo 1, no. 2, oct., p. 60–84). [2746
Popularized and rather slight in style, but includes quotations from documents and is by a master in the field. Mostly sixteenth and seventeenth centuries.

———. Heráldica coahuilense. Notas históricas sobre los escudos de armas del estado de Coahuila, de Zaragoza y de las ciudades de Saltillo y Sabinas. México, D. F. A. del Bosque, imp. 30 p., ilus. [2747
Historical notes on the coats of arms of the State of Coahuila and the cities of Saltillo and Sabinas.

Alfau, Antonio Eugenio. La organización jurídica y administrativa de la Española

durante los años 1520-1600 (*Bol. unión interamer. Caribe*, vol. 5, abril-junio, p. 5-30). [2748]
A compilation of the laws, or abstracts of laws, found in Fabié, *Ensayo Histórico de la Legislación Española en . . . Ultramar.*

Almada, Francisco R. Los primeros pobladores de Santa Eulalia y San Francisco de Cuéllar (*Bol. soc. chihuahuense*, tomo 4, no. 11, abril 20, p. 419-430). [2749]
Data on sixteen men, largely from parish archives.

Artiles, Jenaro. Consideraciones sobre la fecha de la conquista de Cuba (*Univ. Habana*, año 8, no. 50-51, sept.-dic., p. 62-77). [2750]
Early accounts leave the date of the departure of Velásquez for Cuba vaguely in 1511. Modern students, following Irene Wright, have suggested "the end of 1510 or the beginning of 1511." The present article advances grounds for believing the departure to have been not later than June, 1510.

Barón Castro, Rodolfo. Pedro de Alvarado. Madrid. Ed. Atlas. 158 p. [2751]
En 158 páginas de apretada lectura nos ofrece el autor de la *Población del Salvador*, una historia anovelada del conquistador de Guatemala. El prestigio histórico del autor, bien cimentado en su magnífica obra demográfica, que si no lleva el nombre de histórico sobre la nación salvadoreña, nos permite entregarnos en sus manos y aceptar confiados, las afirmaciones que hace de Alvarado, que por la naturaleza de la colección en que ve la luz la obra no pueden ser confirmadas con abundancia de citas.
La escasez de obras monográficas sobre el legendario conquistador y la belleza del estilo hace más apreciable este interesante librito. [C. Sáenz de Santa María]

Barra, Luis L. de la. Apuntes genealógicos sobre los Torres (*Div. hist.*, vol. 4, no. 3, enero 15, p. 123-127). [2752]
Continued from vol. 3, no. 1, Nov., 1942, p. 10-17. Notes on a famous Mexican colonial family, of Navarrese origin.

Bayle, Constantino. Un "Dorado" inglés en el cárcel de la Villa de Madrid (*Rev. Indias*, Madrid, año 4, no. 11, enero-marzo, p. 167-176). [2754]
Summary and extract from lengthy statement made by "Capitán Francisco Sparri, inglés" while imprisoned in Madrid, in hopes of gaining his release. He had been with Raleigh in the search for El Dorado, "the past year of 1592." The documents are of 1600 to 1603, and come from the Archives of the Indies.

Borah, Woodrow. Silk raising in colonial Mexico. Berkeley, Los Angeles. Univ. of California press. (Ibero-Americana series, No. 20). vii, 169 p., illus. [2755]
A very scholarly study, based on a great variety of sources, manuscript and printed. Sericulture flourished in Mexico in the 16th century, and rather unsuccessful efforts were made at revival there in the 18th. It was not otherwise found in Latin America, aside from early experiments in Santo Domingo and a 16th century trial in Peru.

Cabal, Juan. Balboa, descubridor del Pacífico. Barcelona. Ed. Juventud. (Col. vidas y memorias). 220 p. [2756]
Popularized, and no indication of sources.

Calderón Quijano, José Antonio. El fuerte de San Fernando de Omoa. Su historia e importancia que tuvo en la defensa del golfo de Honduras (*Rev. Indias*, Madrid, año 4, no. 11, enero-marzo, p. 127-163). [2757]
Continued from earlier issues. This installment begins in 1768 and ends with the British attack of 1779-1780. Documents from the Archive of the Indies, and 13 maps. All but one of the maps are contemporary.

Camacho, Ramiro. El obispo Alcalde, benemérito de Guadalajara (*Estud. hist.*, año 1, no. 1, enero, p. 61-68). [2758]
Fray Antonio Alcalde, Dominican friar, formerly bishop of Cartagena and of Yucatan, born in Spain in 1701, bishop of Guadalajara from 1771 until his death in 1792. An outstanding enlightened and philanthropic prelate.

Carreño, Alberto María. Arte colonial. Opulencia y pobreza de Borda (*Div. hist.*, vol. 4, no. 11, sept. 15, p. 593-611). [2759]

———. Los misioneros en México. Los padres Salvatierra y Kino y la península de California (*Div. hist.*, vol. 4, no. 12, oct. 15, p. 635-641). [2760]
Largely by use of a manuscript account by Salvatierra, of his labors from 1699-1701, shows that the latter was the real "discoverer" that Lower California was a peninsula, though Kino had foreseen it.

———. La primera biblioteca del continente americano (*Div. hist.*, vol. 4, no. 8, junio 15, p. 428-431; no. 9, julio 15, p. 488-492). [2761]
Refers to the library left by Bishop Zumárraga to the Franciscan monastery in Mexico City.

Castellanos, J. Humberto R. Labor y disciplina, de los religiosos en la colonia (*Bol. mus. bibl.*, Guatemala, segunda época, año 3, no. 1, abril, p. 19-31). [2762]
An appreciation rather than a factual study, but by a very well informed writer.

Castillo, Ignacio B. del. Diario biográfico (*Div. hist.*, vol. 4, no. 1, nov., 1942, p. 23-28; no. 2, dic., 1942, p. 98-106; no. 3, enero 15, p. 132-142; no. 4, feb. 15, p. 192-197; no. 5, marzo 15, p. 255-262; no. 6, abril 15, p. 309-314; no. 7, mayo 15, p. 363-369; no. 8, junio 15, p. 407-423; no. 9 ,julio 15, p.

471–482; no. 10, agosto 15, p. 534–543; no. 11, sept. 15, p. 587–592; no. 12, oct. 15, p. 660–665). [2763
Brief but valuable biographic data on Mexicans from 16th century to living men, arranged by day and month of birth (or of death). So far, through March 5.

Castro y Tosi, Norberto de. Fundadores de casas hidalgas en Costa Rica (*Rev. arch. nac.,* Costa Rica, año 7, no. 1–2, enero-feb., p. 105–108; no. 3–4, marzo-abril, p. 186–193; no. 5–6, mayo-junio, p. 325–330; no. 7–8, julio-agosto, p. 434–443; no. 9–10, sept.-oct., p. 507–514). [2764
Completed from earlier issues in 1942. See *Handbook, no. 8, 1942,* item 2979.

Chamberlain, Roberto S. La controversia entre Cortés y Velázquez sobre la gobernación de la Nueva España, 1519–1522 (*An. soc. geog. hist. Guatemala,* año 19, tomo 19, no. 1, sept., p. 23–56). [2765
A careful study of the voluminous documentation, including some manuscript. Discusses Spanish as well as colonial aspects.

Chávez, Ezequiel A. El ambiente geográfico, histórico y social de fray Pedro de Gante, hasta el año de 1523. México. Ed. Jus. 197 p. [2766
An excellent discussion of the life of the famous Mexican educator-friar, prior to his arrival in Mexico. The style is rather popularized, and the notes are interpolated in the text.

———. El primero de los grandes educadores de la América, fray Pedro de Gante. Segunda ed. México. Ed. Jus. 148 p. [2767
Reprinted from the first edition of 1934. With the item just above, furnishes the reading public with a full biography of Gante, which is as interesting as it is scholarly.

Chávez Hayhoe, Arturo. Guadalajara de 1560 a 1600 (*Bol. junta aux. jalis.,* tomo 8, no. 1, abril, p. 13–49; no. 2, oct., p. 63–100). [2768
Notes gathered from a vast range of printed sources, and arranged under subject heads. The latter have no obvious order, but the work is readable and valuable.

Chávez Orozco, Luis. Las instituciones democráticas de los indígenas mexicanos en la época colonial (*Amér. indígena,* vol. 3, no. 1, enero, p. 73–82; no. 2, abril, p. 161–171; no. 3, julio, p. 265–276; no. 4, oct., p. 365–382). [2769
A scholarly study of the transformation of the *cacicazgo* into the 16th century system of *gobernación.* Mexico City had four Indian *barrios* with elected Indian officials. (Later eras, and other areas, are also studied).
Based on documents from the national archives in Mexico City.

Chevalier, François. Les cargaisons des flottes de la Nouvelle Espagne (*Rev. Indias,* Madrid, año 4, no. 12, abril-junio; p. 323–330). [2770
El autor ha reunido una serie de interesantes datos sobre la composición cualitativa de las flotas de ida y de vuelta que hacían el comercio entre España y su virreinato de la Nueva España. Es un estudio interesante y representa una concienzuda elaboración sobre datos documentales del Archivo de Indias. [C. Sáenz de Santa María]

Cook, S. F. The conflict between the California Indian and white civilization. Berkeley. Univ. of California. 4 pts. (c. 400 p.) [2771
The first and longest part deals with the demoralization and decline of the Indians under the Spanish missions. Part two deals with the non-mission Indians prior to 1848.

Crouse, Nellis M. The French struggle for the West Indies, 1665–1713. New York. Columbia univ. press. iv, 324 p., illus. [2772
A good chronological summary of international politics and warfare, based on printed works mostly of a secondary nature. In view of the large part that the struggle with the Dutch and Spanish plays in the story, it is amazing that the author seems unaware of the dangers inherent in neglecting their side of the story.

Cuevas, Mariano. Monje y marino. La vida y los tiempos de Fray Andrés de Urdaneta. México. Ed. Layac. xv, 417 p., ilus., mapas. [2773
Emphasizes the times rather than the life (1508–1568) of the famous navigator; shows considerable bias in discussing personages of the period, and gives insufficient indication of sources. But there is an excellent bibliography, and the sources came from Lima as well as from Mexico City and Sevilla.

Dávila, Vicente. Visión de México colonial (*Rev. javeriana,* tomo 19, no. 94, mayo, p. 170–177; no. 95, junio, p. 208–217). [2774
A highly appreciative glorification of the accomplishments of the Church as the fountainhead of culture in colonial Mexico.

Debien, G. Le plan et les débuts d'une caféitère à Saint-Domingue. La plantation La Merveillère aux Anses-à-Pitres (*Rev. soc. hist. géog. Haïti,* vol. 14, no. 51, oct., p. 9–32). [2775
Notes from a family archive and from various departmental archives, in France.

Delanglez, Jean. The authorship of the Journal of Jean Cavelier (*Mid-America,* vol. 25, no. 3, July, p. 220–223). [2776
In 1938 the author published a manuscript in the hand of Lahontan, which purported to be a copy of a journal by the brother of La Salle. He now prints a document and mentions other reasons which he

has for doubting Jean Cavelier's authorship.

———. El Río del Espíritu Santo (*Mid-America*, vol. 25, no. 3, July, p. 189–219; no. 4, Oct., p. 231–249). [2777
A thoroughly critical study of maps and other evidence, as to whether the Río del Espíritu Santo on maps of the 16th and 17th centuries was intended to represent the Mississippi. The portions so far printed cast doubt on that identity. To be continued.

———. The sources of the Delisle map of America, 1703 (*Mid-America*, vol. 25, no. 4, Oct., p. 275–298). [2778
A critical and scholarly commentary on the sources, as listed by Delisle himself in manuscript, of his *Carte du Canada . . . 1703*. This has as its bottom half a *Carte du Mexique et de la Floride . . . et des Antilles . . . 1703*, which was the first scientific mapping of the lower Mississippi, and the earliest extant accurate delineation of the Gulf Coast from Apalachee Bay to the Mississippi.

Díaz del Castillo, Bernal. Historia verdadera de la conquista de la Nueva España. Ed. modernizada. Prólogo y notas de Ramón Iglesia. México. Ed. Nuevo Mundo. 2 vols. xvi, 399; 399 p. [2779
The editor, a recognized authority on Díaz del Castillo and Cortez, has punctuated the original and eliminated the redundancies, to improve the readableness of the work.

Díaz Durán, José Constantino. Historia de la Casa de moneda del Reino de Guatemala, desde 1731 hasta 1773 (*An. soc. geog. hist. Guatemala*, año 18, tomo 18, marzo, p. 191–193). [2780
A chronological history of the building which housed the Guatemala mint. It was begun in 1733 and finished in 1759. A contemporary plan is reproduced.

Favrot, H. Mortimer. Colonial forts of Louisiana (*La. hist. quart.*, vol. 26, no. 2, April, p. 722–754; no. 3, July, p. 722–755). [2781
A useful, chronological series of extracts and abstracts from English and French language works, dealing with French and Spanish forts in the whole Mississippi valley, from the Lakes to the Gulf, and east to Mobile and Apalachicola, about 1670 to 1803.

Galíndez, Jesús. Los Vascos en la audiencia de Santo Domingo (*Clío*, año 10, no. 57–58, enero–abril, p. 232–237). [2782
Of about 3,000 names in an index for the 18th century of persons in the Spanish Antilles, 136 have Basque names. The author adds intersting comments.

García Guiot, Silvano. Rodrigo de Albornoz, contador real de la Nueva España. México. Ed. de la Soc. mex. de geog. y estad. (Temas de México, Serie hist., 1). 278 p. [2783
A useful, though hardly definitive, biography of one of the *oficiales reales* who disputed for power with Cortez and others of his period.

García Peláez, Francisco de P. Memorias para la historia del antiguo reino de Guatemala. Segunda ed. Guatemala. Tip. Nacional. 1943–1944. (Bibl. Payo de Rivera). 3 vols., ilus. [2784
Reprinted from the first edition (3 vol., Guatemala, 1851–1852), with an introduction by Víctor Miguel Díaz. The introduction deals especially with the life of Archbishop García Peláez (1785–1867) and points out that the work was begun at the suggestion of the *prócer* Mariano Gálvez when the latter was head of the state. It was finished after seven and one half years study of the archives and other sources, and delayed in printing.

González, Luis Felipe. Origen y desarrollo de las poblaciones de Heredia, San José y Alajuela durante el régimen colonial. San José. Imp. La Tribuna. 50 p. [2785

Guthrie, Chester L. Trade in colonial Mexico City (*Mexican life*, vol. 19, no. 11, Nov., p. 19–21). [2786

Guzmán Lozano, Emilio. Breve historia de las alcabalas en México (*Jus*, tomo 10, no. 54, enero, p. 17–62; tomo 11, no. 60, julio, p. 21–41). [2787
The *alcabala* was ordered by Junta de Ministros in 1568, and by Royal *cédula* of November 10, 1571. Collection started January 1, 1575. These installments discuss story only to 1821.

Herrera Carrillo, Pablo. Fr. Junípero Serra, civilizador de las Californias. México. Ed. Xochitl. (Col. Vidas mexicanas, tomo 8). 233 p. [2789
Popularized and appreciative, but quotes extensively from documents, and cites the sources in the text. Used some manuscript.

Herrera S., Julio Roberto. Anotaciones y documentos para la historia de los hospitales de la ciudad de Santiago de los Caballeros de Guatemala (*An. soc. geog. hist. Guatemala*, año 18, tomo 18, marzo, p. 225–272). [2790
Excellent documentation and data, but arranged hospital by hospital. with no overall synthesis.

Juárez Muñoz, J. Fernando. El obispo Cortés y Larraz (*An. soc. geog. hist. Guatemala*, año 18, tomo 18, marzo, p. 273–278). [2792
Dr. Pedro Cortés y Larraz, 1768–1779. There is a contemporary portrait.

Lamadrid, Lázaro. Los estudios franciscanos en la antigua Guatemala (*An. soc.*

geog. hist. Guatemala, año 18, tomo 18, marzo, p. 279–305). **[2793**
Notes for the history of the subject stated, 16th to 18th centuries and mostly from the Guatemalan archives.

Lardé, Jorge. Orígenes de San Salvador Cuscatlán (*Ateneo,* Salvador, año 31, no. 158, junio, p. 13–21; no. 159, sept., p. 3–16; no. 160, dic., p. 22–27). **[2794**
The eighteenth century historian Juarros said that San Salvador was founded on its first site on April 1, 1528 and moved to its present site eleven years later. Modern research has proved that it was in existence by May, 1525, but left the precise dates undecided.
In an article unfinished up to the end of 1943, Señor Lardé proceeds to examine the true date.

Lascurain y Zulueta, Carlos. Localización de las ruinas de la primitiva Villa Rica de la Veracruz, fundada 1519 (*Bol. soc. mex. geog. estad.,* tomo 58, no. 1–2, enero–abril, p. 191–202). **[2795**
The ruined walls of the first Veracruz were found in 1933, fifty kilometers north of the present city of that name, after three earlier expeditions (the first in 1890) had failed to discover the site.

Le Riverend Brusone, Julio J. Comentario en torno a las ideas sociales de Arrate (*Rev. cub.,* vol. 17, no. 2, abril.–dic., p. 326–341). **[2796**
A carefully organized examination of the social thought of José Martín Félix de Arrate, the eighteenth century Cuban historian and municipal officer. Based to a considerable degree upon the municipal archives.

Lewis, Samuel. La Iglesia de San Francisco de Veraguas (*Bol. acad. panameña hist.,* segunda época, no. 1, enero–junio, p. 37–41). **[2797**
An artistic appreciation, with a little history, of a famous churrigueresque church, built probably in the late seventeenth or early eighteenth century. See also item no. 2744 above.

López de Gómara, Francisco. Historia de la conquista de México. Introducción y notas por Joaquín Ramírez Cabañas. México, D. F. Ed. P. Robredo. 2 vols. **[2798**
The *notas* correct or clarify the text. The introduction deals, among other things, with the controversy over the validity of the López de Gómara interpretation of Cortez' personality.

López-Portillo y Weber, José. Los cronistas de la conquista de Nueva Galicia (*Mem. acad. mex. hist.,* tomo 2, no. 3, julio–sept., p. 209–230). **[2799**
Criticism of the various contemporary accounts.

Lunardi, Federico. Lempira, el héroe de la epopeya de Honduras (*Rev. arch. bibl. nac.,* Tegucigalpa, tomo 21, no. 8, feb., p. 501–515; no. 9, marzo, p. 561–591; no. 11, mayo, p. 433–447, 691–709). **[2800**
Concluded from earlier issues. A scholarly study of documents, traditions and geography. Lempira's death permitted the founding of Comayagua. He was killed in late July or early August, 1538.

McCarthy, Edward J. Spanish beginnings in the Philippines, 1564–1572. Washington, D. C. Catholic univ. of America. 145 p. **[2801**
Scholarly and readable.

Martínez Cosío, Leopoldo. Ensayo sobre heráldica mexicana (*Mem. acad. mex. hist.,* tomo 2, no. 4, oct.–dic., p. 372–388). **[2802**
A generalized discussion, essentially of the ideas that underlay heraldry as it developed in the Mexican conquest.

Martínez del Río, Pablo. Ante la Inquisición (*Div. hist.,* vol. 4, no. 5, marzo 15, p. 266–272). **[2803**
A rather successful effort to clarify the *modus operandi* of the Holy Tribunal, based on the *procesos* in the Mexican national archives.

———. La aventura mexicana de Sir John Hawkins (*Mem. acad. mex. hist.,* tomo 2, no. 3, julio–sept., p. 241–295). **[2804**
A carefully worked out narrative, based on the voluminous English and Spanish sources, some of the latter in manuscript. There are more or less contemporary illustrations.

Mateu y Llopis, Felipe. Navíos ingleses en el puerto de Veracruz en 1763 (*Rev. Indias,* Madrid, año 4, no. 14, oct.–dic., p. 683–708). **[2805**
Como contribución al estudio de las relaciones angloespañolas en América presenta el autor este pequeño incidente que dió mucho que hablar a los vecinos de Veracruz y llegó a ser uno de los capítulos de cargo en la residencia del Virrey. Hasta cinco navíos procedentes de la Habana, entonces bajo pabellón británico, fueron llegando a puerto de Veracruz, con el pretexto de repatriar prisioneros y bajo los preliminares de la Paz de París y en realidad con el objeto de colocar mercancías y de entrar un auténtico espionaje hasta el corazón del virreinato. La desconfianza de las autoridades españolas hizo abortar el plan. [C. Sáenz de Santa María]

Maza, Francisco de la. Enrico Martínez; cosmógrafo e impresor de Nueva España. México. Ed. de la Soc. mex. de geografía y estadística. (Temas de México, serie historia 2). 174 p., facsíms. **[2806**
A study of the life and work of the famous printer, scholar, and engineer in Mexico. He was born in Hamburg about 1550–1560, lived in Spain from his eighth

to his nineteenth year, and after some more time in Europe, reached Mexico in 1589. *Apéndice I:* La biblioteca de Enrico Martínez (p. 151-161); *Bibliografía:* (p. 165-169).

Mendizábal, Miguel O. de. La conquista espiritual de la "Tierra de Guerra" y su obstrucción por los conquistadores y pobladores (*An. soc. geog. hist. Guatemala,* año 19, tomo 19, no. 2, dic., p. 132-140). [2807
Deals with Lacandones, about 1537-1558, from standard printed sources.

Menéndez, Carlos R. La obra educativa de los jesuítas en Yucatán y Campeche durante la dominación española, 1618-1767 (*Div. hist.,* vol. 4, no. 4, feb. 15, p. 176-183; no. 5, marzo 15, p. 232-239). [2808
Detailed and valuable data, but sources very incompletely indicated.

Molina Solís, Juan Francisco. Historia del descubrimiento y conquista de Yucatán. Con una reseña de la historia de los mayas. Prólogo de Antonio Médiz Bolio. México, D. F. Ed. Mensaje. 2 vols. [2809
First edition: Mérida, 1896.

Molina-Téllez, Félix. La conversión del cacique Juan de las tierras de Guatemala (*Rev. hist.,* Buenos Aires, tomo 2, no. 1, julio, p. 37-44). [2810
A journalistic but documented account of an incident in Guatemala of 1537.

Monterde García Icazbalceta, Francisco. El temor de Hernán Cortés y otras narraciones de la Nueva España. Prólogo de Luis González Obregón. México. Imp. Universitaria. 343 p. [2811
Imaginative recreations of situations and actions with a factual foundation.

Moreyra P. S., Manuel. Portobelo y la travesía del Istmo en la época colonial (*Mercurio peruano,* año 18, vol. 25, no. 196, julio, p. 319-329). [2812
A journalistic account, apparently entirely from well known sources and dealing mostly with the eighteenth century. There is no real discussion of the *travesía.*

Mowat, Charles L. East Florida as a British province, 1763-1784. Berkeley and Los Angeles. Univ. of California. (Univ. of California, Publ. in hist., vol. 32). 237 p. [2813
A thoroughly scholarly study of certain aspects of a non-Spanish interlude in the history of a long time Spanish colony. Considerable parts have at least passing value for students of the preceding or succeeding Spanish period.

LA NOBLEZA COLONIAL, ÚLTIMO TERCIO DEL SIGLO 18 (*Bol. arch. gen.,* México, tomo 14, no. 2, abril-junio, p. 289-315; no. 3, julio-sept., p. 441-476). [2814
Continued from an earlier issue. A list of titles with comment as to the legal status for purposes of taxation. Some of the titles were *radicado* in Spain, the Philippines, Habana, Peru or elsewhere outside Mexico.

Ochoa, Ángel S. Los misioneros en México. Los franciscanos en la provincia de Jalisco (*Div. hist.,* vol. 4, no. 3, enero 15, p. 117-122; no. 7, mayo 15, p. 340-344; no. 10, agosto 15, p. 511-517). [2815
Completed from an earlier issue. A chronicle of events in the history of the famous Franciscan monastery of Guadalajara, to 1596. (The building was gutted by fire in 1936).

O'Connor, Thomas F. An alleged Spanish "entrada" into New York (*Mid-America,* vol. 25, no. 4, Oct., p. 130-138). [2816

Orozco, Luis Enrique. San Juan Cozalá (*Estud. hist.,* año 1, no. 1, enero, p. 13-30). [2817
A visit to an ancient Franciscan center, with historical notes and a plan of the church.

Orozco Casorla, Raúl. Genealogía de la familia Soto. San Martín y Soto (*Rev. arch. nac.,* Costa Rica, año 7, no. 3-4, marzo-abril, p. 135-143; no. 5-6, mayo-junio, p. 306-321). [2818
Ancestry, beginning in the seventeenth century, of a prominent Costa Rican family.

Osborne, Lilly de Jongh. Influencias de la época colonial sobre la indumentaria indígena de Guatemala (*An. soc. geog. hist. Guatemala,* año 18, tomo 18, no. 4, junio, p. 425-435). [2820
An earnest effort to trace the effect of the coming of the Spanish, before the invention of the Jacquard loom (early nineteenth century). Data is scanty before the eighteenth century.

Palm, Erwin Walter. La atarazana de Santo Domingo de Guzmán (*Bol. inst. invest. hist.,* año 21, tomo 27, no. 93-96, julio, 1942-junio, 1943, p. 42-48). [2821
A treasure of architecture in Ciudad Trujillo, much overlooked. It was started before 1516 and had its present three naves by 1540, but was not then roofed.

Pardo, J. Joaquín. Efemérides para escribir la historia de la muy noble y muy leal ciudad de Santiago de los Caballeros del Reino de Guatemala (*An. soc. geog. hist. Guatemala,* año 18, tomo 18, marzo, p. 359-408; no. 4, p. 468-483; año 19, tomo 19, no. 2, dic., p. 150-154). [2823
Chronologically arranged data, from August 29, 1541 to (in last installment here) November 7, 1667.
Apparently from archival documentation.

Pérez Valenzuela, Pedro. Los recoletos. Apuntes para la historia de las misiones en la América central. Guatemala. Tip. nacional. xxiii, 127 p. [2824

A publication in connection with the second centennial of the establishment of the archbishopric of Guatemala. Displays an understandable warmth of appreciation of the work of the Franciscan missions in Guatemala. The study is based on excellent printed and manuscript sources.

Pichardo Moya, Felipe. La edad media cubana (*Rev. cub.*, vol. 17, no. 2, abril-dic., p. 288-325). [2825

A survey of certain aspects of Cuban life, prior to 1762.

Ramírez Cabañas, Joaquín. La estimación y los odios que inspiró Cortés (*Div. hist.*, vol. 4, no. 4, feb. 15, p. 198-205). [2827

An analysis of motivations.

Recinos, Adrián. Dos expediciones del gobernador de Guatemala don Pedro de Alvarado (*An. soc. geog. hist. Guatemala*, año 19, tomo 19, no. 1, sept., p. 62-68). [2828

Two expeditions against royal orders: to Peru, 1534-1535, and to Honduras and on to Spain, 1535-1536.

Ríos, Eduardo Enrique. Fray Juan de San Miguel, fundador de pueblos (*Ábside*, vol. 7, no. 3, julio-sept., p. 318-338). [2829

A popularized account of the labors of one of the earliest Franciscans in Mexico, associated especially with Uruapan.

Rodríguez Demorizi, Emilio. La imprenta y los primeros periódicos de Santo Domingo (*Clío*, año 10, no. 60, julio-oct., p. 98-109; no. 61, nov.-dic., p. 115-180). [2830

Reproduction of texts, with facsimiles of title pages of first issues.
El Telégrafo Constitucional de Santo Domingo and *El Duende*, both of 1821, are treated in the November-December installment.

Romero, Fernando. El negro en Tierra Firme durante el siglo 16 (*Bol. acad. panameña hist.*, segunda época, no. 1, enero-junio, p. 3-34). [2831

First part of a study, primarily upon Panama. Chronological in form; cites no sources, but apparently from the standard printed works.

Romero de Terreros, Manuel. El Conde de Regla, Creso de la Nueva España. México. Ed. Xochitl. (Vidas mexicanas, 9). 175 p. [2832

An excellent narrative biography of the eighteenth century Mexican Croesus, though somewhat over-romanticized.
Bibliografía: (3 unnumbered leaves at back).

Roys, Ralph Loveland. The Indian background of colonial Yucatan. Washington. Carnegie inst. of Washington. (Publ. 548). 244 p. [2833

A very scholarly work, dealing with what the Spanish found in Yucatan, and with the cacique system in Yucatan under the Spanish. An appendix treats of the land treaty of Mani.

Salazar, Buenaventura. Los doce primeros apóstoles franciscanos en México. México. Imp. mexicana. vi, 212 p. [2834

Devout popularizations, but interesting and not without value to historians.

Saravia, Atanasio G. Los misioneros muertos en el norte de Nueva España. Segunda ed., corr. y aumentada. México. Ed. Botas. 253 p. [2836

First edition, Durango, 1920. This second edition reproduces the text exactly, with additions or clarifications clearly marked.
The work is essentially a compilation of the relevant data in standard printed works, mostly contemporary, but is a useful guide to North Mexican martyrdoms of the colonial period.

Simpson, Lesley Byrd. Transport in colonial Mexico (*Mexican life*, vol. 19, no. 12, Dec., p. 21-22). [2837

Smith, Robert Sidney. Shipping in the port of Veracruz, 1790-1821 (*Hisp. amer. hist. rev.*, vol. 23, no. 1, Feb., p. 5-20, tables). [2837a

Based on national archives of Mexico City, and municipal archives of Veracruz and Jalapa.

Steck, Francis Borgia. Education in Spanish North America during the sixteenth century. Washington. Dept. of educ., National Catholic welfare conference. 39 p. ("Reprinted from The Catholic educational review, January, February, 1943.") [2839

An appreciative survey, which naturally deals in large part with Mexico.

Torquemada, Juan de. Monarquía indiana. Tomos 1-2. Tercera ed. México. Ed. Salvador Chávez Hayhoe. 2 vols.: 40, 768, 71; 14, 623, 56 p., ilus. [2840

A facsimile reproduction of the edition of Madrid, Nicolás Rodríguez Franco, 1723. The only additions are a title page for this "third edition," and a colophon, in each volume.

Torre, Josefina Muriel de la. El Convento de la Concepción (*Humanidades*, México, tomo 1, no. 1, julio, p. 22-28). [2841

A sketch of the history of what is believed to have been the first convent (e.g., for nuns) in Mexico. It may have been established in the 1530's, it was royally authorized in 1541, and it was closed finally only in 1863.

Troncoso de la Concha, M. de J. Don Juan Sánchez Ramírez y la reconquista

(*Clío*, año 11, no. 59, mayo-junio, p. 58-61). **[2842**

Sánchez, born 1762 and died 1811, was the hero of the reconquest from France in 1808-1809, of Spanish Santo Domingo.

Ugarte de Brusiloff, María. Publicación de la ley en Santo Domingo durante el período de la dominación española (*Bol. arch. gen.*, Ciudad Trujillo, año 6, vol. 6, no. 28-29, mayo-agosto, p. 121-141). **[2843**

A study of the methods by which laws were legally "published" in Hispaniola, chiefly in the eighteenth and early nineteenth centuries. Printing was used from 1814. Sources include the municipal archives of Bayaguana and Monte Plata.

Universidad de la Habana. Facultad de ciencias sociales y derecho público. Cuba en los inicios histórico-institucionales, 1511-1537. Habana. Ed. González y cía. (Publ. de la Cátedra de historia de las institucienes locales de Cuba). 42 p. **[2844**

An interesting though not profound group of twelve papers by students of history in the University. Sources are not cited.

Valle Matheu, Jorge del. Páginas inéditas de la Antigua (*An. soc. geog. hist. Guatemala*, año 18, tomo 18, marzo, p. 313-326). **[2845**

Discusses the *memorias* of P. Fray Antonio de Molina, written 1677 and 1678, continued by Fray Agustín Cano and P. Fray Bartolomé de Viveros. They became incorporated into the well known history of Fray Francisco Ximenes, without the care for citation called for by modern historical ethics.

Vargas, Fulgencio. La ciudad de Dolores Hidalgo, Guanajuato (*Bol. soc. mex. geog. estad.*, tomo 58, no. 1-2, enero-abril, p. 148-190). **[2846**

Historical notes on various subjects.

White, Leslie A. Punche: tobacco in New Mexican history (*New Mex. hist. rev.*, vol. 18, no. 4, Oct., p. 386-393). **[2848**

Without pretending to solve them, discusses the questions as to what sort of tobacco was used in colonial New Mexico, and whether the Indians used any tobacco before the Spanish came.

Yglesias Hogán, Rubén. Las siete ciudades doradas de Cíbola (*Rev. arch. nac.*, Costa Rica, año 7, no. 7-8, julio-agosto, p. 372-384). **[2849**

A popularized appreciation of Coronado's work.

Addenda

Bens Arrarte, José M. Inicio del urbanismo colonial en Hispanoamérica (*Bol. unión interamér. Caribe*, no. 3, enero-dic., 1942, p. 77-102). **[2850**

A commentary upon the provisions of the Leyes de Indias (which are reprinted) concerning cities.

[Documentos para la historia de Cuba, 1764-1823] (*Rev. arch. nac.*, Bogotá, tomo 4, no. 39, mayo, 1942, p. 207-243). **[2851**

For contents, of which the most valuable is a *Descripción del puerto y ciudad de la Habana, año 1764*, see *Handbook no. 8, 1942*, p. 52.

Documentos sobre panamá (*Rev. arch. nac.*, Bogotá, tomo 5, no. 44, nov.-dic., 1942, p. 1-62). **[2852**

A miscellany of documents for the history of the 16th to 18th centuries.

Dunne, Peter Masten. The padre of the magic shoes. (*Mid-America*, vol. 24, no. 4, Oct., 1942, p. 272-285). **[2853**

Deals with the Jesuit Francis Hermann Glandorff, a semi-legendary figure even in his own day, born Osnabruck in 1687; early noted for study and teaching. To Mexico in 1718; took fourth vow in 1721, and became a great missionary among the Tarahumara Indians in the region of Chihuahua from 1722 to his death in 1763.

Malagón Barceló, Javier. El distrito de la audiencia de Santo Domingo en los siglos 16 á 19. Ciudad Trujillo. Ed. Montalvo. 1942. (Univ. de Santo Domingo, Publ., vol. 23). 134 p., ilus. **[2854**

An attempt to determine the territorial jurisdiction of the audiencia de Santo Domingo, as affected by creation of other governments, foreign encroachments, etc. Sources are not adequate for most of the study. The discussion of the period 1809-1821 shows what the author could have done under better working conditions. Eight documents at back, 1511-1861.

Meade, Joaquín. El plan primitivo o traza del Pueblo de San Luís Minas del Potosí en el año de 1593 (con un plano) (*Bol. soc. mex. geog. estad.*, tomo 57, no. 3-4, sept.-dic., 1942, p. 389-415). **[2855**

Pueblo founded in 1592, following the finding of a mine. Existence of the map has long been known, but its location was unknown until the author discovered it in the Archivo General de la Nación, *Tierras* 2777. The article includes several documents.

Rubio Mañé, J. Ignacio. Archivo de la historia de Yucatán, Campeche y Tabasco. III. Documentos: 1559-1560; Apéndices: documentos relativos á instrucción pública. 1782-1805. México. Imp. Aldina, 1942. l, 331 p. **[2857**

A new volume of this valuable series. The items of 1559-1560 are inquisitorial *procesos* concerned with charges of blasphemy.

Ruiz Sánchez, A. Antonio Alcalde, el fraile de la Calavera. Guadalajara. Tall. gráf.

de la Univ. de Guadalajara. 1942. 157 p. [2858

Alcalde was bishop of Guadalajara from 1771 till his death in 1792. This work includes data from the Archive of the old Hospital de San Miguel (now Hospital Civil), now in process of reorganization.

Strickland, Rex W. Moscoso's journey through Texas. An effort to solve a long debated question (*Southw. hist. quart.*, vol. 46, no. 2, Oct., 1942, p. 109–137). [2859

Concerns the route of Luis de Moscoso's *entrada* of 1542. Uses no new documentation. Should be read in connection with the articles on the same subject by J. W. Williams and Albert Waldert, in the same issue of the magazine, p. 138–157, 158–166.

SOUTH AMERICA
BY
JAMES F. KING

DOCUMENTARY INDICES AND GUIDES

Cartagena. Museo histórico. Catálogo del Museo histórico de Cartagena, 1943. Cartagena. Ed. Bolívar. 194 p. [2860

CAUSAS DE INFIDENCIA. TOMO 22 (*Bol. arch. nac.*, Caracas, tomo 29, no. 116, mayo–junio, p. 425–430). [2861

COMPAÑÍA GUIPUZCOANA. TOMOS 9, 10 Y 11 (*Bol. arch. nac.*, Caracas, tomo 29, no. 114, enero–feb., p. 281–286; no. 115, marzo–abril, p. 346–352; no. 116, mayo–junio, p. 405–411; tomo 30, no. 117, julio–agosto, p. 28–34; no. 118, set.–oct., p. 100–106; no. 119, nov.–dic., p. 163–170). [2862

ENCOMIENDAS. TOMO 32 (*Bol. arch. nac.*, Caracas, tomo 29, no. 114, enero–feb., p. 264–269; no. 115, marzo–abril, p. 329–334; no. 116, mayo–junio, p. 387–392; tomo 30, no. 117, julio–agosto, p. 10–15; no. 118, set.–oct., p. 81–87; no. 119, nov.–dic., p. 142–148). [2863

GOBERNACIÓN Y CAPITANÍA GENERAL. TOMOS 18 Y 19 (*Bol. arch. nac.*, Caracas, tomo 29, no. 114, enero–feb., p. 270–274; no. 115, marzo–abril, p. 335–339; no. 116, mayo–junio, p. 393–398; tomo 30, no. 117, julio–agosto, p. 16–21; no. 118, set.–oct., p. 95–99; no. 119, nov.–dic., p. 149–154). [2864

Hernández de Alba, Guillermo. El cedulario del cabildo de Bogotá (*Bol. hist. antig.*, vol. 30, no. 342–343, abril–mayo, p. 367–385). [2865

Reproduces an index, made by the secretary of the Cabildo of Santa Fe de Bogotá in 1761, which lists royal *cédulas* of the period 1532–1760 once preserved in the municipal archives. The contents of this *cedulario*, as well as other documents, were destroyed by fire in 1900. Though it gives only short descriptive titles and the years in which the *cédulas* were issued, this hitherto unpublished index permits the reconstruction of much of the contents of the municipal *cedulario* from duplicates existing in Colombia and Spain.

HOJAS MILITARES. TOMO 10 (*Bol. arch. nac.*, Caracas, tomo 29, no. 114, enero–feb., p. 294–299; no. 115, marzo–abril, p. 359–362; no. 116, mayo–junio, p. 419–424; tomo 30, no. 117, julio–agosto, p. 41–45; no. 119, nov.–dic., p. 177–182). [2866

ÍNDICE DEL ARCHIVO NACIONAL DEL PERÚ. SECCIÓN ARCHIVO DE LA REAL JUNTA DE TEMPORALIDADES. TÍTULOS DE LA HACIENDA DE SAN JOSÉ DE LA NASCA (*Rev. arch. nac. Perú*, tomo 16, entrega 2, julio–dic., p. 221–238). [2867

Lists *cuadernos* covering the years 1763–1804.

ÍNDICE DEL ARCHIVO NACIONAL DEL PERÚ. SECCIÓN ARCHIVO DE LA REAL JUNTA DE TEMPORALIDADES. TÍTULOS DE LA HACIENDA MACACONA (*Rev. arch. nac. Perú*, tomo 16, entrega 1, enero–junio, p. 101–112). [2868

The manuscript *cuadernos* here listed cover the years 1767–1818.

INTENDENCIA DE EJÉRCITO Y REAL HACIENDA. TOMOS 18, 19 Y 20 (*Bol. arch. nac.*, Caracas, tomo 29, no. 114, enero–feb., p. 287–293; no. 115, marzo–abril, p. 353–358; no. 116, mayo–junio, p. 412–418; tomo 30, no. 117, julio–agosto, p. 35–40; no. 118, set.–oct., p. 119–124; no. 119, nov.–dic., p. 171–176). [2869

Lohman Villena, Guillermo. Índice del "Libro becerro de escrituras" (*Rev. arch. nac. Perú*, tomo 16, entrega 1, enero–junio, p. 59–100; entrega 2, julio–dic., p. 175–219). [2870

Lists documents of the period 1535–1537.

REALES PROVISIONES. TOMOS 22 Y 23 (*Bol. arch. nac.*, Caracas, tomo 29, no. 114, enero–feb., p. 275–280; no. 115, marzo–abril, p. 340–345; no. 116, mayo–junio, p. 399–404; tomo 30, no. 117, julio–agosto, p. 22–27; no. 118, set.–oct., p. 88–94; no. 119, nov.–dic., p. 155–162). [2871

Torre Revello, José. El cedulario que formó Benito de la Mata Linares (*Bol. inst. invest. hist.*, año 21, tomo 27, no. 93–96, julio, 1942–junio, 1943, p. 363–365). [2872

Mata Linares was *regente* of the audiencia of Buenos Aires, and his *cedulario* is preserved by the Academia de la Historia of Madrid. The present short note indicates the years covered (1493–1808) in each of the volumes of this chronologically arranged MS *cedulario*.

Documents

Actas del cabildo de Caracas. Tomo 1, 1573–1600. Caracas. Ed Elite. 565 p. [2873

Actis, Francisco C. Un plano "eclesiástico" de Buenos Aires (*Archivum,* tomo 1, cuad. 1, enero–junio, p. 226–228). [2874
"Es por muchos conceptos notable el "Plano . . ." que reproducimos en facsímile: con más propiedad debiera titularse Plano de la División Eclesiástica de Buenos Aires, aún cuando su interés edilicio es evidente también por la minuciosidad de varios detalles curiosos que su autor creyó oportuno consignar" (p. 226). The date of the map seems to be about 1775.

Acuerdos del extinguido cabildo de Montevideo. Anexo, vol. 18. Montevideo. Tall. gráf. Botella. (Archivo general de la nación). 304, xxii p. [2875
"El presente volumen, tercero de los anexos y XVIII de la serie, reproduce los acuerdos comprendidos entre el 6 de enero de 1792 y el 20 de julio de 1795, dando fin de esta manera a la reproducción de todas las actas que por razones que se ignoran, no fueron incluidas en su oportunidad en los lugares en que le correspondía hacerlo." Note in *Rev. hist. Amér.*, no. 16, dic., 1943, p. 249.

Archivo de Indias. Descripción de la ciudad de Tunja, sacada de las informaciones hechas por la justicia de aquella ciudad en 30 de mayo de 1610 años (*Bol. hist. antig.*, vol. 30, no. 342–343, abril–mayo, p. 451–488). [2876

Autos que se comenzaron por mandado del Excmo. Señor Duque de la Palata, Virrey destos Reinos, para trasladar la villa de Pisco a un paraxe más seguro y alexado de la mar. Año de 1688 (*Rev. arch., nac. Perú,* tomo 16, entrega 1, enero–junio, p. 27–57; entrega 2, julio–dic., p. 143–174). [2877

Bromley, Juan (ed.). Libros de cabildos de Lima. Libro duodécimo, años 1593–1597. Lima. Imp. Torres Aguirre. 688 p. [2878

El cabildo de la ciudad de Valencia pide la remoción de un teniente (*Bol. arch. nac.,* Caracas, tomo 30, no. 119, nov.–dic., p. 135–141). [2879
Documents of the year 1785, including a *real provisión* of the Audiencia of Santo Domingo, directing the Governor and Captain General of Caracas to remove the *teniente justicia mayor* of Valencia, José Ignacio Toro, for various abuses described in a petition of the said city.

Capitulación con el mariscal Diego de Almagro para descubrir y poblar 200 leguas en el mar del sur hacia el estrecho de Magallanes (*Rev. bibl. nac.,* Buenos Aires, tomo 9, no. 28, cuarto trim., p. 366–374). [2880
Dated in Toledo, May 21, 1534.

Descripción corográfico-mixta de la provincia Guayana en que se da razón de los ríos que la bañan y facilitan sus comunicaciones; de su población, tierras de labor útiles de sus frondosos montes, frutos y comercio; y se proponen algunos medios los mas asequibles y conducentes a su vivificación y aumento (*Bol. arch. nac.,* Caracas, tomo 29, no. 115, marzo–abril, p. 311–328). [2881
Don Miguel Marmión, author of this report, was governor of Guiana from 1784 to 1790. The document is dated in Guiana, July 10, 1788.

Documentos inéditos relativos a la universidad nacional mayor de San Marcos (*Bol. bibliog.,* Lima, año 16, vol. 13, no. 3–4, dic., p. 173–197). [2882
These documents cover the years 1770 to 1818 and concern the establishment of the Colegio de San Carlos in Lima.

Encomiendas (*Bol. arch. hist. prov. Mérida,* año 1, no. 5, oct., p. 79–82; no. 6, dic., p. 97–101). [2883

Febres Cordero, Tulio. Noticia histórica y jurisdicciones de Mérida (*Bol. arch. hist. prov. Mérida,* año 1, no. 1, feb., p. 2–4). [2884

Fundación de la villa de Nuestra Señora de la Palma (*Rev. arch. nac.,* Bogotá, tomo 5, no. 53–56, sept.–dic., p. 376–397). [2885

Garcés G., Jorge A. (ed.). Documentos históricos. Sublevación de Quito (*Bol. acad. nac. hist.,* Quito, vol. 23, no. 61, enero–junio, p. 133–136). [2886
Documents of 1775 and 1776 concerning an investigation carried out by Viceroy Pedro Messía de la Cerda in Santa Fe de Bogotá concerning a revolt that occurred in Quito in the former year.

Gonzalo Jiménez de Quesada (*Rev. arch. nac.,* Bogotá, tomo 5, no. 53–56, sept.–dic., p. 359–375). [2887

Gutiérrez Valenzuela, Alfredo. Un interesante litigio sucesorio en el año 1785 (*Rev. bibl. arch. nac.,* no. 24–30, junio, p. 1–13). [2888
Documents concerning a lawsuit instituted by the sister of the priest Juan Ciriaco Murillo to prevent the latter from willing his property to his natural son, Pedro Murillo, who later became the proto-martyr of Bolivian independence. Among the documents here published is a baptismal record showing that Pedro Murillo was christened in La Paz on October 13, 1758.

Información hecha por Bernardino Balderrama en nombre de Francisco Pizarro

Sobre Nueva Castilla (*Rev. bibl. nac.*, Buenos Aires, tomo 9, no. 28, cuarto trim., p. 382-390). [2889
A sub-title reads: "Información hecha á petición de Francisco Pizarro, sobre los límites de su gobernación, en que aparece como testigo el piloto Juan Fernández. Lima, 24 Septiembre de 1537."

Informe de Pedro Esteban Dávila, Gobernador del Río de la Plata al Rey de España, manifestando el número y la clase de reducciones de indios existentes en el virreinato y dando cuenta del estado de pobreza en que viven los descendientes de los conquistadores (*Rev. bibl. nac.*, Buenos Aires, tomo 9, no. 28, cuarto trim., p. 326-335). [2890

Informe sobre el estado de la provincia de Maracaibo y manera de remediar su decadencia, dirigido al secretario de estado y del despacho universal de las Indias por el coronel Francisco de Arce, gobernador de la misma provincia, año 1784 (*Bol. arch. nac.*, Caracas, tomo 29, no. 114, enero-feb., p. 249-254). [2891

Jueces que vinieron a la provincia (*Bol. arch. nac.*, Caracas, tomo 30, no. 117, julio-agosto, p. 1-4). [2892
Documents of 1689 concerning steps taken by Governor and Captain General Diego Jiménez de Enciso of the Province of Venezuela to prevent judges sent by the Audiencia of Santo Domingo from interfering with officials in the city of Coro.

Libro de matrícula de estudiantes de los Reales Estudios del Colegio de San Carlos de Buenos Aires, 1773-1818 (*Rev. bibl. nac.*, Buenos Aires, tomo 8, no. 25, primer trim., p. 194-198; no. 26, segundo trim., p. 466-470; tomo 9, no. 27, tercer trim., p. 179-184; no. 28, cuarto trim., p. 449-453). [2894
Continued from the 1942 issues of the *Revista*. See *Handbook, no. 8, 1942*, item 3053. To be continued.

El licenciado Matienzo al licenciado Castro, gobernador del Perú. Carta referente a desórdenes en Cuzco y otros lugares (*Rev. bibl. nac.*, Buenos Aires, tomo 9, no. 28, cuarto trim., p. 391-395). [2895
Dated in La Plata, January 10, 1567.

Martín Moreno, Ángel. La explotación minera del valle del Supia en el siglo 18 (*Rev. Indias*, Madrid, año 4, no. 11, enero-marzo, p. 117-126). [2896
Un alegato hallado por el autor en el archivo de Indias, en que los vecinos del valle piden justicia contra los abusos de su alcalde ordinario D. Augustín de Castro, resulta una magnífica exposición de la situación geográfica del valle (Popayán) de sus riquezas mineras, de sus vías de comunicación, de los modos de vivir y de trabajar . . . todo completado por un croquís de la región. El artículo lo reproduce en su totalidad precedido de un pequeño prólogo. [C. Sáenz de Santa María]

Martínez, Juan. Real cédula fecha en Valladolid a 9 de junio de 1549, por la cual se aprueban y confirman los términos señalados por el licencido Gonzalo Jiménez de Quesada a los pueblos que el ganó y conquistó en el Nuevo Reino de Granada (*Rev. arch. nac.*, Bogotá, tomo 5, no. 53-56, sept.-dic., p. 359-360). [2897

"Memorias curiosas" o "Diario" de Juan Manuel Beruti (*Rev. bibl. nac.*, Buenos Aires, tomo 8, no. 25, primer trim., p. 179-193; no. 26, segundo trim., p. 449-465; tomo 9, no. 27, tercer trim., p. 159-178; no. 28, cuarto trim., p. 442-448). [2898
Continued from the 1942 numbers of the *Revista*. See *Handbook, no. 8, 1942*, item 3058. To be continued.

Noticias de América que manda el padre Miguel Alejo Schabel, misionero de la Sociedad de Jesús al muy reverendo padre Miguel Ángel Tamburino prepósito y vicario general de la misma sociedad, el 9 de abril del año de 1705, de la nueva misión en las islas de Curazao, Bonaire, Aruba y del Río Apure en la tierra firme india en el Reino de Nueva Granada (*Bol. centro hist. larense*, año 2, no. 6, segundo trim., abril-junio, p. 36-46). [2899

Observaciones sobre la importancia del istmo de Panamá y sus riquezas naturales (*Rev. arch. nac.*, Bogotá, tomo 5, no. 53-56, sept.-dic., p. 398-405). [2900

O'Higgins, Tomás. Diario de viaje de Lima a Chiloé, 1796-1797 (*Rev. chil. hist. geog.*, no. 103, julio-dic., p. 30-82). [2901
This day-by-day account of an official reconnaisance expedition places particular emphasis upon details of military and naval importance, including the situation and attitudes of the south Chilean Indians.

Padrón general del vecindario de la parroquia de San Josef de Cúcuta, que por orden del excelentísimo señor virrey de este reino formó el teniente corregidor de Pamplona en el mes de noviembre del año de 1792, y consta de tres mil ochocientos cincuenta y cinco almas (*Rev. arch. nac.*, Bogotá, timo 5, no. 48-49, abril-mayo, p. 242-279). [2902

El primer puente sobre el arroyo Caroata (*Bol. arch. nac.*, Caracas, tomo 30, no. 119, nov.-dic., p. 129-134) [2903
Documents of 1736 concerning the completion of a stone bridge on a main Venezuelan travel route.

Provanza de servicios de Rodrigo de Santander, contador de S. M. en las provincias de Antioquia (*Rev. arch. nac.*, Bogotá, tomo 5, no. 47, marzo, p. 161-204). [2904
Under this title are published fourteen documents of 1576 and 1577, most of them *declaraciones* that shed light on the career and services of this crown servant.

Reales cédulas (*Bol. arch. hist. prov. Mérida*, año 1, no. 2, abril, p. 23-28; no. 3, junio, p. 41-42; no. 4, agosto, p. 58-59; no. 6, dic., p. 91-94). [2905

Reales decretos y reales órdenes (*Bol. arch. hist. prov. Mérida*, año 1, no. 2, abril, p. 28-31). [2906

Reales provisiones (*Bol. arch. hist. prov. Mérida*, año 1, no. 2, abril, p. 31; no. 3, junio, p. 42-46; no. 4, agosto, p. 60-61; no. 6, dic., p. 94-97). [2907

Reconstrucción de las casas reales (*Bol. arch. nac.*, Caracas, tomo 30, no. 117, julio-agosto, p. 5-9). [2908
Royal *cédula* of December 11, 1697 and related documents concerning the renovation of government buildings in Caracas with funds derived from vacant *encomiendas*.

Relación hecha al virrey del Perú por don Francisco Álvarez sobre el carácter y la organización de los indios (*Rev. bibl. nac.*, Buenos Aires, tomo 9, no. 28, cuarto trim., p. 336-365). [2909
The sub-title reads: "Informe . . . relativo al trabajo de los indios en las explotaciones mineras de Potosí.—Carácter y costumbres de aquéllos; su situación antes de la Conquista y después de ella; los primeros ensayos de agricultura y ganadería; régimen de trabajo en las minas; jornales y descansos; reales cédulas y ordenanzas.—Organización de la industria minera; rendimiento de ésta." Dated in Lima, June 1, 1670.

Relación histórica que de su viaje a Cocorote - Barquisimeto - Araure - Guanare - Tucupío - Barinas y el Real hace el misionero jesuíta Miguel Alejo Schabel en el año de 1704 (*Bol. centro hist. larense*, año 2, no. 6, segundo trim., abril-junio, p. 33-35). [2910

La Rioja en la época colonial. Actas de cabildo de la Rioja (*Rev. junta hist. let. La Rioja*, año 2, no. 1, enero-marzo, p. 17-36; no. 2, abril-junio, p. 13-30; no. 3, julio-agosto, p. 19-32). [2911
The *actas* and related documents here published date for the most part from the first years of the seventeenth century.

Testamento otorgado por don Pedro de Mendoza (*Rev. bibl. nac.*, Buenos Aires, tomo 9, no. 28, cuarto trim., p. 375-381). [2912
Signed in San Lúcar de Barrameda on August 21, 1535, before sailing for the Río de la Plata.

Título de lugarteniente de gobernador para la conquista de los indios de guerra de la provincia de los Cumanagotos, expedido por el gobernador y capitán general don Juan Orpín, a favor del alférez Francisco de Brea Lezama (*Bol. arch. nac.*, Caracas, tomo 29, no. 114, enero-feb., p. 247-248). [2913
Dated Nueva Barcelona, September 22, 1644.

Título de "muy noble, valerosa y leal villa" dado a la parroquia de San Josef de Guasimal del Valle de Cúcuta (*Rev. arch. nac.*, Bogotá, tomo 5, no. 48-49, abril-mayo, p. 227-242). [2914
The *expediente* here reproduced covers the period 1792-1793.

Torre Revello, José. Documentos relativos a Antonio Valle y Manuel Moreno Argumosa, abuelo materno y padre, respectivamente, de Mariano Moreno (*Bol. inst. invest. hist.*, año 21, tomo 27, no. 93-96, julio, 1942-junio, 1943, p. 309-334). [2915

Vestigios de cultura en la provincia de Salta antes de su conquista (*Rev. bibl. nac.*, Buenos Aires, tomo 9, no. 27, tercer trim., p. 105-118). [2916
This document is published under the following sub-title: "Informe expedido por don Filiberto de Mena, a requerimiento de don Ramón García Pizarro, sobre los monumentos y vestigios de cultura y progreso industrial existentes antes de la conquista de la provincia de Salta." It is dated in Salta, November 22, 1791.

El virrey caballero de Croix al bailío fray Antonio Valdés, sobre inconveniencia de aplicación de las ordenanzas de intendentes, año 1790 (*Rev. bibl. nac.*, Buenos Aires, tomo 8, no. 25, primer trim., p. 105-141). [2917
The following summary precedes this lengthy document: "Expone los numerosos inconvenientes derivados del régimen de las Intendencias, especialmente por el menoscabo de la autoridad del Virrey, el ejercicio del Vice Patronato, la correcta percepción de las rentas y los abusos de todo género a que su autoridad sin límites daba lugar.—En substitución de aquéllas propone el establecimiento de corregidores que usarán el título de gobernadores, en las ciudades, capitales y provincias de cabecera; requisitos que deben reunir estos funcionarios y régimen a que deben sujetarse.—Reglamento de los sueldos de los gobernadores y corregidores según el nuevo plan propuesto."

Zevallos Quiñones, J. Para la historia de la imprenta en Lima (*Rev. arch. nac. Perú,* tomo 16, entrega 1, enero-junio, p. 5-16). [2918

The titles of the documents here presented are: "Concierto de impresión: Gerónimo de Contreras con el alférez Thomás Velásquez de Medrona, 1625" and "Arrendamiento recibo y entrega de imprenta: el convento de Santo Domingo a Pedro de Cabrera, 1645."

———. Pedro de Quirós. Traslado de la licencia que le dió el presidente para andar por estos reynos (*Rev. arch. nac. Perú,* tomo 16, entrega 2, julio-dic., p. 123-126). [2919

License of President Pedro de la Gasca, dated in Lima, January 27, 1550.

OTHER WORKS

RÍO DE LA PLATA

Acarette du Biscay. Relación de un viaje al Río de la Plata y de allí por tierra al Perú, con observaciones sobre los habitantes, sean indios o españoles, las ciudades, el comercio, la fertilidad y las riquezas de esta parte de América.... Buenos Aires. Alfer y Bays, ed. 132 p. [2920

"La obra de Acarette du Biscay, impresa en francés por primera vez en París en 1672 y traducida al inglés y editada en 1698 y 1716, había sido vertida al castellano por Daniel Maxell y divulgada en la benemérita *Revista de Buenos Aires,* en 1867." "Para esta edición se ha hecho nueva traducción, mas ajustada al texto original y se acompaña de 59 notas eruditas y documentales, que aclaran y enriquecen el texto de tan importante relato, debidas al profesor Julio César González...." Note in *Rev. hist. Amér.,* no. 16, dic., p. 344-345.

Andreozzi, Manuel. Refracción de los acontecimientos históricos (*Sustancia,* año 4, no. 15-16, junio-julio, p. 487-497). [2921

Interpretive notes on the personalities among the Spanish explorers and settlers of Tucumán, the Indians of the area, and the laws and spirit of the Spanish conquest. Philosophical, rather than severely factual.

Argañaras, Héctor D. La epopeya del Tucumán. Romance de la entrada de Diego de Rojas, 1543. Santiago del Estero. Tucumán. Ed. La Raza. 232 p. [2922

Azara, Félix de. Descripción e historia del Paraguay y del Río de la Plata. Tercera ed. Buenos Aires. Ed. Bajel. (Bibl. hist. colonial, 2). 383 p., ilus. [2923

A Spanish soldier engaged in official business in Paraguay and the Río de la Plata at the end of the eighteenth century, Azara laboriously committed to paper his acute eyewitness observations of the geography, flora and fauna, and human inhabitants of these regions. To these he added a summary but critical account of the Spanish conquest and colonization, to about the end of the sixteenth century based on the Spanish *cronistas.* The work was first put in orderly shape in 1790 at the request of the Cabildo de Asunción (the pertinent documents are published as an appendix to this edition), and after the author had further elaborated his work upon his return to Spain it was finally published by his nephew in Madrid in 1847. It was republished in Asunción in 1896. The present third edition, containing a useful introduction by Julio César González, once more makes this important work easily available to scholars.

———. Memoria sobre el estado rural del Río de la Plata y otros informes. Buenos Aires. Ed. Bajel. (Bibl. hist. colonial, 2). 306 p., ilus. [2924

"Esta esmerada reimpresión va precedida de una introducción que firma el director de la colección, profesor Julio César González, en donde traza documentalmente la biografía de Azara y en la cual ha utilizado nuevos documentos que al mismo personaje se refieren. Se acompaña además de la bibliografía e iconografía de don Félix de Azara...." Note in *Rev. hist. amér.,* no. 16, dic., 1943, p. 299.

Cárdenas, Bernardino de. Informe sobre la expulsión de los jesuítas (*Kollasuyo,* año 5, no. 45, enero-feb., p. 72-75). [2925

Apology, written in 1649 by the bishop-governor of Asunción, for his expulsion of the Jesuits from their college and from the city in general. Accuses the Jesuits of arrogance and refusal to recognize episcopal authority (see item 2930a).

Carrizo, Juan Alfonso. Somera noticia de la entrada de Diego de Rojas al Tucumán (*Sustancia,* año 4, no. 15-16, junio-julio, p. 441-457). [2926

Short synthesis of the main facts of Diego de Rojas' *entrada* in the Tucumán area in 1543, based upon new documentation published by Roberto Levillier and upon a reexamination of the colonial *cronistas.* The writer reconstructs the story in the light of first-hand knowledge of Tucumán geography.

Córdoba, Antonio S. C. Descubrimiento del Tucumán. La "entrada" de Diego de Rojas (*Rev. junta hist. let. La Rioja,* año 2, no. 3, julio-sept., p. 117-124). [2927

Against the background of the *entrada* of 1543, the author sketches the first introduction of Christianity into Tucumán. "En esta expedición al Tucumán, tan solo se vieron los primeros destellos del Cristianismo; pués las circunstancias adversas de aquella hora nefasta, no permitieron a los dos virtuosos sacerdotes capellanes desempeñar las tareas propias de su augusto ministerio ..." (p. 124).

Domínguez, Manuel Augusto. Buenos Aires colonial. Buenos Aires. Imp. A. y J. V. Calvo. 68 p. [2928

Public lecture given in the Ateneo Ibero-Americano de Buenos Aires in 1942.

Facil, Aníbal D. La guerra de fronteras en la pampa del coloniaje. Buenos Aires. Ed. J. P. Castagnola. (Junta de estudios históricos de San José de Flores, vol. 10). 31 p. [2929

Fasolino, Nicolás. El maestro D. Pedro Rodríguez (*Archivum*, tomo 1, cuad. 1, enero–junio, p. 16–58). [2930
Born in 1690, Maestro Rodríguez was ordained in 1713; and before his death in 1761 or 1762, he held a succession of important ecclesiastical positions such as those of canon and vicar general of Córdoba. The present short biography, founded largely upon church archives, is designed to rescue from oblivion the name of a deserving priest.

FRAY BERNARDINO DE CÁRDENAS (*Kollasuyo*, año 5, no. 45, enero–feb., p. 69–71). [2930a
The subject of this short editorial sketch was born in La Paz in 1579 and became bishop of Asunción sixty years later. Chosen governor there by popular acclamation, he led a movement to expel the Jesuits from the city. The essay is published as background for a better understanding of Cardenas' "Informe sobre la expulsión de los jesuítas" (see item 2925).

Furlong, Guillermo. El colegio del Salvador en la Plaza de mayo (*Estudios*, año 33, tomo 70, no. 382–383, oct.-nov., p. 255–273). [2931

Gargaro, Alfredo. Las "Aclaraciones históricas" del señor Morales Guiñazú (*Bol. inst. invest. hist.*, año 21, tomo 27, no. 93–96, julio, 1942–junio, 1943, p. 105–113). [2932
Caustic rebuttal of criticisms made in the previous issue of this publication (*Handbook, no. 8, 1942*, item 3091) by Fernando Morales Guiñazú of the author's article, "Los primeros descubridores de Cuyo" (*Handbook, no. 7, 1941*, item 3066). The points at issue include the date of Francisco de Villagrá's first expedition through Cuyo, when the Cuyo Indians were granted in *encomienda*, and whether Pedro de Castilla or Juan Jufré was the real founder of the town of Mendoza.

González, Julio César. Datos estadísticos acerca de la población de los pueblos de Misiones en los años 1802 y 1803 (*Bol. inst. invest. hist.*, año 21, tomo 27, no. 93–96, julio, 1942–junio, 1943, p. 334–344). [2934
These detailed census returns are accompanied by scholarly comment and interpretation based on a variety of sources.

Lafuente Machaín, R. de. Los conquistadores del Río de la Plata. Buenos Aires. Ed. Ayacucho. 705 p. [2935
Revised and enlarged edition of a dictionary of sixteenth-century *conquistadores* of the Río de la Plata, which first appeared in 1937. See item 2279, *Handbook, no. 3, 1937*.

Ledesma Medina, Luis A. El conocimiento del Tucumán y la expedición descubridora de Diego de Rojas (*Sustancia*, año 4, no. 15–16, junio–julio, p. 505–517). [2936
Discusses the antecedents of Diego de Rojas' *entrada* in the Tucumán country. The writer believes Francisco de César, lieutenant of Sebastián Cabot, reached the region in 1529; and that the elder Almagro skirted it on the way to Chile in 1535. Concludes with comments on Diego de Rojas' expedition and its background in Peru in the time of Vaca de Castro.

Levillier, R. La Argentina del siglo XVI. Descubrimiento y población del norte argentino por españoles del Perú, desde la entrada al Tucumán hasta la fundación de Santiago del Estero, 1543–1553. Buenos Aires. Tall. gráf. Porter. 190 p. [2937
"Síntesis de otros trabajos anteriores del autor, relacionados con la conquista del Tucumán. En el título de la obra, queda condensado el período que abarca el volumen, el cual se complementa con la reproducción de algunos documentos que atañen al tema y diversos croquis relativos a los acontecimientos históricos que se exponen." Note in *Rev. hist. amér.*, no. 16, dic., 1943, p. 273.

Lizondo Borda, Manuel. Descubrimiento del Tucumán. El pasaje de Almagro, la entrada de Rojas, el itinerario de Matienzo. Tucumán. Univ. nacional de Tucumán, Inst. de historia, lingüística y folklore, 11). 99 p., mapa. [2938

"MATERIA MÉDICA MISIONERA" DEL HERMANO PEDRO MONTENEGRO (*Rev. bibl. nac.*, Buenos Aires, tomo 8, no. 25, primer trim., p. 142–178; no. 26, segundo trim., p. 429–448; tomo 9, no. 27, tercer trim., p. 119–158; no. 28, cuarto trim., p. 396–441). [2939
Continued from the 1942 numbers of the *Revista*. See *Handbook, no. 8, 1942*, item 3090. To be continued.

Montero Bustamante, Raúl. Apuntes de historia eclesiástica del Uruguay (*Rev. nac.*, Montevideo, año 6, tomo 21, no. 63, marzo, p. 405–429). [2940
First chapter of a projected history of the church in Uruguay written thirty years ago. This chapter concerns only the colonial era. [C. H. Haring]

Moyano, Pedro. El obispo fray Cristóbal de la Mancha. Un aspecto discutido de actuación en Buenos Aires (*Archivum*, tomo 1, cuad. 1, enero–junio, p. 244–254). [2941
Poses rather than answers a number of questions concerning the anti-Jesuit attitude of this mid-seventeenth-century bishop.

Muñoz, José María. Rectificaciones necesarias (*Archivum*, tomo 1, cuad. 1, enero-junio, p. 240-244). [2942

Sharp criticism of Manuel V. Figuerero for alleged inaccuracies and anti-Jesuit bias in his work, *Lecciones de Historiografía de Corrientes*, Primera parte, (Buenos Aires, 1929), particularly in his treatment of the late colonial period.

Ocampo, Armando R. La capilla de San Sebastián de Sañogasta (*Rev. junta hist. let. La Rioja*, año 2, no. 2, abril-junio, p. 85-113). [2943

Notes on the founding of a chapel by Pedro Nicolás de Brizuela about 1628, and on its subsequent vicissitudes throughout the colonial period. Also presented here are transcriptions and facsimiles of pertinent documents.

Padilla, Francisco E. La expedición de Rojas y el destino del Tucumán descubierto (*Sustancia*, año 4, no. 15-16, junio-julio, p. 473-478). [2944

Parras, P. J. de. Diario y derrotero de sus viajes, 1749-1753, España-Río de la Plata-Córdoba-Paraguay. Buenos Aires. Ed. argen. Solar. 251 p. [2945

"Rica en episodios pintorescos de la vida colonial del siglo XVIII, esta obra publicada como tal por primera vez ofrece al lector hermosos trozos de historia americana. Contiene una nota preliminar de José Luis Busaniche con datos interesantes sobre esta crónica de viaje, y algunos datos biográficos del autor." Note in *Rev. hist. amér.*, no. 17, junio, 1944, p. 220.

Pedemonte, Juan Carlos. Hombres con dueño. Crónica de la esclavitud en el Uruguay. Montevideo. Ed. Independencia. (Col. obras históricas). 156 p., ilus. [2946

Written in light style and intended for a popular audience, this little book is nevertheless founded on documents and presents a valuable, if not overly detailed, account of Negro slavery in Uruguay. It discusses the introduction of the first slaves into the Banda Oriental some time before the middle of the eighteenth century and describes the slave trade and slave markets, social and economic aspects of Negro servitude, and slave participation in the wars of independence. The latter half of the book is concerned with the suppression of the slave trade, including Great Britain's part therein (though apparently without reference to the published British documents), and with the emancipation process, which only reached fruition because of the need for slave soldiers in the struggle between *blancos* and *colorados* in the fifth and sixth decades of the nineteenth century.

Pillado, José Antonio. Buenos Aires colonial. Estudios históricos. Nueva ed. rev. y corr. por Luis Antúnez Vilgre. Buenos Aires. Ed. Bonaerense. [2947

Convenient new edition of a work first published in Buenos Aires in 1910, devoted to lengthy and erudite essays on important physical features of colonial Buenos Aires and on selected aspects of the life of the city.

Porto, Aurelio. História das missões orientais do Uruguai. Vol. 1. Rio de Janeiro. Imp. nacional. (Serviço do patrimônio histórico e artístico nacional, Publ. 9). ix, 624 p. [2948

A detailed study of the socio-economic organization and development of Jesuit missions in Rio Grande do Sul and Uruguay based upon Brazilian documentary sources and secondary works. The second volume of the series is given over to a study of art in the missions. [Ed.]

Ramírez Juárez, Evaristo. Fundación de las Reducciones de Nuestra Señora de Dolores, San Bernardo el Vertiz y Ciudad de Nuestra Señora de la Concepción del Bermejo (*Bol. com. nac. mus. mon. hist.*, año 5, no. 5, p. 117-139). [2949

Riego, Manuel Luis del. El imperio jesuítico del Paraguay (*América*, Habana, vol. 17, no. 3, marzo, p. 27-30). [2950

Short, popular synthesis of well known facts.

Sorondo, Miguel. Procedencia del nombre de "El Retiro" (*Bol. inst. invest. hist.*, año 21, tomo 27, no. 93-96, julio, 1942-junio, 1943, p. 192-226). [2951

Denies the popular story that the *barrio* of El Retiro in Buenos Aires is so called from the name that the South Sea Company gave its local factory there when it held the Negro slave *asiento* in the early eighteenth century. Presents evidence to show that the property acquired by the *asiento* company already possessed this name in the seventeenth century.

Torre Revello, José. Crónicas del Buenos Aires colonial. Buenos Aires. Ed. Bajel. (Bibl. hist. colonial, 3). 333 p. [2953

"The present volume brings together a series of articles, many of which, subsequently modified, have appeared in the Sunday sections of the great newspapers of Buenos Aires, *La Prensa* and *La Nación*. ... These historical essays, begun in 1927, were prepared with the present book in mind and their present assembling between two covers is not merely an afterthought designed to enlarge a personal list of publications. Preceded by an introduction of some forty pages outlining the general social and cultural setting of colonial Buenos Aires, the chapters following are twenty articles arranged in a somewhat chronological pattern and describing such diverse aspects of life in the Rio de la Plata capital as: the public reception of royal administrative officers, the festival of the Patron Saint, the Corpus Christi processions, ceremonies attending the proclamation of new Spanish monarchs and state mourning at their decease, bull fights, lampoons and pasquinades, dances, the theater, cards and other games of chance, the lottery, gypsies and other elements of society, etc." Review in *Hisp. amer. hist. rev.*, vol. 24, no. 2, Feb., 1944, p. 310-312.

――――. Esteco y Concepción del Bermejo. Dos ciudades desaparecidas. Buenos Aires. Tall. Casa Jacobo Peuser. (Univ. nac. de Buenos Aires, Facultad de filosofía y letras, Insto. de investigaciones históricas, 85). xxxiii, 180 p. [2954
"Este estudio realizado con ayuda de un gran aparato documental y bibliográfico tiene gran interés para el conocimiento de la penetración española en las provincias del norte de la actual República Argentina. Se trata en él de dos ciudades fundadas en el siglo XVI—una en Tucumán, otra en Asunción—y que desaparecen en menos de un siglo a consecuencia de su posición fronteriza y de la escasez de trabajadores indios. . . ." Review in *Rev. hist. Amér.*, no. 17, junio, 1944, p. 153-154.

――――. Los primeros impresos estampados en Buenos Aires (*Bol. inst. invest. hist.*, año 21, tomo 27, no. 93-96, julio, 1942–junio, 1943, p. 173-191). [2955
Reproduces facsimiles and presents other evidence to show that a small press was turning out broadsides, etc., in Buenos Aires shortly before 1780, the year in which the first examples of printing hitherto known were produced by the press of the Casa de los Niños Expósitos.

Vera Vallejo, Juan Carlos. San Francisco Solano en la evangelización del Tucumán (*Rev. junta hist. let. La Rioja*, año 2, no. 3, julio–sept., p. 111-116). [2956
Notes on the works and miracles of this sixteenth-century saint, with special reference to Tucumán.

Zabala, Rómulo, and **Enrique de Gandía.** Buenos Aires en el nacimiento de Montevideo (*Rev. nac.*, Montevideo, año 6, tomo 21, no. 62, feb., p. 249-278). [2957

CHILE

Almeyda, Aniceto. El doctor don Santiago de Tordesillas (*Rev. chil. hist. geog.*, no. 102, enero–junio, p. 120-157). [2958
Tordesillas was born in Chile in the early eighteenth century and died there in 1766. The present article is concerned with his career as an outstanding creole scholar, jurist, and professor in the University of San Felipe. Appended are his will and a list of the books in his library at the time of his death.
Also published separately.

Graham, Robert Bontine Cunninghame. Pedro de Valdivia, conquistador de Chile. Su biografía y epistolario. Buenos Aires. Ed. Inter-americana. 253 p. [2959
Translation of this author's well-known popular biography, *Pedro de Valdivia, Conqueror of Chile* (London, 1926).

Mujica de la Fuente, Juan. Antigüedades curicanas. Curicó. Imp. "La Prensa." 310 p. [2960
Lamenting the failure to give due attention to regional history in Chile, the author seeks to remedy this alleged defect, at least so far as his own *patria chica* about the town of Curicó is concerned. After presenting a glowing "Panorama general de la provincia," the writer chronicles aspects of Curicó life from Conquest days to the mid-nineteenth century, with emphasis upon the colonial period. Preoccupation with provincial genealogies and a tendency to multiply antiquarian detail with little attempt at organization or interpretation make the book of limited interest to readers lacking an intimate and sentimental interest in Curicó.

UPPER PERU

(*See also item* 474)

La historia de Potosí por Arzanz y Vela (*Rev. bibl. arch. nac.*, no. 24-30, junio, p. 103-111). [2961
Following a brief editorial note deploring the lack of resources to publish in entirety a recently discovered manuscript of the work cited, two chapters corresponding to the years 1571 and 1572 are here presented.

Otero, Gustavo Adolfo. La educación y la universidad colonial (*Rev. jurídica*, año 5, no. 22, marzo, p. 19-25). [2963
Popular lecture concerning the colonial history of the University of San Francisco Xavier, said to have been founded in Chuquisaca about 1624. Emphasizes such aspects as the University's constitution, degrees, professorial chairs, and courses of instruction. Recognizes the revolution wrought in academic life in the latter part of the eighteenth century by the influence of the Enlightenment.

――――. Génesis y evolución del mestizaje. Las clases sociales en la colonia (*Rev. jurídica*, año 5, no. 22, marzo, p. 14-19). [2964
A short analysis, in the form of a public lecture, of the sociological factors involved in race crossing in Upper Peru. "Aunque aparezca el mestizaje como amparado legalmente, la unión de blancos e indios durante el coloniaje no fué un hecho reconocido socialmente, sino que fué una expresión de la vida en una época vitanda y clandestina, ajena a las leyes del honor, a las normas de la familia y al margen de la aprobación ética y divina" (p. 15).

――――. El trabajo y la tierra. La economía en la colonia (*Rev. jurídica*, año 5, no. 22, marzo, p. 25-32). [2965
This public lecture defines *encomienda* and *repartimiento* as used in Upper Peru. "La diferencia esencial entre 'repartimiento' y 'encomienda' de indios es que el repartimiento era un derecho que se tomaban los conquistadores sin más título que la fuerza y por tiempo limitado, mientras que

la encomienda, era el mismo derecho consagrado y regulado por un instrumento jurídico y formalista que entregaba el repartimiento de indios de por vida y con derecho de sucesión" (p. 26). States that land grants were separate from and complementary to *encomiendas;* and traces the process whereby great latifundia were built up. Analyzes the position and economic rôle of *mitayos, yanaconas, pongos,* and other types of Indian workers.

Paredes, M. Rigoberto. Las misiones de mojos y chiquitos (*Rev. bibl. arch. nac.,* no. 24-30, junio, p. 22-29). [2966
Outlines the history of these two groups of mission Indians, from the time of their conquest by Spaniards of Santa Cruz de la Sierra between 1557 and 1562 until the end of the colonial period. Ascribes to the Jesuits, who took over Mojos in 1671 and Chiquitos in 1691, the credit for making them into extraordinarily successful mission communities. Concludes with a brief survey, mission by mission, in the period of decay following the expulsion of the Jesuits.

Vignale, Pedro Juan. Historiadores y cronistas de la Villa Imperial (*Bol. inst. invest. hist.,* año 21, tomo 27, no. 93-96, julio, 1942-junio, 1943, p. 114-130). [2967
This scholarly article adds substantially to the bibliographical data which has resulted from recent interest among Bolivian and other South American students in the so-called *Anales de Potosí.* The writer concludes, mostly from internal evidence in the various copies he has examined, that the *Anales* really represent the following various titles and authorship: "Don Bartholomé Arzay Sánchez y Vela: *Historia de Potosí en los siglos XVI y XVII y Apuntes para los primeros treinta y seis años del siglo XVIII;* don Diego [Arzay] Abranes: *Notas para los años 1736-1760;* don Bartolomé Martínez y Vela: *Anales de Potosí, 1546-1702* e *Historia de Potosí . . . ;* Autor desconocido: *Los sucesos de 1810, 11 y 12 en Potosí,* y Pedro Rincón: *Anales de Potosí, 1830-1870. . . .*"
The author deplores the tendency of certain modern writers to judge the good work of the first of these chroniclers by the superficial product of his followers, pointing out among other things that Bartolomé Arzay Sánchez y Vela preserved the gist of many colonial histories since lost.

PERU

(*See also items* 713, 714)

Baudin, Louis. El imperio socialista de los Incas. Trad. de José Antonio Arze. Santiago. Ed. Zig-Zag. 461 p. [2968
This translation makes available in Spanish Baudin's scholarly *L'Empire Socialiste des Inka* (Université de Paris, *Travaux et Memoires de l'Institut d'Ethnologie,* vol. 5, Paris, 1938).

Carreño, Ángel. Origen de los nombres de las calles del Cuzco colonial (*Rev. univ.* Cuzco, año 32, no. 84, segundo semestre, p. 198-248). [2969
An appendix to an unpublished work, "Tradiciones del Cuzco," the present study explains in brief paragraphs the historic origins of the names of the streets in colonial Cuzco, which are grouped for treatment within the various sections of the city.

Cieza de León, Pedro de. Del señorío de los incas. Prólogo y notas de Alberto Mario Salas. Buenos Aires. Ed. argen. Solar. 340 p., mapas. [2970
This modern edition of a famous colonial chronicler's work is a "reimpresión de la que hiciera Jiménez de la Espada, en 1880." Note in *Rev. hist. amér.,* no. 17, junio, 1944, p. 207.

MacLean y Estenós, Roberto. Escuelas, colegios, seminarios y universidades en el Virreynato del Perú (*Letras,* Lima, no. 24, primer cuatrimestre, p. 14-63). [2973
Scholarly synthesis of a wide variety of documentary and secondary sources concerning colonial education from the mid-sixteenth century until the end of the colonial period. The author is particularly concerned with secondary and higher education and with the Church's rôle therein. One intersting section of the essay deals with race in higher education, notably with the position of mulattoes in the study of medicine. The author states his major conclusions in the following general terms: "El clasismo, la religiosidad, el dogmatismo, el memorismo rutinario, la disciplina garantizada por los castigos corporales, la heterogeneidad y la inconexión, he ahí los principales caracteres de la educación de la colonia" (p. 61). He fails to note any signs of the impact of the Enlightenment upon eighteenth and early nineteenth-century Peruvian education.

Pincherle, Alberto. Notas acerca de un manuscrito inédito del P. Leonardo de Peñafiel (*Bol. bibliog.,* Lima, año 16, vol. 13, no. 1-2, julio, p. 155-169). [2974
Descriptive notes on a manuscript commentary on the *Metaphysics* of Aristotle, which presumably dates from the 1630's. The manuscript was given to Peru by the government of Great Britain in 1942.

Quintana, M. J. Vida de Francisco Pizarro. Buenos Aires, México. Ed. Espasa-Calpe argen. (Col. Austral, 368). 170 p. [2975

Salas, A. M. Pedro Cieza de León. Buenos Aires. Imp. López. 50 p. [2977
"El presente trabajo destinado al estudio de la vida de Cieza de León y su obra, figura como prólogo en el libro de este cronista, titulado: Del Señorío de los Incas. . . . La nueva edición ha sido divulgada por la Editorial "Solar." Note in *Rev. hist. Amér.,* no. 17, junio, 1944, p. 207. See item 2970 above.

Sánchez Cantón, F. J. El convento de San Francisco en Lima (*Rev. Indias,* Madrid, año 4, no. 13, julio-sept., p. 527-551). [2978
El artículo es la reproducción de un impreso rarísimo en el que en estilo barroco,

como corresponde al edificio que se trata de ensalzar se historía la reconstrucción de este convento, con su iglesia y claustro, uno de los monumentos más representativos del arte colonial en la ciudad de los Reyes. Toda la historia gira en torno a la prócer figura de Fr. Luis Cervela cuyo retrato y jeroglífico alusivo aparecen en el artículo juntamente con otras fotografías del plano primitivo y de las realizaciones tales cuales ahora se conservan. [C. Sáenz de Santa María]

Sierra, Vicente D. Don fray Jerónimo de Loaysa (*Archivum*, tomo 1, cuad. 1, enero-junio, p. 93-127). [2980

Loaysa, first bishop of Lima, later became archbishop there, the first churchman of such rank in all South America. The present article sketches sympathetically the early life of this Dominican pioneer and tells in greater detail of his activities in Peru from the time of its pacification by Pedro de la Gasca to Loaysa's death in 1575. Scholarly references to the documentary and secondary sources used.

Whitaker, Arthur Preston. Huancavelica and historical synthesis (*Proc. eighth amer. scien. cong.*, vol. 9, p. 135-142). [2981

After recalling briefly aspects of the history of the Huancavelica mercury mine which he has presented in detail elsewhere (see item 3117, *Handbook no. 7, 1941*), the writer uses them to illustrate the need for related disciplines in historical synthesis. He suggests how such fields of knowledge as toxicology, metallurgy, economics, etc., are vital to an understanding of the decline of productivity of the famous mine from the 1560's to the present.

──────. Las minas de mercurio de Huancavelica (*Mercurio peruano*, año 18, vol. 25, no. 193, abril, p. 151-160). [2982

A translation of Chapter III of the author's *The Huancavelica Merceury Mine*. See *Handbook, no. 7, 1941*, item 3117.

PRESIDENCY OF QUITO

Huerta Rendón, F. El padre Velasco ante la crítica histórica moderna (*Prorsus*, año 2, no. 1, sept., 145-150). [2983

Iglesias, A. Estudio de la ubicación geográfica de la ciudad de Tomebamba (*Rev. centro estud. hist. geog. Cuenca*, entrega 38, marzo, p. 101-113). [2984

Seeks to clarify the meaning of two Quechua place-names, Paucarbamba and Tomebamba, both of which have been cited as the names of the Indian settlement where Cuenca was founded in 1557. Presents evidence to show that Paucarbamba was the name of the Indian *asiento* in question, while Tomebamba was the region in which the town was located. To be continued.

Márquez T., Ricardo. Ecuador amazónico (*Rev. centro estud. hist. geog. Cuenca*, entrega 38, marzo, p. 125-164). [2985

Account of the exploration and temporary settlement of the trans-Andean area of the Kingdom of Quito in the second half of the sixteenth century.

"Con esta breve relación histórica, queda plenamente comprobado que el oriente del Austro Ecuatoriano, fué descubierto y poblado, por los heróicos y patriotas hijos de Cuenca y de Loja, los primeros civilizadores del Oriente Amazónico; y que jamás el Virreinato del Perú proporcionó soldados, armas y más medios necesarios para el engrandecimiento de la Corte de Castilla" [p. 128].

Navarro, José Gabriel. Fundación de conventos en la América española. El convento franciscano de Quito (*Bol. acad. nac. hist.*, Quito, vol. 23, no. 61, enero-junio, p. 5-44). [2986

After a survey of the history of the origins of the regular orders in the Spanish Indies, the author describes in greater detail the establishment of the Franciscans in Quito. Points out that a Franciscan, Fray Marcos de Niza, accompanied Benalcázar to Quito in the first Spanish penetration of that country, and that others of the order participated in the founding of Spanish society there.

Paz y Miño, Luis Telmo. Mapas coloniales del Ecuador (*Bol. acad. nac. hist.*, Quito, vol. 23, no. 62, julio-dic., p. 165-187). [2987

Descriptive notes and comments on the value of "los mapas coloniales dedicados exclusivamente a la representación del territorio ecuatoriano." These are individually listed and treated. At the end of the study is a list, without comments, of colonial physical and political maps of South America in which the territory of Ecuador figures only incidentally.

NEW GRANADA

Acevedo Latorre, Eduardo. Breve noticia sobre los lugares donde existieron San Sebastián de Urabá y Santa María la Antigua del Darién (*Bol. hist. antig.*, vol. 30, no. 349, nov., p. 1096-1105). [2988

Presents the results of researches made in the field while the author was engaged in an official survey of the economic geography of the Intendency of El Chocó. After correlating contemporary accounts with the topography of the country, the writer concludes that San Sebastián was founded near the river Cañaflechal, just south of Punta Arenas, on the east coast of the Gulf of Urabá; while Santa María was established on a branch of the river Tanela near the mouth of the Atrato on the west side of the Gulf. The article is accompanied by a useful map.

Aitken, W. Ernest. La familia Jaramillo de Andrade en el Tolima (*Bol. hist. antig.*,

vol. 30, no. 344-345, junio-julio, p. 603-606). [2989
Genealogical rectifications concerning an important provincial family during the period from the late seventeenth to the first years of the nineteenth century.

Cuervo, Luis Augusto. El inquieto vivir de los días coloniales (*Bol. hist. antig.*, vol. 30, no. 344-345, junio-julio, p. 561-573). [2991
In this public lecture, the writer attacks the sentimental idea, allegedly common in Colombia, that life in colonial New Granada was peaceful and idyllic. Recounts numerous episodes to show that modern traits making for stormy existence, such as greed, ambition, and passion, were also characteristic of the colony.

———. El primer año de la imprenta en Santafé (*Bol. hist. antig.*, vol. 30, no. 347-348, sept.-oct., p. 874-877). [2992
Presents evidence to show that 1711, rather than 1738, the date hitherto accepted, may have witnessed the first printing in Bogotá.

Flórez de Ocáriz, Juan. Autoridad y distrito de la real audiencia y sus poblaciones (*Rev. arch. nac.*, Bogotá, tomo 5, no. 50-52, junio-agosto, p. 294-342). [2994
A chapter from this colonial writer's *Genealogías del Nuevo Reino de Granada*.

Hernández de Alba, Guillermo. La primera cátedra de medicina en el Nuevo Reino de Granada (*Bol. hist. antig.*, vol. 30, no. 347-348, sept.-oct., p. 843-847). [2995
Discusses the beginnings of professional medicine and medical education in Bogotá. States that the "indiscutible primer catedrático de medicina" was the licenciado Rodrigo Enríquez de Andrade, who gave the first lectures on the subject in the Colegio Seminario de San Bartolomé in Bogotá in 1636. Quotes extensively from contemporary documents.

Miramón, Alberto. La brujería en la colonia (*Bol. hist. antig.*, vol. 30, no. 347-348, sept.-oct., p. 805-824). [2997
After commenting briefly on medieval witchcraft in Spain, the writer presents a selection of colorful stories concerning the alleged doings of witches in New Granada, as recounted by Rodríguez Fresle and other colonial writers.

Ortíz, Sergio Elías. Miguel Cabello de Balboa (*Bol. hist. antig.*, vol. 30, no. 342-343, abril-mayo, p. 517-520). [2998
Short notes concerning the sixteenth-century *cronista* of this name, especially in connection with his services as *cura* of the Indian town of Funes following 1572.

Otero D'Costa, Enrique. Museo epigráfico de la Academia (*Bol. hist. antig.*, vol. 30, no. 349, nov., p. 1084-1095). [2999
Description of some of the more interesting epigraphic exhibits preserved in the collection of the Colombian Academy of History. Comments on the historical value of these inscriptions. Illustrated.

Restrepo Canal, Carlos. Erección del virreinato de Santa Fe (*Bol. hist. antig.*, vol. 30, no. 347-348, sept.-oct., p. 982-1024). [3000
This lengthy and substantial article re-examines the history of the preliminary establishment of the Viceroyalty of New Granada in 1717 and its definitive creation in 1739. The writer has used such new material as that appearing in the documentary appendixes of Jerónimo Becker and José María Rivas Groot, *El Nuevo Reino de Granada en el Siglo XVIII* (Vol. I, Madrid, 1921). But because of the lack of the necessary archival materials, he has not been able to add substantially to older accounts.

Restrepo Tirado, Ernesto. Apuntes sobre la quina (*Bol. hist. antig.*, vol. 30, no. 347-348, sept.-oct., p. 912-925). [3002
Discusses the scientific investigation of quinine in eighteenth-century New Granada and the measures taken by the Spanish government to foster its cultivation and protect its monopoly.

———. Espolio del obispo de Cartagena Fray Luis de Córdova Ronquillo (*Bol. hist. antig.*, vol. 30, no. 342-343, abril-mayo, p. 410-415). [3003
Concerns the settlement of the estate left by a bishop of Cartagena who died in Spain in 1640. Based on documents from the Archives of the Indies.

———. Nueva Salamanca de la Ramada (*Bol. hist. antig.*, vol. 30, no. 347-348, sept.-oct., p. 859-862). [3004
Extracts from an *información* concerning a small coastal village between Santa Marta and Río de la Hacha, perpared on April 28, 1578, in accordance with royal commands to forward to Spain descriptions of the communities of the Indies.

Reyes Archila, Carlos. Figuras de la conquista. Doña Inés de Atienza (*Rep. boyacense*, año 19, no. 128-130, enero, p. 885-895). [3005

Rosa, Moisés de la. La fundación de El Banco (*Bol. hist. antig.*, vol. 30, no. 349, nov., p. 1077-1083). [3006
This *"informe oficial"* submitted to the Colombian Academy of History by one of its members, concludes that the physical founding of the Magdalena River town of El Banco took place in 1680 or 1681, and that its legal establishment occurred between April 30, 1744 and March 26, 1746.

VENEZUELA

Antolínez, Gilberto. Aporte etnográfico de la relación geográfica de Nueva Segovia, 1579 (*Acta amer.*, vol. 1, no. 4, Oct.-Dec., p. 442-447). [3007

Carrocera, Cayetano de. Los templos de el Tocuyo (*Bol. centro hist. larense,* año 2, no. 8, cuatro trim., oct.–dic., p. 3–21). [3008

Describes individually the founding and colonial history of the seven churches that have given El Tocuyo the title of "La Ciudad de los Siete Templos." There are footnote indications of the major sources consulted.

Febres Cordero G., Julio. El primer mestizo venezolano (*Bol. centro hist. larense,* año 2, no. 8, cuarto trim., oct.–dic., p. 21–31). [3009

This short sketch of Francisco Fajardo, *mestizo* conquistador of the mid-sixteenth century, is based upon the works of the colonial *cronistas,* available documents, and pertinent modern histories.

——. La real hacienda en Venezuela (*Rev. nac. cultura,* año 5, no. 38, mayo–junio, p. 36–47). [3010

Short account of the development of royal fiscal administration from the time of its beginnings in Venezuela under Juan Martínez de Ampués at Coro throughout the period of the conquest. Based upon a substantial selection of archival and published materials.

Perera, Ambrosio. El Tocuyo conquistado y conquistador (*Rev. nac. cultura,* año 5, no. 40, sept.–oct., p. 58–84; año 6, no. 41, nov.–dic., p. 45–65). [3011

In five chapters, this study gives an account of the expeditions that penetrated the valley of El Tocuyo from the Welser base of Coro, describes the founding of the city of El Tocuyo by Juan de Carbajal in 1545, and discusses the subsequent rôle of the city as a base of operations for the establishment of other Spanish settlements in Venezuela. Ably discusses the often contradictory evidence concerning these matters in the works of the *cronistas* and in available documents, though without footnote references.

ADDENDA

Briceño Iragorry, Mario (ed.). Orígenes de la hacienda en Venezuela. Documentos inéditos de la época colonial. Publicación ordenada por el señor general Isaías Medina Angarita, presidente de la república, en la conmemoración centenaria del traslado de los restos del Libertador a Caracas. Caracas, Imp. nacional. 1942, xx, 219 p. [3012

Text of the first *Libro de Acuerdo de los Oficiales de la Real Hacienda de la Provincia de Venezuela, Coro, 1535.* Reprinted from no. 173 of the *Boletín del Archivo Nacional.* [J. B. Childs]

HISTORY: SPANISH AMERICA
THE REVOLUTIONARY PERIOD

BY

CHARLES C. GRIFFIN

Vassar College

GENERAL STATEMENT

During 1943 historical scholarship relating to the field covered by this section followed lines similar to those recorded in previous issues of the *Handbook*. During the war years extensive works breaking new ground have not been numerous, but in those countries where research in this field has been most active the production of articles and the publication of documents has continued apace.

A few new developments are worth noting here, however. There has been an increase in the study of economic history, especially the history of commerce. In Cuba, Mexico, Chile and the United States material has appeared which throws light on trade and commercial policy in the era of Spanish American independence. See items 3029, 3032, 3037, 3090, and 3095. Local history and the use of local history in the study of regionalism have also flourished. In the following pages, including the Addenda, items will be found dealing with provincial and regional attitudes in Argentina and Colombia and local studies of considerable interest have appeared in Venezuela (on Maracaibo, Cumaná) and in Mexico (Chihuahua) and Argentina (Entre Ríos).

The unfortunate controversy aroused by the publication in 1940 of the work appearing under the name of Colombres Marmol on the Interview of Guayaquil has been definitely ended. The view of the Academia Nacional de la Historia, Caracas, that the documents on which the study was based were forgeries has now been accepted by most historical circles in Argentina, Chile, Colombia, Cuba and Mexico and the United States. The continuing publication of books which reflect historical controversies of long standing is to be noted, however. Books and articles listed below keep alive the problem of interpretation of the career of General Santander; still others discuss the thorny problem of responsibility for the assassination of Sucre. Both Flores and Obando are still being pointed to as morally guilty of inspiring the "Crimen de Berruecos." Current political tendencies are reflected by a work on San Martín and the Logia Lautaro published in Argentina which impugns the liberal-masonic connections imputed to San Martín during the period prior to the liberation of Peru by many earlier writers.

The publication of documentary material of considerable volume and importance has gone forward, largely conducted by official agencies in Venezuela, Colombia, Mexico, Uruguay and Argentina. It is now possible to make tentative studies of a wide variety of subjects on the basis of printed sources. Insofar as this encourages the study by foreigners of topics previously dealt with almost exclusively in a nationalistic atmosphere it is a welcome trend. At the same time, progress in archival and library organization and operation will greatly facilitate the primary research in manuscript material which is still necessary if important results are to be obtained.

The writer would like to make a comment that is also an apology in connection with the present survey. As mentioned in the last issue of the *Handbook*, the coverage for 1942 was inadequate. Something has been done to make up in this year's list of Addenda for the previous omissions. It has been found, however, that many items which might well have been included in this section have been listed in other sections of the 1942 volume. Such items are not relisted here, but the reader is urged to keep in mind that, owing to inevitable overlapping between colonial, revolutionary and national history, it is necessary to use the other historical sections in connection with this one if anything like adequate coverage is expected. In addition the sections on Archives and on International Relations will be found to contain much material significant for the history of the independence movement in Spanish America.

BIBLIOGRAPHY

(*See also sections on* Archives; History: Colonial Period; History: National Period; International Relations; *and* Spanish American Literature)

GENERAL

Delgado, Luis Humberto. Bolívar, Perú y Bolivia. Lima. Ed. Latino América. 271 p. [3013

A book which is primarily polemical and uses historical themes in order to influence present day international relations in South America.

Grases, Pedro. La trascendencia de la actividad de los escritores españoles e hispanoamericanos en Londres (*Bol. inst. cult. ven.-brit.*, vol. 2, no. 18, agosto, p. 101–175). [3014

Discussion of the hispanic writers who visited London during the independence movement in Spanish America with a view to determining the effect of English ideas on them. Among those treated are Miranda, Zea, Bolívar, José Fernández Madrid, San Martín, Rivadavia, O'Higgins as well as certain Spanish authors.

Also published separately, Caracas, 1943.

Lizondo, Estraton J. Monteagudo, el pasionario de la libertad. Su vida y sus obras. Tucumán. Ed. La Raza. 225 p. [3015

A highly laudatory biography. The author defends Monteagudo against each and every imputation made against him by his many detractors and attempts to justify his early radicalism, his moderate political views when associated with San Martín and his final collaboration with Bolívar.

Menéndez, Oriel. Bernardo Monteagudo. Actividades e ideas de un gran revolucionario. Prólogo por Juan Trilla Ibáñez. Buenos Aires. Ed. Ebro. 151 p., ilus. [3016

Millán, Enrique. Génesis de la emancipación hispanoamericana (*Rev. Indias*, segunda época, tomo 18, no. 56, agosto, p. 233–253). [3017

A thoughtful and interesting essay on the origins and character of the Independence movement in Spanish America. Not strikingly original in detail, the article is well worth reading for its breadth of view.

Mosquera, Joaquín. La política del general San Martín, protector del Perú, respecto a la ciudad y provincia de Guayaquil (*Bol. acad. nac. hist.*, Caracas, tomo 26, no. 103, julio-set., p. 165–170). [3018

Reprint of an essay written shortly after the event by a Colombian diplomat defending the Bolivarian position in the controversy over the status of Ecuador.

Pritchett, John Perry. Selkirk's views on British policy toward the Spanish American colonies, 1806 (*Can. hist. rev.*, vol. 24, Dec., p. 381–396). [3019

A meticulously edited document indicating the desire of this prominent British imperial administrator to cooperate with the United States for the liberation of Spanish America with a view to securing British economic advantages there.

MEXICO AND CENTRAL AMERICA

Almada, Francisco R. Sucesos y recuerdos de la independencia en Chihuahua (*Bol. soc. chihuahuense*, tomo 4, no. 8, enero 20, p. 295–301, 334; no. 9, feb. 20, p. 335–340). [3020

Chronicle of military and political developments in Chihuahua from 1810 to 1821. Chiefly concerned with the trial and punishment of Hidalgo and those captured with him. Other topics include production of munitions, the workings of the Constitution of 1812, plots and minor uprisings. The royalists controlled the area throughout the period.

Barnoya Gálvez, Francisco. Fray Ignacio Barnoya, un prócer ignorado (*An. soc. geog. hist. Guatemala,* año 19, tomo 19, no. 2, dic., p. 84–102). [3021

Bellegarde, Dantès. Alexandre Pétion, a pioneer of Pan Americanism (*Bull. pan amer. union,* vol. 77, no. 5, May, p. 245–252). [3022
An urbane sketch of the career of the great Haitian leader and collaborator of Bolívar. A popular essay on a man who should be better known.

Bravo Ugarte, J. El clero y la independencia. Adiciones al ensayo estadístico de los clérigos y religiosos que militaron durante la guerra de independencia en las filas insurgentes, en las trigarantes, y en las realistas (*Ábside,* tomo 7, no. 3, julio–sept., p. 406–409). [3023

COPIA DEL JUICIO SUMARIO DE D. MIGUEL HIDALGO Y COSTILLA (*Bol. soc. chihuahuense,* tomo 4, no. 1, junio 20, p. 25–29, 39–40; no. 2, julio 20, p. 57–59, 81–82; no. 3, agosto 20, p. 93–98; no. 4, sept. 20, p. 135–141; no. 5, oct., p. 182–185, 202–203; no. 6, nov., p. 225–227, 247; no. 7, dic., 1942, p. 268–269, 279, 290–291; no. 8, enero 20, p. 302–303, 334). [3024
This concludes publication of the document which began with no. 1, 1942.

DIARIO DEL VIAJE QUE HIZO EL VIRREY ITURRIGARAY A VERACRUZ, 1805 (*Bol. arch. gen.,* México, tomo 14, no. 1, enero-marzo, p. 153–169). [3025
Gives some details about travel conditions and the character of the country.

DOCUMENTOS DE LA GUERRA DE INDEPENDENCIA (*Bol. arch. gen.,* México, tomo 14, no. 3, julio–sept., p. 379–408). [3026
Papers relating to the execution of Hidalgo and other patriot leaders and the subsequent public exhibition of some of their remains.

ÍNDICE DE LA SECCIÓN COLONIAL DE LOS ARCHIVOS NACIONALES DE COSTA RICA (*Rev. arch. nac.,* Costa Rica, año 7, no. 1–2, enero–feb., p. 589–604; no. 3–4, marzo–abril, p. 605–620; no. 5–6, mayo–junio, p. 621–636; no. 9–10; sept.–oct., p. 653–668; no. 11–12, nov.–dic., p. 669–680). [3027
The documents listed in this installment of the *Indice* are dated from June 4, 1812, to December 11, 1819.

INDICE DE LOS DOCUMENTOS EXISTENTES EN EL ARCHIVO GENERAL DEL GOBIERNO (*Bol. arch. gen.,* Guatemala, tomo 8, nos. 1–4, marzo, junio, sept., dic., a few pages separately numbered at the back of each issue). [3028
Mostly dated 1804–1821. The last issue lists items concerned with the Real Sociedad Económica, 1796–1798. [R. D. Hussey]

Le Riverend Brusone, Julio. La economía cubana durante las guerras de la revolución y del imperio franceses, 1790–1808 (*Rev. hist. Amér.,* no. 16, dic., p. 25–64). [3029
An important study of the commercial and industrial history of Cuba at the end of the colonial period when the trade of the island was subject to the changes and uncertainties of war conditions. The position of sugar producers and merchants is analysed and the economic ideas, especially toward trade regulation, of various groups and individuals is studied. A significant contribution.

Mariscal, Mario. Un motín estudiantil motivado por la declaración de la independencia de México (*Fil. letras,* tomo 5, no. 10, abril–junio, p. 239–244). [3030

Medina Ascensio, Luis. La Santa Sede y la emancipación mexicana (*Estud. hist.,* año 1, no. 2, julio, p. 5–42). [3031
A summary of efforts made by the insurgents of Mexico to make contact with the Vatican through Bishop Carroll of Baltimore. The first part of a longer study. This section covers 1810–15. None of the projects led to anything concrete. Based on printed sources and the principal authorities on the period in Mexico.

Mexico. Secretaría de hacienda y crédito público. Dirección de estudios financieros y Archivo histórico de hacienda. La libertad del comercio en la Nueva España en la segunda década del siglo XIX. Introducción por Luis Chávez Orozco. México. 201 p. [3032
Documents opposing the proposed liberalization of commerce. See review in *Rev. hist. Amér.,* no. 16, dic., p. 182–183.

Olea, Héctor R. La primera imprenta en las provincias de Sonora y Sinaloa. México. Imp. A. Villegas. 68 p. [3033
Established late in 1825 or early in 1826, but the first book appeared in 1826 [R. D. Hussey]

Price-Mars. La coopération haïtienne dans la lutte des peuples américains, pour la conquête de leur indépendance (*Rev. soc. hist. géog. Haïti,* vol. 14, no. 51, oct., p. 1–11). [3035

Salit, Charles R. Anglo-American rivalry in Mexico, 1823–1830 (*Rev. hist. Amér.,* no. 16, dic., p. 65–84). [3036
Rehearses the well known story of the Ward-Poinsett era but makes a new contribution in support of the view that British predominance in Mexico at the time was less due to Poinsett's activities than to the

Smith, Robert Sidney. Shipping in the port of Veracruz 1790–1821 (*Hisp. amer. hist. rev.*, vol. 23, no. 1, Feb., p. 5–20). [3037

An important contribution to the commercial history of the era of Spanish American independence. The statistics given tend to show the small extent of legally recognized foreign trade in Vera Cruz and in general the commercial insignificance of the port. The fluctuation in trade during this period of continual war, revolution and crisis is very interesting.

Teja Zabre, Alfonso. Morelos and his political achievements (*Mexicana rev.*, vol. 3, no. 2, summer, p. 9–15). [3038

Título de villa al pueblo de san cristóbal de alvarado, 1816 (*Bol. arch. gen.*, México, tomo 14, no. 1, enero–marzo, p. 171–174). [3039

A document issued as a reward for resistance by the village to patriot forces during the independence struggle.

NORTHERN SOUTH AMERICA

(*See also item* 11)

Academia colombiana de historia. Las ciudades confederadas del valle del Cauca en 1811. Introd. de Laureano García Ortíz. Bogotá. Ed. Voluntad. (Bibl. de hist. nac., vol. 66). xiv, 235 p., ilus. [3040

Refers to the alliance between the cities of Cali, Buga, Cartago, Caloto, Toro and Santa Ana against the royalists in Popayán. The volume contains the records of the *Junta* of the allied patriot cities. A useful contribution to the clearer understanding of regional forces in New Granada during 1810–1812.

Arias, Juan de Dios. El colegio de San José de Guanenta de San Gil. Primera época, 1787–1824 (*Bol. hist. antig.*, vol. 30, no. 342–343, abril–mayo, p. 386–409). [3041

Details concerning this school or academy during the wars for independence. Quotations from contemporary documents throwing light on the educational policy of the Colombian government.

Arocha, Manuel. Iconografía ecuatoriana del Libertador. Quito. Lit. Romero. 126 p., estampas, retratos, fotos. [3042

An interesting contribution to the iconography of Bolívar and to the study of the art of the period in Quito.

Barriga Alarcón, Julio. Juicio contra el general Santander por la conspiración de septiembre (*Bol. hist. antig.*, vol. 30, no. 344–345, junio–julio, p. 623–685). [3043

A study of the legal aspects of the trial of Santander for conspiracy against the dictatorship of Bolívar in 1828. Discusses the laws in force at the time and use of evidence by the court. The author concludes that the sentence was politically inspired and could not be justified on legal grounds.

Blanco Fombona, Rufino. El espíritu de Bolívar. Ensayo de interpretación psicológica. Caracas. Imp. unidos. [3044

A collection of essays by the well known Venezuelan author and critic. Topics dealt with are: Bolívar's health, his Spanish inheritance, his military qualifications, his imagination, sensibility, and intellectual calibre, his work as writer and political speaker, as well as other miscellaneous related topics.

The author believes that the character of Bolívar corresponds to the "hyperemotive temperament" which is marked by "reactions which are rapid, excessive, and lasting."

See comment by José Nucete Sardi in *Rev. nac. cultura*, no. 40, p. 143–149.

Briceño-Iragorry, Mario. Sentido y ámbito del Congreso de Angostura. Caracas. Ed. Vargas. 24 p. [3045

Camacho Montoya, Guillermo. Santander, el hombre y el mito. Prólogo de Laureano Gómez. Caracas. Ed. Cecilio Acosta. (Bibl. de escritores y asuntos venezolanos, vol. 29). 238 p. [3046

As might be expected by the choice of the conservative Colombian leader as sponsor, this book is a counterblast to the many recently published adulatory biographies of Santander. By selecting divergent aspects of the subject's character and career it is possible to write contradictory but equally documented biographies of this general whose life has become part of Colombian politics for a century.

Conferencias pronunciadas por sus autores en el seno de la academia en el año 1943. Bogotá. Ed. Voluntad. 351 p. [3048

Among the topics relating to the independence period are the following: Análisis Crítico de un Ruidoso Proceso (trial of R. Hand); Causas Económicas de la Independencia de América, by José Forero; Influencia de la Revolución Americana y de la Revolución Francesa en la Independencia de la América Latina, by N. García Samudio.

Copiadores del libertador (*Bol. acad. nac. hist.*, Caracas, tomo 26, no. 101, enero–marzo, p. 80–88). [3049

The continuation of the publication of the letterbooks which has been proceeding at intervals in this journal. This installment contains facsimiles of the Pérez letters bearing on the interview of Guayaquil. All the letters date from 1822.

Estrada Monsalve, Jesús. Simón Bolívar en Santo Tomás de Aquino (*Rev. colegio Rosario*, tomo 38, nos. 373–374, agosto–sept., p. 254–296). [3050

Figueroa, Marco. Don Juan Antonio Paredes, ilustre prócer de la independencia, general de la Gran Colombia. Caracas. Imp. Unidos. [3051]
Paredes was a member of a well known family from Mérida.

Foncillas Andreu, Gabriel (ed.). Un importante documento inédito de Mons. Videla del Pino (*Archivum*, tomo 1, cuad. 1, enero–junio, p. 195–225). [3052]

García Hernández, M. Bolívar, realidad continental. Prólogo de Juan Pinto. Buenos Aires. Soc. impresora americana. [3054]
An Argentine view of the Liberator.

Gironza, Telmo. Claridad sobre Barruecos. Compilación de artículos relacionados con el asesinato del gran mariscal do Ayacucho. Cali. Imp. deptal. 65 p. [3055]
Polemics concerning the statement by the author that Juan José Flores was responsible for the assassination of José Antonio Sucre. [Ed.]

Graterón, Daniel. Vida del general Juan Bautista Rodríguez (*Bol. centro hist. larense*, año 2, no. 5, primer trim., enero–marzo, p. 17–32). [3056]

LA GUERRA DE INDEPENDENCIA EN LA PROVINCIA DE VERACRUZ, SEGÚN EL MANUSCRITO INÉDITO DE UN TESTIGO OCULAR CON ANOTACIONES Y COMENTARIOS. México, D. F. Ed. Cossio. (Publ. históricas). 158 p. [3057]

Hernández de Alba, G. (ed.). Archivo epistolar del General Diego Caycedo, Tomo I, 1804–1830. Bogotá. Ed. ABC. (Bibl. de historia nacional, tomo 67). xxiii, 308 p. [3058]
Collection of papers of a prominent New Granadan soldier and politician.

Jiménez M., Gabriel. Los mártires de Cartagena de 1816 ante el consejo de guerra y ante la historia (*Bol. hist.*, Cartagena, año 8, no. 80–81, enero–feb., p. 3–35). [3059]

Jos, Emiliano. Juan Vicente Bolívar (*Bol. acad. nac. hist.*, Caracas, tomo 26, no. 102, abril–junio, p. 130–151). [3060]
Reprint of an article published earlier in Spain by a member of the staff of the Instituto González de Oviedo. It exploits Spanish archival sources to indicate the desire of the brother of the Liberator to effect a reconciliation between Caracas and the Spanish liberal government in 1811. The move came to nothing owing to the death of Juan Vicente.

JOSÉ DE BOQUI Y LA EMANCIPACIÓN DEL PERÚ (*Rev. arch. nac. Perú*, tomo 16, entrega 1, enero–junio, p. 17–25). [3061]

Lecuna, Vicente (ed.). Cartas del libertador (*Bol. acad. nac. hist.*, Caracas, tomo 26, no. 102, abril–junio, p. 108–129). [3062]
The continuation of the periodical publication of letters of Bolívar that have come to light since the 1930 edition was printed.

———. La conferencia de Guayaquil (*Bol. acad. nac. hist.*, Caracas, tomo 26, no. 101, enero–marzo, p. 30–80). [3063]
The leading student of Bolivariana presents a detailed study of the conference. Dr. Lecuna rejects the interpretation given by Lafond and followed later by Mitre.

———. Descomposición del Perú (*Bol. acad. nac. hist.*, Caracas, tomo 26, no. 104, oct.–dic., p. 271–347). [3064]
Another in the series of articles that have appeared over a period of years in this journal in which the author provides a careful and detailed story of the career of the Liberator. Unrivalled for intimate knowledge of the unpublished documentary material in Caracas.

———. Gobierno del sur. El Perú llama al Libertador, 1822–1823 (*Bol. acad. nac. hist.*, Caracas, tomo 26, no. 103, julio–set., p. 176–228). [3065]
See comment on item no. 3064 above.

Luciani, Jorge. El máximo turbulento de la Gran Colombia y otros estudios. Caracas. Ed. Artes gráficas. [3066]
Concerns Rafael Diego Mérida.

Mallo, Nicanor. El maestro de Bolívar (*Bol. hist. antig.*, vol. 30, no. 347–348, sept.–oct., p. 949–964). [3067]
A brief but useful summary of the life of Simón Rodríguez, the tutor of Bolívar in his early years.

Matos Hurtado, Belisario. Apuntaciones y documentos para la historia de Pamplona (*Bol. hist. antig.*, tomo 30, no. 344–345, junio–julio, p. 574–591). [3068]
Contains data on the educational history of the era and particularly on the part played therein by General Santander.

Medina Chirinos, Carlos. Por los surcos de antaño. Maracaibo. [3069]
Interesting product of research in the local history of Maracaibo and its environs. The author gives attention to the social significance of uprisings before and during the wars for independence.

Naranjo Martínez, Enrique. Alejandro Macaulay. Un héroe norteamericano en la liberación de Colombia (*Bol. hist. antig.*, vol. 30, no. 342–343, abril–mayo, p. 495–508). [3070]
A Colombian diplomat recalls for a North American audience the romantic and warlike adventures of one of these compatriots in the early days of the war for independence in New Granada. A popular account bringing together material from a number of scattered sources.

Nuevos documentos sobre la revolución de agosto (*Bol. acad. nac. hist.*, Quito, vol. 23, no. 62, julio-dic., p. 253-259). [3071]

Nuevos y desconocidos documentos para la historia de la conspiración del 25 de septiembre de 1828 (*Rev. arch. nac.*, Bogotá, tomo 5, no. 47, marzo, p. 205-224). [3072]

Letters from Santander dating from June-December, 1828. The most important is a long one to Bolívar in which he defends himself at length against the charges made at his trial.

Otero D'Costa, Enrique. Noticias bibliográficas relativas a obras raras escritas por autores ingleses sobre historia y viajes por Colombia (*Bol. hist. antig.*, vol. 30, no. 347-348, sept.-oct., p. 848-858). [3073]

An interesting article giving descriptive and critical comment on works chiefly relating to the period of independence and dating from 1820 to 1827. Written for the most part by British volunteers in the army of Colombia.

Otero Muñoz, Gustavo. Archivo Santander. Erratas sustanciales en los veinticuatro tomos (*Bol. hist. antig.*, vol. 30, no. 339-340, enero-feb., p. 1-222). [3074]

An extremely valuable set of corrections to the published papers of Santander which are known to have been poorly edited. The list of *errata* given here fills an entire issue of the *Boletín* and bears witness to the carelessness of the early editing. Most errors are misreadings of the MS handwriting and are usually brief. In some instances, however, they seriously modify the text. Those who use the *Archivo Santander* from now on will have to refer to this list, particularly valuable because it is not likely that the proposed new edition of the *Archivo* will soon see the light.

Parra-Pérez, C. Páginas de historia y de polémica. Caracas. Lit. del Comercio. vii, 349 p., ilus. [3075]

A collection of the shorter occasional articles relating to American history which have come from the pen of this leading Venezuelan scholar. The major part of the volume relates to Miranda and to Bolivarian topics. Of much interest to those interested in controversial aspects of the lives of these Venezuelan leaders.

Posada, Eduardo. Apuntes sobre Vargas Tejada (*Bol. hist. antig.*, vol. 30, no. 341, marzo, p. 251-326). [3076]

Notes on the literary production and life of a poet and dramatist of the independence era. Some of the writings quoted reflect in an interesting way the spirit of the times. The author of the commentary was one of the founders of the Academia Colombiana de la Historia.

Restrepo Tirado, Ernesto. Nariño y el duque de Frías (*Bol. hist. antig.*, vol. 30, no. 347-348, sept.-oct., p. 926-929). [3077]

Exploits a document from Spanish Archives, a report to his government by the Spanish ambassador in London concerning an interview with the Colombian leader. The Duke was unsuccessful in getting Nariño to return to Spain. The latter, though showing personal friendliness, told the Spaniard that no compromise peace was possible.

Robertson, William Spence. The so-called apocryphal letters of Colombres Mármol on the interview of Guayaquil (*Hisp. amer. hist. rev.*, vol. 23, no. 1, Feb., p. 154-155). [3078]

One of the leading authorities in the United States on the period of Spanish American independence ratifies the view of the Venezuelan Academy of History as to the spuriousness of the documents on which the work in question was based.

Roig de Leuchsenring, Emilio. Bolívar y la fraternidad americana (*Rev. bim. cub.*, vol. 51, no. 2, marzo-abril, p. 184-198). [3079]

An address commemorating various aspects of inter-American cooperation in the past with special reference to Spanish American interest in Cuban independence. Of little interest for historians. Published also in *Rev. Habana*, año 1, tomo 2, no. 8, abril, p. 122-136.

Rueda Vargas, Tomás. Nariño (*Rev. Indias*, segunda época, tomo 18, no. 55, julio, p. 24-34). [3080]

A charming essay on the latter years of the "Precursor." The author, a Colombian man of letters who recently died, has the ability to make even a slight piece of work remarkably vivid.

Sanabria, Alberto. Evocaciones y recuerdos. Prólogo de J. A. Cova. Caracas. Ed. C. Acosta. [3081]

Deals with leaders and figures of the city of Cumaná and with the life of the region in the independence period. The comments of visitors such as Humboldt, Bello and Páez are given. Based on documentary sources.

Tejera, Humberto. Bolívar contra la esclavitud (*Rev. nac. cultura*, año 5, no. 36, enero-feb., p. 3-10). [3082]

A brief but judicious summary of the topic.

Uprimny, Leopoldo. Santo Tomás de Aquino, Simón Bolívar y la democracia (*Rev. colegio Rosario*, tomo 38, no. 367-368, feb.-marzo, p. 3-16; no. 369-370, abril-mayo, p. 85-114). [3083]

Vallarino Jiménez, José. Diario de la Barranquilla cuando estuve cerca del Libertador (*Bol. acad. nac. hist.*, Caracas, tomo 26, no. 104, oct.-dic., p. 258-265). [3084]

Record of conversations with Bolívar not long before his death, 1830.

Vernaza, José Ignacio. Antonia Santos (*Bol. hist. valle*, Cali, entrega 86, feb., p. 22-26). [3085]

Vetancourt, Manuel Norberto. José Francisco Pueblo (*Rev. nac. cultura,* año 5, no. 38, mayo–junio, p. 13–35). [3086]
The career of the patriot general Bermúdez, prominent in eastern Venezuela. Covers the chronology of his career in some detail. Bermúdez was one of the most popular and jacobinical leaders in that region and though tumultuous and unruly showed great courage and public spirit. No references to the sources used are given but there is some evidence of the use of primary sources by the author.

Warren, Harris Gaylord. Xavier Mina's invasion of Mexico (*Hisp. amer. hist. rev.,* vol. 23, no. 1, Feb., p. 52–76). [3087]
The best acccount extant of the final stages of the career of the ill fated Spanish liberal leader. It is to be noted that Mina was successful in making contact with Mexican patriot forces and that his defeat was primarily due to the weakness of the revolutionary movement at the time he came to Mexico. He also seems to have had serious difficulty in holding his foreign troops together and to have shown serious weaknesses as a military leader.

Zawadzky C., Alfonso. Comentario al libro *Las ciudades confederadas del Valle del Cauca en 1811.* Bogotá. Ed. Voluntad. (Acad. colombiana de la hist., Bibl. de hist. nac., vol. 66). 79 p. [3088]
A broad interpretive essay on the movement for independence in the Cauca. The author believes that "there was a well defined revolutionary surge from south to north, from Quito into the upper Cauca with Cali playing a major role." (J. F. King in *Hisp. Am. Hist. Rev.*, February.)

Zevallos Quiñones, J. Poderes de pretenciones y para testar, del señor doctor don Toribio Rodríguez de Mendoza (*Rev. arch. nac. Perú,* tomo 16, entrega 2, julio–dic., p. 127–142). [3089]
Documents of 1803 and 1818, respectively, concerning a precursor of Peruvian independence. [J. F. King]

SOUTHERN SOUTH AMERICA

Amunátegui Solar, D. Origen del comercio inglés en Chile (*Rev. chil. hist. geog.,* no. 103, julio–dic., p. 83–95). [3090]
Touches on the trade of the independence period.

Arce, F. A. Entre Ríos y la revolución de Mayo. Santa Fe. Imp. de la Univ. nac. del Litoral. 56 p. [3091]
An objective study based on documents, 1809–1811. See *Rev. hist. Amér.,* no. 17, p. 201.

Barros Borgoño, Luis. San Martín y la medalla de Baylén (*Rev. chil. hist. geog.,* no. 102, enero–junio, p. 5–11). [3092]
Refers to the medal won by San Martín in the Peninsular War prior to his return to America.

Bowers, Claude G. Thomas Jefferson and South America (*Bull. pan amer. union,* vol. 77, no. 4, April, p. 183–191). [3093]
Apparently based almost exclusively on the printed editions of Jefferson's letters and not showing any use of recent monographic literature. Chiefly a work of propaganda to stress Jefferson's interest in South America and Mexico.

Bunster, Enrique. Lord Cochrane. Un estudio con variaciones. Santiago. Ed. Zig-Zag. (Vidas extraordinarias). 208 p., ilus. [3094]
The author claims to have written the first study of Cochrane by a Chilean. On the whole sympathetic to the celebrated adventurer, but maintains a cautious attitude in connection with the disputes between Cochrane and San Martín. The author feels that Cochrane was unjustly treated. Not a full biography, the work covers only the period of the subject's activity in Chile and Peru.

Centner, Charles W. Relaciones comerciales de Gran Bretaña con Chile, 1810–1830 (*Rev. chil. hist. geog.,* no. 103, julio–dic., p. 96–107). [3095]
Though it deals with a more extended period the article covers the commercial predominance of Great Britain in Chile during the independence era. This situation is held to grow out of British supremacy in textile and metal industry and to the size and efficiency of its merchant marine.

Chiriboga N., Ángel Isaac. El prócer General don Antonio Farfán (*Bol. acad. nac. hist.,* Quito, vol. 23, no. 62, julio–dic., p. 149–164). [3096]
CORRESPONDENCIA DEL DEÁN FUNES CON EL LIBERTADOR BOLÍVAR Y EL MARISCAL ANTONIO JOSÉ DE SUCRE, REFERENTE AL CONGRESO DE PANAMÁ, SITUACIÓN DE COLOMBIA, GUERRA DEL BRASIL CON LAS PROVINCIAS UNIDAS DEL RÍO DE LA PLATA (*Rev. bibl. nac.,* Buenos Aires, tomo 8, no. 25, primer trim., p. 209–222). [3097]
Continuation of item 3155, *Handbook, no. 8, 1942.*

Cova, Jesús Antonio. Sucre, ciudadano de América. Vida del gran mariscal de Ayacucho. Caracas. Ed. Cecilio Acosta. (Bibl. de escritores y asuntos venezolanos, vol. 32). 317 p., ilus. [3098]
A book written in the Bolivarian tradition. Sucre appears as a somewhat impossible Galahad. Well written summary of the subject's career but not an original contribution. The author has used the standard printed sources extensively. He takes for granted the guilt of Obando for the death of Sucre and is hostile to Santander.

Díaz, Adolfo M. D. Gervasio Posadas ¿historiador eclesiástico? (*Archivum,* tomo 1, cuad. 1, enero–junio, p. 236–239). [3100]
Transcription and facsimile of a fragment of a manuscript in the hand of Posa-

das, possibly written in 1809, but concerning events from 1796 to 1807, including the English invasions of the Río de la Plata. The editor in an introductory note expresses the hope that when the rest of the manuscript is found it will prove to be an important account of political and ecclesiastical events. [J. F. King]

Díaz, Antonio, and **Eduardo Acevedo Díaz.** Artigas y los siete jefes engrillados (*Rev. nac.,* Montevideo, año 6, tomo 22, no. 65, mayo, p. 282–308). [3101

An extract from the memoirs of Antonio Díaz, one of Alvear's officers, who was handed over by the latter's successors to Artigas, but who with his fellow prisoners was generously treated by the Uruguayan caudillo.

Draghi Lucero, Juan. Cuando retornó a su patria el Protector del Perú (*An. inst. invest. hist.,* Mendoza, tomo 1, 1941 [i.e. 1943], p. 525–532). [3102

———. El diario de O'Higgins en Cuyo (*An. inst. invest. hist.,* Mendoza, tomo 1, 1941 [i.e. 1943], p. 537–550). [3103

———. San Martín, su chacra, su molino y la ubicación de su primer monumento (*An. inst. invest. hist.,* Mendoza, tomo 1, 1941 [i.e. 1943], p. 551–622). [3104

EL ECO DE LOS ANDES. Reimpresión facsimilar publicada por el Instituto de Investigaciones históricas, Universidad Nacional de Cuyo. Mendoza. 246 p. [3105

Covers the files of this paper from 1820 to 1824.

Edwards, Alberto. La organización política de Chile, 1810–1833. Santiago. Ed. Difusión chilena. 165 p. [3106

A thoughtful discussion of political evolution during the era of national formation written from a conservative point of view. Emphasis is placed on social and economic forces rather than on political ideas. The work of Portales is praised as truly national and above party.

Elordi, Guillermo F. Mariano Moreno, ciudadano ilustre. Buenos Aires. Ed. El Ateneo. 317 p. [3107

Second edition, revised, of a work published in 1938. Contains a list of works that can be authoritatively ascribed to Moreno over which there has been considerable controversy.

Fasolino, N. Francisco Javier Echagüe y Andía (*Rev. junta estud. hist. Santa Fe,* tomo 9, oct., p. 9–22). [3108

Biographical data on a friend of San Martín who was dean of Lima cathedral 1821–1822.

Feliú Cruz, Guillermo (ed.). Expediente relativo al desgraciado suceso de las armas reales en Maipó, el 5 de abril de 1818. Santiago. Tall. La Nación. (Bibl. nac., Col. de historiadores y de documentos relativos a la independencia de Chile, tomo 31). 460 p., ilus. [3109

A very important document dealing with the situation in Chile on the eve of the liberation of the country by the forces of San Martín. Throws light on the political and military problems of the royalists in Chile and their relations with Peru.

LAS INSTRUCCIONES DADAS A LOS DIPUTADOS DE LA PLATA A LA ASAMBLEA DE 1813 (*Rev. hist.,* Montevideo, segunda época, año 37, tomo 14, no. 40–42, dic., p. 331–343). [3110

Ives, Mabel Lorenz. He conquered the Andes. The story of San Martín, the liberator. Boston. Little, Brown and co. 241 p., illus. [3111

Designed for school use. A well written, balanced and objective brief biography that is probably the best work of its kind on the subject.

Jáuregui Rosquellas, Alfredo. Síntesis de la vida y la obra patriótica del dr. Jayme de Zudáñez. Sucre. Ed. Rotary club. 149 p. [3112

An appreciation of a hitherto little known Bolivian patriot. The essay is well documented. [Ed.]

MEMORIAS CURIOSAS. "DIARIO" DE JUAN MANUEL BERUTI (*Rev. bibl. nac.,* Buenos Aires, tomo 8, no. 26, segundo trim., p. 449–465; tomo 9, no. 27, tercer trim., p. 159–178). [3114

Miscellaneous notes and observations relating to the era of the British attack on the River Plate region and the "reconquista." Contemporary posters and verses, comments on Liniers.

Montenegro, Carlos. Los pasquines en la Revolución de julio (*Kollasuyo,* año 5, no. 49, junio–julio, p. 3–14). [3115

Moreno, Mariano. Escritos. Prólogo y ed. crítica de Ricardo Levene. Buenos Aires. Ed. Estrada. (Bibl. de clásicos argentinos, vol. 6). [3116

Selections from the writings of Mariano Moreno have several times been published. The first serious edition was prepared by Norberto Piñero in 1896, and reprinted in 1915. Dr. Levene in 1942 edited a volume similar to the above, *El Pensamiento Vivo de Mariano Moreno,* published by Losada. [C. H. Haring]

Otero, Gustavo Adolfo. El mundo social y político de don Pedro Domingo Murillo (*Bol. soc. geog.* La Paz, año 54, no. 65, junio, p. 55–75). [3117

Otero D'Costa, José María. Obando (*Bol. hist. antig.,* vol. 30, no. 344–345, junio–julio, p. 592–602). [3118

A brief defense of the general and liberal politician against the attacks of those who accuse him of complicity in the assassination of Sucre. Contains references to a number of early polemical writings of the nineteenth century on the "Crimen de Berruecos."

Pérez-Acosta, Juan F. Peligrosas actividades de la quinta columna en Buenos Aires y Asunción, 1811 y 1812 (*Bol. inst. invest. hist.*, año 21, tomo 27, no. 93-96, julio, 1942-junio, 1943, p. 155-172). [3119
Chiefly concerned with intrigues of Portugal in Paraguay and with reactionary Spanish plots in Buenos Aires.

Pinto, Manuel María. La revolución de la intendencia de La Paz (*Kollasuyo*, año 5, no. 49, junio-julio, p. 58-69). [3120

Pivel Devoto, Juan E., and **Rodolfo Fonseca Muñoz** (eds.). La diplomacia de la patria vieja, 1811-1820. Montevideo. Imp. El Siglo ilustrado. (Archivo histórico diplomático del Uruguay, tomo 3). xvi, 407 p. [3121
Documents previously published in the *Boletín del Ministerio de Relaciones Exteriores.* The documents include the essential core of the correspondence between Artigas and his government and foreign authorities, among them those of Buenos Aires, Paraguay, Portugal, Spain. For comment see *Hisp. amer. hist. rev.*, vol. 23, no. 4, November, 1943, p. 767-768.

Pizarro, Orlando. El libertador San Martín en Santiago de Chile, 1817-1818 (*Atenea*, año 20, tomo 74, no. 220, oct., p. 70-77). [3122
Details of San Martín's daily life during his residence in Santiago.

Ravignani, Emilio. Acuerdos secretos de la secretaría de guerra del poder ejecutivo, entre los años 1813 y 1817 (*Bol. inst. invest. hist.*, año 21, tomo 27, no. 93-96, julio, 1942-junio, 1943, p. 344-361). [3124
Covers such topics as: army discipline, secret funds, munitions productions and purchase, propaganda, desertions, prisoners of war, relations with the United States and with Great Britain, as well as general domestic politics.

Sáenz Valiente, José M. Aspectos de la vida municipal porteña: como funcionaba el cabildo después de la revolución (*Rev. der. admin. munic.*, no. 164, oct., p. 989-1002; no. 165, Nov., p. 1084-1102). [3125
A legal study of the powers, privileges, organization, and procedure of the *cabildo* of Buenos Aires during the independence period. The colonial *reglamento* of 1695, the later decrees of 1814 and following years are compared.

Tonelli, Armando. El general San Martín y la masonería. Buenos Aires. Tall. gráf. A. Arcella. 168 p. [3126
A polemical work designed to combat the previous work of Zúñiga and to deny that the Logia Lautaro was masonic in character. The author makes much of the absence of positive evidence about the matter. Undoubtedly mainly political, the famous lodge's exact relations to international masonry will probably never be fully cleared up.

Torre Revello, José. El aula de la escuela de la Villa de Luján en 1797 (*Bol. inst. invest. hist.*, año 21, tomo 27, no. 93-96, julio, 1942-junio, 1943, p. 1-6). [3127
Case study, based upon original documents, of the methods, furnishings, etc., of an elementary school for boys at the end of the eighteenth century. [J. F. King]

ÚLTIMOS AÑOS DEL GENERAL SAN MARTÍN (*Rev. bibl. nac.*, Buenos Aires, tomo 9, no. 28, cuarto trim., p. 316-325). [3128
Letters from Balcarce in France to a friend in Argentina dating from 1850 to 1888, to some extent relating to the later career of San Martin in Europe and his attitude toward political developments in Argentina.

Valencia Avaria, Luis. La declaración de la independencia de Chile. Santiago. Ed. El Esfuerzo. [3129
Contains text and facsimile of the original document issued by O'Higgins.
From *Boletín de la Academia Chilena de la Historia.*

Vázquez Machicado, José, and **Humberto Vázquez Machicado.** La biblioteca de Pedro Domingo Murillo, signo de la cultura intelectual (*Kollasuyo*, año 5, no. 49, junio-julio, p. 75-91). [3130

Vilardi, Julián A. La fundación del Museo público de Buenos Aires (*Bol. inst. invest. hist.*, tomo 27, no. 93-96, julio, 1942-junio, 1943, p. 299-307). [3131
The foundation of the museum was related to that of the Biblioteca Nacional and owed much to the initiative of Rivadavia, both in 1812 and later when he was at the helm of the province in 1826.

———. El primer cabildo patriota. El 17 de octubre de 1810 (*Estudios*, año 33, tomo 70, no. 384, dic., p. 428-433). [3132

Villaroel, M. Una Juana de Arco americana, doña Juana Azurday de Padilla (*La Nación*, dic. 19). [3133
A woman who rose to the rank of colonel, it is held, in the wars of independence in upper Peru. A native of Chuquisaca.

ADDENDA

Alba, Pedro de. Simón Bolívar y José Cecilio del Valle (*Rep. amer.*, año 23, tomo 39, no. 10, mayo 23, 1942, p. 152-159). [3134
Draws parallels between the two patriot leaders.

Álvarez Rubiano, P. Los indígenas de Méjico en 1820, según un testimonio epistolar (*Rev. Indias*, Madrid, año 3, no. 7, enero-marzo, 1942, p. 125-130). [3135

Blanco Fombona, Rufino. Bolívar y la guerra a muerte. Época de Boves, 1813-1814. Caracas. Imp. Unidos. 1942. [3136

Canter, Juan. Las sociedades secretas, políticas y literarias, 1810–1815. Buenos Aires. Imp. de la Universidad. 1942. [3137]

CARTAS DE LLIBERTADOR, 1815–1830 (*Bol. acad. nac. hist.*, Caracas, tomo 25, no. 97, enero–marzo, 1942, p. 38–56). [3138]
Continuation of the publication of additional original letters of Bolívar as they come to light. These serve to supplement Dr. Lecuna's edition of the *Cartas de Bolívar* published in 1930. This installment contains, chiefly, material from 1816–1820 and a few letters of 1830.

COPIADORES DEL LIBERTADOR, 1821–1822 (*Bol. acad. nac. hist.*, Caracas, tomo 25, no. 98, abril–junio, p. 183–196; no. 99, julio–set., 1942, p. 249–275). [3139]
Continues the systematic publication of the letterbooks of Bolívar. The originals are preserved in the Casa Natal del Libertador in Caracas.

Cortázar, Roberto, and **Luis Augusto Cuervo** (eds.). Congreso de 1824. Cámara de Representantes: Actas. Bogotá. Ed. Voluntad. (Acad. colombiana de la historia, Biblioteca de historia nacional, tomo 75). 1942. p. xxiv, 362. [3140]
Important documents for the study of civil affairs in this agitated era of Colombian history under the constitution of Cúcuta. Includes an index.
See *Hisp. Am. Hist. Rev.*, Nov., p. 759–760.

LOS DOS SITIOS DE VALENCIA, RELACIÓN DE LO OCURRIDO EN LOS DOS SITIOS QUE SUFRIÓ VALENCIA EN EL AÑO DE 1814 POR UN JEFE REPUBLICANO QUE SE HALLÓ EN ELLOS (*Bol. acad. nac. hist.*, Caracas, tomo 25, no. 100, oct.–dic., 1942, p. 137–158). [3141]
A detailed diary of military operations written by the officer who commanded the patriot forces in the city, Juan de Escalona.

Espinosa, José María. Memorias de un abanderado. Recuerdos de la patria boba, 1810–1819. Bogotá. Bibl. popular de cultura colombiana. 1942. 228 p. [3142]
A reprint by the Ministry of Education of Colombia of an interesting memoir of the early period of the revolution in New Granada. The author was a native of Bogotá.

Lecuna, Vicente. Campaña de Bomboná, 1822 (*Bol. acad. nac. hist.*, Caracas, tomo 25, no. 99, julio–set., 1942, p. 215–248). [3143]
Military history of the campaign which culminated with the setback suffered by the patriot forces at Bomboná. The author holds, that the campaign paved the way for the subsequent capitulation of Pasto and Quito. A documentary appendix contains source material on which the essay is based.

———. Las cartas apócrifas de Colombres Mármol. Contestación al Sr. Rómulo D. Carbia (*Bol. acad. nac. hist.*, Caracas, tomo 25, no. 97, enero–marzo, 1942, p. 3–28). [3144]
Dr. Lecuna here rebuts the allegations of Carbia, chiefly supporting his views by additional details in line with his original attack on these documents, see *Handbook, no. 6, 1940*. He demonstrates quite effectively that handwriting, signatures, paper, spelling, as well as content clearly indicate the spuriousness of the documents in question.

———. El Congreso de Cúcuta, consecuencias políticas y militares de la batalla de Carabobo (*Bol. acad. nac. hist.*, Caracas, tomo 25, no. 98, abril–junio, 1942, p. 162–178). [3145]
A chronicle of the year 1821 in Venezuela, centering on the plans and problems of Bolívar. The article also contains material on the Independence of Panama. As usual the author has published a documentary appendix. Some of this material has been previously published but new documents are also printed.

———. La cuestión de Guayaquil y la campaña de Pichincha (*Bol. acad. nac. hist.*, Caracas, tomo 25, no. 100, oct.–dic., 1942, p. 336–389). [3146]
The policy of the Liberator in the southern provinces of Colombia is analyzed sympathetically with new light on certain aspects of the Guayaquil separatist question derived from the Archivo Sucre, recently acquired by the Academy at Caracas. The article is followed by a documentary appendix.

Márquez T., Ricardo. El capellán del mariscal Sucre, Sr. Dr. Miguel Custodio Veintimilla. Cuenca. 1942. [3147]

Millares Carlo, Agustín. Las cartas apócrifas. Demostración de Profesor Millares Carlo (*Bol. acad. nac. hist.*, Caracas, tomo 25, no. 97, enero–marzo, 1942, p. 29–37). [3148]
The author, a Spanish paleographer of renown, confirms the opinion of Dr. Lecuna in this technical study. Valuable because of its clear impartiality and objectivity.

Montbas, Hugues Barthon de. Las revoluciones de Francia y la Independencia de Hispano-América (*Bol. acad. nac. hist.*, Caracas, tomo 25, no. 98, abril–junio, 1942, p. 105–136). [3149]
A somewhat rambling essay tracing relationships and parallels between the political history of France and that of Hispanic America in the revolutionary era. Magnifies the importance and the influence of France. Few facts are presented to buttress assertions made, but the parallels drawn are interesting.

Paz Soldán, Luis F. Los peruanos en la batalla de Ayacucho (*Peruanidad*, vol. 2, no. 11, nov.–dic., 1942, p. 874–875). [3150]
Stresses the contribution of Peruvian troops in the final battle of the Revolution.

RECUERDOS DE FERNANDO BOLÍVAR (*Bol. acad. nac. hist.*, Caracas, tomo 25, no. 100, oct.-dic., 1942, p. 296-314). [3151

Memoirs of the early life of a nephew of the Liberator who was near him as secretary in the last months of his life. Reports some conversations and opinions of this final period. The author was the son of Juan Vicente Bolívar.

Travieso, Carmen Clements. Luisa Cáceres de Arizmendi, 1799-1866 Caracas. 1942. (Bibl. femenina venezolana, tomo 7, Publicaciones de la Asociación cultural interamericana). [3152

A study of one of the principal patriot heroines of the war of independence in Venezuela. Wife of the leader from Margarita Island.

Vilardi, J. A. Ordenanzas provisionales para el cabildo de Buenos Aires (*Bol. inst. invest. hist.*, año 20, tomo 26, no. 89-92, 1942, p. 113-116). [3153

The first changes in the basic legislation during the revolution.

HISTORY: CARIBBEAN AREA
THE NATIONAL PERIOD

BY

DANA MUNRO

Princeton University

GENERAL STATEMENT

From the standpoint of those interested in the history of Mexico and the Caribbean republics, the year was an unprofitable one. Relatively few substantial scholarly works appeared. The absence of publications by North American scholars was especially striking.

As is usually the case, the items from Mexico and Cuba are far more numerous than those from any of the other republics. The Mexican output reflects a somewhat greater interest in documentary material, while Cuban historians have been more concerned with national heroes. The centenary of Maceo's birth brought forth at least four full length biographies of that leader and there were several shorter studies dealing with phases of Martí's career. Few books of general interest were published in Central America or the other West Indian republics.

BIBLIOGRAPHY

(See also sections on Archives; History: Revolutionary Period;
and International Relations)

MEXICO

(See also items 71, 115)

Barnes, Nancy. Carlota, American empress. New York. Julian Messner, inc., 214 p., illus. [3154]
Popular, romantic biography.

Basch, Samuel. Maximiliano de Méjico. Madrid. Ed. Atlas. (Col. Cisneros, 21). 195 p. [3155]
An abridgement of Basch's story of the final months of Maximilian's career. Basch was the Emperor's personal physician.

Bravo Ugarte, José. Las cuatro primeras constituciones de México independiente (1824, 1836, 1843, 1857) y el acta de reformas constitucionales de 1847 (*Estud. hist.*, año 1, no. 1, enero, p. 69–79). [3156]
Comparative study of the governmental framework established in the various Mexican constitutions down to 1847.

Esquivel Obregón, Toribio. Dato importante acerca del triunfo de la revolución de Ayutla (*Jus*, tomo 10, no. 59, junio, p. 419–429). [3158]
Suggests that Santa Anna withdrew from the presidency of Mexico in 1855 because of the hostility of the Government of the United States. Quotes a long despatch from Gadsden, the American Minister, to the Secretary of State at Washington showing Gadsden's violent disapproval of Santa Anna's régime.

Gómez de Orozco, Federico. Las publicaciones del extinto ayuntamiento y del departamento del Distrito federal. Reseña histórica. México. Bibl. de la Segunda feria del libro. 13 p. [3159]
An interesting sketch of the history of the archives of Mexico City from the time of Cortés.

Guzmán, Martín Luis. El águila y la serpiente. Memorias de la revolución mexicana. Ed. by Ernest Richard Moore. New York. W. W. Norton & co. 309 p. [3160]
An annotated abridgement for use in classes in Spanish or Latin American history.

Irigoyen, Ulises. El coronel Miguel Ahumada, gobernante educador (*Bol. soc. chihuahuense*, tomo 5, no. 1, dic. 20, p. 10–30). [3161]
What Colonel Ahumada accomplished in the field of public instruction as governor of Chihuahua under Díaz.

Murray, Paul V. La necesidad de una actitud revisionista ante la historia de México en el siglo diecinueve. México. Ed. Jus. (Rev. de derecho y ciencias sociales). 25 p. [3162
Urges that more historians pay attention to the 19th century in Mexico.

Núñez y Domínguez, José de Jesús. Semblanza biográfica del señor licenciado F. Javier Gaxiola. México. Soc. mex. de geog. y estad. 42 p. [3163
A brief biography of a Mexican historian.

Pérez Galaz, Juan de D. Primer gobernador de Yucatán después de su independencia (*Yikal maya than,* año 4, tomo 4, no. 41, enero, p. 23–25). [3164
A very short note.

Ramírez Cabañas, Joaquín. Un historiador del siglo pasado (*Fil. letras,* tomo 5, no. 9, enero–marzo, p. 121–129). [3165
Brief biographical sketch of Ángel Núñez Ortega (1838–1890).

Secretaría de relaciones exteriores. La misión confidencial de don Jesús Terán en Europa, 1863–1866. Prólogo de Gabriel Saldívar. México. (Archivo histórico diplomático mexicano, segunda serie, no. 1). xxiii, 107 p. [3167
The correspondence of Juárez' representative in Europe during the French intervention. Important.

Sotelo Inclán, Jesús. Raíz y razón de Zapata. Investigación histórica. México. Ed. Etnos. 236 p. [3168
Explains Zapata's revolt in terms of the history of the village where he was born. The village's long struggle for its lands, from the time of the conquest, is illustrated by documents. An interesting case study.

Velázquez, Primo Feliciano. D. Joaquín García Icazbalceta (*Mem. acad. mex. hist.,* tomo 2, no. 2, abril–junio, p. 101–157). [3169
An essay on the work of a great Mexican historian.

CENTRAL AMERICA

ADMINISTRACIÓN DEL GENERAL FRANCISCO MORAZÁN (*Rev. arch. nac.,* Costa Rica, año 7, no. 3–4, marzo–abril, p. 193–198). [3170
One document of 1841.

DATOS SOBRE LA VIDA DEL GENERAL FRANCISCO MORAZÁN, TOMADOS LITERALMENTE DE LAS MEMORIAS DE DON JOSÉ ANTONIO VIJIL (*Rev. arch. bibl. nac.,* Tegucigalpa, tomo 21, no. 7, enero, p. 448–455; no. 8, feb., p. 516–520). [3170a
Of possible interest to a biographer of Morazán.

García, Miguel Ángel. Diccionario histórico-enciclopédico de la república de El Salvador. Tomo 6. San Salvador. Imp. Nacional. 541 p. [3171

Hill, Roscoe R. Marinos americanos en Nicaragua (*Rev. arch. nac.,* Costa Rica, año 7, no. 1–2, enero–feb., p. 20–34). [3172
The history of the Legation Guard at Managua. Published also in English in *Hisp. amer. essays,* p. 341–360.

LIBRO COPIADOR DE COMUNICACIONES DEL MINISTRO GENERAL SARAVIA (*Rev. arch. nac.,* Costa Rica, año 7, no. 1–2, enero–feb., p. 109–112; no. 3–4, marzo–abril, p. 168–185; no. 9–10, sept.–oct., p. 542–558). [3173

Lizano Hernández, Víctor. Colegio de San Luis Gonzaga. Primera época, año de 1870. Segunda época, años 1871 y 1872 (*Rev. arch. nac.,* Costa Rica, año 7, no. 5–6, mayo–junio, p. 295–306; no. 7–8, julio–agosto, p. 403–423). [3174
A detailed history of the school's activities during the periods indicated.

Polakowsky, H. La república de Costa Rica en Centro-América, 1877 (*Rev. arch. nac.,* Costa Rica, año 7, no. 1–2, enero–feb., p. 40–56). [3175
A translation of a German description of conditions in Costa Rica in 1877, with special reference to agriculture.

Reina Valenzuela, José. D. Francisco Cruz y la botica del pueblo (*Rev. arch. bibl. nac.,* Tegucigalpa, tomo 21, no. 7, enero, p. 472–484; no. 8, feb., p. 525–538; no. 9, marzo, p. 592–602; no. 11, mayo, p. 710–721; no. 12, junio, p. 777–790; tomo 22, no. 1, julio, p. 11–22; no. 2, agosto, p. 78–92; no. 3, sept., p. 137–150; no. 4, oct., p. 217–228; no. 5, nov., p. 276–284; no. 6, dic., p. 339–352). [3176
Biography of a 19th century Honduran statesman.

Reyes Testa, Benito. Combatiendo la fábula. Remembranzas del 3 de noviembre. Panamá. Imp. Nacional. 64 p., ilus. [3177

Rippy, J. Fred. Relaciones entre los Estados Unidos y Guatemala durante la época de Justo Rufino Barrios. (*Rev. arch. nac.,* Costa Rica, año 7, no. 5–6, mayo–junio, p. 286–294). [3178

Rosa, Ramón. Biografía de don José Cecilio del Valle. Tegucigalpa. Tip. Aristón. 115 p., ilus. [3179
A brief biography, written in 1882.

Thompson, Emmanuel. Defensa de Carrillo. Tercera parte (*Rev. arch. nac.,* Costa Rica, año 7, no. 9–10, sept.–oct., p. 454–474). [3180

Turcios R., Salvador. El ciudadano D. José Antonio Vijil (*Rev. arch. bibl. nac.*, Tegucigalpa, tomo 21, no. 11, mayo, p. 722–723). [3181]
A short note.

Valle, Rafael Heliodoro. Gral. Francisco Morazán, héroe y reformador (*Rev. arch. bibl. nac.*, Tegucigalpa, tomo 21, no. 7, mayo, p. 459–467). [3182]
A brief panegyric.

CUBA

Aguirre, Sergio. Seis actitudes de la burgesía cubana en el siglo 19 (*Dialéctica*, año 2, vol. 2, no. 6, marzo–abril, p. 153–177). [3184]
The attitude of the Cuban bourgeoisie toward Spanish rule varied from period to period during the 19th century. At times it advocated simply reform, at other times it sought independence, and on occasion it favored annexation to the United States.

Angulo y Pérez, Andrés. Curso de historia de las instituciones locales de Cuba. Primera parte. Orígenes. Tomo I. Havana. Ed. Cultural. [3185]
This first volume traces the history of local government in Spain from the earliest times through the period of the Reconquest.

Archivo nacional. Correspondencia diplomática de la delegación cubana en Nueva York durante la guerra de independencia de 1895 a 1898. Tomo primero. Prefacio de José Agustín Martín. Habana. Imp. "El Siglo XX." (Archivo nac., Publ., no. 2). xlviii, 171 p., ilus. [3186]
Estrada Palma's letters from New York to agents of the Cuban revolutionary movement in other countries. Dr. Martínez' preface gives an account of the diplomatic history of the revolutionary movement.

Asociación nacional de hacendados de Cuba. Exposición dirigida en julio 8, 1894, por el círculo de hacendados y agricultores de la isla de Cuba a los cortes del reino español en la cual se señalaban las principales causas que por su continuidad producían la excesiva gravedad de la crisis que atravesaba la industria azucarera y las soluciones que había que aplicar entonces con toda urgencia para evitar su inminente ruina. Habana. F. Solana y cía. 164 p. [3187]
An interesting document, dealing not only with the condition of the sugar industry but also with other social and economic problems on the eve of the War for Independence.

Brown Castillo, Gerardo. La Sociedad cubana en 1831 (*Rev. mex. soc.*, año 5, vol. 5, no. 2, segundo trim., p. 191–199). [3188]
Sketches very briefly the outstanding characteristics of the various classes in Cuban society in 1831. Appends a brief bibliography.

Caturla Brú, Victoria. Caracteres de Enrique Piñeyro como historiógrafo (*Univ. Habana*, año 8, no. 49, julio–agosto, p. 81–95). [3189]
Brief study of the outstanding characteristics of Piñeyro's historical work.

Chacón y Calvo, José María. Evocación de Justo de Lara. Habana. Ateneo de la Habana. (Publ., 4). 23 p. [3190]
An essay on the life and work of a Cuban publicist.
From *Revista de la Habana*, no. 13, sept., 1943.

Córdova, Federico de. Luis Victoriano Betancourt, 1843–1885. Habana. Imp. Siglo XX. (Acad. de la historia de Cuba, publ. 146). 26 p. [3191]
A tribute to the Cuban poet and revolutionary leader.

———. Martí, americanista (*Univ. Habana*, año 8, no. 46–48, enero–junio, p. 83–102). [3192]
A lecture, portraying Martí as an ardent exponent of inter-American solidarity and a warm admirer of North America.

Fernández de Castro, José Antonio. Ensayos cubanos de historia y de crítica. Con una carta de Fernando Ortíz. Habana. Ed. J. Montero. (Bibl. de historia, filosofía y sociología, vol. 13). 178 p. [3193]
Essays on various subjects. The longest one deals with José Fernández Madrid's connection with the movement for Cuban independence in the early 19th century; others with a French traveller's account of Habana in 1825, with the poetry of Heredia, and other historical and literary subjects.

Gay-Calbó, Enrique. Varela revolucionario (*Rev. bim. cub.*, vol. 51, no. 1, enero–feb., p. 73–110). [3194]
An account of Félix Varela's political views and activities.

Griñán Peralta, Leonardo. Martí líder político. Habana. Ed. Jesús Montero. 177 p. [3195]
An analytical study of Martí's philosophy and qualities as a revolutionary leader.

Hernández Travieso, Antonio. Primera comisión pacificadora en campo revolucionario. Un episodio de la guerra del 68 (*Rev. bim. cub.*, vol. 51, no. 3, mayo–junio, p. 387–394). [3196]
A brief account of an unsuccessful effort to make peace early in the Ten Years' War.

Horrego Estuch, Leopoldo. Antonio Maceo. Héroe y carácter. Habana. Ed. Luz-Hilo. 289 p. [3197
A substantial bibliography.

Mañach y Robato, Jorge. Miguel Figueroa, 1851-1893. Habana. Imp. Siglo XX. (Acad. de la historia de Cuba, Publ. no. 148). 37, vii p., ilus. [3198
Biographical sketch of a Cuban autonomist leader.

———. La nación y la formación histórica. Habana. Acad. de la historia de Cuba. 74 p. [3199
Address delivered on the occasion of his admittance to the Academy of History. Dr. Emeterio Santovenia's reply, a tribute to Dr. Mañach, is printed in the same pamphlet.

Marquina, Rafael. Antonio Maceo, héroe epónimo. Habana. Ed. Lex. 447 p. [3200
A full treatment of Maceo's career and personality.

Pérez-Beato, Manuel. Rectificaciones históricas. Fascículo primero. Habana. Ed. del Archivo histórico Pérez-Beato. 86 p. [3202
Notes correcting errors in papers presented to the Inter-American Conference on Municipal History.

Pérez Cabrera, José Manuel. José María Aguirre. Habana. Imp. El Siglo XX. (Acad. de la historia de Cuba). 56 p., ilus. [3203
Sketch of the career of a hero of the Ten Years' War and of the revolt of 1895.

Rodríguez Morejón, G. Maceo, héroe y caudillo. Habana. Ed. Cultural. 220 p. [3204
The biography of Maceo which was awarded the Bacardi prize.

Roig de Leuchsenring, Emilio. Algunos conceptos martianos de la República (Arch. José Martí, año 3, no. 1, enero-dic., 1942 [i.e., 1943], p. 60-79). [3205
Martí's political ideals and their application to Cuba's problems of today.

Santovenia y Echaide, Emeterio Santiago. Martí, legislador. Buenos Aires. Ed. Losada. (Col. Cristal del tiempo). 156 p. [3206
This is another study of Martí's political philosophy, as it appears in his ideas about law-making.

———. Política de Martí. Habana. Tall. de Seoane, Fernández y cía. 156 p. [3207
An interpretation of Martí's political and social philosophy.

———. Raíz y altura de Antonio Maceo. Habana. Ed. Trópico. 146 p. [3208
A brief biography.

Sociedad cubana de estudios históricos e internacionales. El obispo Martínez Dalmau y la reacción anticubana. Habana. Arrow press. 117 p. [3209
A series of articles defending the Bishop in connection with an historical address in which the Bishop criticized the Spanish régime in Cuba.

Tejera y García, Diego Vicente. Un párrafo de la historia de Cuba (Rev. bim. cub., vol. 51, no. 3, mayo-junio, p. 395-417). [3210
The story of an effort by the autonomist party to reach an agreement with the republican revolutionists on the eve of the American intervention in Cuba.

Vega Cobiellas, Ulpiano. La personalidad y la obra del general Fulgencio Batista Zaldívar, presidente de la república de Cuba. Habana. Ed. Cultural. 161 p. [3211
A laudatory account of General Batista's political career.

DOMINICAN REPUBLIC

Despradel y Batista, Guido. La municipalidad de Santo Domingo ante el golpe libertador del 27 de febrero (Bol. arch. gen., Ciudad Trujillo, año 6, vol. 6, no. 26-27, enero-abril, p. 3-27). [3212
An account of the work of the municipal administration which functioned in Santo Domingo City in the final months of Haitian rule and the first months of independence.

Rodríguez Demorizi, Emilio. Correspondencia del cónsul de Francia en Santo Domingo, 1844-1846 (Bol. arch. gen., Ciudad Trujillo, año 6, vol. 6, no. 28-29, mayo-agosto, p. 142-146; no. 30-31, sept.-dic., p. 273-403). [3214
Interesting and important letters, dealing especially with the consul's intrigues, both before and after the declaration of Dominican independence, in an effort to obtain Samaná Bay and establish a French protectorate.

———. Expedición de Sánchez y de Cabral. Apuntes y documentos para su estudio (Clío, año 10, no. 57-58, enero-abril, p. 203-231). [3215
A brief account of an unsuccessful attempt by Sánchez and Cabral to prevent the annexation of the Dominican Republic by Spain in 1861. The author prints several hitherto unpublished documents.

———. La revolución de 1843 (Bol. arch. gen., Ciudad Trujillo, año 6, vol. 6, no. 26-27, enero-abril, p. 28-110). [3216
A brief account, accompanied by several documents dealing with the revolution against Boyer which paved the way for Dominican independence.

ADDENDA

Álvarez, Miguel Ángel. De cómo perdimos las provincias de Nicoya y Guanacaste. Primera parte. Granada, Nic. Tip. Salesiana. 1942. 104 p. [3217

A history of the boundary dispute between Nicaragua and Costa Rica, with special reference to the provinces of Nicoya and Guanacaste.

Ocaranza, Fernando. Juárez y sus amigos. Colección de ensayos. Segunda serie, 1860. México, D. F. Ed. Stylo. (Inst. panamericano de geografía e historia. Publ. no. 65). 251 p. 1942. [3218

Selections from Juárez' personal correspondence, with explanatory material.

Rippy, J. Fred. Justo Rufino Barrios (*Hisp. amer. essays*, 1942, p. 280–298). [3219

The political career of the Guatemalan dictator.

HISTORY: SPANISH SOUTH AMERICA
THE NATIONAL PERIOD

BY

CLARENCE H. HARING
Harvard University

AND

MIRON BURGIN
Department of Commerce

GENERAL STATEMENT

The historical bibliography for the year on Argentina since independence, as usual more extensive than that of any other South American country, calls for little comment. Much of it continues to be given to a discussion pro and con of the career and times of the dictator Rosas. Two works call for special mention: Dr. Ramón J. Cárcano's interesting memoirs, *Mis Primeros 80 Años* (no. 3232), and Ricardo Piccirilli's two volume biography of Bernardino Rivadavia (no. 3268).

Chile's celebration in 1943 of the centenary of the formal occupation of the Strait of Magellan became the occasion for several important publications on the subject (nos. 3299–3301, 3306). The contemporary literary movement of the year 1842 is also represented by a capital study from the pen of Norberto Pinilla (no. 3305). It is interesting to note in passing that a Chilean gentleman rises to the defense, in a substantial volume, of Bolivia's claim to a territorial outlet (presumably through Chile) to the Pacific (no. 3297).

The death in October, 1942 of the Colombian historian, Eduardo Posada, one of the founders of the Academia Colombiana de Historia, called forth a notable issue of the *Boletín de Historia y Antigüedades* (vol. 30, no. 341) devoted entirely to his personality and career. Two noteworthy articles on Colombian history should also be mentioned: one on the political career of José María Obando by Enrique Otero D'Costa (no. 3315); the other by Miguel Aguilera relating to the assassination of General José María Córdoba (no. 3309).

A new bi-monthly journal of Lima, *Historia*, presented several outstanding articles on Peruvian history: two by Jorge Basadre, on the antecedents of the War of the Pacific (no. 3330), and on more recent domestic politics (no. 3331); and another by Watt Stewart concerned with the collapsing fortunes of the great railway impresario, Henry Meiggs (no. 3335). Fernando Schwalb López Aldana also contributes an important essay on the Peru-Bolivian Confederation of Santa Cruz (no. 3296).

Historiography in Uruguay is rather better represented than usual. The centenary of the beginning of the Guerra Grande has called forth a considerable number of publications on both banks of the River Plate. The Academia Nacional de Historia in Buenos Aires issued a facsimile reproduction of *La Nueva Era*, one of the fugitive periodicals published by the defenders of Montevideo in 1846 (no. 3340); Claudio María Braconnay contributed a volume on the part played by the French Legion (no. 3341); and articles in the *Revista Nacional* by Raúl Montero Bustamente and José Salgado (nos.

3353, 3358) bear upon the same general subject. Perhaps the most important historical publication of the year in Uruguay is the two volume *Historia de los Partidos Políticos en el Uruguay* by the distinguished director of the Museo Histórico, Juan E. Pivel Devoto (no. 3356).

BIBLIOGRAPHY

(See also sections on Archives; History: Revolutionary Period; and International Relations)

ARGENTINA

(See also items 95, 3131)

Álvarez, Juan. Historia de Rosario (1689–1939). Buenos Aires. Imp. López. 658 p., ilus. [3220

A chronicle of the political, social and economic development of the second largest city in Argentina, with special attention to the last ninety years.

ARCHIVO DE FÉLIX FRÍAS. CORRESPONDENCIA CON JOAQUÍN TOCORNAL, JUAN M. GUTIÉRREZ, ANDRÉS LAMAS Y OTRAS PERSONALIDADES SOBRE ORGANIZACIÓN NACIONAL Y ESTADO POLÍTICO DEL PAÍS (*Rev. bibl. nac.*, Buenos Aires, tomo 9, no. 27, tercer trim., p. 73–104). [3221

Seven letters written by Félix Frías between October 1, 1853 and May 17, 1859.

Arenas Fraga, Abelardo. Relación histórica de las misiones diplomáticas argentinas. Embajadas y legaciones (*Rev. bibl. nac.*, Buenos Aires, tomo 8, no. 25, primer trim., p. 199–208; no. 26, segundo trim., p. 471–480; tomo 9, no. 27, tercer trim., p. 217–240; tomo 9, no. 28, cuarto trim., p. 454–465). [3222

Lists of chiefs of missions to all countries with which Argentina has had diplomatic relations since 1810.

Beltrán, Oscar R. Historia del periodismo argentino. Pensamiento y obra de los forjadores de la patria. Buenos Aires. Ed. Sopena argentina. 359 p. [3223

An annotated list of the periodicals published in Argentina since the beginning of the nineteenth century, with emphasis upon Buenos Aires before 1853. Only 58 pages are devoted to the years following Monte Caseros, and 73 pages to the provinces.

Besio Moreno, Nicolás. Rosario de Santa Fe. Cartografía y población. 1744–1942. La Plata. Univ. nac. de La Plata, Inst. del Museo. 298 p. [3224

Bilbao, Manuel (ed.). Antonino Reyes. Memorias del edecán de Rosas. Nueva ed., con noticia biográfica por Jorge Bilbao e importantes agregados y documentos. Buenos Aires. Ed. Americana. 535 p. [3225

First published in Buenos Aires in 1883 as volume I of *Vindicación y Memorias de don Antonino Reyes*. Volume II never appeared. The book was the first serious attempt at a dispassionate discussion of Rosas and his régime, and stirred up the bitterest hostility at the time.

Bosch, Beatriz. El estatuto provisorio constitucional de Entre Ríos (*Bol. inst. invest. hist.*, año 21, vol. 27, no. 93–96, julio 1942–junio 1943, p. 227–253). [3226

Relates the circumstances attending the formulation of the temporary constitution of 1822 in Entre Ríos, after the death of Francisco Ramírez and the seizure of the provincial government by Lucio Mansilla, and emphasizes the important rôle of Casiano Calderón in these events. Followed by the text of the constitution.

Bravo, Mario. El gigante Amapolas (*Libertad creadora*, tomo 1, no. 1, enero-feb., p. 17–40). [3227

An appreciation of Juan Bautista Alberdi, with special reference to Alberdi's writings in the periodical *La Moda* published in Buenos Aires in the late 'thirties.

Bucich Escobar, Ismael. Museo histórico Sarmiento (*Rev. hist. Amér.*, no. 16, dic., p. 85–122). [3228

A brief statement of the antecedents of the foundation of the Museum, followed by a descriptive list of its contents, principally the personal effects, furniture and archives belonging to President Sarmiento. A slightly abbreviated version appears in *Bol. com. nac. mus. mon. hist.*, año 5, no. 5, p. 47–102.

Cady, John Frank. La intervención extranjera en el Rio de la Plata, 1838–1850. Estudio de la política seguida por Francia, Gran Bretaña y Norteamerica con respecto al dictador Juan Manuel de Rosas. Trad. de Juan M. Uteda. Introd. de Luis A. Podestá Costa. Buenos Aires. Ed. Losada. (Bibl. de la Soc. de historia argentina, 14). 307 p. [3229

Caldcleugh, Alexander. Viajes por América del Sur. Río de La Plata, 1821. Trad.

y prólogo de José Luis Busaniche. Buenos Aires. Ed. argentinas Solar. 255 p. [3230

Cánepa, Luis. Antecedentes históricos y tradicionales de los símbolos argentinos. La bandera, el escudo, la escarapela, la banda presidencial. Buenos Aires. Tall. Linari. 155 p. [3231

Relates the history of the national flag, the seal, the cockade, and the presidential sash.

Cárcano, Ramón J. Mis primeros 80 años. Buenos Aires. Ed. Sudamericana. 445 p. [3232

Spirited reminiscences of one of Argentina's most distinguished political figures, with interesting comments upon the political mores of his country. Especially important for the Revolution of the Year 90 and for the presidency of Roque Sáenz Peña.

Carrasco, Jacinto. D. Juan Manuel de Rosas y el obispado del deán don Diego Estanislao Zavaleta (*Archivum*, tomo 1, cuad. 1, enero-junio, p. 127-135). [3233

The main portion of the article consists of a letter from Rosas to Estanislao López, in which the governor of Buenos Aires explains why he must reject Alejandro Heredia's request that Diego Estanislao Zavaleta be named bishop of Córdoba.

Comisión de homenaje al Dr. Pedro Goyena en el centenario de su nacimiento. El doctor Pedro Goyena. Juicios sobre la personalidad del esclarecido ciudadano e insigne maestro. Buenos Aires. 62 p., ilus. [3234

Dr Pedro Goyena (1843-1892) was a distinguished orator and legislator, and for many years professor of Roman Law in the University of Buenos Aires.

Comisión nacional de museos y monumentos históricos. Boletín, año 5, no. 5. Buenos Aires. 599 p. [3235

Includes, among other items, the annual report of the president of the Comisión, Dr. Ricardo Levene, detailed descriptions of the Museo Histórico Sarmiento and the Museo Mitre, and a variety of current information regarding other historical monuments and museums of the republic.

Corbazzo, Alberto P. El dictador Rosas y las islas Malvinas (*América*, Habana, vol. 17, no. 1-2, enero-feb., p. 49-53). [3236

Only the first few paragraphs refer to the Falkland Islands. The rest of the article reviews the brutal and tyrannical aspects of the Rosas régime.

Cúneo, Dardo. Juan B. Justo. Buenos Aires. Ed. Americalee. 313 p. [3237

An eloquent political biography of one of the founders of the Socialist Party in Argentina, comprising, however, more history than biography.

Dana Montaño, Salvador M. La constitución de 1853 y sus autores e inspiradores. Santa Fe. Univ. nac. del Litoral. Inst. social. 43 p. [3238

A review of the ideological and political considerations which animated the protagonists of the constitution of 1853. The influence of the constitution of the United States and of French political thought is minimized.

Domínguez, Wenceslao N. Ferré, Paz y el ejército de reserva después de Caá-Guasú (*Bol. inst. invest. hist.*, año 21, tomo 27, no. 93-96, julio, 1942-junio, 1943, p. 49-81). [3239

Defends the actions of Governor Ferré of the province of Corrientes in his relations with General Paz during the revolt of Corrientes against the dictator Rosas in 1841.

Estrada, José Manuel. Problemas argentinos. Prólogo de Martín Aberg Cobo. Buenos Aires. Imp. de la Univ. (Univ. de Buenos Aires, Facultad de derecho y ciencias sociales). 218 p. [3240

"A collection of three works, *Signum Foederis*, *Problemas Argentinos*, and *Notas Sobre la Crisis Política del 90*, illustrating the orientation of the author's political and sociological thought."

Fleitas, Odin E. Vidal, el último mazorquero. Buenos Aires. Ed. Iguazú. 58 p. [3241

A vitriolic attack upon Juan Ramón Vidal who at the age of 26 became governor of Corrientes (1889) and who for nearly five decades dominated the political life of the province. Vidal died in 1940.

Font Ezcurra, Ricardo. La revisión de la historia (*Rev. inst. inv. hist. J. M. Rosas*, no. 11, marzo-abril, p. 5-22). [3242

Contrasts Rosas' policy of national consolidation with the alleged "treasonable" disregard of the unitaries for the territorial integrity of the Argentine Confederation.

———, San Martín y Rosas. Su correspondencia. Buenos Aires. Ed. La Mazorca. 100 p. [3243

Letters exchanged between Rosas and San Martín between August 1838 and the latter's death, twelve years later; reprinted from earlier collections, with a running commentary by one of the foremost exponents of the Rosista school of historiography.

Gabriel, José. Lucio V. Mansilla, porteño ejemplar (*Sustancia*, año 4, no. 14, marzo-abril, p. 281-290). [3244

A charming essay on the life and works of L. V. Mansilla. Mansilla was the son of a general in the early civil wars and a nephew of the dictator Rosas, a traveler, writer, soldier, politician, skilled duelist and famous conversationalist; one of the most interesting figures of nineteenth century Argentina.

Gaceta de la provincia oriental. Canelones, 1826-1827. Reproducción facsimilar dirigida por los señores Ariosto D. González, Simón S. Lucuix y Arturo Scarone. Prólogo del señor S. S. Lucuix. Montevideo. [3245
Only 16 issues of this weekly are known to have been published. Simón S. Lucuix in an introductory essay notes that the political orientation of the *Gaceta* was unitary.

Gadea, Wenceslao S. Don Justo. La tragedia de Entre Ríos de 1870. San José y Concordia. Buenos Aires. Imp. López. 234 p. [3246
A detailed description of Justo José de Urquiza's residence and an account of the assassination of Urquiza and his two sons, Justo Carmelo and Waldino. Well documented.

Gandía, Enrique de. Los estudios históricos en la Argentina. Buenos Aires. Ed. El Ateneo. 170 p. [3247
Discusses the historical writings of Lucas Ayarragaray and Ramón J. Cárcano.

Gobierno i ajentes diplomáticos de la república argentina en Chile, 1836-1847 (*An. inst. invest. hist.*, Mendoza, tomo 1, 1941 [i.e. 1943], p. 3-523). [3248
Diplomatic documents touching upon relations between Argentina and Chile.

Gómez Ferreyra, Avelino Ignacio. El abate Sallusti. Su desconocida personalidad y su opinión sobre el carácter de los argentinos (*Archivum*, tomo 1, cuad. 1, enero-junio, p. 158-194). [3249

González Arrilli, Bernardo (comp.). La tiranía y la libertad. Juan Manuel de Rozas según 127 autores. Buenos Aires. Ed. La Vanguardia. 640 p. [3250
In this extensive volume the compiler assembled excerpts culled from the writings of over one hundred authors, all of them opponents of Rosas and his régime. The purpose of the volume, according to the compiler, is to demonstrate once more that all tyranny is an outrage. The material is arranged under forty-four headings corresponding to the various events and general characteristics of the administration of Rosas. There is also an index of authors quoted in the volume.

Iconografía de Mitre. Prólogo de Rómulo Zabala. Buenos Aires. Inst. Mitre. [3251
Three pages of text and 58 illustrations.

Intervención europea en el Río de la Plata (*Rev. bibl. nac.*, Buenos Aires, tomo 8, no. 25, primer trim., p. 223-240). [3252
Three letters from Valentín Alsina to Félix Frías and to J. Le Long written between May 22, 1849 and August 17, 1850.

Irazusta, Julio. Vida política de Juan Manuel de Rosas a través de su correspondencia. Tomo 2, 1835-1840. Buenos Aires. Ed. Albatros. 307 p. [3253
Volume I was published in 1941. See *Handbook, no. 7, 1941,* item 3447.

Isabèlle, Arsenio. Viaje a Argentina, Uruguay y Brasil en 1830. Noticia biográfica del autor por Ernesto Morales. Trad. de Pablo Palant. Buenos Aires. Ed. Americana. 454 p. [3254
Translation of a very interesting and informative book of travel and description by a native of Havre, published in 1835.

Latzina, Eduardo. Francisco Latzina en el centenario de su natalicio 2 de abril de 1943. Su labor intelectual de 50 años en la Argentina memorada por su hijo. Buenos Aires. Ed. Peuser. 79 p., ilus. [3255
A brief biography followed by a detailed bibliography both published and unpublished.

Levene, Ricardo. Notas para la historia de las ideas sociales y jurídicas argentinas (*Rev. univ. Buenos Aires*, tercera época, año 1, no. 1, julio-sept., p. 35-46). [3256
Dr. Levene sustains his well-known thesis that the ideological sources of the Revolution of 1810 and of the later constitutional organization of the republic were predominantly Spanish and Argentine.

Límites entre Salta y Santiago del Estero (*Rev. bibl. nac.*, Buenos Aires, tomo 8, no. 25, primer trim., p. 102-104). [3257
A letter from Manuel Solá, governor of Salta, to Felipe Ibarra, dated September 3, 1839, in which the former proposes a boundary between the two provinces.

Martínez, Yolanda (ed.). El pensamiento de Echeverría. Buenos Aires. Ed. Lautaro. (Bibl. del pensamiento argentino). 167 p. [3258
The selections are arranged under the following headings: Fundamentos de la democracia; La Revolución de Mayo; El Partido unitario; El Partido federal; La Unidad nacional; La Reorganización nacional; Educación y democracia; Literatura nacional; Revolución de Febrero en Francia.

Mitre, Adolfo. Mitre, periodista. Buenos Aires. Ed. Peuser. (Inst. Mitre). 253 p. [3259
Traces the journalistic career and activities of the Argentine statesman and founder in Buenos Aires of "La Nación," one of the world's greatest newspapers.

———— (ed.). El pensamiento de Mitre. Buenos Aires. Ed. Lautaro. (Bibl. del pensamiento argentino, 3). 156 p., foto. [3260
Selections from the historical and political writings of the great Argentine statesman.

Montero Bustamante, Raúl. Un testigo de la batalla de Ituzaingó (*Rev. nac.*, Monte-

video, año 6, tomo 22, no. 64, abril, p. 116–120). [3261
Interesting details of the battle drawn from the *Diario de la Guerra del Brasil* of the Uruguayan General José Brito del Pino.

LAS MONTONERAS DEL CAUDILLO GENERAL ÁNGEL VICENTE PEÑALOZA (EL CHACHO) 1863 (*Rev. bibl. nac.*, Buenos Aires, tomo 8, no. 25, primer trim., p. 15–101). [3262
Correspondence between Juan A. Gelly y Obes and General Wenceslao Paunero, comprising thirty letters written during the months May–November, 1863.

Mota del Campillo, Eduardo. El Congreso constituyente de 1853. Sus componentes, su obra. Buenos Aires. Tall. Alfonso Ruiz. 52 p. [3263

Ocampo, Armando R. La Rioja de ayer y de hoy. Buenos Aires. Ed. Calinto Perlado. 360 p. [3264
Historical survey of the press in that province between 1854 and 1940.

Orlandi, Héctor Rodolfo. El pacto federal como constitución argentina, 1831 (*Rev. col. procuradores Buenos Aires*, año 22, no. 80, enero–marzo, p. 25–44). [3265
The federal pact was a political alliance of the participating provinces, but produced no unity on economic and juridical questions.

Ortiz de Rozas, Alfredo. Rosas y el odio mitrista (*Rev. inst. inv. hist. J. M. Rosas*, no. 11, marzo–abril, p. 23–64). [3266
A defense of Rosas as an administrator and statesman by a descendant of the dictator.

Palcos, Alberto. Nuestra ciencia y Francisco Javier Muñiz. El sabio—el héroe. La Plata. Facultad de humanidades y ciencias de la educación. (Bibl. humanidades, tomo 29). 349 p. [3267
The life and work of one of Argentina's earliest scientists, a physician who from the time of Rosas to the Paraguayan War rendered important services to his country.

Piccirilli, Ricardo. Rivadavia y su tiempo. Buenos Aires. Ed. Peuser. 2 vols.: 529, 632 p. [3268
The first well-documented, full scale biography of one of the founders of the Argentine nation; a superb example of the printer's art as well.

POLÍTICA INTERNA ARGENTINA (*Rev. bibl. nac.*, Buenos Aires, tomo 9, no. 28, cuarto trim., p. 263–299). [3269
Scattered correspondence over the years 1860–1906 dealing with the political problems of the republic, by Sarmiento, Gorostiaga, Roca, Mitre, Rawson and others.

Ratto, Héctor C. Vida de Brown. Buenos Aires. Ed. Emecé. 77 p., 28 ilus. [3270
A short popular account of the founder of the Argentine navy.

REBELIÓN DE ENTRE RÍOS. RICARDO LÓPEZ JORDÁN, 1870 (*Rev. bibl. nac.*, Buenos Aires, tomo 9, no. 27, tercer trim., p. 11–72). [3271
Forty-two letters from the archive of General Juan A. Gelly y Obes, most of them addressed to him, and all relating to the military campaign against López Jordán, May 14–December 28, 1870.

REFUGIADOS ARGENTINOS EN BOLIVIA. JUICIOS Y COMENTARIOS SOBRE LA DICTADURA DE ROSAS (*Rev. bibl. nac.*, Buenos Aires, tomo 9, no. 28, cuarto trim., p. 300–308). [3272
A letter written by Félix Frías, unitary exile in Chuquisaca, to Miguel Piñero, January 7, 1843.

Rodríguez, Carlos J. Irigoyen. Su revolución política y social. La Unión cívica radical. Buenos Aires. Ed. La Facultad. 238 p. [3273
By means of copious excerpts from Irigoyen's speeches and programmatic statements the author endeavors to reconstruct the political, economic and social philosophy of the leader of Unión Cívica Radical who was twice president of Argentina.

Rojas Paz, Pablo (ed.). El pensamiento de Alberdi. Buenos Aires. Ed. Lautaro. (Bibl. del pensamiento argentino, 2). 166 p., foto. [3274
Includes a brief study of Alberdi's political ideas by Adolfo Posada and a discourse by Jean Jaurés.

Rosa (h.), José María. Alberdi y las ideas constitucionales del 53 (*Rev. inst. inv. hist. J. M. Rosas*, no. 11, marzo–abril, p. 65–84). [3275
In the author's view the political and economic programs of Alberdi and his *correligionarios* were anti-national since they opened the country to races and influences of non-Hispanic origin.

Ruiz y Ruiz, Raúl A. El tratado del Litoral de 1831 (*Rev. junta estud. hist. Santa Fe*, tomo 9, oct., p. 23–42). [3276
A brief discussion of the quadrilateral treaty and of the activities of the Comisión Representativa. The author notes that Rosas must accept the responsibility for the Comisión's failure to accomplish its purpose and for its untimely dissolution. The author believes, however, that powerful interests in Buenos Aires forced Rosas' hand. Unfortunately, these powerful interests are not identified.

Sagarna, Antonio. Entre Ríos. Paraná. Imp. oficial de la Provincia de Entre Ríos. 47 p. [3277
A brief and rather hasty review of the social and economic history of the province since independence.

Sánchez Zinny, Eduardo F. La revolución inconclusa. Esquema para una interpretación del contenido social argentino. Buenos Aires. Imp. López. 321 p. **[3278**

An analysis of the political and social evolution of Argentina since emancipation in which the author argues that up to June 4, 1943, the objectives of the revolutionary movement of 1810 were being sacrificed on the altar of expediency and greed. In the opinion of the author the June revolution opens a new era in Argentina's history, an era in which the Revolution of 1810 will at last be completed.

Tonda, Américo A. Los apoderados del deán Funes en la corte de Madrid a la luz de su correspondencia inédita (*Archivum*, tomo 1, cuad. 1, enero-junio, p. 136-158). **[3279**

Torre Revello, José. Museo Mitre (*Bol. com. nac. mus. mon. hist.*, año 5, no. 5, p. 103-115). **[3281**

A brief statement of the history, contents, and publications of the Museo Mitre.

Torres, Arturo. La constitución de Córdoba. Estudio histórico. Buenos Aires. Ed. Ideas. 318 p. **[3282**

A comparative study of the constitutions of the Province of Córdoba since 1821. The constitution now in force is analyzed article by article, each of which is compared with the corresponding provisions of previous constitutions.

Universidad nacional de Cuyo. Instituto de investigaciones históricas. El Eco de los Andes. Nos. 1-61, 23 de septiembre de 1824-25 de diciembre de 1825. Mendoza. Tall. gráf. Atlas, J. Belmonte. 1 vol., facsíms. **[3283**

El Eco de los Andes was a liberal, anticlerical weekly of Mendoza supporting the general program of Bernardino Rivadavia. This is a facsimile reproduction with an introductory essay by Juan Draghi Lucero.

Vanasco, Luis Ángel. Ensayo histórico de San José de Flores. Buenos Aires. Ed. J. P. Castagnola. (Junta de estudios históricos de San José de Flores, vol. 9). 28 p. **[3284**

Vega Díaz, D. de la. Las primeras montoneras riojanas durante la guerra del Paraguay (*Rev. junta hist. let. La Rioja*, año 2, no. 1, enero-marzo, p. 87-98). **[3285**

An account of the activities of Governor Julio Campos and the liquidation of the *montonera*. Lacks documentation.

Ygobone, Aquiles D. Juan Francisco Seguí y el congreso del año 53 (*Rev. colegio abogados Buenos Aires*, tomo 21, no. 2, p. 103-124). **[3287**

A dithyrambic account of the public career of the secretary of the Constituent Congress of 1852, later prominent in the public life of his native province of Santa Fe.

Zeballos, Estanislao S. Rosas y la soberanía argentina de los ríos (*Rev. inst. inv. hist. J. M. Rosas*, no. 11, marzo-abril, p. 85-100). **[3288**

Reprint of a speech delivered in the Chamber of Deputies on December 15, 1915 relating to the boarding of the Argentine steamer "Bartolomé" by H. M. S. "Orama." In the course of the discourse Zeballos reviewed in eulogistic terms Rosas' defense of the principle of national sovereignty over Argentine rivers.

Zorilla, Manuel M. Al lado de Sarmiento y de Avellaneda (Recuerdos de un secretario). Segunda ed. Buenos Aires. Ed. Ayacucho. 332 p. **[3289**

Somewhat disappointing. Much general history, and fewer "revelations" than one might expect.

Zorraquín Becú, H. De aventurero yanqui a cónsul porteño en los Estados Unidos. Buenos Aires. **[3290**

Concerns the career of David C. DeForest, prosperous Yankee merchant in Buenos Aires, who returned to the United States in 1818 with an appointment as "consul general" of the United Provinces, but was never so recognized by the Department of State.

BOLIVIA

Aguirre, Nataniel. Unitarismo y federalismo (*Rev. jurídica*, año 6, no. 25, dic., p. 8-27). **[3291**

First published in 1877. A critical analysis of the political and economic program of the unitary party in Bolivia and an exposition and defense of the federalist doctrine.

Díaz A., Julio. Fastos militares de Bolivia. La Paz. Escuela tip. Salesiana. (Bibl. del Min. de defensa nac., vol. 13). 568 p., mapas. **[3292**

A detailed study of the more important military campaigns in which Bolivia was involved since independence down to the Chaco war. Bolivia lost over 20 per cent of its territory as a result of military defeats.

Montenegro, Carlos. Nacionalismo y coloniaje. Su expresión histórica en la prensa de Bolivia. La Paz., Ed. Autonomía. xvii-xxiii, 250 p., ilus. **[3293**

A thoughtful review of the political history of Bolivia as reflected in the contemporary press.

Otero, Gustavo Adolfo. Figuras bolivianas del siglo 19 (*Kollasuyo*, año 5, no. 47, abril, p. 167-175). **[3294**

Discusses Evaristo Valle, Ricardo Mariano Terragas, and Gabriel René Moreno as representative figures in the history of Bolivian thought.

Santa Cruz, Víctor. Treinta años de historia paceña, 1825-1855. La Paz. Ed. Universo. 332 p. **[3295**

An intimate history of the capital of Bolivia, with special emphasis upon political development. The study is based largely upon secondary material. The volume closes with short biographical notes on Santa Cruz, Ballivián and Belzú, a list of the prefects of the Department of La Paz, and a list of municipal presidents.

Schwalb López Aldana, Fernando. Estudio panorámico de la Confederación Perú-Boliviana (*Rev. peruana der. int.*, tomo 3, no. 8, abril-junio, p. 139-166). [3296

A very interesting and suggestive discussion of the forces behind the grandiose political design of the president of Bolivia, Andrés Santa Cruz.

Vergara Vicuña, Aquiles. Contesto a un general de Chile. La Paz. Lit. e imp. Unidas. 434, xv p. [3297

Former Chilean deputy and Minister of Justice and Education defends Bolivia's demand for a free access to the Pacific and justifies his position on historical, economic and geographic grounds.

Zalles, Juan María. Nuevas crónicas. Santiago. Imp. univ. 172 p. [3298

The first volume, *Crónicas*, was published in 1942. The second, like the first, consists chiefly of short biographical sketches of some of the outstanding figures in the political history of Bolivia, with a few papers on contemporary problems.

CHILE

(*See also item* 3106)

Aguirre Humeres, Alfonso. Relaciones históricas de Magallanes. La toma de posesión del Estrecho y fundación de una colonia por la república de Chile en 1843. Santiago. Imp. Chile. 316 p. [3299

A comprehensive and well documented account of a neglected chapter in the history of Chilean expansion in the southernmost part of the continent.

Astorquiza Sazzo, Juan. "Una tragedia en la colonia." Crónicas de los albores de Punta Arenas (*Atenea*, año 20, tomo 71, no. 213, p. 168-180). [3300

A circumstantial but undocumented account of the murder of Bernardo Philippi, governor of Punta Arenas, by Patagonian Indians in 1852.

Braun Menéndez, Armando. Fuerte Bulnes. Buenos Aires. Ed. Emecé. 353 p. [3301

An account of the formal occupation of the Strait of Magellan by the Chilean government in 1843 and the vicissitudes of the settlement until its transfer to Punta Arenas six years later.

Fuenzalida Grandón, Alejandro. Don Valentín Letelier y su labor intelectual. Don José Toribio Medina. Mitre en Chile. Santiago. Prensas de la Univ. de Chile. 44 p. [3303

Three essays by the distinguished historian, author of *Lastarria y su Tiempo* and other works, who died in April 1942. Published in his memory by the University of Chile.

Orrego Barros, Carlos. Don Diego Barros Arana, rector del Instituto nacional, 1863-1873. Santiago. Prensas de la Univ. de Chile. 62 p. [3304

An account of the positivist principles and policies of the rector of Instituto Nacional, and an examination of his place in Chile's political and social development.

Published also in *An. univ. Chile*, no. 45-46, p. 15-72.

Pinilla, Norberto. La generación chilena de 1842. Santiago. Ed. de la Univ. de Chile. 227 p. [3305

This volume comprises "the most thorough and carefully documented study to date" of the intellectual renaissance in Chile of the Year '42 and the origins of the famous Literary Society. See review in *Hisp. amer. hist. rev.*, May, 1944, p. 301.

Valdés A., Benjamín. ¿Pretendió el gobierno francés tomar posesión del estrecho de Magallanes? (*Rev. chil. hist. geog.*, no. 103, julio-dic., p. 5-16). [3306

The author shows that there is no contemporary evidence to support the common belief that France planned to seize the Strait in 1843 when it was occupied by Chile, or that Chileans thought so at the time.

Valencia Avaria, Luis (ed.). Memorias íntimas de don Pedro Félix Vicuña Aguirre. Santiago. Imp. El Esfuerzo. 100 p. [3307

Very interesting and pungent commentaries by a prominent Chilean liberal upon political events from the beginning of the independence movement in 1810 to the election of President Bulnes in 1841.

COLOMBIA

Academia colombiana de historia. Archivo epistolar del general Domingo Caycedo. Tomo 1. Bogotá. Ed. ABC. (Bibl. de historia nacional, vol. 67). 308 p. [3308

A selection of 310 letters written to General Caycedo during the years 1804-1830, all but 38 of which date from 1819 and after. Published to commemorate the centenary of the death of one of Colombia's most prominent figures in the struggle for independence and during the early days of the republic.

Aguilera, Miguel. Análisis crítico de un ruidoso proceso. Bogotá. Ed. Voluntad. (Acad. colombiana de historia, Conferencias). p. 223-288. [3309

Penetrating analysis of the recently published evidence in the trial of Rupert Hand for the assassination of General José María Córdoba at the battle of El Santuario, October 17, 1829.

Cortázar, Roberto. Elogio de los historiadores Henao y Arrubla (*Bol. hist. antig.*, vol. 30, no. 346, agosto, p. 777–794). [3310
Interesting biographical information concerning the authors of the distinguished textbook on the history of Colombia.

Elías Ortiz, Sergio. Bibliografía de Eduardo Posada (*Bol. hist. antig.*, vol. 30, no. 341, marzo, p. 357–365). [3311
See following item.

García Samudio, Nicolás. La vida y la obra del doctor Eduardo Posada (*Bol. hist. antig.*, vol. 30, no. 341, marzo, p. 233–250). [3312
Dr. Posada, one of the founders of the Academia Colombiana de Historia and its first president, died on October 31, 1942. This issue of the *Boletín* is devoted entirely to his "life and works."

Guzmán Esponda, Eduardo. Aventuras del palacio de San Carlos. De Bolívar a Reyes. Las alfombras del general Salgar. El lujo de Holguín. Mosquera y Núñez (*Bol. hist. antig.*, vol. 30, no. 347–348, sept.–oct., p. 938–948). [3313
Interesting essay on the dramatic occurrences in this picturesque old colonial mansion which served as the official residence of the president of the republic from the time of Bolívar to that of Rafael Reyes.

INVESTIGACIÓN ADELANTADA AL GENERAL EDUARDO BONITTO. DOCUMENTOS OFICIALES. Bogotá. Imp. nacional. 72 p. [3314
Report of a military court concerning the participation of General Bonitto in the revolutionary plot against President Alfonso López.

Otero D'Costa, Enrique. José María Obando (*Bol. hist. antig.*, vol. 30, no. 344–345, junio–julio, p. 592–602). [3315
A vigorous defense of the romantic and tempestuous career of one of the great figures in the early history of the republic of Colombia.

Restrepo, José Manuel. Historia de la revolución de la República de Colombia en la América meridional. Tomo 3. Bogotá. Imp. nacional. (Bibl. popular de cultura colombiana, Historia, vol. 14). 299 p. [3316
First published in Paris in 1827. Volumes 1 and 2 of the present edition appeared in 1942.

Rippy, J. Fred. Dawn of the railway era in Colombia (*Hisp. amer. hist. rev.*, vol. 23, no. 4, Nov., p. 650–663). [3317
A very interesting essay on railway development down to the outbreak of the first World War.

Robertson, William Spence. An early threat of intervention by force in South America (*Hisp. amer. hist. rev.*, vol. 23, no. 4, Nov., p. 611–631). [3318
Refers to a thorny dispute between Colombia and France which grew out of apparently high-handed treatment of a Frenchman claiming diplomatic privileges as a consul (1834–1835). The dispute almost led to the use of force. [C. C. Griffin]

Salazar, Víctor M. Memorias de la guerra (1899–1902). Bogotá. Ed. A B C. 406 p. [3319
An account, from the Conservative angle, of the bitter civil "War of the thousand days," by a prominent general in the Conservative ranks, recently deceased.

ECUADOR

Albornoz, Víctor M. Don Rafael Torres (*Rev. centro estud. hist. geog. Cuenca*, vol. 10, entrega 38, marzo, p. 165–186). [3320

Luna, Miguel M. La casa solariega de los Larreátegui, 1878–1895. Guayaquil. Lib. de E. A. Uzcátegui. 80 p., ilus. [3321

Parks, Lois F., and **Gustave A. Nuermberger.** The sanitation of Guayaquil (*Hisp. amer. hist. rev.*, vol. 23, no. 2, May, p. 197–221). [3322
An historical account of the yellow fever scourge in Ecuador's principal seaport, and of the efforts, chiefly by the United States Government and the Rockefeller Foundation, to achieve its elimination.

PARAGUAY

Amarilla Fretes, Eduardo. Independencia del Paraguay. Asunción. Imp. El Arte. (Inst. paraguayo de investigaciones históricas). 26 p. [3323
A brief statement of 14 pages tracing the events from 1810 leading to the Declaration of Independence of November 25, 1842, followed by documents.

Benítez, Justo Pastor. Estigarribia. El soldado del Chaco. Buenos Aires. Ed. Difusam. 234 p. [3324
A very sympathetic biography of the much lamented leader of the Paraguayan armies in the Chaco War, later president of Paraguay, by a lifelong friend who was closely associated with his political career.

Bray, Arturo. Hombres y épocas del Paraguay. Segunda ed. Prólogo de Higinio Arbo. Buenos Aires. Ed. Ayacucho. 186 p., ilus. [3325
Brief biographical sketches of eight presidents of Paraguay, including José Gaspar Francia, Carlos Antonio López and Francisco Solano López.

Ministerio de relaciones exteriores. Lista de ministros de relaciones exteriores del Paraguay desde la época de su independencia. Asunción. Imp. Nacional. 8 p. [3326

Ramos, R. Antonio. El Paraguay y el Brasil durante la dictadura de Francia (*Bol. inst. invest. hist.*, año 21, tomo 27, no. 93-96, julio, 1942-junio, 1943, p. 254-298). [3327
The author traces the relations between Brazil and Paraguay after 1810, and the reasons for the severance, by the dictator Francia, of commercial relations with Brazil through Mato Grosso.

Soler, Juan José. Hacia la unión nacional. Cuarenta años de vida pública. Buenos Aires. Imp. del Plata. 299 p. [3328
The general theme of the volume is Paraguay. The chapters are in reality essays on a variety of historical and current topics. The following chapters are of interest to the historian: El ajetreo de la política (Ch. II); El mariscal Estigarribia (Ch. IV); La democracia paraguaya (Ch. X).

PERU

Alayza y Paz Soldán, Luis. El mariscal Nieto, figura epónima de Moquegua (*Rev. escuela mil.*, Perú, año 18, no. 206, feb., p. 71-78). [3329
A brief review of the early years of Peruvian independence and of Nieto's political activities. Nieto is represented as the champion of democracy and constitutionality.

Basadre, Jorge. 5 de abril de 1879 (*Historia*, Lima, vol. 1, no. 4, set.-oct., p. 401-412). [3330
A detailed analysis, on the basis of new evidence, of the diplomatic background of the War of the Pacific.

———. En torno al Perú de 1900 a 1939 (*Historia*, Lima, vol. 1, no. 1, marzo-abril, p. 45-50). [3331
An extremely interesting and suggestive interpretative essay on Peruvian politics since the administration of President Piérola.

Lazo, Raimundo. Vigil, Palma, González Prada (*Univ. Habana*, año 8, no. 50-51, sept.-dic., p. 90-113). [3332
A very interesting essay on the personality and the intellectual contribution of three directors of the National Library in Lima.

Mariátegui, José Carlos. 7 ensayos de interpretación de la realidad peruana. Segunda ed. Lima. Bibl. Amauta. 275 p. [3333
A collection of articles which appeared originally in *Mundial* and *Amauta*. Published in book form in 1928 and several times since.

Martínez, Santiago. Prefectos de Arequipa, 1825-1943. Arequipa. Tip. Valverde. 212 p., ilus. [3334

Stewart, Watt. El último negocio de Meiggs en el Perú (*Historia*, Lima, vol. 1, no. 3, julio-agosto, p. 238-251). [3335
Frantic efforts of Henry Meiggs to save his railway enterprises in Peru from financial ruin and to resume construction, in face of the fiscal crisis in the republic in the years 1875-1877.

Ugarteche, Pedro, and Evaristo San Cristóval. Mensajes de los presidentes del Perú. Vol. 1, 1821-1867. Lima. Lib. Gil. 486 p. [3336
The volume opens with the address of San Martín when he resigned the supreme command to the Congress of 1822, and ends with the message read by Gen. Mariano Ignacio Prado at the opening of the Constituent Assembly of 1867.

Ulloa, Alberto. El Perú y el Japón (*Rev. peruana der. int.*, tomo 3, no. 8, abril-junio, p. 111-134). [3337
Traces diplomatic relations with Japan from their inception in 1870 to the present time, with reference especially to the problems created after 1895 by Japanese immigration.

Vegas Castillo, Manuel. El primer ferrocarril del Perú (*Peruanidad*, vol. 3, no. 14, junio-agosto, p. 1116-1119). [3338
A brief account of the antecedents of the steam railway between Lima and Callao from the first proposal of the project by the government of Bolívar in May, 1826 to the opening of the road on May 17, 1851.

URUGUAY

(*See also item* 98)

ACTUACIÓN DE DON ANDRÉS LAMAS EN EL BRASIL. ARCHIVO DE FÉLIX FRÍAS (*Rev. bibl. nac.*, Buenos Aires, tomo 9, no. 27, tercer trim., p. 185-216). [3339
Seventeen letters to Félix Frías in Buenos Aires from Andrés Lamas in Rio de Janeiro and Petrópolis, all but two falling within the dates, July 7, 1855-Oct. 13, 1856.

Argentina. Academia nacional de la historia. La Nueva Era. Reproducción facsimilar. Homenaje al Instituto histórico y geográfico del Uruguay, en el centenario de su fundación. Introducción de Ricardo Levene. Buenos Aires. Ed. Peuser. (Bibl. de la Acad. nac. de la historia, tomo 21). 29, 10, 11, 8 p. [3340
La Nueva Era, directed by Andrés Lamas and having as its outstanding contributor Bartolomé Mitre, appeared in three issues between February 11 and March 8, 1846, just before the Revolution of April First led by General Rivera.

Braconnay, Claudio María. La Legión francesa en la defensa de Montevideo.

Montevideo. Ed. C. García. 305 p., ilus. [3341
The part played by the French Legion in the last years of the Guerra Grande, especially during the siege of Montevideo. The story covers the period from February 1843 to the fall of Rosas. Raúl Montero Bustamante wrote a brief introduction.

De María, Isidoro. La Guerra Grande (*Rev. nac.*, Montevideo, año 6, tomo 21, no. 61, enero, p. 133-139). [3342
Brief review, from the Uruguayan angle, of relations between Argentina and Uruguay, 1828-1843, leading to the siege of Montevideo by Oribe. A reprint of the Prologue by De María of "Anales de la defensa de Montevideo."

Díaz, César. Memorias, 1842-1852. Arroyo grande. Sitio de Montevideo. Caseros. Prólogo de José M. Fernández Saldaña. Buenos Aires. Ed. argentinas Solar. 320 p. [3343
Reprint of the *Memorias* of the Uruguayan general, first published by his nephew, Adriano Díaz, in Buenos Aires in 1878.

Erserguer, Enrique V. Cosas del Uruguay. En torno a la década 1933-1942. Montevideo. Ed. A. Monteverde. 313 p. [3344
Comments and notes on current politics and national issues.

Frugoni, Emilio. Génesis y formación de un destino democrático (*Nosotros*, segunda época, año 8, no. 84, marzo, p. 238-253). [3345
The author finds the sources of the predominantly democratic sentiment of the people of Uruguay in the character of the early colonists, the pastoral environment, the democratic mentality of the leader of independence, José Artigas, and in the later current of immigration from Europe.

Galain, Ramón L. Al servicio del partido. Hilvanando recuerdos. Montevideo. Ed. C. García. 143 p. [3346
Memoirs by an active member of the Partido Blanco, covering the years from 1885 to 1930.

González, Ariosto Domingo. ¿Orientales o uruguayos? Montevideo. Imp. El Siglo ilustrado. 70 p. [3347
In reply to the assertion of Ángel H. Vidal the author assembles evidence to show the antiquity and universality of the term *uruguayo*. González argues that the term *oriental* was used rather infrequently in the early years of independence. Inclusion of the term *oriental* in the official name of the republic was not a spontaneous act which condensed the glories of the revolutionary period. The author then proceeds to show that the term *uruguayo* is at least as valid as the one advocated by Vidal.

Herrera y Thode, Daniel. El Dr. Lucas Obes en los esplendores de su época. Montevideo. Ed. Archivo general de la nación. 131 p. [3348
A sympathetic sketch of an Uruguayan statesman active during the first half of the 19th century. Undocumented.

Jáureguy, Miguel Ángel. El carnaval de Montevideo en el siglo 19 (*Rev. nac.*, Montevideo, año 6, tomo 22, no. 66, junio, p. 368-395). [3349
Evocation of popular customs in the River Plate countries during the past century.

Lamas, Andrés. Escritos. Tomo 2. Montevideo. Imp. L. I. G. U. (Inst. histórico y geográfico del Uruguay). xxx, 350 p. [3350
The title of the volume is somewhat misleading since it contains only one of Lamas' writings, the famous declaration written in Brazil entitled "Andrés Lamas a sus compatriotas" (p. 1-90). In an appendix are reproduced letters to and by Lamas which serve to throw light on certain points discussed in the declaration (p. 91-172). The rest of the volume is given over to the reproduction of three pamphlets dealing with contemporary political problems.

Magariños de Mello, Mateo J. La misión de Florencio Varela a Londres, 1843-1844 (*Rev. hist.*, Montevideo, segunda época, año 37, tomo 14, no. 40-42, dic., p. 1-281). [3351
A detailed study of Varela's efforts to secure British support in Montevideo's struggle against Rosas.

Martínez, José Luciano. José Cándido Bustamante (*Rev. nac.*, Montevideo, año 6, tomo 21, no. 63, marzo, p. 393-404). [3352
Biographical sketch of an eminent Uruguayan journalist, soldier and politician, 1832-1885.

Montero Bustamante, Raúl. La Guerra Grande (*Rev. nac.*, Montevideo, año 6, tomo 21, no. 62, feb., p. 161-200). [3353
The battle of Arroyo Grande, December 6, 1842, in which the foes of Rosas under General Rivera were routed by General Oribe; and the subsequent refusal by Rosas to permit Oribe to proceed to the capture of Montevideo.

———. 1828 (*Rev. nac.*, Montevideo, año 6, tomo 21, no. 61, enero, p. 118-132). [3354
Dithyrambic account of the conquest of Misiones by General Fructuoso Rivera in 1828 during the war against Brazil. Reveals the bitter personal jealousies among the Uruguayan leaders.

Palomeque, Alberto. Juan Carlos Gómez y Artigas (*Rev. nac.*, Montevideo, año 6, tomo 22, no. 64, abril, p. 5-18). [3355
Chapter from an unpublished book written in 1922, defending José Artigas against the censures of Juan Carlos Gómez in *La Tribuna* in April, 1857.

Pivel Devoto, Juan E. Historia de los partidos políticos en el Uruguay. Montevideo. Tip. Atlántida, 1942-1943. 2 vols. [3356

REVOLUCIÓN DEL DOCTOR BERNARDO BERRO EN EL URUGUAY (*Rev. bibl. nac.*, Buenos Aires, tomo 9, no. 28, cuarto trim., p. 482-490). [3357
Letters of Félix Frías to Gustavo Heber, written in Buenos Aires, February 25-March 11, 1868.

Salgado, José. El primer centenario del Sitio Grande (*Rev. nac.*, Montevideo, año 6, tomo 21, no. 62, feb., p. 244-248). [3358
Reflections inspired by the centenary of the beginning of the eight years' siege of Montevideo by Oribe, 1843-1851.

VENEZUELA

Álamo, Antonio. Referencias para la historia (*Bol. centro hist larense*, año 2, no. 6, segundo trim, abril-junio, p. 3-15). [3360
Reminiscense of the "War of Liberation" against President Cipriano Castro in 1902.

Perera, Ambrosio. Historia orgánica de Venezuela. Caracas. Ed. Venezuela. 326 p. [3362
A brief survey in 258 pages of the political, judicial and territorial organization of Venezuela from the sixteenth century to the present, over two-thirds of the space being devoted to the years since 1821. In an index of 58 pages are inserted many long explanatory notes regarding historical details not included in the body of the text. A very useful book of reference.

Pinzón, Rafael. La evolución del caudillo en Venezuela (*Bitácora*, vol. 2, cuad. 6-7, agosto-sept., p. 14-35). [3363
A somewhat lyrical commentary on the phenomenon of *caudillismo* in Venezuela.

Zubrillaga Perera, Cecilio. Jacinto Lara y la política regional de hace un siglo, vista en documentos inéditos (*Bol. centro hist. larense*, año 2, no. 7, tercer trim., julio-set., p. 33-44). [3364
Traces the activities of general Lara in Barquisimeto in 1842-1843, and adduces evidence to show that Lara's political ideology as leader of the regional party "Unidos" corresponded to the program of the national conservative party.

ADDENDA

Acevedo, Eduardo. Manual de historia uruguaya después de Artigas. Tomo segundo. Período de organización nacional. La acción de nuestros partidos políticos desde la primera presidencia constitucional en 1830 hasta el golpe de estado de 1933. El Uruguay a través de un siglo en seis de sus aspectos principales. Montevideo. Tall. gráf 33. (Univ. de la República Oriental del Uruguay, Anales, año 49, entrega no. 151). 1942. 991 p., ilus. [3365
The first four chapters are a reprint of chapters in Acevedo's *Historia del Uruguay*, tomo II, published in 1919. They are followed by a historical sketch (270 p.) of Uruguayan history from the election of Rivera in 1830 to the *coup d'état* of President Terra in 1933, with special reference to freedom of the press. Thereafter 478 pages are devoted to a survey throughout the same century of population, public education, money and banking, commerce and industry, public health, and finance.

Buceta Basigalup, Juan Carlos. Apuntes para la historia del periodismo argentino. Segunda ed. Buenos Aires. Imp. de Niños expósitos. 1942. 127 p. [3366
Brief notes on the growth and development of Argentina's daily and periodical press since its early beginnings. There is an index of names and of titles of publications mentioned in the text.

Duprey, Jacques. Alejandro Dumas, escritor al servicio de Montevideo y adversario de Rosas. Trad. de Isabel Gilbert de Pereda. Buenos Aires. Ed. Giles. 1942. 253 p. [3367
An extensive critical analysis of *Montevideo ou une Nouvelle Troie* and other writings of Alexandre Dumas bearing upon the relations between Uruguay and Juan Manuel de Rosas.

Font Ezcurra, Ricardo. Rivadavia y el proletariado. Buenos Aires. Ed. de la Rev. del Inst. de investigaciones históricas Juan Manuel de Rosas. 1942. 48 p. [3368
Makes Rivadavia responsible for the provision in the Constitution of 1826 which denied to wage earners the right to vote.

Ibarguren, Federico. Rosas y la tradición hispanoamericana. Buenos Aires. 1942. 28 p. [3369
In the view of this writer Rosas is hated because he fought against the ideology of the French Revolution, because he symbolized the mentality, the mores and the political conceptions inherited from Catholic and Imperial Spain, and because he was the Restorer of the Hispanic American tradition in Argentina.

HISTORY: BRAZIL

BY

ALEXANDER MARCHANT

GENERAL STATEMENT

Two works on the Jesuits and a synthesis of Brazilian life stand out among the year's books in history. Serafim Leite completed the third and fourth volumes of his history of the Company of Jesus in Brazil. Fittingly enough, they were handsomely printed in the Imprensa Nacional and published under government auspices. Aurélio Porto's study of the Jesuits on the southern border is the first volume of a valuable contribution, and reflects much credit on the publishing policy of the Serviço do Patrimônio Histórico e Artístico Nacional. Of wider interest, and reflecting an historical temperament of a high order, is Fernando de Azevedo's *A Cultura Brasileira*, the first of the introductory volumes of the 1940 census. While it is more an interpretation than, strictly speaking, a history, it remains one of the most considered and inclusive syntheses that has appeared in recent years.

The level of scholarship shown in the use of documentary sources and in the careful weighing of evidence unfortunately has not been maintained by most of the authors of the rest of the year's work. Biography continues to be popular and is reaching out to deal with a number of exceedingly interesting but hitherto neglected personages, but only too seldom do biographers make use of adequate documentation. One of the most interesting trends is a slight increase in the number and quality of editions of diaries and correspondence of eminent or interesting people. Provided that the published texts are faithful to the originals, these volumes should do a good deal to stimulate the search for, and competent use of this occasionally refractory but generally interesting material. Translations of travellers' account continue to bring texts in Portuguese within the reach of the inquisitive reader. Possibly because the war has indirectly made access to books and documents more difficult, not all editors of translations have seized the opportunity to take into account in their annotations the bibliography that has accumulated around a book or a subject since the time of the writing of the original text. Another trend that is obvious and threatens to become painful is the rise in the price of all books, accompanied by progressive deterioration in the quality of paper and printing.

Keeping track of new books in history has always been a problem, especially for the student outside Brazil, but that task may now be lessened somewhat by the prospective appearance of a bibliography devoted exclusively to the history of Brazil. By an administrative order of March 27, 1943, the Minister of Foreign Relations created a Committee for the Study of Texts concerning the History of Brazil,[1] which has the duty of keeping abreast of

---

[1] The committee, which published its first report and list in 1944 to cover the second half of 1943, was composed originally of Rodolfo Garcia, Heitor Lyra, E. F. de Souza Docca, Hélio Vianna, and Luiz Camillo de Oliveira Netto, with Roberto Luiz Assumpção de Araújo as secretary.

historical writing concerning Brazil, published in Brazil and abroad; of issuing a list of such works periodically; of indicating any errors that may be found; and of undertaking such historical studies as the Minister of Foreign Relations may desire.

In the United States, *Mid-America* has succeeded in publishing a considerable body of material emphasizing political and religious aspects of Brazilian colonial history, and it is to be hoped that the intention of publishing the articles in book form is carried out.

BIBLIOGRAPHY

(*See also sections on* Archives, Brazilian Art, *and* International Relations)

GENERAL

Bevilaqua, Clovis. Revivendo o passado. No. 7: Figuras e datas, 1892. Rio de Janeiro. Ed. Borsoi. 25 p. [3370

Caetano, Marcelo. Do Conselho ultramarino ao Conselho do império. Lisboa. Div. de publ. e bibl., Agência geral das colónias. 122 p. [3371
General outline of the development of Portuguese colonial administration from 1580 to 1937. Chapter 3, Creation of the Conselho ultramarino (1643), and chapter 4, The Conselho ultramarino. primeiro período (1643-1833) provide background for Brazilian colonial history. Appendix of documents.

Calmon, Pedro. História do Brasil. 3 vols. São Paulo. Cia. ed. nacional. (Bibl. ped. bras., série 5, Brasiliana, vols. 176, 176A, 176B.) 476 p., 495 p., 448 p. [3372
Vol. 1 was published in 1939 (incorrectly listed in *Handbook no. 6*, item 3569, as having appeared in 1940); vol. 2 in 1941; vol. 3 in 1943.
A general history, to stand beside this prolific author's *História da Civilização Brasileira* and *História Social do Brasil*, written on the premise that the volume of recent Brazilian historiography makes possible "the integral revision of Brazilian history." Devotes a volume to a century, with subtitles that characterize each period: vol. 1, As origens (1500-1600); vol. 2, A formação (1600-1700); vol. 3, A organização (1700-1800). A fourth volume is now in preparation on the Empire (1800-1900).

Carmo, J. A. Pinto do. Bibliografia de Capistrano de Abreu. Rio de Janeiro. Imp. nacional. (Min. da educação e saúde, Inst. nac. do livro, Col. B 1, Bibliog. 3). 133 p., ilus. [3373
An indispensable work as much to students of Brazilian history as to those of Brazilian hisoriography. The compiler, who also contributes a biographical sketch of Capistrano, explains why his list is not entirely complete. First list gives Capistrano's own articles and books; the second, the prefaces, annotations and introductions that he contributed to books by other authors; the third, translations by him: the fourth, selected articles about Capistrano and reviews of some of his books. Reproductions of sample pages and manuscripts.

Chandler, Charles Lyon. O Brasil e os Estados Unidos de 1774 a 1820 (*Rev. inst. Brasil-Estados Unidos*, vol. 1, no. 3, set., p. 63-77). [3374
To demonstrate that the Good Neighbor policy between Brazil and the United States goes back to the colonial period of both countries.

Costa, Didio I. A. da. História marítima do Rio de Janeiro (*Bol. min. trab. ind. com.*, ano 9, no. 102, fev., p. 243-265). [3375
Gonçalo Coelho founded a factory in Guanabara Bay; this was the establishment to which the natives gave their word signifying "casa de branco," transcribed by the Portuguese as "carioca."

D'Alessandro, Alexandre. A Escola politécnica de São Paulo. Histórias da sua história. São Paulo. Ed. Revista dos tribunais. 306 p., ilus. [3376
The first volume of several to come.

Garcia, Rodolfo. Exotismos franceses originários da língua tupí (*Rev. acad. bras. let.*, ano 42, vol. 65, jan.-junho, p. 157-202). [3377
Though more a study in etymology, this well-annotated word-list should be brought to the attention of historians for the light it casts on words of Tupí origin in early written sources, especially of the XVI and XVII centuries.

Goycochêa, Castilhos. Fronteiras e fronteiros. São Paulo. Cia. ed. nacional. (Bibl. ped. bras., série 5, Brasiliana, vol. 230). 298 p. [3378
Studies of Brazilian boundary settlements, with interesting and revealing sidelights on the people and issues involved. Chapter 8, "O fronteiro mór do Império," calls attention to the contributions of Duarte da Ponte Ribeiro (Conselheiro and later Barão da Ponte Ribeiro), who made the study of the national boundaries a matter of prime concern in the Foreign Office and who created the *mapoteca* of the Itamaraty.

Lima Júnior, Augusto de. A capitania de Minas Gerais. Prefácio de Dr. Jaime Cortesão. Rio de Janeiro. Livr. Zélio Valverde. 334 p., ilus. [3379]
Second edition.

Lobo, Luiz. História militar do Pará. Rio de Janeiro. Ed. Bedeschi. (Bibl. militar, vol. 65). 144 p. [3380]
An aspect of the history of the Province of Pará, mainly between 1801 and 1889. Documents.

Moya, Salvador de (ed.). Instituto genealógico brasileiro. Anuario genealógico brasileiro, ano 4, 1942. São Paulo. 1943? 364 p. [3381]
Invaluable reference annual, giving genealogical and biographical information on royal families connected with Brazil; the Brazilian episcopate; holders of titles under the Empire, with corrections and amplification of information given in earlier numbers; foreign nobility; and certain Brazilian families of distinction. The great number of photographs, some of considerable age, gives added interest.

Pirassinunga, Adailton Sampaio. Ensino militar no Brasil (*Rev. inst. hist. geog. Rio Grande do Sul*, ano 23, no. 89, primer trim., p. 55–123). [3382]
Concentrates on the Real Academia da Artilharia, Fortificação e Desenho da Cidade do Rio de Janeiro, founded 1793; much interesting detail and quotation from documents of the time, with the statutes of the Academy and a musterroll for 1795 in an appendix.

Poliano, Luis Marques. Ordens honoríficas do Brasil. História, organização, padrões legislação. Rio de Janeiro. Imp. nacional. 324 p., ilus. [3383]
Invaluable specialized reference work, issued under the joint auspices of the Minister of Foreign Relations and the Minister of War.

Sanmartin, Olinto. Aspectos econômicos da velha Porto Alegre (*Rev. inst. hist. geog. Rio Grande do Sul*, ano 23, no. 89, primer trim., p. 125–137). [3384]
Brief notes of value of properties, commercial movement, and living costs in the city, mainly between 1810 and 1850.

Serrano, Jonathas. Resumen de la historia del Brasil. Rio de Janeiro. Imp. Nacional. (Min. de relaciones exteriores, Div. de cooperção intelectual, Col. de estudios bras., no. 2.) 127 p. [3385]
Spanish text of a summary outline of Brazilian history issued by the government for the edification of the Spanish-reading republics.

Trindade, Raimundo. Genealogias da zona do Carmo. Ponte Nova. Est. gráf. Gutenberg, Irmãos Pena. 568 p. [3386]
Detailed genealogies, invaluable as a checklist of names and personages in a long-settled part of Minas.

Vidal, Barros. Bento Manuel. Paisagem humana de heroismo e bravura (*Cultura política*, año 3, no. 24, fev., p. 64–73). [3387]
Sketch of Bento Manuel Ribeiro, 1783–1855, whose military career is associated with the history of the Brazilian army in Cisplatine affairs.

COLONIAL AND REVOLUTIONARY PERIODS

(*See also items* 490, 4141)

Almeida, Aluísio de. Araritaguaba (*Rev. arq. mun.*, São Paulo, ano 9, vol. 91, julho, p. 123–133). [3388]
Biographical notice of António Cardoso Pimentel, born 1630, with description of Araritaguaba, his holdings in São Paulo.

Azevedo, Victor de. Manuel Preto, o moço (*Rev. arq. mun.*, São Paulo, ano 8, vol. 90, maio–junho, p. 119–139). [3389]
Bandeirante history, with genealogical comment on the family of Manuel Preto.

Belmonte. No tempo dos bandeirantes. Terceira ed. São Paulo, Rio de Janeiro. Cia. Melhoramentos de São Paulo. [3390]
This revised and augmented edition of a highly colorful and valuable historical work is announced as the definitive one. It has illustrations by the author, who is well known as an artist. For the original edition, see *Handbook, no. 5, 1939*, item 3893. [S. Putnam]

Belo, L. de Oliveira. Algumas verdades acêrca do descobrimento do Brasil (*Rev. soc. geog. Rio de Janeiro*, tomo 50, p. 50–75, mapas). [3391]
Lecture given in the Gabinete Português de Leitura do Rio de Janeiro, April 28, 1943, and repeated, with maps and slides in the Sociedade de Geografia do Rio de Janeiro, May 28, 1943. Discusses whether Brazil was discovered accidentally or purposefully. Assumes the existence of a policy of secrecy and concludes that discovery was purposeful. With reference to the last anchorage of Cabral, concludes that Cabral anchored on the morning of April 23 opposite the mouth of the Rio Cramimuam and on the morning of the 25th within the Baía da Santa Cruz, in the stretch at present named Cabrália, i.e., between 16° 16' and 16° 19' S. lat. Points out the confusion surrounding the name Porto Seguro, which he suggests could be cleared up by archival research.

Bezerra, Alcides. A filosofia na fase colonial (*An. soc. bras. fil.*, ano 3, no. 3, 1942, 1943, p. 18–41). [3392]
Brief outline of a large and neglected subject, summarizing the work in philosophy of Padre Vieira, Diogo Gomes Carneiro, Manoel do Desterro, Frei Matheus d Encarnação Pina, Nuno Marques Pereira, Mathias Aires, Frei Gaspar da Madre d Deus, Francisco Luiz Leal, and Fre Caneca.

Butler, Ruth Lapham. Duarte da Costa, second governor-general of Brazil (*Mid-America*, vol. 25, new series, vol. 14, no. 3, July, p. 163–179). [3394

Careful study of the principal events in the short governorship of the "unhappy, inept, and unimaginative da Costa, whose governorship can best be summarized as a somewhat sterile interlude" between those of Tomé de Sousa and Mem de Sá.

Casal, Manuel Ayres de. Corografia brasílica, ou Relação histórico-geográfica do reino do Brasil. São Paulo. Ed. Cultura. (Série brasílica, 1–2). 2 vols. [3395

A reprinting of Padre Casal's famous descriptive geography of Brazil, with his historical footnotes and commentaries; first published in Rio de Janeiro, Impressão Régia, 1817. The present edition is in the Série Brasílica, directed by José Peres, but has no annotations and no indication of who prepared the text for this printing.

Cortesão, Jaime (ed.). A carta de Pero Vaz de Caminha. Com um estudo de Jaime Cortesão. Rio de Janeiro. Ed. Livros de Portugal. (Col. clássicos e contemporâneos, no. 1). 354 p. [3396

Fine photographic reproduction of the original letter, with a transcription and a translation into modern Portuguese; biographical and historical chapters give background; appendix of documents relating to Pero Vaz.

Coutinho, Gago. Descobrimento do Brasil. Coordenação em mapa das rotas de descobrimento no Atlântico Sul, especialmente a de Cabral (*Cultura política*, ano 3, no. 30, agôsto, p. 85–102). [3397

Maintains that Cabral reached Brazil by design, because Brazil had already been discovered before 1497 by Portuguese exploring the sea-lane that Vasco da Gama used in going to India. Insists that the Portuguese kings had a "policy of secrecy."

Espinosa, J. Manoel. José de Anchieta: "Apostle of Brazil" (*Mid-America*, vol. 25, new series, vol. 14, no. 4, Oct., p. 250–274). [3398

First part; second part appears in *Mid-America*, January, 1944. Though brief, the two parts of this article provide one of the few biographic sketches in English of one of the most attractive figures among the early Jesuits in Brazil. It is to be hoped that this article will grow into a full-length book on Anchieta—something that is much needed and that would be especially valuable if published in English.

Fouquet, Karl. O cêrco de Igaraçú, 1549. São Paulo. Tip. Gutenberg. (Soc. Hans Staden, folheto no. 6.) 31 p., ilus. [3399

Interesting re-examination of the sources, resulting in the conclusion that the commonly accepted date of the siege (1548) is incorrect.

Franco, Arthur Martins. Diogo Pinto e a conquista de Guarapuava. Curitiba. Tip. João Haupt & cia. 270 p., ilus. [3400

The first volume of a new series begun by the Conselho Administrativo do Museu Paranaense as a place of publication for regional history. Because publication of this volume coincides with the 250th anniversary of the founding of the city of Curitiba, the Historical Section of the Museu makes it a tribute to the occasion. A study of the work of Diogo Pinto de Azevedo Portugal, of the expedition of 1809–1810 to drive the hostile natives from the Campos de Guarapuava, and of the re-establishment by Diogo Pinto of settlement in that region. Large numbers of documents interpolated in the text; appendix of documents; reproductions of old maps. On the whole, an attractive and interesting study of a neglected phase of the history of white settlement, based on archival and secondary sources.

Greenlee, William B. The first half-century of Brazilian history (*Mid-America*, vol. 25, new series, vol. 14, no. 2, April, p. 91–120). [3401

Useful succinct summary, sketching the discovery by Cabral and subsequent early voyages to Brazil; the effect on Portuguese policy produced by attempts of the French to occupy Brazil; the general characteristics of settlement by the *donatários;* and the political and religious policy of John III, as reflected in his sending Tomé de Sousa as governor in 1549.

Jaeger, Luis Gonzaga. História da introdução do gado no Rio Grande do Sul. Cristóvão de Mendoza ou Manuel Gonçalves Ribeiro? (*Rev. inst. hist. geog. Rio Grande do Sul*, ano 23, no. 90, segundo trim., p. 217–245). [3402

Result of a debate elaborated in several papers before the Instituto Histórico e Geográfico do Rio Grande do Sul on the questions of when, and by whom, cattle was introduced into Rio Grande do Sul and of how the cattle men should be described (*estancieiro, fazendeiro,* or *criador*). Expresses the conclusion of the Instituto that the year is 1634, the man is Christóvão de Mendoza (the anniversary of whose death is suggested as an appropriate date for celebration in this connection), and the proper term is *estanceieiro*.

Leite, Serafim. História da Companhia de Jesús no Brasil. Tomos 3–4. Rio de Janeiro. Imp. nacional. Lisboa. Livr. Portugália. 2 vols.: xxviii, 487; xxv, 440 p., ilus. [3404

Vols. 1 and 2 appeared in 1938; see *Handbook, no. 4, 1938,* item 3411a. At the suggestion of Afrânio Peixoto and Rodolfo Garcia, publication of vols. 3 and 4 was undertaken by the Instituto Nacional do Livro of the Ministry of Education of Brazil. Typography and format have been carefully and successfully considered to make them consistent with the first two volumes.

A superb work, maintaining the high

level of masterly organization of material, command of archival sources, distinction of style, and fine workmanship in controlling a formidable mass of footnotes and appendixes that made vols. 1 and 2 so notable. Vols. 3 and 4 concern Jesuit work in the north of Brazil. Vol. 3 is subtitled: *Norte—1) Fundações e entradas, séculos XVII–XVIII,* and deals with Ceará, Maranhão, Pará, and Amazonas, with the spreading out of the Jesuits there and with the organization of their work. Vol. 4 is subtitled: *Norte—2) Obra e assuntos gerais, séculos XVII–XVII.* Its five books deal with A magna questão da liberdade; aldeamento e catequese dos índios; o grave assunto das subsistências; regime interno e apostolado externo; and ciências, letras e artes.

Machado, José de Alcántara. Vida e morte do bandeirante. Introdução de Sérgio Milliet. São Paulo. Livr. Martins. (Bibl. de literatura brasileira, 5). 236 p., ilus. [3405]

Attractive edition, with illustrations by J. Wasth Rodrigues, of what has become a standard work on the material culture of the *bandeirantes;* first published 1929.

Marchant, Alexander. Do escambo à escravidão. As relações económicas de portugueses e indios na colonização do Brasil, 1500–1580. Trad. de Carlos Lacerda. São Paulo, Rio de Janeiro, etc. Cia. ed. nacional. (Bibl. pedagógica bras., Serie 5, Brasiliana, vol. 225). 205 p. [3406]

Excellent translation by Carlos Lacerda.

Martins, Francisco Pires. A propósito de Afonso Sardinha (*Rev. arq. mun.,* São Paulo, ano 9, vol. 92, agôsto-set., p. 99–111). [3407]

Biographical notice of Afonso Sardinha (fl. 1550–1600), *fazendeiro* in São Paulo, armateur and dealer in the African slave trade, and an early developer of mining.

Melo, Mário. Pródromos da independência em Pernambuco (*Cultura política,* ano 3, no. 24, fev., p. 39–45). [3408]

Text, with explanatory notes, of a letter of the governor of Pernambuco to the Viceroy of Brazil, March 6, 1821, concerning the revolution in Bahia, February 10.

———. Rebelião de frades no século 17 (*Cultura política,* ano 3, no. 26, abril, p. 110–113). [3409]

Brief notes, drawn mainly from the collection *Documentos Históricos,* of the movement among Brazilian religious to declare their independence from their European brethren.

Millares Carlo, Agustín. Más datos sobre el Apóstol del Brasil (*Fil. letras,* tomo 5, no. 10, abril-junio, p. 245–249). [3410]

Brief bibliographical notes, by the author of the *Ensayo de una Bibliografía de Escritores Naturales de las Islas Canarias* (Madrid, 1932), with reference to documents of a lawsuit involving Juan de Anchieta (nephew of José).

Moreira, Albertino G. Iguapé e outras cidades mortas (*Rev. arq. mun.,* São Paulo, ano 9, vol. 93, out.-dez., p. 61–73). [3411]

Notes on an ancient São Paulo city, in existence before 1647, once alive, but now, like a number of others, only a shadow.

ORDENS RÉGIAS (*Rev. arq. mun.,* São Paulo, ano 8, vol. 88, jan.-fev., p. 217–222; vol. 89, março-abril, p. 205–210; vol. 90, maio-junho, p. 149–154; ano 9, vol. 91, julho, p. 135–139; vol. 93, out.-dez., p. 89–93). [3412]

Concerning the Senado da Câmara da Cidade de São Paulo, 1739–1740.

Ott, Fidelis. Um autógrafo de frei Antônio de St. Maria Jaboatão (*Rev. arq. mun.,* São Paulo, ano 9, vol. 92, agôsto-set., p. 119–136). [3413]

Text of two dissertations by the author of the *Orbe Seráfico,* entitled "Se há na América a planta sensitiva" and "Se é certo produzir-se também na América a herva que abranda o ferro como afirma certo autor." Excerpted from a MS of Jaboatão's works found by Pe. Ott in the Arquivo do Convento de São Francisco in Baía, "Obras académicas e outras várias, prozas e versos, feitas e recitadas na Academia Brasílica dos Renascidos . . . 6 de junho, dia, em que fazia annos o Fidelissimo Rey e Senhor D. Joseph I ano de 1759." For the background of the history of ideas against which these excerpts should be placed, see Alberto Lamego, *A Académia Brasílica dos Renascidos* (Paris, Gaudio, 1923), and A. P. Whitaker, *Latin America and the Enlightenment* (New York, Lippincott, 1942).

Pinto, Luiz de Aguiar Costa. Lutas de famílias no Brasil. Éra colonial (*Rev. arq. mun.,* São Paulo, ano 8, vol. 88, jan.-fev., p. 7–125). [3415]

Excellent study of a well-known but, curiously enough, little-studied phase of the early days of great and powerful families who, in the absence of effective rule by representatives of the king, governed themselves, administered their own justice, generally conducted their affairs to further family interests and to satisfy family honor, and (perhaps the most striking aspect) "went a-feudin'" in inter-family vendettas. Part 1 is general background: chap. 1, "A vingança privada e a solidariedade da família"; chap. 2, "O declínio da vingança privada" (showing the rise of political power and the decline of *direito interfamilial*); chap. 3, "A sociedade brasileira, a família, e o estado." Part 2 is *estudos de casos:* chap. 4, "Os Pires e Camargos" (the most famous and best-known case of inter-family war); chap. 5, "Os Montes e Feitozas" (a case-study from the Northeast); and chap. 6, "A justiça interna da família." Appendix of documents to each chapter. See also *Handbook, no. 8, 1942,* item 3444.

Pôrto, Aurélio. História das missões orientais do Uruguai. Rio de Janeiro. Imp.

nacional. (Serv. do Pat. hist. artíst. nac., publ. no. 9). 624 p., ilus. [3416
The first volume of two; the history of the region and people, and of the entry of the Jesuits, based on a wide range of documentary sources; many hitherto unused; see General Statement.

Sommer, F. Os Schetz da Antuerpia e de S. Vicente (*Rev. arq. mun.*, São Paulo, ano 9, vol. 93, out.–dez., p. 75–86). [3417
Excellent study of the wealthy Antwerp capitalist family which invested in São Vicente (São Paulo) sugar in the sixteenth century.

Varnhagen, Francisco Adolfo de. História das lutas com os holandeses no Brasil de 1624 a 1654. São Paulo. Ed. Cultura. (Série brasílica, no. 3). 345 p. [3418

Vasconcelos, Simão de. Vida do veneravel padre José de Anchieta. Prefácio de Serafim Leite. Rio de Janeiro. Imp. Nacional. (Min. da educação e saúde, Inst. nacional do livro, Bibl. popular bras., 3). 2 vols. [3419
Very handy re-edition (6.5 by 5 in.) of this classic. Brief bio-bibliographical sketch by Pe. Leite. Based on first edition, Lisbon, 1672; modernized spelling and punctuation; omits the Latin poem in praise of Our Lady and the "Recopilação da vida do Padre José de Anchieta."

THE EMPIRE AND THE REPUBLIC

(*See also item* 4919)

Antunes, Dioclécio de Paranhos. Andrade Neves, o vanguardeiro! Rio de Janeiro. Ed. Bedeschi. (Bibl. Militar, vol. 64). 156 p. [3420
Biography of José Joaquim de Andrade Neves, Barão do Triunfo, 1807–1869, the brilliant cavalry officer of the Farroupilhas, Uruguayan, and Paraguayan wars, who died in 1869 after being wounded in the battle of Lomas Valentinas.

Armitage, João. História do Brasil desde o período da chegada da família de Bragança em 1808 até a abdicação de d. Pedro I. em 1831. Compilada à vista dos documentos públicos e outras fontes originais formando uma continuação da *História do Brasil* de Southey. Terceira ed. brasileira com anotações de Eugenio Egas e Garcia Júnior. Rio de Janeiro. Ed. Zelio Valverde. 389 p. [3421
A compound re-edition, consisting of the translation, published in 1837, signed "Por um Brasileiro," who is presumed to be Joaquim Teixeira de Macedo; amplified by the notes and additional material by Eugênio Egas to the second Brazilian edition, published in 1914; and rounded out by notes prepared especially for this version by Garcia Júnior.

Besouchet, Lídia (ed.). Correspondência política de Mauá no Rio da Prata, 1850–1885. São Paulo. Cia. ed. nacional. (Bibl. ped. bras., série 5, Brasiliana, vol. 227). 251 p., ilus. [3422
Apparently the first volume of two. This one is taken up almost entirely with correspondence with Andrés Lamas, and a few letters exchanged with other Uruguayans. The next volume is to cover correspondence with Argentines, such as Mitre and Urquiza. The present collection is one made by Miss Besouchet in the course of writing her "Mauá y Su Época" and is of the greatest value and interest to students of the nineteenth century in Brazil. Her preface (p. 6–50) is good background setting for the letters themselves, and her notes are helpful. No index; presumably one will be supplied when the volumes are complete.

Biblioteca nacional. Guerra dos farrapos. Ordens do dia do general Barão de Caxias, 1842–1845. Rio de Janeiro. Imp. nacional. (Bibl. Rio-grandense). 430 p. [3423
Text based on an authenticated copy of the Livro de Ordens do Dia do Comando em Chefe do Exército na Província do Rio Grande do Sul, November 7, 1842, to November 9, 1945, given to the Biblioteca Nacional by General E. F. Sousa Docca, president of the governing board of the Biblioteca Militar. Separate from vol. 63 of the *Anais da Biblioteca Nacional;* no notes or explanatory material.

Boiteux, Henrique. O marquês de Tamandaré. Um indígete brasiliense. Rio de Janeiro. Livr. Zélio Valverde. (Bibl. de grandes biografias, 4). 598 p., ilus. [3424
Full length biography of Joaquim Marques Lisboa, emphasizing his services to Brazil during war.

Boiteux, Lucas Alexandre. Marinha imperial versus Cabanagem. Rio de Janeiro. Imp. naval. (Ed. do Min. da marinha). 410 p., ilus. [3425
History of the way in which the Brazilian navy was used in suppressing the Cabanagem (or Cabanada) revolt in Pará in the 1830's.

Calmon, Pedro. Vida de dom Pedro primeiro, o rei cavaleiro. Segunda ed. aumentada. São Paulo. Cia ed. nac. (Bibl. pedagógica bras., Serie 5a, Brasiliana, vol. 226). 312 p., ilus. [3426
Second edition, with additional notes and documents, of this popular work, first published in 1933.

Chagas, Paulo Pinheiro. Teófilo Otoni e a colônia de Mucurí (*Rev. imig. col.,* ano 4, no. 3, set., p. 404–415). [3427
Sketch of Otoni's interest, 1848–1860, in the Companhia de Comércio e Navegação do Rio Mucurí, which, in connection with plans for colonization, was to open up eastern Minas Gerais.

Chediak, Antonio J. Carlos de Laet, o polemista. Rio de Janeiro. Ed. Valverde. [3428

Second series, mainly on political and literary themes, of the vitriolic polemics of this articulate and pugnacious conservative.

COLÔNIA DE PETRÓPOLIS 1846–1847 (*Rev. imig. col.*, ano 4, no. 3, set., p. 417–432). [3429

Reports of 1846 and 1847 presented to the Assembléia Legislativa Provincial of the State of Rio de Janeiro concerning the development of this colony established by Swiss settlers.

AS COLÔNIAS MERIDIONÁIS EM 1846. RELATÓRIOS APRESENTADOS AO BARÃO DE CAIRÚ, EM 1846, POR LUIZ FREDERICO KALKMANN (*Rev. imig. col.*, ano 4, no. 2, junho, p. 236–252). [3430

Documents, including a report of November 11, 1846, on the colony of São Pedro de Alcántara and one of November 28, 1846, on the colony of São Leopoldo, describing the conditions in each since 1830. Followed by a memorial by Kalkmann and Júlio Frederico Koeler to the Emperor, January 12, 1847, relative to the creating of a company to further German colonization in Brazil. Koeler is familiar as one of the leaders in the establishment of Petrópolis.

Costa, Renato. Síntesis de una vida, Mauá. Buenos Aires. Tall. gráf. Augusta. (Col. problemas americanos, 12). 59 p. [3431

Lectures given on December 27, 1941, on the occasion of the unveiling of the bust of Mauá in the Palace of Commerce of the Commercial Association of Pôrto Alegre. Based on Lídia Besouchet's interpretation, but goes farther in ascribing to Mauá a desire to exclude foreign capital from the development of the River Plate region, and consequently makes Mauá appear more "Americanist" than is perhaps the case.

DEBATES PARLAMENTARES SOBRE A COLÔNIA DONA FRANCISCA, 1850 (*Rev. imig. col.*, ano 4, no. 3, set., p. 446–463). [3432

Extracts from the *Anais da Câmara dos Deputados do Império* concerning the foundation of this early colony in Santa Catarina.

DEBATES PARLAMENTARES SÔBRE COLONISAÇÃO EM 1870 (*Rev. imig. col.*, ano 4, no. 2, junho, p. 334–350). [3433

Extracts from the *Anáis do Senado do Império*, September 15–16, 1870.

DOCUMENTOS HISTÓRICOS SÔBRE COLONISAÇÃO, 1847 (*Rev. imig. col.*, ano 4, no. 3, set., p. 433–445). [3434

Extract from the report of 1847 of the Repartição dos Negócios do Império, presented to the Assembléia Geral, advocating legislation to aid colonization.

Dutra, José Soares. Cairú. Precursor da economia moderna. Rio de Janeiro. Ed. Vecchi. 171 p. [3435

Rather slight study, emphasizing economic aspects, of a most interesting figure, José da Silva Lisboa, Visconde de Cairú, whose effect on Brazil in the first half of the nineteenth century has yet to be evaluated.

Egas, Eugenio. Libertação dos escravos (*Rev. acad. paulista let.*, ano 6, no. 22, junho, p. 48–64). [3436

Sketch of the circumstances leading to the abolition of slavery in Brazil in the period 1871–1888. [S. Mosk]

EMIGRAÇÃO PARA O BRASIL (*Rev. imig. col.*, ano 4, no. 2, junho, p. 253–263). [3437

Proposals by Dr. Oscar von Kopff, who had been in Brazil from 1851 to 1854, concerning German mass emigration to Brazil, accompanied by documents by José António Saraiva and Joaquim Maria Nascentes de Azambuja.

Goycochêa, Castilhos. Gumercindo Saraiva na guerra dos maragatos. Rio de Janeiro. Ed. Alba. 199 p. [3438

Short study of one of the final episodes of social and political separatism in the revolt of 1893 in the South.

IMIGRAÇÃO NORTE-AMERICANA PARA O BRASIL (*Rev. imig. col.*, ano 4, no. 2, junho, p. 264–333). [3439

Documents, 1866–1867, concerning Confederate migration to Brazil. Includes reports, letters, and memoranda of Joaquim Maria Nascentes de Azambuja, José António Saraiva, António Francisco de Paula e Souza, and Frank McMillan. Concerns Ballard Dunn (author of *Brazil, a Home for Southerners*), the brig *Derby* from Galveston, which was wrecked on the Cuban coast, and the projects of McMillan himself.

Kidder, Daniel P. Reminiscências de viagenes e permanência no Brasil (Províncias do Norte), compreendendo notícias históricas e geográficas do Império e das diversas províncias. São Paulo. Livr. Martins. (Bibl. hist. bras., no. 12). 266 p., ilus. [3440

Translation by Moacir N. Vasconcellos. The first part of this translation, covering Rio de Janeiro and the province of São Paulo, appeared in 1940; see *Handbook, no. 6, 1940*, item 3641. The "northern provinces" of this second part are Baía, Sergipe, Pernambuco, Rio Grande do Norte, Ceará, Piauí, Maranhão, and Pará.

Leclerc, Max. Cartas do Brasil. São Paulo. Cia. ed. nac. (Brasiliana, vol. 215). [3441

Translated, with notes, by Sergio Milliet; articles on Brazil in 1889–1890 by this celebrated correspondent of the *Journal des Débats*.

Lima Sobrinho, Barbosa. Centenário do Almirante Jaceguai (*Rev. acad. bras. let.*, ano 42, vol. 65, jan.–junho, p. 68–95). [3442

Sketch of Artur Silveira da Mota, Baron of Jaceguai, Brazilian sailor who distinguished himself at Humaitá.

Lopes, Valdemar. Varnhagen e a mudança da capital (*Cultura política*, ano 3, no. 32, set., p. 158–166). [3443

Varnhagen's inclinations toward an interior rather than a maritime capital, as set forth in his *Memorial Orgânico* (1849; later editions).

Mangabeira, João. Rui, o estadista da república. Rio de Janeiro. Ed. José Olympio. (Col. docs. bras., no. 40). [3444
Not intended to be a biography; concentrates on the political career of Rui in the Republic. Rich anecdotal treatment, grouped around episodes in his career under various presidents. Strongly pro-Rui.

Mauá, Irineu Evangelista de Sousa, Visconde de. Autobiografia. Rio de Janeiro. Ed. Valverde. 370 p., ilus. [3445
Second edition, with slightly amplified annotations. See *Handbook, no. 8, 1942,* item 3510.

Mello, Geraldo Cardoso de. A Barão Mambucaba. Aspectos de sua vida, sua personalidade e sua grande decendência. Piracicaba. Tip. Aloisi. 90 p. [3446
Short biographical notes of José Luiz Gomes, born in Piraí (Province of Rio de Janeiro), 1791, died 1855; created Barão of Mambucaba, 1854; large landholder and local political figure. Genealogical information about his numerous descendants takes up the bulk of the work.

Oliveira, Albino José Barbosa de. Memórias de um magistrado do império. Revistas e anotadas por seu bisneto Américo Jacobina Lacombe. São Paulo. Cia. ed. nacional. (Bibl. pedagógica bras., Série 5a, Brasiliana, vol. 231). 378 p., ilus. [3447
The autobiography of the celebrated lawyer and judge, Conselheiro Albino (1809–1889), kept by him in notebooks in the form of letters addressed to his children. Most of the entries appear to have been prepared in 1882. Describes family matters, his education and early advances in the law, his appointment to the Supremo Tribunal in 1864, and subsequent career. Sr. Lacombe's annotations are abundant and illuminating.

Pinho, Vanderlei. Salões e damas do segundo reinado. São Paulo. Livr. Martins. [3448
Well-done social history, reflecting political and literary interest, centering around the salons and conversationalists of the Empire; many illuminating early photographs of the people discussed.

A PRIMEIRA MISSÃO A ROMA DO BARÃO DE PENEDO. O 46° ANIVERSÁRIO DO CONDE D'EU NO "CORREIO IMPERIAL" (*Cultura política*, ano 3, no. 28, junho, p. 205–206). [3449
Text of the letter of credence of Francisco Inácio de Carvalho Moreira, later Barão de Penedo.

Rio Branco, José Maria da Silva Paranhos, Barão de. O Visconde do Rio Branco. Rio de Janeiro. Ed. A Noite. 347 p., ilus. [3450
A biography of the Visconde by his son, the Baron; reprinted by Renato de Mendonça, with brief notes and a short introduction entitled "A missão Paranhos e a integridade do Paraguai." Most interesting reading, especially when taken in conjunction with the biography of the Baron by his own son, the Ambassador Raul do Rio-Branco. See *Handbook, no. 8, 1942,* item 3530.

Santos, Francisco Marques dos. O casamento de dom Pedro II (*Estud. bras.,* ano 5, vol. 10, no. 29–30, março–junho, p. 166–222). [3451
Detailed description of the festivities and decorations connected with the marriage of D. Pedro II, with a brief sketch of the diplomatic negotiations to arrange the alliance.

Schlichthorst, Karl. O Rio de Janeiro como é. 1824–1826. Huma vez e nunca mais. Rio de Janeiro. Ed. Getúlio Costa. 301 p., ilus. [3452
Translation by Emy Dodt and Gustavo Barroso, with notes by the latter; description of the city and its life by a German mercenary soldier.

Serpa, Phocion. Miguel Couto, uma vida exemplar. Rio de Janeiro. Gráf. Sauer. 461 p. [3453
A biography, in familiar style and emphasizing human interest, of this celebrated physician and medical professor (1865–1934), who devoted much of his life to a campaign for popular education. Annex of appreciations (academic discourses) by Miguel Osório de Almeida, Afonso Arinos, and Mário de Alencar. Somewhat diffuse, but casts sidelights on a neglected phase of a recent period.

Serra, Astolfo. Caxias e o seu govêrno civil na província do Maranhão. Rio de Janeiro. (Bibl. militar, vol. 68). 176 p. [3454
A brief study (*apontamentos para estudos mais autorizados*) of Caxias' governorship, February, 1840, to May, 1841; appendix of documents.

Tenório, Oscar. As idéias de Tavares Bastos sôbre a imigração (*Rev. imig. col.,* ano 4, no. 3, set., p. 395–404). [3455
A slight but illuminating sketch of the ideas of this exponent of liberalism who (1862–1870) urged the Imperial government to aid immigration and who was interested, among other matters, in Chinese coolie immigration in the Amazon.

Vargas, Netto. General Vargas. Rio de Janeiro. Ed. Bedeschi. 58 p. [3457
A laudatory little booklet about General Manuel de Nascimento Vargas, active in Brazilian affairs half a century ago, but whose chief claim to fame lay in begetting the present president. [R. H. Fitzgibbon]

Viana, Hélio. A pequena imprensa da regência de Araújo Lima, 1837–1840 (*Cultura política,* ano 3, no. 33, out., p. 124–146). [3458
Pamphlets: "O Progresso," "A Pepineira," "O correios de petas," "O popular,"

"O 22 de abril," "A Rôlha," "O pregoeiro," "O sova," "Dois de dezembro," "O monarquista do século XIX," "A verdade nua e crua," and "O grito da razão."

―――. A pequena imprensa da regência de Feijó, 1835-1836 (*Rev. Brasil,* terceira fase, ano 6, no. 55, set., p. 71-82). [3459

Brief bibliographic notes with comments on the contents of these rare pamphlets: "A novidade extraordinaria," "O sapateiro político," "O compadre do Itú a seu compadre do Rio," "O sorvete de bom gosto," "A nova caramuruada" and "O barriga."

―――. A pequena imprensa dos últimos meses do primeiro reinado (*Cultura política,* ano 3, no. 30, agôsto, p. 114-120). [3460

Comments on more rare pamphlets: "O Buscapé," "O doutor Tirateimas," "O narcisco," "O novo conciliador," "O enfermeiro dos doudos."

―――. A revolução de 7 de abril em quatro pasquins de 1831 (*Rev. Brasil,* terceira fase, ano 6, no. 54, junho, p. 67-76). [3461

Examples of the pamphleteering and pasquinade writing of the 1830s as shown in the rare "Cartas ao povo," "Os dois compadres liberais," "O velho cazamenteiro," and "O médico dos malucos."

―――. Visconde do Sepetiba. Petrópolis. Tip. Ipiranga. 209 p. [3462

Separate from vol. 7 of the "Centenário de Petrópolis. Trabalhos da Comissão." Biographical study of Aureliano de Sousa e Oliveira Coutinho (1800-1855), created Visconde de Sepetiba in 1855. Rehabilitation of one of the Conservative ministers of the early reign of D. Pedro II, generally attacked or briefly dismissed as an ill-understood behind-the-scenes politician.

ADDENDA

Reis, Artur Cesar Ferreira. A conquista espiritual da Amazonia. São Paulo. Escolas profissionais salesianas. 1942? 130 p. [3463

Preface by Pedro Calmon.

INTERNATIONAL RELATIONS SINCE 1830

BY

BRYCE WOOD

Swarthmore College

GENERAL STATEMENT

Perhaps because the Battle of the Atlantic turned in favor of the United Nations in 1943, publications in the field of Latin American international relations showed less concern over problems of hemisphere defense than in 1942, and displayed renewed interest in such perennial topics as Pan Americanism, boundary questions and the Monroe Doctrine. Nevertheless, several important publications emphasized the continuing danger to the Americas presented by Axis activity. The Comisión Investigadora of the Argentine Chamber of Deputies, formerly known as the Taborda Committee, published one of its last reports, an analysis of "tourism" as a method of Axis penetration (item 3531); two opposing views are offered on the nature of *Hispanidad* (items 3534 and 3536); and the Institute of Pacific Relations presents a useful study of the Japanese in South America (item 160).

The outstanding publications in the field of Pan Americanism are two documentary collections; that of the Division of International Law of the Carnegie Endowment for International Peace (item 3486), and the mimeographed volumes of the Pan American Union entitled: *Improvement and Coordination of Inter-American Peace Instruments* (items 4506–3508). Among commentators, the writings of Drs. Cravioto González (item 3488), Ordóñez Fetzer (item 3502), and Whitaker (item 3516), are of more than usual interest. An important step in the worsening of United States-Argentine relations is marked by the Storni-Hull diplomatic exchange (item 3496).

Latin America is not usually looked upon as a field for the examination of power politics in action, at least on the part of the Latin American states themselves, but studies of a power-political slant are being made of what so far may be only incipient drives for influence in the River Plate region by Argentina and Brazil. The articles by Drs. Bernstein (item 3539), and Whitaker (item 3541) and the Pan American Union's summary of the new Argentine-Bolivian railroad treaty (item 3555), draw attention to a line of development which can be traced back through the River Plate Conference of 1941 and the Chaco War, and beyond.

In the United States, the Good Neighbor Policy was vigorously attacked by Senator Butler and defended by a battery of officials led by Secretary of State Hull (item 3524). The Senator from Nebraska alleged waste in the government's expenditures in Latin America (item 3521), but the charges did not lead to a Congressional investigation of the policy of the administration.

Among other entries worthy of special note are the first report of the Advisory Committee for Political Defense (item 3528), the expression of faith in *Free Men of America* by the Mexican Foreign Minister (item 164), the analysis of the Olney Corollary by G. B. Young (item 3517) which leads to speculations different from those of S. F. Bemis (item 3518) in regard to intervention, and the eloquent attack upon the policy of ex-President Castillo of Argentina by the veteran Socialist leader, Nicolás Repetto (item 3473).

BIBLIOGRAPHY

(See also sections on Archives and History)

GENERAL

(See also items 106, 2534)

Barros, Jaime de. A política exterior do Brasil, 1930-1942. Segunda ed. correta e aumentada. Rio de Janeiro. Ed. Valverde. 308 p. [3464]
The second edition of this work is very considerably changed as compared to the first edition. (See *Handbook, no. 7, 1941,* item 3708). A review of the important years 1941 and 1942 is added, with special attention to the Rio Conference, Brazil's entry into the war, and the Peru-Ecuador dispute. Some of the original material has been condensed.

Bernstein Harry. The land that seeks a sea (*The Pan American,* vol. 4, no. 3, June, p. 5-8). [3465]
A good, brief analysis of the nature of Bolivia's relations with Argentina, Brazil and Chile.

Caldwell, R. G. Exile as an institution (*Pol. sci. quart.,* vol. 58, June, p. 239-262). [3466]
Political exile in Latin America examined primarily from a legal point of view.

Escobar, Adrián C. Palabras americanas. Tres discursos sobre política internacional. Buenos Aires. Imp. López. 31 p. [3467]
Three speeches, interpretive of Argentine foreign policy by the ambassador of Argentina to the United States.

Fabela, Isidro. Las relaciones entre los Estados Unidos de Norteamérica y México (*Mundo libre,* México, tomo 2, no. 12-13, enero-feb., p. 7-16). [3468]
A survey of Mexican-United States relations. The author expresses great sympathy for the good-neighbor policy, and hope for collaborative relations in the future.

Gandía, Enrique de. La amistad argentino-venezolana desde Bolívar a la doctrina Drago (*Rev. hist.,* Buenos Aires, tomo 2, no. 1, julio, p. 17-28). [3469]
An Argentine historian emphasizes the friendly character of Argentine-Venezuelan relations from the time of the meeting of Bolívar and San Martín. Dr. Gandía quotes from Bolívar's letters to show Bolívar's high opinion of the "Héroe del Sur." The doctrine of Luis María Drago and its relation to the "pacific blockade" of Venezuela in 1902 is given prominence, as are Spanish and Argentine backgrounds of the Monroe Doctrine.

González Garza, Federico. México y los Estados Unidos de América a la luz de las nuevas ideas internacionales. México, D. F. Asociación nac. de abogados. 24 p. [3470]
Text of a speech before the National Bar Association. In a lengthy introduction, the author explains that, having been invited to give a speech at a meeting of the Council on Foreign Relations in New York on March 11, 1919, having submitted the manuscript of his speech, and being present at the banquet, he was not called upon by the Chairman to speak. After this introduction, Sr. González Garza delivered to the National Bar Association the speech he was to have given to the Council on Foreign Relations in 1919. In what now seem relatively restrained terms, he criticized imperialistic policies and suggested the substitution of policies of confidence and mutual respect. The author closes with an expression of great satisfaction over the theme of the conversations between Presidents Camacho and Roosevelt at their meeting in Monterrey.

Murray-Jacoby, H. The diplomacy of President Trujillo. Introd. by R. Comprés Pérez. New York. 18 p. [3471]
A eulogy of President Trujillo's policies of peace and Pan Americanism by a United States banker and diplomat.
Reprinted from *Cooperación,* August, 1943.

A POLÍTICA DO BRASIL COM OS ESTADOS UNIDOS (*Cultura política,* ano 3, no. 31, agôsto 22, p. 77-84). [3472]
An unsigned article, tracing the course of Brazilian-United States relations, and concentrating on the continuity and strength of Brazilian solidarity with the policy of the United States.

Repetto, Nicolás. Política internacional. Buenos Aires. Tall. La Vanguardia. 236 p. [3473]
A valuable collection of speeches on foreign policy and other subjects by the Argentine Socialist leader. Of special interest is the eloquent statement of liberal Argentine opinion concerning the part played by the Argentine Government at the Rio de Janeiro Conference. In this speech, made in the Chamber of Deputies in June, 1942, in support of an interpellation on foreign policy, Dr. Repetto said: "The real reasons for the international policy of the president [Castillo] reside in the deep sympathy which is felt by him and the men around him, for totalitarian political methods; and his unshakeable conviction that the Axis states will win the war."

Rippy, J. Fred. Relations of the United States and Costa Rica during the Guardia era (*Bull. pan amer. union*, vol. 77, no. 2, Feb., p. 61–68). [3474
This article traces the economic development of Costa Rica in the period 1870–1885, with special reference to the role played by Minor C. Keith.

Rodríguez Cerna, José (comp.). Colección de tratados de Guatemala. Vol. 2. Parte primera: Pactos con países americanos. Parte segunda: Pactos inter-americanos. Guatemala. Tip. nacional. (Sría. de relaciones exteriores). 2 vols.: 637, 722 p. [3475
Part 1 brings the treaties with all American States down to 1941. See *Handbook*, no. 5, *1939*, item 3276 for Vol. 1. Part 2 contains texts of conventions, resolutions, etc., of the Panama Congress of 1826, and of the eight Pan American Conferences.

Shaw, Albert. International bearings of American policy. Baltimore. The Johns Hopkins press. x, 492 p. [3476
The author, formerly editor of the *Review of Reviews*, calls this a "medley" of reminiscence and opinion. Four chapters discuss inter-American affairs: X. The Monroe Doctrine and Pan American accord; XI. Boundary settlements by agreement, Oregon, Brazil, Venezuela; XII. Cuban independence and the Panama Canal; XIII. We cultivate relations with Canada and Mexico.

Stuart, Graham H. Latin America and the United States. Fourth. ed., thoroughly revised. New York, London. D. Appleton-Century. (The Century political science series). 509 p. [3477
The fourth edition of this text brings it abreast of events through 1942.

Ulloa y Sotomayor, Alberto. El Perú y el mundo. Lima. Ed. Relieves americanos. (Discursos y conferencias, 4). 14 p. [3478
A lecture, dealing with Peruvian foreign affairs in general terms.

Unión democrática centroamericana. Departamento editorial. Por qué lucha Centro América. México. Gráf. Panamericana. 75 p. [3479
A group of antifascist, Central American exiles, and others, publishes its program and objectives, together with a series of letters to Vice-President Henry A. Wallace and Under Secretary of State Sumner Welles. The Unión declares the regimes of Honduras, Guatemala, Nicaragua and Salvador to be unconstitutional, and, after a frank statement of the economic and cultural backwardness of Central America, pleads for the application of the Atlantic Charter to Central America.

Whitaker, Arthur P. The Inter-American system (*Int. amer. affairs*, *1942*, p. 10–40). [3480
A survey of the political year by the editor of this valuable yearbook, with special reference to the Rio de Janeiro Conference and to the development of synarchism in Mexico.

White, John W. Our good neighbor hurdle. Milwaukee. Bruce publ. co. 209 p. [3481
A book by the well-known correspondent, amplifying the thesis as stated in the preface that: "The one most serious obstacle to closer friendship and understanding between the people of the United States and those to the South of us is the proselytizing activity of the army of North American Protestant missionaries who have been sent to the southern republics 'to bring Christianity to them.'"

PAN AMERICANISM

Aguiar, R. José. Hacia la comunidad democrática americana. Montevideo. Ed. Comini. 46 p., ilus., mapa. [3482
A fervent expression of faith in the unity of the Americas, and an argument for the fourth term because of President Roosevelt's indispensability in the task of realizing this ideal.

Aranha, Oswaldo. El panamericanismo en el desenvolvimiento histórico-político del Brasil (*América*, Habana, vol. 18, no. 1–2, abril-mayo, p. 19–24). [3483
Translation of an unidentified speech by the former Minister of Foreign Relations of Brazil. Dr. Aranha eulogizes the cause of Pan Americanism and dwells on the part played by Brazil in its development. "Pan Americanism today is not a great and growing movement of continental solidarity, but a real union of all the American Republics...."

Blanco, Julio Enrique. Razonamientos sobre el panamericanismo. Fascículo primero (*Rev. mus. Atlán.*, no. 2–3, abril, suplemento, p. 1–59). [3484

Cáceres, Julián R. Datos sobre el arbitraje en América (*Proc. eighth amer. scien. cong.*, vol. 10, p. 263–291). [3485
A brief history of arbitration in the Americas, with particular attention to the contributions of Central America, by the Minister of Honduras in Washington.

Carnegie endowment for international peace. Division of international law. Conferencias internacionales americanas. Primer suplemento, 1938–1942. Washington. xxxviii, 501 p. [3486
The supplement to *Conferencias Internacionales Americanas, 1889–1936*; not the Spanish edition of *The International Conferences of American States, First Supplement, 1933–1940*. This contains texts of final acts of the Eighth Conference, and of the Conferences of Ministers of Foreign Affairs at Panama, Havana and Rio de Janeiro. In two long appendices are synopses of Pan American Conferences of all types, and of Pan American organizations; the list in each case is more complete than in the comparable English lists.

Cortés Medina, Hernán. Ibero-americanismo y pan-americanismo. Hacia una verdadera comprensión americana. México. 76 p. [3487

A thesis presented to the Facultad de Derecho of the Universidad de Mexico. With considerable frankness and penetration the author analyzes the development of Pan Americanism and its attendant problems. He distinguishes three stages of Pan Americanism: 1. Latin American initiatives; 2. North American hegemony; 3. A Pan Americanism of understanding.

Cravioto González, Joaquín. El panamericanismo a través de las tres reuniones de consulta entre los ministros de relaciones exteriores de las repúblicas americanas. México, D. F. Imp. "Gallarda."—I. Franco. 84 p. [3488

A Mexican views with sympathy the recent course of inter-American relations, and emphasizes his country's role in their development.

Culbertson, Ely. Pan American federation now (*The Pan American*, vol. 4, no. 4, July–Sept., p. 12–14). [3489

The author of *Total Peace* describes the organization of the American Federation, one of the eleven regional groups in his plan for World Federation.

Fernandini de Alvarez-Calderón, Anita. Creación de una mesa redonda de paz interamericana (*Proc. eighth amer. scien. cong.*, vol. 10, p. 245–262). [3490

A proposal, by the Vice-President of the National Council of Peruvian Women, for the creation of an inter-American agency to keep the peace, with powers roughly comparable to those of the Council of the League of Nations.

Finlayson, Clarence. Confederation of the Americas (*Commonweal*, vol. 38, July, p. 339–341). [3491

A sweeping view of the American scene, with suggestions for future development ranging from internationalization of the Panama Canal, to "an economic congress with jurisdiction for the whole continent to draw up legislation."

García Robles, Alfonso. Latinoamericanismo y panamericanismo (*Mundo libre*, México, tomo 1, no. 11, dic., 1942, p. 31–36; tomo 2, no. 12–13, enero–feb., p. 39–43). [3492

The author suggests that there are real and growing bonds linking Anglo-Saxon and Latin America.

Gómez Reinoso, Teófilo. El tribunal de justicia interamericana y las conferencias panamericanas (*Rev. der. int.*, año 22, tomo 44, no. 87, sept., p. 119–124). [3493

A review of the initiatives for an inter-American Court of Justice, and the expression of a hope that they may be successfully renewed after the war.

Hazelton, Alan Weaver. Eloy Alfaro, apostle of Pan Americanism. Forest Hills, N. Y. Las Americas publ. co. (Andhra research univ. pamphlets). 47 p., illus. [3494

An enthusiastic tribute to the former president of Ecuador, through whose efforts a Pan American conference attended by several American States was held in Mexico in 1896. The author is General Secretary and Deputy Dean for Latin America of the International Faculty of Andhra Research University. A bibliography of works on General Alfaro is included.

Inman, S. G. Steps to unity: proposed association of American nations (*Int. amer.*, vol. 2, no. 7, July, p. 14–16). [3495

An attack upon Mr. Henry Luce's notion of an "American Century" as applied to Latin America, and suggestions for the formation of a stronger association of the American nations than now exists.

THE INTERNATIONAL POSITION OF ARGENTINA. Correspondence between the Secretary of state and the Argentine Foreign minister (*Dept. state bull.*, vol. 9, no. 220, Sept. 11, p. 159–166). [3496

Text of the exchange of notes in which the implicit request for munitions via Lend-Lease by the Argentine Foreign Minister was pointedly refused by the Secretary of State.

Kull, Robert I. The Pan American Union, an international secretariat (*Agenda*, vol. 2, on. 2, May, p. 114–123). [3497

A useful description of the organization and working of the Pan American Union. The author examined the Union to see how far it might serve as a model for a secretariat of international agencies outside the Americas. He concludes that "a system more far-reaching organically is necessary for problems such as world security."

Lazcano Mazón, Andrés María. Armonía constitucional del nuevo mundo. Panorama panamericanadiense (*Rev. der. int.*, año 22, tomo 44, no. 87, sept., p. 7–42). [3498

Basing his study on an article by George Jaffin (*Handbook, no. 8, 1942*, item 3619), Dr. Lazcano Mazón points to constitutional similarities among the American states on many points, and suggests the acceptance of a Pan American-Canadian Super-Constitution, with provisions for common citizenship, currency and right to trade.

Loewenstein, Karl. Pan Americanism in action. Committee for political defense (*Curr. hist.*, vol. 5, no. 27, Nov., p. 229–236). [3499

A survey of the work of the Emergency Advisory Committee for Political Defense by the author of *Brazil under Vargas*.

Medeiros, J. Paulo de. Aspectos do panamericanismo e uma tradicão da política

brasileira (*Cultura política,* ano 3, no. 23, jan., p. 31-36). [3500
Argument and quotations emphasizing the firmness of the policy of the Brazilian Government in support of Pan Americanism.

Muniz, João Carlos. El momento de América (*Rev. bim. cub.,* vol. 51, no. 3, mayo-junio, p. 321-335). [3501
An address by the Brazilian Ambassador to Ecuador, emphasizing, in opposition to German ideas and aspirations, the American principles of the unity of peoples, and equality of races.

Ordóñez Fetzer, Marco Tulio. Panamericanismo. Guatemala. Centro editorial. 90 p. [3502
A thesis presented to the Facultad de Ciencias Juridicas y Sociales of the Universidad de Guatemala. The author, sympathetic to the growth of Pan Americanism, considers that the simultaneous development of movements such as *centroamericanismo, hispanoamericanismo,* or *indoiberoamericanismo* would not be inconsistent with the aims of the larger grouping.

Pan American union. Medidas adoptadas por la Unión panamericana para llevar a efecto las resoluciones aprobadas por la octava conferencia internacional americana y las tres reuniones de consulta de los ministros de relaciones exteriores de las repúblicas americanas. Washington. (Série sobre congresos y conferencias, No. 44). ii, 57 p. [3503
The Spanish text of item 3504.

―――. Steps taken by the Pan American union in fulfillment of the resolutions adopted at the eighth international conference of American states and the three meetings of the Ministers of foreign affairs of the American republics. Report submitted to the members of the Governing board, by the Director general, October, 1943. Washington. (Congress and conference series, No. 44). ii, 58 p. [3504
The official summary of the multifarious activities of the Pan American Union in pursuance of the responsibilities entrusted to it by the Lima Conference and the meetings of Foreign Ministers. This is an indispensable record of Pan Americanism in action.

―――. **Executive committee on postwar problems.** El sistema interamericano. Elementos para el estudio de los problemas de organización de la post guerra. Washington. iii, 56 p. [3505
A general survey of the Pan American "system" with a description of fundamental principles, and of the functioning of various inter-American organizations.

―――. **Juridical division.** Aperfeiçoamento e coordenação dos instrumentos internacionais de paz. Resolução 15 de la Oitava conferencia internacional americana. Washington, D. C. 1941?-1943. 5 vols. [3506
Tomo 1, primeira parte. Exposição sôbre os projetos apresentados à Oitava conferência internacional americana relativos ao aperfeiçoamento e coordenação dos instrumentos interamericanos de paz. 1941? 71 p.
Tomo 1, segundo parte. Published in Spanish only. See item 3508.
Tomo 2. Textos dos projetos sôbre aperfeiçoamento e coordenação dos instrumentos interamericanos de paz submetidos à Oitava conferência internacional americana. 1941. 173 p.
Tomo 3. Convênios e acordos interamericanos de paz existentes e outros convênios de paz assinados pelos estados americanos. 1941. 162 p.
Tomo 4. Texto dos documentos relativos ao estabelecimento de uma Associação de nações americanas apresentados à Oitava conferencia internacional americana. 1941. 11 p.
Tomo 5. Texto dos documentos relativos a identificação do agressor e aplicação de sanções apresentados à Oitava conferência internacional americana. 1943. 25 p.
Portuguese version of item 3508, q. v.

―――. Improvement and coordination of Inter-American peace instruments. Resolution 15 of the Eighth international conference of American states. Washington, D. C. 1941-1943. 4 vols. [3507
Vol. 1, part 1. Report on the documents presented to the Eighth international conference of American states relative to the improvement and coordination of Inter-American peace instruments. 1941. 94 p.
Vol. 1, part 2. Published only in Spanish. See item 3508.
Vol. 2. Text of the projects on improvement and coordination of the Inter-American peace instruments submitted to the Eighth international conference of American states. 1943. 167 p.
Vol. 3. Existing Inter-American peace instruments and other general peace treaties signed by the American states. 1941. 142 p.
Vol. 4. Text of the draft treaty on the establishment of an Association of American nations submitted to the Eighth international conference of American states. 1941. 14 p.
English version of item 3508, q. v.

―――. Perfeccionamiento y coordinación de los instrumentos interamericanos de paz. Resolución 15 de la Octava conferencia internacional americana. Washington, D. C. 1940. 5 vols. [3508
Tomo 1, primera parte. Informe sobre los proyectos presentados a la Octava conferencia internacional americana relativos al perfeccionamiento y coordinación de los instrumentos de paz. 1940. 89 p.
Tomo 1, segunda parte. Estudio comparado de los proyectos presentados a la Octava conferencia internacional americana sobre el perfeccionamiento y coordinación

de los instrumentos interamericanos de paz. 1940. 108 p.

Tomo 2. Texto de los proyectos sobre perfeccionamiento y coordinación de los instrumentos inter-americanos de paz sometidos a la Octava conferencia internacional americana. 1940. 187 p.

Tomo 3. Convenios y acuerdos interamericanos de paz existentes y otros convenios de paz suscritos por los estados americanos. 1940. 140 p.

Tomo 4. Texto de los documentos relativos al establecimiento de una Asociación de naciones americanas sometidos a la Octava conferencia internacional americana. 1940. 26 p.

Tomo 5. Texto de los documentos relativos a la identificación del agresor y a la aplicación de sanciones sometidos a la Octava conferencia internacional americana. 1940. 28 p.

An indispensable series for students of inter-American efforts to keep the peace. The American peace machinery as a whole is documented, and official plans for its improvement are described and annotated. These volumes provide a basis for understanding the issues of inter-American organization which will be raised at future Pan American Conferences.

Santos Muñoz, Pablo. Posibilidad de la incorporación de Canadá a la Unión panamericana. Buenos Aires. Imp. de la Univ. 17 p. [3509]

A speech before the Argentine Institute of International Law on June 15, 1943 by the Consejero Político Legal of the Ministry of Foreign Relations, formerly Argentine minister to Canada. Dr. Santos Múñoz reviews the question methodically and impartially and finds there is no legal reason why Canada could not join the Pan American Union. He notes that there is less interest than in the recent past on the part of Canadians for such incorporation.

Sayán de Vidaurre, Alberto. Réplica a las antidemócratas y antipanamericanistas. Buenos Aires. p. 40. [3510]

An Argentine publicist justifies his previous attack on British imperialism (see item 3553), defends the United States against the charge that it is a "Carthaginian conglomeration," attacks a pro-Hispanidad policy for Argentina and eloquently defends Pan-Americanism.

Turlington, Edgar. The general principles of inter-American organization (*Proc. eighth amer. scien. cong.*, vol. 10, p. 149-152). [3511]

A chatty, pithy statement of some practical truths about the American international organization, which is called a "cooperative association." Speaking of rhetorical fictions, Mr. Turlington says: "I do not see that they do any harm in declarations signed by all the Americas, provided everybody who signs knows that fictions are being used."

Ulloa, Alberto. Principios generales de organización interamericana. Nueva organización de la Unión panamericana (*Proc. eighth amer. scien. cong.*, vol. 10, p. 141-147). [3512]

A suggestion that the various agencies of inter-American cooperation in the social, economic, educational and medical fields should be centralized under the control of the Pan American Union.

Urquidi, José Macedonio. El panamericanismo: sus bases, principios y fines. ¿Cómo cabe conceptuarlo y que debe esperarse de él? (*Proc. eighth amer. scien. cong.*, vol. 10, p. 161-173). [3513]

A general discussion of Pan Americanism by a Bolivian international lawyer.

MONROE DOCTRINE

Davis, Jr., Thomas B. Carlos de Alvear and James Monroe: New light on the origin of the Monroe Doctrine (*Hisp. amer. hist. rev.*, vol. 23, no. 4, Nov., p. 632-649). [3514]

A review of the impressions of the Monroe Doctrine obtained by the first Argentine Minister to the United States. It is interesting to learn that "Monroe assured Alvear that his declaration constituted an unequivocal promise to protect South America."

Pôrto, L. de Almeida Nogueira. Um episódio da doutrina de Monroe. A fórmula Nabuco na 4ª conferência internacional americana (*Cultura política*, ano 3, no. 28, junho, p. 39-42). [3515]

An account, with contemporary press comments, of the rejection, at the Pan American Conference of 1910, of a Brazilian resolution expressing the gratitude of the Latin American countries for the policy of the Monroe Doctrine.

Whitaker, Arthur P. Our Pan American policy and the post-war world (*Harvard educ. rev.*, Oct., p. 285-300). [3516]

An important article, deserving a wider audience than it will probably obtain in this publication. Professor Whitaker argues that the time is close at hand when the Monroe Doctrine will be abandoned as a specialized foreign policy of the United States toward Latin America. The reason for this is that "our policy towards other parts of the world is being assimilated to our policy towards Latin America as this has evolved on the basis of the Monroe Doctrine." The United States, in this view, will not attempt to form a bloc of American States "against the world."

Young, G. B. Intervention under the Monroe Doctrine. The Olney corollary (*Pol. sci. quart.*, vol. 57, June, p. 247-280). [3517]

After a careful re-examination of Secretary Olney's policy in the British Guiana dispute, Mr. Young adduces the Olney Corollary to the Monroe Doctrine: "If grounds exist sufficient to persuade the United States that the political or territorial integrity of an American state is threatened by a non-American power, the

United States regards the Monroe Doctrine as automatically implicated, and claims the right to intervene between the two disputing states. Termination of the dispute through a settlement reached by the free consent of both states will be considered as satisfying the Doctrine. If, however, no such settlement is reached, the United States may suggest, and impose impartially, such a composition of the dispute as seems in its sole judgment reasonable and just." Intervention has now been abandoned by the United States but Mr. Young suggests the Olney Corollary might again obtain, "if at a critical juncture a stubborn European-Latin American dispute should sometime jeopardize hemispherical solidarity."

GOOD NEIGHBOR POLICY

Bemis, Samuel Flagg. The Latin American policy of the United States. An historical interpretation. New York. Harcourt, Brace & co. (Yale univ., Inst. of international studies). xiv, 470 p., illus. [3518
A full length study based on the general theme that the policy of the United States toward Latin America has been determined by considerations of self-defense. Therefore, with the possible exception of the method by which Panama was taken the policy of the United States is largely justified. This is a vigorous and controversial book. It censures Woodrow Wilson for opening "full wide the sluiceways" of the Mexican Revolution. It claims that it is the citizens of the United States and not the Latin American governments, who have been the victims of economic exploitation in the Western Hemisphere. In view of recent United States policy toward Argentina it would seem that Professor Bemis was overoptimistic in titling one of his chapters "The Triumph of Absolute Nonintervention."

Butler, Hugh Alfred. Our deep dark secrets in Latin America (*Readers' digest*, vol. 43, Dec., p. 21-25). [3519
The popular, greatly condensed version of Senator Butler's charges of good-neighborly extravagance. See item 3521.

EMBASSIES REPLACE LEGATIONS (*Bull. pan amer. union*, vol. 77, July, p. 381-386). [3520
This article comments upon the completion of the process by which the United States has come to exchange ambassadors, rather than ministers, with all the Latin American republics. Selections are quoted from the speeches made on the occasion of the presentation of letters of credence to President Roosevelt by the new ambassadors of Guatemala, El Salvador, Nicaragua, the Dominican Republic, Honduras and Haiti.

EXPENDITURES AND COMMITMENTS BY THE UNITED STATES GOVERNMENT IN OR FOR LATIN AMERICA. Report by Hon. Hugh Butler . . . and the reply to such report made by Hon. Kenneth McKellar . . . together with accompanying papers from the heads of departments verifying same. Washington. U. S. Government print. office. (U. S. Senate, Seventy-eighth congress, First session, Document no. 132). 170 p. [3521
The text of the tempest-provoking report of Senator Butler, together with the rebuttal of the administration, sponsored by Senator McKellar.

Herring, Hubert. Senator Butler and Latin America (*New republic*, vol. 109, no. 25, Dec. 20, p. 872-874). [3522
A critical analysis of Senator Hugh Butler's report on the United States' expenditures in Latin America. Mr. Herring concludes that the Senator has harmed both his party and his country by his "ill natured and ill informed outburst." (See item 3521).

Manger, William. The United States and Latin America. A survey of recent changes in the relations of the United States with the other American republics. Washington, D. C. Pan American union. 27 p. [3523
A useful summary of United States policy since 1933.

STATEMENT BY THE SECRETARY OF STATE. ATTACK BY SENATOR BUTLER ON THE GOOD-NEIGHBOR POLICY (*Dept. state bull.*, vol. 9, no. 234, Dec. 18, p. 430-431). [3524
The official reply to Senator Butler's charges that the United States government was wasting money on its policy in Latin America.

HEMISPHERE DEFENSE

Amador, Armando C. México en la contienda mundial. México, D. F. Publ. España con honra. 48 p. [3525
A useful review of the attitude of the Mexican government toward the incidents of the "world crisis" since 1931, with quotations from government spokesmen. There is a chronology and a bibliography.

Barros, Jaime de. A diplomácia brasileira e a defesa da América (*Cultura política*, ano 3, no. 34, nov., p. 107-111). [3526
A review of Brazilian foreign policy from 1930 to 1943, with emphasis upon Brazil's role of opposition to the totalitarian states. The author is Chief of the Section of Publications of the Ministry of Foreign Relations.

———. A diplomácia brasileira e a guerra (*Cultura política*, ano 3, no. 31, agôsto 22, p. 65-76). [3527
An account of incidents leading up to Brazil's participation in World War II, with special reference to the close cooperation between Brazil and the United States.

Inter-American emergency advisory committee for political defense,

Montevideo. Annual report submitted July, 1943. With an appendix containing the recommendations approved from April 15, 1942 to July 15, 1943. Montevideo. (English ed. distributed by the Pan American union, Washington, D. C.). xii, 287 p. [3528

This important document is the Committee's first report. It includes materials on the origin and organization of the Committee, recommendations on measures of political defense and some account of action taken by the American states. Comments on such action, however, indicate that the Committee feels that a great deal remains to be done to assure adequate political defense of the hemisphere.
Published also in Spanish.

Padilla, Ezequiel, Mário de Pimentel Brandão, and José L. Chouhy Terra. The political defense of the Americas. México. Ed. La Nación. (Dept. of state for foreign affairs, Bureau of international news service, National and international problems series, no. 18). 46 p. [3529

Speeches made by the Mexican Foreign Minister, a Vice-President of the Emergency Advisory Committee for Political Defense, and the Committee's Secretary General, on the occasion of the visit of a delegation of the Committee to Mexico to discuss the best means for carrying out the Committee's recommendations.

Pimentel, José Francisco. El Comité consultivo de emergencia para la defensa política (*Rev. der. int.*, año 22, tomo 44, no. 87, sept., p. 116–118). [3530

A note on the work of the Advisory Emergency Committee for Political Defense.

AXIS INFLUENCE

Argentina. Cámara de diputados. Comisión investigadora de actividades antiargentinas. Formas y medios de la penetración totalitaria. Oficina de información de los ferrocarriles alemanes. Buenos Aires. 134 p., ilus. [3531

The latest publication of the Taborda Committee (under the presidency of Juan Antonio Solari). This is a documentary exposé of Nazi "tourism" on a grand scale. The Comisión concludes: "The Oficina de Información de los Ferrocarriles Alemanes, which operated until May, 1942 . . . constituted one of the principal centers for the diffusion of national socialist propaganda in Argentina via the press, radio and cinema." It also operated in Uruguay, Paraguay and Chile. There are 55 pages of photostatic reproductions of documents.

Bradford, Saxtone E. The battle for Buenos Aires. New York. Harcourt, Brace & co., publ. vi, 307 p. [3532

A racy account of the propaganda battle for Argentina between the Axis and the United States. The battle so far as propaganda is concerned was being lost by the United States, in Mr. Bradford's opinion, because of governmental ineptitude, because Americans in Argentina took no interest in the struggle, and because we appeared to have been maneuvered into a defensive position. Interesting reading.

Chase, Allan. Falange. The axis secret army in the Americas. New York. G. P. Putnam's sons. x, 278 p., ilus. [3533

A vivid and documented account of the activities of the Nazi-inspired Falange in Latin America, the Philippines and the United States. The author concludes that "if the Iberian Peninsula emerges from this war as the Fascist bastion that it is at this hour, then all our dead will have died in vain."

Diffie, Bailey W. The ideology of *hispanidad* (*Hisp. amer. hist. rev.*, vol. 23, no. 3, Aug., p. 457–482). [3534

A well-documented and pungent article. Professor Diffie distinguishes between *Hispanismo*, "largely a liberal movement based on the principles of the Enlightenment," and *Hispanidad*. Of the latter, the author states: "Unless its advocates misrepresent it, it is Roman Catholic Fascism, the official foreign policy of the Falange Española, designed to reunite the Hispanic peoples around the concept of privilege, hierarchy, autocracy, and intolerance. How much real strength it has in Spain and America only time can tell."

Fernández Artucio, Hugo. La organización secreta nazi en Sudamérica. México, D. F. Ed. Minerva. 315 p. [3535

The Spanish edition of Professor Fernández Artucio's *The Nazi Underground in South America* (*Handbook, no. 8, 1942*, item 3765). It is dedicated to Víctor Raúl Haya de la Torre.

Kenny, Michael. Hispanidad (*The Catholic world*, vol. 157, Sept., p. 596–603). [3536

Hispanidad "implies no political ties or ambitions in either hemisphere, merely pride in a common cultural heritage by peoples who speak the same tongue and in their ways of Catholic and social life stem from the same root." The author comments upon the resurgence of *Hispanidad* subsequent to the attainment of power by the present Spanish government.

Loewenstein, Karl. Legislation against subversive activities in Argentina (*Harvard law rev.*, vol. 56, no. 8, July, p. 1261–1306). [3537

A detailed survey, which covers more ground than its title indicates, of anti-Axis and anti-Communist legislation in Argentina. The tone of the article is unsympathetic to Argentine governments since the retirement of President Ortiz.

POLITICAL QUESTIONS

Alfaro, Ricardo Joaquín. Los acuerdos entre Panamá y los Estados Unidos.

Panamá. Imp. el Panamá América. 12 p., ilus. [3538
Reproduction of a letter by Dr. Alfaro, ex-president of Panama, to Mr. Drew Pearson, the columnist, protesting the latter's assertions that the United States was buying friendship in Panama by means of recent United States-Panama treaties. Dr. Alfaro states that both countries were acting in their own interests and in a spirit of cooperation. The letter was originally printed in *La Estrella de Panama*, Dec. 10, 1942.

Bernstein, H. Power politics on the Río de la Plata (*Int. amer.*, vol. 2, no. 9, Sept., p. 10–13). [3539
A valuable introduction to the conflicting interests of Argentina and Brazil in the Plata basin. Can we begin to use the term "conflicting imperialisms" as applicable to Latin American states in Latin America?

Instituto ecuatoriano-venezolano de cultura. Fuerza presente de la doctrina bolivariana. La visita al Ecuador del canciller de Venezuela Dr. C. Parra Pérez. Quito. Imp. de la univ. (Comisión ecuatoriana de cooperación intelectual, Publ., no. 3). 274 p. [3540
A collection of newspaper articles, speeches, etc., relating to the visit to Ecuador in November, 1942, of the Venezuelan Minister of Foreign Relations. The various contributions indicate the existence in Ecuador, and possibly in Venezuela, of a desire for a reconstitution in one form or another of the union once called Gran Colombia. The development of special forms of collaboration between these states and Colombia may be receiving serious consideration.

Whitaker, A. P. Power politics in South America. Brazil gives Bolivia an outlet to the sea (*Curr. hist.*, vol. 4, no. 24, August, p. 382–387). [3541
An article dealing with the issues raised by the Brazilian offer to Bolivia of free port facilities in Santos. It should be read in conjunction with Dr. Harry Bernstein's article, item 3539.

POST WAR PROBLEMS

Comité jurídico interamericano. Recomendación sobre problemas de la postguerra (*An. fac. cien. jur. soc.*, Chile, vol. 9, no. 33–36, enero–dic., p. 85–115). [3542
The text of the Committee's Recommendation of September 5, 1942.

Latin American juridical committee. Preliminary recommendations on postwar problems. Formulated at the request of the Third meeting of ministers of foreign affairs of the American republics, Rio de Janeiro, January, 1942 (*Int. conciliation*, no. 387, Feb., p. 101–129). [3543
The English text of recommendations intended to be of world wide application for the coming peace.

Pan American union. Executive committee on post-war problems. The basic principles of the inter-American system. Washington. vi, 40 p. [3544
An important publication, presenting a synthesis of the ideas embodied in many resolutions and conventions of the American Republics.
A Portuguese version of the text was published under the title *Os Princípios Fundamentais do Sistema Interamericano*.

BOUNDARIES

Barcia Trelles, Camilo. El problema de las islas Malvinas. Madrid. Ed. nacional. 114 p. [3545
The author of *Doctrina de Monroe y Cooperación Internacional* (Madrid, 1931) reviews the history of the Falkland Islands dispute, and warns Argentina that the United States, following the policy of the "destroyer deal" with Britain, intends to obtain control of the Falklands. The writing of the book was completed in July, 1941.

Chaves, Omar Emir. Fronteiras do Brasil. Límites com a república da Colombia. Os tratados. Rio de Janeiro. Ed. Bedeschi. (Bibl. militar, vol. 63). 219 p., ilus. [3546
A running account, together with twenty-nine documents from the Bull of Alexander VI to the exchange of notes approving the minutes of the last session of the Mixed Boundary Commission, of the course of frontier negotiations between Brazil and Colombia. The author was a technical adviser to the Commission. Three detailed maps which may incidentally interest students of the eastern frontiers of Peru and Ecuador, are included.

Colombia. Ministerio de relaciones exteriores. Oficina de longitudes y fronteras. Arreglo de límites entre la república de Colombia y la república de los Estados Unidos de Venezuela. Bogotá. Ed. lit. Colombia. 227 p., mapas. [3547
The documentary history of the Colombian-Venezuelan boundary. The editor of this series, Julio Garzón Nieto, contributes an introduction. The texts are supplemented by 33 maps. For earlier volumes in this excellent series, see *Handbook, no. 7, 1941*, items 3782–3784.

Cravioto, Adrián. La paz de América. Guatemala y Belice. México. Ed. Cultura. (Grupo América de México). 56 p., ilus., mapa. [3548
A Mexican colonel states the case of Guatemala vs. Great Britain in the dispute over Belize. Col. Cravioto states that as one form of compensation for the cooperation of the American nations against the Axis, the remaining colonies in America should become autonomous, and Belize should be returned to Guatemala.

Guatemala. Ministry for foreign affairs. Continuation of the White book. The question of British Honduras (Belize question). Guatemala. [3549

First series, no. 8. Bordering territories of the Captaincies General of Guatemala and Yucatan during the Colonial period. The Anglo-Mexican treaty of 1893, defense by the Minister of foreign affairs, Lic. Ignacio Mariscal. Cordial and solidary attitude of the government of the United States of Mexico. 389-424 p.

First series, no. 9. The United States and British occupancy in Central America, by Dr. Luis Anderson. 427-482 p.

Second series, no. 1. Annual report of the Executive for the previous constitutional year. 42 p.

Second series, no. 2. The British Empire and the Republic of Guatemala, the contending parties. Defense of the Guatemalan government's viewpoint, by Roberto Piragibe da Fonseca. 45-84 p.

Second series, no. 3. Commentary by Lic. Toribio Esquivel Obregón upon the study of the Anglo-Guatemalan controversy, by Dr. Roberto Piragibe da Fonseca. 87-99 p.

Second series, no. 4. Arbitraje sobre Belice por Sinforoso Aguilar. 117-158 p.

Further publications of the Guatemalan ministry for Foreign Affairs presenting the Guatemalan case in the Belize controversy.

López Jiménez, Ramón. Belice, tierra irredenta. México. Ed. Mundo actual. 232 p. [3550

The author, formerly under-secretary of the Salvadorean ministry of foreign affairs, asserts that the Anglo-Guatemalan treaty of 1859 was invalid because Guatemala could not, by herself, recognize British sovereignty in territory which belonged jointly to all the Central American states. The solution of the present "problem" of Belize should, therefore, be found in the transfer of Belize to all the Central American states; they in turn should surrender it to Guatemala.

Pozuelo A., José. Por la patria y por el amigo. Testimonio relativo a los hechos que culminaron con el definitivo y feliz arreglo del problema fronterizo entre Costa Rica y Panamá. San José. Imp. La Tribuna. 27 p., ilus., mapas. [3551

An interesting account, by a Costa Rican journalist, of how he and a Panamanian colleague arranged a meeting in 1940 between President Arias of Panama, and President-elect Calderón of Costa Rica in an endeavor to arrange the settlement of the boundary dispute between the two countries. It was this interview, Sr. Pozuelo states, which laid the basis of agreement and goodwill resulting in the boundary treaty of May 1, 1941.

Sayán Álvarez, Carlos. Política nacional e internacional del Perú. Lima. Ed. Relieves americanos. 51 p. [3552

A collection of speeches by the President of the Chamber of Deputies of Peru, of which the most important concern is the boundary settlement with Ecuador, and the 1941 commercial treaty with Chile.

Sayán de Vidaurre, Alberto. Para la inmediata restitución de las Malvinas. Prólogo de Alfredo L. Palacios. Buenos Aires. Unión nacional y democrática interamericana. 30 p., ilus. [3553

The author prints the text of a letter of January 29, 1943 to the United States Ambassador to Argentina, requesting the United States Government to undertake, "as leader of Pan Americanism," negotiations with Great Britain for "the prompt re-establishment of Argentine sovereignty over the Falklands." Support for the author's views is found, oddly enough, both in a preface by Dr. Alfredo L. Palacios, the eminent Argentine Socialist, and in an editorial reproduced from the rightist paper *Cabildo*.

Vásquez Machicado, Humberto. El ocaso de Villamil de Rada (*Kollasuyo*, año 5, no. 47, abril, p. 184-198; no. 48, mayo, p. 276-289). [3554

A biographical sketch of the Bolivian engineer and author, the first part of which relates to boundary negotiations between Bolivia and Brazil in the period 1860-1875.

ADDENDA

Alekseyev, V. Fashistskaya ugroza Latinskoy Amerike. Moskva. Ogiz. 1942. 39 p. [3554a

An exposé of the activities of Nazi, Fascist and Falange elements in various Latin American countries. [Ed.]

ARGENTINE-BOLIVIAN RAILROAD TREATY; ARGENTINE-BOLIVIAN AGREEMENT ON HIGHWAY CONSTRUCTION (*Bull. pan. amer. union*, vol. 76, June, 1942, p. 354-355). [3555

Summaries of two recent transport agreements between these two Plata region states.

Volkov, A. Latinskaya Amerika v borbye protiv hitlerisma. Moskva. Gospolitizdat. 1942. 47 p. [3555a

A survey of the efforts of Latin America to assist the United Nations in the war against the Axis. [Ed.]

TREATIES, CONVENTIONS, INTERNATIONAL ACTS, PROTOCOLS, AND AGREEMENTS

BY

MANUEL S. CANYES

Pan American Union

GENERAL STATEMENT

The negotiation, approval, ratification, and promulgation of international instruments, both bilateral and multilateral, by the Latin American countries in 1943 showed a slight increase as compared with the previous year.

As will be observed, a great many of the treaties and agreements listed deal with matters connected with the war. Most of them were concluded between the Latin American States themselves, or with the United States. Only seven were concluded with non-American states.

The sources utilized in the preparation of this summary, as in the previous five summaries, are the official documents available in the Library or the Juridical Division of the Pan American Union. Occasionally publications of a non-official character have been relied upon. As some of the official publications for the year 1943 have not as yet been received at the Pan American Union, there is no assurance that the information is complete. As in previous years, a section has been inserted, entitled *Addenda*, to include treaties which appeared in publications received after the list was printed.

The brief abstracts of the contents of the bilateral agreements are given for the purpose of identifying the general nature of each treaty. This treatment is not accorded the world treaties, as the texts of these instruments are more readily accessible.

In accordance with Resolution XXIX approved by the Eighth International Conference of American States held at Lima in 1938, a number of the Governments, members of the Pan American Union, have continued to register with the Pan American Union the treaties, conventions or agreements which they have concluded or ratified. The majority of the registrations were made by the Government of the United States, but many of these have not been reported in the summary because they relate to agreements between the United States and non-American powers.

With respect to the approval and ratification of world treaties and conventions, there was relatively little activity, whereas there was marked activity in connection with Pan American agreements. The action taken by the Latin American countries on Pan American Treaties and conventions is not included in this report. This information appears in the chart which is inserted at the end of the summary.

BILATERAL TREATIES

ARGENTINA—BOLIVIA

Rubber Agreement, signed at La Paz on July 23, 1943.

Argentina promises to buy 250 tons of Bolivian rubber a year at the rate of 9 Argentine pesos per kilogram, and 10.60 Argentine pesos for rolled gum (laminated rubber) placed in Villazón.

The Argentine Government will permit the exportation to Bolivia of machines and live stock for reproduction on a par with the value of Bolivian rubber.

The agreement is to last four years, and is to be retroactive to January 1, 1943.
Reported in: *Revista Argentina de Derecho Internacional*, Buenos Aires, 2ª serie, tomo 7, no. 1, enero–marzo, 1944, p. 69–70 (Spanish).

ARGENTINA—BOLIVIA

Supplement to the Boundary Treaty of July 8, 1925 and Subsequent Notes, effected by exchange of notes signed at Buenos Aires on June 25, 1943.

Provides that the terms set forth in the notes of October 14 and 16, 1925, for the registration of the titles to property which had changed nationality, shall be interpreted in such a way that the date indicated in the exchange of notes of November 9, 1942 shall be extended to September 1, 1945.
Reported in: *Revista Argentina de Derecho Internacional*, Buenos Aires, 2ª serie, tomo 7, no. 1, enero–marzo, 1944, p. 69 (Spanish).

ARGENTINA—BRAZIL

Agreement Regarding the Construction of an International Bridge between the Brazilian City of Santana do Livramento and the Argentine City of Paso de Los Libres, effected by exchange of notes signed at Rio de Janeiro, July 16, 1943.

Because of the shortage of materials due to war, Argentina agrees to furnish gasoline and other items, while Brazil agrees to supply iron and wood, etc. to the respective construction committees responsible for building the bridge.
Reported in: *Boletim do Ministério das Relações Exteriores*, no. 8, 31 de agôsto, 1943, p. 518 (Portuguese); *Revista Argentina de Derecho Internacional*, Buenos Aires, 2ª serie, tomo 7, no. 1, enero–marzo, 1944, p. 69 (Spanish).

ARGENTINA—BRAZIL

Treaty of Commerce and Navigation of January 23, 1940, amended by exchange of notes signed at Rio de Janeiro, July 23, 1942 and January 22, 1943.

Corrects item 240 of Table A regarding Brazilian tariffs on grains and vegetables.
Text of notes in: *Boletim do Ministério das Relações Exteriores*, no. 3, 31 de março, 1943, p. 174–175 (Portuguese).

ARGENTINA—CHILE

Agreement on Frozen Meats established by notes of December 27, 1940, extended for two years by exchange of notes signed at Buenos Aires, March 23, 1943.

Reported in: *Revista Argentina de Derecho Internacional*, Buenos Aires, 2ª serie, tomo 7, no. 1, enero–marzo, 1941, p. 69 (Spanish).

ARGENTINA—CHILE

Agreement to Supply the Argentine Market with Chilean Sodium Nitrate, effected by exchange of notes signed at Buenos Aires, April 12, 1943.

The agreement is to be effective for ten years from the date of signature, and may be renewed at that time.
Summary in: *Informaciones Argentinas*, Buenos Aires, no. 73, 15 de abril, 1943, p. 4 (Spanish).
Reported in: *Revista Argentina de Derecho Internacional*, Buenos Aires, 2ª serie, tomo 7, no. 1, enero–marzo, 1944, p. 69 (Spanish).

ARGENTINA—CHILE

Treaty on the Bases for a Customs Union, signed at Buenos Aires, August 24, 1943.

Provides for a Mixed Commission to study and report on the bases for a customs union within at least a year from the date of signing of this treaty. Besides agreeing on a payments system suitable for mutually advantageous trade, the two governments will immediately abolish or reduce duties and modify their customs systems as soon as possible.
This agreement on the plan of procedure to conclude a customs union, which will be open to adherence by any border country, is intended as the first step toward a continental economic organization in which customs barriers would be reduced or abolished.
Text in: *Argentine News*, no. 54, September, 1943, p. 14 (English); *Informaciones Argentinas*, Buenos Aires, no. 78–79, septiembre-octubre, 1943, p. 18–20 (Spanish).

ARGENTINA—CHILE

Treaty on Traffic and Transit, signed at Buenos Aires, August 24, 1943.

In accordance with the terms of the Argentine-Chilean Commercial Treaty of

June 3, 1933, and the Additional Protocol of February 18, 1938, this treaty provides for customs regulations and defines transit activities for the purpose of facilitating movement of goods in transit through Argentina and Chile and destined for a third country.

Contains special regulations for private traffic subject to the international rules of the Paris Convention of 1926, modifying that of 1909, and for public traffic, subject to the laws of the country through which it is to pass.

Text in: *Argentine News*, Buenos Aires, no. 54, September, 1943, p. 9, 12–13 (English); *Informaciones Argentinas*, Buenos Aires, no. 78–79, septiembre–octubre, 1943, p. 14–15, 18 (Spanish); *Revista Oficial de la Cámara Argentina de Comercio*, Buenos Aires, septiembre, 1943, p. 4–5, 32–33 (Spanish).

ARGENTINA—CHILE·

Treaty on Transandine Railways and International roads, signed at Buenos Aires, August 24, 1943.

Taking into account the notes signed at Mendoza, February 2, 1933 and at Santiago de Chile, March 29, 1933, and the final note of the first meeting of the Joint Committee for the Study of Transandine Railways and Communications signed at Santiago, April 8, 1936, the Governments of Argentina and Chile have agreed to expedite and complete construction on specific sections of the Transandine railroads; to complete the international road between Los Andes and Caracoles and to extend the international road to Santiago and Valparaíso; to commence immediately the surveys not yet started, and to initiate construction or improvements on specific international highways.

Each Government will provide the funds necessary for carrying out inside its territory construction mentioned in this agreement. The loans for this purpose may be launched in both countries, and the Governments will grant one another the necessary authority.

Text in: *Argentine News*, Buenos Aires, no. 54, September, 1943, p. 14 (English).

ARGENTINA—ECUADOR

Commercial Treaty, signed at Buenos Aires on September 1, 1943.

Provides for reciprocal unconditional and unlimited most-favored-nation treatment in export, import and customs relations. This most-favored-nation treatment extends also to nationals of either high contracting party intending to reside, travel, develop business or professions in either country, with certain specified reservations. Article XI binds the respective parties to settle whatever disputes may arise by pacific means according to international law.

Will take effect thirty days after the exchange of ratifications in Quito.

Text in: *Revista Argentina de Derecho Internacional*, Buenos Aires, 2ª serie, tomo 6, no. 4, octubre–diciembre, 1943, p. 377–381 (Spanish); *Argentine News*, Buenos Aires, no. 54, September, 1943, p. 22–23 (English).

ARGENTINA—GREAT BRITAIN

Commercial Agreement Regarding the Purchase of Surplus Argentine Meat, effected by exchange of notes signed at London on August 26, 1943.

The Government of Great Britain promises that all excess exportable Argentine meat, including frozen and dried products, shall be purchased by the British and United Nations Governments until September 30, 1944. Britain will pay in pounds sterling, and other countries will pay in dollars.

Reported in: *Boletim do Ministério das Relações Exteriores*, no. 12, 31 de dezembro, 1943, p. 874 (Portuguese); *The Times*, London, September 27, 1943, p. 4 (English); *New York Times*, September 27, 1943, p. 9 (text of British statement); *American Journal of International Law*, Washington, vol. 38, no. 1, January, 1944, p. 128 (English).

ARGENTINA—PARAGUAY

Act Relative to the Achievement of a Customs Union, signed by the Argentine and Paraguayan Ministers of Foreign Affairs at Buenos Aires, December 15, 1943.

In accordance with Article I of the Commercial Treaty signed on November 17, 1943, this act provides for the establishment of a Mixed Commission to study all available means for achieving a customs union between the two countries. This Commission is to be composed of six representatives of each country.

The Governments agree to take immediate steps to promote commercial interchange between the two countries.

Text in: *Revista Argentina de Derecho Internacional*, Buenos Aires, 2ª serie, tomo 7, no. 1, enero–marzo, 1944, p. 94–95 (Spanish).

ARGENTINA—PARAGUAY

Agreement on Postal Service between Buenos Aires and Asunción and vice-versa, signed at Buenos Aires on December 15, 1943.

Provides for the employment of postal clerks of both countries on trains carrying mail between Buenos Aires and Asunción, and establishes regulations for the handling and distribution of mail.

After the exchange of ratifications in Asunción, this agreement will continue in force unless denounced by either party with six months' notice.

Text in: *Revista Argentina de Derecho Internacional*, Buenos Aires, 2ª serie, tomo 7, no. 1, enero–marzo, 1944, p. 98–99 (Spanish).

ARGENTINA—PARAGUAY

Agreement on the Establishment of Air Communications with Asunción, effected by exchange of notes signed at Buenos Aires, December 15, 1943.

Argentina agrees to extend the northeast air route to Asunción by initiating a transport service for passengers and mail between Buenos Aires and Iguazú with stops at Colonia Yeruá, Monte Caseros and Posadas.

Paraguay agrees to develop an adequate landing field with all the necessary airdrome services, and to aid the work of the personnel stationed in Asunción.

Text in: *Revista Argentina de Derecho Internacional*, Buenos Aires, 2ª serie, tomo 7, no. 1, enero–marzo, 1944, p. 102–103 (Spanish).

ARGENTINA—PARAGUAY

Agreement on the Exchange of Postal and Communications Officials, signed at Buenos Aires on December 15, 1943.

Provides for the travel, study and remuneration of postal and communications officials making surveys in either country.

After the exchange of ratifications in Asunción, this agreement will remain in effect indefinitely unless denounced by either party with six months' notice.

Text in: *Revista Argentina de Derecho Internacional*, Buenos Aires, 2ª serie, tomo 7, no. 1, enero–marzo, 1944, p. 99–100 (Spanish).

ARGENTINA—PARAGUAY

Agreement on Unlawful Publications, signed at Buenos Aires on December 15, 1943.

Provides that the postal administration of either high contracting party shall inform the country of origin of all publications that cannot be legally distributed by mail; and that after such communication, all possible steps shall be taken to prohibit such use of the postal system. For five days after the notification of prohibition, such publications shall be returned to the country of origin. Thereafter, any illegal publications shall be destroyed by the postal administration discovering them.

The agreement shall remain in effect indefinitely unless denounced by either country with six months' notice.

Text in: *Revista Argentina de Derecho Internacional*, Buenos Aires, 2ª serie, tomo 7, no. 1, enero–marzo, 1944, p. 101 (Spanish).

ARGENTINA—PARAGUAY

Agreement Regarding the Establishment of Free Ports in Buenos Aires and Rosario for Paraguayan Goods, signed at Buenos Aires on December 15, 1943.

Provides for the deposit, storage and distribution of Paraguayan goods in Buenos Aires and Rosario; defines the customs regulations on merchandise bound to or from Paraguay; and prescribes reservations on the export and import of arms and munitions.

This agreement will become effective thirty days after the exchange of ratifications in Asunción, and is to continue in force for one year from the day on which either power denounces it. But it may not be denounced until it has been in force for two years.

Text in: *Revista Argentina de Derecho Internacional*, Buenos Aires, 2ª serie, tomo 7, no. 1, enero–marzo, 1944, p. 96–98 (Spanish).

ARGENTINA—PARAGUAY

Commercial Treaty, signed at Buenos Aires, November 17, 1943.

Provides for a Mixed Commission to prepare the way for a complete customs union in keeping with the Agreement signed in Asunción July 8, 1916, and reiterated at Regional Conferences of the Countries of the River Plate.

Establishes regulations for the payment of duties on products passing through either country.

This treaty must be in force at least two years before either party may denounce it, in which case it will continue in effect until one year from the day of denouncement.
Argentina: Ratified by decree of December 3, 1943.
Ratifications exchanged at Buenos Aires December 16, 1943. At that time, additional measures were adopted to facilitate highway, river and air transport, and to establish free port zones in Buenos Aires and Rosario for use by Paraguay.
English text in: *Argentine News*, Buenos Aires, no. 56, November, 1943, p. 4–7, 10–12.
Spanish text in: *Informaciones Argentinas*, Buenos Aires, no. 81, 15 de diciembre, 1943, p. 30–31, 36–39; *Revista Argentina de Derecho Internacional*, Buenos Aires, 2ª serie, tomo 7, no. 1, enero–marzo, 1944, p. 73–91.
Ratification and additional measures in: *Informaciones Argentinas*, Buenos Aires, no. 81, 15 de diciembre, 1943, p. 15 (Spanish); *Boletín de la Cámara de Comercio Argentino-Paraguaya*, Buenos Aires, año 4, no. 12, diciembre, 1943, p. 25–28 (Spanish); *Newsletter of the Chamber of Commerce of the United States of America in the Argentine Republic*, Buenos Aires, Newsletter, no. 482, December 16, 1943, p. 1 (English).

ARGENTINA—PARAGUAY

Convention on the Revision of Texts for the Teaching of History and Geography, signed at Buenos Aires, December 15, 1943.
Provides that statistics and attitudes regarding peoples of the Americas represented in history and geography text books be brought up-to-date.
After the exchange of ratifications in Asunción, this convention shall remain in effect indefinitely unless denounced by either country with six months' notice.
Text in: *Revista Argentina de Derecho Internacional*, Buenos Aires, 2ª serie, tomo 7, no. 1, enero–marzo, 1944, p. 102 (Spanish).

ARGENTINA—PARAGUAY

Exchange of Notes, signed at Asunción November 5, 1943, extending the Supplementary Boundary Treaty of July 5, 1939.
Both Governments agree to extend for one more year the terms set forth in Article 4 of the Supplementary Boundary Treaty of July 5, 1939, in order that the Mixed Commission may complete its work and present its report.
Reported in: *Revista Argentina de Derecho Internacional*, Buenos Aires, 2ª serie, tomo 7, no. 1, enero–marzo, 1944, p. 70 (Spanish).

ARGENTINA—PARAGUAY

Payment Agreement, signed at Buenos Aires, November 17, 1943.
Supplements the Argentine-Paraguayan trade treaty signed November 17, 1943, and provides that from the day this treaty becomes effective a statistical account shall be opened where the c.i.f. value of Argentine exports to Paraguay and the f.o.b. value of Paraguayan exports to Argentina will be registered. Procedures will be controlled by the Central Bank of the Argentine Republic and the Bank of the Republic of Paraguay. The Argentine Government agrees to encourage the investment of Argentine capital to further the development of the Paraguayan industry and production, and will send a technical mission to study on the spot the economic possibilities.
Effective for two years, the present agreement will come into force thirty days after the exchange of ratifications in Buenos Aires. The agreements between the banks for the management of funds shall become effective the same day.
Text in: *Argentine News*, Buenos Aires, no. 56, November, 1943, p. 12 (English); *Informaciones Argentinas*, Buenos Aires, no. 81, 15 de diciembre, 1943, p. 39, 42 (Spanish); *Revista Argentina de Derecho Internacional*, Buenos Aires, 2ª serie, tomo 7, no. 1, enero–marzo, 1944, p. 92–93 (Spanish).

ARGENTINA—SPAIN

Agreement on the Exchange of Official Publications, effected by exchange of notes signed at Buenos Aires, April 12, 1943.
Continues in force the cultural agreement of September 7, 1942, and provides for a more complete exchange of the national literature of either country within the other.
Becomes effective one month after the date of signature, and remains in force indefinitely unless denounced with six months' notice by either party.
Summary in: *Informaciones Argentinas*, Buenos Aires, no. 73, 15 de abril de 1943, p. 3–4 (Spanish).
Reported in: *Revista Argentina de Derecho Internacional*, Buenos Aires, 2ª

serie, tomo 7, no. 1, enero–marzo, 1944, p. 69 (Spanish).

ARGENTINA—UNITED STATES OF AMERICA

Agreement Concerning Military Aviation Instructors, effected by exchange of notes signed at Washington, June 23 and September 2, 1943.
Renews the Agreement of June 29, 1940, as renewed by the Agreement of May 23 and June 3, 1941.
Effective for two years beginning June 29, 1943.
Registered with the Pan American Union by the Government of the United States of America, November 15, 1943.
Reported in: *The Department of State Bulletin*, vol. 9, no. 222, September 25, 1943, p. 216 (English).
Text in: *U. S. Executive Agreement Series*, no. 340 (English).

BOLIVIA—BRAZIL

Agreement on the Regulation of Frontier Commerce, signed at Rio de Janeiro in 1943. (No exact date given.)
Provides that commerce between the frontier populations of the two countries shall be freed from all current and future obligations of inspection. This dispensation shall relate only to products destined for markets catering to immediate and daily consumption, in the frontier zones. Such products may not be shipped inland.
This agreement shall enter into force 30 days after the exchange of ratifications at La Paz, and shall continue in effect for one year, unless previously denounced with three months' notice. It may be renewed for yearly periods by tacit consent.
Reported in: *Boletim do Ministério das Relações Exteriores*, no. 7, 31 de julho, 1943, p. 406 (Portuguese).

BOLIVIA—BRAZIL

Agreement on Tourist Traffic and Granting of Entry Facilities to Nationals of Either Country, signed at Rio de Janeiro in 1943.
Provides certain exemptions from entry fees or taxes for either country's nationals traveling as tourists, or for scientific observations, art, sports, or business interests, on condition that they do not remain more than twelve months at a time. These travelers shall carry consular visas stamped "Temporary."
The Convention shall enter into force sixty days after the exchange of ratifications at La Paz.
Reported in: *Boletim do Ministério das Relações Exteriores*, no. 7, 31 de julho, 1943, p. 406 (Portuguese).

BOLIVIA—URUGUAY

Agreement on Radio-Telegraphic Communications, signed at La Paz, April 28, 1943.
Provides for direct radio-telegraphic service between the two countries.
Summary in: *Boletín oficial del Ministerio de Relaciones Exteriores*, Montevideo, vol. 15, no. 7, mayo, 1943, p. 31–32 (Spanish).

BRAZIL—CHILE

Treaty of Commerce and Navigation, signed at Rio de Janeiro, March 1, 1943.
Provides for unconditional and unlimited most-favored-nation treatment, effective for one year from the date on which ratifications are exchanged. If not denounced with three months' notice prior to the date of expiration, it will continue in force another year.
Replaces the treaty signed at Santiago, November 18, 1941.
Brazil: Approved by decree-law no. 5,331 of March 18, 1943.
Text in: *Diário Oficial*, Rio de Janeiro, 26 de março de 1943, secção 1, p. 4441, 4443–4445, tables (Portuguese and Spanish).
Summary in: *Boletim do Ministério das Relações Exteriores*, no. 3, 31 de março, 1943, p. 142–143 (Portuguese).

BRAZIL—CHINA

Treaty of Friendship, Cancelling Extraterritoriality, signed at Rio de Janeiro, August 20, 1943.
Based on the principles of the treaty of friendship, commerce and navigation signed at Tien-Tsin, October 3, 1881.
Abolishes certain privileges enjoyed by occidental powers in Chinese territory.
Reported in: *Christian Science Monitor*, Boston, August 21, 1943, p. 8 (English); *American Journal of International Law*, Washington, vol. 38, no. 1, January, 1944, p. 126 (English).
Summary in: *Boletim do Ministério das Relações Exteriores*, no. 9, 30 de setembro de 1943, p. 624–625 (Portuguese).

Brazil—Paraguay

Convention for the Promotion of Tourist Traffic, and Granting of Entry Facilities to Nationals of Either Country, signed at Rio de Janeiro, May 10, 1943.

Both governments agree to exempt from entry fees or taxes one another's nationals traveling as tourists, or for scientific observations, art, sports, of business interests, on condition that they do not remain in the visited country more than twelve months at one time.

Both countries bind themselves to make further agreements on related services, such as:

a) Transit of travel vehicles
b) Transit of passenger and mail planes
c) Favorable customs schedule for travelers' baggage

The convention shall enter into force sixty days after exchange of ratifications in Asunción.

Brazil: Ratified September 27, 1943.

Text in: *Boletim do Ministério das Relações Exteriores*, no. 6, 30 de junho de 1943, p. 315–316 (Portuguese).

Reported in: *Diário Oficial*, Rio de Janeiro, 29 de setembro de 1943, secção 1, p. 14483.

Brazil—Paraguay

Treaty of Commerce and Navigation, signed at Rio de Janeiro, May 10, 1943.

Provides unconditional and unlimited most-favored-nation treatment for commerce between the two signatory states. Merchant ships of either country shall have equal privileges in the territorial waters of Brazil and Paraguay, especially in the use of port facilities for loading and unloading passengers and cargo.

The treaty provides for many other reciprocal facilities.

Partial text in: *Boletim do Ministério das Relações Exteriores*, no. 6, 30 de junho de 1943, p. 314–315 (Portuguese).

Brazil—Portugal

Agreement Regarding the Establishment of a Telegraph Service, signed at Rio de Janeiro, April 30, 1943.

In conformity with Article XIII of the International Convention on Radiocommunications signed at Madrid in September, 1932, and as a complement to the Postal Agreement signed by Brazil and Portugal at Lisbon, April 30, 1942, this agreement establishes regulations and rates for regular and coded messages.

To be effective on the date decided by the interested administrations, and to continue in force indefinitely.

Brazil: Approved by decree-law no. 5,536, June 1, 1943.

Text in: *Diário Oficial*, Rio de Janeiro, 3 de junho de 1943, secção 1, p. 8641 (Portuguese).

Brazil—United States of America

Agreement for the Intensification of Rubber Production in the State of Mato Grosso, signed at Rio de Janeiro, April 19, 1943.

The State of Mato Grosso undertakes to stimulate the production of rubber in unworked lands with the financial assistance of the Rubber Development Corporation. The agreement is to remain in effect until December 31, 1946.

Brazil: Approved by decree-law no. 5,476, May 11, 1943.

Text in: *Diário Oficial*, Rio de Janeiro, 13 de mayo de 1943, secção 1, p. 7349–7350 (Portuguese).

Brazil—United States of America

Agreement for the Prosecution of the Cooperative Public Health and Sanitation Program in Brazil, Provided for by Resolution XXX, Approved at the Third Meeting of Ministers of Foreign Affairs held at Rio de Janeiro in January, 1942, signed at Rio de Janeiro, November 25, 1943.

Provides that the Brazilian Ministry of Education and Health and The Institute of Inter-American Affairs shall continue to maintain the technical service known as Serviço Especial de Saúde Pública (SESP), which shall formulate and execute the health and sanitation program.

The agreement also establishes a schedule for the deposit of funds in the Banco do Brasil for use by SESP, and provides that the Institute of Inter-American Affairs may maintain a field party of technicians in Brazil to consummate the program consisting of individual projects.

Effective January 1, 1944, and in force until December 31, 1948.

Text in: *Boletim do Ministério das Rela-*

ções Exteriores, no. 12, 31 de dezembro de 1943, p. 960–967 (Portuguese and English).

BRAZIL—UNITED STATES OF AMERICA

Agreement on the Recruitment, Transportation and placement of Workers in the Amazon, signed at Rio de Janeiro, September 6, 1943.

Provides that the Rubber Development Corporation shall deposit $2,400,000 in the Banco do Brasil at the disposal of the Brazilian Government. $300,000 will be available immediately and the rest will become available in similar amounts at definite periods.

Brazil: Ratified September 14, 1943, by decree-law no. 5,813.

Text in: *Boletim do Ministério das Relações Exteriores,* no. 10, 31 de outubro de 1943, p. 719–721 (Portuguese).

BRAZIL—UNITED STATES OF AMERICA

Agreement Regarding Health and Sanitation Projects in the Rio Doce Valley, signed at Rio de Janeiro, February 10, 1943.

Brazil: Approved by decree-law no. 5,592, June 18, 1943.

Reported in: *Diário Oficial,* Rio de Janeiro, 12 de julho de 1943, secção 1, p. 10609 (Portuguese).

BRAZIL—UNITED STATES OF AMERICA

Agreement Regarding Military Service, effected by exchange of notes signed at Washington, January 23, April 28, and May 24, 1943.

Effective April 30, 1943.

Provides a method under which Brazilian citizens may elect to serve in the forces of their own country, in lieu of service in the armed forces of the United States.

Registered with the Pan American Union by the Government of the United States on August 27, 1943.

Text in: *U. S. Executive Agreement Series,* no. 327 (Portuguese and English).

Reported in: *Boletim do Ministério das Relações Exteriores,* no. 7, 31 de julho de 1943, p. 450–451 (Portuguese).

BRAZIL—UNITED STATES OF AMERICA

Financial Agreement, signed at Rio de Janeiro, March 18, 1943.

The Export-Import Bank of Washington provides a credit of $14,000,000 in favor of the Companhia Vale de Rio Doce, S. A., to finance the production, sale and transportation of minerals.

Brazil: Ratified May 24, 1943.

Text in: *Diário Oficial,* Rio de Janeiro, 26 de maio de 1943, seeção 1, p. 8145 (Portuguese).

BRAZIL—VENEZUELA

Commercial Modus Vivendi, effected by exchange of notes signed at Caracas, June 11, 1943.

This agreement extends for the period of one year the commercial *modus vivendi* signed at Caracas on June 11, 1940.

It will continue in effect until June 11, 1944, unless suspended in accordance with the stipulations of the 1940 agreement.

Text of notes in: Ministerio de relaciones exteriores. *Libro amarillo de los Estados Unidos de Venezuela ... 1944.* Caracas. Tipografía americana. 1944. p. 226–227 (Spanish).

CHILE—ECUADOR

Convention on Cultural Relations and the Exchange of Professors and Students in the Fields of Science, Letters and Arts, signed at Quito, October 30, 1943.

Text in: *Boletín Informativo,* Ministerio de relaciones exteriores, 25 de noviembre de 1943, p. 1–3 (Spanish).

CHILE—MEXICO

Protocol Extending for One Year the Commercial Modus Vivendi of March 23, 1942, signed at Mexico City, October 13, 1943.

The *modus vivendi* will continue in force for three months after one government has notified the other that it wishes to terminate the agreement.

Reported in: *Revista del Comercio Exterior,* México, tomo 8, no. 11, noviembre, 1943, p. 370 (Spanish).

CHILE—UNITED STATES OF AMERICA

Agreement Renewing the Agreement of April 23, 1940, Relative to a Military Aviation Mission, effected by exchanges of notes signed at Washington, November 27 and December 23, 1942, and April 14, 1943.

Original agreement reported in *Handbook, no. 6, 1940.*

Effective April 23, 1943.

Registered with the Pan American Union by the Government of the United States of America, June 21, 1943.
Text in: *U. S. Executive Agreement Series*, no. 315 (Spanish and English).

CHILE—UNITED STATES OF AMERICA

Mutual Aid Agreement, effected by an exchange of notes, signed at Washington, March 2, 1943.

This agreement on the principles of mutual aid applicable to the common defense of the American continent was negotiated under the authority of and in conformity with the Lend-Lease Act of March 11, 1941.
Reported in: *The Department of State Bulletin*, vol. 8, no. 193, March 6, 1943, p. 208 (English).

CHILE—URUGUAY

Convention Facilitating the Importation of Books and Printed Matter, signed at Montevideo, August 31, 1943.

Establishes duty-free entry for unbound or paper-bound books and pamphlets, such as newspapers, magazines, and musical compositions, provided they are printed by presses established in the signatory states, and provided they are not de luxe editions. In both countries, such publications shall be entitled to price-scales equivalent to 50 per cent of the general rate formerly allowed such publications.

Newspapers, magazines and other publications of definite frequency not exceeding three months shall benefit by internal postal rates.

This agreement does not include publications of propaganda destined to affect the political, social or moral order of the signatory states.

Ratifications are to be exchanged as soon as possible at Santiago, and the convention is to remain in force indefinitely unless denounced with six months' notice by either party.

Text in: *Boletín del Ministerio de Relaciones Exteriores*, Montevideo, segunda época, tomo 16, no. 3, setiembre, 1943, p. 39–40 (Spanish).

CHILE—URUGUAY

Convention Regarding the Revision of Educational Texts, signed at Montevideo, August 31, 1943.

Provides for the periodic revision of texts used in teaching the national history of either country to develop understanding and cooperation between the two countries, especially in matters of inter-American solidarity, the pacific relations of states, the growth of national and international juridical relations, and the general influences of moral, scientific, intellectual and artistic values.

Both governments agree to revise periodically the statistics of geographic texts.

Revision of texts is to be entrusted to the National Committees for Intellectual Cooperation.

Ratifications shall be exchanged as soon as possible in Santiago, and the convention is to remain in force indefinitely, unless denounced with six months' notice by either party.

Text in: *Boletín del Ministerio de Relaciones Exteriores*, Montevideo, segunda época, tomo 16, no. 3, setiembre, 1943, p. 40–42 (Spanish).

CHILE—URUGUAY

Travel and Tourist Convention, signed at Montevideo, August 31, 1943.

To facilitate travel, this convention provides that a citizen of one country may enter and remain up to three months in the other country with no requisite other than that showing his identification card to the authorities, and proving by a pass certified by his national consular officials that there will be no difficulty in his returning to his country of origin.

A resident alien of at least five years' standing in either country may also enjoy these travel privileges, provided the proper authorities certify that there will be no difficulty in his returning to his country of residence.

Both States agree to facilitate the movement of automotive tourist traffic in accordance with the provisions of the automotive traffic convention signed at Paris, April 24, 1936, as long as there is no similar inter-American treaty.

Ratifications are to be exchanged as soon as possible at Santiago, and the convention is to remain in force indefinitely, unless denounced with three months' notice by either party.

Text in: *Boletín del Ministerio de Relaciones Exteriores*, Montevideo, segunda época, tomo 16, no. 3, setiembre, 1943, p. 37–39 (Spanish).

Chile—Venezuela

Commercial Modus Vivendi, effected by Exchange of notes signed at Caracas, November 5, 1943.

Renews for a period of one year the commercial *modus vivendi* signed at Caracas, October 11, 1941, and renewed at Santiago de Chile, November 5, 1942.

Effective from the date of signature, this agreement shall be applied provisionally until it is ratified by the Chilean Government.

Text in: Ministerio de relaciones exteriores. *Libro amarillo de los Estados Unidos de Venezuela . . . 1944.* Caracas. Tipografía americana. 1944. p. 233–234 (Spanish).

Colombia—Ecuador

Additional Protocol to the Treaty of Commerce of July 6, 1942, signed at Quito, October 14, 1943.

This protocol modifies the list of Colombian and Ecuadorian products to be admitted duty-free to either country, as stated in Article V of the Treaty of Commerce of July 6, 1942.

Text in: *Comercio Ecuatoriano,* Quito, no. 30, marzo, 1944, p. 5 (Spanish).

Colombia—Spain

Payment Agreement, signed at Madrid, July 26, 1943.

To expedite reciprocal trade and commercial relations, the two governments have established a "clearing" system for merchandise coming from one another's countries, and have agreed that credit shall be furnished by the Instituto Español de Moneda Extranjera and by the Banco de la República de Colombia to facilitate the handling of exports. The debtor nation shall reimburse the appropriate bank within six months after drawing on these funds.

This agreement shall continue in force for two years after the day it becomes effective, and by tacit consent may be renewed for two-year intervals, unless denounced with three months' notice by one of the high contracting parties.

Text in: *Boletín Comercial, Órgano Oficial de la Cámara de Comercio de Medellín,* no. 222, noviembre, 1943, p. 2–4 (Spanish).

Colombia—United States of America

Agreement Renewing a Naval Mission, effected by exchange of notes signed at Washington, July 23 and August 7, 1943.

Continues in effect the agreement of November 23, 1938 as modified by the supplementary agreement of August 30, 1941, and extended by the agreement of September 22 and November 5, 1942.

Registered with the Pan American Union by the Government of the United States of America, October 16, 1943.

Text in: *U. S. Executive Agreement Series,* no. 337 (English and Spanish).

Colombia—Venezuela

Agreement Concerning Frontier Commercial Air Traffic, effected by exchange of notes signed at Caracas, March 20, 1943.

Permits straight-line flying between certain points, regardless of the national borders, by the commercial airplanes of either country, and grants mutual landing privileges.

Effective indefinitely, unless terminated with 30 days' notice.

Text in: *Gaceta Oficial,* Caracas, marzo, 1943, p. 140.501 (Spanish); *Boletín de la Cámara de Comercio de Caracas,* marzo, 1943, p. 8744–8746 (Spanish).

Colombia—Venezuela

Commercial Treaty, effected by exchange of notes signed at Caracas, March 13, 1943.

Original agreement reported in *Handbook, no. 8, 1942.*

This treaty renews for the period of one year from the date of signing the convention of March 14, 1936, which was extended for additional periods of one year each in 1937, 1938, 1939, 1940, 1941 and 1942. It may be extended for an additional year at the time of expiration.

Text in: Ministerio de relaciones exteriores. *Libro amarillo de los Estados Unidos de Venezuela . . . 1944.* Caracas. Tipografía americana. 1944. p. 229–232 (Spanish); *Gaceta oficial,* Caracas, 16 de marzo, 1943, p. 140.405, 140.408–140.409 (Spanish).

Costa Rica—United States of America

Agreement Concerning Cooperative Rubber Investigations in Costa Rica, effected by exchange of notes signed at San José, June 21 and July 1, 1943.

Continues in force after June 30, 1943 the agreement of April 19 and June 16, 1941, as amended by the supplementary agreement of April 3, 1943. (See also: Supplementary agreement.)

Registered with the Pan American Union by the Government of the United States of America, October 11, 1943.

Text in: *U. S. Executive Agreement Series*, no. 335 (Spanish and English).

Costa Rica—United States of America

Supplementary Agreement Concerning Cooperative Rubber Investigations in Costa Rica, effected by exchange of notes signed at San José, April 3, 1943.

Establishes procedures to be followed in connection with the sale of rubber products and with respect to accounting and disbursements. It is to be an integral part of the agreement effected by an exchange of notes dated April 19, 1941 and June 16, 1941.

Registered with the Pan American Union by the Government of the United States of America on July 14, 1943.

Text in: *U. S. Executive Agreement Series*, no. 318 (Spanish and English).

Cuba—United States of America

Agreement Regarding Military Service by Nationals of Either Country Residing in the Other, effected by exchanges of notes signed at Washington, November 6, 1942, January 9 and February 1, 1943.

Reported in *Handbook, no. 8, 1942*.

Provides a method under which Cuban citizens may elect to serve in the forces of their own country, in lieu of service in the armed forces of the United States.

Registered with the Pan American Union by the Government of the United States of America, August 19, 1943.

Text in: *U. S. Executive Agreement Series*, no. 321 (Spanish and English).

Cuba—United States of America

Agreement Regarding the 1943 Cuban Sugar Crop, effected by exchange of notes signed at Havana, April 2 and 3, 1943.

Provides that the Cuban Sugar Stabilization Institute shall sell to the Commodity Credit Corporation 2,700,000 tons of the 1943 Cuban sugar crop, in the form of raw sugar; that the 300,000 tons of the 1943 Cuban sugar to be marketed to other than United States markets shall be offered first to the CCC; and that sugar not needed for local consumption shall be offered to the CCC before being offered to other purchasers.

Also provides for the disposition of the 1942-crop molasses owned by the Defense Supplies Corporation.

Reported in: *The Department of State Bulletin*, vol. 8, no. 200, April 24, 1943, p. 355 (English).

Cuba—United States of America

Agreement Regarding the 1944 Cuban Sugar Crop, signed at Washington, September 22, 1943.

Through the Commodity Credit Corporation the United States agrees to purchase a minimum of 4 million short tons of the 1944 Cuban sugar crop to supply the requirements of the United States and of the other United Nations.

Reported in: *The Department of State Bulletin*, vol. 9, no. 222, September 25, 1943, p. 216 (English).

Cuba—United States of America

Supplementary Military and Naval Cooperation Agreement with Cuba, signed at Havana, on February 1, 1943.

Supplements the agreement of June 19, 1942 and the supplementary agreement of September 7, 1942.

Reported in: *The Department of State Bulletin*, vol. 8, no. 206, June 5, 1943, p. 501 (English).

Dominican Republic—United States of America

Agreement Approving the Memorandum of Understanding Dated May 20, 1943, Relative to the Purchase by the United States of Exportable Surpluses of Dominican Rice, Corn and Peanut Meal, effected by ex-

change of notes signed at Ciudad Trujillo, June 10, 1943.
Registered with the Pan American Union by the Government of the United States of America, February 25, 1944.
Text in: *U. S. Executive Agreement Series,* no. 350 (English and Spanish).

DOMINICAN REPUBLIC—UNITED STATES OF AMERICA

Agreement Regarding a Health and Sanitation Program, effected by exchanges of notes signed at Ciudad Trujillo, June 19 and July 7, 1943.
Provides that the Government of the United States of America shall contribute a sum not to exceed $100,000 and a group of public health technicians to cooperate with Dominican Government officials in the execution of a program of health and sanitation.
The Dominican Republic will contribute such personnel, services and funds for local expenditures as it may consider necessary for the efficient development of the program.
Registered with the Pan American Union by the Government of the United States of America, January 11, 1944.
Text in: *U. S. Executive Agreement Series,* no. 346 (English and Spanish).

DOMINICAN REPUBLIC—UNITED STATES OF AMERICA

Agreement Regarding a Naval Mission to the Dominican Republic, signed at Washington, January 25, 1943.
The mission is to cooperate with the Dominican Ministry of War and Marine in increasing the efficiency of its coast guard and aviation, and will continue for a period of four years from the date of signing this agreement, unless extended or previously terminated.
Registered with the Pan American Union by the Government of the United States of America, June 19, 1943.
Text in: *U. S. Executive Agreement Series,* no. 312 (English and Spanish).

DOMINICAN REPUBLIC—UNITED STATES OF AMERICA

Agreement Regarding Workmen's Compensation in Connection with Certain Projects under Construction or Operation in the Dominican Republic, effected by exchanges of notes signed at Ciudad Trujillo, October 14 and 19, 1943.
Provides for the payment of compensation benefits under United States Law in case of claims by American citizens employed on projects under construction or operation by cost-plus contractors with the Government of the United States in the Dominican Republic.
Registered with the Pan American Union by the Government of the United States of America, May 23, 1944.
Text in: *U. S. Executive Agreement Series,* no. 353 (English and Spanish).

ECUADOR—UNITED STATES OF AMERICA

Agreement Concerning Detail of a Military Officer to Serve as Technical Director of the Eloy Alfaro Military College of Ecuador, signed at Washington, September 13, 1943.
This agreement came into force on the date of signature, and is to continue for a period of four years unless previously terminated.
Registered with the Pan American Union by the Government of the United States of America, November 11, 1943.
Text in: *U. S. Executive Agreement Series,* no. 338 (English and Spanish).

EL SALVADOR—UNITED STATES OF AMERICA

Agreement Extending the Agreement of March 27, 1941 Concerning the Detail of Military Officer to Serve as Director of the Military School and of the Military Academy of El Salvador, effected by exchange of notes signed at San Salvador, March 25, 1943.
Original agreement reported in *Handbook, no. 7, 1941.*
Effective March 27, 1943.
Registered with the Pan American Union by the Government of the United States of America, July 15, 1943.
Text in: *U. S. Executive Agreement Series,* no. 316 (Spanish and English).

EL SALVADOR—UNITED STATES OF AMERICA

Agreement Regarding Military Service, effected by exchanges of notes signed at Washington, April 3, May 14 and May 31, 1943.
Effective May 15, 1943.
Provides a method whereby Salvadorean

citizens may elect to serve in the forces of their own country, in lieu of service in the armed forces of the United States.
Registered with the Pan American Union by the Government of the United States of America, September 22, 1943.
Text in: *U. S. Executive Agreement Series*, no. 325 (English and Spanish).

EL SALVADOR—UNITED STATES OF AMERICA

Agreement Regarding the Detail of Military Officer to Serve as Director of the Military School and of the Military Academy of El Salvador, signed at San Salvador, May 21, 1943.

This agreement came into force on May 21, 1943, and is to continue in force for a period of two years, unless extended or previously terminated.
Registered with the Pan American Union by the Government of the United States of America, October 16, 1943.
Text in: *U. S. Executive Agreement Series*, no. 328 (English and Spanish).

GUATEMALA—UNITED STATES OF AMERICA

Agreement Concerning the Detail of a Military Officer to serve as Director of the Polytechnic School of Guatemala, signed at Washington, July 17, 1943.

This agreement became effective on the date of signature, and is to continue in force for a period of one year, unless previously terminated.
Registered with the Pan American Union by the Government of the United States of America, September 16, 1943.
Text in: *U. S. Executive Agreement Series*, no. 329 (Spanish and English).

GUATEMALA—UNITED STATES OF AMERICA

Agreement Regarding the Construction of the Inter-American Highway, effected by exchange of notes signed at Guatemala, May 19, 1943.

Provides for certain financial and technical arrangements to improve the Guatemalan section of the Inter-American Highway.
Registered with the Pan American Union by the Government of the United States of America, January 11, 1944.
Text in: *U. S. Executive Agreement Series*, no. 345 (English and Spanish).

HAITI—UNITED STATES OF AMERICA

Supplementary Agreement Regarding Haitian Finances, signed at Port-au-Prince, August 28, 1943.

Provides for certain modifications of the provisions of Articles I and II of the Executive Agreement of September 30, 1942, and for the continuance of those provisions in effect from and after October 1, 1943 to and including September 30, 1944, with some exceptions.
Registered with the Pan American Union by the Government of the United States of America, May 23, 1944.
Text in: *U. S. Executive Agreement Series*, no. 378 (English and Spanish).

HAITI—VENEZUELA

Commercial Modus Vivendi Agreement, effected by exchange of notes signed at Port-au-Prince, May 29, 1943 and at Caracas, July 10, 1943.

This agreement is in accordance with the Haitian decree-law of May 19, 1943, whereby the President of Haiti decided to grant to all American republics the benefits of the lowest rates of import duties.
The present *modus vivendi* will be in force for a period of one year, and at the time of expiration may be extended for a similar period.
Text in: Ministerio de relaciones exteriores. *Libro amarillo de los Estados Unidos de Venezuela . . . 1944.* Caracas. Tipografía americana. 1944. p. 244–245 (Spanish).

HONDURAS—UNITED STATES OF AMERICA

Agreement Regarding Plantation Rubber Investigations, effected by exchanges of notes signed at Tegucigalpa, June 18 and 28, 1943.

Continues in force the agreement of February 28, 1941, providing for the development of a source of crude rubber in Honduras.
Registered with the Pan American Union by the Government of the United States of America, May 23, 1944.
Text in: *U. S. Executive Agreement Series*, no. 358 (English and Spanish). Also contains the text of the agrement of February 28, 1941.

MEXICO—UNITED STATES OF AMERICA

Agreement on the Temporary Migration of Mexican Agricultural Workers to the United States, effected by exchanges of notes signed at Mexico City, April 26, 1943.

Revises the agreement of August 4, 1942, which was reported in *Handbook, no. 8, 1942*.

Registered with the Pan American Union by the Government of the United States of America, May 23, 1944.

Text in: *U. S. Executive Agreement Series*, no. 351 (English and Spanish).

Reported in: *The Department of State Bulletin*, vol. 9, no. 215, August 7, 1943, p. 86 (English).

MEXICO—UNITED STATES OF AMERICA

Agreement Regarding a Health and Sanitation Program, effected by exchange of notes signed at Mexico City, June 30 and July 1, 1943.

Both Governments agree to provide certain sums of money and technical personnel to collaborate in a program for the development of health and sanitation in Mexico.

Registered with the Pan American Union by the Government of the United States of America, February 25, 1944.

Text in: *U. S. Executive Agreement Series*, no. 347 (English and Spanish).

MEXICO—UNITED STATES OF AMERICA

Agreement Regarding Military Service, effected by exchange of notes signed at Mexico City, January 22, 1943.

Regulates certain aspects of the performance of military service by nationals of either country residing in the territory of the other country.

Registered with the Pan American Union by the Government of the United States of America, September 16, 1943.

Text in: *U. S. Executive Agreement Series*, no. 323 (English and Spanish); *The Department of State Bulletin*, vol. 8, no. 186, January 23, 1943, p. 87–90 (English).

MEXICO—UNITED STATES OF AMERICA

Agreement Regarding Plantation Rubber Investigations, effected by exchanges of notes signed at Mexico City, July 10 and September 20, 1943.

Effective July 1, 1943.

Continues in force the agreement of April 11, 1941, as supplemented by the agreement of July 14, 1942 and the agreement of March 3, 4 and 29 and April 3, 1943, providing for the development of a source of crude rubber in Mexico.

May be terminated by six months' written notice from either government.

Text in: *U. S. Executive Agreement Series*, no. 364 (English and Spanish). Also contains the texts of the earlier agreements.

MEXICO—UNITED STATES OF AMERICA

Agreement Regarding the Recruiting of Mexican Non-Agricultural Workers, effected by exchange of notes signed at Mexico City, April 29, 1943.

Provides certain principles, procedures and conditions under which unskilled non-agricultural workers will be recruited in Mexico for non-agricultural work in the United States.

Registered with the Pan American Union by the Government of the United States of America, May 23, 1944.

Text in: *U. S. Executive Agreement Series*, no. 376 (English and Spanish).

MEXICO—UNITED STATES OF AMERICA

Convention for the Protection of Migratory Birds and Game Mammals, signed at Mexico City, February 7, 1936.

United States of America: On October 9, 1943 the President proclaimed an amendment to this convention. It relates to the open seasons on mourning or turtle dove.

Reported in: *The Department of State Bulletin*, vol. 9, no. 225, October 16, 1943, p. 267 (English).

Text of treaty in: *U. S. Treaty Series*, no. 912, 1937 (English and Spanish).

MEXICO—UNITED STATES OF AMERICA

Lend-Lease Agreement, signed at Washington, March 18, 1943, to replace the agreement of March 27, 1942.

Original agreement reported in *Handbook, no. 8, 1942*.

This agreement on the principles of mutual aid applicable to the common defense of the American continent was negotiated under the authority of and in conformity with the Lend-Lease Act of March 11, 1941.

Reported in: *The Department of State Bulletin*, vol. 8, no. 195, March 20, 1943, p. 251 (English).

NICARAGUA—UNITED STATES OF AMERICA

Agreement Concerning Detail of a Military Officer to Serve as Director of the Military Academy of the National Guard of Nicaragua, effected by exchange of notes signed at Washington, October 22 and 25, 1943.
Continues in force the agreement of May 22, 1941.
Registered with the Pan American Union by the Government of the United States of America, January 11, 1944.
Text in: *U. S. Executive Agreement Series*, no. 344 (English).

NICARAGUA—UNITED STATES OF AMERICA

Agreement Regarding Plantation Rubber Investigations, effected by exchanges of notes signed at Managua, June 23 and 26, 1943.
Continues in force the agreement of January 11, 1941 providing for the development of rubber plantations in Nicaragua.
Registered with the Pan American Union by the Government of the United States of America, May 23, 1944.
Text in: *U. S. Executive Agreement Series*, no. 357 (English and Spanish). Contains the text of the agreement of January 11, 1941.

PANAMA—UNITED STATES OF AMERICA

Agreement Regarding the Inter-American Highway, effected by exchange of notes signed at Panama, May 15 and June 7, 1943.
The Government of Panama agrees to assume one-third of the total cost of the construction of the Inter-American Highway within the limits of the Panamanian section under Public Law 375 of December 26, 1941 of the Congress of the United States of America. The Panamanian share of the cost will amount to approximately $2,200,000.
Registered with the Pan American Union by the Government of the United States of America, May 23, 1944.
Text in: *U. S. Executive Agreement Series*, no. 365 (English and Spanish).

PANAMA—UNITED STATES OF AMERICA

Agreement Renewing Agreement for the Detail of a United States Army Officer as Adviser to the Minister of Foreign Affairs of Panama, effected by exchange of notes signed at Washington, July 6, and August 5, 1943.
Renews for a period of one year the agreement signed July 7, 1942, which was reported in *Handbook, no. 8, 1942*.
Effective July 7, 1943.
Registered with the Pan American Union by the Government of the United States of America, October 16, 1943.
Text in: *U. S. Executive Agreement Series*, no. 336 (English and Spanish).
Reported in: *Department of State Bulletin*, vol. 9, no. 217, August 21, 1943, p. 117 (English).

PARAGUAY—PERU

Convention Regarding the Promotion of Cultural Relations, signed at Lima, July 9, 1943.
Provides that, beginning in 1944, both Governments shall stimulate the exchange of students and professors, official publications, photographs, films of historical and geographic interest, and particularly those dealing with hygiene, physical education, social welfare, etc.; establish scholarships and fellowships for students in the universities and special schools in Lima and Asunción; hold institutes in both capitals, and promote investigations in science and the arts.
Both governments agree to organize through their respective offices of cultural relations an exchange of periodicals and clippings on technical, economic, social and cultural affairs of their people, and to maintain radio programs on official broadcasting stations.
Ratifications shall be exchanged as soon as possible in either Lima or Asunción. The convention shall continue in force indefinitely unless denounced by six months' notice from either high contracting party.
Text in: *El Comercio*, Lima, 10 de julio, 1943, p. 2, 4 (Spanish).
Reported in: *El País*, Asunción, 13 de julio, 1943, p. 2 (Spanish).

PARAGUAY—UNITED STATES OF AMERICA

Agreement Regarding a Military Aviation Mission to the Republic of

Paraguay, signed at Washington, October 27, 1943.

The mission is to continue for a period of four years from the date of the signing of the agreement, unless previously terminated or extended, and is to cooperate with the Commander in Chief of the Armed Forces of the Republic of Paraguay and with the personnel of the Paraguayan Air Force with a view to enhancing the efficiency of the Paraguayan Air Force.

Registered with the Pan American Union by the Government of the United States of America, January 11, 1944.

Text in: *U. S. Executive Agreement Series,* no. 343 (English and Spanish).

PARAGUAY—UNITED STATES OF AMERICA

Agreement Regarding a Military Mission, signed at Washington, December 10, 1943.

The Mission is to continue for a period of four years from the date of the signing of the Agreement, unless extended or previously terminated, and is to cooperate with the Commander in Chief of the Armed Forces of the Republic of Paraguay and to serve as instructors at the Paraguayan Superior School of War and for such purposes as may be agreed upon by the Chief of the Mission and the Commander in Chief of the Armed Forces.

Registered with the Pan American Union by the Government of the United States of America, February 25, 1944.

Text in: *U. S. Executive Agreement Series,* no. 354 (English and Spanish).

PERU—UNITED STATES OF AMERICA

Agreement on the Establishment of the Inter-American Cooperative Food Production Service in Peru, effected by exchanges of notes signed at Lima, May 19 and 20, 1943.

Peru: Ratified May 20, 1943.

Text in: *U. S. Executive Agreement Series,* no. 385 (English and Spanish).

Reported in: *Department of State Bulletin,* vol. 9, no. 263, July 9, 1944, p. 55 (English).

Ratification reported in: *Revista de Legislación Peruana,* Lima, año 4, no. 41, mayo, 1943, p. 2884 (Spanish).

PERU—UNITED STATES OF AMERICA

Agreement Regarding the Sale of Strategic Metals and Minerals to the Metals Reserve Company, signed at Lima, July 20, 1943.

Provides for further exploration of mines and the purchase and export of strategic metals and minerals by the Metals Reserve Company to meet the demands of the United Nations in the war effort.

Effective from date of signature until June 30, 1944.

Text in: *Revista de Legislación Peruana,* Lima, año 4, no. 43, julio, 1943, p. 3099-3103 (Spanish); *Economista Peruano,* Lima, año 33, no. 59, tercera era, agosto, 1943, p. 217-219.

Reported in: *Boletim do Ministério das Relações Exteriores,* no. 9, 30 de setembro de 1943, p. 589 (Portuguese).

PERU—UNITED STATES OF AMERICA

Agreement Relative to the Detail of a Military Adviser to Remount Service of Peruvian Army, effected by exchange of notes, signed at Washington, November 23 and December 20, 1943.

Renews the agreement of April 15, 1941 reported in *Handbook, no. 7, 1941.*

Registered with the Pan American Union by the Government of the United States of America, May 23, 1944.

Text in: *U. S. Executive Agreement Series,* no. 363 (English and Spanish).

PERU—UNITED STATES OF AMERICA

Amendment to the Rotenone Conventions of May 7, 1942 and August 18, 1942, signed at Lima, June 16, 1943.

By the Convention of August 18, 1942 the Defense Supplies Corporation transferred its responsibilities in the Convention of May 7, 1942 to the Commodity Credit Corporation. This Amendment to the Rotenone Conventions, signed by the Commodity Credit Corporation and the Republic of Peru, provides fixed prices for rotenone in roots or in powdered form of definitely stipulated chemical content. These prices shall be applied to contracts made between May 12, 1943 and May 7, 1944, and shall be paid by the Commodity Credit Corporation.

The Government of Peru shall determine the time necessary to dry and grind the roots to meet the specifications of quality set forth in the treaty of May 7, 1942, and shall require that all rotenone in root or powdered form in excess of the normal crop shall be sold to the Commodity Credit Corporation.

Text in: *Revista de Legislación Peruana*, Lima, año 4, no. 46, octubre, p. 3389-3390 (Spanish).

PERU—UNITED STATES OF AMERICA

Convention with the Defense Supplies Corporation Regarding Aviation, signed at Lima, February 12, 1943.

Supplements the rubber agreement of April 23, 1942.

Provides for financial arrangements with the Defense Supplies Corporation in constructing certain airport facilities, supplying certain airplanes, and improving communications in the remote rubber areas.

Text in: *Revista de Legislación Peruana*, Lima, año 4, no. 44, agosto, 1943, p. 3145-3150 (Spanish).

Reported in: *Department of State Bulletin*, vol. 8, no. 191, February 20, p. 175, 1943 (English).

PERU—UNITED STATES OF AMERICA

Quinine Convention of October 19, 1942 and Memorandum to the Convention, signed at Lima, June 19, 1943.

Principal convention: Provides for augmenting the output of cinchona bark, for establishing permanent plantations and installations for the treatment of the bark in Peru, and gives chemical specifications and price scales for products destined for the United States.

The United States of America acting through the Defense Supply Corporation and the Republic of Peru together with the Permanent Quinine Committee, agree that this convention shall be in force for three years from the date of signature, and may be extended for yearly periods thereafter.

Memorandum to the convention: The signatories of the principal convention agree that the Peruvian Government's plantation called "Sinchono" near Tingo María is adequate for the cultivation of cinchona trees, and determine the plantation's program. Of the $300,000 provided for the promotion of cinchona cultivation and the output of antimalarial products in Peru, up to $100,000 shall be set aside to run this plantation until October 19, 1945, and other funds shall come from the Permanent Quinine Committee. After that date all matters of conservation, administration and improvement and expansion shall revert to the Peruvian Permanent Quinine Committee or other designated agency. Clauses 5 and 6 pertain to cinchona production and shipments to the armed forces of the United Nations.

This convention shall be effective from the date of signing until October 19, 1958. Clauses 5 and 6 shall not lapse before December 31, 1965.

Peru: Ratified by law no. 9806 of June 12, 1943.

Text in: *Revista de Legislación Peruana*, Lima, año 4, no. 46, octubre, 1943, p. 3359-3369 (Spanish).

Summary in: *Economista Peruano*, Lima, año 33, no. 50, 10 de noviembre de 1942, p. 111 (Spanish).

VENEZUELA—CANADA

Commercial Modus Vivendi, effected by exchange of notes signed at Caracas, April 9, 1943.

Renews without any modifications for the period of one year, the commercial *modus vivendi* signed at Caracas, March 26, 1941.

This agreement will continue in force until April 9, 1944.

Text of notes in: Ministerio de relaciones exteriores. *Libro amarillo de los Estados Unidos de Venezuela . . . 1944.* Caracas. Tipografía americana. 1944. p. 227-228 (Spanish).

VENEZUELA—SPAIN

Commercial Modus Vivendi, effected by exchange of notes signed at Caracas, September 17, 1943.

Extends for one year the commercial *modus vivendi* signed September 17, 1942.

Text in: Ministerio de relaciones exteriores. *Libro amarillo de los Estados Unidos de Venezuela . . . 1944.* Caracas. Tipografía americana. 1944. p. 234-235 (Spanish).

VENEZUELA—SWITZERLAND

Commercial Modus Vivendi, effected by exchange of notes signed at Caracas, March 16, 1943.

This agreement extends until February 27, 1944, the provisions of the commercial *modus vivendi* concluded February 27, 1942. It may be suspended before that date, however, in accordance with the terms of the aforesaid convention.

Text in: Ministerio de relaciones exteriores. *Libro amarillo de los Estados Unidos* de Venezuela . . . *1944*. Caracas. Tipografía americana. 1944. p. 246–247 (Spanish).

VENEZUELA—UNITED STATES OF AMERICA

Agreement Concerning the Development of Foodstuffs Production in Venezuela, effected by exchange of notes signed at Caracas, May 14, 1943.

Provides a plan whereby in the Venezuelan Ministry of Agriculture a special office shall be created to stimulate the production of the most necessary foodstuffs of vegetables and animal origin.

This agreement is to be in force one year, but may be extended an additional year by the Venezuelan government.

Registered with the Pan American Union by the Government of the United States of America, October 27, 1943.

Text in: *U. S. Executive Agreement Series*, no. 333 (English and Spanish); *Gaceta Oficial*, Caracas, 15 de mayo, 1943, p. 21012 (Spanish); Ministerio de relaciones exteriores. *Libro amarillo de los Estados Unidos de Venezuela . . . 1944*. Caracas. Tipografía americana. 1944. p. 235–243 (Spanish).

VENEZUELA—UNITED STATES OF AMERICA

Agreement Regarding a Health and Sanitation Program, effected by exchange of notes signed at Caracas, February 18, 1943.

Both Governments agree to provide certain sums of money and technical personnel to collaborate in the anti-malaria campaign in Venezuela.

Registered with the Pan American Union by the Government of the United States of America, February 26, 1944.

Text in: *U. S. Executive Agreement Series*, no. 348 (English and Spanish).

VENEZUELA—UNITED STATES OF AMERICA

Convention Regarding Rubber (Caucho) Production in Venezuela, effected by exchange of notes signed at Caracas, October 13, 1943.

Extends for a period of one year the *modus vivendi* agreement on the trade and development of rubber, signed at Caracas, October 13, 1942.

Text in: Ministerio de relaciones exteriores. *Libro amarillo de los Estados Unidos de Venezuela . . . 1944*. Caracas. Tipografía americana. 1944. p. 243–244 (Spanish).

ADDENDA

ARGENTINA—CHILE

Agreement on the Interchange of Teachers, Publicists, Artists, Scientists and Technicians, Journalists and University Students of Advanced Courses, signed at Buenos Aires, June 3, 1938.

Argentina: Approved the agreement by decree no. 74,795 M.208 of October 16, 1940.

President's message No. 31 to Congress on August 22, 1941 accompanied the proposal of a law setting aside ten thousand pesos to cover travel expenses of the Argentine delegation abroad.

Ratified by presidential decree September 20, 1943.

Ratification decree in: *Argentine News*, Buenos Aires, no. 53, November, 1943, p. 18 (English).

BOLIVIA—PERU

Protocol on Safe-Conducts, Modifying the Agreement of July 22, 1940, signed at Lima, October 18, 1941.

Provides for the issuance of safe-conducts to natives and small merchants, nationals of either country, who pass over the frontier.

After one year, the agreement may be terminated on three months' notice.

Text in: *Revista Jurídica*, Cochabamba, diciembre, 1942, p. 70–71 (Spanish).

BOLIVIA—UNITED STATES OF AMERICA

Agreement Regarding the Production and Purchase of Bolivian Rubber and Chestnuts, signed July 15, 1942.

The Rubber Reserve Company agrees to establish an agency and a fund to assist the Bolivian Government in developing its rubber lands, and to acquire all rubber and rubber products in excess of domestic needs as well as 150 tons to be exported annually to neighboring countries.

Bolivia agrees to increase production of rubber, and to sell 500 tons of chestnuts to the United States.

This agreement will remain in force until December 31, 1946.

Text in: *Revista Jurídica*, Cochabamba, año 5, no. 21, diciembre, 1942, p. 74–78 (Spanish).

Reported in: *Department of State Bulletin*, vol. 7, no. 160, July 18, 1942, p. 633 (English).

BRAZIL—CANADA

Trade Agreement, signed at Rio de Janeiro, October 17, 1941.
Reported in *Handbook, no. 6, 1941* and *no. 7, 1942.*
Provides unconditional and unrestricted most-favored-nation treatment in all matters concerning customs duties and subsidiary charges, and in the method of levying duties.
The present agreement shall be effective 30 days after the exchange of ratifications, and shall remain in force for two years. Thereafter it may be renewed for yearly periods unless terminated with six months' notice by either country.
Brazil: Ratified May 19, 1942. Promulgated by presidential decree no. 12.419 of May 13, 1943.
Ratifications exchanged at Ottawa, March 17, 1943.
Text in: *Diário Oficial*, Rio de Janeiro, 15 de maio de 1943, secção 1, p. 7476–7478 (English and Portuguese).
Reported in: *Boletim do Ministério das Relações Exteriores*, no. 4, 30 de abril de 1943, p. 198–199 (Portuguese).

BRAZIL—CHILE

Convention on Cultural Interchange, signed at Santiago, November 18, 1941.
Provides for student-professor exchange between the two countries, as well as for the establishment of chairs of history and literature at the national universities for exchange professors, and for ten yearly scholarships to enable students of either country to study in professional schools, or institutions of higher learning.
Provides for an interchange of books, and a series of publications presenting the best literature, history and biographies of either country, and also for special national sections to be developed in the national and leading libraries of either country.
Chile: Ratified by decree no. 1680 of November 13, 1943.
Ratifications exchanged at Rio de Janeiro, September 8, 1943.
Text in: *Diario Oficial*, Santiago, año 66, no. 19,719, 27 de noviembre de 1943, p. 2704–2705 (Spanish).
Summary in: *Boletim do Ministério das Relações Exteriores*, no. 9, 30 de setembro, 1943, p. 610–611.

BRAZIL—COLOMBIA

Agreement on Cultural Interchange, signed at Rio de Janeiro, October 14, 1941.
Provides for centralizing cultural intercourse in permanent organizations with seats in Rio de Janeiro and Bogotá, and for granting five annual scholarships in each country to students of the other country—three in university studies and two in agricultural institutes.
Becomes effective 90 days after the exchange of ratifications, and will continue in force until one year after denunciation by either party.
Brazil: Approved by decree-law no. 5,378 of April 5, 1943.
Text in: *Diário Oficial*, Rio de Janeiro, 8 de abril, 1943, secção 1, p. 5.273, 5.275 (Portuguese and Spanish).

BRAZIL—DOMINICAN REPUBLIC

Convention on Cultural Interchange, signed at Rio de Janeiro, December 9, 1942.
Reported in *Handbook, no. 8, 1942.*
Brazil: Approved by decree-law no. 5,245 of February 12, 1943.
Ratified March 23, 1943.
Promulgated by presidential decree no. 12.950 of July 20, 1943.
Dominican Republic: Approved by the Senate, January 14, 1943; by the House of Representatives January 20, 1943; and promulgated by presidential decree of January 22, 1943.
Ratifications exchanged at Ciudad Trujillo, June 17, 1943.
Text in: *Diário Oficial*, Rio de Janeiro, ano 82, no. 38, 15 de fevereiro de 1943, secção 1, p. 2137–2139; no. 169, 22 de julho de 1943, secção 1, p. 11123–11124 (Portuguese and Spanish); *Boletim do Ministério das Relações Exteriores*, no. 8, 31 de julho de 1943, p. 542–544 (Portuguese and Spanish); no. 2, 28 de fevereiro de 1943, p. 110–112 (Portuguese); *Gaceta Oficial*, Ciudad Trujillo, año 64, no. 5864, 3 de febrero de 1943, p. 3–7 (Spanish).

BRAZIL—UNITED STATES OF AMERICA

Agreement Regarding a Health and Sanitation Program, effected by exchange of notes signed at Washington, March 14, 1942.
Provides for collaboration between the Health and Sanitation Division of the Office

of the Coordinator of Inter-American Affairs and the Brazilian Government in a specific health and sanitation program initially designed for the Amazon Basin area. At the desire of the Government of Brazil the agreement can be extended to other areas.

The United States agrees to provide an amount not to exceed $5,000,000 for this program, and Brazil will furnish expert personnel, materials, services and funds for local expenditures.

Text in: *U. S. Executive Agreement Series,* no. 372 (English).

BRAZIL—UNITED STATES OF AMERICA

Agreement Regarding a Project to Increase the Production of Rubber in Brazil, effected by exchange of notes signed at Washington, March 3, 1942.

The Rubber Reserve Company will cooperate with the Brazilian Government in developing rubber in the Amazon Valley and adjacent regions and will establish a five-million dollar fund for that purpose.

Text in: *U. S. Executive Agreement Series,* no. 371 (Portuguese and English).

BRAZIL—UNITED STATES OF AMERICA

Agreement Regarding the Mobilization of Productive Resources of Brazil, effected by exchange of notes signed at Washington, March 3, 1942.

The United States of America agrees to provide financial and technical assistance to Brazil for the purpose of increasing the production of strategic materials essential to hemisphere defense.

Text in: *U. S. Executive Agreement Series,* no. 370 (Portuguese and English).

BRAZIL—URUGUAY

Agreement on the Legalization of Consular Manifests, signed at Montevideo, January 8, 1942.
Reported in *Handbook, no. 8, 1942.*
Ratifications exchanged at Rio de Janeiro, September 24, 1942.
Uruguay: Promulgated by the President of Uruguay, November 12, 1942.
Text in: *Boletín del Ministerio de Relaciones Exteriores, Montevideo,* segunda época, tomo 14, no. 3, setiembre de 1943, p. 24–26 (Spanish).

BRAZIL—VENEZUELA

Convention for Cultural Interchange, signed at Rio de Janeiro, October 22, 1942.
Reported in *Handbook, no. 8, 1942.*
Brazil: Ratified November 25, 1942.
Reported in: *Diário Oficial,* Rio de Janeiro, 27 de novembro de 1942, secção 1, p. 17290 (Portuguese).

CHILE—PERU

Commercial Modus Vivendi, signed November 26, 1938.
Reported in *Handbook, no. 3, 1938.*
Extended, by exchange of notes signed December 31, 1942, until January 31, 1943, or until the exchange of ratifications takes place regarding the Commercial Treaty and Protocol signed at Santiago, October 17, 1941.
Reported in: *Boletín de la Cámara de Comercio de Lima,* año 15, vol. 14, no. 163, enero de 1943, p. 2 (Spanish).

CHILE—PERU

Treaty of Commerce and Additional Protocol, signed at Santiago, October 17, 1941.
Reported in *Handbook, no. 7, 1941.*
Peru: Ratified October 1, 1942.
Chile: Ratified February 10, 1943.
Text in: *Diario Oficial de la República de Chile,* Santiago, año 66, no. 19485, 15 de febrero de 1943, p. 441–443 (Spanish).
Reported in: *Economista Peruano,* Lima, 10 de noviembre de 1942, p. 115–118 (Spanish); *Boletín de la Cámara de Comercio de Lima,* año 15, vol. 14, no. 167, mayo de 1943, p. 221–223 (Spanish).

COLOMBIA—UNITED STATES OF AMERICA

Parcel Post Agreement, signed at Bogotá January 31, 1939, and at Washington, February 7, 1939.
States postal and insurance regulations.
United States: Ratified February 14, 1939.
Colombia: Approved by the Senate and the House of Representatives, February 24, 1943.
Ratified March 11, 1943.
Text in: Cámara de representantes, Bogotá. *Anales,* serie 1, no. 30, 5 de abril de 1943, p. 268–273 (Spanish).
Ratification in: *U. S. Treaty Information*

Bulletin, no. 113, February, 1939, p. 34 (English).

COLOMBIA—UNITED STATES OF AMERICA

Supplementary Convention to the Extradition Treaty of May 7, 1888, signed at Bogotá, September 9, 1940.
Reported in *Handbook, no. 6, 1940* and *no. 8, 1942*.
Colombia: Approved by law no. 8 of March 8, 1943.
Promulgated by decree no. 1291 of July 2, 1943.
United States: Proclaimed by the President, June 26, 1943.
Instruments of ratification exchanged at Washington, June 23, 1943.
Registered with the Pan American Union by the Government of the United States of America, October 22, 1943.
Text in: *U. S. Treaty Series,* no. 986 (English and Spanish); *Diario Oficial,* Bogotá, 12 de julio de 1943, p. 130 (Spanish).

COLOMBIA—URUGUAY

Conciliation and Arbitration Convention, signed at Montevideo, November 21, 1941.
Provides for a conciliation commission of three members, and for the arbitration of all disputes regardless of the cause.
Colombia: Approved by the Congress of Colombia, February 24, 1943, by law no. 14 of March 11, 1943.
Text in: Colombia. Cámara de representantes. Bogotá, *Anales,* series 1, no. 30, 5 de abril de 1943, p. 280–281 (Spanish); Senado. *Anales,* Bogotá, serie 1, no. 34, 6 de abril de 1943, p. 316–317 (Spanish).
Reported in: *Boletín del Ministerio de Relaciones Exteriores,* Montevideo, tomo 15, no. 6, abril de 1943, p. 34 (Spanish).

CUBA—CHINA

Treaty of Friendship, signed at Havana, November 11, 1942.
Reported in *Handbook, no. 8, 1942*.
Cuba: Ratified March 31, 1943.
Promulgated by the Cuban President, April 10, 1943.
Ratifications exchanged at Havana, December 18, 1943.
Text in: *Gaceta Oficial,* Habana, 24 de diciembre de 1943, p. 21603 (Spanish); *Cuba Económica y Financiera,* Habana, vol. 19, no. 214, enero de 1944, p. 11 (Spanish).

DOMINICAN REPUBLIC—HAITI

Modus Operandi Agreement, signed at Port-au-Prince, November 21, 1939.
Provides that a traveler from one country to the other must carry an identification card and special permits from the consulate or legation of the country to be visited, and from the national police authorities of his own country.
Travelers entering either country illegally shall be denied such papers thereafter, and shall be repatriated as soon as possible.
Effective as soon as published in the official papers of either country, and will continue in force indefinitely unless denounced with six months' notice by either high contracting party.
Text in: *Le Moniteur,* Port-au-Prince, 95ème année, no. 5, 15 janvier 1940, p. 33–36 (Spanish and French).

EL SALVADOR—GUATEMALA

Treaty of Free Commerce, signed October 14, 1941. Additional Protocol, signed December 29, 1941. Second Additional Protocol, signed November 13, 1942.
Reported in *Handbook, no. 8, 1942*.
Guatemala: Approved the Second additional protocol by decree no. 2705 of April 8, 1943.
El Salvador: Denounced the treaty by note of March 9, 1943, whereby it notified the Government of Guatemala that it did not wish to renew the treaty of free commerce which would normally expire November 6, 1943.
Reported in: *Diario de Centro América,* Guatemala, tomo 40, no. 15, 15 de marzo de 1944, p. 144 (Spanish).

MEXICO—UNITED STATES OF AMERICA

Consular Convention, signed at Mexico City, August 12, 1942.
Reported in *Handbook, no 8, 1942*.
Mexico: Ratified March 26, 1943.
Registered with the Pan American Union by the Government of the United States of America, October 6, 1943.
Text in: *U. S. Treaty Series,* no. 985 (English and Spanish).
Reported in: *The Department of State Bulletin,* vol. 8, no. 196, March 27, 1943, p. 264–265 (English).

PANAMA—UNITED STATES OF AMERICA

Agreement and Exchanges of Notes on the Lease of Defense Sites, signed at Panamá, May 18, 1942.

Reported in *Handbook, no. 8, 1942.*
Effective May 11, 1943.
Panama: Approved by Congress by law no. 141, May 11, 1943.
Text in: *Gaceta Oficial,* Panamá, año 40, no. 9105, 21 de mayo de 1943, p. 1–4 (Spanish); *U. S. Executive Agreement Series,* no. 359 (English and Spanish).
Reported in: *The Department of State Bulletin,* vol. 11, no. 263, July 9, 1944, p. 55 (English).

PERU—UNITED STATES OF AMERICA

Convention on the Purchase of Peruvian Hemp and Sacking, signed at Washington, May 14, 1942.

Through the Commodity Credit Corporation, the United States agrees to purchase all Peruvian hemp up to, but not exceeding 4,000 tons of 2,240 pounds each during each twelve-month period beginning September 15, 1942 and ending September 14, 1944. In case of armistice, certain regulations shall govern the remaining sales to the CCC. The Peruvian Government promises that all deliveries of hemp from Peruvian crops will be sold to the CCC for the duration of this agreement.

The CCC will lend the Peruvian Government the machinery necessary for improving and cleaning the sacking in accordance with the convention's sacking specifications and terms of export to the United States.

Peru: Ratified April 2, 1943.
Text in: *Revista de Legislación Peruana,* Lima, año 4, no. 40, abril de 1943, p. 2751–2753 (Spanish).
Ratification in: *Revista de Legislación Peruana,* Lima, año 4, no. 46, octubre de 1943, p. 3371–3372 (Spanish).

PERU—UNITED STATES OF AMERICA

Convention Regarding Cotton, signed at Washington, April 22, 1942.

The U. S. Department of Agriculture, through the Commodity Credit Corporation, agrees to buy up to 1,000,000 quintals of the 1942 Peruvian cotton crop. In following years, and through December 31st after the cessation of hostilities, the CCC will buy of each crop all cotton in excess of domestic consumption and exports to other customers.

This agreement also sets forth the terms for storage, protection of property, prices and transportation fees, and establishes the size of areas under cultivation, fiber lengths and grades of cotton effected by this convention.

Text in: *Revista de Legislación Peruana,* Lima, año 4, no. 40, abril de 1943, p. 2737–2740 (Spanish).

PERU—UNITED STATES OF AMERICA

Convention Regarding the Experiment Station at Tingo María, Peru, signed at Washington, April 21, 1942.

Defines the scientific and educational aims of the Tingo María Experiment Station in developing basic and strategic tropical agriculture in the Amazon Valley in Peru and cooperating with other hemisphere institutions encouraging tropical agriculture through interchange of information and scientific personnel.

From the day of signature, this convention shall continue in force for ten years, unless the Congress of either country fails to appropriate the necessary funds. In such a case, the convention shall be terminated seventy days after written notice from either government.

Text in: *Revista de Legislación Peruana,* Lima, año 4, no. 40, abril de 1943, p. 2733–2737 (Spanish).

PERU—URUGUAY

Convention on Coastal Trade, signed at Lima, July 28, 1922.

Peru: Ratified by Legislative Resolution No. 4893, January 10, 1942.
Reported in: *Revista de Legislación Peruana,* Lima, año 4, no. 40, octubre de 1943, p. 3354 (Spanish).

PERU—VENEZUELA

Convention for the Advancement of Historical Studies, signed at Lima, November 11, 1942.

Reported in *Handbook, no. 8, 1942.*
Ratifications exchanged at Caracas, November 27, 1943.
Summary in: *The Department of State Bulletin,* vol. 7, no. 182, December 19, 1942, p. 1013 (English).
Reported in: *The Department of State Bulletin,* vol. 10, no. 244, February 26, 1944, p. 212 (English).

MULTILATERAL TREATIES AND CONVENTIONS

I. WORLD TREATIES AND CONVENTIONS

In 1943, the Latin American Republics ratified or adhered to the world treaties and conventions indicated below:

1. **International Telecommunications Conventions and Acts, signed at Cairo, April 8, 1943.**

   Colombia: Ratified by law no. 9 of March 8, 1943.

   Text in: *Anales de la Cámara de Representantes,* Bogotá, serie 1, no. 30, 5 de abril de 1943, p. 266–268 (Spanish).

2. **Agreement for United Nations Relief and Rehabilitation Administration, signed at Washington, November 9, 1943.**

   Western hemisphere signatories: Bolivia, Brazil, Canada, Costa Rica, Dominican Republic, El Salvador, Haiti, Honduras, Panama, Paraguay, United States of America.

   Signatories subject to ratification or legislative approval: Chile, Colombia, Cuba, Ecuador, Guatemala, Mexico, Nicaragua, Peru, Uruguay, Venezuela.

   Mexico: Ratified November 15, 1943.

   El Salvador: Ratified December 23, 1943.

   Reported in: *The Department of State Bulletin,* vol. 9, no. 229, November 13, 1943, p. 335–336; vol. 10, no. 249, April 1, 1944, p. 305 (English); *Diario Oficial,* México, 7 de enero de 1944, p. 1 (Spanish).

ADDENDA

1. **International Convention for the Suppression of the Illicit Traffic in Dangerous Drugs, signed at Geneva, June 26, 1936.**

   Colombia: Approved by law 12, March 11, 1943.

   Text in: Senado, *Anales,* Bogotá, serie 1, no. 34, Sesiones extraordinarias de 1943, p. 309–313 (Spanish).

2. **International Load Line Convention, signed at London, July 5, 1930.**

   Uruguay: By a decree of February 26, 1942, the Government of Uruguay established certain modifications of this convention in accordance with a proposal made in 1941.

   By a decree of May 5, 1943, the Government of Uruguay extended the modifications established by the decree of February 26, 1942, until six months following the conclusion of the present armed conflict.

   Reported in: *The Department of State Bulletin,* vol. 8, no. 296, June 5, 1943, p. 503 (English).

II. STATUS OF PAN AMERICAN TREATIES AND CONVENTIONS

The present status of the treaties, conventions, protocols and agreements concluded at the special and general Pan American Conferences is shown by the chart of July 1, 1944 inserted below:

STATUS OF THE PAN AMERICAN TREATIES AND CONVENTIONS
(Revised to July 1, 1944 by the Juridical Division of the Pan American Union)

Symbols.—S: Signatory. Sr: Signed with reservations. NS: Non-signatory. A: Adherence subject to ratification. Ad: Adherence deposited. Ar: Adherence with reservations. AR: Adherence ratified. ARd: Adherence ratified and deposited. ARdr: Adherence ratified and deposited with reservations. ARr: Adherence ratified with reservations. D: Denounced. R: ratified. Rd: Ratification deposited. Rdr: Ratification deposited with reservations. Rp: Ratified provisionally.

	Argentina	Bolivia	Brazil	Colombia	Costa Rica	Cuba	Chile	Ecuador	El Salvador	United States	Guatemala	Haiti	Honduras	Mexico	Nicaragua	Panama	Paraguay	Peru	Dominican Republic	Uruguay	Venezuela

FIRST CONFERENCE (Washington, 1889–1890)
No Treaties or Conventions signed.

SECOND CONFERENCE (Mexico, 1901–1902)

1. Pecuniary Claims (In force 5 years)
2. Extradition
3. Practice of Learned Professions
4. Formation of Codes of International Law
5. Protection of Literary and Artistic Copyright
6. Exchange of Publications
7. Patents, Industrial Drawings and Models and Trade-Marks
8. Rights of Aliens
9. Obligatory Arbitration

THIRD CONFERENCE (Rio de Janeiro, 1906)

10. Status of Naturalized Citizens
11. Pecuniary Claims (Expired December 31, 1912)
12. Patents, Trade-Marks, Literary and Artistic Property
13. International Law (Codification)

FOURTH CONFERENCE (Buenos Aires, 1910)

14. Patents
15. Trade-Marks
16. Literary and Artistic Copyright
17. Pecuniary Claims

FIFTH CONFERENCE (Santiago, 1923)

18. Prevention of Conflicts (Gondra Treaty)
19. Publicity of Customs Documents
20. Trade-Marks and Commercial Names
21. Nomenclature for the Classification of Merchandise

STATUS OF THE PAN AMERICAN TREATIES AND CONVENTIONS—Continued

	Argentina	Bolivia	Brazil	Colombia	Costa Rica	Cuba	Chile	Ecuador	El Salvador	United States	Guatemala	Haiti	Honduras	Mexico	Nicaragua	Panama	Paraguay	Peru	Dominican Republic	Uruguay	Venezuela
SIXTH CONFERENCE (Habana, 1928)																					
22. Status of Aliens	S	S	Rd	Rd	Rd	S	Rd	Rd	S	Rdr	Rd	S	S	Rdr	Rd	Rd	S	S	Rd	Rd	S
23. Asylum	S	S	Rd	Rd	S	Rd	S	Rd	S	NS	S	S	R	Rd	Rd	Rd	S	S	Rd	Rd	S
24. Consular Agents	S	S	Rd	Rd	S	Rd	S	Rd	S	R	S	S	S	S	Rd	Rd	S	Rd	Rdr[1]	Rd	Rd
25. Diplomatic Officials	S	S	Rd	Rd	Rd	Rd	Rdr	Rd	S	Rdr	S	Rd	S	S	Rd	Rd	S	S	Rd	Rd	S
26. Maritime Neutrality	S	S	S	Rd	Rd	S	S	Rd	S	S	S	S	S	Rd	Rd	Rd	S	S	Rd	S	S
27. Rights and Duties of States in Event of Civil Strife	S	Rd	Rd	S	Rd	S	S	Rd	Rd	Rd	S	Rd	S	S	Rd	Rd	S	S	Rdr	S	S
28. Treaties	S	S	S	S	S	S	S	Rd	NS	S	Rd	Rd	S	Rd	Rd	Rd	S	S	S	S	S
29. Commercial Aviation	S	S	Rd	R	Rdr	Rd	Rdr	Rd	S	Rd	S	S	S	S	Rd	Rd	S	S	Rd	S	S
30. Literary and Artistic Copyright	S	S	S	S	Rd	S	S	Rd	S	NS	Rd	S	Rd	S	Rd	Rd	S	S	S	S	NS
31. Private International Law	S	Rdr	Rdr	S	Rdr	Rd	Rdr	Rdr	Rdr	Rd	Rd	Rdr	Rd	Rd	Rd	Rd	S	Rd	Rd	S	Rdr
32. Pan American Union	S	S	Rd	S	Rd	Rd	Rd	Rd	S	Rd	Rd	S	S	Rd	Rd	Rd	S	S	Rd	Rd	Rd
SEVENTH CONFERENCE (Montevideo, 1933)																					
33. Nationality of Women	S	S	Rd	Rd	NS	Rd	Rd	Rd	S	Rdr	Rd	S	Rdr	Rdr	R	Rd	S	S	S	S	NS
34. Nationality	NS	NS	ARdr	NS	NS	NS	Rd	Rd	NS	NS	NS	NS	Rdr	Rd	NS	Rd	NS	NS	NS	S	NS
35. Extradition	S	NS	S	Rd	NS	S	Rdr	Rd	Rdr	Rdr	Rd	S	Rdr	Rdr	R	Rd	NS	Rdr	Rd	S	NS
36. Optional Clause annexed to the Convention on Extradition	S	NS	Rd	Rd	NS	Rd	NS	NS	Rd	NS	Rd	NS	NS	NS	NS	NS	NS	NS	Rd	S	NS
37. Political Asylum	S	NS	Rd	Rd	NS	Rd	Rd	S	Rd	NS	Rd	S	Rd	Rd	R	A	S	S	Rd	S	NS
38. Revision of History Textbooks	S	NS	NS	Rd	NS	NS	Rd	Rd	NS	S	Rd	S	Rd	Rd	R	Rd	ARd	NS	Rd	S	NS
39. Additional Protocol to the Conciliation Convention (1929)	NS	NS	NS	ARd	NS	NS	Rd	R	NS	Rd	ARd	R	Rd	Rd	R	Rd	S	S	Rd	S	ARdr
40. Rights and Duties of States	S	NS	Rdr	Rd	ARd	Rd	Rd	Rd	Rd	Rdr	Rd	Rd	Rd	Rd	Rd	Rd	S	Sr	Rd	S	Rd
EIGHTH CONFERENCE (Lima, 1938) — No Treaties or Conventions signed.																					
CONFERENCE FOR THE MAINTENANCE OF PEACE (Buenos Aires, 1936)																					
41. Maintenance, Preservation and Reestablishment of Peace	S	S	Rd	Rd	Rd	Rd	Rd	Rdr	Rd	Rd	Rd	Rd	Rdr	Rd	Rd	Rd	Rd	S	Rd	S	Rd
42. Protocol Relative to Non-Intervention	S	S	Rd	Rd	Rd	Rd	Rd	Rdr	Rd	NS	Rd	Rd	Rd	Rd	Rd	Rd	S	S	Rd	S	Rd
43. Prevention of Controversies	S	S	S	Rd	Rd	Rd	Rd	Rd	Rd	Rdr	Rd	Rd	Rd	Rd	Rd	Rd	S	Sr	Rd	S	S
44. Good Offices and Mediation	S	S	Rd	Rd	Rd	Rd	Rd	Rd	Rdr	Rdr	Rdr	Rd	Rdr	Rdr	Rd	Rd	Sr	Rd	Rd	S	S
45. Fulfillment of the Existing Treaties	Sr	S	S	Rd	S	S	S	S	Rd	S	Rd	S	Rd	Rd	Rd	Rd	Rd	Rd	S	S	S
46. Pan American Highway	S	S	Rd	Rd	Rd	S	Rd	S	Rd	Rd	Rd	Rd	Rd	Rd	Rd	Rd	S	Rd	Rd	S	Rd
47. Promotion of Inter-American Cultural Relations	S	S	Rd	Rd	Rd	S	Rd	S	S	Rd	Rd	Rd	Rd	S	Rd	Rd	S	Rd	Rd	S	Rd
48. Interchange of Publications	S	S	Rd	Rd	Rd	S	Rd	S	Rd	NS	Rd	Rd	Rd	Rd	Rd	Rd	S	Rd	Rd	S	Rd
49. Artistic Exhibitions	S	S	Rd	Rd	Rd	S	Rd	S	Rd	NS	Rd	Rd	Rd	Rdr	Rd	Rd	S	S	Rd	S	Rd
50. Peaceful Orientation of Public Instruction	S	S	Rd	Rd	Rd	S	Rd	S	Rd	NS	Rd	Rd	Rd	Rd	Rd	Rd	S	Rd	Rd	S	Rd
51. Facilities for Educational and Publicity Films	S	S	Rd	Rd	Rd	S	Rd	S	Rd	NS	Rd	Rd	Rdr	Rdr	Rd	Rd	S	Rd	Rd	S	Rdr

[1] Reservations not accepted by the United States.

STATUS OF THE PAN AMERICAN TREATIES AND CONVENTIONS—Continued

CONVENTIONS SIGNED AT OTHER PAN AMERICAN CONFERENCES	Argentina	Bolivia	Brazil	Colombia	Costa Rica	Cuba	Chile	Ecuador	El Salvador	United States	Guatemala	Haiti	Honduras	Mexico	Nicaragua	Panama	Paraguay	Peru	Republica Dominicana	Uruguay	Venezuela
52. Inter-American Conciliation (Washington, 1929)	NS	S	Rd	Rd	S	Rd	Rd	Rd	Rd	Rd	Rd	Rd	Rd	Rd	Rd	Rd	Rd	Rd	Rd	Rd	Rd
53. Inter-American Arbitration (Washington, 1929)	NS	Sr	Rd	Rdr	Sr	Rd	Rdr	Rdr[2]	Rdr	Rdr	Rdr	Rd	Rdr	Rdr	Rd	Rd	Sr	Rd	Rdr	Sr	Rdr
54. Progressive Arbitration Protocol (Washington, 1929)	NS	S	S	S	S	R	Rd	Rd	RR	S	Rd	Rd	Rd	Rd	Rd	S	S	S	Rd	S	Rd
55. Anti-War Pact (Rio de Janeiro, 1933)[1]	Rd	AR	Rd	ARdr	A	ARd	Rdr	ARdr	ARdr	ARdr	ARd	ARd	ARdr	Rd	ARd	ARd	Rd	ARdr	ARd	Rd	ARdr
56. Trade-Mark and Commercial Protection (Washington, 1929)	NS	S	S	Rd	S	Rd	S	S	NS	Rd	Rd	Rd	Rd	S	Rd	Rd	Rd	Rd	S	S	S
57. Registration of Trade-Marks—Protocol (Washington, 1929)	NS	S	S	S	S	Rd	NS	S	NS	Rd	NS	Rd	Rd	S	S	Rd	S	Rd	S	NS	S
58. Electrical Communications (Mexico, 1924)	S	NS	S	S	S	S	NS	S	S	NS	S	NS	NS	Rd	S	Rd	Rd	S	Rd	S	NS
59. Sanitary Code (Habana, 1924)	Rd	ARd	Rd	Rd	Rd	Rd	Rd	ARd	Rd	Rd	Rd	Rd	Rd	Rdr	AR	Rd	Rd	Rd	Rd	Rd	Rd
60. Additional Protocol to the Sanitary Code (Lima, 1927)	Rd	S	Rd	Rd	S	S	ARd	Rd	NS	Rd	S	S	S	ARd	S	Rd	R	Rd	Rd	Rd	Rd
61. Regulation of Automotive Traffic (Washington, 1930)	S	S	S	S	S	NS	S	Rd	S	S	S	NS	Rd	Rd	S	S	S	Rd	Rd	S	S
62. Most-Favored-Nation Clause in Commercial Treaties (Washington, 1934)[3]	....	....	....	S	....	Rd	....	....	....	Rd	S	....	....	....	S	S	....	....	....	....	....
63. Artistic Institutions and Historic Monuments—Roerich Pact (Washington, 1935)	S	S	Rd	Rd	S	Rd	Rd	S	Rd	Rd	Rd	S	R	Rd	S	S	S	S	Rd	S	Rd
64. Movable Property of Historic Value (Washington, 1935)	....	....	....	....	....	....	Rdr	S	Rd	....	Rd	....	....	Rd	Rd	S	....	....	....	S	....
65. Declaration Relative to Foreign Companies (Washington, 1936)	....	....	....	....	....	....	Sr	S	S	Rdr	....	....	....	....	S	....	....	S	Sr	....	Rd
66. Repression of Smuggling (Buenos Aires, 1935)	S	S	Rd	S	S	S	Rd	Rd	S	S	S	S	S	S	S	S	S	S	S	Rd	S
67. Tourist Passport and Transit Passport for Vehicles (Buenos Aires, 1935)	S	S	S	S	S	NS	S	S	S	NS	S	S	S	S	S	S	Rd	S	S	Rd	S
68. Transit of Airplanes (Buenos Aires, 1935)	S	S	S	S	S	S	Rdr	Rd	S	S	S	S	S	Rd	S	S	S	S	S	Rd	S
69. Pan American Commercial Committees (Buenos Aires, 1935)	S	S	R	S	S	S	S	S	S	S	S	S	S	S	S	S	S	S	Rd	Rd	S
70. Protocol on Powers of Attorney (Washington, 1940)[4]	....	Sr	S[1]	Rdr	....	....	....	....	Rdr	Rd	....	....	....	....	S	S	....	....	....	....	Rdr
71. Inter-American Bank (Washington, 1940)	....	S	S	S	....	....	....	S	....	S	....	....	....	R	S	....	S	....	S	....	....
72. Convention on European Colonies and Possessions (Habana, 1940)	Rdr	S	Rd	Rd	Rd	S	Sr	Rd	Rd	Rd	Rd	Rd	Rd	Rd	Rd	Rd	S	Rd	Rd	Rd	Rd
73. Nature Protection and Wild Life Preservation (Washington, 1940)	Sr	S	S	S	S	S	S	S	Rd	Rd	Rd	Rd	....	Rd	S	....	....	R	Rd	S	Rd
74. Inter-American Coffee Agreement (Washington, 1940)	....	....	Rd	Rd	Rd	Rd	....	Rd	Rd	Rd	Rd	Rd	Rd	Rd	Rd	....	....	Rd	Rd	....	Rd
75. Protocol to the Inter-American Coffee Agreement (Washington, 1941)[5]	....	....	S	S	S	S	....	S	S	S	S	S	S	S	S	....	....	S	S	....	S
76. Inter-American Indian Institute (Mexico, 1940)	....	S	....	ARd	R	R	....	Rd	Rd	Rd	....	....	Rd	Rd	Rd	ARd	Rd	Rd	ARd	A	....
77. Regulation of Automotive Traffic (Washington, 1943)	....	S	S	....	S	S	....	S	S	Sr	S	S	S	....	S	....	....	S	Sr	....	....
78. Inter-American Institute of Agricultural Sciences (Washington, 1944)	....	....	....	....	S	S	S	S	Rd	R	S	....	S	....	S	S	....	....	S	S	....
79. Convention on the Inter-American University (Panama, 1943)	Sr	S	S	S	S	S	S	S	S	Sr	S	S	S	S	S	S	S	S	S	S	S

[1] Ar: Greece, Italy, Norway. AR: Portugal. ARr: Turkey. ARd: Spain. ARdr: Bulgaria, Czechoslovakia, Finland, Rumania, Yugoslavia.

[2] Abandons the first two reservations made when signing the treaty.

[3] Rd: Greece. S: Economic Union of Belgium and Luxemburg.

[4] The Protocol is effective from the date of signature unless signed *ad referendum*. Brazil did not sign *ad referendum*.

[5] The Protocol became operative on the day following the date of signature.

STATUS OF THE PAN AMERICAN TREATIES AND CONVENTIONS—Continued

APPENDIX A

Conventions Signed at the Inter-American Radio Congresses

	Argentina	Bolivia	Brazil	Colombia	Costa Rica	Cuba	Chile	Ecuador	El Salvador	United States	Guatemala	Haiti	Honduras	Mexico	Nicaragua	Panama	Paraguay	Peru	Republica Dominicana	Uruguay	Venezuela	Canada	Newfoundland	Bahamas	España
1. South American Regional Agreement on Radio-communications (Buenos Aires, 1935)	Rd	Rd	Rd				Rd										Rd			Rd					
2. South American Regional Agreement on Radio-communications (Buenos Aires, 1935) [Revision of Rio de Janeiro, 1937]	S	S	Rd	S			S				S				S	Rd	S	S	S	S	S				
3. South American Regional Agreement on Radio-communications (Buenos Aires, 1935) [Revision of Santiago, 1940]			S				Rd	S									Rd								
4. Radiocommunications Convention (Habana, 1937)	Rd		Rdr	S		Rd	S			Rd	S	Rd		Rd	S	Rd	A[1]	Rd	Rd	S	S	Rd		ARd	
5. Arrangement concerning Radiocommunications (Habana, 1937)			Rdr	S		S	Rd			Rd	S	Rd		Rd	S	Rd		Rd	Rd	S	S	Rd			
6. North American Regional Broadcasting Agreement (Habana, 1937)						Rd				Rd				Rd					Rd			Rd	ARd	ARd	
7. Arrangement concerning Radiocommunications (Habana, 1937) [Revision of Santiago, 1940]	Rd				NS	S	Rd		S	Rd	S Rd	NS	R	S	S Rd	NS S			S			ARdr			D
8. Regional Radio Convention (Guatemala, 1938)	S	S	Rd	Rd	S	S	S	S		Rd[2]	S	Rd	Rd	S	Rd	S	S	Rd	Rd	S	S				Ad

APPENDIX B

Conventions Signed at the American Postal Congresses

1. Spanish American Postal Convention (Madrid, 1920)	Rd	Rd	Rd	Rd	Rd	S	S	Rd	Rd		S	A	Rd	S	Rd	S	Rd	Rd	Rd	S	S				Rd

Pan American Postal Union

2. Principal Convention (Buenos Aires, 1921)	Rd	Rd	Rd	S	Rd	Rd	Rd	Rd	Rd	Rd	Rd		Rd	Rd	Rd	Rd	S	S	Rd	Rd	Rd				Rd
3. Parcel Post Convention (Buenos Aires, 1921)	Rd	Rd	Rd	S	Rd	Rd	Rd	Rd	Rd	Rd	Rd		Rd	Rd	Rd	Rd	S	S	S	Rd	Rd				Rd
4. Money Order Convention (Buenos Aires, 1921)	Rp	S	Rd	S	Rd	S	Rd	Rd	Rd	Rd	Rd	A	Rd	Rd	Rd	Rd	S	Rd	Rd	S	S				
5. Principal Convention (Mexico, 1926)	Rp	Rd	Rd	R	Rd	Rd	Rd	Rd	S	Rd	Rd		Rd	Rd		Rd	S	Rd	Rd	Rd	Rd	Ad			Rd
6. Parcel Post Convention (Mexico, 1926)	Rp	Rd	Rd	R	Rd	Rd	Rd	Rd	S	Rd	Rd		Rd	Rd		Rd	S	Rd	S	Rd	Rd	Ad			Rd
7. Money Order Convention (Mexico, 1926)	Rp	Rd			Rd		Rd	S	S	Rdr	Rd		Rd	Rd		Rd	S	Rd	Rd	S	S				Rd
8. Agreement Concerning Money Orders (Madrid, 1931)	Rp	Rd	Rd	Rd	Rd	S	Rp	S	Rd	Rdr	Rd	S	S	Rd	S	S	Rp	S	Rd	S	Rd				Rd
9. Convention, Protocol and Regulations, and Provisions on Correspondence by Air (Madrid 1931)	Rp	Rd	Rd	Rd	Rd	S	Rp	Rd	Rd	Rd	Rd	S	Rd	Rd	Rd	Rd	Rp	Rp	Rd	Rp	Rd	Rd			Rd
10. Parcel Post Agreement (Madrid, 1931)	Rp	Rd	Rd	Rd	Rd	S	Rp	Rd	Rd	Rd	Rd	S	Rp	Rd	Rd	Rd	Rp	Rp	Rd	Rp	Rd	Rd			Rd
11. Convention, Final Protocol and Regulations of Execution (Panama, 1936)	Rp	Rd	Rd	S	S	S	S	Rd	Rd	Rd	Rd	Rd	S	Rd	S	Rd	Rp	Rd	Rd	Rd	Rd	Rd			Rd
12. Parcel Post Agreement and Final Protocol (Panama, 1936)	Rp	Rd	Rd	S	S	S	S	Rd	Rd	Rd	Rd	S	S	Rd	Rd	Rd	Rp	Rd	S	Rd	Rd	Rd			Rd
13. Transportation of Correspondence by Air (Panama, 1936)	Rp	Rd	Rd	S	S	S	S	Rd	Rd	NS	S	S	Rp	Rd	S	Rd	Rp	Rd	S	Rd	Rd	Rd			Rd
14. Agreement Relative to Money Orders and Final Protocol (Panama, 1936)	Rp	Rd	Rd	S	S	S	Rd	S	Rd	Rd	S	Rd	Rp	Rd	Rd	Rd	Rp	Rd	S	Rd	Rd	Rd			Rd

[1] Paraguay adhered *ad referendum*, and is applying the Convention provisionally.
[2] In behalf of the Canal Zone.

LABOR AND SOCIAL WELFARE

BY

GUSTAVO-ADOLFO ROHEN Y GÁLVEZ

BIBLIOGRAFÍA

(See also sections on General Works and Economics)

AMERICA LATINA

GENERAL

(*Véanse también los items* 984, 991, 991a)

Oficinia internacional del trabajo. Anuario de estadísticas del trabajo. Year-book of labour statistics. Annuaire de statistiques du travail. Montreal. Oficina internacional del trabajo. xii, 222 p., cuads. [3556
Publicación anual, en edición trilingüe, con información estadística internacional, de 1929 a 1942, sobre población activa, empleo y paro, horas de trabajo, salarios, presupuestos familiares, migración, accidentes del trabajo, costo de la vida y precios al por menor. Todos los países de América Latina están representados.

Pan american union. Division of labor and social information. Labor trends and social welfare in Latin America, 1941 and 1942. Washington, D. C. 153 p., illus. [3557
Están representados todos los países latinoamericanos, con excepción de Guatemala y Honduras.

Rohen y Gálvez, Gustavo-Adolfo. A selective guide to the material published in 1942 on labor and social welfare in Latin America (*Handbook of latin american studies*, no. 8, *1942*, p. 338–357). [3558
UNDÉCIMA CONFERENCIA SANITARIA PANAMERICANA (*Bol. ofic. sanit. panamer.*, año 22, no. 3, marzo, p. 193–201). [3559
Esta Conferencia (Rio de Janeiro, septiembre 6 a 18 de 1942) aprobó los votos, resoluciones y recomendaciones siguientes: Defensa continental y sanidad pública (mejoramiento e intercambio de recursos médicos; Encuestas sobre necesidades médicas y sanitarias); Ingeniería sanitaria (intercambio de materiales para obras sanitarias; estímulo de la producción de cemento en regiones escogidas); Nutrición (producción planificada y distribución equitativa de alimentos; educación en materia de nutrición; planes nacionales de alimentación basados en colaboración internacional; higiene de la leche; investigaciones sobre costo de la vida) y Vivienda (estudio de la habitación en todos sus aspectos y creación de comisiones nacionales sobre la materia).

Texto inglés en *Bull. pan amer. union*, vol. 22, no. 1, Jan., p. 26–34.

Valle, Rafael Heliodoro. Bibliografía de la sociología en Hispano-América (*Rev. mex. soc.*, año 5, vol. 5, no. 4, cuarto trim., p. 569–580). [3560
Algunas de estas fichas bibliográficas, de 1938 a 1943, se refieren a trabajo y previsión social en general.

DERECHO Y LEGISLACIÓN DEL TRABAJO

Unión panamericana. Oficina de información obrera y social. Muestras de legislación social americana. Washington, D. C. 71 p. [3561
Resúmenes de la siguiente legislación en vigor en 1941: Argentina: Trabajo a domicilio; Bolivia: Cooperativas de consumo; Brasil: Protección del trabajo de menores; Colombia: Enseñanza vocacional agrícola e industrial; Costa Rica: Seguro social; Cuba: Conciliación de los conflictos de trabajo; Chile: Salario mínimo en la industria salitrera; Ecuador: Participación en las utilidades; El Salvador: Horas de trabajo y descanso semanal; Guatemala: Terminología del trabajo; Haití: Inspección del trabajo; Honduras: Ahorro escolar; México: Habitación obrera; Nicaragua: Descanso semanal; Panamá: Código del trabajo; Paraguay: Ahorro obligatorio; Perú: Tribunales del trabajo; República Dominicana: Vacaciones anuales de los empleados de comercio y otros; Uruguay: Accidentes del trabajo y enfermedades profesionales; Venezuela: Control de precios. Bibliografía.

ORGANISMOS OFICIALES, ASOCIACIONES PATRONALES Y OBRERAS

Álvarez, Juan. ¿Qué quiere Lombardo? (*Economista*, año 5, tomo 9, no. 108, agosto 16, p. 33–37). [3562
Requisitoria "contra la propaganda disolvente" del líder obrero en la jira abajo mencionada (item 3563).

LA CONFEDERACIÓN DE TRABAJADORES DE AMÉRICA LATINA (*Rev. int. trab.*, vol. 27, no. 3, marzo, p. 458–459). [3563
Síntesis del Informe presentado en diciembre de 1942 a los trabajadores de

México por Vicente Lombardo Toledano, Presidente de la Confederación de Trabajadores de América Latina, sobre su jira a Bolivia, Colombia, Costa Rica, Cuba, Chile, Ecuador, El Salvador, Guatemala, Honduras, Nicaragua y Perú, en cumplimiento del mandato del Primer Congreso de dicha C.T.A.L. (véase *Handbook, no. 8, 1942*, item 3671).
Texto inglés en *Int. lab. rev.*, vol. 47, no. 3, March, p. 397-398.

Empleo y desocupación

(*Véanse también los items* 141, 3556)

Oficina internacional del trabajo. Empleo, paro y duración del trabajo (*Rev. int. trab.*, vol. 27, no. 3, marzo, p. 462-472; no. 6, junio, p. 912-922; vol. 28, no. 3, sept., p. 468-478; no. 6, dic., p. 932-942, cuads.). [3564]
En estas estadísticas (ya descritas en los *Handbook, no. 7, 1941*, item 3841 y *Handbook, no. 8, 1942*, item 3673) se encuentran representados Chile y México (número de parados); Argentina (Buenos Aires) y Colombia (trabajadores ocupados en las minas, la industria, los transportes y el comercio); Argentina, Colombia (Bogotá), Chile, México y Uruguay (trabajadores ocupados en la industria); Colombia (por primera vez, con horas totales de trabajo) Argentina y México (horas de trabajo efectivo).
Texto inglés en *Int. lab. rev.*, vol. 47, no. 3, March, p. 410-413; no. 6, June, p. 797-807; vol. 48, no. 3, Sept., p. 401-411; no. 6, Dec., p. 801-811.

Migración y colonización

(*Véase también el item* 3556)

Relación sucinta de las resoluciones aprobadas por el pleno del Primer Congreso Demográfico Interamericano (*Economista*, año 5, no. 10, nov. 10, p. 10-13, 36). [3565]
Celebrado en México, D. F., de octubre 12 a 23 de 1943, aprobó las siguientes resoluciones: Comisión de demografía: Coordinación de los movimientos migratorios; Levantamiento del censo continental, incluyendo estadísticas económicas y sociales; Uniformización de las investigaciones sobre movimientos demográficos y migratorios. Comisión de etnología y eugenesia: Impulso de la educación para mejorar las condiciones de vida de las poblaciones afroamericanas; Elevación de los niveles de vida sociales, económicos y culturales de la población indígena; Educación y adaptación de los inmigrantes. Comisión de política demográfica: Desenvolvimiento individual para elevar el nivel de vida de los trabajadores y para absorber corrientes migratorias; Realización de encuestas sobre presupuestos familiares según la técnica de la Oficina Internacional del Trabajo (véase *Handbook, no. 8, 1942*, item 3690); Aplicación de las recomendaciones de otras conferencias sobre la materia. Migración: Financiamiento internacional de la migración.

Salarios, Horas, Descansos y Costo de la Vida

(*Véase también el item* 3556)

Mekler, Ana. El costo de la vida obrera en América. Washington. Unión panamericana, Oficina de información obrera y social. 139 p., mimeogr. [3566]
Recopilación de series, fuentes y métodos de las estadísticas del costo de la vida en los países latinoamericanos, exceptuando Honduras.

Oficina internacional del trabajo. Índice de comparación internacional del costo de la alimentación en octubre de 1941 (*Rev. int. trab.*, vol. 27, no. 2, feb., p. 307-309, cuadro). [3567]
Habiéndose suprimido Colombia de esta encuesta anual (véase *Handbook, no. 8, 1942*, item 3674), América Latina queda representada por tres países: Argentina, Chile y México.
Texto inglés en *Int. lab. rev.*, vol. 47, no. 2, Feb., p. 269-271.

———. Índices del costo de la vida y precios de la alimentación (*Rev. int. trab.*, vol. 27, no. 1, enero, p. 147-152; no. 4, abril, p. 617-623; vol. 28, no. 1, julio, p. 146-152; no. 4, oct., p. 633-639, cuads.). [3568]
Índices de Argentina, Brasil, Colombia, Costa Rica, Cuba, Chile, México, Perú, Uruguay y Venezuela, ya descritos (véanse *Handbook, no. 7, 1941*, item 3847 y *Handbook, no. 8, 1942*, item 3675).
Texto inglés en *Int. lab. rev.*, vol. 47, no. 1, Jan., p. 125-131; no. 4, April, p. 539-545; vol. 48, no. 1, July, p. 124-130; no. 4, Oct., p. 542-548.

———. Salarios (*Rev. int. trab.*, vol. 27, no. 2, feb., p. 294-306; no. 5, mayo, p. 768-778; vol. 28, no. 2, agosto, p. 302-314; no. 5, nov., p. 791-803, cuads.). [3569]
El alcance geográfico de estas series (véanse *Handbook, no. 7, 1941*, item 3848 y *Handbook, no. 8, 1942*, item 3678) quedó reducido a los siguientes países: Argentina, Colombia, Chile, México y Uruguay.
Texto inglés en *Int. lab. rev.*, vol. 47, no. 2, Feb., p. 256-268; no. 5, May, p. 672-684; vol. 48, no. 2, August, p. 259-271; no. 5, Nov., p. 677-689.

Quirós, Juan B. El contenido laboral en los códigos negros americanos (*Rev. mex. soc.*, año 5, vol. 5, no. 4, cuarto trim., p. 473-510). [3570]
En los códigos negros franceses y españoles, se establecen los siguientes "standards": descanso dominical y días feriados para su observancia religiosa; jornadas largas con fines hacia la "máxima" (!?) producción; ausencia de medidas relativas al salario, pues el trabajo es remunerado en especie; importancia concedida a la alimentación "comparable al pienso de un animal de labor" y asistencia obligatoria para prevenir la "gran pérdida productiva y pecuniaria del esclavo."

Seguro Social

Altmeyer, A. J. Primera conferencia interamericana de seguridad social (*Bol. unión panamer.*, vol. 77, no. 3, marzo, p. 143-147). [3571
Breve reseña de la Conferencia ya citada (véanse *Handbook, no. 7, 1941*, item 3864 y *Handbook, no. 8, 1942*, item 3686). Texto inglés en *Bull. pan amer. union*, vol. 77, no. 1, Jan., p. 12-16.

INTER-AMERICAN HEALTH PLAN. IT'S NOW GOING FORWARD ON BIG SCALE (*For. com. weekly*, vol. 11, no. 9, March 29, p. 8-9, 39-40, illus.). [3572
Los Ministros de Relaciones Exteriores de América, reunidos por tercera vez en Rio de Janeiro, aprobaron un plan sanitario a desarrollar cooperativamente entre las autoridades competentes latinoamericanas y la División de Salud y Sanidad de la Oficina del Coordinador de Asuntos Interamericanos en Washington, D. C. Aunque su objetivo inmediato es asegurar la producción de caucho, fibras, minerales y otros productos estratégicos, este plan perdurará después de la guerra bajo la forma de hospitales, dispensarios, casas-cuna, escuelas de enfermeras, instalaciones sanitarias.

Vivienda, Nutrición y Otros Standards de Bienestar Obrero

(*Véanse también los items* 1013, 3556, 3559, 3565, 3570)

ACUERDOS INTERNACIONALES CENTROAMERICANOS SOBRE EDUCACIÓN (*Rev. int. trab.*, vol. 27, no. 2, p. 255-256). [3573
En una conferencia sobre educación (San José de Costa Rica, septiembre de 1942), Costa Rica, El Salvador, Guatemala, Honduras, Nicaragua y Panamá firmaron 2 convenios y 17 recomendaciones que establecen bases comunes para programas de enseñanza profesional, vocacional y agrícola.
Texto inglés en *Int. lab. rev.*, vol. 47, no. 2, Feb., p. 223.

Jones, Robert C. Low-cost housing in Latin America. Washington, D. C. Pan american union, Division of labor and social information. 20 p., illus. [3574
Legislación y práctica sobre la vivienda obrera en los países latinoamericanos a excepción de Haití y Honduras.

Trabajo de Mujeres y Menores y Otras Categorías Especiales de Trabajadores

Cannon, Mary M. Women's organizations in Ecuador, Panama and Peru (*Bull. pan amer. union*, vol. 77, no. 11, Nov., p. 601-607). [3575
Datos sobre asociaciones de empleadas y obreras.

ARGENTINA

General

Departamento nacional del trabajo. División de estadística. Investigaciones sociales 1942. Buenos Aires. (Serie A, no. 7). xv, 65 p., cuads., diagr., gráfs. [3576
Un nuevo volumen de esta importante síntesis anual (véanse *Handbook, no. 7, 1941*, item 3887 y *Handbook, no. 8, 1942*, item 3693).

ÍNDICE GENERAL 1921-1943. REVISTA DEL COLEGIO DE ABOGADOS DE BUENOS AIRES (*Rev. colegio abogados*, Buenos Aires, tomo 21, no. 6, p. 913-1132). [3577
Entre las materias de este índice de los 21 volúmenes de la *Revista* figuran las siguientes: Accidentes de trabajo; contratos de trabajo; despido; días feriados, empleados de comercio; empleados públicos; inmigración; jubilación de abogados, ferroviarios; legislación y jurisprudencia nacional, provincial y extranjera sobre trabajo y previsión social; locación de servicios; mujeres y menores; riesgos profesionales; salario familiar y trabajo.

ÍNDICES DE LA ECONOMÍA ARGENTINA (*Véritas*, año 13, no. 157, abril 1, p. 409-439, cuads.). [3578
Capítulo I: *Territorio y población* incluye población urbana y rural; aumento de la población y crecimiento migratorio; Capítulo III: *Finanzas* incluye ahorros en la Caja Nacional de Ahorro y otras instituciones bancarias; Capítulo VII: *Transportes y comunicaciones* incluye migración; Capítulo IX: *Social* incluye beneficios acordados por la Caja Nacional de Jubilaciones y Pensiones Civiles, de Empleados Ferroviarios y de la Caja de Accidentes del Trabajo; Capítulo X: *Trabajo y salario* incluye costo de la vida; huelgas, jornada de trabajo; ocupación y salarios en la industria; Capítulo XI: *Censos* incluye Censo Industrial de 1940.

INFORMACIÓN SOCIAL (*Rev. cien. econ.*, año 31, serie 2, no. 258, enero, p. 81-89; no. 259, feb., p. 187-190; no. 261, abril, p. 353-366; no. 262, mayo, p. 455-465; no. 263, junio, p. 576-584; no. 264, julio, p. 669-680; no. 265, agosto, p. 773-779; no. 266, sept., p. 849-902; no. 268, nov., p. 1273-1283; no. 269, dic., p. 1383-1390). [3579
Véase *Handbook, no. 7, 1941*, item 3889.

SEGUNDO CONGRESO SANITARIO DE MEDICINA SOCIAL Y GREMIAL EN ARGENTINA (*Rev. int. trab.*, vol. 27, no. 1, enero, p. 114-115). [3580
En este congreso (Buenos Aires, julio 8 a 11 de 1942), convocado por la Federación Médica Argentina, se aprobaron resoluciones técnicas tendientes a mejorar la actual situación de la población obrera en cuanto a salarios, higiene y medicina, seguro social, vivienda, nutrición y protección de mujeres y menores.
Texto inglés en *Int. lab. rev.*, vol. 47, no. 1, Jan., p. 99-100.

Derecho y Legislación del Trabajo

(*Véanse también los items* 3577, 3760)

Legislación nacional (*Protec. soc.*, año 6, no. 60, enero, p. 44–53; no. 61, feb., p. 37–69; no. 62, marzo, p. 74–101; no. 63, abril, p. 65–75; no. 64, mayo, p. 79–97; no. 65, junio, p. 57–65; no. 66, julio, p. 44–55; no. 67, agosto, p. 69–94; no. 68, sept., p. 49–56; no. 69, oct., p. 45–85; no. 70, nov., p. 33–37). [3581
Compilación ya anotada (véase *Handbook, no. 7, 1941,* item 3998).

Unsain, Alejandro M. Ordenamiento de las leyes obreras argentinas. Buenos Aires. Ed. Losada. (Acad. de ciencias económicas, ediciones especiales, no. 2). 106 p. [3582
Compilación anotada y comentada de la principal legislación social promulgada de 1905 a 1943.

Organismos Oficiales, Asociaciones Patronales y Obreras

(*Véase también el item* 3588)

Segundo congreso de la confederación general del trabajo de la república argentina (*Rev. int. trab.*, vol. 27, no. 4, abril, p. 614–615). [3583
Celebrado en Buenos Aires, de diciembre 15 a 19 de 1942.
Texto inglés en *Int. lab. rev.*, vol. 47, no. 4, April, p. 537.

Relaciones Industriales

(*Véanse también los items* 3578, 3588, 3596)

Despontin, Luis A. Normas de procedimientos para conflictos colectivos e individuales del trabajo en la Provincia de Córdoba (*Rev. univ. nac. Córdoba*, año 30, no. 5–6, julio–agosto, p. 529–567). [3584
Los procedimientos conciliatorio, arbitral y administrativo establecidos en el nuevo Código de Procedimientos Civiles de la Provincia de Córdoba de 1943 para la solución de conflictos colectivos e individuales resultantes de juicios por indemnización de accidentes de trabajo y de despido, constituyen, según el entendido autor, una "punta de lanza" en el derecho procesal del trabajo de toda da Nación.

Empleo y Desocupación

(*Véanse también los items* 3564, 3577, 3578, 3593)

Establishment of national employment system in Argentina, 1943 (*Month. labor rev.*, vol. 57, no. 5, Nov., p. 946–949). [3585
Cumpliendo con el convenio sobre desocupación de la primera Conferencia Internacional del Trabajo (Washington, 1919), ratificado por Argentina en 1933, el gobierno decretó en julio 21 de 1943 el establecimiento de un Registro Nacional de Colocaciones y su coordinación con las agencias de empleo públicas y privadas existentes en el país.

Losanovscky Perel, Vicente. La desocupación en las profesiones liberales (*Rev. cien. econ.*, año 31, serie 2, no. 266, sept., p. 821–845). [3586
Analiza las causas de esta desocupación y sugiere soluciones permanentes del problema.

Migración y Colonización

(*Véanse también los items* 3565, 3577, 3578)

Pinto, Víctor. La nueva ley de inmigración argentina (*Rev. cien. econ.*, año 31, serie 2, no. 261, abril, p. 295–308). [3587
Análisis de las modalidades y factores del movimiento inmigratorio para establecer una política racional en la materia.

Salarios, Horas, Descansos y Costo de la Vida

(*Véanse también los items* 991, 3564, 3566–3569, 3577, 3578, 3580, 3603)

Buenos Aires (provincia). Departamento del trabajo. Condiciones de vida de la familia obrera. La regulación colectiva del trabajo. La Plata. 192 p., diagr., cuads. [3588
Resultados estadísticos, debidamente anotados y comentados, de dos encuestas (agosto de 1938 y agosto de 1942) sobre presupuestos familiares e índices del costo de la vida basados en ellas para varias poblaciones de la Provincia. Legislación provincial sobre asociaciones profesionales. Datos sobre contratos colectivos.

Casiello, Francisco. Protección a la familia argentina (*Rev. econ. arg.*, año 25, tomo 42, no. 296, feb., p. 46–53). [3589
Exposición de motivos de la Comisión de Legislación del Trabajo de la Cámara de Diputados sobre "asignaciones familiares."

Costo de la vida (*Rev. econ. arg.*, año 25, tomo 42, no. 295, enero, p. 35; no. 296, feb., p. 67; no. 297, marzo, p. 99; no. 298, abril, p. 141; no. 299, mayo, p. 182; no. 301, julio, p. 325; no. 302, agosto, p. 363; no. 303, sept., p. 393; no. 304, oct., p. 421; no. 305, nov., p. 449; no. 306, dic., p. 477). [3590
Véase *Handbook, no. 7, 1941,* item 3924.

El costo de la vida (*Rev. econ. arg.*, año 25, tomo 42, no. 298, abril, p. 117–122, cuads.). [3591
Fuentes y métodos de compilación de los índices del costo de la vida antes citados (item 3590).

Descanso semanal en la República Argentina (*Rev. int. trab.*, vol. 27, no. 4, abril, p. 589). [3592
Aumento de la jornada de trabajo para contrarrestar la escasez de obreros calificados en la industria ferroviaria.
Texto inglés en *Int. lab. rev.*, vol. 47, no. 4, April, p. 514–515.

Empleo y salarios. costo de la vida (*Véritas*, año 13, no. 145, enero 15, p. 78; no. 146, feb. 15, p. 153; no. 147, abril 1, p. 407; no. 148, abril 15, p. 561; no. 149, mayo 15, p. 655; no. 150, junio 15, p. 735; no. 151, julio 15, p. 829; no. 153, sept. 15, p. 1008; no. 154, oct. 15, p. 1096; no. 155, nov. 15, p. 1182; no. 156, dic. 15, p. 1299). [3593
Índices de empleo, salarios pagados en la industria y costo de la vida en Buenos Aires (véase item 3590).

Ministerio del interior. Departamento nacional del tlabajo. División de estadística. Adaptación de los salarios a las fluctuaciones del costo de la vida. Problemas que suscita, normas de aplicación práctica. Buenos Aires. (Serie B, Estadísticas y censos, no. 12). 86 p., mimeogr. [3594
Estudio comparativo (1939 a 1943) de las fluctuaciones de los salarios fijados en los contratos colectivos y del costo de la vida, preparado para la aplicación de la legislación de 1943 sobre aumentos de salarios.

Política de salarios en la República Argentina (*Rev. int. trab.*, vol. 27, no. 6, junio, p. 870). [3595
Adaptación automática de los salarios al costo de la vida.
Texto inglés en *Int. lab. rev.*, vol. 47, no. 6, June, p. 761–762.

Rolandi, Renato D. El sistema de arbitraje obligatorio y el salario mínimo (*Rev. cien. econ.*, año 31, serie 2, no. 268, nov., p. 1231–1258; no. 269, dic., p. 1313–1343). [3596
Antecedentes oficiales y privados. Notas bibliográficas.

Seguro Social

(*Véanse también los items* 3577, 3578, 3580, 3599, 3601)

Los seguros sociales en Argentina (*Rev. int. trab.*, vol. 27, no. 3, marzo, p. 446–449). [3597
Descríbense los siguientes progresos: Para cubrir el déficit de la Caja de Pensiones Ferroviarias, la ley de septiembre 30 de 1942 introdujo radicales reformas (ya preconizadas en el *Handbook, no. 7, 1941*, items 3949, 3951 y 3952) en el régimen de cotizaciones y prestaciones de dicha Caja; por ley no. 12822 de septiembre 30 de 1942 se autorizó a la Caja de Jubilaciones y Pensiones Bancarias a otorgar a sus afiliados préstamos en efectivo; la legislación sobre indemnización de los accidentes de trabajo (véase *Handbook, no. 7, 1941*, items 3946, 3950 y 3953) fué modificada por decreto no. 136,439 de noviembre 24 de 1942 con objeto de garantizar un mejor pago de las prestaciones actuales; finalmente, en la Provincia de Santa Fe fué promulgada la ley no. 3072 de septiembre 21 de 1942 sobre seguro de invalidez y muerte y la vivienda para empleados públicos.
Texto inglés en Int. lab. rev., vol. 47, no. 3, March, p. 387–390.

Vivienda, Nutrición y Otros Standards de Bienestar Obrero

(*Véanse también los items* 1013, 1394, 3574, 3577, 3578, 3580, 3597)

Cofferata, Juan F. Algunas consideraciones sobre la ley 9679 y el problema de la vivienda propia (*Rev. econ. arg.*, año 25, tomo 42, no. 300, junio, p. 230–231). [3598
La acción privada, y no únicamente el Estado, debe colaborar en la obra de la Comisión Nacional de Casas Baratas.

Korn Villafañe, Adolfo. La justica social y el problema de la denatalidad (*Rev. der. admin. munic.*, no. 55, enero, p. 33–40). [3599
No será posible obtener una "natalidad próspera" mientras no tengan vigencia jurídica en la Argentina los derechos sociales de la vivienda, la alimentación, el seguro social, "la enseñanza científica" y la educación moral, descritos brevemente en este artículo.

Social services for residents of low-cost housing in argentina (*Month. labor rev.*, vol. 57, no. 3, Sept., p. 508–509). [3601
Financiamiento, prestaciones y administración de los nuevos servicios sociales (seguro mutualista de muerte, servicios clínicos, visitadoras sociales, centros de recreación, enseñanza doméstica, etc.) otorgados en Buenos Aires por la Comisión Nacional de Casas Baratas en virtud de las resoluciones nos. 9331 y 9332 de octubre 31 de 1942.

Trabajo de Mujeres y Menores y Otras Categorías Especiales de Trabajadores

(*Véanse también los items* 459, 3561, 3577, 3580)

Coghlan, Eduardo A. El trabajo de los menores (*Rev. econ. arg.*, año 26, tomo 42, no. 304, oct., p. 401–406). [3602
Medidas para mejorar la actual situación en cuanto a delincuencia, educación y trabajo de menores.

Olmo Castro, Amalo. La angustiosa economía actual del empleado (*Véritas*, vol. 13, no. 146, feb. 15, p. 95–96). [3603
Datos y cifras sobre condiciones de vida y trabajo en Santiago del Estero.

BOLIVIA

General

Andrade, Víctor. Elementos generales sobre las condiciones de trabajo, de legislación y de otros problemas sociales de la República de Bolivia (*Protec. soc.*, año 6, no. 62, marzo, p. 6–27; no. 63, abril, p. 7–26; no. 64, mayo, p. 6–18; no. 65, junio, p. 6–19; no. 66, julio, p. 7–9; no. 67, agosto, p. 7–42; cuads. plegadizos). [3605
Aprovechando la legislación y estadísticas de su país con un criterio científico y práctico a la vez, el autor—ampliamente conocido como experto en la materia—ataca la solución de los angustiosos problemas bolivianos de trabajo y previsión social. Documento básico.

Índice bibliográfico de Protección social (*Protec soc.*, año 6, no. 67, agosto, p. 66–68; no. 68, sept., p. 57–67; no. 69, oct., p. 39–44; no. 70, nov., p. 39–44). [3606
Índice bibliográfico, por orden cronológico, de los editoriales, artículos, legislación nacional y síntesis mensuales (item 3609) a partir del primer número, febrero de 1938.

Informe de la Comisión Mixta Boliviano-Estadounidense del Trabajo. Montreal. Oficina internacional del trabajo. 105 p. [3607
Véase el item siguiente, 3608.

Informe y recomendaciones de la Comisión Magruder sobre las condiciones de trabajo en Bolivia (*Protec. soc.*, año 6, no. 61, feb., p. 70–83). [3608
Aspirando "a lograr un standard de vida compatible, que proporcione alimentación suficiente, vivienda adecuada y educación a la familia, y se ofrezca seguridad en aquellos períodos en que el individuo haya perdido transitoria o permanentemente su capacidad de producir," esta Comisión (véanse items 3607, 3610) hizo recomendaciones bajo los siguientes rubros: I. Condiciones de vida de los trabajadores. II. Educación. III. Libertad de asociación y negociación colectiva. IV. Regulación del salario mínimo. V. Regulación de horas de trabajo. VI. Seguro social. VII. Servicio público y gratuito de colocaciones. VIII. Vivienda. IX. Sanidad. X. Organización de la cooperación norteamericano-boliviana.

Síntesis mensual (*Protec. soc.*, año 6, no. 60, enero, p. 27–33; no. 61, feb., p. 13–18; no. 62, marzo, p. 35–42; no. 63, abril, p. 30–35; no. 64, mayo, p. 33–39; no. 65, junio, p. 27–31; no. 66, julio, p. 15–22; no. 67, agosto, p. 49–53; no. 68, sept., p. 19–23; no. 69, oct., p. 14–19; no. 70, nov., p. 14–17; no. 71, dic., p. 17–21). [3609
Notas sobre trabajo y previsión social ya comentadas (véase *Handbook, no. 7, 1941*, item 3993).

La situación en Bolivia. Misión de expertos del trabajo de los Estados Unidos (*Rev. int. trab.*, vol. 27, no. 3, marzo, p. 411–412). [3610
A petición del Gobierno de La Paz se creó en enero de 1943 una Comisión Mixta Americano-Boliviana de Expertos del Trabajo, con representantes gubernamentales, patronales y obreros, encargados de estudiar *in situ* la situación de los trabajadores del país con objeto de mejorar sus condiciones de vida y trabajo y de aumentar la producción de minerales estratégicos teniendo en cuenta salarios, horas, seguridad, higiene, etc. Esta Comisión—hasta ahora única en su género en América Latina—presentó, como informe, el item 3608.
Texto inglés en *Int. lab. rev.*, vol. 47, no. 3, March, p. 359–360.

Watt, Robert J. Bolivian puzzle (*Int. amer.*, vol. 2, no. 7, July, p. 17–19, illus.). [3611
Análisis de los complejos problemas sociales bolivianos, preparado por el representante obrero en la Comisión Magruder (item 3610).

Derecho y Legislación del Trabajo

(*Véanse también los items* 3605, 3608, 3610, 3624)

Amendments to Bolivian labor code (*Month. labor rev.*, vol. 56, no. 4, April, p. 732–733). [3612
El Código del Trabajo, promulgado por decreto supremo de mayo 24 de 1939, fué declarado ley por el Congreso Nacional a fines de 1942, haciéndosele modificaciones en cuanto a la compensación por despido, indemnización de accidentes profesionales y huelgas en servicio público.

Gutiérrez, José María. Breve anotación sobre el Código del trabajo (*Protec. soc.*, año 6, no. 60, enero, p. 17–26). [3613
El autor afirma que en el nuevo código (véanse items 3614 y 3615) no se ha tenido en cuenta el grado incipiente de la industria boliviana y que el código en vez de ser "sencillo y lacónico" es "una legislación bastante extensa, complicada y de difícil manipulación."

Ley general del trabajo (*Protec. soc.*, año 6, no. 61, feb., p. 45–69). [3614
En diciembre 8 de 1942, el Congreso Nacional elevó a la categoría de ley, el Código General del Trabajo promulgado por Decreto supremo de mayo 24 de 1939. Contiene los siguientes capítulos: Disposiciones generales; contrato de trabajo; categorías especiales de trabajadores; condiciones generales de trabajo; seguridad e higiene; asistencia médica y otras medidas de previsión social; riesgos profesionales; seguro

social obligatorio; organizaciones de trabajadores y patronos; conflictos y lockouts; prescripciones y sanciones.

REGLAMENTACIÓN DE LA LEY GENERAL DEL TRABAJO (*Protec. soc.*, año 6, no. 67, agosto, p. 69–94). [3615
Promulgada por decreto supremo de agosto 13 de 1943 (véase item 3614).

RESÚMEN INFORMATIVO DE DISPOSICIONES LEGALES DE ÍNDOLE ECONÓMICA Y SOCIAL (*Bol. banco central Bolivia*, año 15, no. 59, enero–marzo, p. i–xx; no. 61, julio–sept., p. i–xlii; no. 62, oct.–dic., p. i–xv). [3616
Leyes, decretos y resoluciones sobre trabajo y previsión social.

SALARIOS, HORAS, DESCANSOS Y COSTO DE LA VIDA

(*Véanse también los items* 991, 3556, 3608, 3610, 3614, 3754)

Banco central de Bolivia. 15ª memoria anual correspondiente a la gestión del año 1943 presentada al sr. ministro de hacienda y estadística. La Paz. Ed. artística. 110 p., cuads., gráfs. [3617
Índices mensuales (diciembre 1936=100) del costo de la vida, alimentación, etc. en La Paz, preparados por la Dirección General de Estadística.

ÍNDICE DEL COSTO DE LA VIDA EN LA REPÚBLICA (*Bol. banco central Bolivia*, año 15, no. 59, enero–marzo, p. 29–31; no. 61, julio–sept., p. 30–35; no. 62, oct.–dic., p. 35–40). [3618
Índices mensuales (1931=100) de alimentación, combustible, vestido, servicios, habitación y total en La Paz y otras 8 ciudades del país.

PRECIOS EN LA CIUDAD DE LA PAZ (*Bol. banco central Bolivia*, año 15, no. 59, enero–marzo, p. 26–28; no. 61, julio–agosto, p. 27–29; no. 62, oct.–dic., p. 27–29, cuads.). [3619
Cifras absolutas mensuales de precios de artículos alimenticios, vestido, servicios, combustible y habitación.

PRECIOS Y COSTO DE VIDA (*Bol. banco central Bolivia*, año 15, no. 59, enero–marzo, p. xiv; no. 60, abril–junio, p. xiv; no. 61, julio–sept., p. xiii; no. 62, oct.–dic., p. xvi, cuads.). [3620
Estadísticas y comentarios sobre los índices de alimentos, combustibles, vestido, servicios, habitación y total de costo de la vida (diciembre de 1936=100) en La Paz.

SEGURO SOCIAL

(*Véanse también los items* 3608, 3610, 3614, 3754)

Andrade, Víctor. Una visión de los problemas sociales de post-guerra en Bolivia (*Protec. soc.*, año 6, no. 60, enero, p. 6–13). [3621
El autor señala el seguro de invalidez y vejez para los obreros mineros, la ampliación de los servicios sociales existentes y, en general, la seguridad social, como una de las soluciones bolivianas de post-guerra.

CAJAS DE CRÉDITO Y PREVISIÓN SOCIAL (*Bol. banco central Bolivia*, año 15, no. 59, enero–marzo, p. 17; no. 60, abril–junio, p. 17; no. 61, julio–sept., p. 17; no. 62, oct.–dic., p. 22, cuads.). [3622
Balances mensuales de la Caja de Seguros y Ahorros Obreros, Caja de Crédito Popular y Caja de Jubilaciones Ferroviarias.

EL MOVIMIENTO DE LA SEGURIDAD SOCIAL EN BOLIVIA (*Rev. int. trab.*, vol. 27, no. 6, junio, p. 902). [3623
Nombramiento de una comisión para la reorganización de las cajas de jubilación (ya anunciada en los *Handbook, no. 7, 1941*, items 4012, 4013, 4015 y 4019 y *Handbook, no. 8, 1942*, item 3716) y la legalización de la Caja de Seguro y Ahorro Obrero (véanse *Handbook, no. 7, 1941*, items 4003–4005 y *Handbook, no. 8, 1942*, item 3712).
Texto inglés en *Int. lab. rev.*, vol. 47, no. 6, June, p. 788–789.

ORGANIZACIÓN Y REGLAMENTO DE LA CAJA DE SEGURO Y AHORRO OBRERO. OTRAS DISPOSICIONES PERTINENTES (*Protec. soc.*, año 6, no. 69, oct., p. 45–85). [3624
Compilación de leyes, decretos y resoluciones, de 1935 a 1942.

VIVIENDA, NUTRICIÓN Y OTROS STANDARDS DE BIENESTAR OBRERO

(*Véanse también los items* 3561, 3574, 3608, 3610, 3614, 3618–3620, 3754)

Puente, Carlos. Plan de edificación social para vivienda (*Protec. soc.*, año 6, no. 71, dic., p. 23–27). [3625
Política de edificación de la Caja de Seguro y Ahorro Obrero en sus aspectos técnico, administrativo y financiero.

TRABAJO DE MUJERES Y MENORES Y OTRAS CATEGORÍAS ESPECIALES DE TRABAJADORES

(*Véanse también los items* 3608, 3610, 3614, 3754)

Pereyra, Diómedes de. America's tin industry (*Int. amer.*, vol. 2, no. 7, July, p. 20–27, photogr.). [3626
Condiciones sociales en la industria boliviana del estaño, documentadas histórica y fotográficamente.

PROYECTO DE LEY DE PROTECCIÓN A LA INFANCIA Y CÓDIGO DE MENORES (*Protec. soc.*, año 6, no. 62, marzo, p. 52–66; no. 63, abril, p. 50–

64; no. 64, mayo, p. 66-78; no. 65, junio, p. 45-52). **[3627**
Del patronato nacional de menores y huérfanos de guerra y de los jueces de menores y organismos auxiliares.

Sobre catastro radiográfico de torax. Observaciones realizadas en la ciudad de La Paz (*Bol. ofic. sanit. panamer.*, año 22, no. 9, sept., p. 790-793). **[3628**
Ponencia de la delegación de Bolivia a la XI Conferencia Sanitaria Panamericana (item 3559). Datos provisionales, 1940–1943, sobre exámenes radioscópicos y radiofotográficos en maestros de escuela y obreros industriales.

BRASIL

GENERAL

(*Véanse los items* 1708a, 3556, 3557)

Derecho y Legislación del Trabajo

Consolidación de la legislación del trabajo en Brasil (*Rev. int. trab.*, vol. 28, no. 6, dic., p. 878-882). **[3629**
La abundante legislación sobre trabajo y previsión social, promulgada desde 1930, fué "consolidada" en un solo cuerpo en mayo de 1943.
Texto inglés en *Int. lab. rev.*, vol. 48, no. 6, Dec., p. 755-758.

Ministério do trabalho, industria e comércio. Commissão técnica de orientação sindical. Consolidação das leis do trabalho. Rio de Janeiro. 262 p. **[3630**
Texto de la legislación arriba mencionada.

Monteiro, Luis Augusto Rego, José de Segadas Viana, Dorval Lacerda, y Arnaldo Sussekind. Consolidação das leis de proteção do trabalho (*Bol. min. trab. ind. com.*, ano 9, no. 101, jan., p. 105–128). **[3631**
Dictámen de la comisión encargada de elaborar el anteproyecto de Consolidação das Leis do Trabalho, finalmente adoptada en mayo de 1943 (items 3629, 3630).

Organismos Oficiales, Asociaciones Patronales y Obreras

Sindicatos e federações em 1943 (*Bol. min. trab. ind. com.*, ano 9, no. 104, abril, p. 85-89, quads.). **[3632**
Federaciones y sindicatos nacionales y locales de trabajadores y empleados, por regiones geográficas.

Empleo y Desocupación

(*Véanse también los items* 1635, 3636)

Industrial distribution of workers in Brazil, 1940 (*Month. labor rev.*, vol. 56, no. 4, April, p. 682, table). **[3633**
Distribución, por industrias, de 825,425 trabajadores.

La movilización económica y los problemas relativos a la mano de obra en Brasil (*Rev. int. trab.*, vol. 27, no. 6, junio, p. 824-834). **[3634**
Siguiendo la entrada de Brasil a la gueerra, el gobierno dispuso por decreto-ley no. 4750 de septiembre 28 de 1942 la movilización de los recursos nacionales. Ella comprende la organización económica del país, de la mano de obra y de la enseñanza vocacional.
Texto inglés en *Int. lab. rev.*, vol. 47, no. 6, June, p. 721-730.

Migración y Colonización

(*Véase el item* 3565)

Salarios, Horas, Descansos y Costo de la Vida

(*Véanse también los items* 991, 3566, 3568, 3646)

Duración del trabajo en época de guerra en Brasil (*Rev. int. trab.*, vol. 27, no. 1, enero, p. 109). **[3635**
Aumento de la duración normal de la jornada de trabajo en las empresas de servicios públicos y defensa nacional según decreto legislativo no. 4639 de agosto 31 de 1942.
Texto inglés en *Int. lab. rev.*, vol. 47, no. 1, Jan., p. 94-95.

Employment and wages in São Paulo, Brazil, 1942 and 1943 (*Month. labor rev.*, vol. 57, no. 3, Sept., p. 581-592, tables). **[3636**
Número de trabajadores en la industria y los servicios públicos de la ciudad de São Paulo y el resto del Estado en 1943 y tarifas mínimas y máximas en diversas ocupaciones en 1942-1943.

Increased minimum-wage rates in Brazil, 1943 (*Month. labor rev.*, vol. 56, no. 3, March, p. 592). **[3637**
Según resolución de enero 8 de 1943.

Minimum monthly wage rates in Brazil, 1943 (*Month. labor rev.*, vol. 57, no. 2, Aug., p. 349). **[3638**
Nueva fijación de salarios mínimos para los obreros industriales, 1943-1946, según el decreto-ley no. 5473 de mayo 11 de 1943.

Números índices mensais do custo da alimentação (*Bol. min. trab. ind. com.*, ano 9, no. 10, jan., p. 340-353; no. 102, fev., p. 306-316; no. 103, março, p. 298-314; no. 104, abril, p. 330-357; no. 105, máio, p. 337-364). **[3639**
El número de localidades cubiertas por estas series (véanse *Handbook, no. 7, 1941*, item 4075 y *Handbook, no. 8, 1942*, item 3726) ha aumentado a unas 1520.

Preços dos gêneros de primeira necessidade (*Bol. min. trab. ind. com.*, ano 9, no. 101,

jan., p. 335–339; no. 102, fev., p. 301–305; no. 103, março, p. 293–297; no. 104, abril, p. 325–329; no. 105, máio, p. 332–336). **[3640**
Continuación de las series ya descritas en los *Handbook, no. 7, 1941,* item 4076 y *Handbook, no. 8, 1942,* item 3727.

Higiene y Seguridad del Trabajo

Estatística de accidentes do trabalho (*Bol. min. trab. ind. com.,* ano 9, no. 101, jan., p. 240–255, quads.). **[3641**
Cifras de enero a junio de 1941. Continua las cifras del *Handbook, no. 8, 1942,* item 3728.

Ribeiro, Adalberto Mário. A defesa da saúde do trabalhador nacional (*Rev. serv. públ.,* ano 6, vol. 4, no. 3, dez., p. 64–75). **[3642**
Describes the Divisão Higiene e Segurança do Trabalho created in December, 1942. [J. B. Childs]

Seguro Social

Aniversario del Instituto de Retiros y Pensiones Marítimos del Brasil (*Rev. int. trab.,* vol. 27, no. 1, enero, p. 114). **[3643**
Cifras sobre reservas y prestaciones, 1934–1942.
Texto inglés en *Int. lab. rev.,* vol. 47, no. 1, Jan., p. 99.

Santos, Evaristo dos. Incorporação e fusão de caixas (*Bol. min. trab. ind. com.,* ano 9, no. 103, março, p. 220–226). **[3644**
Esta reforma disminuirá el número de cajas de previsión de 81 a 48.

Los seguros sociales en Brasil (*Rev. int. trab.,* vol. 27, no. 4, abril, p. 601–604). **[3645**
Se relatan progresos legislativos y administrativos de las varias cajas de previsión social.
Texto inglés en *Int. lab. rev.,* vol. 47, no. 4, April, p. 525–528.

Los seguros sociales en Brasil (*Rev. int. trab.,* vol. 28, no. 3, set., p. 453). **[3646**
Progresos recientes en cuanto a indemnización por accidentes de trabajo y asignaciones familiares.
Texto inglés en *Int. lab. rev.,* vol. 48, no. 3, Sept., p. 388–389.

Vivienda, Nutrición y Otros Standards de Bienestar Obrero

(*Véanse también los items* 1633, 3574)

Cooperativas fundadas de 1902 a 1941 (*Bol. min. trab. ind. com.,* ano 9, no. 104, abril, p. 333–334, quads.). **[3647**
Clasificadas por tipo y estado.

Duncan, Julian S. Rice and feijoada (*Int. amer.,* vol. 2, no. 10, Oct., p. 19–24, illus.). **[3648**
"Brazil strives to raise her standards of living, to correct deficient natural diet of rice and beans, and to improve the health of the masses."

Trabajo de Mujeres y Menores y Otras Categorías Especiales de Trabajadores

(*Véase el item* 3561)

Miscelánea

Ribeiro, Adalberto Mário. A defesa da criança no Brasil (*Rev. serv. públ.,* ano 6, vol. 1, no. 3, março, p. 84–115). **[3650**
Describes the Departamento Nacional da Criança, created February 17, 1940 by decree law 2,024. [J. B. Childs]

———. O Serviço de asistência a menores (*Rev. serv. públ.,* ano 6, vol. 1, no. 2, feb., p. 83–106). **[3651**
The Instituto Sete de Setembro (created in 1932) was by decree 3,799, November 5, 1941, transformed into the Serviço de Asistência a Menores. [J. B. Childs]

CHILE

General

Labor conditions in Chile, 1942 (*Month. labor rev.,* vol. 57, no. 4, Oct., p. 716–719, tables). **[3652**
Legislación sobre horas y empleados privados; paros y otros conflictos industriales; salarios, costo de la vida, y control de precios; seguro social.

Empleo y Desocupación

(*Véanse también los items* 3564, 3659, 3660, 3661)

Asistencia a los desocupados y a los inadaptados sociales en Chile (*Rev. int. trab.,* vol. 28, julio, p. 115–116). **[3653**
Organismos encargados de dicha asistencia.
Texto inglés en *Int. lab. rev.,* vol. 48, no. 1, July, p. 98–99.

Bolsa del trabajo (*Estad. chil.,* año 16, no. 12, dic., p. 684). **[3654**
Cifras mensuales y anuales de obreros, empleados particulares y domésticos solicitando trabajo, de 1932 a 1943. Véase *Handbook, no. 7, 1941,* item 4135.

La colocación y la lucha contra el paro en Chile (*Rev. int. trab.*, vol. 27, no. 4, abril, p. 575). [3655
Para contrarrestar el paro causado por los efectos de la guerra en la economía nacional, fué creada una comisión para estudiar la desocupación y la redistribución de la mano de obra.
Texto inglés en *Int. lab. rev.*, vol. 47, no. 4, April, p. 503.

Regulations on unemployment benefits for salaried employees in Chile (*Month. labor rev.*, vol. 57, no. 6, Dec., p. 1174). [3656
Según el decreto no. 42 de enero 12 de 1943, con notas bibliográficas sobre la legislación chilena de seguro contra el paro.

Salarios, Horas, Descansos y Costo de la Vida

(*Véanse también los items* 3561, 3567, 3569, 3652)

Costo de alimentación (*Estad. chil.*, año 16, no. 12, dic., p. 737–738, cuads.). [3657
Cifras absolutas del costo de la alimentación, vestido, combustible y luz en varias ciudades de Chile (véase *Handbook, no. 7, 1941*, item 4140).

Costo de la vida (*Estad. chil.*, año 16, no. 12, dic., p. 738–739). [3658
Estadísticas ya anotadas (véase *Handbook, no. 7, 1941*, item 4141).

Industria del cemento (*Estad. chil.*, año 16, no. 12, dic., p. 693). [3659
Estadísticas sobre empleados ocupados y jornales, 1930–1943 (véase *Handbook, no. 7, 1941*, item 4144).

Industria manufacturera del azúcar (*Estad. chil.*, año 16, no. 12, dic., p. 692). [3660
Estadísticas de ocupación obrera, empleados, jornales, sueldos y prestaciones sociales, 1941–1943.

Jornales (*Estad. chil.*, año 16, no. 12, dic., p. 683–684). [3661
Número de empleados y obreros ocupados, días trabajados, salarios totales y por día, y jornales medios en varias industrias, 1937–1943. Continua el *Handbook, no. 7, 1941*, item 4137.

Seguro Social

(*Véase también el item* 3652)

Control de las instituciones de seguro social en Chile (*Rev. int. trab.*, vol. 28, no. 1, julio, p. 135–136). [3662
A partir de enero 1 de 1943, el Departamento de Previsión Social del Ministerio de Salud, Previsión y Asistencia Social vigilará el perfeccionamiento técnico, administrativo y financiero de unas 40 instituciones chilenas de seguro social (véase *Handbook, no. 8, 1942*, item 3752).
Texto inglés en *Int. lab. rev.*, vol. 48, no. 1, July, p. 115–116.

El funcionamiento de la caja de seguro obligatorio (*Rev. int. trab.*, vol. 27, no. 4, abril, p. 598–601). [3663
Creación del Servicio Médico Nacional para los Trabajadores No Manuales y estadísticas sobre movimiento económico, morbilidad, invalidez y muerte en la Caja de Seguro Obligatorio.
Texto inglés en *Int. lab. rev.*, vol. 47, no. 4, April, p. 522–525.

Grove, Eduardo. Seguro social en Chile (*Bol. unión panamer.*, vol. 77, no. 6, junio, p. 315–323, ilus.). [3664
Legislación y estadísticas sobre medicina preventiva y asistencia médica a los obreros industriales, los empleados públicos y privados y la población en conjunto; proyectos sobre seguros sociales.

Social insurance for journalists in Chile, 1941 (*Month. labor rev.*, vol. 56, no. 4, April, p. 690–692, tables). [3665
Campo de aplicación, prestaciones y administración de la Sección Periodistas de la Caja Nacional de Empleados Públicos y Periodistas.

Social security in Chile (*For. com. weekly*, vol. 10, no. 6, Feb. 6, p. 6–7, 9, illus.). [3666
Notas descriptivas y cifras estadísticas sobre seguro social, asistencia médica, vivienda y nutrición.

Trabajo y previsión social (*Estad. chil.*, año 16, no. 12, dic., p. 685–688, cuads.). [3667
Cifras de 1928 a 1943 sobre ingresos, gastos, prestaciones, inversiones y reservas de las cajas de previsión social (véase *Handbook, no. 7, 1941*, item 4179).

Vivienda, Nutrición y Otros Standards de Bienestar Obrero

(*Véanse también los items* 1013, 3574, 3666)

Caja de la habitación popular (*Estad. chile.*, año 16, no. 12, dic., p. 685–687, cuads.). [3668
Continua, para los años 1940 a 1943, las estadísticas sobre habitación popular ya citadas (véase *Handbook, no. 7, 1941*, item 4180a).

Harrison, Lewis K. Chile plans low-rent houses (*For. com. weekly*, vol. 13, no. 2, Oct. 9, p. 5, 28). [3669
Dentro de un programa de vivienda barata, la Caja de la Habitación Popular construía, de 1943 a 1953, 12,000 viviendas anualmente.

COLOMBIA

General

(*Véanse los items* 3556, 3557, 3561)

Organismos Oficiales, Asociaciones Patronales y Obreras

Comité sindical de planificación económica en colombia (*Rev. int. trab.*, vol. 27, no. 6, junio, p. 911). **[3670**
Creado dentro de la Confederación de Trabajadores de Colombia.
Texto inglés en *Int. lab. rev.*, vol. 47, no. 6, June, p. 795–796.

Salarios, Horas, Descansos y Costo de la Vida

(*Véanse también los items* 991, 3564, 3566, 3568, 3569)

Price control legislation in colombia, 1943 (*Month. labor rev.*, vol. 57, no. 1, July, p. 40–41). **[3671**
Resúmen de la ley no. 7 de marzo 2 de 1943 para impedir la especulación con productos alimenticios, farmacéuticos y de consumo general entre las clases trabajadoras.

Prima movil sobre las asignaciones de los empleados nacionales en colombia (*Rev. int. trab.*, vol. 28, no. 3, sept., p. 444). **[3672**
Ordenada por decreto de junio 22 de 1943.
Texto inglés en *Int. lab. rev.*, vol. 48, no. 3, Sept., p. 381.

Seguro Social

Caja de previsión social de la navegación en colombia (*Rev. int. trab.*, vol. 28, no. 1, julio, p. 136–137). **[3673**
Creada por fallo arbitral. Cubre los riesgos de enfermedad, invalidez y muerte.
Texto inglés en *Int. lab. rev.*, vol. 48, no. 1, July, p. 116.

Herrnstadt, Ernesto. Colombia ante el problema de la seguridad social (*Rev. int. trab.*, vol. 27, no. 4, abril, p. 489–514). **[3674**
La seguridad social en Colombia se basa actualmente en numerosas disposiciones sobre accidentes del trabajo y seguro de enfermedad, maternidad, vejez, muerte y cesantía diseminadas incoherentemente en la legislación del trabajo, los contratos colectivos y aun las sentencias arbitrales. Analizando estas medidas desde el punto de vista técnico, el autor demuestra la urgente necesidad de unificar y extender los servicios existentes por medio de la implantación del seguro social obligatorio y describe los principios generales que habrán de aplicarse a este fin. En una nota final se enumeran las principales leyes colombianas sobre previsión social.
Texto inglés en *Int. lab. rev.*, vol. 47, no. 4, April, p. 426–447.

COSTA RICA

General

(*Véanse también los items* 3565, 3568, 3573, 3574)

Reingreso de costa rica en la organización internacional del trabajo (*Rev. int. trab.*, vol. 27, no. 1, enero, p. 70). **[3675**
Goza "de todos los derechos inherentes a la calidad de Miembro de la Organización Internacional del Trabajo" a partir de noviembre 12 de 1942.
Texto inglés en *Int. lab. rev.*, vol. 47, no. 1, Jan., p. 62.

Social guarantees in costa rica by constitutional amendment, 1943 (*Month. labor rev.*, vol. 57, no. 6, Dec., p. 1175–1176). **[3676**
Estas "garantías sociales" sobre trabajo y previsión social (anunciadas en el *Handbook, no. 8, 1942*, items 3771 y 3773) quedaron definitivamente incorporadas a la Constitución en julio 7 de 1943.

Organismos Oficiales, Asociaciones Patronales y Obreras

El movimiento sindical en costa rica (*Rev. int. trab.*, vol. 27, no. 6, junio, p. 910, vol. 28, no. 6, dic., p. 931). **[3677**
Notas sobre su estructura y organización.
Texto inglés en *Int. lab. rev.*, vol. 47, no. 6, June, p. 794–795; vol. 48, no. 6, Dec., p. 800.

Seguro Social

(*Véase también el item* 3561)

Reglamento de aplicación del seguro social en costa rica (*Rev. int. trab.*, vol. 27, no. 4, abril, p. 595–597). **[3678**
Por decreto no. 8 de agosto 25 de 1942 se modificó en cuanto al campo de aplicación y los riesgos cubiertos, la legislación sobre seguro social en vigor (véase *Handbook, no. 8, 1942*, items 3774–3778).
Texto inglés en *Int. lab. rev.*, vol. 47, no. 4, April, p. 520–521.

CUBA

General

(*Véanse los items* 3565, 3568, 3574)

Organismos Oficiales, Asociaciones Patronales y Obreras

(*Véase también el item* 3561)

Reconocimiento de las federaciones sindicales en cuba (*Rev. int. trab.*, vol. 28, no. 3, sept., p. 414–415). **[3679**
Las restricciones al registro legal de federaciones y confederaciones sindicales im-

puesta por decreto legislativo en noviembre 7 de 1933 fueron suprimidas por decreto de abril 9 de 1943.
Texto inglés en *Int. lab. rev.*, vol. 48, no. 3, Sept., p. 356.

Tercer congreso nacional de la confederación de trabajadores de Cuba (*Rev. int. trab.*, vol. 27, no. 3, marzo, p. 459–460). [3680
Breve reseña de este Congreso (La Habana, diciembre 9 a 12 de 1942). En cuanto al Segundo Congreso, véase *Handbook, no. 7, 1941,* item 3834 y 4239.
Texto inglés en *Int. lab. rev.*, vol. 47, no. 3, March, p. 398.

Empleo y Desocupación

Medidas contra el paro en Cuba (*Rev. int. trab.*, vol. 27, no. 1, enero, p. 96–97). [3681
Legislación sobre reempleo de trabajadores llamados al servicio militar y de conductores de autobuses y asistencia de paro para trabajadores portuarios.
Texto inglés en *Int. lab. rev.*, vol. 47, no. 1, Jan., p. 84–85.

Seguro Social

Caja de indemnizaciones por accidentes de guerra marítima en Cuba (*Rev. int. trab.*, vol. 27, no. 4, abril, p. 604–605). [3682
Establecida por decreto no. 6163 de noviembre 4 de 1942.
Texto inglés en *Int. lab. rev.*, vol. 47, no. 4, April, p. 528–529.

Miscelánea

Allen, Devere. Child welfare de luxe (*Int. amer.*, vol. 2, no. 9, Sept., p. 23–27, ilus.). [3683
En el Instituto Cívico Militar de Ceiba del Agua, creado por el ex-presidente Fulgencio Batista, 1250 niños y jóvenes de ambos sexos aprenden artes y oficios.

ECUADOR

General

(*Véanse también los items* 3561, 3565, 3574, 3575)

Caja del seguro de empleados privados y obreros. Informe que presenta el gerente de la Caja del seguro al Consejo de administración acerca de las labores desarrolladas en el año de 1942. Quito. 104 p., cuads. [3684
Contiene la documentación ya anteriormente anotada (véanse *Handbook, no. 7, 1941,* items 4250 y 4251 y *Handbook, no. 8, 1942,* item 3976).

Organismos Oficiales, Asociaciones Patronales y Obreras

El sindicalismo en Ecuador (*Rev. int. trab.*, vol. 27, no. 6, junio, p. 910–911; erratum: vol. 28, no. 1, julio, p. 162). [3685
Según esta información exclusiva, la unidad sindical en el Ecuador fracasó, en marzo de 1943, principalmente en vista de la oposición a la participación de los dirigentes de los trabajadores extranjeros de la Confederación de Trabajadores de América Latina.
Texto inglés en *Int. lab. rev.*, vol. 47, no. 6, June, p. 795.

Seguro Social

Meneses Pallares, Arturo. La nueva ley del seguro social en el Ecuador (*Bol. unión panamer.*, vol. 77, no. 5, mayo, p. 263–269, ilus.). [3686
Resúmen de la ley de julio 25 de 1942 (véase *Handbook, no. 8, 1942,* item 3798).
Resúmen en inglés en *Bull. pan amer. union,* vol. 77, no. 6, June, p. 332–337.

Progreso de la caja de pensiones del Ecuador en 1942 (*Rev. int. trab.*, vol. 28, no. 2, agosto, p. 297–298). [3687
Datos sobre afiliados, ingresos, prestaciones e inversiones, en 1942, de la Caja de Pensiones del Instituto Nacional de Previsión, reformada por la ley de julio 26 de 1942 (véase *Handbook, no. 8, 1942,* item 3798).
Texto inglés en *Int. lab. rev.*, vol. 48, no. 2, August, p. 254–255.

EL SALVADOR

Miscelánea

(*Véanse también los items* 1122, 3556, 3557, 3561, 3565, 3573, 3574)

Government measures for improvement of living standards in El Salvador (*Month. labor rev.*, vol. 57, no. 2, August, p. 233–236). [3688
Estudio panorámico del progreso reciente de los standards de vida y producción del trabajador salvadoreño obtenidos con la política de vivienda, colonización y cooperativismo encomendada al Banco Hipotecario, la Junta de Mejoramiento Social y la Junta Nacional de Defensa Social.

La ley sobre el crédito rural en El Salvador (*Rev. int. trab.*, vol. 28, no. 1, julio, p. 143–144). [3689
Esta ley, de enero 7 de 1943, prevee la creación de una "Cooperativa de cajas de crédito rural limitada" que tenderá a mejorar las condiciones de vida y trabajo de sus miembros.
Texto inglés en *Int. lab. rev.*, vol. 48, no. 1, July, p. 121–122.

Mejoramiento social en el salvador (*Rev. int. trab.*, vol. 28, no. 6, dic., p. 882). [3690
A través de "Mejoramiento Social, S. A.," institución encargada de la construcción, venta o arrendamiento de casas baratas y de la creación, conservación y perfeccionamiento de empresas, obras y servicios para el mejor aprovechamiento de la tierra o para mejorar las condiciones sociales y económicas del país.
Texto inglés en *Int. lab. rev.*, vol. 48, no. 6, Dec., p. 758.

GUATEMALA

Miscelánea

(*Véanse también los items* 3556, 3557, 3561, 3565)

Decreto no. 3064—decree no. 3064 (*Rev. econ. nac.*, año 7, no. 79–80, julio–agosto, p. 37–39). [3692
Decreto de julio 27 de 1943, en español e inglés. Fija modalidades para el pago de salarios mínimos en los establecimientos manufactureros.
Resumen del decreto en *Rev. int. trab.*, vol. 28, no. 6, dic., p. 907; texto inglés del resumen en *Month. labor rev.*, vol. 57, no. 5, Nov., p. 970.

HAITI

Miscelánea

(*Véanse también los items* 3556, 3557, 3561, 3573, 3574)

Establishment of social security bureau in haiti (*Month. labor rev.*, vol. 57, no. 2, August, p. 277). [3693
Se autorizan la indemnización de accidentes profesionales, el establecimiento de hospitales y hogares para trabajadores accidentados y la realización de proyectos agrícolas, industriales y otros de carácter social, según decreto-ley de mayo 15 de 1943.

Minimum-wage legislation in haiti (*Month. labor rev.*, vol. 56, no. 3, March, p. 593). [3694
Esta legislación, la primera en su género en Haiti, se aplica a los empleados públicos y a los trabajadores en empresas privadas industriales, comerciales y agrícolas.

HONDURAS

Miscelánea

(*Véanse también los items* 3556, 3561)

Honduras. economic conditions (*For. com. weekly*, vol. 10, no. 9, Feb. 27, p. 24–25). [3695
Esta reseña económica incluye notas sobre mano de obra, empleo y control de precios.

MEXICO

General

(*Véanse también los items* 3556, 3557)

Aspectos económicos y sociales de méxico durante la . . . quincena del presente mes (*Economista*, tomo 8, año 4, no. 93, enero 1 a tomo 10, año 5, no. 116, dic. 16, cuads.). [3696
Esta sección bisemanal incluye notas sobre derecho y legislación del trabajo; relaciones industriales; empleo y desocupación; salarios y costo de la vida; migración y colonización; seguridad e higiene y seguro social.

Secretaría del trabajo y previsión social. Anuario de estadísticas del trabajo. México, D. F. 171 p., cuads. [3697
Estadísticas, brevemente explicadas y comentadas, sobre agrupaciones sindicales, empresas industriales, número de personas ocupadas, accidentes del trabajo, enfermedades, profesionales, conflictos del trabajo, huelgas, paros, desocupación, salarios y tiempo trabajado, salario mínimo y costo de la vida (véase *Handbook, no. 7, 1941*, item 4276).

———. Memoria de labores. Septiembre de 1942–agosto de 1943. México, D. F. Tall. gráf. de la nación. 279 p., cuads., algunos plegadizos, diags. [3698
Véanse referencias anteriores: *Handbook, no. 7, 1941*, item 4277 y *Handbook, no. 8, 1942*, item 3807.

Organismos Oficiales, Asociaciones Patronales y Obreras

(*Véase también el item* 3697)

Pallares, Eduardo. La CTM y la suprema corte (*Economista*, año 5, tomo 10, no. 108, agosto 16, p. 13–15). [3699
Refutación a un memorandum dirigido por la Confederación de Trabajadores de México a la Suprema Corte con objeto de obtener una sentencia favorable en un juicio sobre pago de salarios caídos, según el artículo 122 de la Ley Federal del Trabajo.

Tercer congreso de la confederación de trabajadores de méxico (*Rev. int. trab.*, vol. 27, no. 6, junio, p. 908–910). [3700
Celebrado en México, D. F., marzo 28 a abril 1 de 1943. Reseña.
Texto inglés en *Int. lab. rev.*, vol. 47, no. 6, June, p. 793–794.

Workers' organizations in mexico (*Month. labor rev.*, vol. 57, no. 3, Sept., p. 535–536, table). [3701
Una breve compilación, basada en fuentes gubernamentales y obreras, de las discutidísimas estadísticas y estimaciones del número y los afiliados de los sindicatos en

las industrias bajo jurisdicción federal. Cubre los años de 1933 a 1941.

Relaciones Industriales

(*Véanse también los items* 3696, 3697)

Reglamento de la inspección local del trabajo en el distrito federal (*Trab. prev. soc.*, tomo 18, no. 70, nov., p. 5-13). [3702
Reglamento de agosto 20 de 1943.

Reglamento de la junta federal de conciliación y arbitraje (*Trab. prev. soc.*, tomo 17, no. 66, julio, p. 75-93). [3703
De julio 21 de 1933.

Empleo y Desocupación

(*Véanse también los items* 3564, 3696, 3697)

Loyo, Gilberto. Profesiones y ocupaciones para la juventud de México (*Rev. econ.*, México, vol. 6, no. 6, junio 30, p. 27-33). [3704
En este magnífico cuadro de la situación económica y social del país y su futuro hasta 1950, se exponen las amplias posibilidades de empleo de la juventud en carreras técnicas en la agricultura, ganadería, forestería y pesca; minas y petróleo; industrias, comunicaciones y transportes; comercio; administración pública y profesiones liberales.

Migración y Colonización

(*Véanse también los items* 3564, 3565, 3696)

El éxodo de nuestros braceros mexicanos (*Rev. econ.* México, vol. 6, no. 2, feb. 28, p. 24-26). [3705
Estima el autor que "es a todas luces inconveniente impedir en forma total la salida de braceros mexicanos [a Estados Unidos] y que lo más adecuado es una reglamentación rigurosa y una observación continua acerca de las repercusiones que sobre nuestra economía tenga el éxodo de nuestros nacionales."

McWilliams, Carey. They saved the crops (*Int. amer.*, vol. 2, no. 8, August, p. 10-14, illus.). [3706
Otra reseña ilustrada sobre los satisfactorios resultados de la migración planificada por los gobiernos de México y Estados Unidos (véanse items siguientes).

Migración temporal de los trabajadores mexicanos a los estados unidos (*Rev. int. trab.*, vol. 28, no. 3, sept., p. 437-439). [3707
Resúmen de las clausulas principales del acuerdo entre México y los Estados Unidos de abril 29 de 1943 y del reglamento respectivo de la Comisión Americana de Mano de Obra de Guerra de junio 17 de 1943 sobre la migración temporaria de trabajadores no agrícolas y del nuevo acuerdo de abril de 1943 sobre reclutamiento de trabajadores agrícolas.
Texto inglés en *Int. lab. rev.*, vol. 48, no. 3, Sept., p. 375-377.

Roller Issler, Anne. Good neighbors lend a hand. Our Mexican workers (*Survey graphic*, vol. 32, no. 10, Oct., p. 389-393, illus.). [3708
"This is the story of Mexican nationals on the farms of one Californian county during the harvest of 1943. It concerns an arranged migration with guaranteed working conditions supervised by the United States government, under a cooperative plan satisfactory to farmer employers."

Rules for admission of Mexican workers as railroad track laborers (*Month. labor rev.*, vol. 57, no. 2, August, p. 240-241). [3709
Reglamentación de los derechos y deberes de patronos americanos y trabajadores mexicanos no agrícolas ("braceros"), establecida por la U. S. Manpower Commission (Junta Americana para la Mano de Obra de Guerra) en virtud del convenio méxiconorteamericano de abril 29 de 1943 sobre la inmigración temporaria de trabajadores no agrícolas.

Temporary migration of Mexican agricultural workers. Agreement between the United States and Mexico. Washington, D. C. U. S. Department of state. (Executive agreement series no. 278). 13 p. [3710
Este convenio, firmado en agosto 4 de 1942, fija condiciones de vida y trabajo.

Salarios, Horas, Descansos y Costo de la Vida

(*Véanse también los items* 991, 3566-3569, 3696, 3697)

Decreto que ordena el aumento de sueldos y salarios de los empleados públicos civiles de la federación (*Trab. prev. soc.*, tomo 18, no. 69, oct., p. 21-27). [3711
De septiembre 27 de 1943.

Decreto que reforma y adiciona la ley de compensación de emergencia al salario (*Trab. prev. soc.*, tomo 18, no. 69, oct., p. 31-35). [3712
De octubre 11 de 1943.

Hernández, Manuel A. Observaciones al informe del gerente de petróleos mexicanos (*Economista*, año 5, tomo 10, no. 99, abril 1, p. 6-8, 34-38; no. 101, mayo 1, p. 7-8, 34-38; no. 103, junio 1, p. 8, 33-38). [3713
En esta severa crítica de la administración de Petróleos Mexicanos se demuestra que los salarios y las prestaciones sociales pagados actualmente son menores de las que percibirían los obreros si no se hubiere

decretado la expropiación petrolera de marzo de 1938 y que la construcción y reparación de viviendas obreras ha sido insuficiente desde entonces.

Ley de compensación de emergencia al salario insuficiente (*Trab. prev. soc.*, tomo 17, no. 69, oct., p. 5–15). [3714
De septiembre 23 de 1943.

Minimum wage rates in mexico (*Month. labor rev.*, vol. 56, no. 1, Jan., p. 153–155). [3715
Salarios mínimos, por regiones e industrias, aprobados por las Juntas Centrales de Conciliación y Arbitraje para 1942 y 1943.

Texto de la carta del señor presidente de la república al sindicato de trabajadores ferroviarios de la república mexicana y texto de la contestación de éstos al primer magistrado (*Economista*, año 5, tomo 9, no. 99, abril 1, p. 29–31). [3716
Correspondencia cambiada en marzo de 1943 sobre la colaboración de los empleados y obreros en el mejoramiento de los ferrocarriles del país y en particular sobre puestos de confianza, disciplina y vacaciones pagadas en caso de enfermedades profesionales.

Higiene y Seguridad del Trabajo

(*Véase también el item* 3696)

Conclusiones y recomendaciones (*Trab. prev. soc.*, tomo 17, no. 68, sept., p. 35–62). [3717
Autores, títulos y texto suscinto de las ponencias aprobadas por el Segundo Congreso Nacional de Higiene y Medicina del Trabajo, clasificadas como sigue: enfermedades profesionales, accidentes del trabajo, higiene y seguridad, centros de atención para trabajadores, legislación, economía, estadísticas y educación en el trabajo.

Convocatoria y programa para la primera convención de seguridad industrial del distrito federal, organizada por el departamento del distrito federal y la secretaría del trabajo y previsión social (*Trab. prev. soc.*, tomo 17, no. 66, julio, p. 57–62). [3718
Bases, temario y lista de conferencias y sus autores.

Organización, funcionamiento y competencia de las comisiones de seguridad e higiene (*Trab. prev. soc.*, tomo 16, no. 64, mayo, p. 69–85). [3719
Compilación de las disposiciones respectivas contenidas en la Ley Federal del Trabajo y el Reglamento de Medidas Preventivas de Accidentes del Trabajo, seguida de un "Prontuario para las Comisiones de Seguridad e Higiene."

Primera convención de seguridad del distrito federal (*Economista*, año 5, tomo 10, no. 107, agosto 1, p. 2, 41–42). [3720
Convocada por la Secretaría del Trabajo y Previsión Social (México, D. F., julio 20–23 de 1943).

Segundo congreso nacional de higiene y de medicina del trabajo en méxico (*Rev. int. trab.*, vol. 27, no. 6, junio, p. 904). [3721
Celebrado en México, D. F., en julio de 1943. Programa y convocatoria.
Texto inglés en *Int. lab. rev.*, vol. 47, no. 6, June, p. 789–790.

Segundo congreso nacional de higiene y medicina del trabajo (*Trab. prev. soc.*, tomo 16, no. 65, junio, p. 53–61). [3722
Bases reglamentarias y temario.

Seguro Social

(*Véanse también los items* 3696, 3697)

Alanís Patiño, Emilio. El seguro social ante el seguro privado (*Rev. econ.*, México, vol. 6, no. 1, enero 20, p. 26–28). [3723
Sobre el discutido problema de las repercusiones favorables y adversas de la implantación del seguro social obligatorio en los seguros privados de vida.

Corson, John J. Security in Mexico (*Survey graphic*, vol. 32, no. 9, Sept., p. 354–355, 364–365). [3724
Otro análisis de la ley del seguro social dentro del ambiente económico y social del país.
Texto español en *Rev. econ.*, México, vol. 6, no. 10, 31 oct., p. 22–25.

El instituto mexicano del seguro social (*Rev. econ.*, México, vol. 6, no. 5, mayo 31, p. 30–34). [3725
El Instituto, como órgano administrativo de la ley del seguro social.

Instituto mexicano del seguro social. El seguro social en México. México, D. F. Tall. gráf. de la nación. 540 p., ilus. [3726
La recopilación más completa sobre seguro social en México. Contiene los antecedentes, anteproyectos, proyectos de la ley y sus reglamentos, así como artículos y conferencias de propaganda que precedieron a su promulgación.

Ley del seguro social en méxico (*Rev. int. trab.*, vol. 27, no. 2, feb., p. 283–285). [3727
Otro resúmen de la ley arriba citada.
Texto inglés en *Int. lab. rev.*, vol. 47, no. 2, Feb., p. 246–248.

Mingarro y San Martín, José. El seguro social (*Investig. econ.*, tomo 3, no. 1, primer., p. 45–62; no. 4, cuarto trim., p. 327–335). [3728
Estudio de caracter general sobre seguro social con algunos ensayos de interpretación sobre campo de aplicación, obligatoriedad y riesgos cubiertos por la ley mexicana.

Palacios, Manuel R. La influencia del seguro social en la economía (*Rev. econ.,* México, vol. 6, no. 1, enero 20, p. 24-26). [3729]
El seguro social dentro del movimiento revolucionario mexicano y de la economía nacional.

Reglamento de la ley de seguro social (*Trab. prev. soc.,* tomo 16, no. 64, mayo, p. 5-10). [3730]
Reglamento de abril 25 de 1943 (véase item 3726).

Rohen y Gálvez, Gustavo-Adolfo. The Mexican social insurance law (*Soc. sec. bull.,* vol. 9, no. 3, March, p. 11-16). [3731]
Contenido: Antecedentes históricos, adopción, bases legales, campo de aplicación, riesgos asegurados, prestaciones, organización financiera, administración y aplicación de la nueva ley mexicana del seguro social.

Santos Guajardo, Vicente. El seguro social y la convención de seguridad social (*Rev. econ.,* México, vol. 6, no. 7, julio 31, p. 26-27). [3732]
Características principales de la Ley del Seguro Social, descritas por el Director del Instituto Mexicano del Seguro Social ante la Primera Convención de Seguridad Industrial del Distrito Federal (item 3718).

Vivienda, Nutrición y Otros Standards de Bienestar Obrero

(*Véanse también los items* 1013, 1088, 3561, 3574, 3713)

Fligelman, Belle. Mexico's dinner guests (*Int. amer.,* vol. 2, no. 7, July, p. 28-29, photo.). [3733]
Descripción ilustrada de un comedor familiar para obreros.

Franco, José Felipe, y Antonio Y. García I. Contribución al estudio de la alimentación del obrero mexicana (*Trab. prev. soc.,* tomo 17, no. 67, agosto, p. 39-50). [3734]
Resultado de una encuesta entre 966 obreros mineros de Pachuca, Estado de Hidalgo: 54 obreros trabajando a media intensidad estan sobrealimentados, pero su régimen está desequilibrado; 601 obreros trabajando intensamente y 311 trabajando muy intensamente están subalimentados y su régimen está tambien desequilibrado. "El alcoholismo es general y más acentuado a medida que aumenta la intensidad del trabajo." Estos resultados confirman los datos de una encuesta anterior (véase *Handbook, no. 7, 1941,* item 4331).

Trabajo de Mujeres y Menores y Otras Categorías Especiales de Trabajadores

Reglamentación del trabajo a domicilio en las pequeñas industrias en México (*Rev. int. trab.,* vol. 27, no. 2, feb., p. 281-283). [3736]
En los talleres de costura, pequeñas industrias y trabajo a domicilio del Distrito Federal, según decreto de septiembre 11 de 1942.
Texto inglés en *Int. lab. rev.,* vol. 47, no. 2, Feb., p. 245-246.

NICARAGUA

Miscelánea

(*Véanse también los items* 3556, 3557, 3561)

Nicaragua. economic conditions (*For. com. weekly,* vol. 10, no. 9, Feb. 27, p. 27-28). [3737]
Dentro de las condiciones económicas descritas, hay referencias al empleo, la desocupación, la actividad industrial y el costo de la vida.

PANAMÁ

Miscelánea

(*Véanse también los items* 3556, 3557, 3561, 3574)

Caja de seguro social. Informe anual del gerente a la Junta directiva, enero 1 de 1943. Panamá. 24 p., diag. [3738]
Primer informe acerca del número de asegurados, financiamiento, prestaciones pagadas y otros resultados de la aplicación administrativa del seguro contra enfermedad, maternidad, invalidez, vejez y muerte para empleados de empresas privadas en Panamá y Colón y empleados públicos en la República (véase *Handbook, no. 8, 1942,* item 3845).

Reforma del seguro social en Panamá (*Rev. int. trab.,* vol. 28, no. 1, enero, p. 133-135). [3739]
El régimen de seguro social establecido en 1941 (véase *Handbook, no. 8, 1942,* item 3845) fué modificado por ley no. 134 de abril 27 de 1943 en cuanto a su campo de aplicación, administración y financiamiento.
Texto inglés en *Int. lab. rev.,* vol. 48, no. 1, Jan., p. 115-116.

PARAGUAY

General

(*Véanse también los items* 3556, 3557)

Martínez Díaz, Nicasio. Breve reseña de política agraria en el Paraguay (*Véritas,* año 13, no. 157, abril 1, p. 364-367). [3740]
Selección y control de la inmigración y la colonización, control de precios y enseñanza agrícola.

Salarios, Horas, Descansos y Costo de la Vida

Fixing of minimum wages authorized in paraguay, 1943 (*Month. labor rev.*, vol. 57, no. 6, Dec., p. 1223–1224). **[3741**
Disposiciones del decreto-ley no. 620 de octubre 2 de 1943 sobre fijación de salarios mínimos para los obreros y empleados de la industria privada y las empresas estatales, municipales y de servicio público.

Pay increases in paraguay (*Month. labor rev.*, vol. 56, no. 1, Jan., p. 155–156). **[3742**
Para obreros y empleados en la industria y el comercio, según decreto-ley no. 15011 de octubre 8 de 1942.

Miscelánea

(*Véanse también los items* 3561, 3574)

Cody, Morrill. Refuge in the Chaco (*Int. amer.*, vol. 2, no. 7, July, p. 10–13, illus.). **[3743**
Inmigración y colonización menonita en Paraguay.

Creación del seguro social en paraguay (*Rev. int. trab.*, vol. 27, no. 6, junio, p. 899–900). **[3744**
La legislación social sobre ahorro obligatorio (véase *Handbook, no. 7, 1941*, item 4347) y sobre accidentes del trabajo fué reemplazada por un sistema de seguro social promulgado por decreto-ley de abril 13 de 1943.
Texto inglés en *Int. lab. rev.*, vol. 47, no. 6, June, p. 585–586.

PERÚ

General

(*Véanse los items* 3565, 3574)

Relaciones Industriales

(*Véase también el item* 3561)

La colaboración entre el gobierno, los empleadores y los asalariados del perú (*Rev. int. trab.*, vol. 27, no. 3, marzo, p. 420–422). **[3745**
La implantación del arbitraje obligatorio (véase *Handbook, no. 8, 1942*, item 3851) y la organización de comisiones tripartitas encargadas de solucionar problemas sociales y económicos de las industrias textil, panificadora, etc., constituyen "progresos notables" de la reglamentación de las condiciones de trabajo.
Texto inglés en *Int. lab. rev.*, vol. 47, no. 3, March, p. 367–369.

Salarios, Horas, Descansos y Costo de la Vida

(*Véase también el item* 3568)

Regulation of profit sharing and dismissal compensation in peru, 1943 (*Month. labor rev.*, vol. 57, no. 1, July, p. 64–65). **[3746**
Breve resúmen de la legislación en vigor, 1928–1943.

Seguro Social

Extension of social insurance in peru, 1942 (*Month. labor rev.*, vol. 57, no. 3, Sept., p. 512). **[3747**
El campo de aplicación del magnífico sistema peruano de seguro social (documentado en los *Handbook, no. 7, 1941*, items 4369–4377 y *Handbook, no. 8, 1942*, items 3853–3857) fué ampliado por decreto de octubre 28 de 1942 para cubrir trabajadores mayores de 60 años, conductores de automóviles de servicio público en Lima y Callao y obreros textiles a destajo.

Vivienda, Nutrición y Otros Standards de Bienestar Obrero

(*Véase el item* 1013)

Trabajo de Mujeres y Menores y Otras Categorías Especiales de Trabajadores

(*Véase también el item* 3575)

Chueca, Felipe. Primer congreso peruano de protección a la infancia (*Bol. unión panamer.*, vol. 77, no. 11, nov., p. 609–613, ilus.). **[3748**
Temas tratados en este Congreso (Lima, julio 3 a 10 de 1943): Sección de higiene social (asistencia social y el núcleo familiar; asistencia prenatal) y Sección de higiene mental y de la legislación sobre la infancia (alcance y reforma de la legislación social sobre el niño).

REPÚBLICA DOMINICANA

Miscelánea

(*Véanse los items* 3556, 3557, 3561)

URUGUAY

Miscelánea

(*Véanse también los items* 3556, 3557, 3561, 3564, 3565, 3568, 3569, 3574)

JUBILACIÓN PARA LOS EMPLEADOS DOMÉSTICOS EN URUGUAY (*Rev. int. trab.*, vol. 27, no. 4, abril, p. 604). [3749
Establecida obligatoriamente por decreto de julio 22 de 1942.
Texto inglés en *Int. lab. rev.*, vol. 47, no. 4, April, p. 528.

RETIREMENT BENEFITS FOR DOMESTIC SERVANTS IN URUGUAY (*Month. labor rev.*, vol. 56, no. 6, June, p. 1116-1117). [3750
Según decreto-ley de julio 22 de 1942.

URUGUAY. ECONOMIC CONDITIONS (*For. com. weekly*, vol. 10, no. 13, March 27, p. 20-21). [3751
Situación en algunas industrias manufactureras y de la construcción, mano de obra y empleo.

VENEZUELA

GENERAL

(*Véanse los items* 3556, 3557, 3561, 3568)

VIVIENDA, NUTRICIÓN Y OTROS STANDARDS DE BIENESTAR OBRERO

(*Véase también el item* 3574)

Cabrera Malo, R. y J. M. Bengoa Lecanda. La alimentación en Venezuela (*Rev. san. asist. soc.*, vol. 8,. no. 1, feb., p. 131-139). [3752
Costo y consumo de productos alimenticios en relación con la organización y funcionamiento del programa nacional de nutrición, según Informe presentado a la XI Conferencia Sanitaria Panamericana (item 3559). Bibliografía.

CONSIDERACIONES SOBRE LA ALIMENTACIÓN EN VENEZUELA (*Bol. ofic. sanit. panamer.*, año 22, no. 8, agosto, p. 673-680). [3753
Los numerosos estudios venezolanos sobre nutrición (cuya lista bibliográfica se incluye) llegan todos a la misma conclusión: las trabajadores no están bien alimentados, pués debido a salarios insuficientes, consumen carbohidratos en exceso en relación con proteínas y vitaminas.

ADDENDA

Capriles Rico, Remberto, y Gastón Arduz Eguía. Proyecto de código del trabajo. La Paz. Ed. del estado. 1942. xxxvii, 345 p. [3754
Preparado por dos eminentes expertos del Ministerio de Trabajo, Sanidad y Previsión Social teniendo en cuenta los standards mínimos de la legislación internacional del trabajo y la previsión social. Contiene los capítulos convencionales sobre asociaciones obreras y patronales; relaciones industriales; salarios, horas, descansos y otras condiciones del contrato de trabajo; higiene y seguridad industriales; seguro social; vivienda, nutrición y otros standards de bienestar obrero en la industria, el comercio y la agricultura y trabajo de mujeres y niños, doméstico, a domicilio, etc.

Martí Escasena, Manuel. Legislación obrera de la República de Cuba. La Habana. Ed. Cultural. 1942. 2 vols.: 508; 486 p. [3755
Segunda edición del *Handbook, no. 7, 1941*, item 4226. Puesta al día hasta mayo de 1942.

Peña, Lázaro. La unidad es victoria. Habana. Confederación de trabajadores de Cuba. 1942. 43 p. [3756
Política sindical presente y futura de la Confederación y llamamiento a la unidad sindical. Presentada al Tercer Congreso Nacional de la Confederación de Trabajadores de Cuba (item 3680).

Ravard, Francisco Alfonso. La cuestión social. Caracas. Ed. C. A. artes gráficas. 1942. xxxi, 454 p. [3757
Pasa en revista las doctrinas económicas y sociales a través del tiempo, dándole énfasis al problema obrero, especialmente desde el punto de vista católico.

Ruiz de Gamboa A., Alberto, y Juan Díaz Salas. Legislación social. Código del trabajo. Santiago. Ed. Nascimento. 1942. 2 vols.: 1046; 760 p. [3758
Código del trabajo de 1931 (véase *Handbook, no. 8, 1942*, item 3739) y legislación y jurisprudencia conexas, hasta diciembre de 1942. Anotado y comentado. Índice por materias.

Soifer, J., M. A. Carou, y L. Ureta Sáenz Peña. Compendio de la legislación del trabajo. Buenos Aires. Ed. cía. publicitaria argentina. 1942. 338 p. [3759
Compendio de legislación internacional y nacional y de contratos colectivos.

Unsain, Alejandro M. Trabajo a domicilio. Exposición y comentario a la ley no. 12713. Buenos Aires. Ed. Valerio Abeledo. 1942. 371 p. [3760
Véanse *Handbook, no. 7, 1941*, items 3978 y 3986 y *Handbook, no. 8, 1942*, item 3711.

SPANISH AMERICAN LITERATURE: THE COLONIAL PERIOD

BY

IRVING A. LEONARD

University of Michigan

GENERAL STATEMENT

In a world at war it is not surprising that the publication of materials relating to the literature of a remote and seemingly placid era in human history such as that of colonial Hispanic America is comparatively small. It is, perhaps, remarkable that the number of such items available continues so large and that their variety is so wide. The fundamental section 'Texts' contains as many titles as the preceding year, and it includes two new editions of the Inca Garcilaso de la Vega's *Comentarios Reales* (items 3774, 3775), suggesting that the simple prose and nostalgic narrative of the first important American writer is finding, more than three centuries later, a widening audience. The most curious item of the year is that extraordinary example of baroque scholarship, *El Paraíso en el Nuevo Mundo*, a ponderous, two-volume study of Antonio de León Pinelo, now printed for the first time. Of more genuine literary interest and merit are the poems of the talented eighteenth century Jesuit of Ecuador, Juan Bautista de Aguirre, whose life and reprinted writings are studied in different publications (items 3763, 3784, 3804). Among the individual figures, however, the Cuban patriot, José Martí, continues to inspire an apparently inexhaustible production of books, articles and essays on all aspects of his great personality and works.

The current literature of a more miscellaneous character tends to center about three general themes, viz., the colonial printing press, the colonial theater, and the colonial book trade. Under the last mentioned topic the increasing number of book-lists appended to studies clearly shows the wide choice of Spanish and European authors to whom colonial readers and writers had easy access, and these documents permit a broadening base for an investigation of the cultural and intellectual atmosphere of colonial life.

BIBLIOGRAPHY

(*See also section on* History: Colonial Spanish America)

BIBLIOGRAPHICAL WORKS

(*See also items* 9, 15, 91)

BIBLIOGRAFÍA HISPANOAMERICANA. LITERATURA. ÉPOCA COLONIAL (*Rev. hisp. mod.*, año 9, no. 1-2, enero-abril, p. 161-163, 254-255). [3761]

Porras Barrenechea, Raúl. Los cronistas del Perú, 1528-1650 (*Mercurio peruano*, año 8, vol. 25, no. 197, agosto, p. 361-378). [3761a]

The preliminary essay of a forthcoming book on the chroniclers of Perú, discussing the various materials classified as chronicles and distinguishing the latter from formal histories.

William, Edwin B. Literature in Spanish America (*Publ. mod. lang. assoc.*, vol. 58, supplement). [3762]

TEXTS

Aguirre, Juan Bautista de. Poesías y obras oratorias. Estudio preliminar de Gonzalo Zaldumbide, texto establecido por Gonzalo Zaldumbide (verso) y por Aurelio Espinosa Pólit (prosa). Quito. Imp. del Min. de educación. (Inst. cultural ecuatoriano, Clásicos ecuatorianos, vol. 3). lxii, 126 p. [3763
Cf. item 3804.

Alzate, José Antonio de. Se reprueba con un estilo burlesco el estudio de la peripatética (*Cult. México*, año 2, no. 1, enero–junio, p. 69–78). [3764
Text of the eighteenth century Mexican scholar's satirical attack on Aristotelian philosophy published in the November 30, 1790, number of the *Gaceta de Literatura*.

Arjona, Doris King, and **Carlos Vázquez Arjona.** Siglo de aventuras. Narratives of Spanish exploration in America. New York. Macmillan co. 177 p. [3765
A reading text for classes in Spanish, composed of selections adapted from sixteenth century chroniclers such as Columbus, Garcilaso de la Vega, el Inca, Pigafetta, Díaz del Castillo, Cabeza de Vaca, Gaspar de Carvajal, Valdivia and Francisco Vázquez.

Fernández de Castro, José Antonio (ed.). Varona. México, D. F. Sría. de educación pública. xxxvi, 234 p., ilus. [3766
The Cuban philosopher, Enrique José Varona (1849–1933).

Landívar, Rafael. Libro tercero de la *Rusticatio mexicana*. Las cataratas guatemaltecas. Trad. de Melecio Morales López (*An. soc. geog. hist. Guatemala*, año 18, tomo 18, no. extraordinario, marzo, p. 306–312). [3767
Spanish translation of Latin original of part of the 15 canto poem on the marvels of America by the Guatemalan Jesuit (1731–1793).

Loayza, Francisco A. de (ed.). La verdad desnuda, o las dos faces de un Obispo. Escrita en 1780 por un imparcial religioso. Lima. (Los pequeños grandes libros de historia americana, Serie 50, vol. B). 276 p. [3768

Martí, José. Escenas mexicanas. Habana. Ed. Trópico (Obras completas, 48–50). 1942–1943. 3 vols. [3769

———. Un viaje a México (*Arch. José Martí*, año 4, no. 1, enero–abril, p. 230–240). [3770

Porras Barrenechea, Raúl (ed.). Antonio de León Pinelo, *El paraíso en el nuevo mundo: comentario apologético, historia natural y peregrina de las Indias Occidentales* . . . Publícalo con un prólogo . . . bajo los auspicios del Comité del Cuarto centenario del descubrimiento del Amazonas. Lima. Imp. Torres Aguirre. 2 vols., ilus., facs. [3771
First printing of a voluminous manuscript, preserved in the Royal Library of the late Alphonso XIII, whose original was written by the celebrated Portuguese Jewish bibliographer (1596–1660). In five books totalling 93 chapters the author seeks to prove the location of the Biblical Eden as the Amazon basin. Its chief interest is that of a curious manifestation of the baroque in scholarship. The 43 page prologue of the editor admirably introduces this bibliographical curiosity.

Robles, Oswaldo (ed.). Fray Alonso de la Vera Cruz. *Investigación filosófico-natural. Los libros del alma*. México, D. F. Imp. universitaria. (Bibl. de filosofía mexicana, vol. 1). 144 p. [3772
A translation with notes of a philosophical treatise by the first occupant of the Chair of Scholastic Theology at the University of Mexico (1504–1584).

Rodríguez Demorizi, Emilio (ed.). Del romancero dominicano. Santiago, R. D. Ed. El Diario. 115 p., ilus. [3773
Eight ballads of historical interest, mostly unpublished hitherto, by Dominican poets from the little known Luis José Peguero (?–1792) to Eulogio C. Cabral (1868–1928), with a brief introduction on the ballad in Hispaniola.

Rosenblat, Ángel (ed.). Garcilaso de la Vega, el Inca. *Comentarios reales de los Incas*. Prólogo de Ricardo Rojas. Glosario de voces indígenas. Buenos Aires. Emecé ed. 2 vols.: xxi, 288; 334 p. [3774

Urteaga, Horacio H. (ed.). Garcilaso de la Vega, el Inca. *Los comentarios reales de los Incas*. Anotaciones y concordancias con las *Crónicas de Indias*. Segunda ed. Lima. Imp. Gil. (Col. de historiadores clásicos del Perú, tomo 1–3). 1941–1943. 3 vols. [3775

Vargas Ugarte, Rubén. De nuestro antiguo teatro. Colección de piezas dramáticas de los siglos dieciseis, diecisiete y dieciocho. Lima. Univ. católica del Perú. (Bibl. histórica peruana). xlii, 275 p. [3775a
A collection of unpublished dramatic writings of colonial Peru: *El Dios Pan*, a pastoral eclogue by Diego Mexía de Fernangil, about 1608; *Decuria de Santa María Egipcíaca*, a short piece for Jesuit classes in declamation, attributed to Salvador de Vega (first half of 18th century); *Amar en Propia Muerte*, a three act comedia by Juan de Espinosa Medrano (1632–1688); *Auto del Nacimiento del Hijo de Dios*, an anonymous piece of the first part of the 18th century; *Decuria muy Curiosa que Trata de los Diferentes Efectos que Causa en el Alma el que Recibe el San-

tísimo Sacramento by Salvador de Vega 1723); *Coloquio a la Natividad del Señor* by the nun, Sor Juana María a Josefa de Azaña Llano; *Loa al Cumplimiento de Años de la Sra. Princesa de Asturias;* and the *Entremés de la Justicia y el Litigante* by the famous blind poet Francisco del Castillo (1716–1772).

Zaldumbide, Gonzalo (ed.). Gaspar de Villaroel, *Gobierno eclesiástico-pacífico, 1656.* Quito. Imp. del Min. de gobierno. (Clásicos ecuatorianos, vol. 1). 304 p. [3776

A partial reprint of the 1738 edition of an important colonial work by a writer and clergyman associated with Ecuador, Peru and Chile.

INDIVIDUAL FIGURES

(See also item 4894)

Alfau de Solalinde, Jesusa. El barroco en la vida de Sor Juana (*Humanidades*, Mexico, vol. 1, no. 1, julio, p. 9–21). [3777

The authoress, in this study published posthumously, believes that the amatory and erotic verses in some of the poetry of the Mexican nun, Sor Juana Inés de la Cruz (1651–1695). are reflections of the baroque spirit of her time and do not express her personal experience.

Andrade Coello, Alejandro. Un sabio americano: Francisco J. de Caldas (*América*, Habana, vol. 18, no. 1-2, abril-mayo, p. 47–48). [3778

Brief sketch of Colombian scholar (1771–1811) with special reference to his scientific work in Ecuador.

Benvenuto, Ofelia M. B. de. Los versos sencillos de José Martí (*Arch. José Martí*, año 3, no. 1, enero-dic., 1942 [i.e., 1943], p. 43–53). [3779

Blanco Villalta, J. G. Uno de los primeros cronistas del Río de la Plata: Francisco Villalta (*Universidad*, Santa Fe, no. 8, p. 189–205). [3780

An account with quotations of the "Carta" written by Villalta. He was in the expedition of Don Pedro de Mendoza who arrived at the Isla de San Gabriel in 1536.

Bosch, Mariano G. Lavardén y el teatro (*Bol. estud. teatro*, año 1, no. 1, enero, p. 15–20). [3781

Cabrices, Fernando. Mateo Rosas de Oquendo, poeta satírico de la conquista (*Rev. nac. cultura*, año 5, no. 40, sept.-oct., p. 10–16). [3782

A descriptive review of Alfonso Reyes' work on the same subject in which the author takes exception to the statement that Rosas de Oquendo representa "una de las primeras manifestaciones de la picaresca popular americana."

Caparroso, Carlos Arturo. Fernández Madrid y Vargas Tejeda (*Rev. Indias*, segunda época, tomo 17, no. 53, mayo, p. 272–278). [3783

Two minor Colombian poets José Fernández Madrid (1789–1830) and Luis Vargas Tejeda (1802–1829). The first was unsuccessful in his odes to Bolívar, but possessed delicacy and charm in his lighter verse. The second was a gifted and versatile poet whose short, hectic life left unfulfilled his early promise. Though romantics in political action, both reflect contemporary neoclassic influences.

Carilla, Emilio. Un olvidado poeta colonial. Buenos Aires. Inst. de cultura latinoamericana. 94 p. [3784

A collection, preceded by a critical essay, of *Versos Castellanos, Obras Juveniles, Miscelánea*, by an Ecuadorian Jesuit, Juan Bautista Aguirre (1725–1786), the manuscript of which was discovered in Guayaquil by the nineteenth-century Argentine critic, Juan María Gutiérrez. Graceful facility, sensitiveness and deep feeling occasionally expressed in these verses on themes both sacred and profane reveal an authentic minor poet.

Castro Leal, Antonio. Juan Ruiz de Alarcón. Su vida y su obra. Presentación de Alfonso Reyes. México. Tall. de la cultura (Ed. Cuads. americanos, 2). 270 p. [3785

Chávez, Ezequiel A. ¿Sor Juana Inés de la Cruz forjó, a lo menos implícitamente, una teoría del conocimiento de todas las cosas? ¿Tuvo clara idea de lo que son y de lo que significan las intuiciones? (*Rev. univ.*, Guadalajara, tomo 1, no. 3, agosto-oct., p. 14–17). [3786

Córdova, Federico de. Martí escritor (*Univ. Habana*, año 8, no. 50–51, sept.–dic., p. 114–132). [3787

———. Martí idealista (*Univ. Habana*, año 8, no. 49, julio–agosto, p. 23–42). [3788

An imaginary conversation between the Cuban apostle and a countryman, Nicolás Heredia, a pragmatic novelist, revealing the idealistic faith of Martí in the redemption of his people.

Delgado Fernández, Gregorio. Martí, y la "Guerra chiquita" (*Arch. José Martí*, año 3, no. 1, enero-dic., 1942 [i.e., 1943], p. 11–39). [3789

Gómez Orozco, Alicia. Don Antonio Alzate y Ramírez (*Humanidades*, México, vol. 1, no. 2, dic., p. 169–177). [3791

A short, documented sketch of the eighteenth-century Mexican scientist and philosopher (1738–1799).

Lizaso, Félix. Martí y la utopía de América. Habana. Col. Ensayos. 46 p. [3792

Words and thoughts of the Cuban hero, José Martí, on the "Continent of human hope."

López, Casto Fulgencio. Relación muy breve y elogiosa de la vida y la obra de Garcilaso Inca de la Vega, primer escritor criollo del Perú. Caracas. C. A. de artes gráficas. 87 p., ilus., facs. [3793
Commentary designed to popularize the *mestizo* chronicler (1540–1616), emphasizing the Americanism in his work.

Luque Colombres, Carlos A. El deán doctor don Gregorio Funes. Arraigo de su familia en América. Córdoba. Imp. de la Universidad (Inst. de estudios americanistas, Cuad. de historia, 6). 62 p. [3794
Antecedents of ecclesiastical writer, historian and patriot of Argentina (1749–1829).

Martínez Bello, Antonio. Ideas sociales y económicas de José Martí (*América*, Habana, vol. 19, no. 1, julio, p. 66–68). [3795
Author refutes criticism of his book of the same title as article made by Lucio Pabón Núñez.

Maza, Francisco de la. Mujeres distinguidas. La vida conventual de Sor Juana (*Div. hist.*, vol. 4, no. 12, 15 de oct., p. 666–670). [3796
Brief sketch of Sor Juana Inés de la Cruz (1651–1695) in the convent of San Gerónimo in Mexico City.

Millares Carlo, Agustín. Algunas noticias acerca del escritor domínico Fray Alonso de Espinosa (*Fil. letras*, tomo 5, no. 9, enero–marzo, p. 85–93). [3797

Paredes, Jaime. El caballero de las estrellas (*Rev. Indias*, segunda época, tomo 18, no. 55, julio, p. 94–104; no. 56, agosto, p. 189–198). [3798
Essays or fragments of an overly rhetorical biography of the creole scientist, executed by the Spaniards in New Granada, Francisco J. de Caldas (1771–1811).

Piedra-Bueno, Andrés de. Martí americanista (*Arch. José Martí*, año 3, no. 1, enero–dic., 1942 [i.e., 1943], p. 104–125). [3799

Porras Barrenechea, Raúl. El padre Bernabé Cobo (*Historia*, Lima, vol. 1, no. 2, mayo–junio, p. 98–104). [3800
Sketch of Peruvian chronicler and Jesuit (1582–1657).

Quesada y Miranda, Gonzalo de. La juventud de Martí. Habana. Imp. Siglo XX. 23 p. [3801

Romero, Emilia. El indio santo del Perú. Apostillas a un libro antiguo (*Bol. bibliog.*, Lima, año 16, vol. 13, no. 1-2, julio, p. 11–24). [3802
An annotated, biographical sketch of the Indian saint Nicolás de Ayllón (1632–1677), derived from a rare seventeenth-century work, *Vida Admirable y Muerte Prodigiosa de Nicolás de Ayllón* . . . (Madrid, 1684), a copy of which is in the library of Federico Gómez de Orozco of Mexico City. The cover and frontispiece of this rare volume are reproduced.

Vela, David. Landívar (*An. soc. geog. hist. Guatemala*, año 18, tomo 18, no. extraordinario, marzo, p. 327–358). [3803
The Guatemalan Jesuit, Rafael Landívar (1731–1793), who imitated Virgil's *Georgics* in his *Rusticatio Mexicana*.

Zaldumbide, Gonzalo. El único gran poeta de nuestro pobre siglo 18 (*Rev. Indias*, segunda época, tomo 16, no. 49, enero, p. 145–189). [3804
A more extended critical study of the Ecuadorian Jesuit Juan Bautista Aguirre (1725–1786) than that which preceded the edition of his verse by Emilio Carilla (cf. no. 3784).

ESSAYS, CRITICISM, MISCELLANEOUS STUDIES

(*See also items* 2958, 2991, 3014)

Almeyda, Aniceto. El autor del *Purén indómito* (*Rev. chil. hist. geog.*, no. 103, julio–dic., p. 175–196). [3805
Discusses in detail the various theories concerning the disputed authorship of the historical poem, *Purén Indómito*. Concludes that the two main rivals, "Hernando Álvarez de Toledo y Diego Arias de Saavedra vinieron a juntarse en la guerra de Arauco, donde ambos pelearon en las mismas batallas y cantaron en octavas reales las hazañas de sus heróicos compañeros. . . .
"Arias de Saavedra ingresó por matrimonio a la familia de su amigo, sin dejar descendencia, en tanto que los Álvarez de Toledo son raíz y origen de toda nuestra antigua aristocracia; el poema de Álvarez de Toledo se ha perdido, y ha circulado con su nombre el de Arias de Saavedra; a Álvarez de Toledo lo recuerdan todos nuestros historiadores, y Arias de Saavedra se encuentra "sepultado en las oscuras aguas del olvido" (p. 195–196). [J. F. King]

Arrom, José Juan. Representaciones teatrales en Cuba a fines del siglo 18 (*Hisp. rev.*, vol. 11, no. 1, Jan., p. 64–73). [3807
Brief discussion of theater in Havana in 1791 with a list of titles and dates of performances compiled from the *Papel Periódico de La Havana*. Comparison with offerings of contemporary colonial theaters elsewhere in Spanish America, particularly Mexico City and Lima, would have increased the interest and value of this article.

———. Voltaire y la literatura dramática cubana (*Romanic rev.*, vol. 34, no. 3, Oct., p. 228–234). [3808
Zaïre was translated in Cuba as early as 1800; José María Heredia (1803–1839), in his translation of *Mohamed o El Fanatismo*, and Joaquín Lorenzo Luaces (1826–1867)

in his *Aristodemo* (1867), also betray the influence of the French philosopher.

Beltroy, Manuel. La literatura peruana precolombina (*Rev. hisp. mod.*, año 9, no. 3, julio, p. 199–208). [3809

A lecture reviewing theories concerning possible Incan literature which concludes that it was "incipient" in an oral tradition of folkloric poetry, drama and music; though unwritten, it survives in subject matter and spirit.

Corbató, Hermenegildo. La emergencia de la idea de nacionalidad en el México colonial (*Rev. iberoamer.*, vol. 6, no. 12, mayo, p. 377–392). [3810

From colonial writers including Cortés, Bernal Díaz, Cervantes de Salazar, Valbuena, Sigüenza y Góngora, Landívar and expelled Jesuits, the author finds evidence of a dawning sense of Mexican nationality.

Escalante, Hildamar. Juan Pablos, primer impresor de América (*Rev. nac. cultura*, año 6, no. 37, marzo–abril, p. 76–84). [3812

Discussion of Cromberger's contract with Juan Pablos for the establishment of the first printing press in Mexico City, and of works printed on it up to 1561, the year of Pablo's death.

García Chuecos, Héctor. Primera imprenta y primer libro venezolano (*Bitácora*, vol. 1, cuad. 3, mayo, p. 50–57). [3813

A recently discovered document indicates that in 1795 there was "una imprenta de camino" in Venezuela. Author finds evidence that a tariff list and almanac were authorized for publication in 1810 at Caracas. No product of this press is known.

Heras, Carlos. Orígenes de la Imprenta de niños expósitos, con una introducción sobre los primeros trabajos de la Imprenta de niños expósitos. La Plata (Publ. del archivo histórico de la Provincia de Buenos Aires, Documentos del archivo, vol. 10). xxiii, 363 p. [3814

Publication of two bundles of documents relating to the concession of printing press to José de Silva y Aguiar in Buenos Aires and its operation from 1780 to 1783, affords data of economic interest on costs of manufacture, paper, wages, etc. The press was chiefly for "job-printing" of almanacs, catechisms, pastoral letters, proclamations, and school primers. The introduction and indices greatly facilitate understanding and use of this material.

Jiménez Rueda, Julio. Santa Teresa y Sor Juana, un paralelo imposible. Discurso de ingreso en la Academia mexicana ... y respuesta del académico de número Genaro Fernández Macgregor. México, D. F. 54 p. [3815

The inspired Mexican poetess, Sor Juana Inés de la Cruz (1651–1695), had none of the mysticism of the Spanish Saint of Ávila.

Leonard, Irving A. A frontier library, 1799 (*Hisp. amer. hist. rev.*, vol. 23, no. 1, Feb., p. 21–51). [3816

The auction sale of the effects of the Governor of Spanish Louisiana, Don Manuel Gayoso de Lemos, included the disposal of some 411 volumes representing about 165 different works. These included titles on engineering, medicine, jurisprudence, geography and travel, religion, history, and particularly *belles lettres*, etc., in Spanish, English, French, Portuguese and Latin. All attest to the catholic tastes of a cultivated gentleman, and further prove the relatively free circulation of books in the Spanish colonies shortly before the wars of independence. List of books and selling prices appended.

―――. *Guzmán de Alfarache* in the Lima book trade, 1613 (*Hisp. rev.*, vol. 11, no. 3, July, p. 210–220). [3817

A notarial document recording a transaction of two Lima merchants relating to some 155 books, of which copies of Mateo Alemán's famous picaresque novel represent nearly half of the total, affords convincing evidence both of the circulation of light literature in the colonies and of the popularity of this particular fictional work in the early seventeenth-century viceroyalty of Peru.

―――. Light reading in sixteenth-century Spanish America (*Bull. pan amer. union*, vol. 77, no. 9, Sept., p. 493–499). [3818

Essay on the importation of books into the Spanish colonies, emphasizing the allegedly forbidden romances of chivalry and including an account of the arrival of the first copies of *Don Quixote*. Article translated in the Portuguese (vol. 45, no. 10, p. 483–489) and Spanish (vol. 78, no. 3, p. 145–151) editions of the *Bulletin*.

―――. Montalbán's *El valor perseguido* and the Mexican Inquisition, 1682 (*Hisp. rev.*, vol. 11, no. 1, Jan., p. 47–56). [3819

Proceedings associated with the banning by the Holy Office of Mexico City of the Spanish playwright's *comedia* after a performance in the public theater of the viceregal capital.

Lohmann Villena, Guillermo, and Raúl Moglia. Repertorio de las representaciones teatrales en Lima hasta el siglo 18 (*Rev. filol. hisp.*, año 5, tomo 5, no. 4, oct.–dic., p. 313–343). [3820

Interesting list of plays and authors performed in colonial Lima, collected from many sources, and further proving colonial Spanish America had access to much of the literary culture of the mother country.

Miguel i Vergés, J. M. Aspectos de las andanzas del padre Mier: una rectificación histórica (*Cuad. amer.*, año 2, vol. 11, no. 5, sept.–oct., p. 143–164). [3821

Notes from unpublished manuscripts of the Mexican patriot, Fray Servando Teresa Mier, Noriega y Guerra, whose activities in behalf of the separation of Mexico from

Spain led to frequent imprisonment and travels in Spain and the United States. His *Memorias*, with their commentary on Mexican society are a mixture of romantic and *costumbrista* elements.

Moglia, Raúl. Representación escénica en Potosí en 1663 (*Rev. filol. hisp.*, año 5, tomo 5, no. 2, abril–junio, p. 166–167). [3822
A *Relación de la grandiosa fiesta que el sr. Gob. D. Luis de Andrade y Sotomayor, alcalde ordinario de la imperial villa de Potosí hizo a la renovación del Santísimo Sacramento a 4 de marzo de 1663* indicates a loa, which mentions Lope de Vega, was performed on the public square. An edition of this rare work was printed in Seville in 1899, composed of 50 copies.

Ortiz, Fernando. La hija cubana del iluminismo. Con numerosos datos, documentos, notas bibliográficas y grabados. Havana. Ed. Molina y cía. 72 p. [3823
A speech given at the sesquicentenial of the foundation of the Sociedad Económica de Amigos del País de La Habana, describing the reflection of the eighteenth century "Enlightenment" in Cuba encouraged by Luis de las Casas, Captain General of Cuba and founder of the Sociedad. Annotations fill the pages from 27 to 72.

Peiser, Werner. El barroco en la literatura mexicana (*Rev. iberoamer.*, vol. 6, no. 11, feb., p. 77–93). [3824
A discussion of the characteristic elements of the baroque in colonial Mexican literature illustrated particularly by the writings of Sor Juana Inés de la Cruz (1651–1695), Carlos de Sigüenza y Góngora (1645–1700), and Muñoz de Castro.

Porras Barrenechea, Raúl. La biblioteca de un revolucionario: Sánchez Carrión, prócer civil del Perú (*Mercurio peruano*, año 18, vol. 25, no. 193, abril, p. 119–130). [3825
Inventario of the library of an intellectual leader in Peruvian struggle for independence who died in 1825 while campaigning with Bolívar. List includes some 146 works of Greek and Latin classics, chronicles of Spain, some 15 works in French including Montesquieu and Buffon and Condorcet, and mathematical works. Works in English limited to *belles lettres*, including *Paradise Lost* of Milton; also works in Italian, including Tasso.

Santovenia, Emeterio S. La cultura cubana en la segunda mitad del siglo 16 y principios del 17 (*América*, Habana, vol. 19, no. 1, julio, p. 15–16). [3826
Brief notes on the education, literature, theater, music, sculpture, painting, etc., at turn of the seventeenth century, from a book in preparation.

Schwab, Federico. Los textos millcayac del P. Luis de Valdivia y la antigua biblioteca de los jesuítas del Cuzco (*Bol. bibliog.*, Lima, año 16, vol. 13, no. 3–4, dic., p. 267–277). [3827
Discovery in the library of the University of Cuzco of a copy of a work on some Indian dialects of the Province of Cuyo, now within Argentina, definitely establishes the fact of the publication of this work by the first rector of the Jesuit college in Chile in 1607 at Lima. This discovery resulted from the examination of an inventory of books in the Jesuit library totalling some 4,500 volumes, mostly theological but including works of Grotius, Solórzano Pereira, Gaspar de Villaroel, and Latin and Greek historians, and poets.

Serrano Redonnet, Antonio E. Prohibición de libros en el primer sínodo santiagueño (*Rev. filol. hisp.*, año 5, tomo 5, no. 2, abril–junio, p. 162–166). [3828
Bishop Fernando de Trejo of Tucumán, Argentina, summoned a diocesan synod on September 9, 1597, which ordained that all books entitled Diana, by whatever author, the Celestina, the novels of chivalry and "poesías torpes y deshonestas" should be gathered up and burned. There is no evidence that this decree was rigorously observed and it is of more interest as an indication of the wide diffusion in the Spanish Indies of the allegedly banned *libros profanos*.

Zevallos, J. (ed.). Concierto de impresión, Gerónimo de Contreras con el alférez Thomas Velásquez de Medrano. Arrendamiento reciuo y entrega de imprenta, el convento de Santo Domingo a Pedro de Cabrera, 1645 (*Rev. arch. nac.*, Perú, tomo 16, entrega 1, enero–junio, p. 9–11). [3829
Documentary materials for the history of seventeenth century printing in Peru.

ADDENDA

Bayle, Constantino. Un libro nuevo de Gonzalo Ximénez de Quesada (*Rev. Indias*, Madrid, año 3, no. 7, 1942, p. 111–120). [3830
An account of a recently published manuscript *Apuntamientos y Anotaciones sobre la Historia de Paulo Jovio* by the Conqueror of Nueva Granada from an original preserved in the library of the Universidad de Valladolid. In this work Jiménez de Quesada refutes the statements of the Bishop of Nochera, injurious to the good name of the conquistadores.

Rodríguez Demorizi, Emilio. Hostos en Santo Domingo. Vol. 2. Ciudad Trujillo. Imp. J. R. Vda Garcia. 1942. [3831
Vol. 1 was published in 1939. See *Handbook, no. 5, 1939*, item 2848.

SPANISH AMERICAN LITERATURE: THE NATIONAL PERIOD

BY

STURGIS E. LEAVITT

University of North Carolina

AND

FRANCISCO AGUILERA *

Library of Congress

GENERAL STATEMENT

The year 1943 was not a notable one for imaginative literature in Spanish America. A number of Spanish American entries for the Farrar and Rinehart award were published, but strangely enough none of them had been deemed worthy of the prize, although the Argentine entry, Ernesto L. Castro's *Los Isleros*, must have seemed well worthy of consideration. The prize went to a novel in French, which is mentioned in this bibliography, but it must be confessed that this production by Philippe Thoby-Marcelin and Pierre Marcelin is not a great piece of work. It is confused, sordid, and unrelieved by humor or noble aspirations. During the year a good deal of earlier material was made available, the most important of which were selections from the works of Horacio Quiroga, edited by J. A. Crow, and *Flor de Tradiciones* of Ricardo Palma, edited by George W. Umphrey and Carlos García-Prada. An edition of Uribe Piedrahita's *Toa* in 1942 is also deserving of special mention.

The world of scholarship held its own against the record of previous years. Among numerous important articles were Gilberto González y Contreras' study of the social novel in Spanish America, R. E. McNicoll's "Intellectual Origins of Aprismo," Otis Green's analyses of the ideology of Manuel Gálvez, and Josefina Lerena Acevedo's life of Carlos Reyles. Norberto Pinilla made important contributions to our knowledge of the intellectual movement of 1842 in Chile; R. U. Pane contributed a bibliography of Latin American books in English translation; and Enrique Finot brought out a history of the literature of Bolivia, about which little was available before.

The year 1943 saw the death of a number of important Spanish American writers: Tomás Gatica Martínez, Chilean novelist; Enrique Geenzier, Panamanian journalist, poet, diplomat and statesman; José Eduardo Guerra, Bolivian poet and novelist; Rafael López, Mexican poet; Daniel Samper Ortega, whose name will always be associated with the great collection of Colombian literature, the "Biblioteca Aldeana"; Rogelio Sotela, Costa Rican poet; Froylán Turcios, Guatemalan poet; and Guillermo Valencia, the eminent Colombian poet so well known throughout the Spanish world. [S. E. Leavitt]

Not a single new work of outstanding value in the field of poetry has come to our attention. Publishers contented themselves with issuing anthologies,

---

* Mr. Aguilera is responsible for the poetry items. [Ed.]

some of which will prove to be very useful; such is the case of Yunque's anthology of Argentine "social poets" and Contín Aybar's anthology of the poetry of the Dominican Republic. The publication of volumes of selected poems by individual figures such as Andrade, Othón, Tablada, and Borges was quite the fashion. The criticism of poetry did not fare any better than did its creation, with the exception of Concha Meléndez' searching essay on César Vallejo. In the biographical genre mention should be made only of the life of Herrera y Reissig by his sister, Herminia. One promising sign, however, creatively speaking, was the founding in the Dominican Republic of a restless poetry magazine, *La Poesía Sorprendida*. [F. Aguilera]

BIBLIOGRAPHY

BIBLIOGRAPHICAL WORKS

(*See also items* 66, 77)

Fitz-Gerald, John D. Spanish American literatures (*New international year book*, 1942, p. 660–663). [3832]
A review of the year by countries.

Jones, Willis Knapp. Latin American drama. A reading list (*Books abroad*, vol. 17, no. 1, winter, p. 27–31; no. 2, spring, p. 121–125). [3833]
A useful list of critical material and original works.

Leavitt, Sturgis E. Theses dealing with Hispano-American language and literature —1942 (*Hispania*, Washington, vol. 26, no. 2, May, p. 180–183). [3834]
This list of masters' and doctors' theses includes the contributions of the Universities of Havana, Puerto Rico, and Mexico.

———, and **Francisco Aguilera**. A selective guide to the material published in 1941 on Spanish American literature: the national period (*Handbook, no. 8, 1942*, p. 364–378). [3835]

Mapes, E. K. Bibliografía de tesis sobre literatura iberoamericana preparadas en las universidades de Iberoamérica (*Rev. iberoamer.*, vol. 6, no. 11, feb., p. 203–206). [3836]
This list, though incomplete, is valuable in the orientation of graduate studies. It includes theses from 1935 to 1940.

Moore, Ernest R., and **James G. Bickley.** Rafael Delgado. Notas bibliográficas y críticas (*Rev. iberoamer.*, vol. 6, no. 11, feb., p. 155–200). [3837]
An excellent list of the works of Delgado, including critical studies about the man and his production.

Ortiz, Sergio Elías. Bibliografía de Eduardo Posada (*Bol. hist. antig.*, vol. 30, no. 341, marzo, p. 357–365). [3838]
Includes books, pamphlets, compilations, magazine and newspaper articles. 228 items.

Pane, Remigio U. Two hundred Latin American books in English translation (*Mod. lang. jour.*, vol. 27, no. 8, Dec., p. 593–604). [3839]
A revision and extension of "A Selected Bibliography of Latin American Literature in English Translation" (item 3981).

Stowell, Ernest L. More Mexican writers and pseudonyms (*Hisp. rev.*, vol. 11, no. 2, April, p. 164–174). [3840]
Additions to Grismer's *Reference Index* (*Handbook, no. 5, 1939*, item 3623) and M. A. Yancey "Some Mexican Writers and Their Pseudonyms" (*Handbook no. 8, 1942*, item 3968), taken from J. B. Iguíniz, *Catálogo de seudónimos* . . . México, 1913.

Williams, Edwin B. Literature in Spanish America (*Publ. mod. lang. assoc.*, vol. 58, supplement, part 2, p. 1276–1297). [3841]
A yearly survey of books and articles published by North American scholars.

LITERATURE OTHER THAN POETRY

Essays, Criticism and Biography

(*See also items* 2537, 3014, 3305, 3808, 3312, 3332)

Alegría, Fernando. La épica de la literatura latinoamericana (*Atenea*, año 20, tomo 71, no. 213, marzo, p. 151–167). [3842]
A review of Torres-Ríoseco's *Epic of Latin American Literature* (see *Handbook, no. 8, 1942*, item 4039) and sufficiently extensive to receive mention here.

Arce, Magda. Mariano Latorre, novelista chileno contemporáneo (*Rev. iberoamer.*, vol. 6, no. 11, feb., p. 103–119; no. 12, mayo, p. 303–334). [3843]
Continuation of a previous study (*Handbook, no. 8, 1942*, item 3973). Also published in *Rev. hisp. mod.*, año 9, no. 1–2, enero–abril, p. 21–58.

Bello, Andrés. [Selections]. Prólogo del doctor Gabriel Méndez Plancarte. México.

Sría. de educación pública. xlvi, 197 p. [3845]
An excellent presentation of different phases of Bello's work, with an illuminating introduction.

Caballero Calderón, Eduardo. Don Tomás Rueda Vargas (*Rev. Indias*, segunda época, tomo 18, no. 55, julio, p. 8–17). [3846]
Personal recollection of the man as teacher and scholar.

Caro, Miguel Antonio. José Fernández Madrid (*Rev. Indias,* segunda época, tomo 18, no. 57, sept., p. 407–423). [3847]
Biography and criticism written in 1889.

Casanovas, Domingo. Ensayo crítico sobre Dámaso Velázquez (*Rev. nac. cultura,* año 5, no. 40, sept.–oct., p. 110–121). [3848]
An extensive analysis of A. Arraiz' novel (item 3918).

Danieri, Erly. Esta tierra de América. Buenos Aires. Univ. de Buenos Aires, Facultad de filosofía y letras. 105 p. [3849]
Seven essays in which the life and literature of the United States and Latin America are compared. Without attempting any profound analysis, the author gives orientation to an interesting topic.

Duplessis, Gustavo. Cuatro novelas de la naturaleza en Sud América (*Rev. Habana,* año 2, tomo 3, no. 16, dic., p. 363–371). [3850]
Consideration of Alcides Arguedas' *Raza de Bronce;* Jaime Mendoza's *Páginas Bárbaras;* J. E. Rivera's *La Vorágine;* and Diómedes de Pereyra's *El Valle del Sol.*

ESCRITOS DEL DOCTOR EDUARDO POSADA (*Bol. hist. antig.,* vol. 30, no. 341, marzo, p. 251–352). [3851]
An excellent study of the work of a great Colombian writer.

Fernández MacGregor, Genaro (ed.). Vasconcelos. México. Ed. de la Sría. de educación pública. xxvi, 229 p. [3852]
Selections from José Vasconcelos' pedagogical, sociological and philosophical writings, with an excellent introduction.

Finot, Enrique. Historia de la literatura boliviana. México. Lib. Porrúa hnos. xix, 474 p., ilus. [3853]
This volume is particularly valuable as a reference book because practically every figure of importance is mentioned, with information not readily available elsewhere. The critical material suffers from too much dependence upon other writers.

García-Prada, Carlos. De hispano-americanismo literario (*Rep. amer.,* año 24, tomo 40, no. 16, marzo 13, p. 248–251). [3854]
Previously published in *Hispania* and *Univ. cat. bolivariana* (*see Handbook, no. 8, 1942,* item 3998).

Garmendia, Hermann. El tema urbano en una novela de fin de siglo (*Rev. nac cultura,* año 5, no. 39, julio–agosto, p. 56–64). [3856]
The importance of a little known Venezuelan novel, written by Miguel Eduardo Pardo, who is also not very well known.

Gómez Restrepo, Antonio. Semblanza del señor Caro (*Rev. Indias,* segunda época, tomo 18, no. 57, sept., p. 328–339). [3857]
A speech delivered at the unveiling of a statue to Miguel Antonio Caro in 1917.

González, Manuel Pedro. Trayectoria del gaucho y su cultura. El hombre y su medio. Su expresión artística. Habana. Ed. Ucar, García y cía. 135 p. [3858]
After a frank introduction which analyses the spirit of the capital of Argentina, the author gives a comprehensive introduction to an understanding of the gaucho and his literary significance. These two studies were presented as lectures before the Institución Hispano-Cubana de Cultura.

———. Trends in Hispanic American literature (*Books abroad,* vol. 17, no. 1, winter, p. 16–21). [3859]
Helpful orientation for the beginner in this field.

González Prada, Alfredo. Manuel González Prada. A son's memories (*Books abroad,* vol. 17, no. 3, July, p. 201–207). [3860]
Intimate details of the life of one of the great figures of Peru.

González y Contreras, Gilberto. Aclaraciones a la novela social americana (*Rev. iberoamer.,* vol. 6, no. 12, mayo, p. 403–418). [3861]
A brilliant analysis of the tendencies of the Latin American noval, with abundant examples of the different classifications.

Gorostiza, Celestino. Lo blanco y lo negro. Carta a Xavier Villaurrutia (*Letras de México,* año 7, vol. 1, no. 1, enero, p. 6, 8). [3862]
An exposition of the attitude of the Mexican public toward a national theater, with encouragement to Villaurrutia to persevere in his efforts to write original Mexican plays.

Grases, Pedro. Del porqué no se escribió el "Diccionario matriz de la lengua castellana" de Rafael María Baralt. Caracas. Tall. de artes gráfs. 86 p. [3863]
Baralt's grandiose project met with the downright disapproval of Bartolomé José Delgado and it was abandoned after the publication of the prospectus.

———. Proyección continental de la cultura venezolana (*Bitácora,* vol. 1, cuad. 2, abril, p. 21–29). [3864]
Comments on an edition of J. M. de Larra published in Caracas in 1839.

———. La singular historia de un drama y de un soneto de Andrés Bello. Caracas. Insto. pedagógico de Caracas. 94 p. [3865
Interesting facts and speculations about an allegorical play entitled *"La España Restaurada"* and the sonnet *"A la Victoria de Bailén."*

Green, Otis H. Manuel Gálvez, 'Gabriel Quiroga,' and *La maestra normal* (*Hisp. rev.*, vol. 11, no. 3, July. p. 221-252). [3866
The relation between *El Diario de Gabriel Quiroga*, the first work of Gálvez, and his later production. This study and others in the series are essential to an understanding of Gálvez' work.

———. Manuel Gálvez, 'Gabriel Quiroga,' and *El mal metafísico* (*Hisp. rev.*, vol. 11, no. 4, Oct., p. 314-327). [3867
The second of a series of excellent articles dealing with the ideology of Gálvez.

Grismer, Raymond L., and John T. Flanagan. The cult of violence in Latin American short fiction (*Hispania*, Washington, vol. 26, no. 2, May, p. 161-170). [3868
The authors conclude that violence is the most impressive feature of this type of fiction.

Guerrero, Jorge. Cinco modernos cuentistas del Ecuador (*Rev. Indias*, segunda época, tomo 16, no. 50, feb., p. 358-368). [3869
Brief mention of a number of earlier writers of prose fiction, who are almost unknown, and praise of the work of José de la Cuadra, Alfonso Cuesta y Cuesta, Ángel F. Rojas, Eduardo Mora Moreno, and Pablo Palacio. Their principal productions are mentioned, but specific criticism is somewhat lacking.

Johnson, Harvey Leroy. Una contrata inédita, dos programas y noticias referentes al teatro en Bogotá entre 1838 y 1840 (*Rev. iberoamer.*, vol. 7, no. 13, nov., p. 49-67). [3870
Interesting information regarding the state of the theater in the Colombian capital in the early nineteenth century.

Kurz, Harry. Constancio Vigil, writer of children's stories (*Hispania*, Washington, vol. 26, no. 3, Oct., p. 295-301). [3871
Summaries of representative stories of a writer famous in Spanish America for the spiritual treatise, *El Erial*, but little known in the United States.

Latorre, Mariano. La Facultad de filosofía y la literatura chilena (*Atenea*, año 20, tomo 74, no. 221, nov., p. 116-129). [3872
The large part that the early days of the Universidad de Chile had in the development of Chilean literature.

Leo, Ulrich. *Las lanzas coloradas* (*Bitácora*, vol. 2, cuad. 6-7, agosto-sept., p. 58-82). [3874
An analysis of the most important stylistic features of Arturo Uslar Pietri's famous novel.

Lerena Acevedo de Blixen, Josefina. Reyles (*Rev. nac.*, Montevideo, año 6, tomo 21, no. 62, feb., p. 206-228; tomo 22, no. 65, mayo, p. 174-207; tomo 23, no. 67, julio, p. 49-82; no. 69, sept., p. 433-455; tomo 24, no. 70, oct., p. 90-125). [3875
A detailed and interesting account of the life and personality of Carlos Reyles, with comment on his works.

Magaña Esquivel, Antonio. Usigli en el teatro (*Letras de Mexico*, año 7, vol. 1, no. 2, feb. 15, p. 4). [3877
An excellent characterization of Rodolfo Usigli's work, and its significance to the modern Mexican theater.

Martínez, José Luis. La literatura mexicana en 1942 (*Letras de México*, año 7, vol. 1, no. 2, feb. 15, p. 9-10). [3878
An excellent survey of the production for the year.

Maya, Rafael. Marco Fidel Suárez, clásico de América (*Rev. iberoamer.*, vol. 6, no. 11, feb., p. 23-39). [3879
The character of the man and his literary work, with especial reference to his style.

Medinaceli, Carlos. José Eduardo Guerra, novelista (*Kollasuyo*, año 5, no. 48, mayo, p. 261-275). [3880
The importance of Guerrra's *El Alto de las Ánimas* (1919), with an analysis of its principal character.

———. Nataniel Aguirre. Cuentista, poeta y dramaturgo (*Kollasuyo*, año 5, no. 51, oct.-dic., p. 181-210). [3881
Rather general treatment, but with some facts of interest.

Montenegro, Ernesto. The Latin American literary prizes for 1943 (*Books abroad*, vol. 17, no. 4, autumn, p. 309-311). [3882
Principally a review of the prize winning novel *Canapé Vert* (see item 3945), with brief mention of the winner for non-fiction, Argentina Díaz-Lozano's *Peregrinaje*.

Monterde, Francisco. Sobre una nota de bibliografía mexicana (*Ábside*, vol. 7, no. 2, abril-junio, p. 297-298). [3883
Letter to E. R. Moore, calling his attention to an English novel translated into Spanish in Mexico before *Bianina*, mentioned by Moore in *Ábside*, vol. 6, no. 4, p. 459 (see *Handbook, no. 8, 1942*, item 3882). Reference is to a translation of Sophie Lee's *The Recess*, Mexico, 1833.

Morales, Adolfo. La herencia y el medio en *Juan de la Rosa* (*Kollasuyo*, año 5, no. 51, oct.-dic., p. 215-222). [3884
The ancestry of Nataniel Aguirre, author of this important Bolivian novel.

Núñez, Estuardo. La literatura actual del Perú (*Rep. amer.*, año 24, tomo 40, no. 6, sept. 11, p. 89–90). [3885
A rapid survey from 1916 on, with but little critical comment.

Onetti, Carlos María. Alberdi escritor (*Sur*, año 12, no. 107, sept., p. 42–62). [3886
A study of the literary qualities of one of the "worst" writers of his generation.

Ortega Torres, José J. Tomás Rueda Vargas (*Bol. hist. antig.*, vol. 30, no. 350, dic., p. 1131–1136, port.). [3887
A tribute to the man as academician, writer, and director of the National Library.

Otero, Gustavo Adolfo. Notas sobre Gabriel René Moreno (*Rev. Indias*, segunda época, tomo 19, no. 59–60, nov.–dic., p. 239–267). [3889
An interesting analysis of the personality and many-sided work of the great Bolivian scholar.

Otero D'Costa, Enrique. Daniel Samper Ortega (*Bol. hist. antig.*, vol. 30, no. 350, dic., p. 1137–1140, port.). [3890
A tribute to the compiler of one of the great collections of America, the Biblioteca Aldeana.

Pérez Petit, Víctor. Obras completas. Crítica. V. Las tres catedrales del naturalismo. Montevideo. Ed. Claudio García y cía. 448 p. [3891
Los hermanos Goncourt.—Emilio Zola.—Alfonso Daudet.

Phillips, Walter T. Chilean customs in Blest Gana's novels (*Hispania*, Washington, vol. 26, no. 4, Dec., p. 397–406). [3892
A summary of the findings of a Ph. D. thesis (Univ. of Southern California, 1943) by the same title. This article includes a valuable bibliography of Blest Gana's works and of source material on Chilean customs.

Picón-Salas, Mariano. Viaje al amanecer. Prólogo de E. Abreu Gómez. México. Ed. Mensaje. (Selecciones hispanoamericanos). 202 p. [3893
Recollections of boyhood days told in a pleasing style and with sincere feeling. They give a clear picture of life in Mérida, Venezuela, and of the author's temperament.

Pinilla, Norberto. Mariano Latorre. Introducción (*Rev. hisp. mod.*, vol. 9, no. 1–2, enero–abril, 17–21, ilus.). [3895
Mention of the various phases of Latorre's literary career.

———. La pólemica del romanticismo en 1842. Buenos Aires. Ed. Americalee. 141 p. [3896
A compilation of the articles published in Chile by Vicente Fidel López, Salvador Sanfuentes, Domingo Faustino Sarmiento, and others. These are of especial importance to the history of Chilean literature.

Plath, Oreste. Literatura chilena moderna (*Rev. Brasil*, ano 6, terceira fase, no. 56, dez., p. 37–42). [3897
A bit of literary reportage in which a great deal of information is compressed into small space. [S. Putnam]

Portuondo, José Antonio. Tarjetero: Cuba literaria, 1942 (*Rev. bim. cub.*, vol. 52, no. 1, julio–agosto, p. 71–81; vol. 52, no. 2, sept.–oct., p. 275–281). [3898
A review of the year, with especial comment on the outstanding items.

Posadas, Rosa Margarita. Las novelas de Angélica Palma. Estudio crítico-biográfico, con una síntesis de sus novelas. Lima. Ed. La Prensa. iv, 90 p. [3899
A thesis for the degree of Doctor of Philosophy in the Catholic University of Peru. It is not a penetrating study by any means, but it does contain useful information about the daughter of the great Peruvian author of *Tradiciones*.

Ramos, Samuel (ed.). Rodó. México. Ed. de la Sría. de educación pública. xxvii, 171 p. [3900
This collection includes the famous essay *Ariel*, and representative selections from Rodó's other works. The preface by Samuel Ramos is an excellent introduction to a study of Rodó.

Riva Agüero, José de la. Los veinticinco años de nuestro *Mercurio* (*Mercurio peruano*, año 18, vol. 25, no. 197, agosto, p. 348–360). [3901
More a history of the tendencies of this magazine than a history of the magazine itself.

Salgado, José. Florencio Varela (*Rev. nac.*, Montevideo, año 6, tomo 24, no. 71, nov., p. 289–298). [3902
Biography, with particular mention of his assassination and the trial that followed.

Sánchez, Luis Alberto. Rafael Maluenda, novelista de almas (*Rev. nac. cultura*, año 5, no. 38, mayo–junio, p. 58–68). [3903
The literary career of one of the famous literary group, Los Diez.

Silva Castro, Raúl. La literatura de Chile. Examen y refutación de un libro de don Mariano Latorre (*Rev. iberoamer.*, vol. 7, no. 13, nov., p. 103–128). [3904
A severe indictment of Latorre's *La Literatura de Chile* (see *Handbook, no. 7, 1941*, item 4625).

Spell, Jefferson Rea. Mexican society of the twentieth century as portrayed by Mariano Azuela (*Int. amer. intel. interchange*, p. 49–61). [3905
A chapter from a series of studies in Spanish American literature published by the University of North Carolina Press in 1944.

Suárez, Marco Fidel. Elogio de Don Miguel Antonio Caro (*Rev. Indias*, segunda época, tomo 18, no. 57, sept., p. 297-327). **[3906]**

A tribute read before the Academia Colombiana de Historia, October 12, 1909.

Torres-Ríoseco, Arturo. Grandes novelistas de la América Hispana. Berkeley, Los Angeles. Univ. of California press. vi, 206 p. **[3907]**

Chapters from *Novelistas Contemporáneos de América* (see *Handbook*, no. 6, 1940, item 4116a) dealing with Eduardo Barrios, Manuel Gálvez, Joaquín Edwards Bello, Manuel Díaz Rodríguez, Pedro Prado, and Rafael Arévalo Martínez. A number of changes have been made in this collection, the first volume of which, *Los novelistas de la Tierra*, was published in 1941. See *Handbook, no. 7, 1941* (item 4726).

Tovar y R., Enrique D. Al márgen de la solidaridad americana. Un episodio de la vida de desterrado de Ricardo Palma (*Rev, Habana*, año 1, tomo 1, no. 6, feb., p. 540-546). **[3908]**

Presentation of the facts about Palma's defense of President Castilla when Palma was an exile in Chile, with important additions to the bibliography of Palma. Of particular interest is the identification of a play *Rodil* published in 1851.

Trías Monge, José. Características generales de la literatura portorriqueña (*Rev. Indias*, segunda época, tomo 17, no. 53, mayo, p. 211-220). **[3909]**

An excellent survey.

Ugarte, Manuel. Escritores iberoamericanos de 1900. Santiago de Chile. Ed. Orbe. 271 p. **[3910]**

Casual recollections of many writers, including Delmira Agustini, Francisco Contreras, José Santos Chocano, Rubén Darío, Enrique Gómez Carrillo, José Ingenieros, Leopoldo Lugones, Amado Nervo, Belisario Roldán, Florencio Sánchez, Alfonsina Storni, and José María Vargas Vila.

Umphrey, George W. Spanish American literature compared with that of the United States (*Hispania*, Washington, vol. 26, no. 1, Feb., p. 21-34). **[3911]**

A general study which will serve as an introduction to the uninitiated in Spanish American literature.

Vela, David. Literatura guatemalteca. Guatemala. Unión tipografía. 2 vols.: xvii, 308; 440 p. **[3912]**

The first volume deals with pre-Colombian and colonial literature, the second with the nineteenth century.

Vitoria, Marcos. El humorismo en la literatura argentina actual (*Cuad. amer.*, año 2, vol. 11, no. 5, sept.-oct., p. 206-221). **[3913]**

An instructive article with mention of numerous examples of a quality not generally associated with Spanish American literature.

PROSE FICTION

Aguilera Malta, Demetrio. La isla virgen. Con un prólogo de Ángel F. Rojas. Guayaquil. Ed. Vera y cía. 313 p. **[3914]**

The struggle of civilization against the jungle on the Ecuadorian coast, with numerous cases of conflicts between classes.

Aldao, Martín. La vida falsa. Buenos Aires. Imp. Belmonte. 358 p. **[3915]**

A story of the empty life of the Latin American colony in Paris after the first World War. Neither characters nor situations arouse particular interest.

Alegría, Fernando. Lautaro, joven libertador de Arauco. Santiago. Ed. Zig-zag. 238 p. **[3916]**

A novelized account of one of the Araucanian chieftains of Ercilla's *Araucana*. Like the original it spares no details of the atrocities on either side in the conflict between Spaniards and Indians. It was awarded first prize in the Farrar and Rinehart contest, juvenile section.

Alemán Bolaños, Gustavo. Novelas. Buenos Aires. Ed. Atlántida. 94 p. **[3917]**

Of the seven short stories that comprise this book, one, "Burguesía," is worthy of note because of its local color.

Arráiz, Antonio. Dámaso Velázquez. Buenos Aires. Ed. Progreso y cultura. 290 p. **[3918]**

This novel dealing with the coast of Venezuela is more interesting for its local color and minor characters than for its torrid plot, principal characters, or sensational ending.

Barletta, Leónidas. La señora Enriqueta y su ramito. Buenos Aires. Soc. imp. americana. 129 p., ilus. **[3919]**

Twelve stories simply told and full of feeling. The illustrations by A. I. Vallmitjana add no little to the attractiveness of the collection.

Bazán, Armando. Prisiones junto al mar. Buenos Aires. Ed. Claridad. (Col. Claridad, vol. 196). 127 p. **[3920]**

The life of political prisoners on the Island of San Fernando in Peru. The novel is lacking in precise details about the life of the prisoners and contains too many discussions of politics.

Bertomeo, Carlos A. El valle de la esperanza. Una historia de Gales y Chubut. Buenos Aires. Ed. El Ateneo. 270 p. **[3921]**

This account of colonization in Southern Argentina by a religious group from England presents a new and interesting subject, but a lack of specific detail detracts from its value.

Castro, Baltazar. Piedra y nieve. Prólogo de Alberto Romero. Santiago. Ed. Talamí.

(Col. Nuevos novelistas de Chile). 133 p. [3922
Six stories of rough life in Chile, told with picturesque and effective detail.

Castro, Ernesto L. Los isleros. Buenos Aires. Ed. Losada. 231 p. [3923
This novel deals with a universal theme; it presents an unusual side of Argentine life, it makes mention of World War II; and it does not end in tragedy. It was the selection of the Argentine committee for the Farrar and Rinehart prize for 1942, and received special mention from the American committee. It ranks high in the Spanish American production for 1943.

Crow, John A. (ed.). Horacio Quiroga. Sus mejores cuentos. México, D. F. Ed. Cultura. (Clásicos de América, Ed. del Inst. internacional de literatura iberoamericana, 3). lii, 290 p. [3924
An excellent selection of stories, with a full introduction and bibliography. One of the most important publications of the year.

Díaz-Solís, Gustavo. Llueve sobre el mar. Caracas. Tip. La Nación. (Cuadernos literarios de la Asociación de escritores venezolanos, 41). 74 p. [3925
Three stories full of interest and related in a straightforward manner.

Donoso, Armando (ed.). Algunos cuentos chilenos. Buenos Aires, México. Ed. Espasa-Calpe argentina. (Col. Austral, 376). 152 p. [3926
One selection each from the short stories of Baldomero Lillo, Federico Gana, Augusto D'Halmar, Rafael Maluenda, Fernando Santiván, Eduardo Barrios, Joaquín Edwards Bello, Mariano Latorre, Marta Brunet, and Manuel Rojas, with a brief prologue and notes.

Edwards Bello, Joaquín. En el viejo almendral. Santiago, Chile. Ed. Orbe. 635 p. [3927
Recollections of figures, types, and customs in Valparaíso, Viña del Mar, Quillota, and Santiago before the modernizing of present times. Full of tremendous vitality, it could be improved by cutting. Apparently this book is an extension of *Valparaíso, La Ciudad del Viento*, published in 1931.

Gallegos, Gerardo. Beau Dondón conquista un mundo. Habana. Ed. La República. 232 p. [3928
A historical novel dealing with Santo Domingo in the early nineteenth century. The plot is exciting and the scenes are picturesque, but character analysis is lacking.

García, Serafín J. (comp.). Panorama del cuento nativista del Uruguay. Montevideo. Ed. Claridad. (Bibl. de escritores uruguayos, 11). 319 p., ilus. [3929
Twenty-six stories by as many authors, preceded by brief biographical sketches.

García Roel, Adriana. El hombre de barro. México. Ed. Porrúa hnos. 343 p. [3930
This account of country life in Mexico gives a great deal of insight into the customs and beliefs of the people, but it can hardly be classified as a novel. Still, it received the Lanz Duret novel prize for 1942.

Koenenkampf, Guillermo. Azul del sur. Santiago, Chile. Ed. Orbe. 218 p. [3931
Although the scene of this novel is a German settlement in Chile, the author fails to introduce more than superficial local color. The story itself is not convincing and the merit of the whole book is not to be compared with the author's earlier *Casa con Tres Patios*.

Laña Santillana, Pilar. Más allá de la trocha. Lima. Imp. Gmo. Lenta. 328 p. [3932
A simple story of a visit to the interior of Peru, with abundant and interesting details of customs and scenery.

López y Fuentes, Gregorio. Acomodatio. Novela de un político de convicciones. México. Ed. Botas. 301 p. [3933
This satire on Mexican politics is loosely constructed and is lacking in characterization. It is not representative of López y Fuentes at his best.

Mallea, Eduardo. Las águilas. Buenos Aires. Ed. Sudamericana. (Col. Horizonte). 266 p. [3934
A story of frustration that might well happen anywhere. There is little that is characteristic of Argentina in the book, nor is the novel equal to Mallea's previous work.

Miranda, Marta Elba. Aposento de brujos. Santiago, Chile. Ed. Orbe. 134 p. [3935
A series of sketches of life in a country town in Chile, with particular attention to scenery, customs and types of people. The scenes and groups presented are more pleasing than the title would indicate.

Monterde, Francisco. Novelistas hispanoamericanos. Del prerromanticismo a la iniciación del realismo. México. Unión distribuidora de ediciones. (Selecciones hispanoamericanas). 219 p. [3936
Selections from the work of José Joaquín Fernández de Lizardi, J. V. Lastarria, José Mármol, Jorge Isaacs, Manuel de J. Galván, and Clorinda Matta de Turner, with brief introductory statements.

Nascentes, Antenor (ed.). Antologia espanhola e hispano-americana. Rio de Janeiro. Livr. Zélio Valverde. [3937
This anthology of Spanish and Spanish American poets and prose writers has been prepared for the use of schools, by a professor of the Colégio D. Pedro II. Latin American countries represented are Argentina, Chile, Colombia, Cuba, Ecuador, Guatemala, Mexico, Nicaragua, Paraguay, Peru, the Dominican Republic, Salvador, Uruguay, and Venezuela. The editor con-

fesses that haste prevented his adding "um esboço histórico da literatura espanhola, notícias bio-bibliográficas e anotações." [S. Putnam]

Palma, Ricardo. Flor de tradiciones. Introducción, selección y notas de George W. Umphrey y Carlos García-Prada. México. Ed. Cultura. (Clásicos de América, Ed. del Inst. internacional de literatura iberoamericana). xxvii, 272 p. [3938

Among the many editions of selections from work of the great Peruvian *tradicionalista* this collection stands out on account of its comprehensive introduction and up-to-date bibliography.

Ramírez Cabañas, Joaquín (comp.). Antología de cuentos mexicanos (1875-1910). Buenos Aires. Ed. Espasa-Calpe argentina. (Col. Austral, 358). 154 p. [3939

Selections from Vicente Riva Palacio, José María Roa Bárcena, Justo Sierra, Juan de Dios Peza, José López Portilla y Rojas, Rafael Delgado, Manuel Gutiérrez Nájera, Carlos Díaz Dufóo, Amado Nervo, Cayetano Rodríguez Beltrán, and Victoriano Salado Álvarez, with brief introduction and notes.

Ramos, Dinoran. Seis mujeres en el balcón. Caracas. Ed. La Nación. (Bibl. femenina venezolana, 8). 67 p. [3940

This collection of short stories was awarded first prize in the Third Literary Contest for women, Venezuela, 1942. The stories reveal a sincerity and depth of feeling unusual in Spanish American prose fiction.

Revueltas, José. El luto humano. México. Ed. México. 299 p. [3941

A series of tragic circumstances which have a cumulative effect of intense depression. The story embraces many sides of Mexican life, all of which are presented in the same gloomy vein. This novel was the first selection of the Mexican committee for the Farrar and Rinehart prize.

Rojas, Manuel. El bonete maulino. Santiago, Chile. Ed. Cruz del sur. (Col. de autores chilenos). 191 p. [3942

Three regional stories simply told, with more attention to characterization than anything else.

Salvador, Humberto. Prometeo. Quito. Tall. gráf. de educación. 336 p. [3943

This novel sets forth graphically the trials of the teaching profession in Latin America, but the story is weakened by a certain lack of continuity and too many plots.

Santa Cruz, Rosendo. Cuando cae la noche. Guatemala. 280 p. [3944

This novel of country life in Guatemala has fine possibilities but it lacks the intensity one would expect from the situations presented. It was the first choice from Guatemala for the Farrar and Rinehart Prize.

Thoby-Marcelin, Philippe, and **Pierre Marcelin.** Canapé-vert. New York. Ed. de la Maison française. 255 p. [3945

Winner of the Farrar and Rinehart prize. It is a novel of low life in Haiti, with many elements of sorcery and other superstitions. It is striking on account of the novelty of its setting, but not notable otherwise. Written in French, but included here because it was entered in the competition.

Urrutia, Alberto F. Música del más allá y otros cuentos. Rosario. Tall. La Capital. 133 p. [3946

Twelve short stories written in clear and forceful style, with a care for plot, situation and characters. Some of these stories would rank high in any collection.

Villarino, María de. Pueblo en la niebla. Buenos Aires. Ed. Losada. 166 p. [3947

Thirteen short stories written in a delightful and familiar style, and characterized by delicacy of feeling.

Wernicke, Rosa. Las colinas del hambre. Buenos Aires. Ed. Claridad. (Bibl. de escritores argentinos, Obras de autores clásicos y contemporáneos, 11). 265 p., ilus. [3948

Dealing with an unusual side of provincial life in Argentina, this novel is notable for its vivid descriptions, but is marred by lack of objectivity. The author is too evidently pleading a cause.

DRAMA

Payró, Roberto Jorge. Sobre las ruinas. Drama en cuatro actos. Ed. C. K. Jones and Antonio Alonso. Boston. D. C. Heath and co. (Spanish American series). xxii, 151 p. [3949

A school text of a well known Argentine play, with an excellent introduction.

Villaurrutia, Xavier. Autos profanos. México. Ed. Letras de México. 209 p. [3950

Five one act plays, three previously published, but now out of print, and two hitherto unpublished. The plays are notable for their dialogue, humor and psychology.

——. La mujer legítima. Pieza en tres actos. México. Ed. R. Loera y Chávez. 131 p. [3951

A well written play, with plot, characters, and dramatic situations. It well deserves the high praise given it by Enrique Díez-Canedo in the prefatory pages.

NEW EDITIONS

(*See also item* 3160)

Aldao, Martín. El caso de *La gloria de don Ramiro*. Nueva ed. corr. y aumentada.

Buenos Aires. Ed. Atlas, J. Belmonte. 355 p. **[3952**
A devastating criticism of Enrique Larreta's famous novel, sparing neither plot, characters, style, nor vocabulary. The first edition of Aldao's study, published in 1913 under the pseudonym "Luis Vila y Chaves," is rare.

Alegría, Ciro. El mundo es ancho y ajeno. Santiago. Ed. Ercilla. 509 p. **[3953**
Fifth edition of the winner of the Farrar and Rinehart contest for 1941.

Altamirano, Ignacio M. La navidad en las montañas. México. J. Porrúa e hijos. 156 p., ilus. **[3954**
A modern edition of a famous Mexican classic.

Barrett, Rafael. Obras completas. Buenos Aires. Ed. Americalee. (Col. universal de estudios sociales). 688 p. **[3955**
A timely edition of the works of a talented Paraguayan author who deserves to be better known.

Cané, Miguel. Juvenilia. Buenos Aires. Ed. Molino. (Clásicos americanos, 6). 142 p. **[3956**
This account of student life is one of the classics of Argentine literature.

Edwards Bello, Joaquín. La chica del Crillón. Quinta ed. Santiago. Ed. Ercilla. (Col. contempóraneos). 236 p. **[3957**
A well known novel dealing with contemporary life in Santiago, Chile.

Gallegos, Rómulo. La trepadora. Buenos Aires. Ed. Espasa-Calpe. (Col. Austral, 126). 180 p. **[3958**
One of the early novels of the famous Venezuelan author.

Larreta, Enrique. La gloria de Don Ramiro. Tercera ed. Buenos Aires. Ed. Espasa-Calpe. (Col. Austral, 74). 301 p. **[3960**
A new edition of a famous historical novel dealing with Spain.

Latorre, Mariano. Cuna de cóndores. Prólogo de Emilio Vaïsse. Estudio de Eliodoro Astorquiza. Santiago, Chile. Ed. Nascimento. 241 p. **[3961**
This notable collection of short stories was first published in 1918.

———. Ully. Segunda ed. Santiago, Chile. Ed. Nascimento. 99 p. **[3962**
This short novel by the well known Chilean novelist was first published in 1923.

———. Zurzulita. Segunda ed. Prólogo de Benjamín Subercaseaux. Santiago, Chile. Ed. Nascimento. 366 p. **[3963**
This extensive novel of country life in Chile was first published in 1920.

Lillo, Baldomero. Sub sole. Santiago, Chile. Ed. Nascimento. 250 p. **[3964**
Third edition of a famous collection of short stories. Pages 185–250 are devoted to the life of Lillo, with a bibliography, by J. S. González Vera.

Martínez Zuviría, Gustavo. Todas las novelas. Madrid. Imp. Rivadaneyra. 2006 p. **[3965**
A monster edition of the works of "Hugo Wast."

Mejía de Fernández, Abigail. Historia de la literatura dominicana. Quinta ed. del resumen, corregido y aumentado. Santiago, Dom. Rep. Ed. El Diario. 162 p. **[3966**
This volume is intended to be a text book, but it is a useful guide for the general reader.

Quiroga, Horacio. Los arrecifes de coral. Montevideo. Ed. Claudio García. (Bibl. Rodó, 93). 128 p., port. **[3967**
This collection of prose and verse is preceded by "Horacio Quiroga y su pueblo" by Carlos A. Herrera MacLean, and "El sentido de la vida de Horacio Quiroga" by Antonio M. Grampone.

Reyes, Oscar Efrén. Juan Montalvo. Quito. Tall. gráf. de educación. 494 p., ilus. **[3968**
A serious and detailed study of the great Ecuatorian essayist. This is the second edition. The first was published in 1935.

Rubió y Lluch, Antonio. Don Miguel Antonio Caro (*Rev. Indias*, segunda época, tomo 18, no. 57, sept., p. 347–375). **[3969**
This study of the work of Caro was originally published in vol. 4 of the *Obras Completas* of Caro.

TRANSLATIONS

Alegría, Ciro. The golden serpent. Trans. by Harriet de Onís. New York, Toronto. Farrar and Rinehart. 242 p. **[3970**
One of the great novels of Peru, and indeed of Spanish America.

Amorim, Enrique. The horse and his shadow. Trans. by Richard L. O'Connell and James Graham Luján. New York. Charles sons, publ. x, 252 p. **[3971**
This novel of Uruguayan country life was first published in 1941. See *Handbook, no. 7, 1941*, item 4689.

González Peña, Carlos. History of Mexican literature. Revised ed. Trans. by Gusta Barfield Nance and Florene Johnson Dunstan. Introduction by Ángel Flores. Dallas. Southern Methodist univ. press. 398 p., port. **[3972**
A timely and excellent translation of one of the best histories of literature in Spanish America.

Thoby-Marcelin, Philippe, and **Pierre Marcelin.** Canapé-vert. Trans. by Edward LaRocque Tinker. New York. Farrar & Rinehart. 225 p. [3973
See item 3945.

Vigil, Constancio C. Seeds. Trans. by Nina Bull. Forest Hills, N. Y. Las Américas publ. co. viii, 61 p., port. [3974
Sententious sayings from *El Erial, Amar es Vivir, Las Verdades Ocultas,* and *Vidas que Pasan.*

ADDENDA

Bazán, Armando (ed.). Antología del cuento peruano. Santiago, Chile. Ed. Zig-Zag. 1942. 258 p., port. [3975
One or more well chosen selections from Ricardo Palma, Clemente Palma, Abraham Valdelomar, Ventura García Calderón, Manuel Beingolea, Enrique López Albújar, César Vallejo, María Wiesse, Héctor Velarde, Fernando Romero, José Díez-Canseco, Armando Bazán, Arturo Burga Freitas, Ciro Alegría, Rosa Arciniega, and José María Arguedas, with a brief introduction by the editor.

Gallegos, Rómulo. El forastero. Caracas. Ed. Elite. 1942. 289 p. [3976
Second edition within the year of a novel which falls below the standard of the author's earlier works. It presents an imposing array of secondary characters, but is lacking in atmosphere, situations, and plot.

García Velloso, Enrique. Memorias de un hombre de teatro. Prólogo de Ricardo Rojas. Buenos Aires. Ed. Guillermo Kraft. 1942. xix, 296 p., ilus. [3977
Anecdotes of the theater and personal recollections of writers and artists written by a man who was very close to the Argentine stage.

Gutiérrez, Juan María. Cartas de un porteño. Polémica en torno al idioma y a la Real academia española, sostenida con Juan Martínez Villegas, seguida de "Sarmienticidio." Buenos Aires. Ed. Americana. 1942. xxviii, 286 p., ilus. [3978
The documentation of one of the most interesting episodes of the intellectual life of Spanish America—J. M. Gutiérrez' refusal to accept election to the Spanish Academy—followed by a spirited attack on Sarmiento.

Isaacs, Jorge. María. Santiago, Chile. Ed. Zig-Zag. 1942. 406 p., ilus. [3979
This edition of Isaacs' famous novel includes a "vocabulario de provincialismos" and his *Poesías Completas.*

Latorre, Mariano. Mapú. Santiago, Chile. Ed. Orbe. 1942. 313 p. [3980
Twenty regional stories saturated with local color. A glossary of fifteen pages explains the difficult terms.

Pane, Remigio U. A selected bibliography of Latin American literature in English translation (*Mod. lang. jour.,* vol. 26, no. 2, Feb., 1942, p. 116-122). [3981
A list of Latin American works available in English translation.

Picón Febres, Gonzalo. El sargento Felipe. Ed. by Guillermo Rivera. Boston D. C. Heath and co. 1942. viii, 213 p., ilus. [3982
A school edition of a well known Venezuelan novel.

Sarmiento, Domingo Faustino. Estados Unidos. Buenos Aires. Emecé, ed. (Col. Buen Aire). 1942. 97 p., ilus. [3983
Selections from *Viajes por Europa, África y América,* first published in 1849. The comments on life in the United States are of perennial interest.

Tario, Francisco. La noche. México. Antigua libr. Robredo. 1942. 211 p. [3984
Fifteen stories of uneven merit. Those that deal with unusual themes are the best.

Uribe Piedrahita, César. Toa. Narraciones de caucherías. Buenos Aires, México. Ed. Espasa-Calpe. (Col. Austral, 314). 1942. 152 p. [3985
Second edition of a rare and important Colombian novel dealing with the jungle.

POETRY

BOOKS OF VERSE

Andrade, Olegario V. Obras poéticas. Estudio y texto de Eleuterio F. Tiscornia. Buenos Aires. Acad. argentina de letras. (Serie Clásicos argentinos, vol. 2). lxxv, 242 p. [3986
This new edition of the works of "the true national poet" of Argentina, published under the auspices of the Academia Argentina de Letras, includes the first dependable biography of Andrade and the first satisfactory text. However, its distinguished editor, Eleuterio F. Tiscornia, thinks that further research is still imperative. Dr. Tiscornia establishes that the poet was born in Brazil in 1839, and not two years later in Argentina, as asserted in all literary histories so far. He also proves that the poem *La Creación* was not Andrade's work but that of the Chilean Luis Rodríguez Velasco, and that the poem *Al General Lavalle* should be entitled *Al General Ángel Vicente Peñaloza.*

Arce y Valladares, Manuel José. Romancero de Indias. Guatemala. Tip. América. 180 p. [3987
Sixty narrative poems written in old Spanish, evoking the main protagonists of the Spanish conquest of America. An amazing *tour de force,* both philologically and artistically, worthy of widespread diffusion.

Arrazola, Roberto (ed.). Antología poética de Colombia. Buenos Aires. Ed. Colombia. 263 p. [3988

Thirty-three poets, from José Fernández Madrid (1789–1830) to Rafael Maya (born in 1897). If we were to take Carlos García-Prada's *Antología de Líricos Colombianos* (1937) as a norm, by virtue of its unquestionable authority, this new anthology, in one-third the space, fares commendably well. It is more liberal with the minor celebrities of the nineteenth century and it includes a smaller number of living poets than García-Prada's collection. Recommended as an adequate introduction to the subject.

Ballagas, Emilio. Nuestra Señora del Mar. Entrega de "Fray Junípero." Habana. 39 p. [3989

Beautiful series of poems inspired by the traditional cult of the Virgen de la Caridad in Cuba. This is a new phase in the work of Ballagas, a poet who has distinguished himself both as a cultivator of Afrocuban themes and as an "abstractionist."

Blanco, Andrés Eloy. Sus mejores poemas. Caracas. Lit. y Tip. Vargas. (Hojas de poesía, no. 1). 6 p. [3990

This noted Venezuelan poet and statesman was born in 1898. One of the five poems offered in this selection is from a volume to be published soon, *Giraluna*.

Borges, Jorge Luis. Poemas (1922–1943). Buenos Aires. Ed. Losada. 181 p. [3991

The distinguished Argentine poet and critic, Jorge Luis Borges, born in 1900, has published three books of verse. Nearly all his poems are reprinted here (70 out of 85). The new material is confined to six compositions, two of which are in English.

Buzó Gomes, Sinforiano (ed.). Índice de la poesía paraguaya. Asunción. Buenos Aires. Ed. Tupã. 384 p. [3992

An inclusive anthology, whose editor preferred to be hospitable rather than selective, for the very good reason that Paraguayan poetry is practically unknown outside the country. Ninety poets are chronologically divided into three groups: 1860–1910, 1911–1932, and the last decade. Early poetry is succinctly referred to in an initial chapter. A number of the selections are in Guaraní, a language which many Paraguayans use not only in daily life but also in their writings. A few women poets are included. The compiler deserves praise for including so many poets, for recognition accorded to Guaraní, as well as for his excellent biographical and bibliographical notes.

Capdevila, Arturo. Primera antología de mis versos. Buenos Aires, México. Ed. Espasa-Calpe argentina. (Col. Austral, 352). 251 p. [3993

Selections from the ten books of verse so far published by this prolific writer of poetry, fiction, non-fiction, and drama. Included also are five poems from a forthcoming book. The general impression is that Capdevila has failed to fulfill the promise of great poetry held out in his second work, *Melpómene* (1912).

Contín Aybar, Pedro René (ed.). Antología poética dominicana. Santiago, Dom. Rep. Ed. El Diario. xvii, 310 p. [3994

The compiler divides his forty-six poets into three groups: men poets born between 1845 and 1900; men poets born in the twentieth century; and women poets, with no dates mentioned, out of chivalry. Even though he admits that the country "has not produced a great poet," he insists that the Dominican Republic is "a mother of poets." His critical notes, more informing than is customary in most anthologies, and the selection of poets and poems reveal a man of taste, who has the courage of his convictions. To this merit must be added the fact that this is the first comprehensive anthology of Dominican poetry published since Osvaldo Bazil's *Parnaso Dominicano* (Barcelona, 1915).

Cordero y Torres, Enrique (ed.). Poetas y escritores poblanos (por origen o adopción), 1900–1943. Puebla, Mexico. Ed. Nieto. 562 p. [3995

Seventy-seven writers from the state of Puebla, two-thirds of whom are still living, are represented in this anthology, mostly by poetry. The literary quality of the selections is rather questionable; nevertheless, the book is valuable as a Who's Who, thanks to the thorough biographical information furnished by the editor.

Correa, Julio. Cuerpo y alma. Buenos Aires. Ed. Difusam. 86 p. [3996

First book by a Paraguayan poet still in his literary novitiate. A friend of the author writes a prologue containing some useful data on Paraguayan poetry.

Corvalán, Stella. Palabras. Santiago, Chile. Imp. Universitaria. 77 p. [3997

The spontaneity of *Sombra en el Aire* (1940) has here disappeared, leaving little of poetic significance.

Domínguez, María Alicia. Campo de luna. Buenos Aires. Tall. A. y J. V. Calvo. 96 p. [3998

Tenth book of verse by a woman poet who has also distinguished herself for her work in the field of fiction. This new book does not, however, do justice to her past achievements.

D'Sola, Otto. El viajero mortal. Caracas. Lit. y Tip. del Comercio. 58 p. [3999

In this fourth book Otto D'Sola reveals new qualities which make him stand out as one of the most interesting personalities in Venezuelan poetry.

Esténger, Rafael (ed.). Cien de las mejores poesías cubanas. Habana. Ed. Mirador. 261 p. [4000

One hundred "of the best" Cuban poems, by thirty-eight poets no longer living, from Manuel de Zequeira y Arango (1764–1846) to Rubén Martínez Villena (1899–1934). For chronological reasons the so-called "poesía afrocubana" is not represented.

Estrada Paniagua, Felipe. Vértice. Managua. Ed. Nuevos horizontes. 80 p. [4001

Skilfully written verse that takes one back to the distant days of Nervo's elegiac poems.

Geenzier, Enrique. Viejo y nuevo. Panamá. 219 p. [4002

Panamá's poet-laureate gathers in one volume his two popular books, *Crepúsculos y Sombras* (1916) and *Corazón Adentro* (1925), and most of his 1926-1942 production. Throughout a lifetime his poetry has safely remained on the margin of esthetic experimentations and emotional fervor.

González Tuñón, Raúl. Himno de pólvora. Santiago, Chile. Ed. Nueva América. 230 p. [4004

Prose and poetry bearing on the war, especially on its ideological aspects. The thirty-one poems included in pages 165-230 reveal an uncompromising innovator in poetry and an unconditional supporter of the Soviet cause. González Tuñón was born in Buenos Aires in 1905. This is his tenth book.

Hays, H. R. (ed.). 12 Spanish American poets. An anthology. English translations, notes, and introduction by the editor. New Haven: Yale univ. press; London: H. Milford, Oxford univ. press. vi, 336 p. [4005

Ten of this round dozen of leading poets admirably exemplify both the robust creativeness and the vagaries of Spanish American poetry in the last twenty-five years. They are: Jorge Luis Borges (Argentina); Vicente Huidobro, Pablo de Rokha, and Pablo Neruda (Chile); Eugenio Florit and Nicolás Guillén (Cuba); Jorge Carrera Andrade (Ecuador); José Gorostiza (Mexico); César Vallejo (Peru); and Jacinto Fombona Pachano (Venezuela). The two other poets, Ramón López Velarde (Mexico) and Luis Carlos López (Colombia), belong to an older generation. The original Spanish text and Mr. Hays' translations are printed side by side. The translator—as he himself declares—"has tried to render the images faithfully and to preserve in every case the character of the original meter and to add nothing of his own." This procedure is particularly adequate in translating those poets in this anthology who really write prose fancifully printed as verse. Informing, discerning introduction and notes by the editor.

Hernández, Efrén. Entre apagados muros. México. Imp. Universitaria. 150 p. [4006

A return to the musical idiom of some early bards of the Spanish golden age, with some traces of cultism; real inspiration and well defined poetic personality.

Loudet, Enrique (ed.). Letras argentinas en Centro América. Poetisas, poetas y prosistas argentinos. San José, C. R. Imp. Nacional. 281 p. [4007

Brief selections from the works of about two hundred poets and seventy prose writers. The compiler, a diplomat representing Argentina in Central America, was handicaped by the lack of materials.

Mármol, José. Cantos del peregrino. Prólogo y edición crítica de Rafael Alberto Arrieta. Buenos Aires. Ed. Estrada. (Clásicos argentinos, vol. 8.) liv, 312 p. [4008

José Mármol (1818-1871), under the influence of Byron's *Childe Harold*, wrote between 1844 and 1846 these autobiographical cantos.

Mata, G. Humberto. Ecuador en el hombre. Cuenca, Ecuador. Bibl. Cenit. 77 p. [4009

White-heat political poetry.

Mel, Solón de (pseud.). Sinfonía de los cuatro elementos. México, D. F. Ed. Prisma. 63 p. [4010

Pantheism, nationalism, eroticism in dazzling prosodical arrangements. This is an enlarged edition of *Tetralogía Elemental* (1933). Author's real name: Guillermo de Luzuriaga y Bribiesca.

Mitre, Bartolomé (tr.). Horacianas de Mitre. Publicación facsímil de los originales. Dirigida y prologada por Ricardo Levene. Buenos Aires. Tall. gráf. Guillermo Kraft. (Inst. Mitre). xliii, 588 p. [4011

Facsimile edition of Mitre's original manuscript of his ambitions undertaking in the fields of scholarship and poetry, a Spanish translation of all the odes of Horace. Originally published in book form in two separate parts, dated 1895 and 1896 respectively.

Morales, Ernesto (ed.). Antología poética argentina. Buenos Aires. Ed. Americana. 476 p. [4012

The editor has intended to compile a collection of the best Argentine poetry "from its earliest utterances to the present ones," with emphasis on lyric poetry. The colonial period is represented by one name only (Manuel de Lavardén); the eight living poets included have been writing for over a quarter of a century. The thirty other poets represented reflect the country's turbulent history during the first half of the nineteenth century, the rise of an earthy nationalism, and the influence of European literary movements.

Morales Lara, Julio. En la honda un lucero. Caracas. Tip. La Nación. (Cuads. lit. de la Asociación de escritores venezolanos, no. 42.) 78 p. [4013

Selections from *Savia* (1930) and *Múcura* (1935) and later works by a poet in the modern manner whose authentic inspiration springs from the soil.

Navarro Luna, Manuel. Poemas mambises. Manzanillo, Cuba. Imp. El Arte. 12 p. **[4014**
Four noble songs of Cuban independence.

Neruda, Pablo. Nuevo canto de amor a Stalingrado. México. Comité de ayuda a Rusia en guerra. 14 p. **[4015**
The most quoted war poem in Spanish. Neruda found it necessary to scan and rhyme his hendecasyllables—not always in an orthodox manner.

———. Selección. Recopilación y notas de Arturo Aldunate. Santiago. Nascimento. 352 p. **[4015a**
Extensive selection from Neruda's poetry; most of his limited prose production; a few commentaries by brother poets (the one by García Lorca is here published for the first time); several photographs; and brief but informing notes. Books represented: *Crepusculario* (1923), *20 poemas de Amor y una Canción Desesperada* (1924), *Anillos* (1925), *Tentativa del Hombre Infinito* (1926), *El Habitante y su Esperanza* (1926), *Residencia en la Tierra, Primera Parte* (1934), *Residencia en la Tierra, Segunda Parte* (1935), *España en el Corazón* (1937), *Las Furias y las Penas* (1939). Of special interest are 13 poems from his ambitious work in progress, *Canto General de Chile*, and four other poems published singly in Mexico in 1941–1942.

Ortíz Saralegui, Juvenal. Las dos niñas y otros poemas. Buenos Aires. Ed. Losada. **[4016**
Fine example of modernism which does not spurn the ageless tradition of medieval and classical Spanish poetry. A new departure for this distinguished Uruguayan poet.

Othón, Manuel José. Breve antología lírica. Prólogo y selección de Jesús Zavala. San Luis Potosí, México. Univ. potosina autónoma. 113 p. **[4017**
Symptomatic of a revived interest in Othón (1858–1906) is the editor's prediction that some day Othón will be considered one of the great poets in the Spanish language. The selections in this volume seem to support such claim. Excellent biographical sketch appended.

Pardo García, Germán. Sacrificio. México, D. F. Ed. Cultura. 118 p. **[4018**
In his ninth book in thirteen years this distinguished Colombian poet shows that he has capitulated, at least partially, to certain logogriphic tendencies in current poetry. He persists, however, in writing alexandrines of faded elegance.

Rivero, Pedro. El mar de las perlas. Caracas. Ed. Elite. (Cuads. lit. de la Asociación de escritores venezolanos, no. 39.) 122 p. **[4019**
Eighty-one sonnets written according to the most exacting cannons. Their external marble-like coldness often encloses deep sentiment, as in the case of the sonnet entitled *Ambición*.

Rojas, René. Silabario de amor. Prólogo de Augusto d'Halmar. Santiago? Chile. Ed. Orbe. 138 p. **[4020**
Very uneven first book by a promising poet.

Silva Valdés, Fernán. Antología poética 1920–1940. Buenos Aires. Ed. Losada. 163 p. **[4021**
Selected poems by the popular and distinguished Uruguayan poet whose "nativism" springs from within and is not restricted to the picturesque.

Tablada, José Juan. Los mejores poemas de . . . Ed. por. J. M. González Mendoza. México. Ed. Surco. 159 p. **[4021a**
Born in 1871, Tablada published, between 1899 and 1928, six books which, notwithstanding their extremely limited circulation, started fashions such as the imitation of Japanese verse forms and have given him a legendary reputation as an exotic and a cosmopolite. This poorly edited book includes selections from all his works. Outstanding even today are his nineteenth-century poem *Onix* and his "jaikais" of 1919 and 1922.

Tinoco, Juan. Paisajes y retratos. Habana. Ed. Seoane, Fernández. 97 p. **[4022**
A Venezuelan poet of great talent writes fifty sonnets relating to a corner of his country's history. What might have been fine poetry is marred by the excessive use of unusual words bordering on the pedantic.

Valle, Rafael Heliodoro. Contigo. México. Ed. R. Loera y Chávez. 58 p. **[4023**
The distinguished writer from Honduras offers a sheaf of poems which by contrast with the poetry of his contemporaries seem almost revolutionary because of their purity of form and sanity of content. The introduction by Enrique González Martínez is a warm tribute to Valle as a man and writer.

Vidal, María Antonia (ed.). Cien años de poesía femenina española e hispano-americana, 1840–1940. Barcelona. Ed. Olimpo. 220 p. **[4024**
The following Spanish American women poets are included: Gertrudis Gómez de Avellaneda, María E. Vaz Ferreira, María Enriqueta, Delmira Agustina, Alicia Lardé, Gabriela Mistral, Juana de Ibarbourou, and Alfonsina Storni. Spain is represented by twelve poets.

Villalobos, Héctor Guillermo. Jagüey: romances regionales guayaneses. Caracas. Ed. Bolívar. 128 p. **[4025**
Prize-winning poems which occasionally succeed in ringing true to their subject, namely the customs and scenes of the Venezuelan Guiana.

Yunque, Álvaro (ed.). Poetas sociales de la Argentina (1810–1943). Buenos Aires. Ed. Problemas. 2 vols.: 241; 198 p. **[4026**
The compiler, himself a poet and a social reformer, was admittedly more concerned with the documentary value of the material

collected than with its purely esthetic quality. However, the results are commendable even from a literary standpoint. The ninety poets included represent all degrees of protest and non-conformity, from mere disquietude to militant leftism. Of the eight sections into which the work is divided, those devoted to the "Boedo" group, the Jewish poets, and the redeemers of the peasant class are the largest and most significant.

BIOGRAPHY AND CRITICISM

(*See also items* 3294, 3860, 3878, 3910)

Alba, Pedro de. Tono y ruta de la poesía mexicana (*Cuad. amer.*, año 2, vol. 11, no. 5, sept.–oct., p. 245–251). [4027]
To suggest that Mexican poetry cannot be adequately described as being typically melancholy, the critic emphasizes López Velarde's "robust" quality.

Arango, Daniel. Carta a Pablo Neruda (*Rev. Indias*, segunda época, tomo 18, no. 56, agosto, p. 207–216). [4028]
Serious objections to Neruda's "political" poetry.

Arango Ferrer, J. Germán Pardo García o el poeta de la desolación (*Rev. nac.*, Montevideo, tomo 23, no. 69, sept., p. 421–432). [4029]
The critic considers Pardo García "one of the greatest Colombian poets of all times."

Baeza Flores, Alberto. Conducta y poesía (*Atenea*, año 20, tomo 73, no. 218, agosto, p. 162–167). [4030]
Oneirocritical account of the young surrealist poets constituting the "Mandrágora" group of Chile.

Bazil, Osvaldo. Tarea literaria y patricia. Habana. Ed. La Verónica. 220 p. [4031]
Two-thirds of the articles or speeches collected in this book deal with literature, mostly Dominican poetry and Rubén Darío. The remaining third is a eulogy of the President of the Dominican Republic.

Bietti, Oscar. La poesía de González Carbalho (*Nosotros*, segunda época, año 8, tomo 23, no. 93, dic., p. 303–308). [4032]
Poetry in minor tone, clearly expressed, unlike that of many of the poet's contemporaries.

———. Rafael Alberto Arrieta (*Nosotros*, segunda época, año 8, tomo 20, no. 83, feb., p. 165–172). [4033]
In praising Arrieta's sensible and sensitive poems the critic laments what he calls "chaos" in present-day poetry.

Bollo, Sarah. La poesía de Amado Nervo (*Rev. nac.*, Montevideo, año 6, tomo 23, no. 68, agosto, p. 219–224). [4034]
Emphasis on the religious, ethical and sentimental aspects of Nervo's poetry.

Carbonell, Diego. Lo morboso en Rubén Darío. Ensayos de interpretación científica. Prólogo de J. A. Cova. Caracas. Ed. Cecilio Acosta. 219 p. [4035]
Despite its diffuseness and excessive display of erudition, often irrelevant, this book brings together much interesting biographical material.

Carías Reyes, Marcos. Juan Ramón Molina. Tegucigalpa. Imp. Calderón. 38 p. [4036]
No objectivity was intended by the author in this encomiastic appraisal of one of the most celebrated poets of Honduras, Juan Ramón Molina (1875–1913).

Carilla, Emilio. Mármol y Espronceda (*Nosotros*, segunda época, año 8, tomo 22, no. 88, julio, p. 78–81). [4037]
José Mármol's *Canto del Poeta* is a servile imitation of Espronceda's *Canción del Pirata*.

Carrera Andrade, Jorge. El americano nuevo y su actitud poética (*Cuad. amer.*, año 2, vol. 7, no. 1, enero–feb., p. 205–228). [4038]
Interesting remarks on Spanish America's vital contribution to world poetry, with emphasis on Darío, Neruda, Guillén, and Gorostiza. Translated by H. R. Hays for *Poetry*, Chicago, vol. 62, no. 2, p. 88–104.

———. Edades de mi poesía (*Rev. Indias*, segunda época, tomo 19, no. 59–60, nov.–dic., p. 268–281). [4039]
The distinguished Ecuadorian poet traces his own poetic development from 1915 to 1940.

Castañeda, Daniel. Entre el haikai y la copla (*Letras de México*, año 7, vol. 1, no. 5, mayo, p. 4–5). [4040]
A Japanese verse form transplanted to Mexico, where it has been successfully cultivated by Tablada, Villalobos, Romero, and Duvalier.

Castro Leal, Antonio. Guillermo Valencia ha muerto (*Cuad. amer.*, año 2, vol. 11, no. 5, sept.–oct., p. 241–244). [4041]
Brief but cogent appraisal of Valencia's significance within the modernist movement.

Centurión, Carlos. La generación intelectual del 23 (*Rev. ateneo paraguayo*, año 2, no. 7, enero, p. 15–43). [4042]
Most of the thirty-one Paraguayan writers sketched and quoted in this study were poets.

Díez-Canedo, Enrique. Rubén Darío, Juan Ramón Jiménez y los comienzos del modernismo en España (*Hijo pródigo*, año 1, vol. 2, no. 9, dic., p. 145–151). [4043]
Interesting recollections of Darío's influence in Spain at the end of the nineteenth century.

Dougé, Joubert. Essai sur José Martí. Port-au-Prince. 172 p. [4044]
Fifty pages of this essay by a Haitian admirer of Martí deal with the latter's poetry.

Escala, Víctor Hugo. Cuatro jóvenes poetas del Ecuador. Panamá. Ed. Estrella de Panamá. 21 p. **[4045]**
The four poets touched upon in this rather casual paper are Medardo Ángel Silva, Arturo Borja, Ernesto Noboa Caamaño, and Humberto Fierro. All four had a brief hour of fame in the early twenties and committed suicide within a year of each other.

Fernández de Castro, José Antonio. Tema negro en las letras de Cuba (1608–1935). Habana. Ed. Mirador. 95 p. **[4046]**
A weighty essay, notwithstanding its brevity, on the Cuban literary works, largely in verse form, related to the Negro, as author or subject.

Fernández Moreno, César. Informe sobre la nueva poesía argentina (*Nosotros*, segunda época, año 8, tomo 23, no. 91, oct., p. 71–93). **[4047]**
An important report—factual and well-documented—on a "new generation" of Argentine poets (those who are between twenty and thirty years of age). The author, himself one of these younger poets, is the son of the "Fernández Moreno" we all know.

Figueira, Gastón. Un gran poeta colombiano (*Sustancia*, año 4, no. 14, marzo-abril, p. 328–334). **[4048]**
A review of the several books published by Germán Pardo García in the decade 1930–1940.
Also published in *América*, Habana, vol. 20, no. 1–2, oct.–nov., 1943, p. 53–56.

———. Poesía y antillanidad de Manuel del Cabral (*Sustancia*, año 4, no. 17, oct., p. 836–842). **[4049]**
A poet from the Dominican Republic whom the critic persuasively places among "the great American poets of the present day."

———. Un recuerdo para la poesía de Andrés Héctor Lerena Acevedo (*Rev. nac.*, Montevideo, año 6, tomo 22, no. 66, junio, p. 396–403). **[4050]**
The critic claims that Lerena (1895–1918?), one of Uruguay's forgotten modernist poets, deserves a place next to Herrera y Reissig and Juana de Ibarbourou.

Finlayson, Clarence. Notas en torno a la poesía chilena (*Rev. Indias*, segunda época, tomo 19, no. 58, oct., p. 90–100). **[4051]**
Principal Chilean poets of the present century.

García-Prada, Carlos. Zurce que surce líricos chismes (*Rev. iberoamer.*, vol. 6, no. 11, feb., p. 207–212). **[4052]**
On the Colombian Luis Carlos López and his unique brand of humor in poetry.
Also published in *Rep. amer.*, vol. 40, no. 10, junio 12, 1943, p. 145–147.

Gil-Albert, Juan. América en el recuerdo y la poesía de Octavio Paz (*Letras de México*, año 7, vol. 1, no. 1, enero, p. 5, 11). **[4053]**
A Spanish vanguard poet discusses one of his Mexican peers.

Gulla, Luis Alberto. Exégesis. Montevideo. 94 p. **[4055]**
All but one of the five penetrating articles in this book deal with contemporary Uruguayan poets. Special mention should be made of the paper on Emilio Oribe, the poet-philosopher.

Hays, H. R. Jorge Carrera Andrade, magician of metaphors (*Books abroad*, vol. 17, no. 2, spring, p. 101–105). **[4056]**
Carrera Andrade, born in 1903, "is the leading contemporary poet of Ecuador and belongs in the front rank of Latin American literature."

Hernández de Mendoza, Cecilia. Miguel Antonio Caro. Diversos aspectos de un humanista colombiano. Bogotá. Prensa de la Univ. nac. 88 p. **[4057]**
A doctoral dissertation on Colombia's most representative man of letters in the nineteenth century. The author's fervid admiration for the distinguished poet and humanist seems to have prevented her from being explicit about her facts.

Herrera y Reissig, Herminia. Vida íntima de Julio Herrera y Reissig (*Rev. nac.*, Montevideo, año 6, tomo 21, no. 63, marzo, p. 371–380; tomo 23, no. 69, sept., p. 375–390; tomo 24, no. 70, oct., p. 73–82). **[4058]**
The poet's life recalled by his sister, thirty-three years after his premature death. Most important biographical source.

Holguín, Andrés. Traducciones poéticas de Guillermo Valencia (*Rev. Indias*, segunda época, tomo 17, no. 54, junio, p. 436–446). **[4059]**
Translating was an important poetic activity of Valencia.

Jiménez, Juan Ramón. ¿América sombría? (*Rep. amer.*, vol. 40, no. 14, agosto 14, p. 209–211). **[4060]**
Mostly on Neruda, whose alleged indianism is denounced by Jiménez as a pose.
Also published in *Letras de México*, año 7, vol. 1, no. 10, oct., 1943, p. 5, 9.

Lacau, María Hortensia. Guillermo Valencia (*Nosotros*, segunda época, año 8, tomo 23, no. 92, nov., p. 167–180). **[4061]**
Detailed, though brief, biographical and critical notes on the great Colombian poet who died in 1943 at the age of seventy.

Martínez, José Luis. Situación de Amado Nervo (*Letras de México*, año 7, vol. 1, no. 11, nov., p. 1–2). **[4063]**
Even though Nervo is still a favorite with the Mexican public at large, the intelligentsia seems to have disowned him.

Meléndez, Concha. Muerte y resurrección de César Vallejo (*Rev. iberoamer.*, vol. 6, no. 12, mayo, p. 419–453). **[4064**
Searching analysis of the difficult poetry of a Peruvian writer who has become a symbol of revolutionary neo-Indianism in life and literature. Rather than reaching for conclusions the critic seems to have been interested in verifying the facts about a life, an aesthetic credo, and a syntax which were as tortured as those of any Spanish American writer of the last twenty-five years.

Menéndez y Pelayo, Marcelino. Historia de la poesía argentina y uruguaya. Buenos Aires. Publ. del Liceo de España. 219 p. **[4065**
Reprint of the chapters on Argentine and Uruguayan poetry included in Menéndez y Pelayo's *Historia de la Poesía Hispano-Americana* (Madrid, 1911–1913). This epoch-making work was completed in 1892 and included only poets no longer living.

Moncada, Raúl. Al que le venga el sayo ... (*Rep. amer.*, vol. 40, no. 13, julio 31, p. 194–195). **[4067**
Neruda's side on the controversy over his poem *Dura Elegía*, written on the death of Prestes' mother.

Ortiz de Montellano, Bernardo. Figura, amor y muerte de Amado Nervo. México. Ed. Xochitl. (Vidas mexicanas, no. 10). 168 p. **[4068**
Sympathetic evocation of a poet, an epoch, and a "poetic climate," done in rhapsodic fashion with a minimum of biographical data and a maximum of well-chosen quotations.

Oyarzún, Mila. La poesía femenina en Chile (*Atenea*, año 20, tomo 73, no. 218, agosto, p. 168–194). **[4070**
Brief characterizations of a great many women poets of Chile, from Mercedes Marín del Solar to the latest Sapphos.

Pagés Larraya, Antonio. El poeta Antonio Lamberti. Contribución al estudio del ambiente literario de su época. Buenos Aires. Imp. de la Univ. (Inst. de literatura argentina, publ., Sección de crítica, vol. 2, no. 7, p. 543–611). **[4071**
Lamberti (1845–1926), born in Uruguay of Italian parents, settled in Buenos Aires, where he became one of the most successful minor poets and most beloved public figures. His posthumous book, *Poesías* (1929), published by the Universidad de Buenos Aires, contains most of the poems with which he delighted magazine readers and literary audiences for a quarter of a century. This monograph on his life and work (the former much more significant than the latter) charmingly reconstructs certain aspects of literary life in Buenos Aires, especially at the time of the arrival of Rubén Darío.

Paz, Octavio. Respuesta a un cónsul (*Letras de México*, año 7, vol. 1, no. 8, agosto, p. 5). **[4072**
A "victim" of Pablo Neruda victimizes the undiplomatic Chilean diplomat.

Pedro, Valentín de. Naufragio y salvación de Fernández Moreno (*Sustancia*, año 4, no. 14, marzo–abril, p. 296–313). **[4073**
Born in 1896 of Spanish parents, Fernández Moreno (he never signs his Christian name) was born in Argentina, was taken to Spain at the age of six, and returned to Buenos Aires eight years later, to become the urbane poet of the *urbis*.

Pinilla, Norberto. El soneto *Roma*. Santiago. Publ. de la "Revista de educación." 18 p. **[4074**
Brief article about the exact text of a sonnet written in collaboration by Rubén Darío and Antonio Lamberti.

——— (ed.). La polémica del romanticismo en 1842: V. F. López, D. F. Sarmiento, S. Sanfuentes. Buenos Aires. Ed. Americalee. 142 p. **[4075**
The Chilean scholar, Norberto Pinilla, brings together in this book the articles published in Chilean periodicals, in 1842, by two eminent Argentine exiles, López and Sarmiento, and three Chilean upholders of classicism, on the subject of romanticism. Most of these articles had been buried for a century in rather inaccessible newspaper files. Professor Pinilla, author of noteworthy critical studies about the so-called "literary movement of 1842" in Chile, has performed a great service in making these memorable articles available.

Plácido, A. D. Leopoldo Lugones. Su formación, su espíritu, su obra. Montevideo. Imp. El Siglo ilustrado. 25 p. **[4076**
Biographical sketch of "one of the most representative figures of the Spanish American intelligentsia" and rapid review of his many works in various fields, principally poetry.
Reprinted from *Revista del Instituto Histórico y Geográfico del Uruguay*, vol. 17.

Prudencio, Roberto. José Eduardo Guerra: siguiendo la huella de un poeta (*Kollasuyo*, año 5, no. 48, mayo, p. 231–245). **[4077**
Better known for a searching study of Bolivian letters, *Itinerario Espiritual de Bolivia*, José Eduardo Guerra (1893–1943) wrote two books of verse, *Del Fondo del Silencio* and *Estancias*.

Roa Bastos, Augusto. "Canto secular" de Eloy Fariña Núñez (*Rev. ateneo paraguayo*, año 2, no. 7, enero, p. 50–52). **[4078**
One of the outstanding Paraguayan poems.

Ronald. Reencuentro con Parra del Riego (*Nosotros*, segunda época, año 8, tomo 22, no. 90, sept., p. 292–300). **[4079**
Juan Parra del Riego, born in Peru in 1894, died in Montevideo in 1925. He became identified with Uruguayan life. A street in Montevideo has been named after him and the Ministry of Education published his complete works in verse and prose.

Sabat Ercasty, Carlos. Un viaje por el alma de María Eugenia (*Rev. nac.*, Monte-

video, año 6, tomo 22, no. 64, abril, p. 95–108). **[4080**
On María Eugenia Vaz Ferreira (1875–1924).

Santaella Murias, Alicia. Fausto Burgos, el poeta del ensueño y del alba (*Sustancia*, año 4, no. 17, oct., p. 825–833). **[4081**
Fausto Burgos, of Tucumán, is an outstanding representative of regionalism in Argentine poetry.

Tovar y R., Enrique D. Luis Benjamín Cisneros (*Mercurio peruano*, año 18, vol. 25, no. 190, enero, p. 30–35). **[4082**
Cisneros (1837–1904) was made poet laureate by the Ateneo de Lima in 1901.

Undurraga, Antonio de. La órbita poética de Jorge Carrera Andrade (*Rep. amer.*, vol. 40, no. 1, enero 9, p. 9–11). **[4084**
The Chilean critic considers the Ecuadorean poet a genuine Indo-American voice.

———. Zodíaco de la poesía chilena en 1941 (*Atenea*, año 20, tomo 71, no. 211–212, enero–feb., p. 83–109; no. 213, marzo, p. 247–257). **[4085**
Concluding parts of an excellent survey of Chilean poetry in 1941.

Vásquez, Rafael. La poesía de León de Greiff (*Rev. Indias*, segunda época, tomo 16, no. 50, feb., p. 394–403). **[4086**
The contemporary Colombian poet León de Greiff strives to identify poetry with music.

Villegas García, Leonor. Algunos caracteres de la poesía romántica mexicana. México. 84 p. **[4087**
The Mexican romantic poets analyzed by this pupil of the distinguished critic, Francisco Monterde, are: Fernando Calderón, Ignacio Rodríguez Galván, Guillermo Prieto, Ignacio Ramírez ("El Nigromante"), Ignacio Manuel Altamirano, Manuel M. Flores, Manuel Acuña, Agustín F. Cuenca, Manuel Gutiérrez Nájera ("Duque Job"), and Luis G. Urbina.

Xammar, Luis Fabio. Derrotero de la nueva poesía peruana (*Rev. Indias*, segunda época, tomo 17, no. 51–52, marzo–abril, p. 82–88). **[4088**
From Chocano, Eguren and Vallejo stems the poetry of the modern Peruvian poets.

———. Escuela lírica de Alfonso Reyes (*Letras de México*, año 7, vol. 1, no. 9, sept., p. 5, 8). **[4089**
The distinguished Mexican humanist's abundant poetry production ought to be better known.

Zavala, Jesús. Mis recuerdos de Urbina (*Rep. amer.*, vol. 40, no. 5, marzo 13, p. 73–74). **[4090**
Luis G. Urbina as seen in the 'nineteen-twenties by a young admirer.

NEW EDITIONS

Bernárdez, Francisco Luis. Cielo de tierra. Buenos Aires. Ed. Sudamericana. 144 p., ilus. **[4091**
Poetry which suffers from prosiness in its least felicitous moments, but attains sometimes a rare distinction. The several poems in which Bernárdez departs from formal metrics remind one of the later phase of the Brazilian poet, Jorge de Lima. But this is a mere coincidence, since the latter's *A Túnica Inconsútil* did not precede the first edition of this work (1937).

Guillén, Nicolás. Sóngoro cosongo y otros poemas. Con una carta de don Miguel de Unamuno. Segunda ed. Habana. Ed. Páginas. 120 p. **[4092**
A welcome reissue.

Hernández, José. Martín Fierro. Nueva ed. notablemente aumentada. Estudio, notas y vocabulario de Eleuterio F. Tiscornia. Buenos Aires. Ed. Losada. 420 p. **[4093**
Third edition of Dr. Tiscornia's abridged work, not to be confused with his more exhaustive *Martín Fierro comentado y anotado* of 1925.

Martínez Villena, Rubén. La pupila insomne. Con un bosquejo biográfico de Raúl Roa. Segunda ed. Habana. Ed. Ucar, García y cía. 166 p. **[4094**
Reprint of a posthumous work which revealed the promise of a fine poet. Martínez Villena (1899–1934) was the acknowledged leader of Cuban students and workers of the extreme left, and has since his death been honored as a martyr of the cause. Roa's 60-page biography is a significant document.

Perdomo, Apolinar. Cantos de Apolo. Ciudad Trujillo. Ed. Montalvo. 165 p. **[4095**
Memorial edition of the one book of Apolinar Perdomo (1889–1918), first published posthumously in 1923. He was a belated romantic whose poetry showed defective schooling.

TRANSLATIONS

Allen, John Houghton (tr.). A Latin-American miscellany. 77 p. **[4096**
Privately printed.
About half of the text includes English translations of Spanish American poetry, selected apparently at random.

Hays, H. R. (tr.). 12 Spanish American poets. An anthology. English translations, notes, and introduction by the editor. New Haven: Yale univ. press; London: H. Milford, Oxford univ. press. vi, 336 p. **[4097**
See item 4005.

POETRY, A MAGAZINE OF VERSE. Chicago, Illinois. Vol. 62, no. 2, May, p. 61-120. [4098
Fourteen of the sixteen poets in this "Latin American" issue are Spanish Americans. Six of the fourteen cannot be said to be representative figures.

ADDENDA

Andrade y Cordero, César. Ventana al horizonte. Cuenca, Ecuador. Ed. Austral. 1942. 239 p. [4100
An important work by a poet whose intellectual preciosity does not mar his true poetic instinct.

Barrenechea, Julio. Rumor del mundo. Santiago, Chile. Ed. Nascimento. 1942. 106 p. [4101
One of the most beautiful books of verse to come out of Chile in the last few years. Barrenechea should be more widely known; the spotlight should not be directed exclusively in the direction of his compatriots Mistral, Rokha, Huidobro, and Neruda. (See article by Gabriela Mistral, "Recado para Julio Barrenechea," in *Nosotros*, segunda época, año 8, tomo 22, no. 88, julio 1943, p. 42-46.)

CANTOS A SEBASTOPOL. Homenaje de los poetas aiapeanos: 22 de julio de 1942. Montevideo. Ed. Claudio García & cía. 1942. 54 p. [4102
Twenty poets, members of the society of arts and letters "A.I.A.P.E.," pay homage to one of the Red Army's epic feats. Included among the poets is the Brazilian writer, Jorge Amado, who contributes a poem in Portuguese.

Caraballo, Isa. Celebración de los sentidos. Habana. Ed. Selecta. 1942. 162 p. [4103
Eminent writers have lavished praise on Isa Caraballo's earlier book, *Vendimia de Huracanes*. In the present work she ambitiously explores new pastures. She emerges as a singer of the "body electric" and a grandiloquent ode-maker, in addition to her other poetic activities in the fields of love, death, and foreign travel.

Córdova, Ramiro de. Neurosis en la literatura centroamericana. Managua. Ed. Nuevos horizontes. 1942. 86 p. [4104
This "contribution to the study of *Modernismo* in Guatemala, El Salvador, Honduras, Nicaragua, and Costa Rica" is a most interesting study, rich in unusual information and sound literary doctrine. Notwithstanding the title there is no psychoanalytical approach; it is simply unadulterated literary history and criticism.

Cova, J. A. (ed.). Máximos y menores poetas venezolanos. Prólogo de J. Natalicio González. Caracas. Ed. Cecilio Acosta. 1942. 2 vols.: 452 p. [4105
From Bello's *Silva a la Agricultura de la Zona Tórrida* to Lazo Martí's *Silva Criolla*, the sixteen poets in the first volume show a high degree of attachment to their native soil. In the second volume, eighteen poets explore the no-man's land of romanticism and modernism. The youngest poets represented are the distinguished fortyish group made up of Paz Castillo, Andrés Eloy Blanco, Fombona Pachano, Sotillo, and Arraiz. Brief notes on each poet, generally adequate.

Frugoni, Emilio. La elegía unánime. Introducción por Roberto Ibáñez. Buenos Aires. Ed. Losada. 1942. 169 p. [4106
The ninth book in forty-two years of a distinguished Uruguayan poet whose work never fails to reflect a noble concern for man and society. (Reviewed by Roberto F. Giusti in *Nosotros*, segunda época, año 8, tomo 20, no. 83, feb. 1943, p. 157-164.)

Miró, Rodrigo. Bibliografía poética panameña. Panamá. Imp. Nacional. 1942. 61 p. [4107
The author of *Indice de la Poesía Panameña Contemporánea* (Chile, Ercilla, 1941) has compiled this useful bibliography of the poetry published by Panamanians or in Panamá from 1872 to 1942. The work is divided into two parts: "Indice alfabético" (subdivided into national authors and foreigners) and "Indice cronológico."

Silva, José Asunción. Prosas y versos. Ed. por Carlos García-Prada. México, D. F. Ed. Cultura. 1942. xxxv, 215 p. [4107a
Two-thirds of the selections are poems. Informative introduction and notes; extensive bibliography. Second volume in the series "Clásicos de América" published under the auspices of the Instituto Internacional de Literatura Iberoamericana.

Soto-Hall, Máximo. La niña de Guatemala. El idilio trágico de José Martí. Guatemala. Tip. Nacional. 1942. 164 p. [4108
Well documented and reverently written account of Martí's stay in Guatemala, where he arrived on March 26, 1877, and met María García Granados, "la niña de Guatemala" of his unforgettable poem. Máximo Soto-Hall knew both Martí and María.

Vallejo, César. Antología de . . . Ed. por Xavier Abril. Buenos Aires. Ed. Claridad. 1942. 175 p. [4108a
About fifty pages of introductory material by various authors who see in this Peruvian poet (1894-1938) one of the most representative voices of Spanish America. Selections from *Los Heraldos Negros*, *Trilce*, *Poemas humanos*, and *España, aparta de mí este cáliz*.

BRAZILIAN LITERATURE

BY

SAMUEL PUTNAM

GENERAL STATEMENT

If the year 1942 in literary Brazil was, in a manner of speaking, one of subterranean travail,[1] the year 1943 by contrast is one that begins to show a brilliant fruition, particularly in the field of fiction. In the domain of the novel, indeed, this is the most interesting season since the mid-thirties. Jorge Amado's *Terras do Sem Fim*, Érico Verissimo's *O Resto é Silencio*, Tito Batini's *Entre o Chão e as Estrelas*, José Lins do Rego's *Fogo Morto*, Lúcio Cardoso's *Dias Perdidos*, Guilherme Figueiredo's *Rondinella*, and João Alphonsus' short story collection, *Eis a Noite!*—this is a creative harvest that would be a notable one at any time. And in addition to these well known names there are certain newcomers or comparative newcomers whose offerings are most promising. One might mention Sra. Leandro Dupré's second novel, *Eramos seis*, and Lia Corrêa Dutra's prize-winning volume of tales, *Navio sem Porto*. Sylvia Leão makes her début, with *White Shore of Olinda*, by writing not in Portuguese but directly in English. Two other new writers of talent are revealed by the contest for the Prêmio Humberto de Campos, Eliezer Burlá (*Os Braços Suplicantes*) and Leda Maria Albuquerque (*A Semana de Miss Smith*). In *O Futuro Nos Pertenece*, by Amilcar Dutra de Menezes, we have an attempt to put the ideology of the Estado Novo into a novel of the "new generation."

It is perhaps significant that the work which appeared to arouse the greatest interest on the part of the cultivated reading public was the anthology of Brazilian short story masterpieces edited by Edgard Cavalheiro and Almiro Rolmes.[2] Donatello Grieco also gives us a collection of this kind. While this interest may in part be explained by a concern, that is always present, with the literary patrimony as a whole (thus we have an anthology of lyrical masterpieces, as well, this year), there can be no doubt that the serious writers and readers of Brazil are intensely desirous of seeing the broad-teeming and tremendously diversified life of their country captured and set down in fictional form. This it is that accounts for the perennial fervor with which they turn to novelists of the past, such as Graça Aranha, whose epoch-marking *Canaã* appears in a new edition this year, and Aluízio Azevedo, whose *Obras Completas* are in course of publication.

In the realm of contemporary verse, while there are a number of volumes to be inspected, the gleanings are by no means comparable to those in the novel. Brazilian poetry at the moment appears to be of a distinctly religious-mystical trend. This impulse, always a prominent one, in recent years has been strengthened by the influence of highly skilled craftsmen like Jorge de Lima, Murilo Mendes, and others, who have found inspiration in Maritain, Bergson,

---

[1] See General Statement, *Handbook, no. 8, 1942.*
[2] See item 4234.

and similar sources.[3] In this connection attention may be drawn to the *Canto de Libertação* of Paulo Corrêa Lopes, a poet who has won the enthusiastic praise of distinguished fellow practitioners of the art. Vincius de Morais gives us his *5 Elegias.*

Mention has been made of the anthology, *As Obras Primas da Lírica Brasileira.* There are, besides, a number of important reprints of individual poets; these include the complete works of Castro Alves, Cruz e Souza, Fagundes Varela, Alvares de Azevedo, Moacir de Almeida, and Gregório de Matos, and the love poems (the *Glaura*) of Manoel Ignácio da Silva Alvarenga.

While speaking of poetry, we may note Roger Bastide's *A Poesia Afro-Brasileira,* a study of the African influence on Brazilian verse.

Another creative work of the year that is a bit hard to classify, lying as it does somewhere between the novel, poetry, and the province of folklore, is the first volume of Oswald de Andrade's *Marco Zero.* This marks the definite return to the literary scene of a writer who is by way of being the Ramón Gómez de la Serna of Brazil.[4]

In the field of the essay and literary criticism the indefatigable and almost always provocative Sra. Lucia Miguel Pereira provides us with *A Vida de Gonçalves Dias,* and M. Nogueira de Silva undertakes to sum up the Gonçalves Dias-Castro Alves controversy. The novelist, Marques Rebêlo, contributes a study of the mid-nineteenth-century writer, Manoel Antonio de Almeida, who, dying prematurely, was mourned by José Verissimo as "a talvés mais promissora esperança do romance brasileiro." Among the important critical articles in magazines may be noticed: José Vieira's on Lima Barreto; Jaime Cardoso's on Mário de Alencar; and João Dornas Filho's on Uriel Tavares. Gilberto Freyre's monumental and history-making work, the *Casa Grande & Senzala,* now goes into its fourth and definitive edition and an English translation is under way.

An outstanding bibliographical event of 1943 was the publication of the third edition of Silvio Romero's *História da Literatura Brasileira,* under the editorship of his son, Prof. Nelson Romero. Among the noteworthy reprints of early works is that of *Diálogos das Grandezas do Brasil.*

* * * *

And now it may be asked: what are the cultural trends of the year as manifested in literature? For one thing, there continues to be a good deal of interest in the literature of the mother country, Portugal, although this is not so pronounced as it has been in the past and has, possibly, more of a distinctly political tinge. We find the Portuguese writer, Vitorino Nemésio, in a letter to the Brazilian novelist, José Lins do Rego, urging "uma república das letras para Portugal e Brasil." Manuel Anselmo, well known man of letters and Portuguese consul at Recife, significantly makes use of the title, "Família literária luso-brasileira." The works of Garrett are reprinted at São Paulo; Guilherme Auler writes a book on Antônio Sardinha; and Gustavo Barroso collects *Os Melhores Contos de Portugal.* The *Revista do Brasil* has a regular department, "Letras Portuguesas," conducted by Lucia Miguel Pereira; and the continuing presence in Brazil of the great Portuguese scholar and critic, Fidelino de Figueiredo is in itself a potent cultural influence.

[3] See *Handbook, no. 1, 1935,* p.212 and item 2195.
[4] See note on item 4228.

Meanwhile, cultural relations between Portuguese-speaking and Spanish-speaking America would appear to be growing constantly more cordial. Antenor Nascentes edits an *Antologia Espanhola e Hispano-americana* for the benefit of Brazilian readers,[5] and Ronald de Carvalho's *Pequena História da Literatura Brasileira* appears in Spanish dress, at Buenos Aires. We find Oreste Plath writing on modern Chilean literature in the *Revista do Brasil*,[6] while the Argentinian Braulio Sánchez-Saes makes Carlos Drummond de Andrade known in the pages of *Sustancia*. A countryman, Paulo Ronai, performs a similar service for this poet in *Universidad Católica Bolivariana*. In *Cultura Política*, Brito Broca discusses Héctor Varela's *Elisa Lynch*, and under the auspices of the Instituto Brasileiro-Chileno de Cultura, Angyone Costa publishes his *Paisagens de Chile*. José Lins do Rego makes a lecture tour of Uruguay.

The most pronounced influence, however, upon the writing scene in Rio de Janeiro, São Paulo, and Porto Alegre would appear to be the one coming from the United States of America. "Estamos em plena voga das letras ianques," declares Broca Brito in *Cultura Política*. One is not surprised that the Livraria Martins of São Paulo publishes a short history of North American literature by Bueno Silveira (*Pequena História da Literatura Norte-americana*). Most significant of all, it may be, is the volume entitled *Vida Intelectual nos Estados Unidos*, (São Paulo, Editora Universitária. 1943? 226 p.) a remarkable symposium, with sixteen Brazilians and North Americans collaborating. As usual, numerous North American authors are brought over in translation, among the works thus rendered being William Saroyan's *Human Comedy*, Carl Van Doren's *Benjamin Franklin*, and excerpts from Franklin's own writings. A decided increase in the number of Portuguese-English, English-Portuguese dictionaries is to be noted, and is doubtless due in part to the presence of United States troops in Brazil. The cultural exchange of visitors between the two countries likewise keeps up, the novelist, Viana Moog, being one of our latest guests—he is reported to be at work upon a book of "impressions."

Translations continue to bulk large, and so far as first-rate works are concerned, it is probably safe to say that they outnumber the native product.

* * * *

A number of literary prizes were awarded during the year 1943. The Prêmio Humberto de Campos (Livraria José Olympio) for the best volume of short stories went to Lia Corrêa Dutra for *Navio sem Porto*, with Leda Maria Alburquerque (*A Semana de Miss Smith*) and Eliezer Burlá (*Os Braços Supplicantes*) receiving honorable mention. The Brazilian Academy of Letters' Ramos Paz Prize for the best novel of 1942 by a Brazilian or Portuguese writer was awarded to Afonso Schmidt for his *Irmão sem Nome*.[7] The Academy's Prêmio José Verissimo for criticism and literary history was conferred upon Afonso Arinos de Melo Franco for his introduction and notes to the

---

[5] See item 3937.

[6] See item 3897.

[7] This work and several others mentioned below in connection with prize awards had not as yet been published—or copies, at least, had not been received here—at the time this General Statement went to press. This is true of the volumes by Jacques Raimundo, Tenório de Alququerque, Gastão Cruls, and Sérgio Buarque de Holanda. These books will be noticed, as they appear, in subsequent issues of the *Handbook*.

Cartas Chilenas.[8] The Francisco Alves awards for works on the Portuguese or Brazilian language produced in 1942 were: first prize of 10,000 cruzeiros to Francisco Fernandes for his *Dicionario de Verbos e Regimes;* second prize of 5,000 cruzeiros to Jacques Raimundo for *A Lingua Portuguesa no Brasil;* third prize of 3,000 cruzeiros to A. Tenorio de Alburquerque for *A Evolução das Palavras.*

In connection with the Brazilian entries in the second Latin American Prize Contest conducted by the North American publishing house of Farrar & Rinehart, the awards in the field of the novel went to Jorge Amado (*Terras do Sem Fim*) and Oswald de Andrade (*Marco Zero*); in the field of the essay, to Gastão Cruls (*Heléia Amazônica*) and Sergio Buarque de Hollanda (*Caminhos e Fronteiras*); in the field of juvenile fiction to Marques Rebêlo and Arnaldo Tabaía (*Pequena História de Amor*).[9] In connection with the entries for the novel prize. José Lins do Rego received one vote for his *Agua Mãe*,[10] and Affonso d' E. Taunay was given one vote for his biography, *Bartolomeu de Gusmão*.[11]

In commemoration of the centenary of the author of *Inocência*, the Prêmio Taunay of the Biblioteca Militar was awarded to Manuel Cavalcanti Proença for his *Ribeira de São Francisco*. The Prêmio Raúl de Leoni of the Academia Carioca de Letras was bestowed upon J. G. de Araujo Jorge for his book of poems, *Eterno Motivo.*

Brazil had at least three literary centennials to observe in 1943, those of the birth of the Visconde de Taunay and Teófilo Braga (the latter passed practically unnoticed) and that of the death of Robert Southey. The anniversary that received the most attention, however, was that of a book, the *Urupês* of Monteiro Lobato, the short story collection of a quarter of a century ago that remains a milestone in Brazilian literature. (See the article by Gilberto Freyre in the *Revista do Brasil*.) During the year two leading Brazilian writers celebrated their fiftieth birthdays; they were Tristão de Ataide (Alceu Amoroso Lima) and Mário de Andrade.

Deeply mourned in Brazil was the death of the Argentine translator, Benjamín de Garay. Awarded the Ordem do Cruzeiro do Sul by the Brazilian government for his services to Brazilian culture, Benjamín de Garay was a vital link between intellectuals of his own country and language and those of Brazil. Among the numerous works that he had rendered into Spanish was Euclides da Cunha's *Os Sertões*. In writing of him, Gilberto Freyre observes that for this Argentinian "um escritor brasileiro, mesmo mediocre, era quasi como se fosse um rei. Mais que um embaixador, que um ministro, que um general. A literatura ha trinta anos que era sua Passargada. Uma Passargada onde êle foi amigo de reis. Onde conheceu Euclides da Cunha, Bilac, Coelho Neto." [12]

Announcement was made this year that the Stefan Zweig heirs had presented the Brazilian government with a complete collection of Zweig's works in the original German and in various foreign language editions, along with the books in his library, his letters, diaries, notes, etc., as well as his house-

---

[8] See *Handbook, no. 6, 1940*, items 4293 and 4321.
[9] See *Handbook, no. 8, 1942*, item 4484.
[10] See *Handbook, no. 7, 1941*, item 4976.
[11] See *Handbook, no. 8, 1942*, item 4169.
[12] See note in the *Revista do Brasil*, ano 6, tercera fase, no. 54, junho, p. 126.

hold furnishings, personal belongings, his paintings and other works of art, photographs of the author and his friends, etc. This material will be in charge of the Brazilian Educational Association, and the plan is to install it as a museum in the house where Zweig and his wife committed suicide. Two well known writers, Dr. Menotti del Picchia and Dr. Osório de Almeida, were elected to the Brazilian Academy of Letters in 1943. Of interest to bibliophiles is the founding of A Sociedade dos Cem Bibliófilos do Brasil, which will issue one de luxe volume a year. The one chosen for 1943 was the *Memórias Póstumas de Braz Cubas* of Machado de Assis, with illustrations by Portinari.

In a most unusual poll taken by a Rio de Janeiro newspaper, one-hundred-eighty Brazilian writers cast their ballots to determine the ten greatest novelists that the country has produced. The novelists thus selected were: Machado de Assis, Aluizio Azevedo, Graciliano Ramos, José Lins do Rego, Lima Barreto, Jorge Amado, Raul Pompéia, José de Alencar, Manoel Antônio de Almeida, and Raquel de Queiroz. It will be seen that only four living novelists are included: Amado, Ramos, Lins do Rego, and Raquel de Queiroz. The greatest number of votes given to a single work went to *Dom Casmurro*, by Machado de Assis.

Perhaps the most interesting literary controversy of the year was the one provoked by an attack on Gilberto Freyre that was made by certain members of the Law Faculty of Recife. Students and others promptly came to Freyre's support.

BIBLIOGRAPHY

LINGUISTICS, DICTIONARIES, ENCYCLOPEDIAS, BIBLIOGRAPHIES

Ackerman, Fritz. Bibliografia de Gonçalves Dias (*Bol. bibliog.*, São Paulo, ano 1, vol. 1, out.–dez., p. 53–56). [4109
   For other Gonçalves Dias items of this year, see the works by Lucia Miguel Pereira (item 4189) and M. Nogueira da Silva (item 4210).

Binns, Harold Howard. Dicionário inglês-português. São Paulo. (Col. O Livro de bolso). 287 p. [4110

Campos, Ipê de. Vocabulário ortográfico moderno. Segunda ed. São Paulo. (Col. O Livro de bolso, no. 7). 431 p. [4111
   A dictionary with the new approved spelling, in convenient pocket size.

Christie, Christina. African influence in the Brazilian-Portuguese language and literature (*Hispania*, Washington, vol. 26, no. 3, Oct., p. 259–266). [4112
   Informative article on a philological question that has been the subject of considerable research in recent years.

Fernandes, Francisco. Dicionário de verbos e regimes. Terceira ed. Porto Alegre. Ed. Globo. 623 p. [4114
   For the first edition of this work, see *Handbook, no. 6, 1940,* item 4416. For a review of the third edition, by Valdemar Cavalcanti, see *Revista do Brasil*, ano 6, terceira fase, no. 54, junho, p. 106–107. "Na bibliografia brasileira," says Sr. Cavalcanti, "não existe nenhum livro similar.... Trabalho paciente, de chinês, executado com o necessario método e espírito de sistema.... O sr. Francisco Fernandes é um impenitente conquistador de verbos; um d. Juan terrivel e sempre insatisfeito." The critic finds that the praise originally given the work in the *Revista do Brasil* (ano 3, terceira fase, no. 25, julho, 1940, p. 72–73) was fully merited: "excelente realização"; "obra valiosíssima"; "obra madura"; etc. The author himself tells us that this is a "longo e exhaustivo trabalho de vários anos." One especial merit is that Sr. Fernandes has drawn upon contemporary writers as well as those of the past for his examples, although, as Cavalcanti points out, he could profitably go still further in this direction.

Gonçalves, Francisco. A palavra *Qué*, Funções. Observações. Concordância. Exercícios práticos. Rio de Janeiro. Coed. brasílica. 202 p. [4115

Leão, Múcio. Bibliografia de João Ribeiro (*Bol. bibliog.*, São Paulo, ano 1, vol. 1, out.–dez., p. 1–7, 112). [4116
   Bibliography of the nineteenth-century historian and critical essayist.

Lima, Carlos Henrique de. Teoria de análise sintática. Prefácio do professor

Antonio Honaiss. Rio de Janeiro. Livr. Francisco Alves. 103 p. [4117

Lima, Hildebrando de, and **Gustavo Barroso.** Pequeno dicionário brasileiro da lingua portuguesa. Revisto por Manuel Bandeira e José Batista da Luz. Redigido nas ortografias simplificada e mista. Quarta ed. São Paulo. Ed. Civilização brasileira. 1,234 p. [4118
This fourth edition has been basically revised and augmented by a number of collaborators: Antenor Nascentes; Aurelio Buarque de Holanda Ferreira; C. Delgado de Carvalho; Fernando de Azevedo; Francisco Venâncio Filho; José Batista da Luz; Leonor de Azeredo Pena; Oscar Monte; Rene Laclette; and Tales Melo Carvalho.

Machado Filho, Aires da Mata. A gramática e o ensino da lingua (*Rev. Brasil,* ano 6, terceira fase, no. 53, março, p. 24–28). [4119
On the place of grammar in language study.

Magalhães, Alvaro. Dicionário enciclopédico brasileiro. Porto Alegre. Ed. Globo. 1943? 1557 p. [4120
In the preparation of this work, Professor Magalhães has been assisted by a staff of more than fifty specialists, including Francisco Fernandes, Érico Veríssimo, Everardo Backheuser, Aroldo de Azevedo, Balduino Rambo, Amaral Fontoura, and others. Illustrated.

Nabuco, Joaquim. Bibliófilos versus bibliófagos. Rio de Janeiro. Livr. J. Leite. 87 p. [4121
The eloquent and biting title of this brochure speaks for itself. The author is concerned with the conservation of Brazilian libraries and archives. There is a preface by Prof. Artur Neiva. Illustrated with engravings.

Oliveira, J. Lourenço de. Tratado de acentuação gráfica ou topológia diacrítica. Belo Horizonte. Imp. oficial de Minas Gerais. 61 p. [4122
This is based upon the vocabulary of the Brazilian Academy of Letters and the law (no. 5,186) of January 13, 1943.

Prazeres, Rimus; Almir da Câmara de **Matos** Peixoto; and **Lídio Costa.** Dicionário geográfico, gramatical e biográfico ilustrado. Rio de Janeiro. Ed. Brasileira artística. 32 p. [4123

Putnam, Samuel. A selective guide to the material published in 1942 on language and literature: Brazil (*Handbook, no. 8, 1942,* p. 379–400). [4124

Reis, Antônio Simões dos. Pseudônimos brasileiros. Pequenos verbetes para um dicionário. Primeira série. Segundo vol. Rio de Janeiro. Ed. Zélio Valverde. 63 p. [4125

Silva Neto, Serafim. Crítica serena. Erros e confusões e atrasos do Sr. Cândido Jucá Filho. Postscriptum. Rio de Janeiro. 8 p. [4126
A postscript to the author's *Miscelânea Filológica* (*Handbook, no. 7, 1941,* item 5126). For Cândido Jucá Filho's work, see *Handbook, no. 3, 1937,* item 3584. A philological controversy.

Torres, Artur de Almeida. Questões filológicas. Rio de Janeiro. Ed. Irmãos Pongetti. 118 p. [4127
On a variety of philological topics.

CRITICISM, ESSAYS, BIOGRAPHIES, MEMOIRS, TRAVEL BOOKS, ANTHOLOGIES, MISCELLANEOUS PROSE, COLLECTED WORKS (PROSE AND POETRY)

(See also items 900, 901, 3419, 3428)

A. A. [Athayde, Austregesilo de]. Maurois e o jardim (*Rev. Brasil,* ano 6, terceira fase, no. 53, março, p. 138–139). [4128
An acerb but merited note on what might be termed the Ivory-Towerism of André Maurois with respect to the struggle against fascism on the cultural plane, based upon Maurois' own memoirs.

Andrade, Gilberto Osório de. América hispânica e América saxônica. Recife. Diretório acadêmico da Faculdade de direito de Recife. 58 p. [4129
Lecture delivered at the Recife Law School on November 21, 1942, in the presence of the consular corps of the various American republics. A graceful gesture designed to promote good-neighborliness. Dedicated to Gilberto Freyre. Gaston Figueira thinks the title might better have been: *América Ibérica e América Saxônica.*

Andrade, João Pedro de. A poesia da modérníssima geração. Génese duma atitude poética. Porto Alegre. Livr. Latina. (Cads. azuis, Literatura e arte, no. 7). 58 p. [4130
For understanding the poets of today.

Andrade, Mário de. Aspectos de literatura brasileira. Rio de Janeiro. Americ-ed. 256 p. [4131
This book contains essays on Tristão de Ataide, Luis Aranha, Machado de Assis, Castro Alves, and others.

———. O baile dos quatro artes. São Paulo. Livr. Martins. [4132
A collection of five essays: "A arte e o artezão"; "Romantismo musical"; "A fantasia de Walt Disney"; "O romanceiro do lampeão"; and "Chopin." The volume is of particular interest to music lovers, while "O romanceiro do lampeão" touches on native folklore.

———. Os filhos da Candinha. São Paulo. Livr. Martins. [4133
Collected articles on literary and artistic subjects, from 1929 to the present time. The author has been termed "the Pope of Brazilian modernism" and he did, indeed, make literary history in the 1920's.

Anselmo, Manuel. Família literária luso-brasileira. Rio de Janeiro. Ed. José Olympio. [4134
Essays on literature and aesthetics, by the Portuguese consul at Recife who happens to be at the same time a well known man of letters. On the *Família Literária Luso-brasileira,* see General Statement. The essays are classified under the headings: "A poesia e alguns problemas"; "O ensáio, a crítica e a crônica"; and "O romance e as personalidades." They consist of reviews and articles that have previously appeared in periodical publications.

ANUÁRIO BRASILEIRO DE LITERATURA, 1942. No. 6. Rio de Janeiro. Ed. Irmãos Pongetti. 249 p. [4135
Brazil's distinguished literary annual has some while since become an institution. It is as usual rich in literary and artistic material and is attractively illustrated.

Auler, Guilherme. Antônio Sardinha. Recife. Ciclo cultural luso-brasileiro. 273 p. [4135a
On the Portuguese "integralist" writer who was the leader of the early century literary school in his country that opposed democracy and espoused the cause of monarchy. He died in 1925.

Barbosa, Francisco de Assis. Cronologia de Hipólito José da Costa (*Rev. Brasil,* ano 6, terceira fase, no. 55, set., p. 41–51). [4136
For the as yet to be written biography of the famous early-nineteenth-century publisher and editor of the *Corréio Brasiliense.*

Barros, Jaime de. A formação da literatura brasileira (*Cultura política,* ano 3, no. 23, jan., p. 101–106). [4137
The author's point of view is set forth in his opening paragraph: "Erro inicial e frequente em alguns historiadores literários é separar a literatura de um povo da sua história ecônomica, política, social, de que ela constitue apenas uma das manifestações." However, the brief space at his command makes it possible for him here to do little more than scrape the surface of his theme.

Bastide, Roger. A poesia afro-brasileira. São Paulo. Livr. Martins. (Col. Mosáico, no. 4). 151 p. [4138
A study of the African influence in Brazilian poetry, by a professor of the University of São Paulo. Mulatto writers of the eighteenth century, Caldas Barbosa, Silva Avarenga, and others are briefly considered, more space being given to such nineteenth century figures as Gonçalves Dias, Gonçalves Crespo, and the great symbolist poet, Cruz e Souza. At least one critic, Hélio Vianna, expresses a slight feeling of dissatisfaction with the volume: ". . . seus julgamentos são feitos mais *de fóra* que *de dentro.* Isto é, partem de quem julga um caso exótico, não de quem compreende uma questão interna. . . ."

Bloch, Pedro. Grande era o Couto! Rio de Janeiro. Est. de artes gráf. C. Mendes Junior. 156 p. [4139
Described as a "romance-biografia" of Miguel Couto, the Brazilian physician and professor (1865–1934). He was noted, among other things for his studies of yellow fever.

Braga, Rubem. A lira contra o muro. [4140
This, the author's second book of *crônicas,* has a most unusual dedication: "Dedico este livro aos companheiros do *Corréio do Povo* e da *Folha da Tarde,* e aos amigos de Pôrto Alegre, com um forte abraço de gratidão. Esta é a minha dedicatória a favor, mas como andamos em tempo de guerra quero fazer uma dedicatória contra. E comece por Hitler, mas não fique nesse grande cão escandaloso nem nos que latem e mordem de sua banda. Atinja, aquí e alí, todos os que, no claro e no escuro, trabalham mesquinhamente contra o amanhã. Aos carniceiros prudentes e ás velhas aves de rapina barrigudas e todavia insensatas; aos constructores de brejos e aos vendedores de agua podre; aos que separam os homens pela raça e privilégios; aos que aborrecem e temem a voz do homem simples e o vento do mar; e aos urubús, aos urubús."

Brandão, Ambrosio Fernandes (ed.). Diálogos das grandezas do Brasil. Rio de Janeiro. Dois mundos ed. 318 p. [4141
Reprint of the classic early-seventeenth-century work, with an *"apresentação"* by Jaime Cortesão, a preliminary note by Afrânio Peixoto, an introduction by Capistrano de Abreu, and notes by Rodolfo Garcia. This is truly a distinguished assemblage of editorial names. Sr. Garcia has added more notes to those that he provided for the previous edition by the Brazilian Academy under the editorship of Peixoto. This is a critical edition in the true sense of the word, and an authoritative one.

Broca, Brito. A literatura da guerra no Brasil (*Cultura política,* ano 3, no. 31, agosto 22, p. 310–317). [4142
A study of the literature to which war has given rise in Brazil from the time of the Visconde de Taunay and his *Retirada da Laguna* down through Euclides da Cunha and *Os Sertões* to the present era. There is a section on "Machado de Assis e a guerra do Paraguai," one on José de Alencar and *A Guerra dos Mascates,* one on the war theme in romantic poetry, etc. An informative and valuable article.

———. O livro de Héctor Varela (*Cultura política,* ano 3, no. 23, jan., p. 109–112). [4143
On the Argentine writer's *Elisa Lynch.*

———. O romance de Diamantina (*Cultura política,* ano 3, no. 30, agosto, p. 137–142). [4144
On the *Memórias do Distrito Diamantina e da comarca de Serro Frio* of Joaquim

Felício, revolving about the ancient and legendary city of Diamantina in the northern part of Minas Gerais.

Calmon, Pedro. História do Brasil no poesia do povo. Rio de Janeiro. Ed. A. Noite. 1943? 333 p. [4145
An interesting and important treatise by a historian and novelist who is well fitted to deal with the subject.

Cardoso, Jaime. Mário de Alencar, Ateniense (*Rev. Brasil*, ano 6, terceira fase, no. 53, março, p. 32-50). [4146
A study of the son of the famous nineteenth-century novelist, José de Alencar, a son who as poet and prose writer and in his intellectual attitudes contrasted so vividly with his father. Jaime Cardoso sees in Mário de Alencar "todas as virtudes estéticas que so as longas civilizações possibilitam ... um fidalgo de espírito ... um heleno cuja heráldica de processos remontava, em plena conciência, ao jardim ateniense de Platão...."

Carpeaux, Otto Maria (pseud.). Aspectos sociais da história literária brasileira (*Rumo*, terceira fase, ano 1, vol. 1, no. 2, terceiro trim., p. 17-21). [4147
Much attention has been given in recent years to the economic side of Brazilian literary history. The present writer is concerned with the social.

Carvalho, Ronald de. Pequeña historia de la literatura brasileña. Buenos Aires. Imp. Mercatali. (Bibl. de autores brasileños traducidos al castellano, no. 10). 441 p. [4148
This standard brief history of Brazilian literature, first published in 1919 (Rio de Janeiro, F. Briguiet & cia.), has been rendered into Spanish by Prof. Julio E. Payró and has been provided with a foreword by Rómulo Zabala. A sixth Brazilian edition appeared in 1937 (F. Briguiet & cia.) and in the same year an Italian translation was published in Florence (*Handbook, no. 3, 1937*, item 3481).

Cavalcanti, Povina. Ausência da poesia. Rio de Janeiro. Ed. A. Coelho Franco F.º 229 p. [4149
A critical consideration.

Docca, Souza. Visconde de Taunay (*Estud. confer.*, no. 19, abril, p. 5-16). [4150
Interesting paper by a modern military man on the author of the *Retirada da Laguna*.

Dornas Filho, João. A influência social do negro brasileiro. Curitiba. Ed. Guaíra. [4151
It is of interest to compare this treatise with the various works of Gilberto Freyre, Arthur Ramos, and others, and the researches represented by the participants in the Afro-Brazilian Congresses held in recent years.

———. A vida silenciosa e atormentada de Uriel Tavares. Alguns versos inéditos do poeta-lavrador de Muzambinho (*Rev. Brasil*, ano 6, terceira fase, no. 55, set., p. 52-57). [4152
On the tragic life of the poet Minas Gerais who was "discovered" by the late Jackson de Figueiredo in his book, *Humilhados e Luminosos*. Born in 1891. Uriel Tavares died in 1938.

Figueira, Gaston. Visión de la nueva poesía del Brasil, II (*Rev. iberoamer.*, vol. 7, no. 13, nov., p. 81-101). [4153
An Uruguayan poet on the poetry of Brazil.

Figueiredo, Fidelino de. Criteriology and literature (*Books abroad*, vol. 17, no. 2, spring, p. 112-115). [4154
A paper contributed from the University of São Paulo, where the eminent Portuguese scholar is at present stationed.

Figueiredo, Guilherme. Os cliches da comdéia brasileira (*Rev. Brasil*, ano 6, terceira fase, no. 54, junho, p. 117-121). [4155
An article that will appeal to all those interested in the Brazilian theater.

Freitas, Bezerra de. O pensamento social na literatura brasileira (*Cultura política*, ano 3, no. 35, dez., p. 243-247). [4156
A brief schematic study of value to the literary historian. Bezerra de Freitas is the author of a school-text, the *História da Literatura Brasileira* (see *Handbook, no. 5, 1939*, item 3911).

Freitas Júnior, Otávio de. Ensaios de nosso tempo. Rio de Janeiro. Ed. da Casa do estudante do Brasil. 125 p. [4157
Essays in contemporary sociology. With a preface by Mário de Andrade, one of the leaders of the modernist movement of the 1920's.

Freyre, Gilberto. Atualidade de Euclides da Cunha. Segunda ed. Rio de Janeiro. Ed. de C. E. B. 63 p. [4158
See *Handbook, no. 7, 1941*, item 4881.

———. Casa grande & senzala. Formação da família brasileira sob o regime de economia patriarcal. Quarta ed., definitiva. Rio de Janeiro. Ed. José Olympio. 2 vols., 780 p. [4159
This truly epoch-marking work was first published in 1933, in Rio de Janeiro (Maia & Schmidt, Ltda.). See the review by Manoel da Silva Soares Cardozo, *Books Abroad*, vol. 8, no. 4, Oct., 1934, p. 478-479. A second edition appeared in 1936 (see *Handbook, no. 2, 1936*, item 1635). A third edition was published in 1938. On the storm occasioned by *Casa Grande e Senzala* in certain reactionary circles, see the General Statement, *Handbook, 2, 1936*). This attack has from time to time been renewed, but Freyre has found warm defenders. (See General Statement.) For his own view of his work and the reception accorded it, see his article "A propósito de um livro

em terceira edição," *Revista do Brasil*, ano 1, no. 1, terceira fase, julho, 1938, p. 33–40. For Freyre's background, the reader may be referred to Dr. Lewis Hanke's article, "Gilberto Freyre: Brazilian Social Historian," *Quart. Journ. Inter-Amer. Rels.*, vol. 1, no. 3, July, 1939, p. 24–44. (A Spanish version of this article appeared in the *Revista Hispánica Moderna*, año 5, no. 2, abril, 1939, p. 98–120.) For further background material, of a personal nature, see Dr. Robert C. Smith's review of Freyre's *Região e Tradição*, in the *Inter-Amer. Quart.*, vol. 3, no. 4, Oct., 1941, p. 110–114. See also, Dr. W. Rex Crawford's *A Century of Latin American Thought* (Harvard University Press, 1944), p. 203–217. An English translation of *Casa Grande & Senzala*, by the editor of this section, is at present in course of preparation. A Spanish translation was made by the late Benjamín de Garay of Argentina, translator of Euclides da Cunha's *Os Sertões* (see *Handbook, no. 8, 1942*, item 4207).

———. Continente e ilha. Rio de Janeiro. Ed. da C. E. B. 69 p. [4160]
Lecture given in the State Library of Rio Grande do Sul, November 19, 1940.

———. Vinte e cinco anos depois (*Rev. Brasil*, ano 6, terceira fase, no. 55, set., p. 136–137). [4161]
Reprint of an article published in *O Jornal*, on the twenty-fifth anniversary of the appearance of the *Urupês* of Monteiro Lobato (see item 4251) and the significance of this work for Brazilian letters. See General Statement.

Fusco, Rosário. A literatura brasileira no começo do século 19 (*Cultura política*, ano 3, no. 23, jan., p. 107–108). [4162]
On the relation of early-century Brazilian writing to European movements. On the author of this article, see *Handbook, no. 6, 1940*, p. 376 and items 4308 and 4309.

Goyochêa, Castilhos, and **Ivan Lins.** Orações. Rio de Janeiro. Gráf. Sauer. (Bibl. da Acadêmia carioca de letras, cad. 6). 67 p. [4163]
Addresses before the Acadêmia Carioca de Letras.

Grieco, Agrippino. Ai dos livros! (*Rev. Brasil*, ano 6, terceira fase, no. 55, set., p. 137–140). [4164]
A bitingly witty article on the sins (ignorance) of translators and the fate of foreign books in Brazil. Reprinted from *O Jornal*.

Hamilton, D. Lee. A vida e as obras de José de Anchieta (*Hispania*, Washington, vol. 26, no. 4, Dec., p. 407–427). [4165]
A comprehensive view, in some twenty pages, of the life and works of Brazil's great Jesuit missionary, pioneer, and pioneer writer, Anchieta. Cf. the work by Simão de Vasconcelos (item 4218) and the biography by Jorge de Lima (Rio de Janeiro, Civilização Brasileira, 1934).

LANTERNA VERDE. No. 7. Rio de Janeiro. Sociedade Felipe d'Oliveira. 191 p. [4166]
This compilation, representing the contributions of a number of writers, is always an interesting one, and the seventh issue lives up to its predecessors.

Leão, Antônio Carneiro. Meus heróis. Rio de Janeiro. Ed. A Noite. 1943? 261 p. [4167]
Biographical sketches. Drawings by Armando Pacheco.

Lima, Alceu Amoroso. A igreja e o novo mundo. Problemas de cultura contemporânea. Rio de Janeiro. Livr. Zélio Valverde. xv, 194 p. [4168]
By the well known Catholic intellectual, who also writes under the name of Tristão de Athayde.

Lima, Hermes. O pensamento vivo de Tobias Barreto. São Paulo. Livr. Martins. 1943? (Bibl. do Pensamento vivo). 193 p. [4169]
Cf. the lecture by Nelson Romero (item 4198).

Lima, Medeiros. O homem na obra de Graciliano Ramos (*Rumo*, terceira fase, ano 1, vol. 1, no. 1, primeiro trim., p. 71–74). [4170]
Brief study of the human element in the work of one of Brazil's most significant present day novelists.

Lins, Álvaro. Jornal de crítica. Segunda série. Rio de Janeiro. Ed. José Olympio. 360 p. [4171]
On Lins and his *Jornal de Crítica*, see *Handbook, no. 7, 1941*, item 4895.

Lins, Ivan Monteiro de Barros, and **Carlos Süssekind de Mendonça.** Orações. Rio de Janeiro. Gráf. Sauer. (Bibl. da Acadêmia carioca de letras, cad. 4). 117 p. [4172]
Addresses delivered before the Acadêmia Carioca de Letras.

Lopes, Luciano, and **Carlos Süssekind de Mendonça.** Orações. Rio de Janeiro. Graf. Sauer. (Bibl. da Acadêmia carioca de letras, cad. 8). 96 p. [4173]
Addresses delivered before the Acadêmia Carioca de Letras.

Lousada, Wilson. Notas sobre literatura infantil (*Cultura política*, ano 3, no. 27, maio, p. 131–137). [4174]
Some fresh observations on the subject.

Magalhães, Basílio de. As primas obras de filosofia e de ficção, de autoria brasileira (*Rumo*, terceira fase, ano 1, vol. 1, no. 3, quarto trim., p. 47–52). [4175]
Study in the beginnings of Brazilian prose by a recognized authority.

Martins, Wilson. Literatura do Paraná (*Cultura política*, ano 3, no. 32, set., p. 88-91). [4176
In which the author confesses that he is writing about something that does not exist. He sets forth the reasons.

Maul, Carlos. A marquesa de Santos. Segunda ed. Rio de Janeiro. Ed. Zélio Valverde. [4177
This work, portraying the subject as "um modelo de matrona," has been rightly described as a eulogy rather than a biography. The second edition has additional notes and engravings.

Menucci, Sud. Machado de Assis. São Paulo. 61 p. [4178
A lecture on the subject, now issued in pamphlet form.

Moniz, Edmundo. Francisco Alves de Oliveira. Rio de Janeiro. (Publ. da Acad. brasileira, 3. Bibliografia.) 139 p. [4179
On the work of the Brazilian publisher and writer. The bibliographical notes are by Osvaldo Melo Braga. Sixteen illustrations.

Montelo, Josué. Como Aluísio Azevedo se fez romancista (*Cultura política*, ano 3, no. 26, abril, p. 180-183). [4180
The literary "*formação*," as the Brazilians would call it, of one of their outstanding novelists of the nineteenth century.

———. Machado de Assis e a literatura nacional (*Cultura política*, ano 3, no. 32, set., p. 92-95). [4181
A study of Machado de Assis' stylistic contributions.

Moog, Clodomir Viana. Uma interpretação da literatura brasileira. Rio de Janeiro. Casa do estudante do Brasil. 80 p. [4182
Brief essay by a prominent creative writer of today, author of *Um Rio Imita o Reno* (*Handbook, no. 5, 1939*, item 3977), *Novas Cartas Persanas* (*Handbook, no. 3, 1937*, item, 3511), etc. His critical works include *Eça de Queiroz e o Século 19*, of 1938 (see *Handbook, no. 5, 1939*, item 4081a), and *Heróis de Decadência* (*Handbook, no. 5, 1939*, item 3933a).

Nemésio, Vitorino. Uma república das letras para Portugal e Brasil. Carta a José Lins do Rêgo (*Rev. Brasil*, ano 6, terceira fase, no. 55, set., p. 20-23). [4183
On the significance of this letter, see General Statement.

Ornellas, Manoelito de. Símbolos bárbaros. Porto Alegre. Ed. Globo. 166 p. [4184
Collection of essays by a well known journalist and lecturer. There are half a dozen in all. Among the more interesting ones are: "Caminhos do modernismo"; "O cisne branco do simbolismo"; and "Tradições e símbolos." The first mentioned deals with the modern art movement ("*modernismo*") that started about the year 1922. A number of famous personages of the twenties, some of them all but forgotten now, live again in these pages.

Passos, Alexandre. A nova geração intelectual de Baia. Rio de Janeiro. Ed. Irmãos Pongetti. 27 p. [4185
This little pamphlet is an addition to the author's essay, *Letras Baianas*. For the literary-cultural historian.

Pereira, Lucia Miguel. Ainda Antero de Quental (*Rev. Brasil*, ano 6, terceira fase, no. 53, março, p. 105-106). [4186
On Antero de Quental, see *Handbook, no. 8, 1942*, General Statement and works cited.

———. Letras portuguesas (*Rev. Brasil*, ano 6, terceira fase, no. 54, junho, p. 111-112). [4187
On the edition of the *Obras Completas* of Gonçalves Crespo (Edições Libros de Portugal). Sra. Miguel-Pereira stresses the essentially Brazilian character of the poet's work.

———. Letras portuguesas (*Rev. Brasil*, ano 6, terceira fase, no. 55, set., p. 112-114). [4188
On the edition (Edições Dois Mundos) of selections from *As Farpas* by Ramalho Ortigão and Eça de Queiroz. "*As Farpas* não deviam sobrevivir aos seus autores. Não são, afinal, nenhuma obra prima. Mas não só não morreram, como estão bem vivas."

———. A vida de Gonçalves Dias. Contendo o diário inédito da viagem de Gonçalves Dias ao Rio Negro. Rio de Janeiro. Ed. José Olympio. 424 p. [4189
An important biographical-critical study of one of the leading Brazilian poets of the last century, by a distinguished critic of today. While sympathetic to her subject, the author has a rigorous respect for the truth and endeavors to let the poet speak for himself in so far as is possible. The work is richly documented. On Sra. Miguel Pereira, see *Handbook, no. 4, 1938*, items 4168, 4169, 4232, and 4232a. Her *Machado de Assis*, published in 1937, occasioned a lively critical controversy (see *Handbook, no. 3, 1937*, item 3507). Cf. the work by M. Nogueira da Silva (item 4210).

Pontes, Eloi. Machado de Assis. São Paulo. Ed. Cultura. (Vidas luminosas). 91 p. [4190
A brief biographical sketch by the author of *A Vida Contradictória de Machado de Assis* (see *Handbook, no. 5, 1939*, item 3946). With a portrait of the subject.

Portela, Bastos. Cenas da nossa vida literária (*Cultura política*, ano 3, no. 24, fev., p. 115-118; no. 32, set., p. 103-107). [4191
On the disappearance of the *vie de Bohème* in the Brazilian capital. The author quotes the dictum of a Rio journalist: "Foi o futebol que desferiu o golpe de morte na boêmia literária do Rio."

Putnam, Samuel. Dom Pedro of Brazil (*Int. amer.*, vol. 2, no. 1, Jan., p. 32–33). **[4192]**
Review of Sergio Corrêa da Costa's *As Quatro Coroas de d. Pedro I.* (*Handbook*, no. 7, *1941*, item 4871a); Christivano de Camargo's *O Principe Galante* (*Handbook*, no. 7, *1941*, item 4989a); and the *Cartas de d. Pedro I. a d. João VI.*, edited by Augusto de Lima Junior (*Handbook*, no. 7, *1941*, item 3611).

———. Race and nation in Brazil (*Science and society*, vol. 7, no. 4, fall, p. 321–337). **[4193]**
A consideration of the views of Euclides da Cunha as set forth in *Os Sertões*.

Rangel, Alberto. Trasanteontem. São Paulo. Livr. Martins. 242 p., ilus. **[4194]**
Another charming book by the now famous author of *Inferno Verde*. Rich in picturesque details out of Brazil's forgotten past.

Rebêlo, Marques. Vida e obra de Manoel António de Almeida. Rio de Janeiro. Imp. Zélio Valverde. (Min. da educação e saúde, Inst. nac. do livro, Col. B 3, Biografia, 1). 132 p. **[4195]**
When Manoel António de Almeida died in a shipwreck at the age of thirty, in 1861, José Verissimo wrote of him: "Com êle pode dizer-se, naufragou a talvés mais promissora esperança do romance brasileiro." It is, accordingly, altogether fitting that he should be studied as he is here by one of Brazil's leading contemporary novelists. Speaking of Almeida's *Memórias de um Sargento de Milicias*, Verissimo referred to it as "essa obra até então a mais original e a mais viva da nossa ficção." Silvio Romero termed this same work "um dos livros mais garbados das letras brasileiras." Rebêlo gives an interesting account of the various editions of the *Memorias*, including the famous bowdlerised seventh edition. Almeida was in a sense *homo unius libri*; his other writings, such as they are, find due consideration in the present volume. His labors as a translator and critic are also discussed. The Rebêlo essay gives evidence of minute and exhaustive research and represents a real contribution to the history of Brazilian literature.

Ribeiro, Maria Rosa Moreira. O teatro no estado nacional (*Estud. confer.*, no. 19, abril, p. 59–70). **[4196]**
Lecture given on February 20, 1943, at the Instituto Nacional de Ciência Política.

Rodrigues, Lysias A. Roteiro do Tocantins. Rio de Janeiro. Ed. José Olympio. **[4197]**
The author of this decidedly unliterary work from the point of view of style, which none the less holds its literary interest, was a member of the exploring expedition of 1931, preliminary to the opening of the Tocantins air route in the states of Goias, Maranhão, and Pará. As an aviator he later explored the same region by air, in 1935. The account is written in a simple unaffected manner, but the author's enthusiasm, which has led him to be compared to Saint-Exupéry, livens the pages of the factual narrative. There are a number of contributions to regional folklore.

Romero, Nelson. Tobias Barreto. Rio de Janeiro. Of. gráfs. O Globo. 29 p. **[4198]**
This is the address delivered by Sr. Nelson at the Instituto Brasileiro de Cultura on June 13, 1939, in commemoration of the Tobias Barreto centenary (see *Handbook*, no. 5, *1939*, p. 355). Cf. the work of Hermes Lima (item 4169).

Romero, Sílvio. História da literatura brasileira. Terceira ed. Rio de Janeiro. Ed. José Olympio. (Col. Documentos brasileiros, no. 24, 24-A, 24-B, 24-C, 24-D). 5 vols.: 337; 370; 385; 358; 481 p. **[4199]**
One of the literary-bibliographical events of the year in Brazil is the publication of this new and greatly enlarged edition of Sílvio Romero, the turn-of-the-century critic and historian of Brazilian literature. This edition has been prepared by the author's son, Prof. Nelson Romero. Where previous editions were in two volumes, this one, it will be noted, is in five. At the time of his death Sílvio Romero had gathered the material for a third volume; and in addition, the son has collected other writings of his father to make two more volumes. This work, running to nearly 2,000 pages, is truly a monumental one. An anonymous commentator in *Cultura Política* observes: "Hoje, principalmente, com a nova edição, temos nessa obra verdadeira suma do Brasil mental."

Rónai, Paulo. Letras del Brasil, no. 4. Carlos Drummond de Andrade. *Poesía* (*Univ. cat. bolivariana*, vol. 9, no. 29, feb.–marzo, p. 97–104). **[4200]**
Cf. the article by Sánchez-Saes (item 4209).

———. Letras del Brasil, no. 5. Aurélio Buarque de Hollanda, *Dois mundos* (*Univ. cat. bolivivariana*, vol. 9, no. 30–31, abril-junio, p. 292–296). **[4201]**

———. A poesia de Carlos Drummond de Andrade (*Rev. Brasil*, ano 6, terceira fase, no. 56, dez., p. 26–32). **[4202]**
Important study of one of the most important of modern Brazilian poets.

Salgado, Álvaro F. Vida e poesia de Alberto de Oliveira (*Cultura política*, ano 3, no. 30, agôsto, p. 147–152). **[4203]**
Study of a nineteenth-century poet.

———. Vida e poesia de Carvalho Júnior (*Cultura política*, ano 3, no. 32, set., p. 96–102). **[4204]**
Study of a poet who, according to the author, was one of the precursors of the Parnassian school in Brazil.

———. Vida e poesia de Emílio de Meneses (*Cultura política*, ano 3, no. 29, julho, p. 55–61). **[4205]**
Nineteenth century poet on the fringes of the Parnassian movement.

———. Vida e poesia de Machado de Assis (*Cultura política*, ano 3, no. 34, nov., p. 302–308). [4206
The stress here is on the poetry of Machado de Assis.

———. Vida e poesia de Teófilo Dias (*Cultura política*, ano 3, no. 27, maio, p. 138–144). [4207
On the nineteenth-century Parnassian.

———. Vida e poesia de Vicente de Carvalho (*Cultura política*, ano 3, no. 24, fev., p. 110–114). [4208
Another poet of the second phase of Parnassianism.

Sánchez-Saes, Braulio. Carlos Drummond de Andrade, poeta enfocado al mundo (*Sustancia*, ano 4, no. 15–16, junio–julio, p. 689–696). [4209
Cf. the articles by Paulo Rónai (items 4200 and 4202).

Silva, M. Nogueira da. Gonçalves Dias e Castro Alves. Rio de Janeiro. Ed. A. Noite. 164 p. [4210
A contribution to a literary controversy that has been going on for some time between the partisans of Gonçalves Dias and those of Castro Alves, in which the author ends by siding with the former in bestowing the title of "o major poeta" on the bard of Maranhão. The two principal chapters are entitled: "Gonçalves Dias e os recursos verbais e simbólicos da poesia nacional"; and "O influxo gonçalvino na poesia de Castro Alves." Cf. the work by Lucia Miguel Pereira (item 4189). See the edition of the *Obras Completas* of Castro Alves (item 4274).

Sodré, Nelson Werneck. Influência da terra na literatura brasileira (*Cultura política*, ano 3, no. 24, fev., p. 104–109). [4211
On the geographic influence in Brazilian literature.

———. Sentimento de nacionalidade na literatura brasileira (*Cultura política*, ano 3, no. 27, maio, p. 118–130). [4212
On the nationalist impulse in relation to Brazilian writers.

———. Síntese do desenvolvimento literário no Brasil. São Paulo. Livr. Martins. 118 p. [4213
Brief but important work by the author of the *História da Literatur Brasileira; Seus Fundamentos Econômicos* (*Handbook, no. 4, 1938*, item 4199).

Souza, Claudio de. O humorismo de Machado de Assis. Rio de Janeiro. Ed. Civilização brasileira. 1943? 34 p. [4214
Lecture given before the Brazilian Academy of Letters, with two additional chapters "acerca do laconismo e da impassibilidade de Machado de Assis." On Machado de Assis, cf. the work by Luis Paula-Freitas, *Handbook, no. 8, 1942*, item 4206.

Souza, J. B. Mello e. Estudantes do meu tempo. Rio de Janeiro. Ed. Alba. 212 p. [4215
Memories of student days at the Colégio Pedro II.

Taunay, Affonso de Escragnolle. O encilhamento. Terceira ed. Rio de Janeiro. Ed. Melhoramentos. 1943? 303 p. [4216
Scenes from the life of Rio de Janeiro in the early 1890's, by a writer who is one of the formative influences in the Brazilian novel.

Tollens, Paulo. Fundamentos do espírito brasileiro. Porto Alegre. Ed. Globo. 296 p. [4217
A study in national psychology.

Viana Filho, Luiz. A vida de Rui Barbosa. Segunda ed. São Paulo. Cia. ed. nac. (Bibl. do espírito moderno, Serie terceira, História, vol. 17). 301 p., ilus. [4219

Vieira, José. O Lima Barreto que eu conhecí (*Rev. Brasil*, ano 6, terceira fase, no. 56, dez., p. 43–47). [4220
Interesting personal reminiscences by one who knew the subject well.

Vítor, Edgar d'Almeida. Ad immortalitatem. Síntese histórica da Academia brasileira de letras. Bio-bibliografia de seus membros. Rio de Janeiro. Ed. Irmãos Pongetti. 165 p. [4221
Of historical, biographical, bibliographical, and literary interest.

NOVELS, SHORT STORIES, PROSE SKETCHES

Albuquerque, Leda Maria. A semana de Miss Smith. Rio de Janeiro. Ed. José Olympio. [4222
This collection of short stories received honorable mention in the contest for the Prêmio Humberto Campos. See General Statement.

Alencar, José de. O guarani. Rio de Janeiro. Ed. H. Antunes. 1943? 390 p. [4223
New edition of one of the most famous novels in Brazilian literature.

———. A guerra dos mascates. Crónica dos tempos coloniais. Primeira parte. São Paulo. Ed. Melhoramentos. 1943? 307 p. [4224

———. As minas de prata. Rio de Janeiro. Ed. Melhoramentos. 1943? 1050 p. [4225
Reprint of a classic work by the nineteenth-century novelist who here gives a picture of Brazilian colonial society.

Alphonsus, João. Eis a noite! Contos e novelas. São Paulo. Livr. Martins. 1943? 166 p. [4226
Short stories and novelettes by the winner of the Prêmio Machado de Assis of

1936, for his novel, *Totônio Pacheco* of 1935 (see *Handbook, no. 1, 1935*, p. 212 and item 2203). His novel, *A Gallinha Cega*, was published in 1937 (*Handbook, no. 3, 1937*, item 3586), his *Rola Moça* in 1938 (*Handbook, no. 4, 1938*, item 4212). Cover design and illustrations by Percy Deane.

Amado, Jorge. Terras do sem fim. São Paulo. Livr. Martins. [4227

Jorge Amado is not only one of the leading novelists of present day Brazil; his name would have to be mentioned well up in any list of the half-dozen of the most important writers in the genre that Latin America has to show. Born at Pirangi, in the municipality of Ilhéus, Baía, on August 10, 1912, he began writing at the age of nineteen. While in his teens he had been a worker in the cacao fields of the Ilhéus region, and it was to this locale that he first looked for the subject-matter of his stories, and to it he today returns in *Terras do Sem Fim*. His first novel, *O Pais do Carnaval*, was published in Rio de Janeiro, in 1932. This was followed by *Cacáu* (Rio de Janeiro, Ariel, 1933; second edition, 1934), which is based upon his own experiences as a plantation hand. In 1934 he gave us *Suór*, the story of an unspeakable slum tenement in Baía, in which the tenement itself, in a manner, becomes the protagonist. (See *Handbook, no. 1, 1935*, p. 211). See a review of *Cacáu* and *Suór* by the present editor (*Books Abroad*, vol. 9, no. 2, spring, 1935, p. 166). In 1935 came *Jubiabá*, with a Negro worker of Baía as the hero. (See *Handbook, no. 1, 1935*, item 2204). In *Mar Morto* (1936) and *Capitães da Areia* (1937), Amado turns to the Baian waterfront for inspiration, the former novel dealing with sea-going men, their loves and light-o'-loves, while the latter is a story of "dead-end kids." (See *Handbook, no. 2, 1936*, item 2926; *Handbook, no. 3, 1937*, p. 409 and item 3532. For an extract from the *Mar Morto* in English translation, see *Fiesta in November*, edited by Angel Flores and Dudley Poore, Boston, Houghton Mifflin Company, 1942, p. 384–397, and General Statement, *Handbook, no. 8, 1942*.) It was with his *Jubiabá* in the mid-thirties that Amado appeared to shift somewhat from the proletarian theme to what might be described as "genre" writing, or to the exciting adventure tale, as in *Capitães da Areia*. (See an article by the present editor, "The Brazilian Social Novel (1935–1940)," *The Inter-American Quarterly*, vol. 2, no. 2, April, 1940, p. 5–12; on Amado, see p. 9–10. Cf. what the same writer has to say of Amado, *Science and Society*, vol. 6, no. 1, winter, 1942, p. 41 and 49–50. Amado himself, however, would deny that any such change has occurred; see his foreword to the present work.) The *Terras do Sem Fim*, then, is Amado's seventh novel to date. As he tells us, in the past ten years he has written "seven novels, two biographies, a number of poems" and has given "dozens of lectures." He is the biographer of Luiz Carlos Prestes, the Brazilian Communist leader. In the novel here under consideration, the author, as has been said, goes back to the theme of his miniature novel of ten years ago, *Cacáu*, in the prefatory note to which, he had posed the question, as if to himself: "Será um romance proletário?" But where *Cacáu* endeavored to picture the lives of plantation workers, *Terras do Sem Fim* has to do with the big plantation owners of those early-century days when something very like a "gold-rush" occurred from the northern part of the State of Baía to the city of Ilhéus, where, rumor had it, the streets were "paved with gold." The scene, accordingly, is one that is highly reminiscent of our own "wild west" frontier days. There is the same disregard of human life, the same premium that is put on physical courage, the same unscrupulousness in the acquisition of wealth, while a number of the characters likewise remind one of certain stock figures out of the "westerns," such as the professional frock-coated gambler, the prostitute with her fluffy lace parasol, etc. There is plenty of excitement, a world of "color," much poetry, and a deeply moving love story that is all the more appealing by reason of its quaint 1890 flavor. Amado has always been a good deal of a poet in the novel; he has even been criticized for this; and as a result, the *Terras do Sem Fim* ends by being a production that is brilliantly unclassifiable. In his *Brazilian Literature* (New York, Macmillan, 1944), Erico Verissimo alludes to this work as "a panoramic novel full of pathos and drama," and he adds: "It is in my opinion one of the most daring and impressive novels ever published in Brazil. It is a barbaric parade of heroes and bandits, potentates and underdogs, whores and saints, common people and ghosts. The book is at the same time a prose poem, a folkloric tale, a crude story, a libel, and a work of art." Elsewhere, Verissimo has said that this is "o livro mais impressionante e corajoso da moderna literatura brasileira"; and again: "I look upon *Terras do Sem Fim* as the most vigorous, the most alive novel that has ever been written in Brazil." In another reviewer's opinion, it is: "um livro estranho, desigual e bárbaro, cheio de acentos dissonantes, esplêndido de belezas inesquecíveis, rudo e por vezes primário, com um misterioso poder de sugestão mágica, que é o principal elemento encantatório desse romancista do mar e da mata, das multitudões e das plantações de cacáu, das grandes vozes, dos grandes coros, das grandes melopéias–das grandes sinfonias humanas." (See *Revista do Brasil*, ano 6, terceira fase, no. 56, dez., p. 104.) For a good deal less favorable view, see *Cultura Política*, ano 3, no. 35, dez., p. 259–260. This anonymous commentator finds that Amado is possessed of "uma obsessão de fazer poesia" and that the result is "uma forma de lirismo palavroso . . . grandiloqüência *chevrotante*." Dr. W. Rex Crawford finds that the characters are not clearly drawn and fail to develop. From all of which it may be seen that the critics are far from agreed as to the merits of this book, but in any case, its provocative quality is obvious. An English translation by the present editor is in course of preparation. Two of Amado's novels have been translated into Spanish: *Cacáu* (see *Handbook, no. 2, 1936*, item 2927); and *Mar Morto* (*Handbook, no. 6, 1940*, item 4361;

translated by Benjamín de Garay). Amado himself is the translator of the *Doña Bárbara* of Rómulo Gallegos (*Handbook, no. 6, 1940*, items 4179 and 4434). His *Jubiabá* has been done into French under the title of *Bahia de Tous les Saints* (*Handbook, no. 5, 1939*, item 3960). There can be no doubt that, in his poetic-creative inspiration, Amado is under the influence of Castro Alves (see his *ABC de Castro Alves*, *Handbook, no. 7, 1941*, item 4852). For his views on modern Brazilian literature, see his article published in the *Nueva Gaceta* of Buenos Aires (*Handbook, no. 7, 1941*, item 4853).

Andrade, Oswald de. Marco Zero. 1. A revolução melancôlica. Rio de Janeiro. Ed. José Olympio. [4228

For the past sixteen years at least, ever since the first number of his *Revista de Antropofagia* appeared, in May, 1928, with its "*Manifesto Antropófago*," Oswald de Andrade has been one of the best known and most picturesque figures on the Brazilian literary scene. Previous to that, however, he had published five volumes of verse and prose, beginning with his novel, *Os Condenados*, of 1922. From the start he would seem to have been rather heavily under the French modernist influence, that of Cocteau being particularly evident in his "anthropophagite" period (around 1928). For a time his work fell into the stream of *modernismo* of the late twenties; but he soon emerged as a distinctly individual personality, one who, in his perennial playboy aspect, may be compared to the Spanish Ramón Gómez de la Serna. (He did not, for example, become identified with *modernismo* in the manner, say, of Mário de Andrade.) From both the literary and the political point of view, his career has been a stormy one. His pro-Communist play, *O Homem e o Cavalo*, created a scandal in 1934 (see *Handbook, no. 1, 1935*, p. 211). After that Andrade was in eclipse for some time and made a journey to Europe, where he remained for a number of years, returning to make his reappearance in literary circles of Rio in 1937 (see *Handbook, no. 4, 1938*, item 4213). Since then, he has turned to safer themes in the rich folklore material of Brazil, the present work being based upon the cyclic romance of Marco Zero, of the São Paulo region. An excerpt was published, under the title of "Perigo Negro," in the *Revista do Brasil*, terceira fase, ano 1, no. 4, out., p. 383-415; see *Handbook, no. 4, 1938*, item 4213. The work is characterized by the employment of cinematographic technique, and the idiosyncracies of dialect and popular speech. Political implications once again are not lacking. With Oswald de Andrade, as with Ramón Gómez de la Serna, one has the feeling, always, that anything may happen. A collection of the author's plays was published in 1937 (see *Handbook, no. 4, 1938*, item 4280).

Aranha, Graça. Canaã. Nova ed. revista. Rio de Janeiro. Ed. F. Briguiet. 276 p. [4229

Reprint of an epoch-marking early-century classic.

Azevedo, Aluízio. O cortiço. Nona ed. Rio de Janeiro. Ed. F. Briguiet. (Obras completas). 304 p. [4230

This tale of a slum tenement is one of the classics of late-nineteenth-century Brazilian literature. Drawings by Marian Colonna.

———. Demônios. Rio de Janeiro. Ed. F. Briguiet. (Obras completas, vol. 13). 175 p. [4231

Preface by M. Nogueira da Silva. Drawing by Marian Colonna.

———. Uma lágrima de mulher. Quinta ed. Rio de Janeiro. Ed. F. Briguiet. (Obras completas, vol. 1). xi, 138 p. [4232

The publishing house of Briguiet for a number of years has been engaged in putting out the complete works of this important late-nineteenth-century novelist. (The volumes are not published in numerical order. See *Handbook, no. 4, 1938*, item 4118.) Certain volumes are reprinted in answer to public demand. The present one has a foreword by M. Nogueira da Silva.

———. Philomena Borges. Quarta ed. Rio de Janeiro. Ed. F. Briguiet. (Obras completas, vol. 6). 219 p. [4233

Contains the preface written for the third edition by M. Nogueira da Silva. Drawing by Marian Colonna.

Barbosa, Almiro Rolmes, and **Edgard Cavalheiro** (eds.). As obras primas do conto brasileiro. São Paulo. Livr. Martins. (Col. A marcha do espírito, vol. 9). xii, 356 p., illus. [4234

Twenty-eight Brazilian short story writers are included in this collection, among them many of the best known names. The selection of authors has been made with critical taste, and the introduction, notes, and bibliography are valuable. See the review by Dudley Poore, *The Inter-American*, vol. 3, no. 2, Feb., 1944, p. 35.

———. As obras primas do conto universal. Segunda ed. São Paulo. Livr. Martins. (Col. A marcha do espírito, vol. 6). 1943? 381 p. [4235

This collection contains twenty-three stories in all, by world-famous writers. There are portraits specially designed for this edition by Urban. Review by Valdemar Cavalcanti, *Revista do Brasil*, ano 6, terceira fase, no. 53, março, p. 94-95.

Barreto, Lima. Recordações do escrivão Isaias Caminha. Terceira ed. Algumas palavras de Eloi Pontes. São Paulo. Ed. O livro de bolso. 233 p. [4236

Modern classic by a turn-of-the-century writer who died in the early 1920's.

Barroso, Gustavo (ed.). Os melhores contos históricos de Portugal. Rio de Janeiro. Dois mundos ed. 305 p. [4237

The Portuguese authors included in this collection are: Herculano Conde de Sabugosa; Eça de Queiroz; Antoninho Sardinha; Henrique Lopes de Mendonça; Júlio Dantas; Pinheiro Chaga; D. João de Castro; Rebêlo da Silva; and Jaime Cortesão.

Batini, Tito. Entre o chão e as estrelas. Rio de Janeiro, São Paulo. Ed. Civilização brasileira. 266 p. [4238

Tito Batini, by profession a São Paulo journalist of Italian descent, began his novel-writing career in 1941 with *E Agora que Fazer?* (See *Handbook, no. 7, 1941*, p. 464 and item 4950.) Dealing with a theme that is new in Brazilian literature, the building of a great railway and its tremendous cost in human lives, *E Agora Que Fazer* won almost extravagant praise from the reviewers. Yet most critics are agreed that in *Entre o Chão e as Estrelas,* the author has written an even better book. In his first story Batini had been concerned with the rôle of the anonymous worker-hero. In the present one, still adhering to the proletarian theme, he depicts the wretched yet hope-filled lives of the poor in their zinc-roofed hovels amid the muddy lanes on the outskirts of a large city. The city's lights are for them the stars of hope as they grub for a bare existence and dream of better things to come. With the war they are rendered conscious of the meaning of fascism and the threat it holds for their dreams. They accordingly mobilize their efforts and do all they can to bring about an anti-fascist victory. That in brief is the story, which cannot be told in a few words. The book has a wealth of fully drawn and life-like characters.

Borba, Jenny Pimentel de. Paixão dos homens. Rio de Janeiro. Borba, ed. [4239

A novel by the author of *40° a Sombra* (see *Handbook, no. 6, 1940*, item 4364). Dealing with the life of refugees in Brazil.

Burlá, Eliezer. Os braços suplicantes. Rio de Janeiro. Ed. José Olympio. [4240

Short story volume that won honorable mention in the contest for the Prêmio Humberto Campos. See General Statement.

Campos, Eduardo. Aguas mortas. Ceará. Ed. CLA. [4241

Short stories, dealing for the most part with provincial themes.

Cardoso, Lúcio. Dias perdidas. Rio de Janeiro. Ed. José Olympio. [4242

Tale of life in a small provincial town, by one of Brazil's leading novelists. On Cardoso, see *Handbook, no. 7, 1941*, item 4991. Sérgio Milliet finds that this novel is written "numa linguagem densa, por vezes pesada." The author has been seen as the Brazilian Julien Green.

Diniz, Júlio. Os fidalgos da casa mourisca. Rio de Janeiro. Ed. Dois mundos. 415 p. [4243

Novel dealing with provincial life.

Dupré, Leandro. Éramos seis. São Paulo. Cia. ed. nac. 277 p. [4244

Second book by a young woman novelist whom Brazilian critics look upon as most promising, although some (Monteiro Lobato, for example) have criticized her grammar, punctuation, dialogue, etc. Sra. Dupré made her literary debut in 1941, with *O Romance de Teresa Bernard* (see *Handbook, no. 7, 1941,* item 4956). There can be no doubt that her second novel shows considerable progress, in the matter of language and otherwise. See the review by Valdemar Cavalcanti, *Revista do Brasil*, ano 6, terceira fase, no. 54, junho, p. 104–106. Strongly anti-fascist and pro-democratic in tone.

Dutra, Lia Corrêa. Navio sem pôrto. Rio de Janeiro. Ed. Josá Olympio. [4245

Collection of short stories that was unanimously awarded the Prêmio Humberto de Campos. The critics find that the author is in the classic Maupassant tradition, rather than that of Katherine Mansfield. Poetry, irony, pity, humor, and a sense of tragedy as well as a distinguished prose style are among the qualities they have discerned in her work. See General Statement. The title story has to do with Jewish refugees.

Figueiredo, Guilherme. Rondinella. Rio de Janeiro. Ed. O Cruzeiro. [4246

A novel (*Rodinella*) and twenty short stories. One of the important fiction volumes of the year. See the review by Valdemar Cavalcanti, *Revista do Brasil*, ano 6, terceira fase, no. 56, dez., p. 96–97. The author has been compared to Chekhov and Gogol, but Sr. Cavalcanti feels that more justice can be done him by an attempt to strike a critical balance.

Garrett, João Baptista da Silva Leitão de Almeida. Obras completas. São Paulo. Ed. Cultura. 2 vols. [4247

The works of the early-nineteenth-century Portuguese romanticist (1799–1854).

Grieco, Donatello (ed.). Antologia de contos brasileiros. Rio de Janeiro. Ed. A Noite. [4248

Sixteen short story writers in all are represented, five of them dead, eleven living. A number of well known names are represented, among them Machado de Assis, Lima Barreto, Afonso Arinos, and António de Alcântara Machado. Cf. item 4234.

Lamego, Luis. Dom Pedro I, herói e enfermo. Rio de Janeiro. Ed. Zélio Valverde. 188 p. [4248a

Another view of the monarch who led the struggle for Brazilian independence. The work contains a bibliography.

Leão, Sylvia. White shore of Olinda. New York. The Vanguard Press. [4249

Here is a Brazilian writer who produces her first novel directly in English, without benefit of translator! A realistic, lyrical, extremely sympathetic tale dealing with the lives of fishermen in northern Brazil.

Lima, Jorge de. Calunga. Segunda ed. Rio de Janeiro. Alba ed. (Col. Romance brasileiro). 241 p. [4250

For the first edition of this well known novel by Brazil's leading contemporary poet, see *Handbook, no. 1, 1935*, p. 212 and item 2213. Cover design by Luis Jardim.

Lobato, Monteiro. Urupês, outros contos e coisas. São Paulo. Cia. ed. nac. [4251

This is the edition commemorative of the twenty-fifth anniversary of the appearance of Monteiro Lobato's *Urupês,* which marked a turning point in the evolution of the modern Brazilian short story. See General Statement. In addition to *Urupês* and other stories in the original volume, there are selections from *Cidades Mortas, Negrinha,* and *O Macaco Que se Fez Homem* as well as excerpts from the author's more recent work, including articles and stories for children. There are interesting biographical and critical notes by Arthur Neves. All in all, a highly suitable memorial for the grand old man of Brazilian letters while he is still alive.

Macedo, Joaquim Manuel de. O moço loiro. São Paulo. Ed. Cultura. [4252

———. A moreninha. Rio de Janeiro. Livr. H. Antunes. (Col. Excelsior, no. 19). 158 p. [4253

A *roman de moeurs* of the second half of the nineteenth century that has delighted a number of generations of Brazilians.

Menezes, Amilcar Dutra de. O futuro nos pertenece. Rio de Janeiro. Ed. José Olympio. [4254

A novel of the "new generation" that has grown up under the Estado Novo of Getúlio Vargas. Written by a captain in the Brazilian army, it was given wide advance publicity. It is distinctly a novel with political intentions, and, while strongly anti-Nazi in tone, it exhibits a certain anti-intellectualistic bias. Illustrations by Santa Rosa.

Nery, Adalgisa. Og. Rio de Janeiro. Ed. José Olympio. 135 p. [4255

Collection of short stories by the famous poet. Cover design by Santa Rosa.

Oliveira, Alvarus de. Crónicas da metropole. São Paulo. Cia. Brasil ed. 177 p. [4256

A book of metropolitan sketches by one of Brazil's best-selling popular writers, the author of *Romance Que a Propria Vida Escreveu, Grito do Sexo,* etc. Cf. his short story collection, *Hoje* (*Handbook, no. 5, 1939,* item 3980).

Picchia, Menotti del. Salome. Segunda ed. Rio de Janeiro. Ed. A Noite. 1943? 394 p. [4257

For the first edition of this prize-winning novel, see *Handbook, no. 6, 1940,* item 4377. See also, *Handbook, no. 4, 1938,* item 4377; *Handbook, no. 3, 1937,* item 2778; and *Handbook, no. 1, 1935,* item 1284.

Potiguara, José. Sapopema. Contos amazônicos. Rio de Janeiro. Ed. Henrique Velho. 215 p. [4258

A book of short stories to be added to the growing literature of the Amazon region. Cover design by Alves de Meneses.

Queiroz, Amadeu de. Sabina. São Paulo, Rio de Janeiro. Ed. Guaíra. (Col. Caderno azul). 73 p. [4259

A well told little love story, touching in its simplicity. Published in the Coleção Caderno Azul, under the general editorship of Sergio Milliet, De Plácido e Silva, and Luis Martins. Attractively bound in boards.

Queiroz, Raquel de. As três Marias. Segunda ed. Rio de Janeiro. Ed. José Olympio. [4260

On this work, see *Handbook, no. 5, 1939,* item 3983.

Ramalho, Ortigão, and Eça de Queiroz. As farpas. Seleção e prefácio de Gilberto Freyre. Rio de Janeiro. Dois Mundos ed. (Col. Clássicos e contemporâneos, no. 9, 9 A). 1943? 2 vols.: 303; 304 p. [4261

Raposo, Inácio. A mulher que foi papa. Rio de Janeiro. Ed. Pan-Americana. 1943? 451 p. [4262

Historical novel on an internationally known theme.

Rego, José Lins do. Fogo morto. Rio de Janeiro. Ed. José Olympio. [4263

One of the outstanding novels of the year, by one of Brazil's most important writers. This work has a certain affinity to the author's "sugar-cane cycle" on the one hand, and on the other hand, to a work like his *Pedra Bonita.* We are given a glimpse of the decadence of the old rural aristocracy and, at the same time, there is a strong fanciful element in this tale. Popular superstitions are vividly depicted and a number of highly picturesque types emerge. The critics (e.g., Hélio Vianna) are still finding fault with José Lins do Rego's style. Brazilians are comparing Lins do Rego to our Steinbeck, but he impresses this reviewer as being more nearly akin to the late Thomas Hardy.

Teles, Leonor. Porteira velha. Rio de Janeiro. 182 p. [4264

A collection of short stories.

Verissimo, Érico. Caminhos cruzados. Sexta ed. Porto Alegre. Ed. Globo. 355 p. [4265

On this, Verissimo's masterpiece, now in its eighteenth thousand, see *Handbook, no. 1, 1935,* General Statement and item 2223. For a review by the present editor, see *Books Abroad,* vol. 10 (1936), p. 302.

———. Crossroads. Translated by L. C. Kaplan. New York. The Macmillan co. 373 p. [4266

An expert English version that succeeds remarkably well in capturing the beauty and subtle nuances of the original.

———. O resto é silêncio. Porto Alegre. Ed. Globo. [4267

One of contemporary Brazil's three or four most important novelists, Érico Verissimo here returns, more or less, to the manner of his *Caminhos Cruzados*, the work by which he definitely established his reputation (see note on item 4265). There is the same interweaving of human destinies in the life of a provincial city, in this case Porto Alegre, set off by the author's unfailingly beautiful prose style and his deep fund of sympathy and human emotion. *O Resto é Silêncio* is particularly remarkable for its well drawn and full-bodied characters. Érico Verissimo knows people, above all those of the smaller towns. His gift for keen observation and rapid and accurate assimilation of impressions was shown to North Americans by the book he wrote about us some years ago, *Gato Preto em Campo de Neve* (*Handbook, no. 7, 1941*, item 4939). The truth is that he is always the novelist, whatever the genre at which he may try his hand. This may be seen from his marvelously understanding life of Jeanne d'Arc (*A Vida de Joanna d'Arc*) of eight years ago (1935), one of the best books that have been written on the Maid (see *Handbook, no. 1, 1935*, item 2225; see the present editor's review, *Books Abroad*, vol. 10 (1936), p. 168–169). It is his novelist's gift combined with his exceptional ability as a *prosateur* that makes of Verissimo so admirable a translator for difficult English language writers like Thomas Wolfe and others. (His labors as a translator have been many and distinguished.) On the other hand, his gift of fantasy and true poetic feeling has enabled him to become, also, one of Brazil's most popular writers of tales for children, of which he has any number to his credit. Verissimo's talent is a delicate one, especially in his earlier novels, like *Clarissa* (1933) and *Música ao Longe* (see *Handbook, no. 1, 1935*, item 2224). It was with *Caminhos Cruzados* and *A Vida de Joana d'Arc*, both published in 1935, that his work began to take on more substantial dimensions. In *Um Lugar ao Sol* (*Handbook, no. 2, 1936*, General Statement and item 2950) and *Olhai os Lírios do Campo* (*Handbook, no. 4, 1938*, item 4248a), he appears to go back to the mood, and to a large extent the style, of *Clarissa* and *Música ao Longe*, while in his Spanish War story, *Saga* (*Handbook, no. 6, 1940*, item 4388), what we have is a rather curious combination of the two moods and styles, which results in something of a breakdown in the center of this, perhaps the author's least successful novel, though one that is well worth reading. It is this reviewer's opinion that Sr. Verissimo's visit to and sojourn in the United States, as revealed in his *Gato Preto*, has led to the still further broadening and deepening of his insights and sympathies, until now, even when dealing with the life of his native Porto Alegre, he comes more and more to take on the stature of an international writer, even though he may remain, as he does, profoundly Brazilian in his roots. Any excursion into the domain of the modern Brazilian novel is incomplete unless one has made the acquaintance of Érico Verissimo. Some have compared him to Thornton Wilder, and *O Resto e Silêncio* has even been seen as "a sort of *Bridge of San Luis Rey*, set in Porto Alegre."

Vieira, José Geraldo. A quadragésima porta. Porto Alegre. Ed. Globo. [4268

José Geraldo Vieira is a novelist with a cosmopolitan background and outlook. The present work contains a caricature of a well known Brazilian literary figure.

Warin, Reinaldo de. Romeu e Julieta. São Paulo. Ed. Cultura. 1943? 190 p. [4269

Novelized version of the Shakespearean drama.

VERSE

Accioli, João. Olho d'agua. Segunda ed. Rio de Janeiro. Ed. Civilização brasileira. 141 p. [4270

For the first edition, see *Handbook, no. 3, 1937*, item 3563.

Almeida, Moacir de. Poesias completas. Voz do abismo, Soluções do deserto, Clamor dos séculos, e outros poemas. Rio de Janeiro. Ed. Zélio Valverde. (Col. Grandes poetas do Brasil). 1943? viii, 152 p. [4271

The work of a poet who belongs to the second phase of the Parnassian movement of the nineteenth century. The edition has been revised by Pádua de Almeida and has a preface by Atílio Milano.

Alvarenga, Manoel Ignácio da Silva. Glaura, poemas eróticos. Prefácio do Afonso Arinos de Melo Franco. Rio de Janeiro. Imp. nac. (Bibl. popular brasileira, no. 16). xxvii, 255 p. [4272

The "Biblioteca Popular Brasileira," under the auspices of the Instituto Nacional do Livro, is devoted to the reprinting of rare works of a literary and historical nature. The present text of the *Glaura* is based upon the extremely rare edition of 1799. In his preface Arinos de Melo Franco provides the necessary background, both biographical and bibliographical.

Alves, Amil. O canto da liberdade e outros poemas. Rio de Janeiro. Ed. Borsoi. 111 p. [4273

Poems animated by a love of freedom and humanity.

Alves, António de Castro. Obras completas. Rio de Janeiro. Ed. Zélio Valverde. (Col. Grandes poetas do Brasil, no. 5–6). [4274

A new and revised edition of the "Poet of the Slaves," with a preface by Agrippino Grieco. Cf. the edition put out by the Companhia Editora Nacional of São Paulo (see *Handbook, no. 4, 1938*, item 4251; cf. *Handbook, no. 7, 1941*, item 4988). See Jorge Amado's *A B C de Castro Alves* (*Handbook, no. 7, 1941*, item 4852). On the Castro Alves—Goncalves Dias controversy, see the work by M. Nogueira da Silva (item 4210).

Azevedo, Alvares de. Obras completas. Rio de Janeiro. Ed. Zélio Valverde. 2 vols. [4275

Vol. 1 contains the "Lyra dos vinte anos" and has been revised by Atílio Milano, who provides a preface. Vol. 2 has the "Poesias diversas," the "Poema do frade," and "O conde Lopo." The second volume has been revised, with a preface, by Edgard Cavalheiro. For another edition of the *Obras Completas*, of last year (1942), see *Handbook, no. 8, 1942,* item 4184a.

Bandeira, Manuel, and **Edgard Cavalheiro** (eds.). As obras primas da lírica brasileira. São Paulo. Livr. Martins. (Col. A marcha do espírito). [4276
One of the series of anthologies devoted to Brazilian masterpieces in the various literary genres put out by this publishing house. (Cf. the *Obras Primas do Conto Brasileiro,* item 4234). Among the criticisms made of this collection is that disproportionate space is accorded the moderns; it has also been pointed out that not all the selections by any means properly may be classified as lyrics.

Barata, Rui Guilherme. Anjos dos abismos. Rio de Janeiro. Ed. José Olympio. 84 p. [4277
Poems of a melancholy cast.

Cearense, Catulo da Paixão. Poemas bravios. Rio de Janeiro. Ed. Bedeschi. 270 p. [4278
Verse of the *sertões*. New edition, definitively revised by the author.

———. Sertão em flor. Prefácio de Mário de Alencar. Sétima ed. Rio de Janeiro. Ed. Bedeschi. 256 p. [4279
As may be seen, this poet is popular with the public.

Faria, Maria Adail Philidory de. Jasmins. Rio de Janeiro. Ed. Rodrigues. 60 p. [4280
Collection of verse highly feminine in flavor.

Garros, José Boadella. La caravana de los elefantes. Rio de Janeiro. Ed. Irmãos Pongetti. 115 p. [4281
The importance of this poet is perhaps indicated by the fact that Carlos Drummond de Andrade has written an introduction for the volume. Sr. Garros has something new to say, and a new way of saying it. Portrait of the author.

Jorge, J. G. de Araujo. Eterno motivo. Rio de Janeiro. Ed. Vecchi. 1943? 128 p. [4282
A pleasing poet on the poet's older themes.

Kemps, Emilio. Cantos de amor ao céu e à terra. Porto Alegre. Ed. Globo. 1943? 194 p. [4283
Well done verse in the conventional manner.

Lopes, Paulo Corrêa. Canto de libertação. Porto Alegre. Tip. do Centro. 52 p. [4284
Perfervid poems of religious mysticism. The volume includes translations from Mallarmé, André Spire, André Germain, and others. This is the author's third book of verse. His work has been praised by Jorge de Lima, Cecilia Meireles, Manuel Bandeira, Carlos Drummond de Andrade, and other poets of high reputation.

Mangabeira, Edila. O que ficou de mim. Rio de Janeiro. Ed. Irmãos Pongetti. 74 p. [4285
Love poems.

Martins, Ataide. Nilza. Rio de Janeiro. Ed. Irmãos Pongetti. 82 p. [4286
This little volume of verse has a highly laudatory preface by a member of the Academy of Letters of Minas Gerais, Plínio Mota.

Matos, Gregório de. Obras completas. Sacra. Lírica. Graciosa. Tomo 1. São Paulo. Ed. Cultura. (Os mestres da lingua, no. 9). 389 p. [4287
Edition of the classic seventeenth-century poet.

Maul, Carlos. A marcha de gigante. Quinta ed. Rio de Janeiro. Ed. Bedeschi. 46 p. [4288
Special edition of a popular poet, with wood-blocks by Odete Barcelos.

Meneses, J. Alves de. Atura de ritmos. Rio de Janeiro. Ed. Coelho Branco. 128 p. [4289
Volume of verse with cover design and pen-and-ink sketches by the author.

Morais, Vincius de. 5 elegias. Rio de Janeiro. Ed. Irmãos Pongetti. 43 p. [4290
A slender offering from one of Brazil's most important modern poets, winner of the Felippe d'Oliveira prize for 1935 (see *Handbook, no. 1, 1935,* item 2198).

Reis Júnior, Pereira. Canções do infinito. Rio de Janeiro. Ed. Borsoi. 103 p. [4291
This poet is presented, in the form of a prefatory letter, by the distinguished critic, Agrippino Grieco.

Souza, Cruz e. Obras completas. São Paulo. Ed. Cultura. 2 vols. [4292
Works of the late-nineteenth-century bard whom Andrade Muricy has termed the "maior poeta moderno do Brasil" (*A Nova Literatura Brasileira,* Porto Alegre, Ed. Globo, 1936, p. 399). Cruz e Souza, a Negro and the son of a slave, signalled the beginning of Brazilian symbolism, with his collection *Broqueis* (1893).

Varela, Fagundes. Obras completas. São Paulo. Ed. Cultura. (Col. Os mestres da lingua, no. 8). 624 p. [4293
For another edition of the *Obras Completas,* see the one put out last year (1942) by Zélio Valverde, in the "Grandes Poetas do Brasil" series. See review by Valdemar Cavalcanti, *Revista do Brasil,* ano 6, terceira fase, no. 54, junho, p. 106; cf. Cavalcanti's review of the Valverde edition, *ibid.,* ano 6, terceira fase, no. 53, março, p. 91–94. On the rediscovery of Varela, see *Handbook, no. 4, 1938,* p. 348 and item 4164.

Veiga, Vincius da. Poemas antigos. Rio de Janeiro. Ed. Irmaõs Pongetti. 102 p. [4294
Capable poet in the older forms.

DRAMA

Abreu, Modesto de. O ermitão da gloria. Rio de Janeiro. Papelaria e tip. Coelho. (Col. Ópera nac., no. 1). 63 p. [4295
An opera libretto in three acts.

Mesquita, Alfredo. Os priâmidas. Rio de Janeiro. Ed. José Olympio. 158 p. [4296
Play in three acts.

Messina, Felipe. Os homens!—Que horror! Rio de Janeiro. Ed. da Papelaria e tip. Coelho. (Col. Teatro nac., no. 12). 90 p. [4297
Comedy in three acts.

Pena, Martins. Teatro cômico. São Paulo. Ed. Cultura. [4298
Collection of the dramatic works of the early nineteenth-century novelist, journalist, and playwright (1815–1848), concerning whom modern critical opinion is divided. Carlos Süssekind de Mendonça, for example, is warm in his praise; Agrippino Grieco is a good deal more reserved; for a summary, see the latter's *Evolução da Prosa Brasileira* (Rio de Janeiro,, Ed. Ariel, 1933), p. 74–77.

Tojeiro, Gastão. Sai da porta, Deolinda! ou um sobrinho igual ao tio. Rio de Janeiro. (Col. Teatro nac., no. 13). 89 p. [4299
A light comedy in three acts.

TRANSLATIONS

Anet, Claude. Ariane. Rio de Janeiro. Ed. José Olympio. (Romances para a mulher, vol. 10). [4300
A typical Anet novel: "Romance de amor. De muito amor," as a Brazilian paragrapher puts it. Translation by Manuelito de Ornelas.

Annunzio, Gabriele d'. Episcopo & cia. O martir. Os anais de Ana. Rio de Janeiro. Ed. Irmãos Pongetti. 197 p. [4301
Translations by Sodré Viana.

Armstrong, Margaret. Vida e morte de Trelawny. Porto Alegre. Ed. Globo. [4302

Aurélio, Marco. Os doze livros de sabedoria. Rio de Janeiro. Ed. Vecchi. (Os grandes pensadores, no. 10). 132 p. [4303
Translated by Persiano da Fonseca.

Baldwin, Faith. Este homem é meu. São Paulo. Ed. Universitária. 1943? 221 p. [4304
Translated by Iolanda Vieira Martins.

Balzac, Honoré de. Um caso tenebroso. São Paulo. Livr. Martins. (Col. Excelsior, vol. 23). 1943? 250 p. [4305
Translated by Tarsila do Amaral and Luis Martins.

Baring, Maurice. Daphne Adeane. Rio de Janeiro. Ed. José Olympio. (Fogos cruzados, vol. 15). 1943? 424 p. [4306
Translated, with a preface, by Oscar Mendes.

Baudelaire, Charles. Arabescos filosóficos. Rio de Janeiro. Ed. Vecchi. 1943? 105 p. [4307
Translated by Dírio Gorgot.

Brophy, John. Sargento imortal. São Paulo. Livr. Martins. (Col. Contemporânea). 1943? 293 p. [4308
Translated by Maslowa Gomes Venturi.

Butler, Samuel. Destino da carne. Rio de Janeiro. Ed. José Olympio. [4309
Translation of *The Way of All Flesh*.

Cather, Willa. Safira e a escrava. Porto Alegre. Ed. Globo. [4310
Translation by Miroel Silveira.

Cervantes Saavedra, Miguel de. O curioso impertinente. São Paulo. Ed. Cultura. (Novelas de coração, no. 9). 185 p. [4311
Translation by A. F. de Castilho.

———. Dom Quixote de la Mancha. Segunda parte. Vol. 2. São Paulo. Ed. Cultura. (Os mestres do pensamento, vol. 21). 586 p. [4312

Chamfort (Sébastien Roch Nicolas). Caracteres e anedotas. Rio de Janeiro. Ed. Veechi. (Os grandes pensadores, vol. 8). 1943? 125 p. [4313
Translated by Persiano da Fonseca.

Chateaubriand, François René. Atalá e Renato. São Paulo. Ed. Cultura. (Novelas do coração, no. 5). [4314

Conrad, Joseph. Tufão. Porto Alegre. Ed. Globo. 1943? 283 p. [4315
Translation by Queiroz Lima. Cf. *Handbook, no. 5, 1939*, items 4017 and 4018.

De la Roche, Mazo. Herança de Whiteoac. Rio de Janeiro. Ed. José Olympio. [4315a
Translated, with a preface, by Herman Lima.

Defoe, Daniel. As confissões de Moll Flanders. Rio de Janeiro. Ed. José Olympio. (Col. Fogos cruzados). [4316
Translation by the well known novelist, Lúcio Cardoso.

Dekobra, Maurice. Macau, inferno do jogo. Rio de Janeiro. Ed. Vecchi. 1943? 229 p. [4317
Translated by Abelardo Romero.

Dickens, Charles. A vida do Nosso Senhor. Rio de Janeiro. Ed. José Olympio. 142 p. [4318]
Translation by Costa Neves. Illustrations by Luiz Jardim.

Dostoiewsky, F. Alma da criança. Rio de Janeiro. Ed. Criança. 1943? 202 p. [4319]

———. Diário de um escritor. Rio de Janeiro. Ed. Vecchi. 1943? 485 p. [4320]
Translation by Frederico dos Reis Coutinho.

Dumas, Alexandre. Mestre Adão, o calabrês. Rio de Janeiro. Ed. Vecchi. 229 p. [4321]
Translated by J. Dubois Júnior.

———. Os três mosqueteiros. São Paulo. Ed. Cultura. [4322]

———. A tulipa negra. São Paulo. Ed. Cultura. (Novelas universais, no. 4). 289 p. [4323]

Dumas, fils, Alexandre. A dama das camélias. Rio de Janeiro. Ed. Vecchi. 225 p. [4324]
Complete and definitive edition in Portuguese. Translated by Flávio Goulart de Andrade. Prologue by Jules Janin.

Dumesnil, René. A alma do médico. Rio de Janeiro. Ed. Vecchi. 1943? 223 p. [4325]
Translated by Flávio Goulart de Andrade.

Feer, Léon. O Buda. São Paulo. Ed. Cultura. [4326]
Translated by Heitor Ferreira Lima.

Fiedler, Arkady. Esquadrão 303. Rio de Janeiro. Ed. Pan-americana. 1943? 171 p. [4327]
Translated by Japi Freire.

Fischer, Louis. Alvorada da vitória. São Paulo. Ed. Prometeu. 238 p. [4328]
Translated and revised by Lívio Xavier.

France, Anatole. O senhor Bergeret em Paris. Rio de Janeiro. Ed. Vecchi. 1943? 235 p. [4329]
Anatole France finds a distinguished translator in Eloi Pontes.

Franklin, Benjamin. Breviário do homem de bem. Rio de Janeiro. Ed. Vecchi. (Os grandes pensadores, vol. 7). 1943? 125 p. [4330]
Translated by Dr. Dério Gorgot.

Funck-Brentano, Frantz. Lutero. Rio de Janeiro. Ed. Vecchi. (Col. Vidas extraordinárias). 318 p. [4331]
Translation by the distinguished hand of Eloi Pontes.

Glaspell, Susan. A madrugada se aproxima. Rio de Janeiro. Ed. José Olympio. (Grandes romances para a mulher, vol. 9). [4332]
Translation by Maluh de Ouro Preto, revised by Eugénia Celso.

Goethe, J. W. Fausto. Primeira parte. São Paulo. Cia. ed. nac. [4333]
Translation by Jenny Klabin Segall.

Goldsmith, Oliver. O vigario de Wakefield. Rio de Janeiro. Ed. Irmãos Pongetti. [4334]
The *Vicar of Wakefield* has previously been published in Brazil in mediocre translations. The present careful rendering is by Sra. Cira Neri and has been revised by the novelist and translator, Marques Rebêlo.

Gorki, Maximo. Tormenta sobre a cidade. Rio de Janeiro. Ed. Vecchi. 1943? 188 p. [4335]
Translation by J. da Cunha Borges.

Gutiérrez, Eduardo. Juan Moreira. São Paulo. Livr. Martins. (Col. Excelsior, vol. 18). [4336]
Translation of an Argentine work which has been described by a Brazilian reviewer as "um romance à margem duma biografia." The hero is a Robin-Hood-like champion of the weak. Portuguese rendering by Carlos Maul.

Hamsun, Knut. Pan. São Paulo. Livr. Martins. (Col. Excelsior). [4337]
This work, which won the Nobel Prize, has been translated by Augusto Sousa. The Brazilian reading public in the past has become acquainted with *Hunger* and other Hamsun novels.

Harris, Frank. Minha vida e meus amores. Porto Alegre. Ed. Meridiano. 275 p. [4338]
Translated by Elias Davidovich.

Hermant, Abel. Horas de amor de um guerreiro. Rio de Janeiro. Ed. Civilização brasileira. 400 p. [4339]
Translation by Godofredo Rangel.

Hilton, James. Na noite do passado. Rio de Janeiro. Ed. José Olympio. 1943? 329 p. [4340]
Translation by Pedro Dantas and Aurélio Gomes de Oliveira.

Hoffman, Charles. Ainda serás minha. Rio de Janeiro. Ed. Pan-americana. 1943? 340 p. [4341]
Translation by Alex Viany.

Huxley, Aldous. Admiravel mundo novo. Porto Alegre. Ed. Globo. (Col. Nobel, vol. 36). 1943? 346 p. [4342]
Translation by Vidal de Oliveira. With a portrait of the author.

———. Eminência parda. Porto Alegre. Ed. Globo. 1943? 303 p. [4343]
Translated by Paulo Moreira da Silva.

Ibáñez, Blasco. A catedral. Rio de Janeiro. Ed. Irmãos Pongetti. [4344]
Translation revised by the novelist, Marques Rebêlo.

Johnson, Hewlett. O poder soviético. Prefácio de Dom Carlos Duarte da Costa,

bispo de Maura. Rio de Janeiro. Ed. Calvino. xxiii, 463 p. [4345
The translation is by Daví J. de Castro. The original drawings by Nowell Mary Hewlett Johnson are retained.

Juvenal. Satiras. São Paulo. Ed. Cultura. [4346
Selected by José Peres, who writes the introduction.

Kelly, Judith. A felicidade vem depois. Rio de Janeiro. Ed. Civilização brasileira. 400 p. [4347
Translated by Godofredo Rangel.

Lagerlöf, Selma. Lendas cristãs. Rio de Janeiro. Ed. A Noite. 1943? 221 p. [4348
Translation by Rosinha de Mendonça Lima. Preface by Pedro Calmon. Illustrations by Armando Pacheco.

Lamartine, Alphonse de. Graziela. São Paulo. Ed. Cultura. (Novelas do coração, no. 4). 1943? 164 p. [4349

Lewis, Sinclair. Dr. Arrowsmith. Porto Alegre. Ed. Globo. 445 p. [4350
This work, that won the Nobel Prize in 1930, is translated by Juvenal Jacinto. With portrait of the author.

Lin, Yu-t'ang. Minha terra e meu povo. Rio de Janeiro. Ed. Irmãos Pongetti. 387 p. [4350a
Translated by Carlos Domingues.

Louys, Pierre. O amor de Bilitis. Rio de Janeiro. Ed. José Olympio. (Col. Rubayat). [4351
Rendering of the *Chansons de Bilitis*, by Guilherme de Almeida.

Macinnes, Helen. Insuspeitos. Rio de Janeiro. Ed. José Olympio. 1943? 402 p. [4352
Translation by M. P. Moreira Filho.

MAHABHARATA. São Paulo. Ed. Cultura. [4353
Reconstruction of the Hindu epic, based upon the original texts, transcribed with notes by Melo Noronha e Faro.

Mann, Thomas. A montanha mágica. Rio de Janeiro. Ed. Pan-americana. 538 p. [4354
Portuguese rendering by Otto Silveira.

Maria, Gra-Duquesa da Russia. Memórias (Educação de uma princesa). Rio de Janeiro. Ed. José Olympio. (O Romance da vida, vol. 23). 1943? 324 p. [4355
Translation by Gulnara de Morais Lobato. Contains André Maurois' preface to the French edition.

Maritain, Jacques. Os direitos do homem e a lei natural. Rio de Janeiro. Ed. José Olympio. 1943? 152 p. [4356
Translated by Afrânio Coutinho.

Marlitt, Suzanna. A voz do coração. São Paulo. Emp. ed. Brasileira. 1943? 216 p. [4357
Translated by Ana Wey Meyer.

Mason, Van Wyck. A morte dansa na Rumânia. Porto Alegre. Ed. Globo. (Col. Amarela, vol. 107). 1943? 256 p. [4358
Translated by Amilcar de Garcia.

Maugham, W. Somerset. O destino de um homem. Porto Alegre. Ed. Globo. (Col. Nobel, vol. 48). 1943? 288 p. [4359
Translation by Moacir Werneck de Castro.

———. Meu diário de guerra. Rio de Janeiro. Ed. Pan-americana. 1943? 194 p. [4360
Translation of "Strictly Personal," by Fernando Tude de Sousa.

Maupassant, Guy de. Bel ami. São Paulo. Livr. Martins. [4361

———. Contos. Pôrto Alegre. Ed. Globo. [4362
Selections from the best of the Maupassant tales, most of them translated by Mário Quintana.

———. Pierre et Jean. Rio de Janeiro. Ed. Pan-americana. [4363
Portuguese translation by Alvaro Gonçalves.

Mauriac, François. Uma gota de veneno. Rio de Janeiro. Ed. Irmãos Pongetti. [4364
Brazilian version of *Thérèse Desqueyroux*. M. Mauriac is fortunate in having as his translator the fine poet, Carlos Drummond de Andrade, who also provides a preface.

Nietzsche, F. O crepúsculo dos ídolos. Rio de Janeiro. Ed. Vecchi. (Os grandes pensadores, no. 5). 1943? 122 p. [4366
Translated by Persiano da Fonseca.

Norris, Kathleen. Algemas de ouro. Rio de Janeiro. Ed. José Olympio. (O romance para você, vol. 4). 1943? 309 p. [4367
Translation by Dora Alencar de Vasconcelos.

Photiades, Constantin. As múltiplas vidas do Conde de Cagliostro. Rio de Janeiro. Ed. Vecchi. (Col. vidas extraordinárias, vol. 2). 365 p. [4368
Translated by Robert Pessoa.

Poe, Edgar Allan. O mistério de Marie Roget. Rio de Janeiro. Ed. Vecchi. 1943? 255 p. [4369
Translated by Líbero Rangel de Andrade and Frederico dos Reis Coutinho.

Redier, Antoine. São Vicente de Paulo. O apóstolo da caridade. Rio de Janeiro. Ed. Vecchi. 247 p. [4370
Translated by Anita Martins de Sousa.

Roberts, Kenneth. Cara ou caroa. Rio de Janeiro. Cia. ed. nac. [4371]
Translation of *Oliver Wiswell.* The translator is Gulnara de Morais Lobato.

Ruck, Berta. Dinheiro do céu. São Paulo. Cia. ed. nac. (Bibl. das moças, vol. 108). 254 p. [4372]
Translation by Albertina Pinheiro.

Saint-Pierre, Jacques Henri Bernadin de. Paulo e Virginia. São Paulo. Ed. Cultura. (Novelas do coração, no. 1). [4373]

Sand, George. Êle e ela. Rio de Janeiro. Ed. Vecchi. [4374]
Translation by Abelardo Romero.

Saroyan, William. Comedia humana. Rio de Janeiro. Ed. Pan-americana. [4375]
Translated by Alex Viany.

Scott, Walter. Ivanhoé. São Paulo. Ed. Cultura. (Novelas do coração, no. 7-8). 1943? 2 vols.: 250; 239 p. [4376]

Seghers, Anna. A sétima cruz. São Paulo. Livr. Martins. (Col. Contemporânea). 1943? 355 p. [4377]
Translation by Otávio Mendes Cajado.

Seneca. Aira. Rio de Janeiro. Ed. Vecchi. (Os grandes pensadores, no. 11). 127 p. [4378]
Translated by Antero Barradas Barata.

Spence, Hartzell. Com um pé no céu. Rio de Janeiro. Ed. Irmãos Pongetti. 1943? 308 p. [4379]
Translated by Sodré Viana.

Stendhal (Henri Beyle). A cartuxa de Parma. São Paulo. Ed. Océano. [4380]
Translated by Antônio Rino.

———. O vermelho e o negro. Porto Alegre. Ed. Globo. (Bibl. dos Séculos, vol. 4). 1943? 471 p. [4381]
Translated by Sousa Júnior and Casemiro Fernandes.

Stevenson, Robert Louis. A flecha preta. Rio de Janeiro. Ed. Vecchi. 234 p. [4382]
Translated by Edison Carneiro.

Stowe, Harriet Beecher. A cabana do Pai Tomaz, ou a vida dos negros na América. São Paulo. Ed. Cultura. (Novelas universais, no. 2). 418 p. [4383]

Tácito (Publius Cornelius Tacitus). Germania. Rio de Janeiro. Livr. para todos. [4384]
For an extremely interesting commentary on this translation, put out by a popular publishing house that usually goes in for material of quite a different sort, see the leading article in the *Revista do Brasil* for June: "Tácito no cordel," by Paulo Rónai (*Revisto do Brasil,* ano 6, terceira fase, no. 54, p. 1–13). Sr. Rónai sees this as a phenomenon of the times, and also as a testimony to the "'atualidade' permanente da civilização antiga."

Tahan, Malba. O homem que calculava. Oitava ed. Rio de Janeiro. Ed. Getúlio Costa. 287 p. [4385]
Translation and notes by Prof. Breno Alencar Bianco. Illustrations by Felicitas Barreto. Drawings by Horácio Rubens.

———. O livro de Aladim. Rio de Janeiro. Ed. Getúlio Vargas. 1943? 190 p. [4386]
Collection of oriental tales. Translated, with notes, by Prof. Brenco Alencar Bianco.

Totheroh, Dan. Vales profundos. Rio de Janeiro. Ed. Pan-americana. 325 p. [4387]
Translated by V. Coaracy.

Van Doren, Carl. Benjamin Franklin. Porto Alegre. Ed. Globo. 1943? 596 p. [4388]
This work, which won the 1939 Pulitzer Prize has been translated by J. de Matos Ibiapina.

Vance, Ethel. Represália. São Paulo. Livr. Martins. [4389]

Vergilio. Obras completas. Bucólicas. Geórgicas. Eneida. São Paulo. Ed. Cultura. (Os mestres do pensamento, vol. 26). 390 p. [4390]
The translation of the *Bucolics* is by Leonel da Costa Lusitano; the *Georgics* by Antonio Feliciano de Castilho; the *Aeneid* by Odorico Mendes.

Voltaire (Jean François Marie Arouet). A princesa de Babilônia. São Paulo. Livr. Martins. 307 p. [4391]
This volume includes the three *nouvelles:* A princesa de Babilônia; O ingênuo; and Micromegas. Translated by Miroel Silveira.

Werfel, Franz. Céu roubado. Rio de Janeiro. Ed. José Olympio. (Col. Fogos cruzados). 1943? 351 p. [4392]
Translated by Sodré Viana.

Zola, Émile. Por uma noite de amor. Rio de Janeiro. Ed. Pan-americana. 173 p. [4394]
Translation revised by Inácio Raposo.

CHILDREN'S BOOKS

Acquarone, Francisco. História maravilhosa da arca de Noé. Terceira ed. São Paulo. Ed. Melhoramentos de São Paulo. 48 p. [4395]
The old Noah's ark story. For the very young.

Almeida, Lúcia Machado de. O mistério do polo. Rio de Janeiro. Ed. Criança. 57 p. [4396]
Arctic adventures, told for children.

BAIANINHA. Segunda ed. São Paulo. Ed. Melhoramentos de São Paulo. (Histórias de tio Damião). 1943? 16 p. [4397]
For very young children. Close to life material.

Barreto, Arnaldo Oliveira. Ali-Baba e os quarenta ladrões. São Paulo. Ed. Melhoramentos. (Bibl. Infantil, no. 23). [4398
A classic children's tale.

———. A barboleta amarela. Oitava ed. São Paulo. Ed. Melhoramentos de São Paulo. (Bibl. infantil, no. 20). 1943? 48 p. [4399
For younger readers.

———. O califé cegonha. Nona ed. São Paulo. Ed. Melhoramentos de São Paulo. (Bibl. Infantil, no. 8). 1943? 56 p. [4400

———. A gata borralheira. Oitava ed. São Paulo. Ed. Melhoramentos. (Bibl. Infantil, no. 22). 48 p. [4401
A story that is a favorite with the Brazilian young.

———. O sargento verde. Nona ed. São Paulo. Ed. Melhoramentos de São Paulo. (Bibl. Infantil, no. 14). 1943? 56 p. [4402

Busch, W. Corococó e Caracacá. São Paulo. Ed. Melhoramentos. 32 p. [4403
A brief tale for children, translated by Guilherme de Almeida.

Espinheira, Ariosto. Viagem através do Brasil. Vol. 4. Brasil Leste. 2. Minas Gerais. Segunda ed. São Paulo. Ed. Melhoramentos. 135 p. [4404
Brazilian geography for the young.

Ferreira, Barros. A conquista da cidade sagrada. Quarta ed. São Paulo. Ed. Melhoramentos de São Paulo. 1943? 54 p. [4405
A popular tale for children that has already run through three editions.

Fleury, Renato Seneca. Santos Dumont. São Paulo. Ed. Melhoramentos. 248 p. [4406
Story of Brazil's famous aviation pioneer, told for younger readers.

A GALINHA RUIVA. Segunda ed. São Paulo. Ed. Melhoramentos de São Paulo. (Série Horas felizes). 1943? 10 p. [4407
For the very young.

Guimarães, Vicente. A princezinha do castelo vermelho. Belo Horizonte. Ed. "Era uma vez." Gráf. Queiroz Breiner. 58 p. [4408
Drawings by Rodolfo.

Hummel, A. História de Jacinto. Sexta ed. São Paulo. Ed. Melhoramentos de São Paulo. (Bibl. Infantil, no. 29). 48 p. [4409

Mosley, Zack. Jack do Espaco, campeão dos ares. Rio de Janeiro. Ed. Globo juvenil. (Col. Gibi, no. 18). 1943? 427 p. [4410
An ambitious book for children, in translation. Illustrated.

Munchausen, Barão de. As histórias fantásticas do Barão de Munckhausen. São Paulo. Ed. Melhoramentos de São Paulo. 1943? 56 p. [4411
An edition for children.

PAPAGAIO REAL. São Paulo. Ed. Melhoramentos de São Paulo. (Histórias de tio Damião). 1943? 16 p. [4412
For the very young.

Picchia, Menotti del. Viagens de João Peralta e Pé de Moleque. Quarta ed. São Paulo. Ed. Melhoramentos de São Paulo. 1943? 111 p. [4413
Children's book by a well known man of letters.

ADDENDA

Abreu, Casimiro de. Obras completas. Rio de Janeiro. Ed. Zélio Valverde. (Col. Grandes poetas do Brasil). 1942. [4414
See review by Valdemar Cavalcanti, *Revista do Brasil*, ano 6, terceira fase, no. 53, março, 1943, p. 91–94. Cf. *Handbook, no. 6, 1940*, item 4390. Cf. the edition of the *Poesias Completas, Handbook, no. 4, 1938*, item 4249. For Renato Almeida's verdict on Casimiro de Abreu, see *Handbook, no. 5, 1939*, General Statement and item 3877.

ANAIS DA BIBLIOTECA NACIONAL DO RIO DE JANEIRO. Vol. 63, de 1941. Rio de Janeiro. Impr. nac. 1942. [4415
This volume, published under the supervision of the Director of the National Library, Rodolfo Garcia, contains the "Ordens do dia do general Barão de Caxias," and so is of especial interest to the student of Brazilian history.

Aranha, Graça. Machado de Assis e Joaquim Nabuco. Comentários e notas à correspondência entre estes dois escritores. Segunda ed. Rio de Janeiro. Ed. F. Briguiet. (Obras completas, vol. 4). 1942. [4416
This is vol. 4 of the *Obras Completas* of Graça Aranha in course of publication by Briguiet. The correspondence given here begins in 1865, when Nabuco was fifteen years of age, and ends with a letter written by the great abolitionist from the United States under date of September 3, 1908. (Machado de Assis died on September 29 of the same year.) In his final letter Nabuco says: "V. é a mocidade perpétua cercada de todas as afetações de velhice. . . ." In his introduction Graça Aranha dwells on the two complementary sides of Brazilian literature as represented by these two writers.

Conde, Hermínio de Brito. A tragédia ocular de Machado de Assis. Com um prefácio do dr. João Alfredo Lopes Braga. Rio de Janeiro. Ed. A. Noite. 1942. [4417
A study of Machado de Assis' myopia, which amounted to near-blindness, and which, along with other disadvantages from which he suffered, tended to make his life a secluded and unhappy one. The preface is by the president of the League for the Prevention of Blindness.

Martins, Cyro. Mensagem errante. Porto Alerge. Ed. Globo. 1942. 263 p. [4418
By one of the veterans of the regional novel in Brazil.

Peixoto, Afrânio. O príncipe perfeito. Lisboa-Porto. 1942. [4419
A new interpretation of the life of John II.

Varela, Fagundes. Obras completas. Rio de Janeiro. Ed. Zélio Valverde. (Col. Grandes poetas do Brasil). 1942. 3 vols. [4420
See review by Valdemar Cavalcanti, *Revista do Brasil,* ano 6, terceira fase, no. 53, março, 1943, p. 91–94.

LAW

BY

HELEN L. CLAGETT

Library of Congress

AND

ANYDA M. MARCHANT

Library of Congress

GENERAL STATEMENT

The output of legal literature in Latin America has apparently diminished but little in spite of wartime curtailments and shortages of paper, machinery and labor. It is true that the quality of the paper used in the printing is very inferior, but the quantity of material issued seems unaffected. It has been particularly noted that there has been little or no change in the format and frequency of publication of the legal periodicals and serial publications issued by our southern neighbors, contrary to the fate suffered by a great many of the law periodicals in our own country, which have in many instances been forced to change from monthly to quarterly, and in a few cases to cease publication altogether.

Reciprocity in interest and ideas continues among the lawyers of the Western Hemisphere. A focus for this interest, and a forum for this interchange of ideas has been supplied during the past few years by the Inter-American Bar Association. The work of this important association has gained momentum since its first meeting in Havana in 1941, and intensification of interest was noted at the second conference in Rio de Janeiro in 1943 and the third in Mexico City in 1944. At the Rio de Janeiro conference, Dr. Eduardo J. Couture, famous Uruguayan legal author and member of the law faculty of Montevideo, pointed out the importance of a sympathetic attitude among American lawyers toward each other's systems of law, and this note has been sounded over and over in the papers presented and addresses delivered at all of the conferences. This attitude naturally affects the interest in the comparative law of our countries in the production of legal literature although even yet the tendency toward comparison with the law of European countries prevails.

In two fields of law have the lawyers and legislators of Latin America especially set ambitious goals for their countrymen in laying the legal framework for the material betterment of their people. Their awareness of the social problems underlying the political structure of their countries has led them to discuss and adopt new and modern sociological and psychological principles of criminal law and labor law. Their interest in these two subjects continues to overshadow the more traditional aspects of law. The trend noted in the past few years in the development of the various phases of administrative law and procedure was even more intensified in 1943. The legal scholars and lawmakers have turned their attention to the study of problems arising directly from the rapidly growing industrialization and urbanization of their countries. Public utilities and tax legislation have been subjects of a constantly increasing number of articles and books.

Probably the most important single piece of legislation passed during the last few years in Latin American republics is the new Lei de Introdução to the Brazilian Civil Code. This new law, which formulates the general principles to be used in the interpretation of the Code, was adopted by decree-law no. 4707 of September 17, 1942. Speaking of the old Introductory Law, which has thus been superseded, Clovis Bevilaqua, distinguished draftsman of the Civil Code, defined its purpose in these words: "It is not a component part of the Code; it is, so to speak, an annexed law, which is published together with the Code to facilitate its application. Its provisions include material relative to public law, to hermeneutics and to private international law." The most striking change made by the new Lei de Introdução is in the field of private international law or conflict of laws. Three articles in particular may be cited: Article 7 which now provides for the non-recognition of foreign divorces in Brazil, if the parties are Brazilians; this is the clarification of a much discussed and debated point. Article 10 of the new law provides for the application of the law of the domicile of the deceased in cases of inheritance of property. The former law provided for the application of the law of the country of which the deceased was a national. Article 12 makes definite provision for the use of exequaturs and letters rogatory, another sphere in which the former law was vague and variously interpreted. Elaborate studies of this new Introductory Law had not yet appeared in 1943, but articles, such as that published in the March issue of the Brazilian periodical, *Revista Forense*, contributed by Percival de Oliveira, had opened the discussion.

During the years 1943–44, the countries of the Western Hemisphere lost several of their more distinguished jurists. Foremost among these was Clovis Bevilaqua, the draftsman of the Brazilian Civil Code, who died on July 26, 1944. The death of two other Brazilians has also been regretted, i.e,. Rodrigo Octávio de Langaard Menezes, whose long and brilliant career in national and international affairs terminated on February 29, 1944; and José de Paula Rodrigues Alves, one of Brazil's most distinguished diplomats, who at the time of his death on May 6, 1944, held the position of his country's ambassador to Argentina. Dr. José Gil Fortoul, a former President of Venezuela and the author of an important work on the Constitutional history of Venezuela, died June 15, 1943, at the age of 81. Among North Americans, the death of Dr. James Brown Scott on June 23, 1943, one of the most eminent international lawyers of his period, should be especially noted. He was a founder of the American Institute of International Law and took an active part in most of the international societies and congresses affecting the Western Hemisphere during the last forty years.

A departure from the routine of former "Law" sections of the *Handbook* is initiated in this issue, consisting of the inclusion of annotated and unannotated editions of codes and laws. It is hoped that thus a connection may be established between the *Handbook*, and the series of legal guides published by the Law Library of Congress, by which the *Handbook* will bring up to date the material contained in the Guides.

BIBLIOGRAPHY

(*See also sections on* Government, Labor and Social Welfare, *and* Philosophy)

COLLECTIONS OF LAWS AND BIBLIOGRAPHIES

Argentina

Gil Navarro, Orlando (ed.). Novísima recopilación de leyes usuales de la República Argentina y decretos reglamentarios, revisada y puesta al día. Buenos Aires. Casa ed. Rodríguez Giles. 4 vols. [4421

Índice ediar y códigos argentinos. Vol. 2. Buenos Aires. Cía. argentina de editores. 2746 p. [4422
An extremely useful and very extensive digest-index of the provisions of the civil code of Argentina, with citations to the articles where the provisions can be found. The original text of the code with the notes of its drafter, Vélez Sarsfield, is found at the back of the volume. The texts of amendatory legislation are also appended. The first volume, containing an index-digest to the Constitution and other codes has not yet been published.

Restoy, Eugenio, and **Arturo Doeste** (comps.). Compilación de leyes, decretos y resoluciones. Vols. 2, 3. Buenos Aires. [4423
Covers the legislation under a topical classification.

Chile

Orden público. disposiciones legales y reglamentarias sobre la materia. Ed. oficial. Santiago. Ed. Zig-Zag. (Ministerio del interior). 582 p. [4424
Contains the text of the Constitution, pertinent articles from the Penal Code, the press law, election law, regulations governing aliens, etc.

Costa Rica

Disposiciones legales atinentes a la defensa nacional. San José. Imp. nacional. 35 p. [4425
A pamphlet containing a compilation of emergency war legislation.

Cuba

Sánchez Roca, Mariano. Legislación de transportes . . . Conforme a los textos oficiales, concordada, puesta al día, anotada con la jurisprudencia del Tribunal supremo y completos sumarios alfabéticos é índices legislativos. Habana. Ed. Lex. (Manuales Lex, 14). 656 p. [4426
An annotated compilation of legislation on all types of transportation, including railroads, air and maritime navigation, as well as general and special regulations thereon, all annotated with case law.

Mexico

Andrade, Manuel. Leyes y reglamentos sobre comunicaciones y transportes. México. Información aduanera de México. Loose-leaf. [4427
Another of the author's valuable loose-leaf services covering legislation and departmental orders, circulars and regulations on such subjects as transportation by air, rail, highway, and sea; postal service, radio, telegraphs, etc.

Legislación de emergencia relativa a propiedades y negocios del enemigo. México. Junta de administración y vigilancia de la propiedad extranjera. 234 p. [4428
An unannotated compilation of war legislation, including laws and executive decrees suspending temporarily constitutional rights, the administration of property of enemy aliens, enacted in 1942 and 1943.

Nicaragua

Leyes de emergencia 1941–1943. Managua. Tall. nacionales. (Publ. del Ministerio de hacienda). 319 p. [4429
A compilation of legislative and executive decrees and laws from June 23, 1941 to August 28, 1943.

Peru

León Garaycochea, C. P. Legislación de aeronáutica. Lima. Imp. Segrestán. 2 vols. [4430
The first two volumes of a very useful compilation of legislation on Peruvian aviation, by the compiler of the more extensive work on naval and aviation law. The compilation includes not only legislation, but also departmental and executive orders, regulations, provisions from other related legislation, from the Constitution, the national budget, codes, and extracts or digests from council regulations.

PHILOSOPHY OF LAW; HISTORY OF LAW; JURISPRUDENCE

General

Vance, John T. The background of Hispanic American law; legal sources and

juridical literature of Spain. New York. Central book co. 296 p. **[4431**
A commercial edition of a dissertation submitted in 1937 which was described in the *Handbook, no. 3, 1937* (nos. 2208 and 3623). Corrections, a few additions and an index to authors cited are found in this edition.

ARGENTINA

(*See also items* 4964, 4973)

Borga, Ernesto Eduardo. Ciencia jurídica; ó jurisprudencia técnica. Buenos Aires. Ed. Sociedad bibliográfica argentina. 516 p. **[4432**
A contribution in the field of philosophy and history of law by a professor at the Universidad de La Plata. The influence of the theories of well-known legal philosophers, such as Kelsen, Scheler, Kant, Recasens Siches, del Vecchio and others, is discussed in the various chapters.

Bustos Fierro, Raúl. Iniciación al derecho. Córdoba. Ed. "Assandri." 126 p. **[4433**
A general discussion of the development of law.

Carbone, M. Filosofía del derecho. Buenos Aires. Ed. Sanná. 403 p. **[4434**
A textbook in use by the Facultad de Derecho y Ciencias Sociales de Buenos Aires. This material follows the general trend of such works published in Latin America, i.e., it gives a general survey of the philosophy of law from ancient Greece to modern times. A discussion of the various schools of thought, particularly those developed in Italy and Germany, is included, followed by chapters on theory of law, positive law, and applied law.

BRAZIL

Ribeiro, C. J. de Assis. História do direito brasileiro. Vol. 1, 1500–1822. Rio de Janeiro. Liv. Zélio Valverde. 208 p. **[4437**
This first volume of an ambitious work considers the history of penal law in primitive and colonial Brazil under three aspects: penal law among the Indians at the time of the discovery of Brazil; as applied in the villages into which the early missionaries attempted to gather and settle the Indians; and in the colony, up to the time of the Independence. In the first two parts the author utilizes the testimony of the Jesuit fathers and of the explorers and travellers who left accounts of the sixteenth and seventeenth centuries. The third part concerns the colonial law of Portugal.

COLOMBIA

Sánchez, J. G. Legal system of Colombia (*Law notes*, vol. 47, May, p. 5–15, 18–22). **[4438**

DOMINICAN REPUBLIC

Mejía Ricart, Gustavo Adolfo. Historia general del derecho. Santiago, Dom. Rep. Ed. El Diario. 378 p. **[4439**
A very valuable contribution, in a field that is practically untouched. It is apparently a companion volume to the author's *Historia General de Derecho e Historia del Derecho Dominicano* (1942). The discussion is arranged in five parts: the pre-Hispanic; the period of Spanish conquest (1492–1680); the Colonial (1680–1821); the period of Haitian domination, when French law was applied to the island (1822–1844); and the Dominican (1884–1943). The last chapter deals with the French codes and important laws adopted in the last period. The author points out that, because of this abrupt break in the evolution of the national legal system, the Dominican Republic has French laws. Nevertheless, Spanish influence lingers "in many aspects of our juridical tradition."

MEXICO

(*See also item* 4967)

Esquivel Obregón, Toribio. Apuntes para la historia del derecho en México. Vol. 3. México. Publicidad y ediciones. 768 p. **[4440**
The fine detail of this scholarly work by the eminent Mexican jurist is carried on in this third volume of a compendious history of law. The present volume deals with private law and legislation enacted during the period of transition following the end of the colonial régime. The first volume was noted in *Handbook, no. 3, 1937*, no. 3647.

EVOLUCIÓN DEL DERECHO MEXICANO, 1912–1942. México. Ed. Jus. (Publ. de la Escuela libre de derecho, Serie B, Vol. 6). 2 vols. **[4441**
An important symposium by well-known jurists. The work covers the various branches of law and their development over a period of 30 years. Included are studies on philosophy of law, constitutional law, administrative law, private and public international law, labor law, penal legislation and penal procedure, civil laws and civil procedure, commercial law, and some general topics, such as development of the legal profession, legal culture and general theories of law. Among the contributors are Felipe Tena Ramírez, José Ángel Ceniceros, Pablo Macedo, and Germán Fernández del Castillo.

Ramos, Samuel. Historia de la filosofía del derecho. México. Imp. universitaria. 186 p. **[4443**
The subject of philosophy of law is treated chronologically. The second part of the book concerns the introduction of various philosophical theories in Mexico, and deals particularly with the work of several Mexican authors.

Peru

Alvarado Sánchez, José. Las fundaciones en nuestro derecho. Lima. Cía de impresiones y publicidad. 108 p. [4444
Reviewed in *Revista Peruana de Derecho*, April–June, 1943.

Venezuela

Herrera Mendoza, Lorenzo. La escuela estatutoria en Venezuela y su evolución hacia la territorialidad. Caracas. 122 p. [4445
Reviewed in the *Boletín de la Facultad de Derecho y Ciencias Sociales* (Córdoba), July–August, 1943, and also in *Revista de Derecho Internacional* (Havana, Cuba), December 31, 1943.

COURTS AND JUDICIAL PROCEDURE (CIVIL AND CRIMINAL)

Argentina

Alsina, Hugo. Tratado teórico-práctico de derecho procesal civil y comercial. Vol. 3. Buenos Aires. Cía. argentina de editores. [4447
The first and second volumes of this compendious treatise on procedure appeared in 1941 and 1942, respectively. The present volume concerns the various types of procedure in both the civil and commercial fields, treated from a comparative point of view. The work contains extensive footnotes and case law of the Argentine courts.

Ayarragaray, Carlos Alberto. Introducción a la ejecución de sentencias. Buenos Aires. Ed. V. Abeledo. 263 p. [4448
The author gives a synthesis of his lectures over a period of years. This volume contains an excellent foreword by the author on how legislation for a nation should be formulated and developed in this field. There are also numerous footnotes, while various chapters include individual bibliographies relating to the subject discussed.

Código de procedimientos en lo civil y comercial de la provincia de Buenos Aires. Contiene además las leyes sobre términos judiciales para dictar sentencia, impuesto de justicia, etc. Buenos Aires. Ed. J. Lajouane y cía. (Códigos de la provincia de Buenos Aires). 214 p. [4449

Código de procedimientos en material civil y comercial de la capital de la república, completado con las leyes sobre organización de los tribunales de la capital. Buenos Aires. Ed. J. Lajouane y cía. (Códigos y leyes usuales de la República Argentina). 286 p. [4450

Colombo, Carlos J. La Corte nacional de casación. Buenos Aires. Ed. V. Abeledo. 2 vols. [4451
An extensive discussion on cassation, giving its general historical antecedents, with particular reference to Argentine legislation and practice. The various types of cassation cases are discussed, including civil and criminal, in labor and administrative law, and the system as practiced in the provinces. A section is devoted to comparative law. There are two appendices which contain a comprehensive bibliography by countries, and a draft for new legislation for Argentina.

Guía de los tribunales. Buenos Aires. Imp. Mercur. 114 p. [4452
The type of information included in this handbook is generally difficult to ascertain, such as the location of the various courts, the names and addresses of the judges, and the location of government agencies. It also contains the text of pertinent provisions of the Constitution and related legislation.

Imaz, Esteban, and Ricardo E. Rey. El recurso extraordinario. Buenos Aires. Ed. Revista de jurisprudencia argentina. 298 p. [4453
A treatise on federal procedure dealing with the extraordinary remedy available to individuals in upholding the supremacy of the Constitution. It contains a discussion of constitutional and administrative law, with references to North American practice.

Lazcano Colodrero, Raúl. Ley orgánica del poder judicial de la Provincia de Córdoba. Buenos Aires. Ed. Jurídica Argentina. 330 p. [4454
This volume contains not only the well-annotated text of the provincial law regulating the local judiciary, but also the texts of the Constitution and by-laws of various organizations including the Bar Association of Córdoba, the Association of Notaries, the Association of Accountants, and others.

Persegani, Primo. Causa Fernando D. Orecchia versus "La Continental compañía de seguros generales, s.a." . . . Buenos Aires. Ed. Caporaletti hnos. 287 p. [4455
A discussion and study of a case decided by the courts in the capital of Buenos Aires, where the insurance company refused to pay on a policy of 100,000 pesos upon the death of the insured, because of fraud. The insured was killed by relatives, the beneficiaries, to secure this sum. An excellent legal study on fraud and the provision in insurance policies in point is included.

Procedimiento y recursos ante la justicia federal por aplicación de leyes especiales . . . Buenos Aires. (Facultad de derecho de la Universidad de Buenos Aires, Investigaciones del Seminario de ciencias jurídicas y sociales, Publ. 41). 397 p. [4456
A composite work by students of the Seminar under the direction of Professor Jantus. The topic covers federal procedure

and appeals in the field of customs law, domestic taxation and patents.

Sabaté, Domingo. Régimen procesal de menores. Buenos Aires. Ed. La Facultad, 78 p. **[4457**

An article by article comment on the Law of Juvenile Courts of 1939. The author also includes opinions and decisions rendered in cases in point; statistics on juvenile delinquency for the years 1940–1942, arranged by the types of crimes committted; and an appendix of suggested amendments to the law.

BRAZIL

CÓDIGO DE PROCESSO PENAL. DECRETO-LEI NO. 3689 DE 3 DE OUTUBRO DE 1941. Rio de Janeiro, São Paulo. (Códigos e leis do Brasil, Coleção Freitas Bastos). 435 p. **[4458**

Contains in addition a few other pertinent decrees and an index prepared by Serrano de Andrade.

Braga, António Pereira. Exegese do código de processo civil. Vol. 2, tomo 2. Rio de Janeiro. Ed. Max Limonad. 527 p. **[4459**

An ambitious treatise on the new Code of Civil Procedure, with much attention given to theory. The present volume discusses articles 1 and 2. The preceding volume, published in 1942, was purely introductory, discussing the historical problems of procedural law.

Buzaid, Alfredo. A ação declaratória no direito brasileiro. São Paulo. Livr. Acadêmica, Saraiva & cia. (Coleção de estudos de direito processual civil. 199 p. **[4460**

A good study, in which the author has given adequate attention to the origin of the declaratory judgment, its position in comparative law and in international law, and finally its use, scope and purpose under the new Brazilian Code of Civil Procedure.

Cunha, Hamilton Pinheiro da. Sustação da execução. Errônea aplicação do decreto-lei no. 4,598 de 29/8/1942, sôbre alugueres. São Paulo. Departamento jurídico da prefeitura de São Paulo. Procuradoria judicial. 41 p. **[4461**

The *mandado de segurança* is a new institution of the Brazilian law, first projected in the 1920's and first formulated in the 1934 Constitution. It is a writ which owes much to the writs of Anglo-American law and which bears some resemblance to the Mexican *amparo*. Its use and development is of the first importance and any petitions for its protection therefore of greatest interest. In this case the City of São Paulo sought it against what was alleged to be a manifestly illegal action of the judge of the inferior court. The argument prepared by the City's lawyer here published, rehearses the important elements of and grounds for the use of the writ.

Espinola Filho, Eduardo. Código de processo penal. Vol. 5. Rio de Janeiro. Livr. Freitas Bastos. 547 p. **[4462**

The latest volume in this important commentary concerns arts. 503 to 620, on special actions and appeals in general. Reviewed in *Direito*, ano 4, vol. 21, p. 143.

Nunes, Castro. Teoria e prática do poder judiciario. Rio de Janeiro. Ed. "Revista forense." 698 p. **[4463**

Picanço, Melchiades. Das ações de divisão e demarcação de terras. Rio de Janeiro. Ed. A. Coelho Branco F°. (Biblioteca jurídica brasileira, 48). 163 p. **[4464**

The first part is a commentary on the articles of the new Code of Civil Procedure which concern boundaries and partition of land. A large proportion of the book consists of an appendix containing portions of the old codes of civil procedure for the Federal District, the States of São Paulo, Minas Gerais, and the judicial code of the State of Rio de Janeiro which govern the subject.

Raitani, Francisco. Prática de processo civil. São Paulo. Ed. Guaíra. 376 p. **[4465**

A lawyer's form book and manual, to accompany the new code.

Souza Neto, José Soriano de. Pareceres. Recife. Ed. Saraiva. (Separata de *Revista académica da Faculdade de direito do Recife*, vol. 49). 249 p. **[4466**

Opinions on questions of law, some of them hypothetical questions and some actual cases. One of the most interesting cases concerns payment and protest of international bills of exchange.

CHILE

CÓDIGO ORGÁNICO DE TRIBUNALES. Edición oficial. Santiago. Imp. Universo. (Códigos de la República de Chile). 189 p. **[4467**

Aylwin Azocar, Patricio. El juicio arbitral. Santiago. Imp. El Imparcial. 347 p. **[4468**

This dissertation, presented to the Facultad de Derecho de la Universidad de Chile, is a careful study of an important phase of labor law.

Fontecilla Riquelme, Rafael. Derecho procesal penal, naturaleza del proceso penal y las normas que lo regulan en la doctrina, en la ley, en la jurisprudencia de nuestros tribunales. Santiago. Ed. El Imparcial. 2 vols. **[4469**

A two-volume text on penal procedure. Each chapter is divided into sub-topics printed in bold-face type. The first volume discusses the legal history of criminal procedure. The second treats principally of the rules of procedure in force in various countries, and especially in Chile. Both are extensively documented, and contain digests of case-law. These notes in many instances include the entire text of the judge's opinion. The work also has fine alphabetical subject and author indexes, as well as an index to the Latin phrases used, with Spanish equivalents, index to cases cited, and to the legal provisions and codes cited.

Melo, Guerrero, Mariano. Competencia y procedimientos de la Corte suprema en materia internacional. Valparaíso. Tip. Salesiana. 327 p. [4470

A comprehensive treatment.

COLOMBIA

Peña Dávila, Juan Manuel. La prueba en derecho procesal civil. Bogotá. Ed. Centro. 143 p. [4471

A brief comment on the law governing the introduction of evidence in civil causes. The author includes a handy index to the pertinent articles of the judicial code.

CUBA

Aguilar Almeida, Fernando Leopoldo. Ley de enjuiciamiento civil, comentada y algunos juicios críticos. Vol. 1. Habana. Ed. Cultural. [4472

The author has annotated each article of the Cuban Code of Civil Procedure, not only with case-law and decisions of his own rendering, but also with comments and suggestions from his own experience on the bench. An important discussion on what the modern judge should know, consider and apply, is found on the first 23 pages.

Caneda y Acosta, Cecilio Abelardo. El amparo y su jurisprudencia; comentarios a la Orden 362 de 1900. Habana. Ed. Cultural. 414 p. [4473

The author has commented at length upon each article of the Cuban writ of *amparo,* and cited case-law in point. This writ is not to be confused with the comprehensive constitutional suit of Mexico of the same name. In Cuba, this protective suit is limited to the recovery of property unlawfully seized or held.

Castroverde, Salvador W. de. La expropiación forzosa en nuestro derecho positivo y en la jurisprudencia. Habana. Ed. Jesús Montero. (Bibl. jurídica de autores cubanos y extranperos, vol. 70). 121 p. [4474

An illuminating treatise on eminent domain legislation and practice in Cuba. Reviewed in *Revista de Derecho Internacional* (Havana), issue of December 31, 1943.

GUATEMALA

Coronado Aguilar, Manuel. Curso de derecho procesivo penal. Guatemala. Tip. Sánchez y De Guise. 425 p. [4475

If this is not the first comprehensive treatise on criminal procedure in Guatemala, it is the first in many years.

HAITI

CODE D'INSTRUCTION CRIMINELLE, AVEC LES DERNIÈRES MODIFICATIONS. Port-au-Prince. Ed. Henri Deschamps. 199 p. [4476

A. Rigal, former director of L'École Nationale de Droit, has provided annotations.

MEXICO

NUEVO CÓDIGO FEDERAL DE PROCEDIMIENTOS CIVILES, PUBLICADO EN EL *Diario oficial,* TOMO 136, NO. 45, CORRESPONDIENTE AL 24 DE FEBRERO DE 1943, CON EXPOSICIÓN DE MOTIVOS. México. Antigua libr. Robredo. 193, 147 p. [4477

An unannotated edition of the new federal code of civil procedure. The first 193 pages are devoted to the *exposición de motivos,* and the last 147 to the text of the code.

Burgoa, Ignacio. El juicio de amparo. México. Ed. Minerva. 673 p. [4478

A detailed history of the famous Mexican writ of *amparo.* The author's introduction dealing with the philosophical basis of the writ is in itself worthy of notice. He then traces the origin and development of this constitutional suit.

Canudas y Orezza, Luis Felipe. Nuevo código federal de procedimientos civiles ... con una monografía sobre el Ministerio público federal por el lic. José Aguilar y Maya. México. Ed. Porrúa hnos. y cía. [4479

The new federal code of procedure supersedes that of 1908, and the text, annotated by the author, is included herein, as is that of the new organic law on the office of Federal Government Attorney. The study includes an informative *exposición de motivos.*

Pina, Rafael de. Temas de derecho procesal. México. [4480

The author is a Spanish authority on procedure and former professor at the University of Seville, now domiciled in Mexico. The work is general in nature, but a great part of it is devoted to Mexican legislation and practice.

URUGUAY

Couture, Eduardo J. El procedimiento verbal ante los jueces de paz. Segunda ed. Montevideo. Ed. Claudio García y cía. 63 p. [4481

A reprint from the *Revista de Estudios Jurídicos y Sociales,* dealing with the subject of oral procedure in cases coming before the courts of justices of the peace in Uruguay.

Macedo, Álvaro F. Sentencias: derecho civil, derecho comercial, derecho procesal.

Montevideo. Ed. C. García y cía. 390 p. **[4482**
A collection of decisions rendered by the author during three years on the bench. These cover civil and commercial problems, such as domestic relations, legal capacity to contract, sales, succession, copyright, negotiable instruments, agency, as well as various branches of the procedural field.

VENEZUELA

Acuña, Alfredo. Jurisprudencia ordenada de la Corte federal y de casación de Venezuela. Caracas. Ed. "Las Novedades." 299 p. **[4483**
A digest of case law compiled from the reports of the Federal Court covering the period from 1935 to 1942. A useful tool for the research worker.

EXPOSICIÓN DE MOTIVOS Y PROYECTO DE CÓDIGO DE PROCEDIMIENTO CIVIL. 1943. Caracas. Boletín de la Comisión codificadora nacional, Publ. extraordinaria no. 40. 214 p. **[4484**

ADMINISTRATIVE AND CONSTITUTIONAL LAW

ARGENTINA

Adrogué, Carlos A. Poderes impositivos federal y provincial sobre los instrumentos de gobierno. Buenos Aires. Ed. G. Kraft. 711 p. **[4484a**
A treatise on taxation, with emphasis on administration.

Álvarez, Juan C. Derecho federal y municipal. Buenos Aires. Ed. Sanná. 530 p. **[4485**
The contents refer to Argentine material. Each chapter is headed by a summary of its contents.

Berçaitz, Miguel Ángel. Régimen de créditos a empleados y obreros de la administración pública. Buenos Aires. Ed. L. J. Rosso. 139 p. **[4486**
A distinguished contribution to the field of administrative law with respect to the subject of government employees.

Jarach, Dino. El hecho imponible; teoría general del derecho tributario sustantivo. Buenos Aires. Revista de jurisprudencia argentina. 184 p. **[4487**
The author stresses the juridical viewpoint, and includes extensive footnotes with references to foreign works.

BRAZIL

Cavalcanti, Themistocles Brandão. Tratado de direito administrativo. Vols. 2–4. Rio de Janeiro. Livr. Freitas Bastos. **[4488**
Volume I appeared in 1942. Volume II to IV, *Dos Serviços Públicos, Execução Diréta, Autarquias, Economia Mixta, Concessões,* are of considerable practical value, since it is the most rapidly developing phase of administrative law.

Fonseca, Tito Prates da. Lições de direito administrativo. Rio de Janeiro. **[4489**
The work of this jurist in public law is well known in Brazil for solidity and usefulness. This volume improves on his older work, *Direito Administrativo,* by including more interpretative matter.

Pinto, Carlos Alberto A. de Carvalho. Discriminação de rendas. Segunda ed. São Paulo. Prefeitura do município de São Paulo. 193 p. **[4490**
One of the studies presented by this author to the Conferência Nacional de Legislação Tributária in 1941. He gives a technical discussion of the administration of the Brazilian tax system, with some comparative matter.

Sousa, Rubens Gomes de. A distribuição da justiça em matéria fiscal. São Paulo. Ed. Martins. 112 p. **[4491**
The author suggests the setting up of an administrative council to supervise the administration of the fiscal laws, the decisions of the council to be subject to review by the ordinary courts.

CHILE

Zañartu Irigoyen, Hugo. Recopilación de leyes y reglamentos administrativos, especialmente sobre el servicio de obras públicas. Santiago. Tall. graf. Héctor Benaprés. 2 vols. **[4492**
The first volume contains the text of the Constitution and of the *ley de emergencia,* besides the organic laws of many governmental agencies. Volume two includes the *ley orgánica de obras públicas,* as well as laws and regulations on public roads, bridges, railroads, etc. The compilation is not annotated.

CUBA

Gutiérrez Sánchez, Gustavo. Código electoral. Habana. Ed. Lex. 469 p. **[4493**
An annotated text of the new electoral law of 1943, which, among other innovations, makes voting by the citizens compulsory, and failure to do so punishable. The code is preceded by a lengthy discursive introduction of 64 pages by the compiler. The consultation of the material is greatly facilitated by the marginal notes and the various elaborate indexes and digests.

Lazcano y Mazón, Andrés María. Ley de jubilaciones de funcionarios y empleados públicos de 25 de junio de 1919 y sus modificaciones. Habana. Ed. Lex. 409 p. **[4494**
The text of the law is followed by lengthy annotations to each provision with historical background material, definitions in the

constitution and civil service legislation. A second part of work is devoted to case-law from 1919 to 1942, in a convenient alphabetical arrangement. The third part of the volume relates principally to the text of the retirement law of 1919, but inserts also entire texts, or pertinent provisions, of related legislation up to 1943. The fourth part includes legal and judicial forms, and there is at the end a brief alphabetical subject summary of the pension law.

Pozo, Justo L. Dictámen sobre el proyecto de ley de los oficios públicos. Habana. Imp. P. Fernández y cía. 169 p. [4495

A report by a member of the Senate Committee on Political and Constitutional Law, dealing with the regulations of services of public officials and employees.

Ramírez Olivella, Gustavo. Legislación contencioso-administrativa con toda la jurisprudencia establecida por el Tribunal supremo de Cuba desde su creación hasta la fecha. Segunda ed. notablemente aumentada. Habana. (Biblioteca jurídica de autores cubanos y extranjeros, vol. 121.) 394 p. [4496

The first edition of this compilation appeared in 1931. The material covers administrative law and procedure, particularly the latter, with citations and excerpts from cases decided by administrative tribunals.

Vidal de la Torre, Luis, and **Miguel A. Pérez León.** Apremios administrativos. Habana. Ed. Lex. 557 p. [4497

The joint authors, both Government officials, have set forth herein the legislation and procedure for compelling the payment of national and municipal taxes by the citizens. The articles of the laws appear in large type, and the authors' comments follow in smaller type, while the extensive footnotes, including related legislation and case law, are printed in italics. Various forms are found at the back of the volume. The specific laws treated are decree-laws nos. 113 of July 31, 1935, and no. 773 of April 4, 1936.

Mexico

Codificación de las disposiciones administrativas vigentes cuya aplicación corresponde al Departamento del Distrito Federal. Publicación oficial. México. Imp. Acción. 2 vols. [4498

A comprehensive compilation of laws, regulations, decrees, circulars, administrative decisions and other legal provisions related to the government of the Federal District of Mexico.

Uruguay

Estrázulas, Hugo. La administración pública en el estado moderno (poder discrecional, recurso por desviación de poder). Montevideo. Ed. Rex. 57 p. [4499

This study deals with the discretionary power granted to administrative bodies, and appeals against abuse of this power.

Venezuela

Hernández Ron, J. M. Tratado elemental de derecho administrativo. Segunda ed. Caracas. Ed. "Las Novedades." 431 p. [4500

The first edition of 1935, besides being out of print, has also had its contents superseded in many respects by the new legislation which Venezuela has enacted in recent years. The principal emphasis in this treatise is placed on local law, but the author includes much foreign material for comparative purposes, both in the text and in the extensive footnotes.

CIVIL LAW

Argentina

Código civil. edición facsimilar de los manuscritos del Dr. Dalmacio Vélez Sársfield. Buenos Aires. Tall. graf. de la Penitenciaría nacional. 141 p. [4501

An analytically annotated edition of the civil code officially approved by the Ministerio de Justicia é Instrucción Pública. At the end of the book are found facsimile reprints of various manuscript notes by Vélez Sársfield.

Proyecto de reforma de 1936. concordancias de antecedentes y de textos legales nacionales y extranjeros. Tomo 1. Buenos Aires. Seminario de ciencias jurídicas y sociales. 646 p. [4502

Under the supervision of Professor Enrique Torino, the Seminario de Ciencias Jurídicas y Sociales of the Universidad de Buenos Aires has studied the proposed amendments to the Civil Code of Argentina. Each article of the draft is carefully compared with similar provisions in preceding legislation, in proposed and drafted provisions, and in foreign legislation. This is an excellent research tool. The present volume covers only the first 332 articles of the draft.

Alsina Atienza, Dalmiro A. El principio de la buena fe en el Proyecto de reforma de 1936. Vol. 2. Buenos Aires. (Facultad de derecho civil comparado, Seminario de ciencias jurídicas y sociales). [4503

The first volume, published in 1942, was concerned with the general principles of the topic of "good faith" in all instances in which it appears in the civil code. This second volume covers the point in relation to the purchase, transfer and other methods of acquisition, and to contracts, successions, persons, and other legal acts.

Carniol, S. Enrique. Manual teórico y práctico de sucesiones y filiación. Buenos Aires. Ed. Lavalle. 2 vols. [4504

A complete handbook on cases, law and practice in the broad field of succession, including wills, testaments, partition, guardianship, taxation, administrators and testators, and proof. The extensive footnotes contain the text of legislation and of learned opinion on the points involved in each case. The author's notes on the amendments which he considers necessary in law are also included. Numerous forms for documents and procedure will be found in these volumes.

Legón, Fernando. Tratado de los derechos reales en el código y en la reforma. Tomo 7: Síntesis de la propiedad. Buenos Aires. Ed. Valerio Abeledo. [4505

An extensive treatise on real rights as they are covered in the Argentine civil code, and the revision of same which was proposed in 1936. The first six volumes have covered possession, protection of possessory rights, and property rights. The present volume deals with restrictions and limitations on property and ownership. Every volume is extensively annotated with references to national and foreign sources, notes to foreign legislation and excerpts from other authorities.

Saravia, Guillermo Alberto. La adopción, estudio de doctrina y de legislación comparadas y del proyecto de reforma del Código civil argentino... Buenos Aires. Ed. Depalma. (Biblioteca jurídica, Sección: Derecho civil, dirigida por el Dr. Alfredo Orgaz, 1). 312 p. [4506

A general comparative study of legislation on adoption covering the legislation of ancient Greece and the Orient up to the modern Argentine code. The legislation proposed in 1942 for a code on minors is discussed in the last chapter.

Yorio, Aquiles. Tratado de la capacidad jurídica de la mujer. Buenos Aires. Ed. El Ateneo. 493 p. [4507

A comprehensive treatise on the legal capacity of women in contracts, commercial affairs, wills and succession, property, and guardianship of children. The greater part of the work is devoted to Argentine legislation since the enactment of law No. 11.357 in 1926.

Brazil

Espinola, Eduardo, and Eduardo Espinola Filho. A lei de introdução ao código civil brasileiro. (Decreto-lei no. 4,657 de 4 de setembro de 1942). Vol. 1, arts. 1–7. Rio de Janeiro, São Paulo. Liv. Freitas Bastos. 639 p. [4508

The purpose of such a law is to state the general principles which must govern the interpretation of the code. This commentary by the Chief Justice of the Supreme Court and his son is a thorough study of the first seven articles of the law, with considerable attention given to comparative law.

Fernandes, Adaucto D'Alencar. Cláusula de não responsabilidade. Rio de Janeiro. Ed. A. Coelho Branco F°. (Bibl. jurídica brasileira, no. 49). 279 p. [4509

The first two parts of this study discuss the theory of the law of contracts and orients the clause limiting liability in the general background. Part 3 concerns the practical application of limiting clauses in various types of contracts, notably carriers' contracts, including air carriers.

Lopes, Miguel Maria Serpa. Comentário teórico e prático da lei de introdução ao código civil. Rio de Janeiro. Liv. Jacintho. 375 p. [4510

The first volume of a two-volume study of the new introductory law to the civil code. It covers the first six articles and is of equal interest to the commentary noted above.

Monteiro, Osvaldo de Carvalho. Cláusula "rebus sic stantibus" (*Rev. forense*, ano 40, vol. 94, fasc. 479, p. 242–255). [4511

A competent study of a technical problem of contract law. The author gives about equal attention to the comparative law on the principle and its acceptance and application in Brazilian law.

Rosa, Alcides. Noções de direito civil. Rio de Janeiro. Liv. Zélio Valverde. 263 p. [4512

The author says that this is "all the civil law in one volume." As a bird's-eye view of this branch of the law, this is a remarkably succinct little volume.

Chile

Alessandri Rodríguez, Arturo. De la responsabilidad extracontractual en el derecho civil chileno. Santiago. Imp. Universitaria. 716 p. [4513

A discussion of Title 35, Book IV, of the Chilean civil code by one of Chile's most renowned jurists. Its usefulness is increased by an index to the laws and code articles cited, as well as the usual alphabetical index to subject-matter.

Colombia

Cediel Ángel, Ernesto. Ineficacia de los actos jurídicos. Bogotá. Escuelas grafs. Salesianas. 269 p. [4514

A comprehensive treatment of a fundamental and frequently discussed aspect of law.

Cuba

Acevedo Laborde, René. Menores é incapacitados, preceptos legales y jurisprudencia sobre enajenación y gravámenes de sus bienes y transacciones acerca de sus derechos, con notas y comentarios. Habana. Ed. Lex. 160 p. [4515

The pertinent provisions found in the Cuban constitution, civil code, code of civil procedure, notarial code, commercial code and the mortgage law and its regulations, with respect to minors and persons legally incapacitated, are collected in this volume, and annotated with comments and case-law. Forms are also inserted where related to the point regulated in the provision.

Brito y Mederos, Lincoln E. Ley de alquileres; comentarios sobre la ley de 23 de marzo de 1939 y sus prórrogas. La Habana. Ed. Cultural. 208 p. [4516

This is a comparative study on landlord and tenant relations in Cuba and Spain by a distinguished member of the bench. Much of the case law cited is from decisions rendered by the author himself.

Machado, José. Los contratos sobre bienes con ocasión del matrimonio. Manzanillo. Ed. "El Arte." 259 p. [4517

The new Cuban constitution of 1940 occasioned considerable change in the field of domestic relations and community property, which had been regulated by the civil code provisions and their amendments. The author of this work, a municipal judge, was authorized by the Minister of Justice to publish this unofficial study. The details of the relations between husband and wife, particularly with reference to property, are well illustrated, and a discussion of the draft law drawn up by a Codification Commission is also included in this work.

Núñez y Núñez, Eduardo Rafael. Código civil hecho extensivo a Cuba por Real Decreto de 31 de julio de 1889, tal como rige después de las modificaciones introducidas por la constitución de 1940. La Habana. Ed. J. Montero. (Colección legislativa de bolsillo, vol. 3). 399 p. [4518

A small volume containing the text of the civil code of 1889, as amended to date, with annotations to certain articles to be harmonized with the changes made therein by the new Constitution of 1940.

Valle Moré, José del. La capacidad de la mujer casada para contratar y ejercer el comercio después de la Constitución de 1940. Habana. Ed. Lex. 61 p. [4519

A monograph dealing with recent progress in the field of women's right and capacity to enter contracts and other legal situations in her own name.

Mexico

Gomís Soler, José, and **Luis Muñoz.** Elementos de derecho civil mexicano. Tomo 2. México. 584 p. [4520

This most outstanding modern treatise on civil law commenced publication in 1942. The second volume covers real rights only. Each subdivision of the subject is treated historically.

Rojina Villegas, Rafael. Teoría general de las obligaciones o derecho de crédito. México. Ed. El nacional. 2 vols. [4521

A comprehensive treatise on the subject of obligations and contracts in general. The law and practice in Mexico are particularly stressed throughout, with comparative commentaries on foreign laws.

Uruguay

Oddo, Julio Armando. La adopción, estudio del instituto en la doctrina, en nuestro derecho positivo y en otras legislaciones. Montevideo. Imp. Moderna. 184 p. [4522

A comparative study on adoption in Roman law and in the modern legislation of France, Switzerland, Prussia and other countries, Particular emphasis, however, is given to local legislation and practice, as regulated by the provisions of the various codes and special laws of Uruguay.

Venezuela

Adrián-La Rosa, Mariano. Estudio comparativo del código civil, vigente, con él de 1922. Caracas. Ed. Egry. 502 p. [4523

An important and scholarly work, containing the text of the recently enacted civil code of Venezuela printed on one side of the page, and the corresponding provisions of the superseded code of 1922 on the other side, for purposes of comparison. The changes in wording are noted in italics in the former code. Besides 140 entirely new articles, there are also many changes, principally of terminology. A valuable reference tool.

Código civil de los estados unidos de Venezuela. Edición oficial. Caracas. Imp. Nacional. 548 p. [4524

An unannotated official edition of the recently enacted civil code of Venezuela.

CRIMINAL LAW

Argentina

Bernaqui Jaureguy, Carlos Alberto. El delito de estafa y sus principios doctrinarios. Buenos Aires. Libr. jurídica V. Abeledo. 648 p. [4525

This work is an enlarged and improved edition of the author's dissertation, which was awarded a gold medal by the Facultad de Derecho de La Plata. It is a very detailed and scholarly study covering all phases of the crime of fraud, comparing Argentine legislation with that of other countries, including France, Spain, Germany, and with Anglo-Saxon practice, as well as with that of other American republics.

Gallegos, Jorge L. El menor ante el derecho penal, estudio comparativo del problema argentino del abandono en la minoridad. Buenos Aires. Ed. A. López. 517 p. [4526]

An extensive treatise on a favorite subject—juvenile delinquency.

Matti, Carlos Horacio. Elementos de derecho penal; Parte general. Vol. 1. Buenos Aires. Ed. Dovile. [4527]

The first volume of a comprehensive treatise on penal law in general, with references to local legislation and practice.

Monacelli, Gualterio. Derecho penal fiscal; régimen de los impuestos internos; la doctrina, legislación y jurisprudencia. Bahía Blanca. "Casa Muñiz." 318 p. [4528]

A monograph on the criminal law in the field of taxation, including some background material, and discussing the different types of taxes imposed in Argentina, what constitutes liability and punishable acts, and the procedure for trying and punishing these acts.

Porto, Jesús Edelmiro. La pena de muerte. Buenos Aires. Sociedad bibliográfica argentina. 471 p. [4529]

A most interesting and comprehensive work on capital punishment. The author gives a general and local historical survey, discusses Argentine and foreign legislation from the philosophical point of view, and gives arguments in favor and against capital punishment.

Ure, Ernesto J. El delito de apropiación indebida. Buenos Aires. Ed. Ideas. 419 p. [4530]

A treatise on unjust enrichment and restitution. This topic is included in the Argentine penal code along with crimes of fraud, abuse of confidence, cheating, theft, etc. The work contains extensive footnotes with reference not only to the national legislation, but to Argentine case-law and to foreign treatises in the field.

BRAZIL

CÓDIGO PENAL. DECRETO-LEI NO. 2,848 DE 7 DE DEZEMBRO DE 1940. Rio de Janeiro, São Paulo. Liv. Freitas Bastos. (Códigos e leis do Brasil. Coleção Freitas Bastos). 363 p. [4531]

Contains also the *lei das contravenções penais;* the *lei de introdução ao código penal e da lei das contravenções penais.* Index provided by Serrano de Andrade.

Americano, Odin S. do Brasil. Dos crimes contra os costumes. São Paulo. Ed. Revista dos tribunais. [4532]

A well-documented work on a section of the new penal code.

Baldessarini, Francisco de Paula. Dos crimes contra a incolumidade pública, dos crimes contra a paz pública, dos crimes contra a fe pública. Rio de Janeiro. Livr. Jacinto. (Tratado de direito penal, vol. 9). 291 p. [4533]

A volume in this monumental commentary on the new penal code, each subject being treated by a different author.

Carvalho, Beni. Crimes contra a religião, os costumes e a família. Rio de Janeiro. Livr. Jacinto. (Tratado de direito penal). 384 p. [4534]

Another volume in this many-volumed treatise.

Duarte, José. Da ação penal, da extinção, da punibilidade. Rio de Janeiro. Livr. Jacinto. 272 p. [4535]

A treatise on articles 102 to 120 of the new penal code. The author admittedly leans heavily on the Italian commentators on the Italian penal code, to which the Brazilian criminal code is much indebted.

Noronha, Edgard Magalhães. Crimes contra os costumes. Comentários aos arts. 213 a 226, e 108 no. viii do Código penal. São Paulo. Livr. Acadêmica, Saraiva & cia. 364 p. [4536]

A public defense attorney (*promotor público*) discusses the field of law known to American lawyers as "sex crimes."

Ribeiro, Jorge Severiano. Do crime, da responsabilidade, da co-autoria. Rio de Janeiro. Livr. Jacinto. (Tratado de direito penal, vol. 2). 438 p. [4537]

This well-known commentator on penal law contributes an important volume to the compendium on the new code being issued by this publisher.

Silva, A. J. da Costa e. Código penal. (Decreto-lei no. 2848, 7 de dezembro de 1940). Vol. I, arts. 1 a 74. São Paulo. Cia. ed. nacional. 422 p. [4538]

One of the most trustworthy, if conservative, commentaries on the new code. The author, a former São Paulo judge whose treatises on the old penal code were authoritative, died July 8, 1943. He had been invited by the Minister of Justice to assist the members of the commission named to draft the 1940 code. Many of his observations on the changes made in the new law are included in this work.

Sousa, Iéte Ribeiro de, and José Luiz Ribeiro de Sousa. O novo direito penal. São Paulo, Ed. revista dos tribunais. 501 p. [4539]

A practical guide, with many forms, to the penal code and the code of criminal procedure.

Vergara, Pedro. Delito de homicídio. Vol. I. O dolo no homicídio. Rio de Janeiro. Livr. Jacinto. 520 p. [4540]

The author considers the concept of homicide in the new penal code. Such reconsideration of the fundamental principles of the criminal law are necessary, in the light of the new attitudes towards crime and criminals implicit in the modern legislation that served as a model for the Brazilian code.

COLOMBIA

Mesa Prieto, Guillermo (ed.). Código penal colombiano. Segunda ed. Bogotá. Ed. Cromos. (Codificaciones J. A. Archila). 480 p. [4541

Ortega Torres, Jorge. Código penal y de procedimiento penal. Bogotá. Ed. Centro. (Ediciones librería jurídica). 415 p. [4542
The text, with annotations.

CUBA

González Enríquez, Pablo F. El código de defensa en la jurisdicción correccional. Habana. Ed. Lex. 330 p. [4543
The articles of the new penal code are discussed at length. The texts of the articles are inserted in small type and are followed by numbers which indicate citations to *jurisprudencia* of the criminal chamber of the Supreme Court, 1939–1942, in the fifth part of the volume. The text of recent legislation is found in the various appendices, while the previous legislation is commented upon in connection with the main part of the work.

Maza y Rodríguez, Emilio. La legítima defensa en la jurisprudencia cubana. La Habana. Ed. Jesús Montero. (Bibl. jurídica de autores cubanos y extranjeros, vol. 73). 268 p. [4544
Reviewed in *Revista de Derecho Internacional* (Havana), issue of December 31, 1943.

Sánchez Roca, Mariano. Leyes penales de la República de Cuba y su jurisprudencia. Conforme a los textos oficiales. Vol. 1. Habana. Ed. Lex. [4545
The first volume of the compilation of Cuban penal legislation follows the style instituted by Sánchez Roca in his previous collections on administrative and civil laws. These constitute up-to-date research tools. In the present volume, the new code of social defense is extensively annotated with case-law and digests of prior legislation. An unannotated text of the military criminal code is also included. The compiler includes individual indexes to the two codes and to the legislation cited.

PERU

Cuba Torres, Sergio. Código penal del Perú. Ley no. 4868, anotado y concordado con la jurisprudencia de los tribunales. Trujillo, Perú. Imp. Gamarra. 176, lxvi p. [4546
An annotated edition of the 1924 Criminal Code, containing references to pertinent provisions of other legislation and to case-law in point. A lengthy appendix includes the texts of other special laws complementing the code such as those on vagrancy, aliens, police zoning, military courts, use of explosives, etc.

URUGUAY

Rompani, Santiago I. Delitos de difamación e injuria y legislación sobre imprenta. Montevideo. Ed. Claudio García. 459 p. [4547
A good treatise on the subject.

COMMERCIAL LAW

ARGENTINA

Bosch, Felipe. Derecho comercial marítimo. Buenos Aires. Ed. El Ateneo. 311 p. [4548
An interesting work on maritime commercial law, with special reference to Argentine legislation, covering such topics as the crew, contracts for transportation of persons and goods, risks, international legal aspects, and customs. An appendix of approximately 35 pages includes short articles by various authors on related points. The author is an expert attached to the Cámara Sindical de Aseguradores Marítimos.

Molinari, Antonio Manuel, and **Ernesto Paulero.** Sociedades de responsabilidad limitada. Buenos Aires. Ed. El Ateneo. 352 p. [4549
An exhaustive treatise on comparative legislation on the limited liability business association which is similar to the English private company. The authors discuss at length the comparative legislation as well as the historical background, and the function in detail of this type of business organization in Argentina.

Pella Ratell, Roberto F. Digesto de aduana. Buenos Aires. Ed. Bernabé y cía. 3 vols. [4550
A comprehensive compilation of legislation and case law in the field of customs administration. The various topics are extensively annotated, principally with excerpts from learned opinion. Although the material is limited to legislation in force, citations are given to antecedent legislation, and this makes the work an excellent source for reference in the field.

BRAZIL

Avellar, Pedro de Alcántara. Promissórias e duplicatas. Rio de Janeiro. Liv. Jacinto. 505 p. [4551
The author eschews the idea that his book is a treatise. It is intended merely as a guide and form book for the law on this type of negotiable instrument.

Brasil, Avio. Reserva de domínio. Rio de Janeiro. Liv. Jacinto. 315 p. [4552

Nelson Hungria, in his preface to this study, calls it the most complete made in Brazil of this type of sales contract. The author includes a good selection of pertinent laws, with explanatory notes.

CHILE

Allú Fernández, Ricardo. Juntas de accionistas en sociedades anónimas. Valparaíso. Imp. universo. 110 p. [4553

Although a dissertation presented to the University of Chile, this monograph is of considerable value in view of the dearth of material available on the subject of business associations in Chile.

Somarriva Undurraga, Manuel. Tratado de las cauciones. Santiago. Ed. Nascimento. 611 p. [4554

This treatise on suretyship grew out of law school lectures at the Universidad de Chile. The author has added to it and developed it into an excellent general treatment of the subject.

Zuloaga Villalón, Antonio. Derecho industrial y agrícola. Santiago. Ed. Nascimento. 604 p. [4555

A law school text, but valuable as a modern treatment of the subject.

COLOMBIA

Angulo, Juan B.; Miguel A. Garavito; and Alfonso Sánchez Nieto. Navegación marítima y fluvial. Bogotá. Ed. Antena. 622 p. [4556

Contains the text of the Code of Maritime and River Commerce, the Pan American Sanitary Code and Resolutions, and a compilation of laws, decrees and administrative orders on transport by sea and on inland waters, customs, etc. The compilation, made by the two first named authors, was revised and arranged by Sánchez Nieto.

Castillo, Antonio del. Comentarios de derecho comercial. Bogotá. Ed. Santafé. 140 p. [4557

Up-to-date notes on an important branch of law, in the form of lectures.

Gil Sánchez, Alberto. Estudio comparado sobre quiebras. Medellín. Ed. Teoría. 163 p. [4558

On discussing decree no. 750 of 1940, which modernized the Colombian law on bankruptcy, the author includes much historical material, as well as comparative law on the subject.

Uribe-Holguín, Ricardo. El caso fortuito y la inculpabilidad en la no ejecución de las obligaciones contractuales. Bogotá. Ed. Antena. 197 p. [4559

A careful study of the problem presented when a debtor fails to pay his debt, his default being caused by a fortuitous event or accident.

CUBA

Aguirre, Agustín. Publicidad inmobiliaria. La Habana. Ed. J. Montero. (Biblioteca jurídica de autores cubanos y extranjeros, vol. 72). 210 p. [4560

A treatise on Cuban practice and legislation on the subject of registration of real property and mortgages. The author discusses many of his points from a comparative viewpoint, with particular emphasis on the English and Australian system.

Suárez Blanco, José. Prontuario legal de la vida marítima. Habana. Ed. Lex. 320 p. [4561

A very complete handbook containing all necessary information on the legal aspects of shipping, such as papers, registration, taxation, coastwise trade, insurance, pleasure cruises, minor passengers, lights, salvage, shipwreck, sanitation, etc., compiled from the pertinent Cuban legislation. This includes not only the text of laws, decrees, and orders, but also forms.

MEXICO

Andrade, Manuel. Código de comercio reformado. Quinta ed. México. Información aduanera de México. (Ed. Andrade). Loose-leaf. [4562

Not only the text of the 1889 code, as amended to date, but also the annotated texts of legislation on banks, money, customs, corporations, and insurance, are included in this handy loose-leaf volume. This is kept up to date with subscriptions to loose-leaf additions and substitutions.

———. Nuevo código agrario. México. Información aduanera de México. 169 p. [4563

Besides the text of the new agrarian code of 1943, the compiler has also included related legislation, and the resolutions of the Claims Commission with respect to the small agricultural plots distributed among the natives at the time the landed estates were expropriated and divided up.

Barrera Graf, Jorge. El desapoderamiento de la quiebra. Análisis de las disposiciones relativas en el código de comercio y en el anteproyecto de ley de quiebras. México. Ed. Stylo. 178 p. [4564

This monograph is one of a series issued by the Seminario de Derecho Privado of the Universidad Nacional Autónoma. The author treats his subject with respect to the provisions in the commercial code and the new bankruptcy law of 1942.

Hinojosa Ortiz, Manuel. Nuevo código agrario; concordancias y comentarios. México. 269 p. [4565

The text of the agrarian code enacted in December 1942 is annotated and commented upon by the author, with citations and references to antecedent legislation.

LEGISLACIÓN BANCARIA. México. Asociación de banqueros de México. **[4566**
A compilation of banking and credit legislation, which includes the resolutions of the National Banking Commission. These form a body of administrative decisions in this field.

Rodríguez y Rodríguez, Joaquín. Ley de quiebras y de suspensión de pagos de 31 de diciembre de 1942. Concordancias, anotaciones, exposición de motivos y bibliografía. México. Ed. Porrúa y hnos. 468 p. **[4567**
An invaluable reference tool, giving not only the text of the newly enacted bankruptcy law of Mexico, but also comments and annotations, citations to pertinent provisions of other legislation, and the statement of purposes for the enactment. The author has also compiled a bibliography on bankruptcy.

PERU

Castañeda, Jorge Eugenio. La letra de cambio ante los tribunales peruanos. Lima. (Biblioteca de derecho y ciencias sociales). 83 p. **[4568**
A monograph on bills of exchange in the case-law of Peru. Reviewed in the *Revista Peruana de Derecho*, julio–diciembre 1943.

Cornejo, Lino. Derecho marítimo comercial. Lima. Ed. Gil. 150 p. **[4569**
The stenographic notes taken in the author's class on maritime commercial law have been compiled into a textbook for the Facultad de Derecho of the Universidad de San Marcos. The material is elaborated by the addition of various forms and models.

URUGUAY

Asociación de agrimensores del Uruguay. Código rural. Ley no. 10.024. Montevideo. Ed. Milton Reyes & cía. 195 p. **[4570**
The text is preceded by laws and decrees governing its application and followed by the decree-law of February 13, 1943, classifying the roads in the country and settling the jurisdiction over them, according to locality.

INTERNATIONAL LAW PRIVATE

ARGENTINA

Romero del Prado, V. N. Tratado de derecho internacional privado. Tomo 2. Córdoba. Imp. de la universidad. 577 p. **[4571**
A timely treatise on conflict of laws, in which the author criticizes many of the policies followed in such fields as extra-territoriality of law, which he declares is open to arbitrariness and caprice in its clauses of reciprocity and courtesy. Other chapters discuss the application of foreign laws in Argentina and the codification of private international law. The volume is well-documented and contains copious footnotes. This second volume is reviewed in the issue for June 30, 1944 of the *Revista de Derecho Internacional*, Havana, Cuba.

BRAZIL

Costa Netto, Benedicto. A unificação do direito privado. Ensáio de uma tese. São Paulo. Emp. gráf. da "Revista dos Tribunais." 103 p. **[4572**
A study presented to the Segunda Conferência Interamericana de Advogados of the Congresso Jurídico Nacional. The author attempts to redefine the sphere of private law.

COLOMBIA

Jaramillo Vélez, Lucrecio. La nulidad en derecho privado. Medellín. Ed. Teoría. 202 p. **[4573**
An excellent review of the subject.

ECUADOR

Jácome Moscoso, Rodrigo. Nacionalidad y extranjería. Quito. Imp. de educación. 204 p. **[4574**
This treatise on private international law relative to the rights of aliens in Ecuador is most instructive. Very little has been written on this subject in Ecuador.

MEXICO

Arce, Alberto G. Manual de derecho internacional privado mexicano. Guadalajara. Lib. Font. 521 p. **[4575**
This thorough study on conflict of laws deals particularly with Mexican legislation and practice on the various points treated therein, but it also touches upon the general aspects of the subject. This type of work should be of great interest to the North American lawyer.

VENEZUELA

Herrera Mendoza, Lorenzo. Nociones preliminares sobre extra-territorialidad de leyes y sentencias. Caracas. Emp. El Cojo. 107 p. **[4576**
A monograph on conflict of laws on the point of extraterritoriality of laws and court decisions. The author also discusses the systems of England, France and the United States.

INTERNATIONAL LAW PUBLIC

ARGENTINA

Podestá Costa, L. A. Manual de derecho internacional público. Buenos Aires. Ed. El Ateneo. 524 p. [4577
An intelligently written work on international law.

Ruiz Moreno, Isidoro. Manual de derecho internacional público. Buenos Aires. Ed. J. Castagnola. 553 p. [4578
The subject is developed from general principles and historical development to the present inter-American programs and contributions in the field. Some of the subjects covered deal with neutrality, maritime and terrestrial warfare, the society of nations, and the place of persons therein, and international administrative law.

Velasco Ibarra, José María. Derecho internacional del futuro. Buenos Aires. Ed. Americalee. 209 p. [4579
The author's views on international law in the post-war world.

CHILE

Álvarez, Alejandro. Después de la guerra. Buenos Aires. Imp. de la Universidad. (Universidad de Buenos Aires, Facultad de derecho y ciencias sociales). 544 p. [4580
A collection of three addresses delivered by the author, dealing with the contribution of America to the new international order, the comparison of the old and new orders and the need of revision in the courses in law and political science.

DOMINICAN REPUBLIC

Sánchez y Sánchez, Carlos. Curso de derecho internacional público americano. Ciudad Trujillo. Ed. Montalvo. 729 p. [4581
A very scholarly and valuable contribution in the field of public international law, as it has been developed in the Western Hemisphere. The author discusses the work of the many international and inter-American conferences and their influence upon international law. Two appendices contain the status of multilateral and bilateral treaties and conventions.

OTHER TOPICS

ARGENTINA

Argüero, Luis Eduardo, and **Mario Alberto Cichero.** El decreto no. 1580 sobre rebaja de alquileres. Buenos Aires. Ed. Scio. 158 p. [4582
A commentary on recent Argentine legislation on rent control and low-cost housing (decree no. 2175). The joint authors have compiled herein the various laws and decrees on the subject, adding their own comments. Forms are also included.

Lemoine, Luis de. Inventos y marcas. Buenos Aires. Estudios Lemoine. 261 p. [4583
A treatise on the history and recent trends in legislation on patents and trademarks.

PRIMERA CONFERENCIA DE ABOGADOS DE LA CIUDAD DE BUENOS AIRES, 4 A 7 de mayo de 1943. Buenos Aires. 345 p. 4584
The proceedings of the first Conference of the city bar association. The program of the conference is outlined, and the membership of the committees named, as well as a list of the delegates, texts of the resolutions adopted, etc. Discussion concerned principally the judicial organization of the Federal Capital, legislation on misdemeanors, adoption, and procedure in cases of support and alimony.

Ray, José Domingo, and **Horacio Solari.** Notas de estudio de legislación de minas y petróleo. Buenos Aires. El Centro de la Facultad de derecho. 84 p. [4585
Notes and comments on the important legislation dealing with mining law.

Tristán Rossi, Francisco. El Decreto-ley de locación. Buenos Aires. Ed. "Verbo." 158 p. [4586
An interesting commentary on the Argentine rent control law of 1943, and on landlord-tenant relations in general. The text of the law, and of subsequent and preceding federal and provincial decrees are included in the first chapter.

BRAZIL

Lopes, Alexandre Monteiro. Novo dicionário jurídico brasileiro. Rio de Janeiro. A. Coelho Branco Filho. (Biblioteca jurídica brasileira, no. 15). 294 p. [4587
The present volume is not the definitive Brazilian legal dictionary. But since it has only meager and out-of-date rivals, its importance is beyond question. It may be compared to, although it does not equal, Henri Capitant's *Vocabulaire Juridique*.

Medici, Fernando Penteado. Consolidação do regulamento da Ordem dos advogados do Brasil. São Paulo. Ed. Saraiva & cia. (Biblioteca da Livraria acadêmica). 184 p. [4588
A useful little handbook containing all the up-to-date legislation concerning the Brazilian Bar Association and the code of ethics for lawyers.

COLOMBIA

Arias Mejía, Gerardo. Lecciones sobre derecho minero colombiano. Medellín. Lib. Siglo XX. 710 p. [4589
Eduardo Arias Robledo assisted in the compilation of this text, and Germán Orozco Ochoa added the interpretative case-law.

Mexico

The mineral survey. THE MINING LAWS OF MEXICO. México. 211 p. [4590]
This compilation contains the translations of laws and regulations on mining up to the time of publication. A valuable source book for the research worker lacking language facilities.

Uruguay

CÓDIGO DE MINERÍA. DECRETO-LEY NO. 10,527. Ed. oficial. Montevideo. Imp. nacional. 89 p. [4591]
Promulgated January 28, 1943, to go into effect April 20, 1943.

Venezuela

Bertorelli C., Francisco José. Manual consultivo de la ley de impuesto sobre la renta. Caracas. Lib. del Comercio. 303 p. [4592]
Besides the text of the recent income tax law, with marginal notes, the compiler also includes pertinent provisions from other codes and legislation.

Cover, Gilbert Grace (ed.). Regulations governing the law of hydrocarbons of 1943. Caracas. Cía. artes gráficas. 144 p. [4593]
English and Spanish texts, with indexes in both languages.

LIBRARIES

BY

ARTHUR E. GROPP

American Library in Montevideo

NOTES OF EVENTS AND TRENDS

INSTRUCTION IN LIBRARY SCIENCE

The growing interest in the organization of libraries in Latin America has revealed the pressing need for training in librarianship. Here and there library schools have sprung up to relieve this need. Schools in operation prior to 1943 are located in Havana, São Paulo, Rio de Janeiro, Buenos Aires, and Santiago. A Summer School for librarians was held under the auspices of the American Library Association and the National Library of Colombia in Bogotá in 1942, and a course in school libraries was given in the International Summer University in San José, Costa Rica, in 1941. Centers which joined this list in 1943 are: Montevideo, Uruguay, Lima, Peru, and Trinidad, B.W.I. Furthermore, plans are being laid for instruction in Library Science in Quito, Ecuador, and in Mexico.

In Montevideo the School is operating under the auspices of the Engineers' Association of Uruguay, established there on March 23, with an enrollment of 56 students selected from 150 applicants, who met two times each week through November 27. Instruction was in charge of the editor of this section, assisted by Jeanne H. Williams, graduate of the Library School of Louisiana State University, and Dorothy M. Gropp, graduate of the Library School of Kansas State Teachers College of Emporia. It included: history of books and printing; history of libraries in ancient and medieval times and in America, with special emphasis on libraries in Latin America and in Uruguay; bibliography; types of libraries and their services; the ideal library; acquisition of library materials; classification and cataloging with laboratory work; services to the public; and binding. The forty students who completed the course were presented with a diploma. The examining board at the end of the course was composed of two visiting librarians, J. Frederic Finó and Carlos Víctor Penna, professors of Library Science in Buenos Aires; the teachers of the course; Secundino Vázquez, Director of the Legislative Library; and Juan B. Silva Vila, Sub-Director of the National Library.

During the year a bill was presented in the National Congress to create an official library school. The bill also proposes to create a National Board of Librarians for the purpose of standardizing library practices, and to collect and disseminate library and bibliographic information.

In Lima, the Library School, established under the auspices of the National Library, opened its enrollment on November 20. Twenty-five from 305 applicants were accepted. The program of study includes library administration; bibliography with special reference to Perú; cataloging and classification; history of books; paleography; history of libraries and library associations. It is planned for a six-month period with 16 hours of instruction weekly.

The staff includes Raymond Kilgour, graduate of the University of Michigan, Jorge Aguayo, specialist in library science from Cuba, Margaret Bates, graduate of the University of Columbia, Elizabeth Sherier, graduate of the George Washington University, Josefina Fabilli, of Stanford University, and Víctor Barriga, Alberto Pincherle, Carmen Ortiz de Zeballos, and Carmen Andráca, of Lima.

In both schools preference was given to librarians and to persons having not less than a secondary school education. A knowledge of foreign languages and of office procedure was also considered. The library group in Peru was organized in close cooperation with the American Library Association.

In Trinidad, the Central Library Scheme, directed by Helen Gordon Stewart, opened a preliminary training course on September 1.

PUBLICATIONS

During the year a number of excellent manuals on organization and procedure in libraries appeared. These are the direct result of the need for such books in the teaching of library science throughout Latin America. Manuel Selva of Buenos Aires reports his considerably enlarged second edition of *Manual de Bibliotecnia* in preparation and Carlos Víctor Penna has in preparation a guide to cataloging and a catalogers' code.

Two manuals are products of Cuban librarians. One is a condensed, useful and practical manual on classification and cataloging by Jorge Aguayo; the other by José Antonio Ramos, wider in scope, emphasizes the decimal classification system. In Brazil, the Instituto Nacional do Livro has begun the publication of manuals for Brazilian librarians in its series on Library Science. It published a treatise on various systems of classification by José Soares de Souza and has in press a manual on the decimal classification system and on subject headings. In Tucumán, Argentina, Juan M. Ligoule of the Agricultural Experiment Station Library published a detailed explanation and a history of the decimal classification system used in that Library. The manner of presentation makes this a useful tool in teaching decimal classification. In Buenos Aires, Eduardo Mújica Farías, reissued in considerably augmented form his manual for use in organizing and administering archive material.

ACTIVITIES IN THE UNITED STATES

Due to the war effort in the United States the widespread interest in Latin American libraries and library relations has been limited to a few organizations.

The Library of Congress had several of its staff in the field and continued the development of the Hispanic Foundation under the direction of Lewis Hanke. In the death of John T. Vance, Librarian of the Law Library in the Library of Congress, on April 13, 1943, soon after his return from extensive study in Latin America, the program of inter-American library relations lost a staunch and ardent supporter.

The American Library Association opened its International Relations Office in Washington with Dr. Harry M. Lydenberg as its Director. This Office in October undertook the supervision and operation of the three American libraries in Latin America: the Benjamin Franklin Library in Mexico City, the American Library in Managua, and the Artigas-Washington Library in Montevideo, as the result of an agreement of the American Library Association and the

Department of State. The Association closed the first year of its project of donating books to libraries in Latin America. Approximately $125,000 worth of books were distributed, including 579 periodical subscriptions. A total of 453 libraries had been invited to participate. This project, by resolution of the advisory committee of the American Library Association, is being continued for another year.

The Committee on Library Cooperation with Latin America of the Association, clearing through the International Relations Office, announced its membership as Rudolph Gjelsness, Chairman, Lewis Hanke, Vice-Chairman, Eileen Cunningham, Charles J. Gosnell, and Sarita Robinson.

The Inter-American Bibliographical and Library Association met in Washington on February 20 jointly with the District of Columbia Library Association. Two sessions were held, attended by approximately 300 members and visitors.

ACTIVITIES IN LATIN AMERICA

Library activities and the attention given to libraries and librarianship in print make it impossible to report completely from all sections of Latin America. Consequently, in the following paragraphs it is aimed to give only a resumé of the outstanding develpoments.

In Argentina the Escuela de Servicio Social continued to give its course in library science first begun in 1937. This year two professors were in charge of instruction. J. Frederic Finó gave instruction on the history of books and libraries, and Carlos Víctor Penna on cataloging and classification. Laboratory work was initiated in connection with the latter.

The Comité Argentino de Bibliotecarios de Instituciones Científicas y Técnicas, presided over by José A. Trillo with Mario Maveroff, secretary-treasurer, and Ernesto G. Gietz, technical director, at the end of 1943 had a membership of 31 affiliated and 68 supporting institutions. This organization during 1942, having completed its catalog, listing the holdings of scientific and technical periodicals in the various affiliated and supporting institutions, distributed 1,077 copies of the catalog to foreign and national libraries. It arranged for the selection of government publications of the United States for donation to several libraries in Argentina. It set up a union card catalog of periodicals totalling 24,000 entries, arranged by subject, by country of origin, and by title. At the end of 1942 it had received, supplementing the printed catalog, 2,533 additional titles from 20 of its affiliated and supporting institutions. In addition to the periodical holdings, the Comité received a mass of information through the circulation of a six-page questionnaire on the services, hours of service, date of foundation and type of library, type of catalog used, rules followed in cataloging procedure, description and extent of the book collection, system of classification, finances, and personnel from the various member institutions.

The Instituto Bibliotecológico, created in the Universidad de Buenos Aires, has undertaken, with assistance from the Rockefeller Foundation, to compile a union catalog of the holdings in the various libraries of the University. The project is being carried out through the microfilming of the catalogs and then the copying of the entries in accord with standard cataloging rules. Ernesto G. Gietz is director of the Institute and Carlos Víctor Penna assistant director.

The government of Argentina is spending about 700,000 pesos for the development of popular libraries. A law was proposed for the creation of an office of libraries, thus centralizing library information and organization. The proposal includes the establishment of library schools in the universities of La Plata, Santa Fe, Córdoba and Tucumán.

The Municipality of Buenos Aires reported a book collection of 2,556,089 in 189 libraries. In these libraries 2,058,040 readers consulted 3,122,328 books.

Several library conventions took place in various cities of Argentina. The first congress of popular libraries of the Province of Santa Fe took place in Santa Fe in April. Plans were being laid for a congress of librarians in Córdoba in 1944. In December 1942 the first congress of librarians of popular libraries of the Province of Buenos Aires took place in La Plata. In Rosario Librarians are planning a library association.

The University of La Plata on January 18, 1943 founded its Ibero-American Institute, headed by Ataúlfo Pérez Aznar. One of the aims of this Instituto is to develop a library of Ibero-American materials. It is located on the second floor of the library of the University.

In Brazil the Instituto Nacional do Livro reports that 1,330 public and semi-public libraries have been registered with that body. Of these, 510 are in the Province of São Paulo. The Instituto continued to issue serviceable manuals for use in Brazilian libraries and to offer a printed card service.

In São Paulo the Municipal Library in May opened services in its new quarters. The library has a collection of about 150,000 volumes and is loaning books at the rate of about 25,000 volumes monthly.

In Cuba, Jorge Aguayo of the General Library of the Universidad de la Habana is on leave of absence to assist in the Library School of Peru.

Fermín Peraza y Sarausa, director of the Municipal Library of Havana, reported 38,312 readers during 1942 who read 38,036 volumes. The Library acquired 717 titles of books and 385 titles of magazines. A total of 21,479 volumes have been catalogued. It employs nine persons at the central library and three each at the two branch libraries. The project for the construction of a new building would locate the library in the park bordered by San Rafael, San Miguel, Aramburú, and Hospital streets. The building is planned for a capacity of 150,000 volumes and a reading room for 100 readers.

In Ecuador Sra. Rosa Boya de Icaza became the Director of the National Library to replace Enrique Terán, retiring Director. Sra. de Icaza is the third woman to direct a national library in Latin America. The other two are Srta. Trini Medal in Nicaragua, who was succeded in December 1938 by Sra. Rosaura Tijerino.

In Guatemala the Director of the National Library, Rafael Arévalo Martínez, reports participation in an exhibition of Guatemaltecan imprints which took place in the Museum of History and Fine Arts in November 1942. Of the 2,000 books exhibited 702 were from the National Library. During 1942 the Library acquired 172 books and 12,000 periodical publications. Readers numbered 48,308. Six persons are in the employ of the Library.

In Honduras, Miguel Ángel Ramos, Director of the National Library and Archives, reports the following statistics for the year 1941–1942: receipts of 22 newspapers, 210 magazines, 149 bulletins, 348 pamphlets, and 358 books. It distributed on an exchange basis 538 collections of the *La Gaceta*, 336 of the *Boletín Legislativo,* 1,286 pamphlets, 372 official reports, 1,732 periodical publications, 626 *boletines,* and 85 books. A total of 3,450 readers consulted 4,951 volumes. The collection numbers 16,608 volumes cataloged and 2,000 volumes in forèign languages uncataloged.

In Panama, Ernesto J. Castillero, Director of the National Library, visited the United States as a guest of the Department of State for a three-month period.

The Panama Canal Zone authorities allocated $25,000 for the acquisition of books in the Canal Zone.

In Peru the Biblioteca Nacional and the Sociedad Geográfica de Lima suffered an irreparable loss by fire of their collections during the night of May 9 to 10. An inventory after the fire reveals that only 29 of the valuable pieces and some 1,009 other items were saved. The knowledge of this disaster brought about immediate sympathetic reaction in all parts of the continent. Committees were organized to collect material to form the basis for a new collection in the National Library. The Government of Peru provided funds for the construction of a new building with a capacity of 1,000,000 volumes. The new Director, Jorge Basadre, replacing C. A. Romero, retiring Director, indicated the basic needs for a new collection, as follows: classics of other languages translated into Spanish; reference books; library science and books on library administration; foreign authors who have written about Latin America, particularly about Peru; books on the teaching of English and periodicals. He declared that duplicate copies of any material will be gladly received for allocation to other Peruvian libraries. Under his direction the National Library began the publication of a *Boletín,* the first issue appearing in October.

The Biblioteca of the Universidad Mayor de San Marcos received donations from the British Council and from the American Library Association. It reported 20,444 books consulted during the months of September and October.

The Library of the Chamber of Deputies in Peru began the publication of its *Boletín bibliográfico* in November. Its hours of service are, 9 a.m. to 11 p.m. daily. The number of readers totalled 5,954 during the month of September. It acquired the library, of Dr. Ángel Gustavo Cornejo, one time professor in the Universidad Mayor de San Marcos, consisting of about 2,000 volumes.

In El Salvador the National Library, directed by Julio César Escobar, acquired the private library of Dr. Adrián García. It reports the following statistics for the year 1942: 56,424 persons, of whom 45,360 were men, 1,060 women, and 10,004 children, came to the Library and consulted 69,517 volumes in the Library and borrowed 9,268 volumes for home reading. It participated in the exhibitions of books in Santa Ana and in the Escuela Normal "España" in San Salvador.

The Trinidad Public Library in Port of Spain formulated the following aims: to secure a standard book collection; to provide an efficient service for children; to encourage adult reading; and to transform the library into a more progressive community organization. Registration of readers totalled 4,163, which is 1,128 more than the previous year. It circulated 74,992 volumes. It maintains a collection of 34,130 volumes. According to the plan of disposing unused materials it discarded 1,151 books.

Also in Trinidad, the Central Library Scheme sponsored by the Carnegie Corporation and directed by Dr. Helen Gordon Stewart has: 1) set up the Scheme in Trinidad and Tobago and has experimented in extension work with clubs and schools in rural areas; 2) Secured acceptance of the regional library Scheme in all of the British colonies; 3) Nearly finished reorganization of three libraries in the area and has begun the reorganization of four others; 4) Established a preliminary library training course beginning on September 1 with the majority of students from other Islands; 5) Compiled a union catalog of about 6,000 entries; 6) Drafted a five year plan to continue the Scheme after the completion of the present period under the Carnegie Corporation. The Central Library Scheme has a stock of 5,735 volumes at headquarters, circulating 7,712 volumes during the year. The Director visited Antigua, British Guiana, Barbados, and Grenada.

In Uruguay a contract was let for the construction of a new National Library building, planned for housing also the Historical Museum. In this case the book capacity is 800,000 volumes. If the Historical Museum is not transferred the building will have a capacity of 1,600,000 volumes. In December the National Library exhibited reorganization plans of the Library. Lectures formed a part of the exhibition program, some as follows: explanation of the reorganization plans, by Juan B. Silva Vila, Sub-Director of the National Library; Technical library practices, by Arthur E. Groop; History of art and binding, by Cándido Bordolli Danero; Notable books in the National Library, by J. M. González Larrieta; and Plans for a children's division, by Albana Larrinaga. The Library received as a gift a collection of José Enrique Rodó documents and manuscripts from a sister of this outstanding Uruguayan literary personality. The cataloging and calendaring are in charge of Roberto Ibáñez, poet and literary critic. The National Library entered into exchange relations with various libraries in Argentina and continued its assistance to public libraries in the interior through its exchange division.

In accord with the resolution of the Comisión Municipal de Cultura of the city of Montevideo, all libraries under its jurisdiction are to bear the name of an illustrous national personality. In this connection the library in the Union District became the Biblioteca Municipal "Dr. Francisco A. Schinca."

On August 23, 1943 the Biblioteca Artigas-Washington was inaugurated with special ceremonies at which the President of the Republic and other government officials and foreign representatives were present. This Library is one of the three American libraries administered by the American Library Association.

Various popular libraries and libraries of social, student, and athletic clubs were inaugurated. The total of the libraries in Uruguay now numbers well over 600. Of the libraries inaugurated special mention can be made of the Biblioteca "Pbro. Dr. Manuel Pérez Castellanos" in Carmelo, Uruguay, which was inaugurated on May 26 under the auspices of the Women's Patriotic Committee of that City. From the date of its founding through August, 1943 it reported that 1,173 readers had come to the Library. Of these about 75 percent are from the secondary and the industrial schools.

In Venezuela, the National Library sent a collection of books to Ecuador, also to the National Library in Lima.

A law under consideration by the Venezuelan legislature would require the deposit in the National Library of two copies of every printed piece. An office of bibliography was created in the National Library. Thirty-three persons are on the staff of the library.

The Library of the Archivo Nacional is continuing the cataloging of the volumes, historically important to America. Other items which do not properly belong to the specialty of the National Archives are being transferred to the National Library.

In the Virgin Islands of the United States the Saint Thomas Public Library has adopted the closed stack system, but applicable only to school students. It further adopted a set of rules and regulations on the services of the Library. The supervising librarian, Enid Baa, is on leave of absence to study library science at Columbia University. The Library initiated a story hour for children, having an attendance of 45 in each session. During the year 1942–1943 it circulated 13,909 volumes to adults and 23,011 to juvenile readers. It added 606 new books to its collection.

BIBLIOGRAPHY

(*See also item* 73)

Aguayo, Jorge. La función de la biblioteca en la universidad (*Univ. Habana*, año 8, no. 46–48, enero–junio, p. 103–122). **[4594**
Originally printed in the *Revista de Derecho y Ciencias Sociales*, Habana, abril–mayo, 1942. Published also in *Bol. bibliog.*, Lima, año 16, no. 3–4, dic., p. 229–241.

———. Manual práctico de clasificación y catalogación de bibliotecas. Habana. Ed. Jesús Montero. (Bibl. de historia, filosofía y sociología, vol. 12). 142 p. **[4595**
One of the most practical manuals published to date in the field of cataloging and classification in the Spanish language. The author treats in 8 chapters: Indispensible knowledge of bibliography; Library classification and cataloging; the Dewey classification system; Some cataloging rules; Norms for composing a catalog card; The catalog; Filing rules; and Use of printed cards. In two appendices he gives the most used abbreviations in cataloging, and a glossary of terms.

Arce, Magda. Los cursos de administración y la biblioteca del D. A. S. P. en la biblioteca de Itamaraty. Santiago. Prensas de la Univ. de Chile. 14 p. **[4596**

Argentina. Biblioteca del Congreso de la nación. Clave técnica de la clasificación. Buenos Aires. Imp. del Congreso nacional. 31 p. **[4597**
An outline of the classification scheme in the library of the Argentine congress. [J. B. Childs]

———. Memoria correspondiente al año 1942. Buenos Aires. 3 p. **[4598**
Mimeographed report of the activities of the Committee. Lists a total of 92 institutions, affiliated with the Committee.

———. **Jockey Club. Biblioteca.** Boletín. No. 49, enero—no. 50, oct. **[4599**
No. 53 is identified as año 9. Issued in enero, marzo, mayo, julio, octubre.

———. **Córdoba. Dirección general de bibliotecas.** Boletín de bibliotecas. Córdoba. Año 1, no. 1, feb.—. **[4600**
This bulletin contains the law creating the Dirección de Bibliotecas in Córdoba, the set of by-laws proposed for putting the law into operation, and preliminary proceedings leading up to the passage of the law. Of particular interest is the list of libraries of the Province of Córdoba, in the capital and in the interior on p. 9–10.

———. **Museo social argentino. Escuela de servicio social.** Curso de biblioteconomía. Buenos Aires. 1943? 10 p. **[4601**
The program of studies includes 19 parts of lectures and 14 parts of practice and observational work.

———. **Universidad nacional del Litoral. Facultad de ciencias jurídicas y sociales. Biblioteca.** Catálogo metódico de la biblioteca. Santa Fe. Imp. de la Univ. nac. del Litoral. (Supl. no. 2, 1940–1943). 270 p. **[4602**
This is the second of the supplement series of the catalog. The original *Catálogo Metódico* was published in 1937. The catalog is supplied with an alphabetical index of authors.

Azevedo, Francisco José de. Biblioteca municipal de São Paulo (*Acrópole*, ano 6, no. 68, dez., p. 207–214). **[4603**
Highly illustrated article showing views of the surroundings, exterior, and interior of the new municipal library building.

Basadre, Jorge. Hacia una política bibliotecaria (*Bol. bibliog. bibl. cám. dip.*, año 1, no. 1, nov., p. 2–3). [4604
Peru needs 1) a national library law, 2) a system of popular libraries, 3) rural library service, 4) a committee working in behalf of libraries, 5) a national library association.

LA BIBLIOTECA PÚBLICA DE LA SOCIEDAD ECONÓMICA DE AMIGOS DEL PAÍS (*Rev. bim. cub.*, vol. 52, no. 2, sept.–oct., p. 161–171). [4605

BIBLIOTECARIO. Director: Bartolomé Curletto. Santa Fe. No. 16, enero/marzo—no. 18, julio/set. [4606
Carries short articles and general library news of the Americas, particularly of Argentina, in newspaper format. Contained in No. 16: "Quién gobierna una biblioteca?," by Arthur E. Bostwick; "Un tema sobre bibliotecas populares en las poblaciones rurales," by José A. Napoli; "Las bibliotecas populares y los bibliotecarios," by Julio A. Giampietro; in No. 17: Report of Bibliotecas Infantiles y Escolares: "Introducción al curso de instrucción bibliotecaria para bibliotecas infantiles y escolares," broadcast under name of Hora Escolar; and, proposed law for the creation of Dirección Nacional de Bibliotecas; in no. 18: "Bibliotecas públicas populares del Consejo de educación," by Nelly L. de Anganuzzi; "El bibliotecario," by Juana Manrique de Lara; "El escritor, el lector, y el bibliotecario," by Juan R. Stagno, and "Biblioteca pública municipal de Paysandú."

BOLETÍN DE INFORMACIONES DE LA BIBLIOTECA. Centro social y biblioteca popular "Villa Colón." Villa Colón, Montevideo. No. 15, enero—no. 25, dic. [4607
A three- to four-page mimeographed bulletin with illustrations, giving information about new acquisitions and notes about books and library activities.

BOLETÍN DE LA BIBLIOTECA. Instituto cultural anglo-uruguayo. Montevideo. No. 1, Junio—. [4608
Contains notes on books, lending rules of the library, list of new books and the installments of the library catalog. The bulletin plans to give a full listing of books in the library and of the monthly acquisitions.

BOLETÍN DE LA BIBLIOTECA PÚBLICA "MÁRTIRES DE LA LIBERTAD." Habana. No. 20. [4609
Carries summary of work done during 1942.

BOLETÍN DE LA COMISIÓN PROTECTORA DE BIBLIOTECAS POPULARES. Buenos Aires. Año 10, no. 47, enero/marzo–año 11, no. 50, set./dic. [4610
Each number is a 6 page sheet, and carries articles on libraries and on bibliography.

Bondeli, Elsa de. Back stage; behind the scenes of the Biblioteca Benjamin Franklin, Mexico City (*Libr. jour.*, vol. 68, no. 2, Jan. 15, p. 57–60). [4611

Bordoni, Mario G. Biblioteca "Doctor Francisco Alberto Schinca" (*El Día*, Montevideo supl., año 12, no. 553, agosto 22, p. 2–3, ilus.). [4612
Description of the Municipal Library of Montevideo in the Union District, where it was established on May 11, 1929.

Brazil. Escola livre de sociologia e política. Escola de biblioteconomia. Letivo, 1943. São Paulo. Ed. Rev. dos tribunais. 17 p. [4613
Gives Roster of faculty and staff, general information and description of courses: Cataloging and classification; Organization and administration of libraries; Reference and bibliography; History of the book.

———. **São Paulo (estado). Conselho estadual de bibliotecas e museus.** Decreto-lei no. 13,411, de 10 de junho de 1943. São Paulo. Emp. gráf. da Revista dos tribunais. 113 p. [4614

Buonocore, Domingo. Elementos de bibliotecología; formas de libro (*Libri*, año 1, no. 7, oct., 1942, p. 175–176; año 2, no. 3, junio, 1943, p. 70–71). [4615
Transcription of that part of the textbook, published under the same title, referring to the book in relation to book-dealers and publishers.

Calabrese Leonetti, R. Nuestras bibliotecas y el bibliotécnico (*Rev. asoc. cult. bibl.*, año 2, no. 5, marzo, p. 4–6). [4616
Plea for raising library standards and for elevating the position of librarian.

Cuba. Habana. Biblioteca municipal. Memoria de los trabajos realizados de 1940 a 1942. Habana. Ed. Molina y cía. (Bibl. municipal, Serie A, Memorias, no. 6). 39 p., ilus. [4617
Contains statistics on readers of library, hours of service and volumes read; acquisitions; cataloging, binding and correspondence; publications; and finances, with an appendix on the needs of the library and an explanation of the projected new library building.

Doria, Irene de Menezes. Guia de classificação decimal. Prefácio de Rubens Borba de Morais. São Paulo. Livr. Martins. (Escola de biblioteconomia de São Paulo, Série de biblioteconomia, no. 1). 107 p. [4618

Forero, Manuel José. Apuntaciones para la historia de la biblioteca nacional (*Bol. hist. antig.*, vol. 30, no. 342–343, abril-mayo, p. 509–516). [4619

Franco, Alberto. La Biblioteca del Teatro Colón (*Bol. com. prot. bibl. pop.*, año 10, no. 47, enero–marzo, p. 2). [4620
A music library.

García, Germán. Actualidad de Sarmiento y otros ensayos bibliotecarios. Bahía Blanca. Ed. Pampa-Mar. 70 p. [4621
Contains: Actualidad de Sarmiento; ¿Qué se lee en la Argentina?; Ética bibliotecaria; Autonomía; El bibliotecario; Bibliotecas viajeras; Organización; Literatura bibliotecaria.

Gietz, Ernesto G. Catálogos centralizados (*Bol. com. prot. bibl. pop.*, año 11, no. 50, set.-dic.). [4622
Cites places and standards of union catalogs in use, and indicates the plans of the Instituto Bibliotecológico of the Universidad de Buenos Aires.

Gropp, Arthur E. School of library science in Montevideo, Uruguay (*Bull. La libr. assoc.*, vol. 7, no. 2, Dec., p. 13–15). [4623
Summary of the establishment and first year of operation.

Jáuregui Rosquellas, Alfredo. Las bibliotecas y la democracia (*Rev. bibl. arch. nac.*, no. 24–30, junio, p. 33–37). [4624
An expression on the place of the library in the future of universal culture.

Ligoule M., Juan. La Biblioteca de la Estación experimental agrícola de Tucumán; su organización. Tucumán. Estación experimental agrícola de Tucumán. (Publ. miscelánea, no. 2). 137 p. [4625
Gives historical data and objectives of the library; description of the library, its catalogs, and its publications. An excellent account of the decimal classification system and its application to the library is given This portion of the volume is one of the best treatments in Spanish of the Decimal Classification System.

Marasso, Arturo. La lectura. Buenos Aires. Comisión protectora de bibliotecas populares. 32 p. [4626
The article is written by the Vice-president of the Comisión Protectora de Bibliotecas Populares. Emphasizes the need of book selection for the guidance of reading.

Moraes, Rubens Borba de. O problema das bibliotecas brasileiras. Prefácio de Gilberto Freyre. Palavras de Francisco de Assis Barbosa. Rio de Janeiro. Casa do estudante do Brasil. Conferências, Série Itamaratí). 64 p. [4627
Lecture given in the Library of the Ministry of Foreign Relations, September 23, 1943 on the problems of Brazilian libraries.

Obregón, Rodolfo. La rica colección de la Biblioteca municipal del Subte. (*El día*, nov. 28, ilus.). [4628
Description of the new library opened in the Subterranean exhibition rooms of the Municipality of Montevideo. The collection gives emphasis to reference and art books.

Ocampo, María Luisa, and Salvador Ortiz Vidales. Guía de las bibliotecas en el Distrito federal. México. Tall. El nacional. 26 p. [4629
93 libraries are accounted for in this guide.

Ortiz de Zevallos, Carmen. Esquema de clasificación decimal para una biblioteca pequeña (*Bol. bibliog.*, Lima, año 16, vol. 13, no. 1–2, julio, p. 103–109). [4630
Divides scheme into 10 classes, subdivided by the next 10 divisions, with expansion to third division in Education, Spanish language, Spanish literature, Geography, and History, with extension to one point in Peruvian history.

Palma, Ricardo. Apuntes para la historia de la Biblioteca de Lima (*La prensa*, Lima, 14 de mayo). [4631
Reprinted notes on the history of Peru's Biblioteca Nacional.

Penna, Carlos Víctor. Algunas aplicaciones de la micro-fotografía en las bibliotecas (*Bol. com. prot. bibl. pop.*, año 10, no. 47, enero-marzo, p. 5). [4632

———. Bibliografías y bibliotecas como impulsoras de la industria del libro. (Reprint from *Argentina Gráfica*, Buenos Aires, nov.-dic., 1943, 6 p.). [4633
Refers to the lack of complete bibliographic information of book production and to the potentiality of the more than 2,999 libraries to stabilize and enhance the book trade in Argentina. Sets down the requirements of good, bibliographic compilation.

Peraza y Sarausa, Fermín. Bibliotecas del Caribe. Notas de viaje acerca de las bibliotecas de República Dominicana, Puerto Rico, Curaçao, La Guaira y Caracas, Barranquilla, Panamá, San José, Guatemala, y San Salvador. Habana. Ed. Anuario bibliográfico cubano. 40 p., ilus., fotos. [4634

———. Directorio de bibliotecas de Cuba. Habana. 51 p. [4635

Peru. Biblioteca nacional. Boletín. Lima. Año 1, no. 1, oct.—. [4636
Printed in 62 pages by the Librería e Imprenta "El Cóndor." It is directed by Jorge Basadre. It outlines the objectives of the National Library. Gives inventory of books saved after the fire: 29 valuable pieces, some 1,009 other pieces.

PROYECTO DE UNA ESCUELA DE BIBLIOTECNIA (*Diario of.*, Uruguay, tomo 153, no. 11,152, 29 nov., p. 290A–291A). [4637
The project would create a library school in Uruguay. It is here approved for inclusion in the budget by the Ministry of Education and presented for consideration in the Senate. It specifies a program of studies on history of the book and bibliography; history, administration, cataloging and classification of libraries; and national and international library cooperation. The

School would be governed by a Board of Librarians which also would appoint a Library and Bibliographical Committee.

Ramos y Aguirre, José Antonio. Manual de biblioeconomía. Clasificación decimal, catalogación metódico-analítica y organización funcional de bibliotecas. Habana. Imp. P. Fernández. (Corp. de bibliotecarios, archiveros y conservadores de museos del Caribe, Publ. 1). xiii, 469 p., ilus. [4638

Treats in separate chapters in the first 200 p.: classifications, cataloging with model illustrations of cards, and organization and administration. In the last 269 p. gives decimal classification tables, accompanied by an alphabetical index.

UNA REUNIÓN DE BIBLIOTECARIOS. Buenos Aires. 23 p. [4639

Gives account of the meeting of officials and librarians of Buenos Aires and of neighboring cities, the meeting taking place in the headquarters of the Comisión Protectora de Bibliotecas Populares on December 16, 1942.

REVISTA DE LA ASOCIACIÓN CULTURAL DE BIBLIOTÉCNICOS. Buenos Aires. Año 1, no. 2, mayo, 1942—ano 2, no. 5, marzo. [4640

The Association dedicates itself to the "culture of our country and the dignity of the library profession." Each number carries short articles on libraries, librarianship, bibliography, and notes about library events. Membership is limited to the graduates of the Library Course of the Museo Social Argentino.

Sambaquy, Lydia de Queiroz. Como a biblioteca pode e deve servir ao Brasil. Rio de Janeiro. Imp. Nacional. 10 p. [4641

Schwab, Federico. Las bibliotecas y los lectores (*Bol. bibliog. bibl. cám. dip.*, año 1, no. 1, nov., p. 4–6). [4642

Stresses the service angle.

Selva, Manuel. La enseñanza de la biblioteconomía en nuestro país y en Estados Unidos (*Bol. mus. soc. arg.*, año 31, no. 249–250, marzo–abril, p. 65–72). [4643

A comparison of library conditions and library school instruction in the United States with those in the Argentine Republic. The author points out the varied standards which exist in the United States, in large part due to the non-existence of a centralized body. He feels that librarians should be especially prepared for the organization and management of libraries.

Souza, José Soares de. Classificação. Sistemas de classificação bibliografica. Rio de Janeiro. Imp. nacional. (Min. da educação e saúde, Instituto nacional do livro, Col. B-2, Biblioteconomia, 4). 163 p. [4644

The volume begins with chapters listing the technical terms used in its preparation and giving a treatment of classification, rules for classifying and an explanation of the Cutter author tables. It follows with an explanation of the classification schemes of Brunet; Dewey; Cutter Expansive System; Library of Congress; Bliss; and that developed by Shiali Ramamrita Ranganathan of India.

Tauro, Alberto. Pasado y futuro de la biblioteca (*Bol. bibliog., bibl. cám. dip.*, año 1, no. 1, nov., p. 6–9). [4645

Envisaging the role of a well organized National Library to contribute to Peru's cultural and intellectual life.

Valle, Adrián del. Treinta años en la biblioteca de la Sociedad económica de amigos del país (*Rev. bim. cub.*, vol. 51, no. 3, mayo–junio, p. 340–359). [4646

ADDENDA

Argentina. San Juan. Sociedad Franklin biblioteca popular. Memoria. 1 de julio 1941—30 de junio 1942. San Juan. 1942. 57 p. [4647

Barbieri, Honorio. Bibliotecas sin bibliotecarios (*Rev. asoc. cult. bibl.*, año 1, no. 2, mayo, 1942, p. 3–4). [4648

A plea for elevating the position of librarians in Argentina.

Calabrese Leonetti, Rogelio. Condición social del bibliotecario (*Rev. asoc. cult. bibl.*, año 1, no. 2, mayo, 1942, p. 23–24). [4649

Refers to the position of the Argentine librarian.

LA CREACIÓN DE LAS BIBLIOTECAS POPULARES (*Bol. educ.*, San José, año 1, no. 7, abril, 1942, p. 6). [4650

Cites law no. 10 passed by the Congress of Costa Rica on October 16, 1941, and signed by the President on October 17, 1941, creating a system of popular libraries in Costa Rica. The Dirección General de Bibliotecas and Biblioteca Nacional are named for the execution of the law. Libraries are to be established in the capitals of all the cantons of the country.

Colombia. Biblioteca nacional. Exposición del libro, 26 de julio a 26 de agosto 1942, auspiciada por la Dirección de extensión y bellas artes del Ministerio de la educación nacional y la Biblioteca nacional. Bogotá. Prensas de la Bibl. nac. 1942. 82 p., ilus., facsims. (part col.). [4651

The publication was compiled under the direction of Juan Bueno Medina and the Director of the National Library.

Gallardo, Domingo V. Evocación histórica de la Biblioteca popular "Benjamin Franklin," de la ciudad de San Juan (*Rev. asoc. cult. bibl.*, año 1, no. 3, agosto, 1942, p. 4–5). [4652

History of the Popular Library of San Juan, Argentina, founded in 1866, and today having over 27,000 volumes.

Guterbock, Bruno. La biblioteca mecanizada; un método mecánico de fichado y cataloguización (*Rev. asoc. cult. bibl.*, año 1, no. 3, agosto, 1942, p. 6–10). [4653
Written in favor of mechanizing the library procedure, i.e., the adoption of labor saving devices to enhance the usefulness of the library.

Kreibohm, Enrique. Menosprecio y valoración de la clasificación decimal. Tucumán. Ed. Yussem. (Soc. de bibliotecarios de Tucumán, Publ., Serie mínima, no. 1). 1942. 15 p. [4654
Defense of the decimal classification system, especially against the deprecatory comments of Domingo Buonocore of Santa Fe and Alfredo Cónsole of Buenos Aires.

Martínez Acosta, Orlando. Función social de la biblioteca pública (*Más luz*, año 7, no. 1, marzo 6, 1942, p. 5–7). [4655
Speaks of problems of the public library and outlines the purposes: to reach the soul of the people.

Mújica Farías, Eduardo. Doctrinas y sistemas administrativos de las modernas organizaciones. Buenos Aires. Ed. La Facultad. 1942. 2 vols. [4656
Manual for use in organizing, administering, classifying, and filing books, papers, documents, correspondence, etc. Treats concretely the procedure and is amply illustrated with samples of forms, guides, furniture, etc. One chapter is devoted to libraries in other countries. The manual is primarily intended for use by archivists.

Romero Sosa, Carlos Gregorio. Los orígenes de la Biblioteca pública en Salta (*Rev. asoc. cult. bibl.*, año 1, no. 4, dic., 1942, p. 19–20). [4657
Description with historical notes of the public library in Salta, Argentina, which was created in 1862.

Sabor Vila, Sara. Fichado de incunables (*Rev. asoc. cult. bibl.*, año 1, no. 2, mayo, 1942, p. 15–18). [4658
Outlines the data that should comprise a description of an incunabula, namely, bibliographical notes, typographical description, textual description and physical description. Also gives a list of abbreviations found used in incunabula, and a model illustrating a description of a 1479 Sermons of Michael de Carcano.

Sambaqui, Lidia de Queiroz. A acão social da biblioteca pública. Rio de Janeiro. Imp. Nacional. 1942. 8 p. [4659

SARMIENTO. Boletín de la Asociación Biblioteca popular, Domingo F. Sarmiento. Buenos Aires. Cuarta época, no. 6/8, enero/marzo, 1942—no. 11/12, junio/julio, 1942. [4660
Contains articles on authors, on general subjects and notes on the library.

Torre Revello, José. Archivo general de la nación (*Rev. asoc. cult. bibl.*, año 1, no. 3, agosto, 1942, p. 27–41). [4661
A good description of the National Archives of Argentina.

MUSIC

BY

CHARLES SEEGER

Pan American Union

GENERAL STATEMENT

Music in Latin America has been so newly distinguished as a field of study that a selective bibliography for any one year, or even for several consecutive years, has as yet no basic body of texts to which it may offer continuity. With publication, long overdue, of two substantial contributions now in preparation—*A Guide to Latin American Music*, by Gilbert Chase, Editor of this section of the *Handbook* for 1940-42, and the *Diccionario de la Música Latinoamericana*, by Otto Mayer-Serra—the foundation will at last be laid for the bibliography of the field.

Of prime concern to the builders of such aids and to students who consult them must be the criteria upon which selection is made. Traditionally, a single set, which we may designate as intrinsic, served in such undertakings. Musical value was found in terms of music as a thing in itself. Dominated by the notion "highest artistic values" (of the European past), professional musicians and musicologists alike discounted or ignored colonial and contemporary music. It could only bid for, but scarcely hope to gain, the interest of scholars.

Around 1900, this tradition began to lose its position of dominance. Music of other high cultures was found to have values that could not be fitted into the single standard of European prestige music. At the same time, music was increasingly found to be a tangible and important element in total culture. From viewpoints of anthropology, psychology, education, social studies and even of politics, music was found to serve functions irrespective of whether professional musicians said it was "good" or not. Many people began to value in music not so much what the professional musicians said was "good," but what they found it was "good *for*." Music activity in the Americas became worthy of study.

Thus, in a way opposed to the older criticism based upon intrinsic criteria alone, but certainly imposed upon it, a newer criticism based upon extrinsic criteria emerged. It is still well below the stage of formulation reached by its older counterpart. Its higher elaboration must probably await the devising of improved statistical apparatus of quantitative analysis, since it concerns the preferences not of a few highly vocal arbiters of taste but those of millions of ordinary people whose tastes are not so much to be discerned in speech as in acts—acts of diverse kinds, such as turning dials, purchasing records, sheet music, instruments, and gathering for performance of music by themselves, without ministrations of professional musicians.

The following list represents an adjustment of these two sets of criteria. It follows a precedent set by the former editors of this section, William Berrien and Gilbert Chase, though here carried, perhaps, to a greater extreme. Accordingly, in a subject in which a fairly high level of accomplishment has been maintained, as in the composition of fine-art or concert music, listing of publication of presumably moderate merit has been omitted. In a subject or in a country where production has been at a minimum, publication appearing to be of moderate or even of slight merit may be required reading.

It is important to call the attention of the student to: (1) the probable inadequacy of coverage of the survey of publications upon which the list for the year is made; and (2) the certain inadequacy of coverage of the total estimated field by the total estimated publication.

As to the first of these, there was felt in the year 1943 the full force of war restrictions upon such surveys as the present. The shortage of materials, the virtual stoppage of transportation of music materials, and the black-list, to mention only a few of the items, have caused the ADDENDA to mount to a number which might reflect upon the industry of the preceding editor, had he not, in turn, experienced similar embarrassment by war conditions. This temporary decrease of available published materials has been compensated for, it is true, by an increase in radio broadcasting, in composition, and in concert performance, that even without wartime restrictions might have left us with a coverage problem. The forms in which these activities leave material trace are, however, peculiarly diffuse and fugitive—advertisements and notices in newspapers, typed scripts, unique direct sound-recordings in the files of private companies, concert programs and manuscripts on music paper which is often of poor quality. No pretense to coverage of any of these is made here.

As to the second concern—the certain inadequacy of coverage of the total estimated field by the total estimated publication—the problem here is one of content rather than of form. Of the three main music traditions—Amerindian, European and African—that have gone into the making of present-day music activity in Latin America, survival of each, without discernible trace of acculturation with the others is generally recognized. The kind of systematic studies which might enable us clearly to distinguish between these contemporary survivals have, however, barely been begun. And while we have elaborate history of European music, we have none of Amerindian or African. Therefore, when we come to study the hybrids formed among these traditions, which comprise the bulk of the music materials of our field, we are without some of the prerequisites for study. Data are entirely lacking in some important areas, and techniques of analysis are embryonic. Yet, nearly every author writes freely of the "autochthonic," the "classic" and the "negro" elements in Latin American music. This free use of labels encourages vague and prejudiced theorizing that only too easily becomes translated into action. The very Latin-American-ness of the music found in Latin America is open to question. The music-nationalism and -racism, which figure so extensively in published writings, are often without musicological foundation, either scientific or critical, though almost anyone can distinguish a typical Brazilian from a typical Mexican song or dance. Like the old-time preacher, we "argify and sputify but do not" and cannot "show wherein."

The situation is complicated by the fact that hybridization of the three main traditions has taken place upon four distinct levels of social life, giving us four distinct types of music idiom, primitive or tribal art, fine art, folk art and popular art, serving four distinct social functions, though, by further hybridization, they appear to shade off into one another in myriad undetectable ways.

Coverage of this field is partly, then, deficient from a strictly music-technical (intrinsic) viewpoint. We do not possess the scientific and critical apparatus to support implications of broad inclusion. An equally large deficiency is due to critical bias—the conservatory-trained writer who sees only the "classic" in music, the folkloristically inclined who sees only the strange hybrid *música elevada*, the moralist who sees only the "sincere," the school-man who sees only teaching material, the music-business-man who sees only what pays, etc. The total field—a complex of many interdependent, though often conflicting data, viewpoints, and objectives—is contemplated by few. Yet that, if anything, is the field of study—unless we are careful to define some part of it more clearly *as a part*—a thing rarely done.

The total field of music should not be conceived entirely apart from the concept of total culture. But the study of total culture, still in its infancy, helps us not at all with music, a small, though not entirely insignificant element in that total. The essential problem—even the clear statement of it, the push outward, as it were, by music upon its environment and the pressing in upon it of that environment—still eludes us, though it is in the interaction of these two that operations in the field must, eventually, be accounted for.

One area of prime importance has been knowingly slighted here, that of popular or commercial music, *música populachera*. Once ignored on principle by the serious student, it has recently been recognized as the only music idiom in which the New World has distinguished itself. With the recognition of the fact, however, there has not been evolved a technique for handling it for purposes of scholarship either as a separate subject or in conjunction with conventional subjects. By its nature a hybrid of fine art and folk art idioms, it has received such forced growth through "plugging" on the radio, juke-box, film and in "café society," that an attempt to give it adequate coverage here would double the space needed and completely confuse the customary appearance of a scholarly bibliography. Some way of handling this twentieth century wonder-child must be found by musicology, and that quickly. To say that most of its production is mediocre and is forgotten almost as soon as it is made public, is merely to repeat what can be said of its parent idioms. To an understanding of contemporary music activity and to history, due regard for the mediocre, especially when functioning upon a very large scale, is essential. The contemporary popular commercial idiom holds the public attention and interest of uncounted millions. The hold is not maintained alone by the comparatively small number of "bests," but also by the general run of the presses. A Latin American "Hit Parade" would be a convenience in our study of the idiom from an intrinsic viewpoint, but could serve only as an introduction to the field. For the present, the best initiation to the mysteries are the dance floor and the record catalogue. But few have the courage to mix the two and the strength to live and tell us about it. Inquiries disclose, for instance, that the Radio Corporation of America, Victor Division, released 79 Latin American discs during the year 1943. Few releases of Latin American firms have been received. Unfortunately, phonograph records, like so much printed music, are mostly undated. Company files will reward the diligent student, but for the first steps in this direction the shelves of a few private collectors offer the best start. The Latin American catalogue of Southern Music Publishing Company of New York is worth consulting also.

Coming to be of prime importance in the study of music in any part of the world are the so-called direct recordings made in the field with portable sound-recording equipment, often by independent initiative of enthusiastic individuals, though increasingly with institutional and government assistance. There are three main depositories of such recordings of interest to the student of music in Latin America. The first was established by Carlos Vega, Chief of the Section of Musicology, in the Argentine Museum of Natural Sciences in Buenos Aires, and contains records from many areas in South America. The Department of Anthropology of Columbia University, New York, maintains an archive under direction of George Herzog, which specializes in scientific recordings of primitive music. The Archive of American Folk Song in the Music Division of the Library of Congress, Washington, D. C., has been adding field recordings of all kinds from Latin America to its already large body of Anglo-American material. Collections are acquired by exchange, by gift, and through cooperative projects with institutions in the other American republics as, for instance, the University of Brazil (Luiz Heitor Corrêa de Azevedo), the University of Panama (Myron Schaeffer), the Instituto Indigenista Interamericano of Mexico City (Henrietta Yurchenco). The Music Division of the Pan American Union holds several hundred copies of the afore-mentioned discs, together with some originals. National collections have been made by Juan Liscano (Venezuela), by the Discoteca Municipal of São Paulo, Brazil, and by the University of Chile. Duplicates of these have been, or are expected to be, made available to the Library of Congress through exchange. A second, revised edition of George Herzog's "Research in Primitive and Folk Music in the United States" (American Council of Learned Societies, Bulletin No. 24, April 1936), now in preparation, will probably give more detailed information upon material of this type.

Attention of the student should be called to the fact that in the preparation of this list no survey of general periodical literature has been made. And for the ADDENDA section (publications of 1942 which came to the notice of the Editor of the *Handbook* after the volume for that year was already in press) music magazines were not surveyed. It is also worth while pointing out that a considerable body of the writing about music in Latin America is upon the music of Europe, particularly upon European musicians. Materials of this sort are not listed here, nor are translations into Spanish of books and articles by European authors about European music contained in Latin American music magazines or published by New World presses.

BIBLIOGRAPHY

MUSIC

GENERAL

Baron, Maurice (arr.). Calypso songs of the West Indies, by Massie Patterson and Lionel Belasco. New York. M. Baron co., publ. 25 p. [4662

12 songs for voice and piano. For popular use.

Charles, Hubert, Raymond Quevedo, and **Rupert Grant.** Victory calypsoes, 1943 souvenir collection, published by Lion and Atilla [pseuds.]. Port of Spain, Trinidad. The Caribbee printerie. 22 p. [4663

Words only.

Cugat, Xavier (ed.). Meet Mr. Cugat, bringing "Latin America" to you in music and rhythms. New York. Irving Berlin inc., publ. 79 p., illus. [4664

19 popular songs for voice and piano, with English and Spanish words. Prefatory text includes instructions for playing instruments such as *maracas, bongo, güiro* and *claves.*

Darcy, Thomas F. (arr.). Anthems of the United nations. New York. Irving Berlin, inc., publ. [4665
Compiled and arranged for band by the leader of the United States Army Band. 32 instrumental parts and conductor part (1st Bb cornet) for each anthem. Includes the anthems of Bolivia, Brazil, Costa Rica, Cuba, Dominican Republic, El Salvador, Guatemala, Haiti, Honduras, Mexico, Nicaragua, and Panama.

Henius, Frank (arr.). Songs and games of the Americas. New York. Charles Scribner's sons. 56 p., illus. [4666
Compilation of 38 songs from all countries, for popular use. Simple piano accompaniments. Sources, except for country of origin, not given.

Kramer, Alex M. (ed.). United nations folk songs and dances. New York. Edwards music co., publ. 64 p. [4667
Piano arrangements, for popular use; some with words in original language and English. Includes the following Latin American music: *Morena, morena* (Brazil); *Lolita* (Costa Rica); *En Cuba* (Cuba); *Himno de Capotillo* (Dominican Republic); *Madrecacaos en flor* (El Salvador); *Himno a Barrios* (Guatemala); *By a shady lane* (Haiti); *Himno al pino* (Honduras); *La golondrina* (Mexico); *Hermosa soberana* (Nicaragua); *En lo frondoso* (Panama); *Amor maldito* (Puerto Rico).

Labastille, Irma (arr.). Recuerdo latinoamericano. New York. Edward B. Marks music corp. 64 p., ilus. [4668
21 songs from 5 countries (Argentina, Chile, Cuba, Ecuador and Peru) arranged for piano or voice and piano, for popular use. Spanish and English words.

Treharne, Bryceson (arr.). National anthems of the United Nations and associated powers. Boston. Boston music co. 132 p. [4669
For voice and piano. Words in original language and English. Includes the anthems of Bolivia, Brazil, Chile, Colombia, Costa Rica, Cuba, The Dominican Republic, Ecuador, El Salvador, Guatemala, Haiti, Honduras, Mexico, Nicaragua, Panama, Paraguay, Peru, Uruguay, and Venezuela.

ARGENTINA

Aretz-Thiele, Isabel. Primera selección de canciones y danzas tradicionales argentinas. Buenos Aires. Ed. Ricordi americana. 62 p. [4670
Contains 22 songs with piano accompaniment. Preface by Carlos Vega under whom author studied and worked in the Sección de Musicología of the Museo Argentino de Ciencias Naturales. Both Prof. Vega and the author have collected folk material extensively with sound-recording equipment in the provinces of Argentina and in Bolivia, Peru, Chile and Uruguay. The accompaniments are said to consider the characteristics of the harp, guitar and bombo with which some of the songs are traditionally accompanied. Additional stanzas are taken from collectanea of Juan Alfonso Carrizo and Carlos Vega.

Castro, Sergio de. Dos canciones. Montevideo. Ed. coop. interam. de compositores. (Publ. no. 22). 3 p. [4671
For voice and piano, with Spanish words. Composed in 1940. Includes brief biography and list of works.

Engelbrecht, Richard. Tres poemas de Rainer Maria Rilke. Montevideo. Ed. coop. interam. de compositores. (Publ. no. 26). 9 p. [4672
For medium voice and piano, with Spanish, German and English words. Composed 1942. Includes brief biography and list of works.

Paz, Juan Carlos. Cuarta composición en los doce tonos. Montevideo. Ed. coop. interam. de compositores. (Publ. no. 27). 8 p. [4673
Violin solo, op. 37. Includes brief biography and list of works.

―――. Tercera composición en los 12 tonos (*New music*, vol. 16, no. 2, Jan., 12, 4 p.). [4674
For Bb clarinet and piano. Score and part. Includes brief biographical note and list of works.

Sammartino, Luis R. Sendas de nostalgia. Buenos Aires. Ed. Ricordi americana. 3 p. [4675
A *vidalita* for voice and piano, with Spanish words.

Videla, Heriberto. Canciones de mi tierra; quince canciones y danzas mendocinas; refundición y armonización por Alberto Rodríguez. Mendoza, Argentina. Ed. Bermejo & Fucci. 101 p., music. [4676
Songs of the celebrated guitarist and singer of folk-popular music, known as "El Pichón" (1883–1942), a provincial Hans Sachs, drawn out of a 25-year retirement by the arranger. Videla belonged to a family of musicians. He neither wrote nor read music, but was eclectic in his musical taste. The arranger "has undertaken the sympathetic and patriotic task of giving unity and rhythm to the 'canciones errabundas' created by Videla. . . ." By "unity" is meant "literary and music-theoretical unity." 15 songs with piano accompaniment.

BRAZIL

Abreu, Zequinha. Tico-tico. New York. Chas. K. Harris music publ. co. 8 p., and 47 pts. [4677
Arrangement for full band of popular "hit." Conductor's score with instrumental indications.

Cosme, Luiz. Canção do tio Barnabé. Montevideo. Ed. coop. interam. de compositores. (Publ. no. 18). 3 p. **[4678**
Piano solo. Composed 1930. Includes brief biography and list of works.

Fernândez, Óscar Lorenzo. Noite cheia de estrêlas. São Paulo. Ed. Irmãos Vitale. 3 p. **[4679**
New edition of the composer's op. 17, no. 1, for voice and piano. Portuguese, Spanish and English words.

Guarnieri, Camargo. Canto no. 1. New York. Associated music publishers. 5, 1 p. **[4680**
For violin and piano. Score and part.

Mignone, Francisco. Canto de negros. New York. Edward B. Marks music corp., publ. 5 p. **[4681**
For voice and piano. Portuguese and English words.

———. Crianças brincando. New York. Edward B. Marks music corp. (Latin American series of contemporary composers). 8 p. **[4682**
Piano solo.

———. Dorme-dorme. New York. Edward B. Marks music corp. 5 p. **[4683**
For women's chorus (SSA) a cappella. Portuguese and English words.

———. Miudinho. New York. Edward B. Marks music corp. (Latin American series of contemporary composers). 6 p. **[4684**
Piano solo.

———. Passarinho está cantando. New York. Edward B. Marks music corp. 5 p. **[4685**
For voice with ingenious piano accompaniment. Portuguese and English words.

Pereira, Artur (arr.). Na Baia tem (*Resenha musical*, ano 6, no. 63–64, nov.–dez., suplemento musical 16, 2 p.). **[4686**
For 4-part mixed chorus, a cappella.

Santoro, Claudio. Invenções a duas vozes, no. 1–2 (*Resenha musical*, ano 5, no. 53–54, jan.–fev., suplemento musical 12, 1 p.; no. 55–56, março–abril, suplemento musical 13, 1 p.). **[4687**
For piano. Reproduced from manuscript copy.

Villa-Lobos, Heitor. Moreninha (The little paper doll) from A próle do bébé, no. 1; arranged for 2 pianos, 4 hands, by Arthur Whittemore and Jack Lowe. New York. Associated music publishers. 8, 8 p. **[4688**
Two scores for piano 1–2.

BOLIVIA

Martínez Arteaga, Julio. Ajjllan-quiritua. Buenos Aires. Ed. musicales Ramón Sopena. 3 p. **[4689**
Piano solo based upon Aymara Indian theme. Verses in Spanish and Aymara are appended.

CHILE

Ejército. Jefatura de bandas. [Publicaciones]. Santiago. 3 vols. **[4690**
A collection of band scores. Issues during 1943 include *Himno de Yungay*, by José Zapiola, *A las Américas*, by Jovino Chacón Ramírez, and *Plegaria del soldado*, by Francisco Piccione Blasi. Some of the contributors to the series are officers in the Army Bands.

Letelier Llona, Alfonso. Cuatro canciones de cuna. Montevideo. Ed. coop. interam. de compositores. (Publ. no. 30). 22 p. **[4691**
Score for woman's voice and orchestra of flute, clarinet, harp and strings. Composed in 1939. Includes brief biography and list of works.

Negrete, Samuel. Rítmica. Montevideo. Ed. coop. interam de compositores. (Publ. no. 21). 5 p. **[4692**
Piano solo. Includes brief biography and list of works.

Universidad de Chile. Instituto de extensión musical. Departamento de investigación folklórica. Chile. Santiago. 53 p., ilus., música. **[4693**
Initial effort of the Departamento, under the leadership of Domingo Santa Cruz and Eugenio Pereira Salas, each of whom contributes a preface. Other contributors are: Carlos Lavin, Vicente Salas Viu, Carlos Isamitt, Jorge Urrutia and Filomena Salas. There are 23 songs with music notations and descriptions of songs and dances.

COLOMBIA

Murillo, Egeilio (?). Estudio no. 29. New York. Southern music publ. co. (Inter-American band series, Latin-American dances, no. 2). 10 p., and pts. **[4694**
For band. Conductor's condensed score with instrumental indications. Composer's name on cover is "Egeilio," probably error for Emilio Murillo (1880–1942).

Posada Amador, Carlos. Cinco canciones medioevales. Montevideo. Ed. coop. interam. de compositores. (Publ. no. 20). 9 p. **[4695**
Some twelfth and thirteenth-century melodies harmonized in conservative diatonic style, in 1938 and 1939. Score: SATB, a cappella. Includes brief biography and list of works.

Costa Rica

Zúñiga Zeledón, José Daniel. La patria canta. San José. Ed. Danzuni. 8 p. **[4696**
Four songs with piano accompaniment, *El boyero, Mis canciones, Caña dulce, La carreta tica,* and one piano solo, *Danza india.*

Cuba

Ardévol, José. Dos sonatas a tres. Montevideo. Ed. coop. interam. de compositores. (Publ. no. 28). 15 p. **[4697**
Primera sonata: score for oboe, clarinet and violoncello. Segunda sonata: score for two flutes and viola. Composed in 1938. Includes brief biography and list of works.

García Caturla, Alejandro. Dos canciones corales cubanas. Montevideo. Ed. coop. interam. de compositores. (Publ. no. 29). 10 p. **[4698**
Score for 6-part mixed chorus (SSATBB) a cappella. Composed in 1931 and 1937. Includes brief biography and list of works.

Hernández Gonzalo, Gisela. Preludio y giga. Habana. 7 p. **[4699**
Piano solo.

———. Sonata no. 1 en do. Habana. 11 p. **[4700**
Piano solo.

Lecuona, Ernesto. Album no. 1. Danzas para piano. Habana. Ed. C. G. Galdo. **[4701**
10 *danzas* for piano solo. Full name of composer: Ernesto Lecuona y Casado.

———. Rapsodia negra. New York. Dorset publ. 13 p. **[4702**
For piano.

———. Tres miniaturas. New York. Dorset publ. 11 p. **[4703**
For piano.

Dominican Republic

Mena, Luis E. Elila. New York. Alpha music. (Concert music of the Americas). 3 p. **[4704**
Caprice for piano. Contains list of popular airs of the Dominican Republic, "just published."

El Salvador

Alas, Ciriaco de Jesús. Himno de la ciudad de San Salvador (*Símbolos de la ciudad de San Salvador,* San Salvador, p. 5-7, ilus.). **[4705**
For voice and piano. Spanish words, by Carlos Bustamante.

Baratta, María de. La yegüita (*Rev. min. instr. públ.,* vol. 2, no. 7, julio–sept., p. 125-129, música). **[4706**
Score of folk *son* (for *pito,* or reed flute, and *tambor*) together with speculations upon its origin and with a stylisation for piano.

Mexico

Amézquita Borja, Francisco. Colección de cantos y bailes regionales. Puebla. Imp. cinematográfica Lux. 22 p., música. **[4707**
Contains 15 tunes and dance routines.

Gomezanda, Antonio. "Mariache," primera ópera ranchera mexicana, en tres actos y un intermedio bailable; letra y música. México, D. F. Inst. musical Gomezanda. 187 p. **[4708**
Vocal score: Spanish words.

Orientación musical. México. Vol. 2, no. 19, enero–no. 24, junio; vol. 3, no. 25, julio–no. 30, dic. **[4709**
Each issue contains a short composition.

Ponce, Manuel M. Intermezzo (*Bol. sem. cult. mex.,* tomo 1, no. 1, julio, p. 46-47). **[4710**
For piano.

———. Seis canciones arcaicas. Montevideo. Ed. coop. interam. de compositores. (Publ. no. 19). 17 p. **[4711**
Six songs for voice and piano, with Spanish words: *Más quiero morir por veros, Zagaleja del casar, De las sierras, Sol, sol, gi, gi, Desciende el valle, Tres morillas.* Caption title: Seis poemas arcaicos. Includes brief biography and list of works.

———. Tres poemas de Enrique González Martínez. Montevideo. Ed. coop. interam. de compositores. (Publ. no. 23). 10 p. **[4712**
For voice and piano: *Nocturno de las rosas, Onda, La despedida.* Spanish and English words. Includes brief biography and list of works.

Nicaragua

Delgadillo, Luis A. Cantos escolares nicaragüenses. Managua. Tall. nacionales. 88 p. **[4713**
A collection of 34 songs, some popular, some folk, many composed for school children, to which are appended 11 songs by Alejandro Vega Matus. The compiler (b. 1887) is dean of Nicaraguan composers.

Uruguay

Lanao de la Haza, Ulises. Alegre domingo (*Bellas artes,* suplemento musical no. 2, 3 p.). **[4714**
Marinera for violin and piano. Score.

VENEZUELA

ALBUM DE MÚSICA FOLKLÓRICA DEL ESTADO TÁCHIRA. Caracas? Min. de relaciones interiores. 40 p. [4715
A collection of 17 songs and piano music, some composed, some traditional.

Ministerio de educación nacional. Dirección de cultura. Archivo de música colonial venezolana. Montevideo. Inst. interamericano de musicología. 8 vols. [4716
A collection comprising scores for mixed voices and orchestra. Date on title-page (nos. 1, 2, 3, 5): 1942. Date on cover, all issues: 1943. For historical comments, see no. 4828. Contains *Pésame a la Virgen*, by Juán José Landaeta; *Tres lecciones para el Oficio de Difuntos*, by José Ángel Lamas; *Tristis est*, by Cayetano Carreño; *Salve*, by Juan Manuel Olivares; *Salve Regina*, by José Ángel Lamas; *In Monte Oliveti*, by Cayetano Carreño; *Popule meus*, by José Ángel Lamas; *Christus factus est*, by Caro de Boesi.

———. Tercer cuaderno de canciones populares venezolanas. Caracas. (Bibl. venezolana de cultura). 57 p. [4717
20 popular and folk-popular songs with piano accompaniment. According to preface, this "música de la clase media" appears here in print for the first time, transcribed direct from oral tradition. Some songs are anonymous; others carry name of composer or arranger. The piano accompaniments, by V. E. Sojo, are patterned after the traditional guitar figures, but are "purificadas de errores armónicos."

Plaza, Juan B. Seven Venezuelan songs on poems by Luis Barrios Cruz. New York. Associated music publ. 2 vols. [4718
This first printing contains so many errors that corrections are being made on the plates. A second edition will be issued and distributed with the request that all copies of the first printing be destroyed. Piano accompaniments. Contents.—v. 1. *Yo me quedé triste y mudo. La noche del llano abajo. Cuando el caballo se para. Hilando el copo del viento.*—v. 2. *Por estos cuatro caminos. La sombra salió del monte. Palma verde, garza blanca.*

Sojo, Vicente Emilio. Joropo. Caracas. Ed. Egry. 8 p. [4719
For voice and piano. Spanish words.

RECORDS

BIBLIOGRAPHY

(See also items 4739, 4760 and 4777)

LATIN AMERICAN MUSIC ON RECORDS (*The Gramaphone shop, inc., Record Supplement*, New York, vol. 6, no. 5, May, p. 6–10). [4720
An excellent list of concert, popular and folk music currently available through the Gramaphone shop, New York, with prices.

Radio corporation of America. RCA Victor division. The music America loves best. Camden, N. J. 501 p. [4721
Recordings of Mexican popular music listed on p. 498–501.

United States. Library of congress. Recording laboratory. Catalog of phonograph records; selected titles from the Archive of American folk song issued to January, 1943. Washington, D. C. 18 p. [4722
"Spanish religious songs and game songs, edited by Alan Lomax," p. 14–15.

RECORDS

Boulton, Laura C. Indian music of Mexico. Victor album P-94. [4723
Field recordings of Zapotec, Otomi and Yaqui Indian music, and of the playing of instruments from Ticui and Mérida, Yucatán.

CARNIVAL IN RIO. Fon-Fon and his orchestra, Carlos Galhardo with orchestra, and Patrício Teixeira with orchestra. Three 10-inch records. Victor album P-137. [4724
Contains six popular dance tunes: *Samba-le-lê; Abre a janella; Lig, lig, lig, le; Oh! Senhora viuva; Não tenho lágrimas;* and *Olá, Seu Nicolau.*

Labastille, Irma (comp.). Bailes nacionales, Latin-American folk dances. Five 10-inch records. Bost album ES4. [4725
Includes *Los Viejitos* and *Chiapanecas* of Mexico, and an example of *pasillo* and *bambuco* of Colombia, *marinera* of Peru, *joropo* of Venezuela, *huella*, *firmeza* and *zamba* of Argentina, and the *pericón* of Uruguay.

Lecuona, Ernesto. Dame de tus rosas; and Mala noche, by Domínguez. Carlos Ramírez with the Victor concert orchestra, conducted by Alfred Cibelli. One 10-inch record. Victor 10-1043. [4726
Examples of the song-form *canción bolero* sung by the Colombian baritone.

SOUTH AMERICAN FIESTA. Various orchestras and singers. Three 10-inch records. Victor album P-135. [4727
Contents: *Alma llanera*, Venezuelan *joropo* by Pedro E. Gutiérrez, performed by Lorenzo Herrera and his orchestra; *Ay! Dame tu corazón*, Ecuadorian *pasacalle* by Marco T. Hidrobo, performed by Rubén and Plutarco Uquillas; *Guabina chiquinquireña*, Colombian folk dance by Alberto Urdaneta F., sung by Pedro Vargas; *Las mirlas*, Colombian *bambuco* by Jesús M. Trespalacios, sung by Elena and Lucia with guitar accompaniment; *Lejos de mi bien*, Argentine *zamba* played by Maldonado-Infante folklore orchestra; and *Amargura*, Argentine *tango-canción* by Le Pera-Gardel, sung by Carlos Gardel with orchestra.

SOUTH AMERICAN MELODIES. Carlos Molina and his orchestra, Leon and his Rumba

Boys, Sotero San Miquel y sus Rancheros. Five 10-inch records. Continental album CON-6. [4728]
Popular music interpreted by Latin American dance orchestra experts.

Villa-Lobos, Heitor. The baby's family: Rag doll, Cardboard doll, and China doll. Guiomar Novaes, pf. One 10-inch record. Columbia 17355D. [4729]
First three of the eight movements of his suite *Prole de bebê, no. 1* (composed 1918); played by the Brazilian pianist.

PUBLICATIONS

(*See also section on* Folklore)

GENERAL

Chase, Gilbert. Americanismo musical (*Modern music*, vol. 20, no. 3, March–April, p. 214–215). [4730]
Describes the organization and content of the *Boletín Latinoamericano de Música*.

———. Materials for the study of Latin American music (*Music and libraries*, Washington, Music library association, p. 14–21). [4731]
Useful information by the outstanding U. S. authority on the music of Spain and Latin America.

———. Music of the new world (*Music educators journal*, vol. 30, no. 2, Nov.–Dec., p. 17–18, 49). [4732]
Discussion of the radio programs of that name arranged by the author for the radio broadcast series "Inter-American University of the Air" of the National Broadcasting Co. See also no. 4738.

———. La música de España. Buenos Aires. Ed. Hachette. (Col. Numen). 410 p., ilus., música. [4733]
Translation of "The Music of Spain." See *Handbook of Latin American Studies, no. 7, 1941*, no. 5506.

Fern, Leila. Origin and functions of the Inter-American music center (*Notes music libr. assn.*, vol. 1, no. 1, Dec., p. 14–22). [4734]
The Inter-American Music Center was established in 1941 to serve as the Music Division of the Pan American Union.

———. Selected list of Latin American song books and references for guidance in planning fiestas. Third ed., enlarged. Washington, D. C. Pan american union, Music division. 11 p., mimeographed. [4735]
A list of material available from United States publishers, suitable for club and school use.

González, Manuel Pedro. Latin American music (*Mexican life*, vol. 19, no. 1, Jan., p. 37–38, 51–53). [4736]
Popular discussion.

Loewenberg, Alfred. Annals of opera, 1597–1940. Introduction by Edward J. Dent. Cambridge. W. Heffer & sons, publ. 879 p. [4737]
Chronology of operatic performances. Includes the following Latin American operas: Argentina: *Nazdah*, by Athos Palma; *El Matrero*, by Felipe Boero; 4 operas by Ettore Panizza; *Huemac*, by Pascual de Rogatis; *Cayo Petronio*, by Constantino Gaito; *Tabaré*, by Alfredo Schiuma; *Tarass Bulba*, *Pampa*, and *Gli Eroi*, by Arturo Berutti.
Brazil: *Noite do Castello*, *Il Guarany*, *Fosca*, *Salvator Rosa*, and *Lo Schiavo*, by Antonio Carlos Gomez [sic].
Chile: *La Fioraia di Lugano*, by Eleodoro [sic] Ortiz de Zárate.
Cuba: *Dolorosa*, by Eduardo Sánchez de Fuentes.
Mexico: *Ildegonda* and *Cleopatra*, by Melesio Morales; *Keofar*, by Felipe Villanueva.

National broadcasting company. Music of the new world. Broadcast series of the NBC Inter-American university of the air. . . . Handbook, vols 2–3. New York. Southern music publ. co. 2 vols. [4738]
Syllabus written by Gilbert Chase for his half-hour broadcast of "Music of the Americas." Contains much information not otherwise available.

Pan American union. Sources for Latin American popular music (*Documentary material for the Good neighbor tour*, Washington, D. C., vol. 1, p. 28–33). [4739]
List of songs, music for orchestra and band, and phonograph records available in the U. S. Mimeographed.

Pereira Salas, Eugenio. Notes on the history of music exchange between the Americas before 1940. Washington, D. C. Pan American union, Music division. (Music series, no. 6). 37 p., mimeographed. [4740]
Pioneer survey. Appendix I contains information, not appearing elsewhere in print, upon the Pan American Association of Composers (1929–1935). Appendix II is a list of Latin American artists appearing in concerts at the Pan American Union (1924–1939). Appendix III comprises notes upon Latin American music awards at three North American expositions. Includes bibliography. Spanish edition is Music series no. 7.

Rothe, Friede. Music strengthens Pan-American ties (*Musical America*, vol. 63, no. 3, Feb. 10, p. 174, illus.). [4741]
Informative.

Seeger, Charles. Review of inter-American relations in the field of music, 1940–1943. Washington, D. C. Pan American union, Music division. 13 p., mimeographed. [4742]
Discussion.

Argentina

Hurtado, Leopoldo. Below the equator (*Modern music*, vol. 20, no. 2, Jan.–Feb., p. 121–124). [4743]
A review of recent music activities in Argentina.

SADAIC. Revista de la Sociedad argentina de autores y compositores de música. Buenos Aires. Año 6, no. 42, julio–dic., 204 p., ilus. [4744]
Special issue commemorating the 25th anniversary of SADAIC.

Schiuma, Oreste. Música y músicos argentinos. Segunda ed. Buenos Aires. Imp. M. Lorenzo Rañó. 237 p. [4745]

Serrano Plaja, Arturo (comp.). Hijo del alba. Villancicos, canciones, ensaladillas y coloquios pastoriles de nochebuena. Buenos Aires. Imp. López. 103 p. [4746]

EL TAMBORIL. Boletín mensual de información musical. Buenos Aires. Año 1, no. 1, feb.—. [4747]
Contains notices, news and comments.

Williams, Alberto. Amancio Alcorta, compositor. Buenos Aires. 18 p., ports. [4748]
Elsewhere Williams refers to Alcorta (1805–1862) as the "dean of Argentine composers."

Bolivia

ECO DE BOLIVIA (*Eco musical*, año 2, no. 8, mayo, p. 25). [4749]
Review of a concert of the music of Julio Martínez Arteaga, young Bolivian composer who has followed "el ritmo popular sin introducir ninguna inovación."

Núñez del Prado, Nilda. Danzas de Bolivia (*Bol. unión panamer.*, vol. 77, no. 2, feb., p. 77–82, ilus.). [4750]
Informative, non-technical.
Published also in the English edition of the *Bulletin of the Pan American Union* for July under the title, "Bolivian dances," and in the Portuguese edition for September under the title, "Dansas da Bolivia."

Brazil

Alvarenga, Oneyda. O movimento de consultas da discoteca pública municipal durante 1941 e 1942. São Paulo. Depto. de cultura. 53–72 p. [4751]
Circulation statistics for this public library of phonograph records.
Separate from *Rev. arq. mun.*, São Paulo, ano 9, vol. 92, agôsto–set., 1943.

Andrade, Mário de. Popular music and song in Brazil. Translated by Luiz Victor Le Cocq d'Oliveira. Rio de Janeiro. Imp. nacional. (Min. of state for foreign affairs of Brazil, Div. of intellectual co-operation, Resumé no. 2). 23 p. [4752]
Reprint, in English, of mimeographed article in Portuguese issued in 1936.

Barreto, Ceição de Barros. Estudo sôbre hinos e bandeira do Brasil. Rio de Janeiro. Carlos Wehrs, publ. 72 p., ilus. [4753]
Numerous music examples, including anthems by Francisco Manuel da Silva, Francisco Braga, Dom Pedro I, and Leopoldo Miguez.

Castro e Silva, Egydio de. A course in Brazilian music (*Teachers college record*, vol. 45, no. 2, Nov., p. 103–108). [4754]
Report upon a course given by the author at the Horace Mann-Lincoln School, N. Y., during the summer of 1943.

Chase, Gilbert. Camargo Guarnieri (*Int. amer.*, vol. 2, no. 1, Jan., p. 30–31, port.). [4755]
Brief biographical and critical notes upon this Brazilian composer, with facsimile of his music MS.

CONCURSO AO PRÊMIO LUIZ ALBERTO PENTEADO DE REZENDE (PARA SINFONIA) (*Resenha musical*, ano 6, no. 63–64, nov.–dez., 1 p.). [4756]
Contains the rules for competition offering a first prize of 10,000 cruzeiros and a second prize of 5,000 cruzeiros.

CONCURSO MUSICAL INTER-AMERICANO (*Resenha musical*, ano 6, no. 61–62, set.–out., p. 39–40). [4757]
Contains the rules of the contest conducted by the Chamber Music Guild of Washington, D. C., for two string quartets. In Portuguese.

Corrêa de Azevedo, Luiz Heitor. José Maurício Nunes Garcia (1767–1830), ensáio histórico (*Resenha musical*, ano 6, no. 63–64, nov.–dez., p. 4–13, port.). [4758]
Brief, authoritative biography of the "father of Brazilian music." To be continued.

———. O "recortado" na "moda" goiana (*Cultura política*, ano 3, no. 33, out., p. 201–203, ilus.). [4759]
Discussion of the relationship between the rural dance-song (*moda*) and the *recortado*, a separate piece traditionally joined to it. Includes plate of Adolfo Mariano, celebrated *violero* (guitarist) and *dansador*.

———. Violas de Goiaz (*Cultura política*, ano 3, no. 34, nov., p. 293–296, ilus.). [4760]
Scholarly discussion of the stringing, tuning, fretting, and terminology of varieties of guitars found in Goiaz by the author.

Luper, Albert T. The music of Brazil. Washington, D. C. Pan American union, Music division. (Music series, no. 9). 40 p. [4761]
Syllabus, for popular use. Contains 5 pages of bibliography, 2 pages of titles of

recordings of Brazilian music, and 16 pages of titles of Brazilian music available in the U. S., comprising, in large part, the only published listing of holdings of Brazilian music in the Pan American Union.

Machado Filho, Aires da Mata. O negro e o garimpo em Minas Gerais. Rio de Janeiro. Livr. José Olympio. (Col. documentos brasileiros, 42). 138 p., música. **[4762**
Carefully documented study of songs of Afro-Brazilian workers in the diamond mines. "*Garimpo,* more specifically, was the clandestine mining of diamonds, and the *garimpeiro* he who did it. We know of the severe punishment meted to *garimpeiros.*" 68 music notations and a vacabulary of the dialect.

Pedrosa, Mário. Camargo Guarnieri (*Bol. união panamer.,* vol. 45, no. 2, fev., p. 63–67). **[4763**
The present article was written upon the occasion of the first visit of the Brazilian composer Camargo Guarnieri (b. 1907) to the United States during the season of 1942–1943. A translation from the Portuguese appears in the April issue of the English edition of the *Bulletin of the Pan American Union.*

Peppercorn, Lisa M. Some aspects of Villa-Lobos' principles of composition (*Music rev.,* vol. 4, no. 1, Feb., p. 28–34). **[4764**

Sinzig, Pedro. Sêlo postal e música (*Cultura política,* ano 3, no. 34, nov., p. 297–301, ilus.). **[4765**
Urges use of musical subjects on stamps for propaganda purposes. Plate reproduces two Brazilian postage stamps issued in 1936 to celebrate centenary of birth of Carlos Gomes—one a profile portrait; the other, some measures from his opera *O Guarani.*

CHILE

(*See also item* 1879)

Barlow, Samuel L. M. Chilean travels (*Modern music,* vol. 20, no. 4, May–June, p. 270–273). **[4766**
Information, with comments, upon contemporary music activities.

COLOMBIA

(*See also item* 1893)

Lima, Emirto de. Apuntes sobre el folklore de la costa atlántica de Colombia (*Bol. unión panamer.,* vol. 77, no. 1, enero, p. 23–27, música). **[4767**
Appreciations of the role of singing in Colombia, especially in the rural occupations of farming, herding cattle, boating, and merry-making at Christmas time. 3 short music notations.

COSTA RICA

Zúñiga-Tristán, Virginia. Music in the schools of Costa Rica. Lexington, Ky. 155 p. **[4768**
Master's thesis, University of Kentucky. Typewritten copy.

CUBA

Ardévol, José. Hacia una escuela cubana de composición (*Conservatorio,* oct.–dic., p. 3–5). **[4769**
By the leader of a group of talented young composers who have formed the Grupo de Renovación Musical.

BOLETÍN DEL GRUPO DE RENOVACIÓN MUSICAL. Habana. No. 1, feb.—. **[4770**
The group is formed almost entirely of graduates of the Conservatorio Municipal de Música, but *más concretamente* of the pupils of maestro José Ardévol. See also no. 4769.
Director: Serafín Pró. Published irregularly.

Chase, Gilbert. Nin-Culmell, Cuban international (*Int. amer.,* vol. 2, no. 3, March, p. 32, port.). **[4771**
Brief biographical note about this composer and pianist.

CONSERVATORIO. Conservatorio municipal de música de La Habana. Habana. Oct.–dic.—. **[4772**
First issue. Contains articles, news and reviews.

Martín, Edgardo. El problema de los compositores en América (*Conservatorio,* oct.–dic., p. 6–9). **[4773**
By one of the leaders of the Grupo de Renovación Musical, a critic and composer.

MUSICALIA. Revista de arte y crítica editada por la Sociedad coral de la Habana. Habana, Cuba. Segunda época, año 3, no. 7, julio/agosto–no. 9, nov./dic. **[4774**
The three issues for 1943 contain articles upon music activities, especially those of *La Coral de la Habana,* together with reviews of books and phonograph recordings.

Tolón, Edwin T., and Jorge A. González. Operas cubanas y sus autores. Prólogo de Eduardo H. Alonso. Habana. Ed. Ucar, García. 472 p., ilus. **[4775**
Reviews history of opera during colonial times. Contains some information upon Luis Moreau Gottschalk's two unfinished operas, "Carlos IX" and "Isaura de Salerno." Author considers Gaspar Villate y Montes (1851–1891) "el precursor" of José Mauri y Esteve (1856–1937), Hubert de Blanck (1856–1932) and Eduardo Sánchez de Fuentes (1874–1944).

DOMINICAN REPUBLIC

(*See item* 3773)

ECUADOR

Cevallos García, Gabriel. Intención y paisaje de la música nacional ecuatoriana. Cuenca. Ed. Reed & Reed. 16 p. [4777
Dissertation read to the Rotary Club of Cuenca. Informative. Contains list of 41 RCA Victor records of folk and popular music of Ecuador.

Muñoz Sanz, Juan Pablo. La educación musical en la nueva cultura de América (*América*, Quito, año 18, no. 77, mayo–agosto, p. 402–407). [4778
The author believes that the decadence of music in nearly all the Indo-American countries is due to condescending instrumentalists, bad professors and false folklorists. Urges more rigorous self-criticism and makes specific recommendations. Thoughtful and challenging.

Salgado, Gustavo. Indian music in ancient Ecuador (*Etude*, vol. 61, no. 4, April, p. 244, 272, illus.). [4779
Informative travelogue.

GUATEMALA

Castellanos, J. Humberto R. Breve historia de la música en Guatemala (*Bol. mus. bibl.*, Guatemala, segunda época, año 3, no. 3, oct., p. 112–121). [4780
Quotes extensively from previous histories of Sáenz Poggio, Díaz and Jesús Castillo. This installment covers the period to 1773. To be continued.

Ley, Salvador. Actuales posibilidades del arte musical en Guatemala (*Orientación musical*, vol. 2, no. 19, enero, p. 8–9, 17; no. 20, feb., p. 3–6). [4781
Notes on contemporary professional musicians in Guatemala.

MEXICO

(*See also items* 1857, 1884, 1896–1899)

Altamirano, Ignacio M. Don Melesio Morales (*Rev. mus. mex.*, tomo 3, no. 1, 7 enero, p. 10–13; no. 2, 7 feb., p. 35–38; no. 3, 7 marzo, p. 63–65; no. 5, 7 mayo, p. 110–112; no. 8, 7 agosto, p. 180–182; no. 9, 7 sept., p. 206–207; no. 10, 7 oct., p. 228–232). [4782
Melesio Morales, Mexican musician and composer, was one of the most active influences in the operatic, concert, and music-pedagogic life of his day (1838–1908). This biographical essay, written before his death by one of his contemporaries, is reprinted from *El Renacimiento*, tomo 1, May 22, 1869.

Amézquita Borja, Francisco. Música y danza; algunos aspectos de la música y danza de la sierra norte del estado de Puebla. Puebla. 101 p., ilus., música. [4783
Contains 44 tunes, among others music for the *Danza de los Quetzales* and for the *Danza de los Voladores*. Some notations are marked with author's or arranger's names. Others are credited to Juan Bonilla, blind singer of traditional songs.

Barajas, Manuel. Himno nacional mexicano ... Cómo cantarlo correctamente. Lección grabada por su autor ... en discos de la R. C. A. Víctor mexicana, con la cooperación del Coro de madrigalistas acompañado por el pianista Eduardo Munōz. México. Sría. de educación pública. 10 p. [4784
Numerous music notations.

———— (comp.). Coros escolares. México. Ed. de la Sría. de educación pública. 47 p. [4785
14 songs intended for use in primary and secondary schools. The editor points out certain errors in the music and text of the national anthem (see also no. 4784). Piano accompaniment and Spanish words.

Bermejo, Manuel M. Errores sobre nuestro nacionalismo musical (*Orientación musical*, vol. 3, no. 28, oct., p. 6–7, 20; no. 30, dic., p. 6–8). [4786
Author believes that sincerity is the prime criterion for the definition of music nationalism. Rejects folklorism, indianism, popularism, the belief that music has specific effects upon national psychology, etc.

Buitrón, Juan B. Historia de una reforma (*Schola cantorum*, Morelia, año 5, no. 5, mayo, p. 66–69; no. 6, junio, p. 84–87; no. 10, oct., p. 146–148). [4787
Installments 1 and 2 appeared in the August and October issues for the year 1939. "Desaparecidos los motivos de la interrupción—al menos en parte—reanudamos hoy nuestra tarea." The aim is first, to discuss the reform of "música sagrada" in the Archbishopric of Morelia and second, to present a brief synthesis of the music of Michoacán as a whole—its ecclesiastical and secular aspects. Copious historical allusion. To be continued.

Carrillo, Julián. Nueva gráfica musical (*Bol. sem. cult. mex.*, tomo 1, no. 1, julio, p. 90–106). [4788
Brief presentation of a numerical, single-line music notation.

Flores, Sabino. Documentos relativos a la solemne instalación de la Sociedad filarmónica guanajuatense, en 1856 (*Rev. mus. mex.*, tomo 3, no. 6, 7 junio, p. 131–134; no. 8, 7 agosto, p. 178–179). [4789
The program, given in a private residence, before an audience of 200 people, comprised selections from such Italian

operas as "I Puritani" and "Lucia." The formal address is included.

Guerrero, José E. El teatro litúrgico y las pastorelas en México (*Orientación musical,* vol. 2, no. 19, enero, p. 7, 15; no. 20, feb., p. 7; no. 21, marzo, p. 4–5, iii; no. 22, abril, p. 10–11). [4790]

The Spanish religious drama, of which a brief history is given, was welcomed by the Aztec people. Little change is to be noted in present traditions from the colonial practice. The *dramatis personae* are about the same: the shepherds Bato and Gila, the hermit, Luzbel, la Astucia, el Pecado, la Diosa, Bras and others. Comparison is made between a pastorela described by Padres Ponce and Motolinía, in the sixteenth century, by Antonio García Cubas in the nineteenth, and by the author himself recently in Guanajuato.

Guisa, Marcelina. Escuelas diocesanas de música sagrada en la República Mexicana (*Schola cantorum,* Morelia, año 5, no. 2, feb., p. 27–31). [4791]

Schools were founded and have been maintained as follows: Aguascalientes (1938–); Querétaro (1892–1924 and 1942–); Guadalajara (dates not given); Jalapa (1940–); Mexico (1940–); Morelia (1914–); León (1904–1914, 1930 intermittently until 1941, 1941–); Oaxaca (1941–); Tulancingo (1939–?).

Mayer-Serra, Otto. Información, no crítica (*Tiempo,* vol. 2, no. 2, abril 25, p. 58). [4792]

Under this title the author begins his column of "Cine—Música—Radio—Teatro."

——. Mexican musical folklore (*Etude,* vol. 61, no. 1, Jan., p. 17, 58, 72; no. 2, Feb., p. 89, 137, 139, illus.). [4793]

For the general reader. Treats of the *corrido.* 7 music notations. The contents page for March lists the continuation of this article, but text is lacking.

——. Panorama de la música hispanoamericana. México, D. F. Ed. Atlante. 379–440 p., ilus. [4794]

Separate of vol. 2 of *Enciclopedia de la Música* (México, D. F. Ed. Atlante. 1943. 3 vols.).

Mendoza, Vicente T. El grupo musical mexicano llamado "Mariachi" (*Rev. univ.,* Guadalajara, tomo 1, no. 2, mayo–julio, p. 87–89). [4795]

The *mariachi* is "un género de música de origen español . . . actualmente la manifestación musical criolla más clara y precisa," grafted into the states of Nayarit, Jalisco, Michoacán, Guerrero, part of Oaxaca, and beyond. This music became known as such at least by the end of the eighteenth and beginning of the nineteenth centuries. It had been prohibited by the Inquisition during the Colonial period.

Mariachi music is played by an orchestra of 2 violins, 1 jarana (small guitar), 1 guitar (or vihuela), 1 large guitar, and 1 harp. Sometimes a clarinet is included. Doubling of instruments is common. In Guerrero, a tambor is added. When a drum is lacking, sounding-board of the harp is slapped with hand or fingers. *Sones, gustos, jarabes, malagueñas, chilenas, valonas, corridos, zambas, relaciones, barcarolas,* etc., are played. The rhythm of the melody is obviously European, but the accompaniment is not. Singing may be added, sometimes by the players.

One music notation (rhythmic symbols only).

——. Un juego español del siglo 16 entre los otomíes (*An. inst. invest. est.,* vol. 3, no. 10, p. 59–74, música). [4796]

Investigation made by the author in company with Gabriel Saldívar in the Valley of Mezquital, Hidalgo. Informants were mostly children from 7–14 years of age. The game is one of question and answer. [It is related to the Spanish version of the game of *pez pecigaña (pipirigaña,* etc.). It is about a girl killed by snake-bite and ends with some religious allusion.—R. S. Boggs]. The title adopted is "El cuento de la araña." Five complete notations of five separate versions are given. Otomí and Spanish words. Comparative study (words only) is made with version found in Puerto Rico, Colombia, Argentina and Spain.

Ponce, Manuel M. Lo popular y lo vulgar en la música (*Bol. sem. cult. mex.,* tomo 1, no. 2, oct., p. 85–88). [4797]

Discussion.

Romero, Jesús C. Melesio Morales, estudio bibliográfico (*Rev. mus. mex.,* tomo 3, no. 11, 7 nov., p. 248–252). [4798]

Bio-bibliographical list. See also no. 4782.

——. Música precortesiana; estudio histórico-crítico de nuestra protohistoria musical (*Orientación musical,* vol. 2, no. 19, enero, p. 12–13; no. 20, feb., p. 8–10, 16; no. 21, marzo, p. 8–9; no. 22, abril, p. 12–13; no. 23, mayo, p. 8–9, 17, iii; no. 24, junio, p. 7–8, 20). [4799]

——. Reseña histórica de la fundación del Conservatorio nacional de música (*Orientación musical,* vol. 3, no. 25, julio, p. 9; no. 26, agosto, p. 7; no. 27, sept., p. 6–7, 20; no. 28, oct., p. 8; no. 29, nov., p. 13–14; no. 30, dic., p. 11, 15). [4800]

Sandi, Luis. Struggle in Mexico (*Modern music,* vol. 20, no. 4, May–June, p. 273–276). [4801]

Up-hill work in school music education in Mexico, by the man responsible for its administration, who is also a composer and conductor of the outstanding choral group.

SCHOLA CANTORUM. Revista de cultura sacromusical. Morelia. Año 5, no. 1, enero–no. 11/12, nov./dic. [4802]

Besides the several articles and music listed under author in this *Handbook,* the periodical contains monthly news about ecclesiastical music activities in the State of Michoacán.

Vásquez, Nabor. Breve historia de las bandas de música en México (*Orientación musical*, vol. 3, no. 25, julio, p. 14; no. 26, agosto, p. 11; no. 27, sept., p. 9–10; no. 29, nov., p. 10–11; no. 30, dic., p. 10, 20). [4803
To be continued.

Yurchenco, Henrietta. La música indígena en Chiapas, México (*Amér. indígena*, vol. 3, no. 4, oct., p. 305–311). [4804
Report upon an expedition under the auspices of the Inter-American Indian Institute with cooperation of the Music Division of the Library of Congress, which made sound-recordings on discs of the music of the Zoque, Tzotzil, Chiapaneco and Tojolobal Indian groups. 100 *sones* were recorded and 700 feet of 16 mm. film made. One music notation.

NICARAGUA

Delgadillo, Luis A. Historia de la música en Nicaragua (*Eco musical*, año 2, no. 8, mayo, p. 14–17, port.). [4805
Brief notes by the dean of Nicaraguan composers.

PANAMA

ARMONÍA. Órgano del Conservatorio nacional de música y declamación. Panamá. Año 1, vol. 1, no. 1, agosto—. [4806
Notes and comments on current music activities. Director: Luis A. Delgadillo. Monthly.

Castillero R., Ernesto J. Orígenes del Himno nacional panameño (*Armonía*, año 1, vol. 1, no. 4, nov., p. 7–10). [4807

Zozaya, Ricardo. Santos Jorge, autor de la música del Himno de la República de Panamá (*Armonía*, año 1, vol. 1, no. 4, nov., p. 5–6, port.). [4808

PARAGUAY

Hensler, Haven. The music of the Paraguayan people. [4809
Negative photostat of 39 pages of typewritten, single-spaced manuscript, containing 18 short music examples, bibliography, and list of commercial phonograph records of Paraguayan folk-popular music. The author believes "it is the first systematized effort at any collection of material on the heretofore little-known and scattered folk music of Paraguay."

Moreno, Juan Carlos. Datos para la historia de la música en el Paraguay (*Rev. ateneo paraguayo*, año 2, no. 8, nov., p. 6–22). [4810
Divides history of music in Paraguay into three periods (1) of the conquest, with retrospective glance into pre-Columbian epoch; (2) colonial period to the war of 1864–1870; (3) modern period. A pioneer effort by the editor of the *Revista*.

PERU

(*See also items* 517, 526)

Baudizzone, Luis M. (ed.). Poesía, música y danza inca. Buenos Aires. Ed. Nova. (Col. mar dulce). 91 p., ilus., música. [4810
The 6 music notations for piano, contained in pages 75–86, are reduced facsimiles excerpted from *El Canto Popular* (Instituto de literatura argentina. Sección folklore, t. 1. Buenos Aires, 1923). Six fine photographs.

Bustamante, Manuel E. Apuntes para el folklore peruano. Ayacucho. Imp. "La Miniatura." 178, iv p., ilus. [4811
"Bailes y cantos. Música indígena. Instrumentos musicales. El toro corneta. El jarahui. Breves referencias sobre la música vernacular": p. 134–145. Contains wood-cut of *toro corneta*.

Caballero F., Policarpo. El tusuy o la danza incaica (*Eco musical*, año 2, no. 7, abril, p. 25–27). [4812
Continuation of article which appeared in nos. 1 and 2 (1942). Consists of reflections based upon information found in "legend and tradition." Some quotations from chroniclers and missionaries.

Figueroa, Rosa E. Rosa Mercedes Ayarza de Morales (*Eco musical*, año 2, no. 9, junio, p. 3–6, ilus.). [4814
Biographical notes on this collector and arranger of traditional Peruvian music.

Holzmann, Rodolfo. Ensáio analítico da obra musical do compositor peruano Teodoro Valcárcel (*Resenha musical*, ano 5, no. 57–58, máio–junho, p. 13–18; no. 59–60, julho–agosto, p. 18–19). [4815
Translation into Portuguese of the author's article which first appeared in the March issue of *Eco Musical* (Buenos Aires) (see no. 4818). The musical supplement which accompanies that issue is also contained in this Brazilian periodical.

——— (comp.). Catálogo de las obras de Daniel Alomía Robles (*Bol. bibliog.*, Lima, año 16, vol. 13, no. 1–2, julio, p. 25–78). [4816
This Peruvian composer (1871–1942) produced a considerable body of work, most of it "folkloristic" in character. There are over 200 compositions, some printed, most in MS; an additional 125 piano arrangements of folk-songs, works for theatre and cinema, and the famous collection "Folklore del Perú" containing 650 melodies notated at dictation, here classified according to type. The words to many tunes in this collection are missing, as is often all documentation of informant, date, place. Province or Department is usually given, which allows an "índice por departamentos."

———. Catálogos de las obras de Alfonso de Silva y Vicente Stea (*Bol. bibliog.*, Lima, año 16, vol. 13, no. 3–4, dic., p. 242–252). [4817
Author considers Silva (1903–1937) "como el peruano que más genio poseía." None of

his important works is published. There are approximately 65 titles in all, some songs, some piano solos, some works for chamber ensembles and 15 for orchestra. Vicente Stea (1884–1943) was born in Italy but lived in Lima from 1917. "Músico de profundos conocimientos técnicos, no tenía, sin embargo," according to this author, "una inspiración muy flúida." There are listed about 42 mature works, 17 for orchestra, and many songs and chamber music works.

HOMENAJE A LA MEMORIA DEL COMPOSITOR PERUANO THEODORO VALCÁRCEL (*Eco musical*, año 2, no. 6, marzo, p. 1–33, retratos). [4818
Memorial issue containing a biography and list of works of Valcárcel (1900–1942); "Un prefacio a las estampas del ballet Suray-Surita," by Luis E. Valcárcel; "¿Qué significa Suray-Surita?"—an explanation by Theodoro Valcárcel; "Ensayo analítico de la obra musical del compositor . . ." by Rodolfo Holzmann; and a musical supplement of examples of Valcárcel's works.

HOMENAJE A LA MEMORIA DEL COMPOSITOR Y FOLKLORISTA PERUANO DANIEL ALOMÍA ROBLES EN EL PRIMER ANIVERSARIO DE SU FALLECIMIENTO (*Eco musical*, año 2, no. 10, julio, p. 1–30, ilus., retratos, música). [4819
Memorial issue including testimonials of contemporaries of Robles (1871–1942), biographical sketch by Rodolfo Holzmann, and a musical supplement containing the song "Camino del cielo" with piano accompaniment.

URUGUAY

Ayestarán, Lauro. Crónica de una temporada musical en el Montevideo de 1830. Montevideo. Ed. Ceibo. 108 p., ilus. [4821
Research on music activity during 1830, the year of the first operatic performance in Montevideo. One music notation.

Correa Luna, Carlos. Luis Sambucetti, 1860–1926 (*Eco musical*, año 2, no. 9, junio, p. 9–12, port.). [4822
Appreciative biographical note upon career of celebrated violinist, conductor and composer, promoter and organizer of the National Orchestra and Chamber Music Society of Montevideo.

Muller, María V. de. Luis Sambucetti (*Rev. nac.*, Montevideo, año 6, tomo 24, no. 70, oct., p. 30–53, ilus., música). [4823
Biographical. See also no. 4822.

VENEZUELA

(*See also* 1907)

Liscano, Juan. Baile de tambor (*Bol. soc. venez. cien. nat.*, tomo 8, no. 55, abril-junio, p. 245–251). [4824
Information upon Afro-Venezuelan folk traditions in song and dance in the coastal region from Zulia to Sucre.

Olivares Figueroa, R. Canciones de corro populares en Venezuela (*Educación*, Caracas, año 4, no. 27, oct.–nov., p. 17–19). [4825
Urges utilization of traditional children's game songs in education.

———. Villancicos de Noche Buena (*Onza, tigre y león*, año 6, no. 54, dic., p. 4–5, 12). [4826
Words for "Corred, pastorcitos"; no music.

Plaza, Juan Bautista. Don Bartolomé Bello, músico (*Rev. nac. cultura*, año 5, no. 39, julio–agosto, p. 5–14). [4827
The father of Andrés Bello, Venezuelan writer, is found to have been for 13 years a singer in the Cathedral of Caracas.

———. Music in Caracas during the colonial period, 1770–1811 (*Musical quarterly*, vol. 29, no. 2, April, p. 198–213, illus.). [4828
In 1935 a wooden box in the cellar of the National School of Music in Caracas was opened, disclosing, in a state of excellent preservation, a quantity of music manuscripts dating from the period 1770–1811 (the year the Independence Act of Venezuela was signed). Juan B. Plaza arranged and classified them, later selecting and editing some for publication, together with other works of the period which began, on account of awakened public interest, to be deposited in the archives of the School and in the National Library. The story is that a young priest, Don Pedro Palacios y Sojo, made a trip to Rome and Madrid in 1770, bringing back with him contemporary instruments and scores. Juan Manuel Olivares, a well-trained musician of an older generation, and José Ángel Lamas, of a younger, together with other composers whose works are published in this series, gathered around Father Sojo, creating a colonial school of music which flourished until changed political conditions stopped their activity. Juan José Landaeta, one of the group and composer of the song "Gloria al Bravo Pueblo" (later adopted as the national anthem of Venezuela) was shot by Royalists in 1814. Selected works are published by the Ministry of Education. See also no. 4716.

PUERTO RICO

Cadilla de Martínez, María. La conga (*Alma latina*, año 14, no. 409, oct. 2, p. 6). [4829
Brief study of music acculturation processes leading to formation of present dance.

ADDENDA

MUSIC

GENERAL

CANCIONES PANAMERICANAS, SONGS OF THE AMERICAS. New York. Silver Burdett, publ. 1942. 42 p. [4830
28 songs from 21 republics and Canada. Piano accompaniment. Words in the original language and English.

Guenther, Felix (arr.). La hora del canto (The hour of singing). New York. Edward B. Marks, publ. 1942. 55 p. [4831
Compilation of 26 songs from Argentina, Chile, Cuba and Mexico, with piano accompaniment, for practical use. Spanish words only. Sources, other than country of origin, not noted.

Novoa, Sofía (arr.). Cantares españoles. Hastings-on-Hudson, N. Y. Gessler publ. co. 24 p. [4832
Compilation of 26 songs, most of them with simple piano accompaniment, for popular use. Spanish words. Sources not given.

Wilkes, Josué Teófilo (arr.). Colonial songs from Latin America (from 12 colonial songs of the 17th century). Boston. C. C. Birchard, publ. 1942. 4 vols. [4833
Four songs for mixed chorus (SSATB) a cappella. Original collection was by Fray Gregorio de Zuola, Franciscan monk (16..–1709). Each song published separately with Spanish and English words. Contents: *A cierto galán su dama, Don Pedro a quien los crueles, Malograda fuentecilla, Pardos ojos de mis ojos*.

ARGENTINA

García Morillo, Roberto. Conjuros. Montevideo. Ed. coop. interam. de compositores. (Publ. no. 17). 1942. 17 p. [4834
Suite for piano, op. 3. Includes brief biography and list of works.

Ginastera, Alberto E. Impresiones de la Puna. Montevideo. Ed. coop. interam. de compositores. (Publ. no. 12). 1942. 13 p. [4835
Score for flute and string quartet. Composed 1934. Includes brief biography and list of works.

Iglesias Villoud, Héctor. Catamarqueña. Montevideo. Ed. coop. interam. de compositores. (Publ. no. 15). 1942. 5 p. [4836
Piano solo, from the series "Provincianas." Includes brief biography and list of works.

Paz, Juan Carlos. Tercera sonatina. Montevideo. Ed. coop. interam. de compositores (Publ. no. 10). 1942. 9 p. [4837
Piano solo. Composed in 1933. Includes brief biography and list of works.

Wilkes, Josué Teófilo. Evening bells (No hei querio eso, vidit'ay). Cleveland. Sam Fox, publ. 1942. 7 p. [4838
For mixed chorus (SATB) and piano. Spanish and English words.

———. Green trees (Arboles verdes). Cleveland. Sam Fox, publ. 1942. 7 p. [4839
For mixed chorus (SATB) and piano. Spanish and English words.

BOLIVIA

Patiño, Jr., Adrián. "Thokontañaañittiscuntañaani" (Bailaremos—brincaremos). Danza aymara-pasacalle. Cochabamba. Depto. de educación musical y artística. 1942. 2 p. [4840
Piano solo.

Roncal, Simeón. Marcha 3 de febrero, Bolivian concert march. New York. Boosey, Hawkes, Belwin, publ. (Boosey Hawkes standard band no. 27). 1942. [4841
Conductor's score and instrumental parts for band.

BRAZIL

Barrozo Netto, Joaquim Antônio. O ferreiro (The blacksmith). Chicago. Clayton F. Summy, publ. 1942. 8 p. [4842
For women's chorus (SSA) a cappella. Portuguese and English words.

———. Two canons. Chicago. Clayton F. Summy, publ. 1942. 4 p. [4843
For two equal voices, a cappella, with vocalise syllables. Contents: *Canon sem palavras, O sino da egrejinha*.

Braga, Francisco. Toada. Boston. Cundy-Bettoney. 1942. 7, 2 p. [4844
For bassoon and piano. Score and part.

Cantú, A. Cantiga de Jatobá (das margens do Rio S. Francisco). São Paulo. Ricordi americana, publ. 1942. 16 p. [4845
For mixed chorus (SATB) a cappella. Portuguese words.

Fernândez, Óscar Lorenzo. Canção da fonte. São Paulo. Ed. Irmãos Vitale. 1942. 2 p. [4846
For medium voice and piano. Portuguese words.

———. Coração inquieto. São Paulo. Ed. Irmãos Vitale. 1942. 3 p. [4847
For medium voice and piano. Portuguese words.

———. Pirilâmpos. São Paulo. Ed. Irmãos Vitale. 1942. 4 p. [4848
Piano solo. No. 5 of his suite Prelúdios do crepúsculo, op. 15.

———. Primeira suite brasileira. São Paulo. Ed. Irmãos Vitale. 1942. 3 vols. [4849
In three movements, for piano: *Velha modinha, Suave acalanto, Saudosa seresta*.

———. Segunda suite brasileira. São Paulo. Ed. Irmãos Vitale. 1942. 3 vols. [4850
In three movements, for piano: *Ponteio, Moda, Cateretê*.

———. Terceira suite brasileira. São Paulo. Ed. Irmãos Vitale. 1942. 3 vols. [4851
In three movements, for piano: *Toada, Seresta, Jongo*.

———. Visões infantís, op. 22. São Paulo. Ed. Irmãos Vitale. 1942. 2 vols. **[4852**
Suite for piano in three movements, of which no. 1, *Pequeno Cortejo* and no. 2, *Ronda nocturna*, appeared in this edition.

Guarnieri, Camargo. Canção sertaneja. Boston. Cundy-Bettoney, publ. 1942. 6, 1 p. **[4853**
Composed in 1928. This arrangement for oboe and piano. Score and part. Also published for Bb clarinet and piano.

Koellreutter, H. J. Música 1941. Montevideo. Ed. coop. interam. de compositores. (Publ. no. 14). 1942. 11 p. **[4854**
Piano solo. Composed in 1941. Includes brief biography and list of works.

McKinney, Howard D. (arr.). Tutú Marambá. New York. J. Fischer, publ. 1942. 7 p. **[4855**
Brazilian folk-song arranged for women's chorus (SSA) and piano. English words only.

Mignone, Francisco. Cantiga de ninar. Chicago. Clayton F. Summy, publ. 1942. 8 p. **[4856**
Brazilian slumber song arranged for women's chorus (SSA) with optional accompaniment. English and Portuguese words.

———. Cateretê. Philadelphia. Theodore Presser, publ. 1942. 12 p. **[4857**
Brazilian dance, arranged for mixed chorus (SATB, divided) a cappella. English words only.

———. Quasi modinha. New York. Edward B. Marks, publ. (Latin American series of contemporary composers). 1942. 6 p. **[4858**
Piano solo.

Nepomuceno, Alberto. O baile na flor (The dance in the flower). New York. Carl Fischer, publ. 1942. 5 p. **[4859**
For women's chorus (SSA) a cappella. English and Portuguese words.

PIANO MUSIC OF BRAZIL (*New music*, vol. 16, no. 1, Oct., 1942, 22 p.). **[4860**
Collected, and with an introduction by Nicolas Slonimsky. Contents: *Moda*, by Óscar Lorenzo Fernández; *Valsa*, by Camargo Guarnieri; *Chôro*, by Radamés Gnattali; *Melodia da montanha*, and *New York sky-line*, by Heitor Villa-Lobos; and *Lenda sertaneja no. 9*, by Francisco Mignone.

ROBBINS PRESENTA UNA SERIE BRASILEÑA DE SAMBAS Y MARCHAS PARA ORQUESTA. Habana. Robbins music co. of Cuba. 1942. 8 vols. **[4861**
A collection of currently popular Brazilian music arranged for dance orchestra. Spanish and Portuguese words. Issues in 1942 include *Bahiana* (*Que é que a bahiana tem?*) by Dorival Caymmi; *Helena! Helena!* by António Almeida and Constantino Silva; *Brasil*, by Benedicto Lacerda and Aldo Cabral; *Dansa do bóle-bóle*, by João de Barro and Alcyr Pires Vermelho; *Carinhoso*, by A. Vianna; *Lloro tu despedida*, by Benedicto Lacerda and Aldo Cabral; *Cáe, cáe*, by Roberto Martins; and *Linda flor*, by H. Vogeler.

CHILE

Casanova Vicuña, Juan. 4 esquisses sinfónicos. Santiago, Chile. Ed. Casa Amarilla. 1942. 26 p. **[4862**
Orchestral score for suite in 4 movements: *El afilador de cuchillos, Tarde de otoño, Machitún, Así es mi tierra.*

Piccione Blasi, Francisco. Obras militares. Santiago, Chile. Ed. Casa Amarilla. 1942. 4 vols. **[4863**
Full band scores. Works in this series for 1942 include *Juventud militar*, "*Ejército de Chile*," "*Infantería*," and "*Marcha fúnebre*." These works form part of the major series listed under no. 4690.

COSTA RICA

Fonseca, Julio. Gran fantasía sinfónica sobre motivos folklóricos. San José. Litografía nacional. 1942. 16 p. **[4864**
Arranged for piano.

Quesada, José. Mi ñata. Providence, R. I. Axelrod, publ. (Two Costa Rican dances, no. 2). 1942. **[4865**
Arranged for full and symphonic band by Ángel del Busto. Conductor's score and instrumental parts.

———. El son de la luna. Providence, R. I. Axelrod, publ. (Two Costa Rican dances, no. 1). 1942. **[4866**
Arranged for full and symphonic band by Ángel del Busto. Conductor's score and instrumental parts.

DOMINICAN REPUBLIC

García, Juan Francisco. Sambumbia no. 1 (Dominican rhapsody). New York. Alpha, publ. (Concert music of the Americas). 1942. 8 p. **[4867**
For piano.

MEXICO

Chávez, Carlos. Concerto for the piano with orchestra; arrangement for two pianos, four-hands. New York. G. Schirmer, publ. 1942. 96 p. **[4868**
Score.

———. Three poems for voice and piano. New York. G. Schirmer, publ. 1942. 3 vols. **[4869**
Songs, published separately. English and Spanish words. Contents: *Segador, Hoy no lució la estrella de tus ojos, Nocturna rosa.*

Lerdo de Tejada, Miguel. Gay fiesta (Corrido del sol). New York. H. Flammer, publ. 1942. 6 p. [4870
Mexican folk-song arranged for two- and three-part treble voices and piano. English words only.

Ponce, Manuel M. Cantos infantiles. México. Sría de educación pública. 1942. 26 p. [4871
Contains the Mexican National Anthem and 10 songs with piano accompaniment by Ponce. Spanish words, by Rosaura Zapata.

PERU

Carpio Valdés, Roberto. Suite para piano. Montevideo. Ed. coop. interam. de compositores. (Publ. no. 13). 1942. 11 p. [4872
Composed in 1939. Includes biography and list of works.

PUERTO RICO

Busto, Ángel del. Reminiscencias (Caribbean concert dance no. 6). ·New York. Alpha, publ. (Concert music of the Americas). 1942. 5 p. [4873
For piano.

URUGUAY

Ascone, Vicente. Montes de mi Queguay. Montevideo. Ed. coop. interam. de compositores. (Publ. no. 11). 1942. 8 p. [4874
Score for voice, string quartet and piano. Includes brief biography and list of works.

Peyrallo, Félix. Holiday (Día de fiesta). Boston. Boston music co. 1942. 14 p. [4875
For men's chorus (TTBB) a cappella. Spanish and English words.

Santórsola, Guido. Agonía. Montevideo. Ed. coop. interam. de compositores. (Publ. no. 16). 1942. 9 p. [4876
Composed in 1937, for contralto and orchestra. This score for voice and piano with indications of instrumentation. Includes brief biography and list of works.

PUBLICATIONS

(See also items 549, 2002)

Andrade, Mário de. The music of carnival (Travel in Brazil, vol. 2, no. 3, 1942, p. 1-7). [4877
Brief, authoritative article on the carnival in Brazil, for the general reader. 7 fine photographs.

Barajas, Manuel. El Himno nacional mexicano; su historia y la búsqueda del original; las deformaciones sufridas. México. Ed. de la Sría. de educación pública. 1942. 8 p. [4878
Brief history of the anthem with note on corruptions of the original texts of words and music, which have been made apparently in the course of "communal modification," resulting from almost a century of currency of the anthem in the oral tradition.

Marchena, Enrique de. Del Areito de Anacaona al poema folklórico; Brindis de Salas en Santo Domingo. Ciudad Trujillo. Ed. Montalvo. 1942. 95, 2 p. [4880

Montes de Oca, José G. La navidad en Querétaro. Forest Hills, N. Y. Las Americas publ. co. 1942. 67 p., ilus. [4881
6 music notations.

Sá Pereira, Antônio. Mobilização musical da juventude americana. Rio de Janeiro. Univ. do Brasil, Escola nacional de música. 1942. 29 p. [4882
Report of the author's trip to the United States to investigate music education in 1942.

Sociedad argentina de autores y compositores de música, Buenos Aires. Memoria correspondiente al ejercicio 1941/42; balance general e inventario; presupuesto de gastos y cálculo de recursos para el próximo ejercicio 1942/43. Buenos Aires. Ed. Garrot, Tasso & Vita. 1942. 144 p. [4883
Financial papers of the largest rights society in Latin America.

PHILOSOPHY [1]

BY

RISIERI FRONDIZI [2]

Universidad Nacional de Tucumán, Argentina

OJEADA GENERAL

Hace cinco años que iniciamos desde esta sección un balance anual de la producción filosófica con el propósito de que se adquiriera conciencia en la América Latina de las posibilidades, tendencias y limitaciones del propio pensamiento, y se conociera en los demás países la orientación y los valores de la filosofía latinoamericana actual. Acaso no estaría demás completar cada cinco años dicho balance anual con una visión de conjunto que destaque lo más importante de ese período.

Sin lugar a dudas, el último lustro pertenece a una etapa de rápido crecimiento de la producción filosófica latinoamericana. Cinco años antes, nuestra tarea hubiera sido sencilla por la escasez de producción, y complicada por las dificultades que había que vencer para lograr una información precisa. En cambio, desde que se inició esta sección han figurado en ella todos los años más de cien publicaciones, a pesar de que se excluyen deliberadamente las de escaso valor filosófico y los artículos que se refieren a doctrinas o pensadores ajenos a la América Latina. Se han publicado ya obras de reconocido valor teórico que revelan vocaciones filosóficas genuinas, además de ensayos sobre el propio pensamiento latinoamericano que ponen de manifiesto la existencia de una conciencia histórica imprescindible para que el pasado obre como impulso y no como lastre del presente y del futuro.

Todas las tendencias importantes del pensamiento filosófico contemporáneo están representadas en la bibliografía latinoamericana. Si bien la fenomenología y el neo-tomismo son las dos corrientes predominantes, las obras originales de mayor valor no pertenecen a ninguna de estas dos tendencias. Las cuestiones de orden metafísico y ético son las que han predominado conjuntamente con las que se refieren a filosofía jurídica y social. La producción bibliográfica revela poco interés por los problemas lógicos y epistemológicos: la ciencia y la filosofía continúan alejadas en la América Latina.

Entre las obras referentes a cuestiones metafísicas se destacan, en la Argentina, la de Miguel Ángel Virasoro, *La Libertad, la Existencia y el Ser* (Instituto de Filosofía, Universidad de Buenos Aires, 1942), [*Handbook, no. 8, 1942*, item 4897], la de Alberto Rougés, *Las Jerarquías del Ser y la Eternidad*, (Universidad Nacional de Tucumán, 1943) [item 4960] y la de Ángel Vassalo,

---

[1] Dada la naturaleza del *Handbook* sólo se analizan aquí las obras y artículos originales o que se refieren a pensadores latinoamericanos, excluyéndose las reseñas bibliográficas y las publicaciones de escaso valor filosófico o que tengan por objeto principal estudiar doctrinas o pensadores ajenos a la América Latina. A fin de suplir esta última limitación se agrega un *Apéndice* con la nómina de las obras de filosofía publicadas en 1943 y excluídas de la sección de crítica bibliográfica por las razones señaladas.

[2] Agradecemos la colaboración de Rafael Carrillo (Colombia), R. P. Leonel Franca (Brasil) y José Gaos (México).

Elogio de la Vigilia, (Buenos Aires, Ed. Losada, 1939) ; y en México el sugestivo trabajo de Samuel Ramos, *Hacia un Nuevo Humanismo,* (La Casa de España en México, 1940) [*Handbook, no. 6, 1940,* item 5007]. Los problemas de filosofía jurídica han logrado un puesto destacado gracias a la contribución de Carlos Cossio en la Argentina y Eduardo García Maynes en México. El primero es autor de *La Plenitud del Orden Jurídico y la Interpretación Judicial de la Ley,* (Buenos Aires, Ed. Losada 1939) [*Handbook, no. 5, 1939,* item 4441], *El Substracto Filosófico de los Métodos Interpretativos,* (Universidad del Litoral, 1940) [*Handbook, no. 6, 1940,* item 5043], *La Valoración Jurídica y la Ciencia del Derecho,* (Universidad del Litoral, 1941) [*Handbook, no. 7, 1941,* item 5680], y *Las Lagunas del Derecho,* (Universidad de Córdoba, 1942) [*Handbook, no. 8, 1942,* item 4502]. El profesor García Maynes ha publicado, a su vez, diversos artículos de filosofía jurídica además de una importante aunque breve obra titulada *Libertad, como Derecho y como Poder,* (Compañía General Editora, 1941) [*Handbook, no. 7, 1941,* item 2480]. Sobre filosofía social deben mencionarse los trabajos de Sebastian Soler, *Ley, Historia y Libertad,* (Buenos Aires, Ed. Losada, 1943) [item 4973], P. Leonel Franca, *A Crise do Mundo Moderno,* (Rio de Janeiro, Livr. José Olympio Editora, 1942) [*Handbook, no. 8, 1942,* item 4906], y Antonio Caso, *La Persona Humana y el Estado Totalitario,* (Universidad Nacional de México, 1941) [*Handbook, no. 7, 1941,* item 5679]. Entre las obras de carácter general deben citarse el *Fermentario* de Carlos Vaz Ferreira (Buenos Aires, Edit. Losada, 1940) [*Handbook, no. 6, 1940,* item 5013], *Seis Temas do Espírito Moderno de Euryalo Cannabrava* (São Paulo, Ed. Sep, 1941) [*Handbook, no. 7, 1941,* item 5631] y los diversos escritos de Francisco Romero.

Los mejores ensayos de indagación del pasado filosófico se han publicado en México. En primer lugar debe figurar el extenso trabajo de Leopoldo Zea, *El Positivismo en México,* (El Colegio de México, 1943) [item 4921], y el ensayo de Samuel Ramos sobre *Historia de la Filosofía en México* (Universidad Nacional de México, 1943) [item 4912]. Se han editado algunas obras fundamentales para el conocimiento de las ideas del siglo pasado entre las que se destacan, por la seriedad de la edición y los estudios que la acompañan, el *Curso Filosófico* de Juan C. Lafinur y *Los Principios de Ideología* de Juan M. Fernández de Agüero, ambas publicadas por el Instituto de Filosofía de la Universidad de Buenos Aires. Debemos recordar, finalmente, la publicación de numerosas traducciones de obras clásicas y contemporáneas que saldaron algunas deudas importantes de la bibliografía filosófica en castellano.

Los españoles llegados últimamente a América, y en particular el conjunto excepcional que se halla radicado en México, nos han brindado valiosos ensayos filosóficos. Por la calidad y la influencia que han tenido deben mencionarse las siguientes obras: Joaquín Xirau, *Amor y Mundo;* Juan D. García Bacca, *Introducción al Filosofar; Invitación a Filosofar,* I y II; y *Tipos Históricos del Filosofar Físico;* Luis Recasens Siches, *Vida Humana, Sociedad y Derecho;* José Medina Echavarría, *Sociología: Teoría y Técnica;* José Ferrater Mora, *Diccionario de Filosofía;* etc. . . . . Sin contar las numerosas traducciones de clásicos y contemporáneos que bastarían para asegurar un permanente agradecimiento de los lectores de lengua española.

Este esquemático balance de la producción filosófica del último lustro es suficiente para explicar el interés despertado por la filosofía latinoamericana dentro y fuera de sus fronteras. Fuera de la América Latina, Estados Unidos es el país que más se ha interesado por nuestro pensamiento. *Philosophic Abstracts y Philosophy* and *Phenomenological Research* han abierto sus páginas a la filosofía latinoamericana, y en algunas universidades norteamericanas se han dictado cursos sobre el desarrollo de nuestras ideas filosóficas. Con la realización del First Inter-American Congress of Philosophy, que tuvo lugar en la Universidad de Yale en mayo de 1943, acaso se haya iniciado una nueva etapa en el proceso de acercamiento de quienes tienen la responsabilidad de la cultura filosófica de América.

BIBLIOGRAFÍA

(*Véase también la sección* Derecho)

REEDICIONES Y ESTUDIOS CRÍTICOS

(*Véanse también los items* 3258, 3392)

ANUARIO DE FILOSOFÍA DEL SEMINARIO DE INVESTIGACIONES FILOSÓFICAS DE LA FACULTAD DE FILOSOFÍA Y LETRAS. México. Univ. nac. autónoma de México. 158 p. [4884]
Es el primer volumen del Seminario de Investigaciones Filosóficas. "El Seminario se propone analizar . . . la historia de la filosofía mexicana a través de sus más destacados exponentes." El presente volumen trae los siguientes trabajos: "La Filosofía Natural de los Vivientes en Fray Alonso de la Vera Cruz," por Lourdes Ortiz del Castillo; "Fray Francisco Naranjo," por Alfonso Zahar Vergara; "Breve Nota sobre Fray Juan de San Anastasio y su Glosario Escolástico," por Oswaldo Robles; "Antonio Caso y su Escuela," por Francisco Gil Villegas; "Temas de Filosofía Jurídica en la Obra de Clemente de Jesús Munguía," por Salvador Guandique.

Barreiro, José P. (ed.). El pensamiento de Domingo Faustino Sarmiento. Buenos Aires. Ed. Lautaro. 160 p. [4885]

BIBLIOGRAFÍA ARGENTINA DE PUBLICACIONES FILOSÓFICAS. Años 1937 a 1943. Buenos Aires. Comisión nacional de cooperación intelectual. 31 p. [4887]
Este fascículo da una idea de la producción filosófica argentina de los últimos siete años. Si bien se advierten omisiones, errores y repeticiones injustificadas, él puede servir de base a un futuro repertorio bibliográfico de la filosofía de ese país.

BOLETÍN BIBLIOGRÁFICO DEL CENTRO DE ESTUDIOS FILOSÓFICOS. México. Facultad de filosofía y letras de la Univ. nacional de México. Año 3, no. 10–no. 11/12; año 4, no. 13. [4888]
Cf. *Handbook, no. 6, 1940*, item 4961.

Brightman, Edgar Sheffield. Personalism in Latin America (*The Personalist*, vol. 24, no. 1, spring, p. 147–162). [4889]
Es un artículo muy general en el que se toma el término personalismo—o personismo—en un sentido amplio. Se advierte la falta de algunos pensadores de jerarquía —Antonio Caso, por ejemplo—y la inclusión de otros de poco valor. Se trata, sin embargo, de un esquema informativo de utilidad para quienes deseen acercarse a la filosofía latinoamericana.

———. Structure and transcendence in the thought of Francisco Romero (*Phil. phenom. research*, vol. 4, no. 2, Dec., p. 134–141). [4890]
El conocido filósofo norteamericano expone las líneas generales del pensamiento filosófico del profesor Romero destacando, con razón, los conceptos de estructura y trascendencia.

Caso, Antonio. México. Apuntamientos de cultura patria. México. Imp. Universitaria. 162 p. [4891]
Esta obra, que constituye una continuación de los temas tratados en *Discursos a la Nación Mexicana*, se divide en tres partes. La primera está dedicada al estudio de los problemas sociales y políticos de México, la segunda a la evolución de su cultura y la tercera nos ofrece un esquema de la geografía intelectual de ese país. En la segunda parte encontrará el lector una exposición del filósofo mejicano Juan Benito Díaz de Gamarra de quien el autor se ha ocupado ya en otra oportunidad.
Esta nueva obra de Caso es una contribución a la historia de la cultura mejicana.

Coutinho, Afranio. Some considerations on the problem of philosophy in Brazil (*Phil. phenom. research*, vol. 4, no. 2, p. 186–193). [4892]
Breve esquema de la actual filosofía brasileña.

Farver, Marvin. The significance of phenomenology for the Americas (*Phil. phenom. research*, vol. 4, no. 2, p. 208–216). [4893]
Se exponen las ideas fundamentales de la fenomenología para destacar, en líneas muy generales, lo que ha significado para América y lo que puede significar en el futuro.

Fernández de Castro, José A. Ubicación de Varona (*Univ. Habana*, año 8, no. 49, julio–agosto, p. 43–80). [4894]
Artículo informativo sobre la vida y obra del gran pensador cubano.

Francovich, Guillermo. Dos filósofos bolivianos (*Rev. ateneo paraguayo*, año 2, no. 7, enero, p. 7-11). [4895

———. Filósofos brasileños. Buenos Aires. Ed. Losada. 151 p. [4896
Esta obra nos ofrece un panorama de la filosofía brasileña, desde la colonia hasta nuestros días y en tal carácter llena una sentida necesidad que las obras de Silvio Romero y Leonel Franca no lograban satisfacer. Los capítulos centrales están dedicados a la exposición de las ideas de Luis Pereira Barreto, Tobías Barreto y Farías Brito, y la parte final a la consideración de los pensadores actuales.

Freyre, Gilberto. En torno do problema de uma cultura brasileira (*Phil. phenom. research*, vol. 4, no. 2, p. 167-171). [4897
El joven pensador brasileño señala en esta breve comunicación la necesidad de que la cultura de su país ofrezca una personalidad propia al no limitarse a su fuente europea sino recoger también la contribución de las culturas indoamericana, africana y asiática. El artículo está seguido de su traducción inglesa y de breve comentario del profesor Glenn R. Morrow.

Frondizi, Risieri. Contemporary Argentine philosophy (*Phil. phenom. research*, vol. 4, no. 2, p. 180-186). [4898
Panorama de la filosofía argentina contemporánea incluido, con ligeras modificaciones, en el trabajo del autor titulado *Tendencies in Contemporary Latin-American Philosophy*.

———. A selective guide to the material published in 1942 on Latin American philosophy (*Handbook of latin american studies, no. 8, 1942*, p. 440-448). [4899

———. Tendencies in contemporary Latin-American philosophy (*Int. amer. intel. interchange*, p. 35-48). [4900
Es éste, acaso, el primer estudio de conjunto sobre la filosofía latinoamericana contemporánea. Trae la bibliografía esencial sobre el tema.

Gandolfo, Rafael. El aporte de la filosofía europea a la cultura americana (*Estudios*, Santiago, no. 128, p. 10-18). [4901
Basado en un esquema muy incompleto de la influencia de la filosofía europea sobre Iberoamérica, el autor extrae precipitadamente algunas conclusiones. Afirma, por ejemplo, que "el americano actual no siente necesidad del espíritu" y habla luego de "síntomas de degeneración precoz." Propone la vuelta al realismo aristotélico acrecentado por "una fenomenología y un existencialismo purificados."

Gaos, José. Significación filosófica del pensamiento hispano-americano (*Cuad. amer.*, año 2, vol. 8, no. 2, marzo-abril, p. 63-86). [4902

González del Valle, Francisco. Filosofía en La Habana (*Rev. bim. cub.*, vol. 51, no. 1, enero-feb., p. 111-121). [4903
Se refiere a la polémica sobre el eclecticismo de Cousin que tuvo lugar en La Habana en los años 1938-1940 y en la que intervinieron José de la Luz y Caballero por una parte y los hermanos González del Valle y Cañizo, por otra.

———. Un trabajo inédito del padre José Agustín Caballero (*Rev. cub.*, vol. 17, no. 2, abril-dic., p. 143-210). [4904
Reproducción facsimilar del *Curso de Filosofía Electiva* del Padre Caballero escrito para el curso de filosofía que se inició en 1797 en el Real Colegio Seminario de San Carlos de La Habana. Trae una introducción del Dr. González del Valle en la que se expone brevemente la historia del manuscrito publicado ahora por primera vez.

Hernández Travieso, Antonio. Historia del pensamiento cubano hasta Félix Varela (*Phil. phenom. research*, vol. 4, no. 2, p. 141-145). [4905
Brevísimo esquema de las ideas del Padre Varela precedido de algunas referencias a sus dos maestros, José Agustín Caballero y Bernardo O'Gaván.

Millares Carlo, Agustín. Registro bibliográfico. Primero y segundo semestres de 1942. México. Univ. nac. autónoma de México, Facultad de filosofía y letras. 87 p. [4907
Es el suplemento al tomo 4 de la revista *Filosofía y Letras*. Cfr. *Handbook, no. 7, 1941*, item 5643.

Mota, Fernando de Oliveira. Compreensão de Farias Brito. Vol. 1. Recife. Ed. Caderno acadêmico. 141 p. [4908
Se propone el autor desentrañar las ideas filosóficas del ilustre pensador brasileño movido por un propósito de valorización y, al mismo tiempo, de divulgación de esas ideas.

Orfila Reynal, Arnaldo. Alejandro Korn, argentino ejemplar. Bahía Blanca. Filial del Colegio libre de estudios superiores. 25 p. [4909

Pérez-Marchand, Lina. La filosofía en la América Latina (*Sustancia*, ano 4, no. 15-16, junio-julio, p. 596-604). [4910
Breve artículo informativo sobre los estudios filosóficos en la América Latina. Trae una corta bibliografía en la que faltan obras fundamentales incluyendose otras que poco tienen que ver con el tema.

Picón-Salas, Mariano. Rousseau en Venezuela (*Phil. phenom. research*, vol. 4, no. 2, p. 195-201). [4911
Se estudia la resonancia que tuvo Rousseau en la cultura venezolana. El artículo está seguido de su versión al inglés.

Ramos, Samuel. Historia de la filosofía en México. México. Imp. Universitaria. 187 p. [4912

Las obras de Agustín Rivera y Emetrio Valverde Téllez, publicadas a fines del siglo pasado y principios del actual, no logran satisfacer las necesidades de quienes intentan penetrar en el pensamiento filosófico de México. El trabajo que comentamos supera las deficiencias de aquellas obras, que en parte utiliza, y nos ofrece un acertado panorama de conjunto, al estudiar la filosofía mejicana desde la época colonial hasta nuestros días. Las páginas dedicadas al período anterior a la independencia constituye lo mejor de la obra, mientras que la exposición del período positivista resulta insuficiente. En la parte dedicada al pensamiento contemporáneo se advierten algunas omisiones un tanto injustificadas—como la de Ezequiel Chávez—o referencias demasiado breves a hombres que encabezan un sector importante del pensamiento mejicano, como Oswaldo Robles, por ejemplo. Llama la atención también el poco reconocimiento de la contribución indiscutible del grupo selecto de pensadores españoles radicados en México en la última década. El autor no pretende darnos, por cierto, un panorama acabado del pensamiento mejicano sino un cuadro histórico provisional que sirva de guía y de acicate a la investigación referente al desenvolvimiento de la cultura de su país. Y no hay duda alguna que ha logrado plenamente este propósito fundamental.

Esperamos que la publicación de esta obra ponga de manifiesto la necesidad de trabajos similares en los demás países latinoamericanos que cuentan tan sólo con estudios fragmentarios o exposiciones superficiales.

Roa, Armando. Introducción a una filosofía sudamericana (*Estudios,* Santiago, no. 128, p. 4–14). [4913

Afirma el autor que el sudamericano ve en el ser el elemento material, que tiene una imagen táctil del mundo, que acepta sin reservas la existencia del mundo físico. Por eso, dice, es ajeno a los problemas gnoseológicos. Este hecho y muchos otros que el autor señala en su breve artículo, son muy discutibles, lo mismo que el supuesto "materialismo" del iberoamericano.

Rodríguez-Embril, Luis. Religión y filosofía de Martí (*Nueva dem.,* vol. 24, no. 12, dic., p. 30–32). [4914

Romero, Francisco. Breve noticia sobre Alejandro O. Deustua (*Luminar,* vol. 6, no. 3–4, p. 310–317). [4915

———. Enrique José Varona (*Cursos y conferencias,* año 11, vol. 22, no. 131–132, feb.–marzo, p. 415–436). [4916

Trás algunas consideraciones generales sobre la filosofía en Iberoamérica, el autor expone el pensamiento del ilustre filósofo cubano en base, principalmente, a su *Lógica* y su *Psicología.*

———. Tendencias contemporáneas en el pensamiento hispano-americano (*Phil. phenom. research,* vol. 4, no. 2, p. 127–134). [4917

Esquema general de la filosofía hispanoamericana contemporánea.

———. Tiempo y destiempo de Alejandro Korn (*Libertad creadora,* tomo 1, no. 2, abril–junio, p. 258–262). [4918

Estudia a grandes trazos las razones del silencio en torno a Korn durante su vida, y la proyección de la obra del gran filósofo argentino en la cultura de su país.

Torres, João Camilo de Oliveira. O positivismo no Brasil. Petrópolis. Ed. Vozes. 336 p. [4919

Medulosa obra en la que se expone con fino espíritu crítico el desarrollo del positivismo en el Brasil. Se estudian las condiciones políticas, sociales y religiosas que hicieron posible el surgimiento del positivismo y se muestra por qué razones no se trató de un movimiento especulativo sino más bien político-religioso.

Vitier, Medardo. El P. José Agustín Caballero (*Univ. Habana,* año 8, no. 50–51, sept.–dic., p. 78–89). [4920

Texto de una conferencia sobre la personalidad e ideas filosóficas fundamentales del Padre Caballero.

Zea, Leopoldo. El positivismo en México. México. Ed. El Colegio de México. 254 p. [4921

El joven pensador mejicano nos ofrece en esta obra un notable estudio de las condiciones históricas, sociales y políticas que explican el surgimiento y ulterior desarrollo del positivismo en su país.

La obra comprende una Introducción y cinco secciones que tratan, respectivamente, del nacimiento, orígenes, desarrollo—en Gabino Barreda (III) y sus discípulos (IV)— y utopía del positivismo mejicano. En sus páginas se advierte una visión amplia y profunda de un importante período de la cultura de México, basada en material de primera mano.

La tesis central del autor, que subscribimos enteramente, es que el positivismo mejicano no consiste en un sistema conceptual con validez y sentido en el plano puramente filosófico sino un instrumento al servicio de ideas políticas, sociales y educativas. El surgimiento del positivismo con Barrega es un ejemplo claro de esta tesis.

A lo largo de toda la obra se advierte la influencia de Ortega y Gasset recibida, acaso, a través de José Gaos que tanto ha tenido que ver con la formación filosófica del autor y la estructuración de este trabajo en particular. Zea demuestra aquí su vocación por los estudios filosóficos y una extraordinaria capacidad de captación del sentido de los momentos históricos que investiga. La obra es de suma utilidad para el conocimiento de la cultura mejicana y un verdadero ejemplo de investigación en su género.

OBRAS GENERALES Y MISCELÁNEA

Alarco, Luis Felipe. El problema de la trascendencia (*Historia,* Lima, vol. 1, no. 2, mayo-junio, p. 79-82). [4922

Barboza, Enrique. Fundamentación de las ciencias espirituales (*Letras,* Lima, no. 24, primer cuatrimestre, p. 64-87). [4922a

Bouts, Paul, y Camille Bouts. A psicognomia. (Caracterología). Rio de Janeiro. Ed. Vera Cruz. 432 p. [4923

Centro de estudios de filosofía y humanidades. Estudios de filosofía: 1942. Córdoba. Univ. nac. de Córdoba. 114 p. [4924
Este volumen contiene los siguientes trabajos: *La enseñanza de la filosofía,* por Emile Gouiran (p. 7-12); *Innatismo de Formas,* por Alfredo Fragueiro (p. 15-52); *Campanella y Descartes,* por Rodolfo Mondolfo (p. 55-62); *El error. Sus fundamentos metafísicos y psicológicos,* por Expedito I. Granero (p. 65-71); *Un comentario sobre "El Fedón,"* por Juan Bernardo Videla (p. 75-86); *Tipos psicológicos,* por Carlos R. Echegoyen (p. 89-109).

Chapman, Emmanuel. O tomismo vivo (*Estudos,* ano 3, no. 3). [4925

Ferrão, V. A. Argolo. Pesquisa do vocábulo filosofia (*An. soc. bras. fil.,* ano 3, no. 3, 1942-1943, p. 41-49). [4926

Fragueiro, Alfredo. Introducción a los problemas de la filosofía. Primera parte: Preliminares—gnoseología. Córdoba. Imp. de la Universidad. 260 p. [4927
Es una obra elemental basada en la versión taquigráfica del curso que dictó el autor en el Instituto de Filosofía de la Universidad de Córdoba.
Los problemas generales de la filosofía y de la relación de ésta con las ciencias constituyen los *Preliminares.* La parte central de la obra está dedicada al problema del conocimiento, estudiandose principalmente las cuestiones acerca de su origen, objeto y valor.
Se advierte, desde un principio, la orientación neo-tomista del autor que llega a limitar la perspectiva de los problemas estudiados.

Franca, Leonel. A história da filosofia na doutrina de Santo Tomaz de Aquino (*Estudos,* ano 3, no. 4-5, p. 3-21). [4928

García Bárcena, J. R. Esquema de un correlato antropológico en la jerarquía de los valores. Habana. Ed. del autor. 17 p. [4929
Es un breve ensayo orientado en la teoría de los valores de Max Scheler.

Kuri Breña, Daniel. Metafísica de la persona humana (*Ábside,* vol. 7, no. 2, abril-junio, p. 201-218). [4930

Mangabeira, Francisco. Qué e o homem? Rio de Janeiro. Ed. José Olympio. [4931
A mystical-philosophical study of man's rôle on the earth and the objectives for which he should strive. With renewed vigor, the author enters upon the old discussion of faith versus reason, with the purpose of showing that there is no essential contradiction between the two. He sees Christianity as providing the supreme wisdom for a way of life. [S. Putnam]

Menéndez Samará, Adolfo. Iniciación en la filosofía. Por problemas y en forma histórica. México. Antigua lib. Robredo. 405 p. [4932
Más que una introducción a la filosofía esta obra parece una historia de la filosofía, aunque en este carácter adolecería de omisiones injustificadas. En la primera parte se estudian las clásicas cuestiones del concepto y método de la filosofía, y otras de interés actual: "La diversidad de los sistemas y la definición de la filosofía," "El peligro del filosofar," etc.

Millas, Jorge. Idea de la individualidad. Santiago. Prensas de la Univ. de Chile. 224 p. [4933
Se estudia en esta obra el ser del hombre proponiendose una doctrina que el autor llama personalismo. Con la intención de apartarse de toda teoría preconcebida, el señor Millas intenta "una descripción pulcra, exacta, de los hechos de la experiencia inmediata de nuestra individualidad psicológica." Considera que la temporalidad, la libertad y la racionalidad son los supuestos esenciales de la persona humana.
El libro contiene agudas observaciones y no es el producto de una fría preocupación intelectual sino la expresión de una experiencia humana plenamente vivida.

Miró Quesada C., Francisco. El espíritu objetivo y el campo proprio de la historia (*Historia,* Lima, vol. 1, no. 3, julio-agosto, p. 207-214). [4933a

———. Rasgos fundamentales de la filosofía contemporánea (*Letras,* Lima, no. 24, primer cuatrimestre, p. 101-104). [4934

Monserrat, Santiago. Esencia de la filosofía (*Educación,* Córdoba, no. 2, nov., p. 1-16). [4935

Mueller, Leonardo. O ponto de partida da motivação crítica da certeza natural (*Estudos,* ano 3, no. 3). [4936

Nobrega, Clovis da. Concepção racional do universo (*An. soc. bras. fil.,* ano 3, no. 3, 1942-1943, p. 53-64). [4937

Reyna, Alberto Wagner de. La historia de la filosofía (*Estudos,* ano 3, no. 3). [4938

Robles, Oswaldo. Propedéutica filosófica. México. Lib. de Porrúa hnos. 222 p. [4939
Es una introducción a la filosofía sistemática escrita desde un punto de vista neo-tomista. Sus diversos capítulos tratan, re-

spectivamente, de la filosofía, su división y método, teoría del conocimiento, metafísica, teodicea y óntica existencial, filosofía de la naturaleza, lógica, y filosofía moral.
Cómo sucede con muchos otros libros de igual género, esta obra del representante más destacado del neo-tomismo mejicano es de poca utilidad pues resulta casi ininteligible a los neófitos y escasamente original, en su tratamiento histórico y sistemático, para despertar el interés de los estudiosos de la filosofía.

Romero, Francisco. A mundi incunabulis (*Sur*, año 12, no. 101, feb., p. 21–40). [4940
Notas sobre las primeras historias de la filosofía incluídas posteriormente en su obra *Sobre la Historia de la Filosofía*.

———. La filosofía de la cultura (*Univ. Antioquía*, tomo 15, no. 58, abril–mayo, p. 243–250). [4941
Reproducción del trabajo que, bajo el mismo título, aparece en el volumen *Curso Colectivo de Filosofía del Derecho*. Cfr. item 4964.

———. El presente inviolable (*Cuad. amer.*, vol. 7, no. 1, enero–feb., p. 79–88). [4942
Se muestra en que sentido el presente es incognoscible—("todo saber es retrospectivo"—), inasible—("ya no está al alcance de la mano cuando ésta se cierra para atraparlo"), impensable por las paradojas a que da lugar.

———. Sobre la historia de la filosofía. Tucumán. Univ. nac. de Tucumán, Facultad de filosofía y letras. 99 p. [4943
La parte central de la obra está dedicada al estudio de la naturaleza de la historia de la filosofía. Se ofrecen algunos casos en que el juicio histórico no ha podido cristalizar en una opinión satisfactoria, para mostrar las dificultades de la historia de la filosofía y la íntima conexión que tiene el juicio histórico con las ideas filosóficas y la concepción del mundo del historiador. Se reproducen, en la parte final del volumen, tres trabajos publicados con anterioridad: *A Mundi Incunabulis, Concepción del Mundo y Método;* y *Fausto, Sánchez, Descartes*.

Serra Moret, Manuel. Los fundamentos de la historia y de la filosofía. Buenos Aires. Ed. Americalee. 258 p. [4944

Van Acker, Leonardo. Filosofía e progresso moral da humanidade (*A ordem*, vol. 23, no. 1, jan., p. 41–49). [4945

Vasconcelos, José. El realismo científico. México, D. F. Facultad de filosofía y letras, Centro de estudios filosóficos. 170 p. [4946

LÓGICA Y EPISTEMOLOGÍA

Bustos Fierro, Raúl. Filosofía, matemáticas y ciencias de la naturaleza. Córdoba. Univ. de Córdoba, Inst. de filosofía. 61 p. [4947

Toranzos, Fausto. Introducción a la epistemología y fundamentación de la matemática. Buenos Aires. Ed. Espasa-Calpe argentina. 239 p. [4948

GNOSEOLOGÍA Y METAFÍSICA

Alzamora Valdez, Mario. La ontología del conocer (*Rev. univ. cat. Perú*, tomo 11, no. 4–5, julio–agosto, p. 192–209). [4949

Astrada, Carlos. Temporalidad. Buenos Aires. Ed. Cultura viva. 202 p. [4950

Bazzano, Oreste G. Crítica cognitionis. Buenos Aires. Ed. Espasa Calpe argentina. 198 p. [4951

Estiú, Emilio. Las bases ontológicas del saber y de la educación (*Rev. educ.*, enero–feb.). [4952

Finlayson, Clarence. Algunas observaciones metafísicas sobre la muerte (*Estudios*, no. 130, p. 54–66). [4953
El autor estudia el problema de la muerte a la luz de la distinción neo-tomista de individuo y persona.

———. Los nombres metafísicos de Dios o el constitutivo formal de la Divinidad (*Univ. cat. bolivariana*, vol. 9, no. 30–31, abril–mayo, p. 203–231; no. 33, julio–sept., p. 378–409). [4954

Gouirán, Emile, y otros. Seminario de metafísica: El problema de la causalidad. Córdoba. Univ. nacional de Córdoba, Inst. de filosofía y humanidades. 115 p. [4955

Haas, João Nepomuceno. Os problemas fundamentais da metafísica (*Estudos*, ano 3, no. 4–5, p. 22–42). [4956

Labrousse, Rogelio P. Trascendencia y causalidad (*Sustancia*, año 4, no. 14, marzo–abril, p. 234–262). [4957
Si bien el autor promete estudiar el problema de la causalidad dentro de la hipótesis de un Dios trascendente, omnipotente, lo central de artículo lo constituyen agudas observaciones sobre los diversos tipos de experiencia y los problemas que surgen de la relación de ésta con la trascendencia.

Martínez, Raúl V. La nada, el infinito, Dios. Córdoba. Imp. de la univ. nacional de Córdoba. (Publ. del Inst. de humanidades, 1941, no. 27). 19 p. [4958

Quiles, Ismael. Metaphisica generalis sive ontologia summa philosophica argentinensis. Vol. 3. Buenos Aires. Ed. Espasa-Calpe argentina. 416 p. [4959

Rougés, Alberto. Las jerarquías del ser y la eternidad. Tucumán. Univ. nacional de Tucumán, Facultad de filosofía y letras. 155 p. [4960

Esta obra es el producto de largos años de meditación sobre los problemas capitales del espíritu humano. El autor opone la realidad física a la espiritual. En su opinión el ser del mundo físico se agota en el instante pues carece de pasado y de futuro. El mundo espiritual, en cambio, se caracteriza por la coexistencia en el presente de "un pasado que supervive y de un futuro que se anticipa." Es decir, por ser, esencialmente, un mundo de "totalidades sucesivas." Por eso su pasado no es irrevocable, mientras que el pasado del devenir físico se anonada y su futuro no puede anticiparse en forma alguna.

El hombre está en medio del mundo físico, que tan sólo "vive" en el instante, y la eternidad, que es un presente que incluye todo el pasado y el futuro. La jerarquía de cada ser dependerá de la dimensión temporal de su presente. El hombre se siente arrastrado, por un lado, hacia la inmimalidad que es el camino del presente instantáneo de la realidad física; y por el otro siente el impulso ascendente hacia la eternidad, que es la vocación suprema del espíritu humano.

Sin ánimo de poner en duda la versación científica del autor, creemos necesario anotar que la imagen del mundo exterior que nos ofrece en esta obra parece estar inspirada en una concepción científica que la física actual repudia. El ser físico es también un acontecer y, por lo tanto, tiene su raíz en el tiempo, resistiéndose a que se le considere en la inmovilidad del instante.

Inspirada en las ideas de Plotino entre los antiguos y de Bergson entre los contemporáneos, esta obra del Dr. Rougés revela una madurez espiritual, una vocación filosófica y un sentido moral poco comunes en la América Latina.

Virasoro, Miguel Ángel. Filosofía del espíritu. El espíritu subjetivo (*Rev. univ. Buenos Aires*, tercera época, año 1, no. 1, julio–sept., p. 55–68). [4961

Meduloso artículo del autor de *La Libertad, la Existencia y el Ser* en el que, apoyado en parte en la concepción fenomenológica, señala tres estratos de la subjetividad: fenomenológico, existencial y metafísico. Propone finalmente una intuición absoluta o metafísica que nos permite ascender "a la comprensión de la libertad como raíz primera y condición incondicionada de toda realidad."

———. Filosofía del espíritu absoluto (*Sustancia*, año 4, no. 17, oct., p. 773–799). [4962

Después de exponer y criticar suscintamente la concepción hegeliana del espíritu absoluto, el autor caracteriza a éste como "el proceso hacia la unidad." La parte final del artículo contiene atrayentes reflexiones sobre la naturaleza de Dios en quien el autor ve la síntesis en acto de la finitud e infinito.

ÉTICA, Y FILOSOFÍA SOCIAL Y POLÍTICA

Aftalión, Enrique R. El derecho como objeto y la ciencia del derecho. Buenos Aires. Ed. del autor. 30 p. [4963

Alsina, Ramón M., y otros. Curso colectivo de filosofía del derecho. Buenos Aires. Univ. de Buenos Aires, Facultad de derecho y ciencias sociales. 131 p. [4964

Este "curso colectivo," dictado en mayo y junio de 1942, contiene los siguientes trabajos: *Introducción a la problemática jurídica actual* (Ramón M. Alsina); *La filosofía de la cultura* (Francisco Romero); *El sentido del derecho para la vida humana* (Juan Llambías de Azevedo); *El derecho como objeto y la ciencia del derecho* (Enrique R. Aftalión); *Las especies del saber jurídico* (Manuel Río); *Posición cultural de las orientaciones políticas* (Martín T. Ruiz Moreno).

Borga, Ernesto Eduardo. Principios materiales del conocimiento jurídico (*Universidad*, Santa Fe, no. 15, p. 25–134). [4965

Casanovas P., Domingo. Vigencia y cumplimiento de la ley. Contribución a la fenomenología jurídica (*An. univ. cent. Venezuela*, tomo 28, oct.–dic., 1942 [i.e. 1943], p. 127–155). [4966

Este artículo del joven pensador español comprende tres partes, que tratan respectivamente de "Norma y normalidad," "Instituciones y figuras," y "Vigencia y cumplimiento."

Fuentes Mares, José. Ley, sociedad y política. México. Imp. Universitaria. [4967

En este opúsculo intenta el autor realizar una valoración de la doctrina de San Agustín de acuerdo a la perspectiva jurídico-política actual. Las pasiones políticas empañan, a ratos, la vista al pensador.

Larroyo, Francisco. Los principios de la ética social. México. Lib. de Porrúa hnos. 230 p. [4968

Mingarro San Martín, José. Fundamentos de la filosofía del derecho (*Univ. Habana*, año 8, no. 50–51, sept.–dic., p. 281–304). [4969

Se propone el autor desentrañar la naturaleza del derecho partiendo de una concepción filosófica inspirada en Ortega y Gasset.

Miraglia, Luis. Filosofía del derecho. Buenos Aires. Ed. Impulso. 590 p. [4970

Nieto Arteta, Luis Eduardo. La lógica jurídica y la reflexión trascendental (*Universidad*, Santa Fe, no. 14, p. 53–149). [4971

Romano Muñoz, José. El secreto del bien y del mal. Segunda ed. México. Antigua Lib. Robredo. [4972

A través de las páginas de este manual se advierte la vocación filosófica y la capacidad crítica de su autor, catedrático de la Facul-

tad de Filosofía y Letras de la Universidad Nacional de México.
Lo central de la obra está formado por una teoría de los valores inspirada en Max Scheler y Nicolai Hartmann y con la vista puesta en la filosofía existencial. El autor considera que "el conocimiento del valor es lo único capaz de entregarnos el secreto del bien y del mal."

Soler, Sebastián. Ley, historia y libertad. Buenos Aires. Ed. Losada. 250 p. [4973
Se analiza en esta obra del conocido jurista argentino la actual crisis política y jurídica desde un punto de vista liberal y a la luz de la historia. Se estudia en particular la situación en la época iluminista, para terminar con un análisis de los problemas más importantes de la actualidad y una incitación a la militancia democrática que asegure la supervivencia de la libertad.

APÉNDICE

Filosofía Antigua y Medieval

Aristóteles. Metafísica. Trad. por Patricio de Azcárate. Buenos Aires. Ed. Espasa-Calpe argentina. 312 p. [4974

———. La política. Tercera ed. Buenos Aires. Ed. Espasa-Calpe argentina. 282 p. [4975

Boecio, Severino. La consolación de la filosofía. Trad. de Fray Alberto de Aguayo. Edición e introducción del P. Luis G. Alonso Getino. Buenos Aires. Ed. Espasa-Calpe argentina. 183 p. [4976

Festugier, A. J. Sócrates. Trad. y prólogo de Nimio de Anquín. Buenos Aires. Ed. Inter-americana. 173 p. [4977

Fouillée, Alfredo. La filosofía de Platón. Trad. de Edmundo González Blanco. Buenos Aires. Ed. Mayo. 557 p. [4978

———. Historia general de la filosofía. Trad. de Gallach Palés. Buenos Aires. Ed. Anaconda. 641 p. [4979

García Bacca, Juan David (ed.). El poema de Parménides. México. Univ. nacional autónoma, Facultad de filosofía y letras, Centro de estudios filosóficos. xv, 234 p. [4980

Guyau, J. M. La moral de Epicuro. Trad. de Hernández Almanza. Buenos Aires. Ed. Américalee. 305 p. [4981

Los presocráticos. Vol. I: Jenófanes-Parménides-Empédocles. Trad., prólogo y notas de Juan D. García Bacca. México. Ed. El Colegio de México. 210 p. [4982

Merani, Alberto L. Los filósofos del medioevo. Buenos Aires. Ed. Progreso y cultura. 188 p. [4983

Mondolfo, Rodolfo. El genio helénico y los caracteres de sus creaciones espirituales. Trad. de Ducezio Licitra. Tucumán. Univ. nacional de Tucumán, Facultad de filosofía y letras. 149 p. [4984

Séneca. Tratados Morales. Trad. de Pedro Fernández Navarrete. Buenos Aires. Ed. Espasa-Calpe argentina. 168 p. [4985

Suárez, P. Francisco. Introducción a la metafísica. Trad. de J. Adúriz. Buenos Aires. Ed. Espasa-Calpe argentina. 230 p. [4986

Tredici, J. Historia de la filosofía. Buenos Aires. Ed. Difusión. 329 p. [4987

Filosofía Moderna

Caso, Antonio. Filósofos y moralistas franceses. México. Ed. Stylo. [4988

Cassirer, Ernst. Filosofía de la ilustración. Trad. de Eugenio Imaz. México, D. F. Fondo de cultura económica. 343 p. [4989

Croce, Benedetto. Lo vivo y lo muerto de la filosofía de Hegel. Trad. de Francisco González Ríos. Buenos Aires. Ed. Imán. 344 p. [4990

Dujovne, León. Spinoza. Tomo 3: La obra de Baruj Spinoza. Buenos Aires. Univ. de Buenos Aires. Inst. de filosofía de la Facultad de filosofía y letras. 325 p. [4991

Kant, Manuel. Crítica de la razón pura. Tomo 2. Buenos Aires. Ed. Sopena argentina. 201 p. [4992

———. Lo bello y lo sublime. La paz perpétua. Buenos Aires. Ed. La Barca. 140 p. [4993

———. Principios metafísicos del derecho. Nota preliminar de Francisco Ayala. Buenos Aires. Ed. Américalee. 215 p. [4994

Masson-Oursel, Paul. Historia de la filosofía. Vol. 3. La filosofía en Oriente. Trad. de Demetrio Náñez. Buenos Aires. Ed. Sudamericana. 177 p. [4995

Mondolfo, Rodolfo. Rousseau y la conciencia moderna. Trad. de Vicente P. Quintero. Buenos Aires. Ed. Imán. 133 p. [4996

Nietzsche, Friedrich. El origen de la tragedia. Trad de Eduardo Ovejero y Maury. Buenos Aires. Ed. Espasa-Calpe argentina. 168 p. [4997

Ravá, Adolfo. La filosofía europea en el siglo XIX. Buenos Aires. Ed. Depalma. 202 p. [4998

Romero, Francisco, y Carlos Jesinghaus. La cultura moderna. La Plata, Argentina. Univ. nacional de La Plata. 106 p. [4999

Vinci, Leonardo da. Aforismos. Selección, trad. y prólogo de E. García de Zúñiga. Buenos Aires. Ed. Espasa-Calpe argentina. 151 p. [5000

Windelband, Wilhelm. Historia de la filosofía. Tomo 4: La filosofía del Renacimiento. Trad. de Francisco Larroyo. México. Ed. Antigua lib. Robredo. [5001

―――. Historia de la filosofía. Tomo 5: La filosofía del iluminismo. Trad. de Francisco Larroyo. México. Ed. Antigua lib. Robredo. 192 p. [5002

Filosofía Contemporánea

Alarco, Luis Felipe. Nicolai Hartmann y la idea de la metafísica. Lima. Bibl. de la Sociedad peruana de filosofía. 88 p. [5003

Bergson, Henri. Materia y memoria. Trad. de Martín Navarro. La Plata, Argentina. Ed. Calomino. 269 p. [5004

―――. La risa. Segunda ed. Trad. de Amalia Haydée Raggio. Buenos Aires. Ed. Losada. 154 p. [5005

Boutroux, Emile. William James y su filosofía. Trad. de Mario Falcao Espalter. Montevideo. Ed. Claudio García. 96 p. [5007

Burckhardt, Jacob. Reflexiones sobre la historia universal. Trad. de Wenceslao Roces. México. Ed. Fondo de cultura económica. xlv, 390 p. [5008

Croce, Benedetto. Aesthetica in nuce. Trad. de Italia Questa de Marelli. Estudio preliminar de Gherardo Marone. Buenos Aires. Ed. Inter-americana. 157 p. [5010

Delle Piane, A. L. William James. Montevideo. Ed. A. Monteverde. 249 p. [5011

Donovan, M. Tratado de filosofía. Segunda ed. Buenos Aires. Ed. Lacort. 330 p. [5012

García Morente, Manuel. La filosofía de Henri Bergson. Montevideo. Ed. Claudio García. 136 p. [5013

Góngora Perea, César. El espíritu y la vida en la filosofía de Max Scheler. Lima. Lib. e imp. D. Miranda. 133 p. [5014

Liard, Luis. Lógica. Trad. de Atilio E. Torrassa. Buenos Aires. Ed. Araujo hnos. 419 p. [5015

Lida, Raimundo. Belleza, arte y poesía en la estética de Santayana. Tucumán. Univ. nacional de Tucumán, Facultad de filosofía y letras. 159 p. [5016

Maritain, Jacques. Introducción general a la filosofía. Trad. de Leandro de Sesma. Segunda ed. Buenos Aires. Ed. Club de lectores. 240 p. [5017

Meinecke, Friedrich. El historicismo y su génesis. Trad. de José Mingarro y San Martín, y Tomás Muñoz Molina. México. Fondo de cultura económica. 525 p. [5018

Náñez, Demetrio (comp.). Boutroux. Selección de textos precedidos de un estudio de A. P. Lafontaine. Buenos Aires. Ed. Sudamericana. 217 p. [5018a

―――. Comte. Selección de textos precedidos de un estudio de René Hubert. Buenos Aires. Ed. Sudamericana. 226 p. [5018b

Poincaré, Henri. La ciencia y la hipótesis. Trad. de Alfredo B. Besio y José Banfi. Buenos Aires. Ed. Espasa-Calpe argentina. 232 p. [5019

Rickert, H. Ciencia cultural y ciencia natural. Trad. de Manuel G. Morente. Buenos Aires. Ed. Espasa Calpe argentina. 231 p. [5020

Sánchez Villaseñor, José. José Ortega y Gasset. México. Ed. Jus. [5021

Santayana, George. Tres poetas filósofos: Lucrecio, Dante, Goethe. Trad. de José Ferrater Mora. Buenos Aires. Ed. Losada. 199 p. [5022

Scheler, Max. El puesto del hombre en el cosmos. Trad. de José Gaos. Segunda ed. Buenos Aires. Ed. Losada. 140 p. [5023

Vossler, Carlos. Filosofía del lenguaje. Ensayos. Trad. y notas de Amado Alonso y Raimundo Lida. Buenos Aires. Ed. Losada. 281 p. [5024

Windelband, W., and H. Heimsoeth. Historia de la filosofía. Tomo 7: La filosofía en los siglos diecinueve y veinte Trad. de Francisco Larroyo. México. Antigua lib. Robredo. [5025

ADDENDA

Brugger, Ilse. Filosofía alemana traducida al español. Repertorio bibliográfico a cargo de Ilse Brugger, con la colaboración de Luis Juan Guerrero y Francisco Romero. Buenos Aires. Univ. de Buenos

Aires, Facultad de filosofía y letras, Inst. de estudios germánicos. 1942. 195 p. [5026

Casanovas, Domingo. Fenomenología del lenguaje (*Bol. acad. ven.,* año 9, no. 35-36, julio-dic., 1942, p. 89-112). [5027

Reflexiones generales, inspiradas en la filosofía de Husserl, sobre el lenguaje y la gramática.

Derisi, Octavio N. Lo eterno y lo temporal en el arte. Buenos Aires. Ed. C.E.P.A. 1942. 185 p. [5028

Francovich, Guillermo. Los ídolos de Bacon. Sucre, Bolivia. Univ. de San Francisco . Xavier. 1942. 135 p. [5029

ABBREVIATIONS

A

Aberdeen-Angus	Órgano Oficial de la Corporación Argentina de Aberdeen-Angus. Buenos Aires, Argentina.
Ábside	Revista de Cultura Mexicana. México, D. F. Mexico.
Acción económica	Buenos Aires, Argentina.
Acrópole	Revista Mensal. Arquitectura, Urbanismo, Decoração. São Paulo, Brazil.
Acta amer.	Acta Americana. Review of the Inter-American Society of Anthropology and Geography. Washington, D. C.
Actas acad. nac. cien. exac. fis. nat. Lima	Actas de la Academia Nacional de Ciencias Exactas, Físicas y Naturales de Lima. Lima, Peru.
Actas primera sesión 27 cong. int. amer.	Actas de la Primera Sesión celebrada en la Ciudad de México en 1939 del Vigésimoséptimo Congreso Internacional de Americanistas, Instituto Nacional de Antropología e Historia. Secretaría de Educación Pública. México, D. F., Mexico.
Actas trab. cient. del 27 cong. int. amer.	Actas y Trabajos Científicos del Vigésimoséptimo Congreso Internacional de Americanistas, Lima, 1939. Lima, Peru.
Agenda	A Quarterly Journal of Reconstruction. The London School of Economics and Political Science. Oxford, England.
Agric. Americas	Agriculture in the Americas. United States Department of Agriculture. United States Office of Foreign Agricultural Relations. Washington, D. C.
Agric. costarricense	El Agricultor Costarricense. Revista de Ganadería, Agricultura e Industria. San José, Costa Rica.
Agric. hist.	Agricultural History. Washington, D. C.
Agric. ven.	El Agricultor Venezolano. Caracas, Venezuela.
Agricultor	Concepción, Chile.
Agricultor mex.	El Agricultor Mexicano. Ciudad Juárez, Chihuahua, Mexico.
Agronomía	Órgano del Centro de Estudiantes de Agronomía. Escuela Nacional de Agricultura y Veterinaria. Lima, Peru.
Algodón	Boletín de la Cámera Algodonera del Perú. Lima, Peru.
Alma latina	Semanario de Cultura Hispánica al Servicio de la Raza. San Juan, Puerto Rico.
Alpha	Revista Universitaria. Universidad Nacional de San Marcos. Facultad de Letras y Pedagogía. Lima, Peru.
Amer. anthrop.	American Anthropologist. New York, N. Y.
Amer. antiquity	American Antiquity. Menasha, Wisconsin.
Amer. collector	American Collector. New York, N. Y.
Amer. econ. rev.	American Economic Review. Evanston, Illinois.
Amer. forests	American Forests. The American Forestry Association. Washington, D. C.
Amer. heart jour.	American Heart Journal for the Study of the Circulation. St. Louis, Missouri.
Amér. indígena	América Indígena. Órgano Oficial del Instituto Indigenista Interamericano. México, D. F., Mexico.
Amer. jour. orthodontics and oral surgery	American Journal of Orthodontics and Oral Surgery. St. Louis, Missouri.
Amer. jour. phys. anthrop.	American Journal of Physical Anthropology. Washington, D. C.
Amer. jour. soc.	The American Journal of Sociology. The University of Chicago Press. Chicago, Illinois.
Amer. year book	American Year Book. New York, N. Y.
América, Habana	América. Revista de la Asociación de Escritores y Artistas Americanos. Habana, Cuba.
América, Quito	América. Publicación Trimestral del Grupo América. Quito, Ecuador.
An. acad. nac. artes let.	Anales de la Academia Nacional de Artes y Letras. Habana, Cuba.
An. arq. Bol.	Anales de Arqueología de Bolivia. Con anexo de la Revista de Lingüística y Farmacopea Indiana. Órgano Oficial de la Sociedad Arqueológica de Bolivia. La Paz, Bolivia.

An. econ. estad.	Anales de Economía y Estadística. Bogotá, Colombia.
An. escuela nac. cien. biol.	Anales de la Escuela Nacional de Ciencias Biológicas. Secretaría de Educación Pública. Instituto Politécnico Nacional. México, D. F., Mexico.
An. fac. cien. jur. soc., Chile.	Anales de la Facultad de Ciencias Jurídicas y Sociales. Universidad de Chile. Santiago, Chile.
An. fac. educ. ciên. let. Pôrto Alegre	Anais da Faculdade de Educação, Ciências e Letras de Pôrto Alegre. Pôrto Alegre, Brazil.
An. fac. filos. educ., sec. filol.	Anales de la Facultad de Filosofía y Educación de la Universidad, Sección de Filología. Santiago, Chile.
An. inst. biol.	Anales del Instituto de Biología. Universidad Nacional de México. México, D. F., Mexico.
An. inst. etnog. amer.	Anales del Instituto de Etnografía Americana. Universidad Nacional de Cuyo. Instituto de Etnografía Americana. Mendoza, Argentina.
An. inst. ing. Chile.	Anales del Instituto de Ingenieros de Chile. Santiago, Chile.
An. inst. invest. est.	Anales del Instituto de Investigaciones Estéticas. México, D. F., Mexico.
An. inst. invest. hist., Mendoza	Anales del Instituto de Investigaciones Históricas. Universidad Nacional de Cuyo. Mendoza, Argentina.
An. Missouri botanical garden	Annals of the Missouri Botanical Garden. Galesburg, Illinois.
An. mus. arg. cien. nat.	Anales del Museo Argentino de Ciencias Naturales "Bernardino Rivadavia." Buenos Aires, Argentina.
An. paulistas medicina e cirurgia	Anais Paulistas de Medicina e Cirurgia. São Paulo, Brazil.
An. soc. bras. fil.	Anais da Sociedade Brasileira de Filosofia. Rio de Janeiro, Brazil.
An. soc. cient. arg.	Anales de la Sociedad Científica Argentina. Buenos Aires. Argentina.
An. soc. folk. México.	Anuario de la Sociedad Folklórica de México. México, D. F., Mexico.
An. soc. geog. hist. Guatemala	Anales de la Sociedad de Geografía e Historia de Guatemala. Guatemala, Guatemala.
An. univ. cent. Ecuador.	Anales de la Universidad Central del Ecuador. Quito, Ecuador.
An. univ. cent. Venezuela.	Anales de la Universidad Central de Venezuela. Caracas, Venezuela.
An. univ. Chile.	Anales de la Universidad de Chile. Santiago, Chile.
An. univ. Santo Domingo.	Anales de la Universidad de Santo Domingo. Ciudad Trujillo, Dominican Republic.
Andean quart.	Andean Quarterly. Chile-United States Cultural Institute. Santiago, Chile.
Applied anthrop.	Applied Anthropology. Problems of Human Organization. The Society for Applied Anthropology. Boston, Massachusetts.
Arch. español arte.	Archivo Español de Arte. Consejo Superior de Investigaciones Científicas. Instituto Diego Velázquez. Madrid, Spain.
Arch. José Martí.	Archivo José Martí. Ministerio de Educación. Dirección de Cultura. Habana, Cuba.
Architect. record	The Architectural Record. New York, New York.
Archivum	Revista de la Junta de Historia Eclesiástica Argentina. Buenos Aires, Argentina.
Armonía	Órgano del Conservatorio Nacional de Música y Declamación. Panamá, Panama.
Arq. mus. nac.	Arquivos do Museo Nacional. Rio de Janeiro, Brazil.
Arq. pol. civil São Paulo.	Arquivos da Policia Civil de São Paulo. Diretoria Geral da Secretaria da Segurança Pública. São Paulo, Brazil.
Arq. serv. assist. menores.	Arquivos do Serviço de Assistência a Menores. Rio de Janeiro, Brazil.
Arquitectura, Habana	Arquitectura. Órgano Oficial del Colegio Nacional de Arquitectos. Habana, Cuba.
Arquitectura, México	Arquitectura. México, D. F., Mexico.
Ars. México	México, D. F., Mexico.
Art in America	Springfield, Massachusetts.
Art news	New York, N. Y.
Asia and the Americas.	New York, N. Y.
Atenea	Concepción, Chile.
Ateneo, Salvador	Ateneo. Revista del Ateneo de El Salvador. San Salvador, El Salvador.

Atlântico	Revista Luso-Brasileira. Edição do Secretariado da Propaganda Nacional, Lisboa, e do Departamento de Imprensa e Propaganda. Rio de Janeiro, Brazil.

B

Bellas artes	Revista de la Sociedad de Bellas Artes del Perú. Lima, Peru.
Biblos	Órgano Oficial de la Cámara Argentina del Libro. Buenos Aires, Argentina.
Bitácora	Caracas, Venezuela.
Bol. acad. arg. let.	Boletín de la Academia Argentina de Letras. Buenos Aires, Argentina.
Bol. acad. dom. lengua	Boletín de la Academia Dominicana de la Lengua. Ciudad Trujillo, Dominican Republic.
Bol. acad. nac. cien., Córdoba	Boletín de la Academia Nacional de Ciencias. Córdoba, Argentina.
Bol. acad. nac. hist., Caracas	Boletín de la Academia Nacional de la Historia. Caracas, Venezuela.
Bol. acad. nac. hist., Quito	Boletín de la Academia Nacional de Historia. Quito, Ecuador.
Bol. acad. panameña hist.	Boletín de la Academia Panameña de la Historia. Panamá, Panama.
Bol. acad. ven.	Boletín de la Academia Venezolana, Correspondiente de la Española. Caracas, Venezuela.
Bol. arch. gen., Ciudad Trujillo	Boletín del Archivo General de la Nación. Ciudad Trujillo, Dominican Republic.
Bol. arch. gen., Guatemala	Boletín del Archivo General del Gobierno. Guatemala, Guatemala.
Bol. arch. gen., México	Boletín del Archivo General de la Nación. México, D. F., Mexico.
Bol. arch. hist. prov. Mérida	Boletín del Archivo Histórico de la Provincia de Mérida. Mérida, Venezuela.
Bol. arch. nac., Caracas	Boletín del Archivo Nacional. Caracas, Venezuela.
Bol. arch. nac., Habana	Boletín del Archivo Nacional. Habana, Cuba.
Bol. asoc. internac. perm	Boletín de la Asociación Internacional Permanente. Congreso Sudamericano de Ferrocarriles. Buenos Aires, Argentina.
Bol. banco central Bolivia	Boletín del Banco Central de Bolivia. Departamento de Estadística y Estudios Económicos. La Paz, Bolivia.
Bol. bibl. archivo nac.	Boletín de la Biblioteca y Archivo Nacionales. Tegucigalpa, Honduras.
Bol. bibliog., Lima	Boletín Bibliográfico. Universidad Mayor de San Marcos. Biblioteca Central. Lima, Peru.
Bol. bibliog., São Paulo	Boletim Bibliográfico. Publicação da Biblioteca Pública Municipal de São Paulo. São Paulo, Brazil.
Bol. bibliog. antrop. amer.	Boletín Bibliográfico de Antropología Americana. Instituto Panamericano de Geografía e Historia. Tacubaya, D. F., Mexico.
Bol. bibliog. bibl. cám. dip.	Boletín Bibliográfico de la Biblioteca de la Cámara de Diputados. Lima, Peru.
Bol. bibliog. yucateca	Boletín de la Bibliografía Yucateca. Yucatán, Mexico.
Bol. cám. comercio Caracas	Boletín de la Cámara de Comercio de Caracas. Caracas, Venezuela.
Bol. centro hist. larense	Boletín del Centro Histórico Larense. Barquisimeto, Estado Lara, Venezuela.
Bol. com. nac. mus. mon. hist.	Boletín de la Comisión Nacional de Museos y Monumentos Históricos. Buenos Aires, Argentina.
Bol. com. prot. bibl. pop.	Boletín de la Comisión Protectora de Bibliotecas Populares. Buenos Aires, Argentina.
Bol. con. nac. geog.	Boletim do Conselho Nacional de Geografia. Instituto Brasileiro de Geografia e Estatística. Rio de Janeiro, Brazil.
Bol. consorcio centros agríc. Manabí	Boletín del Consorcio de Centros Agrícolas de Manabí. Portoviejo, Provincia de Manabí, Ecuador.
Bol. cont. dept.	Boletín de la Contraloría Departamental. Departamento de Santander. Bucaramanga, Colombia.
Bol. coop. inst. pecuária Bahia	Boletim da Cooperativa Instituto de Pecuária da Bahia. Bahia, Brazil.
Bol. dir. gen. agric. ganad.	Boletín de la Dirección General de Agricultura y Ganadería. Lima, Peru.

Bol. educ., San José........Boletín de Educación. Al Servicio de la Cultura Nacional. Secretaría de Educación Pública. Secretaría de la Jefatura Técnica de Educación Primaria. San José, Costa Rica.
Bol. escuela nac. ing........Boletín de la Escuela Nacional de Ingenieros. Instituto Politécnico Superior. Lima, Peru.
Bol. estud. teatro..........Boletín de Estudios de Teatro. Comisión Nacional de Cultura. Instituto Nacional de Estudios de Teatro. Buenos Aires, Argentina.
Bol. filol., Montevideo......Boletín de Filología. Sección de Filología y Fonética Experimental. Instituto de Estudios Superiores de Montevideo. Montevideo, Uruguay.
Bol. folklore, folkvisa y folkway......Boletin de Folklore, Folkvisa y Folkway. Anexo al Revista de Antropología de Bolivia. Órgano Oficial del Instituto "Tihuanacu" de Antropología, Etnografía y Prehistoria. La Paz, Bolivia.
Bol. hist., Cartagena.......Boletín Historial. Órgano de la Academia de la Historia de Cartagena de Indias. Cartagena, Colombia.
Bol. hist. antig.............Boletín de Historia y Antigüedades. Bogotá, Colombia.
Bol. hist. valle, Cali........Boletín Histórico del Valle. Centro Valle-Caucano de Historia y Antigüedades. Cali, Colombia.
Bol. hon. concejo deliberante......Boletín del Honorable Concejo Deliberante. Buenos Aires, Argentina.
Bol. inform. petrol.........Boletín de Informaciones Petroleras. Buenos Aires, Argentina.
Bol. inst. Brasil-Estados Unidos......Boletim do Instituto Brasil-Estados Unidos. Rio de Janeiro, Brazil.
Bol. inst. cult. ven.-brit.....Boletín del Instituto Cultural Venezolano-Británico. Caracas?, Venezuela.
Bol. inst. invest. hist.......Boletín del Instituto de Investigaciones Históricas. Buenos Aires, Argentina.
Bol. inst. soc...............Boletín del Instituto de Sociología de la Facultad de Filosofía y Letras de la Universidad de Buenos Aires. Buenos Aires, Argentina.
Bol. inst. sudamer. petról...Boletín del Instituto Sudamericano del Petróleo. Montevideo, Uruguay.
Bol. junta aux. jalis........Boletín de la Junta Auxiliar Jalisciense de la Sociedad Mexicana de Geografía y Estadística. Guadalajara, Mexico.
Bol. mens. dir. econ. rural..Boletín Mensual de la Dirección de Economía Rural. Secretaría de Agricultura y Fomento. México, D. F., Mexico.
Bol. mens. junta nac. algodón......Boletín Mensual de la Junta Nacional de Algodón. Buenos Aires. Argentina.
Bol. min. agric., Rio.......Boletim de Ministerio da Agricultura. Rio de Janeiro, Brazil.
Bol. min. trab. ind. com.....Boletim do Ministerio do Trabalho, Industria e Commercio. Rio de Janeiro, Brazil.
Bol. minas petról., Lima....Boletín de Minas y Petróleo. Ministerio de Fomento y Obras Públicas. Lima, Peru.
Bol. minas petról., México..Boletín de Minas y Petróleo. México, D. F., Mexico.
Bol. mus. arq. Col..........Boletín del Museo Arqueológico de Colombia. Ministerio de Educación Nacional. Extensión Cultural y Bellas Artes. Servicio de Arqueología. Bogotá, Colombia.
Bol. mus. bibl., Guatemala..Boletín de Museos y Bibliotecas. Órgano de Publicidad y Difusión Cultural, Etnológica, Arqueológica y Bibliográfica. Guatemala, Guatemala.
Bol. mus. hist. nat. "Javier Prado"......Boletín del Museo de Historia Natural "Javier Prado." Universidad Nacional Mayor de San Marcos. Lima, Peru.
Bol. mus. nac., Chile......Boletín del Museo Nacional. Museo Nacional de Historia Natural. Santiago, Chile.
Bol. mus. nac., Rio........Boletim do Museu Nacional. Ministério da Educação e Saúde. Rio de Janeiro, Brazil.
Bol. mus. soc. arg..........Boletín del Museo Social Argentino. Buenos Aires, Argentina.
Bol. of. policía, San Salvador......Boletín Oficial de la Policía. Órgano Mensual de la Dirección General del Cuerpo. San Salvador, El Salvador.
Bol. ofic. sanit. panamer....Boletín de la Oficina Sanitaria Panamericana. Washington, D. C.
Bol. oficial bolsa com. Rosario......Boletín Oficial de la Bolsa de Comercio del Rosario. Rosario, Argentina.
Bol. sec. inv. geog.........Boletín de la Sección de Investigaciones Geográficas. Instituto de Estudios Superiores del Uruguay. Montevideo, Uruguay.

ABBREVIATIONS

Bol. sem. cult. mex.........Boletín del Seminario de Cultura Mexicana. México, D. F., Mexico.
Bol. serv. soc. menores, São Paulo   Boletim do Serviço Social dos Menores. São Paulo, Brazil.
Bol. soc. arg. antrop.......Boletín de la Sociedad Argentina de Antropología. Buenos Aires, Argentina.
Bol. soc. biol. Concepción..Boletín de la Sociedad de Biología de Concepción. Concepción, Chile.
Bol. soc. chihuahuense......Boletín de la Sociedad Chihuahuense de Estudios Históricos. Chihuahua, Mexico.
Bol. soc. geog. La Paz......Boletín de la Sociedad Geográfica de La Paz. La Paz, Bolivia.
Bol. soc. geog. Lima........Boletín de la Sociedad Geográfica de Lima. Lima, Peru.
Bol. soc. geog. Sucre.......Boletín de la Sociedad Geográfica "Sucre." Sucre, Bolivia.
Bol. soc. geol. Perú........Boletín de la Sociedad Geológica del Perú. Lima, Peru.
Bol. soc. mex. geog. estad..Boletín de la Sociedad Mexicana de Geografía y Estadística. México, D. F., Mexico.
Bol. soc. venez. cien. nat....Boletín de la Sociedad Venezolana de Ciencias Naturales. Caracas, Venezuela.
Bol. sup. serv. café........Boletim de Superintendência dos Serviços de Café. São Paulo, Brazil.
Bol. trim. depto. nac. criança   Boletim Trimestral do Departamento Nacional de Criança. Rio de Janeiro, Brazil.
Bol. união panamer.........Boletim da União Pan Americana. Washington, D. C.
Bol. unión interamer. Caribe   Boletín de la Unión Interamericana del Caribe. Habana, Cuba.
Bol. unión panamer.........Boletín de la Unión Panamericana. Washington, D. C.
Bolivia ....New York, N. Y.
Books abroad ....Norman, Oklahoma.
Bras. açucar. ....Brasil Açucareiro. Instituto de Açucar e do Alcool. Rio de Janeiro, Brazil.
Bull. amer. paleontology...Bulletin of American Paleontology. Ithaca, New York.
Bull. bur. amer. ethnol......Bulletin of the Bureau of American Ethnology. Washington, D. C.
Bull. bur. d'ethnologie......Bulletin du Bureau d'Ethnologie de la République d'Haïti. Port-au-Prince, Haiti.
Bull. geol. soc. amer........Bulletin of the Geological Society of America. New York, N. Y.
Bull. La. libr. assoc.........Bulletin of the Louisiana Library Association. New Orleans, Louisiana.
Bull. nat. hist. soc. Maryland   Bulletin of the Natural History Society of Maryland. Baltimore, Maryland.
Bull. pan amer. union......Bulletin of the Pan American Union. Washington, D. C.
Burlington mag. ....Burlington Magazine. London, England.

C

Campesino ....El Campesino. Órgano Oficial de la Sociedad Nacional de Agricultura. Santiago, Chile.
Can. hist. rev..............Canadian Historical Review. Toronto, Canada.
Carnegie mag. ....Carnegie Magazine. Pittsburgh, Pennsylvania.
The catholic world.........New York, N. Y.
Ceres ....Revista Bi-Mensal de Divulgação de Ensinamentos Teóricos e Práticos sobre Agricultura, Veterinária, Industrias Rurais. Escola Superior de Agricultura do Estado de Minas Geraes. Viçosa, Brazil.
Christian science monitor..Boston, Massachusetts.
Chron. bot. ....Chronica Botanica. Waltham, Massachusetts.
Ciencia ....Revista Hispano-Americana de Ciencias Puras y Aplicadas. México, D. F., Mexico.
Ciencia y técnica..........Revista del Centro Estudiantes de Ingeniería. Buenos Aires, Argentina.
Cinófono ....Lima, Peru.
Clío ....Revista Bimestre de la Academia Dominicana de la Historia. Ciudad Trujillo, Dominican Republic.
Comercio ....El Comercio. Lima, Peru.
Comments on arg. trade....Comments on Argentine Trade. Buenos Aires, Argentina.
Commer. Amer. ....Commercial America. The Commercial Museum. Philadelphia, Pennsylvania.

Commer. pan Amer........Commercial Pan America. Washington, D. C.
Commonweal ....New York, N. Y.
Conservatorio ....Conservatorio Municipal de Música de La Habana. Habana, Cuba.
El consultor práctico de   Santiago, Chile.
  las leyes
Contrib. amer. anthrop.   Contributions to American Anthropology and History. Car-
  hist.   negie Institution of Washington. Washington, D. C.
Coopecarril ....Órgano Oficial de la Institución Cooperativa del Personal de los Ferrocarriles del Estado, Ltda. Buenos Aires, Argentina.
La crónica médica.........Lima, Peru.
Cuad. amer. ....Cuadernos Americanos. México, D. F., Mexico.
Cuad. cult. teatral..........Cuadernos de Cultura Teatral. Instituto Nacional de Estudios de Teatro. Buenos Aires, Argentina.
Cuad. tall. San Lucas......Cuaderno del Taller San Lucas. Granada, Nicaragua.
Cult. bras. ....Cultura Brasileira. Serviço Gráfico do Instituto Brasileiro de Geografia e Estatística. Rio de Janeiro, Brazil.
Cult. México ....La Cultura en México. Boletín de la Comisión Mexicana de Cooperación Intelectual. México, D. F., Mexico.
Cultura ....Órgano de la Biblioteca Popular "Bernardino Rivadavia." Cañada de Gómez, Argentina.
Cultura peruana ....Lima, Peru.
Cultura política ....Revista Mensal de Estudos Brasileiros. Rio de Janeiro, Brazil.
Curr. hist. ....Current History. New York, N. Y.
Cursos y conferencias......Revista del Colegio Libre de Estudios Superiores. Buenos Aires, Argentina.

D

D. N. C..................Revista do Departamento Nacional do Café. Rio de Janeiro, Brazil.
Darwiniana ....Revista del Instituto de Botánica Darwinion. Academia Nacional de Ciencias Exactas, Físicas y Naturales de Buenos Aires. Buenos Aires, Argentina.
Dept. state bull...........The Department of State Bulletin. United States Department of State. Washington, D. C.
Design ....Columbus, Ohio.
El Día, Montevideo ....El Día. Montevideo, Uruguay.
Dialéctica ....Revista Continental de Teoría y Estudios Marxistas. Habana, Cuba.
Diario de hoy.............San Salvador, El Salvador.
Diario de la marina........Habana, Cuba.
Diario de noticias, Rio.....Diario de Noticias. Rio de Janeiro, Brazil.
Diario of. Uruguay........Diario Oficial de la República Oriental del Uruguay. Montevideo, Uruguay.
Diario rural ....Montevideo, Uruguay.
Direito ....Direito; Doutrina, Legislação e Jurisprudência. Rio de Janeiro, Brazil.
Div. agric. ....Divulgaciones de Agricultura. Ministerio de Agricultura. Dirección de Agricultura. Lima, Peru.
Div. hist. ....Divulgación Histórica. México, D. F., Mexico.
Dom Casmurro ....Rio de Janeiro, Brazil.
Dyn ....The Review of Modern Art. Coyoacan, D. F., Mexico.

E

Eco musical ....Buenos Aires, Argentina.
Econ. bol. ....Economía Boliviana. Revista de Economía y Finanzas. La Paz, Bolivia.
Econ. finan. ....Economía y Finanzas. Revista Mensual de Circulación Panamericana. Santiago, Chile.
Econ. geog. ....Economic Geography. Clark University. Worcester, Massachusetts.
Economista ....El Economista. Órgano del Instituto de Estudios Económicos y Sociales. México, D. F., Mexico.
Educación, Caracas ....Revista para los Maestros. Editada por el Ministerio de Educación Nacional. Dirección de Cultura. Caracas, Venezuela.

ABBREVIATIONS

Educación, Córdoba ...... Educación. Córdoba, Argentina.
Engin. mining jour. .... Engineering and Mining Journal. New York, N. Y.
Estad. chil. .... Estadística Chilena. Revista de la Dirección General de Estadística. Santiago, Chile.
Estadística .... Journal of the Inter-American Statistical Institute. México, D. F., Mexico.
Estud. bras. .... Estudos Brasileiros. Rio de Janeiro, Brazil.
Estud. confer. .... Estudos e Conferências. Rio de Janeiro, Brazil.
Estud. educ. .... Estudos Educacionais. Florianópolis, Brazil.
Estud. educ., Santa Catarina   Estudos Educacionais. Santa Catarina, Brazil.
Estud. hist. .... Estudios Históricos. Guadalajara, México.
Estudios .... Buenos Aires, Argentina.
Estudios, Santiago .... Estudios. Mensuario de Cultura General. Santiago, Chile.
Estudos .... Pôrto Alegre, Brazil.
Etude .... Philadelphia, Pennsylvania.
Excelsior, México .... Excelsior. El Periódico de la Vida Nacional. México, D. F., Mexico.
Export trade and shipper .. New York, N. Y.

F

F. N. F. .... Publicação da Faculdade Nacional de Filosofía. Rio de Janeiro, Brazil.
Fil. letras .... Filosofía y Letras. Revista de la Facultad de Filosofía y Letras. Universidad Nacional Autónoma de México. México, D. F., Mexico.
Flora .... Quito, Ecuador.
Folklore .... Boletín del Departamento de Folklore del Instituto de Cooperación Universitaria de los Cursos de Cultura Católica. Buenos Aires, Argentina.
Folklore Americas .... Chapel Hill, North Carolina.
For. affs. .... Foreign Affairs. Council on Foreign Relations, Inc. New York, N. Y.
For. agric. .... Foreign Agriculture. United States Department of Agriculture. United States Office of Foreign Agricultural Relations. Washington, D. C.
For. com. weekly .... Foreign Commerce Weekly. United States Department of Commerce. Bureau of Foreign and Domestic Commerce. Washington, D. C.
For. pol. rep. .... Foreign Policy Reports. Foreign Policy Association. New York, N. Y.
Formação .... Rio de Janeiro, Brazil.
Fortune .... New York, N. Y.

G

Gaceta of., Cuba .... Gaceta Oficial. Habana, Cuba.
Gaea .... Anales de la Sociedad Argentina de Estudios Geográficos. Buenos Aires, Argentina.
Garcilaso .... Órgano del Centro Inca Garcilaso. Cuzco, Peru.
Gazette des beaux arts ..... New York, N. Y.
Geog. jour. .... Geographical Journal. London, England.
Geog. mag. .... The Geographical Magazine. London, England.
Geog. rev. .... Geographical Review. New York, N. Y.

H

La hacienda .... New York, N. Y.
Handbook, no. 8, 1942 ...... Handbook of Latin American Studies, no. 8, 1942. Cambridge, Massachusetts.
Harper's mag. .... Harper's Magazine. New York, N. Y.
Harvard educ. rev. .... Harvard Education Review. Harvard University. Cambridge, Massachusetts.
Harvard law rev. .... Harvard Law Review. Harvard University. Law School. Cambridge, Massachusetts.
Hijo pródigo .... El Hijo Pródigo. México, D. F., Mexico.

Hisp. amer. essays	Hispanic American Essays. A Memorial to James Alexander Robertson, Edited by A. Curtis Wilgus. The University of North Carolina Press. Chapel Hill, North Carolina.
Hisp. amer. hist. rev	Hispanic American Historical Review. Durham, North Carolina.
Hisp. rev.	Hispanic Review. A Quarterly Journal Devoted to Research in the Hispanic Languages and Literatures. University of Pennsylvania. Philadelphia, Pennsylvania.
Hispania, Washington	A Journal Devoted to the Interests of Teachers of Spanish. American Association of Teachers of Spanish. George Washington University. Washington, D. C.
Historia, Lima	Historia. Revista Bimestral. Lima, Peru.
Hoy	México, D. F., Mexico.
Humanidades, México	Humanidades. Órgano de los Alumnos de la Facultad de Filosofía y Letras. Universidad Nacional Autónoma de México. México, D. F., Mexico.

I

Ilus. bras.	Ilustração Brasileira. Rio de Janeiro, Brazil.
Ind. azuc.	La Industria Azucarera. Órgano del Centro Azucarero Argentino. Buenos Aires, Argentina.
Inform. arg.	Informaciones Argentinas. Ministerio de Relaciones Exteriores y Culto. Dirección de Información al Exterior. Buenos Aires, Argentina.
Ingeniería	Buenos Aires, Argentina.
Int. amer.	The Inter-American. Washington, D. C.
Int. amer. affairs, 1942	Inter-American Affairs, 1942. Edited by Arthur P. Whitaker. Columbia University Press. New York, N. Y.
Int. amer. bibliog. rev	Inter-American Bibliographical Review. Washington, D. C.
Int. amer. intel. interchange	Proceedings of the Inter American Conference on Intellectual Interchange. University of Texas. Institute of Latin American Studies. Austin, Texas.
Int. conciliation	International Conciliation. New York, N. Y.
Int. lab. rev	International Labour Review. Geneva, Switzerland.
Investig. econ.	Investigaciones Económicas. Escuela Nacional de Economía. Universidad Nacional Autónoma de México. México, D. F., Mexico.

J

O Jornal	Rio de Janeiro, Brazil.
Jornal do commercio	Rio de Janeiro, Brazil.
Jour. amer. folklore	Journal of American Folklore. New York, N. Y.
Jour. farm econ	Journal of Farm Economics. Menasha, Wisconsin.
Jour. geog.	Journal of Geography. Chicago, Illinois.
Jour. geol.	Journal of Geology. Chicago, Illinois.
Jour. Jamaica agric. soc.	The Journal of the Jamaica Agricultural Society. Kingston, Jamaica.
Jour. land. pub. util. econ	The Journal of Land & Public Utility Economics. University of Wisconsin. Madison, Wisconsin.
Jour. negro hist.	Journal of Negro History. Washington, D. C.
Jour. pol.	The Journal of Politics. University of Florida. Gainesville, Florida.
Jour. roy. inst. British architects	Journal of the Royal Institute of British Architects. London, England.
Jus	Revista de Derecho y Ciencias Sociales. México, D. F., Mexico.

K

Kiva	The Kiva. University of Arizona. Arizona Archaeological and Historical Society. Arizona State Museum. Tucson, Arizona.
Kollasuyo	Revista Mensual de Estudios Bolivianos. La Paz, Bolivia.

L

L. A. social econ. trans.	Proceedings of the Conference on Latin America in Social and Economic Transition. Inter-American Short Papers. The University of New Mexico Press. Albuquerque, New Mexico.
La. hist. quart.	Louisiana Historical Quarterly. New Orleans, Louisiana.
Land pol. rev.	Land policy review. Bureau of Agricultural Economics. Department of Agriculture. Washington, D. C.
Law Notes	Brooklyn, N. Y.
Lawyers guild rev.	Lawyers Guild Review with which is combined International Juridical Association Bulletin. Washington, D. C.
Letras, Lima	Letras. Universidad de San Marcos. Lima, Peru.
Letras de México	México, D. F., Mexico.
Libertad creadora	Revista Trimestral publicada por los Amigos de Guillermo Korn. La Plata-Buenos Aires, Argentina.
Libr. jour.	Library Journal. New York, N. Y.
Libri	Buenos Aires, Argentina.
Liturgical arts	Liturgical Arts Society. Concord, New Hampshire.
Luminar	México, D. F., Mexico.

M

Magazine of art	The American Federation of Arts. Washington, D. C.
Man	A Record of Anthropological Science. The Royal Anthropological Institute. London, England.
A Manhã	Rio de Janeiro, Brazil.
Más luz	Órgano Oficial de la Asociación "Más Luz." Santiago de las Vegas, Cuba.
Masterkey	The Masterkey. Los Angeles, California.
Mem. acad. mex. hist.	Memorias de la Academia Mexicana de la Historia. México, D. F., Mexico.
Mercados del mundo	Información Agroeconómica. Ministerio de Ganadería y Agricultura. Dirección de Agronomía. Sección Economía y Estadística Agraria. Montevideo, Uruguay.
Mercurio peruano	Lima, Peru.
Méx. agrario	México Agrario. Revista Sociológica. México, D. F., Mexico.
Mex. amer. rev.	Mexican-American Review. México, D. F., Mexico.
Mexican life	México, D. F., Mexico.
Mexicana rev.	Mexicana Review. New York, N. Y.
México antig.	El México Antiguo. México, D. F., Mexico.
Mid-America	An Historical Quarterly. Loyola University. Institute of Jesuit History. Chicago, Illinois.
Middle amer. research records	Middle American Research Records. Middle American Research Institute. New Orleans, Louisiana.
Mod. lang. jour.	Modern Language Journal. Washington, D. C.
Modern music	New York, N. Y.
Mon. educ. común	El Monitor de la Educación Común. Órgano del Consejo Nacional de Educación. Buenos Aires, Argentina.
Month. labor rev.	Monthly Labor Review. United States Department of Labor. Bureau of Labor Statistics. Washington, D. C.
Mundo libre, México	Mundo Libre. Revista Mensual de Política y Derecho Internacional. México, D. F., Mexico.
Museum news	American Association of Museums. Washington, D. C.
Music educators journal	Chicago, Illinois.
Music rev.	The Music Review. Cambridge, England.
Musical America	New York, N. Y.
Musical quarterly	New York, N. Y.

N

La Nación	Buenos Aires, Argentina.
Nat. geog. mag.	National Geographic Magazine. Washington, D. C.
Nat. hist.	Natural History. American Museum of Natural History. New York, N. Y.
New international year book, 1942	The New International Year Book. A Compendium of the World's Progress for the Year 1942. New York-London.

New Mex. anthrop	New Mexico Anthropologist. Santa Fe, New Mexico.
New Mex. hist. rev	New Mexico Historical Review. Santa Fe, New Mexico.
New Mexico quart. rev	New Mexico Quarterly Review. Albuquerque, New Mexico.
New music	A Quarterly of Modern Compositions. New York, New York.
New pencil points	East Stroudsburg, Pennsylvania.
New republic	The New Republic. New York, N. Y.
New world guides to the Latin American republics	The New World Guides to the Latin American Republics. Edited by Earl Parker Hanson. Sponsored by the Office of the United States. Coordinator of Inter-American Affairs. Duell, Sloan and Pearce. New York, N. Y.
Nosotros	Buenos Aires, Argentina.
Notas mus. La Plata	Notas del Museo de La Plata. Instituto del Museo de la Universidad Nacional de La Plata. Buenos Aires, Argentina.
Notes latin amer. studies	Notes on Latin American Studies. The Joint Committee on Latin American Studies. Washington, D. C.
Notes music libr. assn	Notes of the Music Library Association. Rochester, New York.
Notes on middle amer. arch. ethnol.	Notes on Middle American Archaeology and Ethnology. Carnegie Institution of Washington. Division of Historical Research. Washington, D. C.
Noticioso	Ministerio de Agricultura de la Nación. Dirección de Propaganda y Publicaciones. Buenos Aires, Argentina.
Nueva dem.	La Nueva Democracia. New York. N. Y.

O

Oasis	Órgano Oficial del Centro Cultural Árabe. Quito, Ecuador.
Obs. econ. fin.	O Observador Econômico e Financeiro. Rio de Janeiro, Brazil.
Onza, tigre y león	Revista para la Infancia Venezolana. Editada por la Dirección de Cultura del Ministerio de Educación Nacional. Caracas, Venezuela.
Orbe	Universidad de Yucatán. Mérida, Mexico.
A ordem	Revista de Cultura. Rio de Janeiro, Brazil.
Orientación musical	Revista Mensual. Órgano del Ateneo Musical Mexicano. México, D. F., Mexico.
Ouro branco	Mensario Técnico-Informativo do Algodão. São Paulo, Brazil.

P

Pac. art. rev	Pacific Art Review. M. H. De Young Memorial Museum. San Francisco, California.
Pac. hist. rev	Pacific Historical Review. University of California Press. Los Angeles, California.
Palacio	El Palacio. Santa Fe, New Mexico.
The Pan American	New York, N. Y.
The personalist	The University of California. Los Angeles, California.
Perú	Revista Mensual Ilustrada al Servicio del Intercambio Argentino Peruano. Buenos Aires, Argentina.
Peruanidad	Órgano Antológico del Pensamiento Nacional. Dirección de Propaganda e Informaciones. Lima, Peru.
Phil. phenom. research	Philosophy and Phenomenological Research. Published for the International Phenomenological Society by the University of Buffalo. Buffalo, New York.
Planificación econ.	Planificación Económica. Secretaría de la Economía Nacional. México, D. F., Mexico.
Pol. sci. quart	Political Science Quarterly. New York, N. Y.
La Prensa	Buenos Aires, Argentina.
La Prensa, Lima	La Prensa. Lima, Peru.
Prev. segur.	Previsión y Seguridad. Almanaque Anual para el Taller, el Hogar y el Campo Mexicanos. Recopilaciones de Manuel L. Barragán. Séptima edición. Monterrey, Mexico.
Prev. soc., Quito	Previsión Social. Boletín del Ministerio de Previsión Social y Trabajo. Quito, Ecuador.
Primitive man	Washington, D. C.
Proc. agric. soc. Trinidad Tobago	Proceedings of the Agricultural Society of Trinidad and Tobago. Port of Spain, Trinidad.
Proc. amer. phil. soc	Proceedings, American Philosophical Society. Philadelphia, Pennsylvania.

Proc. eighth amer. scien. cong.	Proceedings of the Eighth American Scientific Congress, held in Washington, D. C., May 10-18, 1940. United States Department of State. Washington, D. C.
Proc. U. S. nat. mus.	Proceedings of the United States National Museum. Washington, D. C.
Prorsus	Órgano del Instituto Superior de Pedagogía y Letras. Guayaquil, Ecuador.
Protec. soc.	Protección Social. Órgano de la Caja de Seguro y Ahorro Obrero. La Paz, Bolivia.
Publ. mod. lang. assoc.	Publications of the Modern Language Association of America. Baltimore, Maryland.
Publ. mus. etnog., Buenos Aires	Publicaciones del Museo Etnográfico. Universidad Nacional de Buenos Aires. Facultad de Filosofía y Letras. Buenos Aires, Argentina.
Public management	International City Managers' Association. Chicago, Illinois.

Q

Quart. jour. econ.	Quarterly Journal of Economics. Cambridge, Massachusetts.

R

Railway gaz.	Railway Gazette. London, England.
Razón y fe	Madrid, Spain.
Readers digest	Pleasantville, New York.
Reg. cult. yuc.	Registro de Cultura Yucateca. México, D. F., Mexico.
Reg. oficial	Registro Oficial. Quito, Ecuador.
Rel. soc. arg. antrop.	Relaciones de la Sociedad Argentina de Antropología. Buenos Aires, Argentina.
Rep. amer.	Repertorio Americano. San José, Costa Rica.
Rep. boyacense	Repertorio Boyacense. Órgano del Centro de Historia de Tunja. Tunja, Colombia.
Resenha musical	São Paulo, Brazil.
Rev. acad. bras. let.	Revista da Academia Brasileira de Letras. Rio de Janeiro, Brazil.
Rev. acad. col. cien. exact. fís. nat.	Revista de la Academia Colombiana de Ciencias Exactas, Físicas y Naturales. Bogotá, Colombia.
Rev. acad. paulista let.	Revista da Academia Paulista de Letras. São Paulo, Brazil.
Rev. agric., Costa Rica.	Revista de Agricultura. San José, Costa Rica.
Rev. agric., Cuba.	Revista de Agricultura. Habana, Cuba.
Rev. agric., Dom. Rep.	Revista de Agricultura. Ciudad Trujillo, Dominican Republic.
Rev. agríc., Guatemala.	Revista Agrícola. Secretaría de Agricultura. Guatemala, Guatemala.
Rev. agric. com., Panamá.	Revista de Agricultura y Comercio. Ministerio de Agricultura y Comercio. Panamá, Panama.
Rev. agron.	Revista Agronômica; Agricultura e Criação. Pôrto Alegre, Brazil.
Rev. arch. bibl. nac., Tegucigalpa	Revista del Archivo y Biblioteca Nacionales. Tegucigalpa, Honduras.
Rev. arch. nac., Bogotá.	Revista del Archivo Nacional. Bogotá, Colombia.
Rev. arch. nac., Costa Rica.	Revista de los Archivos Nacionales. San José, Costa Rica.
Rev. arch. nac. Perú.	Revista del Archivo Nacional del Perú. Lima, Peru.
Rev. arq. mun., São Paulo.	Revista de Arquivo Municipal. Órgão da Sociedade de Etnografia e Folclore e da Sociedade do Sociologia. Departamento de Cultura. Prefeitura do Município de São Paulo. São Paulo, Brazil.
Rev. asoc. cult. bibl.	Revista de la Asociación Cultural de Bibliotécnicos. Buenos Aires, Argentina.
Rev. asoc. méd. arg.	Revista de la Asociación Médica Argentina. Buenos Aires, Argentina.
Rev. asoc. rural Uruguay.	Revista de la Asociación Rural del Uruguay. Montevideo, Uruguay.
Rev. ateneo paraguayo.	Revista del Ateneo Paraguayo. Asunción, Paraguay.
Rev. bibl. arch. nac.	Revista de la Biblioteca y Archivo Nacionales. Sucre, Bolivia.
Rev. bibl. nac., Buenos Aires	Revista de la Biblioteca Nacional. Buenos Aires, Argentina.
Rev. bim. cub.	Revista Bimestre Cubana. Habana, Cuba.
Rev. bolsa cereales.	Revista de la Bolsa de Cereales. Buenos Aires, Argentina.

Rev. bras.	Revista Brasileira. Academia Brasileira de Letras. Rio de Janeiro, Brazil.
Rev. bras. estat.	Revista Brasileira de Estatística. Rio de Janeiro, Brazil.
Rev. bras. geog.	Revista Brasileira de Geografia. Rio de Janeiro, Brazil.
Rev. Brasil	Revista do Brasil. Rio de Janeiro, Brazil.
Rev. cám. agric. primera zona	Revista de la Cámara de Agricultura de la Primera Zona. Quito, Ecuador.
Rev. centro estud. hist. geog. Cuenca	Revista del Centro de Estudios Históricos y Geográficos de Cuenca. Cuenca, Ecuador.
Rev. chil. hist. geog.	Revista Chilena de Historia y Geografía. Santiago, Chile.
Rev. cien. econ.	Revista de Ciencias Económicas. Universidad Nacional. Buenos Aires, Argentina.
Rev. ciên. econ., São Paulo	Revista de Ciências Econômicas. São Paulo, Brazil.
Rev. cien. jur. soc.	Revista de Ciencias Jurídicas y Sociales. Universidad Nacional del Litoral. Santa Fe, Argentina.
Rev. ciencias, Lima	Revista de Ciencias. Lima, Peru.
Rev. col. procuradores Buenos Aires	Revista del Colegio de Procuradores de la Ciudad de Buenos Aires. Buenos Aires, Argentina.
Rev. colegio abogados Buenos Aires	Revista del Colegio de Abogados de Buenos Aires. Buenos Aires, Argentina.
Rev. mex. estud. antrop.	Revista Mexicana de Estudios Antropológicos. Sociedad Mexicana de Antropología. Mexico, D. F., Mexico.
Rev. colegio Rosario, Bogotá	Revista del Colegio Mayor de Nuestra Señora del Rosario. Bogotá, Colombia.
Rev. cub.	Revista Cubana. Habana, Cuba.
Rev. der. admin. munic.	Revista de Derecho y Administración Municipal. Buenos Aires, Argentina.
Rev. der. int.	Revista de Derecho Internacional. Órgano del Instituto Americano de Derecho Internacional. Habana, Cuba.
Rev. econ.	Revista Económica. Buenos Aires, Argentina.
Rev. econ., México	Revista de Economía. México, D. F., Mexico.
Rev. econ. arg.	Revista de Economía Argentina. Buenos Aires, Argentina.
Rev. econ. estad.	Revista de Economía y Estadística. Córdoba, Argentina.
Rev. econ. nac.	Revista de la Economía Nacional. Publicación Mensual editada por el Banco Central de Guatemala. Guatemala, Guatemala.
Rev. educ.	Revista de Educación. Dirección General de Escuelas de la Provincia de Buenos Aires. Buenos Aires, Argentina.
Rev. educ., Goiâna	Revista de Educação. Goiâna, Brazil.
Rev. educ., Medellín	Revista de Educación. Medellín, Colombia.
Rev. educ. públ., Rio	Revista de Educação Pública. Órgão da Secretaria Geral de Educação e Cultura da Prefeitura do Distrito Federal. Rio de Janeiro, Brazil.
Rev. escuela mil., Perú	Revista de la Escuela Militar. Chorillos, Peru.
Rev. fac. agron., Montevideo	Revista de la Facultad de Agronomía. Universidad de la República. Montevideo, Uruguay.
Rev. fac. cien. econ.	Revista de la Facultad de Ciencias Económicas. Universidad Mayor de San Marcos. Lima, Peru.
Rev. fac. cien. econ. adm.	Revista de la Facultad de Ciencias Económicas y de Administración. Montevideo, Uruguay.
Rev. fac. nac. agron., Medellín	Revista de la Facultad Nacional de Agronomía. Medellín, Colombia.
Rev. filol. hisp.	Revista de Filología Hispánica. New York, N. Y.-Buenos Aires, Argentina.
Rev. fomento	Revista de Fomento. Ministerio de Fomento. Caracas, Venezuela.
Rev. forense	Revista Forense. Rio de Janeiro, Brazil.
Rev. ganadera, Habana	Revista Ganadera. Habana, Cuba.
Rev. geog. amer.	Revista Geográfica Americana. Sociedad Geográfica Americana. Buenos Aires, Argentina.
Rev. Habana	Revista de La Habana. Habana, Cuba.
Rev. hacienda, Venezuela	Revista de Hacienda. Caracas, Venezuela.
Rev. hisp. mod.	Revista Hispánica Moderna. Columbia University. New York, N. Y.
Rev. hist., Buenos Aires	Revista de Historia. Buenos Aires, Argentina.
Rev. hist., Montevideo	Revista Histórica. Publicación del Museo Histórico Nacional. Montevideo, Uruguay.

Rev. hist. Amér.	Revista de Historia de América. Instituto Panamericano de Geografía e Historia. México, D. F., Mexico.
Rev. iberoamer.	Revista Iberoamericana. México, D. F., Mexico.
Rev. imig. col.	Revista de Imigração e Colonização. Rio de Janeiro, Brazil.
Rev. Indias	Revista de las Indias. Bogotá, Colombia.
Rev. Indias, Madrid	Revista de Indias. Madrid, Spain.
Rev. inst. antrop. univ. nac. Tucumán	Revista del Instituto de Antropología de la Universidad Nacional de Tucumán. Tucumán, Argentina.
Rev. inst. Brasil-Estados Unidos	Revista do Instituto Brasil-Estados Unidos. Rio de Janeiro, Brazil.
Rev. inst. defensa café Costa Rica	Revista del Instituto de Defensa del Café de Costa Rica. San José, Costa Rica.
Rev. inst. etnol. nac.	Revista del Instituto Etnológico Nacional. Bogotá, Colombia.
Rev. inst. hist. geog. Rio Grande do Sul	Revista do Instituto Histórico e Geográphico do Rio Grande do Sul. Pôrto Alegre, Brazil.
Rev. inst. inv. hist. J. M. Rosas	Revista del Instituto de Investigaciones Históricas Juan Manuel de Rosas. Buenos Aires, Argentina.
Rev. inst. sanmartiniano Perú	Revista del Instituto Sanmartiniano del Perú. Lima, Peru.
Rev. inst. soc. bol.	Revista del Instituto de Sociología Boliviana. Sucre, Bolivia.
Rev. int. soc.	Revista Internacional de Sociología. Consejo Superior de Investigaciones Científicas. Sección de Sociología del Instituto "Sancho de Moncada." Madrid, Spain.
Rev. int. trab.	Revista Internacional del Trabajo. Oficina Internacional del Trabajo. Ginebra, Switzerland-Montreal, Canada.
Rev. javeriana	Revista Javeriana. Bogotá, Colombia.
Rev. junta estud. hist. Santa Fe	Revista de la Junta de Estudios Históricos de Santa Fe. Santa Fe, Argentina.
Rev. junta estud. hist. Santiago del Estero	Revista de la Junta de Estudios Históricos de Santiago del Estero. Santiago del Estero, Argentina.
Rev. junta hist. let. La Rioja	Revista de la Junta de Historia y Letras de La Rioja. Museo Inca Huasi. La Rioja, Argentina.
Rev. jurídica	Revista Jurídica. Órgano de la Facultad de Derecho, Ciencias Sociales, Políticas y Económicas de la Universidad Autónoma de Cochabamba. Cochabamba, Bolivia.
Rev. ling. farm. ind.	Revista de Lingüística y Farmacopea Indiana. Anexo a Anales de Arqueología de Bolivia. Sociedad Arqueológica de Bolivia. La Paz, Bolivia.
Rev. marina mercante nac.	Revista de la Marina Mercante Nacional. Santiago?, Chile.
Rev. médica, San José	Revista Médica. San José, Costa Rica.
Rev. mex. geog.	Revista Mexicana de Geografía. México, D. F., Mexico.
Rev. mex. soc.	Revista Mexicana de Sociología. Universidad Nacional Autónoma. Instituto Investigaciones Sociales. México, D. F., Mexico.
Rev. militar, Buenos Aires	Revista Militar. Buenos Aires, Argentina.
Rev. min. agric. com. ind.	Revista del Ministerio de Agricultura, Comercio e Industrias. Asunción, Paraguay.
Rev. min. instr. públ.	Revista del Ministerio de Instrucción Pública. San Salvador, El Salvador.
Rev. minería, Medellín	Revista Minería. Medellín, Colombia.
Rev. mun., Guayaquil	Revista Municipal. Guayaquil, Ecuador.
Rev. mus. Atlán.	Revista del Museo del Atlántico. Dirección Departamental de Educación Nacional. Barranquilla, Colombia.
Rev. mus. hist. nac. Chile	Revista del Museo Histórico Nacional de Chile. Santiago, Chile.
Rev. mus. La Plata	Revista del Museo de La Plata. Instituto del Museo de la Universidad Nacional de la Plata. Buenos Aires, Argentina.
Rev. mus. mex.	Revista Musical Mexicana. México, D. F., Mexico.
Rev. mus. nac., Lima	Revista del Museo Nacional. Lima, Peru.
Rev. nac., Habana	Revista Nacional de Ciencias Político-Económico-Sociales. Habana, Cuba.
Rév. nac., Montevideo	Revista Nacional. Ministerio de Instrucción Pública. Montevideo, Uruguay.
Rev. nac. agric.	Revista Nacional de Agricultura. Bogotá, Colombia.
Rev. nac. cultura	Revista Nacional de Cultura. Caracas, Venezuela.
Rev. parlamentaria	Revista Parlamentaria. Buenos Aires, Argentina.
Rev. peruana der. int.	Revista Peruana de Derecho Internacional. Órgano de la Sociedad Peruana de Derecho Internacional. Lima, Peru.

Rev. prob. arg. amer........Revista de Problemas Argentinos y Americanos. Universidad Nacional de La Plata. La Plata, Argentina.
Rev. san. asist. soc..........Revista de Sanidad y Asistencia Social. Ministerio de Sanidad y Asistencia Social. Caracas, Venezuela.
Rev. semana ....Revista da Semana. Rio de Janeiro, Brazil.
Rev. serv. patr. hist. Revista do Serviço do Patrimônio Histórico e Artístico Nacional. Rio de Janeiro, Brazil.
art. nac.
Rev. serv. públ..............Revista do Serviço Público. Rio de Janeiro, Brazil.
Rev. soc. cient. Paraguay..Revista de la Sociedad Científica del Paraguay. Asunción, Paraguay.
Rev. soc. cub. ing..........Revista de la Sociedad Cubana de Ingenieros. Habana, Cuba.
Rev. soc. geog. Cuba........Revista de la Sociedad Geográfica de Cuba. Habana, Cuba.
Rev. soc. geog. Rio de Revista da Sociedade de Geographia do Rio de Janeiro. Rio de Janeiro, Brazil.
Janeiro
Rev. soc. hist. géog. Haïti..Revue de la Société d'Histoire et de Géographie d'Haïti. Port-au-Prince, Haiti.
Rev. trabalho ....Revista do Trabalho. Rio de Janeiro, Brazil.
Rev. univ., Cuzco...........Revista Universitaria. Cuzco, Peru.
Rev. univ., Guadalajara....Revista Universitaria de la Asociación de Post-Graduados y ex-Alumnos de la Universidad Autónoma de Guadalajara. Guadalajara, Mexico.
Rev. univ. Buenos Aires....Revista de la Universidad de Buenos Aires. Buenos Aires, Argentina.
Rev. univ. cat. Perú........Revista de la Universidad Católica del Perú. Lima, Peru.
Rev. univ. Cauca...........Revista de la Universidad del Cauca. Popayán, Colombia.
Rev. univ. Guayaquil......Revista de la Universidad de Guayaquil. Guayaquil, Ecuador.
Rev. univ. nac. Córdoba....Revista de la Universidad Nacional de Cordóba. Córdoba, Argentina.
Rev. univ. Puebla..........Revista de la Universidad de Puebla. Puebla, Mexico.
Rio Grande odontológico..Pôrto Alegre, Brazil.
Romanic rev...............The Romanic Review. A Quarterly Publication of the Department of Romance Languages in Columbia University. Columbia University Press. New York, N. Y.
Rumo ....Propriedade da Casa do Estudiante do Brasil. Rio de Janeiro, Brazil.
Rural sociology ....Baton Rouge, Louisiana.

S

Saber vivir ....Buenos Aires, Argentina.
Sat. rev. lit................The Saturday Review of Literature. New York, N. Y.
Schola cantorum, Morelia..Schola Cantorum. Revista de Cultura Sacro-Musical. Morelia, Mexico.
Sci. month. ....Scientific Monthly. New York, N. Y.
Science and society........New York, N. Y.
Simiente ....Órgano de la Sociedad Agronómica de Chile. Santiago, Chile.
Soc. sec. bull..............Social Security Bulletin. Social Security Board. Washington, D. C.
Sociologia ....Revista Didática e Científica. São Paulo, Brazil.
South. folk. quart..........Southern Folklore Quarterly. The University of Florida in cooperation with the Southeastern Folklore Society. Gainesville, Florida.
Southw. hist. quart.........Southwestern Historical Quarterly. Austin, Texas.
Studio ....London, England.
Sur ....Buenos Aires, Argentina.
Surco ....San José, Costa Rica.
Survey graphic ....New York, N. Y.
Sustancia ....Tucumán, Argentina.

T

Teachers college record.....Columbia University. Teachers College. New York, New York.
Tecné ....Técnica, Arquitectura, Urbanismo. Buenos Aires, Argentina.
Texas folk. soc. pub........Texas Folklore Society Publications. Austin, Texas.
Think ....International Business Machines Corporation. New York, N. Y.
Tiempo ....Semanario de la Vida y la Verdad. México, D. F., Mexico.
Tierras y aguas............Bogotá, Colombia.
Tiras de colores............México, D. F., Mexico.

Tlalocan	A Journal of Source Materials on the Native Cultures of Mexico. Published by the House of Tlaloc. Sacramento, California.
Trab. prev. soc.	Revista del Trabajo y Previsión Social. México, D. F., Mexico.
Travel	New York, N. Y.
Travel in Brazil	Rio de Janeiro, Brazil.
Trim. econ.	El Trimestre Económico. México, D. F., Mexico.
Tropical agric.	Tropical Agriculture. The Imperial College of Tropical Agriculture. Trinidad, British West Indies.
Tzunpame	Órgano de Publicidad del Museo Nacional de El Salvador. San Salvador, El Salvador.

U

Unión agríc. sur	Unión Agrícola del Sur. Una Revista para los Agricultores del Sur de Chile. Concepción, Chile.
Univ. Antioquia	Universidad de Antioquia. Medellín, Colombia.
Univ. cat. bolivariana	Universidad Católica Bolivariana. Medellín, Colombia.
Univ. Habana	Universidad de La Habana. Habana, Cuba.
Univ. mus. bull.	University Museum Bulletin. University of Pennsylvania. The University Museum. Philadelphia, Pennsylvania.
Universidad, Potosí	Universidad autónoma "Tomás Frías." Potosí, Bolivia.
Universidad, Santa Fe	Universidad. Publicación de la Universidad Nacional del Litoral. Santa Fe, Argentina.

V

Venezuela	Revista de Informaciones Venezolanas. Caracas, Venezuela.
Véritas	Buenos Aires, Argentina.
Vida agríc.	La Vida Agrícola. Lima, Peru.
Vida médica	Rio de Janeiro, Brazil.
Vida rural	La Vida Rural. Revista Mensual Ilustrada de Agricultura, Ganadería e Industrias. Bogotá, Colombia.

W

Waman puma	Revista Mensual de Cultura y Folklore. Cuzco, Peru.
Weekly statis. sugar trade jour.	Weekly Statistical Sugar Trade Journal. New York, N. Y.
World affairs	The American Peace Society. Washington, D. C.
World econ.	World Economics. Bulletin of the Institute of World Economics. Washington, D. C.

Y

Yikal maya than	Mérida, Mexico.

Z

Zeit. ethnol.	Zeitschrift für Ethnologie. Berlin, Germany.

INDEX

A

A. A. (Athayde, Austregesilo de), 4128.
Abad, Luis V., 1127, 1128.
Abad, Plácido, 746.
Abadío Arango, Sergio, 1185.
Aberastury, Marcelo F., 1006.
Aberg Cobo, Martín, 3240.
Abreu, Capistrano de, 4141.
Abreu, Casimiro de, 4414.
Abreu, D. Frois, 2312.
Abreu, Modesto de, 4295.
Abreu, Zequinha, 4677.
Abril, Xavier, 4108a.
Acarette du Biscay, 2920.
Accioli, João, 4270.
Acevedo, Eduardo, 3365.
Acevedo Díaz, Eduardo, 3101.
Acevedo Laborde, René, 4515.
Acevedo Latorre, Eduardo, 2988.
Ackermann, Fritz, 4109.
Acosta, Jorge R., 257.
Acosta Solís, M., 2208, 2294.
Acquarone, Francisco, 4395.
Actis, Francisco C., 2874.
Acuña, Alfredo, 4483.
Adame, Enrique Bautista, 2508.
Adames, George E., 1750, 1751.
Adrián-LaRosa, Mariano, 4523.
Adrogué, Carlos A., 4446.
Adúriz, J., 4986.
Aftalión, Enrique R., 4963.
Aguayo, Alberto de, 4976.
Aguayo, Jorge, 4594, 4595.
Agüero, Luis Eduardo, 4582.
Aguiar, R. José, 3482.
Aguilar, Francisco de, 2699.
Aguilar, Juan María, 2744.
Aguilar Almeida, Fernando Leopoldo, 4472.
Aguilar Revoredo, J. F., 2209.
Aguilera, Francisco, 3835.
Aguilera, Miguel, 3309.
Aguilera Malta, Demetrio, 3914.
Aguirre, Augustín, 4560.
Aguirre, Juan Bautista de, 3763.
Aguirre, Nataniel, 3291.
Aguirre, Sergio, 3184.
Aguirre González, Juan Manuel, 958.
Aguirre Humeres, Alfonso, 3299.
Aitken, W. Ernest, 2989.
Álamo, Antonio, 3360.
Alanís Patiño, Emilio, 1038, 3723.
Alarco, Luis Felipe, 4922, 5003.
Alarcón M., Adolfo, 959.
Alas, Ciriaco de Jesús, 4705.
Alayza y Paz Soldán, Luis, 105, 3329.
Alba, Pedro de, 3134, 4027.
Albán Mestanza, Ernesto, 1485.
Alberts, H. W., 1589, 2134.
Albornoz (h.), Alejandro, 1.
Albornoz, Víctor M., 3320.
Albuquerque, Leda Maria, 4222.

Alcívar Castillo, Gonzalo, 1579.
Aldao, Martín, 3915, 3952.
Aldunate, Arturo, 4015a.
Alegría, Ciro, 3953, 3970.
Alegría, Fernando, 3842, 3916.
Alekseyev, V., 3554a.
Alemán Bolaños, Gustavo, 3917.
Alemar, Luis E., 2745.
Alencar, José de, 4223–4225.
Alencar, Mario de, 4279.
Alencar, Meton de, 1776.
Alessandri Rodríguez, Arturo, 4513.
Alessio Robles, Vito, 2746, 2747.
Alexander, J. L., 2335.
Alfarc, Ricardo Joaquín, 3538.
Alfaro Siqueiros, David, 770, 820.
Alfau, Antonio Eugenio, 2748.
Alfau de Solalinde, Jesusa, 3777.
Allen, Devere, 106, 3683.
Allen, John Houghton, 4096.
Allú Fernández, Ricardo, 4553.
Almada, Francisco R., 2, 2749, 3020.
Almazán Rodríguez, Ángel, 1315.
Almeida, A. Tavares de, 1605.
Almeida, Aluísio de, 3388.
Almeida, Fernando Flávio Marques de, 2313.
Almeida, Guilherme de, 4351, 4403.
Almeida, Horácio de, 900.
Almeida, Lucia Machado de, 4396.
Almeida, Moacir de, 4271.
Almeida, Pádua de, 4271.
Almeida, Renato, 1994, 1995.
Almeida, Rômulo de, 1606.
Almeyda, Aniceto, 2958, 3805.
Alonso, Amado, 5024.
Alonso, Antonio, 3949.
Alonso, José, 1316.
Alphonsus, João, 4226.
Alsina, Hugo, 4447.
Alsina, Ramón M., 4435.
Alsina Atienza, Dalmiro A., 4503.
Altamirano, Ignacio M., 3954, 4782.
Altmeyer, A. J., 3571.
Altolaguirre, Manuel, 838.
Alvarado Sánchez, José, 4444.
Alvarenga, Manoel Ignácio da Silva, 4272.
Alvarenga, Oneyda, 1996, 4751.
Álvarez, Alejandro, 4580.
Álvarez, José, 550.
Álvarez, Juan, 3220, 3562.
Álvarez, Juan C., 4485.
Álvarez, Miguel Ángel, 3217.
Álvarez Álvarez, Manuel, 2460.
Álvarez Basurto, Herminio, 2509.
Álvarez González, H. (Pedro J. Vargas A.), 1441.
Álvarez Lejarza, Emilio, 390.
Álvarez López, Enrique, 2635.
Álvarez Rubiano, P., 3135.
Álvarez Urquieta, Luiz, 685.
Álvarez Vázquez de Prada, Enrique, 1442.
Alves, Amil, 4273.

Alves, António de Castro, 4274.
Alves, José, 2303.
Alzamora Valdez, Mario, 4949.
Alzate, José Antonio de, 3764.
Amadeo, Octavio R., 2619a.
Amadeo, Santos P., 2385.
Amado, Jorge, 4227.
Amador, Armando C., 3525.
Amaral, F. Pompeu do, 1706.
Amaral, Tarsila do, 4305.
Amarilla Fretes, Eduardo, 3323.
Americano, Odin S. do Brasil, 4532.
Amézquita Borja, Francisco, 4707, 4783.
Amorim, Enrique, 3971.
Amunátegui Lecaros, Miguel Luis, 2461.
Amunátegui R., Miguel Luis, 107.
Amunátegui Solar, Domingo, 2210, 2592, 3090.
Anaya, Laureano O., 1317.
Anderson, Edgar D., 196, 231.
Andia, Teófilo, 2211.
Andicoechea, José A., 1406.
Andrade, Almir de, 2424.
Andrade, Carlos Drummond de, 4281, 4364.
Andrade, César D., 1486.
Andrade, Flávio Goulart de, 4324, 4325.
Andrade, Gilberto Osório de, 4129.
Andrade, João Pedro de, 4130–4133.
Andrade, Líbero Rangel de, 4369.
Andrade, Manuel, 4427, 4562, 4563.
Andrade, Mário de, 4157, 4752, 4877.
Andrade, Olegario V., 3986.
Andrade, Oswald de, 4228.
Andrade, Rodrigo Melo Franco de, 860–864.
Andrade, Serrano de, 4458.
Andrade, Theophilo de, 1665.
Andrade, Víctor, 3605, 3621.
Andrade Coello, Alejandro, 3778.
Andrade y Cordero, César, 4100.
Andrea, Miguel de, 2386.
Andreozzi, Manuel, 2387, 2921.
Andrews, Edward Wyllys, 285.
Anet, Claude, 4300.
Angarita R., Roberto, 1180.
Angelelli, Victorio, 1318.
Angulo, Juan B., 4556.
Angulo A., José, 1878, 1879.
Angulo Iñíguez, Diego, 686.
Angulo y Pérez, Andrés, 3185.
Annunzio, Gabriele d', 4301.
Anquín, Nimio de, 4977.
Anselmo, Manuel, 4134.
Antezana Paz, Franklin, 1415, 1416, 1496.
Antolínez, Gilberto, 538, 539, 3007.
Antonioletti, Mario, 960, 1443, 1444.
Antunes, Dioclécio de Paranhos, 901, 3420.
Antúnez Echegaray, Francisco, 2047.
Aparicio, Francisco de, 450.
Apenes, Ola, 258.
Apocalipse, Geraldo G. M., 1707.
Aquino, Ivo d', 1777.
Arámburu, Marcelo G., 1060.
Arango, Daniel, 4028.
Arango, Rodolfo, 1276.
Arango Ferrer, J., 4029.
Aranha, Graça, 4229, 4416.
Aranha, Oswaldo, 3483.
Araujo, Alfonso, 1162.
Araujo, Juan, 2048.
Araujo, Oscar Egídio de, 1609, 1684, 1685.
Arbo, Higinio, 3325.
Arboleda, José Rafael, 497.
Arca Parró, Alberto, 1502, 1503.
Arce, Alberto G., 4575.
Arce, F. A., 3091.
Arce, Henrique J., 2593.
Arce, Magda, 3843, 4596.
Arce y Valladares, Manuel José, 3987.
Arcila Vélez, Graciliano, 587.
Arciniegas, Germán, 2636.
Ardévol, José, 4697, 4769.
Ardissone, Romualdo, 2015.
Arduz Eguía, Gastón, 3754.
Arenas Betancur, Rodrigo, 671.
Arenas Fraga, Abelardo, 3222.
Aretz-Thiele, Isabel, 4670.
Arévalo Martínez, Rafael, 2595.
Argañaras, Héctor D., 2922.
Argentina:
 Academia Nacional de Bellas Artes, 687–689.
 Academia Nacional de la Historia, 3340.
 Administración General de Vialidad Nacional, 1314.
 Banco Central de la República Argentina, 1321.
   Oficina de Investigaciones Económicas, 1407.
 Banco de la Nación Argentina, 1322, 1396.
 Biblioteca del Congreso de la Nación, 4597.
 Biblioteca Nacional, 644.
 Buenos Aires (ciudad). Jockey Club. Biblioteca, 4599.
 Buenos Aires (prov.), 1328.
   Departamento del Trabajo, 3588.
   Ministerio de Gobierno, 1329.
 Cámara de Diputados. Comisión Investigadora de Actividades Antiargentinas, 3531.
 Catamarca (prov.). Gobernador, 2391.
 Comisión Nacional de Museos y Monumentos Históricos, 3235.
 Comité Argentino de Bibliotecarios de Instituciones Científicas y Técnicas, 4598.
 Contaduría General de la Nación, 1336.
 Córdoba (prov.). Dirección General de Bibliotecas, 4600.
   Gobernador, 2392.
 Corporación Argentina de Productores de Carnes, 1337.
 Departamento Nacional del Trabajo, 1340, 1341.
   División de Estadística, 3576.
 Dirección General de Ferrocarriles, 1343.
 Dirección General de Navegación y Puertos, 1344.
 Dirección General del Impuesto a los Réditos, 1345.
 Federación Argentina de Cooperativas de Consumo, 1349.
 Instituto Agrario Argentino, 1373.
 Instituto de Estudios Económicos del Transporte, 1374.

Instituto de Estudios de Filosofía del Derecho, 4435.
Instituto Geográfico **Militar, 2171.**
Instituto Movilizador de Inversiones Bancarias, Buenos Aires, 1375.
Junta Reguladora de Granos, 1376.
Mendoza (prov.). Gobernador. 2402.
Ministerio de Economía, Obras Públicas y Riego, 1382.
Ministerio de Agricultura, 13, 1562.
Ministerio de Hacienda, 1383.
Dirección General de Estadística y Censos de la Nación, 1384–1387.
Ministerio de Justicia e Instrucción Pública. Comisión Nacional de Cooperación Intelectual, 17.
Ministerio de Relaciones Exteriores y Culto, 108.
Ministerio del Interior, 2403.
Departmento Nacional del Trabajo. División de Estadística, 3594.
Museo Social Argentino. Escuela de Servicio Social, 4601.
Rosario. Dirección General de Estadística del Municipio, 1398.
Salta (prov.). Gobernador, 2408.
San Juan. Sociedad Franklin Biblioteca Popular, 4647.
Santa Fe (prov.). Gobernador, 2409.
Unión Cívica Radical, 2414.
Universidad de Buenos Aires. Facultad de Filosofía y Letras. Instituto de Sociología, 113.
Universidad Nacional de Córdoba. Biblioteca Mayor, 4.
Centro de Estudios de Filosofía y Humanidades, 4924.
Escuela de Ciencias Económicas, 1029.
Universidad Nacional de Cuyo. Biblioteca, 16.
Instituto de Investigaciones Históricas, 650, 2629, 3283.
Universidad Nacional de La Plata, 188.
Universidad Nacional del Litoral. Biblioteca "Estanislao S. Zeballos," 40.
Facultad de Ciencias Económicas, Comerciales y Políticas, 1412.
Facultad de Ciencias Jurídicas y Sociales. Biblioteca, 4602.
Instituto de Investigaciones Jurídico-Políticas, 2415.
Argerich, Guillermo, 1554.
Argos (pseud.), 690.
Arias, Juan de Dios, 3041.
Arias F., José Abdiel, 1110.
Arias Mejía, Gerardo, 4589.
Arias Robledo, Eduardo, 4589.
Aristóteles, 4974, 4975.
Ariza, Gustavo, 692.
Arjona, Doris King, 3765.
Armellada, Cesáreo de, 540.
Armendaris, Luis A., 2212.
Armijo, Leoncio, 1039.
Armitage, João, 3421.
Armour Research Foundation, Chicago, 1320.
Armstrong, Margaret, 4302.
Arocha, Manuel, 3042.

Arouet, Jean François Marie. See Voltaire.
Arrais, Monte, 2425–2427, 2457.
Arráiz, Antonio, 3918.
Arrazola, Roberto, 3988.
Arrendondo, Alberto, 1129, 1130.
Arriagada H., Carlos, 1445.
Arrieta, Rafael Alberto, 4008.
Arrom, José Juan, 3807, 3808.
Arruda, Joy, 1778.
Arrús, Oscar F., 1504.
Artigas Soriano, Rosa, 1446.
Artiles, Jenaro, 2750.
Ascone, Vicente, 4874.
Aslakson, Carl I., 2213.
Asociación de Agrimensores del Uruguay, 4570.
Asociación Folklórica Argentina, 1833.
Asociación Nacional de Hacendados de Cuba, 3187.
Astorquiza, Eliodoro, 3961.
Astorquiza Sazzo, Juan, 3300.
Astrada, Carlos, 4950.
Athayde, Austregesilo de [A. A.], 4128.
Aubert de la Rue, 2092.
Augusto, José, 1611, 1612.
Auler, Guilherme, 4135a.
Aurélio, Marco, 4303.
Auza Arce, Carlos, 510.
Avellaneda, Jacinto, 2214.
Avellar, Pedro de Alcántara, 4551.
Avellar Marques, J. Q. de, 1588.
Ávila, Bastos de, 451a.
Ávila, Federico, 109.
Ávila, J. Bastos d', 588, 589.
Avila, Jefferson, 922.
Ayala, Francisco, 4994.
Ayarragaray, Carlos Alberto, 4448.
Ayestarán, Lauro, 4821.
Aylwin Azocar, Patricio, 4468.
Ayrosa, Plínio, 477, 478.
Azara, Félix de, 2923, 2924.
Azarola Gil, Luis Enrique, 2546.
Azcárate, Patricio de, 4974.
Azevedo, Aldo M. de, 1671.
Azevedo, Aluízio, 4230–4233.
Azevedo, Alvares de, 4275.
Azevedo, Fernando de, 109a, 847, 1779.
Azevedo, Francisco José de, 4603.
Azevedo, Luiz Heitor Corrêa de. See Corrêa de Azevedo, Luiz Heitor.
Azevedo, Raúl de, 1752.
Azevedo, Victor de, 3389.
Aznárez, Julio Gregorio, 1529.

B

Bach, Federico, 1079.
Backheuser, Everardo, 1780.
Badel, Dimas, 2102.
Baeza Flores, Alberto, 4030.
Báguena Visconti, Enrique, 1447.
Bahr, Carlos, 1781.
Baldessarini, Francisco de Paula, 4533.
Baldus, Herbert, 479, 507.
Baldwin, Faith, 4304.
Baldwin, Leland Dewitt, 2597.
Ballagas, Emilio, 3989.
Ballesteros Gaibrois, Manuel, 2638.

Ballivián C., René, 1417, 1418.
Balzac, Honoré de, 4305.
Bancroft, Huldah, 621.
Banda C., Francisco, 2215.
Bandeira, Manuel, 4118, 4276.
Banfi, José, 5019.
Bangoa Lecanda, J. M., 3752.
Barahona López, Ernesto, 2523.
Barajas, Manuel, 4784, 4785, 4878.
Barata, Antero Barradas, 4378.
Barata, Mário, 1968.
Barata, Rui Guilherme, 4277.
Baratta, Augusto, 286.
Baratta, María de, 4706.
Barbieri, Honorio, 4648.
Barbosa, Almiro Rolmes, 4234, 4235.
Barbosa, Enrique, 413.
Barbosa, Francisco de Assis, 4136.
Barbosa, M. A. Caldas, 1782.
Barbosa, Octavio, 2304, 2314.
Barboza, Enrique, 4922a.
Barcia Trelles, Camilo, 3545.
Barcos, Julio R., 961.
Baring, Maurice, 4306.
Barletta, Leónidas, 3919.
Barlow, R. H., 231–233, 2685, 2703.
Barlow, Samuel L. M., 4766.
Barnes, Nancy, 3154.
Barnoya Gálvez, Francisco, 3021.
Baron, Maurice, 4662.
Barón Castro, Rodolfo, 2751.
Barra, Luis L. de la, 2752.
Barrau, José, 1323.
Barreda Laos, Felipe, 2639.
Barreiro, José P., 4885.
Barrenechea, Julio, 4101.
Barrera Graf, Jorge, 4564.
Barrera Vásquez, Alfredo, 318, 377, 1943.
Barres, Francisco, 1324.
Barreto, Arnaldo Oliveira, 4398–4402.
Barreto, Castro, 1699, 1700.
Barreto, Ceição de Barros, 4753.
Barreto, Emilio G., 1518.
Barreto, Lima, 4236.
Barrett, Rafael, 3955.
Barrientos R., Juvenal, 610, 611.
Barriga Alarcón, Julio, 3043.
Barro y Segura, Antonio, 1131.
Barros, Jaime de, 3464, 3526, 3527, 4137.
Barros, Richomer, 1614.
Barros Borgoño, Luis, 3092.
Barros Hurtado, César, 2388.
Barroso, Gustavo, 4118, 4237.
Barrozo Netto, Joaquim Antônio, 4842, 4843.
Bartholomeu, Hermes, 1783, 1784.
Basabe Castellanos, Carlos, 1531.
Basadre, Jorge, 110, 2640, 3330, 3331, 4604.
Basch, Samuel, 3155.
Bassewitz, Maria Pavão V., 1785.
Bastida R., Luis, 1568.
Bastide, Roger, 1786, 4138.
Bastos, A. M., 1753.
Batini, Tito, 4238.
Baudelaire, Charles, 4307.
Baudin, Louis, 551, 2968.
Baudizzone, Luis M., 4810.
Bay Sevilla, Luis, 691.
Bayle, Constantino, 2641, 2754, 3830.

Bazán, Armando, 3920, 3975.
Bazil, Osvaldo, 4031.
Bazzano, Oreste G., 4951.
Beals, Carleton, 111, 112.
Beals, Ralph L., 347, 348, 351–353, 1872.
Becker, Henry F., 1096.
Beeche Cañas, L., 612.
Beesley, Claude A., 1834.
Behrendt, Richard F., 5, 962–964, 984, 2598.
Belasco, Lionel, 4662.
Belaúnde, C. H., 1555.
Bellani Nazeri, Rodolfo, 1835.
Bellegarde, Dantès, 965, 3022.
Bello, Andrés, 3845.
Bello, José Luis, 692.
Belmont Arias, Jorge, 1422.
Belmonte, 3390.
Belo, L. de Oliveira, 3391.
Beltrán, Oscar R., 3223.
Beltrán, P. P., 1287.
Beltroy, Manuel, 3809.
Belzoni, Guido C., 966.
Bemis, Samuel Flagg, 3518.
Benisovich, Michel, 866.
Benítez, Justo Pastor, 3324.
Benítez Delorme, Carlos, 2043.
Benítez Gámez, Santos, 1080.
Bennett, Wendell C., 197, 427.
Bens Arrarte, José M., 2850.
Bentenmüller, Gustavo Linhares, 1615.
Benvenuto, Ofelia M. B. de, 3779.
Berçaitz, Miguel Ángel, 4486.
Bergamín, José, 839.
Bergeiro, José M., 2295.
Bergson, Henri, 5004, 5005.
Berlin, Heinrich, 235, 339a, 2704.
Bermejo, Jaime, 1389.
Bermejo, Manuel M., 4786.
Bermúdez Plata, Cristóbal, 2682.
Bernaqui Jaureguy, Carlos Alberto, 4525.
Bernárdez, Francisco Luis, 4091.
Bernaschina G., Mario, 2462, 2463.
Bernstein, Harry, 3465, 3539.
Berrios, R. H. A., 1284.
Berro, Román, 747.
Berro García, A., 2016.
Bertoméo, Carlos A., 3921.
Bertorelli C., Francisco José, 4592.
Besio, Alfredo B., 5019.
Besio Moreno, E., 2172, 3224.
Besouchet, Lídia, 3422.
Besson, Juan, 2599.
Betancourt, Félix, 2374.
Bevilaqua, Clovis, 3370.
Beyer, Hermann, 319–321.
Beyle, Henri. See Stendhal.
Bezerra, Alcides, 3392.
Bianco, Breno Alencar, 4385, 4386.
Bickley, James G., 3837.
Bidwell, Percy W., 967.
Bielsa, Rafael, 2389.
Bietti, Oscar, 4032, 4033.
Bilbao, Jorge, 3225.
Bilbao, Manuel, 3225.
Biloni, José Santos, 2173.
Binns, Harold Howard, 4110.
Bird, Junius B., 410.
Biró de Stern, Ana, 1927.

Bittencourt, H. V. de C., 1754.
Blaisten, Raúl J., 1325.
Blanco, Andrés Eloy, 3990.
Blanco, Julio Enrique, 3484.
Blanco Fombona, Rufino, 3044, 3136.
Blanco Villalta, J. G., 3780.
Blasco Ibáñez, Vicente, 4344.
Blasques L., L., 2049.
Bloch, Pedro, 4139.
Boavista, Paulo T., 923.
Bobadilla, Perfecto H., 2086.
Boecio, Severino, 4976.
Boggs, Ralph Steele, 1836-1838, 1969.
Boggs, Stanley H., 287-289.
Boisson, Cardoso Ofélia, 1787.
Boiteux, Henrique, 3424.
Boiteux, Lucas Alexandre, 3425.
Boliva:
  Archivo General de la Nación, 622.
  Banco Central de Bolivia, 3617.
  Banco Hipotecario Nacional, 1419.
  Banco Mercantil, La Paz, 1420.
  Banco Minero de Bolivia, 1421.
  Biblioteca Nacional, 622.
  Dirección General de Presupuesto, 1428.
  Ministerio de Hacienda. Dirección General de Estadística, 2216, 2217.
  Presidente, 2419.
  Superintendencia de Bancos, 1438.
Bollo, Sarah, 4034.
Bondeli, Elsa de, 4611.
Borah, Woodrow, 2755.
Borba, Jenny Pimentel de, 4239.
Bordoni, Mario G., 4612.
Borga, Ernesto Eduardo, 4432, 4965.
Borges, J. da Cunha, 4335.
Borges, Jorge Luis, 3991.
Bormida, Alfredo, 1326.
Bosch, Beatriz, 2175, 3226.
Bosch, Felipe, 4548.
Bosch, Mariano G., 3781.
Bose, Walter B. L., 1327.
Boudot, Eugenio, 1640.
Boulton, Laura C., 4723.
Bourgeois, Julia F., 236.
Boutroux, Emile, 5007, 5018a.
Bouts, Camille, 4923.
Bouts, Paul, 4923.
Bowers, Claude G., 3093.
Bracaccini, O., 2174.
Braconnay, Claudio María, 3341.
Bradford, Saxtone E., 3532.
Bradley, David H., 1104, 1104a.
Braga, Antonio Pereira, 4459.
Braga, Francisco, 4844.
Braga, João Alfredo Lopes, 4417.
Braga, Ruben, 4140.
Branco, Plinio A., 2586.
Brand, Donald D., 199, 259, 332, 354, 354a, 969.
Brandão, Ambrosio Fernandes, 4141.
Brandão, Antonio Fernandes, 3393.
Brandão, Mário de Pimentel, 3529.
Brannon, Maximiliano P., 1117.
Brasil, Avio, 4552.
Braun Menéndez, Armando, 3301.
Bravo, Carlos, 1839.
Bravo, Mario, 3227.
Bravo Ugarte, José, 3023, 3156.

Bray, Arturo, 3325.
Brazil:
  Acre (território). Departmento Estadual de Geografia e Estatística, 1679.
  Amazonas (estado). Departmento Estadual de Estatística, 2422.
  Interventor Federal, 2423.
  Banco do Brasil, 1613.
  Biblioteca Nacional, 653, 3423.
  Conselho Nacional de Estatística, 1743.
  Conselho Nacional de Geografia, 1744, 2428.
  Coordenação da Mobilização Econômica, 1735.
  Curitiba, 2432.
  Departamento Administrativo do Serviço Público, 2433, 2434.
  Departamento Nacional de Educação. Divisão de Educação Física, 1796.
  Departamento Nacional de Imigração, 1701.
  Departamento Nacional do Café, 1739.
  Escola Livre de Sociologia e Política.
  Escola de Biblioteconomia, 4613.
  Espírito Santo (estado). Interventor Federal, 2435.
  Goiânia. Colégio Santa Clara, 1799.
  Instituto Brasileiro de Geografia e Estatística, 2587.
    Conselho Nacional de Estatística, 1721.
    Conselho Nacional de Geografia, 1730.
  Instituto do Açucar e do Alcool, 1737, 1757.
  Instituto Histórico e Geográphico Brasileiro, 2351.
  Instituto Nacional do Mate, 1731.
  Instituto Nacional do Sal, 1722.
  Maranhão (estado). Interventor Federal, 2441.
  Minas Gerais (estado). Departamento Estadual de Estatística, 1681.
  Ministério da Agricultura. Serviço de Informação Agrícola, 1732, 1734.
  Ministério da Educação e Saúde, 943.
  Ministério da Fazenda. Diretoria de Rendas Aduaneiras, 1723.
    Serviço de Estatística Econômica e Financeira, 1726.
  Ministério das Relações Exteriores, 1616.
    Conselho de Imigração e Colonização, 1746.
  Ministério de Justiça e Negócios Interiores. Imprensa Nacional, 20.
  Ministério do Trabalho, Industria e Comércio. Commissão Técnica de Orientação Sindical, 3630.
    Serviço de Estatística da Previdência e Trabalho, 1733.
  Pará (estado). Interventor Federal, 2443.
  Rio de Janeiro. Bibliotheca Nacional, 4415.
  Rio Grande do Sul (estado), 2450.
  Santa Catarina (estado). Interventoria Federal, 2452.
  São Paulo (cidade). Arquivo Municipal, 645.
    Biblioteca Pública Municipal de São Paulo, 12.

São Paulo (estado). Associação Comercial, 1736.
Conselho Estadual de Bibliotecas e Museus, 4614.
Departamento Estadual de Estatística, 1659-1661, 1720.
Diretoria de Estatística, Indústria e Comércio, 1724, 1725, 1727.
Federação das Indústrias do Estado de São Paulo, 1646.
Instituto Geográfico e Geológico, 2319.
Secretaría da Agricultura, Indústria e Comércio. Departamento da Produção Animal, 1728.
Diretoria de Publicidade Agrícola, 1766.
Secretaria da Fazenda do Estado de São Paulo. Superintendência dos Serviços do Café, 1729.
Sergipe (estado), 2453.
Serviço do Patrimônio Histórico e Artístico Nacional, 889.
Sociedade Brasileira de Estatística, 1743.
Superintendência dos Serviços do Café, 1666, 1669.
Uruguaiana. Prefeitura Municipal, 2455.
Vitória. Prefeitura Municipal, 2459.
Brazilian Government Trade Information Bureau, 1738.
Brenner, Anita, 115.
Briceño Iragorry, Mario, 3012, 3045.
Brightman, Edgar Sheffield, 4889, 4890.
Brineman, Jr., John H., 2059, 2107.
Brito y Mederos, Lincoln E., 4516.
Broca, Brito, 2336, 4142-4144.
Brodkorb, Pierce, 2050.
Broggi, Jorge A., 2218-2223.
Bromley, Juan, 2878.
Brondo Whitt, E., 1882, 1913.
Brophy, John, 4308.
Brown Castillo, Gerardo, 3188.
Bruet, Edmond, 2092.
Brüggen, Juan, 2224, 2225.
Brugger, Ilse, 5026.
Bryan, C. R., 970.
Buceta Basigalup, Juan Carlos, 748, 3366.
Bucich Escobar, Ismael, 3228.
Bueno, Zei, 1642.
Buentello, Humberto, 1952.
Buero, Juan Antonio, 2226.
Buitrón, Juan B., 4787.
Bull, Nina, 3974.
Bullón Noroña, Gustavo, 2227.
Bulnes Aldunate, Luis, 1451.
Bundy, P. A., 2103.
Bunge, Alejandro Ernesto, 1330.
Bunster, Enrique, 3094.
Buonocore, Domingo, 4615.
Burbano, Jaime, 1580.
Burckhardt, Jacob, 5008.
Burden, W. A. M., 116.
Burgaleta, Vicente, 1423.
Burgin, Miron, 22.
Burgoa, Ignacio, 4478.
Burgos, Joaquín, 1105.
Burlá, Eliezer, 4240.
Busaniche, José Luis, 3230.
Busch, W., 4403.
Buschiazzo, Mario J., 693, 706, 749.
Bustamante, Manuel E., 4811.
Busto, Ángel del, 4873.
Bustos Fierro, Raúl, 4433, 4947.
Bustos Pérez, Vicente, 2228.
Butler, Hugh Alfred, 3519, 3521.
Butler, Ruth Lapham, 3394.
Butler, Samuel, 4309.
Buvelot, Louis-Auguste, 902.
Buzaid, Alfredo, 4460.
Buzó Gomes, Sinforiano, 3992.

C

Cabal, Juan, 2756.
Caballero Calderón, Eduardo, 2027, 3846.
Caballero F., Policarpo, 4812.
Cabeza de Vaca, 355.
Cabrera la Rosa, Augusto, 2024.
Cabrera Malo, R., 3752.
Cabrices, Fernando, 3782.
Cáceres, Julián R., 3485.
Cáceres Freyre, Julián B., 1970.
Cadilla de Martínez, María, 4829.
Cady, John Frank, 3229.
Caetano, Marcelo, 3371.
Caillet-Bois, Horacio, 773.
Caillet-Bois, Teodoro, 462.
Cajado, Otávio Mendes, 4377.
Calabrese Leonetti, Rogelio, 4616, 4649.
Calasans, José, 1939.
Calcagno, Alfredo D., 2176, 2177.
Caldcleugh, Alexander, 3230.
Calderón Quijano, José Antonio, 2757.
Caldwell, R. G., 3466.
Callado, A. C., 926.
Calmon, Pedro, 3372, 3426, 4145, 4348.
Calzadilla Valdez, Fernando, 1302.
Camacho, José María, 472, 2025.
Camacho, Ramiro, 2758.
Camacho Montoya, Guillermo, 3046.
Camargo Gámez, Eduardo, 1181.
Campanella, Andrés, 2017.
Campos, Eduardo, 4241.
Campos, Ipê de, 4111.
Campos, Luis Felipe Gonzaga de, 2316.
Campos, Mauricio M., 694.
Canal Feijóo, Bernardo, 1971.
Canals Frau, Salvador, 398, 451, 463, 464.
Candela, P. B., 600.
Cané, Miguel, 3956.
Caneda y Acosta, Cecilio Abelardo, 4473.
Cánepa, Luis, 3231.
Cannon, Mary M., 3575.
Canoutas, Seraphim G., 2642.
Canter, Juan, 3137.
Cantú, A., 4845.
Canudas y Orezza, Luis Felipe, 4479.
Caparroso, Carlos Arturo, 3783.
Capdevila, Arturo, 3993.
Capriles Rico, Remberto, 3754.
Caraballo, Isa, 4103.
Caracas, Raúl de, 1788.
Carbajales, Eduardo, 1331.
Carbia, Rómulo D., 2601.
Carbone, M., 4434.
Carbonell, Diego, 4035.
Cárcano, Ramón J., 3232.

Cardenal Argüello, Salvador, 1883.
Cárdenas, Bernardino de, 2925.
Cárdenas, Fortunato E., 2229.
Cárdenas C., Luis A., 1206.
Cardoso, Jaime, 4146.
Cardoso, Joaquim, 867.
Cardoso, Lúcio, 4242, 4316.
Cardozo, Antonio M., 2471.
Carías Reyes, Marcos, 4036.
Carilla, Emilio, 3784, 4037.
Carlson, Fred A., 2026.
Carmo, J. A. Pinto do, 3373.
Carnegie Endowment for International Peace. Division of International Law, 3486.
Carnegie Institution of Washington, 223.
Carneiro, Edison, 1972, 4382.
Carneiro Leão, A., 117.
Carniol, S. Enrique, 4504.
Caro, Miguel Antonio, 1164, 3847.
Carou, M. A., 3759.
Carpeaux, Otto Maria, 4147.
Carpio Valdés, Roberto, 4872.
Carral Tolosa, Esther W. de, 2296.
Carranza Pérez, R., 1332.
Carrasco, Jacinto, 3233.
Carreño, Alberto María, 2759–2761.
Carreño, Ángel, 1867, 2969.
Carrera Andrade, Jorge, 2230, 4038, 4039.
Carrillo, Alfonso, 1093.
Carrillo, Julián, 4788.
Carrizo, Juan Alfonso, 1997, 2926.
Carrizo Valdés, Jesús María, 2011.
Carrocera, Cayetano de, 3008.
Carroll, Charles D., 1928.
Carson, James S., 972.
Carter, J. E. L., 409.
Carulla, Juan E., 2390.
Carvalhal, José Francisco, 1789.
Carvalho, Beni, 4534.
Carvalho, Daniel de, 1617.
Carvalho, João Luiz, 1618.
Carvalho, José Zacarias de Sá, 1790.
Carvalho, Maria Conceição Vicente de, 2337.
Carvalho, Mário Orlando de, 1619.
Carvalho, P. P. de, 1755.
Carvalho, Ronald de, 4147a.
Casal, Manuel Ayres de, 3395.
Casanova, Eduardo, 405.
Casanova Vicuña, Juan, 4862.
Casanovas, Domingo, 3848.
Casanovas P., Domingo, 4966, 5027.
Cascudo, Luiz da Câmara, 1840, 1873, 1988.
Cash, M. C., 672, 774.
Casiello, Francisco, 3589.
Caso, Alfonso, 237, 238.
Caso, Antonio, 4891, 4988.
Cassirer, Ernst, 4989.
Castañeda, Daniel, 1884, 4040.
Castañeda, Jorge Eugenio, 4568.
Castellanos, Alfredo, 582.
Castellanos, J. Humberto R., 2762, 4780.
Castilho, A. F. de, 4311.
Castilho, Antonio Feliciano de, 4390.
Castillero R., Ernesto J., 2593, 4807.
Castillo, Antonio del, 4557.
Castillo, Ignacio B. del, 2763.
Castillo de Luca, Antonio, 2010.

Castillo Jácome, Julio, 193.
Castillo V., Julio, 2231.
Castillo Vélez, Othón, 1490.
Castillo y Piña, José, 2051.
Castro, Baltazar, 3922.
Castro, Christovam Leite de—See Leite de Castro, Cristovam.
Castro, Daví J. de, 4345.
Castro, Ernesto L., 3923.
Castro, Luis Gabriel, 2093.
Castro, Martha de, 696, 697.
Castro, Moacir Werneck de, 4359.
Castro, Sergio de, 4671.
Castro e Silva, Egydio de, 4754.
Castro Leal, Antonio, 3785, 4041.
Castro y Tosi, Norberto de, 2764.
Castroverde, Salvador W. de, 4474.
Catalano, Luciano R., 1333.
Catharino, José Martins, 1686.
Cather, Willa, 4310.
Caturla Brú, Victoria, 3189.
Cavalcanti, Carlos de Lima, 1620.
Cavalcanti, Povina, 4148.
Cavalcanti, Themistocles Brandão, 4488.
Cavalheiro, Edgard, 4234, 4235, 4275, 4276.
Cavero-Egusquiza, Ricardo, 2232.
Cearense, Catulo da Paixão, 4278, 4279.
Cebreiro Blanco, Luis, 2643.
Ceccatto, G. do N., 1756.
Cediel Ángel, Ernesto, 4514.
Celso, Eugénia, 4332.
Ceniceros, José Ángel, 4441.
Centner, Charles W., 3095.
Centurión, Carlos, 4042.
Cerda Silva, Roberto de la, 356–358.
Cervantes Saavedra, Miguel de, 4311, 4312.
Cervera Andrade, Alejandro, 2602.
Cevallos García, Gabriel, 4777.
Chacón, Gabriel, 537.
Chacón, Lucas Raúl, 1097.
Chacón y Calvo, José María, 1774a, 3190.
Chagas, Paulo Pinheiro, 3427.
Chalmers, Henry, 973.
Chamberlain, Henry, 904.
Chamberlain, Roberto S., 2765.
Chamfort (Sébastien Roch Nicolas), 4313.
Chandler, Charles Lyon, 3374.
Chanetón, Abel, 2644.
Chaparro Ruminot, Leoncio, 1569.
Chapman, Emmanuel, 4925.
Charles, Hubert, 4663.
Chase, Allan, 3533.
Chase, Gilbert, 4730–4733, 4755, 4771.
Chateaubriand, Assis, 928.
Chateaubriand, François René, 4314.
Chaves, Omar Emir, 3546.
Chavez, Arlindo, 1707a.
Chávez, Carlos, 4868, 4869.
Chávez, Cástulo, 1424.
Chávez, Ezequiel A., 2766, 2767, 3786.
Chávez, Tobías, 25.
Chávez González, Rodrigo A., 1929.
Chávez Hayhoe, Arturo, 2768.
Chávez Orozco, Luis, 2769.
Chediak, Antonio J., 4149.
Cheesman, E. E., 1581.
Chevalier, François, 2770.
Chicago Public Library, 26.

Childs, James B., 27.
Chile:
Banco Central de Chile, 1447a, 1448, 1450.
Banco Hipotecario de Chile. Consejo de Administración, 1449.
Biblioteca Nacional, 118.
Caja Autónoma de Amortización de la Deuda Pública, 1452, 1453.
Caja de Crédito Agrario, 1453a.
Caja de Crédito Hipotecario, 1454.
Confederación de la Producción y del Comercio, 1455a.
Corporación de Fomento de la Producción, 1456.
Dirección General de Estadística, 1458, 1459, 1462.
Secretaría General del Censo, 1460.
Ejército. Jefatura de Bandas, 4690.
Instituto de Fomento Minero e Industrial, 1466.
Instituto Geográfico Militar, 2233.
Ministerio de Hacienda, 1468.
Museo de Bellas Artes, 673.
Oficina Meteorológica, 2234.
Partido Socialista, 2465, 2466.
Presidente, 2467.
Senado, 2589.
Sindicato Nacional Vitivinícola, 1577.
Superintendencia de la Casa de Moneda y Especies Valoradas, 1479.
Universidad de Chile. Instituto de Extensión Musical. Departamento de Investigación Folklórica, 4693.
Chilean Nitrate Sales Corporation, 1454a.
Chillida, Luis Alberto, 583.
Chira, Magdaleno C., 2235.
Chiriboga N., Ángel Isaac, 3096.
Chouhy Terra, José L., 3529.
Christie, Christina, 4112.
Christophersen, Ricardo, 1533.
Chueca, Felipe, 3748.
Cichero, Mario Alberto, 4582.
Cidade, F. de Paula, 2338.
Cieza de León, Pedro de, 2970.
Cifuentes S., Alberto, 1455.
Cirerol Sansores, Manuel, 239, 340.
Claremont Colleges, 28.
Clark, J. M., 1582.
Clark, Oscar, 1791.
Clothier, II, William J., 428.
Clozel, José, 1792.
Coaracy, V., 4387.
Cock A., Víctor, 1186.
Cody, Morrill, 3743.
Cofferata, Juan F., 3598.
Coghlan, Eduardo A., 3602.
Coiscou Henríquez, Máximo, 2706.
Colán Secas, Hermógenes, 1945, 1989.
Colbacchini, Antonio, 549.
Collier, Donald, 397, 426.
Colman, Narciso R., 2023.
Colombia:
Academia Colombiana de Historia, 651, 3040, 3308.
Antioquia (depto.). Gobernador, 2468.
Secretaría de Gobierno, 2469.
Archivo Nacional, 628.
Biblioteca Nacional, 4651.
Bogotá. Contraloría Municipal, 1163.
Bolívar (depto.). Secretaría de Gobierno, 2470.
Cartagena. Museo Histórico, 2860.
Contraloría General de la República, 1177, 1182, 2094.
Federación Nacional de Cafeteros, 974.
Instituto Etnológico Nacional, 212.
Medellín. Oficina de Caminos, Catastro y Estadística, 1169.
Ministerio de Fomento. Dirección General de Estadística, 1184.
Ministerio de Gobierno, 2473, 2474.
Ministerio de Minas y Petróleos, 1188.
Ministerio de Relaciones Exteriores. Oficina de Longitudes y Fronteras, 3547.
Museo Arqueológico de Colombia, 198.
Presidente, 2476.
Revisoría Fiscal de Instituciones Oficiales de Crédito, 1178a, 1178b.
Santander (depto.), 2479.
Secretario de Agricultura y Fomento, 1299.
Superintendencia Nacional de Cooperativas, 957.
Tolima (depto.). Gobernador, 2480, 2481.
Universidad del Cauca, 171.
Valle del Cauca (depto.). Secretaría de Agricultura y Fomento, 1300.
Colombo, Carlos J., 4451.
Colombo, Luis, 1334.
Colón, Ramiro L., 2135.
Comas, Juan, 200, 201, 360, 573, 574, 613-615.
Comisión de Homenaje al Dr. Pedro Goyena en el Centenario de su Nacimiento, 3234.
Comité Jurídico Interamericano, 3542.
Comprés Pérez, R., 3471.
Comte, August, 5018b.
Concha, Carlos, 2536.
Conde, Hermínio de Brito, 4417.
Coney, Donald, 120.
Congreso de la Economía de las Provincias de Tarapacá y Antofagasta, Primero, 1472, 1473.
Congreso Panamericano de Carreteras, Cuarto, 1034.
Congresso Pan-Americano da Criança, 1794, 1816.
Conrad, Joseph, 4315.
Consejo Permanente de Asociaciones Americanas de Comercio y Producción, 975, 976, 1335.
Comisión Ejecutiva, 977.
Constanzó, María de las Mercedes, 584.
Contín Aybar, Pedro René, 3994.
Contreras y López de Ayala, Juan, Marqués de Lozoya, 698, 750.
Conway, George Robert Graham, 2711.
Cook, S. F., 2771.
Cooke, C. Wythe, 2044.
Corbató, Hermenegildo, 3810.
Corbazzo, Alberto P., 3236.
Corbett, John M., 436, 438.
Cordero y Torres, Enrique, 3995.
Córdoba, Antonio S. C., 2927.
Córdoba, Juan de, 395.
Córdoba Flores, Cristina, 29.

Córdova, Federico de, 3191, 3192, 3787, 3788.
Córdova, Ramiro de, 4104.
Cornejo, Lino, 4569.
Cornejo Bouroncle, Jorge, 429, 511.
Coronado Aguilar, Manuel, 4475.
Corral, José Isaac, 2118.
Correa, Julio, 3996.
Correa Arango, Iván, 1165.
Correa Ávila, Carlos, 1556.
Corrêa de Azevedo, Luiz Heitor, 1880, 1881, 4758–4760.
Correa Luna, Carlos, 4822.
Correa Vergara, Luis, 1570.
Correia, Jonas, 1795.
Correia Filho, Virgilio, 1643.
Corson, John J., 3724.
Cortázar, Augusto Raúl, 1842, 1973, 1974.
Cortázar, Roberto, 3140, 3310.
Cortés González, J. J., 662.
Cortés Medina, Hernán, 3487.
Cortés Vargas, Carlos, 661.
Cortesão, Jaime, 3379, 3396, 4141.
Corvalán, Stella, 3997.
Cosio, J. B., 1132.
Cosío, Ricardo, 1535.
Cosme, Luiz, 4678.
Costa, Angyone, 859.
Costa, Carlos Duarte da, 4345.
Costa, Didio I. A. da, 3375.
Costa, Fernando, 1621.
Costa, J. Wilson, 1708.
Costa, João Angyone, 122, 455, 480–482.
Costa, Lidio, 4123.
Costa, Odorico, 2430, 2431.
Costa, Renato, 3431.
Costa Filho, Miguel, 1622.
Costa Netto, Benedicto, 4572.
Costa Rica:
  Archivos Nacionales, 629.
  Dirección General de Estadística, 1098–1100.
  Secretaría de Gobernación, 2082.
Council of the Corporation of Foreign Bondholders, 979.
Coutinho, Afrânio, 4356, 4892.
Coutinho, Frederico dos Reis, 4320, 4369.
Coutinho, Gago, 3397.
Couture, Eduardo J., 4481.
Cova, Jesús Antonio, 3098, 4035, 4105.
Covarrubias, Miguel, 261.
Cover, Gilbert Grace, 4593.
Cravioto, Adrián, 3548.
Cravioto González, Joaquín, 3488.
Crawford, D. M. 1223.
Crespo, Eduardo, 1338.
Crist, Raymond E., 2028, 2104.
Cristiá, Pedro J., 1339.
Croce, Benedetto, 4990, 5010.
Croce, Francisco M., 1557.
Crouse, Nellis M., 2772.
Crow, John A., 3924.
Cruz, Manuel, 483, 484.
Cruz, Salviano, 1688.
Cruz-Coke, Eduardo, 1457.
Cuadra, Pablo Antonio, 1924.
Cuadros, Alfredo, 1426.
Cuadros E., Manuel E., 430.

Cuarto Congreso Panamericano de Carreteras, 1034.
Cuba:
  Archivo Nacional, 630, 631, 2687, 3186.
  Colegio Nacional de Maestros Agrícolas, 1275.
  Comisión Cubana de Cooperación Intelectual, 119.
  Dirección General del Censo, 1134.
  Habana. Biblioteca Municipal, 4617.
  Junta de Economía de Guerra, 1138.
  Ministerio de Agricultura, 1280.
  Oriente (prov.), 2488.
  Senado. Comisión de Derecho Político y Constitucional, 2490.
  Sociedad Económica de Amigos del País de la Habana, 1144.
  Universidad de la Habana, 1145, 2844.
Cuba Torres, Sergio, 4546.
Cuervo, Luis Augusto, 2991, 2992, 3140.
Cuevas, Mariano, 2773.
Cugat, Xavier, 4664.
Culbertson, Ely, 3489.
Cúneo, Dardo, 3237.
Cunha, Hamilton Pinheiro da, 4461.
Cunha, Lourenço Pereira da, 1642.
Cúrio, Nestor Wanderley, 869.

D

Dahlberg, A. C., 1252, 1266–1268.
D'Alessandro, Alexandre, 3376.
Dana Montaño, Salvador M., 3238.
Danieri, Erly, 3849.
Dantas, Pedro, 4340.
Darcy, Thomas F., 4665.
D'Ascoli, Carlos A., 1207.
Daus, Federico A., 2178.
Davalillo, Clemente, 1427.
Davidovich, Elias, 4338.
Dávila, Vicente, 2774.
Dávila, Víctor M., 512.
Dávila Garibi, J. Ignacio, 1953.
Dávila Garibi, José Ignacio, 2713, 2714.
Davis, Harold E., 2511.
Davis, Jr., Thomas B., 3514.
Dé Carli, Gileno, 1644, 1645.
De la Roche, Mazo, 4365.
De María, Isidoro, 3342.
Deasy, George F. 2179, 2180.
DeBaylé, León, 1107.
Debien, G., 2688, 2775.
Deevey, Jr., Edward S., 224.
Defoe, Daniel, 4316.
Dekobra, Maurice, 4317.
Delanglez, Jean, 2776–2778.
Delboy, Emilio, 1930.
Delgadillo, Luis A., 4713, 4805.
Delgado, Luis Humberto, 3013.
Delgado Barrenechea, José C., 2236.
Delgado Fernández, Gregorio, 3789.
Delgado Flores, Carmen, 431.
Delgado Vivanco, Edmundo, 1998.
Delle Piane, A. L., 5011.
Denison, Jr., John H., 303.
Derisi, Octavio N., 5028.
Descartes, S. L., 1157.
Despontin, Luis A., 3584.

Despradel y Batista, Guido, 3212.
Deutschman, Z., 2045.
Dewey, L. H., 980.
Díaz, Adolfo M., 3100.
Díaz, Antonio, 3101.
Díaz, César, 3343.
Díaz, Juvenal A., 2297.
Díaz, Severo, 2052.
Díaz A., Julio, 3292.
Díaz-Bolio, José, 396.
Díaz de León, Francisco, 751, 752.
Díaz del Castillo, Bernal, 2779.
Díaz Doin, Guillermo, 125, 2394.
Díaz Durán, José Constantino, 2646, 2780.
Díaz Morales, Ignacio, 775.
Díaz-Pacheco, Santiago, 2136, 2137.
Díaz Rodríguez, Justo, 1289, 1290.
Díaz Salas, Juan, 3758.
Díaz-Solís, Gustavo, 3925.
Dickens, Charles, 4318.
Dieseldorff, E. P., 322.
Díez-Canedo, Enrique, 4043.
Diffie, Bailey W., 3534.
Diniz, Júlio, 4243.
Docca, Souza, 4150.
Doeste, Arturo, 4423.
Domingues, Carlos, 4350a.
Domínguez, Manuel Augusto, 2928.
Domínguez, María Alicia, 3998.
Domínguez, Wenceslao N., 3239.
Dominican Republic:
  Archivo General de la Nación, 633.
  Dirección General de Estadística, 1146.
  Sección de Producción y Economía, 1147–1151.
  Registro Público, 1153.
  Santo Domingo (distrito), 2494.
  Secretaría del Tesoro y Comercio, 2125.
Dóndoli, César, 2095.
Donoso, Armando, 3926.
Donovan, M., 5012.
Dorfman, Adolfo, 981, 982, 1346, 1347.
Doria, Irene de Manezes, 4618.
Doria, João, 1914.
Dornas Filho, João, 4151, 4152.
Dorta, Enrique Marco, 699, 700.
Dostoiewsky, F., 4319, 4320.
Dougé, Joubert, 4044.
Draghi Lucero, Juan, 3102–3104.
Drucker, Philip, 262, 263.
Drumond, Carlos, 485.
D'Sola, Otto, 3999.
Du Solier, Wilfrido, 264.
Duarte, José, 4535.
Dubois Júnior, J., 4321.
Dufourcq, Lucila, 1843.
Dujovne, León, 4991.
Dumas, Alexandre, 4321–4323.
Dumas, fils, Alexandre, 4324.
Dumesnil, René, 4325.
Duncan, David D., 2113.
Duncan, Julian S., 3648.
Dunne, Peter Masten, 2853.
Dunstan, Florence Johnson, 3972.
Duplessis, Gustavo, 3850.
Dupont Aguiar, Mario, 1536.
Dupré, Leandro, 4244.
Duprey, Jacques, 3367.

Dupuy, Daniel Hammerly, 2181.
Duque, L., 592.
Duque Gómez, Luis, 414, 415.
Durán, Fernando, 1461.
Durón, Jorge Fidel, 30.
Dussan de Reichel, Alicia, 423.
Dutra, José Soares, 3435.
Dutra, Lia Corrêa, 4245.
Dutton, Bertha P., 290.

E

Eça, Raúl d', 2630.
Echeverría, Ruperto, 1308.
Eckert, Georg, 552.
Ecuador:
  Banco Central del Ecuador, 1487, 1488.
  Caja del Seguro de Empleados Privados y Obreros, 3684.
  Cámara de Comercio de Guayaquil, 1489.
  Contraloría General, 1491.
  Instituto Superior de Pedagógica y Letras de Guayaquil, 167.
  Ministerio de Agricultura, 1584.
  Ministerio de Gobierno, 2496, 2497.
  Ministerio de Hacienda, 1492.
  Ministerio de Previsión Social, 506.
  Partido Socialista, 2590.
  Presidente, 2498.
  Superintendencia de Bancos, 1495.
Edwards, Alberto, 3106.
Edwards Bello, Joaquín, 3927, 3957.
Egas, Eugenio, 3436.
Eguiguren, Luis Antonio, 2237.
Ekholm, Gordon F., 225.
El Salvador:
  Dirección General de Estadística, 1118.
  Federación de Cajas de Crédito, 1119, 1120.
  Ministerio de Hacienda, Crédito Público, Industria y Comercio, 1121.
  Presidente, 2544.
  San Salvador. Alcaldía Municipal, 2545.
Elhueta G., Manuel, 2238.
Elías Ortiz, Sergio, 3311.
Elordi, Guillermo F., 3107.
Encina, Juan de la, 753.
Enciso, Jorge, 265, 701.
Encyclopedia Americana, 126.
Engel, Walter, 818.
Engelbrecht, Richard, 4672.
Englekirk, John, 42.
Ernesto Tornquist & Co., Ltda., 1348.
Erserguer, Enrique V., 3344.
Escala, Víctor Hugo, 4045.
Escalante, Carlos Manuel, 1101.
Escalante, Hildamar, 3812.
Escalante, José Ángel, 473, 553.
Escalona Ramos, Alberto, 240, 323, 702.
Escobar, Abelardo, 1224.
Escobar, Adrián C., 3467.
Escobar M., Gabriel, 531.
Escobar V., Ismael, 2239, 2240.
Espinheira, Ariosto, 4404.
Espinola, Eduardo, 4508.
Espinola Filho, Eduardo, 4462, 4508.
Espinosa, J. Manoel, 3398.
Espinosa, José María, 3142.

Espinosa Pólit, Aurelio, 3763.
Espinosa Saldaña, Antonio, 776.
Esquivel Obregón, Toribio, 3158, 4440.
Esténger, Rafael, 4000.
Estevão, Carlos, 451a.
Estiú, Emilio, 4952.
Estrada, Gonzaga-Duque, 930.
Estrada, José Manuel, 3240.
Estrada Monsalve, Jesús, 3050.
Estrada Paniagua, Felipe, 4001.
Estrázulas, Hugo, 4499.
Etchegoyen, Félix E., 931.

F

Fabela, Isidro, 3468.
Fabra Ribas, A., 984, 985.
Facil, Aníbal D., 2929.
Facio, Rodrigo, 1102.
Fairbanks, João Carlos, 2344.
Falcao Espalter, Mario, 5007.
Fanda, Lorenzo, 934.
Farfán, José M. B., 514–516, 554.
Faria, Maria Adail Philidory de, 4280.
Faro, Melo Noronha e, 4353.
Farver, Marvin, 4893.
Fasolino, Nicolás, 2930, 3108.
Faulkner, O. T., 2114.
Favrot, H. Mortimer, 2781.
Fayt, Carlos S., 2396.
Fazenda, Viera, 870.
Febres Cordero, Tulio, 2884.
Febres-Cordero G., César, 1209.
Febres Cordero G., Julio, 3009, 3010.
Feer, Léon, 4326.
Fein Pastoriza, Delia, 2018.
Fejos, Paul, 517.
Felipe, Luis, 2105.
Feliú Cruz, G, 655, 3109.
Feliú Cruz, René, 624.
Fennell, Thomas A., 2126, 2127.
Fenoglio Preve, Simón, 1350, 1351.
Fergusson, Erna, 2241.
Fern, Leila, 4734, 4735.
Fernandes, Adaucto D'Alencar, 4509.
Fernandes, Casemiro, 4381.
Fernandes, Francisco, 4114.
Fernández, Justino, 703, 704, 778, 779, 822, 825, 826, 830, 831, 833, 2722.
Fernández, Miguel Ángel, 291, 341.
Fernández, Óscar Lorenzo, 4679, 4846–4852.
Fernández, Ramón, 1082.
Fernández Artucio, Hugo, 3535.
Fernández de Castro, José Antonio, 3193, 3766, 4046, 4894.
Fernández de Córdoba, Joaquín, 32.
Fernández del Castillo, Germán, 4441.
Fernández MacGregor, Genaro, 3815, 3852.
Fernández Moreno, César, 4047.
Fernández Navarrete, Pedro, 4985.
Fernández Saldaña, José M., 3343.
Fernández Usubillaga, Jorge, 2298.
Fernandini de Álvarez-Calderón, Anita, 3490.
Ferrão, V. A. Argolo, 4926.
Ferrari Rueda, Rodolfo de, 2604.
Ferrario, Benigno, 547.
Ferrater Mora, José, 5022.
Ferreira, Barros, 4405.

Ferrer, Juan M., 1352.
Ferrero, Rómulo A., 1512, 1513.
Ferreyra, Miguel A., 1353.
Festugier, A. J., 4977.
Fiedler, Arkady, 4327.
Fiedler, Reginald H., 2242.
Figueira, Gastón, 4048–4050, 4153.
Figueiredo, Fidelino de, 4154.
Figueiredo, Gastão de, 1799.
Figueiredo, Guilherme, 4155, 4246.
Figueiredo, Lima, 127, 1680.
Figueroa, Marco, 3051.
Figueroa, Rosa E., 4814.
Figuerola, José, 1354.
Finlayson, Clarence, 3491, 4051, 4953, 4954.
Finot, Enrique, 3853.
First National and Pan American Press Congress, 128.
Fischer, Louis, 4328.
Fischlowitz, Estanislau, 129, 1689, 1690.
Fisher, Kurt A., 312.
Fisher, Reginald, 717.
Fitz-Gerald, John D., 3832.
Flanagan, John T., 3868.
Fleitas, Odin E., 3241.
Fleury, Renato Seneca, 4406.
Fligelman, Belle, 3733.
Flores, Ángel, 3972.
Flores, Sabino, 4789.
Flores, Teodoro, 2053.
Flores Araoz, José, 705.
Flores Zavala, Leopoldo, 1083.
Flórez de Ocariz, Juan, 626, 2994.
Fogelquist, Donald F., 1885.
Foncillas Andreu, Gabriel, 3052.
Fonseca, Julio, 4864.
Fonseca, Persiano da, 4303, 4313, 4366.
Fonseca, Tito Prates da, 4489.
Fonseca Muñoz, Rodolfo, 659, 3121.
Font Ezcurra, Ricardo, 3242, 3243, 3368.
Fontecilla Riquelme, Rafael, 4469.
Forero, Manuel José, 4619.
Fornaciari, Mario, 1355.
Fornaguera, M., 592.
Fouillée, Alfredo, 4978, 4979.
Fouquest, Karl, 3399.
Fragueiro, Alfredo, 4927.
Franca, Arí, 2345.
Franca, Leonel, 4928.
France, Anatole, 4329.
Franchelli, R. A., 1558.
Franck, Harry A., 2030.
Franco, Afonso Arinos de Melo, 851, 4272.
Franco, Alberto, 1999, 2000, 4620.
Franco, Alejandro, 553.
Franco, Arthur Martins, 3400.
Franco, José Felipe, 3734.
Franco Inojosa, José María, 555.
Francovich, Guillermo, 4895, 4896, 5029.
Frank, Waldo, 130.
Franke, H., 1672.
Franklin, Albert B., 131.
Franklin, Benjamin, 4330.
Fray Junípero (Miguel José Serra), 3989.
Freire, Japi, 4327.
Freire, Omar R., 1537.
Freitas, Bezerra de, 4156.
Freitas, Carlos A., 445.

Freitas, M. A. Teixeira de, 2305.
Freitas, Newton, 486, 1887.
Freitas, Rita de, 1623.
Freitas Júnior, Octávio de, 4157.
Frenguelli, Joaquín, 2182.
Freyre, Gilberto, 4158–4161, 4261, 4897.
Friede, Juan, 498.
Frola, Francisco, 1084.
Frondizi, Risieri, 4898–4900.
Frugoni, Emilio, 3345, 4106.
Fuentes Mares, José, 4967.
Fuenzalida Grandón, Alejandro, 3303.
Fuenzalida Villegas, Humberto, 2243.
Funck-Brentano, Frantz, 4331.
Furlong, Guillermo, 706, 2605, 2931.
Fürnkorn, Dívico Alberto, 1357.
Fusco, Rosário, 4162.

G

Gabaldon Márquez, Joaquín, 2565.
Gabriel, José, 3244.
Gadea, Wenceslao S., 3246.
Galain, Ramón L., 3346.
Galán Gómez, Mario, 1291.
Galarza, Ernesto, 986.
Galíndez, Jesús, 2782.
Galindo Mendoza, Alfredo, 2054.
Gallagher de Parks, Mercedes, 780, 842.
Gallardo, Domingo V., 4652.
Gallegos, Gerardo, 2606, 3928.
Gallegos, Jorge L., 4526.
Gallegos, Rómulo, 3958, 3976.
Galván de del Río, Carmen, 1888.
Gamio, Manuel, 2607.
Gámiz, Abel, 1863.
Gándara, Raúl, 2138.
Gandía, Enrique de, 132, 456, 518, 2647, 2683, 3247, 3469.
Gandolfo, Rafael, 4901.
Gangotena y Jijón, Cristóbal de, 2608.
Gann, Thomas, 292.
Gaos, José, 4902, 5023.
Garavito, Miguel A., 4556.
Garcés, V. Gabriel, 133, 504.
Garcés Bedregal, Miguel, 556.
Garcés G., Jorge A., 2886.
Garcia, Amilcar de, 4358.
García, Antonio, 1166, 1167.
García, Germán, 4621.
García, Juan Crisóstomo, 707.
García, Juan Francisco, 4867.
García, Miguel Ángel, 3171.
Garcia, Rodolfo, 3377, 4141.
García, Secundino, 557.
García, Serafín J., 3929.
García Bacca, Juan David, 4980, 4982.
García Bárcena, J. R., 4929.
García Cadena, Alfredo, 1168.
García Castellanos, Telasco, 2183.
García Caturla, Alejandro, 4698.
García Chuecos, Héctor, 3813.
García de León, Jr., Porfirio, 1226.
García de Zúñiga, E., 5000.
García Franco, Salvador, 2648.
García Granados, Rafael, 324.
García Guiot, Silvano, 2783.
García Hernández, M., 3054.

García-Mata, Carlos, 1358.
García-Mata, Rafael, 1359, 1380, 1558.
García Méndez, Carlos A., 2244.
García-Molinare, 2134.
García Montes, Oscar, 987.
García Morente, Manuel, 5013.
García Morillo, Roberto, 4834.
García Payón, José, 266, 267.
García Peláez, Francisco de P., 2784.
García-Prada, Carlos, 3854, 3938, 4052, 4107a.
García R., José María, 1292.
García Robles, Alfonso, 3492.
García Roel, Adriana, 3930.
García Samudio, Nicolás, 3312.
García Vázquez, Ricardo, 2120.
Garcia Velloso, Enrique, 3977.
García y García, Elvira, 1976.
Garcilaso de la Vega, el Inca, 3774.
Gargaro, Alfredo, 2932.
Garmendia, Hermann, 3856.
Garrett, João Baptista da Silva Leitão de Almeida, 4247.
Garrido, Pablo, 1889.
Garrido Alfaro, Vincent, 134.
Garros, José Boadella, 4281.
Gastón, Francisco José, 2121.
Gay Calbó, Enrique, 2649, 3194.
Gaya, Ramón, 754.
Gayne, Jr., C., 781.
Geenzier, Enrique, 4002.
Gerbi, Antonello, 160, 1514.
Getino, Luis P. Alonso, 4976.
Gho Elizondo, Sigifredo, 1571.
Gibson, Christopher H., 2346.
Gibson, William Marion, 2472.
Gietz, Ernesto G., 4622.
Gil, Enrique, 1360.
Gil-Albert, Juan, 4053.
Gil Navarro, Orlando, 4421.
Gil Sánchez, Alberto, 4558.
Gilbert de Pereda, Isabel, 3367.
Gillan, Crosby Lee, 317.
Gillin, John, 384.
Gillmor, Frances, 1925.
Giménez Lanier, Joaquín, 755.
Ginastera, Alberto E., 4835.
Giovanetti, Bruno, 2347.
Girard, Rafael, 616.
Girón Cerna, Carlos, 988.
Gironza, Telmo, 3055.
Giuffra, Elzear Santiago, 2031.
Glaspell, Susan, 4332.
Gleason Álvarez, Miguel, 1063.
Glover, Tomás B., 1361.
Godwin, Francis W., 1362.
Goethe, J. W., 4333.
Goggin, John M., 268.
Goison, Christopher H., 2184.
Goldsmith, Oliver, 4334.
Goldstein, Marcus S., 575, 576.
Gollán (h.), Josué, 2397, 2398.
Gomes, Antônio Osmar, 871.
Gomes, Tapajoz, 905, 936, 937.
Gómez, Eugenio J., 1178.
Gómez, Hernán F., 669.
Gómez de Orozco, Federico, 33.
Gómez Ferreyra, Avelino Ignacio, 3249.
Gómez Haedo, Juan Carlos, 135, 2019.

Gómez Orozco, Alicia, 3791.
Gómez Reinoso, Teófilo, 3493.
Gómez Restrepo, Antonio, 3857.
Gómez Robleda, José, 577.
Gomezanda, Antonio, 4708.
Gomís Soler, José, 4520.
Gonçalves, Álvaro, 1709a, 4363.
Gonçalves, Francisco, 4115.
Góngora Perea, César, 5014.
Gonzaga, Antônio Galvão, 1702.
González, Ariosto D., 3245, 3347.
González, J. Natalicio, 4105.
González, Julio César, 2934.
González, Luis Felipe, 2785.
González, Manuel Pedro, 3858, 3859, 4736.
González, N., 1977.
González, Pedro A., 2055.
González, Silvino N., 34.
González Alegría, Luis, 585.
González Arrilli, Bernardo, 3250.
González Arzac, Rodolfo A., 1363.
González Blanco, Edmundo, 4978.
González Couttin, H., 1195.
González del Valle, Francisco, 4903, 4904.
González Enríquez, Pablo F., 4543.
González Galé, José, 1364.
González Gallardo, Alfonso, 1042.
González Garaño, Alejo B., 708, 756, 2005.
González Garza, Federico, 3470.
González H., Gonzalo, 1227.
González Martínez, Enrique, 4023.
González Mendoza, J. M., 4021a.
González Ortega, José, 2056.
González Padilla, José, 1085.
González Peña, Carlos, 3972.
González Prada, Alfredo, 3860.
González Ríos, Francisco, 4990.
González Rodríguez, Miguel, 1135.
González Ruiz, Ricardo, 2139.
González Sol, Rafael, 1943a, 2090.
González Tuñón, Raúl, 3004.
González Vera, J. S., 3964.
González Vidart, Arturo, 1600.
González y Contreras, Gilberto, 3861.
Goodwin, Philip L., 849, 938.
Gorgot, Dério, 4330.
Gorgot, Dírio, 4307.
Gorki, Maxim, 4335.
Gorostiza, Celestino, 3862.
Gouirán, Emile, 4955.
Govantes, Evelio, 709.
Goyochêa, Castilhos, 3378, 3438, 4163.
Graham, Robert Bontine Cunninghame, 2650, 2959.
Grain, José María, 558.
Grant, Rupert, 4663.
Grases, Pedro, 1210, 3014, 3863–3865.
Graterón, Daniel, 3056.
Graves, Norma Ryland, 2348.
Greca, Alcides, 2399.
Green, Otis H., 3866, 3867.
Green, Philip L., 136, 137.
Greenbie, Sydney, 2245.
Greenleaf, R., 710.
Greenlee, William B., 3401.
Greslebin, Héctor, 452.
Greve, Ernesto, 2609.
Gridilla, Alberto, 2246.

Grieco, Agrippino, 4164, 4274, 4291.
Grieco, Donatello, 4248.
Griffin, Donald F., 2140.
Griñán Peralta, Leonardo, 3195.
Grismer, Raymond L., 3868.
Gropp, Arthur E., 4623.
Grove, Eduardo, 3664.
Gschwind, Eduardo P., 2485.
Guarnieri, Camargo, 4680, 4853.
Guatemala:
 Archivo General del Gobierno, 634.
 Ministry for Foreign Affairs, 3549.
 Presidente, 2499.
 Secretaría de Agricultura, 1264.
 Secretaría de Gobernación y Justicia, 2500.
 Sociedad de Geografía e Historia, 2084.
Gudin, Eugenio, 1673.
Guedes, Jaime Fernandes, 1667.
Guenther, Felix, 4831.
Guerra, Fermina, 1874.
Guerrero, Jorge, 3869.
Guerrero, José E., 4790.
Guerrero, Luis Juan, 5026.
Guerrero, Raúl G., 1875.
Guerrero Galván, J., 782.
Guest, P. L., 1267a.
Guevara, Darío C., 2212.
Guido, Mario M., 1366.
Guilbert, Henry D., 578.
Guillén, Nicolás, 4092.
Guillén y Tato, Julio, 2651.
Guimarães, Fábio de Macedo Soares, 2318.
Guimarães, Vicente, 4408.
Guisa, Marcelina, 4791.
Gulla, Luis Alberto, 4055.
Gunther, John, 138.
Gusmão, Clovis, 1647.
Guterbock, Bruno, 4653.
Guthrie, Chester L., 2786.
Gutiérrez, Alfredo F., 1086.
Gutiérrez, Eduardo, 4336.
Gutiérrez, José María, 3613.
Gutiérrez, Juan María, 3978.
Gutiérrez, Ricardo, 757.
Gutiérrez Castel, Luis Alberto, 1367.
Gutiérrez Colombres, Benjamín, 1990.
Gutiérrez Forno, María Antonieta, 1463.
Gutiérrez Sánchez, Gustavo, 4493.
Gutiérrez Valenzuela, Alfredo, 2888.
Guyau, J. M., 4981.
Guzmán, Eulalia, 241.
Guzmán, Martín Luis, 3160.
Guzmán Esponda, Eduardo, 3313.
Guzmán Lozano, Emilio, 2787.

H

Haag, Alfred H., 989.
Haas, João Nepomuceno, 4956.
Haiti:
 Banque Nationale de la République d'Haïti. Départément Fiscal, 1154.
Hall, Melvin, 990.
Halmar, Augusto d', 4020.
Hamilton, D. Lee, 4165.
Hamsun, Knut, 4337.
Hanke, Lewis, 139, 2652.

Hanson, Earl Parker, 140.
Hanson, Elliott S., 141.
Harding, Jane, 1152.
Hardy, F., 2155.
Harkness, Jr., Alberto, 2653.
Harrington, Tomás, 465.
Harris, Frank, 4338.
Harris, G. D., 2106.
Harris, Seymour E., 991, 991a.
Harrison, J. V., 2247.
Harrison, Lewis K., 3669.
Harth-Terré, Emilio, 711–716.
Haskins, Caryl P., 2032.
Hatch, D. Spencer, 362.
Hatcher, Evelyn, 353.
Haussmann, Frederick, 992.
Hauzer, René, 1293.
Haydée Raggio, Amalio, 5005.
Hays, H. R., 4005, 4056, 4097.
Hazelton, Alan Weaver, 3494.
Heath, S. Burton, 2141.
Hediger, Ernest S., 1043.
Heilborn, Ott, 2248.
Heimsoeth, H., 5025.
Heller, Frederico, 1710.
Hellmer, Joseph R., 1890.
Henao Jaramillo, J., 1304.
Henckel, Carlos, 590.
Hendrichs, P. R., 269.
Henius, Frank, 2349, 4666.
Hensler, Haven, 4809.
Hepp D., Ricardo, 1572.
Heras, Carlos, 643, 3814.
Heredia Luna, S., 2203.
Hermant, Abel, 4339.
Hernández, A. E., 1251.
Hernández, Carlos, 1136.
Hernández, Efrén, 4006.
Hernández, José, 4093.
Hernández, Juan J., 379.
Hernández, Manuel A., 3713.
Hernández, Timoteo L., 2057.
Hernández Almanza, 4981.
Hernández de Alba, Gregorio, 202, 416, 417, 591, 3058.
Hernández de Alba, Guillermo, 657, 2865, 2995.
Hernández de León, Federico, 148.
Hernández de Mendoza, Cecilia, 4057.
Hernández Gonzalo, Gisela, 4699, 4700.
Hernández Ron, J. M., 4500.
Hernández Ron, Ramón, 1211.
Hernández Travieso, Antonio, 3196, 4905.
Herrán, Alberto L., 1183.
Herrera, F. L., 2249.
Herrera, Moisés, 36.
Herrera Carrillo, Pablo, 2789.
Herrera Gray, Enriqueta, 519.
Herrera Mendoza, Lorenzo, 4445, 4576.
Herrera S., Julio Roberto, 2790.
Herrera y Reissig, Herminia, 4058.
Herrera y Thode, Daniel, 3348.
Herring, Hubert Clinton, 143, 3522.
Herrmann, Lucila, 1623.
Herrnstadt, Ernesto, 3674.
Herron, Francis, 144.
Hewett, Edgar L., 717.
Hickman, C. Addison, 1014.

Higbee, E. C., 1590, 2249a.
Hileret, René, 1368.
Hill, Roscoe R., 663, 3172.
Hilton, James, 4340.
Hinojosa Ortiz, Manuel, 4565.
Hiss, Philip Hanson, 2115, 2155a.
Hobagen, Jorge, 1515.
Hobbs, Hulda R., 290.
Hodge, W. H., 2156.
Hodgson, R. E., 1252, 1266–1268, 1273.
Hoempler, Armin, 2250.
Hoffman, Charles, 4341.
Hoffmann-Harnisch, Wolfgang, 872.
Hoffmann-Harnisch, Júnior, Wolfgang, 873. 1915.
Hoffmannsthal, Emil von, 1369.
Holguín, Andrés, 4059.
Holzmann, Rodolfo, 4815–4817.
Honaiss, Antonio, 4117.
Honduras:
  Archivo Nacional, 635.
  Presidente, 2504.
  Secretaría de Gobernación, 2505.
  Sociedad de Geografía e Historia, 636.
  Tegucigalpa. Distrito Central. Consejo, 2503.
Honig, Edwin, 939.
Hooper, Ofelia, 391, 1269.
Hopkins, J. A., 1565.
Horkheimer, Hans, 520.
Horne, Bernardino C., 145, 993.
Horrego Estuch, Leopoldo, 3197.
Hostos, Adolfo de, 363.
Howard, George Delvigne, 446, 448.
Hrdlička, Aleš, 564, 601.
Huamán Oyague, Noe, 618.
Hubert, René, 5018b.
Huerta Rendón, F., 2983.
Hummel, A., 4409.
Humphreys, Robert Arthur, 147, 2610.
Hunter, Dard, 230.
Hunter, R. V., 783.
Hunziker, O. F., 1273.
Hurtado, Leopoldo, 4743.
Hutchinson, J. B., 2131.
Huxley, Aldous, 4342, 4343.

I

Ibáñez, Bernardo, 1464.
Ibáñez, Roberto, 4106.
Ibáñez C., Donaciano, 2251.
Ibarguren, Federico, 3369.
Ibarra (h.), Alfredo, 1944.
Ibarra Grasso, Dick Edgar, 521.
Ibiapini, J. de Matos, 4388.
Iglesias, A., 2984.
Iglesias, Antonio, 817.
Iglesias Villoud, Héctor, 4836.
Iguíniz, Juan B., 38.
Imaz, Esteban, 4453.
Imaz, Eugenio, 4989.
Imbelloni, José, 204, 242, 243, 559, 565, 617, 1844.
Inchauspe, Pedro, 1978.
Inman, Samuel Guy, 150, 3495.
Instituto Agrario Argentino, 2185, 2186.

Instituto Ecuatoriano-Venezolano de Cultura, 3540.
Instituto Interamericano de Historia Municipal e Institucional, 784.
Instituto Panamericano de Bibliografía y Documentación, 18.
Instituto Sudamericano del Petróleo, 968.
Inter-American Emergency Advisory Committee for Political Defense, 3528.
Inter-American Financial and Economic Advisory Committee, 994, 995.
Inter-American Society of Anthropology and Geography, 195.
Inter-American Statistical Institute, 983, 996.
International Labor Office, 1013, 1432, 3556, 3564, 3567–3569.
Ippisch, Franz, 1262.
Iraizoz, Antonio, 2654.
Irazusta, Julio, 3253.
Ireland, Gordon, 2375.
Iriarte, Agustín F., 674.
Irigoyen, Ulises, 2058, 3161.
Isaacs, Jorge, 3979.
Isabèlle, Arsenio, 3254.
Ives, Mabel Lorenz, 3111.
Ivovich, Esteban, 1466a.
Izquierdo, Luis A., 2143.
Izquierdo, María, 828, 840.

J

Jacinto, Juvenal, 4350.
Jácome Moscoso, Rodrigo, 4574.
Jacovella, Bruno, 1979.
Jaeger, Luis Gonzaga, 3402.
Jakob, Cristofredo, 2033, 2187.
Jakob, Ricardo, 2188.
James, Florence, 41.
Janin, Jules, 4324.
Jarach, Dino, 4487.
Jaramillo, Gabriel Giraldo, 718.
Jaramillo Alvarado, Pío, 505.
Jaramillo Bruce, Rodolfo, 1573.
Jaramillo Vélez, Lucrecio, 4573.
Jarvis, Norman D., 2242.
Jáuregui Rosquellas, Alfredo, 3112, 4624.
Jáureguy, Miguel Ángel, 3349.
Jesinghaus, Carlos, 4999.
Jijena Sánchez, Rafael, 1967, 1993.
Jiménez, Georgina, 1111.
Jiménez, Juan Ramón, 4060.
Jiménez Borja, Arturo, 1945.
Jiménez Correa, Carlos P., 1309, 1516.
Jiménez M., Gabriel, 3059.
Jiménez Rueda, Julio, 3815.
Jirkal H., Juan, 1572, 2238.
Jobim, José, 1624.
Johnson, Frederick, 579.
Johnson, Harvey Leroy, 3870.
Johnson, Hewlett, 4345.
Johnson, Jean Bassett, 364.
Johnson, John J., 2655.
Joint Committee on Latin American Studies, 161.
Jolly, A. L., 2157.
Jones, C. K., 42, 3949.
Jones, Robert C., 3574.
Jones, Willis Knapp, 3833.
Jongh Osborne, Lilly de. See Osborne, Lilly de Jongh.
Jor, J. O. de Souza, 1758.
Jorge, J. G. de Araujo, 4282.
Jorim, Labieno, 1759.
Jos, Emiliano, 2656, 3060.
Juárez Muñoz, J. Fernando, 2792.
Jubé Júnior, J. R. R., 1802.
Juderías y Loyot, Julián, 2657.
Junta de Historia Eclesiástica Argentina, 2594.
Jurandyr, Dalcidio, 1650.
Juvenal, 4346.

K

Kafuri, Jorge, 1713.
Kahn, Máximo José, 1891.
Kamenka, Michel B., 875.
Kant, Manuel, 4992–4994.
Kany, C. E., 1954, 1955.
Kaplan, L. C., 4266.
Katz, Carlos, 2252.
Keidel, J., 2189.
Kelly, Isabel, 226.
Kelly, Judith, 4347.
Kelsey, Vera, 154.
Kemble, John Haskell, 2611.
Kemps, Emilio, 4283.
Kendrick, A. F., 719.
Kennedy, Stetson, 1892.
Kenny, Michael, 3536.
Kernisan, Clovis, 1155.
Kidder II, A. V., 293–295, 307, 432.
Kidder, Daniel P., 3440.
Kiddle, Lawrence B., 43.
King, James Ferguson, 2658, 2726.
Kinnaird, Lucia Burk, 44.
Kirchoff, Paul, 206.
Kirkpatrick, F. A., 2659.
Kirstein, Lincoln, 785, 821, 850.
Klein, Enrique, 2253.
Klinge, Gerardo, 1228, 1592.
Koellreutter, H. J., 4854.
Koenenkampf, Guillermo, 3931.
Korn, Guillermo, 815.
Korn Villafañe, Adolfo, 3599.
Koseritz, Carl von, 851.
Kraft, Guillermo, 45.
Kramer, Alex M., 4667.
Krassa, Pablo, 1467.
Kraus, H. Felix, 786, 813, 819.
Krause, Fritz, 487.
Kreibohm, Enrique, 4654.
Krull, Germaine, 876.
Kubler, George, 720.
Kuczynski-Godard, Máximo H., 207, 2254.
Kühn, Franz, 2190.
Kull, Robert I., 3497.
Kuri Breña, Daniel, 4930.
Kurtz, Benjamin T., 296.
Kurz, Harry, 3871.

L

Labarca Letelier, René, 1574.
Labastille, Irma, 4668, 4725.
Labell, Milton J., 1035.

Labrousse, Rogelio P., 4957.
Lacaille, A. D., 313.
Lacau, María Hortensia, 4061.
Lacayo B., Gilberto, 2525.
Lacerda, Carlos, 3406.
Lacerda, Dorval, 1691, 3631.
Lacerda, Pedro Paulo Sampaio, 1625, 1651.
Lachatañeré, Rómulo, 1980.
Lacombe, A. J., 1804.
Lacombe, Américo Jacobina, 3447.
Ladrón de Guevara, Blanca, 1981.
Lafontaine, A. P., 5018a.
Lafuente Machaín, R. de, 2935.
Lagerlöf, Selma, 4348.
Lamadrid, Lázaro, 2793.
Lamar Roura, Justo, 1278.
Lamartine, Alphonse de, 4349.
Lamas, Andrés, 3350.
Lamego, Luis, 4248a.
Laña Santillana, Pilar, 3932.
Lanao de la Haza, Ulises, 4714.
Landívar, Rafael, 3767.
Lanús, Carlos E., 1377.
Lanz Margalli, Luis, 2633.
Larco Herrera, Rafael, 208.
Larco Hoyle, Rafael, 523.
Lardé, Jorge, 2794.
Lardé y Larín, Jorge, 392.
Larreta, Enrique, 3960.
Larroyo, Francisco, 4968, 5001, 5002, 5025.
Lascurain y Zulueta, Carlos, 2795.
Lastres, Juan B., 1946.
Latcham, Ricardo E., 560.
Latin American Economic Institute, 1124.
Latin American Juridical Committee, 3543.
Latorre, Mariano, 3872, 3961–3963, 3980.
Latzina, Eduardo, 3255.
Latzina, Francisco, 2191.
Lázaro, Juan F. de, 2192.
Lazcano Colodrero, Raúl, 4454.
Lazcano y Mazón, Andrés María, 3498, 4494.
Lazo, Agustín, 676.
Lazo, Raimundo, 3332.
Lazzari de Pandolfi, Carolina, 2193.
Le Riverend Brusone, Julio J., 2796, 3029.
Leão, Antônio Carneiro, 4167.
Leão, Múcio, 4116.
Leão, Sylvia, 4249.
Leavitt, Sturgis E., 155, 3834, 3835.
Leclerc, Max, 3441.
Lecron, James D., 998.
Lecuona, Ernesto, 4701–4703, 4726.
Lecuna, Vicente, 3062–3065, 3143–3146.
Ledesma Medina, Luis A., 45a, 664, 2936.
Legón, Fernando, 4505.
Lehmann, Henri, 418, 453, 592, 721.
Lehmann, Walter, 314.
Lehmann-Nitsche, Robert, 1934.
Leighton, George R., 3157.
Leipziger, Hugo, 677.
Leitão, Cândido de Melo, 2352.
Leite, João Barbosa, 1804, 2436.
Leite, Serafim, 877, 3404, 3419.
Leite de Castro, Cristovam, 2306.
Leiva, Elío, 2612.
Lemoine, 878.
Lemoine, Luis de, 4583.

Leo, Ulrich, 3874.
León, Jorge, 1253, 1254, 2079.
León, Pedro, 678.
León Garaycochea, C. P., 4430.
León Pinelo, Antonio de, 2660, 3771.
Leonard, Irving A., 156, 3816–3819.
Lerdo de Tejada, Miguel, 4870.
Lerena Acevedo de Blixen, Josefina, 3875.
Lermitte, Carlos, 2299.
Lessa, Francisco, 1788.
Letelier Llona, Alfonso, 4691.
Levene, Ricardo, 670, 722, 3256, 3340, 4011.
Levevier, Armando I., 46.
Lévi-Strauss, Claude, 488.
Levillier, R., 2937.
Levín, Enrique, 2194.
Lewin, Boleslao, 2661.
Lewinsohn, Richard, 1626.
Lewis, Beatrice Fleischman, 47.
Lewis, Samuel, 2797.
Lewis, Sinclair, 4350.
Ley, Salvador, 4781.
Liard, Luis, 5015.
Library of International Relations. Chicago, 49.
Licínio, Aluízio, 1652.
Licitra, Ducezio, 4984.
Lida, Raimundo, 5016, 5024.
Liddle, R. A., 2106.
Light, Ann, 984.
Ligoule M., Juan, 4625.
Lillo, Baldomero, 3964.
Lima, Alceu Amoroso, 4168.
Lima, Araújo, 2353.
Lima, Carlos Henrique de, 4117.
Lima, Emirto de, 1893, 2002, 4767.
Lima, Heitor Ferreira, 4326.
Lima, Herman, 1653, 4315a.
Lima, Hermes, 4169.
Lima, Hildebrando de, 4118.
Lima, Jorge de, 4250.
Lima, Medeiros, 4170.
Lima, Queiroz, 4315.
Lima, Rosinha de Mendonça, 4348.
Lima Júnior, Augusto de, 3379.
Lima Sobrinho, Barbosa, 1654, 1655, 3442.
Lin, Yu-t'ang, 4350a.
Lines, Jorge A., 209, 345, 345a.
Linné, Sigvald, 325, 333.
Lins, Álvaro, 4171.
Lins, Ivan Monteiro de Barros, 4163, 4172.
Lira, Jorge A., 524, 2012.
Liscano, Juan, 1894, 4824.
Lisdero, Alfredo, 1378.
Lizano Hernández, Víctor, 3174.
Lizardi Ramos, César, 326, 327.
Lizaso, Félix, 3792.
Lizondo, Estraton J., 3015.
Lizondo Borda, Manuel, 2938.
Llamosa, Rafael, 1065.
Llanos, Luis A., 433.
Llorens, Emilio, 1379, 1380.
Loayza, Francisco A. de, 3768.
Lobato, Gulnara de Morais, 4355, **4371**.
Lobato, Monteiro, 907, 4251.
Lobell, **M. J., 2242.**
Lobet de Tabbush, Bertha J., 1935.
Lobo, Luiz, 3380.

Loewenberg, Alfred, 4737.
Loewenstein, Karl, 3499, 3537.
Lohman Villena, Guillermo, 2870, 3820.
Lombardo Toledano, V., 158. 2515.
Lopes, Alexandre Monteiro, 4587.
Lopes, Luciano, 1805, 4173.
Lopes, Miguel Maria Serpa, 4510.
Lopes, Paulo Corrêa, 4284.
Lopes, R. Paula, 1692.
Lopes, Tomás de Vilanova Monteiro, 1806.
Lopes, Valdemar, 3443.
López, Casto Fulgencio, 3793.
López, Víctor Manuel, 2059, 2107.
López Albújar, Enrique, 561.
López de Gómara, Francisco, 2798.
López Jiménez, Ramón, 3550.
López Portillo y Weber, José, 2613, 2799.
López Ramírez, Tulio, 542, 543, 602.
López y Fuentes, Gregorio, 3933.
Lorca Rojas, Gustavo, 2376.
Lorwin, L. L., 999.
Losanovscky Perel, Vicente, 3586.
Loudet, Enrique, 4007.
Lourenço, João de, 1627.
Lourenço Filho, M. B., 1775.
Lousada, Wilson, 4174.
Louys, Pierre, 4351.
Loyo, Gilberto, 365, 1088, 3704.
Loza Colomer, Carlos A., 2400.
Luciani, Jorge, 3066.
Lucuix, Simón S., 3245.
Luelmo, Julio, 2662.
Luján, E. R., 1255.
Luján, James Graham, 3971.
Lullo, Oreste di, 1846, 1982.
Luna, Lisandro, 1895.
Luna, Miguel M., 3321.
Luna, S. Heredia, 2203.
Lunardi, Federico, 297, 2728, 2800.
Luper, Albert T., 4761.
Luque Colombres, Carlos A., 3794.
Luros, Pablo, 612.
Lusitano, Leonel da Costa, 4390.
Luz, José Batista da, 4118.
Luzuriaga y Bribiesca, Guillermo de ("Solón de Mel"), 4010.

M

M. P. de A., 53.
McBride, George McCutchen, 2164.
Macbride, James Francis, 2255.
McBride, Merle Alexander, 2164.
McCarthy, Edward J., 2801.
McClintock, John C., 1000.
McDougall, Elsie, 298.
Maceda, Álvaro F., 4482.
Macedo, Joaquim Manuel de, 4252, 4253.
Macedo, Pablo, 4441.
Macedo, Roberto, 53a.
Macedonia, Leonardo, 2437.
Machado, Alexandre Marcondes, 2438.
Machado, Anibal M., 942.
Machado, José, 4517.
Machado, José de Alcántara, 3405.
Machado Filho, Aires da Mata, 4119, 4762.
Macieira, Anselmo, 879.
Macinnes, Helen, 4352.
McKellar, Kenneth, 3521.
McKinney, Howard D., 4855.
MacLean y Estenós, Alejandro, 1593.
Mac-Lean y Estenós, Roberto, 159, 525, 1001, 2973.
McNicoll, Robert Edwards, 2537.
McQueen, Charles A., 1002.
McWilliams, Carey, 3706.
Maes, Ernest E., 2165.
Maffry, August, 1003.
Magalhães, Alvaro, 4120.
Magalhães, Amílcar A. Botelho de, 489.
Magelhães, Basílio de, 1847, 1947–1950, 1956, 1983, 1984, 2020, 4175.
Magalhães, Celso de, 2439.
Magalhães, Lucia, 1807, 2440.
Magaña Esquivel, Antonio, 3877.
Magariños de Mello, Mateo J., 3351.
Maglione, Eduardo F., 2377.
Magno, Paschoal Carlos, 852.
Maia, Alvaro, 1760.
Maia, Jacyr, 1808.
Maia, Silvia Tigre, 1809.
Maige Abarca, José, 1575.
Makemson, Maud Worcester, 244, 245.
Malagón Barceló, Javier, 2854.
Malaret, Augusto, 1957, 1958, 1966.
Maldonado, Ángel, 2256.
Mallea, Eduardo, 3934.
Mallo, Nicanor, 3067.
Mañach y Robato, Jorge, 3198, 3199.
Mangabeira, Edila, 4285.
Mangabeira, Francisco, 4931.
Mangabeira, João, 3444.
Mangelsdorf, P. C., 2035.
Manger, William, 3523.
Mann, Thomas, 4354.
Manrique de Lara, Juana, 54.
Manríquez, Cremilda, 1848.
Mantecón, José Ignacio, 65.
Mapes, E. K., 3836.
Marasso, Arturo, 4626.
Marbán, Edilberto, 2612.
Marchant, Alexander, 3406.
Marchant, Annie d'Armond, 2307.
Marchena, Enrique de, 4880.
Margain, Carlos R., 328.
Margain Araujo, Carlos R., 246.
Maria, Grã-Duquesa da Russia. See Romanoff, Maria.
Mariaca, Guillermo, 1433.
Marian, Dagmar, 723.
Marianno Filho, José, 853, 880–882.
Mariátegui, José Carlos, 3333.
Marín García, Segundo, 724.
Marín Madrid, Alberto, 2257.
Marinho, Inezil Pena, 1810.
Marins, Álvaro (Seth), 952.
Mariscal, Federico E., 342.
Mariscal, Mario, 3030.
Maritain, Jacques, 4356, 5017.
Markham, Clemente H., 474.
Marlitt, Suzanna, 4357.
Marmer, H. A., 2036.
Mármol, José, 4008.
Marone, Gherardo, 5010.
Marques, J. de O., 1761.
Márquez, Javier, 2663.

Márquez Blasco, Javier, 1004.
Márquez Miranda, Fernando, 466.
Márquez T., Ricardo, 2985, 3147.
Marquina, Rafael, 3200.
Martí, José, 3769, 3770.
Martí Escasena, Manuel, 3755.
Martín, Edgardo, 4773.
Martín, José Agustín, 3186.
Martín del Campo, Rafael, 247.
Martín Moreno, Ángel, 2896.
Martínez, José Agustín, 2486.
Martínez, José Luciano, 3352.
Martínez, José Luis, 3878, 4063.
Martínez, Juan, 2897.
Martínez, Liborio, 580.
Martínez, Raúl V., 4958.
Martínez, Santiago, 3334.
Martínez, Yolanda, 3258.
Martínez Acosta, Orlando, 4655.
Martínez Arteaga, Julio, 4689.
Martínez Bello, Antonio, 3795.
Martínez Cosío, Leopoldo, 2802.
Martínez Dalmau, Eduardo, 2664.
Martínez de la Torre, Ricardo, 2538.
Martínez del Río, Pablo, 222, 2803, 2804.
Martínez Díaz, Nicasio, 1499, 3740.
Martínez Lamas, Julio, 1538.
Martínez Rivera, E., 2144.
Martínez Sáenz, Joaquín, 1279.
Martínez Syro, Lázaro, 1187.
Martínez Villegas, Juan, 3978.
Martínez Villena, Rubén, 4094.
Martínez y Díaz, José F., 2614.
Martínez Zuviría, Gustavo, 3965.
Martins, Ataide, 4286.
Martins, Cyro, 4418.
Martins, Francisco Pires, 3407.
Martins, Iolanda Vieira, 4304.
Martins, Luis, 4305.
Martins, Wilson, 4176.
Mason, D. I., 1559-1561.
Mason, J. Alden, 210, 227, 228.
Mason, Van Wyck, 4358.
Masson-Oursel, Paul, 4995.
Mata, G. Humberto, 4009.
Maten y Llopis, Felipe, 2805.
Mateos, S. I. F., 2665.
Mateos Higuera, Salvador, 329.
Matley, C. A., 2133.
Matos, Gregório de, 4287.
Matos Hurtado, Belisario, 3068.
Matti, Carlos Horacio, 4527.
Matus Gutiérrez, Carlos, 1483.
Mauá, Irineu Evangelista de Sousa, Visconde de, 3445.
Maugham, W. Somerset, 4359, 4360.
Maul, Carlos, 4177, 4288, 4336.
Maupassant, Guy de, 4361-4363.
Mauriac, François, 4364.
Maurois, André, 4355.
Maya, Rafael, 3879.
Mayer-Serra, Otto, 4792-4794.
Maza, Francisco de la, 725, 726, 2806, 3796.
Maza y Rodríguez, Emilio, 4544.
Meade, Joaquín, 2855.
Means, P. A., 197.
Medeiros, J. Paulo de, 3500.
Medeiros, Océlio de, 2442.

Medici, Fernando Penteado, 4588.
Medina Álvarez, Cesáreo, 1916.
Medina Angarita, Isaías, 2570.
Medina Ascensio, Luis, 3031.
Medina Chirinos, Carlos, 3069.
Medinaceli, Carlos, 3880, 3881.
Meinecke, Friedrich, 5018.
Mejía Baca, José, 2259.
Mejía de Fernández, Abigail, 3966.
Mejía Fernández, Miguel, 1067.
Mejía Ricart, Gustavo Adolfo, 4439.
Mekler, Ana, 3566.
Mel, Solón de (Guillermo de Luzuriaga y Bribiesca), 4010.
Meléndez, Concha, 1849, 4064.
Meléndez, Luis, 787.
Melgarejo Vivanco, José Luis, 270.
Mello, Astrogildo Rodrigues de, 2666, 2667.
Mello, Geraldo Cardoso de, 3446.
Mello, Mario D. Homen de, 1762.
Melo, Carlos R., 2401.
Melo, J. C., 1676, 1677.
Melo, Leopoldo, 1550.
Melo, Mário, 3408, 3409.
Melo Guerrero, Mariano, 4470.
Mena, Luis E., 4704.
Mencher, E., 2107.
Mendes, Amando, 1656.
Mendes, Figueiredo, 1811.
Mendes, J. E. Teixeira, 1305, 1668.
Mendes, Odorico, 4390.
Mendes, Oscar, 4306.
Mendes, Renato da Silveira, 2354.
Méndez Dorich, Rafael, 679.
Méndez Plancarte, Gabriel, 3845.
Mendieta y Núñez, Lucio, 366.
Mendigutía, Fernando, 1139.
Mendive, Pedro I., 1381.
Mendizábal, Miguel O. de, 2807.
Mendonça, Carlos Süssekind de, 4172, 4173.
Mendoza, Vicente T., 1896-1900, 4795, 4796.
Mendoza Zeledón, Carlos, 727.
Menéndez, Carlos R., 2808.
Menéndez, Oriel, 3016.
Menéndez Samará, Adolfo, 4932.
Menéndez y Pelayo, Marcelino, 4065.
Meneses, Djacir, 1628.
Meneses, J. Alves de, 4289.
Meneses, Rómulo, 2260.
Meneses Pallares, Arturo, 3686.
Menezes, Amilcar Dutra de, 4254.
Menucci, Sud, 4178.
Merani, Alberto L., 4983.
Merker, C. A., 2080.
Merla, Pedro, 1089.
Mesa Prieto, Guillermo, 4541.
Mesquita, Alfredo, 4296.
Mesquita, José de, 1629.
Messina, Felipe, 4297.
Mestre, Pedro Cabrer, 2120.
Métraux, Alfred, 457, 458, 467, 508, 2616.
Mexico:
    Archivo General de la Nación, 637.
    Banco Nacional de Crédito Agrícola, 1222.
    Campeche (estado). Gobernador, 2510.
    Departamento Agrario, 55.
    Departamento de Salubridad Pública, 56.

INDEX

Dirección General de Estadística, 1061, 1076, 1081.
Guanajuato (estado), 2512.
Hidalgo (estado). Gobernador, 2513.
Instituto Mexicano del Seguro Social, 3726.
Jalisco (estado). Gobernador, 2514.
Nuevo León (estado). Gobernador, 2517.
Oficina de Estadística y Estudios Económicos, 1040.
Presidente, 2519.
San Luis Potosí (estado), 2520.
Secretaría de Agricultura y Fomento, 1246, 1247.
   Dirección de Economía Rural, 1041, 1248.
Secretaría de Comunicaciones y Obras Públicas, 57.
Secretaría de Hacienda y Crédito Público, 58, 646, 647.
   Dirección de Estudios Financieros y Archivo Histórico de Hacienda, 3032.
Secretaría de la Defensa Nacional, 59.
Secretaría de la Economía Nacional, 60, 1046, 1049.
   Dirección General de Estadística, 1048.
Secretaría de Relaciones Exteriores, 1069, 3167.
Secretaría del Trabajo y Previsión Social, 3697, 3698.
   Departamento de Informaciones Sociales y Estadística. Biblioteca, 61.
Seminario de Cultura Mexicana, 114.
Servicio de Bibliotecas, 62.
Universidad Autónoma de Guadalajara. Asociación de Post-Graduados, 172.
Universidad de Yucatán, 19.
Universidad Nacional Autónoma de México. Centro de Estudios Filosóficos, 4888.
   Facultad de Filosofía y Letras, 146.
   Seminario de Investigaciones Filosóficas, 4884.
Meyer, Ana Wey, 4357.
Meyer L'Epée, Consuelo, 367.
Michaca, Pedro, 1917.
Middle American Information Bureau, 1036, 1037.
Mignone, Francisco, 4681–4685, 4856–4858.
Migone, Raúl C., 1006.
Milano, Atílio, 4271, 4275.
Milans, Jeremías, 1539.
Miles, Cecil W., 2096.
Millán, Enrique, 3017.
Millares Carlo, Agustín, 63–65, 2652a, 3148, 3410, 3797, 4907.
Millas, Jorge, 4933.
Millás, José Carlos, 2122.
Miller, O. M., 2261.
Milliet, Sérgio, 3405.
Mimenza Castillo, Ricardo, 299.
Mineral Survey, 4590.
Mingarro y San Martín, José, 3728, 4969, 5018.
Miquel i Vergés, J. M., 3821.
Mira Restrepo, Jorge, 1170, 1197.
Miraglia, Luis, 4970.
Miramón, Alberto, 2997.

Miranda, Marta Elba, 3935.
Miranda, Nicanor, 1901.
Miró, Rodrigo, 4107.
Miró Quesada C., Francisco, 4933a, 4934.
Mitchell, Julio, 2617.
Mitre, Adolfo, 3259, 3260.
Mitre, Bartolomé, 4011.
Moedano Koer, Hugo, 271, 334.
Moglia, Raúl, 3822.
Molina, Raúl A., 2668.
Molina Solís, Juan Francisco, 2809.
Molina-Téllez, Félix, 2810.
Molinari, Antonio Manuel, 4549.
Molinas, Nicanor, 2404.
Moliner, Israel M., 66.
Moll, Bruno, 1518.
Moll, Roberto, 1212.
Monacelli, Gualterio, 4528.
Monbeig, Pierre, 2355, 2356.
Moncada, Raúl, 4067.
Mondolfo, Rodolfo, 4984, 4996.
Monge Alfaro, Carlos, 2081.
Moniz, Edmundo, 4179.
Monroy, Guadalupe, 54.
Monsanto, Luis E., 1213.
Monserrat, Santiago, 4935.
Montagu, M. F. Ashley, 567.
Montbas, Hugues Barthon de, 3149.
Monteagudo, Pío I., 1379.
Monteiro, Luis Augusto Rego, 3631.
Monteiro, Osvaldo de Carvalho, 4511.
Montellano, Carlos, 2418.
Montellano, Julián V., 2418.
Montelo, Josué, 4180, 4181.
Montenegro, Carlos, 3115, 3293.
Montenegro, Ernesto, 3882.
Monterde García Icazbalceta, Francisco, 2811, 3883, 3936.
Montero Bustamante, Raúl, 758, 2940, 3261, 3353, 3354.
Montes de Oca, José G., 4881.
Montes de Oca, Luis, 1045.
Montesenti, M. Lourdes Macuco, 1812.
Monteverde, Manuel, 1541, 1542.
Montignani, John B., 680.
Montón Blasco, Juan, 2097.
Montoya, Hernán, 1171, 1172.
Moog, Clodomir Viana, 4182.
Moore, Ernest Richard, 2692, 3837, 3160.
Moore, R. E., 1007, 1008, 1594.
Moore, W. Robert, 2159.
Mora, Enrique de la, 788.
Moraes, Rubens Borba de, 904, 4627.
Morais, J. de, 1804.
Morais, Vincius de, 4290.
Morales, Adolfo, 3884.
Morales, Ernesto, 3254, 4012.
Morales Lara, Julio, 4013.
Morales López, Melecio, 3767.
Morales Otero, Pablo, 2145
Moran, Carlos M., 2378.
Morató, Octavio, 1543.
Moravsky, Bernardo, 2262.
Moreau, Louis-Auguste, 902.
Moreira, Albertino G., 3411.
Moreira, J. Roberto, 1813, 1814.
Moreira Filho, M. P., 4352.
Moreno, Delfino C., 2618.

Moreno, Juan Carlos, 4810.
Moreno, Mariano, 3116.
Moreno Quintana, Lucio M., 1388.
Morente, Manuel G., 5020.
Moreyra P. S., Manuel, 2812.
Morillo, Manuel M., 759.
Morley, Sylvanus Griswold, 300, 380.
Mortara, Giorgio, 1009, 1198, 1630, 1714, 1715.
Mosley, Zack, 4410.
Mosquera, Joaquín, 3018.
Mostny, Grete, 411, 412.
Mota, Fernando de Oliveira, 4908.
Mota, Otoniel, 301.
Mota, Plinio, 4286.
Mota del Campillo, Eduardo, 3263.
Moura, Pedro de, 2321, 2322.
Mowat, Charles L., 2813.
Moya, Salvador de, 3381.
Moyano, Pedro, 2941.
Mozo, Sadí H., 1389.
Muelle, Jorge C., 434.
Mueller, Leonardo, 4936.
Mujica de la Fuente, Juan, 2960.
Mujica Farías, Eduardo, 4656.
Müllerried, Friedrich K. G., 272, 2060.
Mullen, A. J., 1310, 1311.
Müller, João Pedro, 2357.
Muller, María V. de, 4823.
Munchausen, Barão de, 4411.
Muniz, João Carlos, 3501.
Muñoz, J. E., 1585.
Muñoz, José María, 2942.
Muñoz, Laurentino, 1173.
Muñoz, Lucila, 1851.
Muñoz, Lumbier, Manuel, 2061.
Muñoz, M. A., 1256.
Muñoz Molina, Tomás, 5018.
Muñoz Sanz, Juan Pablo, 4778.
Muntsch, Alberto, 381.
Murillo, Egeilio (?), 4694.
Murillo, Emilio (?), 4694.
Murra, John V., 426.
Murray, Paul V., 3162.
Murray-Jacoby, H., 3471.
Mussolini, Gioconda, 1623.

N

Nabuco, Joaquim, 4121.
Nadal Mora, Vicente, 728.
Namm, Benjamin H., 2358.
Nance, Gustav Barfield, 3972.
Náñez, Demetrio, 4995, 5018a, 5018b.
Naranjo Martínez, Enrique, 3070
Narizzano, Hugo, 1469.
Nascentes, Antenor, 3937.
Nass, Hermann, 1306.
National Broadcasting Company, 4738.
National Policy Committee, 1010.
Navarro, Guillermo, 1195.
Navarro, José Gabriel, 2986.
Navarro, Martín, 5004.
Navarro Bolandi, Edwin, 1255.
Navarro del Águila, Víctor, 435, 526, 603, 2021.
Navarro Luna, Manuel, 4014.

Navarro Tomás, Tomás, 1959.
Navarro y Noriega, Fernando, 2729.
Negrete, Samuel, 4692.
Negrón Pérez, Porfirio, 382.
Nehgme Rodríguez, Elías, 1470.
Neira Martínez, Policarpo, 1199.
Neiva, Alvaro, 1815.
Neiva, Artur, 4121.
Nel Gómez, Pedro, 681.
Nemésio, Vitorino, 4183.
Nepomuceno, Alberto, 4859.
Neri, Cira, 4334.
Neruda, Pablo, 824, 4015, 4015a.
Nery, Adalgisa, 4255.
Neves, Costa, 4318.
New England Institute of Inter-American Affairs, 67.
Newell, Norman D., 2263.
Newman, Marshall T., 604.
Neyra, Joaquín, 816.
Nicaragua:
  Dirección General de Estadística, 1108.
  Granada, 2524.
  Junta de Control de Precios y Comercio, 1108.
  Ministerio de Gobernación, 2526, 2527.
  Presidente, 2528.
  Recaudador General de Aduanas y Alta Comisión, 1109.
  Superintendencia de Bancos, 1108.
Nicolas, Sébastien Roch. See Chamfort.
Nichols, Madaline W., 42, 44.
Nichols, R. A., 1257.
Nieto, Luis, 1902.
Nieto Arteta, Luis E., 1011.
Nieto Arteta, Luis Eduardo, 4971.
Nietzsche, Friedrich, 4366, 4997.
Nigra, Clemente Maria da Silva, 884.
Niklison, Carlos, A., 2195.
Nobrega, Clovis da, 4937.
Noel, Martín, 749.
Noguera, Eduardo, 211, 229, 273, 335.
Normano, J. F., 160, 1012.
Noronha, Edgard Magalhães, 4536.
Norris, Kathleen, 4367.
Novoa, Sofía, 4832.
Nuermberger, Gustave A., 3322.
Nunes, Castro, 4463.
Nunes, Osório, 945.
Núñez, Estuardo, 3885.
Núñez, José Ramón, 2196, 2197.
Núñez Brian, Joaquín, 1077.
Núñez del Prado, Nilda, 4750.
Núñez Portuondo, Emilio, 2487.
Núñez Valdivia, Jorge E., 2539.
Núñez y Domínguez, José de J., 335a, 1852, 3163.
Núñez y Núñez, Eduardo Rafael, 4518.
Nürenberg, Zacarías, 1390.

O

O'Bourke, Juan E., 729.
Obregón, Rodolfo, 4628.
O'Brien, John A., 162.
Ocampo, Armando R., 2943, 3264.
Ocampo, María Luisa, 4629.
Ocaranza, Fernando, 3218.

Ochoa, Ángel S., 2815.
Ochoa, Raúl, 1544.
Ochoa Campos, Moisés, 274.
Ochoa Sierra, Blanca, 419.
O'Connell, Richard L., 3971.
O'Connor, Thomas F., 2816.
Oddo, Julio Armando, 4522.
Oficina Internacional del Trabajo, 1013, 1432, 3556, 3564, 3567–3569.
O'Gorman, Edmundo 2693.
O'Gorman, J., 760.
O'Higgins, Tomás, 2901.
Oitavo Congresso Pan-Americano da Criança, 1794, 1816.
Olea, Héctor R., 3033.
Olivares Figueroa, R., 1903–1905, 4825, 4826.
Oliveira, Albino José Barbosa de, 3447.
Oliveira, Alvarus de, 4256.
Oliveira, Américo Leónidas Barbosa de, 2323.
Oliveira, Aurélio Gomes de, 4340.
Oliveira, Avelino Inácio de, 2360.
Oliveira, Beneval de, 1703, 1716, 2308, 2361–2363.
Oliveira, Carlos Gomes de, 1632.
Oliveira, J. Lourenço de, 4122.
Oliveira, J. M. Cardoso de, 908.
Oliveira, Olinto, 1817.
Oliveira, Vidal de, 4342.
Olmo Castro, Amalo, 3603.
Olschki, Leonardo, 2159, 2669.
Olson, Paul R., 1014.
Onetti, Carlos María, 3886.
Onetto, Carlos L., 730.
Onís, Harriet de, 3970.
Ontañón, Mada, 761, 843.
Oppenheim, Víctor, 545, 593, 2264–2266.
Oramas, Luis R., 454.
Orantes, José Andrés, 1845.
Ordóñez, Ezequiel, 2062.
Ordóñez Fetzer, Marco Tulio, 3502.
Orfila Reynal, Arnaldo, 4909.
Orico, Osvaldo, 2620.
Orive Alba, Adolfo, 2063.
Orlandi, Héctor Rodolfo, 3265.
Orloski, John A. E., 1152.
Ornellas, Manoelito de, 4184, 4300.
Orozco, José Clemente, 834.
Orozco, Luis Enrique, 2817.
Orozco Casorla, Raúl, 2818.
Orozco Muñoz, Francisco, 275.
Orozco Ochoa, Germán, 4589.
Orrego Barros, Carlos, 3304.
Ortega, Alfredo, 1193.
Ortega Ricaurte, Enrique, 627.
Ortega Ruïz, Francisco J., 1242.
Ortega Torres, Jorge, 4542.
Ortega Torres, José J., 3887.
Ortiz, Fernando, 3193, 3823.
Ortiz, Nair, 1623.
Ortiz, Ricardo M., 1391.
Ortiz, Sergio Elías, 499, 500, 2998, 3838.
Ortiz de Montellano, Bernardo, 4068.
Ortiz de Rozas, Alfredo, 3266.
Ortiz de Zevallos, Carmen, 4630.
Ortiz de Zevallos, Luis, 2267.
Ortiz Dueñas, Jorge, 1985.
Ortiz Fernández, Fernando, 393, 394.
Ortiz, R., Guillermo, 1294.
Ortiz Saralegui, Juvenal, 4016.
Ortiz Vidales, Salvador, 4629.
Osborne, Douglas, 276.
Osborne, Lilly de Jongh, 154, 349, 1932, 1933, 2091, 2820.
Osgood, Cornelius, 447, 448.
Osgood, Wilfred H., 2268.
Osorio, Pedro Miguel, 1960.
Osorio Lizarazo, J. A., 1200.
Ospina Racines, E., 1189, 1190.
Ossandón Guzmán, Carlos, 762.
Otão, José, 1818.
Otero, Gustavo Adolfo, 2963–2965, 3117, 3294, 3889.
Otero D'Costa, Enrique, 2999, 3073, 3315, 3890.
Otero D'Costa, José María, 3118.
Otero Muñoz, Gustavo, 658, 3074.
Othón, Manuel José, 4017.
Otoya Arboleda, F. J., 1295.
Ots Capdequi, José María, 2670.
Ott, Carlos Fidelis, 885.
Ott, Fidelis, 3413.
Ovejero y Maury, Eduardo, 4997.
Oyarzún, Aureliano, 496.
Oyarzún, Mila, 4070.

P

Paalen, Wolfgang, 277.
Pach, Walter, 732, 763.
Pacheco Quintero, Ricardo, 501.
Pacull T., Luis M., 1471.
Padilla, Ezequiel, 164, 3529.
Padilla, Francisco E., 2944.
Padilla D'Onís, Luis, 2621.
Páez Brotchie, L., 665.
Pagano, José León, 810.
Pagés Larraya, Antonio, 4071.
Paiva, Cecilia Castro, 1623.
Paiva, Glycon de, 2304.
Paiva, Ruy Miller, 1762.
Palacios, Alfredo L., 188, 3553.
Palacios, Enrique Juan, 335b, 336.
Palacios, Manuel R., 3729.
Palant, Pablo, 3254.
Palavecino, Enrique, 548.
Palcos, Alberto, 3267.
Palenque Ceballos, Jaime, 1436.
Palés, Gallach, 4979.
Pallares, Eduardo, 3699.
Palm, Erwin Walter, 733, 2821.
Palma, Ricardo, 3938, 4631.
Palomeque, Alberto, 3355.
Paltán, José D., 620.
Pan American Union, 165, 1015, 1016, 1243, 1906, 3503, 3504, 4739.
    Columbus Memorial Library, 70.
    Division of Intellectual Cooperation, 789.
    Division of Labor and Social Information, 3557, 3561.
    Executive Committee on Post-War Problems, 3505, 3544.
    Governing Board, 1017.
    Juridical Division, 3506–3508.
    Oficina de Información Obrera y Social, 1018.
    Travel Division, 2364.

Panama:
  Caja de Seguro Social, 3738.
  Ministerio de Agricultura y Comercio. Sección de Economía Agrícola, 1270.
  Ministerio de Gobierno y Justicia, 2530.
  Ministerio de Hacienda y Tesoro, 1112.
  Oficina del Censo de 1940, 1113, 1114, 2088.
  Presidente, 2531.
Pane, Remigio U., 3839, 3981.
Pani, Mario, 790.
Paraguay:
  Dirección de Hidrografía y Navegación, 2198.
  Dirección General de Estadística, 1498.
  Ministerio de Agricultura, Comercio e Industrias, 1497.
  Ministerio de Relaciones Exteriores, 3326.
  Presidente, 2533.
Pardo, Isaac J., 1907.
Pardo, J. Joaquín, 2823.
Pardo García, Germán, 4018.
Paredes, Jaime, 3798.
Paredes, Manuel Rigoberto, 2296, 2966.
Pareja Paz Soldán, José, 1519, 2270.
Parks, Lois F., 3322.
Parodi, L. R., 2199.
Parra-Pérez, C., 3075.
Parras, P. J. de, 2945.
Parsons, Elsie Clews, 1853.
Partido Comunista del Perú, 2591.
Partido de la Revolución Mexicana, 71, 2518.
Pasquel, Leonardo, 2379.
Passin, Herbert, 368, 1918.
Passos, Alexandre, 4185.
Pastor, R. A., 2634.
Patiño, Adrián, 4840.
Patrón Taura, Pedro, 2540.
Patterson, Gardner, 1019.
Patterson, Massie, 4662.
Paucke, Florián, 468.
Paulero, Ernesto, 4549.
Paulet, Pedro E., 1520.
Paulotti, Osvaldo L., 585.
Pavón Abreu, Raúl, 248.
Payró, Julio E., 811, 812.
Payró, Roberto Jorge, 3949.
Paz, Ataliba de Figueiredo, 1763.
Paz, Juan Carlos, 4673, 4674, 4837.
Paz, Octavio, 4072.
Paz Estenssoro, Víctor, 1434.
Paz Soldán, Luis F., 3150.
Paz y Miño, Luis Telmo, 2987.
Pearce, Thomas M., 1961.
Pearl, Raymond, 1020.
Pedemonte, Juan Carlos, 2946.
Pedro, Valentín de, 4073.
Pedrosa, Mário, 4763.
Peiser, Werner, 3824.
Peixôto, Afrânio, 886, 1854, 4141, 4419.
Peixoto, Almir da Câmara de Matos, 4123.
Peixoto, Sílvio, 72.
Pella Ratell, Roberto F., 4550.
Pellerano, Glorialdo, 2200
Peltzer, Ernesto, 1214.
Peña, Lázaro, 3756.
Pena, Martins, 4298.
Peña, Moisés T. de la, 1244.
Peña Dávila, Juan Manuel, 4471.
Peña Guzmán, Solano, 1392, 1551.
Peñaloza, Luis, 1435.
Penna, Carlos Víctor, 4632, 4633.
Peón Aloy, Pura, 2123.
Peppercorn, Lisa M., 4764.
Peraza y Sarausa, Fermín, 73–76, 104, 2622, 4634, 4635.
Perdomo, Apolinar, 4095.
Pereda, José A., 1393.
Pereda Valdés, Ildefonso, 1951.
Pereira, Altamirano Nunes, 2365.
Pereira, Antônio Sá. See Sá Pereira, Antônio.
Pereira, Artur, 4686.
Pereira, Dulcidio, 1788.
Pereira, Lucia Miguel, 4186–4189.
Pereira, Moacir Soares, 1657.
Pereira Salas, Eugenio, 1940, 4740.
Perera, Ambrosio, 3011, 3362.
Peres, José, 4346.
Pereyra, Diómedes de, 3626.
Pérez, A. R., 1586.
Pérez, Aquiles, 2272.
Pérez-Acosta, Juan F., 3119.
Pérez-Beato, Manuel, 3202.
Pérez Cabrera, José Manuel, 3203.
Pérez de Barradas, José, 420.
Pérez Estrada, Francisco, 1924.
Pérez Galaz, Juan de D., 77, 78, 383, 3164.
Pérez León, Miguel A., 4497.
Pérez-Marchand, Lina, 4910.
Pérez Martínez, Héctor, 78, 666, 2695.
Pérez Montero, Carlos, 764.
Pérez Petit, Víctor, 3891.
Pérez Valenzuela, Pedro, 2824.
Perotti, J., 791.
Persegani, Primo, 4455.
Peru:
  Archivo Nacional, 638, 668.
  Asociación Peruana de Ingenieros Agrónomos, Lima, 1549.
  Banco Central de Reserva del Perú, 1505, 1508.
  Banco Central Hipotecario del Perú, 1506.
  Banco del Perú y Londres en Liquidación, 1507.
  Biblioteca Nacional, 4636.
  Cámara de Diputados, 1509. Biblioteca, 14.
  Departamento de Estadística General de Aduanas, 1510.
  Dirección de Caminos y Ferrocarriles, 1511.
  Dirección Nacional de Estadística, 1552.
  Junta Nacional de la Industria Lanar, 1517.
  Presidente, 2541.
  Rimac, 2542.
  Sociedad de Bellas Artes del Perú, 772.
  Sociedad Nacional Agraria, Lima, 1523.
  Superintendencia de Bancos, 1524, 1525.
  Universidad Mayor de San Marcos, 15.
Pesce, Vicente, 1595.
Pessoa, Robert, 4368.
Pessôa Sobrinho, Eduardo Pinto, 2444.
Petersen, George, 2274.
Peyrallo, Félix, 4875.

Philadelphia Museum of Art, 792.
Phillips, Walter T., 3892.
Photiades, Constantin, 4368.
Picado, Teodoro, 1258.
Picanço, Melchiades, 4464.
Picchia, Menotti del, 4257, 4413.
Piccione Blasi, Francisco, 4863.
Piccirilli, Ricardo, 3268.
Pichardo Moya, Felipe, 2825.
Picón Febres, Gonzalo, 3982.
Picón-Salas, Mariano, 3893, 4911.
Piedra-Bueno, Andrés de, 3799.
Pierre, Marcelin, 3945, 3973.
Pierson, Donald, 3649.
Pillado, José Antonio, 2947.
Pimenta, Joaquim, 1693.
Pimentel, José Francisco, 3530.
Pina, Rafael de, 4480.
Pina, Rogelio, 1140.
Pincherle, Alberto, 2974.
Pineda de Castro, Álvaro, 1201.
Pinheiro, Albertina, 4372.
Pinheiro, Maria Esolina, 1694, 1819.
Pinho, Vanderlei, 3448.
Pinilla, Gaspar María de, 544.
Pinilla, Norberto, 3305, 3895, 3896, 4074, 4075.
Pinto, Almir, 947.
Pinto, Carlos Alberto A. de Carvalho, 4490.
Pinto, Estevão, 490.
Pinto, Luis, 2366.
Pinto, Luis C., 1855.
Pinto, Luiz de Aguiar Costa, 3415.
Pinto, Manuel María, 3120.
Pinto, Víctor, 3587.
Pinto Lima, J., 1781.
Pinzón, Rafael, 3363.
Pirassinunga, Adailton Sampaio, 3382.
Pittier, H., 2108.
Pivel Devoto, Juan E., 659, 3121, 3356.
Pizarro, Orlando, 3122.
Pla, Gil, 1141.
Plácido, A. D., 4076.
Plata Uricoechea, Fernando, 2475.
Plath, Oreste, 1962, 3897.
Platt, Raye R., 2038, 2039.
Platt, Robert S., 1021, 2040.
Plaza, Juan Bautista, 4718, 4827, 4828.
Pleiss, Paul, 2166.
Podestá, Roberto A., 2405.
Podestá Costa, Luis A., 3229, 4577.
Poe, Edgar Allan, 4369.
Poincaré, Henri, 5019.
Polakowsky, H., 3175.
Polanía Puyo, Jaime, 421.
Poliano, Luis Marques, 3383.
Pollan, A. A., 1094.
Poma de Ayala, Felipe Huamán, 527.
Ponce, Manuel M., 4710–4712, 4797, 4871.
Ponce de León, Carlos, 1312.
Pontes, Eloi, 4190, 4236, 4329, 4331.
Poore, Charles, 1068.
Popenoe, Wilson, 1259.
Porras Barrenechea, Raúl, 3761a, 3771, 3800, 3825.
Portela, Bastos, 4191.
Portela, Gerardo, 1142.
Portell Vilá, Herminio, 1143.

Pôrto, Aurélio, 3416.
Pôrto, Hannibal, 1764.
Porto, Jesús Edelmiro, 4529.
Pôrto, L. de Almeida Nogueira, 3515.
Portuondo, José Antonio, 3898.
Posada, Eduardo, 3076.
Posada Amador, Carlos, 4695.
Posadas, Rosa Margarita, 3899.
Posnansky, Arthur, 406, 407, 475, 528, 529, 594, 2003, 2006.
Potiguara, José, 4258.
Potsch, Waldemiro, 1634, 1820.
Pough, Frederick H., 2064.
Pound, F. P., 1202, 1296.
Pourchet, Maria Julia, 595.
Powell, Jane Swift, 1260, 1285.
Pozo, Justo L., 4495.
Pozuelo A., José, 3551.
Prati, Edmundo, 765.
Prats, Alardo, 841.
Prazeres, Oto, 2445.
Prazeres, Rimus, 4123.
Prazeres, T. Alves, 1717.
Pressoir, C., 2128.
Preto, Maluh de Ouro, 4332.
Pretto, Julio C., 618.
Price-Mars, 3035.
Priego de A., Mireya, 53.
Prieto, Julio, 793.
Primer Congreso de la Economía de las Provincias de Tarapacá y Antofagasta, 1472, 1473.
Pritchett, John Perry, 3019.
Prudencio, Roberto, 4077.
Puente, Carlos, 3625.
Puerto Rico:
    Institute of Tropical Agriculture, 2142.
    Insular Board for Vocational Education, 1157a.
    Junta de Salario Mínimo. División de Investigaciones y Estadísticas, 1158.
    Minimum Wage Board, 1159.
    Office of Information, 2146, 2147.
    Water Resources Authority, 2152, 2153.
Pulgar Vidal, Javier, 562, 2275.
Putnam, Samuel, 4124, 4192, 4193.

Q

Queiroz, Amadeu de, 4259.
Queiroz, Eça de, 4261.
Queiroz, Raquel de, 4260.
Quesada, José, 4865, 4866.
Quesada y Miranda, Gonzalo de, 3801.
Questa de Marelli, Italia, 5010.
Quevedo, Raymond, 4663.
Quevedo A., Sergio A., 605, 606.
Quijada Jara, Sergio, 1856, 1919, 1986, 2013.
Quijano, Manuel de Jesús, 2532.
Quiles, Ismael, 4959.
Quinn, Vernon, 2065.
Quintana, M. J., 2975.
Quintana, Mário, 4362.
Quintanilla, Luis, 168.
Quintela, Gloria, 1776.
Quintero, Vicente P., 4996.
Quinzio Figueiredo, Jorge Mario, 2671.
Quiroga, Horacio, 3924, 3967.

Quiroga, Oscar, 1521.
Quirós, Alfonso, 361.
Quiroz, Juan B. de, 2671a, 3570.

R

Rabuffetti, Luis Ernesto, 2406.
Radin, Paul, 1876.
Radio Corporation of America. RCA Victor Division, 4721.
Raimondi, Antonio, 2276.
Raitani, Francisco, 4465.
Ramalho, Ortigão, 4261.
Rambo, Balduino, 2324.
Ramírez, Guadalupe, 1857.
Ramírez Cabañas, Joaquín, 2827, 3165, 3939.
Ramírez Juárez, Evarista, 2949.
Ramírez Olivella, Gustavo, 4496.
Ramos, Arthur, 491.
Ramos, Dinoran, 3940.
Ramos, Floriano Augusto, 2447.
Ramos, Ignacio, 2277.
Ramos, Miguel A., 7.
Ramos, R. Antonio, 3327.
Ramos, Samuel, 3900, 4443, 4912.
Ramos Espinosa, Alfredo, 1941.
Ramos G., M. Miguel, 236.
Ramos y Aguirre, José Antonio, 4638.
Rangel, Alberto, 4194.
Rangel, Godofredo, 4339, 4347.
Rangel Couto, Hugo, 1091.
Raposo, Inácio, 1868, 4262, 4394.
Rasmussen, W. D., 81, 1022, 1216.
Ratto, Héctor C., 3270.
Ravá, Adolfo, 4998.
Ravard, Francisco Alfonso, 3757.
Ravignani, Emilio, 3124.
Raw, Frank, 2132.
Ray, José Domingo, 4585.
Real de Azúa, Exequiel M., 794.
Rebêlo, Marques, 4195, 4334, 4344.
Recasens, José, 213.
Recinos, Adrián, 2828.
Redfield, Robert, 348, 385.
Redier, Antoine, 4370.
Reeves, R. G., 2035.
Regal, Alberto, 1522.
Rêgo, José Lins do, 909, 4263.
Reichel-Dolmatoff, Gérard, 422, 423.
Reina Valenzuela, José, 3176.
Reis, António Simões dos, 83–85, 4125.
Reis, Arthur Cézar Ferreira, 888, 3463.
Reis, José, 1769.
Reis Júnior, Pereira, 4291.
Reiser, Hans, 530.
Reissig, Luis, 170.
Repetto, Nicolás, 1394, 3473.
Resende, Antonio, 1765.
Restoy, Eugenio, 4423.
Restrepo, José Manuel, 3316.
Restrepo Canal, Carlos, 3000.
Restrepo Posada, José, 734.
Restrepo Tirado, Ernesto, 3002–3004, 3077.
Reti, Ladislao, 1395.
Revilla Q., Alfredo, 2420.
Revueltas, José, 3941.
Rex González, Alberto, 400, 401.

Rey, Ricardo E., 4453.
Reyes, Alfonso, 173, 3785.
Reyes, Oscar Efrén, 3968.
Reyes Archila, Carlos, 3005.
Reyes Testa, Benito, 3177.
Reyna, Alberto Wagner de, 4938.
Reyna, Margarita, 1079.
Ribadeneira, Jorge A., 2278.
Ribeiro, Adalberto Mário, 2449, 3642, 3650, 3651.
Ribeiro, C. J. de Assis, 4437.
Ribeiro, Carolina, 1822.
Ribeiro, Jorge Severiano, 4537.
Ribeiro, Maria Rosa Moreira, 4196.
Ribón, Segundo Germán, 735.
Rickards, Constantine G., 330, 336a.
Rickert, H., 5020.
Riego, Manuel Luis del, 2950.
Riera Fernández, José, 1436.
Ries, Maurice, 386.
Rigal, A., 4476.
Rino, Antônio, 4380.
Río, Alfonso del, 1869, 1920.
Rio Branco, José Mário da Silva Paranhos, Barão de, 3450.
Ríos, Eduardo Enrique, 2829.
Rippy, J. Fred, 3178, 3219, 3317, 3474.
Risopatrón, Oscar, 2279.
Risopatrón M., Daniel, 1576.
Ritchie, John, 553.
Riva Agüero, José de la, 3901.
Rivas, Guillermo, 766, 795, 796, 829, 832.
Rivas Camacho, Santiago, 1297.
Rivera, Diego, 797, 827.
Rivera, Guillermo, 3982.
Rivera-Santos, Luis, 1159a.
Rivero, Pedro, 4019.
Riveros, Bernabé, 2477.
Rivet, Paul, 174, 213, 424, 502, 503, 545.
Roa, Armando, 4913.
Roa, Raúl, 4094.
Roa Bastos, Augusto, 4078.
Roberts, Jr., Frank H. H., 214.
Roberts, Kenneth, 4371.
Robertson, William Spence, 2624, 3078, 3318.
Robledo, Emilio, 1858.
Robles, Oswaldo, 3772, 4939.
Roca, Blas (Francisco Calderío), 2489.
Roces, Wenceslao, 5008.
Rocha, Federico A., 1437.
Rocha, Germano Carvalho, 2451.
Roche, Jean Cazenave de la, 2160.
Rodó, José Enrique, 3900.
Rodrigues, José Wasth, 890.
Rodrigues, Lysias A., 4197.
Rodríguez, Alberto, 4676.
Rodríguez, Blas E., 337.
Rodríguez, Carlos J., 3273.
Rodríguez (h.), Jesús María, 1106.
Rodríguez, Jorge, 1191, 1192.
Rodríguez Aragón, Ismael, 215.
Rodríguez Arias, Julio C., 1397, 2407.
Rodríguez Cerna, José, 3475.
Rodríguez Demorizi, Emilio, 2830, 3214–3216, 3773, 3831.
Rodríguez-Embril, Luis, 4914.
Rodríguez Goicoa, J., 1023.
Rodríguez Lozano, 835.

INDEX 513

Rodríguez Morejón, G., 3204.
Rodríguez Rivera, Virginia, 1870, 1921, 1942.
Rodríguez y Rodríguez, Joaquín, 4567.
Rohen y Gálvez, Gustavo-Adolfo, 86, 3558, 3731.
Rohmeder, Guillermo, 2190, 2201, 2202.
Roig de Leuchsenring, Emilio, 736, 3079, 3205.
Roigt, Honorio E., 1024.
Rojas, Manuel, 3942.
Rojas, René, 4020.
Rojas, Ricardo, 459, 469, 3774, 3977.
Rojas Carrasco, Guillermo, 1963.
Rojas Coria, Rosendo, 1092.
Rojas Paz, Pablo, 3274.
Rojina Villegas, Rafael, 4521.
Rolandi, Renato D., 3596.
Roller Issler, Anne, 3708.
Romano Muñoz, José, 4972.
Romanoff, Maria, 4355.
Romero, Abelardo, 4317, 4374.
Romero, Emilia, 3802.
Romero, Fernando, 2672, 2831.
Romero, Francisco, 4915–4918, 4940–4943, 4999, 5026.
Romero, Javier, 568.
Romero, Jesús C., 4798–4800.
Romero, Nelson, 4198.
Romero, Sílvio, 4199.
Romero de Terreros y Vinent, Manuel, 737, 738, 767, 2832.
Romero de Valle, Emilia, 2672.
Romero del Prado, V. N., 4571.
Romero Flores, Jesús, 87.
Romero Manrique, Alfonso, 1298.
Romero Sosa, Carlos Gregorio, 4657.
Rompani, Santiago I., 4547.
Rónai, Paulo, 4200–4202.
Ronald, 4079.
Roncal, Simeón, 4841.
Rondón, Cándido M. da Silva, 216.
Rosa, Alcides, 4512.
Rosa (h.), José María, 3275.
Rosa, José Vieira da, 2325.
Rosa, Moisés de la, 3006.
Rosa, Otelo, 2326.
Rosa, Ramón, 3179.
Rosado de la Espada, Diego, 1055.
Rosado Ojeda, Vladimiro, 1864.
Rosen, Edward, 2673.
Rosenblat, Ángel, 3774.
Roses, Mariano, 2136.
Ross, Lee, 1635.
Rosselot Borden, Fernando, 2588.
Rothe, Friede, 4741.
Rougés, Alberto, 4960.
Roumaine, Jacques, 315.
Rowe, John H., 531.
Roxo, Matias G. de Oliveira, 2327.
Royo y Gómez, José, 2098.
Roys, Ralph Loveland, 2833.
Rubens, Carlos, 948.
Rubín de la Borbolla, Daniel F., 619.
Rubio, Ángel, 2625.
Rubio Mañé, J. Ignacio, 2857.
Rubió y Lluch, Antonio, 3969.
Ruck, Berta, 4372.
Rudofsky, Bernard, 949.

Rueda Vargas, Tomás, 3080.
Ruiz Bourgeois, Julio, 1475.
Ruiz de Gamboa A., Alberto, 3758.
Ruiz de Velasco, Tomás, 2066.
Ruiz Moreno, Isidoro, 4578.
Ruiz P., Cristóbal, 1580.
Ruiz Sánchez, A., 2858.
Ruiz y Ruiz, Raúl A., 3276.
Ruppert, Karl, 302, 303.
Rusconi, Carlos, 586.

S

Sá, Carlos, 1823.
Sá, Paulo, 1788.
Sá Pereira, Antônio, 4882.
Saad, Pedro A., 1493.
Saavedra, Alfredo M., 1859, 1860, 1964.
Saavedra Lamas, Carlos, 1399.
Sabat Ercasty, Carlos, 4080.
Sabaté, Domingo, 4457.
Sabogal, José, 768.
Sabor Vila, Sara, 4658.
Saco, Alfredo M., 89.
Sady, Rachel Reese, 369.
Sáenz Valiente, José M., 3125.
Sagarna, Antonio, 3277.
Saint-Pierre, Jacques Henri Bernadin de, 4373.
Saiz de la Mora, Santiago, 2626.
Salas, Alberto Mario, 402, 2977.
Salazar, Buenaventura, 2834.
Salazar, Víctor M., 3319.
Salazar B., Mariano, 612.
Salazar Maza, T. C., 1217.
Saldívar, Gabriel, 88, 278, 3167.
Saleh Sada, Félix, 1476.
Salgado, Álvaro F., 4203–4208.
Salgado, Gustavo, 4779.
Salgado, José, 3358, 3902.
Salinas Alanís, Miguel, 2736.
Salinas Lozano, Raúl, 1075.
Salit, Charles R., 3036.
Salvador, Humberto, 3943.
Samaniego, Juan José, 1494.
Sambaquy, Lydia de Queiroz, 4641, 4659.
Sammartino, Luis R., 4675.
Sampaio, Theodoro, 2310.
San Cristóval, Evaristo, 3336.
Sanabria, Alberto, 3081.
Sanabria M., Víctor, 2677a.
Sánchez, George I., 1775.
Sánchez, J. G., 4438.
Sánchez, Luis-Alberto, 89, 2627, 3903.
Sánchez Cantón, F. J., 2978.
Sánchez de Bustamante, Teodoro, 1400.
Sánchez Gómez, Gregorio, 2478.
Sánchez Miguel, J., 2067.
Sánchez Mouso, J. M., 1281.
Sánchez Nieto, Alfonso, 4556.
Sánchez Roca, Mariano, 4426, 4545.
Sánchez-Saes, Braulio, 4209.
Sánchez Ventura, Rafael, 249.
Sánchez Villaseñor, José, 5021.
Sánchez y Sánchez, Carlos, 4581.
Sánchez Zinny, Eduardo F., 3278.
Sand, George, 4374.
Sandi, Luis, 4801.

INDEX

Sanmartin, Olinto, 3384.
Santa Cruz, Rosendo, 3944.
Santa Cruz, Víctor, 3295.
Santa Rosa, Tomás, 854.
Santaella Murias, Alicia, 4081.
Santamarina, Jorge A., 1401, 1402.
Santayana, George, 5022.
Santelices, Sergio, 1908.
Santiana, Antonio, 620.
Santillán, Luis A., 2203.
Santoro, Claudio, 4687.
Santórsola, Guido, 4876.
Santos, Evaristo dos, 3644.
Santos, Francisco Marques dos, 910, 911, 3451.
Santos, Francisco Martins dos, 1824.
Santos, José de Almeida, 855.
Santos Muñoz, Pablo, 3509.
Santovenia y Echaide, Emeterio Santiago, 2687, 3206–3208, 3826.
Sanz, Rafael, 1991.
Sapahaqui, David F., 476.
Sapahaqui, Manuel, 476.
Sapriza Carrau, Héctor M., 1025.
Saravia, Atanasio G., 2836.
Saravia, Guillermo Alberto, 4506.
Sarmiento, Domingo Faustino, 3983.
Saroyan, William, 4375.
Satterthwaite, Jr., Linton, 250, 304–306, 330a.
Saubidet, Tito, 1861.
Saubidet Bilbao, Eduardo, 1403.
Saunders, G. M., 621.
Sayán Álvarez, Carlos, 3552.
Sayán de Vidaurre, Alberto, 177, 2410, 3510, 3553.
Scarone, Arturo, 3245.
Schaden, Egon, 460.
Schedl, Armando, 532.
Scheler, Max, 5023.
Schiuma, Oreste, 4745.
Schlichthorst, Karl, 3452.
Schmidt, C. B., 1767–1769.
Schmidt, Max, 509.
Schulz, R. P. C., 331.
Schwab, Federico, 90, 91, 533, 3827, 4642.
Schwalb López Aldana, Fernando, 3296.
Schweigger, Erwin, 2280–2282.
Scott, Walter, 4376.
Scott, Warner H. H., 1116.
Scott, Winthrop R., 2109.
Secades, Eladio, 1909.
Seco Villalba, José Armando, 2411.
Seeger, Charles, 4742.
Segall, Jenny Klabin, 4333.
Seghers, Anna, 4377.
Seijas Rodríguez, Antenor, 2283.
Selva, Manuel, 4643.
Seneca, 4378, 4985.
Seoane, Manuel, 179.
Sepp, Antônio, 891.
Serpa, Phocion, 3453.
Serra, Astolfo, 3454.
Serra, Miguel José (Fray Junípero), 3989.
Serra Moret, Manuel, 4944.
Serrano, Antonio, 403.
Serrano, Jonathas, 3385.
Serrano Plaja, Arturo, 4746.
Serrano Redonnet, Antonio E., 3828.

Serrato, José, 2380.
Sesma, Leandro de, 5017.
Sete, Mario, 1827.
Seth (Álvaro Marins), 952.
Seuánez y Olivera, R., 2300.
Sgrosso, Pascual, 2204.
Sharp, Roland Hall, 2129.
Shaw, Albert, 3476.
Shaw, Earl, 2117a.
Shellenberger, J. A., 1403a, 1565.
Shephard, C. Y., 2114.
Sieck Flandes, Roberto, 338.
Siegel, Morris, 1865.
Sierra, Vicente D., 2684, 2980.
Sievers Wicke, Hugo Konrad, 180.
Silva, A. J. da Costa e, 4538.
Silva, Benedicto, 2381.
Silva, Carlos Alberto, 2412.
Silva, Edmundo de Macedo Soares e, 1662.
Silva, Egydio de Castro e. See Castro e Silva, Egydio de.
Silva, J. Félix, 553.
Silva, José Asunción, 4107a.
Silva, M. Nogueira da, 4210, 4231–4233.
Silva, Nogueira da, 892.
Silva, Paulo Moreira da, 4343.
Silva Castro, Raúl, 3904.
Silva Celis, E., 425.
Silva Ferrer, Manuel, 2301.
Silva Neto, Serafim, 4126.
Silva Valdés, Fernán, 798, 4021.
Silveira, Artur Leite, 1663.
Silveira, Miroel, 4310, 4391.
Silveira, Otto, 4354.
Silveira Zorsi, Fermín, 1546.
Simmons, Anna G. E., 2367.
Simoens Arce, F., 1547.
Simón, Raúl, 1477, 1478.
Simonsen, Roberto Cochrane, 1636, 1637.
Simpson, George Eaton, 1877.
Simpson, Lesley Byrd, 2837.
Sinzig, Pedro, 4765.
Skewes, Eduardo, 590.
Slifko, C. W., 1770.
Smisor, George T., 2703.
Smith, A. L., 307.
Smith, Marinobel, 893.
Smith, Nicol, 2110.
Smith, Robert C., 682, 856–858, 912, 953.
Smith, Robert Sidney, 2837a, 3037.
Soares, José Carlos de Macedo, 1638.
Soares, Lúcio de Castro, 2328.
Sociedad Argentina de Autores y Compositores de Música, 4883.
Sociedad Central de Arquitectos, Buenos Aires, 799.
Sociedad Cubana de Estudios Históricos e Internacionales, 3209.
Sociedad Mexicana de Geografía y Estadística, 2068.
Sodré, Nelson Werneck, 4211–4213.
Soifer, J., 3759.
Sojo, Vicente Emilio, 4719.
Solar, Enrique M. del, 1596, 2284.
Solari, Horacio, 4585.
Solari, Juan Antonio, 181.
Soler, Juan José, 3328.
Soler, Sebastián, 4973.

Soler Sanuy, Juan, 1404.
Somarriva Undurraga, Manuel, 4554.
Sommer, F., 3417.
Soper, F. L., 2368.
Sorondo, Miguel, 2951.
Sosa de Quesada, Aristides, 2491.
Sotelo Inclán, Jesús, 3168.
Soto, Jorge N., 1203.
Soto-Hall, Máximo, 4108.
Soto Paz, Rafael, 92.
Sousa, Anita Martins de, 4370.
Sousa, Augusto, 4337.
Sousa, Fernando Tude de, 4360.
Sousa, Henrique Cáper Alves de, 2329, 2330.
Sousa, Iéte Ribeiro de, 4539.
Sousa, José Luiz Ribeiro de, 4539.
Sousa, Rubens Gomes de, 4491.
Sousa Júnior, 4381.
Sousa-Leão (filho), Joaquim de, 894, 895.
Souza, Claudio de, 4214.
Souza, Cruz e, 4292.
Souza, J. B. Mello de, 4215.
Souza, José Soares de, 4644.
Souza, Odorico Machado de, 596.
Souza Neto, José Soriano de, 4466.
Spalding, Walter, 2022, 2331.
Spangenberg, Guillermo, 2205. .
Spell, Jefferson Rea, 3905.
Spence, Hartzell, 4379.
Spicer, Edward H., 370.
Spota, Felipe, 741.
Stadler, Remigio N. D., 1405.
Stark, Harry N., 2154, 2161.
Steck, Francis Borgia, 2696, 2839.
Stefanich, Juan, 2534.
Steggerda, Morris, 569, 2069.
Steinfeld, Eduardo R., 1406.
Stendhal, 4380, 4381.
Sterling, E. A., 2085.
Stevenson, Robert Louis, 4382.
Steward, Julian H., 217, 218.
Stewart, T. D., 570–572, 581, 607, 608.
Stewart, Watt, 3335.
Stirling, Matthew W., 279, 280.
Stockdale, Frank, 183.
Stone, Doris, 316, 346, 2083.
Storni, Horacio Julio, 2413.
Stowe, Harriet Beecher, 4383.
Stowell, Ernest L., 3840.
Strickland, Rex W., 2859.
Strong, William Duncan, 197, 219, 436–438.
Strube E., León, 470.
Stuart, Graham H., 3477.
Suárez, Marco Fidel, 3906.
Suárez, P: Francisco, 4986.
Suárez Blanco, José, 4561.
Suárez Marzal, Julio, 814.
Subercaseaux, Benjamín, 3963.
Sussekind, Arnaldo, 3631.
Susto, Juan Antonio, 2697.
Swanton, John R., 439.
Swick, Clarence H., 2213.
Szaffka, Tihamér, 2009.
Szyszlo, Vitold de, 2285, 2286.

T

Tabbush, Bertha J. Lobet de, 404.
Tablada, José Juan, 4021a.

Tacitus, Publius Cornelius, 4384.
Tahan, Malba, 4385, 4386.
Tamayo, Francisco, 546, 1910, 1936.
Tamayo, Jorge L., 2738.
Tannenbaum, Frank, 184, 2454.
Tapia Villarroel, Noel Guillermo, 1480.
Tappy, Elizabeth B., 1526.
Tario, Francisco, 3984.
Taunay, Affonso de E., 896, 913, 914, 4216.
Tauro, Alberto, 4645.
Tax, Sol, 348.
Taylor, Carl C., 1408, 1567.
Tebboth, Tomás, 471.
Teitelboim, Volodia, 2674.
Teixeira, Emilio Alves, 2332.
Teja Zabre, Alfonso, 3038.
Tejera, Humberto, 3082.
Tejera y García, Diego Vicente, 3210.
Teles, Leonor, 4264.
Teletor, Celso Narciso, 387.
Tello, Julio C., 440.
Telmo, Manacorda, 845.
Tena Ramírez, Felipe, 4441.
Tenório, Oscar, 3455.
Teódulo, José, 954.
Terán Gómez, Luis, 1026, 1313, 1439.
Theaman, John R., 2133.
Thoby-Marcelin, Philippe, 3945, 3973.
Thompson, Emmanuel, 3180.
Thompson, J. Eric S., 251–253, 308–311, 343.
Tinker, Edward Larocque, 3973.
Tinoco, Juan, 4022.
Tinoco Filho, Mário, 597.
Tiscornia, Eleuterio F., 3986, 4093.
Tobar Donoso, Julio, 2675.
Tobell, Milton F., 2117.
Tojeiro, Gastão, 4299.
Tollens, Paulo, 4217.
Tolón, Edwin T., 4775.
Tomlinson, Edward, 185.
Tompkins, John Barr, 331a.
Tonda, Américo A., 3279.
Tonelli, Armando, 3126.
Toranzos, Fausto, 4948.
Torino, Enrique, 4502.
Torquemada, Juan de, 2840.
Torra, A., 2492.
Torrassa, Atilio E., 5015.
Torre, Josefina Muriel de la, 2841.
Torre Revello, José, 94, 95, 2676, 2872, 2915, 2953–2955, 3127, 3281, 4661.
Torres, Ana Palese de, 2206.
Torres, Artur de Almeida, 4127.
Torres, Arturo, 3282.
Torres, João Camilo de Oliveira, 4919.
Torres, José Garrido, 1719.
Torres, Vasconcellos, 1697.
Torres Gigena, Carlos, 1409.
Torres-Ríoseco, Arturo, 3907.
Tortorelli, Lucas A., 1410.
Toscano, Salvador, 254, 281.
Totheroh, Dan, 4387.
Toussaint, Manuel, 683, 742, 743.
Tovar y Ramírez, Enrique Demetrio, 2628, 3908, 4082.
Traucki, Boris, 1361.
Travesari, Pedro P., 1911.
Travieso, Carmen Clements, 3152.

Tredici, J., 4987.
Treharne, Bryceson, 4669.
Trevisán, Egidio C., 1411.
Trías Monge, José, 3909.
Trimborn, Hermann, 220, 563.
Trindade, Raimundo, 3386.
Trinidade, Cônego Raimundo, 897.
Tristán Rossi, Francisco, 4586.
Troncoso de la Concha, M. de J., 2842.
Trotter, Mildred, 609.
Truesdell, Leon E., 1160.
Trumpy, D., 2099.
Tumba Ortega, Alejandro, 96.
Tupí Caldas, J. A. L., 1987.
Turcios R., Salvador, 3181.
Turlington, Edgar, 3511.

U

Ugarte, Manuel, 3910.
Ugarte, Salvador, 2698.
Ugarte de Brusiloff, María, 2843.
Ugarteche, Félix de, 97.
Ugarteche, Pedro, 3336.
Uhle, Max, 408.
Ulloa S., A. G., 1250.
Ulloa y Sotomayor, Alberto, 3337, 3478, 3512.
Umphrey, George W., 3911, 3938.
Undurraga, Antonio de, 4084, 4085.
Unión Democrática Antinazista Dominicana, 2495.
Unión Democrática Centroamericana. Departamento Editorial, 3479.
Unión Panamericana. See Pan American Union.
United States:
  Bureau of Foreign and Domestic Commerce, 2117b.
  Department of Commerce. Bureau of the Census, 1027, 1161, 2151.
  Department of State, 186, 1307, 1771.
    Anglo-American Caribbean Commission. United States Section, 1126.
  Hydrographic Office, 2168.
  Library of Congress, 1027a.
    Division of Bibliography, 97a.
    Hispanic Foundation. Archive of Hispanic Culture, 2008.
    Recording Laboratory, 4722.
  Office of Price Administration. Foreign Information Branch. Latin American Section, 1057, 1501.
  Office of the Coordinator of Inter-American Affairs. 187, 1051.
  Soil Conservation Mission to Venezuela, 1220.
  Tariff Commission, 1028, 1070.
University of New Mexico, Albuquerque. School of Inter-American Affairs, 121.
University of Texas, Austin. Institute of Latin American Studies, 189.
Unsain, Alejandro M., 3582, 3760.
Uprimny, Leopoldo, 3083.
Uranga H., Javier, 2740.
Ure, Ernesto J., 4530.
Ureta Saenz Peña, L., 3759.
Uriarte, Amanda Cajina, 2383.
Uribe-Holguín, Ricardo, 4559.

Uribe Piedrahita, César, 3985.
Uribe Romo, Emilio, 1071.
Urioste, Antero, 98.
Urquidi, José Macedonio, 3513.
Urquidi, Víctor L., 1030, 1072.
Urrutia, Alberto F., 3946.
Urteaga, Horacio H., 3775.
Uruguay:
  Asociación Nacional de Contadores. Instituto de Economía, 1528.
  Banco de la República Oriental del Uruguay, 1530, 1532, 1545.
  Contralor de Exportaciones e Importaciones, 1534.
  Dirección de Agronomía, 1599.
  Ministerio de Ganadería y Agricultura. Dirección de Agronomía, 1540.
  Museo y Archivo Ernesto Laroche, 844.
  Presidente, 2549.
  Universidad. Facultad de Derecho y Ciencias Sociales, 2550.
Uteda, Juan M., 3229.

V

Vaillant, George C., 197, 255, 256, 282.
Vaïsse, Emilio, 3961.
Val, Gorki del, 1923.
Valcárcel, Luis E., 220a, 534, 535, 2287.
Valdés, Octaviano, 836.
Valdés A., Benjamín, 3306.
Valdivia Dávila, Víctor, 2288.
Vale, J. Rodrigues, 1674.
Valencia Avaria, Luis, 3129, 3307.
Valencia Rangel, Francisco, 2070, 2071.
Valentini, F. J. J., 2677.
Valentini, Felipe J., 2677a.
Valenzuela, Eduardo, 1179.
Vallarino Jiménez, José, 3084.
Valle, Adrián del, 4646.
Valle, Cipriano, 283.
Valle, José, 1122.
Valle, Rafael Heliodoro, 99, 2678, 3182, 3560, 4023.
Valle C., Ángel, 1352.
Valle Matheu, Jorge del, 2845.
Valle Moré, José del, 4519.
Vallejo, César, 4108a.
Van Acker, Leonardo, 4945.
Van Doren, Carl, 4388.
Vanasco, Luis Ángel, 3284.
Vance, Ethel, 4389.
Vance, John T., 4431.
Vandellós, José A., 1218.
Varela, Fagundes, 4293, 4420.
Varela Martínez, Raúl, 1301.
Vargas, Fulgencio, 2073, 2846.
Vargas, Getulio, 2456.
Vargas A., Pedro J. (H. Álvarez González), 1441.
Vargas Netto, 3457.
Vargas Ugarte, Rubén, 100, 3775a.
Vargas Viriato, 2457.
Varnhagen, Francisco Adolfo de, 3418.
Varona, Enrique José, 3766.
Várzea, Afonso, 2333, 2370–2372.
Vasconcelos, Dora Alencar de, 4367.
Vasconcelos, José, 3852, 4946.

Vasconcelos, Simão de, 3419.
Vásquez, Juan Ernesto, 1123.
Vásquez, Rafael, 4086.
Vásquez Calcerrada, Pablo B., 2137.
Vassallo Rojas, Emilio, 1483.
Vauthier, Louis L., 898.
Vázquez, Nabor, 4803.
Vázquez Arjona, Carlos, 3765.
Vázquez de Espinosa, Antonio, 2741.
Vázquez Machicado, Humberto, 3130, 3554.
Vázquez Machicado, José, 3130.
Vega, J., 372.
Vega Cobiellas, Ulpiano, 3211.
Vega Díaz, D. de la, 3285.
Vegas, Armando, 2105.
Vegas Castillo, Manuel, 3338.
Veiga, A. César, 2458.
Veiga, Vincius da, 4294.
Vela, David, 3803, 3912.
Velarde, Héctor, 802.
Velasco Ceballos, Rómulo, 101.
Velasco Ibarra, José María, 4579.
Velásquez Carrasco, Luis, 2522.
Velázquez, Primo Feliciano, 3169.
Velázquez Fernández, Raúl, 1261.
Vélez, Martín, 1161a, 2137.
Vellard, J. A., 454a.
Vellard, Juan Alberto, 2014.
Veloz, Ramón, 1219.
Venâncio Filho, Francisco, 1829.
Venezuela:
  Anzoátegui (estado). Presidente, 2551.
  Secretaría General de Gobierno, 2552.
  Araqua (estado). Presidente, 2553.
  Archivo Nacional, 642.
  Banco Central de Venezuela, 1204, 1205.
  Barinas (estado). Presidente, 2554.
  Secretaría General de Estado, 2555.
  Biblioteca Nacional de Venezuela, 11.
  Bolívar (estado). Presidente, 2556.
  Secretaría General de Gobierno, 2557.
  Carabobo (estado). Presidente, 2558.
  Secretaría General de Gobierno, 2559.
  Cojedes (estado). Presidente, 2560.
  Secretaría General de Gobierno, 2561.
  Dirección de Estadística, 1208.
  Distrito Federal. Gobernador, 2562.
  Falcón (estado). Presidente, 2563.
  Secretaría General de Gobierno, 2564.
  Guárico (estado). Presidente, 2566.
  Lara (estado). Presidente,, 2567.
  Mérida (estado). Presidente, 2568.
  Secretaría General de Gobierno, 2569.
  Mérida (prov.). Archivo Histórico de la Provincia de Mérida, 649, 2600.
  Ministerio de Educación Nacional. Dirección de Cultura, 4716, 4717.
  Ministerio de Relaciones Interiores, 2571.
  Miranda (estado). Presidente, 2572.
  Secretaría General de Gobierno, 2573.
  Nueva Esparta (estado). Presidente, 2574.
  Secretaría General, 2575.
  Portuguesa (estado). Presidente, 2576.
  Secretaría General de Gobierno, 2577.
  Presidente, 2578.
  Sucre (estado). Presidente, 2579.
  Secretaría General de Gobierno, 2580.
  Táchira (estado). Presidente,. 2581.
  Secretaría General de Gobierno, 2582.
  Trujillo (estado). Presidente, 2583.
  Secretaría General, 2584.
  Valencia. Archivo Histórico de la Municipalidad de Valencia, 648.
  Zulia (estado). Presidente, 2585.
Venturi, Maslowa Gomes, 4308.
Vera Cruz, Alonso de, 3772.
Vera Vallejo, Juan Carlos, 2956.
Vercesi, D. R., 1604.
Vergara, Pedro, 4540.
Vergara, Roberto, 1484.
Vergara Vicuña, Aquiles, 3297.
Vergilio, 4390.
Verissimo, Érico, 4265–4267.
Vernaza, José Ignacio, 3085.
Vetancourt, Manuel Norberto, 3086.
Viana, Gaspar, 1830.
Viana, Hélio, 3458–3462.
Viana, João de Segadas, 1682.
Viana, José de Segadas, 3631.
Viana, Oliveira, 1698.
Viana, Sodré, 4301, 4379, 4392.
Viana Filho, Luiz, 4219.
Viany, Alex, 4341, 4375.
Vidal, Ademar, 1705, 1773, 2373.
Vidal, Barros, 3387.
Vidal, Bento A. Sampaio, 1670.
Vidal, Esther, 2074.
Vidal, María Antonia, 4024.
Vidal de Battini, Berta Elena, 1992.
Vidal de la Torre, Luis, 4497.
Vidales, Luis, 1175, 2100.
Videla, Carlos J., 1440.
Videla, Heriberto, 4676.
Vidussi, J., 803.
Vieira, Flavio, 1683.
Vieira, Gastão, 492.
Vieira, José, 4220.
Vieira, José Geraldo, 4268.
Vieira, Oldegar, 1831.
Vigil, Constancio C., 3974.
Vignale, Pedro Juan, 2967.
Vignolo Murphy, Carlos, 1527.
Vigo, Salvador C., 2416.
Vijil, José Antonio, 3170a.
Vila, Pablo, 2101.
Vilardi, Julián A., 3131, 3132, 3153.
Villa-Lobos, Heitor, 4688, 4729.
Villablanca, Celestina, 1862.
Villafuerte Flores, Carlos, 1073.
Villalobos, Héctor Guillermo, 4025.
Villar, G. E., 2041.
Villar Córdoba, P. E., 441.
Villarejo, Avencio, 2290.
Villarino, María de, 3947.
Villaroel, Gaspar de, 3776.
Villaroel, M., 3133.
Villaseñor, Eduardo, 1052, 1058.
Villaurrutia, Xavier, 805, 3950, 3951.
Villegas García, Leonor, 4087.
Viñas, Julia MacLean, 744.
Viñas y Mey, Carmelo, 2679.
Vinci, Leonardo da, 5000.
Virasoro, Miguel Ángel, 4961, 4962.
Vitier, Medardo, 4920.
Vítor, Edgar d'Almeida, 4221.
Vitoria, Marcos, 3913.
Vitureira, Cipriano Santiago, 846.
Vivante, Armando, 461, 2004.

INDEX

Viver, G. E., 1587.
Vives Buchaca, Lorenzo, 2680.
Vivó, Hugo, 1283.
Vivó, Jorge A., 373.
Volkov, A., 3555a.
Volpi, Carlos A., 1413.
Voltaire, 4391.
Von Hagen, Victor Wolfgang, 230, 389.
Vossler, Carlos, 5024.
Vuelvas, Luis Matías, 1176.

W

Wagley, Charles, 493, 494.
Wagner, Moritz, 2089.
Waibel, Leo, 2124.
Wainer, Jacobo, 2384.
Waitz, Paul, 2075, 2076.
Wakefield, A. J., 1286.
Walker, Edwin F., 1937.
Wallich, H. C., 1031.
Wardle, H. Newell, 339.
Warin, Reinaldo de, 4269.
Warner, Ruth E., 374a.
Warren, Harris Gaylord, 3087.
Waterman, Thomas Tileston, 745.
Watkins, Frances E., 1938.
Watt, Robert J., 3611.
Wauchope, Robert, 344.
Weberbauer, Augusto, 2291, 2292.
Weiant, Clarence Wolsey, 284.
Weitlaner, R. J., 375.
Weitlaner de Johnson, Irmgard, 375.
Wells, J. W., 2106.
Wenger, Franz, 598.
Werfel, Franz, 4392.
Wernicke, Edmundo, 468, 2042.
Wernicke, Rosa, 3948.
Westheim, Paul, 769, 806.
Wetmor, Alexander, 2077.
Whitaker, Arthur P., 190, 2981, 2982, 3480, 3516, 3541.
Whitaker, Edmur de Aguiar, 599.
White, John W., 3481.
White, Leslie A., 2848.
Whorf, Benjamin Lee, 350.
Wickizer, V. D., 1032.
Wile, Raymond S., 2302.
Wilgus, Alva Curtis, 102, 2630.
Wilkes, Josué Teófilo, 4833, 4838, 4839.
Wille, J. E., 1597.
Willey, Gordon R., 437, 438, 443, 444.
Williams, Alberto, 4748.
Williams, Edwin B., 3762, 3841.
Williams, L., 2162.
Wilson, Charles Morrow, 103, 2163.
Wilson, J. P., 1484a.
Windelband, Wilhelm, 5001, 5002, 5025.
Winning, H. von, 272.

Wirth, D. Mauro, 495.
Witt, Lawrence W., 1774.
Wolnitzky B., Alfredo, 1578.
Wooster, Julia L., 1059.
Wylie, Kathryn H., 1074, 1265, 1272.
Wythe, George, 1033.

X

Xammar, Luis Fabio, 4088, 4089.
Xavier, Lívio, 4328.

Y

Yankas, Lautaro, 684.
Yepes, José, 2207.
Yépez Arangua, Edgar, 537.
Yglesias Hogán, Rubén, 2849.
Ygobone, Aquiles D., 3287.
Yorio, Aquiles, 4507.
Young, Chester W., 1156.
Young, G. B., 3517.
Yriart, Juan F., 1552a.
Yunque, Alvaro, 4026.
Yurchenco, Henrietta, 4804.

Z

Zabala, Rómulo, 2957.
Záferson Macedo, S., 1598.
Zaldumbide, Gonzalo, 3763, 3776, 3804.
Zalles, Juan María, 3298.
Zañartu Irigoyen, Hugo, 4492.
Zanetta, Alberto, 1414.
Zárraga, Ángel, 807, 808, 837.
Zarur, Jorge, 917, 2311.
Zavala, Jesús, 4017, 4090.
Zavala, Silvio, 2681.
Zawadzky C., Alfonso, 3088.
Zbrozek, Jerzy, 1832.
Zea, Leopoldo, 4921.
Zeballos, Estanislao S., 3288.
Zevallos Quiñones, J., 2918, 2919, 3089, 3829.
Zilli, Juan, 2078.
Zink, Sidney, 1664.
Zola, Émile, 4394.
Zorilla, Manuel M., 3289.
Zorraquín Becú, H., 3290.
Zozaya, Ricardo, 4808.
Zubrillaga Perera, Cecilio, 3364.
Zuloaga, Manuel Antonio, 191.
Zuloaga Villalón, Antonio, 4555.
Zum Felde, Alberto, 192, 221.
Zúñiga, Neptalí, 2631.
Zúñiga Huete, Ángel, 2506, 2507.
Zúñiga-Tristán, Virginia, 4768.
Zúñiga Zeledón, José Daniel, 4696.